Sociology

Sociology

THIRD EDITION

Beth B. Hess
COUNTY COLLEGE OF MORRIS

Elizabeth W. Markson
BOSTON UNIVERSITY

Peter J. Stein
WILLIAM PATERSON COLLEGE

MACMILLAN PUBLISHING COMPANY
New York

Macmillan Publishing Company
866 Third Avenue, New York, New York 10022

Collier Macmillan Canada, Inc.

Library of Congress Cataloging-in-Publication Data

Hess, Beth B.
  Sociology.

  Includes index.
  1. Sociology.   I. Markson, Elizabeth Warren.
II. Stein, Peter J.   III. Title.
HM51.H46 1988   301   87-24837
ISBN 0-02-354351-5

Printing: 1 2 3 4 5 6 7   Year: 8 9 0 1 2 3 4

PHOTO CREDITS
Part I: The Stock Market © Roy Morsch/Greenwich St., NYC.
Part II: The Stock Market © Joan Menschenfreund/Puerto Rican Wall Mural, NYC.
Part III: Equitable Life Assurance Society of the U.S. © Thomas Hart Benton/"City Activities with Subway."
Part IV: Insight © Jon A. Renbold, Radcliffe Street in Bristol, PA.
Part V: (Red dot–"used"– Inc.–'85) Live Aid concert.
Part VI: David Anderson Gallery, New York, NY © John Hultberg/ "Apocalypsia" 1971–2.

Preface

Each edition of *Sociology* has differed from its predecessor in important ways. Most of these differences reflect the directions in which our discipline has grown and changed. Some chapters are added, others merged, and within each chapter the material is completely revised as new research comes to our attention. But there are also continuities: the constant focus on structural factors, the tone, and the balance among various perspectives. And, with each attempt, we have sharpened our language to clarify complex concepts without sacrificing the intellectual rigor required of sociological analysis.

Features

ORGANIZATION

The sequence of chapters in *Sociology,* 3rd Edition, is the standard format for major introductory texts: The Study of Society; Self in Society; Social Differences and Inequality; The Institutional Spheres; Contemporary Issues; and Social Change. Individual instructors can construct their own sequence and selection. For example, some instructors prefer to begin with an analysis of culture (Chapter 3) and social structure (Chapter 4), returning later in the course to the material on theory (Chapter 1) and methods (Chapter 2). Many instructors also prefer to discuss crime, punishment, and the criminal justice system (Chapter 16) in sequence with Chapter 6 on conformity and deviance.

Although no completely new chapters have been added to this edition, it does run two chapters longer than its predecessor because we have separated and expanded our coverage of some topics. The chapter on "Gender and Age Stratification" has been replaced by Chapter 8 on "Gender Stratification" and by Chapter 9 on "Age Stratification." The number of sociologists and the quality of their research in these two subfields require that each be given a chapter of its own.

Similarly, the chapter on the Political Economy has been expanded to two chapters: one on the economic system (Chapter 12) and one on the polity (Chapter 13). Much new material has been added in each chapter—an extended discussion of organizations and work in Chapter 12, and sections on war and the military in Chapter 13.

FORMAT

While this edition of *Sociology* has a very different look from earlier editions, it retains important features. For example, instructional aids for students include the universally praised marginal explanations, chapter outlines, chapter summaries, a complete glossary of key concepts, and an extensive and up-to-date bibliography. The illustration and photographs, however, are all new and set in a four-color design. These visuals provide a stimulating and sometimes provocative complement to the text.

A completely new set of *vignettes* describes the research interests of sociologists. These autobiographical perspectives introduce students to an active sociology, one that is committed to creating an awareness of society and a capacity for responsible analysis. The *boxes* describing new research have been updated and include interesting case material and examples that elaborate on text discussion. *Sociology & You* discussion sections also enhance text material with topics that relate to the students' experiences and life choices.

As in previous editions, our commitment to data-based conclusions is reflected in the generous use of *tables, charts,* and *graphs.* Each chapter concludes with a *summary* and list of *suggested readings.* A *glossary* and comprehensive set of *references* are found at the end of the book, along with both a *name* and *subject index.*

SUPPLEMENTS

The text is supported by a full package of instructional materials, including a *Student Study Guide,* an *Instructor's Manual,* a *Test File,* a *Statistical Supplement,* a *computer simulation,* and a *video.* The *Student Study Guide* was carefully prepared by Dr. Ellen Rosengarten of Sinclair Community College in Dayton, Ohio, who brings to the task her substantial experience as a teacher of undergraduates. The Study Guide provides chapter outlines, learning objectives, definitions, sample test questions, and other learning devices, such as glossary terms and exercises, for the student. The *Instructor's Manual* has been prepared by one of the authors, Peter J. Stein, who contributes his extensive experience as an undergraduate instructor. The *Instructor's Manual* benefits from the many helpful suggestions of colleagues who have used earlier editions, and includes chapter summaries, teaching objectives, key concepts and names, discussions of various teaching approaches, suggestions for class exercises, take-home assignments, lecture outlines, and a bibliography of film and media resources.

We are pleased to add two new supplements to the "package" of the Third Edition: a *computer simulation* and a *video.* The simulation describes a situation in which students must involve themselves in decision-making processes that illustrate their underlying sociological perspective. Using the format of interactive fiction, it simulates a famine relief effort. Students must mobilize resources to distribute surplus U.S. grain to the fictitious famine area of the Desert Horn. The software is accompanied by an *Instructor's Manual* which shows how to use the simulation to discuss concepts such as power, authority, networking, and impression management. The manual has been written by Dr. Christina Spellman, a creative teacher and writer.

An exciting educational *video* has been produced to demonstrate how sociology can be used in the analysis of popular culture. Using contemporary rock music as a reflection of American society, class, race, and gender are discussed. The narration has been written by Dr. Reebee Garofalo of the University of Massachusetts who has published and spoken extensively in this area. The *Instructor's Manual* was written by Dr. Michael Kimmel of SUNY at Stony Brook who has also written about contemporary music.

A *Test File* has been prepared by Dr. Paul Brezina from the County College of Morris, New Jersey. The test bank includes multiple-choice, true-false, and essay questions. A computerized version is available for the IBM PC, XT, AT, and all compatibles as well as the Apple II series and the Apple III.

Acknowledgments

We'd like to thank Chris Cardone, our acquisitions editor; Victoria Norman and Beth Jaffe, editorial assistants; Carrie O'Donnell, our marketing manager; Pat Cabeza, our production supervisor who held it all together; and Tony English, the executive editor of the project. We want to express a special word of gratitude to Pat Gadban, our developmental editor, whose devotion to the project was truly extraordinary!

The photographs in this edition are new and innovative, thanks to the photo research and contributions of Judith Burns, and especially Sybille Millard, who worked extensively and unceasingly on the text photos and who was responsible for the cover photo. The design and layout were developed and carried out with painstaking care and creativity by Berta Lewis.

We also wish to acknowledge our debt to our colleagues who reviewed *Sociology* for its third and previous editions:

Barbara Altman	*University of Maryland, College Park*
Kenneth Benson	*University of Missouri*
Reed Blake	*Brigham Young University*
Leo Carroll	*University of Rhode Island*
Michael Chernoff	*Georgia State University*
Jerry Clavner	*Cuyahoga Community College*
Jay J. Coakley	*University of Colorado, Colorado Springs*
Victor Darnell	*Belleville Area College, IL*
Edward J. Duffy	*Marshall University*
Harold D. Eastman	*Northeast Missouri State University*
William Feigelman	*Nassau Community College*
John W. Fox	*University of Northern Colorado*
Clyde W. Franklin	*The Ohio State University*
Harold Guy	*Prince George's Community College, MD*
Thomas C. Hood	*University of Tennessee*

David E. Kaufman	*Central Washington University*	Eric A. Wagner	*University of Ohio*
Michael Kimmel	*SUNY at Stony Brook*	Jules J. Wanderer	*University of Colorado, Boulder*
Marvin R. Koller	*Kent State University*	Robert A. Weyer	*County College of Morris*
Michael Kupersanin	*Duquesne University*	George J. Yelagotes	*Millersville State University*
Bebe F. Lavin	*Kent State University*		
Martin P. Levine	*Bloomfield College*		
Sharon McPherron	*St. Louis Community College*		
James D. Orcutt	*Florida State University*		
Elaine Padilla	*Rockland Community College*		
Fred C. Pampel	*University of Iowa*		
Howard Robboy	*Trenton State College*		
Ellen Rosengarten	*Sinclair Community College*		
Rita Sakitt	*Suffolk Community College*		
Stephen Schada	*Oakton Community College*		
Charles Selengut	*County College of Morris*		
Arthur Shostak	*Drexel University*		
Christopher Sieverdes	*Clemson University*		
David A. Snow	*University of Texas*		
Charles S. Suchar	*DePaul University*		
Kenrick S. Thompson	*Northern Michigan University*		
Charles M. Tolbert II	*Florida State University*		

We also want to thank our colleagues at the County College of Morris, Boston University, and William Paterson College, for their many insightful and helpful comments and suggestions.

In addition, thanks go to Patricia Rizzo, a graduate student at William Paterson College, and Loraine Giordano, a Doctoral candidate at New York University, for research help with the Third Edition.

While this edition is dedicated to the memory of Dick Hess, a wonderfully supportive spouse and dear friend, we must, as always, thank the many others who lighten our task and bring joy to our lives: Michele Murdock and Ralph Markson; Larry Hess, Alison and David Markson, and Michael Murdock-Stein; Emily and Gary Robinson; Gary Robinson, Jr., and the newest addition to the *Sociology* family, Richard Charles Robinson.

B. B. H.
E. W. M.
P. J. S.

About the Authors

Beth B. Hess is professor of sociology at County College of Morris, where she has had extensive experience in teaching Introductory Sociology. A graduate of Radcliffe College in 1950, she entered graduate school in 1962 as one of the early "recycled homemakers." At Rutgers, she studied with Matilda White Riley and became a member of the team that produced three volumes of *Aging and Society* (Russell Sage, 1968, 1970, 1972). She has published several textbooks in social gerontology, becoming a Fellow of the Gerontological Society of America in 1978. Most recently, her work has focused on issues of concern to women, including papers on public policy and older women; a book on the new feminist movement, *Controversy and Coalition* (coauthored with Myra Marx Ferree; Twayne, 1984); a book of essays, *Women and the Family; Two Decades of Change* (coedited with Marvin B. Sussman; Haworth, 1984) and, most recently, *Analyzing Gender: A Handbook of Social Science Research* (coedited with Myra Marx Ferree; Sage, 1987). Beth Hess has devoted much time and energy to professional organizations. She chairs the Behavioral and Social Science section of the Gerontological Society of America, as well as the Journal and Publications Committee of the Society for the Study of Social Problems. She is past president of the Association for Humanist Sociology, President of the Eastern Sociological Society, and President of Sociologists for Women in Society.

Elizabeth W. Markson received her undergraduate education at Bryn Mawr College, and her M.A. and Ph.D. in sociology from Yale University. She has worked in both applied and academic settings and is currently director for social research at Boston University Gerontology Center. She is also research associate professor of sociology and adjunct associate professor of socio-medical sciences and community medicine at Boston University. She has contributed to various scholarly journals. Recent books include *Older Women: Issues and Prospects* (winner of the 1984 "Books of the Year Award" from the American Journal of Nursing), *Public Policies for an Aging Population* (with Gretchen Batra), and *Growing Old in America* (with Beth B. Hess). Her current research interests include medical sociology and health care, gender stratification, the family, and aging. She has been on the Executive Board of the Northeastern Gerontological Society, member of the Publications Committee of the Gerontological Society of America, and has served as an officer of the Massachusetts Sociological Association and the Society for the Study of Social Problems.

Peter J. Stein is professor of sociology at William Paterson College. He received his B.A. degree at the City College of New York and his Ph.D. in sociology from Princeton University. Stein has taught a number of undergraduate and graduate courses over the past twenty years including Introduction to Sociology; Marriage and the Family; Social Problems; Sociology of Adulthood; History of Social Theory, and Sociology of Sports. He has contributed to various scholarly journals in the areas of teaching sociology; men's work and family roles; two-income families; friendship, and models of adulthood. His books include *Single; Single Life: Unmarried Adults in Social Context; The Family: Functions, Conflicts and Symbols* (with Judy Richman and Natalie Hannon); and *The Marriage Game: Understanding Marital Decision Making* (with Cathy Greenblat and Norman Washburne). He has been active in various professional organizations and has served as Vice-President of the Eastern Sociological Society and Chair of the Family Division of the Society for the Study of Social Problems. He lives in New York City with his wife Michele and their son, Michael.

Contents

Part III

Social Differences and
Inequality   161

Part IV

Institutional Spheres   277

Chapter 16
Law, Crime, and the Criminal
Justice System 425

Part V

Contemporary Issues 459

Chapter 17
Health, Illness, and the
Health-Care System 460

Chapter 18
Population: People and Their Environment 491

Part VI
Social Change 585

Boxes

Part I
The Study of Society

We begin by defining sociology and its special subject matter. Chapter 1 locates sociology in historical context and describes the theorists and researchers who established this relatively new field of study. In the second section of the chapter, we discuss major contemporary theoretical perspectives and introduce the reader to terms and concepts that serve as basic tools throughout the text.

Chapter 2 moves from the question of *what* sociologists study to *how* they seek answers to these questions. We follow the research process from its origin in theory to evaluation of its findings. Scientific and nonscientific factors are identified, sources of information described, and ethical dilemmas discussed. A brief section on data analysis prepares students to read tables, graphs, and other figures.

With a grasp of the sociological perspective and enterprise, we can begin to examine our social selves.

1

The Sociological Perspective

WHAT is sociology and how does it differ from other ways of explaining human behavior? Perhaps the best way to begin is with an example from everyday life. Sometime this week you will probably eat at a luncheonette or restaurant. As you pay your bill, you will probably leave a tip. Why do that? Do you have a deep psychological urge to give money to people who provide a service? Is it biological? Do you have a "tipping gene" that programs your actions? Or, has some divine power commanded you to do so? The answer to all three questions is, of course, "no." Then why, in our society, is this behavior almost automatic? Students pondering this ques-

tion typically give such responses as, "It's expected," "I was taught to," "If you don't, they'll spill soup on you the next time you eat there," or "It's the way they make a living because their wages are so low." Some students will point to group pressure and to "wanting to be taken as a big shot" by the restaurant personnel, other customers, or their dates. And some will point out that if the size of the tip is directly related to the quality of service, it serves to motivate high levels of performance.

Notice that all of these answers involve some form of *interaction;* they assume that your behavior is linked to that of other people, and that you are acting within a *context* of expectations and mutual influence. Under some circumstances—when trying to impress someone, or eating in a crowd—we will probably leave larger tips than when dining alone. Tipping also varies according to the eating place—the more expensive the meal, the proportionately higher the tip. In general also, men tend to tip more generously than do women. And if you have traveled across this country or abroad, you will probably have noticed regional and national variations in tipping expectations.

Once you realize that these differences have little to do with how hungry you are or how you were toilet trained, you can begin to grasp the essence of the sociological perspective: human beings live in groups; these groups are characterized by rules that govern behavior; the rules are learned; and we take other people into account when we choose how to behave. In other words, our thoughts and actions are largely shaped by forces *outside* ourselves—by the social context and how we interpret it.

But notice, also, that we can *choose not* to tip, and that the amount we leave can depend on a number of considerations—what we think is customary, a fear of retaliation or of looking like a cheapskate, what we consider a fair reward for service, or a means of adding to the income of low-paid workers. Thus, although there is an outside patterning or *structure* to which we are reacting, human beings are not robots or puppets: we can choose not to react or we can give varying meanings to our actions. Nevertheless, the raw material on which our choices are based also comes from what we have learned as members of the society.

What is Sociology?

Sociology is the study of human behavior, group life, and of societies.

Sociology is the study of both the outside forces and the ways in which experience is given meaning by people in interaction with others. This means that the individual is *not* the appropriate unit of analysis for understanding behavior, because hu-

man beings do not—cannot—exist in isolation from other people. To the contrary, humans have always lived in groups; we are bound to one another by ties of feeling and obligation. Thus, we cannot predict how individuals will behave in groups simply on the basis of what we know about each one. When we interact with others we create a new level of reality—that of the group, whether it be two people or ten million. The group has a particular size, patterns of expectations, rules, a division of labor, a way of maintaining order, of dealing with conflict, and so forth. These are the *social structures* that we will examine in this book.

Sociologists are also concerned with how people define their own behavior, on the assumption that such meanings are not built-in but worked out in agreement with other participants. In the sociological perspective, every aspect of your behavior and your mind has been influenced by your group memberships—in this society, at this historical moment, in a specific family, friendship circles, religious community, race and nationality grouping, and even the college that you are currently attending.

It is through these group memberships that we are able to feel somewhat secure and thereby experience a sense of stability in daily life. How else, for example, can we explain the seven-day week, which does *not* conform to any natural cycle (unlike the month, which is linked to phases of the moon), except as an attempt by ancient Hebrews to impose a socially derived order on a seemingly chaotic world (Zerubavel 1982). Similarly arbitrary interpretations of natural phenomena characterize all societies. For example, as we shall see in later chapters, although sexuality is a fact of nature, every society creates rules that govern its expression. The question of who can marry whom has as many answers as there are human groups. The patterning of social relationships is, above all, an attempt to create and maintain order and predictability in human affairs.

Studying social life, however, is especially difficult because at the same time that people are shaped by their society, they also act in ways that bring change to their social contexts. In other words, social structure is always evolving and being modified by our very experiences in it (Giddens 1986).

Social structure is the ordering of behavior and social relationships in a relatively predictable way.

These marathon runners, seemingly a disorganized mass of people, are behaving according to a very strong set of expectations within a well-defined social context. All human behavior is influenced by the social system in which it takes place. (© R. Janeart/LTD)

SOCIOLOGY AND THE OTHER SOCIAL SCIENCES

Human behavior has been studied from a number of other perspectives within the *social* sciences (as distinguished from the physical sciences such as biology or physics). Historians, economists, political scientists, and psychologists also observe everyday life and try to understand why we behave as we do, but not with the same emphasis on groups and group structure as in sociology. This emphasis on the group as the unit of analysis is shared with *anthropology,* which is primarily the study of nonmodern societies or of distinct subgroups within modern society. Anthropologists usually do research through intensive involvement in the daily life of the people being studied. And, as will be discussed in Chapter 3, anthropologists tend to focus on the group as a total community with a particular design for living and shared meanings. The distinction between sociology and anthropology is often blurred because the two fields borrow theories and research techniques from each other, and draw upon a shared data base. In many colleges and universities, the two disciplines are represented by one department.

Anthropology is the study of nonmodern societies or of subgroups within modern societies.

4

The difference between sociology and *psychology,* however, is the most difficult to explain to introductory students. Most Americans believe that their actions flow directly from individual needs or motivations. How many times have you been urged to "be in charge," "do it your way," or "look out for number one," as if you existed in a vacuum and were the only source of your success or failure. These beliefs reflect a psychological perspective that views behavior as determined by a person's mental and emotional states.

In contrast, the sociologist begins with the *situation* in which the behavior takes place. In the sociological perspective, behavior is seen as being largely influenced by the context in which it occurs, by social rather than internal factors, even though we cannot always identify those social, or external, forces.

To illustrate the basic difference between these approaches, let us take the example of the statistical link between mental depression and unemployment. One noted psychiatrist (Morowitz 1979) called for a massive mental health effort to treat the depressive symptoms of the unemployed so that they could then seek out and maintain steady employment. He assumed that poor emotional health was responsible for their unemployment. A sociologist would argue the contrary, that mental symptoms are more likely the result rather than the cause of being unemployed. Men who cannot function as breadwinners, which is a crucial source of masculine identity in our society, will experience unemployment as a loss of self-worth and become depressed. The solution, therefore, is not more mental health clinics, but more jobs (Liem and Rayman 1982).

Similarly, attitudes of hostility toward members of minority groups are rarely expressions of personal maladjustment—people do not fear Jews or hate blacks because of the way in which they were handled as infants. The particular prejudices of any society are a product of its history and they are learned, (although a tendency to mistrust anyone who looks and acts differently from us could be a basic, intuitive response (Tajfel 1981)). In fact, the link between attitudes and behaviors may be precisely the opposite from that assumed by the psychological perspective. Rather than acting out a previously existing mind-set, people usually

Psychology is the study of individuals' mental and emotional states, needs, motivation, and behavior.

respond to the perceived demands of their situation and then find reasons for justifying their behavior (Acock and Fuller 1984).

To rephrase the difference: In the psychological or individualistic view, a given situation is the vehicle for the expression of personality; from a sociological viewpoint, behavior is determined by the situation.

THE SOCIOLOGICAL IMAGINATION

In introducing the concept of "the sociological imagination," American sociologist C. Wright Mills (1959) drew a distinction between what he called "personal troubles" and "public issues." *Troubles* are private matters, limited to aspects of daily life of which a person is directly—often painfully—aware. By contrast, *issues* arise from factors outside one's personal control, but that ultimately affect daily life such as business cycles, wars, or university policies.

Let's return to the example of unemployment. To be out of work is to experience great personal troubles, but when large numbers of people are unemployed, it becomes a public issue and leads to policy changes designed to relieve private problems. Similarly, one divorce is a personal problem; when one couple out of two marrying today will eventually divorce, we have a public issue. Mills was fascinated by the process whereby private troubles are transformed into social issues. How and when do individuals define their troubles as due to larger impersonal forces rather than to their own personal failings?

> **Personal troubles** are private problems experienced directly by individuals.
>
> **Public issues** are factors outside one's personal control caused by crises in the larger system.

Mills was also acutely aware of the influence of historical factors on personal outcomes, locating sociology at the intersection of biography (an individual's life course) and history (the experience of the group through time). We must never lose sight of the human being whose life unfolds in a social context, even while recognizing the profound impact of history on the whole sequence of life events.

These considerations led Mills to frame the sociological imagination in terms of three questions: (1) How are activities patterned in a given society? (2) Where is that society located in human history? And (3) what kinds of men and women are produced in that society? As you will learn, the answers to these questions are different from one society to another, and from one historical period to another even within the same society. It is this continual variation that alerts us to the inadequacy of any perspective that assumes an unchanging human nature or automatic playing-out of biological tendencies.

THE SOCIOLOGICAL PERSPECTIVE

In the discussion thus far, we have identified several characteristics of the *sociological perspective*:

- A concern with the *totality* of social life; not simply economic behavior, for example, but the links between the economy and other areas of life, including personal problems.
- An emphasis on the *context* or setting of social action; that is, on the outside

> The **sociological perspective** focuses on the *totality* of social life, the *context* of social interaction, and on the individual as part of a *group*.

Unemployment has been found to lead to depression, anger, and a loss of social identity for the breadwinner which in turn impacts on all other family members. (© Douglas Kirkland/Woodfin Camp and Associates)

YOU HENG YOU YU ZH NG ZHONG UA

The government of the People's Republic of China has sought to replace the traditional Confucian value on large families with an "ideal" of one child per family thereby hoping to lower the nation's birth rate. This wall poster is part of their program of public education. (© J. P. Laffont/SYGMA)

forces that shape and channel individual choices.
- A focus on the *group* rather than on isolated individuals. We are interested in the person as someone with patterned relationships with other people.

A perspective is a way of looking, and the sociological perspective is one way of seeing and explaining, based on the assumption that a group has different characteristics from the individuals that compose it. According to Peter Blau (1980), the "... prime objective of sociology is the study of social structure and the processes that generate and change it, which implies that our units of analysis are collectivities, not persons, because only collectivities have social structure." A *collectivity* is a group of people acting together, and its structure is a result of the coordinated actions of its members.

A collectivity is a group of persons acting together.

SOCIAL FACTS

Social facts are characteristics of the group.

These actions produce *social facts,* patterned regularities in behavior that characterize a collectivity and cannot be located in its individual parts. For example, although the decision to have children is made by individuals and couples in relative privacy, the sum of these decisions is a birth rate that is a property of their society as a whole. Birth rates are also important evidence that behavior is not solely guided by biological necessity; if that were the case, then birth rates would not fluctuate

6 systematically with the state of the econ-

omy or even minor changes in the tax structure. Nor would they vary by race, religion, education, and income of the couple. The decision to have children, then, is extremely sensitive to a host of outside influences, including the meaning given to certain holidays. Can you guess why, in the United States, more children are born in late August and early September than at any other time of the year—in both the South and the North (so it is not a matter of climate)? The Christmas/New Year period in our society is a time of "coming together," of family reunions, reconciliations, attempts to "turn a new leaf," start over again, and so forth. If these feelings are expressed in physical closeness, it should be no wonder that the birth rate peaks some nine months later.

Death rates are also social facts. Although people rarely decide on the timing or nature of their death, each society has a characteristic death rate determined by such factors as public health measures, condition of the economy, diet, customs regarding food consumption, and family income. As these factors change, so will the patterning of death rates by age, sex, or occupation.

Or take the example of job hunting. No matter how well you prepare yourself for the interview, you may not get the job. Not because of any personal shortcoming but because of social facts beyond your control or awareness—the state of the labor market, the number of other applicants, or an employer's taste for people of a particular age or color. The best person may not always be chosen, and the definition of "best" will vary from one person or organization to another.

Emile Durkheim on Social Facts. The great French sociologist Emile Durkheim laid the groundwork for modern sociological theory when he held that *social facts must be explained by other social facts*—by reference to the social structure rather than to individuals or their bodies or minds. Durkheim demonstrated this principle in his study of European suicide rates, which varied consistently from one country to another and by subgroups within a given area—differences that could not be explained by climate, religious teachings, or biological factors. How can we explain the lower suicide rates in Catholic than in Protestant communities, of the married than the unmarried, and of parents compared to people without living children? The common factor, according to Durkheim, was *social integration,* the degree to which a person is part of a larger group. Marriage, parenthood, and the communal emphasis of Catholicism (in contrast to Protestantism's focus on the individual) are ties that bind one person to

others. Indeed, recent studies have confirmed Durkheim's findings on the importance of marriage, parenthood, and religious involvement (Stark et al. 1983, Stack 1985, Breault 1986).

Therefore, if we want to predict the likelihood of suicide, information on psychological states will be less useful than knowledge about a person's enduring social ties. Even if every suicide left a note saying, "I'm so depressed, I cannot go on living," we would still have to explain why these feelings of depression are more common among the unmarried, the unchurched, and those without children. The goal of sociologists is to predict the *probability* of certain events, not what any given person will do. Sociological predictions apply to groups, not to individuals. We cannot, for example, identify the specific people who might jump off a bridge, but we can predict what proportion of jumpers will be male or female, be old or young, or do so in January rather than June.

Following Durkheim, let us examine the typical patterning of suicide rates in the United States by age, sex, and race, as shown in Figure 1-1. With only minor vari-

Social integration refers to the degree to which a person is a part of a larger group.

Probability refers to the statistical likelihood of a given event, not to what any one person will do.

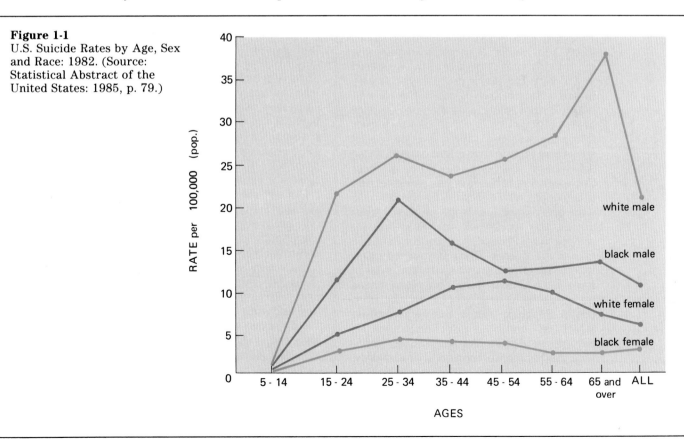

Figure 1-1
U.S. Suicide Rates by Age, Sex and Race: 1982. (Source: Statistical Abstract of the United States: 1985, p. 79.)

ations, these patterns have been consistent for many decades: women are less likely than men to commit suicide, and blacks less likely than whites. Suicide rates peak between ages forty-five to fifty-four for white women, between ages twenty-five to thirty-four for both black males and females, and at age sixty-five and over for white males. Obviously, these differences cannot be explained by biology, early childhood experiences, or mental illness. If the patterns were linked to sex differences, then the shape of the curves for both white and black men or women would be the same. If the causes lie in biologically based racial differences, then the curves for black or white males and females would be roughly similar. But if such social factors as degree of stability in family and work relationships are related to suicide, we can see how these commitments are threatened or weakened at different ages for blacks and whites, females and males.

Another example that supports Durkheim's idea that social facts must be explained by other social facts—by reference to social structure rather than individual attitudes and motivations—comes from research on the relationship between voting and income (Beeghley 1985). As you will see in Chapter 13, in the United States today the higher a person's income the more likely that person is to be registered and to vote. But it was not always this way in our country and it is not the case in many European societies (where the poor have voting rates equal to, if not higher than, the wealthy). What are the social structural factors that might explain these differences? For one, elections in most European countries are on weekends so that people who are paid by the hour or who are exhausted from physical labor during the workweek find it relatively easy to vote. Second, registration requirements are looser than in our country, where all efforts to simplify the system have been defeated in Congress (whose members have been elected by the nonpoor). Beeghley notes that when these structural conditions are changed, voting patterns will also change; and so, then, will the balance of power in the society. The explanation of variations in voting rates, therefore, lies in social factors rather than personality differences.

Social Facts and Reification.   While recognizing social facts, we must be careful *not* to talk about "society" as if it were a person. All too often, even in professional articles, one reads that "society does this" or "says that," but this is the logical fallacy of *reification* (from the Latin "res," meaning "thing"), or making a concrete object out of an abstract concept. Societies are composed of people engaged in patterned behaviors, and we must always specify just who and what we are talking about when we speak of "society": which people, under what circumstances, are doing what to whom.

Social Facts and Subjective Reality.   Thus far, we have discussed social facts as group

Reification is the logical fallacy of treating an abstract concept as a concrete object.

SOCIOLOGY & YOU
Studying Sociology and Making Decisions Knowledgeably

There could be any number of reasons why you're enrolled in this sociology course: it's required, it sounded interesting, one of your friends recommended it, or it meets at a convenient time. But what can you gain from taking another course in sociology or by considering a major in this field? Will it help you to get a better job or have a more successful career in the future? Few college courses can prepare a student for a specific job, since most work requires on-the-job training. But a solid background in sociology has proved valuable for occupational success among recent college graduates. A 1985 study of 800 graduates with sociology majors from four different schools indicates that about one-third are employed in the professions, about one-quarter in service occupations, and another one-quarter in sales or management/administration. In terms of specific occupations, social work, teaching, and retail sales are popular options. Theodore Wagenaar, in his vignette mentions more specific jobs.

However, taking sociology courses is not only useful if directly related to your job choices. These courses can also help to develop an awareness of the society around you and your place in it. This awareness becomes a handy decision-making tool. Sociologists, and psychologists too, suggest that the more we know about a situation, the more capable we are of making a decision we can live with. Saying to yourself, "I'm not going to take this class (buy this car, take this job, date this person) characteristics resulting from many individual acts. Another type of social fact is the *meaning* that people give to their shared experiences. People make sense of their experience through conversation with others. Together we define what is real and not real, good or bad, true or false. Notice how often you look for information from other people about whether or not a party is "really good" or a rock-music group "really exciting." We reinforce our own impressions with the perceptions of others.

In this way, the ideas and feelings that we carry in our heads—our *subjective reality,* in contrast to the world outside ourselves—are largely developed through social interaction. Such shared definitions

Subjective reality is developed through social interaction and refers to the ideas and feelings we have about ourselves and the world.

are social facts just as much as the structural factors we have already discussed.

Sociological Theory

THE IMPORTANCE OF THEORY

The study of society begins with some general ideas of how social life is organized and how membership in different groups affects behavior. A *theory* is a set of logically related statements that explain an entire class of events. Without a theory to guide us, pieces of information remain unconnected items that tell us little about larger patterns. For example, what general statement could you make to link the

A **theory** is a set of logically related statements that seek to explain an entire class of events.

---

just because someone else thinks I should" or "This time around I know what I want to do" are steps in the direction of making *knowledgeable decisions.* To make a knowledgeable decision you have to:

1. Be aware of as many options and alternatives as possible. Then later on you won't regret that you didn't consider all of the avenues open to you when making your decision.
2. Be aware of the social pressures that limit your choices. Recognizing the reality of social pressures, their source and character does not always mean accepting them. But if you decide to make a decision that runs counter to parental, age and gender expectations, you'll be more ready to deal with the possible pressure you'll experience.
3. Clarify your personal values, beliefs and standards. Do this not only rationally by considering the re-

wards and costs, but "emotionally" as well, by being aware of your "gut" reactions. How do you feel about the option you are considering?

4. Be aware of the consequences of choosing each option. Make a list of all the probable positive and negative consequences of each decision you might make.
5. Decide.
6. Recheck the results once you do make a decision and have acted on it. Have things developed for yourself and significant others as you anticipated? How are the results different?
7. Use such information to evaluate future options.

The following figure identifies the points in knowledgeable decision making. Take one or two issues you are currently concerned with and follow the figure point-for-point. What have you learned?

Based on "The Wheel of Knowledgeable Decision-Making" in Nena and George O'Neill, *Shifting Gears: Finding Security in a Changing World.* (New York: Avon, 1974)

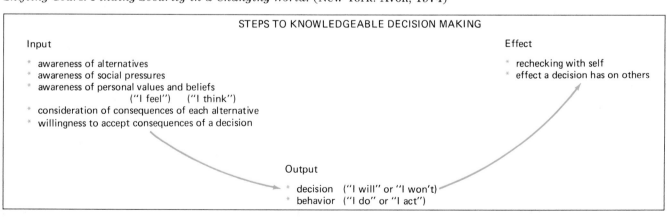

STEPS TO KNOWLEDGEABLE DECISION MAKING

Input
* awareness of alternatives
* awareness of social pressures
* awareness of personal values and beliefs
            ("I feel")   ("I think")
* consideration of consequences of each alternative
* willingness to accept consequences of a decision

Effect
* rechecking with self
* effect a decision has on others

Output
* decision ("I will" or "I won't")
* behavior ("I do" or "I act")

facts that unemployment rates are higher for nonwhites than whites, females than males, and young teenagers than persons fifteen to sixty-four?

This chapter would be easier to write—and much shorter—if there was a single theoretical framework that covered all sociology. But other than recognizing the importance of social structure and the interactive nature of social life, sociologists have used a number of theoretical frameworks (or *models*) to explain the same sets of social facts. Each theory represents a special way of viewing the world and directs our attention to different aspects of society. And indeed, social life is so diverse and all-embracing that any one model would be more limiting than enlightening.

In the remainder of this chapter we will briefly examine some of the guiding ideas and foundations of classical and contemporary sociology. These introductory comments on each theorist are rather short and selective, however, as their major contributions will be discussed in detail throughout the book.

THE ROOTS OF SOCIOLOGY

Sociology as the *systematic* study of people in groups, has its roots in late eighteenth-century Europe, the Age of the Enlightenment. This period followed the collapse of the old medieval order based on unquestioned obedience to kings or other nobles and to religious authorities. In contrast to the "dark ages," the intellectual movement called the Enlightenment emphasized the ideals of progress, political and economic freedom, individualism, the scientific method, and a profound belief in the ability of human beings to solve social problems.

Faith in the divine was to be replaced by reliance on human reason and scientific analysis. The discovery of the individual and of society were major breakthroughs in intellectual history; new ideas were brought into the common language—democracy, self-consciousness, social system. And if all else could be rationally analyzed, why not society itself? Sociology thus emerges at a particular historical moment in response to a need for certain types of information. So, indeed, for that matter, does all knowledge. According to

this view, called the *sociology of knowledge,* what we want to know and what we study are themselves social products, shaped by the historical context of thinkers. The theorists described in this chapter and their particular perspectives are all products of their own time and place.

Enter Sociology—Comte (1798–1857) and Martineau (1802–1876).   August Comte, often called the founder of sociology, coined the word "sociology" from the Latin *socius* (companion, with others) and the Greek *logos* (reason, study of) to describe the new science of social life. The field of sociology would be distinguished by (1) its subject matter—society as something other than the sum of individual actions; and (2) its methods—careful observation, objective measurement, and comparison (the *scientific method*). To the great question of the Enlightenment—"What shall be put in place of the old traditional order?"—Comte replied, "the scientific study of society and group life," by which he meant an approach without any bias on the part of the observer. The idea of science as an absolutely value-free, totally objective activity is called *positivism,* (although Comte himself could not keep religious and philosophical assumption out of his own work (Reinharz 1985)).

We should note at this point that the context in which theories have been created in Western thought has been one dominated by males and their particular way of seeing the world (Reinharz 1985). The structure of the European university system and the limits that were placed on female achievement more or less ensured that few women would enter sociology or have their work taken seriously. Nevertheless, at the same time that Comte was laying the foundations for sociology, an Englishwoman, Harriet Martineau, was making systematic observations of social patterns in England and the United States. Her book *Society in America* is even more theoretically integrated than a similar but more famous study by a French visitor to the United States, Alexis de Tocqueville. And Martineau's essay, *How to Observe Manners and Morals,* has been called the first book on social-research methods (Lipset 1962). Nonetheless, she is best known, not for her original work, but as the English translator of Comte.

In any event, the liberalizing trends of

The **sociology of knowledge** is the study of the way in which the production of knowledge is shaped by the social context of thinkers.

The **scientific method** in sociology involves observation, measurement, and comparison.

Positivism sees science as value-free and totally objective.

The University of Massachusetts has established a chair in Sociology named after Harriet Martineau (shown here). The chair is currently held by Professor Alice Rossi, a distinguished contemporary sociologist. (The Bettmann Archive, Inc., canvas by Richard Evans, 1834)

the Enlightenment with their emphasis on individual freedom and economic justice were soon confronted with opposing tendencies, the counter-Enlightenment. These forces succeeded in suppressing democratic impulses and restoring conservative political, economic, military, and religious ruling groups ("elites"). In this new intellectual atmosphere, the three "giants" of classical sociology—Marx, Durkheim, and Weber—attempted to resist the forces of traditionalism and to preserve the Enlightenment vision of progress toward justice and equality (Seidman 1983).

Karl Marx (1818–1883). Unlike Comte, Marx had little concern with uncovering the basic laws that made social life possible and orderly. He sought, rather, to explain the logic of history in terms of the struggle to end the oppression of the less powerful by the more powerful. Where others saw progress as the supreme law of the universe and marveled at the products of economic development, Marx saw misery, exploitation, and injustice. Marx was struck by the great inequality in wealth and power between those few who con-

trolled the land, factories, educational institutions, and political offices (the "means of producing goods and services") and the many who had only their labor to sell in a market crowded with other workers.

Marx introduced a number of conceptual models, many of which continue to guide sociological analysis regardless of the political viewpoint of the researcher. Even today, Marxist sociology is one of the most dynamic subfields in the discipline. All students of society must reckon with Marx's stunning insights as they have been modified and elaborated by later thinkers. Three of Marx's theoretical models will be referred to throughout this book: the organic totality of the society, the relative importance of the economic sector, and the historical processes of change through conflict (Wacquant 1985).

ORGANIC TOTALITY. The idea of society as an organism similar to the human body where each part performs a distinct function has a long intellectual history, but

Karl Marx (pictured here at age 38) focused on the great inequality in power and wealth in early capitalist societies. His influence upon sociology and for many political movements has been profound. (Archive/Photo Researchers, Inc.)

11

Marx had a much more complex model of how the various areas of social activity influenced one another and together formed a particular kind of society. Tracing the links among educational, religious, political, economic and family arrangements remains a major preoccupation of sociologists, although there is some debate over the relative strength and independence of these sectors.

IMPORTANCE OF THE ECONOMIC SECTOR. For Marx, the basic division in society was between owners and nonowners of the *means of production* (tools, land, factories, knowledge, wealth). This division largely determined the character of the other areas of activity and of the society as a whole at any given historical period. Marx referred to the economic system as the "base" and these other areas—family patterns, political organization, religious beliefs, and educational system—as "superstructure." The superstructure, as Marx pictured it, was built upon the economic base and served to support and maintain the division between elites and the masses. This point has been modified by later theorists who have noted that political structures, family systems, and beliefs can develop and change relatively independently of the economic base and even exert influence on the economic system (Cameron 1985).

Marx also saw that the concept of ownership of the means of production could be extended to the realm of *ideas.* In his own famous phrase, Marx claimed that "the ideas of the ruling class are in every age the ruling ideas" of that society (Marx 1846/1939, p. 39). A Marxist analysis of our society today, for example, would show how the flow of ideas is controlled by the very small circle of wealthy people who own and operate publishing companies, newspapers, magazines, radio and television stations, and who otherwise present audiences with their version of truth. Lacking other sources of information, people will develop a *false consciousness* of the world and themselves, including the belief that hard work accounts for the success of the wealthy.

HISTORICAL CHANGE THROUGH CONFLICT. As you will see in Chapter 22, Marx's model of historical change involves a process of continual struggle between the owners and nonowners, set in motion by built-in strains within the economic system. This conflict, he predicted, will end only when there is no longer a distinction between owners and others—that is, when members of the society as a whole own the means of production. Although Marx saw history as determined by the forces of production, he also believed that events could and should be influenced by human actions. People make history, he said, although not always in the way they had hoped for or intended.

Emile Durkheim (1855–1917). Following Comte, Durkheim viewed society as a reality in its own right. Individual members of society are born, live, and die, but a certain pattern to their experiences exists independently. Individual lives are played out in a society with a preexisting set of rules governing family life, for example, or economic activity. This is the social structure that Durkheim felt to be the proper object of sociological analysis.

Durkheim was very concerned with establishing sociology as a separate academic discipline, hence his emphasis on the uniqueness of society and the impossi-

The **means of production** refers to the tools, land, factories, information, and wealth that form the economic basis of a society.

Ownership of the means of production by the ruling class extends to **ideas** as well as things.

False consciousness of the world develops among people who do not share in the production of ideas.

As well as producing some of the major works in early sociological theory, Emile Durkheim, the French sociologist, worked to establish sociology as a separate academic field. (The Bettmann Archive, Inc.)

bility of reducing it to the study of individuals. Social facts, remember, must be explained with reference to other group-level characteristics. As a consequence, Durkheim was also a pioneer in the use of *social statistics* such as suicide rates. Official records and systematic observations constituted the raw material from which social facts could be deduced and "scientific" statements made.

Social statistics refer to official records and systematic observations from which social facts can be deduced.

As for beliefs and ideas, Durkheim saw these, too, as reflections of society, as a social reality shared by members of the group, and therefore as much a part of the social structure as any behavior. Consistent with the times he could not, however, see that his own ideas about differences in male and female behavior were also socially constructed, assuming them to be basically biologically determined.

Max Weber (1864–1920). Although his lifespan largely overlaps that of Durkheim, the concerns of Max Weber (pronounced "Vey-bear") were closer to those of Marx in many ways. It was obvious by the end of World War I that a new type of society was emerging in Europe based on an industrial economy that would transform existing social structures in ways that could destroy the promise of the Enlightenment.

Weber saw both the up and down side of the modern age. His optimism about the liberating potential of human reason was balanced by a pessimistic realization of its limits (Brubaker 1983): As science uncovers the laws of nature, some of the wonder and mystery of existence is destroyed (Weber's *disenchantment of the world*). Far from liberating the human spirit, Weber saw that technology and modern organizations could become a new type of prison (an "iron cage") without any of the magic that helped people to survive in the past. An emphasis on rationality led, Weber thought, to a separation of feeling from behavior, so that people could avoid responsibility for their own actions.

The **disenchantment of the world** occurs as science replaces faith and fantasy.

Weber shared Marx's organic conception of society and broad sweep of historical analysis. His work on world religions and social structure is notable for the primary emphasis given to the influence of ideas, although Weber, too, was sensitive to the complex interplay among the various areas of social activity.

American sociologists have been influenced by Weber's discussion of the place of

Max Weber's extensive intellectual investigations spanned the diverse fields of economics, law, politics, history, the development of cities, music, and the world's major religions. (The Bettmann Archive, Inc./painting by Otto Neuman)

one's own values and value judgments in sociological analysis. If sociology is to fulfill its claim to be a science of society, researchers must make an effort to be objective observers, without personal bias. But even if this were possible, would it be desirable? Weber, again, could see both sides: the necessity for value-free research but the danger of being without any concern for the uses to which one's knowledge is put. These are dilemmas that still haunt the field, as we shall see in Chapter 2.

Another important contribution to research methods was Weber's insistence that we must understand social reality in the terms of those who are experiencing it. He used the German word *Verstehen* ("understanding") to refer to the ability to imagine the world as other people might see it, to grasp the processes through which they make sense of what happens to them.

Verstehen is the ability to see the world as it might be experienced by others.

Georg Simmel (1858–1916). The German sociologist Georg Simmel, even though a contemporary of Weber, was fascinated by **13**

Features in the Development of American Sociology

The founders of American sociology were also products of their time. Many came from a strongly religious Protestant background with its emphasis on individual responsibility and the obligation to do good in this world (Vidich and Lyman 1985). And many were women. There are at least a dozen women, most associated with the founding of the University of Chicago and its Sociology Department at the turn of the century through World War I, who became recognized scholars and/or activists: Jane Addams, Charlotte Perkins Gilman, Marion Talbot, Florence Kelley, Edith Abbott, Alice Paul, Elsie Clews Parsons, Leta Hollingworth, Jessie Taft, Alice Hamilton, Emily Greene Balch, and Sophonisba Breckinridge (Deegan 1981, Fish 1985, 1986). These women called themselves "sociologists," and most were members of the American Sociological Society (later, Association). Many were doing high-level, quantitative research (urban mapping, consumer surveys, time budgets) at a time when the fashion among their male colleagues at Chicago was for anthropological-type studies of criminals and other unusual types of people. But fashions change, and as sociology became a recognized discipline and various universities sought to "upgrade" their prestige, the women's research efforts ceased to be rewarded, and large numbers left academic life to become activists for social causes in the larger society (Deegan 1986). Of the seventy-seven presidents of the American Sociological Association, four have been women, beginning with Dorothy Swaine Thomas in 1952.

Over time the development of sociological thought in this country was also influenced by the work of refugee scholars from Europe in the 1930s, as well as by the impact of translations of Durkheim, Weber, and Marx. Uniquely American, however, was the dominance of *positivism*, a dependence on objective descriptions of scientifically measured "facts," which, in a reversal of the early choices by members of the "Chicago school" (noted above), has come to be associated with a hard-headed "masculine" approach to social facts. Conversely, the *humanistic* strain in American sociology—in which people's own accounts of their experience are the primary source of information—has over time come to be defined as a softer (i.e., more feminine) form of sociology. This tension between an emphasis on the social structure "out there" and the "inner" reality of individuals has led to the development of very different models for the study of social life.

The history of sociological theory in American society is, therefore, not simple or straightforward, but a continually changing mix of approaches (see Bierstedt 1981, for a full and readable account).

concerns very different from the other classic figures. To answer the basic question, "How is society possible?" Simmel proposed that sociologists focus on people in relationships. Society, for Simmel, was the patterned interactions among members of a group.

Simmel began with the elements of everyday life—playing games, keeping secrets, being a stranger, forming friendships—and arrived at insights into the quality of relationships. Simmel was unlike Durkheim and Weber in both his subject matter and method of study, but like the others, he resisted reducing social behavior to individual personality. Reality he saw as the ways in which we relate to one another and the unity we create together.

George Herbert Mead (1863–1931). The American social psychologist George Herbert Mead also viewed human interaction as the central focus of sociological analysis. Not only society, but "self" and consciousness emerge out of interaction in social settings. Through these ongoing activities with one another, we create and share a world of meanings.

In contrast to an emphasis on social facts "out there," Mead and his followers concentrate on felt experience and the ways in which meaning is constructed through mutual exchange. In this view, all that we know about ourselves and our world is the product of social interaction. Thus, there is always an element of unpredictability and flexibility in social life. Although Mead's emphasis on inner thoughts may appear highly subjective, the individual is never considered apart from others. We will discuss Mead's perspective at greater length in Chapter 5.

Charles Darwin (1809–1882) and Sigmund Freud (1856–1939). Although neither was a sociologist, there are two other towering figures who have left their impact on contemporary sociology: Charles Darwin, a British gentleman-scholar, and Sigmund Freud, an Austrian physician and founder of the field of psychoanalysis. They represent almost opposite poles in the study of human behavior. Darwin's theory of the origins of human beings traced their evolution from the earliest fossil record through the stages of variation and survival experienced by all other living things. What emerged from this process, covering millions of years, was a creature able to speak, to think about itself, and to adapt to any type of environment. This is *Homo sapiens* ("thinking person"), our species.

If Darwin took us back to the origins of life on this planet, Freud led us to the very depths of the human mind, to the *unconscious* forces that often lead people to behave in unpredictable ways. This approach may seem to contradict the rational, orderly, modern mentality proposed by the theorists of the Enlightenment; but through psychoanalytic psychology, Freud applied rational analysis to the nonrational.

Consideration of the origins of species, on the one hand, and of the organization of mental life, on the other, sets the boundaries of the study of human behavior. Between these two poles lies the great bulk of individual experience, played out in patterned relationships with others, within an established social order. The legacy of sociology's founders is that they defined this vast expanse of social life as a field of study in its own right.

With the exception of Comte, each of these earlier thinkers has greatly influenced contemporary sociological thought. The work of Marx, Durkheim, and Weber will reappear frequently throughout the remaining chapters, and the influence of Freud and Mead will be noted in Chapter 5.

Modern Social Theory

Diversity characterizes contemporary sociological theorizing, with several perspectives guiding current research and analysis. In the remainder of this chapter we will discuss several major perspectives, each of which has variations. These are (1) the structural-functional model of society; (2) the conflict model; (3) symbolic-

interaction; (4) the humanistic approach; and (5) the feminist perspective.

THE STRUCTURAL-FUNCTIONAL MODEL

The central focus of the *structural-functional model* is the relationship between two levels of social reality: the whole (the society, a group) and its parts (areas of social activity, members of a group). What do the parts contribute to the maintenance of the whole? And how does the particular structure of the whole affect the behavior of the parts? Success is measured by survival over time.

The main elements of structure at the level of the society as the whole are its economy, its political system, its rules for marriage and family life, techniques for raising children, and a set of rituals and beliefs that unify group members. The specific content of these patterns will vary from one society to another, and will change over time in any one society; but each task—function—must be performed if the whole group is to survive from one generation to another.

The basic question of functional analysis is this: How does any specific element of social structure contribute to the stability of the whole; that is, what is the *social function* of that structural element? Another way of framing this question is to ask, "What are the *consequences* of a given pattern; what happens because people in a given society have this or that way of governing themselves or of arranging marriages, and so forth?"

Talcott Parsons (1902–1975). The American sociologist Talcott Parsons is the best-known theorist of structural-functional analysis. For over four decades, Parsons elaborated an extremely complex and sophisticated conceptual model that we will only sketch briefly.

He began with the concept of a *social system* composed of interrelated parts, each of which must perform an essential function for the maintenance of the whole. The parts are linked by "exchanges" that facilitate task performance. For example, Parsons' (1959) functional analysis of the American family in the 1950s emphasizes the division of labor between husband and wife, which he saw as

The structural-functional model examines the relationship between the parts and the whole of a social system.

The contribution of an element of social structure to the stability of the whole is its **social function.**

A **social system** is a totality composed of interdependent parts.

necessary for family stability. This model portrays the husband as the family's representative to the world of work and the wife as providing emotional support to the family unit, preparing her husband each evening for his daily battles in the big world and training their children for eventually assuming similar duties. In turn, the husband's job provides the income needed to keep family members alive, and both husband and wife receive encouragement for their efforts from the religious and political systems. Furthermore, the children's education is highly supportive of the parents and of the existing social order. Thus, each part maintains the others and all combine to preserve the system over time.

The idea that a group or society is held together by a basic harmony or balance among its parts ("functional relationships") is an important element of the structural-functional perspective. Equally important is Parsons' claim that social order ultimately rests on value consensus among members of the group. *Value consensus* refers to an underlying agreement ("consensus" means to "think together") about the goals of the group and the correct way to achieve those aims. "Values," as will be detailed in Chapter 3, are ideals

Value consensus refers to an underlying agreement about the goals of a group.

of the good and desirable that guide judgments of appropriate conduct.

Criticism of Structural-Functional Analysis.
Finding flaws in this conceptual model, and in Parsons' version in particular, has been a minor industry in academic sociology for many decades. Critics claim that attempts to explain everything with a single model usually tell us little about everyday life; that the ideas are too general; and that real life rarely fits neatly into theoretical boxes. In other words, the theory, they say, is too abstract, too removed from the level of individual experience.

Another target of criticism is the conservative bias of functional theory with its focus on harmony, stability, social order, and "all parts working for the best." If, indeed, the parts are always tending toward balance, then disharmony and conflict will be seen as temporary problems in an otherwise healthy system and not as signals that the system itself may be flawed.

Third, as the example of Parsons' analysis of the American family should suggest, what might have seemed clear in the 1950s is certainly not so today. In his eagerness to find functionality, Parsons overlooked sources of strain within the family, par-

The structural-functional model emphasizes the way in which the various elements of society function for social cohesion. For example, this totem, being carved by Tsimishian Indians of British Columbia, symbolizes the group's identity and helps to unify the tribe. (© Frank Keating/Photo Researchers, Inc.)

Ahistorical functional analysis fails to explore the historical context and change over time of social patterns.

ticularly on the part of its female members. In general, functional analysis has been faulted for being *ahistorical,* that is, failing to trace changes over time, and for overlooking the specific historical context of any social pattern.

From a sociology of knowledge perspective, it is not difficult to see why American sociologists working between 1945 and 1960 would have taken such an optimistic view. These were years of great economic growth, social stability, and what appeared to be widespread value consensus. For other sociologists, however, the conflicts of the 1960s were too widespread to be explained by the functional model, and they turned to different theoretical perspectives in order to understand what was happening in our society.

But functional analysis has not disappeared. Many leading members of the profession were trained in this tradition and still find it extremely useful. Supporters of this perspective claim that its critics have misunderstood the full scope of structural-functional theory. In addition, there are some insights that have stood the test of time, and to which we shall refer throughout this volume. In fact, there is an interesting revival of functional theorizing among a relatively young group of contemporary scholars, led by Jeffrey Alexander (1985, 1986).

Robert K. Merton (1910–   ) and the Refinement of Functional Theory. The power of functional theory lies less in the effort to construct a total model than in much more modest attempts at "theories of the middle range" that can be applied to a limited set of behaviors. In this task, the leading figure is Robert K. Merton, whose work focuses on the *predictable impact* of social structure on human behavior: If this is how the larger system works, then here are the logical alternatives for individuals located in that system.

For example, if immigrants need help in dealing with government agencies where no one speaks their language or appears to care much about them, the situation is ripe for politicians to help the powerless in return for their votes. Here is a social-structural explanation for the rise of political machines in the largest American cities during the late nineteenth and early twentieth centuries. It is an analysis that does not depend on personal characteristics (lust for power on the part of the bosses or

moral weakness on the part of the foreign-born). The political machine was functional for those who became the urban poor, and their loyalty was functional for the machine.

Merton made several refinements of functional analysis that will be used throughout this book. The first is the distinction between *manifest* and *latent functions* (Merton 1968). Manifest refers to "open, stated, or intended goals"; latent function refers to "unexpected and unintended consequences." Every human act, every social pattern has more than one outcome, and many of these consequences will be unforeseen and undesired (Bouden 1982). In some cases, the unintended or latent consequences can undermine the manifest goals of policy, as when urban-renewal projects displace local communities and add to the problems of the poor, or when the military destroys villages in order to save the inhabitants. Such negative outcomes of well-intended policies have also been called "fatal remedies" (Sieber 1981).

Recognition of multiple consequences leads also to the realization that not all behavioral patterns or aspects of social structure are functional; that is, they do not contribute to the maintenance of a society or group. Some patterns may actually reduce the capacity of a system to adapt and survive; these are, therefore, considered *dysfunctional.* When assessing functionality, the questions are: "Does that behavior or structure help or hinder the system as a whole?" and "Are the goals of individuals and groups achieved?"

But not all goals can be achieved, and one group's success may involve another group's failure. Therefore, the sociologist must identify functional *for whom or for what.* Clearly, a war could be functional for a society by reducing outside threats, but highly dysfunctional for many soldiers and civilians. The war will have different consequences for various kinds of people and groups in the society (defense contractors gain, consumer industries lose; generals win promotions, draftees lose several years of employment experience).

Merton's applications of functional analysis to familiar experiences continue to demonstrate the usefulness of this perspective for certain questions. But the model is less helpful in explaining historical processes and change. Just as the functionalist emphasis on stability and order

Manifest functions are open, stated, and intended goals. **Latent functions** are unexpected and unintended consequences.

Dysfunctional patterns reduce the capacity of a system to adapt and survive.

reflected American society in the decades following World War II, the challenges to social order in the 1960s brought an alternative model and a new generation of scholars into prominence.

THE CONFLICT PERSPECTIVE

As its name indicates, *conflict theory* focuses on disorder, disagreement, and open hostility among individuals and groups, and lack of harmony in system parts. From this perspective, it is struggles over power and resources that are normal, and harmonious cooperation that is unusual. Social structure is a temporary and often fragile combination of competing social forces. Conflict can be minimized in periods of economic prosperity, as in the 1950s, but will be intensified during economic downturns.

In the conflict perspective, the task of the social scientist is to examine (1) sources of tension among people and groups with different amounts of power; (2) techniques of conflict control; and (3) the ways in which the powerful maintain and enlarge their influence on all aspects of social structure, including the realm of ideas and values. For example, a functional view of police violence would stress the need for order, while a conflict theorist would note how police violence is typically directed at the least powerful members of the group. In addition, the belief that modern societies are organized ratio-

nally would be considered a myth manufactured by the ruling elite to support their monopoly of high positions.

In the conflict view, the social order at any particular moment is the outcome of struggles among groups of unequal power, and not the result of blind forces of technology or other impersonal historical trends. The conflict question is this: "Who benefits from any given social arrangement?" Conflict within the society is frequently expressed through public protests (Chap. 20), as symptoms of social instability. While a functional analysis would treat the protest as a temporary breakdown of order that can be cured by political tinkering, the conflict approach suggests that the very system requires radical (root) change.

Both the conflict and the functional perspectives focus on the society as a whole, or the *macrosystem* (macro means "large"). Macrosystem analysis is relatively abstract, working from a general model of social structure back to everyday behavior—from "out there" to "down here"; and its theoretical statements are not easy to observe. Describing the functions of religion, for example, is much more difficult than counting how many people attend sacred services.

In contrast to macrosystem analysis, other sociologists, following the path of Simmel and Mead, examine everyday experiences in order to make statements about more abstract structures of action.

The conflict model focuses on the divergent interests of individuals and groups in society. Here American students protest university investments in South Africa. (© Nacke/SYGMA)

The symbolic-interaction model seeks to explain the processes of interaction among people. Here employees of a Tokyo department store greet customers. Would you expect to see this much deference displayed in a U.S. store? (© Eiji Miyazawa/Black Star)

Microsystem analysis focuses on smaller units such as face-to-face interaction.

The **symbolic interaction model** examines how people interact with each other, how they interpret such experiences, and how they organize appropriate responses.

The study of face-to-face interaction is called *microsystem* analysis (micro means "small").

SYMBOLIC-INTERACTION PERSPECTIVE

More of a diversity of approaches than a fully developed theory, *symbolic interaction* refers to the study of how people interact with one another, how we interpret these experiences, and how we organize appropriate responses. The questions of interest are: "How do people make sense of their world, influence one another, and define who they are and what they are doing?" Although the raw material for these interpretations and responses comes from "out there," behavior is not automatic nor always predictable.

The term "symbolic interaction" incorporates two essential features of social life: (1) humans think and communicate in symbols, thus, we can imagine things that do not yet exist, and we can create new meanings; and (2) humans must live in groups. Both of these points will be elaborated throughout this book.

For the symbolic interactionist there is no reality other than that existing in people's minds: what is real is what members of the group agree is real, *including their own identities* (see Chapter 5). In this perspective, then, social life is an uncertain and shifting order reached by talking to one another and held together because it exists in our minds.

Yet individuals do not live in a vacuum but in a set of ongoing relationships within larger social contexts. As stated by W. I. Thomas and Florian Znaniecki, authors of an early classic of American sociology, *The Polish Peasant in Europe and America* (1918–19/1984), social life is "the product of a continual interaction of individual consciousness and objective social reality" (p. 293), that is, between inner reality and the social world "out there."

OTHER MICROLEVEL APPROACHES

Locating sociology in the details of everyday life is also the goal of several variations on the symbolic interaction model. We shall mention two of these: the *dramaturgical approach* of Erving Goffman (1959, 1961, 1971, 1983), and the *ethnomethodology* of Harold Garfinkle (1967).

Goffman's work is called "dramaturgical" because social interaction is viewed as a series of little dramas in which actors present images of themselves, attempt to manipulate the reactions of other people (the audience), protect their identity, and develop rules that guide behavior in daily encounters. Just as an actor has a different "script" for each "stage" on which she or he appears, so does each of us play a different part as we move from one social setting to another in the course of a day. We play many different parts, depending on the context, and at each performance some aspect of our identity is at risk. Thus, social life is a series of challenges, with the outcome never fully predictable. Every encounter is filled with drama.

Some of this uncertainty and excite-

The **dramaturgical approach** sees social interaction as a series of mini-dramas.

19

Ethnomethodology in Action

What, for example, are the hidden, taken-for-granted meanings of the typical dating situation? The best way to find out is to break into these existing understandings by having the woman, at the end of the date, ask her partner how much she owes for her half of the evening's expenses, or by having the man present his partner with a bill for her share of the tab. How does the other react? Why? Gradually, it will become clear that the date involves certain "understood" exchanges, and that the person who pays has greater control over the terms of exchange. Contrast the definition of the situation in a traditional dating relationship to that for "going Dutch," when the partners agree in advance to share the costs.

women's powerlessness? If you were an ethnomethodologist, you would test this possibility by asking probing questions designed to uncover the unspoken assumptions about maleness and femaleness embodied in such rituals as opening doors and helping someone to put on their coat (Richardson 1974).

Other Garfinkle-type experiments include having students act as if they were paying guests in their parents' home. Try it, and see how deeply you have to probe into your parents' reactions before you discover the hidden rules governing the relationships between parents and adult children in our society.

Reflections on Social Theory

Ethnomethodology involves probing beneath the "taken-for-granted" reality.

ment also characterizes Garfinkle's *"ethnomethodology,"* a concept that refers both to the subject matter and the means for gaining information about it (Heritage 1984). Because so much of what we do takes place without conscious awareness, the researcher must dig below the level of "taken-for-granted" reality to discover the basic meaning of social action. For example, when asked why men hold doors for women, most of our students say, "I was taught that it's a form of politeness or way of showing respect." These are taken-for-granted meanings. But suppose it was pointed out that since the other types of persons for whom doors are held are children, the elderly, or the disabled—people thought to be incapable of managing for themselves—might not the deeper meaning of the custom be a reinforcement of

All three major contemporary perspectives try to answer the same question faced by Comte: How is society possible? Functional theorists follow Durkheim in focusing on such macrosystem features as value consensus and interdependence of system parts. Conflict theorists expand on Marx's insights about struggle among owners and nonowners and about the links between economic and political power and ideas. At the microlevel, symbolic interactionists build on Simmel's concepts of human sociability and Mead's analysis of the social act, and on the active, creative capacities of the human being.

Each model helps us understand some aspect of social life. Take the example of unemployment. A functional analysis would explain these rates in terms of the economic system's need for certain types

TABLE 1-1 Models of social theory

	Structural-Functional Model	Conflict Model	Symbolic-Interaction Model
Nature of Society	Integrated, interrelated social structures that together form a system	Competing groups and classes seeking to secure own ends	Interacting individuals, groups and social networks
Basis of Interaction	Consensus on values; shared values	Power, conflict, constraint	Shared meanings via shared symbols
Focus of Study	Social order and how society is maintained	Social change and conflict	Development of self-adaptation to group
Level	Social structure	Social structure	Interpersonal
Social Change	Orderly, moderate change	Change of power and structures of society	Changed meanings and symbols

of workers, on the one hand, and the supply of people with these skills, on the other. A conflict explanation would note that it is not lack of skill but of social power that determines who becomes unemployed and that serves the interests of those who have the jobs. In contrast, symbolic interaction studies would explore the meaning of unemployment to the individual and her/his family. How does a person deal with the identity of being unemployed; how does it affect one's self-image, or one's relationships?

As different as these perspectives are they are all sociological because of their central focus on structured interaction—among individuals, between groups, or across the major areas of social activity. Although no single theoretical model dominates the field today, we can still speak of *a* sociological perspective: a view of how humans behave because they live in groups. Rather than treating these theoretical positions as competing worldviews, the most interesting work in sociological theory today attempts to build bridges across the various models (e.g., Ritzer 1981, Collins 1985).

NEW DIRECTIONS IN SOCIOLOGICAL THEORY

Changes in sociological emphasis will continue to take place as younger scholars ("young Turks"), reflecting the concerns of their historical moment, replace older teachers (Page 1986). Thus, it appears that both the functional perspective, so dominant a few decades ago, and the conflict models of the 1960s may both have run their course. The two perspectives most popular with graduate students and younger sociologists today are ethnomethodology and the "new Marxism," a more complex and sophisticated version, modified by the history of the past 100 years (Burawoy 1982, Skocpol 1980).

Humanist Sociology. There is also a growing interest in *humanist sociology,* which is based on the belief that sociologists must become actively engaged in social change. Humanist sociologists reject the position that social science must or can be "value-free." They maintain that to make such a claim actually serves to reinforce existing inequality (Chap. 2). One's professional goal, they feel, is neither to build a personal reputation nor to search for abstract wisdom, but to use the tools of sociology for the benefit of those deprived of full participation in the society.

Their concern for social justice rather than social order has led most humanist sociologists to the symbolic interactionist perspective in research and to an emphasis on human capacities to resist, challenge, and change social structures. People are seen as active agents rather than as passive reactors. The prime movers behind the establishment of the Association for Humanist Sociology (AHS) in 1975 were Elizabeth Briant Lee and Alfred McClung Lee.

Feminist Sociology. Similar concerns have motivated *feminist* scholars who claim that positivism has produced a world view that separates the researcher from the subjects being studied and imposes the interpretation of the researcher (typically male, white, and middle class) on the actions of others. Thus, the voices of relatively powerless subgroups are either ignored or their experiences defined to fit a male model of appropriateness. Until recently, most research simply left women out, or assumed that they must share the same perceptions as men, or that they were somehow mentally deficient when they had other views. Over the past fifteen years, feminist sociologists have created their own professional organization, Sociologists for Women in Society; built a solid foundation of research on women; and have just launched a new scholarly journal, *Gender & Society.* Although feminist research has used the tools of positivism when necessary, the symbolic-interactionist mode of analysis has been most successful in giving women their own voices.

Anti-Sociological Theory. Throughout its brief history, the sociological viewpoint has been under attack by those who would reduce social life to individual behavior or to biology. We have already discussed the fallacy of using individual-level information to explain group-level phenomena. Another type of *reductionism,* also very popular in our society, comes from students of animal behavior who claim that humans are simply apes that are more developed than those found in zoos. While the differences between animal and hu-

Humanist sociology is based on the belief that sociologists must become actively involved in social change.

Reductionism involves reducing social life to individual behavior or biology.

Teaching Undergraduates About Sociology

THEODORE C. WAGENAAR

Theodore C. Wagenaar is Professor of Sociology at Miami University (Ohio). He took his Ph.D. and M.A. in Sociology at Ohio State University, and his B.A. at Calvin College. He holds elementary certification and has taught every grade from preschool through college. He is editor of Teaching Sociology *and has published in several social scientific and education journals.*

I have always loved teaching and learning about teaching. In college, I took all the coursework for elementary education certification, not necessarily to teach full-time but to better understand the process of becoming a teacher. I also wanted a perspective for understanding teaching and the educational process and structure in this country that was analytically based, not simply normatively or prescriptively based, as the educational perspective is. Most people, both in education and outside, use a psychological perspective to understand the teaching-learning process. Early on, I discovered that the sociological perspective provided a more holistic and structurally-based approach for understanding why people become teachers, why students act and think the way they do, and why schools have come to take on the structures that they have.

I went on to complete a Ph.D. in sociology, with a focus on sociology of education. For my dissertation, I studied the connection between school structure and effectiveness in the elementary schools in Detroit. Since that time, I have studied teacher militancy, school-community relations, the role of the high school counselor, and changes in high school students' values and attitudes. For the last several years, I have done studies for the U.S. Department of Education on changes in the occupations and college fields of study se-

lected by high school seniors, on the nature of students who stop with a high school diploma, and on the role of financial aid in postsecondary education choices. Currently, I am studying a national sample of high school sophomores to compare those who dropped out with those who graduated.

Throughout all my research, the sociological perspective has provided an approach for understanding how the social structures and situations teachers and students find themselves in substantially affect their decisions, actions, and attitudes. For example, research has shown that students drop out because of limited social connectedness to schools; that teachers become militant because of limited participation in decision-making and because of the limited professional status of teaching; and that counselors serve as tracking agents that reinforce traditional career choices among males and females.

In the last decade or so I have turned increasingly to the teaching process at the college level, particularly the teaching of sociology, as a focus of study. Why do professors teach the way they do? What do they know about their students? What factors affect how college students view their professors? What makes for effective lectures and discussions? How do professors and students define the social situation of the classroom? What sex differences exist in teaching and learning? How can professors be encouraged to analyze and improve their teaching? What are the effects on teachers and teaching of the recent national reports citing weaknesses in the college experience? The sociological perspective provides a unique and helpful lens through which to look at these and other education issues. For example, sociologists have discovered that regardless of the size of the college class, about 4–7 students

do most of the discussing. They have also discovered that male and female students are equally likely to say that the sex of the professor makes no difference in how much they talk in class. But when observed, females in classes taught by female teachers definitely do substantially more talking than females who are in classes taught by male teachers.

My persistent use of the sociological perspective and focus on the teaching process have enabled me to assist sociology professors to analyze, assess, and improve their teaching. It's always been surprising to me that professors are quick to use the research in their fields to answer questions on substantive issues such as race relations and organizational effectiveness. But when it comes to teaching, many are quick to say that good teachers are born, not made. They are reluctant to apply the analytical skills of their disciplines to the teaching-learning process, and they seem oblivious to a relatively sound research base on college teaching. My goal has been to present professors with research and analyses on college teaching that will help them to both better understand and improve their teaching. To that end, I have recently become the editor of *Teaching Sociology.*

Some of you may become teachers of sociology or teachers of something else. Teaching at the high school or elementary school level will require state certification. Teaching at the college level requires an advanced degree, typically the Ph.D., but no training in teaching itself. Even today, many Ph.D. programs provide little assistance in learning how to teach. If you make the decision to teach, maintain a very analytical and reflexive approach. Ask lots of "why" questions. As you learn more about teaching techniques, remember the importance of the sociological dimensions of the teaching-learning process.

Some of you may choose to study sociology but choose an occupation other than teaching. A sociology B.A. provides many opportunities in a variety of settings. Jobs held by sociology graduates include probation officer, marketing analyst, public relations specialist, community organizer, staff relations expert, advertising executive, group home administrator, government official, reporter, insurance investigator, attorney, and many others. A sociology degree provides a good background for many jobs requiring skillful interaction with people from various backgrounds and located in various social settings.

Biological determinism is based on the belief that biological factors explain differences in behavior by sex, race, religion, and ethnicity.

Sociobiology is the study of the inheritance of genetically determined behavior.

man behavior are examined in Chapters 3 and 5, it is appropriate to deal with theories of *biological determinism* in this introductory chapter. No matter how often or thoroughly discredited these theories are, a new one appears every decade or so, with the goal of demonstrating that built-in biological differences account for differing abilities between races, sexes, and religious or ethnic groups.

Sociobiology. The most technical theory to date of the inheritance of genetically determined behavior is *sociobiology* (Wilson 1975, Lumsden and Wilson 1981). Just as Darwin traced the evolution of physical characteristics, sociobiologists attempt to do the same for social behaviors. Briefly, this position claims that certain kinds of behaviors—aggression, male sexual dominance, female nurturance, for example—have maximized the survival of the animals or human beings that display them, and therefore, through reproduction over hundreds of thousands of years, these behaviors actually become encoded in the genetic material of the species. It follows, in the view of sociobiology, that these behaviors cannot be greatly modified by social influences except, perhaps, over long periods of time. All the supporting evidence for this theory has come from animal studies, and the leap from these to human behavior has been pure guesswork, a form of arguing by analogy or parallels.

When such claims are subject to careful testing by other scientists they have been found to be basically lacking in demonstrable fact (Lewontin, Rose, and Kamin 1984, Kitcher 1985). Thus, the interesting sociological question is why this theory has enjoyed such widespread success in the popular press. Why do Americans want to believe that human behavior is biologically determined and cannot easily be changed? From a sociology of knowledge perspective, this type of explanation of behavior fits the general climate of political and social conservatism that followed the 1960s. Sociobiology can be used to justify inequality by suggesting that gender and racial differences in achievement reflect genetic and not social structural factors. The theory also provides a rationalization for a greater emphasis on the self, for seeking to protect only one's own family members rather than to work for the welfare of others. In other words, the current popularity of sociobiology appears to be due more to its philosophical attractiveness than to the strength of its scientific basis.

To illustrate the difference between a sociobiological and a sociological interpretation, let us take the fact that the survival of every society requires that its members mate and have children. A sociobiologist would argue that because the people who originally paired off and produced offspring had a stronger inner drive to do so than did other people, their genes were reproduced more successfully, and that over time this has produced a fairly strong genetic tendency in humans toward reproductive behavior (stronger in females than males because they have to invest more in caring for the young). A sociologist would attribute the universality of marriage to social causes. People are taught from one generation to the next to want to marry and have children. Groups that do not figure out some way to motivate members to produce and care for infants will not survive. The tremendous variations in marriage and family customs from one society and one time period to another testify to the creativity and flexibility of human behavior. If mating and reproductive behavior were the result purely of genetic instincts, such variety would not exist.

We do not deny that biology and psychology—and even body chemistry—may affect human behavior. But whatever the direct effect of any of these factors, each person lives in a web of social relationships and an historical context that modify the expression of any act. *All human behavior is mediated* (shaped, channeled, influenced) by social systems. Even if there were such a thing as a mating gene it would not explain variations in marriage rates by education, religion, race, age, or nationality. The answers do not lie in the genes, or the brain, or in the phases of the moon, but in the structure of social life. And that is the subject matter of this book.

Summary

In this chapter we define the field of sociology and distinguish it from the other social sciences. The sociological perspective focuses on the totality of social life, the context of behavior, and the group level of reality (social facts).

The classical sociologists, from Harriet Martineau to George Herbert Mead, were briefly introduced, and their major contributions considered within the framework of the sociology of knowledge that locates thinkers in their historical context. Special attention was paid to the work of Karl Marx, Emile Durkheim, and Max Weber.

Turning to modern sociological theory, we detailed four major perspectives: (1) the *structural-functional* model associated with Talcott Parsons and Robert K. Merton; (2) the *conflict perspective* of a younger generation of neoMarxist scholars such as Theda Skocpol and Michael Burawoy; (3) *symbolic interaction* approaches, built on the work of George Herbert Mead and others concerned with interpersonal processes, including the unique perspectives of Erving Goffman and Harold Garfinkle; and (4) *humanist sociology,* exemplified in the writings of Alfred McClung Lee and Elizabeth Briant Lee.

The chapter touches upon the many women who helped shape the new science of society, especially those linked to the University of Chicago from 1890 to 1920, as well as those who are now producing feminist research and theory. Attention is also paid to antisociological models of self and society, primarily the contemporary emergence of sociobiology.

Suggested Readings

BART, PAULINE, and LINDA FRANKEL. *The Student Sociologist's Handbook,* 4th ed. New York: Random House, 1986. A useful guide for undergraduate and graduate students in sociology that includes chapters on writing term papers, conducting library research, finding appropriate periodicals, resource material, and government data, and using computers for your research.

COLLINS, RANDALL, and MICHAEL MAKOWSKY. *The Discovery of Society,* 3rd ed. New York: Random House, 1984. An articulate account of the development of sociological theory from eighteenth-century France to the contemporary United States, including analyses of the major contributions of Marx, Weber, Durkheim, Cooley, Mead, and Parsons.

FISHMAN, WALDA KATZ, and C. GEORGE BENELLO, eds. *Readings in Humanist Sociology: Social Criticism and Social Change.* Bayside, N.Y.: General Hall, 1986. A collection of the best articles from *Humanity and Society,* the Association for Humanist Sociology Journal.

FREEMAN, HOWARD E., RUSSELL R. DYNES, PETER H. ROSSI, and WILLIAM FOOTE WHYTE, eds. *Applied Sociology: Roles and Activities of Sociologists in Diverse Settings.* San Francisco: Jossey-Bass, 1983. An interesting look at the diverse settings in which sociologists work, including the military, corporate, environmental planning, etc.

GIDDENS, ANTHONY. *Sociology: A Brief But Critical Introduction.* New York: Harcourt Brace Jovanovich, 1983. A brief introduction to some of the major theoretical positions in sociology.

GOFFMAN, ERVING. *The Presentation of Self in Everyday Life.* Garden City, N.Y.: Doubleday/Anchor, 1959. A classic that introduces the dramaturgical perspective to the field of sociology.

HUBER, BETTINA J. *Embarking upon a Career with an Undergraduate Sociology Major.* Washington, D.C.: American Sociological Association, 1982. Useful information about career possibilities in sociology.

KARP, DAVID A., and WILLIAM C. YOELS. *Sociology and Everyday Life*. Itasca, Ill.: Peacock, 1986. A readable overview of sociology full of interesting examples and illustrations using the sociological perspective.

KENNEDY, ROBERT E., JR. *Life Choices: Applying Sociology*. New York: Holt, Rinehart & Winston, 1986. A very useful paperback that answers the question of "what can I get from studying sociology?" by taking readers on a journey through some major life choices, including education, occupation, marriage, parenthood, housing, and retirement.

LEE, ALFRED MCCLUNG. *Sociology for Whom?* 2nd ed. Syracuse, N.Y.: Syracuse University Press, 1986. A challenging call by the past president of the ASA to make sociology involved with the real issues facing humankind. Lee examines the control of sociology and outlines an agenda for humanist sociology.

STRAUS, ROGER H. *Using Sociology: An Introduction from the Clinical Perspective*. Bayside, N.Y.: General Hall Inc., 1985. This book is an introduction to social research methods with an emphasis on practical applications.

2

Doing Sociology

ITEM: In 1976, two doctors published an influential book entitled *Mother—Infant Bonding* (Klaus and Kennell 1976), in which they claimed that there was a crucial period just after childbirth when the newborn should have close physical contact with its mother ("skin-to-skin and eyeball-to-eyeball") in order to have the best chances of physical and emotional development. The book received highly favorable reviews in all the mass media; hundreds of thousands of women were advised to undergo "natural childbirth," so that they could guarantee lifelong advantages to their offspring, and many social scientists hailed this latest scientific evidence of the biological roots of human behavior (Rossi

1977). Yet, in an interview in 1983, the authors admitted that no studies conclusively confirmed either the existence of a critical period or the long-term positive effects of bonding (Brody 1983, Sluckin et al 1983).

Item: Contrary to commonly held beliefs and to some preliminary reports from a major study of schoolchildren, a closer look at the data showed that having divorced parents was not directly or strongly related to low grades (Zakariya 1982).

Item: Although it is generally thought that executives are under extreme occupational stress, heart disease statistics clearly indicate that people who do physical labor and have little control over their work, such as assembly-line workers, have the highest levels of job-related stress and are at the greatest risk for heart attacks (Thoerell and Schwartz 1982).

Item: Because, as you saw in Chapter 1, official statistics show that suicide rates are higher for males than for females, it is assumed that men are somehow more "suicide prone" than women. Yet, if suicide *attempts* were also counted, there would be no difference by sex (Kushner 1985). Females are just as likely as males to try to kill themselves, but they use less effective techniques (knives and pills rather than guns).

These are only four examples of how "common sense" understanding of behavior is influenced by what we would like to believe: that mothering is the key to child development; that divorce should have negative consequences for children; that high-level executives must be under great stress; and that femaleness is naturally associated with life-giving and life-preserving. Notice also how each of these taken-for-granted beliefs supports traditional views of maleness and femaleness and reinforces the existing systems of power and privilege (e.g. Arney 1980): women should stay home and be good mothers; couples ought to stay married; executives deserve their high salaries; men are reckless creatures who need women to tame their destructive tendencies.

The four items are also examples of flawed research. In the studies of infant-mother bonding, for example, the researchers followed only a few cases for a few months before generalizing about all mothers and many years of child development. The first study of divorce and school grades failed to compare single- and two-parent families at the *same* level of income, in which case the differences disappear. Children from low-income families, whether one- or two-parent, perform less well in school than do children from higher-income families, and most female-headed families are relatively poor (see Chapter 7). The original studies of job-related stress simply ignored lower-level employees or were based on information from heart disease specialists who rarely receive office visits from low-income workers. As soon as in-

formation became available from community-wide tests of blood-pressure readings, a more accurate picture emerged. And because official statistics count only completed suicides as testified to by medical authorities, it is possible that many female suicides are mislabeled by physicians who just do not believe that women take their own lives or that are hidden for the sake of respectability.

We must, therefore, carefully examine what we take for granted, where our assumptions come from, and what purposes they serve in legitimating the existing social order. The goal of sociological research is not only to examine the accuracy of our perceptions of reality, but also to suggest the sources of inaccuracy. In this chapter, we consider the need for research and sociology's claim to be a social "science." Then we describe various research strategies: the methods used to gather *data* (the plural of datum, a single piece of information) and the statistics used to describe the data. The chapter closes with a discussion of nonscientific factors in the research process, including the questions of values and of ethical considerations in social research.

Why We Do Research

Because much of sociology deals with everyday life, it might seem that personal observation would be the most accurate source of information. But, as the examples that open this chapter clearly demonstrate, it is precisely our ideas about what is natural or obvious that must be examined. Much of what we believe to be true is simply not correct. In later chapters you will find many more examples of commonly accepted wisdom that are not supported by data, including the following:

- In the past, most Americans grew up in three-generation households characterized by harmonious cooperation and affection (Chap. 11).
- Welfare supports large numbers of able-bodied males too lazy to seek employment (Chap. 7).
- Different races have different intellectual capacities (Chaps. 3, 14).
- The death penalty is a strong deterrent to violent crime (Chap. 16).

Statements like these assume cause-and-effect links that are actually questionable ("problematic") and must be systematically researched rather than accepted as given. It is also important to know why certain assumptions, if not supported by evidence, are nonetheless thought to be true. Why do members of different groups want to believe some things and not others?

Moreover, regardless of the truth of an assumption, those who believe it will behave as if it were true. This is the important sociological concept of the *definition of the situation.* As noted in Chapter 1, meaning is derived from the context of the interaction, and *what people believe to be real is real in its consequences.* If, for example, Americans come to believe that poor women have children in order to receive higher welfare benefits, few citizens will favor increases in such benefits. Thus, the belief has real consequences for these women and their families. In fact, because welfare mothers come into contact with social workers and family-planning information, they are *less* likely to have additional children than are equally poor women outside the welfare system (Moore and Burt 1982).

We do research, then, in order to understand the world about us and to make wise policy choices. How do sociologists investigate the relationships among social facts?

> **Definition of the situation** is a concept indicating that what people believe to be real is real in its consequences.

Ways of Knowing: Subjective and Objective

Human beings arrive at knowledge in both *subjective* and *objective* ways. *Subjective knowledge* comes from the individual's own frame of reference. Some things may be a matter of *faith* ("all things turn out for the best"); others appear to be based on personal *observation* ("kids aren't willing to work hard anymore"); and still other pieces of knowledge are matters of *intuition,* a gut feeling ("I know something just isn't right"). For researchers in the symbolic interaction tradition, these subjective modes of knowing are very important data. To understand how other people see things, we must make that imaginative leap into the mind of others that Max Weber called *Verstehen.* But subjective wisdom, while helpful in making sense of people's definitions of a situation, is

> **Subjective knowledge** derives from an individual's own frame of reference.

not always an accurate guide to broader social systems.

Furthermore, people may not always apply "common sense," even when accurate information is available. For example, although they know how it should be done and are well aware of the costs of ignoring such knowledge, how many of your classmates practice effective study habits or drive carefully? We suspect that you can add many other attitudes and behaviors to the list of things that people do despite "common sense" knowledge of their negative effects. Yet there have been occasions when the common perception has been *more* accurate than prevailing sociological opinion (Pease 1981). For example, in the past several decades, some sociologists have announced the end of political passion, the decline of nationality as an element in self-identity, and the disappearance of religion as a major force in modern life. On these topics, recent evidence (to be discussed in later chapters) indicates that ordinary people probably knew better than the "experts."

Nonetheless, the limitations of subjectivity make it an inappropriate mode of knowledge for the analysis of social facts at the group level of reality. The trend in modern sociology, therefore, is increasingly toward *objective* modes of knowing. Much contemporary research attempts to imitate the methods of such natural sciences as chemistry or physics. Although the rules of science are only one way of organizing knowledge, they are dominant in sociology today (Tudor 1982, Wallace 1983). But we should also realize that the natural sciences have never been free of conflict over which theories come to dominate the various fields (Pickering 1984).

THE SCIENTIFIC METHOD

Ideally, a scientist follows a set of procedures to ensure accuracy and honesty throughout the research process. The *scientific method,* in contrast to faith, common sense, and intuition involves (1) objective observations; (2) precise measurements; and (3) full disclosure of research techniques and results.

Objectivity. Scientists must, as far as possible, be aware of how their own attitudes, expectations, and values might affect their research. They must therefore try to recog-

> The **scientific method** consists of objective observations, precise measurement, and disclosure of results.

nize and then minimize the influence of these factors. They do this by attempting to be aware of the full range of factors involved in a situation and by using research methods that provide safeguards against simply fulfilling their own expectations.

But no method can totally eliminate researcher bias. Even under the most carefully controlled laboratory conditions, the researcher's expectations can affect the outcome of an experiment, as in Rosenthal's experiment where two sets of rats were bred to be the same. When some students were told that their lab animals were brighter than others, those rats ran the maze faster than did absolutely identical animals whose human managers expected them to be a bit slow (Rosenthal and Jacobson 1968).

How much more difficult, then, to measure human beings and their ever-changing thought process. Unlike boiling water, which registers the same temperature from one measurement to the next, people's attitudes and behaviors do not remain constant. For example, just asking someone a question for the first time can subtly influence that person's answer to the same question at a later date. If a researcher asks your opinion of a breakfast food or a presidential candidate, you must stop and think about it. The next time your opinion is sought, it will have been affected by your having already thought about it. There are many ways in which people change from one moment to the next, so that measurements in sociology can never be as exact or consistent as those in the natural sciences.

Precise Measurements. The goal of objectivity is supported by measurement devices that leave as little as possible to guesswork. Research *instruments* such as questionnaires, checklists, and interview forms, allow different observers to obtain similar information. One can thus compare or combine research results to arrive at statements that cover more than one observation at one time.

Deciding *what* to measure is the first problem faced by the researcher. Not everything can be measured directly, especially such abstract concepts as, for example, religiosity, satisfaction in marriage, or student activism. Something that can be counted must be selected to stand for the

Surveys can be conducted in several ways including person-to-person questioning. But in any survey, the quality of information obtained depends on the respondent's willingness to answer. (© Michal Heron/Woodfin Camp and Associates)

abstraction. The items that can be measured and counted are called *empirical referents,* meaning observable acts used as evidence of the abstract concept. In the case of "religiosity," researchers have used a number of empirical referents, including attendance at services (an objective measure) or feelings about the importance of religion in one's own life (a subjective referent). Figure 2-1, on page 30, diagrams these relationships.

There are two major problems in the use of empirical referents. One concerns *reliability:* Does the measuring instrument yield the same result on repeated trials? Reliability is tested by having different researchers use the same instrument in various settings and time periods. If the question, "How often do you attend religious services?" was asked in several separate studies, and similar percentages of respondents answered "weekly," "daily," or "only on major holidays," the question would appear reliable. But does the question really measure what it was designed to, in this case "religiosity"? This is the problem of *validity,* which can be tested by using another set of questions that show the same response pattern. That way you can see if people high or low on one measure are similarly placed on another.

Reliability and validity are never assured; they are goals to which a researcher

Empirical referents are items that can be measured and counted.

Reliability refers to whether the measuring instrument yields the same results on repeated trials.

Validity refers to whether the measuring instrument is really measuring what it was designed to.

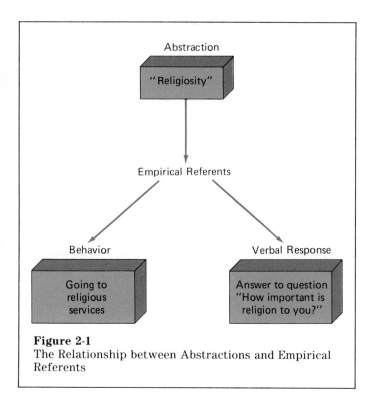

Figure 2-1
The Relationship between Abstractions and Empirical Referents

Full Disclosure. It is a scientific duty to make one's research materials fully available to colleagues. Every published report must provide information on who was studied (the research subjects), what was measured and how, and the statistical procedures used to generate the findings. Researchers should be willing to provide additional information to those who might question the data or seek to replicate the study. In the example described above, other researchers might wish to know how old the sample was (on the average) or if job satisfaction had been measured, two factors that could influence the results as much as having children.

The Science in Social Science

Researchers have had varying success in using the scientific method to explore social life. Every study is somewhat flawed for reasons already mentioned: the essential changeability of human beings, problems of reliability and validity, and the impossibility of total objectivity. Yet sociology is often called a "social science" (along with psychology, political science, and economics). How valid is this claim to scientific certainty?

The basic problem in social science is that when one group of human beings sets out to study other humans, the likelihood of error or misinterpretation exists on *both* sides: in the researcher's bias, and in the possibility that the research subject is responding to cues that the observer overlooks or misunderstands. These difficulties have led some sociologists to suggest that the use of the term "social scientist" implies an exactness that cannot be supported. Nonetheless, the royal road to fame and fortune in contemporary sociology is through *quantitative research,* with all the features of scientific objectivity, including the use of extremely complex statistical techniques.

There are a number of reasons why many sociologists prefer to be thought of as social scientists. Science is associated with numbers and we tend to equate numbers with "hard facts." Think of all the television commercials that feature a man in a white coat pointing to a colorful chart showing that Brand X is 60 percent more

Replication involves repeating a specific study, often with different types of respondents in various settings and at other times.

A sample is a selection from the entire population of interest.

aims. How close one has come to achieving precision and accuracy are for other researchers to decide. One way to test accuracy is to repeat a given study. Such *replication* of research involves using the same research instruments to measure other respondents in various settings and at other time periods.

To provide greater assurance that precise and objective results will be obtained the researcher must also ask questions of or observe the appropriate group of people or *sample.* For instance, suppose one wishes to test the prediction that working women with children will experience more stress than those without children. After designating the empirical referents for feelings of stress (e.g., sleeplessness, reported feelings of anxiety) the researcher must ask who and where are these "working women." It would be impossible, for reasons of time and money, to study the entire population of working women. The researcher will instead sample a portion of it. She might choose, for example, women who work in clerical positions, live in Detroit, and have two children, comparing them to women in the same occupations in Detroit who have no children. (Sampling is discussed in greater detail later in this chapter.)

Quantitative research utilizes scientific objectivity, including complex statistical techniques.

powerful than its nearest competitor, or those automobile ads that measure the capacity of an engine down to the last cubic centimeter. Even though these "authorities" are actors or models, the impression of scientific support for such claims leads buyers to choose one detergent or car over another.

Furthermore, the use of statistics is associated with intellectual toughness (note how often we speak of "hard" facts) in contrast to ideas or impressions (referred to as "soft" data). Numbers are seen as masculine; verbal descriptions as feminine; and in almost all societies, masculinity is highly valued and associated with power (Chap. 8). The idea that the goal of science is to "conquer" nature also reflects a male/female distinction that gives added prestige to scientific claims (Keller 1985, Sayers 1987).

Qualitative research relies primarily on verbal descriptions rather than statistics.

As a consequence of these general beliefs among professionals as well as the public, *qualitative research* that depends on verbal descriptions is frequently ignored and seldom published in the leading journals, even in the field of family studies where feelings, emotions, and intimacy are central topics of examination (LaRossa and Wolf 1985). The belief that quantitative work is more rigorous and "true" than qualitative studies is based on the assumption that scientists can be absolutely impartial and objective. Yet recent work in the sociology of science demonstrates how the researcher's own beliefs and values influence the questions asked, the conclusions arrived at, and the language in which the findings are reported (Keller 1985).

In addition, humanist sociologists would argue, it is not only impossible but undesirable for researchers to consider themselves as something apart from the people whom they are studying; this implies a separateness and superiority by treating research subjects as "others." All researchers, they assert, should be aware of how their own attitudes and beliefs have influenced the way in which they view the world and interpret what they see there. To be objective should mean to recognize one's own biases.

Finally, we must recognize that qualitative studies can also be designed for precision as well as for closeness to the reality of everyday life (Goetz and Le Compte 1984, Hammersley and Atkinson 1983). Is a videotaped encounter any less real than a statistic?

Issues of scientific and nonscientific factors in social research will become clearer as we follow the research process from its origins in theory to its ultimate presentation to colleagues.

The Research Process

Five major steps make up the research process:

1. Selecting and framing the research question
2. Choosing the appropriate time frame and method
3. Gathering the data
4. Analyzing the material
5. Drawing conclusions and reporting the findings.

Americans have great faith in experts, particularly scientists and doctors in white lab coats projecting authority. Is this man a scientist or a well-rehearsed actor? (© Charles Harbutt/Archive Pictures, Inc.)

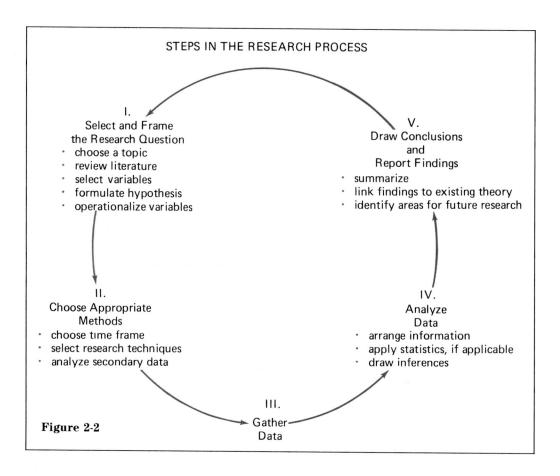

STEPS IN THE RESEARCH PROCESS

I.
Select and Frame
the Research Question
· choose a topic
· review literature
· select variables
· formulate hypothesis
· operationalize variables

V.
Draw Conclusions
and
Report Findings
· summarize
· link findings to existing theory
· identify areas for future research

II.
Choose Appropriate
Methods
· choose time frame
· select research techniques
· analyze secondary data

IV.
Analyze
Data
· arrange information
· apply statistics, if applicable
· draw inferences

III.
Gather
Data

Figure 2-2

Each step involves choices, sometimes dictated by the researcher's conceptual model, and sometimes by practical considerations such as the availability of subjects, funding, and the time needed to do the work. Thus, compromises and selectivity, as well as other nonscientific elements, affect the research process from the very beginning.

WHAT TO STUDY

Step 1: Deciding what to study may be the most nonscientific step of all because researchers are often influenced by their own values in selecting a research topic. The choice of what to study, today, is further complicated by the problem of funding. The more complex the research design, the more financial support is necessary for data gathering and analysis. As few schools can afford to underwrite such expenses, researchers are increasingly dependent on applying for grants from foundations, private research firms, corporations, and government agencies. But this means that one studies what the funding organizations want to know more about. Even so, American scholars still enjoy relative freedom in selecting research topics (Richter 1985). In many countries, this is not the case. Sociology was one of the first disciplines to fall under political control in Nazi Germany and the Soviet Union.

As a mental exercise, ask yourself what questions about social life you would want to explore. Your choice will be influenced by a particular view of the world and what makes it tick. Because most sociologists are interested in the connection between one social fact and another—for example, between receiving welfare and bearing children—think of two social facts that you suspect are related. In our example, the two facts being examined are: (1) whether or not a woman receives welfare and (2) her history of childbearing. These are called *variables* (factors that differ from one group to another or that change over time) in contrast to *constants* (characteristics that do not change from one person or time to another). It is a constant that humans must eat to stay alive, but what they eat, how often, with whom, and

Variables are characteristics that differ from one person or group to another and change over time.

Constants are characteristics that do not change from one person to another and do not change over time.

the meanings attached to food are all variables.

Notice that in this mental exercise you began with *theory* (Chap. 1), which is a conceptual model of how social life is constructed: "If the world works the way I think it does, how would the variables of interest be linked?" This question leads from general theory to specific guesses about the relationship among variables. Such guesses are called *hypotheses* (*hypothesis* in the singular). Because an hypothesis is a specific statement—for example, "if variable Y changes in a given direction, variable X will also change in a predictable way"—it can be tested with evidence gathered from systematic observation.

Before undertaking your own research, however, it is important to conduct a *search of the literature* to find out what is already known about your topic. It may be that your question has been so thoroughly researched that further study is pointless, like reinventing the wheel. More often, the literature search reveals inconsistencies in previous findings. These inconsistencies could guide you to a key aspect of the question that might clarify the previous work and even break new ground. In addition, the literature search today has been vastly simplified by the existence of computerized reference banks.

Having thus clarified your research question, you are now in a position to construct specific hypotheses about how change in one variable may be related to change in another. This relationship is referred to as the *correlation* between or among variables. Knowing, for example, that early marriage is associated with the likelihood of divorce, could lead to the prediction that as the average age at first marriage goes up, the society's divorce rate should level off (all other factors remaining the same). This has been happening recently in the United States (see Chapter 11).

In framing the research question, one's theory also suggests which variable is most likely to cause change in the other. *Independent variables* are those thought to have the greatest impact on the topic under study, or to come first in any chain of events, or to be relatively fixed (but all variables have more than one category or there would be no variation). Typical independent variables in sociological research are age, sex, race, and religion—characteristics that are given rather than chosen. As the word implies, an independent variable stands alone.

Dependent variables, in contrast, are assumed to be influenced by (dependent on) differences in the independent variable. When, for example, we find that whites are more likely than blacks in our society to have a college degree, we conclude that education is the dependent variable and race the independent. It would be difficult to argue that a college education leads to being black or white!

But what in the real world will you measure? As we noted in the discussion of empirical referents, your variable of interest

Hypotheses are specific statements derived from a theory about relationships among variables.

Correlation refers to the effect of one variable on another, how change in one is related to change in another.

Independent variables have the greatest impact, come first in the chain of events *and/or* are relatively fixed.

Dependent variables are influenced by independent variables.

Everything in this scene can be the subject matter of sociology—the people, the quality of the housing, even the grafitti in the wall mural. (© Chuck Fishman/Woodfin Camp and Associates)

must be translated into something that can be observed, counted, measured. This translation is called *operationalizing* the variables. For example, while you might have a clear idea of what constitutes family violence or unemployment, these are by no means simple to measure. Where exactly is the line between some parents' conception of child discipline and abusive behavior? How many weeks or months of nonwork equals "unemployment"? How would you operationalize such abstract variables as "life satisfaction" or "prejudice"? What would you choose to measure? And how could you solve the problem of validity? Each researcher must defend these choices and be prepared for challenges.

Operationalizing the variables translates the abstract into something observable.

DESIGNING THE STUDY

Step 2: In general, the research question dictates the appropriate method for gathering data to test the hypotheses derived from theory. Much depends on whether the information must come from a large number of people or from a particular subgroup; on whether the topic is sensitive or not; and on whether follow-up studies will be needed to measure change, that is, the *time frame* of the study.

Time Frames. *Cross-sectional studies* take place at one time only and can be thought of as slices of life. At a given moment, this is how different kinds of people behaved or responded. The cross-sectional study is like a snapshot, capturing the events of a moment. For information on process and changes—a moving picture, so to speak—we need several cross-sectional studies conducted at different times.

Cross-sectional studies take place at one time only.

Panel or *longitudinal studies* follow a group of respondents over time. It is not always easy to keep track of people for long periods, and those who remain in the study could be quite different from those who drop out, so that the value and the accuracy of the findings may be reduced.

Longitudinal studies follow a group of respondents over time.

With these considerations in mind, let us describe the major research methods of contemporary sociology.

Surveys. The large-scale social *survey* (or *poll*) is designed to yield data from a *representative sample* of respondents. Because it is usually impossible to question each member of the population of inter-

Surveys or polls yield information from a large group of respondents.

est—all voters, for instance, or college students, or hospital employees—some selection is necessary. This smaller group is called a *sample,* and it can be considered representative of the larger population when selected through random sampling.

Random sampling occurs when all possible respondents have an equal chance of being selected. A scientifically selected subgroup drawn from this population is a sample that, within certain statistical limits, reflects the distribution of characteristics in the larger population. Common *random selection* techniques include pulling names from a rotating drum or picking every hundredth (or fifth or tenth) name from a directory. Contrary to its popular usage, the concept of *randomness* in sociology refers to a precise procedure of sample selection.

Random sampling occurs when all possible respondents have an equal chance of being selected.

The survey researcher presents this sample with a pretested set of questions designed to tap the relevant variables. This can be done by mail, telephone, or personal visits, each of which has pros and cons in terms of cost, time, and response rate. In any survey, the amount and quality of information gathered depend on the respondents' willingness to answer. These

Lotteries are based on the process of *random selection,* which gives each player an equal chance of being selected; the probability of winning, however, is very low. For example, your chance of winning the top cash prize in the New York State lottery is 1 in 12,271,512. (© Barbara Rios/Photo Researchers, Inc.)

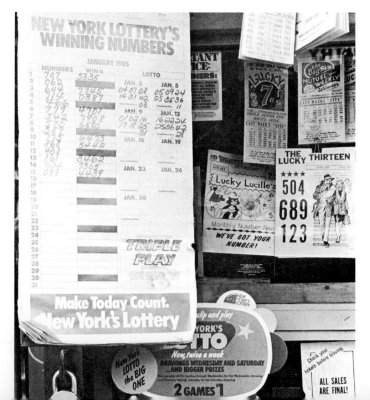

limitations, however, are balanced by the sample survey's advantages in scale and representativeness. Much information can be gathered from many people in a short time, and if the sample is randomly selected, the findings can be generalized to the larger population.

A NEGATIVE EXAMPLE. The best example of how *not* to conduct a survey remains the *Literary Digest* presidential opinion poll of 1936. The magazine sent ten million ballots to people whose addresses could be found in telephone directories, and it received two million responses. On the basis of this 20 percent return rate, the *Digest* confidently predicted the election of Republican Alfred Landon over Democrat Franklin D. Roosevelt, who actually won the November election by one of the largest majorities in history. How had the *Digest* erred so enormously? To begin with, only one-third of American households had telephones in 1936, and these were likely to be homes of the well-to-do, who typically supported Republican candidates. Second, the people who returned the ballots were a self-selected minority who felt very strongly about Landon's election. This negative example illustrates three important principles of research: selecting a sample appropriate to the research question; guarding against the self-selection of respondents; and understanding the characteristics of the total population of interest.

In the decades since the *Literary Digest* fiasco, political polling has become a fine art. The three largest private survey firms—Roper, Gallup, and Louis Harris—regularly predict, within a few percentage points, the outcomes of national elections—each using a base of approximately 1500 randomly selected respondents. The two major political parties are constantly conducting opinion surveys to find out what issues are important to voters and how their candidates are perceived, usually with samples of less than 1000. In fact, the outcome of an election is often known by the participants on the evening before the voting booths are open.

LOADING THE QUESTIONS. To evaluate the findings of survey data, however, it is important to look closely at the way in which the questions are worded. Questionnaires prepared by groups with a specific goal, such as political parties, labor unions, or business organizations, often contain "loaded" questions designed to produce certain responses. For example, an organization called Citizens for Tax Justice, a labor-oriented group working against tax breaks for business, circulated a questionnaire with the following question: "Do you agree or disagree that large corporations should start paying their fair share of taxes before there are any increases in any taxes that ordinary working and middle-income Americans pay?" Conversely, the United States Chamber of Commerce, a business-oriented organization, asked its respondents: "Should Congress enact a tax bill that could hobble economic growth?" (*New York Times,* Apr. 3, 1986: A24).

More commonly, the wording is subtle, acting as a "red flag" that brings particular feelings to the surface. For example, a random-sample survey by a government agency found that the phrase "public welfare" headed the list of services that respondents would cut most severely if government budgets had to be tightened. But most people in the same survey would also place "aid to the needy" ahead of support for colleges, parks, and highway repair. Because public welfare *is* aid to the needy, these responses actually tapped public reaction to the word "welfare" (*New York Times,* Feb. 14, 1983).

Interviews. Sometimes, a large representative sample is not necessary, especially if one is conducting exploratory or *pilot* research before designing a larger study, or if one is seeking intimate information. In these circumstances, a small and nonrepresentative sample is sufficient. Nonrepresentative samples are also appropriate for studies that do not refer to the general public, such as research on influential members of a community. In this case only ***key respondents*** need be interviewed (Merton 1949).

Often, one or two carefully selected cases can provide information on processes that are not easily visible to an observer but are thought to have universal application. Such ***case histories*** are more common in psychology, and particularly psychiatry, than in sociology, although case histories can add the flavor of real life to survey data. For some researchers, especially those in the tradition of ethnomethodology (Chap. 1), an intensive examination of one or a few cases is the only valid method for uncovering the taken-for-granted world. This technique was used by Craig Castleman to study several groups of

Key respondents are carefully selected cases providing information on processes not easily visible but having general application.

Case histories provide in-depth information from a few cases.

The Graffiti Writer

Writers in general are not humble. They tend toward exaggeration when talking of their own abilities and status in the graffiti world, particularly when talking to outsiders or lesser writers. A notable exception to this tendency is the behavior of famous writers, who generally exhibit the sort of quiet dignity that is considered appropriate to those of high position.

Because slow-moving writers tend to get caught by subway conductors or the police, most writers are fast runners. And most possess the physical ability necessary for climbing high fences, vaulting subway turnstiles, or shimmying down el pillars. There are exceptions. OZ, a chubby and slow-moving fifteen-year-old writer, compensated for his lack of speed by wearing a dark blue MTA-regulation-style raincoat and carrying his paint in an attache case whenever he went to the yards. According to Blood Tea, "When a raid came down OZ would just walk away, slowly. Nobody ever stopped him."

Writers frequently have an interest in art. Many develop skills in drawing through their work in the black books, and writers frequently express a desire to go on to careers as cartoonists or animators. They take a greater interest in techniques of illustration, photography, calligraphy, printing, and painting than many other people their age. Writers sometimes are interested in art history, seeking inspiration for new designs for their pieces in art books and museums. In the case of Lee and Fred, such study resulted in a strong feeling of identification with artists of the past. Lee has said:

> I was reading this fat history of art book. I was reading about how the cave men were so advanced

that when they drew animals to show their children how to hunt and to show their type of culture, they knew they couldn't do them in the front of the cave but went to the deepest depths of the cave where they had to crawl. And they'd do it where it would stay forever. And it was like us. Like we go into the tunnels and we'd go all the way to the deepest parts to find the trains and maybe you leave a signature on the wall and it stays there for years. And when you go into the tunnels you say, "Wow, look at that Cliff, look at that IN, look at that Phase." You go into some of those lay-ups. You see a lot of big Cliff pieces and old pieces back there. I look at those pieces and it's like serious.

Many graffiti writers believe that they are beautifying the city with their train painting and consider their writing a public service. Police officer Lesnewski has quoted one captured writer as saying, "You can cut both my hands, you can cut both my arms off, I'll still paint the trains every day because I owe it to the people of New York City to make these trains beautiful."

Although they have much in common with other city kids, graffiti writers as a community are more remarkable for their differences. In a much-fragmented city, writers are among the few young people to reach beyond the bounds of their own neighborhoods and travel throughout the city, meeting and getting to know young people from other boroughs and a variety of ethnic and economic groups.

SOURCE: Craig Castleman. *Getting Up: Subway Graffiti in New York.* Cambridge, Mass.: MIT, 1982, pp. 69–71.

graffiti writers in New York City. Excerpts from his book *Getting Up* demonstrate how the development of confidence and trust between researchers and subjects can produce an intimate view of the subject's world.

Observation and Participant Observation.
Survey and interview data can tell us only what people *say* they do. How can we study what people actually do? Observation is time-consuming, and only a limited number of people and occasions can be studied. Nor can an observer see everything: each of us perceives selectively, tending to recognize what we expect to be

there and overlooking the unexpected. Because the observer must also be careful not to disrupt the activity being examined, observations are confined to places where a researcher will be unnoticed or taken for granted. Otherwise, people might act as they wish to be seen rather than as they would without such self-consciousness.

Many of these observational barriers are reduced when the researcher can become part of the interaction under study, but *participant observation* has its hazards. It may take a long time before the participant observer is fully accepted and the other people behave naturally. There is also the ethical question of furthering

In **participant observation** the researcher becomes part of the interaction under study.

your career by using material gained from those whom you have asked to trust you. Researchers who have used this method typically "debrief" their subjects when the study is completed, asking them to read and comment on the material gathered. There is, however, no way to measure the extent to which the participant observer has subtly changed the group and its interactions.

The classic participant observation study in American sociology was conducted by William Foote Whyte (1943/1984), over four decades ago in a working-class area of Boston. Whyte spent three-and-one-half years hanging out with the "Corner Boys," observing the complex patterns of social relations in what contemporary sociologists had written off as "disorganized slums." At first, Whyte told his subjects that he was writing a book about the history and customs of the area—which was not the full truth. As the research continued, Whyte became more open about what he was doing, but by then, he was fully accepted by most members of the community.

Participant observation has been used most successfully in studying people and places not readily accessible to the general public, and in examining "from the inside" what might not be obvious to an outside observer. Recent participant-observational studies include such diverse settings as a working-class tavern (LeMasters 1975), an illegal abortion clinic (Schlesinger and Bart 1981), medical school (Light 1980), the world of night workers (Robboy 1983), and the Unification Church (Selengut 1983).

For all the difficulties of this method, and the amount of time and emotional energy spent on one small area of activity, participant observation yields the richest type of data: that based on authentic, spontaneous reactions; natural gestures; and all the little details of daily life.

Secondary Analysis. Surveys, interviews, and observations all generate original data—new information. Yet libraries are stocked with material that has already been gathered and can be reused. ***Secondary analysis*** refers to the use of information collected by others.

OFFICAL DATA. The United States government alone produces volumes of information every day; in fact, the United States Government Printing Office is the world's largest publisher. Of special value are the census data gathered from American households every ten years, as well as yearly or monthly random sample surveys on employment, income, family characteristics, housing, voting, and so forth. Each department of government also produces the information needed to plan and evaluate its own programs.

Although the Bureau of the Census and other government agencies have a tradition of being protected from political interference, various adminstrations can influence what topics are covered by special reports and how often certain kinds of data are published. For example, the Reagan Administration was criticized for its plan to stop publishing the government's yearly report on after-tax income (which had shown the rich getting richer, contrary to administration claims). Even though the Bureau of the Census said the Reagan plan was only an effort to cut costs (*New York Times,* July 9, 1985:A16), the report was subsequently issued as usual.

Another potential problem with official statistics arises from the way in which answer categories are constructed. For example, in both Australia and the United

Secondary analysis involves the use of data collected by others.

Official data are collected by government agencies.

Anthropologists often use ethnomethodological techniques. Margaret Mead, shown here talking with one of her respondents on Bali, was an American anthropologist who pioneered in the field. (© Ken Heyman/Gian and Company)

Participant Observation in the Undocumented Community

Nestor P. Rodriguez

Nestor Rodriguez is Assistant Professor of Sociology at the University of Houston and Director of a field study of undocumented Central American migrants in Houston. He has received Ford Foundation grants to study the housing conditions of Hispanics in the U.S. and was an American Sociological Association Minority Fellow from 1976–1980. He has published articles and presented papers about various aspects of Hispanic life in the U.S.

My first experience with fieldwork on undocumented migrants occurred when I joined a field study of undocumented Mexican workers in San Antonio in the summer of 1978. I saw the study as an opportunity to supplement the historical approach I planned to utilize in my Ph.D. dissertation on international labor migration. Just as important at the time, it was an opportunity to earn an income while in graduate school at the University of Texas at Austin.

Unlike historical research, in a field study you meet the people ("subjects") you are studying. When dealing with clandestine populations like undocumented migrant workers this can be a special problem. Entering the country without official permission, undocumented workers are at risk of being detected and apprehended by agents of the Immigration and Naturalization Service (INS). Thus, these workers can be timid about revealing their presence and conditions (e.g., work) of their stay in the United States.

In San Antonio the research crew sought to minimize this problem by recruiting a person who was familiar to many undocumented workers. This central contact person introduced project interviewers to many undocumented workers, employers, and to others who were also familiar with the life experiences of undocumented workers in San Antonio. By the end of the summer, the project met its goal of 100 interviews, with findings of the migrant workers' generally low-paying jobs and low-income life patterns.

The research experience gained in the 1978 study led to the formulation of a larger and more intensive field study of undocumented Mexican workers in Austin in the period 1980–1982. This new field study, however, was initially and methodologically impacted by the concern to help alleviate the problem within Austin's community of undocumented persons, namely that undocumented children would not be permitted by the state to attend public schools.

Even before funding was secured for the research, another field investigator and I planned and organized an "alternative school" for undocumented children in the neighborhood where we anticipated launching the study. After talking with numerous community leaders, we obtained two classrooms in an unused church school, a truckload of bilingual teaching materials from a publishing company that was going out of business, and several teachers who volunteered to work part-time in the alternative school.

Once all the resources were in place, the opening of the school was announced at religious services in a neighborhood church. Since we feared publicizing the school to the extent that it would get the attention of the INS, only a couple of announcements were made, and, thus, we expected only a few children for the first day of class; fifty showed up. Apparently word about the alternative school had spread through social networks of the undocumented community.

While the school was primarily started to help provide an education for undocumented children, it became a key means to gain a research entry into the undocumented community. The study's interviewers, who were heavily identified with the school, gained instant confidence from the undocumented community and direct access to the families of the students. In trying to help obtain health and other services for the children, interviewers interacted intensively with the children's families, achieving an excellent vantage point for the study's focus on the migrants' household and community development.

The interviewers' presence and participation in the undocumented community were further expanded when the undocumented children were finally admitted into public schools, and we converted the school into a program of reading and writing night classes for undocumented workers, many of whom were the parents of our former students. Undocumented workers, men and women, who in our night sessions learned how to write their names became eager supporters of our study of their undocumented migration experiences. By the end of the project's funding in 1983, we had obtained lengthy, detailed observations of sixty undocumented family households, which included 262 household members.

After finishing my dissertation in 1984, I left Austin for a job at the University of Houston. Being a major center in the petro-chemical industry of the world economy, Houston held an even greater attraction for immigrant labor than Austin or San Antonio. My exploratory excursions throughout the city indicated a large presence of Mexican and Central American undocumented migrants. Having already spent over three years in undocumented Mexican research and given the growing importance of Central America for this country, I decided to focus my field research in Houston on the undocumented Central American population, estimated by some observers to number over 100,000 in the metropolitan area.

Starting the fieldwork without funds to hire interviewers, I sought out community organizations that offered services to the many refugees in the undocumented Central American population. This approach, I thought, would put me in contact with many undocumented Central Americans in a few places. From there I could branch out into the undocumented Central American communities through a snowball sample, each person leading me to others.

In my initial contacts with community organizations offering legal, housing, and other services to the undocumented Central Americans, I introduced myself as a sociologist doing an exploratory study of undocumented Central Americans in the city and asked about opportunities to meet some migrants. All community organization directors agreed to my request and promised to call me when they found clients who were willing to be interviewed. I waited for a week at home for the

calls that would start my fieldwork, but the calls did not come.

I realized that the undocumented Central American population presented an added problem in terms of access for research. Unlike undocumented Mexican immigrants, many of those from Central America came from areas of political violence in El Salvador and Guatemala. They feared being associated with political events back home. With this apprehension, it was easy to suspect a sociologist of being a government agent sent to inform on the political attitudes of the migrants. (Informants were common back home and caused many deaths.)

I decided to gain the confidence of leaders in the undocumented Central American communities by planning a small newspaper project that would report on topics and issues important to undocumented Central Americans in the city. One grassroots refugee organization adopted the project, and I quickly found myself accepted by most of the organizational network in the undocumented Central American communities.

With this organizational support, I contacted and interviewed many undocumented Central Americans (Salvadorans, Guatemalans, Hondur-

ans, etc.) and eventually developed a snowball sample of forty migrants in three undocumented communities. For many of the migrants in the sample I acted as an intermediary when they needed to deal with such English-based institutions as hospitals, their children's schools, and courts. The snowball sample became the basis of extending the research to 260 interviews when I obtained funding for a research crew.

There are several approaches to field research. Besides other factors, they differ in the degree to which the researcher interacts with the population under study. Among undocumented immigrants, it has been my experience that the richest observations are made while participating with immigrants in community and household activities. Given the cultural differences and lower socioeconomic conditions of undocumented immigrants, there is a constant need for persons who are knowledgeable about United States society to play an intermediary function between them and the larger host community. This niche provides an exceptional opportunity for participant observation, as well as for accomplishing reciprocity in the research process.

States, in the nineteenth century, the proportion of married women engaged in paid work or production within the household was consistently *undercounted* because the wording of the census classified them as primarily "homemakers" (Deacon 1985, Bose 1987).

Useful information is also gathered by business and trade groups, including labor unions. There is very little in this country that has not been counted at least once by some organization.

HISTORICAL RECORDS. Another type of secondary analysis uses the past as a basis for comparison. Which relationships among variables are relatively constant and which are modified as a society changes over time? The answers lie in letters, archives, and other historical papers. Among the classic works of sociology

is the enormous study *The Polish Peasant in Europe and America,* by W. I. Thomas and Florian Znaniecki (1918–19, 1984) mentioned in Chapter One, who used as primary material the letters exchanged between family members who remained in Poland and those who emigrated to America.

CONTENT ANALYSIS. Books, newspapers, and magazines are often used as source material for *content analysis,* which is a careful counting of how often particular images, words, or ideas appear. From the content analysis, the researcher can test hypotheses about values or social change, for example, trends in sexual behavior between 1940 and 1985, or in the portrayal of women and blacks in the media.

COMPARATIVE STUDIES. A powerful method of testing the universality of rela-

Historical records such as documents, papers, and letters identify relationships among variables over time.

Content analysis counts the number of references to a given item in a sample of publications.

Research can now be done "online" by retrieving information via computer and mod from electronic databases such as Sociological Abstracts. In this photo Miriam Chall, co-founder (with Leo Chall) of Sociological Abstracts, accesses the database. (© Richard Elkins, 1987)

tionships among variables is to compare different societies. Information on other cultures, especially preindustrial and preliterate societies, is contained in *The Ethnographic Atlas* and *Human Relations Area Files* at selected universities, but available to all scholars. These sources provide ready access to anthropological material, coded and indexed for *cross-cultural comparisons* (see Chapter 3).

A favorite topic for cross-cultural comparisons is the generality of sex-linked behaviors. Some researchers, finding a fairly similar division of labor across many societies, have concluded that basic biological and personality differences between men and women account for these social patterns and for the seeming universality of male dominance. More recently, feminist scholars have examined the comparative literature for information specifying the conditions under which women have more or less power. An examination of degrees of difference shifts attention from inflexible characteristics to those social situations that have undergone historical change. Sanday (1981), for example, compared over 150 societies and concluded that male dominance is not an ingrained aspect of human relations but a way of

dealing with survival problems, conflicts, and emotional stresses, which vary from one society to another.

LIMITATIONS OF SECONDARY ANALYSIS. Using available data, although often a great saver of time and money, has certain disadvantages. As the information was originally collected for other purposes, the data are sometimes incomplete, or have been biased by the original researcher, or are in a form inappropriate for use by the secondary analyst.

Experiments. Of all the methods described in this section, *experiments* are the closest to the scientific ideal. The essence of the experimental design is *control over the variables,* a requirement that also makes it the least appropriate and the least used method for sociologists. In everyday life, such control over people or a situation is impossible because behavior stems from the interpretations that people bring to the situation and then modify during the interaction. Yet experimental research, however artificial, *can* clarify relationships that are not easily identified in everyday observation. See Figure 2-3 for a classic experimental design.

THE CLASSIC EXPERIMENT. As described by Riley (1963, p. 612), "the controlled experiment is a powerful design for testing hypotheses of causal relationships among variables. Ideally. . .the investigator throws into sharp relief the explanatory variables. . .[while] controlling or manipulating the independent variable (X), observing its effect on the dependent variable (Y), and minimizing the effects of the extraneous variables." *Extraneous variables* are those that are outside the hypothesis, but that, because they can affect the findings, must be controlled through sample selection:

1. The classic experiment begins with subjects assigned to groups that are as similar as possible in all factors likely to affect the results. This similarity is achieved by matching subjects (by age, sex, or some other variable of possible importance) and then assigning them to one group or another through random selection.
2. Members of both groups are then measured on the dependent variable, an attitude or behavior that the researcher thinks will be influenced by the introduction of the independent variable.

Cross-cultural comparisons examine relationships among variables in different societies.

Experiments come closest to the scientific ideal of control over variables.

Extraneous variables are outside the stated hypothesis.

3. The independent variable, or *causal factor,* is introduced to *one sample only.* This sample becomes the *experimental group* (E), and the sample from which the factor is withheld becomes the *control group* (C).

4. At a later date, members of the experimental and control groups are again measured on the dependent variable. Changes between Time 1 and Time 2 are compared. Any group differences on the dependent variable can then be attributed to the manipulation of the independent variable.

Such a design is most easily carried out where the researcher can control all extraneous elements, as in a social-science laboratory. Experiments are more difficult to conduct in the everyday world, but *field experiments* are possible. For example, social psychologists have devised numerous field experiments to test helping behavior, that is, why people return lost wallets or help someone in distress. In these studies, the causal factor is varied— as when a "victim," thought to be bleeding (red liquid) was helped less often, less quickly, and less directly than one whose collapse was bloodless (Piliavin and Piliavin 1972). If there is a basic similarity in subjects, a control group is not needed because what is crucial is the manipulation of the experimental situation.

> **Field experiments** are designed by social scientists and conducted in the everyday world.

There are also **natural experiments** in which the same population is measured before and after an event that changes their situation, such as a natural disaster or a new law. Studies of the effect of capital punishment often compare murder rates in a state before and after the passage of death penalty legislation. In these cases, the general population is its own control because it is assumed to be the same before and after, with only the independent variable changing.

> **Natural experiments** involve measuring the same population before and after an event that is assumed to change the situation.

Analyzing the Data

Numbers alone rarely permit adequate testing of hypotheses. The many pieces of data must be arranged so that groups or variables may be compared. Sociologists today are trained in **statistics,** numerical techniques for the classification and analysis of data. Some current issues of *The American Sociological Review* and the *American Journal of Sociology* look like the journal of the American Statistical Society. There are, however, many types of research that rely on qualitative rather than statistical analysis.

> **Statistics** are numerical techniques for the classification and analysis of data.

As introductory students, you are not expected to learn most of these analytic procedures. But as a citizen of a society that respects numbers, you should be able to interpret some very basic statistics: percentages, rates, ratios, and measures of central tendency.

PERCENTAGES

The simplest and most important statistic is the *percentage,* or how many in every one hundred, often referred to as the *proportion.* Percentages allow researchers to compare groups of different size. How easily can you tell which is the larger proportion—25 out of 300 cases or 30 out of 400? The use of percentages simplifies such a comparison: 8.3 percent versus 7.5 percent—the larger number, 30, is actually a smaller part of its total.

> A **percentage** indicates how many of an item there are in every one hundred.

RATES AND RATIOS

Rates. Like percentages, *rates* are the number of times a given event occurs in a population. For example, we have already spoken of birth and death rates. The birth rate can be computed on the basis of the whole population: In 1987, in the United

> **Rates** indicate the number of times a given event occurs in a specified population.

Figure 2-3
Classic Experimental Design

States, the birth rate was 14.2 per 1,000 population. But as that population includes males, children, and the very old, a more informative statistic would be based on the population of females between the ages of fifteen and forty-four. In 1987, the rate for this subpopulation was 59.6 per 1,000 women of childbearing ages (down from a high of 118.0 in 1960). It is important, therefore, to note the base on which a rate is computed (National Center for Health Statistics, 1987).

A **ratio** compares one subpopulation to another.

Ratio. A *ratio* compares one subpopulation to another, such as males to females, or suicides to homicides, or legitimate to illegitimate births. For example, the proportion of males to females, or the *sex ratio,* varies over time and with age. In the United States today, among persons under age 14, there are about 104 males for every 100 females, but because male death rates are consistently higher than those for females, by ages 25–44 there are fewer than 97 men for each 100 women. Among those aged 65–69, the ratio is 82 men for every 100 women. And for those aged 85+ there are 40 men for every 100 women (U.S. Senate Special Committee on Aging, 1987). By the year 2000, there may be fewer than 50 men aged 65+ for every 100 older women.

MEASURES OF CENTRAL TENDENCY

Measures of central tendency are single numbers that summarize an entire set of data.

Three of the most common statistics are single numbers that summarize an entire set of data: *measures of central tendency.* These three important summary statistics are the *mean,* the *median,* and the *mode.* Most of you will have heard others speak of "mean test scores," "median income," or "modal family patterns," without knowing precisely what the terms mean. The three measures are very different, as the following example shows:

A group of 100 respondents has taken an "altruism" test to measure their willingness to help another person. The highest score is 10 and the lowest is zero. The 100 scores were distributed as shown in Table 2-1.

The **mean** is the average score for a group of subjects.

Mean. The *mean* is an arithmetical average; in this case, 100 respondents had a total score of 573, for a *group mean* of 5.73 (the total scores divided by the number of respondents).

TABLE 2-1 Altruism among college students

Score	Number of Respondents with That Score
10	6
9	8
8	12
7	14
6	20
5	10
4	9
3	8
2	7
1	3
0	3
	$N = 100$

Total scores: 573

Median. The *median* is the *midpoint* of a distribution of cases, with 50 percent of the cases above and 50 percent below that number. In the preceding example, the midpoint, or fiftieth case, comes somewhere between scores 6 and 7.

The **median** is the midpoint of an entire set of cases.

Mode. The *mode* is the single most common category of cases; in this example, the largest number of respondents (20) had scores of 6. Therefore, 6 is the mode for this group.

If one wants to compare this set of respondents with any other group, only one of these measures of central tendency is needed, rather than the hundred individual scores.

The **mode** is the single most common category of cases.

Reporting the Findings

THE DECISION TO PUBLISH

We have already mentioned the importance of the full disclosure of research techniques, instruments, and findings. But suppose that you, the researcher, have data that you do not want to disclose, that you think might be used against groups with which you are in sympathy. Some researchers do not publish; others try to minimize negative outcomes by interpreting the findings as narrowly as possible.

There are a number of cases in which sociologists have published very controversial reports, for example, Daniel Patrick Moynihan (1965) on the black family and James Coleman (1975) on school desegregation. The Moynihan study was widely interpreted as blaming the educational and economic failures of many urban black males on their being raised in female-headed families. Coleman's report claimed that court-enforced school desegregation, especially when involving crosstown busing, was responsible for "white flight" to the suburbs. Both studies have been refuted by other sociologists, who have also raised what they consider the ethical issue of a more general responsibility of social scientists *not* to increase racism in our society.

PRESENTING THE DATA

Sociologists communicate with one another by publishing in professional journals, by reading papers at professional meetings, and by circulating copies of research papers among friends and colleagues. One major goal is to link one's own study to an existing body of theory and research. Most research reports also point to gaps in the knowledge base, thus generating new questions for other sociologists to explore. In this way, social science becomes cumulative, building a base of data over time.

When reporting their findings, social scientists can claim both too much and too little. Small differences, because they achieve *"statistical significance,"* which is a technical term, are often made to sound as if they also have great social significance. In other cases, an untested correlation, if repeated frequently enough, comes to be generally accepted, as, for example, the belief of many people that student grades have declined because prayers are no longer permitted in public schools. Yet, during these same years, there have been other changes; church attendance has fallen and the consumption of fresh fruits has increased. However no one suggests that these two variables are related.

Simply because two events occur during the same period of time does not prove that one causes the other; they could be unrelated, or both could be the product of some other social trend. This type of incorrect reasoning is called the *particularistic fallacy* because the relationship exists at the level of whole societies (general) and not necessarily at the individual (particular) level. No research yet shows how school prayers affect a

child's grades. A delightful example of this fallacy is the often-noticed fact that birth rates are high in areas with many storks. Can you guess why?

Sociologists may also sound as if they were claiming too little for their findings. Because we deal in general patterns and probabilities, there are many exceptions to every statement. Thus, we often use such words as *many, most, typically, in general, often, perhaps, may, could,* and other terms that allow leeway in predictions. This usage is "probably" safer than dealing in unsupported absolutes or giving the impression that the study of human behavior is more precise than it is.

It is also important to remember that data do not speak for themselves. Numbers become meaningful only when placed in an interpretive context. For example, the fact that 14 percent of all Americans in 1985 were officially designated as poor does not tell us very much unless we know how the poverty level is defined, whether this percentage is more or less than in other years, and how our poverty rate compares with that of other industrial societies. With this other information as the context we can then describe the poverty rate as "high" or "low," "typical" or "atypical," and so forth.

MEDIA MISREPRESENTATION

The vast majority of sociological research goes completely unnoticed by the American public, in part because it is published in very technical terms in professional journals that are read by only a few thousand other social scientists, and in part because what we have to say does not seem to be as compelling or personally relevant as does the work of psychologists or economists. But every now and then a piece of sociological research is picked up by the mass media and conveyed to readers and viewers—with very mixed results.

In the process of making the research accessible to the typical reader, the carefully worded conclusions of the social scientists are oversimplified and often totally distorted. This is precisely what happened to a recently published report on "Marriage Patterns in the United States" (Bennett, et al 1986). The authors correctly noted that since women who graduate from college are less likely to marry than are women who did not attend college, and since the proportion of women who are

Statistical significance is a technical term that indicates how likely a given finding would occur by chance alone.

The **particularistic fallacy** occurs when a correlation at the group level is applied to individuals.

Storks

What was your guess on the relationship between the storks and the birth rates? (Any mention of delivery systems just doesn't count!) Associating the two variables is not only an example of particularistic fallacy, it is also what social scientists call a "spurious correlation." That is, there is really another factor which is creating or causing the association. Storks are found in the rural areas of certain countries. Rural areas are typically characterized by higher birth rates than are urban areas. Thus, the presence of storks and high birth rates seem to go hand in hand, at least to the observer who takes things at face value.

papers and television programs gave a very different and value-laden impression: that college-educated women who had not married by age thirty were doomed to a life of misery and loneliness! Indeed, the *Newsweek* article concluded that the marriage chances of a forty-year-old college-educated woman were so low that she was more likely to be killed by a terrorist than to find a husband. Notice the assumption that all women want to be married or will be forever unfulfilled without a husband.

The authors of the original study have disclaimed these interpretations of their data, noting that they never said anything about the quality of life of nonmarried women, and that they might actually be recording a very positive trend. If women rushed into marriage in the past for social standing and financial security, they now have a choice of what to do with their lives. These points were made on several talk shows and radio interviews by one of the authors of this textbook, a noted expert on single people (Stein 1981), but probably too late to undo the damage of the original misrepresentation of the research.

college graduates has increased in the 1980s, the proportion of never-marrying women will also rise. As you will see in Chapter 11 this is so because these women do not *need* to marry for economic security, and because there will be a shortage of eligible (college-educated) men from which they can choose.

But the way in which these findings were reported in a cover story in *Newsweek* (June 2, 1986) and repeated in news-

This case and similar ones in the past (on IQ, on the black family, and on educational opportunity, for example) illustrate

NBER Working Paper #1701
September 1985

Marriage Patterns in the
United States

ABSTRACT

This paper analyzes cohort marriage patterns in the United States in order to determine whether declining rates of first marriage are due to changes in the timing of marriage, the incidence of marriage, or both. Parametric models, which are well-suited to the analysis of censored or truncated data, are fit separately to information on age at first marriage derived from three data sets which were collected independently and at different points in time. Extended versions of the models are also estimated in which the parameters of the model distributions are allowed to depend on social and economic variables. The results provide evidence that the incidence of first marriage is declining and that there is only a slight tendency for women to delay marriage. In addition, education is the most important correlate of decisions about the timing of first marriage whereas race is the most important correlate of decisions about its incidence.

David E. Bloom
Department of Economics
Harvard University
Cambridge, Massachusetts 02138

Neil G. Bennett
Department of Sociology
Yale University
New Haven, Connecticut 06520

Compare the *Newsweek* cover to the title page of Bennett and Bloom's article. Which is more provocative? Why is the format and design of the mass media so different from that used in presenting scientific research? (© cover and document photographed by Wm. Harris, 1987)

the dilemma of popularizing research findings. To make them understandable to a mass audience, complex ideas and data must be so simplified that they can easily be misinterpreted. Yet without publicity, most research findings are known only to a handful of scholars and their students.

TABLES AND FIGURES

Tables consist of figures arranged to clarify relationships among variables.

Perhaps the most important part of a research report is the presentation of data in tables, charts, graphs, or diagrams.

Reading Tables. A *table* consists of columns and rows of figures, arranged to clarify relationships among variables. A glance at the table should, in most cases, convey information more readily than detailed descriptions. It would take several sentences to tell you what you should be able to read at a glance from Table 2-2.

To interpret a table, start by carefully reading the title, the headings, and the footnotes. Only then will you understand the numbers in the body of the table (called *cells*). In Table 2-2, for example, the title tells you that the cell numbers are the percentages in 1985 of people in the United States aged sixty-five and over who were either single, married, widowed, or divorced. The footnote in this case gives the source as the *Statistical Abstract of the United States* of 1986, which indicates offical Bureau of the Census data.

The cells show the extreme difference between older men and women in the likelihood of their being married rather than widowed. Over half of all elderly women are widowed, whereas over three-fourths of older men have a living wife. Once the cell data have been described, the researcher must explore their meanings. What explains these differences by sex? One clue is the higher death rates of males

TABLE 2-2 Marital status of persons 65+, United States, 1985 (in percents)

	Male	Female
Single	4.9	5.6
Married	77.8	39.7
Widowed	14.0	50.5
Divorced	3.1	4.2

SOURCE: U.S. Bureau of the Census. *Statistical Abstract of the United States,* 1986, p. 28.

than of females of all ages. Another is that women typically marry men older than themselves. What differences do you think being married or widowed makes in terms of satisfaction or standard of living in old age?

Charts and Graphs. Tables are only one way of presenting data. Graphics can be more powerful. Throughout this book, we shall also use other techniques for displaying information. For example, the data in Table 2-2 could be expressed either in *bar graphs* or in *pie-shaped diagrams,* as shown in Figure 2-4 on page 46.

Sociology for What and Whom? Nonscientific and Ethical Considerations

Although most researchers attempt to be objective and systematic in gathering information and analyzing the data, nonscientific factors intrude at each step of the research process. Such factors include: (1) value judgments; (2) increasing reliance on outside funding; and (3) deception by both researchers and subjects.

VALUE JUDGMENTS

One of the foundations of the scientific method is its claim to be *value neutral,* that is, free of researcher bias and personal judgments. But value neutrality is itself a value-laden decision—*not* to accept responsibility for the uses to which one's findings are put. What if studies of the poor lead politicians to reduce assistance programs, or research on Asian peasants is used by the military to destroy resistance movements? Humanist sociologists, among others, believe that if objectivity is an impossible goal, one's values should be openly stated. The potential conflict between the goals of objectivity and engagement that was a central concern of Max Weber continues to spark debate among sociologists. Can one do both good sociology and good deeds?

Although the authors of this introductory textbook have chosen to try to represent fairly the many different points of view in contemporary sociology, they, too, have personal values that ought to be acknowledged so that readers can be aware

Value neutrality, the claim that a researcher can be free of personal bias and judgment, is a foundation of the scientific method in the social sciences.

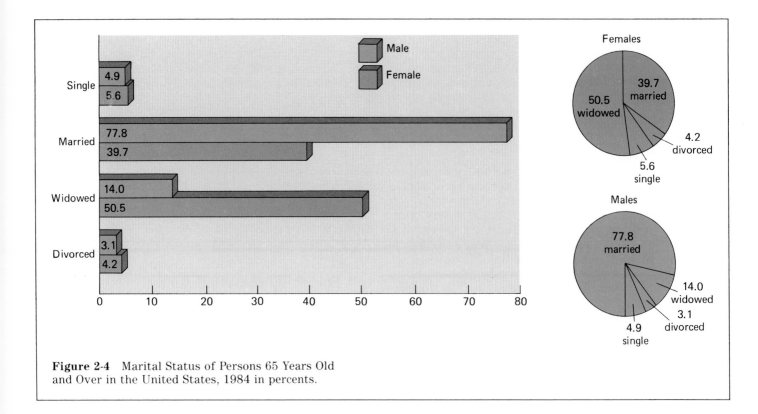

Figure 2-4 Marital Status of Persons 65 Years Old and Over in the United States, 1984 in percents.

FUNDING SOURCES

Does it matter that most large-scale research today is funded by federal or state agencies, private foundations, major corporations, and even foreign governments? There are enough recent examples to suggest that funders influence both what is studied and how the research findings are used. For example, the U.S. Department of Agriculture has funded university-based research projects of great value to national food distributors: artificially colored fruits and chemically treated meats that will be more attractive to consumers, as well as fertilizers and weedkillers that increase crop yield but that may be environmental hazards (Hightower 1972, Busch and Lacy 1983). Drug companies are currently endowing university departments with millions of dollars to discover and test products, but the patent rights are held by the profit-making corporations. This means that the scientific standard of full disclosure must be sacrificed to the secrecy required in commercial research (Stark 1983).

In social science, the research agenda is greatly influenced by the federal government's priorities. In the administration of Lyndon Johnson, for example, research on the causes and conditions of poverty was encouraged; the Reagan administration emphasized civil defense, military technology, drug use, and teenage pregnancy. One of the most controversial cases of government involvement in social science was "Project Camelot," undertaken by the U.S. Army in the 1960s to enlist academic researchers in predicting civil war in South and Central American countries. When it appeared that the information would be used by military dictatorships to wipe out dissent, the resulting protests and publicity helped cancel the program (Horowitz 1965).

DECEPTION

Each research method contains some elements of deception. This is most obvious in experimental and observational studies where the people being observed *must* be unaware of the goals of the research. But even the simplest survey questionnaire invades the respondents' privacy for purposes that they do not know and of which they might not approve.

Ethics in Experiments. All experiments involve the manipulation of human subjects, either placing them in false situations or exposing some but not others to a given stimulus. Suppose that you were testing a new program to reduce drug abuse, how would you justify choosing some adolescents for the new program while leaving others untreated? Or giving the new treatment to those who have not requested it? You could ask for volunteers, but if all subjects were self-selected, the results would be biased.

Another dilemma revolves around how much the researchers need to tell in order to secure "informed consent" from research subjects. Many laboratory-type experiments today are conducted with "captive audiences" such as inmates of institutions and college students. Other studies rely on volunteers who are paid for their time.

Despite protest over the use of deception in experiments, the trend has steadily increased: from 41 percent of studies reported in the *Journal of Personality and Social Psychology* in 1959 to over 60 percent by 1980 (Gross and Fleming 1982). Furthermore, researchers have made value judgments about what kinds of people can be most often deceived: women, students, and people being paid for participation, in contrast to men, volunteers, or people being observed without their knowledge (Gross and Fleming 1982).

Correcting Research Abuses and Misuses. In response to these ethical questions, professional social science organizations have tightened their codes of ethics regarding research on human subjects. Researchers themselves are devising ways of avoiding ethical dilemmas and legal problems through innovative statistical techniques and research designs (Boruch and Cecil 1983).

In addition, most institutions of higher education today have review committees that oversee research on people conducted by faculty or students. These regulations are designed to ensure that no harm will result from subjects' participation.

Government funding is typically regulated by "peer-review" panels of scholars who judge the quality of research proposals. Because peer-review panels are typically drawn from leading figures in a field, there is a tendency to approve projects that support existing conceptual models, as well as a temptation to help friends and colleagues. However, one study of the review process suggests that favoritism was not as important as sheer luck: different panels reviewing the same proposals rated them very differently, with no consistent standards governing the ratings (Cole et al 1981). In addition, heads of government agencies in charge of dispensing millions of research dollars each year can "stack" the peer panels with people known to favor administration goals.

Respondent Bias. Not all deception is on the part of the researcher. It cannot simply be assumed that respondents and research subjects are always aware of, or wish to let others know, what they are doing. Researchers may be deceived if they do not recognize four problems discussed by Douglas (1978):

1. *Misinformation.* Unintended falsehoods when respondents think that they know a "truth" that may not be correct. Examples include the misconceptions cited at the beginning of this chapter.
2. *Evasions.* Intentionally withholding information or turning the question aside.
3. *Lies.* Designed to mislead the questioner. Respondents often give false information about their age or occupation; politicians hide sources of campaign funds; advertisers skirt the truth as an occupational specialty; and even the Boy Scouts of America have padded membership counts for fundraising purposes. These "dirty statistics" are often used to achieve what the subjects consider a higher goal.
4. *Fronts, or Shared Lies About Settings.* Massage parlors that claim to be health spas and banks that exist to "launder" money earned illegally are just two examples of fronts designed to mislead observers.

In other words, the world and its inhabitants are not always what they appear to be, just as a given research study may not be exactly what its investigators claim.

Some kinds of respondent bias are *un-*intentional, as in the general tendency of people to give socially acceptable answers. Researchers have also found that there are persons who are yea-sayers (who tend to agree) and those who are nay-sayers (who tend to disagree) no matter what the issue. In addition, it is possible that some sub-groups have different "response styles" preferring certain response categories or types of questions to others.

Summary

Sociologists test their theories of social life through research. This chapter examines the importance of research, the scientific and nonscientific factors involved in the research process, the methods used, the type of information derived, and the description and analysis of data.

Much of what we think is commonsense knowledge is neither common nor accurate. A systematic examination of the relationships among social facts is crucial for our understanding of the world and for making sound social-policy decisions. Knowledge is gained in different ways. Whereas subjective understanding is based on a person's own perception of the world, or intuition, the scientific method involves objective observation, precise measurement, and the full disclosure of research methods and results. Findings should be capable of replication.

The research process involves five major steps: (1) selecting the research question; (2) choosing the most appropriate method for collecting the necessary information; (3) gathering data; (4) analyzing the data gathered; and (5) drawing conclusions and reporting the findings. Deciding what to study may involve nonscientific factors, such as the researcher's values and attitudes or considerations of time and funding. Framing the research question involves selecting the variables, and making hypotheses about the relationship among the variables. The translation of these hypotheses and abstract variables into ob-servable items is called *operationalizing the variables.*

Selecting the most appropriate research method depends on the respondents sought, the nature of the information, and the type of data required. The methods chosen may involve cross-sectional studies; panel or longitudinal studies; large-scale social surveys; intensive interviews; observational techniques; a secondary analysis of the available official, historical, and comparative data; and/or an experimental design.

The collected information must be arranged so as to compare groups of respondents and variables. Statistics such as percentages, ratios, and measures of central tendency are used to describe the data.

When completed, research findings are published or reported to colleagues at professional meetings. The reporting of findings enables others to evaluate the research and to judge those seeking to influence social policy. Although the research process is guided by the scientific method, the choice of research topics and the decision to report findings are influenced by nonscientific considerations. These considerations involve ethical issues such as the uses to which the data can be put and the extent to which funding agencies shape and control the findings. Sociologists cannot be entirely value-neutral. They can, however, conduct their research in as scientific a manner as possible.

Suggested Readings

BECKER, HOWARD. *Writing for Social Scientists: How to Start and Finish Your Thesis, Book or Article.* Chicago: University of Chicago Press, 1986. This is a very useful guidebook to the organization of scholarship and the components of sound writing. Kai Erickson calls it a "wonderful book—humane, wry, reflective, gentle, and wise."

CAPLOVITZ, DAVID. *The Stages of Social Research.* New York: John Wiley & Sons, 1983. A complete step-by-step guide to qualitative and quantitative research methods, including a chapter on proposal writing.

COLE, STEPHEN. *The Sociological Method,* 3rd ed. Chicago: Rand McNally, 1980. A very clear and concise introduction to the methods and logic of sociological research.

GOULDNER, ALVIN W. *The Coming Crisis of Western Sociology.* New York: Avon Books, 1970. A classic in the field of sociology which discusses the role of politics in the study of social issues.

KUHN, THOMAS S. *The Structure of Scientific Revolutions,* 2nd ed. Chicago: University of Chicago Press, 1962. The book that precipitated the revolution in how social scientists think about their own discipline. A classic that brought the notion of paradigm into common currency.

ROSSI, ALICE C. *Feminists in Politics: A Panel Analysis of the First National Women's Conference.* New York: Academic Press, 1982. An account of the design and implementation of a longitudinal study.

ROSSI, PETER, JAMES WRIGHT, and ANDY ANDERSON, eds. *Handbook of Survey Research.* Orlando, Fla.: Academic Press, 1983. A state-of-the-art handbook on various aspects of survey research, the major method of data collection by sociologists.

SIMMONS, J. L., and GEORGE T. MCCALL. *Social Research: The Craft of Finding Out.* New York: Macmillan, 1985. A compact introduction to the basics of social research: essentials, elements, and modes of research.

WAX, ROSALIE. *Doing Fieldwork.* Chicago: University of Chicago Press, 1978. Includes discussions of student research projects, as well as the moral and practical problems of doing fieldwork in settings like Indian reservations and the detention camps for Japanese-Americans established by our government during World War II.

WHYTE, WILLIAM FOOTE, with KATHLEEN KING WHYTE. *Learning from the Field: A Guide from Experience.* Beverly Hills, Calif.: Sage, 1984. A foremost sociologist draws on his observation and participant observation of street corner society, corporations, restaurants, and Peruvian peasant communities.

Part II
Self in Society

The four chapters in Part II deal with the processes whereby members of human groups create a world of meaning and patterns of behavior that meet their personal needs and permit the group to survive over time. We begin, in Chapter 3, with the study of *culture,* an enveloping context of values, rules, behaviors, and products created through human interactions. In Chapter 4, we examine the *social structures* that embody culture. Social structure consists of those patterned regularities of thought and action that make social life predictable and, therefore, possible.

Chapter 5 deals with *socialization,* the process through which culture is internalized by new members of the group. Socialization also involves the emergence of self-concept. In these ways society becomes part of the person and people become active participants in their society. Although the goal of socialization is conformity to expectations, none of us is so fully socialized that variations in thought and behavior do not occur. Conformity and nonconformity, or *deviance,* are the subject of Chapter 6. Special attention is paid to the functions, dysfunctions, and social control of deviant behavior.

3

The Cultural Context

I MAGINE that during a nuclear attack your classroom has been miraculously transported to a deserted island, and that you and your classmates have forgotten all that you knew before the explosion. You are in the position of the earliest band of humans who had to use their brains to figure out how to survive as individuals and as a group. How do you communicate with one another? Find food? Divide tasks and keep order? Pair off to reproduce new members of the group in a way that minimizes jealousy and conflict? How do you teach the newborn what you have learned and instill a sense of shared responsibility for one another?

These are the essential problems of survival for any group and its individual members. Because human beings are not preprogrammed biologically or psychologically for any one set of responses, each group must work out its own solutions, depending on the resources at hand and the results of trial-and-error attempts to control themselves and their environment. This is the process whereby humans create *culture* and *social structure. Culture,* the subject matter of this chapter, consists of those habits of thinking, believing, and behaving that order our lives. (Chapter 4 will examine how a culture is realized in *social structure,* the actual patterns of social interaction.)

Groups that cannot create and maintain a viable culture will not survive over time. Without the technology to secure sufficient food, people will starve; without self-control, order is impossible; without adequate arrangements for the care of children, the group dies off; and without common beliefs and ceremonies, group members will lack a sense of responsibility for one another. No human group is without culture, and no two cultures are exactly the same.

The Evolutionary Basis of Culture

The need for culture is an outcome of the two to three million years of human evolution during which a number of important changes in the body took place, beginning with the shift to an upright posture. Standing on two feet, in turn, allowed the front paws to develop into hands that could ultimately make tools. A shift to a more varied diet led to changes in the structure of the jaw, leaving more room for brain growth. The placement of the human head at the top of the spinal chord freed space for the development of a voice box in the throat. Major changes in the female reproductive system transformed human sexuality into a predominantly social relationship. Throughout this entire chain of bodily changes, the brain itself was forced to become increasingly complex in order to process new types of information and to control the organism's responses.

At the same time, a narrowing of the birth canal meant that the human infant had to be born when its head and shoulders could easily slip down, long before the nervous system matured—which means long before any fixed responses could be coded into the human brain. The helplessness of the human infant also means that its survival depends on the ability of other humans to care for it over a period of many years.

Furthermore, being born without any preprogrammed or built-in responses, means that one must *learn* how to behave. Here is where the unique complexity of the human brain coupled with the ability to utter a great variety of sounds comes into play—humans create languages of great variety and sophistication through which they share experience and communicate knowledge. Each generation does not need to reinvent the wheel, but can build on the established wisdom of its group—its culture.

Culture began to replace physical evolution as the means of adapting to the environment with the first prehumans who stood upright, perhaps two million years ago. If the behavior of chimpanzees, our closest primate relatives, can be taken as a guide, contrary to mental images you may have of fierce hairy males clubbing wild animals and dragging females into caves, it now appears that the basic group of prehumans consisted of a female and her children who survived by *foraging,* picking readily available foods such as fruits, nuts, and berries, and eating them on the spot (Calvin 1985). At various times, the mother-child unit would be joined by one or more of the adult males who followed them around, and who were selected as mates on the basis of their willingness to share food and help with the young (Tanner 1981).

By 150,000 years ago, populations that could be labeled "human" appeared and spread rapidly from Africa to Southern Europe and across Asia. Called *homo sapiens* ("homo" = human, "sapiens" = wise)—the thinking people—they were characterized by relatively complex brains, skeletons very similar to ours, and a set of simple stone tools. In most bands of *homo sapiens,* containing two or three dozen members, foraging was replaced by *gathering,* a more systematic way of finding foodstuffs, transporting them back to the group, storing and preserving them for later use. Since fire had by now been discovered, it is also likely that both women and men trapped small animals and birds. Large-scale hunting, however, came much later and consisted, at first, of simply driving herds over cliffs and scavenging the remains.

Between 100,000 and 75,000 years ago, a more "modern"-looking *homo sapiens* appeared, and by 35,000 years ago, this new population, *homo sapiens sapiens,* was the dominant species, from which *all* living humans are descended. That is, there are no important differences in evolved potentials or abilities among contemporary racial or ethnic groups. Notice, too, the double emphasis on the ability to think, to create the cultures that have effectively replaced biological evolution as the means

Foraging is the picking for immediate consumption of readily available foods.

Gathering is a more systematic way of finding food, and transporting, storing, and preserving it.

Definitions in Context and Culture: The Experience of Miscarriage

Shulamit Reinharz

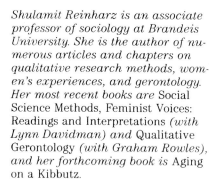

Shulamit Reinharz is an associate professor of sociology at Brandeis University. She is the author of numerous articles and chapters on qualitative research methods, women's experiences, and gerontology. Her most recent books are Social Science Methods, Feminist Voices: Readings and Interpretations *(with Lynn Davidman) and* Qualitative Gerontology *(with Graham Rowles), and her forthcoming book is* Aging on a Kibbutz.

In summer 1973 I found myself "in" three places at once. I was a doctoral candidate in sociology at Brandeis University in Waltham, Massachusetts; I had recently moved to Ann Arbor, Michigan, where I had taken a position as lecturer in the department of psychology at the University of Michigan; and I had taken an eight-month leave of absence from the latter to work in Jerusalem. This array reflects the early stages of many women's academic careers: not quite finishing one's degree, moving, and moving again. In my case at the start of graduate school, I married a graduate student who then finished his degree, received an assistant professorship in history at the University of Michigan, and needed to do archival research in Israel.

Despite my interesting activities, there was one thing missing in my life—a baby. Thinking it would be ideal for me to be pregnant and give birth while on leave, we decided to start a family before going abroad. As is the case with many middle-class working women, I planned my baby, coordinating it with "industrial time," the time frame of the world of work.

Things didn't turn out as planned. About two weeks after arriving in Israel, I began bleeding severely and eventually was hospitalized for a miscarriage. Everything about the experience was bewildering. Since it was my first pregnancy, I was almost oblivious to the possibility of miscarriage. Moreover, as a cultural outsider and geographically uprooted individual, I had not yet made any deep friendships that could provide me with information or support. I was left with no ways of understanding what was happening other than what my doctor told me, which wasn't much.

All I really had to fall back on was my sociological imagination. Thus, shortly after being discharged from the hospital, I began to write extensive fieldnotes. Writing and remembering helped me understand what had occurred, deal with my rage at those who ostensibly were taking care of me, and soften my despair at losing a baby. I recorded in minute detail how my body felt, what I decided to do, what role my husband played, what fantasies I had, what the role of the doctor was, what the hospital layout looked like, what the hospital procedures consisted of, how I interacted with patients and staff, what it meant to recover, and how other people talked to me when I told them what had happened. After finishing my fieldnotes, I wrote an analysis and filed it away. It had served its purpose.

A year or so later, back in the USA, I gave the paper to a friend who was teaching a course on the experience of patienthood. I also showed it to a few other friends, and asked their advice about publishing it. All of them advised me against it, arguing that to express so much anger was "inappropriate" in scholarship. I heeded their advice and turned to the writing of my dissertation, which concerned the socialization of sociologists. Strangely enough, I concluded my thesis with an analysis of how sociologists can use personal experience as a method for social psychological research (Reinharz 1979, 1984).

Three years after the miscarriage and nearly simultaneously with the defense of my dissertation, I gave birth to our first child. Five years after that, our second daughter was born. I had gone on to do more research on women, method, and social psychology—but none on miscarriage. Nevertheless, miscarriage was always in the back of my mind. I still knew almost nothing about it and was constantly surprised about the "invisibility" of this extremely common female experience.

Being in the "back of my mind" meant that I was continuously rethinking my experience and reworking the ideas in my paper, without being completely aware of what I was doing. Two years later (10 years after the miscarriage), I received an invitation to contribute an article to a journal's special issue devoted to the unique stresses faced by women. I didn't know what to contribute, when much to my surprise, my husband reminded me of my long-lost paper on miscarriage. I suppose he too had been thinking about miscarriage. The editors were delighted with the topic and I set to work.

First I scoured the academic literature concerning miscarriage. Finding very little, I wrote an analysis in the tradition of the sociology of knowledge showing how this lack of information reflects the lack of esteem concerning women's experience. I also showed how this sociological and cultural "silence" contributed to my lack of physical and psychological preparation (Reinharz, in press a). In other words, my anger was now put to sociological use.

As a feminist, I try to understand how I am the same as while also being different from, women in other parts of the world. Thus I sought first-hand accounts of miscarriage experiences written by women in different societies. Using the method of interpretive content analysis, I compared these accounts and learned how the meaning of miscarriage varies cross-culturally, leading women to experience the "same" events in completely different ways. Using diaries, essays, and anthropological records, I analyzed the way different social meanings are imbedded in the language with which miscarriage is described. Drawing on feminist theory, I saw how miscarriage is used to define women's moral value, and how miscarriage has been medicalized. In some cultures women control information about miscarriage, and transmit to one another what the experience is and how women can take care of each other when it occurs (Reinharz, in press b).

On the basis of what I now understood about the social dimensions of miscarriage, I undertook a new study about American women's experiences of miscarriage. Moreover, using W. I. Thomas's concept of "definition of the situation" and the method of personal document analysis, I asked if symbolic interactionist theory required modification if the object of

study was miscarriage. This work led me to argue that symbolic interaction theory has a middle-class or male perspective since it presumes an efficacious actor rather than one whose body is beyond her control. The concept of defining a situation implies that people have the ability to define and control. Studying aspects of women's lives reveals how little control women have over their lives and how gaining control so that they can "define the situation" is a continuous struggle. My examination of the role of hospitals in defining the miscarriage experience also led me to question if symbolic interactionists' emphasis on interaction accurately reflects the extent to which social institutions shape behavior (Reinharz 1987).

My next projected study of miscarriage continues to combine my interest in methodology with my interest in women's experiences. I will analyze another researcher's open-ended interview protocols of women who have miscarried. These women

were studied as part of a larger project about pregnancy loss undertaken by Professor Judith Lasker of Lehigh University. I will try to understand the way the experience of miscarriage is defined by these women. Hopefully, all of these studies will help us better understand and value women's experiences in society.

Reinharz, Shulamit. *On Becoming a Social Scientist: From Survey Research and Participant Observation to Experiential Analysis* (San Francisco: Jossey-Bass, 1979; New Brunswick, NJ: Transaction Books, 1984); "What's Missing in Miscarriage?" *Journal of Community Psychology* (in press a); "The Social Psychology of a Miscarriage: An Application of Symbolic Interaction Theory and Method," in Mary Jo Deegan and Michael Hill (eds.) *Women and Symbolic Interaction* (Boston: Allen & Unwin, 1987); "Miscarriage: A Cross-Cultural Study of Women's Experiences," in Dorothy Wertz (ed.) *Research in the Sociology of Health Care* (Westport, CT: JAI Press, in press b).

---

whereby we adapt and change. Body, mind, and culture have all developed together, and the end product is *homo sapiens sapiens,* the creature who is specialized for flexibility.

HUMAN FLEXIBILITY

Relative to body size, the human brain is larger than that of other animals; it also has more pathways and specialized parts. Although other animals can be taught a large number of tricks, humans must rely almost totally on learned responses. The story of evolution and culture is essentially one of progressive weakening of *instinctual behavior* in favor of action that is guided by thought.

In a model of instinctual behavior, as seen in Figure 3-1, the organism (body) experiences arousal of some deep impulse or drive which then leads to a specific tension-relieving act, all as one unbroken chain of behavior.

This is *not* how human beings behave in any important respect. Take, for example,

the sex drive, often described as powerful and irresistible. If this were so, we would be spending our days as well as nights chasing one another. But we do not; we go to classes, do homework, chat with friends, and act sexually only under certain very limited circumstances. We have *learned* the whens, wheres, whys, with whoms, and even the hows of sexual behavior (Remember all those conversations with friends and older siblings?).

Instinctual behavior refers to an unbroken chain of drive arousal leading to tension-relieving action.

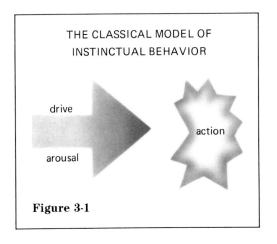

THE CLASSICAL MODEL OF INSTINCTUAL BEHAVIOR

drive

arousal

action

Figure 3-1

In a model of human behavior, then, the link between drive arousal and tension-reducing action is *mediated* (broken into) by the human mind, capable of interpreting the state of the organism and of choosing among the actions acceptable in that culture. That is, we can reflect on what is happening to us and see ourselves as both subject and object. The *reflexive* mind operates on both sides of the model illustrated in Figure 3-2, so that both our sense of our body and our choice of responses are affected by culture.

A classic study of responses to pain among American hospital patients, for example, found that people suffering from the same physical condition showed very different reactions, depending on their religious and ethnic background (Zborowski 1952). Both Jewish and Italian patients were much more emotional than the "old Yankees" who kept a "stiff upper lip" and cried only when they were alone. Yet, although the Jewish and Italian patients were similarly open and vocal about their pain, they were motivated by very different concerns: the Italians by the immediate experience of discomfort, and the Jews by worry over the long-term effects of their illness. Thus, though all patients were exposed to similar levels of pain, their cultural backgrounds had shaped different ways of recognizing and reacting to signals from their bodies.

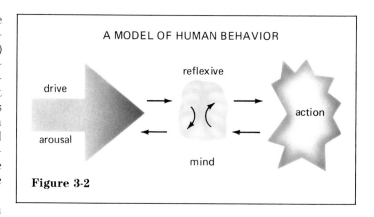

A MODEL OF HUMAN BEHAVIOR

Figure 3-2

will be as many "human natures" as there are cultures (Geertz 1966). In this view, the important aspects of culture are language, beliefs, rituals (ceremonies), art forms, and the customs of daily living. Members of a society use these guideposts to understand what is happening to them and to choose appropriate ways of responding.

Defining Culture

Culture is the blueprint for living of a group whose members share a territory and language, feel responsible for each other, and call themselves by the same name.

Culture is often defined as the blueprint for living of a group whose members share a given territory and language, feel responsible for one another, and call themselves by the same name. The culture of such a group (or society) consists of: (1) solutions to the problems of survival; (2) the ideals and values that shape rules of conduct; and (3) tools and other humanmade objects (*artifacts* or material culture). People become functioning members of the group as they learn and participate in the culture.

Artifacts or material culture consist of tools and other human-made objects.

Another way of looking at culture is to emphasize the way in which it shapes how people experience the world and express meaning (Swidler 1986). Because the human central nervous system develops within a social setting, there can be no human nature independent of culture, and there

SYMBOLS AND LANGUAGE

The key to culture, then, is the evolution of the human capacity for using *symbols*. A symbol is a sound or object or event that has no meaning in and of itself, but only the purely arbitrary meaning that members of a group attach to it. For example, a straight line -|- stands for the number "one" only for people using the arabic numeral system; in other societies that sign could stand for anything on which its members have agreed. When joined at right angles by an intersecting line Christians will recognize it as the sign of the cross with all the emotional attachments that this symbol evokes.

A **symbol** is a sound, object, or event that is given meaning by members of a group.

The most important symbol system is language itself—a set of sounds and gestures whose significance depends on the common understanding of those who use them. *All human communication is symbolic,* through words and actions whose meaning is agreed upon. Our first task on that imaginary deserted island is, therefore, to develop just such a set of shared symbols, a mutual understanding of what is being communicated by particular sounds or gestures. Over time, we will create a language capable of describing the richness of our experience. Although the languages spoken by members of other cultures may seem strange to our ears, just as ours does to them, all human languages are of equivalent complexity and truthfulness and represent the crowning achievement of evolution: the capacity for reflexive thought.

True, animals can be taught the meaning of certain gestures (such as the raised hand for "stay") and to answer to the sound that stands for their name. A few chimpanzees, after many years of training, have mastered some elements of Standard American Sign Language, and one or two have even produced new (untaught) gestures. But such abilities are extremely limited when compared to an average 2½-year-old human's seemingly endless flow of words, sentences and untaught concepts. Furthermore, while apes (and other animals) may communicate effectively among themselves, they have not created cultures that extend across entire groups or that grow more complex over time (Premack 1986). In sum, "human social systems are all mediated by language; perhaps that is why there are no forms of behavior among nonhuman primates that correspond with religion, politics, or even economics" (Washburn 1978, p. 208).

NONVERBAL COMMUNICATION

Not all communication is through speech. Gestures, facial expressions, and body movements are all ways of sending messages. We probably rely more on unspoken than spoken cues to understand what others are really thinking and to adjust our behavior accordingly (Patterson 1983, Goleman 1986).

The study of nonverbal (unspoken) communication is called *kinesics* (Birdwhistle 1970). As with spoken language, the meaning of the gesture depends on the culture. The interpretation of some gestures may vary widely from one society to another; whereas other gestures, such as a smile, seem to have much the same meaning in any culture. Within a society, a given gesture can have different meanings depending on the context: saluting an officer on a military base is a sign of respect; saluting one's parents may be taken as a symbol of disrespect.

In *The Silent Language,* Edward Hall (1959) describes cultural variations in the distance between people speaking to one another: head-to-head in some societies, several feet away in others. Such distances signify general ideas about privacy and the "bubble of personal space" to which a person is entitled. These bubbles also vary

Kinesics is the study of nonverbal communication.

Gestures, facial expressions and body movements send messages, which are often quite clear, without words. (© Costa Manos/Magnum Photos)

within a society according to social power: bosses have more privacy than employees; men are more likely than women to impose on the personal space of people of the opposite sex; and adults have no hesitation in violating the private bubble of a child (Thorne and Henley 1975). Such nonverbal messages tend to reinforce social arrangements (Epstein 1986).

LANGUAGE AND PERCEPTION

Language and gestures reflect the ideals and relationships embedded in culture, because it is through language that members of any society learn to *structure perception.* That is, we see, interpret, and understand the world through the screen of culture embodied in our language.

The idea that language shapes the form and content of one's thought has been most forceably argued by Edward Sapir and Benjamin Whorf and is known as the *Sapir-Whorf hypothesis:*

> Human beings do not live in an objective world alone . . . but are very much at the mercy of the particular language which has become the medium of expression for their society. The "real world" is to a large extent unconsciously built up on the language habits of the group. *No two languages are ever sufficiently similar to be considered as representing the same social reality.* The worlds in which different societies live are distinct worlds, not merely the same world with different labels attached (Sapir 1949, p. 162, emphasis added).

The **Sapir-Whorf hypothesis** states that language shapes the form and content of thought.

57

The Symbolic Significance of Words

In a culture where masculinity is defined as the absence of femininity, the behavior of boys and men can be controlled by the threat of being labeled a sissy. In the U.S. Marine Corps, the process of turning recruits into "real men" begins with the drill instructor referring to his charges as "girls" or "ladies." From then on, the men are motivated to prove that they are anything but such objects of contempt. During the Vietnam war, the distinction between American fighting men and the smaller, more passive Southeast Asians was translated into the difference between heterosexuals and homosexuals, with the Vietnamese being considered "faggots." The definitions of manliness helped maintain high levels of commitment to combat among the Marines.

SOURCE: Charles J. Levy, "ARVN as Faggots: Inverted Warfare in Vietnam," *Society* 8 (1971): 18–27.

Sapir and Whorf derived their hypothesis from studies of how members of various societies perceived such basic aspects of the world as time, space, and color. For example, Whorf reported that the Hopi Indians of the southwest United States had no words for past, present, or future time because the Hopi way is timeless. Therefore, the Hopi sense of time is very different from that of the clock-obsessed American of European ancestry.

To learn another language, therefore, is to enter another way of life, another way of perceiving reality. People who know only one language are probably more narrow-minded than those who can speak more than one language. But such is the adaptive ability of humans, that we can learn other languages and understand other cultures, rather than being limited to only one world-view.

Vocabularies are also useful for understanding aspects of the environment that are important for group survival. The Eskimo have over a dozen words to describe snow because it is essential to know if the snowfall is wet or dry, comes from a certain direction, is likely to be of long or short duration, and so on. Teenage American boys know the year, style, and make of dozens of automobiles because males are

"supposed" to be aware of these subtle differences. In another, less complex society, one word would embrace all "vehicles with four wheels," just as we have one word for "snow," which can be combined with a few descriptive terms.

Words also have an evaluative dimension; some signify "good" things and others "bad." The use of words to arouse emotion and to structure thought is most obvious in politics. Anti-Communists in the United States are fond of describing the Soviet Union as "atheistic," and the Communists of the People's Republic of China used to speak of "capitalist running dogs" when referring to the United States. The symbolic significance of words is well illustrated in the military (see box).

As descendants of the original *homo sapiens sapiens,* all 5.1 billion inhabitants of our planet share a common physical and mental structure. How, then, to account for the many differences in appearance, modes of thought, and behavior? The answer, simply, is culture: the socially constructed beliefs and rules by which people live in human groups. In other words, our common humanity makes us all alike in certain needs and capacities, but because each society has its unique culture, members of that society will share certain characteristics different from those of other societies.

Cultural Development: From Simple to Complex

All known cultures—from the past as well as existing now—can be arranged along a line (a continuum) representing degrees of difference between the *most simple* and the *most complex* in terms of technology, the knowledge base, social structure, and material artifacts. As shown in Figure 3-3, the group's adaptation to its environment (its *mode of subsistence*) provides an economic base able to support a certain size population (Lenski and Nolan 1983).

As more techniques for adaptation are discovered, a division of labor results, with some members performing certain tasks and other members doing another type of work. The food supply becomes more varied and usually more assured so that a larger population can be supported. As the group expands, problems of order lead to increasingly elaborate arrangements

Mode of subsistence refers to the way in which a group adapts to its environment.

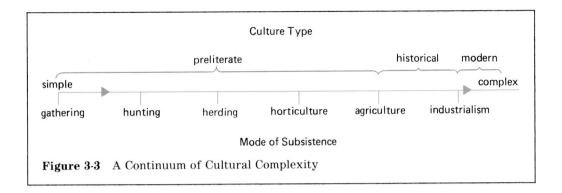

Culture Type

preliterate   historical   modern

simple   complex

gathering   hunting   herding   horticulture   agriculture   industrialism

Mode of Subsistence

Figure 3-3   A Continuum of Cultural Complexity

for making and enforcing rules, for pairing off the unmarried, and for training their young. In all these ways—economic, political, familial, and educational—the group's culture base expands and the society becomes more complex. The more elaborate the division of labor, the greater the differences and inequality among subgroups within the society.

For example, when *hunting* is introduced into a gathering economy, young men tend to specialize in the hunt while the women remain primarily gatherers. Hunting requires new tools: spears and clubs, originally, then bows and arrows—and the skills needed to make and use them effectively. Eventually, members of the group learn how to scrape skins, cook and store meat, and use the bones and sinews to make other tools. All these new traits increase the group's pool of knowledge.

Herding adds such specialties as the care and breeding of animals, and *horticulture* (simple farming) involves learning about plants, how to prepare land, and when to harvest crops. Each of these modes of subsistence is more complex than the preceding one. Settlements become larger; the number and variety of activities increases; and new skills such as basketry, pottery, and weaving are invented or borrowed from other cultures.

The introduction of *agriculture,* some ten to twelve thousand years ago, marked a major shift in social and cultural development. More systematic than horticulture, agriculture involves plowing furrows and irrigating crops, thus ensuring a more dependable food supply. A surplus in good seasons leads to new adaptations such as trading with other societies and building storage facilities. The need for record keeping produces number sys-

The different agricultural technologies of Idaho and Ethiopia give evidence of the existence of both modern and traditional modes of subsistence in the contemporary world. (TOP: © J. P. Laffont/SYGMA; BOTTOM: © M. Phlippot/ SYGMA)

tems and writing to keep track of who owns what.

An equally significant shift in cultural development occurred with the *Industrial Revolution* of the past 150 years. Industrialization led to radical changes in culture and social structure, beginning in Western Europe and then spreading throughout the world. Our society is located at the most complex end of the continuum in a postindustrial era of major technological change.

But there are still a large number of societies located at all points on the spectrum of cultural complexity. How do these groups manage to adapt to their environment and survive over time? What can we learn from contemporary gatherers or gathering/hunting societies?

The **Industrial Revolution** represents a mode of subsistence based on the factory system of production.

THE TASADAY: FROM LEAVES TO LEVIS?

In the mid-1960s, the anthropological world was startled to learn of the accidental discovery of a band of two dozen people, isolated in the rain forests of the Philippines, who had maintained an astonishingly simple way of life. All the elements of culture were there: gathering as a mode of subsistance; shared decision making among all adults; strict rules about who could mate with whom; and an elaborate set of beliefs explaining how they came to the caves and what the future holds (Nance 1982).

Because it is almost impossible today to discover a human group that has not been in contact with other peoples, the appearance of the *Tasaday* was hailed as a major clue to the culture of the earliest human groups. Long before the tools and technology of the hunt were invented, small bands of gatherers similar to the Tasaday must have spread across Africa and Asia. In these groups, both women and men probably performed the same tasks—finding food and tending children—with minimal differences in social power on the basis of gender. Such bands could not survive without high levels of cooperation and food sharing.

Since the 1960s, however, many changes have taken place among the Tasaday, so much so that when revisited recently by journalists from the West, they were discovered wearing Levis and T-shirts, using modern tools, and adopting the customs of a near-by hunting tribe. This radically changed life style has led some scientists to suggest that the original discovery had been a carefully planned trick by the Marcos government to demonstrate a concern for preserving native cultures in the Philippines (Kronholz 1986).

Other anthropologists who have recently visited the band, however, conclude that what has happened is a textbook example of cultural change through contact with more complex societies (Mydans 1986). Such culture contact has become so widespread that we do not expect a similarly isolated group to be discovered, but if one should, the chances are that its culture would be similar to that attributed to the Tasaday.

Fake or real, the story of the Tasaday

These are the Tasaday as they appeared when first "discovered." The question remains: was their "primitive" state a hoax or a reality? (© John Launois/Black Star)

The Lessons of the !Kung San

The !Kung are a gathering/hunting people of Central Africa, whose relatively simple way of life is nonetheless considerably more complex than that of the Tasaday. !Kung peoples (the "!" indicates a clicking sound which is part of their language) once lived on lands full of game for hunting, but have been gradually pushed farther and farther from their original location by white settlers from South Africa.

When first visited by anthropologists in the 1950s, bands of !Kung still followed the customs of their ancestors: the men hunted, the women gathered, and the whole group of thirty adults and children moved from one campsite to another with the change in seasons. Typically, the women gathered in groups, providing 75 percent of the food supply. Although men spent a great deal of time on the hunt, meat was a minor but highly valued part of the !Kung diet, and was shared among all members of the band—as a means of generating group solidarity but also made necessary because meat could not be stored.

As with gathering/hunting groups in general, relations between the sexes were characterized by relative equality, due to the women's major economic contribution as well as the !Kung custom of a husband's coming to live with his wife's relatives. Women as well as men led very active sex lives, frequently outside marriage, although the women's love affairs often brought angry reactions from their husbands.

But changes in the world around them soon overtook the !Kung. The hunting lands were drying up, and the South African government wanted the "natives" on reservations. Some !Kung did move to settlements where they had to change their entire way of life. The women tried growing garden food and the men worked as laborers on roads and farms, or were recruited into the South African army (to fight against other blacks). Missionaries built a church, a school was opened, and a general store replaced the traditional method of distributing food.

When revisited in 1978, the !Kung on the reservation had been transformed from a self-sufficient group to a collection of economically dependent individuals. Families were broken up when young men joined the army or went away to find wage work. Alcoholism became common once the store sold liquor. Disease and death rates have climbed. A cash economy has led to inequality, hoarding, selfishness, and hostility within the settlement. (This pattern could also describe the fate of Native American tribes in the United States.)

In the early 1980s, a small group of !Kung left the reservation and attempted to revive their traditional patterns of hunting and sharing. But most still remain in the settlement, too demoralized to leave. And, behind all these changes, the South African government continues to restrict the movements of all native peoples.

SOURCES: Elizabeth Marshall Thomas, *The Harmless People.* New York: Knopf, 1958; Lorna Marshall, *The !Kung of Nyae Nyae.* Cambridge: Harvard University Press, 1976; Marjorie Shostak, *Nisa: The Life and Words of a !Kung Woman.* Cambridge: Harvard University Press, 1981; Richard B. Lee, *The Dobe !Kung.* New York: Holt, Rinehart & Winston, 1984; Toby Alice Volkman, "The San in Transition," Cambridge: Cultural Survival, Inc., 1986.

will remain one of the most curious episodes in modern anthropology. Could so many experts have been so thoroughly fooled by a make-believe band of tribal people? Or have the media been as quick to reject the idea of such an innocent way of life as they were eager to embrace it in the early 1960s?

If gathering bands are in short supply, there are still a number of gathering/ hunting societies throughout the world. One of the most carefully studied (no hoax here) is the !Kung San of the Kalihari Desert (see box).

The simplicity of the gathering band stands in stark contrast to the life styles of the "super-rich" in our society, where, for example, a New York City real estate developer recently held a coming-of-age party for his three children by inviting 600 guests to an overnight cruise on the ocean liner Queen Elizabeth II (*The New York Times,* Sept. 16, 1986, p. B1 ff). A champagne and caviar reception preceded a dinner of six entrees and three-foot high cakes. Other meals were similarly elaborate. Guests were served by a staff of 1000 and entertained by three orchestras in addition to the ship's own musicians. All the ship's services were available—swimming pools, a movie theater, the health spa, and beauty parlor.

Although members of gathering/hunting societies might recognize the custom of inviting friends to share food in celebration of an important transition in the life course, they could never understand the excessive wastefulness of this event. Nor would the many herding tribes of Africa and Asia, some on the edge of starvation due to overgrazing, climate changes, or civil wars, be able to understand the recent actions of our Department of Agriculture in ordering the immediate slaughter of one million cows in order to maintain the price of milk by cutting down on its supply (Schneider 1986).

TYPES OF CULTURES AND SOCIETIES

Preliterate societies do not have a written language.
Historical societies have left written records.

Modern societies have developed industrial production.

Following our model of cultural development, we will use the terms *simple* and *preliterate* in place of value-laden words such as *primitive* or *uncivilized*. *Preliterate* means before writing and correctly describes most preagricultural societies. Agricultural societies are considered *historical* because some written record has been left, although preliterate people have languages and a vital tradition of spoken history. *Modern* societies are those that have entered the industrial age. All three types of society still exist today. In North America, for example, there are Inuit herders, French-Canadian trappers, Na-

tive American and Mexican horticulturists, and Amish agricultural communities, as well as industrial societies. The general characteristics of different types of preliterate or preindustrial societies are summarized in Table 3-1.

CULTURAL DEVELOPMENT IN A CONFLICT PERSPECTIVE

In taking the mode of subsistence as the determinant of cultural complexity we are following an essentially Marxist view of the crucial significance of the economic base, especially in premodern societies. In modern societies, however, as will be discussed in Chapters 13 and 22, the centralized state can become an independent force in social change.

As our description of gathering and hunting/gathering societies should make clear, equality within the group is possible when most adults perform similar tasks and when there is very little in the way of material culture. Because gathering and hunting require constant movement, people do not accumulate many things, and because the foods must be eaten fresh, sharing is common.

Once the group becomes more geographically settled ("sedentary"), people can hold on to certain possessions—land, animals, and artifacts—and communal sharing is often replaced by private exchanges

TABLE 3-1 Types of preindustrial societies

Type	Size	Mode of Subsistence	Specialization of Labor	Political Structure	Economic Distribution	Degree of Inequality	Integrating Mechanism
Band	20–60 people in one place	Gathering	Very little	Informal, based on skill	Communal sharing	Relatively egalitarian	Kinship (blood and marriage)
Tribe	Hundreds in several residential groups	Hunting Herding Horticulture	Slight, on basis of age and sex	Informal, family- and residence-based	Redistribution of group's goods	Minimal	Residential groups and cross-cutting task groups
Chiefdom	500 to several thousand in large communities	Agriculture and other specializations	Moderate	Chiefs and other recognized leaders	Gift exchange (reciprocity)	Ranked positions	Centralized leadership of chiefs
Early state	Many thousands in cities and towns	Intensive agriculture and professional artisans (special crafts)	Extreme	Formal, legally structured positions, usually hereditary	Market exchange (with a general currency)	Political and economic classes	Monopoly of force by political religious leaders Bureaucracy

niques while fighting the introduction of other aspects of western culture which threaten their total control over their subjects.

Although many industrial societies are similarly marked by wide differences in power, prestige, and wealth among individuals and groups, modern economies also create the conditions under which inequality can be reduced. These are points to which we return in Chapters 7, 10, 21, and 22.

Analyzing Culture

Culture is an *abstraction*; most of its elements cannot be seen or touched; we can describe only what people do and the explanations they give for their conduct. The study of culture provides a "blueprint" for analyzing a given society. We titled this chapter "The Cultural Context" to convey the idea that culture provides a framework for the social arrangements that govern daily life. Some elements of culture are common to all societies and other aspects are limited to only one or a few.

CULTURAL UNIVERSALS AND CULTURAL VARIABILITY

Because every culture must deal with human limitations and possibilities, and because every group must solve the same problems of survival, certain basic elements are found in all cultures. These are the *cultural universals,* or *social institutions* shown in Table 3-2.

But the *content,* the specific details, of such institutions will be different from one society to another, shaped by geography and history. These processes account for *cultural variability* and the astonishing variety of customs, beliefs, and artifacts that humans have devised to meet universal needs. For example, although the need for orderly reproduction has led to rules regulating courtship and marriage in all societies, these can range from a communal ceremony among individuals who may never live together, to arranged marriages and child brides, to the seemingly hit-or-miss choices of contemporary Americans.

Customs that seem "odd" to us are the "natural" way to do things in other soci-

Cultural universals are basic elements found in all cultures.

Cultural variability reflects the variety of customs, beliefs, and artifacts devised by humans to meet universal needs.

The combination of traditional and modern cultures can take some unexpected forms. (© Masami Teraoka/Collection Cray Research and Walker Art Center, 1986)

among individuals or families. As a result, cultural complexity is typically associated with increased inequality, reaching its most systematic form in agricultural societies, especially those based on slavery and/or hereditary ownership.

Conflict over the distribution of goods and services is also common in societies with private ownership of resources but without some overall authority that can resolve disputes between families or among individuals. Indeed, changes in the direction of greater complexity are resisted by those who enjoy power under the existing system (unless they also control the new resources). The sheiks who rule Near Eastern societies, for example, have accepted western oil-producing tech-

TABLE 3-2   Cultural universals

Universal Needs	Group Response (Institutions)
• Adaptation to the environment; food, shelter	• Economic activity: production and distribution of goods and services
• Maintenance of order; rule enforcement; dispute settlement; protection and defense	• Political behavior; lawgiving, policing; defending; judging
• Orderly reproduction and recruitment of new members	• Marriage and family rules
• Training new members in the ways of the group	• Socialization and education
• Constructing beliefs that relieve anxiety and make members feel responsible for one another	• Belief systems

eties. Because every group must transform sexual impulses into patterned and therefore predictable behavior, we find great variability in sexual beliefs and activities among the world's cultures. Some permit open displays of sexuality among children; we find it upsetting. Some allow, even encourage, homosexuality among males; we scorn and try to forbid it. Tibetan monks and Catholic priests are required to remain celibate; in other societies, men are expected to spend their entire lives trying to seduce women. In still other cultures, women are thought to have the stronger sex drive and they behave accordingly. Thus, the same human impulse becomes subject to widely varying rules governing its expression, and in all societies, people are taught that their behavior is "normal" and "natural."

ETHNOCENTRISM AND CULTURAL RELATIVISM

In comparing different cultures, we tend to evaluate the customs of others in the light of our own beliefs and values. Members of all cultures assume that their own design for living is the best and only correct way. Often, the name chosen for the group means "the people," implying that those not sharing the culture are not "people," but "them," outsiders, who are often identified by words that consciously dehumanize (for example, *pig, gook,* and other terms that refer to members of various minorities).

The belief that one's own culture is the only true and good way, as well as the tendency to judge other cultures by those

standards, is called *ethnocentrism* (*ethno* = race, group, people; *centric* = revolving around). Ethnocentrism serves several important functions for individuals and groups: Certainty about the rightness of one's beliefs and behaviors reinforces the tendency to conform and to defend one's society. Ethnocentrism may be essential for social solidarity, the glue that holds the group together.

Ethnocentrism becomes *dysfunctional* (reduces the adaptability of a social system) when beliefs in one's superiority lead to hostility, misunderstandings that provoke conflict, and refusal to find value in other ways of life. Tensions among groups and nations are often heightened by ethnocentrism. If other people are judged less than human, they can be treated differently from those who are "like us." In American history, each new ethnic, religious, or racial group was thought to be inferior to white, Anglo-Saxon Protestants, or the other groups that preceded them, and therefore deserving less than humane treatment.

The social scientist strives to observe all cultures objectively. Aspects of culture should be judged in terms of the meanings attached to them in a given society and not by the standards of another culture. This attempt to understand the world as seen by members of other societies is called *cultural relativism.* Value judgments based on one's own culture are replaced, as far as possible, by an appreciation of the values of other cultures. The social scientist does not ask if cultural elements are good or bad according to some absolute yardstick but, rather, why the element

Ethnocentrism is the belief that one's own culture is the best and the consequent judging of other cultures by that standard.

Cultural relativism involves an effort to understand the world as seen by members of other societies.

Many people in modern societies find the ritual scarification among so-called primitives to be incomprehensible. Yet there are many "moderns" such as this biker in the U.S. and the group of Irezumi in Japan, who undergo elaborate and painful processes to produce "works of art" very central to their identities and social life. (TOP: © Dennis Brack/Black Star; BOTTOM: © Sandi Feldman)

Bodies, Beauty and Pain: A Cross-Cultural Perspective

In a now classic study of cultural relativism demonstrating our own cultural eccentricities and underscoring the idea of cultural relativism, Horace Miner (1956) described the way of life of the Nacirema, a North American group whose chief lives on the banks of the Camotop River. The tribe is obsessed with rituals centered on deforming the human body: changing its color, its smell, and its shape. Under the guidance of "holy mouth men," whom they seek out once or twice a year, the Nacirema engage in a daily ritual of inserting bundles of hogs' hair and magical powders into the mouth and "then moving the bundle in a highly formalized series of gestures." Nacirema ceremonies can be quite painful, as when the men scrape their faces with sharp instruments and the women bake their heads in small ovens.

Described in this way, such customs appear very strange. Perhaps you'd be tempted to call them "primitive." Surely a person from the modern industrial world would not behave in this fashion. Yet Miner was simply looking at American (Nacirema backwards) society from a different perspective. Can you see it? Look at some of our other behaviors. Consider tattooing, a process that is far from painless and is supposed to make the bearer's body both more attractive and somehow more powerful for having endured the pain. Or what of the fairly involved procedures for hair transplants, another painful process designed to counter baldness (and bring on the strength of Samson?).

Of course, we are not alone in these cultural directions. Consider the Irezumi, a subculture of tattooed persons in Japan. Their half and whole body tattoos can take up to ten years to complete and, because they reduce the portions of the skin that breathe, contribute to a shortened life span.

The lessons of cultural relativism teach us that no behavior should be considered out of the context of the culture in which it originates and that what is "natural" to us will not necessarily be so to members of other societies.

SOURCE: Horace Miner, "Body Ritual Among the Nacirema," *American Anthropologist,* Vol. 58 (June 1956), pp. 503–507; Sandi Feldman, *The Japanese Tatoo.* Abbeville Press, NY, 1986.

exists, how it is sustained, and what purpose it serves in that culture. "Does it work for that group?" is the standard for evaluating aspects of culture. The basic assumption (itself a value judgment) in cultural relativism is that each group's solutions to the tasks of survival are as valid as any other's, however unappealing these patterns may seem to someone from another society. Cultural adaptations, therefore, can be compared only in terms of how much they assist the survival of the group. In practice, however, all definitions of what works are bound up in culture-specific values. Perhaps the best one can do is remain aware of the biases brought to any value judgment.

Above all, we must avoid the tendency to think of people in simple societies as being less evolved or intelligent than are members of modern industrial societies. We may appear to be wiser but only because we "stand on the shoulders of giants," that is, we may see further because we can build on the accomplishments of previous cultures. Nor, perhaps, for all our possessions, should we claim moral superiority over the gentle and egalitarian !Kung San.

IDEAL AND REAL CULTURE

Ideal culture reflects the highest virtues and standards of a society.

Within any society, the observer must distinguish cultural *ideals* from the actual beliefs and values that guide everyday life. When asking people to describe their culture, we are likely to receive an answer based on ideals rather than actuality. Nor are ideals always easily realized in everyday life. In our society, for example, the ideal of religious tolerance is frequently violated by attacks on atheists and by attempts to deny tax exempt status to "cults."

Real culture refers to actual behavior.

Every culture provides examples of the gap between what ought to be and what is. Few members of any society can consistently maintain ideal standards of behavior. Thus, *real culture* often consists of justifications for actions that fall short of our highest goals. The excuses still being used to deny equality to American blacks suggest the power of immediate pressures over ideal expectations. Nonetheless, the ideals do serve as targets toward which we must strive and as criteria for evaluating our society as well as our own conduct. The "strain toward consistency" between the real and ideal adds a dynamic tension to culture and society.

NORMS AND VALUES

Social norms are rules of behavior.

Rules of conduct are part of the learned tradition of any group. Rules of behavior are called *social norms.* These are both *prescriptions,* which are definitions of the acceptable (just as a physician's prescription specifies the contents of a medication), and *proscriptions,* which are definitions of acts that are not acceptable (taboos).

Some norms are more important than others. For example, rules involving behavior that is essential to group well-being ("Thou shalt not steal") are typically of greater weight than rules of personal hygiene ("Brush your teeth"). Many norms are simply a matter of taste; others allow little leeway. Yet behaviors thought essential in one society may not be in another. Coloring one's face is optional in America but is essential in Hindu societies, where social position is symbolized by such markings.

Body scars that would be ugly in our society are requirements for becoming an adult among many African tribes. Not very long ago, German students rubbed salt into a face wound to produce a scar that testified to their courage and nobility. In other words, the meaning and strength of a norm must be found within that culture.

How can the social scientist evaluate the strength of a norm? Usually, the members of the society can tell the observer which rules are more important than others, but the confusion between ideal and real culture may be a problem. If you were asked to rank the norms of your society from most to least powerful, could you do so easily? Would you list ideal norms such as playing the game well or real norms such as playing to win at all costs?

Classifying Norms. Following the original classification of William Graham Sumner (1906), we distinguish several types of cultural rules.

FOLKWAYS. Those approved standards of behavior that are passed on from generation to generation as "the way we do things" are called *folkways.* Generally, folkways cover activities that are not necessarily essential to group survival. Eating with a knife and fork, for example, is an American folkway. Our society would not collapse if children threw away their spoons, although parental authority might suffer. Seemingly trivial folkways do, nevertheless, express some societal themes—standards of hygiene in using eating utensils, or standards of appropriate dress in the custom of wearing matching socks.

Folkways are customs transmitted from one generation to the next.

Yet folkways are not considered important enough to be strongly enforced. No court will punish the girl who eats with her fingers or the man who wears two differently colored socks. Violations of the folkways are typically handled in face-to-face interaction, through words and gestures implying disapproval.

Sanctions refer to reactions that convey approval or disapproval of behavior.

All norms are enforced by *sanctions.* Sanctions refer to the reactions of other people that tell you whether or not you are behaving correctly. Positive sanctions reinforce your behavior; negative sanctions indicate that you have violated the norms. Because of their customary character, folkways are typically enforced by *informal sanctions* such as a raised eyebrow, slap on the wrist, or cold shoulder.

MORES. Folkways that have acquired a sense of necessity, of "oughtness," are called *mores.* These norms cover behaviors felt to be important to group stability, so that conformity is not optional. We believe that people should respect authority, help relatives and friends, control sexuality, and observe community standards of appropriate public conduct. Accordingly, violations of the mores meet with more severe sanctions than does failure to follow the folkways. Group scorn and isolation are powerful, though still informal, sanctions because the full force of the community is brought to bear on the offender. Although violations of the mores occur in all societies, group sanctions are most effective among members of small close-knit bands or subgroups.

Mores are folkways that have acquired a sense of necessity.

LAWS. Norms that govern behavior considered most essential to group survival are classified as *laws.* The laws apply to all members of the society, and are enforced by *formal sanctions* exercised by officials with specific responsibility to uphold the law.

Sumner sees *customary laws* as a formalizing of traditional practices, spelling out what is permitted or prohibited and specifying the penalties for nonconformity. *Enacted laws,* in contrast, can represent a departure from custom, and may even go against traditional practices (as when Prohibition was enacted in the United States).

Laws are norms that govern behavior and are considered essential to group survival.

Although laws are designed to ensure public order, they often reflect the ideal culture, setting standards that not everyone can meet. A prime example of such laws are the Ten Commandments of the Old Testament, a minimal set of rules designed to ensure social order: obey authority; reduce jealousy and violence in the group; give honest testimony; and respect property.

Why are certain behaviors governed by laws and not others? In general, the norms of any society are derived from broader ideas about good and bad, right and wrong, and carry a moral dimension. These general concepts are called *values.*

VALUES. Central beliefs about what is important form a standard against which the norms can be judged. Specific rules such as "Thou shalt not kill" reflect both a respect for human life and the group's need to avoid the internal feuding that could follow a murder. There are, however, exceptions to even universal values. Murder is approved when done to the enemy in battle (indeed, medals are given to superior killers), yet death may be the penalty for killing under other circumstances.

Values are the central beliefs of a culture that provide a standard by which norms are judged.

Each culture embodies concepts of the ultimate good, virtue, beauty, justice, and other abstract qualities that are thought to be reflected in the norms. Yet the link between values and norms is not always direct or consistent. For example, the norms—folkways, mores, and laws—that governed white-black relationships in the United States until the 1960s could hardly be reconciled with American values such as equality and justice. And today, resistance to recent gains by blacks is justified by appealing to other values—individualism and freedom from state power.

RITUALS. *Rituals* are culturally patterned ways of dealing with human drives and anxiety-producing events. For example, most societies have highly ritualized courtship and mating patterns that are taught to each generation of young people. Birth, death, and the transition from childhood to adulthood are typically marked by elaborate rituals.

Rituals are culturally patterned ways of dealing with anxiety-producing events.

Public ceremonies that mark some change in a person's position in the society are known as *rites of passage* (Van Gennep 1909/1960). Initiation ceremonies in adolescence (puberty) are among the most common. The precise ceremony varies from culture to culture: Plains Indian boys are left on a mountainside to have a vision; at age thirteen, Jews recite the Holy Scriptures during a Bar/Bat Mitzvah; Christians are confirmed; and in the Andaman Islands, a dance is held in honor of the boy who is soon to become a man, and his back and chest are ritually scarred.

Rites of passage are the ceremonies marking important changes in a person's position in the group.

In every society, certain life changes are recognized as potentially dangerous for the individual and the group—a cultural universal. In each society, the ritual and its symbolism are different—a cultural variation. The function of ritual, everywhere, is to relieve anxiety about the un-

In recent years more minorities and women have gained access to the rites of passage of formerly restricted social institutions such as the military. (© Steiner/SYGMA)

known and to bring human drives and emotions under the control of the group through time-honored ceremonies.

These, then, are the essential elements of culture: symbols, language, norms, values, and rituals. Beliefs, behaviors, attitudes, and artifacts make up the unique adaptations of any human group to its environment.

SUBCULTURES

Subcultures consist of differences in values, beliefs, norms, and behavior among societal subgroups.

We have defined *culture* as a group's response to the conditions of existence, that is, the adaptive, coping solutions to the problems of survival and the effects of history. If subgroups within a society have different experiences, and if needs and opportunities vary from group to group, then we would expect great diversity in life-style among these subgroups. Such differences in values, beliefs, norms, and behaviors are called *subcultural adaptations,* or *subcultures.*

Subcultures appear whenever access to the general culture is different for some members of a society. As all but the most simple societies have division of labor, specialization, and differences in power and prestige, subgroups can be identified in almost every society. The more complex the culture and the more diverse the population, the greater the probability that a society has subcultures.

Subcultures are variations on general cultural themes that permit members of the subgroup to survive under conditions different from those faced by the dominant group. In America, racial, ethnic, and religious minorities have constructed subcultural adaptations to their situation. Keeping some of their Old World customs and language permitted the first generation of immigrants to survive the abrupt change to American ways. For French-speaking Canadians, Hispanic-Americans, and blacks throughout North America, language, skin color, or cultural distinctiveness still provoke discrimination (Chap. 10). As long as this is so, the need for subcultural adaptations and supports will remain strong.

There are also some subgroups whose members prefer to remain relatively isolated from mainstream institutions, in order to preserve their unique life-styles. One thinks immediately of the Amish who have been able to maintain traditional farming communities in the midst of industrialized America, and of Orthodox Jews who have set themselves apart even from other Jewish groups. Such subcultures are preserved by minimizing contact with the "outside" world, especially in the education of their children, which takes place totally within the community.

Conflict between Culture and Subculture. The value dilemma of contemporary Mexican-American youth growing up in the inner city illustrates the conflict that can arise between cultural and subcultural values. As described by Horowitz (1983), there is, on the one hand, the "American Dream" emphasis on education and economic achievement, both of which are difficult for inner city poor to realize. On the other hand are the traditional Hispanic conceptions of masculine "honor," involving the protection of one's reputation through displays of male dominance. The appeal of street gangs as a means of achieving prestige while preserving honor should therefore be understood in the framework of culture conflict.

For young women in the Mexican-American community, the conflict is between traditional family values—virginity before marriage, motherhood, and submission to male authority—and the sexual demands of boyfriends. Because the reality of the streets is not supportive of family values, these women have had to construct new definitions of acceptable behavior that reconcile the conflicting pressures. And over time, the norms of the entire community have expanded to embrace changes in the behavior of their teenagers.

Boundary main-tenance refers to the ways subcultures/subgroups protect themselves from outsiders.

Jargons are special languages of subgroups/subcultures.

Boundary Maintenance. Members of subgroups can protect themselves from outsiders by creating and reinforcing group boundaries. This is the function of special languages, or *jargons.* Just as doctors and lawyers talk to one another in a specialized vocabulary that identifies group members while confusing patients and clients, so also do members of gangs or racial and religious minorities have secret handshakes, special clothes, and other signs of recognition, as well as a jargon that cannot be understood by others. American teenagers have a way of talking and dressing that sets them apart from children and adults. Such barriers reinforce solidarity among the in-group and protect against invasion by out-groups. In some respects, any group that regularly performs a specialized task tends to construct barriers. Athletes, musicians, military personnel, fire fighters, and police officers are among the most thoroughly researched subgroups.

Countercultures represent alternative life-styles for those not conforming to the dominant norms.

Countercultures. Some subcultures also contain elements of clear opposition to the values and beliefs of the larger society (Yinger 1982). A *counterculture* provides an alternative life-style for those who cannot or will not conform to the dominant norms, as for example, the beatniks of the 1950s, the flower children of the 1960s, the members of the 1970s drug scene, and various other cultural dropouts. Similarly, those who live in communes or religious communities cut off from the larger society exemplify a way of life very different from that of the mainstream (Case and Taylor 1979).

Countercultures are distinguished from subcultures by their opposition to the existing social patterns. Subcultural adaptations are attempts to integrate members into the dominant culture while retaining the uniqueness of racial, religious, occupational, or ethnic-group identifications. In

Culture in Everyday Life: Eating

Because culture is the water in our fishbowl, we are usually unaware of its influence on seemingly "natural" activities. The rituals and values surrounding the preparation and eating of food, for example, can tell us a great deal about any culture. This everyday behavior is steeped in context.

Among the strongest of human drives are those aroused by hunger and thirst. Yet seldom does a person eat or drink the first things at hand. Except under the most extreme circumstances, for example, Americans would not drink urine or eat human flesh, although both behaviors have been well documented.

Eating, a simple and universal human activity, is everywhere surrounded by rules, rituals, values, symbols, and taboos. The personal act is transformed into a social event. There are typical foodstuffs for each society: Americans are great consumers of meat, the French of wine, the Tasaday of tadpoles, the Eskimo of blubber, and so forth. A set of values and beliefs develops around these foods; special utensils and behaviors are required; the food has a "meaning" conferred by the group. One need think only of the Thanksgiving turkey in the United States to realize that we are not speaking of unusual customs of preliterate tribes. At this feast, the nation's earliest settlers are remembered; the ideal family is sentimentalized; and the eaters are expected to give thanks to God. In sum, patriotism, family loyalty, and religion are reinforced in this version of the worldwide custom of celebrating the harvest. In other societies, the end of the growing season is an occasion for excesses—overeating and overdrinking, as well as sexual freedoms not otherwise permitted. These releases of energy reward the hard work before the harvest and prepare people for the relatively quiet months ahead while also legitimating a period of deviance.

Within a society, some people are distinguished from others by what and how much they can eat. Most common are different food taboos for men and women, or for children and adults. The well-off have different diets from the poor, and in some societies, strangers are served food different from that eaten by the natives. Women and children are frequently forbidden to eat with the adult males of the group.

You can gain some insights into the relative power and prestige of the members of your own family by observing what happens at the dinner table. Who gets what and in what order? Whose plate is filled first, whose last? Who serves and who doesn't? Who picks the menu?

What kinds of qualities are admired in this Nobel Peace Prize winner who rejects wealth and cares for the poor and this successful trend-setting entertainer who sings "I'm a Material Girl"? (LEFT: © Randi Taylor/SYGMA; RIGHT: © B. Marino/SYGMA)

contrast, those who cannot or will not conform to accepted codes of conduct tend to seek out others who share their views and who will reinforce their opposition to mainstream values and behaviors. This is how countercultures take root.

THE VALUE SYSTEM OF THE UNITED STATES

What can one say of a society in which both Mother Teresa, a nun who ministers to the most impoverished peoples of the world, and the punk rock star Madonna both appear on a list of "most admired women"? Clearly, there is little consistency or agreement on the qualities that Americans value most.

Possibly, no country containing dozens of religious, racial, and ethnic minorities could have a standard culture, one clear set of values and approved behaviors. *Heterogeneity* (the existence of many different subgroups) is an invitation to subcultural development in America. But there is a set of very general values and beliefs that are shared by most members of the society. *Nationalism* and *patriotism,* as the natural outgrowth of ethnocentrism, are powerful factors in all societies as a form of social cement that can unite otherwise different segments of the population. This is the function of national anthems, colorful inauguration ceremonies, and national holidays.

Cultural heterogeneity refers to the existence of many different subcultures and subgroups in a society.

Core Values. Robin Williams, Jr. (1970), identified a set of core values underlying the beliefs and behaviors of Americans. These fifteen value orientations represent a conception of the good life and the goals of social action, of what might be called the *American ethos*:

1. *Achievement and success* as the major personal goals.
2. *Activity and work* favored above leisure and laziness.
3. *Moral orientation,* that is, absolute judgments of good/bad, right/wrong.
4. *Humanitarian motives* as shown in charity and crisis aid.
5. *Efficiency and practicality,* a preference for the quickest and shortest way to achieve a goal at the least cost.
6. *Process and progress,* a belief that technology can solve all problems, and that the future will be better than the past.
7. *Material comfort* as the American Dream.
8. *Equality* as an abstract ideal.
9. *Freedom* as a person's right against the state.
10. *External conformity,* the ideal of going along, joining, and not rocking the boat.
11. *Science and rationality* as the means of mastering the environment and securing more material comforts.
12. *Nationalism,* a belief that American values and institutions represent the best on earth.
13. *Democracy* based on personal equality and freedom.
14. *Individualism,* emphasizing personal rights and responsibilities.
15. *Racism and group-superiority themes* that periodically lead to prejudice and discrimination against those who are racially, religiously, and culturally different from the white northern Europeans who first settled the continent.

This is a bewildering list, combining political, economic, and personal traits, some of which actually conflict with others, as our history shows. Equality is an uneasy partner of beliefs in racial superiority, whereas nationalism often limits the exercise of freedom. The coexistence of such contradictory values accounts for a certain vitality as well as divisions within American society. The content and the

The **American ethos** is a set of core values guiding the beliefs and behaviors of Americans.

importance of any set of value orientations change over time.

The similarity between Williams' list and the values embraced by such founders of our political system as Benjamin Franklin (1784/1970) indicates the enduring strength of concepts described by Max Weber (1904/1958) as forming the core of the Protestant Ethic in the sixteenth century, that is now referred to as the *work ethic*. The work ethic allowed the emerging merchant class to accumulate wealth, to keep their profits, to claim a wide area of personal freedom, and generally to lay the foundation of modern capitalism. (See Chapter 12 for a full discussion of capitalism.)

Central to this ethic are the following values:

Work as a "calling." A *calling* is a sacred task. In most societies throughout history, work has been something people did to survive. To regard physical labor of whatever type as a divine duty is a powerful motive for producing more than what is required just to survive. So strong is the work ethic that even enjoyment of leisure must be presented as an extension of work-related meanings; it must be earned and must present challenges to be overcome (Lewis 1982).

Success as a sign of grace. If work is a sacred task, there must be some way of distinguishing those who perform well from the lazy and the careless. Success in one's chosen occupation seemed a clear and simple sign of divine favor.

Individuals as monitors of their own state of grace. According to early Protestant theology, there should be no intervening group of priests between a human being and God. Martin Luther's revolt against the Catholic Church was primarily an attempt to do away with the layers of churchly authority that interfered with direct communion with God. In this view, the individual, alone, was responsible for his or her own fate. The Protestant symbol was the lonely pilgrim, overcoming the terrors and temptations of earthly life, always anxious and never certain that God's will was being done. The inner fears of eternal damnation served to regulate social behavior.

As Weber notes, while these ideas provide a motivational basis for working hard, striving for success, and accumulating private profits, they could also be used to explain or justify trends that were already under way in the economy (Poggi 1983). How else to persuade people to labor twelve to fourteen hours a day in filthy factories for barely survival wages, except by convincing them that they are doing God's will? And how else to reassure the owners that they are not exploiting workers except to suggest that their success is a sign of grace? Furthermore, if success is due to one's own efforts, then failure must reflect a personal flaw, some lack of moral virtue *within the individual*. If those who fail have brought it upon themselves, the rest of us need feel no responsibility for their situation, although we might choose to offer assistance in the form of charity.

Originally, also, the early Protestants and our Puritan pilgrims stressed *simplicity in life-style*. Vulgar displays of wealth were scorned. Rather, people should practice "worldly asceticism," to deny pleasures and to live in this world as if one had taken a vow of poverty. Clearly, this concept would be extremely important in the early stages of modern economic development. If one works hard, does well, and cannot spend the profit on material possessions, then the money is available for investment. In other words, the practice of worldly asceticism is a precondition for the accumulation of capital required to begin new businesses. (See Chapter 15 for further discussion of the Protestant ethic.)

Just as surely, however, the continued success of profit-making businesses depends on increasingly higher levels of demand for products. While worldly asceticism may be important for generating start-up money, a lot of other people must be willing to part with their earnings in order to buy what is being produced. Thus, a "culture of materialism" is also essential to industrial capitalism (Mukerji 1983). *Materialism* refers to a desire for owning and consuming goods and services. Because materialism is so much a part of our culture, we tend to think of it as a universal aspect of human nature. But the urge to own is no more basic than a willingness to share; both behaviors reflect cultural values.

The culture of materialism is based on the meanings given to the accumulation of worldly goods—as symbols of the "good life" and of the owner's prestige, as the

Materialism refers to a desire for owning and consuming goods and services.

deserved rewards for hard work, and as a means of providing security for one's children. Gradually, then, worldly asceticism has given way to its precise opposite, as both cause and consequence of industrial capitalism (Sussman 1985). The American economist Thorstein Veblen (1899) used the term *conspicuous consumption* to refer to lavish displays of wastefulness designed to impress others with one's ability to throw away money, a thought that would surely shock our Puritan forebears.

These few concepts are the roots of our American emphasis on individualism, on work and achievement, on progress, on a sense of morality for oneself and personal charity for the less fortunate, and, as a consequence, on a sense of righteousness tempered with doubts that must never be openly shown, lest one lose certainty in salvation.

As we shall see in Part III of this book, the work ethic has been used to justify and reinforce great inequalities in our society. The conception of work as a calling permits some forms of exploitation, as when "dirty" work is described as "good for one's soul." By equating success with divine favor, we are led to see the poor as morally flawed. And by placing full responsibility for success or failure on the individual, other reasons for these outcomes—lack of adequate training, discrimination in hiring, a shortage of well-paying jobs—are ignored or treated as personal problems. These considerations suggest that the norms and values of the general culture cannot be assumed to represent complete agreement among all members on what is best for the group.

Cultural Hegemony. In the perspective of conflict theory, values and norms are not neutral; they do not affect all members of a group in the same manner. On the contrary, what is considered good and true and fair benefits some people and not others. Ideas, no less than things, are cultural artifacts—creations of the group and of its most powerful members. The concept of *cultural hegemony* refers to the control over the production of values and norms that is exercised by those who are in a position to create and enforce rules of conduct. We have just seen how the ideology of the work ethic promotes the interests of the successful at the expense of others.

The cultural values of democracy or equality, for example, are assumed to be available to all our citizens, but it would be very difficult to argue that blacks or women, even today, receive equal treatment or are present in decision-making groups in proportion to their numbers in the American population (Chaps. 8 and 10). The laws that are considered so important to democratic culture are not neutral, either. As you will see in Chapter 16, the laws not only protect the interests of the successful but are often unequally enforced, with poor or minority offenders receiving particularly harsh sentences (Unnever 1982).

There is, in other words, a "seamy side of democracy" (Wolfe 1978) in which the value assumptions of our society are used to deny equality to those defined as somehow "less deserving." However, democratic values and ideals can also be used to demand change (Rudé 1980, Gintis 1980), as we will see in Chapter 21.

Changing Values? But surely, some of you may have been saying, there are other ideals and goals that motivate our behavior. What about caring, openness, cooperation, and community? Didn't the 1960s produce another set of values, at least for young adults?

Yes, there is some evidence that the strength of the work ethic has diminished in recent years. Much has been written about young well-educated upwardly mobile professionals—"yuppies"—whose devotion to work is modified by considerations of personal fulfillment, family involvement, and enjoying the good life. Older people, too, appear to be less tied to the work ethic than previously thought, as the data on retirement suggest (Chap. 9). Leisure, once thought to be the breeding ground for sin, is now valued by most adults to the same degree as work.

There is no question, either, that the 1960s left a legacy of openness to new experience; a concern for the environment and its preservation; support for the civil rights of women, racial minorities, and homosexuals; and a strengthened desire for peace.

But "traditional" values of nationalism, individual competition, and materialism are very much alive. One of the most sociologically fascinating characteristics of the 1980s has been the fierce backlash against

Conspicuous consumption is the open display of wastefulness designed to impress others.

Cultural hegemony refers to control over the production of values and norms by those in power.

There has been a definite resurgence of national pride and patriotic values in the '80s. (© Paul Fusco/Magnum Photos)

the ideals of the 1960s. Public opinion polls once more show strong support for the military and expensive weapons systems, as well as increasing opposition to further gains for women and blacks. College students are overwhelmingly enrolled in business-type courses, and describe themselves as more conservative than liberal— a great shift from previous decades. The new cultural heroes are the Rambos and others who take the law into their own hands and rewrite history. The right to personal privacy, a primary goal of the 1960s, is being eroded by opponents of homosexuality, pornography, and drug use.

It is too early to tell whether these backlash trends are the last gasp of the old ethic or its bedrock strength. We can say, however, that there are two competing value orientations today, no longer clearly associated with age. The youngest as well as the oldest adults appear more traditional than do people in their thirties and forties.

TRADITIONAL	NEW RULES
Individualism	Involvement/ commitment
Competition	Cooperation
Achievement	Self-fulfillment
Patriotism	Tolerance
Work	"Good life"

To some extent, this value split reflects a basic dualism that runs throughout our culture. It remains to be seen which set of values—traditional or new rules—dominates the decades ahead. Much depends on the choices made by members of your generation.

Summary

Culture replaces physical evolution as the human adaptation to the natural world. The reflexive mind and capacity for language permit human beings to construct a world of meaning and create rules to govern behavior. The cultures of all human groups consist of: (1) solutions to the problems of survival; (2) values and norms; (3) tools and other material objects. Culture is shared among people who live together, feel responsible for one another, and recognize their common identity.

The ability to manipulate symbols is the central cultural activity. Language, both spoken and nonverbal, structures perception and permits the transmission of knowledge from one generation to another. Culture is thus cumulative. Cultures range from the simple technological base of gathering bands to the complex accumulation of ideas and things in modern industrial nations.

Some elements of culture are universal: a means of adapting to the environment (economy), of maintaining order (political structures), of controlling sexuality and raising children (family systems), and a set of integrating beliefs. But no two societies are alike in the precise content of their culture, giving rise to the great variability of blueprints for living.

In judging the ways of other people, we tend to be ethnocentric, looking through the lens of our own beliefs and customs rather than from the perspective of cultural relativism, whereby traits are interpreted in the context of that culture.

Social norms are prescriptions and proscriptions derived from the central values of the culture that guide our behavior in all situations. The more heterogeneous the society, the more likely it is to have subgroups whose different experiences in the society lead to the development of subcultural variations on the general cultural themes.

The chapter closes with a discussion of the historical roots of the American value system in the Protestant work ethic, and the tension between traditional values and a newer set more relevant to a consumer society.

Suggested Readings

BENEDICT, RUTH. *Patterns of Culture.* Boston: Houghton Mifflin, 1934. An early and still unsurpassed statement of the need to view culture as an integrated whole, reflected in all aspects of social structure and personality. The portraits of Zuni, Dobuan, and Kwakiutl cultures are unforgettable.

HALL, EDWARD. *The Silent Language.* Garden City, NY: Doubleday, 1959. An anthropologist describes how nonverbal communication conveys cultural values, and how these shape the characteristic behaviors of the members of different societies.

KEPHART, WILLIAM. *Extraordinary Groups: The Sociology of Unconventional Life-Styles,* 3rd ed. New York: St. Martin's, 1987. The Amish, the Oneida Community, the Father Divine Movement, the Gypsies, the Shakers, the Mormons, and the modern communes are examined in an interesting and readable style.

MOORE, MACDONALD SMITH. *Yankee Blues: Musical Culture & American Identity.* Bloomington: Indiana University Press, 1985. This work examines the rise of jazz as a musical form in the United States and its perception by "mainstream" musicians as a threat to American culture.

POTTER, DAVID. *People of Plenty: Economic Abundance and the American Character.* Chicago: University of Chicago Press, 1954. This historical analysis of the U.S. since colonial times offers a lively and controversial view of American national character, our value system and behavior patterns.

THOMPSON, E. P. *The Heavy Dancers: Writings on War, Past and Future.* New York: Pantheon, 1985. A series of insightful, rational, and witty political essays on the key issues facing the world today—war and peace.

THORNE, BARRIE, CHERIS KRAMARAE, and NANCY HENLEY, eds. *Language, Gender & Society.* Rowley, MA: Newbury House, 1983. A collection of articles describing and examining the links between gender and language from a feminist perspective.

YANKELOVICH, DANIEL. *New Rules.* New York: Random House, 1981. Based on extensive survey research, Yankelovich identifies recent changes in American values.

YINGER, J. MILTON. *Countercultures.* New York: Free Press, 1982. A comprehensive textbook about the New Left movement of the 1960s: communes, utopias, avant-garde movements in art; hippies, sex, drugs; religious cults, magic, witchcraft; and counterculture education. A first-rate source of information, including a forty-page bibliography.

4

Social Structure, Groups, and Interaction

"BEFORE the disaster, the neighbors, we could look out and tell when one another needed help or when one was sick or something was disturbing that person. . . . If the lights was on late at night, we knew that something unusual was going on and we would go over. . . . People would just know what to do. . . . I don't think there was a better place in the world to live. . . . You'd just have to experience it, I guess, to really know. It was wonderful." (Erikson 1976, p. 190)

These comments, made by residents of Buffalo Creek, West Virginia, describe the close social bonds among the five thousand residents of this mountain mining area. These relationships were suddenly shattered when a makeshift dam, holding 132 million gallons of dirty water used in the mining of coal, gave way after several days of heavy rain. Within a few hours, Buffalo Creek was flooded; four thousand town residents were homeless, and 125 people lay dead in the mud. The once relatively secure, close-knit mining community had been reduced to rubble. The survivors of the flood were so deeply shocked by these events that they withdrew into themselves emotionally, feeling alone and helpless. Not only had the flood de-

Social structure describes the ways in which values, beliefs, attitudes, and rules for behavior are patterned to produce various relationships.

stroyed property, life and peoples' sense of well-being, but it also disrupted the social bonds and relationships that had given the residents a sense of community. The flood that tore apart the physical environment of Buffalo Creek also destroyed its *social structure.* As one survivor commented, "We did lose a community, and I mean it was a good community . . . now everybody is alone. They act like they're lost" (p. 196). Or as Erikson put it, "While both 'I and you' continued to exist physically, 'we' no longer exist as a connected pair or as linked cells in a communal body" (p. 154).

What do we mean by *social structure? Social structure* is a term used by sociologists to describe the ordering of everyday behavior and social relationships in a relatively predictable way. It describes the ways in which values, beliefs, attitudes, and behavior are patterned to produce various relationships. A key concept in sociology, social structure has several components: systems, norms, statuses, roles, interactions, and groups. These components and the ways in which they relate to one another are the subject of this chapter.

Sociologists assume that most social behavior is both orderly and predictable. A society comes into existence and continues to exist because underlying patterns allow its members to know what they should be doing and to anticipate the behavior of other people with some reliability. Otherwise, people could not live with one another. If each of us had to rethink every response every moment, we would be paralyzed with indecision. Humans can live together because they can make rules of behavior (*norms*) that define acceptable behavior in given situations. This chapter will describe the development and the results of the behavioral norms that pattern our social relationships.

Norms are rules of behavior that define acceptable conduct.

The Importance of Social Structure

The reality of social structure is particularly hard for Americans to grasp. We value individualism and support the idea that goals are achieved through individual effort (rather than by luck or group action). Therefore, when trying to explain behavior or situations we look for causes *within* the person rather than at sources external to the individual. For example, studies have shown that women are likely to have lower job aspirations than men. Most Americans have interpreted this finding as proof that something in the "feminine temperament" makes women less interested in success than are men— something like an innate capacity for nurturing others that has no place in the hardhearted world of business, or the presence or absence of certain hormones, or a fear of success because achievement is thought to be unfeminine.

An alternative explanation is that people behave as they do because they are placed in different social positions to begin with, and often, precisely because of their different sex, ethnicity, or culture. For example, research by Kanter (1977) on the behavior of men and women in corporate settings showed that both women and men acted in a "feminine" manner when they were placed in jobs with little chance of promotion. Being male or female was relatively unimportant. Rather, opportunities for advancement, the power associated with the job, and whether the worker was the only male or female in the work group explained the observed differences in attitudes and behaviors between female and male employees. All these factors are external to the personality or temperament of the individual. The facts of working life are still that women are more likely than men to be in dead-end jobs, to have limited power, and to be given only token promotions. Therefore, if they made a realistic appraisal of their situations they would not have great job aspirations. This study illustrated that one's position within a social structure, rather than his or her inborn traits, shapes one's behavior and attitudes.

Further support for the importance of one's place in the social structure comes from laboratory studies of the behavior of men and women who have been assigned to positions of either high or low power within the group. The researchers found no differences in how power was exercised by the high ranking women and men— both behaved in a similar manner. But among the less powerful, men would use whatever power they had against higher ranking women, while the low-power

These two women may have very different chances for advancement as well as different levels of job autonomy. How might you compare and contrast their job aspirations and satisfactions? (© Michal Heron/Woodfin Camp and Associates; © Bill Stanton/Magnum Photo, Inc.)

women made few attempts to assert themselves (Floge and Merrill 1986). One's relative position in the social structure therefore is related both to actual power available and to other sociostructural features that shape the ways in which we behave. In this chapter we will focus on both the social structure and the various ways in which positions in this structure are assigned and played out by each of us.

Components of Social Structure

From a conflict-theory perspective, the most essential aspect of any society is how economic production is organized. Most people in any society work, but only a few control their labor and what they produce. These social arrangements of production, in which some control the labor of others, provide the basis for social structure. In other words, social structure reflects the social relationships of production, such as employer-employee or boss-worker. For example, working on an assembly line creates patterns of relationships different from those created working in an office or on a farm. And even within the same organization, the placement of men and women in the process of production is seen as influencing their behavior. The view that the economic base of a society creates social structure, which, in turn, gives rise to particular forms of behavior, is a far cry from explanations of behavior based on individual motives and characteristics!

The structural-functional approach, in contrast, has focused on what parts make up a structure and on how these are combined to form the total structure, or social system.

SOCIAL SYSTEMS

The concept of a *social system* allows us to perceive one way in which social behavior is patterned. A *system* consists of elements with mutually dependent parts joined in a more-or-less stable manner through time. Change or movement in one part affects the other parts. Systems analysis is a useful way of focusing on how a structure of relationships is put together and how it works. Systems analysis is used in sociology and other fields to describe and identify the whole, its parts, and the way in which the parts are connected. For example, biologists view a living organism as a system of particular arrangements and interactions among various organs. Similarly, physicists see the atom as a system that has a distinctive arrangement of neutrons and protons.

Common to all systems analysis is the idea that "the whole (system) is more than the sum of its parts." That is, the parts relate to one another in an organized and patterned way; this organization gives to the whole some characteristics that are not only different from, but not even found in, those of the separate parts. The whole and its parts can be a society and its institutional spheres, a subsystem such as the family and its members, or any group in which people establish usual ways of acting toward one another over time. In short, a system, because of the organization among its parts, has its own distinctiveness.

A **social system** is a totality composed of interdependent parts.

Systems Theory at Work—The Genogram

A genogram is a diagram that provides a graphic picture of the system of a family and its relationships. Developed by Murray Bowen, a psychotherapist deeply interested in family systems, it is a sort of family tree used by family therapists to collect and organize data about several generations of the family system. It contains names, ages, and geographic location of all family members. It also includes dates of major events such as births, deaths, marriages, divorces, and so forth. Collecting data in this way allows problems or symptoms to be seen in the context of the whole family in addition to the individual who is presented as the problem. The Abbott family genogram gives a systems perspective on Ben as part of his family system. Ben is an 18-year-old college student who is having trouble adjusting to his first year of college, and is seeing someone at the counseling service.

Diagrams such as genograms use certain rules, or conventions, to describe relationships. A square is used to symbolize a male, and a circle a female. Deaths are marked by an "x" and divorce by //. A close relationship is marked by a set of double lines, and a conflictual relationship by wavy lines. As you look at this genogram of the Abbott family,

notice Ben's position. After his parents' divorce in 1983, Ben was very close to his father, Ben Sr., who was recently killed in an auto accident. Ben is not close to his mother or his step-father. He has an older sister, Sue, who has moved to Canada. Note that both he and his family are affected by ascribed and achieved statuses; Ben's parents are of different educational levels and his grandparents were of different ethnicities and religions.

A family therapist who saw Ben as a client would find making a genogram very helpful in understanding Ben's family system as a whole. Ben's difficulties in adapting to college might be seen as a reflection of patterns within the family system. This understanding would provide a basis for counseling. Family-systems theory draws heavily upon sociology and the concept of social systems in treating individuals, couples, or whole families. The basic premise in family-systems therapy is that the behavior and relationships of any part of the family affects the system as a whole. No one member is "good," or "bad," "well," or "sick" but rather some aspect of the family's shared system is out of balance, reducing its effectiveness to function most efficiently as a system.

For example, consider your own family. We couldn't describe your immediate family in terms of each member's unique personality and physical attributes. Every family is more than its individual members; it is an entity unto itself as well. Each family has a division of labor for household tasks, such as buying groceries, balancing the checkbook, doing the laundry, taking out the garbage, washing the dog, deciding on when and where to take a vacation, how money should be spent, which relatives to visit and when, and so forth. It also makes its own rules to govern behavior within the family. These rules may be explicit, such as "don't put your elbows on the table," "you can't drive the car except on special occasions," and "hold the door open for older adults," or they may be implicit or unstated. Moreover, each family has developed a history of its own with symbols, ranging from shared possessions and family photos to a type of home; a special language, such as nicknames, phrases, or stories that have meaning primarily within the family context (stories that begin with, "Remember the time

when . . ."); favorite places to go or ways of spending time together. These are not features of each individual, but patterns developed from the interaction of family members and their particular way of presenting themselves to the outside world.

Each social system, like your own family, has qualities that refer only to the system as a whole. Being a part of a system has effects that cannot be fully understood without reference to the system as a whole. The interconnections between various parts of a social system can be quite complex, as the following box, summarizing one family system, illustrates.

MICRO- AND MACROSYSTEMS. In some respects, then, social life is like a series of Chinese boxes, each nesting within another. Sociologists speak of a microlevel or *microsystem* when referring to face-to-face interaction, that is, to the behavior of people in relationships, such as the Abbott family shown above, or a group of friends, or workers in an office. The macrolevel or *macrosystem* is a social system at a higher level of abstraction, such as *the* American family system rather than a particular

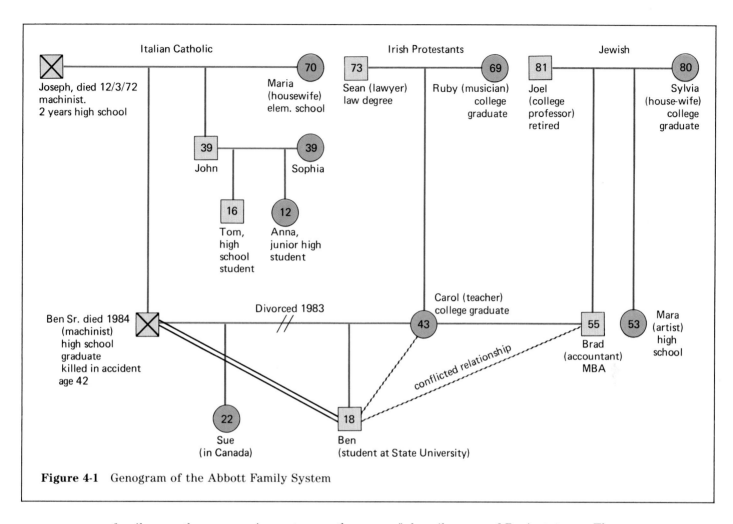

Figure 4-1   Genogram of the Abbott Family System

A **genogram** is a diagram that provides a graphic picture of a family system and its relationships.

family, or the economic system rather than the workers at the local MacDonald's. Each higher level contains the lower ones, however. This is one reason that in the *genogram* age, religion, occupation, and education were noted for each family member. Microsystem information gives clues about links to the macrosystems, and to one's position therein. Each microsystem thus has its own culture and history, values, communication patterns, distribution of power, norms and division of labor, economic level, and so forth. Moreover, it interacts with larger systems, such as other relatives, employers, and community organizations. By looking at a microsystem such as family, we may learn both about that particular family and about the larger social system in which it participates.

Status is a position in a social system.

Status.   The term *status* is used in sociology to mean "position in a social system." Statuses are the building blocks in social structures. To say "Ben is Carol Abbott's

son" describes one of Ben's statuses. Thus statuses are always linked; any particular status implies at least one other to which it is related. The classroom, for example, is composed of two status categories: teacher and student. Without referring to any particular person, we can speak of teacher and student as abstract types. We have, in other words, mental maps of status systems that are populated by particular people. You yourself fill the status of student in various classrooms, with different teachers, but in each case, there are patterned regularities: the teacher in front, the students together, a big desk or table for the teacher, little chair flaps for the students, freedom of speech for the teacher, recognition required for the students, and so on. This structuring of classroom behavior will exist as an arrangement of statuses long after you leave school.

We can now expand the concept of the *social system* to mean a set of linked statuses comprising the whole. Take for

We are socialized from an early age to the statuses and role behavior of the classroom. (© Seth Resnick/Picture Group NR)

ASCRIBED AND ACHIEVED STATUS. Some social positions are based on characteristics that are relatively unchangeable or over which a person has no control. Age, sex, and race, for instance, are not easily changed (although some people may try to disguise them). These are *ascribed* statuses, and they are often associated with positions that are occupied regardless of effort or desire. To be a certain age is to be able to do some things and not others. (See Chapter 9 for further discussion of age.) To be born the daughter of a king is to be a princess. In some societies, the social position of one's parents determines the course of one's life, whether prince or pauper.

In contrast, *achieved statuses* are positions occupied by choice, merit, or effort. Becoming a husband or a wife in our society today is an achieved status. We choose to marry. So, increasingly, is parenthood a matter of choice. One can make many decisions about what kind of work to do or how long to go to school. Still other statuses are filled through election or appointment. Generally, the more complex the society, the more likely are statuses to be occupied through achievement rather than ascription.

While each of us occupies a number of social statuses, some statuses may be more important than others. The most socially important status we occupy is called a *master status* inasmuch as it affects almost every aspect of our lives. It is the status with which we are most identified. A master status has a *generalized* symbolic value, so that people automatically assume that a person with that status possesses a set of other traits associated with it. For example, a nun may occupy a series

Ascribed characteristics are those over which a person has little or no control, such as sex, age, race, ethnicity, and religion.

Achieved statuses are positions occupied as a result of choice, merit, or effort.

Master status is the most important status occupied and one that affects almost every aspect of a person's life.

Status incumbents are people who occupy positions in a social system at a given time.

example, the family system of any society. A family is a recognized unit of *status incumbents,* that is, people who occupy certain positions at a given time. The number and type of statuses making up "the family" will vary from society to society and from one time to another. In some societies, a family is composed of all those related by blood. In the United States, it is most often a married couple and their dependent children. "The family" thus is an abstraction. The Abbott family described earlier is, however, an active group of status incumbents whose behavior may or may not resemble the cultural standard. This distinction is illustrated in Figure 4-2.

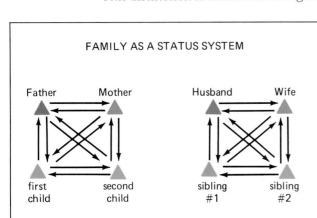

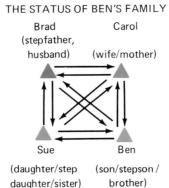

FAMILY AS A STATUS SYSTEM

Father   Mother

first child   second child

Husband   Wife

sibling #1   sibling #2

THE STATUS OF BEN'S FAMILY

Brad (stepfather, husband)   Carol (wife/mother)

Sue (daughter/stepdaughter/sister)   Ben (son/stepson/brother)

Figure 4-2
The family as an abstract unit of status incumbents, and as a specific family (Ben Abbott's). Each person occupies dual statuses in the family (e.g., father/husband, child/sibling). There can also be a difference between the abstract "ideal" incumbent and the actual occupant of the role, as in Ben's family where the "father" is a stepfather.

A physical handicap is often a master status that affects all aspects of a person's life. How is this doctor negating the traits usually associated with being handicapped? How are people likely to treat her when she's in civilian clothes? (© Robert McElroy/Woodfin Camp and Associates)

of both ascribed and achieved statuses: daughter, sister, aunt, teacher, female, age 35, white, social activist, and so forth. But her master status is likely to be that of nun; it is the most visible and most likely to affect the responses of others to her in social interaction. Her other statuses may be ignored. If this nun decides to participate in an anti-nuclear protest and is arrested, it is unlikely that news headlines would read "Aunt Arrested in Demonstration." What would be considered newsworthy is her master status, i.e. nun, which we view as associated with a number of other traits.

If each of us made a list of all the statuses we occupy, the result would be what Merton (1968) has termed our *status set.* Our status sets may be *consistent,* that is, more or less in harmony with each other, or they may be *inconsistent.* When certain statuses are related so that one position tends to reinforce assumptions about other statuses, statuses are consistent. At the personal level, inconsistent statuses lead to disapproval or to anxiety (as may be the case with a military psychiatrist who owes an obligation both to his patients and to the military system). An example of status inconsistency in the United States has been the female physician, who even today may be mistaken for a nurse (Floge and Merrill 1986). Status inconsistency not only creates tension for the individual but could also block opportunities for advancement (see, for example, Lorber 1985) and thus stimulate a desire for social change in power relationships (Goffman 1959).

Role. To know a person's status in a system, whether ascribed or achieved, is also to have some expectations about that person's behavior. For each status there is a code of conduct defining how the incumbent should relate to others. This is what we call *role.*

A role is the dynamic aspect of a status. A central concept in sociology, role describes the patterns of behavior, structured around specific rights and duties that are associated with a particular status in a group or social situation. A person's role in any situation is defined by the set of expectations for behavior in any given status; these expectations are held both by others and by the person. A role thus is the totality of all the cultural patterns associated with a particular status. For example, the status of father calls for a range of behaviors very different from those of a son. Think how surprised we would be if a father went to kindergarten every day or played on the Little League team. We would be equally surprised if his ten-year-old son went to work each morning or coached in the Little League. Both would be violating the rules (norms) for permissible and desirable behaviors, or *role prescriptions,* for their particular status in both the age and family systems. Put differently, the social structure has certain requirements that are reflected in how people are expected to act in a particular status, and how, indeed, they more or less do act. There are differences in the expectations associated with a status, but only within a certain range of culturally acceptable behavior. The fact that behavior is structured by statuses and roles is what makes social life possible. Because members of the same society share similar expectations of people who enact particular roles, they can accurately predict how peo-

Status set consists of all the statuses occupied by a person.

Role is the expected behavior of those who occupy a given status.

Role prescriptions are norms for permissible and desirable behavior.

81

ple will behave and how others will respond to one's own actions. Social order depends on such predictable patterning; otherwise, we would continually be racked by anxiety and uncertainty.

Like statuses, *roles* are organized into *sets* that center on a specific status. Any status involves a person in a number of social relationships usually found to be necessary for people in that particular position. For example, the status of physician contains a number of role sets: doctor/patient; doctor/nurse; doctor/doctor; doctor/hospital administrator; doctor/pharmacist; doctor/social worker; doctor/physical therapist; doctor/patient's relatives; and so forth. The role the physician plays in his or her status will vary according to the role set. For example, in the doctor/patient role set, the physician will play a relatively impersonal role as care-provider to a person playing the role of help-seeker. In the role set of doctor/doctor, both people are more likely to treat each other as equals. In sum, any status incumbent has a set of roles or role set that she or he plays with occupants of

other statuses that establishes expectations for behavior. See Figure 4-3.

The flexibility that each of us has in playing a given role, however, is limited by one's multiple statuses. For example, as Williams (1970) pointed out, everyone is either male or female and of a certain age: thus every other status is influenced by age and gender status. For example, middle-aged adults usually occupy more statuses than the very young or the very old and thus are in more complex role sets. The multiple roles of parent, spouse, employee, son or daughter, and member of civic and religious associations influence one's performance in any one status. Multiple roles may work to one's advantage. As Thoits (1983) noted, the resources provided in one role can often be helpful in the performance of other roles. For example, the social contacts and technical knowledge acquired in one's role as a college student may be useful in other statuses, such as friend, club member, or worker. Multiple statuses also provide acceptable excuses for failing to meet the expected demands of other roles (consider the married student who, overwhelmed by taking care of children and a home, cannot complete a term paper on time). Multiple statuses can also lessen the impact of role loss, so that if one status, such as that of boyfriend, is lost, its impact is reduced if one also occupies the statuses of student, club member, and athlete.

ROLE CONFLICT. Although multiple statuses and roles may bring benefits, in some situations there is *role conflict* when one role contradicts or competes with another. Some of these conflicts arise because different, often contradictory, types of behavior are required. For example, a role that calls for friendship or closeness could also require impersonal judgment or control. Consider the college professor who wants to help students and needs to be on friendly terms with them in order to develop a mutual sense of trust, while treating each one as a unique person. But the role of professor also requires that the students' work be judged and graded, without being influenced by personal considerations. Moreover, the professor's decision could affect students' later careers and opportunities. These conflicting aspects of the role may cause pain to both the professor and the students.

How can role conflict be avoided? Some roles are designed to prevent conflict. For

Role conflict occurs when one role contradicts or competes with another.

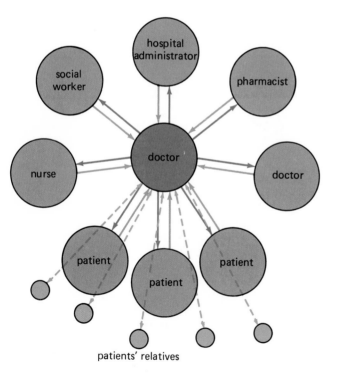

Figure 4-3
Sample role set for a doctor showing reciprocal role expectations. Would role expectations be any different for a doctor who is 40 and female than for one who is 60 and male?

example, physicians are generally not permitted to operate on members of their own family; officers and enlisted men in the military are socially segregated in housing, dining rooms, and in clubs; and some businesses prohibit dating between managerial and line workers. Yet the social distance created by such separation often has negative consequences; in the military, for example, loyalty and willingness to take orders could be reduced. To avoid this type of tension, "bridge positions" or statuses are created, such as the noncommissioned officer, the factory foreman, or the academic counselor. In turn, however, occupants of these bridge statuses are likely to experience role conflict, caught as they are between competing demands.

ROLE STRAIN.   Just as competing expectations within the same role can produce role conflicts, so multiple roles can produce role strain. *Role strain,* as analyzed by William Goode (1960), occurs when the sheer number of a person's roles demand more than she or he can adequately fulfill. One simply does not have the energy or resourcefulness to meet all the expectations of role partners. A current case in point is the employed mother of young children. As a full-time worker, she is paid to devote thirty-five or forty hours to her job, while as a mother she is expected to care for her children. Even where day care is available, a mother is "supposed" to stay home with a sick child. She is also typically responsible for the bulk of housework. In addition, there are older relatives who might require assistance or care. Juggling these multiple roles is very likely to produce role strain.

Are there any solutions to role strain? Alas, there is no magic answer. One way to reduce role strain is to reinterpret or redefine roles. Multiple roles themselves do not necessarily lead to role strain; what is crucial is the amount of time, energy, and commitment required by each role (Marks 1977, Coser and Coser 1974). One might choose to comply with those expectations that carry more severe penalties for nonconforming—a kind of cost-benefit analysis of the amount of time and energy associated with each role versus the rewards or benefits. Thus, the working wife might delegate part of her role to another person in the system, as when her husband agrees to take turns caring for a sick child, or when a sibling assists in caring for the

Role strain occurs when the role demands are more than one can adequately fulfill.

This working mother tried to reduce role strain by carrying on her business at home. Do you think there are any stresses involved in taking this option? (© Rae Russell)

sick parent. When roles are redefined, role strain can be reduced. The success of this strategy, however, depends on mutual agreement among members of the role set involved.

Another type of role strain occurs when the norms governing the performance, and hence the expectations, of role partners are vague or are being revised. This kind of change is happening today in male and female roles in the family, at work, and in society. Although more emphasis has been placed on women's changing roles, men also feel confused about their own roles (Komarovsky 1976, Pleck 1981, 1983, Rubin 1975, Stein 1984). Individual men and women experience the fear and uncertainty associated with this type of role strain, unaware that others have the same feelings. As one of Rubin's respondents, a twenty-nine-year-old husband, complained:

> The worst think is, I've got nobody to talk to about how a guy can be different. The guys at work, all they ever talk about is their cars or trucks. . . . I know Joanie's not so happy, and I worry about what to do about it. But the guys I know, they don't worry about things. . . . They'd think I was nuts . . . people don't talk about these things. (Rubin 1975, pp. 129–130)

83

Context of Social Interaction

DEFINITION OF THE SITUATION

Definition of the situation is the process by which people define, interpret and evaluate the social context to select appropriate attitudes and behaviors.

To a large extent, our behavior is determined not only by our statuses and role sets but by the *definition of the situation.* Behavior in a role is not merely a response but an active effort to define and interpret the social context in which we find ourselves, to assess our interests, and to select appropriate attitudes and behaviors.

As W. I. Thomas pointed out: what people believe to be real is real in its consequences. When others agree with our definition of a situation, we share common understandings and expectations that make interaction easier. Because situations do not define themselves but have meaning conferred on them by the participants, we are continually checking our perceptions with other people.

Roles are essentially dynamic and reflexive. As described by George Herbert Mead, all roles are learned and internalized (Ch. 5). For example, a child who is learning to play baseball must also learn the responses of the other players: "In the game . . . there is a set of responses . . . so organized that the attitude of one calls out the appropriate attitude of the other" (Mead 1946, p. 151). Thus, in learning a role we all see ourselves as others see us, as we are evaluated by others. From the impressions we receive about ourselves, we take a general set of attitudes and behaviors and direct our own behavior accordingly. Thus, there is a constant interplay in role behavior. While general rules exist, considerable improvisation, depending on the responses of others in the role set, allows room for decision, imagination, and initiative. Most of our daily activity takes place in established systems with recognized rules, statuses, and roles. Even when strangers meet, there is a certain pattern to their interaction. For example, consider meeting a new group of people during orientation week for college freshmen. Most students want to know each other's ages, marital or relationship status, ethnic background, home town, high school, and other details that help locate us in relationship to one another. When we identify each other's statuses, we are defining the situation and developing guidelines for interaction. While patterns of defining interaction may vary from culture to cul-

ture (for example, it is considered rude among some groups in Britain to ask new acquaintances, "What kind of work do you do?" but it is a sign of great interest to ask the same question in the United States), no society leaves potentially troublesome encounters to chance. But what about a situation that has never occurred before? How can participants know what is normal?

Anomie. *Anomie* is a French word that means "lack of rules." Émile Durkheim (1897/1966) coined it to refer to situations in which norms are absent, unclear, or confusing, that is, in which no clear nor-

Anomie refers to situations in which norms are absent, unclear, or confusing.

SOCIOLOGY & YOU
Role Overload In Your Future Life

There has been a dramatic increase in the number of two-income families in the U.S. A majority of married women are employed including over 60% of women with school-age children. There are over 26 million two-income couples in the U.S.; in half of these families wives are employed on a full-time basis. When both husband and wife are college graduates they usually form a two-career couple in which both he and she have a full-time career. (A job is a typically salaried position with limited future mobility; a career requires more education, consists of a series of steps leading to advancement within that career.)

As more and more college graduates find themselves in a two-career marriage (estimated at 4.5 million) they find themselves in a new family form. The major advantages of this family form, as reported by wives and husbands, are increased income, more life-style choices and increased satisfaction with marriage. But there are also problems, related to *role strain* and *role overload.* Researchers have identified 5 major *dilemmas* for dual-career couples.

1. *Role Overload* results from the many roles taken on by the couple as spouses, careerists, parents, friends, relatives, community members, etc. The major skills required for coping with the overload involve planning, organizing, training and directing.
2. *Identity Dilemma* results from the confusion between the partners' accumulated and expected roles and behavior and newly acquired roles. Both wives and husbands may experience this, but it is particu-

mative guidance is offered to the role players. For a group to be unified, it must develop a set of norms to regulate behavior. The norms include a clearly defined code of what is expected in the situation.

When the situation itself dissolves or is destroyed, as it was in the Buffalo Creek disaster, the norms disappear as well. The norms are, in other words, deeply embedded in both the physical and social structure. Because people are rule-making and rule-following creatures, they cannot tolerate anomie. We all attempt to create norms to impose meaning and order on anomic situations. In England early in World War II, for example, when people first streamed into air-raid shelters, no clear norms existed; after all, no one had ever before spent night after night sleeping and living underground. But soon, codes of appropriate conduct were developed, and typical divisions of labor emerged. Families occupied the same places each night; leaders, jokesters, comforters, and other role players were acknowledged. Within days, a social system of the air-raid shelter had been constructed; order replaced anomie.

Defining New or Unusual Situations.   In unusual situations as well as in new ones, the members of a group define and redefine

---

larly women who experience tension and conflict that comes from balancing the demands of a career, and managing a home and motherhood.

3. *The Role Cycling Dilemma* is faced when partners want both family life and a career; each of these receives different priorities at different stages of life. There are many questions to resolve: whether or not to have children; when to start a family; how many children should there be; and how far apart should they be spaced?

4. The *Social Network Dilemma* stems from the limited time spouses have to interact with each other. There are questions of whom to include and exclude and from friendship networks and close social contacts.

5. *Normative dilemmas* stem from the tension between traditional expectations for one-breadwinner families, which are still endorsed by family ideology and by some parents, and the expectations of two-career couples.

A diagram of role sets involved in the dual-career family underscores these dilemmas (see figure).

How do people cope with these dilemmas? Research on couples that successfully share responsibilities in breadwinning, domestic chores and decision-making indicates the following 6 major coping strategies:

1. Make a commitment to the relationship;
2. Make a mutual commitment to the goals and careers of both partners;
3. Work for better communication;
4. Redefine and renegotiate roles;
5. Re-examine attitudes and values that interfere with new tasks;
6. If needed, seek professional help.

There is a good chance that, if you marry after receiving your college degree, you too will be in a two-career couple. The experiences of couples that preceded yours

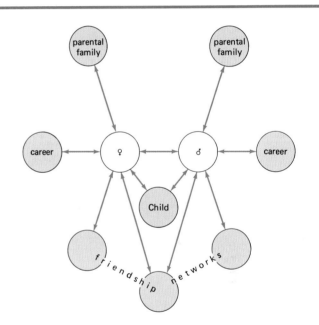

A Dual-Career Family: An example of role overload

should help. Being able to analyze the events in your life can also help to relieve anxieties and frustrations and make solutions more readily recognizable. If you think you will marry (or are married), consider the expectations you have for yourself and your spouse. From what source do these expectations arise? Do you think you'd experience problems in a dual-career marriage? What strategies might ease the stresses? (See Chapter 11 for further discussion of dual-earner families.)

For further reading, see: Rosanna Hertz, *More Equal Than Others: Women and Men in Dual-Career Marriages.* Berkeley, Calif.: Univ. of California Press, 1986.

Rhona Rapoport and Robert Rapoport. *Dual-Career Families Re-Examined: New Integration of Work and Family.* New York: Harper & Row, 1976.

During W.W. II the London Underground (subway) was used as a bomb shelter during night-long raids on the city. British citizens created new norms and behaved in an orderly fashion despite the otherwise anomic situation. (© A/P Wide World Photos)

the situation to maintain order. Weinberg (1968) has described how one nonconforming group, nudists, create definitions that justify their actions, as well as rules that allow them to live together harmoniously even when engaging in behavior that others consider bizarre. In the larger society, modesty is usually defined as keeping one's clothes on and minimizing sexual excitement, which is potentially disruptive. How then can nudist camps enforce standards of self-control and sexual privacy?

The belief system of nonconforming groups provides a new definition of the situation. Nudist camps, for example, maintain that:

1. Nudism and sexuality are unrelated.
2. There is nothing shameful about exposing the human body.
3. The abandonment of clothes can lead to a feeling of freedom and natural pleasure.
4. Nude activities, especially full-body exposure to the sun, leads to physical, mental, and spiritual well-being.

That these definitions are accepted and followed shows how the members of a group can change long-accepted meanings and adopt new behaviors.

How are the new norms maintained? Weinberg pointed to several aspects of the social organization of the nudist camp: (1) screening applicants for admission to eliminate single people, especially young men; (2) maintaining strict rules of interpersonal behavior (no staring, no sex talk, no body contact); (3) forbidding alcoholic beverages; and (4) restricting cameras.

Under these definitions and rules, sexuality is controlled in nudist camps, often more successfully than outside of them. On the outside, clothes are used to arouse sexual interest, as, for example, in ads featuring young women in states of partial undress or men in tight clothing.

If behavior is a response to the situation as perceived by those in it, then situations defined as different are likely to produce variation in behavior. This point is particularly well illustrated by the work of the social psychologist Stanley Milgram (1965), in a set of now-classic experiments. Unknowing subjects were told that as part of a study of learning they would be required to give electric shocks to people who answered questions incorrectly. The experiment was manipulated in several ways. In some situations, the subject saw the "learner" (actually a paid assistant) going into the learning room or could hear the learner's presumed reaction to the electric shock; in some situations, the experimenter stood over the subject or gave orders via headphones or a public-address system. It was found that the subjects' willingness to inflict pain was affected not by their background or by any psychological trait, but by the *experimental situation* itself. That is, when the instructor stood over the subject, it was difficult not to obey; when the authority figure was not present, the subjects were less likely to administer the shocks. The key point here is that people are very strongly influenced by the situations in which they find themselves and by the interpretations that they give to those situations. The tendency to obey, therefore, is not a fixed characteristic of individuals but a variable response to a specific social situation as interpreted by those in it.

Groups

Thus far, we have focused primarily on elements in the social structure, such as status and role, and on the context of social interaction. Yet, a society is also conceptualized as the sum of people who are connected to one another in some patterned way, that is, who live in *groups*. Throughout our lives, we belong to a variety of groups, each of which can influence our actions and our very ideas about ourselves. To be human is to live in groups, although the relationship between individual and group takes various forms.

A *group* is any collection of people bound together by a distinctive set of social relationships. The term *group* is deceptively simple; it is used in everyday conversation to refer to many things. In sociology, however, the word has a specific meaning. A *group,* in the sociological sense, has the following characteristics: (1) a distinctive set of social relationships among the members; (2) interdependence among various people; (3) a feeling that the behavior of each member is relevant to other members; and (4) a sense of membership, or a "we" feeling.

Groups are highly varied, ranging from the members of a family to the workers in an office, from patient and doctor to children attending a summer camp. The membership may be stable or changing, but groups share two common elements: (1) *mutual awareness* of the other members of the group and (2) *responsiveness to the members,* so that actions are shaped in the context of the group.

*A **group** is any collection of people bound together by a distinctive set of shared social relationships.*

GROUP CHARACTERISTICS

Primary Groups.
A basic distinction in sociology is made between small and close-knit groups, on the one hand, and large, impersonal groups, on the other. Charles Horton Cooley (1864–1929) introduced the term *primary group* to describe groups in which the members have warm, intimate, personal ties with one another. Calling the primary group "the nursery of human nature," Cooley saw it as the source of a person's earliest and most nearly complete sense of social unity. The family is our first primary group. Primary groups involve an identity of goals among the members, who share a similar world view and strive for shared goals. Because of their close ties, each person in the primary group is concerned with the welfare of others (Cooley 1902, 1909).

Belonging to a primary group is thus an end in itself; the relationships among the members are valued in their own right, rather than as means to another goal, and are called *expressive.* Because the contacts are usually enjoyable, primary groups are relatively permanent. Face-to-face contacts, spontaneous interaction, involvement with the whole of oneself rather than just a part, and intensity of relationships are hallmarks of the primary group. Human nature does not exist separately in each person but is developed in simple, face-to-face groups.

Secondary Groups.
Unlike primary groups, secondary groups are characterized by few emotional ties among members and by limited interaction involving only part of the person. Formal relationships replace the spontaneity of the primary group. Examples of secondary groups include students in a lecture hall, large work settings, and organizations such as university alumnae associations. All members share one common interest, but otherwise, their goals are different, their contacts with one another are relatively temporary, and their roles are highly structured. Indeed, interaction is viewed as a means to more distant goals: diplomas, wages, the university's financial health. Behavior that is directed toward a more distant goal is called *instrumental* because it is a means to some other end, it is not an end in itself.

Primary groups are often formed within secondary settings, where the friendship circle can influence the larger social system. For example, studies of the behavior of combat soldiers during World War II showed that the average American soldier was driven neither by patriotism nor ha-

*A **primary group** is a small group in which members have warm, intimate, personal ties with one another.*

***Expressive** behavior is valued in its own right.*

***Secondary groups** are characterized by few emotional ties and by limited interaction.*

***Instrumental** behavior is a means to some other goal.*

The bonds that developed under combat conditions remain strong for the survivors as do the memories of fallen brothers, remembered here at the Vietnam Memorial in Washington, D.C. (© Peter Marlow/Magnum Photos)

tred of the enemy but rather by loyalty to his buddies (Stouffer et al. 1949, Shils 1950). The primary group has two functions in combat: first, it establishes group norms for behavior and define roles; second, it supports and maintains soldiers in stressful situations.

Table 4-1 lists those groups that one is most likely to belong to at different points in life. In parentheses are groups that are open to at least some people at a given stage in their lives. For example, in very old age, some people enjoy many of the same primary-group relationships as in old age, although the role partners of most are increasingly likely to be ill or dead.

Gemeinschaft and Gesellschaft. Similar to the difference betwen primary and secondary groups is the distinction made by German sociologist Ferdinand Tönnies (1853–1936) between *Gemeinschaft* (community) and *Gesellschaft* (society). *Gemeinschaft* exists in communities with many primary-group relationships, in which people have known one another for generations and associate in informal ways. These groups are united by common ancestry or geographic closeness.

Gemeinschaft refers to small, traditional communities, characterized by primary-group relationships and intergenerational stability.

In the *Gesellschaft,* relationships are more businesslike and limited. The major social bonds are voluntary and are based on a rational self-interest in achieving a particular goal.

In general, the development of modern societies can be seen as a progressive replacement of the *Gemeinschaft* by the impersonal, fragmented, goal-directed relationships of the *Gesellschaft*. Although Tönnies and others have regretted this shift in contemporary society from a reliance on primary groups to an increasing involvement in secondary groups, the intense, personal nature of the relationships in the *Gemeinschaft* has costs to the individual that are often overlooked. That is, *Gemeinschaft* ties may restrict individuality, spontaneity, and creativity. Personal freedom is cramped when primary-group membership is the only type available. Young people have typically fled such communities to achieve independence.

Because modern society is complex, and most roles and statuses are relatively impermanent, most of us belong both to primary groups and to groups that lie somewhere between primary and secondary groups. These groups, like primary groups, have few members, are informal, and involve the whole person, but they are of

Gesellschaft refers to contractual relationships, where social bonds are voluntary and based on rational self-interest.

Despite the increasing complexity of society, relatively small communities still exist, where people have known each other for generations and share a geographical closeness. This town meeting in Stratford, Vermont brings townspeople together to discuss issues of mutual concern in a forum where they can participate in the political life of their community on a very direct basis. (© Thomas Ames, Jr./F Stop Pictures)

TABLE 4-1 Typical patterns of group membership through the life course

Stage in Life Course	Primary-Group Membership	Secondary-Group Membership
Infancy	Family	None
Preschool	Family Playmates	Distant relatives Neighborhood Church
School	Family Close friends/peers	Student–teacher Classroom/school Distant relatives Neighborhood Church Hobby groups/sports
Adolescence	Family Close friends/peers Work groups	School, plus part-time/summer work groups
Young adult	Family of origin Close friends Lover/spouse Family through marriage and parenthood Work groups	Formal work organization Professional/union group Church Neighborhood Hobby/sports/special-interest groups
Middle-aged adult	Family of origin Close friends Lover/spouse Family of procreation Work groups	Formal work organization Church Neighborhood Civic groups Hobby/sports, etc. Parent groups
Old age	Lover/spouse Children Close friends	Church Neighborhood Civic groups Special-interest groups
Very old age	(Lover/spouse) (Close friends) (Children)	(Church) (Neighborhood) (Civic groups)

limited duration and may not have shared norms, values, and goals. The neighborhood bar, the encounter group, the health club, and the senior citizens' center are examples of such groups. These groups protect people against the impersonality of the larger society without demanding deep emotional involvement. An example is the Oasis, a family tavern in Green Bay, Wisconsin, studied for a year by LeMasters (1975). The Oasis was not really a neighborhood tavern; the patrons came by car, but they were of similar backgrounds, mostly blue-collar workers. Entire families came to the tavern. The Oasis was a center of social life for its regulars, who shared interests in bowling, card games, boating, horseshoes, and gambling. The regulars were also a source of support in times of trouble; they attended funerals, visited each other in the hospital, and collected funds for families in need. Yet, the Oasis customers did not form a primary group. Rather, regular attendance at the Oasis filled some of the needs that these men and women had for a place to gather, to share experiences, and to accept one another before returning to their daily routines.

In-Groups and Out-Groups. In his study, LeMasters noted that only some people participated fully in the many social activities of the tavern and thus formed an *in-group,* with which each member felt a strong identity. Strangers who entered the tavern were treated as outsiders.

The terms *in-group* and *out-group* were coined by William Graham Sumner (1840–1910) and are defined much as they sound. In-groups are ones to which "we" belong; out-groups are ones to which

In-groups are the primary or secondary groups to which we belong; **out-groups** are ones to which we do not belong.

"they" belong. Sumner noted that the amount of hostility directed toward out-groups is related to the degree of in-group closeness. Such hostility is closely allied to *ethnocentrism,* or the belief that one's own group is best, and that it is the standard against which all other groups should be measured. After all, if one's own way of doing things is right, other ways must be wrong!

Strong in-group and out-group feelings reinforce competition. This may be clearly seen at any athletic event, where the fans root fiercely for their teams, sometimes insulting the other side or even destroying property. The members of the in-group are more likely to see their team's defeat as being due to *external* factors, such as unfair referees or poor sportsmanship by the other team, rather than as a result of poor playing on their own side. The strong "we" feeling of the in-group permits its members to interpret events in a way that supports their existing beliefs and that justifies continued membership (Zerubavel 1982).

Reference Groups. Thus far, we have discussed groups to which people belong. There is, however, one specific type of group to which a person need not belong, but that nonetheless influences identity, norms, and values. This is the *reference group.* First described by Herbert Hyman in 1942, the reference group provides a *checkpoint* or *standard* against which one may measure one's own status and role performance, whether or not one is a member of that group. Reference groups are often those in which a person *aspires to gain or maintain acceptance.* The athlete on a Little League team may have the Boston Red Sox as a reference group, modeling his or her playing style and behavior after these unmet heroes.

A reference group also provides a way of organizing one's own experience. As Shibutani (1955) pointed out, this does not necessarily mean that the group is a model for behavior, merely that a person assumes the outlook of the members of that group. Put another way, we all take part in several social worlds simultaneously. Most of you, for example, participate in the world of your parents, the world of your friends, the world of your college or university, the world of your religious group, your ethnic group, and so on. Not all of

> A **reference group** exerts a strong influence on one's identity, norms, and values, whether or not one actually belongs to that group.

these group memberships are compatible, and you may need to divide your life among them. The concept of the *reference group* lets you enter and understand both the world of your parents and that of your peers or of any other group. Thus, you can reconcile the differences among them and choose which norms to follow in each situation.

Group Structure and Processes

Social groups are the building blocks of social structure. Differing widely in size, purpose, and membership, groups nonetheless share several common structural elements and processes that affect their functioning.

GROUP STRUCTURE

Group Formation and Membership. Homans (1950) pointed out that group membership is a circular process. The more people associate with one another, the more they come to share common norms and values, and the more they tend to like one another. This process strengthens group ties through shared activities, friendships, norms, and values. This is not an accidental process, for we gravitate toward groups that reinforce our values and our beliefs. Newcomb (1943) called this gravitation a *need for consensus* that reduces conflict over correct behavior. When people are caught in value differences among groups to which they belong, they generally resolve their discomfort by selecting the group that offers the most immediate rewards of affection, approval, companionship, and participation. In high school and college, many students are caught between competing groups, such as the family and the peer group. To reconcile the differences in norms and values between their family and their peers, some rebel against the family and align more closely with their peers, with whom there is more daily contact and shared activity (Feld 1982). They resolve the conflict by accepting the peer group's definition of families as "old-fashioned" or somehow harmful to personal growth. These shared meanings then draw the peers closer together.

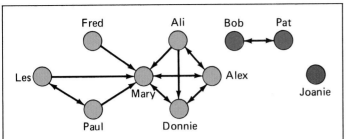

Figure 4-4
Sociogram of student choices of the person with whom each would like to spend free time. (Mutual choices are indicated by double arrows, and one-way choices by arrows pointing from chooser to chosen.)

A **sociogram** identifies interaction patterns in studying group structure.

Perhaps because we participate daily in groups, it seems that what goes on is spontaneous and random. In even the most relaxed and unstructured groups, however, established patterns of interaction develop in which the members are ranked in relationship to one another. Group structure has been studied through the *sociogram* (Moreno 1934). Researchers using the sociogram ask all the members of a group to name those people with whom they would like to work, play, go on a date, and so forth. The choices are then plotted, as were the responses of ten students who were asked with whom they would like to spend free time, shown in Figure 4-4. Mary was the most popular: Six people wanted to spend free time with her. She, however, chose only three of those who chose her. As you look at the sociogram, you will also notice that there were several friendship groupings; Les and Paul; Bob and Pat; and Mary, Donnie, Ali, and Alex. In contrast, Joanie seemed to be a loner, as she neither chose anyone nor was chosen. Although sociograms help describe the structure of the group, asking people with whom they would like to spend time and asking them with whom they actually do spend their spare time may produce very different results. One set of questions taps ideal friendship choices, the other elicits information about actual patterns of interaction. How questions are phrased is thus very important in analyzing the data derived from sociograms.

Group Size. The size of a group is an important aspect of structure that influences interaction within the group and the statuses and roles available. Remem-

ber that primary groups are always relatively small.

The sociologist Georg Simmel (1858–1918) was particularly interested in the effects of the number of people in a group. The smallest unit of sociological analysis is the *dyad,* or two-person group, such as a dating couple. The dyad is characterized by (1) intimacy and a high exchange of information, so that "two can feel as one"; (2) the greatest opportunity for total involvement by each member, but also the greatest possibility of conflict; and (3) joint responsibility. The dyad is extremely fragile, for either person can destroy it by leaving, by withdrawing affection or other needed resources, or by lack of concern for common problems of the dyad (Gupta 1983).

How are role relationships maintained in the highly charged emotional context of the dyad? Pamela Fishman (1978) studied fifty-two hours of taped conversations by three different male–female dyads in their homes. Although the couples could turn the tape recorder off or delete portions of the tape, most of their everyday conversation was recorded. Fishman found an unequal division of labor in making and maintaining conversation between the men and the women. The women tried

The **dyad,** or two-person group, is intimate, has a high exchange of information, and presents great possibilities for total involvement and conflict.

The dating couple, one example of a dyad, provides a setting for intimacy, exchanges of information, good times, and complete involvement. But dyads are also fragile; either partner can withdraw affection, concern or leave, leading to the dissolution of the unit. (© David Burnett/Contact Stock)

harder than the men to keep interaction going; they also failed in this goal more often. The men did little to keep the conversational ball rolling or to make their partner comfortable. The men did, however, decide what was important to talk about. Thus, in a couple, the role of the man was to shape the social reality, whereas that of the woman was to supply support for it.

These findings emphasize the emergence of one role partner in the dyad as the power figure, the other as the worker. That this division of labor was associated with gender is fascinating, as two of the three women were avowed feminists and the other four participants claimed to be sensitive to the goals of the women's movement.

The *triad,* or three-person group, is typically more stable than the dyad. Although the triad usually has less affection and intimacy than the two-person group, it does have a more complex division of labor and more interdependence among the three members. Two members can unite against one member, but the coalitions generally shift, so that unity is maintained, and no one person dominates the triad.

The number of possible combinations of role partners and of roles that may be played in a group increases far faster than the group size. The very fragility of the dyad is caused by the fact that only one interaction or set of roles is possible at one time. That number quadruples, however, in a triad, as you can see in Figure 4-5.

As the size of the group increases, the number of possible combinations increases dramatically. In a family of seven people (mother, father, and five children) there are 120 possible subgroups ranging in size from two to seven people in each group! Clearly, size is related to interaction in groups. Statisticians have developed

The **triad,** *or three-person group, is more stable than the dyad, with a greater division of labor.*

mathematical techniques to calculate the number of possible combinations in a group. If you want to calculate the number of possible role sets in your class, family, or dormitory, you might ask a friend who has taken statistics to help you. The results will probably surprise you, for most of us do not think in these terms.

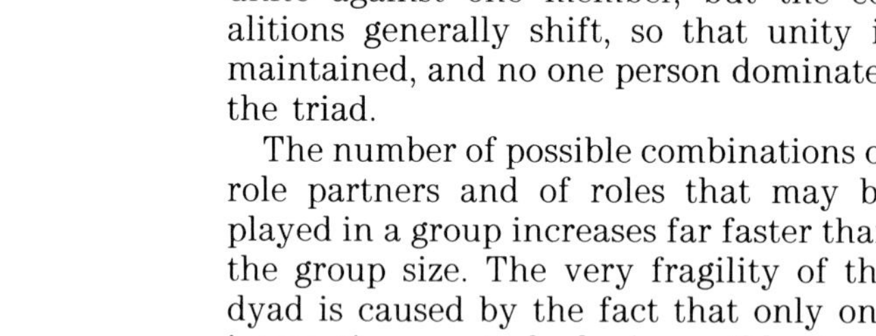

GROUP INTERACTION PROCESSES

Behavior in groups is neither spontaneous nor unstructured. Rather, established interaction patterns evolve even in the most relaxed and unstructured groups. The term *interaction processes* refers to the ways in which role partners agree on the goals of their interaction, negotiate how to reach the goal, and distribute resources. Although each interaction has elements of uniqueness, role partners can interact only in certain ways. These processes can be placed on a continuum, ranging from very willing and positive exchanges of goods, services, or feelings to forced responses. As long as two or more role partners are involved, their potentially conflicting needs and resources must be taken into account.

As groups form, members enact different roles that make up the role structure of any group. Role structures describe the division of labor in social relationships and differ in content and complexity. Two basic role types are particularly important in sociological analysis: *instrumental roles* and *expressive roles* (Bales 1950). *Instrumental* (or *task roles*) are defined much as they sound; their content is oriented toward accomplishing tasks, ranging from pumping gas at a gas station to attempting to win a tennis match. In a classroom situation, for example, the role of the teacher is primarily instrumental: to ensure that students learn certain materials and to maintain control of the class. Similarly, students in a class are expected to play primarily instrumental roles—to master the work and to take tests. In contrast, *expressive roles* involve the expression and release of group tension and emotion through laughter, joking, argument, and other informal actions. In any group, there will be instrumental and expressive behavior; instrumental behavior allows a task to be accomplished, while expressive behavior permits the maintenance of group harmony. The student who cracks a

Interaction processes refer to the ways in which partners agree on the goals of their interaction, negotiate behaviors, and distribute resources.

Task or instrumental roles are oriented toward specific goals.

Expressive roles are oriented toward the expression and release of group tension.

Dyad Role Set

Alan ⟷ Betty

Triad Role Set
Alan

Betty   Chuck

Figure 4-5

joke or whose remarks are greeted with groans is playing an expressive role in the task-oriented classroom. Even in relatively unstructured social situations, such as a party, both instrumental and expressive roles are played; some people organize refreshments, provide the music, or make sure that people meet one another (instrumental roles), and others break self-consciousness and encourage expression of feelings with clowning and horse-play. Each role is essential for group unity.

The Dramaturgical View of Interaction. Each of us attempts to define the situation in ways in which interaction is made predictable. And each of us has a vested interest in presenting ourselves to others in ways that produce the results most beneficial to us. From the *dramaturgical view* developed by Goffman (1959), all role partners may be usefully viewed as actors who perform roles in a physical setting, or stage. Together, the roles we play make up a *social script*. In this sense, all the world is a stage on which we are players, managing impressions of ourselves. When we interact with others, we present a front: our physical appearance, conduct, and definition of the situation. Then we rely on cues from others to orient ourselves to the roles we shall perform. Goffman's dramaturgical model draws from the work of symbolic interactionists such as Mead and Cooley (see Chapter 5) in emphasizing the reflexive nature of interaction and of role playing.

As in the theater, interaction has a *frontstage,* where certain roles are performed, and a *backstage,* where role players are freed from the pressures of public performance. Just as actors in the theater are careful not to let the audience see backstage behavior, so are role players careful to separate their audiences. We can see the usefulness of this model in analyzing interaction in a restaurant. (In fact, setting the stage for the customers' evening out is often taught as part of the course in restaurant management.)

Waiters, waitresses, and customers are actors who use one another as audiences for their performance in their respective roles. Before customers arrive, restaurant personnel set up tables, prepare food for cooking, and play a variety of backstage roles. They also play frontstage roles among themselves—friend, boss, and so forth. When customers arrive, the dining room staff is frontstage in its interaction with customers, taking orders, being polite, and providing services. When dining room staff go into the kitchen, however, they are both backstage and frontstage: for the customers, about whom they are complaining, they are backstage; to the kitchen personnel they are frontstage. Customers who wander unannounced into the kitchen will catch the restaurant workers unaware and engaged in activity very incompatible with the impression that the personnel wish to convey to customers. Thus, as Goffman has noted: "The ... current round of activity of a given

*The **dramaturgical view** of interaction sees all role partners as actors performing roles in a social setting or stage.*

__Frontstage__ interaction occurs in full view of the public; __Backstage__ interaction is free of public-performance constraints.

An evening in your favorite restaurant. What frontstage and backstage behavior can you see in this photograph? (© Katherine Ursillo/Photo Researchers, Inc.)

performer typically contain(s) at least a few facts which, if introduced during the performance, would discredit or at least weaken the claims about self that the performer was attempting to project. . . . When such facts are introduced, embarrassment is the usual result" (1959, p. 209).

In other interactions, the social script is unclear, and role players must negotiate the interaction. Each gives off cues that the other may accept or reject. Once the script is agreed upon, ambiguity is reduced. The dramaturgical approach is useful in understanding the social mechanisms through which we create and maintain impressions of ourselves and cooperate or compete with each other in performance of our roles. As Goffman concluded his analysis of the dramaturgical model: "This report is not concerned with aspects of theater that creep into everyday life. It is concerned with the structure of social encounters. . . . The key factor in this structure is the maintenance of a single definition of the situation, this definition having to be expressed, and this expression sustained in the face of a multitude of potential disruptions" (1959, p. 254).

Principles of Exchange. Elements of exchange also characterize how people interact. In each exchange, one has to give something up to get what one wants. Ideally, a person has a surplus (goods, energy, affection, approval) to exchange for some desired object (love, money, attention) that another person can provide. What is considered a fair exchange depends on each person's own history, needs, resources, and other sources of supply.

As the members bargain for advantage, group relationships emerge, and the system will survive only as long as the exchanges are seen as beneficial. But some participants have more power than others to define the terms of the exchange. The exchange model can be illustrated by patterns of selecting husbands and wives. In many societies, marriage is based on exchanges between families: a cow or land in exchange for a bride or groom. The goal is to preserve the position of the entire family, and young people have little power to choose their marriage partner. In India, parents place newspaper ads that stress a groom-to-be's family background, education, and earning capacity, and the parents of potential brides advertise their daughter's beauty, cooking abilities, and good manners. In the American marriage market (described in Chap. 11), the young people themselves negotiate the exchange.

Short of *coercion* (the unchecked use of force), interaction processes are characterized by some degree of willingness to follow the norms. Cooperation, competition, and compromise are all *modes of exchange,* and the rules of the game are agreed on by the participants for each interaction.

COMPETITION. When individuals or groups define the situation as being one in which scarce resources will go to some and not to others, *competition* results. Usually, the competition is framed as a test of some quality that is unevenly distributed among persons and groups, such as talent, skill, intelligence, strength, or courage. Some decades ago, Waller (1937) coined the term "the rating-dating complex" to

Principles of exchange govern relationships among people as they bargain for desired goods and services.

Coercion is the unchecked use of force to induce compliance.

Competition results when situations are defined as ones in which scarce resources will only go to some.

To the swiftest goes the prize! In what ways are the rules of this kind of athletic competition similar to the rules for behavior in the business world? (© Gerard Vandystadt/Photo Researchers, Inc.)

Does Competing for the Most Toys Make a Winner?

Americans value competition as a process that brings out the best in us. To compete is to test one's self against others, with the goal of defeating an opponent. A noncompetitive society, in this view, was described by former Vice-President Spiro Agnew as, "a bland experience . . . a waveless sea of nonachievers . . . the psychological retreat of a person . . . into a cocoon of false security and self-satisfied mediocrity." (quoted in Kohn 1986, p. 22). But is competition necessary to success? Recent research suggests that competition and achievement may be opposites. For example, a study of business people found an inverse relationship between competitiveness and success; that is, as competitiveness went down among business people, salaries went up. The negative effects of competition have been shown in a variety of fields, ranging from undergraduates to academic psychologists to newsreporters. Competitiveness for space in news reporting has led many science reporters to "hype" their stories—and competition for promotions and tenure has led university scientists to misrepresent their results.

For example, in 1987 a highly controversial article was published in *Nature* (one of the most internationally respected scientific journals) which detailed the numerous falsifications and errors of a young medical researcher who had published over 100 professional papers in less than five years. These errors of omission and commission reflected the fierce competition with colleagues for scarce resources—money and position. To maintain a competitive edge, he had to produce a very large quantity of material in a short time. Furthermore, the senior scientists who cosigned the research reports without reviewing the contents were similarly motivated by the desire to inflate their academic reputations.

There is growing evidence that cooperation, rather than competition, may have better results. First, cooperation allows an efficient sharing of resources, which is almost impossible when people are working against one another. Cooperation allows all the skills of a group to be used, a process that promotes group cohesion. In contrast, competition within a group is likely to promote suspicion, hostility, and conflict. Moreover, competition is often confused with excellence. Producing over 100 scientific articles within a short time certainly gives one a competitive edge against other researchers who may only produce ten. But it would appear that, in the race to do well within the medical research field, this particular scientist sacrificed both honesty and excellence. Doing well became a matter of quantity not quality.

A popular saying today, especially among young upwardly mobile professionals ("yuppies"), is that "The one who dies with the most toys wins." As we think about group processes, it is important to keep in mind that striving for excellence and striving for victory are goals that may not always coincide with each other.

Based in part on Alfie Kohn, "How to Succeed Without Even Vying," *Psychology Today*, September, 1986, pp. 22–28.

describe the almost cutthroat competition for dates that he observed among students at a state university. The most desirable dates belonged to prestige fraternities or sororities, had ample spending money, dressed well, and were active on campus.

Competition is basically social in that the people involved agree to the rules of the game. There is a shared belief that the competition is either necessary or fair, or both. Only thus can the losers accept their failure. Among the college students described by Waller, for example, less popular students accepted the rules of the rating-and-dating game as fair, if not to their advantage. The costs of the competition, for both winners and losers, was often personal strain and tension.

COOPERATION. *Cooperation* occurs when people agree to pool their resources and efforts to reach a common goal. Cooperation involves considering others. The welfare of the group comes before that of each member, although people must perceive that their needs are being met. From an exchange perspective, cooperation is the basis of social order and the most social mode of interaction.

COMPROMISE. *Compromise* is a cooperative effort to minimize the all-or-nothing aspects of competition. Here again, there is a basic agreement among the group members on principles and their shared meanings of fairness. Persons or groups mutually give up extreme demands and settle for a limited goal. The essence of compro-

Cooperation is the sharing of resources in order to achieve a common goal.

Compromise involves giving up extreme demands to achieve limited goals.

mise is that all parties appear to receive some benefits important to them.

Conflict. *Conflict* occurs when parties try to meet their needs by destroying or disabling their opponents. Unlike the other modes of interaction, conflict does not assume approval of the social order. Conflict occurs precisely because such support has been withdrawn, so that the existing order is defined as oppressive or unfair. Conflict aims to defeat and replace those who make and enforce the rules.

Over the past two decades, groups in opposition to official policy have used conflict effectively because of the presence of television cameras and the media's need to present exciting images on the home screen each evening. The antiwar, gay rights, civil rights, Gray Panthers, and women's movements have all used the media to force viewers to face issues and to take sides. The viewers, though, have not always sided with the activists. Gay rights activism gave rise to a backlash crusade against homosexuals; the women's movement produced STOP-ERA and antiabortion demonstrations; antinuclear power groups have activated significant pronuclear lobbies; and the civil rights movement has given new life to the Ku Klux Klan. Conflict presentation, whether in the small group or on a national scale, tends to create extremes of opinion, leading to more conflict and even violence, but often, also, to major change in the social system.

CONFLICT REDUCTION. Each side in a conflict assumes that its goals are correct. This sense of rightness permits people to engage in behavior that might not be acceptable in other situations. Because societal and personal conflict can disrupt social bonds, several ways of reducing conflict are available: (1) *cooptation;* (2) *mediation;* and (3) *ritualized release of hostility.*

Cooptation occurs when the members of the dissenting group are absorbed by the dominant group; as a result, they have a stake in the peaceful settlement of the conflict. Cooptation also occurs when the ideas of the opposition filter into the mainstream, so that there is no longer a need for confrontation. An example of the first form of cooptation would be to appoint consumer activist Ralph Nader to the Federal Trade Commission. An example of the second was extending the vote to women.

Mediation, or the use of a third party to resolve the issues, often occurs in labor-management conflicts within the small group, and more recently, in divorce mediation. (This is another reason why the triad is more stable than the dyad; the dyad has no one to mediate disputes [Simmel 1950].)

A *ritualized release of hostility* is used by some societies and groups to contain conflict. Anthropologists have reported ritualized warfare among groups within a society or between neighboring societies. The hostility is real, but its expression is carefully controlled to preserve both lives and reputations. Among the Tahitians of Polynesia, for example, Service (1963) reported "a sort of moral equivalent of war . . . in the practice of competitive athletes" (p. 263). Nor is ritual conflict found only in traditional societies. Regional conflicts in America are often displaced onto athletic teams: North–South football games, for example, become an occasion for waving the Confederate flag or singing the "Battle Hymn of the Republic."

Conflict occurs when parties try to destroy or disable their opponents.

Cooptation occurs when members of a dissenting group are absorbed by the dominant group.

Mediation refers to the use of a third party to resolve issues.

Ritualized release of hostility occurs when hostility is expressed under controlled situations.

Groups often use forms of theatre to express their protest and to release feelings of hostility in a structured way. Here a demonstrator in South Carolina makes a silent yet dramatic statement. (© Michael Obrien/Archive Pictures)

The **sociology of emotions** demonstrates that emotions are socially constructed, exchanged, and maintained.

The Sociology of Emotions. Sociologists have become increasingly interested in the *sociology of emotions.* (See the vignette in this chapter.) Although we think of emotions as strictly residing within each person, emotions are, in fact, socially constructed, exchanged, and maintained. Put differently, it is one's definition of the social situation that triggers emotional changes and interchanges. Love, jealousy, hate, anger, guilt, sympathy: all are social because they are role-taking feelings. They require another for whom or toward whom to feel (Schott 1979).

Feeling rules shape how, when, with whom, and where an emotion is expressed.

In the process of socialization, each of us acquires a kind of grammar or set of *feeling rules,* which shape how, when, with whom, and where an emotion is expressed (Hochschild 1979). Moreover, display of any emotion is reflexive, that is, it has a feedback loop that affects our power and intimacy relationships with others. How we manage emotion itself varies, of course. We can give, withhold, reject, expect, fake, or "work on" our emotions (Hochschild 1983).

Consider a dating relationship. If, after several dates that were mutually enjoyed by both, one partner announces to the other: "I love you," that person probably has reason to believe that the feeling will be returned. The cues emitted by the role partner may have been misread, but, regardless of the accuracy of this reading, the announcement will affect the course of the relationship. The emotion will either be returned or the role partners will reevaluate their status as a couple. If they share the same "grammar" they can usually expect their feelings to be returned because it is likely that their perceptions of the situation will be similar.

Sharing the same "grammar," however, also allows the role partners to "play the game" instead of really meaning it. Stringing someone along, does, after all, require knowledge of the rules and the cues that bring particular responses. The other party may actually feel obligated to continue responding as if the feelings were real simply to maintain the script.

There are other situations where showing specific emotional responses not really felt by the actors is a normative expectation. Hochschild, in her study of flight attendants, found a deep alienation hidden under the smiles and polite courtesies expected in the job which masked authentic feelings of contempt and dislike. The exchange of money (a salary) for demonstrations of certain emotions apparently generates resentment. This might be extended to apply to the dating situation. The person who is picking up the tab for the evening may think it is legitimate to expect a pleasant response. This may generate resentment from the other party who interprets the dating situation as one wherein it is legitimate for both parties to assess the other and exchange "real" emotions as (and if) desired.

Emotion is thus an interactive exchange. As Hochschild (1983) has pointed out, people build up feeling currencies, which others hold on account, ready to give in the future. "I owe you a favor" is one simple illustration. Failure to follow the rules for emotional exchange can lead to a closed account, at least for certain types of emotional interaction. It is possible, but highly unlikely, that a young man who proposed marriage to his female friend and was greeted with the response of "What? Me marry you? You have to be joking," would keep his love account open with her. Shared emotions provide a basis for social cohesion, as they unite common interests. Moreover, emotions, as Collins (1986) has pointed out, link human action to physical bodies in a dynamic social fashion. The social situation triggers individual emotions and emotional interchanges. These in turn feed back into our bodies on a physiological basis. Much of the research on stress, for example, has indicated that a situation perceived as stressful triggers very specific physiological responses.

We have talked at some length about processes that occur in social systems ranging from the dyad and the small group to whole societies. Similar processes characterize formal organizations, the final aspect of social structure to be discussed in this chapter.

Formal Organizations

Formal organizations are social structures characterized by formality, ranked positions, large size, relative complexity, and long duration.

Formal organizations are an important part of the social system because everyone spends so much time in them; only preschool children and adults who work at home are exempt from being "organization people." Formal organizations (sometimes called *complex organizations*) are characterized by

- Formality
- Ranked positions
- Large size
- Relative complexity
- Duration longer than that of the members composing them.

Examples of complex or formal organizations include such different units as football teams, local school systems, colleges, hospitals, businesses, and government agencies.

Formal organizations are larger and more structured than smaller groups. There is a clear-cut division of labor following an organizational blueprint. Role behavior stems primarily from one's status in the organization and may be less flexible than in informal groups.

The formal organization is an effective and efficient mechanism for doing a large job or many tasks. In any group, as the complexity of tasks increases and as more and more specialization is required, the level of organization and the size of the group also increase. For example, the one-room schoolhouse of the past was much like a small, relatively informal group. A modern school is a formal organization in which various teachers specialize in particular fields, students may move from one classroom to another, and both students and faculty are accountable to the principal, who, in turn, is accountable to a higher level of centralized authority, the superintendent (see Chap. 14).

BUREAUCRACY

Bureaucracy is a formal organization designed to accomplish large-scale administrative tasks through systematic coordination of the work of many people.

One type of formal organization that is common in modern societies is the *bureaucracy.* First described by Max Weber (1922), the bureaucracy is a specific type of organization designed to accomplish large-scale administrative tasks through systematic coordination of the work of many people. According to Weber, the bureaucracy has the following characteristics:

1. The regular activities necessary for the organization to function are assigned as official duties. There is a clear-cut division of labor with a high degree of specialization.
2. Each lower office is under the control and supervision of a higher one; each person is accountable to a supervisor both for his or her own actions and for those of subordinates. (This arrangement is called a *hierarchy.*)
3. Operations and work are governed by a consistent set of rules for specific situations or tasks to ensure uniformity.
4. Officials in the bureaucracy are to perform their tasks impartially, without bias or favoritism.
5. Employment is based on stated qualifications, and employees are protected against unreasonable dismissal.
6. Records are kept of all transactions.

These characteristics indicate how bureaucracies attempt to be impartial and rational. Positions are filled according to technical ability, statuses are achieved rather than ascribed, and the organization aims at efficiency. Do bureaucracies really work that way?

The Bureaucracy at Work: Positive Features. The positive aspects of the bureaucracy include a division of labor that promotes efficiency, clear and specified chains of command and expectations for workers, and the discouragement of favoritism and petty rivalries in promotion. In a complex society such as the United States, the simplicity of the *Gemeinschaft* organization (such as mom-and-pop store) is inappropriate for producing motorcars, breakfast cereals, or large crops of wheat; for ranching; or for treating a heart attack victim. Modern tasks and knowledge are too complex for any one person to master all aspects of even a single specialty such as farming, manufacturing, or hospital administration.

What about the relative security of one's position within the bureaucracy: Is this boon or boondoggle? It is popular to see bureaucrats as concerned only with rules and pay raises. Yet, such job security may be a hidden strength. Comparing people in high-ranking positions in bureaucratic organizations with those in smaller, nonbureaucratic system, Kohn (1971) found that the bureaucrats were *more* creative and had more varied interests, perhaps because the large corporations that he studied had the "pick of the crop" of college graduates. Another explanation is that the relative security of the bureaucratic organization frees executives to explore new ways of doing things without immediate fear of job loss or demotion.

The Bureaucracy at Work: Negative Features. Most Americans have had personal experience with one or more of the negative aspects of the bureaucracy: inefficient communication, buck passing, red tape, and baffling and needlessly complex regulations. In 1987, for example, "simplified" income-tax forms turned out to be more confusing than the barely understandable ones that they replaced. An even more simplified form was ultimately issued. Such complexity and wordiness are related to the nature of bureaucratic organization. That is, because a bureaucracy has written rules specifying appropriate behavior, it tries to make rules for all possible events. This is one of the by-products of "doing things by the book." Rigid rules may sometimes create problems as well as solve them. Thus, errors, when made, tend to be perpetuated and to be difficult to detect and correct. For example, the Social Security Administration discovered in 1983 that over $1 billion had been wrongly paid to dead persons. In most cases, the relatives had reported the deaths to the Social Security Administration, but because of clerical or computer errors, the checks continued to be sent out. One woman who had notified the Social Security Administration of her mother's death in 1975 commented to reporters that she was surprised to see the benefit checks continue to arrive, but "I decided to let them do it until they saw their mistake" (Fialka 1983).

Rewarding incompetence has also been noted by Professor Lawrence Peter, co-author of *The Peter Principle* (1969). With tongue firmly planted in cheek, Peter developed a new science: hierarchiology, or the study of how people rise to their level of incompetence within bureaucracy. This is the Peter Principle:

> Early in life, I faced the problem of occupational incompetence. As a young schoolteacher, I was shocked, baffled, to see so many knot-heads as principals, inspectors, and superintendents. I questioned older teachers. All I could find was that the knot-heads . . . had been capable (once) and that was why they had been promoted. Eventually, I realized the same occurs in all trades and professions . . . a competent employee is eligible for promotion, but incompetence is a bar to promotion. So an employee's final position must be one for which he is incompetent! (p. 8)

Among the negative features of bureaucracy are the growth of rules, regulations, and paperwork necessary to comply with procedures. What do you think will happen to these forms when they're completed and no longer needed? (© John Maramas/Woodfin Camp and Associates)

Another negative feature of bureaucracy that has received wide support is Parkinson's Law: Work expands to fill the number of hours allotted to it (Parkinson 1957). A third criticism is that "officials beget officials," as in the case of many colleges and universities, where the number of Deans and Assistant Deans has grown at a higher rate than faculty positions.

The impersonality of the bureaucracy has also been criticized. Not only may members of the public feel frustrated by the impersonality of an organization such as the employment office, but the absence of flexible and personalized authority can be a straitjacket for many workers. They feel locked into a structure that they are powerless to alter. Yet, few of us would prefer to be judged and treated on the basis of personal qualities such as skin color or religion. And impersonality can guarantee equal treatment: Each client is given the same impersonal treatment.

99

The Sociology of Emotions

ARLIE R. HOCHSCHILD

Arlie Russell Hochschild is professor of sociology at the University of California at Berkeley. She is the author of The Managed Heart: Commercialization of Human Feeling, *a book which was the winner of the Charles Horton Cooley Award, 1984; Honorable Mention, C. Wright Mills Award, 1984; and one of the* New York Times Books of the Year, *1983. She is one of the founders of a new area of research, the sociology of emotions.*

I think my interest in how people manage emotions began when my parents joined the U.S. Foreign Service. At the age of twelve, I found myself passing a dish of peanuts among many guests and looking up at their smiles; diplomatic smiles can look different when seen from below than when seen straight on. Afterwards I would listen to my mother and father interpret various gestures. The tight smile of the Bulgarian emissary, the averted glance of the Chinese consul, and the prolonged handshake of the French economic officer, I learned, conveyed messages not simply from person to person but from Sofia to Washington, from Peking to Paris, and from Paris to Washington. Had I passed the peanuts to a person, I wondered, or to an actor? Where did the person end and the act begin? Just how is a person related to an act?

As a graduate student at Berkeley some years later, I was excited by the writings of C. Wright Mills, especially his chapter in *White Collar* called "The Great Salesroom," which I read and reread, I see now, in search of answers to those abiding questions. Mills argued that when we "sell our personality" in the course of selling goods or services we engage in a seriously self-estranging process, one that is increasingly common among workers in advanced capital-

ist systems. This had the ring of truth, but something was missing. Mills seemed to assume that in order to sell personality, one need only have it. Yet simply having personality does not make one a diplomat, any more than having muscles makes one an athlete. What was missing was a sense of the active emotional labor involved in the selling. This labor, it seemed to me, might be one part of a distinctly patterned yet invisible emotional system—a system composed of individual acts of "emotion work," social "feeling rules," and a great variety of exchanges between people in private and public life. I wanted to understand the general emotional language of which diplomats speak only one dialect.

My search soon led me to the works of Erving Goffman, to whom I am indebted for his keen sense of how we try to control our appearance even as we unconsciously observe rules about how we ought to appear to others. But again, something was missing. How does a person act on feeling—or stop acting on it, or even stop feeling? . . .

We feel. But what is a feeling? I would define feeling, like emotion, as a sense, like the sense of hearing or sight. In a general way, we experience it when bodily sensations are joined with what we see or imagine. Like the sense of hearing, emotion communicates information. It has, as Freud said of anxiety, a "signal function." From feeling we discover our own viewpoint on the world.

We often say that we *try* to feel. But how can we do this? Feelings, I suggest, are not stored "inside" us, and they are not independent of acts of management. Both the act of "getting in touch with" feeling and the act of "trying to" feel may become part of the process that makes the thing we get in touch with, or the thing we manage, *into* a feeling or

emotion. In managing feeling, we contribute to the creation of it.

. . . What gives social pattern to our acts of emotion management? I believe that when we try to feel, we apply latent feeling rules. We say, "I shouldn't feel so angry at what she did," or "given our agreement, I have no right to feel jealous." Acts of emotion management are not simply private acts; they are used in exchanges under the guidance of feeling rules. Feeling rules are standards used in emotional conversation to determine what is rightly owed and owing in the currency of feeling. Through them, we tell what is "due" in each relation, each role. We pay tribute to each other in the currency of the managing act. In interaction we pay, overpay, underpay, play with paying, acknowledge our dues, pretend to pay, or acknowledge what is emotionally due another person. In these ways, we make our try at sincere civility.

. . . Now what happens when the managing of emotion comes to be sold as labor? What happens when feeling rules, like rules of behavioral display, are established not through private negotiation but by company manuals? What happens when social exchanges are not, as they are in private life, subject to change or termination but ritually sealed and almost inescapable?

. . . One sometimes needs a grand word to point out a coherent pattern between occurrences that would otherwise seem totally unconnected. My word is "transmutation." When I speak of the transmutation of an emotional system, I mean to point out a link between a private act, such as attempting to enjoy a party, and a public act, such as summoning up good feeling for a customer.

. . . By the grand phrase "transmutation of an emotional system" I mean to convey what it is that we do privately, often unconsciously, to feelings that nowadays often fall under the sway of large organizations, social engineering, and the profit motive.

. . . This transmutation of the private use of feeling affects the two sexes and the various social classes in distinctly different ways. As a matter of tradition, emotion management has been better understood and more often used by women as one of the offerings they trade for economic support. Especially among dependent women of the middle and upper classes, women have the job (or think they ought to) of creating the emotional tone of social encounters: expressing joy at the Christmas presents others open, creating the sense of surprise at birthdays, or displaying alarm at the mouse in the kitchen. Gender is not the only determinant of skill in such managed expression and in the emotion work needed to do it well. But men who do this work well have slightly less in common with other men than women who do it well have with other women. When the "womanly" art of living up to *private* emotional conventions goes public, it attaches itself to a different profit-and-loss statement.

Similarly, emotional labor affects the various social classes differently. If it is women, members of the less advantaged gender, who specialize in emotional labor, it is the middle and upper reaches of the class system that seem to call for it most. And parents who do emotional labor on the job will convey its importance to their children to prepare them with the skills they will need for the jobs they will probably get.

In general, working-class people tend to work more with things, and middle-class and upper-class people tend to work more with people. More working women than men deal with people as a job. Thus, there are both gender patterns and class patterns to the civic and commercial use of human feeling.

. . . We may well be seeing a response to the transmutation of emotion in the rising approval of the unmanaged heart, the greater virtue now attached to what is "natural" or spontaneous. . . . The high regard for "natural feeling," then, may coincide with the culturally imposed need to develop the precise opposite—an instrumental stance toward feeling. We treat spontaneous feeling, for this reason, as if it were scarce and pre-

cious; we raise it up as a virtue. It may not be too much to suggest that we are witnessing a call for the conservation of "inner resources," a call to save another wilderness from corporate use and keep it "forever wild."

With the growing celebration of spontaneity have come the robot jokes. Robot humor plays with the tension between being human—that is to say, having feeling—and being a cog in a socioeconomic machine. The charm of the little robot R2–D2, in the film *Star Wars,* is that he seems so human. Films like this bring us the familiar in reverse: every day, outside the movie house, we see human beings whose show of feeling has a robot quality. The ambiguities are funny now.

Both the growing celebration of spontaneity and the jokes we tell about being robots suggest that in the realm of feeling, Orwell's 1984 came in disguise several years ago, leaving behind a laugh and the illusion of a private way out.

SOURCE: Arlie Russell Hochschild. *The Managed Heart: Commercialization of Human Feelings,* Berkeley, CA: University of California Press, 1983, p. 15–23.

Goal displacement occurs when the members of an organization are more interested in perpetuating the organization than in performing the tasks for which it was originally designed.

One cause of bureaucratic inefficiency is the tendency of organizations toward *goal displacement,* that is, losing sight of the original goals of the organization, and becoming interested primarily in keeping the organization alive. The survival of the bureaucracy itself and achieving its internal goals of money, status, and prestige become its members' primary product.

INFORMAL GROUPS WITHIN THE BUREAUCRACY

Because the ideals of rationality and discipline are never fully realized in a complex organization, informal social structures develop to fill the gaps. The formal structure is, as we have emphasized, impersonal. Changes in rules, communication patterns, and official leadership lag behind daily events. Furthermore, no matter

how complex the wording, the rules must be general enough to allow for new situations or chance events. The impersonal patterns of relationships within the bureaucracy gives rise to *informal primary-group* relationships among the members of work teams. This kind of informal structure may either reinforce the purpose of the organization (as does the primary group in the military) or work against its goals (as when workers set informal production quotas and punish "rate busters").

Informal groups within the formal organization have several functions: (1) They provide personal satisfaction; (2) they break down barriers in communication within the formal structure; (3) they create discipline within the group; (4) they encourage personal ties that bind a person to the organization because of loyalty to fellow group members (Blau and Scott

Informal primary groups develop within bureaucracies to meet personal needs.

1962). Workers have been known to conduct successful "work-to-rule" protests in which they stick carefully to organizational rules, thus causing work slowdowns, to gain benefits for themselves such as increases in pay or better working conditions. Even relatively low-level informal groups may modify working conditions within the bureaucracy.

THE FUTURE OF BUREAUCRACY

Since around 1900, bureaucracies have become an expanding, ever-present part of the social structure of American society, so that the rationalization of the workplace that Weber detailed is largely complete. Weber (1921) also described bureaucracy as an "iron cage," in which people often feel trapped by rational, impersonal arrangements over which they have no control and which seems to defy all possibilities of flexibility and change. What trends can we foresee for bureaucracies in the future?

As governments and businesses become larger and more complex, so do their organizational structures. But increasing interest in being shown in a less formal hierarchy. In the military, for example, there has been a tendency for patterns of authority to change: from direct orders with no questions asked to persuasion and group agreement about what is to be done, and for more creative, imaginative, and unconventional officers to receive promotion to higher levels (Janowitz 1980). Toffler (1970) suggested that there has been a threefold loosening of bureaucracy, in which permanency, hierarchy, and specialization within the organization decline. Hierarchy has been partially eroded by technical change. With increased automation for routine tasks has come greater organizational flexibility, including job sharing and flexible work hours. Another trend has been the expanding use of professional "experts," who operate in work groups of equals where decisions are made through consensus among members of the work groups rather than in a hierarchical fashion. This participative model enhances communication and work efficiency. *Decentralization* of the bureaucracy is also being evaluated (Kochen and Deutsch 1980).

Although no single remedy for the disadvantages of bureaucratic organization is generally accepted, flexible organizational styles and leadership patterns are constantly evolving. In situations of rapid social change, the emphasis on control within the traditional bureaucracies may be giving way to adaptations that encourage creativity and less rigid structures in both practice and policy (Rothschild and Russell, 1986).

Summary

Social structure is the actual working out of cultural ideals and expectations in the patterned behaviors of people who are linked to one another in some fashion (as kin, neighbors, co-workers, and citizens). The key concepts in the study of social structure are systems, statuses, and roles. The smallest unit of social structure is the role, a set of behaviors expected of a person in a given status. A status is a position in a social system, linked to other statuses by rules or guidelines for behavior (the norms). Together, these patterned statuses form a system, a whole composed of interdependent parts. In other words, members of a status or role system are bound together by predictable actions.

Statuses can be given at birth (ascribed) or gained by one's own effort (achieved). One feature of modern societies is the increasing importance of achievement as compared to ascription in assigning social positions. The roles attached to statuses give shape to human behavior. Most of our daily activity is channeled by the demands and possibilities of the roles we perform. Often, the sheer number of roles causes strain; then, too, the diverse expectations of role partners can lead to conflict both within an individual and between role partners.

But without the guidelines of role expectations, we would not know how to behave. The anxiety of normlessness—anomie—is relieved when people define their situation and develop appropriate rules of behavior. Order is restored in human affairs.

At the level of face-to-face interaction, status and role systems form human groups whose members are aware of or sensitive to the actions of others. Groups are generally described as either primary or secondary, depending on the degree of closeness, formality, intimacy, and totality of the relationships. Industrial societies are characterized by the dominance of secondary groups.

Membership groups provide people with the information and the emotional support required for appropriate role performance. Reference groups—whether or not one is a member—provide the standards against which an individual measures her or his role behavior. Throughout our lives, the various groups in which we are embedded or to which we look for guidance are essential for constructing our definitions of reality, shaping our attitudes, and governing our behavior.

Groups have characteristics of their own, such as size, division of labor, and degree of formality, all of which affect their functioning. Interaction within a group involves elements of exchange, cooperation, competition, and even conflict; and each group varies in its unique mix of these interaction processes. Emotions themselves are interactive processes, governed by a grammar or set of rules and characterized by exchange processes. Groups interact with other units of the society, and these intergroup relationships involve exchange, cooperation, competition, and conflict. In-group solidarity is often enhanced by directing hostility toward out-groups.

Groups are also the building blocks of larger systems called *organizations,* in which a number of smaller units are coordinated in order to achieve some specific goal, such as educating children, defending a society, or dispensing justice. The sum of the organizations in any one sector of a society forms institutions, or institutional spheres, which are the interdependent parts of the society as a whole—its economic system, for example, or its family system.

Social structure, then, encompasses the patterned, normative interaction of systems as small as the dyad and as large as the entire society. In modern societies, small face-to-face groups are often overshadowed by formal organizations, which are also a setting for primary-group relationships among the workers. The bureaucracy is a type of formal organization characterized by a rational specialization of tasks, hierarchical structure, and a merit-tenure system of promotions.

The concepts presented in this chapter—structure, system, status and role, groups, formal organizations and bureaucracies—are important basic tools of sociological analysis. Social structure is the other side of the coin from culture, the enactment of those ideals that form the essence of human societies. In the next chapter, we discuss the link between culture and social structure—the process whereby human beings learn the ways of their culture and the specific groups in which they are embedded.

Suggested Readings

BELLAH, ROBERT N., RICHARD MADSEN, ANNE SWIDLER, WILLIAM SULLIVAN, and STEVEN TIPTON. *Habits of the Heart: Individualism and Commitment in American Life.* Berkeley, California: University of California Press, 1985. A provocative examination of individualism and commitment as well as the shift from "communities of memory" that provided values and identities to more "transient life-style enclaves" focusing on self-interest.

ERIKSON, KAI. *Everything in Its Path: Destruction of Community in the Buffalo Creek Flood.* New York: Simon and Schuster, 1976. What happened when the dam burst at Buffalo Creek, destroying life, property, and the social fabric of an entire community. A very readable, sensitive account of this tragedy and its aftermath.

GARDELL, BERTIL, and GUNN JOHANSSON. *Working Life: A Social Science Contribution to Work Reform.* New York: Wiley, 1981. A collection of papers presenting international perspectives on work reforms and the dilemmas of the bureaucracy.

KANTER, ROSABETH MOSS. *Men and Women of the Corporation.* New York: Basic Books, 1977. How the corporation's own structure, chain of command, and promotion system affect the behavior of employees. It is the job, not gender, that produces different styles of working.

MERTON, ROBERT K. *Social Theory and Social Structure,* revised and enlarged ed. New York: Free Press, 1968. A classic sociological analysis of social structure.

SKOLNICK, JEROME H., and ELLIOTT CURIE. *Crises in American Institutions,* 6th ed. Boston: Little Brown, 1985. A collection of readings on contemporary social problems in the United States. It examines these problems in the context of American institutions and the conflicts and the contradictions inherent within them.

SUDNOW, DAVID. *Passing On: The Sociology of Dying.* Englewood Cliffs, New Jersey: Prentice Hall, 1967. A participant-observation study of the social creation of death and dying in a hospital.

ZURCHER, L. A. *Social Roles: Conformity, Conflict and Creativity,* Beverly Hills, California: Sage Publishing, 1983. A look at the relationship between social roles and personal autonomy.

5

The Social Self

C AN you become a human being without contact with other people? Folklore throughout the world contains stories of lost and abandoned babies who were raised by animals—Tarzan the Ape Man or Mowgli the Jungle Boy—and rumors of such a child periodically fascinate the reading public and intrigue scientists. Yet in no case has the existence of a feral (wild or untamed) child been proved. Human infants cannot be raised to normal adulthood by apes or wolves, but only by other human beings. Indeed, even infant monkeys cannot become effective adults without contact with mature monkeys (Harlow and Harlow 1977).

Human physical and social development do not unfold automatically. Just being born human is not enough. The newborn (neonate) becomes a human being by learning how to behave through interaction with other human beings. In a phrase, human behavior is primarily learned. The learning process is called *socialization* and involves the transmission, by language and gesture, of the culture into which we are born. At the same time, through the same interactions with others, we learn about our "self" and develop a sense of who and what kind of person we are. Essentially, we learn how to behave.

Socialization is the process whereby one learns how to behave in a given society and develops a sense of self.

The first part of this chapter examines socialization as a process of learning the approved behaviors in a given society. The second part presents various theories of personality development, with emphasis on a sociological view of the formation of self-concepts.

Socialization

THE EFFECTS OF EXTREME ISOLATION

In several recent cases of children who grew up without human contact, we can clearly see the effects of extreme isolation. In April 1982, officials in Las Vegas found six children ranging in age from eight months to six years, including two sets of twins, who had been locked in a dark room for most of their lives. They could neither talk (they communicated with grunts and other sounds) nor use eating utensils. Among themselves, they were extremely affectionate, but they were very fearful of other people (*New York Times,* April 24, 1983, p. 23). The fact that they had one another to relate to undoubtedly kept

Physical contact and a warm nurturing environment provide a baseline of trust between parent and child and a foundation upon which social attitudes are built. (© Marilyn Nance)

them from becoming mentally unbalanced.

In other cases, isolated children have had no one with whom to interact. Genie, for example, was thirteen when discovered in 1970. From the time she was twenty months old, she had been kept in a small room, spoken to by no one, and was often severely beaten by her father (Curtiss 1977, Pines 1981). When found, she could neither talk nor walk; she was not toilet-trained and could not chew food, even though she had apparently been a normal baby at birth. Under the care of trained professionals, she was taught how to eat and walk and take care of herself. Slowly, also, she began to talk, but only one or two words at a time. Unlike other children, Genie never experienced the rapid development of language that follows the two-word stage, and her measured IQ remained below average. It seems that there may be a critical period in childhood for developing the capacity for language. Without human contact at that crucial point, a child may lose the opportunity to become fully human (Davis 1940).

In adulthood, too, extreme isolation has severe consequences. Solitary confinement is a cruel and unusual punishment precisely because we need contact with others to maintain a sense of reality, including our own identity. People who are placed in solitary confinement lose their sense of time—that's why they are often portrayed as trying to keep track of days by scratches on the wall—and ultimately come to doubt every aspect of their lives. Among prisoners in Nazi concentration camps in the 1940s, for example, the most isolated men and women experienced the most extreme losses of self-awareness and mental stability (Rose, et al. 1979).

The essential point is that reality is socially constructed, and that without others to help us define reality, we risk "losing our senses," which is the reason why social isolates are so vulnerable to mental problems. The human capacity for social life and our great need to be with other people are the basis of socialization and have roots in the evolutionary development of *homo sapiens.*

THE EVOLUTIONARY BASES

All other animals are instinctively programmed for much of their behavior. But humans are distinguished by their almost

Evolution has produced a creature that can learn and must learn in order to survive.

unlimited ability to learn. Not only *can* we learn, but *evolution* has also produced a creature that *must* learn in order to survive. The human infant, remember, is born at a less developed stage than other animal young; it cannot take care of itself. Hence, one biological basis of socialization is the extraordinary helplessness of the human newborn.

Physical Helplessness. You may have observed newborn kittens or puppies which, within weeks, can get around on their own and even be parted from their mother. In contrast, those animals closest to us on the evolutionary scale, the great apes, have newborns in a manner similar to that of humans: typically one at a time, several years apart, and relatively helpless—clinging to the mother. And, for a year or two, there are many parallels between the infant ape and human child.

In the first two years of life, ape and human infants move in the same order through basic stages of growth, from grasping to self-exploration, followed by reaching out and experimentation, to the higher level of problem solving. A crucial difference, however, is that apes do not follow the human course of language development. Humans have the capacity to learn complex languages and to construct worlds of meaning through speech. The human being is, at birth, a bundle of potentials, unguided by instinct, but capable of learning any language and culture, and totally dependent on its social environment. The infant's mind matures while it is being fed and cared for by others. The term *helpless* in this context refers only to physical dependency; the newborn's brain is actively recording sensations, processing information, and organizing experience.

Dependency. This physical dependence on others is an essential precondition to learning. Because the brain and the nervous system are developed at the same time that an infant is being fed and cared for, a basic sensitivity to the expectations of others is built into our earliest experience. This dependence never leaves us, although the objects may shift—from parents to friends to lovers and even to one's own children. But throughout life, humans need other people to provide them with the affection first experienced in dependent infancy.

The mind that reflects on itself, it seems, is never altogether certain: Who am I? What am I? Am I loved? Am I good? These are the questions that we ask over and over again. One is not born with such knowledge and must seek the answers from others—beginning, of course, with those who take care of one's earliest needs, the nurturers (caregivers) of infancy.

Each society has evolved some relatively stable unit to care for helpless young, typically a group centered on the mother (this is also true of apes). Having carried the infant and given it birth, the mother is the obvious person to care for it. She is also restricted in moving around, somewhat weakened by childbirth, and often limited by the need to breast-feed. There is *no* maternal instinct, but there are many reasons that women behave maternally: the sheer helplessness of the newborn being one, and the mother's own emotional and physical investment in the product of her body being another. But given the very high maternal death rates in most societies throughout history, there is an evolutionary advantage to the human infant's being able to relate to any adult nurturer, and to the willingness of nonrelatives to care for other people's offspring.

The newborn becomes especially sensitive to cues from its caregivers. Over time, the infant discovers that it, too, contributes to the interaction: a wail brings attention, a gurgle thrills an audience, and whining can bring harsh words. An *interdependence* develops between infants and caretakers, although overwhelming power resides in the adults, who can provide or withhold what the infant needs for survival.

Human Needs. Nurturance for physical survival is only one need of the infant. We propose that there are three other responses from others that are essential for well-being across the life course: affection, approval, and some assurance that one is who one claims to be (*validation of self*). A similar set of needs was suggested by W. I. Thomas (1923) in terms of "four wishes"—for new experience, mastery, recognition, and security. The people whose approval and affection we most care about are also those whose failure to like us would hurt most. Throughout our lives we are especially sensitive to the reactions of a few very important people.

Validation of self requires assurance that one is who one claims to be.

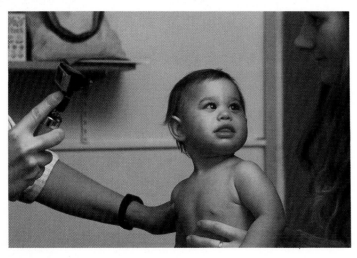

This baby is looking to its mother for both reassurance and cues on how to react to the doctor's advancing stethoscope. (© W. U. Harris)

In infancy, this need for others is physically based. In later years, the ties are almost purely emotional—but are built on the model of the earliest dependency. The cases of Genie and other isolated children are clear evidence of the need for human contact if one is to *become* a human being. Continued interaction is required if one is to *remain* a stable person and, often, to remain alive and healthy. There is increasing evidence of a link between good health and having the support of family and friends. For example, a longitudinal study of the residents of one county in California showed that people without social and community ties were more likely to die in the nine-year follow-up period than were those with many links to other people (Berkman and Syme 1979).

Individual Differences. Although all newborns have undeveloped potential, they are not, of course, identical. Some will learn faster than others, will be musical, will be tall or fat, will be calm or fidgety, and so on through a lengthy list of traits that have some *genetic component*. That is, there may be inherited tendencies toward certain types of behavior or appearance. Each infant is a unique combination of such traits, with the possible exception of identical twins, who share the same genetic material.

But—and this is a crucial point—genetic tendencies do not automatically produce behavior. A tendency is just that, the likelihood that one response will occur

rather than another. Tendencies develop within social structures and can be stifled or encouraged.

Even people born with a great talent—for music, or mathematics, or a sport—do not realize their potential without the support and encouragement of parents and teachers. The environment of the home and the availability of trained instructors are the keys to becoming exceptionally skilled (Pines 1982). Because almost everyone has a special talent, we have to look to these social factors to explain why some young people develop the desire to excel and why others do not.

Bearing in mind that each person is a unique combination of innate and learned traits, we turn now to the process by which people learn the rules of the culture and the particular roles that they are expected to play throughout life.

The Socialization Process

Every newborn can learn any culture, speak any language, and organize experience in different ways as it matures. The function of primary (early) socialization is to present a single world of meaning as the only possible way to organize perceptions (Berger and Luckman 1966). At the micro-level, this information is given through direct training for social roles.

LEARNING ONE'S PLACE

When people occupy a particular status, they must learn the appropriate role behavior. Role learning involves several elements: information, opportunities to rehearse, feedback from role partners, and social supports.

Information. At some point the learner must be given guidance for adequate role performance. The military recruit receives detailed descriptions from a drill instructor; mothers-to-be can attend child-care classes; and children are prepared in advance for kindergarten. There are "how to" books for people interested in everything from being a successful golfer to finding a marriage partner.

Rehearsal. Knowing *what* to do is one thing; doing it is something else. Most performances benefit from practice. Opportunities for trial-and-error learning under relatively safe conditions are usually given to people just entering a role—the "honeymoon" period for newlyweds, political newcomers, and first-year college students.

Another form of rehearsal is called *anticipatory socialization,* involving practice in advance of assuming the role. Thus, little girls play house, and older boys play soldier; high school seniors begin to act like college students; employees expecting a promotion dress more carefully; and older adults take up the hobbies they intend to follow in retirement.

Somewhat related to anticipatory socialization is the behavior called *modeling,* or copying the characteristics of admired persons. Parents, movie stars, and sports figures are common role models for children. It is thought that a shortage of role models in prestige occupations accounts in part for the absence of women and blacks in those fields.

Feedback. Role performances take place before an audience of role partners who transmit messages regarding the performance. *Positive sanctions* are those reactions indicating that the role is well played. *Negative sanctions* involve open criticism or at least the withholding of approval. Depending on the importance of the sanctioner, people will modify their behavior in order to receive positive feedback. The opinions of most people may have little effect, but the judgments of some are crucial. (See discussion of sanctions in Chapter 3 as well.)

Social Supports. Success in a role often depends on the help of people who are willing to train the learner and to tolerate role rehearsals. A growing body of research has documented the crucial importance of supportive social networks, especially in old age (e.g. Peterson and Quadagno 1985, Sauer and Coward 1985). People who have many friends tend to cope with the role changes of retirement and widowhood more successfully than do those who have isolated themselves.

Learning Sexuality. As an example of this learning process—information, rehearsal, feedback, and social supports—let us examine behavior that most Americans assume is the product of a powerful and irresistible "natural" drive. To be sure, there is something that can be called a sex drive, but how it is displayed and interpreted is learned behavior. Because of its great potential for disrupting relationships, sexuality must have been the first human impulse to be brought under control of the group as a basic requirement of social order. (See Chapter 11 for a discussion of how sexuality is controlled by the norms.)

Paradoxically, because the sex drive is so thoroughly socialized, we do seem to be "doing what comes naturally." Yet, if you think about your own experience, you will realize that your entire life has been spent *learning* the what, who, when, where, and why of appropriate sexual conduct.

The flexibility of the human sexual response is most clearly seen in the wide variety of roles and rules, beliefs, and

Anticipatory socialization involves rehearsing prior to assuming a role.

Modeling is the copying of characteristics of admired persons.

Positive sanctions indicate approval of role performance. **Negative sanctions** convey disapproval of role performance.

Anticipatory socialization starts early and involves practicing later roles. In American society, where most adults use phones, children learn about this form of communication at a very young age. What else are these children learning? (© W. U. Harris)

In our society, the beauty contest is still a very important component of the female's sexual script. It articulates the criteria and establishes standards around which women are supposed to build their self image. What do you think is going through the minds of these contestants? (© Jeff Jacobsen/Archive Pictures, Inc.)

Sexual scripts are ways of interpreting events so that responses are either encouraged or suppressed.

behaviors recorded across cultures. What is sexually arousing to a young man or woman in our society may appear hopelessly ugly to a Balinese or Nigerian. In other words, what turns you on is culturally determined, and how you interpret it is socially constructed.

According to the influential work of John Gagnon and William Simon (1973, 1986), humans learn *sexual scripts,* or ways of interpreting events so that certain responses are either encouraged or suppressed. The script and its role requirements allow a person to organize experiences into a recognized pattern. For example, we behave very differently, even with the same role partners, when we define a situation as work, or "just fun," or romantic.

If there is no fixed sexual outcome determined by hormones or early childhood experience, then sexuality is actually a flexible set of responses that can change from one situation to another and across the life course. There are also many *subcultural* variations on the general norms governing sexual behavior in our society. Both what is defined as sexually arousing and how one responds to feelings of arousal vary from one group to another on the basis of race, religion, ethnicity, education, and occupation. And, in our society, though not in all, there are separate scripts for females and males.

SUBCULTURAL DIFFERENCES

Sexuality is only one of the many areas in which young people learn different norms and values according to their parents' income, education, occupation, ethnic background, or religion. For example, chil-

dren from lower-income and blue-collar families tend to begin their sexual experiences at an earlier age, have more partners, and engage in sex more frequently than do the offspring of higher-income and white-collar families (Weinberg and Williams 1980).

Parental Occupation. These findings illustrate the importance of parents' occupations in value formation and transmission. A general discussion of *social class* appears in Part III of this book, but in terms of socialization some mention must be made here of the work of Melvin Kohn and his colleagues (summarized in Kohn and Schooler 1983) on the link between occupation and socialization. Most white-collar occupations require dealing with people, solving problems, and manipulating symbols. These jobs also tend to be non-repetitive and loosely supervised, allowing latitude for *autonomy* (self-direction). In contrast, most blue-collar jobs call for being on time, obeying orders, and dealing with machines. As a consequence, white-collar parents encourage their children to be intellectually curious, flexible, and self-controlled, whereas blue-collar parents reinforce punctuality, obedience to authority, conformity, and technical skills.

In their research, Kohn and his associates show how social structural variables (occupational characteristics) affect parental values that, in turn, influence socialization practices and, ultimately, personality traits of the child.

Kohn's thesis has been supported in comparisons between Polish and American families (Slomczynski, et al. 1981). In both countries, fathers whose occupations call for self-direction place a high value on personal responsibility in their children, whereas men whose work is highly supervised tend to value conformity in their offspring. Similar findings for working women have been reported by Spade (1983).

These differences are also reflected in disciplining techniques. Parents in highly supervised work tend toward physical punishment of children, whereas those in self-directed work favor a more "psychological" approach, especially the threat of the withdrawal of affection. As described in Table 5-1, the two patterns have been labeled *traditional* and *modern*.

The distinction between traditional and modern can be illustrated by the parents' reactions to a child who has broken a neighbor's window. Traditional parents are likely to spank the child for destroying property and to worry about the expense of replacing the window. The "modern" parent tends to focus on the child's state of mind—"why did you do it?" Guilt feelings are reinforced by parental withholding of love. The goal is to teach the child self-control rather than fear of being caught and punished. (In actuality, physical punishment is a relatively ineffective technique for teaching children to control their impulses.) Without necessarily recognizing it, parents are demonstrating that they have lost control (Power and Chapielski 1986); they are relying on force rather than their status as older and wiser.

Similar findings on child disciplining have been reported for a contemporary German sample (Williamson 1984), while a cross-cultural analysis of societies at all stages of complexity found that a cultural emphasis on conformity to rules rather than on self-direction was associated with the use of physical punishments (Peterson, et al. 1982). These data support the general point that socialization practices reflect the parents' experience in the soci-

TABLE 5-1   Two patterns of child-rearing

"Traditional" or Status-Centered	"Modern" or Person-Centered
1. Each member's place in the family is a function of age and sex status.	Emphasis is on selfhood and individuality of each member.
2. Father is defined as boss and more important as agent of discipline: he receives "respect" and deference from mother and children.	Father more affectionate, less authoritative; mother becomes more important as agent of discipline.
3. Emphasis on overt acts—*what* child does rather than *why.*	Emphasis on motives and feelings—*why* child does what he or she does.
4. Valued qualities in child: obedience, cleanliness.	Valued qualities in child are happiness, achievement, consideration, curiosity, self-control.
5. Emphasis on "direct" discipline: physical punishment, scolding, threats.	Discipline based on reasoning, isolation, guilt, threat of loss of love.
6. Social consensus and solidarity in communication; emphasis on "we."	Communication used to express individual experience and perspectives; emphasis on "I."
7. Emphasis on communication from parent to child.	Emphasis on two-way communication between parent and child; parent open to persuasion.
8. Parent feels little need to justify demands to child; commands are to be followed "because I say so."	Parent gives reasons for demands—e.g., not "Shut up" but "Please keep quiet or go into the other room; I'm trying to talk on the telephone."
9. Emphasis on conforming to rules, respecting authority, maintaining conventional social order.	Emphasis on reasons for rules; particular rules can be criticized in the name of higher rational or ethical principles.
10. Child may attain a strong sense of social identity at the cost of individuality, poor academic performance.	Child may attain strong sense of selfhood but may have identity problems, guilt, alienation.

SOURCE: Arlene Skolnick, *The Intimate Environment,* 4th Edition (Boston: Little Brown, 1987), p. 387.

ety as well as central values of their culture (Walters and Walters 1980, Moss and Abramowitz 1982).

Historical Change. Have parental values changed over the past few decades? There is scattered evidence that differences in socialization patterns on the basis of parents' job characteristics have narrowed over the past several decades, and that the overall trend is toward encouraging independence rather than conformity in one's children. Alwin (1984) compared survey data from Detroit parents at three points in time: 1958, 1971, and 1983, and found a constant increase in the value placed on autonomy and a decline in the preference for obedience. The background variable most strongly associated with this trend was *education,* while the influence of occupation appears to have decreased. Alwin also found that the shift toward valuing autonomy was strongest among Catholic parents, suggesting long-term changes in the cultural context of Catholic family life, above and beyond the effects of education.

Gender Differences. Although we will have more to say about the effects of gender socialization in Chapter 8, there is no doubt that mothers and fathers, teachers, and peers behave differently toward boys and girls (reviewed in Block 1984). This differential treatment has clear consequences for personality and for the organization of the mind. For example, Rose Laub Coser (1986) notes that because of their anticipated family roles, girls are encouraged to stay close to home rather than venture into the unknown. This confinement in space and emphasis on personal relationships enhances a girl's verbal skills while limiting her opportunity to develop the abstract thinking skills necessary to do well in mathematics. Coser's analysis is an excellent example of the sociological perspective, moving from the macro (structural) level of socialization practices to the micro (individual) level of personality outcomes, while also providing a sociological explanation for sex differences in verbal and mathematics test scores.

AGENTS OF SOCIALIZATION

If culture is learned, there must be regular channels of transmission. The people and organizations charged with the task of teaching rules and roles are called *agents of socialization.* Chief among these are parents, peers, teachers, and the media.

Parents. The first and most important agents of socialization are the people who care for infants, who are usually also the biological parents. This chapter opened with a discussion of the importance of infant nurturing, and the necessity for stable contacts with adults, whether or not biologically related. In the earliest months and years, information from these nurturers, conveyed by both words and gestures, make up the child's basic understanding of the world around it. This is the infant's introduction to the language that shapes perception and emotions. The child learns the culture as it is interpreted by the socializers. And the desire for continued contact with caregivers, combined with a fear of losing them, motivates the infant to become particularly sensitive to the wishes of those entrusted with her or his care.

Many of these cues are *nonverbal,* matters of mood and feeling expressed in how one is touched or spoken to, played with or held. These impressions are crucial for establishing trust between the child and its socializers. The *quality* of these early interactions is as important as the quantity and content. Especially important is the ability to *empathize,* to put yourself in the place of the other. Empathetic parents and caregivers are also teaching the child to imagine the feelings of others.

Nurturers can also send out contradictory messages, such as screaming "shut up!" or slapping a child to stop it from hitting. The child receives two messages: shouting and slapping are all right for parents, but not oneself. In these *double bind* situations, the child does not know which cue to respond to: the parent's loss of control or the information about one's own shortcomings (Ruesch and Bateson 1951). Hitting people to keep them from hitting is hardly a clear signal. The term *mystification* (Laing 1977) has been used to describe similar problems in parent-child understanding, where a parent says one thing but means another ("Stay out as long as you want; don't mind me!"). Parents can also mystify by placing their own feelings onto the child ("Don't you feel hungry? You *must* be hungry!"), thereby negating the reality of the child's own feelings.

Agents of socialization are people and organizations responsible for teaching rules and roles.

A **double bind** situation develops when the child receives two contradictory messages.

Culture is **internalized** in the mind of the child through parental expectations.

Parents have great potential power. The culture is *internalized* (brought into the mind of the child) through parental expectations. These early learnings are the foundation of later development, and the guilt caused by failure to live up to these expectations is an important motivator of adult performance. Most parents, if not all, attempt to prepare their offspring for what they believe to be success in their society. When parents say, "This is for your own good," they believe that what they are teaching is essential to becoming a capable adult.

In a simple society, parents can probably teach the growing child everything necessary to function as an adult, but in rapidly changing complex societies, where knowledge becomes quickly obsolete, other agents of socialization become important: friends, teachers, and the mass media. In the face of such competition, parents create or support formal organizations—Boy and Girl Scouts, Little League, religiously oriented youth groups—that they hope will socialize their children to approved values.

Although parental controls are weakened in complex societies, many attitudes are transmitted from one generation to another. Such similarity may be the result of direct parental socialization, or the product of *reciprocal socialization* whereby children modify their parents' view of the world. Some continuity is also due to the tendency for parents and children to occupy similar occupational statuses (Glass, et al. 1986).

Through **reciprocal socialization** children modify their parents' view of the world.

Peers.   Another powerful source of information and socialization is the friendship group of *age peers*. Peers are equals, whereas parents are the child's superiors. The greater power of parents makes some kinds of learning difficult. A certain formality must be observed even in the most relaxed homes. In contrast, one can deal with one's peers on a level of equality—tease, insult, rehearse roles, tolerate mistakes, and so on—without the heavy emotional overtones of family relationships.

Children need friends in order to learn many things about being a child, such as how to take turns, share, fight fairly, deal with adults, and prepare for the next stage of growth. At school, the peer group provides vast stores of important knowledge about how to handle authority, manipulate the system, act in and out of school, and approach members of the opposite sex. Even in adulthood, peer groups are important agents of socialization—to marriage, parenthood, retirement, and widowhood. But the adolescent peer group has received the most popular and scientific attention.

ADOLESCENT PEER GROUP.   For several decades, American parents and other adults have looked with amazement and anxiety at the friendship groups of young people between age thirteen and eighteen. Parents fear the power of the group as a challenge to family values and as a rival for the teenager's loyalty.

It would appear, however, that the adolescent peer group is necessary for young people in their journey from dependence

Peers are equals and an important source of information and socialization.

What kinds of values might these children learn belonging to Little League? (© James H. Karales/Peter Arnold, Inc.)

Boy Scouting and the Development of Character

Several recent studies of the Boy Scouts and similar organizations for young males (MacLeod 1983, Magrass 1986) show how scouting represented a response to profound changes taking place in America between 1870 and 1920. Small-town life was giving way to city living, the country was rapidly industrializing, child labor was no longer needed, and middle-class parents became particularly concerned about the moral development of their sons. Adolescence became recognized as a special, and potentially dangerous, period of the life course.

Fearful that their sons' character would be undermined, American middle-class parents welcomed the YMCA (Young Men's Christian Association) and Boy Scout movements that separated the boys from the girls, and that emphasized outdoor activity, team sports, obedience, and self-control. Thus, adolescent males could be prepared for the responsibilities of leadership in industrial society while also learning to accept authority and discipline.

An interesting sociological exercise would be an analysis of contemporary scouting. Have its goals and practices changed in the past sixty-five years? Are there other organizations that fill similar leadership training functions for older males, such as men's service organizations that still resist admitting women as full members?

SOURCES: David I. MacLeod, *Building Character in the American Boy: The Boy Scouts, YMCA, and Their Forerunners, 1870–1920*. Madison, WI: University of Wisconsin Press, 1983; Yale R. Magrass, "The Boy Scouts, the Outdoors, and Empire," *Humanity and Society*, Vol. 10 (February), 1986, pp. 37–57.

and Wiley 1986), other research indicates that while girls were more oriented toward their parents than boys in the 1960s, the pattern did not hold up through the 1980s and may even be reversed today (Sebald 1986).

The process whereby the peer group operates as an agent of socialization parallels that described for infant socialization. Peers, to some extent, replace parents as sources of affection, approval, and validation, and friends are emotionally bound to one another through fear of rejection. But adolescents still need support from their parents, and bonds of affection appear to be much stronger than commonly assumed (Troll and Bengtson 1979). Parents are important socializers to basic values and long-term goals (e.g., finances, education, and career), while peers have most influence on immediate life-style choices, such as appearance, sexual behavior, and leisure activities (Kandel 1982, Sebald 1986).

Although many parents are fearful of the power of the peer group, the major task of adolescence in modern society is precisely to outgrow dependence on one's parents. The strength of the adolescent peer group simply reflects the difficulty of this task. In the extended period when one is too old to be a child but too young to be an adult, a subculture of adolescent roles and attitudes develops, in which a young person can rehearse and prepare for independence. Perhaps the most a parent can do is to try to guide the choice of peers, and hope for the best.

to independence, from childhood to adulthood. The peer group helps adolescents to prepare for adult roles by tolerating one another's attempts to construct an identity (Eisenstadt 1956, Erikson 1963). In a society where people achieve adult statuses primarily by choice or merit, the young person needs the peer group in order to learn how to meet objective ("universalistic") standards of performance, in contrast to the ascribed, unequal, and individualized ("particularistic") criteria of the family. (See Figure 5-1.) Although there is some evidence that girls have more difficulty than boys in separating themselves from the influence of parents (Eskilson

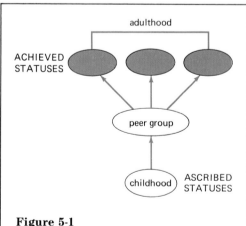

Figure 5-1
The adolescent peer group is a medium for the transition from childhood to adult statuses.

Teachers. Much formal socialization today is in the hands of professionals (see Chapter 14). Teachers, from nursery school on, receive pay for being agents of socialization. Ideally, a teacher has both special knowledge and the skills needed to transmit it. Teachers are also role models for responsible adulthood and for the importance of education. Some may even convey the excitement of learning itself. This is usually the teacher we remember.

In high school and college, many young people form especially close relationships with particular instructors, who become their *mentors* (guides and sponsors). By devoting time and energy to one's students rather than to one's own career advancement, mentors can influence career decisions and open the door to advanced training. Without such a sponsor, many students fail to achieve their full potential. Until recently, it was very difficult for women graduate students to find a mentor willing to further their career goals, and it remains a problem for women seeking high position in the business and professional world.

The Media. To the list of agents of socialization today, we must add several powerful indirect (nonpersonal) channels of communication: radio, movies, television, audio systems, and computer networks. Many people learn about politics, form a vision of the good life, and develop attitudes toward others from what they see on a screen and hear through speakers.

Most research on the socialization influence of the media centers on the effects of television on the beliefs and behaviors of children, who typically spend as much time in front of the set as they do at school—over 50 hours a week. The home video market is another factor here. The influence of the mass media on adults as well as children is discussed in Chapter 20.

> **Mentors** are teachers who act as guides and sponsors.

Formation of the Self

Transmission of the culture is only one aspect of socialization. While people process information about the culture and role expectations, they also learn about their *self*. The self is an organization of perceptions about who and what kind of person one is. Humans are not born with

> **Self** is an organization of perceptions about who and what kind of person one is.

Agnes: The Social Construction of Identity

One of the most-cited case histories in sociology is the study of Agnes, a biological male who had always felt that he was a female. Raised as a male up to age seventeen, Agnes then decided actually to become a woman. Agnes dressed and behaved the way a woman would, became engaged to a young man, and applied to a university clinic for the sex change surgery that would complete the transformation.

Medication and a series of operations could stop the production of male hormones and make Agnes look like a woman. But the hardest part of the sex change was learning how to "be" a woman and to convince others that this was her true identity. What for most women is considered "natural" was for Agnes a problem in the presentation of self. Agnes learned to avoid situations in which others might question her identity, such as all-female gatherings. She also had to construct a believable past history. In other words, Agnes quite literally manufactured a "self."

As we follow Agnes's own story, we realize that each person constructs an identity but is usually unaware of the effort it takes. What is "taken-for-granted" by the rest of us is brought into the open by Agnes. From this one in-depth study, then, we can learn more about the creation of a sexual identity than through any other research design. It is the perfect method for the type of question examined by ethnomethodologists.

SOURCE: Harold Garfinkel, "Agnes," from *Studies in Ethnomethodology* (Englewood Cliffs, N.J.: Prentice-Hall, 1967).

---

this organization nor with this knowledge. It is learned and developed gradually through precisely the same socialization experiences by which the culture is internalized.

Self-concept as a central component of personality has, for the most part, been studied from the symbolic-interaction perspective. For it is through language, the symbol system of culture, and in the intimacy of face-to-face interaction, that messages about the self are conveyed. How the individual interprets and evaluates this information is central to the social construction of identity. Harold Garfinkel has described this process by focusing on a very unique identity problem. (See box.)

JAMES, COOLEY, AND THE SOCIAL SELF

Only gradually does the infant come to distinguish itself from its nurturer. It is, of course, impossible to question a newborn (or even a young child) about its feelings and perceptions. Social scientists can only imagine how it must feel to be an infant. Without more certain knowledge, they have devised this scenario:

> The newborn is totally absorbed in the nurturer–infant system. But the human mind is reflective, and at some point, the infant begins to perceive itself in contrast to the overwhelming other. As the caregiver coos and murmurs, addressing a "you," the infant dimly begins to differentiate (separate) itself, to see itself as being that "you." This is what is meant when the sociologist speaks of the human mind as able to see itself as an object; the infant can reflect on the "you" that is itself, an "I."

And this "you" is what others see you as being. As they talk to you, handle you, and discuss you with others, you learn who you are. The self thus becomes an active participant in its own creation.

The Social Self. The concept of a *social self* was introduced by the psychologist William James (1842–1910), who stated that a person has as many social selves as there are others who recognize that person and carry an image of him or her in their minds. The self, therefore, is not some abstraction; it is rooted in social interaction. People are linked to society through their very self-concept: I am the one who acts and believes and feels in a manner guided by the norms established in a given society at a particular historical moment.

The Looking-Glass Self. Building on James's concept of the social self, Charles Horton Cooley (1864–1929) proposed that the self is composed of a basic self-feeling that is then shaped and given specific content through interactions with important others.

Cooley is best known today for his image of the *looking-glass self.* Just as a mirror reflects a reverse image, one's perception of oneself is never direct. Rather, we see ourselves reflected back in the reactions of others. According to Cooley, our ideas of our self come from (1) our imagining how we appear to other people; (2) how we think they judge our appearance; and (3) how we feel about all this. In other words, our sense of self is more like a process than a fixed object; it is always developing as we interact with others, whose opinions of us are ever-shifting. We can see that the primary group would, therefore, be the crucial location for both socialization and personality development.

Cooley's looking-glass imagery, however, does not imply that the child—or the adult—is a passive receiver of impressions. On the contrary, a person actively manipulates the reactions of others, selects which cues to follow, and judges the relative importance of role partners. Not all reflected images influence the self-process. In general, we tend to accept impressions that reinforce a basic identity and to resist those that do not. Cooley's suggestion that some role partners have

The **looking-glass self** suggests that we see ourselves reflected back in the reactions of others.

Our image of ourself begins to form at an early age and is drawn from reflections in the social world around us. (© Peter Arnold, Inc.)

more effect than others was elaborated by George Herbert Mead (1863–1931).

MEAD AND THE SELF-PROCESS

As we said in Chapter 1, Mead's view of human society was based on the ability of human beings to use symbols to communicate, to create rules, and to adjust their behavior to the expectations of others. A person can do all these things by developing a "self" that can reflect on its own behavior while it is interacting with others. Society is the sum of all these ongoing activities, constantly changing, always becoming something else. Society is also in our minds, through internalized rules, roles, and relationships.

Taking the Role of the Other. If, as Cooley proposed, we learn about ourselves from imagining how we appear to other people, then the reflexive mind not only sees itself as an object but can see into the minds of others! For Mead, this imaginative leap into the mind of others and the taking of that person's attitude toward oneself, is central to the development of self-concept. Mead builds upon and expands Cooley's essential insights, combining concepts of perception and internal reflection, linking these ideas to the tradition of role analysis.

Mead, following Cooley, noted that our first socialization experiences take place within a primary group setting where we learn the shared meanings of our culture. We are able to guess what others are thinking precisely because we have a common language. We share the same set of expectations and standards for role performance.

The child learns by precept (being told how to behave) and practice (trial and error and then feedback). This learning takes place through language, both verbal and nonverbal. Mead used the word ***gesture*** for a symbol that is shared by group members and that is made part of a role performance. Simply put, we internalize the culture and social structure by taking on the role of others, and society thus becomes part of our self.

Significant Other. Particularly important to the formation of self are those specific persons whose approval and affection are especially desired. Parents at first, then

Because of the human need for approval and affection, our significant others have a very strong influence on our attitudes and perceptions. (© Kenneth Rogers/Black Star)

peers, role models, and lovers, can all become *significant others,* with special power to shape one's perceptions.

Generalized Other. For Mead, the term *generalized other* described what is expected of any person in a given status. This is the community's standard of performance. In other words, we must learn both *particular standards* of conduct (from significant others) and *universal norms* (from the generalized other). We learn generalized role expectations from patterned interaction with others.

Stages of Role Taking. Role taking, the central concept in Mead's theory, develops by stages. At first, the child *imitates* others in its immediate environment, primarily family members. This type of activity is relatively disorganized and spontaneous, but it allows the child (up to age three) to differentiate itself from others by becoming another for a moment or two. Even the imaginary playmate that some children persist in talking to, much to their parents' dismay, extends the child's role-taking experience.

According to Mead's developmental theory, at ages three and four, the child expands its repertory to play-act such roles as doctor, letter carrier, fire fighter, in addition to family-based roles. This *play* is actually very serious because the child is learning to take the role of the other in a variety of situations.

A **gesture** is a symbol shared by group members.

Significant others are persons whose affection and approval are particularly desired.

The **generalized other** refers to widely held expectations of any one in a given status.

Play serves to expand a child's repertory of roles.

When children enter school and the society of age-peers, they are exposed to experiences that can lead to even higher levels of generalization. At these ages, *games* become the means by which one learns increasingly complex forms of role-taking. Games, in contrast to play, are organized and often competitive. They have rules and structure and involve a number of specialized role partners. The child must now be able to learn the whole system of interdependent roles. This is the skill we carry into adulthood: the ability to internalize an entire web of role behaviors.

Games are organized and more complex forms of role-taking.

The Emergence of Self. Role-taking is only one aspect of what Mead considered the *process of self*. If internalization were all that was necessary for the formation of a self-image, there would be little novelty or spontaneity in individual behavior. But Mead's "self" is not a mere passive reflection of social norms.

Rather, the self is dynamic, never finished, and always capable of change. Mead distinguished between the *"I"* and the *"me."* The "I" is the creative, acting aspect of self that reflects on and responds to the "me," which is composed of the internalized attitudes of others. This dialogue produces an *organization of perceptions* that forms the self-concept and guides behavior at any one time.

The **"I"** is the creative acting part of self while the **"me"** consists of the internalized attitude of others.

For example, you are constantly engaged in conversations with yourself, in which part of your self is longing to be free of reading assignments and homework, while the other part is reminding you of the expectations of your teacher and the college. Sometimes the "I" will win out, and you will put the books aside in favor of a night out with your friends, and at other times the "me" will triumph because you do have long-range goals that require passing exams and earning a diploma.

Mead saw no necessary conflict between the "I" and the "me," as both are needed to form the social self, although there can also be tension between the meanings derived from experience and those taken from the culture. The assumption that there is minimal conflict between these two sets of meaning, however, may be more true for men than for women (Kaspar 1986). We are only now beginning to see that the male model of experience does not always accurately reflect the female world of meaning (as we will explore in Chapter 8).

According to Mead, society is possible only because human beings can make the imaginative leap into the minds of others and share their world of meaning. In this formulation, "minding" is possible because of the unique human capacity for reflexive thought, so that we can be both subject and object of our own thinking.

GOFFMAN AND THE PRESENTATION OF SELF

Many sociologists view the self as a reflection of the cluster of roles being performed by persons at any point in the life course. For Erving Goffman (1922–1983), personality is actually a *self-presentation,* that is, an impression that we present to others. The self, then, always risks being rejected, and every encounter becomes a drama in which we "manage" the impression we give so that others will accept who we claim to be. In *The Presentation of Self in Everyday Life,* Goffman (1959) showed how carefully we construct a presenting self as the "real me" in order to influence the reactions of role partners and to control the situation.

In this view, there is a self for every situation. Goffman wrote of a *virtual self* that awaits us in every role—what society expects of a person in that role. Whatever innate tendencies and abilities a person may have, each role offers an opportunity to become a particular type of person.

A **virtual self** awaits us in each role we perform.

But some virtual selves are not very appealing to our self-image. For example, many homemakers reject the identity offered by that role, and students who have part-time employment at fast-food counters will resist being thought of as "hamburger helpers." Therefore, there may be a gap between self-image and the virtual self-in-the-role.

Role Distance. Goffman used the term *role distance* to describe the space that a person can place between the self and the self-in-the-role. People use several distancing techniques to warn others not to take them as the virtual self implied in the role. Those of you who have had temporary jobs—busboy, waitress, cashier, stock clerk—that you consider inferior to your true status have probably let others know that you are really a college student or on your way to better things. Perhaps you brought a textbook to the job or did slap-

Role distance is the space placed by a person between the self and the self-in-the-role.

dash work so that no one could possibly take you seriously in such a role. Role distance protects the self and offers some freedom for the expression of personal style.

In many situations, however, we have little choice but to become the self-in-the-role.

The Mind as a Jailor.   In an experiment that has received much publicity, Philip Zimbardo and his colleagues (1973) found that the line between the self and the self-in-the-role can be erased under some circumstances. After answering an ad in local and campus newspapers to participate in "a study of prison life," at fifteen dollars per day for two weeks, twenty-one average, middle-class, college-aged men, carefully screened for physical health, emotional maturity and respect for the law, were accepted. The experimenters randomly assigned the subjects to the status of either prisoner or guard in a "mock prison."

Every step was taken to make the prison as realistic as possible. Both prisoners and guards were ***deindividualized*** through the typical prison processes of removing their civilian identities. The prisoners wore uniforms and had to ask the guards for permission for most normal activities. The guards also had their uniforms: khaki, with nightsticks, handcuffs, whistles, and reflector sunglasses.

Neither group was given much formal instruction in how to play their roles, yet within days each person had *disappeared into the appropriate role*. The guards quickly learned to enjoy unchecked power, and the prisoners began to act in ways that encouraged the guards' dehumanizing treatment. The researchers were amazed at the speed and ease with which the assigned roles and the definition of the situation controlled the behavior of psychologically sound people.

One prisoner was released after a day and a half due to extreme depression, confusion, and uncontrollable crying. On each of the next three days, another prisoner developed similar symptoms and was released. A fifth man broke out in a psychosomatic rash. By the end of six days, the entire experiment was called off, so transformed had these "normal, healthy, educated young men" become. What caused the transformation? Obviously, nothing in the subjects' personality, for all had been

Deindividualization is the process of removing a person's civilian identities.

The military uses deindividuation to create a base on top of which a new identity can be built. The process helps to create loyalty and cohesion among new recruits from varying backgrounds. (© John Hoagland/Gamma Liaison)

carefully screened and randomly assigned. As the experimenters concluded:

> Rather, the subjects' abnormal social and personal reactions are best seen as a product of their transaction with an environment that supported the behavior that would be pathological in other settings, but was "appropriate" in this prison. Had we observed comparable reactions in a real prison, the psychiatrist undoubtedly would have been able to attribute any prisoner's behavior to character defects or personality maladjustment, while critics of the prison system would have been quick to label the guards as "psychopathic." This tendency to locate the source of behavior disorders inside a particular person or group underestimates the power of situational forces. (Zimbardo et al. 1973, p. 41; Zimbardo, Ebbesen, and Maslach 1977.)

This is perhaps the strongest statement of the sociological perspective on personality and behavior.

Other Views of Human Development

The concept of the social self has been very influential in American sociology. Empirical work on the "self-concept," particularly by Morris Rosenberg (1979, 1982), shows the impact of the social environment on how people come to see themselves. Rosenberg (1979) also noted that each person organizes her or his self-concept in different ways at different ages, a finding that suggests a much more complex process than that proposed even by Mead. Not only is the self-concept an intricate system of abilities, tendencies, and identities formed through interaction, it is an active agent in shaping its own environment (Rosenberg and Kaplan 1982).

Indeed, many social scientists claim that the sociological viewpoint too narrowly emphasizes roles and social interaction. In a classic essay, Dennis Wrong (1961) criticized what he called the "oversocialized" view of personality that overlooks the emotional and biological components of behavior. Socialization cannot account for impulsive acts or for many individual differences. Nevertheless, as we saw in Chapter 4, socialization and the context of behavior does have a great deal to do with our emotional experience and expression.

Until the development of the field of sociology of emotion the two major factors in personality development that had not been integrated into sociological models were the *affective* (having to do with feelings and emotions) and the *cognitive* (having to do with how people think and process information). The study of these factors was left largely to psychologists; certain of their basic ideas and theories deserve mention.

Affective personality factors refer to feelings and emotions. **Cognitive** personality factors refer to how people think and process information.

FREUD AND THE STAGES OF PSYCHOSEXUAL DEVELOPMENT

Sigmund Freud (1856–1939), the founder of psychoanalysis, has had a powerful effect on the way Americans think about childhood, sexuality, and the unconscious roots of behavior. Although Freud is often perceived as a culture-bound nineteenth-century theorist whose concepts cannot be empirically tested, several of his insights remain enduring contributions to sociology, especially his analysis of the conflict between self and society, the discovery of the unconscious, and construction of the self as a *psychosocial* process. As with many great thinkers, Freud's ideas are being reformulated from changing historical and social viewpoints.

The Conflict between Society and the Individual. In his essay *Civilization and Its Discontents* (1930/1962), Freud examines the dynamic tension between the individual, who strives to satisfy basic biological drives, and the social order, which requires its members to forego such instant gratification. Humans are born as bundles of desires, but if each person was to satisfy all these urges, social life would be impossible. Society—or as Freud preferred to call it, *civilization*—is based on the control of desire. Socialization means learning to give up (renounce) immediate pleasure. This renunciation is made possible through the manipulation of guilt feelings by the socializers, usually the parents, to whom the infant is bound by powerful emotional bonds. The infant, and then the child, depends on adult nurturers, so that fear of losing their affection becomes a basic anxiety that can be used to force the child to conform to the adults' expectations.

But unlike the child in Cooley and Mead's theories of the social self, Freud's child does not then achieve harmony with the group. Rather, feelings of anger, fear, and guilt must be dealt with through *repression*, that is, placing the unpleasant and unacceptable emotions below the level of consciousness. Civilization, therefore, is built on repressed desires that can, in adulthood, bubble to the surface and cause the symptoms of mental disturbance that require the services of a psychoanalyst.

Repression involves the placing of unpleasant and unacceptable emotions below the level of consciousness.

The Freudian Self. For Freud, as for Mead, the mind, or *psyche,* of the socialized person is a process. In Freud's formulation, this process consists of a dynamic interplay among three elements: (1) "instinctual" desires (the *id*); (2) internalized norms (*superego*); and (3) the aspect of self that is linked to the real world (*ego*). Even though *id, ego,* and *superego* have become part of everyday speech, these are concepts that can never be scientifically tested. But we can all recognize that there are such human traits as desires, internalized standards of conduct, and a sense of location in ongoing social systems.

What Freud has added to our understanding of behavior is the force of the *unconscious,* those mental processes and traces of emotion of which we are not consciously aware. Although Freud ac-

The development of the **psyche** is a process consisting of the interplay among id, ego, and superego. The **id** represents instinctual desires. The **superego** represents internalized norms. The **ego** represents the aspect of self linked to the real world.

knowledged the cultural components in both ego and superego, he also saw that human beings are not always in full control of their emotions or memories.

Stages of Development. The conflict between the individual and society, and the development of the Freudian self, including the unconscious, take place in well-defined phases or *stages* through which each child must travel on the journey to adulthood. At particular moments in childhood, one must renounce a special source of pleasure and deal with the resulting anger and anxiety.

Psychological development for Freud takes place in well-defined phases or stages.

The first such pleasure is being cuddled and fed at the breast or bottle. Like Hostess Twinkies, here are all good things wrapped up in one: love, food, warmth. From a Freudian perspective, being taken off the breast or bottle, that is, being *weaned* destroys this perfect world and generates feelings of extreme hostility. There is little that the infant can do except cry a lot, repress its anger in the subconscious, and learn that the rules are made by others and that life is likely to be full of hard knocks.

In the course of our development we learn that we must sometimes cope with events that are not entirely pleasant or of our own making. The perfect world of infancy cannot last very long. (© W. U. Harris)

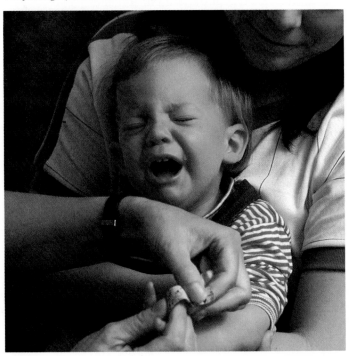

The second major crisis revolves around toilet training. Up to this time, the child has enjoyed the immediate satisfaction of emptying its bladder and intestines at the first sign of discomfort. Now the message is that "your body is no longer yours to do with what you like; you will learn when and where the group considers it appropriate to do certain things." The child now confronts a social system "out there" that can impose its will on one's body. Eventually we give up the struggle for control, but not without another residue of hostility and fear being deposited in the unconscious.

Finally, the child must cope with powerful sexual feelings: an attraction to the parent of the opposite sex, and fierce anger directed toward the same sex parent whom the child perceives as standing in the way of realizing its desires. This is the famous "Oedipal" crises, named after the hero of Greek drama who, unknowingly, killed his father and eventually married his own mother. Freud takes this story as representing "the human condition," with suitable adaptations to cover the situation of female children. The final task of psychosexual development, then, is to renounce the opposite-sex parent as an appropriate sex object while repressing hostile feelings toward the same-sex parent, and thus be freed to become sexually attracted to someone from another family.

Notice that Freud sees gender identity and sexual orientation as *achieved* and not as biologically or psychologically given. In resolving Oedipal feelings, the child becomes self-identified as a girl or boy with sexual feelings typically directed towards a person of the opposite sex. Further, because boys must break away from the all-nurturing mother, they develop a sense of separateness, while the girl's closeness to her mother can never be fully ruptured because she must retain the ability to nurture her own offspring. Here is both a social and psychodynamic explanation of sex differences in personality.

ERIKSON AND EGO DEVELOPMENT

In the decades since Freud's death, the idea of *psychosocial development* has been taken up by other psychologists. Most of them depart from Freud in two major respects. First, Freud's emphasis on the childhood years has proved too limiting;

much personal growth takes place throughout life. Second, Freudian emphasis on the instinctual desires of the id has also been questioned. The newer theories are more concerned with the *ego* as an organized set of self-perceptions. The most influential of these post-Freudian theories of life stages and ego development is that of Erik Erikson.

Erikson extended the stages of personality growth and change to cover the entire life span. By proposing that the life course is composed of a series of challenges that require reorganization of the ego, Erikson opened up the possibility of continual personal change and growth. The potential for personality change and for undoing previous failures makes Erikson's scheme more flexible and liberating than that of Freud.

Erikson (1964) described eight stages, each of which involves a person's ability to adapt to life changes.

Stage 1. From experiences with nurturers, the infant develops a sense either of *basic trust* or of *mistrust.*

Stage 2. In the first three years of life, the child learns and practices all kinds of new skills, emerging with a feeling either of *autonomy* (self-regulation) or of *doubt* and *shame* over its abilities to cope with events.

Stage 3. The four- to five-year-old's success in exploring the environment and in dealing with peers can lead to a sense of *initiative* and self-confidence; failure can produce feelings of *guilt.*

Stage 4. Between the ages of six and thirteen, the focus shifts from family to school, where the child can develop the self-concept either of *industriousness* or of *inferiority.*

Stage 5. In adolescence, the developmental task is *identity formation,* and failure to create a firm sense of self leads to *confusion* about one's identity.

Stage 6. The great challenge of young adulthood is to establish stable love relationships, and the outcome is *intimacy* or *isolation* and loneliness.

Stage 7. Citizenship, work, and family formation are the primary tasks of mature adulthood, and they lead to *generativity,* in contrast to the *self-absorption* and stagnation of those who do not contribute to the well-being of others.

Stage 8. Even the end of life poses a developmental challenge: finding continuity and meaning in one's life—*integrity*—or being unable to break out of isolation and self-absorption, giving way to *despair.*

CRITICISM OF STAGE THEORIES

Erikson's eight stages are best understood as *ideal types,* that is, as descriptions of the characteristics of the very best or the very worst outcomes. Few people go through these precise experiences at just the right ages. Most of us meet life's expected and unexpected challenges with only partial success or failure—some self-confidence, a little guilt, general satisfaction, and continued anxiety. Even the most successful among us is not free of self-doubt.

Although Erikson's model is presented as basically psychological, note that his transition points coincide with major

The **ideal types** of Erikson's eight stages are descriptions of the very best or worst outcomes.

Older adults do not have to lead lives of isolation and despair. A strong sense of self, built in part on sharing with one's peers, produces an integrity that can carry through the full course of a lifetime. (© Ira Wyman/SYGMA)

changes in the person's *social* environment and the sequence of roles one is expected to perform, e.g. from infant to child, from child in the family to student, from student to worker, from nonmarried to married, from nonparent to parent, and from fully involved in family and community to retirement. These are changes in role sets that provide the opportunity for reorganization of the self because the person now interacts with different role partners who have new expectations.

There are several other contemporary versions of stages in personality development (reviewed and popularized by Sheehy 1976). As most of these studies have been based on selected samples of white males, and center on the need to achieve occupational success (Vaillant 1977, Levinson, et al. 1978, Levinson 1986), they have been criticized for ethnocentrism and gender bias (Goghalons-Nicolet and Markson, 1987). Indeed, some critics suggest that the "experts" have created the concept of life stages from their own limited experience as middle-class white male professionals in the late twentieth century (Karp and Yoels 1982, Dannefer 1984). Nonetheless, to the extent that people believe these theories to be true, they will affect how we interpret our own experience.

As with Erikson's model, it is also possible to explain personality development in terms of social role transitions rather than as an inevitable unfolding of a "natural" ground plan. But the concept of stages has great appeal to Americans as a rational and orderly way of organizing perceptions. We share a cultural belief that everything, including our lives, has a simple underlying logic. It is difficult to accept the idea that chance and accidents of history could strongly affect our own personality development.

Although stage theories based on chronological age have had limited value in the study of personality, they have proven illuminating in the study of cognition.

PIAGET AND COGNITIVE DEVELOPMENT

Cognitive development refers to changes over time in how we think.

The concept of *cognitive development* refers to changes over time in how we think, as both mind and body mature. The major figure in this field was Jean Piaget (1896–1980), a Swiss psychologist, who based his theories on observations of children at play and their answers to his questions. From his effort to see the world from their point of view, Piaget concluded that children of different ages had very different understandings of what they were doing.

Not only were there age-related shifts in the complexity of thinking, but Piaget also found changes in *moral reasoning,* that is, the way in which children evaluated situations. As the mind is able to deal with increasingly complicated information, so also does the child learn to handle such abstractions as ideas of fairness and justice.

Moral reasoning involves the application of standards of right and wrong.

In the games of marbles that Piaget observed over and over, very young children accepted the rules absolutely, as written in stone and permitting no changes. Slightly older children were more flexible, modifying the rules to meet unexpected situations. At a more advanced age, youngsters realized that the rules existed only because the players agreed to them, and that the rules could be changed radically and entire new games invented. Notice how these observations tie into Mead's ideas about the importance of games, as well as supporting the basic sociological point that *rules and roles are socially constructed.* Piaget's most cognitively developed subjects were actually amateur sociologists.

Thus do children also learn that absent people do not disappear, that effects have causes, and that the same quantity can take different shapes (for example, that a long string of clay has just as much material as a ball of clay), and so forth. Although Piaget saw cognitive development as age-related, he did not claim that the process was automatic; a child's thinking becomes more complex only when confronted with real-life experiences that encourage such thought. You probably know adults whose rigid thinking resembles that of a Piagetian three-year-old. And as the cases of isolated children mentioned at the start of this chapter remind us, environmental stimulation, trial-and-error attempts to master the task of daily living, and supportive feedback from others are all essential to cognitive growth.

KOHLBERG, GILLIGAN, AND MORAL DEVELOPMENT

Inspired by Piaget's work, Lawrence Kohlberg has spent several decades conducting longitudinal and cross-cultural studies of

Learning From Children

Barrie Thorne

Barrie Thorne taught for many years at Michigan State University; she recently moved to the University of Southern California, with a joint appointment in the Sociology Department and in the Program for the Study of Women and Men in Society. She co-edited Language, Gender and Society *(with Cheris Kramarae and Nancy Henley) and* Rethinking the Family: Some Feminist Questions *(with Marilyn Yalom). She is now writing a book on children's gender arrangements in elementary schools.*

Our research topics sometimes seem to choose us as much as we choose them; there is rich and complicated interplay between living one's life and doing sociology. My first large research project—a participant-observation study of the draft resistance movement of the late 1960s—grew out of my opposition to the Vietnam War and my interest in learning about, and making, political change. I was a draft counselor and helped organize anti-war demonstrations, combining the involved consciousness of a political activist with the more detached outlook of a sociological observer—an uneasy, but provocative mix.

Participating in the radical movements of the late 1960s put me at the origins of the contemporary women's liberation movement. I joined an early consciousness-raising group and became a feminist, a transformation of self and social context that, in turn, shaped the questions I asked as a sociologist. In the early 1970s feminists in many academic fields began to ask "Where are the women?" That relatively simple question led us to see gaps and distortions in traditional knowledge. For example, at that time, sociologists rarely studied housework, the wage gap between men and women workers, or relations of mothers and daughters; and their views of rape echoed the victim-blaming of the surrounding society. Feminists created a new specialty, the sociology of sex and gender, and we showed that attention to gender may alter basic ways of thinking about core sociological topics like inequality, work, social organization, and families.

I had taken a Ph.D. comprehensive exam in sociolinguistics in 1967, but it was not until the women's movement alerted me to issues of gender that I noticed the absence of research on women's patterns of talk and communication. In the early 1970s I worked with feminist colleagues in other disciplines to find out what was known about gender and the differentiation of language and speech. We helped found a new, cross-disciplinary area of research: the study of gender and verbal and nonverbal communication.

After a period of library research, I itched to get back into the "field" and to once again study social life firsthand. I wanted to learn more about interactions between gender and other social divisions—age, race, ethnicity, social class. In my research on communication patterns I was especially interested in studies that found differences in the ways men talk with men, and women with women (several studies, for example, found that women used more mutual head-nodding and "mm hm"'s to indicate that they are listening). I was curious about the dynamics of gender separation and possible differences in the ways women bond with other women, and men with men.

By that time, however, my attention had begun to shift from women and men to boys and girls. I had a four-year-old son who took me into the worlds of children in parks, in our neighborhood, and in day care centers. I noticed a striking fact: even preschool-age children tend to divide by gender; boys play more often with boys, and girls with girls. As a sociologist, I knew such patterns are not "natural," but are so-

cially organized. And as a feminist and a mother, I wondered about the effects of gender separation on children's daily experiences and on their present and future gender relations.

I decided to become a participant-observer in an elementary school and, with a special eye for gender, to find out how children and adults construct their daily worlds. I gained access to a combined fourth–fifth grade classroom in a working-class school in California, where we were living for a year. During the school day I essentially tried to hang out, observing and taking notes in the classroom, the lunchroom, the hallways (where I discovered the intricacies of lining up and defining "cuts"), and on the playground, where I roamed and recorded descriptions of the complex array of activities and groups.

Analyzing the notes I had taken over eight months in the first school and three months in a similar school in Michigan, I found recurring patterns from which I mapped the complexities of children's gender arrangements. Elementary schools are crowded environments and girls and boys share the same formal curriculum; they sometimes interact in relaxed ways. But they also spend a great deal of time in separate groups, occasionally dramatizing gender boundaries with games like "chase and kiss" (also known as "girls chase the boys/boys chase the girls"). Some children cross gender boundaries and participate in activities of the other gender, another part of the complex "gender story" that emerged from watching and being with children. I also found complex interactions among gender, social class, and race. For example, in the California school, when seating was divided by gender, other boys repeatedly maneuvered two nonbilingual Hispanic boys into sitting next to girls, a position the boys saw as contaminating.

Erik Erikson once wrote, "children bring up their parents as much as parents bring up their children." That adage describes my experience not only as a parent, but also as a researcher. I was often surprised by the perceptiveness and social competence of children; they create their own, complex cultural worlds. My surprise alerted me to adult biases. As adults, we often assume that children are incomplete versions of ourselves; we define ourselves by our being, but children (seen as the targets of "socialization"), by their becoming. We tend to ignore children, assuming that their daily actions are trivial and worthy of notice only when they seem cute or irritating. And we may assume that we already know what children are "like," both because they are a familiar part of our environment and because we were once children ourselves.

Adults find it difficult to take children seriously because of the ways our society organizes age divisions. We locate children in families and age-graded schools, excluding them from public life. Children are relatively powerless, although their subordination is extremely complex; treating them like adults may result in their exploitation (this is much truer of younger than older children; note the enormous diversity glossed by the singular term, "the child"). My relatively modest empirical study led me to these much larger concerns. It finally occurred to me that the question, "Where are the children?" may be as compelling as the earlier question, "Where are the women?" We have far to go in understanding children as social actors in varied institutions. To meet that challenge, we will have to wrestle more fully with the complex politics of childhood.

"the child as moral philosopher." In essence, Kohlberg (1981) proposed that, given the necessary experience and stimulation, children go through a sequence of six stages in their ability to handle moral problems.

Between the ages of four and ten, the child's sense of good or bad is linked to obedience to those in positions of power, based on fear of punishment. In adolescence, conformity to the rules is accompanied by the belief that the existing social order is right and true and deserves to be defended. But with the appropriate moral education, older children and young adults can reach the two highest stages of reasoning, in which considerations of community welfare, general rights, and universal ethical principles—such as justice, equality, and the dignity of individuals—become the guides of action and self-judgment.

Although his own cross-cultural studies show some similarities in the early stages of reasoning among children in other modern societies, Kohlberg has been criticized for his ethnocentric value bias in defining what constitutes the highest good—which turns out to be the type of liberal values built into the U.S. Constitution: individual rights, equality of opportunity, equal justice, and so forth (Puka 1983).

The major criticism of Kohlberg's work, however, is that he studied only males. When Kohlberg, like Piaget, discovered early in his work that girls did not make judgments in the same way as boys, he assumed that females were somehow deficient in moral reasoning and proceeded to construct his theories on data from boys and men. While teaching with Kohlberg, the psychologist Carol Gilligan noticed that many women students were dropping his course, and she decided to find out why.

In A Different Voice.   Gilligan's (1982) research found that women brought a different set of values to their moral judgments

Our role performances are constantly evaluated by the important people in our lives. Sometimes we are rewarded and other times not; this affects our feelings of guilt and sense of ethics. How do you think you would react to the situation portrayed in the photo? What effect might that have on the child? (© Erika Stone)

than did men. For example, in one of Kohlberg's favorite moral dilemmas the respondent is asked whether a man named Heinz should steal an expensive medicine that he could not afford to purchase, in order to save the life of his dying wife. Boys tended to define the problem in terms of abstract rights, turning the moral dilemma into a math problem with humans: property rights versus life. In contrast, girls saw the issue in terms of relationships, the needs of all the people involved, and the consequences to husband and wife if he were to be jailed for stealing. Rather than placing one value above another, girls tried to find a third way.

According to Kohlberg's scoring system the girls' answer would rank at about Stage 3, whereas the boys' would be at Stage 6. But, asks Gilligan, by what standard is an "ethic of care" a lower level of moral development than an "ethic of rights"? Or separation a higher value than connectedness? Are these not just two different ways to approach a moral dilemma, with the male pattern rated higher by male researchers? If such gender differences are not innate, but the product of socialization and of life experiences, then they are changeable. If men were to raise children, they would think in terms of attachments, and if women had to spend their lives competing for occupational status, they would think in terms of individual rights.

Although Gilligan's work opened up a new line of research, subsequent studies fail to support her thesis of sex differences in moral development (Walker 1984). There appears to be no clear trend for boys to score higher than girls on Kohlberg's index during childhood or adolescence, and most studies of adults show few differences in moral reasoning that cannot be accounted for by the generally higher levels of education of men compared to women. Nor is there any indication in the sixty-one studies reviewed by Walker (1984) that females and males follow different developmental paths in thinking about abstract moral problems or in their average rates of cognitive development in general (Greeno and Maccoby 1986).

But even if there are no sex differences in how people think about moral problems, men may be less concerned than women with responding to the needs of others, and women may be more fearful

than men at the thought of separation. In this respect, Gilligan's contributions to gender studies illustrate once more the interplay between role expectations, socialization experiences, and personality development.

The theories discussed in this section—of ego development, psychosocial stages, cognition, and moral reasoning—are all concerned with processes going on within the individual, even though prompted by events in the social environment. However, there is also an area of psychological research on learning that is not primarily concerned with egos, emotions, feeling, or the inner workings of the psyche.

B. F. SKINNER AND BEHAVIORISM

Behaviorists, as the name makes clear, concentrate on behavior: observable and measurable actions. The behaviorist who most influenced sociologists is B. F. Skinner (b. 1904). Applying to humans the findings from his years of experiments on pigeons and other laboratory animals, Skinner has claimed that all behavior is shaped by the manipulation of rewards: When an action is rewarded, it is likely to be repeated; when it is not rewarded, it is less likely to be repeated. If a change in behavior is desired, the easiest way to achieve it is to change the conditions under which a reward is available. The sociological implications of Skinner's experiments have been spelled out by Homans (1961) and are one source of contemporary exchange theory. These implications are best understood by the concept of the *Skinner box.*

Skinner Boxes. Skinner achieved some notoriety many decades ago by tending an infant daughter for part of the day in a completely controlled environment that became known as the *Skinner box.* (The child, incidentally, not only survived but thrived, contrary to the expectations of many.) The concept of the environment as a box has important sociological applications. Although humans, unlike pigeons, construct their own environments, they, like pigeons, respond to the rewards in their social world and base later actions on a knowledge of what happened before. The social system can be thought of as one big Skinner box, in which people act within a system of rewards received and withheld.

Behaviorism concentrates on the study of observable activity as opposed to reported or inferred mental and emotional processes.

The **Skinner box** is a completely controlled environment.

It is important to realize that punishments are never as effective as the manipulation of rewards. Punishment may delay—but can never fully erase—a human response; rewards encourage and reinforce the desired actions, which is the reason why physical discipline is a relatively inefficient socialization technique.

Behavior Modification. These principles have been applied to cases in which extreme behavior change is desired by authorities. Prisons and mental hospitals, because they are environments that can be thoroughly controlled twenty-four hours a day (total institutions), have been prime sites for experiments in *behavior modification*. All rewards are withheld until the inmate performs the actions desired by custodians. Over time, *regardless of the internal state of the person* (drives, motives), behavior change takes place. Many contemporary behaviorists, however, take into account a step between the presentation of a stimulus and the response of the individual, as in Figure 5-2. The inclusion of an interpretive element brings behaviorism closer to the symbolic-interaction approach.

In fact, the concepts of behaviorism have been translated to a variety of sociological perspectives. Critics of these approaches claim that this diminishes the importance of the role of human interpretation (meaning) and the social context of behavior. It also suits the political climate of the times, according to one analyst, providing a "cost-effective, reductionist, rational decision-making stereotype of the modern individual . . ." (Denzin 1986).

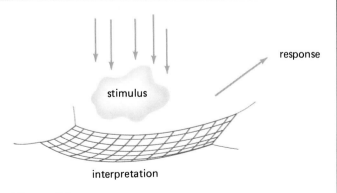

Figure 5-2
A contemporary behaviorist's modification of the classical stimulus-behavior model.

Socialization Across Cultures and the Life Course

THE CULTURAL FACTOR

As described in Chapter 3, each culture is a selection of traits from the range of human possibilities. Some cultures, such as ours, place high value on individualism; others, such as the People's Republic of China, emphasize concern for the group. Fearlessness is admired in some societies, cautiousness in others. And so on, down the long list of human traits. Typically, also, one type of personality is desired for females, another for males; one set of traits for children, another for adults, and even a third for the elderly.

This variety of personality styles is possible because each culture, through its symbol system, creates a particular way of thinking, reinforces certain emotions, and shapes the self-image of its members. The cultural blueprint also determines socialization practices that produce the desired personality types.

What is "normal" for one society may be considered crazy or "sick" in another. In one of the early classics of cultural anthropology, Ruth Benedict (1934) described the inhabitants of the island of Dobu as being deeply mistrustful of one another but especially of close family members—behavior that would be considered "paranoid" in our society where one is supposed to love and trust one's parents or spouse. In contrast to Dobuans, the Zuni Indians of the southwest United States are socialized to a personality style of noncompetitiveness and cooperative sharing, a way of life equally strange to most Americans. Although many of Benedict's details have been challenged by later studies, the major point remains intact: different socialization practices and experiences produce different types of people. Culture, not human nature, shapes our personalities (Shweder and Levine 1985).

SOCIALIZATION

Socialization in childhood cannot prepare a person for the many different roles of adulthood in a modern industrial society. Just think of the major role changes of early adulthood: graduation from school, entry into an occupation, marriage, par-

Desocialization is learning to give up a role. **Resocialization** is learning new ways to deal with old role partners.

enthood, community and civic involvements. These changes require *desocialization* (learning to give up a role) and *resocialization* (learning new ways to deal with the old role partners), as well as *socialization* (learning the new role). And each major role change carries with it the potential for a reorganization of the self.

How many times have you said of someone, "How he's changed since he has married," or "That job certainly made a new person of her," or "My mother's impossible now that she's retired"? These are not new persons, of course, but the same people undergoing important role transitions. Their way of life has been altered and so, accordingly, has their view of themselves and their way of dealing with others.

The transitions of middle and late life have often been thought of as "crises." It was long assumed, for example, that women in midlife are especially vulnerable because they have lost their mother role, and that men in retirement are particularly unhappy at the loss of the worker role. Research, however, does not bear out these predictions, which are based on assumptions about the necessity of parenting to women and of work to men. In fact, most women actually enjoy their freedom from child rearing, particularly

The retirement years are not necessarily filled with stress and crisis. Many people find great contentment and fulfillment as they get older. (© Michael Abramson/ Black Star)

if they are employed (Coleman and Antonucci 1982); many men look forward eagerly to retirement, and those who can afford it are leaving the labor force at increasingly earlier ages (Foner and Schwab 1981).

Most role transitions in adulthood are fairly predictable and can be eased by anticipatory socialization. It also helps if one's friends are going through similar status changes. Just as the peer group of adolescence provides support for role learning at an earlier age, the friends of adulthood help us adjust to later changes. It is the unexpected, "off-time" transitions that are difficult to handle (Neugarten and Hagestad 1983). And people differ in the resources and coping skills that they can call on.

In other words, the popularity of books and articles on the so-called midlife crisis for both men and women greatly exaggerates the effects of the changes that are taking place. Most transitions are relatively gradual and not especially stressful. The differences among individuals are much greater than any similarities in age-based "stages" (Brim and Kagan 1980). Moreover, the very process of aging changes from one age group to another because of the effects of historical change (Riley 1985).

If the self were as fixed as some wish to believe, there would be no point in going to a therapist, or joining an encounter group, or attempting to turn over a new leaf, or engaging in any of the self-improvement schemes that so characterize this society. Paradoxically, Americans believe in the ability to change oneself, while still clinging to a belief in stable personality traits. There is evidence to support both views: Some traits are relatively unchanged over time (McCrae and Costa 1984), and these give us a sense of identity; we can always improve on other traits and come closer to an ideal self.

REFLECTIONS ON THE NATURE OF THE CHILD

Each culture and historical era has its view of the essential nature of the child. Puritans assumed that children were little savages who needed to have evil impulses beaten out of them; Americans in the 1940s and 1950s believed that childhood experiences left an indelible mark on adult personality; and since the 1960s, it has become fashionable for adults to overcome these childhood limitations and discover the "real me" through "self-improvement" therapies.

Professional opinion has also undergone historical change, from an emphasis on fixed traits to a fascination with the idea of biologically determined stages of development, and finally, today, to a recognition of the essential changeability and flexibility of childhood *and* adult personality. In other words, childhood socialization is now thought to be less influential than it was considered to be under the influence of Freud; much can happen all across the life course to lead to reorganization of the self-concept, although some core traits might show considerable stability over time.

Further, according to the child psychologist Jerome Kagan (1984), we should pay less attention to what parents "do" to children than to the meanings that children place on what happens to them. This formulation comes close to the symbolic interactionist emphasis on the person as an active interpreter of experience. Kagan also proposes that there are no *general* cognitive abilities, but only ways of reacting to specific situations; that is, the behavior cannot be understood without consideration of the context!

The earlier debates over the relative effects of "nature" (biology) versus "nurture" (socialization) have been replaced by a more complex understanding of the interplay between individual tendencies and the social environment. Because they are not fully biologically programmed, human beings are characterized by a flexibility of thought and action that allows for change at any point in the life course (Lerner 1984).

All told, it is very difficult to predict behaviors from information about personality. Not only do the components of self-concept change over time, but most behavior is specific to the situation.

Summary

This chapter traces the development of the human being in social context. An infant cannot become a human being without interacting with other humans. Humans differ from all other animals in their capacity to learn rather than being programmed for instinctive action. Human behavior is learned primarily through the process of socialization, which involves the transmission, through language and gestures, of the culture of the society and subgroups into which one is born.

Socialization occurs as people assume roles and learn the rules for interaction with others. They learn roles by acquiring the necessary information, being sensitive to the reaction of others, and receiving social support for role performance.

In America, the major agents of socialization are parents, peers, teachers, and the media. Socialization practices vary within a society among different occupational groups and subcultures.

Socialization also involves the development of self. Cooley proposed that the self is shaped and developed through a "looking-glass" process that reflects the reaction of important others. Mead stressed the capacity to "take the role of the other" toward oneself as being crucial to the development of self. The symbolic-interactionist perspective of Mead has been elaborated by Goffman into the high drama of self-presentations and identity management.

Sigmund Freud focused on the conflict between human drives and the requirements of social life. The Freudian self is characterized by a dynamic interplay between innate desires and social controls on their expression. Erik Erikson has expanded on the Freudian scheme, emphasizing ego development in eight stages across the life course.

Another area of socialization concerns cognitive development, that is, age-related changes in how people process information. Jean Piaget was the pioneer in observational studies of how children perceive and think about their environment. Lawrence Kohlberg has built on Piaget's work to describe stages in moral development: how people make judgments about right and wrong. Carol Gilligan has provided an alternative theory based on the different experiences that females and males bring to their value judgments.

A final psychological model of learning is behaviorism, the study of observable activities. The theory of behavior associated with the work of B. F. Skinner is based on the manipulation of rewards in a controlled environment, without regard to the internal states of the organism.

People perceive major role transitions not necessarily as crises, but often as opportunities for adaptation and change in the self-concept. Although some traits remain relatively constant, others are much more flexible than is commonly believed.

Suggested Readings

ELKIN, FREDERICK, and GERALD HANDEL. *The Child and Society,* 4th ed. New York: Random House, 1984. A well-written overview of the socialization process using both social-psychological and sociological research.

HEWITT, JOHN P. *Self and Society: A Symbolic Interactionst Social Psychology.* 3rd ed.: Boston: Allyn and Bacon, 1983. The concepts of symbolic interaction are clarified as the authors detail how the self develops through social interaction and how social order is created.

LERMAN, HANNAH. *A Mote in Freud's Eye: From Psychoanalysis to the Psychology of Women.* New York: Springer, 1986. This volume provides a contemporary feminist critique of Freud's work.

RIDGEWAY, CECILIA. *The Dynamics of Small Groups.* New York: St. Martin's, 1983. A very fine summary of the sociological research on small groups.

ROSENBERG, MORRIS. *Conceiving the Self.* New York: Morris Books, 1979. A comprehensive look at key concepts of socialization through the analysis of new data and a review of the literature.

RUBIN, LILLIAN B. *Just Friends: The Role of Friendship in Our Lives.* New York: Harper & Row, 1985. A study of the role of friendships and its meanings for women, men, and couples.

SIMON, WILLIAM, and JOHN H. GAGNON. "Sexual Scripts: Permanence and Change." Archives of Sexual Behavior, March, 1986. A comprehensive up-dating and reformulation of one of the most widely used concepts in the field of human sexuality.

SUTTON-SMITH, BRIAN. *Toys as Culture.* New York: Gardner, 1986. An analysis of the ways in which toys reflect contemporary life and shape children's images of social life and social interaction.

ZELIZER, VIVIANA. *Pricing the Priceless Child: The Changing Values of Children.* New York: Basic Books, 1985. A significant historical and sociological contribution to our understanding of the place of children in society. Winner of 1985 C. Wright Mills Award.

6

Conformity and Deviance

JANE is nineteen years old and lives with her family in a New Jersey suburb while attending a local college. Her parents are active in local business and community groups. For the past year, Jane and her friends have bought cocaine from a dealer called "Magic." They "do coke" at one another's houses when their parents are not at home.

RODNEY W. is a middle-aged top executive in a Fortune 500 company. Last year he saw to it that company money was channeled into particular senatorial election campaigns. He also approved the use of corporation funds as "gifts" to foreign

political leaders in return for multi-million dollar contracts. When questioned before a Congressional investigating committee, Rodney claimed that he had not really violated a law. Although both types of contribution were technically illegal, he had found them necessary to "maintaining good business relations and a healthy climate for free enterprise."

ADAM is a college junior majoring in computer science. A straight-A student and secretary of the Student Government Association, Adam has been engaged to his high school sweetheart, Evelyn, for several years. They expect to marry after their graduation, and have agreed to remain virgins until that time. Adam and Evelyn do not smoke, drink liquor, or do coke.

What do these very different people have in common? They are all *deviants.* They illustrate the theme of this chapter: deviants are people who violate generally held norms. To deviate means to depart from the normal, the approved, or the expected. Most often, the concept of deviance is associated with criminals and the mentally ill. But deviance can also describe the acts that are more ambitious, industrious, heroic, or virtuous than generally found or expected, as in the example of Adam and Evelyn. Such individuals as Nobel Prizewinners, self-made millionaires, and war heroes deviate as much from normative behavior as do skid-row alcoholics or bank robbers.

The sociological study of deviance, however, has been almost entirely concerned with *socially disapproved* deviation from the norms, in part because we are fascinated by stories of people who break the rules. Yet social order everywhere depends on people doing what is expected of them by others. But every time a group establishes a norm—a rule of acceptable behavior—another category of actions is automatically created: unacceptable behavior, or deviance. Doob (1971) commented that when the circus was invented, so also was the sideshow. The major function of the sideshow is to reassure viewers of their own normality while ridiculing people who depart from the expected. In this way, conformity is reinforced and anxiety over the unusual is relieved. As deviance can be defined only by reference to conformity, the two are different sides of the same coin; one cannot exist without the other.

Unlike psychologists, sociologists are not primarily concerned with why people, such as those described at the beginning of the chapter, behave in ways that do not conform to rules or expectations. Our interest is in the process whereby behaviors come to be defined as deviant or normal. The sociology of deviance focuses on a series of interrelated questions: (1) How are social norms established? (2) Under what circumstances do violations of the norms occur? (3) What social groups are

Deviants are people who violate norms of expected behavior.

likely to be involved with different types of deviance? (4) How do others respond to nonconforming behavior? and (5) Who has the power to define normal and abnormal?

In this chapter, we examine how group norms are established and internalized. Then we describe the kinds of people and situations most likely to be defined as deviant, and the ways in which authorities attempt to control their behavior. The chapter closes with discussions of residual deviance and changing norms of sexuality.

Conformity and Deviance

As we saw in Chapter 3, norms vary widely across cultures and through historical time. In complex societies, normative agreement becomes very problematic, due to the great number of competing values. For example, people who wish to conserve our natural resources will oppose business interests seeking to expand industrial development—and both can appeal to widely accepted value systems. Legalized abortion is strongly supported by those who value women's rights, but just as fiercely opposed by others who claim to represent the interests of the unborn. Given the extreme diversity of interests within a complex society, how do some norms become more important than others?

Sociological research shows that the relative power of competing groups determines which standards of right and wrong become *the* norms for the group. The content of the rule is less important than the relative strength of its supporters. In seventeenth-century New England, for example, norms were established by the most respected members of the Puritan community. People were brought to court and publicly punished for such threats to Puritan society as swearing at animals, living alone, or walking in a suggestive manner (K. Erikson 1966). No distinction was made between those who violated folkways and those who broke the laws; all behavior was to be governed by a rigid interpretation of the *Bible.* By studying definitions of deviance in any group—seventeenth-century Puritans or twentieth-century Americans—we learn what powerful people find threatening.

It is also tempting for those who make

The ruling members of seventeenth-century New England set very rigid norms. Among the targets of their deep moral zeal were women and girls suspected of being possessed by the devil. How are the rule enforcers depicted in this engraving? (© The Bettmann Archive, after an engraving by Howard Pyle)

the rules to see violators of norms as people who suffer from some personal problem—a sickness of mind or body, or some deep moral flaw—that renders them unable to conform. Yet, from the sociological point of view, deviant behavior differs only in content, but not in its basic nature, from what is called conformity. Indeed, the processes whereby deviant and nondeviant roles are constructed and performed are quite similar, both flowing from group experiences and sanctions.

Issues of deviance and conformity become defined as *social problems* through the same interplay of competing power groups as in the definition of the norms themselves. Those who feel most strongly or who have the most at stake in terms of immediate self interest tend to win out over people less well organized or less fervent or less personally affected. It is important to keep in mind that ideas and behaviors do not exist as good or bad in themselves. Rather, what comes to be called good or bad conduct is the outcome of struggle among those who have the power to shape and define cultural products.

Consider the case of marijuana. Use of marijuana, like any drug, varies by time and place. For example, in India, a country with strong religiously grounded objections to alcohol use, one form of marijuana known as "bhang" is actually prescribed by custom and religion. A liquid form of marijuana mixed with fruit, bhang is expected to be served openly at weddings. In the United States, in contrast, where marijuana is classified as an illegal substance, liquor is freely available to wedding guests. Yet the current definition of marijuana as a *social problem* is relatively recent; in the early 1900s, marijuana was commonly used in over-the-counter medications available in any pharmacy. It was also widely prescribed by physicians for a variety of medical conditions—from headaches and excessive menstrual bleeding to epilepsy, ulcers, and even tooth decay (Snyder 1971). Nor did the medical or scientific community feel that users developed symptoms of addiction or tolerance to marijuana (Clinard and Meier 1985). As late as 1930, only sixteen states had passed laws banning marijuana use.

How did marijuana become a dangerous drug? The answer would seem to lie in vested-interest groups. In 1930 the Federal Bureau of Narcotics (FBN) was established as a separate agency to enforce drug laws. Once created, FBN officials began to look for areas in which it could become involved. Marijuana was one such area. Working in collaboration with the Treasury Department, whose interest was largely financial, the FBN became a "moral entrepreneur" (manager), vigorously enforcing existing laws while also promoting additional anti-drug legislation. More restrictions on the sale and use of "dangerous" substances were essential to the survival and growth of the Bureau, whose budget was dependent on the amount of drug behavior to be regulated: the wider the net, the more money and power it could command. In the 1930s, the FBN conducted a major media campaign to convince Americans that marijuana was an extremely dangerous drug that eroded the will of its users and forced them to crime and depravity. As there was little public opposition from groups favoring marijuana use, the Bureau's definition became the public reality.

Yet attempts to discourage behavior by defining it as a social problem are not **133**

The Economics of Cocaine

Headlines about the use and abuse of cocaine and its derivatives appear almost daily. The stories in 1987 involved a varied cast of "junkies": athletes, police officers, entertainers, stockbrokers, college and high school students. Cocaine use in the United States is now considered a major health problem. The number of regular users is estimated to be as high as 20 million, with an additional 5000 being introduced to cocaine each day. Such wide demand drives up prices and brings huge profits to a complex network of producers, dealers, and distributors. The U.S. government appears powerless to stem the flow; for every carrier or dealer taken out of commission, others step in their place.

Cocaine was not always so popular in our society. Even before being banned in 1908, cocaine had fallen out of favor with people looking for an all-purpose wonder drug. In the 1930s, however, cocaine became the underground "drug of choice" in the subcultures of jazz musicians, criminals, prostitutes, and Hollywood film makers and stars. As the price of cocaine rose, its market became increasingly upscale. Today's cocaine users are typically urban young professionals, many of whom turned to the "rich person's drug" when new laws made it difficult to obtain large quantities of prescription pills.

The availability of sufficient cocaine to meet the rising need was an unintended consequence of the completion of the Pan-American Highway which linked the United States to the sources of coca leaves in Peru and Bolivia. Over time, an extended chain of producers and suppliers has been formed: from the peasant farmers who gather and dry the leaves, to the workers who operate the local laboratories that grind the leaves into paste, to the people who transport the paste down the Amazon River Basin to large South American seaports. Before being shipped abroad, the paste is treated with ether and acids that render it up to ninety-seven percent pure. Then, by plane and ship, the drugs are filtered into the United States. Short of closing off our borders completely, there is no way for drug enforcement officers to capture more than a small proportion of the total flow.

Once in the United States, the cocaine is diluted by adding powdered materials that reduce purity down to twelve percent and sold at current street prices of between $50 and $120 per gram. Thus, what began as 500 kilograms (100 pounds) of coca leaves, worth about $4,000 to the grower in Peru, is now 8 kilos (17.6 pounds) of cocaine valued at half a million dollars in the United States. Overall, the American cocaine business is a $30–50 billion a year industry. Clearly, the financial rewards are very attractive and the risks of capture quite minimal.

Other reasons for the continued flourishing trade in cocaine include the possibility that the drug scene may be functional for our political leaders. Military action in South America can be taken under the cover of a "war on drugs." If Americans can be convinced that our enemies are really drug dealers, they will be more likely to support a military solution than when the conflicts are thought to be ideological. In the United States, drugs have always been a way to keep society's underdogs from rebelling against the system. As Cockburn (1986) notes, it is very difficult to make a revolution while half-stoned.

SOURCES: James Inciardi, "The War on Drugs: Heroin, Cocaine, Crime and Public Policy," *The New York Times*, March 15, 1987, p. 1 ff. Alexander Cockburn, "Some Radical Notions about Fighting Drugs," *Wall Street Journal*, September 11, 1986, p. 31.

always successful. Marijuana continued to enjoy popularity as a recreational drug, and the fact that it was also illegal may have increased its attractiveness to young people who were challenging a broad range of norms in the 1960s and early 1970s. By 1970, survey data showed that 42 percent of college students had smoked pot at least once, and in 1972, a presidential commission declared marijuana use a nationwide threat to the health and morals of American youth. By this time, the drug had become firmly established in the public mind with the "youth movement" of hippies, campus radicalism, changing sexual norms, and protest against the Vietnam War. Marijuana became a symbol of social disorder, and control over its use was elevated to a crusade for law and order. The government's "war on drugs," however, keeps falling victim to other powerful interests, including the conduct of foreign policy, foreign trade, and military considerations. Time and again, the U.S. State Department has approved aid to drug-producing countries in order to

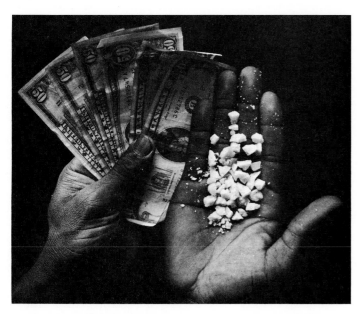

Cocaine is being transformed into "crack" and sold in all major cities of the U.S. Each of these pieces is called a "rock" or a "twenty" and sells for about $20 on the street. The crumbs are called "shake" and are also sold. This dealer pushes enough crack to earn about $2500 a month. (© Leo Hetzel/Photoreporters, Inc.)

achieve diplomatic and military goals. Thus, the power of various interest groups not only influences what is defined as deviant but how vigorously the rules are enforced. Thus, what is considered acceptable or not in any society is the outcome of a political process, in which moral entrepreneurs struggle to impose their view of right and wrong and to expand or maintain their own power.

Structuring Conformity

Many years ago in American society (and in some societies today) deviants were thought to be possessed by devils. In Puritan America, for example, people who deviated from the norms were believed to be witches who had made a contract with the Devil, and who should be imprisoned or killed. The deviant of today is thought to need psychiatric help or punishment (or both). In either case, the deviant has upset ongoing relationships within a system by behaving unpredictably. Before discussing how deviance is possible we must understand how conformity is structured.

HOW NORMS DEVELOP

Norms develop through social interaction and represent a kind of negotiated reality that shapes individual perceptions and behaviors. Even in situations without established norms, members of the group will quickly construct rules that relieve uncertainty and provide guidelines for behavior.

In 1935, Muzafer Sherif, a social psychologist, performed a now-classic experiment that illustrates how norms are formed by people in new and unclear situations. The laboratory experiment used an optical illusion, the so-called autokinetic effect, in which a small fixed point of light that is briefly exposed in a dark room appears to the viewer to move unpredictably in all directions. Not surprisingly, people differed in their estimates of how it moved. Sherif asked people, one at a time and alone, to estimate how far the spot moved. Although there was no objective basis for knowing, each person developed a unique standard or norm of movement. Sherif then organized groups composed of the original subjects divided so that people who had established very different standards in their solitary sessions were placed together. Agreement on a common norm or standard occurred within the groups, although most of the subjects were unaware that they were being influenced by others. In fact, most of the subjects insisted that their individual judgments were made before the others spoke and, furthermore, that they had not been influenced by one another (Sherif 1935)!

Three main factors shape conformity for all of us. First, in an unstructured situation, we distort our perceptions somewhat to reduce the uncertainty of a situation in which we are not sure how to act. Each of us believes that she or he sees an object or event as others do and is unaware of the role of group pressure. Second, group pressure may distort judgment, so that each of us doubts his or her own memory perceptions when others do not agree with us. And last, each of us may decide to agree, even if unconvinced, that our feelings or perceptions are incorrect. After all, who wants to seem different or stupid?

But life is not lived in a laboratory, and despite these pressures toward conformity, complete agreement with all norms

"Just a Case of Ordinary Deviance"

You don't have to go to exotic places or examine extreme behavior to observe deviance. In fact, you need go no further than your favorite classroom. Remember: not all violations of norms and rules are "bad." For example, suppose that on the last exam in one of your difficult courses everyone "bombed-out" except one student who "aced" it. This particular "curvebreaker" did nothing wrong, but the rest of the class lost the ability to criticize the quality of the exam—after all, somebody did well. The one person who does extremely well has not done anything wrong in itself, but she or he has made everyone else look rather ordinary. In other words, the "saint's" very goodness is deviant because it violates the rules of behavior.

Another example of deviance in the classroom involves violation of the rules which may be just as normative as rule-conforming behavior. After all, not all norms and rules are followed. For example, while students are expected to attend classes regularly, you know there are excuses for absence that are considered legitimate by instructors. Given this information, students are expected to offer excuses that will be acceptable to the professor. Included among the excuses usually heard on college campuses for missing class are "My car broke down"; "I was too ill to come to class"; "My alarm didn't go off and I overslept"; or "My roommate became ill and I had to take her to the hospital." All of these excuses reflect accepted values: (1) going to class is important and (2) you show up unless there is compelling physical reason for not going. In reality, of course, students, and occasionally professors, miss classes when other values become more important. The real reasons may be closer to "I was too busy having a good time"; or "I was hung over"; "I couldn't get myself away from my favorite soap"; or "I just didn't feel like it."

But you would tend not to use such an inadequate or unacceptable excuse with your professor. We learn to use the rules required by particular situations even if they are the rules for breaking the rules! It's the possibility of breaking rules and perhaps getting away with it that makes deviance an integral part of social life. Detection and punishment is possible, but not inevitable.

other at some point in our lives, probably even today. Any person's position on the continuum will probably vary from one norm to another and from one social situation to the next. For example, leaders of organized crime can be kindly fathers, while respectable business executives could beat their children. And truthful students may lie to a professor about why they missed a class or failed to hand in an assignment on time.

STRENGTH OF NORMS

Some norms are more important than others. In most complex societies, rules that involve behavior essential to the group's well-being ("Honor thy father and thy mother") typically carry more weight than

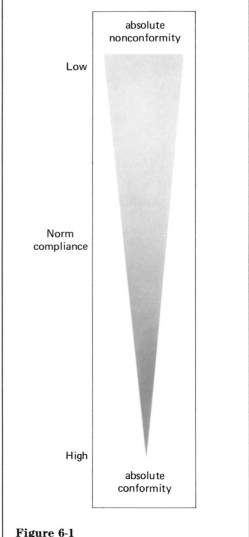

Figure 6-1

is unlikely. Conformity and deviance may be thought of as the opposite ends of a continuum of behavior (see Figure 6-1). Each of us has deviated from one norm or an-

Outrageous dress may result in social sanctions but legal sanctions are not usually applied. Might there be circumstances under which these people's behavior would be considered illegal? (© Steven M. Leonard/ Black Star)

rules of personal hygiene ("Brush your teeth twice a day"). In the United States, deviation from the norm of having only one husband or wife at one time can be prosecuted. In contrast, men who wear polka-dot suits or people who paint a house in zebra stripes may be considered funny or odd but are not fined or put in jail. Similarly, people who refuse to acknowledge introductions or who do not say "thank you" may be considered slobs, but not public menaces deserving punishment. Unlike Puritan New England where the *gemeinschaft* quality of early America required conformity to community norms in all aspects of social life, the complexity of industrialized society guarantees that only those norms considered most important to the group will be severely sanctioned.

Norms may also be either *proscriptive* ("thou shalt not") or *prescriptive* ("thou shalt"). Sociologists have observed that deviations from proscriptive norms are more likely to be severely punished than violations of prescriptive norms.

Yet, all norms are essentially arbitrary. Indeed, there is no one, or eternal, or universal standard of behavior. We are so constantly surrounded by rules we have internalized through socialization that they

Proscriptive norms cover forbidden conduct. **Prescriptive norms** dictate what is expected.

appear to be the "right and proper way of doing things" (Sumner 1909/1940). Yet, what is defined as normative, and therefore what is defined as deviance, changes over time. It also varies from society to society. At one time or another, all of the following activities, currently considered normal or at least not particularly deviant, were defined as criminal deviant acts: printing a book; claiming that the earth is round or not the center of the universe; performing an autopsy on a dead human body; not attending church; and boxing or prizefighting. Indeed, some of these "deviant behaviors" were punishable by death. Even minor deviations might be dealt with harshly; only 150 years ago, in England stealing linen was grounds for being hanged.

Conversely, some behaviors that are harshly condemned in our society today were considered relatively normal in the last century. Opium-based narcotics, for example, were widely available in nonprescription syrups that were even advertised in family magazines. The original Coca-Cola contained a small amount of cocaine to enhance its medicinal properties. It is possible that a higher percentage of Americans were addicted to these "cures" in the nineteenth century than at the present.

Indeed, the typical nineteenth-century "junkie" was a middle-aged, middle-class white woman addicted to over-the-counter medications. Another high use category were children, for whom soothing syrups laced with tranquilizing drugs were frequently prescribed, as seen in the following list of favorite infant remedies of a century ago (Douglas and Waksler 1982):

Dr. James' Soothing Syrup Cordial—Heroin

Children's Comfort—Morphine Sulphate

Dr. Fahey's Pepsin Anodyne Compound—Morphine Sulphate

Dr. Fahrney's Teething Syrup—Morphine and Chloroform

Dr. Miller's Anodyne for Babies—Morphine Sulphate and Chloral Hydrate

Dr. Fowler's Strawberry and Peppermint Mixture—Morphine

Gadway's Elixir for Infants—Codeine

Dr. Grove's Anodyne for Infants—Morphine Sulphate

Kopp's Baby Friend—Morphine Sulphate

Dr. Moffett's Teething (Teething Compound)—Powdered Opium

Victor Infant Relief—Chloroform and Cannabis Indica

In 1893 this French coca wine was available from the local grocery, drug or wine merchant for $1 and was recommended as beneficial for body and brain. Vin Mariani exists today as a wine without the coca added. As our attitudes toward drinking alcohol change, do you think the wine itself could become a thing of the past? (© The Bettmann Archive)

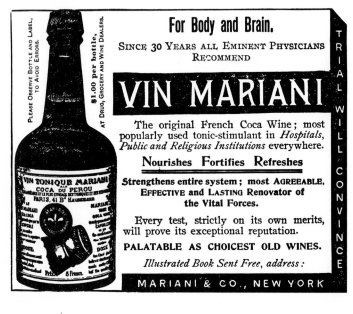

Hooper's Anodyne—The Infant's Friend—Morphine Sulphate

Mrs. Winslow's Soothing Syrup—Morphine Sulphate

In contrast, the typical American addict today is a young, urban, low-income, minority male who lives in a neighborhood where drug use is very common. Another high-risk group is medical professionals—physicians, nurses, dentists, druggists—with easy access to prescription drugs. Although the effects of addiction may not differ, the ways in which addiction is explained, tolerated, or socially controlled will vary from one social group to another.

Definitions of Deviance

In the early 1960s, a study of tolerance toward various nonconforming behaviors found that marijuana users were ranked with prostitutes among the least tolerated deviants (Simmons 1969). In the two-and-a-half decades since, marijuana use has become more common and more accepted. By the early 1980s, as Table 6-1 shows, marijuana use had leveled off at roughly 60 percent of high school students, 64 percent of college students, and 23 percent of all other adults (Akers 1985).

As you can see from Table 6-1, both high school and college students appear to consider marijuana use acceptable enough to admit it to researchers. Nor is smoking pot statistically deviant among these populations. For persons age 26 and over, however, although marijuana use has risen, it is clearly not conforming behavior. Many in the 26-and-over age group are older people who were never introduced to the drug or its subculture. Table 6-1 illustrates a major sociological concept: deviance is measured by the *societal reaction* to an act or lifestyle that violates popular or institutional norms.

In other words, there are no acts that are in and of themselves wrong or evil or deviant. There is only behavior that is defined as unacceptable in a given culture, at a certain historical period, and under particular circumstances. For example, the act of killing another person is called murder only in certain cases; it can be justifiable homicide under other conditions, and even an act of extreme heroism when done by soldiers in wartime.

TABLE 6-1 Trends in using marijuana, 1969–82

	Percentage of Age Group Who Ever Used		
Year	High School Seniors	College Students	Adults Age 26+
1969	21%	22%	(no data)
1974–76	47%	55%	15%
1979	60%	68%	20%
1982	59%	64%	23%

Source: Akers, 1985, Tables 8-1 and 8-2, pp. 198–209 (adapted from longer tables).

Social Functions of Deviance

That deviance resides not in the act itself but in how the act is interpreted by others was noted by Émile Durkheim (1893/1960). Durkheim further proposed that deviance, rather than being destructive or evil, is necessary to societal well-being. To hope to wipe out all sin and waywardness is to ignore the very real functions that deviance plays in maintaining social order. Thus, for the sociologist, behavior that seems unnecessary, irrational, or without purpose is not necessarily so. Durkheim pointed out that crime is a necessary part of all societies. Contradictory as this may sound, crime fulfills an important service by generating *social cohesion* in opposition to it. As the members of a community or a society unite to express outrage and to vent their anger about "criminal" acts, they also develop closer ties to one another. This union in mutual anger creates what Durkheim termed the "public temper," that is, a feeling shared by members of a group and belonging to no one person in particular. Through such group consensus, social order is reinforced. This process is well illustrated by the public temper created in the United States by reports of the mistreatment of the fifty-two persons held hostage in Iran for fourteen months in 1979–81. A wave of shared anger swept the country, creating a sense of solidarity, and defining the Iranians as barbarians and outlaws. Another such wave of public temper occurred in 1986 when the American public discovered that arms had been sent to Iran, the supposed deviant, by the federal government itself to encourage release of American hostages—a plan which, incidentally, did not work.

When deviants are identified and punished, members of the society are united in a common morality that strengthens their own belief system. Thus, deviance has a dual function: *unification of the group* and *boundary setting.* In the Iranian example cited above, some group confusion resulted precisely because of the difficulty of punishing the deviant and defining boundaries between the acceptable and the unacceptable.

Boundary setting is a process by which shared norms and values are established within social groups such as the family, the school, the workplace, a professional association, one's hometown, or the entire society. Within these groups, boundaries are placed at the outer limits of acceptable behavior, so that people's actions are limited and made relatively stable and predictable. In other words, conduct is confined to acceptable forms; behavior outside the boundaries is clearly identified as unacceptable. Kai Erikson (1966) suggested that people learn boundaries through *confrontation.* That is, they constantly test the limits of acceptable behavior to determine the boundary lines. Often, the nature of this confrontation is public, as in demonstrations for gay rights or against family planning clinics where support and opposition are tested.

DEVIANCE AS A SAFETY VALVE

Some deviance, however, is permitted in most societies as a *safety valve,* or a way of releasing frustration, tension, or anger. One example is the current attitude toward prostitution in the United States. Illegal in most states, prostitution nonetheless continues to exist, with only occasional raids and arrests by the police and media crusades. Why?

> **Boundary setting** occurs when shared norms and values set the limits of acceptable behavior.

> **Confrontations** test the limits of acceptable behavior.

> Some deviance serves as a **safety valve** for disruptive tendencies.

This teenage runaway turned to prostitution to survive the streets; Sidney Barrows, called the "Mayflower Madam" because her descendants were among the original colonists, established a high class brothel as a business enterprise. While street walkers are regularly arrested and jailed, Ms. Barrows made an out-of-court settlement and published a book of memoirs which has yielded a great deal of income. (© Stephen Ferry/Gamma-Liaison; © Stephen Shames/Visions)

Many sociologists have argued that prostitution continues to be more-or-less tolerated—although condemned—because it fills certain functions for society. One function is a conservative one. Historically, Americans have distinguished between two types of women: "good" women, whom one marries, and "bad" women, whom a male sleeps with but does not marry. Prostitution has thus reinforced the double standard of morality. Through prostitution, sexual outlet is permitted to men—but not to women—without threatening either family stability or myths about female sexuality. The impersonality and business nature of prostitution also allow men to explore new, sometimes unconventional, sexual practices without involvement or anxiety. Moreover, for many men, prostitution is a convenient way to have sexual intercourse under conditions in which they, as temporary employer, maintain control.

The fact that prostitution is a business also highlights the basic value system of our society. "Call girls" are often used by businesses to help make deals. Many people see a positive value in prostitution, although official morality opposes it. Others view prostitution as not only immoral but criminal. Feminists object to its exploitation of women. But social historians claim that many poor women have found the profession superior to factory work (Rosen 1983). Prostitution today is a multi-million-dollar business, controlled by men, involving male pimps and other employees as diverse as lawyers, law-enforcement personnel, and a cast of thousands, such as madams, organized crime, and business corporations. Prostitution has its own status system, from $1000-a-night call girls who entertain executives to poorly paid streetwalkers (Miller 1986). Wherever she may work, the prostitute is a key person within a social network where she must call on others for special services, as shown in Figure 6-2.

The prostitute depends on others for referrals, services, income, and protection. Often an employee of a pimp who manages her career, she, in turn, produces jobs for others. Her very existence also provides employment for those charged with maintaining and enforcing laws against prostitution (for example, the vice squad of a police force). In general, deviance of all types creates employment and promotion opportunities for agents of social control. In this sense, police depend on crime, just as psychiatrists have a vested interest in mental illness. (See our discussion of role sets in Chapter 4. This concept can be useful when applied to the prostitute and the status incumbents with whom she interacts.)

EXPRESSING DISCONTENT AND PROMOTING SOCIAL CHANGE

Another function of deviance is the expression of discontent with existing norms. The "youth revolt" of the 1960s, for example, involved primarily middle-class youths who openly rejected the values of success and conformity popular in the 1950s. As products of a relatively wealthy society engaged in the Vietnam War, which seemed meaningless to many, the students who demonstrated on campuses, adopted casual dress styles, and rejected conventional behaviors were not only testing boundaries, they were also searching for something beyond the boundaries. Note, also, the closing of ranks among other segments of the society in opposition to the young: hardhats and college administrators, many parents and politicians all created a public temper of shared moral indignation at such ingratitude.

Violation of norms may indicate a flaw in the social system itself. For example, the civil rights activists of the 1960s violated many local norms of conventional behavior and tested the law itself with their nonviolent attempts to gain equal access to seats on buses and at lunch counters. Similarly, university professors are an unlikely group to strike, but many increasingly tend to do so in protests against administration policies, even though such strikes violate conventional norms and disrupt campus routines.

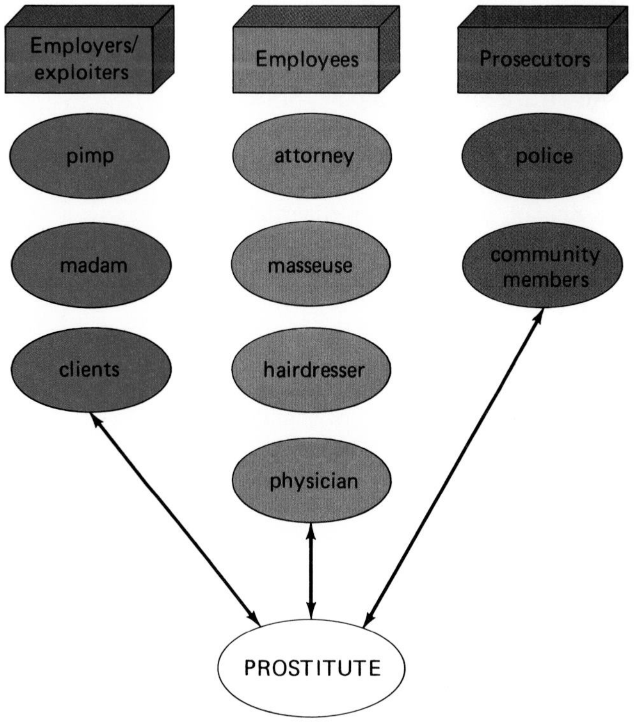

Continued boundary testing can often promote social change, as definitions of deviance are liberalized. For example, continued open challenges to the norms have led to increased tolerance toward dope smoking. But when severe boundary crises occur, members of the community begin to punish activities that were ignored before the crisis. The Salem witch trials in Puritan New England came when the colony was under stress. The Puritan colonists had lost the original sense of purpose that made their society cohesive (Erikson 1966). Searching for witches within society allowed the colonists to reaffirm their shared identity and goals. Only when such zeal in destroying evil threatened the stability of the entire group, as when the governor's wife was accused of witchcraft, did the persecution of "witches" stop.

The example of Puritan New England also shows that what is defined as deviant behavior depends on the social and political context. The definition of deviance also reflects the biases of those in power. The people most likely to be condemned for witchcraft in New England were poor, middle-aged women, usually single or widowed, who had a reputation for nagging or annoying their neighbors (Demos 1983). We can learn much about a group's values by observing who is labeled deviant. As Erikson noted, those people who most fear witches are also most likely to find them in their midst!

PRINCIPLED CHALLENGES TO THE NORMS

Principled challenges are deliberate attempts to confront the norm setters. The challenge is seen as having a moral aspect and is most often an attempt to reform or change a particular part of the society without changing the basic social or normative structure. These protests usually occur when conventional, legitimate means of bringing pressure either have failed or have moved too slowly to satisfy the interests of those seeking change.

For example, within the past few years, there have been dozens of protests against the building and the use of nuclear power plants. In the 1960s and the early 1970s, opposition to nuclear power centered

Principled challenges are deliberate attempts to confront the norm setters.

Figure 6-2
The social network of the prostitute. (Adapted from M. R. Laner, "Prostitution as an Illegal Vocation: A Sociological Overview," in Clifford D. Bryan, ed., *Deviant Behavior: Occupational and Organizational Bases,* Chicago: Rand McNally, 1974.)

The anti-nuclear weapons movement has become very strong in Europe. Here a group of British citizens protest the stationing of cruise missiles in Greenham Common. Such principled challenges to the norms are deliberate attempts to reform or change policies. (© Chris Steele-Perkins/Magnum)

in established groups that used the normal channels of publicity and lawsuits (Barkan 1979). These lawsuits have been slow, costly, and uncertain, leading some people to mount their own principled challenge to nuclear power. In May 1977, fourteen thousand people occupied the construction area of Seabrook, New Hampshire, and were arrested. Suddenly, national publicity was directed toward the movement and its goals. Protests have continued, and the construction of nuclear plants has been halted, partly as a result of these actions. The impact of principled challenges rests on too many outside variables to be predictable (see Chap. 21). At the very least, however, a previously neglected source of discontent is placed on the public agenda.

Social Control

> **Social controls** are techniques for enforcing the norms.

The term *social control* refers to the planned or unplanned processes by which people are taught, persuaded, or forced to conform to norms. Because the survival of any social group depends on most of its members behaving in a predictable manner most of the time, rewards for conform-

ity and negative sanctions for deviant behavior are a crucial aspect of all social systems.

Social controls can be either informal or formal. *Informal mechanisms* include expressions of approval or disapproval by significant others. As we saw in Chapter 5, information on role performance from significant others is a key factor in the internalization of norms. Socialization is every group's first defense against deviance; a person's conscience is the most effective and least expensive form of social control. But few people are so self-controlled that they do not deviate from the norms some time or another. That is the time when informal cues from significant others—a raised eyebrow, a slap on the wrist, the silent treatment—bring us back into line. The fear of losing their affection or approval is usually sufficient to limit further deviance.

When informal sanctions fail, *formal agents of social control* are called upon. Formal agents are people in social roles specifically charged with enforcement of the norms. In our society, formal agents include mental health professionals, law enforcement and criminal justice personnel, welfare workers, and, often, religious leaders. In their roles as formal agents,

> **Formal agents of social control** are people in social roles specifically devoted to norm enforcement.

these people attempt to reduce deviant behavior and reinforce conformity through various rewards and punishments. Mental wellness and interpersonal adequacy are measured by an individual's ability to meet the expectations of others.

As a last step in the process of social control, people whose behavior is so unpredictable or unacceptable that it threatens social order are simply removed from the community. This is the function of prisons and mental hospitals—to ensure orderly group life by warehousing those who cannot otherwise be brought under control. In addition, when violators of the norms are punished, the boundaries of acceptable behavior are clarified.

Although all societies have networks of informal and formal controls, there are variations in the leeway allowed for acceptable role performance and in the severity with which deviation is punished. Currie (1968) identified two basic types of formal control systems: *repressive* and *restrained.* In repressive systems, the agents of social control have extraordinary power to detect and restrain a wide range of forbidden behaviors. Current examples of

Repressive control systems ensure high levels of conformity. **Restrained** control systems involve less intense use of power.

repressive systems include (1) the Republic of South Africa's enforcement of laws that limit the movements of the country's majority black population, or (2) the secret police in Eastern European and South American countries. In contrast, restrained systems of social control are characterized by limits on the invasion of personal privacy, as well as greater tolerance of variation in conformity to the norms. Sweden and the United States, for example, have relatively restrained systems of formal controls.

Theories of Deviance

The first question that most Americans ask about any type of deviance is: Why do they do it? What causes some people to be deviant while others conform?

Several theories attempt to explain why people deviate from the expected, each of which reflects a particular value position with distinct consequences for controlling deviance and dealing with nonconforming people.

Formal enforcement of the law can provide a powerful social control. Why might people pursue criminal activity, as did these crack dealers, knowing they might get caught? What other factors are at work? (© John T. Barr/Gamma Liaison)

Being Disabled in America

MARY JO DEEGAN

Mary Jo Deegan is associate professor in the Department of Sociology at the University of Nebraska–Lincoln. Her coedited book, with Nancy Brooks, Women and Disability: The Double Handicap *has been published by Transaction Press, New Brunswick and Oxford.*

When I was a college sophomore, I entered a hospital for minor surgery on a "trick knee." It had dislocated a number of times after I had injured it doing the "limbo," a Caribbean dance. A cast was put on my leg after the surgery, but it was too tight and within 24 hours it had damaged my circulation, nerves, and muscles. For the next three years, I lived a nightmare. No one wanted to take responsibility for the medical error, no one wanted me to be angry, and very few people wanted to visit me or share my experience. I changed from a typical, fun-loving, apolitical, college woman into a stranger in my everyday life. As a class officer in my community college, I was in the middle of numerous activities. As a "shut-in" in constant pain, with a paralyzed leg and purple foot, my social world shrank to medical personnel who generally tried to convince me my situation was not too bad: I needed to be more mature and cope better; and I was too ambitious.

It took me about two years to come to grips with my radically changed life and view of society. I continued in college, first in a wheelchair and later with crutches and canes. I was in and out of hospitals and became highly critical of medical practices and American society. In 1969, I graduated from college as a chemist, and then searched for work for the next seven months.

Everywhere I went I was confronted with job discrimination as a woman and as a disabled person. After four discouraging months, in desperation, I decided to do something easy and fun. I would go to graduate school for sociology. I am afraid I thought of sociology as a "pud" subject after my training in chemistry.

To my deep surprise, I found that Erving Goffman's STIGMA explained many of my personal struggles during the preceding three years and ASYLUMS revealed many of the medical attempts to strip me of my identity. Caroline Bird's BORN FEMALE told me that my employment discrimination was shared with millions of other women, and that it was illegal. Bird was also the first person to tell me that I was right to be angry.

To my even greater surprise, by the time I entered graduate school, my nerve was rapidly and spontaneously regenerating enough so that I looked as if I was not disabled. For three years, I had been told repeatedly that my injury was permanent and must be accepted, so to appear nondisabled was startling to say the least. (One of the ironic problems at this point was that people kept telling me I was not ambitious enough, there were no limits to my opportunities, and I was too nice.) Over the next two years, the disability became progressively less problematic.

I did my doctoral work as a participant-observer in a rehabilitation hospital. For nine months, I tried to understand the world, experience, and rehabilitation process for the recently and permanently disabled. I understood enough to get my dissertation on "Identity Change in Modern Society: A Case Study of the Physically Disabled" accepted in 1975. I reworked my ideas in a series of articles exploring the lifeworld, or *lebenswelt,* of the physically injured. I emphasize that the reality of this experience is continually being structured, and often denied, by medical personnel, psychologists, family, friends, clergy, educators, and strangers. Thus, a patient cannot express anger without being considered a "difficult patient." The threat of losing needed medical services reinforces "good behavior." Controlling anger often leads to its internalization, and this "quiet anger" is then psychologically explained as part of being disabled instead of being a result of institutional constraints. Similarly, many other experiences are transformed into a medical model. For example, a person with an amputation may feel that the body part that has been removed is still there and often painful. This experience is common among amputees and is called a "phantom limb." I assume that the experience is real and then show that the medical language of a "phantom limb" and the psychological therapy to treat it deny this reality.

In 1979, I saw for the first time that being a woman and being disabled combined into a "multiple minority status." Nancy Brooks (who has her own personal account and encounter with physical disability) and I joined forces to edit a journal issue on disabled women which was published as a book.

Some of my early questions about the world of disability have been answered, but now I have newer questions that need answering. Understanding what it means to be disabled in America is a life-long journey, allowing me to heal as an individual and be creative within a wider community.

BIOLOGICAL AND PSYCHOLOGICAL EXPLANATIONS

Biological Theories. The notion that there is something wrong built into the deviant person is a very old one. Attempts to find biological causes for deviance include studies of head shapes (phrenology), racial types, intelligence, and, most recently, genetics. In all these studies, investigators have looked for relationships between specific body characteristics and deviant behavior, claiming that the body trait causes deviance.

Although a biological explanation for deviance has long appealed to researchers, it has several major flaws, not the least of which are the contradictory findings. For example, one investigator (Hooton 1939) reported that criminals were usually "runty," whereas another (Sheldon 1949) found that husky, athletic types were more often criminals. Furthermore, no evidence has ever been presented to show how any person's biological makeup can cause crime or any other deviant (or conforming) behavior. Most of the studies have based their findings on those few people who have been caught or who have asked for treatment. This sampling bias distorts the findings. Those who are already under treatment for mental illness or for drug addiction or alcoholism, or who have been convicted as criminals, are the unsuccessful deviants. They tell us nothing about the successful ones.

Furthermore, biological explanations reduce the social world to the physical world. That is, feeling and behavior are seen as mere results of people's biological makeup or as master traits, i.e. characteristics which determine and take precedence over other characteristics. Persons who are physically disfigured or disabled usually have to deal with this kind of reasoning in most of their encounters. Yet, human behavior is, as most biologists and other scientists would agree, greatly affected by the social situations that people face.

Psychological Theories. The belief that deviant behavior results from some kind of moral flaw or mental problem in a person remains as popular today as during biblical times. Recent psychological views stress the effects of faulty childhood socialization, so that internal control on behavior has been impaired. But saying that people are thieves because they have weak self-control, the symptom of which is stealing, is akin to saying that people have measles because they have a rash, and that they have a rash because they have measles. The reasoning is *circular*. Moreover, although most of us experience some negative socialization in childhood, not all of us become full-fledged deviants. Individualistic theories of deviance also divert attention from social factors, such as inequality and the power to define appropriate behavior.

SOCIOLOGICAL PERSPECTIVES

Although sociologists note what psychologists, psychiatrists, and biologists say about the origins of deviant behavior, the *social act* is our major concern. Social explanations of deviance must be analyzed both within the context of the society where the behavior occurs and within the framework of social interaction. Neither biological nor psychological theories can predict deviance accurately from a knowledge only of the mind and body of a particular person because both the deviant and those who seek to control or limit deviant behavior are acting within a *social context*. Even conforming behavior may be considered deviant in some social contexts, as the following box illustrates.

Various sociological approaches to the study of deviant behavior have been proposed, most of which complement each other. They shed light on (1) why deviance exists within every known human society; (2) how people become deviant; and (3) what mechanisms for social control are used to limit and punish obvious violations of important social norms.

The Functionalist Approach. Functional theory directs attention to how elements of social structure and behavior *maintain* the stability or the relative equilibrium of societies or groups. Thus, much behavior that we label deviant actually reflects the cultural values of the society in which it occurs—even if only by offending agreed-upon standards of behavior. As Erikson (1966) stated, "The thief and his victim share a common respect for the value of property; the heretic and inquisitor speak much the same language and are keyed to the same religious mysteries; the traitor and the patriot act in reference to the

Being Sane in Insane Places

If you were admitted to a mental hospital today and acted as you normally act, would psychiatrists and hospital staff think you were sane or insane? This is what Rosenhan (1973) and his associates asked. In a now-classic experiment, eight sane people from different backgrounds were admitted at different times, to twelve psychiatric hospitals in different parts of the United States. Each of these "pseudopatients," on arriving at the hospital, presented the same symptoms: a complaint that he or she had heard soft voices saying "empty," "hollow," and "thud." These particular symptoms were chosen as illustrations of the meaninglessness of life, a so-called existential psychosis of which there are no reports in the psychiatric literature. Aside from making up these symptoms and giving a false name and occupation, each pseudopatient behaved as he or she normally would. Yet, none of the hospital staff noticed anything unusual about any of these patients. All but one pseudopatient was diagnosed as schizophrenic. The assumption was that each pseudopatient *must* be mad or he or she would not be there, and his or her activities were interpreted as signs of mental illness. For example, although all the pseudopatients took field notes about their experiences in front of staff and other patients, no staff member ever asked why. Instead, for several pseudopatients, the staff reports noted, "Patient indulges in writing behavior." Each pseudopatient was eventually discharged as improved by the treatment received in the hospital. The other patients, however, were not fooled.

Rosenhan concluded that the hospital itself imposed a special environment in which *all* behavior was made to fit a deviant model—that of mental illness. Behavior was never seen as occurring in response to the environment but rather as indicating individual pathology. It can be very hard to prove you are sane!

The relative stability of offender rates reflects definitions of deviance that roughly match the capacity of the social control mechanisms of the community. Only so many people can be processed at a time without overtaxing the courts and the jails. This pattern is shown in Figure 6-3, which compares the offender rates and the number of convictions in Puritan New England.

When a community's or a society's resources for controlling deviance are overwhelmed by too many violators, social change is likely to occur, and the boundaries of conformity likely to be redefined. This is indeed what happened in New England. When the witch trials threatened to overwhelm the community's capacity to punish witches, the trials for witchcraft ceased. If social change does not occur and the boundaries are not redefined, the social-control system itself must be modified. Something similar is occurring today as our prison system has been severely strained by public demands to "lock 'em up and throw away the key."

The Conflict Theory Approach. According to conflict theory, social harmony is impossible in most existing societies. The roots of conflict lie in the tension between the few who control the means of production and who also have great political influence, on the one hand, and the mass of powerless citizens, on the other. That power is used to enact and enforce laws supporting the interests of the owners against those of the less powerful. Certain kinds of laws and patterns of law enforcement are thus produced by powerful interest groups. As the French author Anatole

same political institutions" (p. 22). Rather than being a symptom of disorganization or conflict, deviance can be seen as promoting group solidarity. Simply put, deviance reinforces the authority of the norms sometimes making them stronger.

Erikson also proposed that the proportion of deviants in the population is likely to stay relatively constant over time. In his studies of Puritan New England, Erikson observed that, although the number of convictions varied from year to year, the offender rate remained fairly constant.

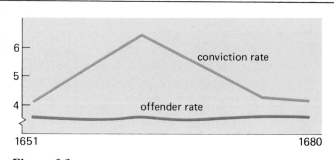

Figure 6-3
Offender rates and conviction rates in Puritan New England. (Source: Kai Erikson, *Wayward Puritans*, New York: John Wiley, 1966, p. 174.)

Where repressive controls are obvious, the conflict model of analysis seems most appropriate. The civil war in El Salvador provides a graphic illustration. (© Bob Nickelesberg/Woodfin Camp and Associates)

France once wrote, "The law in its majestic equality forbids both rich and poor alike to beg in the streets, steal bread, and sleep under bridges."

According to this view, the small groups (elites) who control the economic and political systems set the policies that define legal as well as cultural conformity. Because the goal of elites—to maintain their power—is essentially contrary to the strivings of the less powerful, there is an ongoing "crisis of legitimacy" in which the ruling groups must continually create the impression that the established system is serving the interests of all segments of the population. This is the ultimate goal of "cultural hegemony" as discussed in Chapters 3 and 20: to convince the powerless that their needs are being met. Therefore, in the conflict perspective, the consensus at the root of functional theory is an imposed reality designed to eliminate opposition.

As for the criminal justice system, conflict theorists tend to view the administration of justice as rigged against potentially troublesome populations—the poor, members of minority groups, and others who might challenge the legitimacy of the *status quo*. From this perspective, civil rights marchers in the 1960s broke laws not because they lacked respect for order but because they perceived that order as unjust; union members set up picket lines to protest exploitation; and environmentalists lay down in front of bulldozers to protect public land rather than out of any death wish. In each of these cases, however, the formal forces of social control have been employed against the protesters.

Labeling Theory. Labeling theory asks two basic questions: (1) How is deviance socially produced? and (2) How does labeling affect a person's later behavior? It is the emphasis on the process of defining a person's behavior that has given this approach its name. Labeling does not attempt to explain the basic reasons for individual deviance. Rather, it is concerned with the social processes that encourage and maintain such behavior. In the labeling model, deviance, like beauty, is in the eye of the beholder; it is a quality that lies, not in behavior itself, but in the interaction between the person who commits the act and those who respond to it (Becker 1973). The labeling process is critical to becoming and continuing to be deviant. Thus, a key point in labeling theory is that declaring someone deviant may result in a self-fulfilling prophecy and reinforce the behavior. As Becker argued:

"... deviance is not a quality of the act the person commits, but rather a consequence of the application by others of the rules and sanctions to an 'offender'.... (1963, pp. 8–9). Whether an act is deviant, then, depends on how other people react to it. You can commit clan incest and suffer from no more than gossip as long as no one makes a public accusation, but you will be driven to your death if an accusation is made" (Becker 1963, p. 11).

Although labeling theory developed in the 1950s, its roots go back to earlier symbolic interactionist studies of juvenile delinquency (Tannenbaum 1938) and to the concept of cultural relativism. Deviance is an interactive process between those who

Labeling theory emphasizes the process of defining a person's behavior as deviant.

147

Smoking cigarettes has been a way of life for generations. The public norms are beginning to shift, however, and there are now legal sanctions that can be applied to smokers. Do you consider smokers to be deviant?

violate a norm (or who are believed to have done so) and others who interpret and react to the acts. For example, smoking cigarettes has become increasingly regarded as deviant behavior—so much so that some cities, like Cambridge, Massachusetts, have passed laws to prohibit smoking in any public place. Anyone who smokes in public in Cambridge runs the risk of being labeled a lawbreaker, and a hazard to general health and well-being. If he or she smokes alone and in private, the behavior would not be labeled. The act—in this example, smoking—is the same; what is different is the social construction of the behavior.

Is labeling as important in defining deviance as some sociologists have suggested? Or are deviant labels the result of deviant behavior? Some analysts (Chauncey 1975; Cockerham 1979; Gove 1975, 1979) have suggested that deviant labels are a result, not a cause, of deviant behavior. Others, like Scheff (1966), have proposed that labeling is the single most important cause of a deviant career.

Yet, as recent work has pointed out, labeling can have not one, but several, effects including (1) creating deviant behavior; (2) maintaining deviance; and (3) affecting other areas of life, including jobs, family relationships, and friendships (Link 1983). Critics of labeling theory have focused primarily on whether deviant behavior is created and maintained by

148

labeling, but not on the *effects* of labeling. There is evidence that, although a label may or may not directly affect the specific behavior to which it is attached, the interaction resulting from the label definitely affects other areas of life (Link 1983). A label of mental illness, for example, puts people at a higher risk of job loss and rejection by potential mates, as well as generally undermining their ability to cope. Labeling thus maintains deviance. Rosenhan (1973) observed that to raise questions about normality and abnormality is not to question whether some behaviors are odd: "Anxiety and depression exist. Psychological suffering exists. But normality and abnormality, sanity and insanity, and the diagnoses that flow from them may be less substantive than many believe them to be" (p. 250).

It is not always clear when behavior will be labeled deviant or conforming. The same act can also be viewed differently by different people, as the following description of the returning soldier indicates:

> When the war was over, the soldier came home.
> But he had no Bread.
> Then he saw a man who had.
> He killed him.
> You mustn't kill people, you know, said the judge.
> Why not, asked the soldier. (Borchert 1971)

Likewise the enforcement of a rule depends on several factors: on the *social context,* as the above poem illustrates, and on who violates the rule, who perceives this violation, and whether the perceivers feel that the rule breaking harms them or others in the community.

Deviant Careers and Noncareers

Lemert (1967) has described two types of deviance that relate to the development of a deviant career: primary and secondary deviance. *Primary deviance* originates within the person for one reason or another and is behavior that violates a norm but may either be undetected or excused by others. *Secondary deviance* is a special class of socially defined responses which people make to problems created by the social response to deviance. For example, a person who sees visions or hears voices

Primary deviance is behavior that violates a norm.

Secondary deviance results from the social responses to primary deviance.

while alone is unusual, but if these false-sense perceptions occur in private and are offset by satisfactory performance in other roles, the deviation may be undetected or excused for as long as possible. If, however, the same person holds a conversation with the voices or offers a chair to an invisible creature, he or she is likely to suffer social consequences. Indeed, the questionable behavior could become intensified precisely because others have come to expect it.

Becoming a deviant is a matter not only of labeling but of *social learning* by the rule breaker. Edwin Sutherland (1939) was particularly interested in how one type of deviance, criminal behavior, is learned, and he proposed the theory of *differential association,* which may be summarized as follows:

1. Criminal behavior is learned in social interaction with others and has no unique biological or genetic basis.
2. It is within *primary groups,* rather than from the larger society, that one learns motives and techniques for committing crimes, reasons for conforming to or violating particular rules, and what behavior is permissible in which situation.
3. A person becomes a criminal when definitions favorable to the violation of law outweigh the unfavorable ones; that is, one becomes a criminal because there are more factors favoring such activity than there are opposing it.
4. The differential associations most likely to result in criminal behavior are frequent, long-lasting, and intense, and they occur relatively early in life.
5. Learning criminal behavior is the same as learning any other behavior. For example, people who value money could become robbers, stockbrokers, or physicians. There is thus *no* value or need pattern unique to criminals as opposed to noncriminals. A person becomes criminal when the reinforcement for lawbreaking is stronger than the reinforcement for remaining law-abiding.

Sutherland's theory of differential association shows us that deviance, like any other behavior, may be learned. But not all of us who associate with thieves become thieves, nor do all who associate with alcoholics become alcoholic, and not all of us who associate with fat people get fat.

How does a deviant career begin for some and not others? There are several steps in the process. First, the rule breaker is caught and publicly labeled. One may catch oneself; for example, one may recognize that he or she is overweight and decide voluntarily to join Overeaters Anonymous, or others may brand one as too fat. Second, once tagged, a person's new label is treated as a *master status trait.* (See Chapter 4.) The person's other identities and roles are virtually ignored, and the rule breaker is treated not as John the twenty-year-old student, musician, and chessplayer, but as John the fat man. Third, once a person is perceived as deviant, nothing about her or him is trusted or taken for granted, and the deviant trait seems to color that person's entire being in the eyes of others.

Consider, for example, how fat people are viewed in our society:

> While riding a bus . . . . Barbara became both fascinated and repelled by the sight of a hugely fat passenger. Asked how old the woman was, my friend shrugged her shoulders, as if to say the woman's massive size had somehow made her age . . . irrelevant. . . . Rather than move very far into the bus she sat in a front seat reserved for the elderly and physically handicapped. . . . [In the bus station] Barbara, still curious about the fat woman, was surprised that she dialed a number from memory, as if to a husband or another very close person, for she had imagined during the bus ride that this woman must lead an isolated life. (Millman 1980, p. 69.)

Thus, one deviant trait, obesity, was generalized, so that the viewer automatically assumed that the fat woman had other undesirable traits. A *stigma,* or "sign of moral blemish," attaches to a characteristic that differs from the normal or the normative in a society. Those with this trait are treated as if they bear a mark of disgrace. Thus, the person is *stigmatized,* as others withdraw their acceptance and distort that person's real identity to fit stereotypical expectations (Goffman 1963). In turn, the stigmatized person internalizes part or all of the views of the labelers about the stigma, altering his or her self-concept in the process. As Millman commented about obesity, a generally stigmatized category in our society:

> While most people have a clearer self image and pretty well know what to make of other people's behavior, the fat person is too self-conscious and too marginal. . . . She

---

The theory of **differential association** states that deviant behavior is learned in primary groups and involves the same learning processes as nondeviant behavior.

A **stigma** is a morally undesirable trait that tends to be generalized to other undesirable traits as well.

reasonably comes to doubt her judgments about social situations. . . . The fat individual often finds it easier to give up, to abandon a world that doesn't want her anyway. . . . Everything in her privatized life takes on an illicit or furtive quality. . . . So does she come to feel embattled with her environment. (p. 82)

The last step in a deviant career involves seeking out others who share the stigma. Because interaction with nondeviants is so painful, the deviant avoids their presence. With others who are also stigmatized, the deviant at last finds a supportive peer group. Not only is she or he socially accepted in this group, but a particular world view that explains and supports the stigmatized behavior is created and maintained. This supportive network is called a *deviant subculture.*

Deviant subcultures are supportive peer groups and networks for deviants.

In these subcultures people may try to redefine the stigma in order to counter the majority's perspective on the particular attribute. There are, for example, groups of overweight people who are not devoted to weight loss. Instead, they are supportive of the larger body type and the idea that being heavier is beautiful and, perhaps, healthy. Given that we are a society obsessed with thinness these support groups are an essential for individuals trying to redefine themselves. And certainly these groups may even be one of the first steps towards making changes in the majority's point of view.

In fact, the range of support on this issue has grown over the past ten years. Where at first many of the groups had a feminist emphasis (Orbach 1978, 1982) they have expanded to include a variety of attitudes. This trend has generated several magazines, many stores catering to the need for larger-sized fashions, and books and articles analyzing our cultural obsession with thinness (see, for example, Hillel Schwartz, *Never Satisfied: A Cultural History of Diets, Fantasies and Fat,* New York: Free Press, 1987).

ANOMIE

Anomie, as you will recall from Chapter 4, refers to the disorganization that exists in individuals or society when norms are conflicting, weak, or absent. When one has been socialized to the *norms* and *goals* that govern behavior within a particular culture but is denied access to the *means* of expressing that commitment, anomie may result. Assuming that the goal in American society is to be rich or successful, members of subgroups who are systematically denied the opportunity to achieve this goal by legitimate means will be drawn to alternative means. Robert Merton (1957) proposed five ways in which a person may adapt to the gap between the means and the goals of a culture.

As Table 6-2 shows, there are several adaptive mechanisms, all but one of which does not conform to both the culturally determined goals and the legitimate means of achieving them. The *innovator* will seek new and probably illegitimate means of acquiring wealth and success, for example, racketeering. The *ritualist* is resigned to fate, recognizes that fame and fortune are out of reach, and tends to overconform to the rules for good conduct. The bureaucrat who is more concerned with keeping a job than with upward mobility or achievement, is a type of ritualist. The *retreatist,* however, rejects both the

While dieting continues to be a huge multi-million-dollar business not all women subscribe to the cultural ideal of the slim, trim female body. In a society stressing slimness, organizations like "Women at Large" can provide a source of validation and social support for large women, encouraging them to participate in activities from which they ordinarily feel excluded. (© Sharlyne Powell, Sharon McConnell, Founders of Women at Large, Physical Fitness, Image Enhancement for the Larger Woman, Yakima, Washington)

TABLE 6-2   Merton's typology of individual modes of adaptation to cultural means and goals

Individual Mode of Adaptation		Accepts Cultural Goals	Accepts Institutionalized Means of Attainment
Other Adaptations	Conformity	Yes	Yes
	Innovation	Yes	No
	Ritualism	No	Yes
	Retreatism	No	No
	Rebellion	No/but seeks to replace with other goals	No/but seeks to restructure means of attainment

SOURCE: Adapted from Robert K. Merton, *Social Theory and Social Structure* (New York: Free Press, 1957), p. 140.

means and the goals of the society and drops out—into drug use, mental illness, alcoholism, or life as a street person. Finally, the *rebellious* reject both means and goals while seeking social change. Political radicals, members of some religious cults, and followers of alternative lifestyles (some of which were so popular in the late 1960s) all reject conformity and adopt new goals and means.

Those who are denied access to or who reject the legitimate means and goals of

Retreatism is a mode of adaptation which seems to be increasing in all our major cities. What goals might be out of reach for these men? (© Jim Pozarik/Gamma Liaison)

their society also tend to turn away from former peer and reference groups and to seek out new ones that accept and reward their nonconforming behavior. Hence, subcultures arise for extremely religious people, homosexuals, rock musicians, drug users, political radicals, hustlers, and safecrackers, among many, many others.

Albert Cohen (1955) expanded anomie theory, suggesting that delinquent and law-abiding behavior both depend largely on one's sociocultural environment and social interaction. *Delinquent subcultures* develop primarily among poorer juveniles who are relatively unskilled at competing in a middle-class world. When they enter school, they are measured by middle-class norms that have not been emphasized before in their socialization. Thus, the children of the poor fall short and, being unable to compete successfully in school, seek success elsewhere: in the activities of the gang, where they find validation and excitement.

Opportunity Structure Theory.   Delinquent or criminal subcultures have their roots in the lack of fit between culturally learned aspirations among poor youth and the limited possibilities of attaining success (Cloward and Ohlin 1960). Three types of delinquent subcultures may arise from *blocked opportunity structure*. These subcultures are summarized in Table 6-3. Each of these subcultures stresses a different career pattern and source of gratification: for the criminal, property and wealth; for the conflict-oriented, violence; and for the retreatist, complete withdrawal from both deviant and conformist pressures. All three subcultures can be found today in any major American city.

Delinquent and **criminal subcultures** originate in the differences between aspirations and blocked opportunity structures.

TABLE 6-3 Focus of activity within subculture

Delinquent Subculture Type	Acquisition of Property and Money	Violence and Gang War	Drug Use, Alcohol Use
Criminal	Yes	No	No
Conflict	No	Yes	No
Retreatist	No	No	Yes

ECCENTRIC BEHAVIOR

Although the person who has been labeled as deviant often becomes locked into a deviant career, in certain situations differences are *tolerated,* and the nonconformist is not rejected or isolated from normal social life. The concept of *social distance* is important here. Some types of deviant behavior do not bring extreme stigmatization. A person may be simply considered an "oddball," or *eccentric.* Eccentrics, like deviants, are recognized rule breakers and are observed and defined by others as being unusual. When the behavior is labeled eccentric, however, the rule breaking is not interpreted as either disruptive of or threatening to the social order. Eccentrics may be tolerated for several reasons: (1) They are viewed as unimportant oddities (shopping-bag women); (2) they are members of an in-group that protects them (drunken politicians); or (3) they are protected by their position, wealth, or knowledge (Howard Hughes, for example).

Fame and fortune may protect one from stigma and from being locked into a deviant career even when public labeling has occurred. In 1974, then president Richard Nixon and much of his staff were forced to resign because of the Watergate scandals. Several were charged with and convicted of serious crimes. Yet, their conviction and imprisonment did not ruin their lives, nor were they tracked into criminal careers. Many turned to lecturing and writing, several of them earning hundreds of thousands of dollars, and Nixon has become an "elder statesman."

PETTY AND INSTITUTIONALIZED EVASIONS OF THE NORMS

Petty (trivial, minor) *violations* of the norms are often ignored until they threaten social order. Charging personal expenses to a business account, failing to report all taxable income, stealing office supplies

such as pencils and paper for personal use, parking illegally, and using another student's notes are common petty violations.

Although such rule-breaking carries the risk of negative sanctions, the petty norm-breaker is generally not concerned with the consequences. The rule itself may seem stupid or inconvenient. The acts may not be detected, and if they are, the results are typically not frightening. Breaking these rules may even be justified as fair compensation for an imagined or real loss ("It's OK to cheat on your taxes; the government takes too much anyway").

Institutionalized evasion of norms often occurs within an organization as a permanent, unofficial part of the system. These evasions may be tolerated because they actually help to achieve the goals of the organization, as one study of illegal work practices illustrates (Bensman and Gerver 1963). The researchers focused on how a particular type of illegal work practice—the use of a "tap"—developed and persisted in an aircraft factory. The tap is a tool whose ends are slotted to cut away waste material from the wing plate of an airplane, and it is employed when a nut does not fit easily into its assembly. Rather than hold up the entire production line, a worker reshapes the groove with a tap, but because this procedure reduces the strength of an aircraft's wings, it is the most serious violation of workmanship in the factory. A worker can be fired simply for owning a tap, yet in the factory studied, at least half of the workers owned this tool. Use of the tap was learned within the work group of the factory. The new worker was instructed in the practice by more experienced colleagues. The foreman, too, may have instructed the new worker, but with a warning *never* to get caught.

Inspection was lax. Although everyone in the organization knew that taps were used, the practice was tolerated and encouraged as long as no one was caught,

Eccentric behavior is not viewed as disruptive or threatening to the social order.

Petty violations of norms are trivial and minor violations of rules.

Institutionalized evasion of norms occurs within organizations as a permanent unofficial part of the system which may be tolerated as part of getting the job done.

because when the production line was *not* stopped so that the job could be done correctly, (1) costs were reduced and profits for the company increased; (2) the government got its planes sooner; (3) the work group's productivity earned raises and promotions for the foremen; and (4) the inspector could become "one of the guys" while still meeting the inspection quotas.

In this illustration, institutional deviance in the form of the workers' private, illegal norms allowed the company to fulfill its public, socially valued purpose: the production of airplanes. Thus, the deviant act on the assembly line was conforming in terms of the goal of the larger system. The public, and particularly the pilots of the unsafe aircraft, however, risked the drastic consequences of such institutionalized deviance.

Mental Illness as Residual Deviance

Whereas psychologists focus on the classification, causes, and treatment of mental disorders, sociologists have been interested in (1) the social factors associated with their occurrence and (2) the process by which people are defined as mentally ill. To the sociologist, mental illness is *residual deviance;* that is, it is less obvious and more difficult to define than, say, murder, treason, or bigamy and therefore is not easily classified. Diagnoses of mental illness tend to reflect the norms of the times. In the nineteenth century, physicians considered both masturbation and homosexuality symptoms of mental pathology. Today, neither is regarded as indicating a mental disorder.

It is, however, interesting to note that, whereas the American Psychiatric Association voted to drop homosexuality from its list of mental illness, a new illness has been added: habitual tobacco use. Jaffee (1975) proposed that the habitual teenage smoker probably derives so little esteem from school performance that he or she adopts premature adult behavior such as alcohol use, sexual activity, and smoking. That habitual smoking has emerged as a mental disorder when there is increased awareness that smoking is harmful to one's health emphasizes the importance of contemporary norms in defining exactly what kind of behavior will be labeled as

*Mental illness is **residual deviance** that is less easily identified than more obvious norm violations.*

mental illness. Mental illness, like other forms of social deviance, is defined within a social context.

One of the older sociological hypotheses about mental illness was that it was caused by *social disorganization.* According to Robert Park and most of his coworkers at the University of Chicago in the 1920s, social disorganization was most likely to occur in large, urban centers where *Gemeinschaft* ties were replaced by *Gesellschaft* relationships. The city was thus a source of both mystery and social evil. Noting that almost all types of extreme mental illness were found in the poorest, most rundown areas of the city, these theorists concluded that the illness resulted from the stresses and strains of urban life. Later studies have challenged this view: Neither urban living nor industrialization is directly related to mental illness (Srole 1980, Kadushin 1983). Moreover, each person, whether in the city or not, is embedded in a network of relationships with other people that may lessen or increase the likelihood of being mentally ill. For example, Vietnam veterans who live in large cities and interact with other Vietnam veterans are *less* likely to experience mental distress than those who do not have other veterans as friends (Kadushin 1983).

Do slums breed mental illness? A growing body of research indicates that characteristics such as sex, race, ethnicity, and income are more important in the diagnosis of mental illness than slum residence. In studies where mental health experts are asked to evaluate case histories—the same reports with the sex or age or occupation or race of the patient changed—a diagnosis of severe mental illness is more likely for women than men, older rather than younger people, for low-skill rather than high-skill workers, and for blacks rather than whites.

MENTAL ILLNESS AS A SOCIAL PROCESS

How does residual deviance, regardless of its cause, become labeled as mental illness? Thomas Scheff (1966) proposed that residual rule-breaking stems from different sources. Obviously, people may see, hear, or experience the unusual for many reasons: genetic, family, and stress factors; drugs; infection, starvation, or ex-

Social disorganization, which was more likely to occur in large urban centers, was once thought to explain mental illness.

haustion; or deliberately altered states of consciousness.

Furthermore, most residual rule-breaking is denied or ignored by others until it must be acknowledged. Members of a family or other close-knit group are reluctant to shift their definitions of a person's behavior from "normal" to "sick." Thus, relative to the rate of *treated* residual deviance, the rate of *untreated* rule-breaking is quite high.

Tracking the Patient's Career. According to Erving Goffman (1961), the change in self-concept involved in the process of becoming a mental patient is recognized only after the fact by the person experiencing it. A large role in determining who will actually become a mental patient is played by *career contingencies:* the occupation and income of the rule breaker, the visibility of the rule-breaking, the availability of psychiatric or psychological treatment within the geographic area, and the type of norms that are broken. People who are admitted to psychiatric wards or mental hospitals are usually put there because their behavior, though not illegal, disturbs others who can no longer tolerate it. Thus, a *circuit of agents* is needed to define someone as a mental patient. Such circuits include both *informal social-control agents,* such as family members, friends, and neighbors, and *formal agents,* representing the community, such as the police, the clergy, social agencies, and physicians. These formal agents are sometimes known as *gatekeepers* because they act as guards, regulating the entry of people into a variety of treatments.

Once in the hospital, other social processes lead to further changes in the self-concept. Stripped of outside roles and everyday possessions, such as clothing or pens and paper, patients find that all information about them is recorded and shared by the staff, who discredit any attempts made by the patient to maintain a positive, private, respectable self-concept. Instead, one is asked to face up to one's illness. Patients respond in different ways, but the end result is that the self is no longer private. A new self, adapting to the situation, is gradually reconstructed, but unlike the old self, it "is not a fortress but a small open city" (Goffman 1961). (See also our discussion of self and deindividuation in Chapter 5.)

Career contingencies involve a series of social factors that determine outcomes for people by opening up or closing off certain options.

A circuit of agents includes both informal networks and formal agents.

Gatekeepers regulate entry into treatment agencies.

After Treatment, What? Shedding the label of mental patient is not easy. Most of us have stereotypes of particular kinds of deviants, including mental patients. These are reinforced and continually reaffirmed through ordinary social interaction. "You must be some kind of a nut" indicates social disapproval. Such slogans as "We may be crazy but we've slashed prices to below cost" are common. In the media, the former mental patient who commits an offense is immediately identified as a *mental* patient, although she or he occupies other statuses and roles. "Mental patient" becomes the person's master status trait, and others respond with stereotypes about how a mental patient behaves. People who have ever been treated for mental illness are expected to be irrational, unpredictable, unpleasant, and perhaps violent. Like other stigmatized people, those labeled as mentally ill risk being locked into a deviant role unless they conceal their stigma.

Although the type of mental hospital just described has become increasingly an institution of the past, the process of stigmatization of those labeled as mentally ill continues. As increasing numbers of people once in mental hospitals have been

This woman has been deinstitutionalized and lives in a shelter for the homeless. What kinds of problems do you think she has adapting to social situations? (© George Cohen)

A New Career—Homelessness

Since the mid-1980s, attention has been focused on the growing population of homeless Americans. Almost by definition, the exact number cannot be known; it is a floating population, many of whom find refuge out of the public eye. Some sleep in doorways or subway and train stations; many wander aimlessly in search of food and comfort; others beg for money; and all cause discomfort to those who see them. Emergency shelters have been set up in many towns and cities, but fewer than half of the homeless are likely to have spent any time in such facilities. The National Coalition for the Homeless estimates that approximately 3 million Americans are without shelter, primarily in the major cities on both the East and West coasts, in the North and South. Even small towns in relatively wealthy areas have their homeless.

It is commonly assumed that the recent rapid increase in homelessness is a result of the deinstitutionalization of mental hospital patients, but that movement took place over a decade ago and cannot account for the current cohorts of "street people." Relatively few of today's homeless have ever been hospitalized for psychological problems, nor are they mentally ill, alcoholic, or drug users. Although many do fit the stereotype of being elderly and loners, most are young—children and their mothers, young adults with limited job skills, and temporarily unemployed men. They are not sleeping in doorways out of choice but out of necessity.

The primary cause of homelessness in America today is lack of affordable housing for people with low incomes and limited employment. Most of the homeless for whom information is available had previously lived in urban slum areas where the housing stock has been abandoned by landlords. The tenements and single-room occupancy hotels that once housed large numbers of poor families and single people are rapidly being converted to expensive condominiums with government subsidies to the owners. At the same time, under the Reagan administration, no new public housing was built. In New York City alone, over 100,000 single-room occupancy units were lost between 1971 and 1986. The displaced tenants have nowhere else to go but to the streets or to temporary shelters that are often even less safe and sanitary than no shelter at all. This pattern has been repeated in every major city in America, where housing for the poor has been replaced by luxury apartments and exclusive shops for the wealthy. (See chapter 19 for further discussion of this urban pattern.)

Another major cause of increased homelessness is the surge in unemployment in the 1981–2 recession—about 10 percent—and the slow pace of decline in the years since. The large number of intact families in emergency shelters are almost all accounted for by loss of income due to unemployment and eviction for nonpayment of rent. Yet even when reemployed, many workers will be receiving minimal wages that are not adequate to house a family. As we will detail in Chapter 12, the kinds of jobs available to low-skill workers are very different from those in the past.

Yet rather than tackle these very real and correctable causes of the homelessness epidemic, most federal and state authorities continue to stigmatize street people as mentally ill, lazy, or addicts—a form of blaming the victim. This absolves the government from responsibility for changing the situation. The interpretation is also functional for most citizens: In a nation where owning one's home is a badge of success, the homeless remind us of how fragile our security can be. By defining homelessness as deviance, we are reaffirmed in our righteousness.

Deinstitutionalization involves the release of mental patients into the community.

released to the community *(deinstitutionalized)*, they have found that the label of "mental patient" affects their quality of life. For example, some former mental patients live in special community residences for the mentally ill that are simply mini-institutions where little effort or money is invested in "normalizing" their behavior (Markson 1986). And, as increasing numbers of people, both with and without histories of known mental illness, have become homeless due to social and economic factors (Snow, Baker, and Anderson 1986, Gao 1985, Hombs and Snyder 1982), this new category of people is stigmatized and victimized (Doolin 1986). Shopping-bag women—a category of homeless women who carry their possessions with them—are, for example, the butt of jokes and often physical violence, unless, of course, they are able to "pass" as "normal." But the behavioral adaptations required by street life, where private acts must be conducted in public places, tend to reinforce the development of a new self. Like the self of the long-term mental patient, the self of homeless people becomes "a small open city."

Changing Definitions of Deviance: Sexual Behavior

Sexual scripts suggest appropriate behaviors and attitudes (Simon and Gagnon 1986), and give the answers to questions of who? when? where? and why? They specify appropriate partners; who should lead; how long the encounter should last; and, most importantly, what the activity should mean. Researchers have identified two competing sexual scripts in the United States: the traditional, restrictive, and male-centered script, and an emerging, expressive view of sexuality. The per-

sistence of both has created ambiguity for many people caught between the two. College students, for example, are often caught between their parents' more traditional scripts and the modern scripts supported by the mass media and by peers. Social ambivalence and change are reflected in interpersonal and personal confusion.

What may seem surprising is the fervor and strength with which some people try to persuade others of the correctness of their views. There are, however, political reasons for this: The breaking of any social rule is a threat to its existence: it shows everyone that breaking the rule is at least possible. Douglas and Waksler (1982) formulate four general ideas, stemming from symbolic interaction and labeling theory, regarding sexual conformity and deviance.

1. Humans are capable of a vast array of sexual activities.
2. All societies encourage some and discourage other sexual activities. The

Changes in the norms for sexual expression bring activities into the open which have previously existed, but not in the public eye. (© Theo Westenberg/SYGMA)

range of rules runs from the celibacy of nuns and monks to the permissiveness of advocates of free love. Yet even the most open groups set some restrictions and establish norms.

3. The openly stated reasons for restricting sexual activity are quite varied and may conceal the latent functions of such prohibitions, which are often social and political.

4. A full understanding of sexual behavior requires information about both rule-breakers and rule-makers.

Although accurate statistics on the frequency of premarital intercourse among students are not available, results from numerous studies (Furstenberg 1986, Harris 1986) indicate that college students of the 1980s differ from their counterparts of the 1940s and 1950s in several important ways:

- Male students today are far more likely to have sexual intercourse before marriage; compared to about 45 percent in the 1940s, by the 1980s, about 90 percent had had sexual relations.
- Even more strikingly, female students are almost as sexually active as males. Although only about 25 percent of female students in the 1940s had sexual intercourse before marriage, studies indicate that this number had tripled by the mid-1980s.
- Compared to college males in the 1940s, much of whose sexual activity involved contacts with prostitutes, few college men visit prostitutes today.
- Students are much more likely to live together when unmarried than in past decades.

Have the *norms* regarding premarital sexual relations changed that much? It depends. For example, students at religious colleges, students at schools in the South and the Midwest, students who attend church regularly, and those holding traditional religious beliefs are less likely to have intercourse than those at non-church schools, at colleges in the Northeast or California, or those who do not attend church regularly or who do not hold traditional views about sexuality (Rosen and Rosen 1981). Campus norms, geographic patterns, and one's reference groups clearly set the social context for patterns of sexual behavior.

What one's friends do also influences one's own sexual behavior and seems to be more important than either religious or family rules (Delamater 1981). When norms conflict, students tend to choose the forms of behavior also chosen by their friends. Yet, this choice has a price. When sexual norms are limited and clear, students could feel restricted, but at least the rules are known. When the norms are vague and the options for behavior are greater, students experience anomie and may become sexually involved in order to conform to peer norms. This choice, too, has its price: the disapproval of college administrators, parents, and others.

Has there been a sexual revolution? Recent data indicate that among fifteen-to-sixteen-year-olds 20 percent are sexually active and among seventeen-year-olds a full 50 percent have experienced sexual intercourse (Guttmacher Institute, 1986). However, the evidence suggests that although behavior has changed, there are still multiple norms for premarital sexual conduct (Stayton 1984). Somewhat more than four in ten teenagers, for example, have said that they think teenage values in sexual freedom are too liberal; only about one in four disagree (*Ms.* 1983). Many are caught between competing norms (Zelnick, Kantner, and Ford 1981, Carrera 1984). There are also some countertrends that seem to be influencing the sexual behavior of single women and men. The presence of sexually transmitted diseases, particularly Herpes Simplex Virus Type II among 20 million Americans, and the recent spread of AIDS among heterosexual men and women, is having a strong impact on contemporary sexual scripts. The sexual script advocating permissiveness with or without affection is being reexamined in light of the devastating consequences of AIDS. Chastity, faithfulness, and "safe sex" are increasingly dominant trends in premarital sexual behavior. It would appear that there is another shift in the way sex before marriage is defined; it was seen as deviant before 1960, more and more acceptable in the 1960s, 1970s, and early 1980s, so that abstinence was seen as deviant. Now, as we move into the second half of the 1980s, refraining from sex or at least having sex with only carefully selected partners, is becoming the norm once again. It remains to be seen what the 1990s will bring.

Summary

In every human group some behaviors become defined as appropriate standards of role performance. Once these norms are developed, conformity is encouraged and enforced through agents of social control. Norms set boundaries for acceptable behavior and simultaneously define behavior that is beyond the boundary. The term deviance refers to activities that violate the expectations of others and the accepted rules of appropriateness. A deviant is one whom others define as requiring attention by the agents or agencies of social control.

In general, deviant behavior can be seen as a functional necessity in any society. Deviance mobilizes the community to support community values and norms; it clarifies the boundaries between the accepted and the unacceptable; it provides channels for the release of antisocial feelings; and it can become the cutting edge of long-term changes that enhance the group's adaptability.

A great deal of research has focused on the individual causes of deviance. Theories based on biological differences have not demonstrated a direct link between a particular biological characteristic and a specific form of deviant behavior. Nor have psychological theories established any clear relationship between early childhood experiences or mental states and a given act of nonconformity.

Sociological theories of deviance, by contrast, focus on the deviant act in its full social context: who does what, when, and where, and how others respond. It is not the action that is central, but the response, or the effect that the action has on others and society, that defines the act. Labeling occurs when the behavior is judged to be outside normative boundaries, and when a person is held responsible for that behavior.

Once labeled, the deviant experiences varying degrees of stigmatization. When the label is internalized as one's definition of oneself, a deviant career is launched. The labeled person may seek to avoid negative sanctions by joining a deviant subculture that supports the stigmatized behavior and restores self-esteem.

Another sociological perspective seeks the source of deviance in the social structure rather than in the individual. When commitment to socially approved goals and/or access to legitimate means of achieving these goals are blocked, people may choose nonnormative actions, rejecting either the goals or the means, or seeking to replace these with new ones. The refusal to conform can be a principle challenge to the norms for some higher social good.

Mental illness can be seen as residual deviance, that is, behavior that can be variously defined by different people under different circumstances. Mental illness is a social process involving labeling, stigmatization, internalization, career stages, and treatment. Although the treatment patterns for mental illness are changing, the stigma of being a mental patient remains. Moreover, "mental illness" is used as a term to disqualify other categories of people and to stigmatize them.

Definitions of deviance change slowly and unevenly, and many people are caught between conflicting norms in modern societies.

Suggested Readings

AKERS, RONALD. *Deviant Behavior: A Social Learning Approach,* 3rd ed. Belmont, California: Wadsworth, 1985. A comprehensive undergraduate text that stresses a social-learning approach to understanding deviance.

BECKER, HOWARD S. *The Outsiders: Studies in the Sociology of Deviance.* New York: Free Press, 1963. A classic study in which the labeling perspective is applied to the study of jazz musicians and marijuana smokers.

DOUGLAS, JACK D., and FRANCES CHAPUT WAKSLER. *The Sociology of Deviance: An Introduction.* Boston: Little, Brown, 1982. A comprehensive look at the sociological approaches to deviance, including good analyses of structural, subcultural, interactionist, and neosymbolic interaction.

ERIKSON, KAI. *Wayward Puritans.* New York: Wiley, 1966. Another classic in the labeling tradition, this time a historical analysis of the ways in which deviant behavior was created and dealt with in Puritan New England.

ERICKSON, PATRICIA G., EDUARD M. ADLAF, GLENN F. MURRAY, REGINALD G. SMART. *The Steel Drug: Cocaine in Perspective.* Lexington, Massachusetts: D. C. Heath, 1986. A very informative report on historical and contemporary problems associated with the use of cocaine.

ERMANN, M. DAVID, and RICHARD J. LUNDMAN. *Corporate and Governmental Deviance: Problems of Organizational Behavior in Contemporary Society,* 3rd ed. New York: Oxford University Press, 1987. Twelve essays dealing with the origins, patterns and reactions to corporate and government deviance.

GOFFMAN, ERVING. *Stigma: Notes on the Management of a Spoiled Identity.* Englewood Cliffs, New Jersey: Prentice-Hall, 1963. Goffman's title is self-explanatory. This essay deals with reactions to labeling: The ways in which a stigmatized individual protects her or his self-image and learns to negotiate social interaction.

HOPE, MARJORIE, and JAMES YOUNG. *The Faces of the Homeless.* Lexington, Massachusetts. D. C. Heath, 1987. A compassionate portrait of the growing population of the homeless in the United States.

RYAN, WILLIAM. *Blaming the Victim.* New York: Pantheon, 1971. The classic analysis of how definitions of social problems and the framing of policy debates create a dialogue in which the victims of social injustice are blamed for their fate.

SCHUR, EDWIN M. *Labeling Women Deviant: Gender, Stigma, and Social Control.* New York: Random House, 1984. Interesting examination of how gender behavior is controlled by stigmatizing and labeling undesirable individuals.

Part III
Social Differences and Inequality

The four chapters in Part III describe how personal characteristics such as strength, skill, skin color, age, gender, religion, and ethnicity (national origin) become bases of unequal evaluation and treatment within a society. *Stratification systems* are formed when people are placed in categories that are ranked from high to low on the basis of such traits. Stratification is a key structure in all but the most simple gathering bands, affecting people's life chances and choices.

Assuming that each social system has a limited supply of valued resources—goods, services, honor, affection, power over others—sociologists ask how such resources are distributed. Who gets more or less? And why? The study of stratification explores the links between personal differences and social inequality.

In Chapter 7, we discuss the general principles of social stratification, the distribution of resources in our society today, the consequences of inequality, and the opportunities for upward or downward movement in the stratification hierarchy. Chapter 8 focuses on the importance of gender in understanding the distribution of power, prestige, and property in social systems, and Chapter 9 explores chronological age as a basis of economic and social inequality. Chapter 10 covers race, religion, and ethnicity as determinants of social rank.

7

Social Stratification

WHO should be saved? Although many people might need a heart transplant, the supply of healthy hearts available for this purpose is extremely limited. If you were the hospital administrator with final say, what standards would you use to select which patients receive a transplant and which do not? Suppose that only five of the following eight persons could be chosen, whom would you choose, and why?

- A 50-year-old black male minister
- A 40-year-old white female homemaker
- A 30-year-old white male homosexual physicist
- A 25-year-old white Marxist professor
- A 16-year-old pregnant teenager
- A 60-year-old Hispanic female physician
- The 55-year-old governor of the state
- The 20-year-old disabled son of wealthy parents

Each of these descriptions contains a mix of ascribed and achieved characteristics, some of which are valued more highly in our society than others. Deciding social worth is a complicated process, and this mental experiment is designed to make you aware of your standards of judgment.

When we rank some kinds of people as more deserving than others, we create a *stratification system.* The essence of stratification is captured in one sentence from George Orwell's novel *Animal Farm* (1945): "...all the animals are equal here, but some are more equal than others." Is it always necessary that some people be more equal than others? What are the bases of inequality? And what are its consequences? In the three chapters of Part III we will examine the many theories and research findings on these crucial questions.

> **Stratification systems** rank some individuals and groups as more deserving than others.

Principles of Stratification

In all societies there are three kinds of valued resources: (1) *power*—the ability to impose one's will on others; (2) *prestige*—respect from others; and (3) *property*—wealth, whether measured in land, green paper rectangles, beads, oil, or yams. And in all societies more complex than simple gathering bands, these resources are unequally distributed among individuals and groups.

> **Power** is the ability to impose one's will on others. **Prestige** is measured by respect from others.

Because people who differ in their ascribed and achieved traits are evaluated differently, a *social hierarchy* is formed. A hierarchy is a set of ranked statuses from highest to lowest. Because both the most- and least-valued characteristics are likely to be relatively rare, status hierarchies tend to be diamond-shaped, narrower both at the top and at the bottom.

> **A social hierarchy** is a set of ranked statuses.

Once such a hierarchy is formed, people at different levels or *strata* (plural; the singular is *stratum*) can claim differing amounts of power, prestige, and property. In other words, a set of ranked statuses built on definitions of social worth is transformed into a hierarchy of control over societal resources. Stratification systems are both cause and consequence of inequality.

Although it is possible to imagine a society in which all members are equally valued and equally treated, the human experience appears to be that once a group's economy involves a division of labor beyond gathering, some tasks are considered more important than others, and the people who do different kinds of work are likely to be differentially (unequally) rewarded.

At the very least, labor is divided on the basis of age and sex. The more complex the society, or the more heterogeneous in terms of race, religion, and national origin, the more ways there are to evaluate people differently—by what they are or what they do. Such structures of inequality are typically explained and justified by theories of human nature and social needs.

Theoretical Perspectives

THE FUNCTIONAL THEORY OF STRATIFICATION

The *functional perspective* explains social structures in terms of the consequences of a given arrangement: "What happens because such-and-such a system exists...?" The functional analysis of stratification, in the classic formulation of Davis and Moore (1945), goes like this: Not all persons have the same abilities. Some will have more of those qualities needed and valued by members of a given society at a particular historical moment, such as strength, hunting skills, artistry, wisdom, or ambition. On the other side of the stratification equation is the fact that desired rewards are always limited in quantity, whether naturally or artificially (if everyone can have it, it loses its value as a symbol of superior performance).

Thus, if skills are unequally distributed within a population, it is in the interests of the group that those with the most ability use it for the well-being of all. In return, such persons deserve greater rewards—in admiration, command, or material goods—than do those with less important talents. The assumption is that people will not take risks or use their skills to help the group unless they are promised a reward worth the effort. This being the case, an unequal distribution of resources is functional for group survival.

Meritocracy is a hierarchy of talent.

Functionalists believe that stratification processes produce a hierarchy of talent, called a *meritocracy*—the rule of the most worthy or deserving. In other words, if in our society, the top positions are primarily occupied by white males, the functionalist takes this to reflect the actual distribution of abilities by race and sex. From a functional perspective, therefore, some forms of inequality are inevitable, beneficial to society, and a powerful motive to performance. This point of view is currently popular among writers on the political right (e.g. Gilder 1981, Goldberg 1986).

The functionalist position has been challenged by generations of sociologists. For example, Tumin (1953) immediately pointed out the potential dysfunctions of a system which could breed resentment over blocked opportunity. Moreover, inequality appears to be as much due to scarcity of top slots as to unequal abilities, and many top positions are inherited rather than earned. Furthermore, as Reinharz (1986) suggests in the case of gender, even if inequality were not inevitable, theoretical justifications most certainly are, as those in power try to prove their "natural" superiority.

CONFLICT THEORIES OF STRATIFICATION

In contrast to the functional approach, the conflict perspective, as described in Chapter 1, explains social structure as the outcome of struggles over scarce rewards, in which some individuals and groups may have an original advantage. Those already in power are able to make the rules that set limits on competition. In addition, as Karl Marx pointed out, the dominant ideas of any society are those of its dominant strata. This insight—that ideas are also social products—has been expanded by conflict theorists into the concept of *ideological hegemony* (Gramsci 1959). *Hegemony* means sphere of influence or control, and *ideological hegemony* refers to the control of cultural symbols—beliefs, values, ideals of justice, and so forth (Bourdieu 1985). Because those who own or control the media, educational institutions, and other sources of information come from the higher strata, they are likely to promote definitions of reality that justify their own success (Verba and Orren 1985). In other words, from the conflict perspective, the functional theory of stratification, by emphasizing personal qualities that account for success or failure, can itself be seen as an example of cultural hegemony.

In contrast, conflict explanations of inequality focus on *structural* rather than personal variables. Structural variables include the distribution of occupations in a society, past and present hiring practices, labor markets, the degree of unionization, the organization of the workplace, and the diversity of firms and businesses in a community. These are characteristics of social systems, not of individuals, and they play an important part in creating and maintaining inequality among various groups of workers.

Ideological hegemony refers to control of cultural symbols such as beliefs, values, and ideas.

According to the functionalist point of view how do people come to occupy jobs such as these? From the conflict perspective would the reasoning be the same? (© Michal Heron/Woodfin Camp and Associates; © Peter Arnold, Inc.)

Current research from the conflict perspective locates inequality in the worker's relationship to the productive process, not simply ownership of the means of production, but the range of skills required for a task, control over the pacing of work, and the level of supervision. Different positions in an organization also permit varying degrees of control over the resources of that organization, another important factor (Spaeth 1985). Although linked to many of the same issues raised by Marx over a century ago, conflict analysis today is increasingly sophisticated in both its theory and methods.

A UNIFIED VIEW

The functional and conflict perspectives need not be considered mutually exclusive. The functional model could account for an original stratification hierarchy, while conflict factors maintain inequality long after the basic needs of the group have been met. Thus, people with unusual luck or talents may claim or amass great power and wealth during certain historical periods. Once established, they seek to pass along these advantages to their children, whether or not the offspring have any special skills. The transmission of social status is possible because the members of each generation are unequal in social position from the beginning. One analogy is a foot race in which some runners are naturally faster; some runners have better equipment and training provided by their parents; and some runners are at a disadvantage because of poor diet, lack of training, and inadequate equipment. More important, however, is the fact that the runners do not begin at the same starting line.

Dimensions of Social Stratification

Social stratification refers to hierarchies of statuses based on unequal distribution of power, prestige, and property.

The term *social stratification,* then, refers to hierarchies of statuses in a society that reflect the unequal distribution of power, prestige, and property. For conflict theorists, who view history as the outcome of a struggle between the few who own the means of production (from spears to plows to land to factories) and the many who do

not, it often seems that there is a basic unity in the dimensions of stratification. That is, wealth is power, and both can be used to command respect.

Max Weber, however, emphasized the need to consider three separate types of groupings, even though they cannot always be separated in real life:

1. *Class* refers to people at the same economic level, who may or may not become aware of their common interests and form social classes.
2. *Status groups* are based on the degree of prestige of their members, who tend also to share a common life-style. The honor given a particular status is not necessarily determined by class position; in some societies, the greatest respect is given to those who renounce worldly things.
3. *Parties* are political groupings that may or may not express class interests (see Chap. 13).

In other words, we should examine each dimension separately—political parties, prestige groups, and social classes—before coming to conclusions about the stratification system of any society. Let us turn now to a discussion of the distribution of power, prestige, and property in the United States today.

POWER

Power, defined as the ability to impose one's will on others, is a social resource that is unequally distributed in almost every relationship, group, and society. Some individuals and groups have greater decision-making force than others.

Authority refers to power that belongs to a socially recognized status (e.g. the position of president, police officer, or parent) and which is, therefore, considered legitimate by other members of the society. Although a full discussion of political authority appears in Chapter 13, it is worth noting here that people who hold important government positions tend to come from the upper half of the property hierarchy. Few people leave public office poorer than when they entered, and very few of the poor have ever run for office or been appointed to high posts. Thus, position on one hierarchy can be used to gain status in another—wealth to gain power, and power to gain wealth.

Authority refers to socially legitimated power.

Authority resides in socially recognized status. Corazon Aquino, President of the Philippines, came to power after the overthrow of Ferdinand Marcos whose authority was no longer legitimized by the majority of Philippine citizens. (© Christopher Morris/ Black Star)

Other forms of legitimate power in everyday life include the control that parents exercise over children, that of husbands over wives in many societies, of employers over employees, and of teachers over students. But not all power is considered legitimate; for example, leaders of organized crime enjoy great economic and political power while operating outside of the law (see Chap. 16).

Influence can be defined as the ability to persuade others to follow one's will and is based less on occupying a particular social status than on interpersonal skills. Influential people often also possess unique talents or knowledge, or they may be close to people in authority.

Influence is the ability to persuade others to follow one's will.

PRESTIGE

Prestige (or status honor) depends on the respect given by others. Some societies honor the wise and humble, others the boastful and warlike. In modern industrial societies, prestige is based largely on occupation and income, especially if the occupation requires a long period of training (see Table 7-1). When respondents are asked to judge various occupations in terms of importance and value, the highest ranking is given to *professionals* such as lawyers, doctors, scientists, and professors, who have spent many years training for their jobs, who control the numbers and types of people who can enter their field, and who typically earn high incomes.

Lowest rankings, conversely, are given to people whose jobs require little training, who do "dirty" work, or who must take orders without question. At the bottom of

most prestige-ranking lists, for example, are such occupations as janitor, garbage collector, nursing-home aide, restaurant worker, gas-station attendant, and taxi driver. Although these are not always the lowest paying jobs in the society, they are considered of low prestige.

Occupational rankings are remarkably similar across all modern industrial societies, with professionals highest and unskilled workers lowest. This universal status hierarchy lends itself to a functional explanation: all complex societies have an elaborate division of labor, with occupational roles requiring different levels of skills and control over information. Where skills and information are difficult to obtain and can be restricted to a small group, these few can claim greater rewards (Trieman 1977). What the functional approach does not explain, however, is how occupational rank is transmitted within families from one generation to another.

Although respondents do make a distinction between the economic rewards of an occupation, on the one hand, and its value to the society, on the other, both considerations enter into prestige rankings, so that agreement on social value becomes a justification for economic inequality (Hope 1982). Prestige judgments are also influenced by whether women or men dominate the occupation, with "women's work" typically rated lower.

But the link between occupational prestige and income is not perfect: college professors, whose prestige rank is quite high, tend to have incomes only slightly above the national average. Conversely, lowly rated garbage collectors or dockworkers often benefit from relatively high union-

TABLE 7-1   The prestige ratings of occupations in the U.S.

(Scale runs from 100 (highest) to 1 (lowest); Score = average score for the sample)

Occupation	Score	Occupation	Score	Occupation	Score	Occupation	Score
Physician	82	Registered nurse	62	Foreman	45	Baker	34
College professor	78	Pharmacist	61	Real estate agent	44	Shoe repairman	33
Judge	76	Veterinarian	60	Fireman	44	Bulldozer operator	33
Lawyer	76	Elementary school		Postal clerk	43	Bus driver	32
Physicist	74	teacher	60	Advertising agent	42	Truck driver	32
Dentist	74	Accountant	57	Mail carrier	42	Cashier	31
Banker	72	Librarian	55	Railroad conductor	41	Sales clerk	29
Aeronautical		Statistician	55	Typist	41	Meatcutter	28
engineer	71	Social worker	52	Plumber	41	Housekeeper	25
Architect	71	Funeral director	52	Farmer	41	Longshoreman	24
Psychologist	71	Computer specialist	51	Telephone operator	40	Gas-station	
Airline pilot	70	Stockbroker	51	Carpenter	40	attendant	22
Chemist	69	Reporter	51	Welder	40	Cab driver	22
Minister	69	Office manager	50	Dancer	38	Elevator operator	21
Civil engineer	68	Bank teller	50	Barber	38	Bartender	20
Biologist	68	Electrician	49	Jeweler	37	Waiter	20
Geologist	67	Machinist	48	Watchmaker	37	Farm laborer	18
Sociologist	66	Police officer	48	Bricklayer	36	Maid/servant	18
Political scientist	66	Insurance agent	47	Airline stewardess	36	Garbage collector	17
Mathematician	65	Musician	46	Meter reader	36	Janitor	17
High school teacher	63	Secretary	46	Mechanic	35	Shoeshiner	9

SOURCE: James A. Davis and Tom Smith, *General Social Survey Cumulative File, 1972–1982*. Ann Arbor, Michigan. Inter-University Consortium for Political and Social Research.

negotiated wage scales. Furthermore, many people in low-prestige jobs maintain a sense of self-worth through their

While occupational prestige and income usually correspond, sometimes they don't. Garbage collectors have a low status occupation but in many cities the salary range is substantial. (© Paul Fusco/Magnum)

relationships with family members and coworkers, or through their mastery of whatever skills are required for that occupation, e.g. the bartender with the best memory (Walsh and Taylor 1982).

In other cases, low-ranked occupations associated with illegal drugs bring very high rewards in terms of income and power, and successful criminals could be figures of prestige in their local communities. Generally, however, the distribution of respect within modern societies is related to training, skills, and income. In turn, people in high prestige occupations have the power to impose their particular version of justice and order on the society as a whole (Goode 1977). Although the fit is far from perfect, power, prestige, and property are clearly linked.

PROPERTY

Every society has certain items that signify material success. In the United States, we measure wealth by counting the money value of everything owned by household members, including houses, cars, stocks and bonds, savings accounts, life insurance, and so forth.

Wealth. The actual distribution of property in the United States is very difficult to determine because most very wealthy people have their money in assets that cannot be easily traced (foreign bank accounts, safe-deposit boxes, works of art, and the like). Nonetheless, several recent studies have provided valuable new data on American wealth holders (Bureau of the Census 1986; Joint Economic Committee 1986; Rose 1986).

In 1984, the Bureau of the Census conducted a special study of household wealth and asset ownership based on information from a large national random sample, the first such study since 1963. The percentages of American households at each level of net worth (assets minus debts) is shown in Table 7-2.

As these data indicate, one-third of American households have assets worth less than $10,000. Most of the remainder have some money in the bank, own a car, and are partial owners of their own home. But only 2 percent have assets greater than $500,000.

Asset ownership varies systematically by age, sex, race, education, occupational status, and yearly income. The largest difference is by race, with white households accumulating assets *ten* times those of

The economic differences among wealthy Americans and those with more limited means translate into important differences in life-styles and life chances. The wealthy can spend their money in a number of places including the many boutiques housed in the Trump Tower on Manhattan's fashionable Fifth Avenue. For those interested, apartments are also available, from between $500,000 and $2 million dollars. Others, with more limited economic means, shop in less trendy places such as Orchard Street, on the lower East Side of Manhattan. (© Jeff Perkell/The Stock Market; © Bill Wassman/The Stock Market)

TABLE 7-2 Household net worth: 1984

Net Worth in Dollars	Percent of U.S. Households
Negative or zero	11.0
$1–$4,999	15.3
$5,000–$9,999	6.4
$10,000–$24,999	12.4
$25,000–$49,999	14.4
$50,000–$99,999	19.2
$100,000–$249,999	15.3
$250,000–$499,999	4.0
$500,000 and over	2.0
	100.0

SOURCE: U.S. Bureau of the Census, Current Population Reports, Series P-70, No. 7, *Household Wealth and Asset Ownership: 1984.* U.S. Government Printing Office, Washington, D.C., 1986, p. 10.

black households. Married couples have more assets than the nonmarried; and households headed by persons fifty-five and over are wealthier than those headed by younger persons. According to these data, the top 12 percent of wealth holders account for about 38 percent of total asset ownership in the United States. But the definition of assets in this study did *not* include pension rights, life insurance policies, jewelry, works of art, and home furnishings, nor did the survey include many extremely wealthy households.

Using this broader definition of wealth and assets, Rose (1986: 31) estimates that the top 10 percent of wealth holders own

The Disappearing Middle

Is the United States experiencing a major shift in income distribution? During the 1960s and 1970s, the income gap between rich and poor was narrowing, the proportion in poverty was reduced, and most Americans considered themselves part of the comfortable middle. In the 1980s, however, this trend has been reversed and the income gap between the top and bottom has widened. The number of adults in the Bureau of Labor Statistics "high budget" category has increased by almost 3 percent, and those in the lowest income category increased by over 5 percent (Rose 1986).

Among the factors most commonly cited to explain this U-turn on equality are the following:

- changes in the composition of the labor force with the entry of baby-boom young adults and women, whose earnings are relatively low
- the effects of income losses to workers during the recession of 1981–1982
- the breakdown of union discipline and power
- trade deficits that endanger jobs in the relatively high-paying export manufacturing sector
- federal policies which cut off assistance to lower income families while reducing the tax liabilities of the wealthy

While all these factors have contributed to income inequality, the primary cause, according to one recent analysis (Tilly 1986), lies in deliberate steps taken by major corporations. As real wages for workers grew throughout the 1960s and 1970s, corporate profits were reduced. This problem was worsened by foreign competition in the late 1970s. In response, corporations relocated to nonunionized states, replaced workers with automated equipment, demanded "give-backs" from unions,

increased the use of part-time employees, and ultimately moved manufacturing tasks to less developed countries. In the process, high-paying factory jobs in this country were eliminated, low-pay, part-time jobs increased, as did the ranks of top level managers needed to carry out these policies.

It remains to be seen whether or not the new jobs in service-oriented and high-tech industries will pay as well as the lost ones in heavy-goods manufacturing (auto and steel, especially). Some economists believe that, on average, there will be little slippage in wages (Lawrence 1985), while others see growing polarization of the labor force with white-collar office workers sliding into near poverty (Baillod and Walliman 1985). In addition, because the decline in high-wage blue-collar jobs comes just at the moment that women and blacks finally gained access to them, it is unlikely that current race and gender income gaps will be narrowed.

In the meantime, the 1980s decline in real wages for most employees means that "the American Dream" of bettering oneself may have become "the impossible dream" for previously favored workers as well (Greenhouse 1986).

SOURCES: Baillod, Jurg, and Isidor Walliman, "From Pre-Industrial Office Work to the Age of Micro-Electronics," *Humanity and Society*, 9 (November 1985), 428–442; Bennett Harrison, Chris Tilly, and Barry Bluestone, *Smaller Slices of the Pie*, Center on Budget and Policy Priorities, 1986; Steven Greenhouse, "The Average Guy Takes It on the Chin," *New York Times*, July 13, 1986, Section 3, p. 1 ff.; Robert Z. Lawrence, "The Middle Class is Alive and Well," *New York Times*, June 23, 1985, p. F3; Stephen J. Rose, *The American Profile Poster*, New York: Pantheon, 1986; Lester Thurow, "The Hidden Sting of the Trade Deficit," *New York Times*, January 19, 1986, p. F3; Chris Tilly, "The Great U-Turn," Department of Urban Studies, MIT, 1986.

about 64 percent of the total wealth of the nation, compared to 3 percent of the total owned by the entire bottom *half* of the wealth hierarchy.

A second set of new data on wealth and assets comes from a survey carried out by the Federal Reserve Board in 1983, for which the very wealthy were *over*-sampled and a broad range of sources of wealth was measured. These data indicate an even higher degree of concentration of wealth, with the top 10 percent holding nearly 72 percent of the nation's total privately owned assets (Joint Economic Committee, 1986).

Comparing the distribution of wealth in

1963 and 1983, the congressional Joint Economic Committee also found that the wealth share of the top one-half of one percent of households (the "super rich," with assets of $2.5 million and over) had increased from 25 percent of the total to 35 percent, as seen in Figure 7-1.

The "very" and "super" rich tend to be drawn from the ranks of business, especially banking, insurance, and real estate. And, contrary to earlier data, a greater share of these fortunes comes from accumulated earnings rather than from inherited wealth. Nonetheless, starting with wealth remains the best predictor of staying at the top.

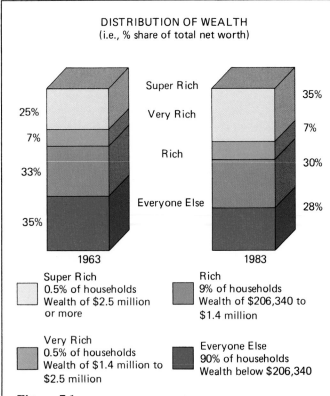

DISTRIBUTION OF WEALTH
(i.e., % share of total net worth)

Super Rich
Very Rich
Rich
Everyone Else

1963 — 25%, 7%, 33%, 35%

1983 — 35%, 7%, 30%, 28%

Super Rich
0.5% of households
Wealth of $2.5 million
or more

Very Rich
0.5% of households
Wealth of $1.4 million to
$2.5 million

Rich
9% of households
Wealth of $206,340 to
$1.4 million

Everyone Else
90% of households
Wealth below $206,340

Figure 7-1
Source: Joint Economic Committee, U.S. Congress, *The Concentration of Wealth in the United States,* July 1986, p. 35 reprinted with the permission of *The Wall Street Journal,* Aug. 15, 1986, p. 1.

Income. Because of the difficulties in measuring personal and family assets, sociologists often prefer to use data on yearly earned income. Income distributions will vary by whether the persons, families, or households are counted. The most accurate measure is *household* income, including both family and single-person units. The distribution of income in the U.S. by race and Spanish origin, by households in 1984 is shown in Table 7-3.

As you can see, household income varies by race and ethnic origin. In 1985, the median income for white households was $29,152, compared to $16,786 for black and $19,027 for Hispanic households (Bureau of the Census, 1986b). While some of this difference is due to the higher proportion of single-parent households among blacks, a great deal is due to the structural factors mentioned earlier: where people are located in the occupational system and the prevailing wage scales.

The median income for households headed by women, no husband present, was $13,660, in contrast to $31,100 for married-couple families. When both husband and wife are in the labor force, median household income rises to $36,431, compared to $24,556 for households where the wife is not employed.

In terms of the income hierarchy, it is best to be white, married, and male. In the

TABLE 7-3   Household income, United States: 1984, by race and Spanish origin, in *percents*

Household Income	All	White	Black	Spanish Origin
Under 5,000	7.9	6.6	18.5	12.4
5,000–9,999	13.2	12.4	20.3	17.3
10,000–14,999	12.1	11.8	15.3	14.8
15,000–19,999	11.4	11.4	11.9	11.7
20,000–24,999	10.4	10.6	8.8	11.5
25,000–29,999	9.2	9.6	6.9	8.8
30,000–34,999	7.7	8.0	4.8	6.5
35,000–39,999	6.3	6.5	3.6	4.8
40,000–44,999	5.2	5.4	3.0	3.9
45,000–49,999	3.9	4.1	2.2	2.5
50,000–59,999	5.2	5.5	2.5	2.5
60,000–74,999	3.8	4.1	1.4	2.0
75,000 and over	3.8	4.1	.8	1.4

Bureau of the Census, Current Population Reports, Special Studies P–23, No. 147, "After-Tax Money Income Estimates of Households: 1984," Washington, D.C.: U.S.G.P.O. July 1986, p. 7–8.

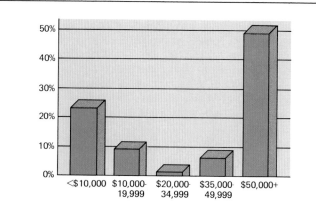

Figure 7-2
Changes in Family Income: 1975–1985 (Percent increase in number of families in each income group, 1975–1985, after adjusting for inflation.) (Source: *American Demographics,* Vol. 8, No. 12, December 1986, p. 14.)

at the higher and lower ends of the income spectrum have increased (Harrison et al. 1986, Rose 1986, Thurow 1986). (See Figure 7-2.)

SOCIOECONOMIC STATUS

Social scientists have long looked for one simplified measure of social rank. The common usage today is to refer to *socioeconomic status (SES)* based on a combination of income, occupational prestige, and education. In most American studies, SES is used as a measure of another abstract concept: *social class.*

Figure 7-3 shows the distribution of American adults on the basis of education, occupation, and income in 1984, from which a rough SES hierarchy can be derived.

Class is perhaps the most powerful variable in the social sciences because almost every other factor of interest to us is influenced by it, from life expectancy to life satisfaction. The measurement of social

Socioeconomic status (SES) is a measure based on a combination of income, occupational prestige, and education.

past several years, however, the proportion of middle-income households appears to have declined, while the percentages

Figure 7-3
Dimensions of SES, 1984

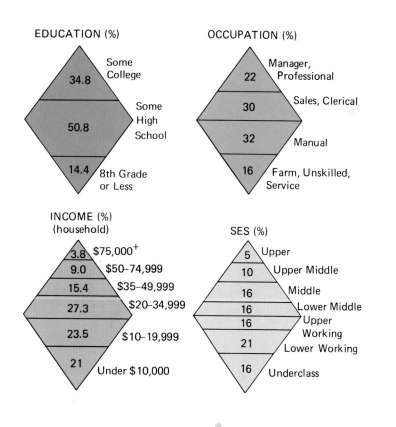

class and the tracing of its effects have been a primary field of sociological inquiry.

Social Class in America

MEASURING SOCIAL CLASS

There are many ways of defining and measuring social class. We have just described the use of an SES index. But many sociologists object to this method because it is based on characteristics of individuals. An alternative approach, from the conflict perspective, focuses on particular features of the job: the *social relations of production* (Wright et al. 1982). Specifically, the relations of production involve the worker's degree of control over decision making, the pacing and sequence of one's own work and that of others.

When these variables—self-direction and supervision—are used to measure social class, the working class becomes the largest category because there are so many employees who do not control the conditions of their own labor or that of other workers. In fact, says one researcher, there is a "... fundamental class cleavage ... between persons with some authority and those with none." When authority is defined as "control over organizational resources ... the lower class [constitutes] a majority of the population." (Spaeth 1985). This is in contrast to the definitions that divide the labor force by white-collar/ blue-collar, or manual (using one's hands)/ nonmanual (using one's brains). Under the relations of production criteria, many white-collar, nonmanual occupations are

really working class, as are women's "pink collar" jobs (hairdressing, waitressing, retail sales, and the like).

Furthermore, people who are in the same job category could have very different degrees of control over their work. For example, a self-employed electrician can choose where and when to work, in contrast to an electrician employed by a utility company. And both types of electrician could have greater control over the conditions of their labor than do white-collar salespersons or office workers.

The class strata produced by the relational perspective are shown in Table 7-4. Not only do workers make up the single largest category, but this working class is disproportionately composed of blacks and women (Wright 1985). (Stratification by gender and race are discussed in Chapters 8 and 10.)

The concept of social class as defined by relations of production owes much to the pioneering work of Karl Marx. As refined and operationalized by contemporary scholars, we can identify two major dimensions of social class depending upon whether one owns the means of production and has control over one's labor. As seen in Figure 7-4, the two variables— ownership and control—can be cross-tabulated to produce a *property space* of four cells describing class location.

Capitalists enjoy both ownership of businesses and control over the labor power of others. *Managers* control the labor of others but are also employees of the owners. *Petit bourgeoise* is a French phrase for small-scale business persons, such as shopkeepers or the self-employed; they own their own places of business, but

TABLE 7-4. Relational model of the American class structure, by sex and race, 1980

Class Category	Men %	Women %	White %	Black %
Employers (large)	2.7	0.8	—	—
Employers (small)	7.4	4.3	—	—
Self-employed (no employees)	6.3	7.4	7.4	1.7
Managers	20.8	12.2	18.4	8.3
Supervisors	14.2	11.2	12.0	11.7
Employees with some self-direction	9.1	9.9	9.5	13.6
Workers	39.6	54.0	43.9	64.0

Adapted from Eric Olin Wright, Cynthia Costello, David Hachen, and Joey Sprague, "The American Class Structure," *American Sociological Review*, 1982, 47; 715, 722.

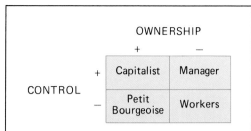

Figure 7-4
A Property Space for Relational Social Class (Adapted from Wright and Perrone, 1977; Robinson, 1984)

do not control the work of others. The true *working class* thus consists of people who are neither owners nor employers.

Another way of looking at social class is to examine *qualitative* or "life-style" differences, as evidenced in leisure activities, clothing, home furnishings, taste in music and art, even preferred foods (Warner 1938, Centers 1949, Bourdieu 1985). These variations both reflect social position and serve to maintain the stratification system, as cultural differences are passed on from one generation to another (see the discussion of *cultural capital* later in this chapter and in Chapter 14).

CLASS AWARENESS AND SELF-PERCEPTION

Class awareness involves recognition of differences in income, occupational prestige, and life-style and one's own class position.

It is relatively simple for a sociologist to select one or more objective indicators of social class—education, income, occupation, degree of control over work, material possessions, and life-style preferences. But how do Americans themselves make class distinctions? In some studies, income was the primary factor (Coleman and Rainwater 1978); in others, education and occupation (Nock and Rossi 1979). Among farmers (Larson et al. 1983), education and income were important but so also was the number of hired workers under one's supervision, a relational variable. And in their analysis of class identification among American blacks, Cannon and Dill (1981) found that respondents placed themselves in the middle or working class on the basis of the social relations of production (managers v. workers) rather than on the prestige ranking of their occupation.

The most extensive recent national study of class awareness in the United States was conducted in the early 1980s by Jackman and Jackman (1983). The researchers found that Americans do indeed distinguish social class, have strong feelings about their own class identification, and tend to associate with status peers (equals). These findings fit Weber's definition of classes as "status groups" originating in common economic interests and resulting in a shared sense of community. Class awareness was strongest among those who characterized themselves as poor (8 percent) or working class (37 percent).

In assigning a class position to themselves and others, respondents used the standard objective variables of income, education, and occupational status, but also included job authority, control over the pacing of one's work, and various life-style factors. As a result, half of the white-collar clerical workers identified themselves as working class, and over 40 percent of blue-collar workers placed themselves in the middle class. It would appear that most Americans consider the appropriate variables and are rather sophisticated amateur social scientists.

CLASS CONSCIOUSNESS

The overall conclusion from recent research is that Americans are very much aware of class differences despite the general tendency to think of oneself as "middle class." There is, however, a critical distinction between *class awareness* and *class consciousness*. People can recognize differences in income, occupational prestige, and life-style but this awareness may not be central to their self-definition or their political orientation.

The myth of classlessness in America is due partly to wishful thinking and partly to the absence of class-based political parties which are common in Europe (Gallie 1983, Rubin 1986). Among the many reasons most often cited for the lack of class consciousness in our society are the following: (1) absence of an hereditary aristocracy, i.e. a privileged class based on blood ties; (2) the ideal of equality that has shaped our political system; (3) the image of America as a nation of immigrants where anything was possible; (4) failure of organized labor to create a sense of work-

Class consciousness occurs when class awareness becomes the central organizing point of self-definition and political actions.

The Working Class Male

DAVID HALLE

Dave Halle received his Ph.D. at Columbia University and is currently assistant professor of sociology at SUNY Stonybrook. He is the author of America's Working Man, 1984, and is currently pursuing research on the sociology of art, with a particular emphasis on the social context of art and photography in the home and in family life.

While my research has been about the American working class, it was in England, where I grew up, that I first became interested in blue-collar life. My father was a scientist employed by a company that manufactured glass in the industrial Midlands. This area was known as the "black country" because of the grime and smoke that its numerous factories produced. When I was a young boy, my father sometimes took me to the factory. I watched in awe as workers poked long, hollow rods into a furnace, withdrew a fiery mass of molten glass, and then blew down the rod, coaxing the shimmering globule into a beautiful, long-stemmed wine glass.

Later, as an undergraduate, I went to Oxford. University life there is lived in colleges; each college has its own green lawns and gardens, shady trees and pleasant benches, all surrounded by gigantic walls to mark off the outside world. The university town is charming and quaint. But on the perimeter of Oxford, at Cowley, are some of the largest factories in the country, producing automobiles. The two settings, university and factory, are very separate, and only the rare student has any contact with the industrial workers just two or three miles away. I disliked undergraduate life at Oxford; it seemed like a cocoon, detached and isolated from real life.

I chose to write my Ph.D. dissertation in Sociology at Columbia University, partly because the location, in the middle of New York City and on the edge of Harlem, was as unlike Oxford as possible. I decided to write about work in a highly automated plant—since there were conflicting theories in the sociological literature about the nature and impact of such work. But getting access to a highly automated plant was difficult. Management were suspicious and unwilling to grant access to outsiders. Finally I found a manager who would allow me to conduct a study. To my delight, the plant was in the industrial heartland of New Jersey, near the largest oil refinery on the East Coast—little chance of being cocooned from real life there!

The plant manager thought I would finish the study in three or four days; luckily, he soon forgot about me, and I had access for a few years. As the study progressed, I realized that if I confined my research to life at work, I would be painting a very one-sided picture of the workers. Life outside the workplace—leisure life, residential and family life—was also crucial. Given my distaste for the sheltered university, I was all too happy to devote my energies to an investigation that kept me far away from it. Eventually, I realized that I had a chance to analyze the entire spectrum of blue-collar life (at least for the better-paid workers I was studying). So I wrote about their jobs, family relations and leisure activities, values and ideology, and views on religion, politics and social class.

But the central theme of the study remained social class and class consciousness. I argued that blue-collar workers such as these have three main forms of class identity. One identity refers to their position in the workplace. Based on the concept of the "working man," it implies a separation between themselves and white-collar workers. They have another identity that refers to life outside of work—their residential setting, leisure and family lives. Based on the concepts of "middle-" and "lower-middle" class, this identity implies important overlaps between blue- and white-collar people. Finally, there is an identity based on the concept of "the American people." This identity is the broadest of all, for it includes everyone except those at the summits of political and economic power. The coexistence of these three class identities in the minds of the workers I studied explains one of the most puzzling problems raised by accounts of the American working class. It explains why those researchers who have found a class-conscious proletariat, and those who have found a working class sufficiently mobile to see themselves as middle class and sufficiently attached to America to respond to certain national symbols and appeals, have both been able to produce enough evidence to sustain their models. Each theory contains part of the truth, but each needs the other for a fully accurate picture.

ing-class solidarity in opposition to owners as a class; (5) the expectation and reality of upward movement in the stratification hierarchy as a result of three centuries of economic growth; and (6) the existence of loyalties and ties that cut across class lines, such as those based on nationality, religion, or race.

For whatever combination of reasons, class consciousness as a basis of political action, in contrast to simple awareness, appears relatively uncommon among most members of the American working and middle class. Nor have the very poor acted upon their consciousness of class. They are too busy dealing with problems of immediate survival. Meanwhile, the upper strata have succeeded in having their class-based interests accepted as the dominant ideology.

SOCIAL CLASS AND SOCIAL ORDER

As we have seen, social resources in American society are unequally distributed and awareness of these differences is widespread. Because inequality can produce discontent and reduce social cohesion, we must ask why our society has remained so stable.

In general, inequality itself does not necessarily produce disorder. Only when inequality is defined as unfair (*inequitable*) is social order threatened. As long as most citizens think that the rules are fair, inequality is tolerated. At some point, the have-nots may withdraw their support and take to the streets, but the monopoly of political force rests with the powerful who typically crush the rebellion. Most of the unrest in Central and South America today is related to extreme inequality in wealth in those nations. Under these circumstances, the appeal of Marxism and its ideology of more equitable distribution of resources is very strong.

Ideological Supports for the American Class Systems. In the United States, beliefs that justify inequality are deeply embedded. Recalling the concept of *ideological hegemony,* it seems logical to expect that the people who control the production of ideas and symbols have constructed a set of beliefs that justify, legitimate, and reinforce the existing distribution of societal resources (Kluegel and Smith 1983). When individuals behave in an unexpected manner—as when wealthy people cheat or po-

These scenes depict two entirely different life-styles in the U.S. What kinds of explanations do we give for the differences in the life-styles shown in these two scenes? (© Mike Maple/Woodfin Camp and Associates; © Nik Wheeler/Black Star)

litical leaders are less than honest—we talk about a few "rotten apples" rather than reexamine the social systems in which they act.

There are several ideological justifications of inequality in our society:

1. *The promise of equal opportunity.* Among the most enduring myths of our culture is the belief that with hard work and a bit of luck, anyone can rise from "rags to riches."
2. *Survival of the fittest,* or "social Darwinism," is based on the belief that society resembles a jungle in which the naturally superior will win out in the struggle for survival. Social inequality, therefore, reflects a law of nature and the inborn differences among people.

3. *Psychological determinism.* As part of our cultural emphasis on individualism, Americans prefer to believe that individual psychological traits—motivation, achievement needs, intelligence, and the like—are responsible for success or failure in the workplace.
4. *The work ethic.* As described in Chapter 3, the American value system is built around the idea that work is a sacred task and that success in one's work can be seen as a sign of divine grace. Failure, therefore, can signify only a lack of good qualities. Some moral flaw within a person accounts for an inability to hold a job and save money, for example, laziness, lack of ambition, or absence of self-control that leads to out-of-wedlock births.
5. *The "culture of poverty."* Many people, including some social scientists (O. Lewis 1959, Banfield 1974, Murray 1985) suggest that a set of values and coping behaviors is transmitted from one generation to another, creating a distinct subculture that reinforces a cycle of poverty. The family, rather than the individual, is to blame, but the result is a personality unfitted for work or for taking responsibility.

All these assumptions have shaped American beliefs about the causes of both wealth and poverty. A number of public opinion surveys have found that most respondents explain poverty in terms of the personal characteristics of the poor (Lewis 1978, Della Fave 1980, Feagin 1975, 1986). As shown in Table 7-5, the general public believes that people are poor because they lack thrift, effort, ability, and morals. By the same reasoning, the wealthy are seen as possessing such positive characteristics as intelligence, a willingness to work hard, and the ability to defer gratification (Cummings and Taebel 1978, Della Fave 1980).

Social scientists themselves often take the individual approach to explaining poverty, largely because the government programs being studied have been exclusively focused on assisting individuals rather than on changing the context in which poor people must make choices (Covello et al. 1980, Kerbo 1981, Goodwin 1983).

Poverty in America

EXPLAINING POVERTY

The Human Capital Approach.   This emphasis on personal qualities comes from classical economic theory that assumes that workers are paid according to their contributions to the productive process. Thus, people who have made investments in themselves through education, training,

TABLE 7-5   Reasons for poverty selected by Americans in national surveys, 1963 and 1980

	Very Important %		Somewhat Important %		Not Important %	
	1963	1980	1963	1980	1963	1980
1. Lack of thrift and proper money management by poor people.	58	65	30	28	11	7
2. Lack of effort by the poor themselves.	55	52	33	38	9	9
3. Lack of ability and talent among poor people.	52	50	33	35	12	15
4. Loose morals and drunkenness.	48	45	31	25	17	28
5. Sickness and physical handicaps.	46	43	39	37	14	20
6. Low wages in some business and industries.	42	39	35	46	20	14
7. Failure of society to provide good schools for many Americans.	36	46	25	26	34	27
8. Prejudice and discrimination against blacks.	33	31	37	40	26	28
9. Failure of private industry to provide enough jobs.	27	34	36	38	31	26
10. Being taken advantage of by rich people.	18	22	30	32	45	44
11. Just bad luck.	8	12	27	27	60	60

SOURCES: Joe R. Feagin, *Subordinating the Poor.* Englewood Cliffs, NJ: Prentice-Hall, 1975, p. 97; and tabulations for the 1980 survey by James R. Kluegel, published in Joe R. Feagin, *Social Problems: A Critical Power-Conflict Perspective,* 2nd Edition. Englewood Cliffs, NJ: Prentice-Hall, 1986, p. 94.

and a willingness to defer immediate rewards possess "human capital" of greater value to employers than that of the less skilled and educated. If women, blacks, and Hispanics generally have less training and more discontinuous work histories than most white male workers, they should expect to earn less. Income inequality, including poverty, is seen as an accurate reflection of the distribution of qualities desired by employers.

Structural Approaches.   In contrast, recent work by sociologists looks not at individuals and their human capital, but at societal-level or structural variables such as items 5–10 in Table 7-5. From this viewpoint, poverty stems from people's location in labor markets and from broad changes in the economic system itself (to be discussed in detail in Chapter 12: see "Labor Segmentation").

That is, the poor are poor in large part because they compete for employment in sectors of the economy that offer little job security and very low wages. High unemployment in certain geographical areas and among certain subgroups are seen as the result of decisions made by owners and investors. Poverty is viewed as the involuntary outcome of unemployment and political powerlessness (Beeghley 1983).

From this perspective, the personality traits so often thought of as causes of poverty—lowered ambition, enjoying what you can now, lack of thrift, and so forth—are logical responses to the realities of unemployment and other insults of "living poorly in America." So long as the structural barriers to steady employment with adequate pay scales persists, so also will the life-styles called the "culture of poverty." But it is not a culture that is consciously transmitted from one generation to the next; it reappears whenever new generations experience the same set of limited options.

WHO ARE THE POOR?

During the Great Depression, one in three Americans lived in poverty. In the early 1960s, despite two decades of economic growth, 30 percent of our population remained impoverished. Figure 7-5 shows the dramatic decline in poverty rates during the "war on poverty" of the mid-1960s, due mostly to programs targeted to the

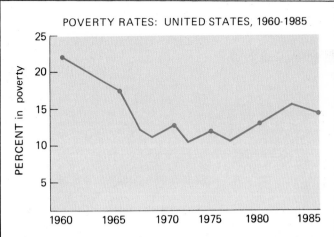

Figure 7-5
Poverty Rates: United States, 1960–1985 (Source: U.S. Bureau of the Census, Current Population Reports, Series P-20, No. 152. *Characteristics of the Population Below the Poverty Level*, 1985, p. 5; Robert Pear, "Poverty Rate Down Slightly in 1985, to Level of '81," *New York Times*, August 27, 1986, p. A17.)

elderly and other "deserving" poor (Appalachian whites and unemployed fathers). Since 1980, however, Reagan administration budget cuts combined with high unemployment and falling wages have pushed the poverty rate upward.

The "New Faces" of Poverty.   In 1985, over 33 million Americans lived in households whose incomes were below the "poverty threshold." This threshold, or *poverty level* is a dollar amount set by the government as the minimum income needed to feed, house, and clothe an individual or family. In 1985, this threshold was about $5500 for a single person, and $8500 for a family of three. If we also include households with incomes slightly above the threshold, the "near poor," the total comes to one in four Americans living in or near poverty.

Although the great majority of the poor are white, the poverty *rate* for whites in 1985 was only 11.4 percent compared to 31.3 percent for blacks and 29 percent for Hispanics. And although over half of poor families are two-parent households, the poverty rate for female-headed families is approximately five times that of married-couple families.

Most seriously affected, however, are children, whose poverty rate has climbed from under 15 percent in 1970 to over 22 percent today. Sixteen percent of white

The poor are often very motivated to find work. It is not personality but structural factors that have to be considered in order to understand poverty. (© Tom Cheek/Stock Boston)

children, almost 40 percent of Hispanic children, and over 43 percent of black youngsters under age 18 live in households with incomes below the minimal survival level. Overall, four out of every ten poor persons are children, and it is they who have been most severely affected by federal spending cuts in the areas of nutrition, health care, and education (Salamon 1985).

The **feminization of poverty** refers to the fact that a majority of the adult poor are women.

The "Feminization" of Poverty. Today's poverty population is also largely female. Women without husbands—unwed teenage mothers, divorced women in general, single parents, displaced homemakers, and elderly widows—are especially likely to have low incomes. Even when they work full-time, their wages tend to be minimal, and most are not covered by unemployment insurance (Pearce 1985).

It is fashionable today to blame all the recent increase in poverty on the rise in female-headed families, but these households have accounted for less than one-third of the new poverty since 1979 compared to 45 percent for married-couple households (Joint Economic Committee,

1986). Low wages and declining employment in manufacturing have had a greater effect on poverty rates than has the increase in female-headed households.

WELFARE PROGRAMS

Despite the growing numbers of the poor and near poor, most federal assistance programs have been reduced or eliminated under the Reagan administration. Especially hard hit are housing, job training, school meals, and health/nutrition supplements for women, infants, and children.

Nor have the largest programs escaped the budget axe. There are four major social welfare programs funded by the federal government:

- *Medicaid* repays physicians and hospitals for the health care expenses of the poor, but the reimbursement rate is so low that patients are often turned away.
- *Food stamps* are available to many below the poverty level, but fewer than half the eligible households receive any stamps. The average monthly value of the stamps, about $90 in 1985, has not been adjusted for rises in the cost of food since 1980. And, in 1986, the government decided to count the rent paid to welfare hotels as income to the tenants, thus reducing their eligibility for food stamps (Harris 1986).
- *Supplemental Security Income (SSI)* covers aid to the blind, disabled, and elderly whose incomes remain well below the poverty threshold. Monthly payments average about $250, or half the poverty level.
- *Aid to Families with Dependent Children (AFDC)* provides income to unemployed single parents, almost all of whom are women. The average monthly AFDC benefit in 1984 was $316, ranging from a low of $91 in Mississippi to a high of $542 in Alaska. AFDC benefits have risen only slightly in comparison to increases in the cost of living.

It is important to note that there are very few able-bodied men receiving federal welfare benefits, and some of these are single-parent fathers. Most recipients, by far, are children and mothers under AFDC (two-thirds of the total), and the blind, disabled and elderly under SSI (26 percent of the total). The small percentage who receive other forms of assistance do so on a temporary basis. In no case do welfare benefits bring a household close to the poverty line.

Also, contrary to another commonly held belief, very few families remain on welfare for more than three to five years. Sixty percent of AFDC families, for example, have been receiving benefits for less than three years, while only 8 percent have been on the welfare rolls for ten years or more. Most families at risk drift in and out of poverty, due to changes in employment, health, and marital status. Job loss, illness, divorce, and separation plunge the unit below the poverty threshold, while reemployment, a return to health, and marriage lift it slightly above (Duncan et al. 1984). Thus, long-term welfare dependency characterizes only a small fraction of the poor, who are most likely to have entered the welfare system as very young unwed mothers and who have found it difficult to develop job skills and find employment that pays enough to raise the family out of poverty. The risk of poverty is somewhat greater for a child growing up in a female-headed family than for a child living in a family with two parents, but this is due less to not having a father in the home than to lack of income and to the stress caused by the family's break-up (McLanahan 1985).

Further, although there are many anecdotes, there is little solid evidence to support the idea that poor women have children in order to increase their welfare benefits. Almost 75 percent of AFDC families have but one or two children, and only 10 percent are composed of four or more children. Nor does the existence of AFDC motivate women to choose to remain unmarried. The prevalence of female-headed families among blacks is due primarily to a shortage of young adult men. Death rates for black males are relatively high, as are the chances of imprisonment; many are in the armed forces; and a disproportionately high percentage are unemployed and underemployed (Darrity and Myers 1984).

Finally, living in poverty is a troubled existence. The poor are more likely than the nonpoor to be ill, feel mental anguish, and commit suicide; to be victims of crime; to fail in marriage; and to see their children suffer from malnutrition and crippling diseases. But poverty is more than being deprived of material things; relationships with others are also affected. The British sociologist Peter Townsend (1983) has constructed a "deprivation index" of social relations that poor children must do without, such as birthday parties, being able to invite friends home to dinner, having a parent's time and attention, or enjoying the security of a stable neighborhood.

The character of our relationships with others is strongly influenced by the nature of our environment. (© Stephen Shames/ Visions)

Workfare. Welfare policy has long been a political battleground. Political conservatives argue that poor people ought to do some form of work—raking leaves or cleaning public buildings, at the very least—in return for their welfare checks. This meets the goals of both reducing public expenditures and of reinforcing the work ethic. Political liberals, while also emphasizing the importance of employment in reducing poverty, claim that the kind of work proposed by the conservatives simply exploits the poor and channels them into low-skill, dead-end jobs. Before 1980, a few states had experimented with forcing some welfare recipients to "work off" their benefits in just such jobs. But these programs were rarely successful in removing large numbers of people from the welfare system or in placing them in jobs that paid over the poverty level. In the last few years, however, several states have developed more sophisticated *workfare* systems designed to train people for positions in the higher-paying private sector of the economy.

The most successful workfare experiment thus far is the Employment and Training Choices (ET) program in Massachusetts. ET meets some liberal criticisms in being primarily voluntary, in providing job training and counseling, child-care and transportation subsidies, and other social support services. In its first two-and-a-half years, the program found jobs for half its clients, lowering the AFDC caseload, saving over $100 million of welfare costs in 1986, and increasing state revenue from taxes paid by the new workers (AFSC 1986).

The ET experiment, however, may not be as successful in states where unemployment rates are considerably higher than in Massachusetts or where there is not a demand for low-skill, low-pay labor. Indeed, the chief criticism of ET is that it has been shaped precisely to prepare workers, at public expense, for local industries to exploit.

Workfare programs are designed to prepare welfare mothers for permanent positions in labor force.

Life-Styles of the Rich and Famous

At the other end of the stratification hierarchy, there are about one million Americans whose assets are valued at $1 million or more. All but a very few are white males or their widows, and most are in their early sixties (*U.S. News and World Report,* Jan. 13, 1986). Their way of life is a source of endless fascination to the tens of millions who regularly watch such television series as *Dynasty, Dallas, The Colbys, Falcon Crest,* and, of course, *Life-Styles of the Rich and Famous.*

Although a number of sports and entertainment personalities are millionaires, at least for a few years, most of the people with new wealth fit the classic mold of the American Dream, having accumulated their assets through hard work, thrift, and risk-taking in business. And according to one recent survey (*U.S. News and World*

The life-styles of the rich and famous provide endless fascination and entertainment for tens of millions of Americans. Here is Malcolm Forbes with guest Elizabeth Taylor at his 1987 birthday party. For the occasion his estate was turned into a castle. (© Maiman/SYGMA)

Report, 1986), not all engage in displays of conspicuous consumption, either as a matter of personal taste or from the realization that a million dollars does not go very far today.

While there may be a million millionaires, the really wealthy, as seen in Figure 7-2, are relatively rare; there are about 42,000 "very rich" households, and a similar number of the "super rich" (wealth of $2.5 million or more). And then there are the great fortunes of America: wealth holdings of hundreds of millions.

One reason why a million dollars might not be sufficient today is that the cost of living for millionaires has risen far more steeply than for the society as a whole. An entire business sector devoted to serving the very rich has emerged in the 1980s, due in part to increasing numbers of high-income households, and in part to the triumph of a consumer ethic. "If you've got it, flaunt it" has replaced the traditional virtues of thrift and modesty. Exclusive shops ("boutiques") catering to the very rich have replaced large department stores, and prices have risen accordingly. The very wealthy tell time with wristwatches that range from $5000 to $1,000,000 (with diamonds), and travel with luggage that could cost $75,000 a set, in genuine crocodile (*Forbes* 1986, Kleinfeld 1986).

In addition, the types of investments open to people of great wealth permit them to avoid taxation. In 1983, for example, 11 percent of the very wealthy managed to pay taxes of 5 percent or less on their total incomes (Internal Revenue Service 1986), and most of the others paid at a rate far below that of the majority of Americans. To some extent, the 1987 tax changes will close many of these loopholes, but at the same time the overall tax rate for the wealthy has been greatly reduced, and the principle of *progressivity* (taxing higher incomes at a higher rate) has been rejected.

Progressivity is the principle of taxing higher incomes at a higher rate.

WEALTH AND CLASS

While wealth can buy you such luxuries as a 52-foot limousine (sleeps six) for only $750,000, it is not an automatic entry card into the upper class. The American upper class is a very exclusive group, consisting of perhaps as many as 60,000 families and individuals, based as much on "blood"

The *Forbes* Four Hundred

For several years, *Forbes* magazine, a business publication, has regularly identified the 400 richest people in America. In the 1986 edition (October 27), these 400 individuals had total assets of $150 billion, which is slightly more than the *total* federal budget on programs for the needy, and only $8 billion less than the total Gross National Product of the country of Mexico. The minimum needed to get on this list in 1986 was $180 million, and the average net worth of the 400 was $390 million.

Forty-two percent of these great wealth holders controlled fortunes that were all or mostly inherited; a similar percentage achieved their wealth without any significant inheritance. The remaining 16 percent built upon modest family resources. In general, however, "old" money (though few family fortunes predate the Civil War) remains the backbone of great fortunes, with most of the "new" wealth coming from oil, real estate, finance, and media ownership.

The "new" rich tend to dominate the list of very top wealth holders—the 23 billionaires—largely because there has not yet been time for their fortunes to become diluted through inheritance to children and grandchildren. Furthermore, because today's very rich tend to have fewer offspring than did the wealthy of the past, their money will remain highly concentrated.

Eighty-one percent of the 400 are white males, and 19 percent are women, all of whom inherited their wealth either as widows or daughters of very rich men. The great majority are of white Anglo-Saxon, Protestant background, including all but a few "old" money families. Non-WASPS, primarily men of Jewish background, are well represented among the "new" fortunes, but this is not a list that comes anywhere close to reflecting the full ethnic diversity of our society.

While a few cases are of the classic "rags to riches" variety, only 3.5 percent were immigrants, and all but 8 percent had some college education; two-thirds are college graduates; and 18 percent earned graduate degrees. Their average age is 62.3 years. Manufacturing, financial operations, media ownership, and oil and gas are the chief bases of today's great fortunes.

SOURCE: *Forbes*, October 27, 1986.

(family background) as on money (Baltzell 1964, Domhoff 1983, Ostrander 1984). Until quite recently, our uppermost stratum was composed almost exclusively of white, Anglo-Saxon, Protestant families whose roots in America go back to the eighteenth century and whose fortunes were accumulated in the nineteenth century. The upper class is still all-white, but a few highly successful individuals from other religions and class origins have managed to win acceptance (a Henry Kissinger and Lee Iacocca, for instance).

The upper class maintains its continuity over time through intermarriage and the socialization of its children in a series of private schools (see Chapter 14) and social activities. As Domhoff (1983) maintains, the upper class is more than a collection of families; it also exists as a set of interrelated social institutions—"patterned ways of organizing the lives of its members from infancy to old age." Private schools and clubs isolate and insulate members of the upper class, providing them with a distinct set of values and behaviors that set them apart from the rest of the stratification system and account for their high level of solidarity.

Despite the glaring differences between the life-styles of this one-half of one percent of our population, on the one hand, and the conditions of poverty or near-poverty that affect 15 to 20 percent of Americans, on the other, few people in the rest of the stratification system express a sense of outrage or even unfairness. On the contrary, public opinion data indicate that most respondents feel that the wealthy are entitled to their success, so long as they played the game according to the rules (Yankelovich and Kaagan 1979). Further, most respondents also feel that with a little bit of luck and more hard work, they, or their children, could someday join the ranks of the rich, if not the upper class itself (Kluegel and Smith 1986).

But just what are these chances for upward movement in the American stratification system?

Social Mobility

Social mobility is the movement of persons and groups within the stratification system.

The term *social mobility* refers to the movement of persons and groups within the stratification system. The distinction between caste systems and class systems is the degree to which status lines can be crossed.

CASTE AND CLASS

In a *caste system,* one's place in the social-stratification system is determined at birth. This ascribed status affects how much education people can have, what occupations they can enter, and whom they can marry. Thus, the hierarchy is preserved over time, with a few exceptions for particularly talented or lucky people. Although caste systems are usually associated with preliterate societies, caste remains an important feature of modern India and South Africa. In the South African case, a system of laws called *apartheid* separates the few whites from the many blacks, ensuring that whites will hold the best land, run the government, and control the economy.

The United States had similar laws up to the 1960s. Our society still has elements of a caste system: in housing, schooling, and occupational structures where there are few, if any, blacks or Hispanics. So it is possible to have features of both closed and open systems in the same society.

Class systems are based on achieved (earned) as well as ascribed (given) traits. When the comparison is between the parents' status and that of their adult children, we speak of *intergenerational (inter* means "between") *mobility.* When the comparison is made between where one begins and where one ends up, it is called

Caste systems are based on ascription, with minimal movement across stratum boundaries.

Apartheid is a system of laws in South Africa that upholds white supremacy and separates the majority of blacks from the minority of whites.

Intergenerational mobility involves status change between parents and their adult children.

Apartheid decrees separation for all types of facilities, thereby affecting both public and private behavior. (© Alon Reininger/ Woodfin Camp and Associates)

Intragenerational mobility involves status changes during a person's own adulthood.

intragenerational (*intra* means "within") or *career mobility*. People and groups can move up or down through the various stratification hierarchies.

The American Dream is based on a belief in upward mobility through talent and hard work. Even those whose hard work has not made them millionaires believe that *upward mobility* is possible for their children. Just as our folklore and children's books are filled with stories of upward mobility through thrift, clean living, and self-discipline, we warn the young against laziness and wastefulness lest they fall in status. *Downward mobility,* that is, losing social status, is portrayed as a disgrace to one's family and a denial of the meaning of our society.

Many people today, perhaps most Americans, change jobs, move from one part of the country to another, divorce, and remarry. In all this movement, some people may experience slight status gains or losses, or *horizontal mobility*.

Social Mobility in the United States

There is a truth to the dream of upward mobility, but it is not a uniquely American reality. All industrial societies with democratic political systems, low birth rates, and an ideology of equal opportunity had high rates of upward mobility between 1945 and 1965. In that period, there was a shift of about 30 percent from manual to nonmanual occupations in the United States, Great Britain, and other modern Western societies (Lenski 1966). Most of this change was intergenerational—based on comparisons of fathers' and sons' jobs—rather than being achieved during the son's lifetime.

The consistency of these findings across industrial societies and the greater importance of intergenerational than intragenerational changes strongly indicate that the structure of the economy determines mobility rates (Hauser et al. 1975, Robinson 1984, Kerckhoff et al. 1985). In other words, most movement in the occupational system, whatever the direction, can be explained in terms of societal-level variables rather than in terms of individual differences among workers.

DEMAND MOBILITY

Demand mobility refers to societal-level factors affecting mobility rates.

The term *demand mobility* refers to the societal-level factors that affect mobility rates. For example, the number and types of jobs available depend on economic system changes, whereas the number and types of people able and willing to fill the jobs depend on the birth rates of different generations. From such data, we can estimate the probabilities of upward or downward movement for various subgroups. As for who *exactly* moves up or down the stratification system, such personal traits as talent, motivation, and luck must be taken into account. But most research on stratification today stresses the effects of structural variables, especially changes in the economic system that open up or close off certain types of jobs.

As seen in Figure 7-6, for example, the proportion of American workers engaged in farming has declined from over 37 percent in 1900 to under 3 percent today. Farm owners may have moved into the petite bourgeoisie class, but farm laborers most likely joined the stratum of manual workers. While farm employment declined, professional and managerial jobs more than doubled, and sales/clerical positions quadrupled over the century. These vast changes are typical of modern societies: from farm to factory in the early stages of industrialization, and then from factory to white-collar "service" jobs in the later stages. Today, nonmanual work accounts for over half the occupational structure compared to 17.5 percent in 1900.

What these structural shifts mean is that most intergenerational occupational mobility is simply forced by circumstances, and that, in general, the trend is toward jobs requiring increasingly higher levels of education and training. Such occupations tend to have higher wage scales than found in the manual and blue-collar sectors if the jobs are filled by men. As we will see in Chapter 8, that which is defined as women's work, at any occupational level, is neither highly valued nor rewarded.

Occupational shifts are not the only structural factor accounting for the spurt in upward mobility between 1945 and 1965. Equally important were the very low birth rates, especially among the middle class, during the Great Depression of the 1930s and early years of World War II. As a

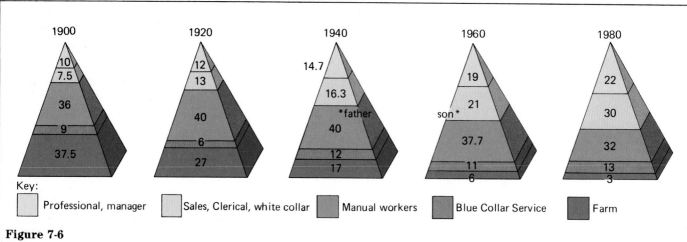

Key:

☐ Professional, manager ☐ Sales, Clerical, white collar ▨ Manual workers ▨ Blue Collar Service ▨ Farm

Figure 7-6
Changing Occupational Structure, U.S.; 1900–1980 (in percents) (Sources: U.S. Bureau of the Census, *Historical Statistics, United States: Colonial Times to Present,* Bicentennial Edition, Part I, p. 139. Washington, D.C.: U.S. Government Printing Office, 1975; *Statistical Abstracts of the United States,* 1986, p. 400. Washington, D.C.: U.S. Government Printing Office, 1986.)

consequence, there was a relatively small pool of job applicants at the very time when the economy was expanding rapidly in the 1950s. White-collar managerial jobs were opening up at a faster rate than children of the middle class could fill them, creating a job vacuum into which young people from the working class could move.

In addition, if they were veterans of World War II, men (and a few women) from working-class backgrounds could take advantage of a program that provided a full four-year college education financed by a grateful nation. This was an option open primarily to whites, as few black youth could afford to stay out of the labor force for four years. Thus, a combination of a free education, a shortage of middle-class youth, and the expansion of the managerial sector accounts for most of the upward mobility experienced by white males in the 1945–1965 period.

ABSOLUTE AND RELATIVE MOBILITY

As they surpassed their fathers in education, occupational prestige, and income, these men enjoyed *absolute social mobility.* But because the entire occupational structure was being upgraded, their position *relative* to other workers might not be so different from that of their father. If, for example, the father was a skilled carpenter (high-level manual worker) and the son an insurance underwriter (white col-

lar), the son's job and educational qualifications and life-style place him in a higher status rank than his father. Yet, if most others in the son's generation also moved into white-collar employment, the positions of father and son compared to all other workers has not greatly changed, as also seen in Figure 7-6.

DISCRIMINATION

Other structural factors that affect mobility include the worker's location in the dual economy (Jacobs 1982, Tolbert 1983), and discrimination in hiring on the basis of race, sex, religion, and ethnic background. From the perspective of the dual-economy concept, women, blacks, and the poor form one labor pool and white males form another. Employers then pick from this split labor market according to their ideas about certain kinds of workers. (See Chapter 12 for further discussion.) Such discrimination is more than a matter of taste (that is, whether or not an employer feels comfortable with certain types of people), it is a means of limiting access to valued resources. *Structured inequality* is the result of systematic exclusion of specific groups on the basis of ascribed characteristics (e.g. Power 1986).

It is only in the past decade or so that American employers have made an effort to hire and promote blacks and women, and only if the federal government is will-

Structured inequality results from the systematic exclusion of specific groups on the basis of ascribed characteristics.

ing to enforce the law. Some gains in equal-employment opportunity were made in the 1970s, when public opinion favored such goals (Burstein 1985), but the public mood and political climate have shifted greatly since 1980, so that the Justice Department now prefers to pursue cases of "reverse discrimination" toward white males, to the extent permitted by the Supreme Court.

Status Attainment

THE RESEARCH EVIDENCE

The assumption of social mobility in modern societies obscures the high level of *class immobility,* that is, the general tendency for social class status to be reproduced from one generation to another. Few individuals rise from the very poorest stratum to fame and fortune, nor do the offspring of the affluent fall very far. Most mobility—both between generations and during one's own career—is a matter of small steps rather than dramatic changes, although these rare instances grab the American imagination as in the example of sports and entertainment stars (see Chapter 20). Success in America, as in other modern societies, is profoundly influenced by the social status of one's family at birth. It also helps to be white, male, an only or first-born child, and to be raised in a home that emphasizes *deferred gratification* (putting off immediate pleasure in order to achieve a future goal) and high achievement expectations. As we noted in Chapter 5, parents' occupation is associated with child-rearing techniques that affect self-control, creativity, intellectual flexibility and interpersonal skills that prepare offspring for different types of jobs. Fathers whose jobs require high levels of self-direction tend to have sons who enter and remain in occupations that allow on-the-job autonomy (Hout 1984).

The Basic Model. The dominant model of *status attainment*—based on extensive studies of men—is shown in Figure 7-7. The father's occupation (as indicator of family SES), and the son's education and first job are the primary determinants of eventual occupation status. Because family SES affects the quality and length of education (see Chapter 14), which, in turn,

Class immobility occurs when social class status is reproduced from one generation to another.

Deferred gratification is the postponing of current pleasure to achieve future goals.

Status attainment research traces the paths by which people reach their ultimate position in the stratification system.

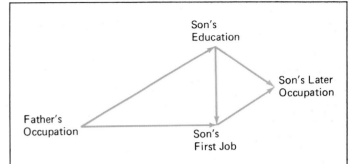

Figure 7-7
The status attainment model. (Source: Adapted from Peter Blau and Otis Dudley Duncan. *The American Occupational Structure,* New York: John Wiley, 1967, p. 170.)

leads to that crucial first job, family background plays the key role (Rumberger 1983).

Families at different locations in the stratification system vary not only in wealth and social power, but in social ties that open occupational doors and encourage the son to develop further social-network resources (Lin et al. 1981). The links between social class and career (intragenerational) mobility are as important as those that influence intergenerational mobility (Snipp 1985).

Nevertheless, to a great extent, the social rank of a married woman continues to be based on that of her husband (Jackman and Jackman 1982), with her mobility measured by the difference between her father's and her husband's occupations or income. As more married women enter the labor force, however, their incomes increasingly raise the household's standard of living. There is already some evidence that a wife's education and income are used to evaluate the family's social status (Nock and Rossi 1979). And in the case of black women, whose employment rates have historically been higher than for white women, a woman's contribution to family well-being has been substantial and well-recognized (Sampson and Rossi 1975).

Who Gets Ahead? In a major reanalysis of all the major status-attainment studies up to 1978, Jencks et al. (1979) concluded that family background variables exert the most powerful influence on a man's eventual occupational status and earnings. This influence operates directly, through

Many young men enter college on athletic scholarships as did the two in the photograph. Since the national trend continues to be toward jobs requiring higher levels of education and a college diploma, finishing their college studies may be more important than playing professionally though briefly. (© James Drake/Time Inc.–Sports Illustrated)

transmission of achievement norms and motivations, and through development of ways of thinking and speaking that prepare one's children for certain types of jobs. Family SES also works indirectly, through education, with higher income households able to afford four years of college *regardless* of their children's intelligence. And a college diploma, no matter what the curriculum or grades, is essential for entering many occupations.

Test scores had some influence on status attainment, but largely through the special encouragement given students who appear to be bright, and not because intelligence always triumphs. The only personality variables that had any effect on mobility outcomes were sociability and leadership in the teenage years, variables which were related to earnings within an occupation but not to occupational prestige level itself (Jencks 1979).

However, it should be added that family background is not all-determining, and that men from similar backgrounds (even the same family) can vary greatly in occupational status. There is always an element of pure chance—luck—that cannot be predicted: being in the right place at the right time, getting a tip from a friend, following a hunch. In addition, because

educational differences are lessening, as almost everyone now has at least four years of high school, the influence of family background should also be reduced.

Some of this effect can be seen in the convergence (coming together) of mobility patterns between black and white men in the 1970s, and in a general weakening of the link between status of origin and destination (Hauser and Featherman 1977, Hout 1984). But these trends appear to have been halted if not reversed in the early 1980s.

CRITICISM OF THE STATUS ATTAINMENT MODEL

As noted, the status-attainment research tradition has until recently been exclusively focused on men, and the model of mobility that emerged was based largely on the history of white males born after 1940. In addition, most studies in this tradition derive from a functionalist perspective that emphasizes the personal characteristics that a worker brings to the economic system (*human capital*)—skills, training, motivation—and the analysis stays at this individual level.

Thus, where human capital qualifications such as education do *not* bring the expected rewards—as when a college degree brings less in occupational prestige and pay for women and blacks than for white males—it is assumed that time and the logic of the marketplace will eventually even things out. Or else some other personal characteristic is used to explain these differences, such as lower work commitment on the part of women, or the quality of schooling for blacks.

From a conflict perspective, however, the focus is on structural barriers to mobility. Inequality, for example, is built into the labor market where women, blacks, and working-class youth are channeled into sectors of the economy where upward mobility is almost impossible (Tolbert 1983). Despite the success of some individual women, blacks, and people from low-income families, their overall distribution in the stratification system has not greatly changed. The ratio of female-to-male or black-to-white earnings has remained virtually constant over the past two and a half decades.

Motivational or attitudinal factors appear to be of little importance in explaining the economic mobility of the poor (Hill et al. 1986). Rather, attitudes of despair and lowered expectations are best interpreted as the *consequences* rather than the causes of poverty. Even decisions about marriage or childbearing that affect poverty status must be looked at in a structural context—the costs and benefits of optional courses of action.

Furthermore, not only are there different barriers to upward mobility for women, the poor, and people of color, than for whites, males, and offspring of the middle class, but different problems even when successful. As noted by Higginbotham and Cannon (1986) in the case of upwardly mobile black women, it is difficult to cut oneself off from the family and community that were so supportive of one's aspirations.

Inequality is also structured when the wealthy transmit accumulated assets from generation to generation, regardless of talent or merit. Robert Merton (1973) describes this aspect of the stratification system as the "Matthew Effect," from the New Testament: "For unto everyone that hath, shall be given in abundance, but from him who hath not, shall be taken away even that which he hath."

As long as ascribed traits such as gender, race, and social class at birth outweigh individual talent and intelligence in determining length of education and type of first job, conflict analysts claim that we really cannot speak of an open class system. But neither can personal characteristics be totally overlooked in trying to predict mobility outcomes. If the conflict model provided an important corrective to functional analysis, the trend in stratification research today is toward an integration of individual and structural variables (Robinson 1985).

Social Status in Everyday Life

From the perspective of symbolic interaction, social statuses are examined at the level of face-to-face encounters. In the give and take of daily interaction, people transmit and receive information about themselves. In Chapter 5, we discussed Goffman's concept of *impression management,* which describes attempts to manipulate the image that we present to others. The goals of impression management are to protect the self-image, save "face," and have our definition of self accepted (validated) by our role partners.

STATUS CUES AND STATUS SYMBOLS

Because people behave differently to those whom they perceive as social superiors, inferiors, or equals, it is important to be able to "locate" others in the prestige hierarchy. We are all rather skilled at picking up *status cues*—speech patterns, dress, hair styles, and the like—and at making status judgments on the basis of gender, age, or race. This information guides our conduct. For example, think of the people whom you call "Sir" or "Ma'am," in contrast to using their first names or just

Status cues such as clothing, speech, and hair styles enable us to locate people in the prestige hierarchy.

Could you make an accurate social assessment of these women based on the status cues available in the photograph? (© Jeff Perkell/The Stock Market; © Joel Gordon/Joel Gordon Photography)

"Hey, you." You address status superiors differently from those you identify as inferiors or equals. These status considerations influence who speaks first or who ends the conversation, who can violate another's personal space, and countless other details of face-to-face encounters.

Status symbols are the outward signs of social rank by which people manage the impression they give. "Keeping up with the Joneses" describes the behavior of people who try to equal the status displays of their neighbors. Appearing to have less means instant loss of prestige. The advertising industry is largely devoted to stimulating people to ever higher levels of consumption so that they can achieve or maintain status in the eyes of others.

Consumption patterns are often used to identify social status. One recent study of blue- and white-collar families with the same income showed two very different patterns of consumption. In comparison with blue-collar families, white-collar families owned smaller cars and television sets, used fewer convenience foods, drank less beer and more vodka, bought furniture one piece at a time rather than as suites, and had a blender rather than an electric frying pan (Schaninger and Sciglimpaglia 1981). Educational level and job prestige had more impact on life-style than did income.

STATUS CONSISTENCY AND INCONSISTENCY

As individuals send and receive status cues, they adjust to one another and select the appropriate response, always protecting their self-image. This is a relatively easy task when role partners present clear and unambiguous status cues, but in modern societies, people are apt to have positions in several status hierarchies.

The term *status consistency* refers to the uniform placement of people across different hierarchies: the ascribed ones of gender, race, age, ethnic background, and family status at birth, as well as the achieved hierarchies of education, occupation, and income. A white male executive ranks high in wealth, prestige, and power. Similarly, a minority cleaning woman has a consistent position at the base of these hierarchies. Status consistency is greatest at both the top and the bottom of the stratification system, having all the features of a caste society.

Industrial societies, however, display relatively high levels of social mobility, particularly at the middle levels of stratification. Thus, the possibility of status inconsistency—occupying a different level of position across hierarchies—is characteristic of modern societies. For example, the head of a crime syndicate may have wealth and power but rank low in prestige. An athlete may have prestige and wealth but little social power.

Status inconsistency has important consequences in interpersonal relationships. The female lawyer or the black doctor, for instance, presents inconsistent cues: a combination of low-ascribed and high-achieved statuses. Some people respond by assuming that the woman or the black must be less qualified, thus creating consistency in their own minds. For the status-inconsistent person, the problem is trying to be accepted in the higher-status role (doctor, lawyer) while his or her role partners are responding to the lower status to maintain their own position. When the male colleague of a woman professional pulls out a chair for her at a board meeting, he is responding to her lower gender status rather than to her equal professional one. Which may be the reason why, in attempting to emphasize their achieved characteristics, upwardly mobile women and people of color are often perceived as "pushy." They are, after all, violating cultural expectations and pushing up against established social boundaries.

At the other extreme are people with high-ascribed but low-achieved statuses such as a white Anglo-Saxon Protestant male who has dropped out of high school and who pumps gas for a living. Believing that their ascribed characteristics entitle them to a better fate than they have actually achieved, such men are likely to feel resentment at the achievements of people they consider their inferiors (Roebeck and Hickson 1982). It is precisely among men of this type that organizations such as the Ku Klux Klan or American Nazi Party find most of their recruits. These organizations emphasize the virtues of whiteness, maleness, and Protestant roots in contrast to the negative traits of nonwhites, Jews, Catholics, communists, homosexuals, and women in general. Notice that we have just given you a purely *structural* explanation of recruitment to the Klan or ANP; it is not prejudice that fuels resentment, but social locations that feed attitudes.

Status symbols are outward signs of social rank.

Status consistency occurs when a person occupies a similar rank across different hierarchies.

Status inconsistency refers to occupying different ranks in different hierarchies.

Summary

With few exceptions, social resources—power, prestige, and property—are unequally divided among people and groups. From a functional perspective, stratification is an inevitable and necessary outcome of individual differences. From the conflict perspective, inequality is culturally structured and transmitted from one generation to another, reinforcing and maintaining the stratification system.

Weber's distinction among class, status, and parties is used to frame our discussion of power, prestige, and property as distinct though interrelated dimensions of stratification. Power can be exercised legitimately (authority) or through interpersonal influence. Prestige refers to respect received from others, typically on the basis of occupation. Property is measured by wealth and income.

A socioeconomic index based on some combination of occupational prestige, income, and education is used by some social scientists to place people and groups within a hierarchy of social classes. Other sociologists prefer to use variables that measure relations of production—control over one's own work and that of others. Recent data suggest that, contrary to the myth of "classlessness," most Americans are aware of social class and have a relatively high degree of class consciousness.

But social inequality is not a threat to social order unless it is also perceived as unfair. In our society, there are strong ideological and institutional supports for inequality, and, hence, little pressure for change.

Poverty remains a major social problem, primarily affecting women, children, and members of racial and ethnic minority groups. Most social scientists locate the sources of poverty in structural rather than personality factors, interpreting the latter as responses to, rather than causes of, poverty. Welfare and workfare programs are described. Despite the long-term negative effects of poverty on people and the society as a whole, there is no public pressure today for redistribution of resources.

At the other end of the income scale, the wealthy enjoy a unique life-style that combines conspicuous consumption with institutional arrangements that preserve their status.

In contrast to caste societies, most modern industrial societies are characterized by relatively high levels of upward mobility both between generations and within a person's own work career. Most of this mobility, however, can be accounted for by changes in the economic system and fluctuations in birth rates. Although absolute mobility has occurred, there has been little change in the relative position of people and groups in the SES hierarchy.

Studies of status attainment—the paths that lead from social placement at birth to adult occupational level—focus on individual-level variables, among which family background and education are the primary determinants. Conflict theorists are beginning to explore the effects on status attainment of the occupational structure itself, hiring practices, and differential wage scales between and within job categories.

Social rank influences everyday interaction. Status cues and status symbols are guides to behavior and impression management. In modern societies, people are likely to display status inconsistencies that create problems in self-presentation and social interaction.

Suggested Readings

BLUMBERG, PAUL. *Inequality in an Age of Decline*. New York: Oxford University Press, 1981. This work examines the recent economic decline and its impact on different social classes in America.

BRAVERMAN, HARRY. *Labor and Monopoly Capital: The Degradation of Work in the Twentieth Century*. New York: Monthly Review Press, 1974. The development of the class structure in the United States and the prevalence of alienation in many occupations are thoroughly described.

FORM, WILLIAM. *Divided We Stand: Class Stratification in America*. Urbana, Illinois: University of Illinois Press, 1985. This work analyzes the political consequences of economic segmentation on the working class in American society and discusses the factors that have created the shifts to a more politically polarized group of workers.

HARRINGTON, MICHAEL. *The New American Poverty*. New York: Penguin Books, 1984. This book documents the different groups in American society that are increasingly facing poverty—unemployed blue-collar workers, undocumented immigrant workers, and women raising children on their own.

HELLER, CELIA. *Structured Social Inequality*, 2nd ed. New York: Macmillan, 1987. An excellent collection of articles dealing with various aspects of stratification in the United States and other societies.

HERLEMANN, HORST G. *The Quality of Life in the Soviet Union*. Boulder, Colorado: Westview Press, 1986. A critical view of Soviet life as a "classless" society.

JACKMAN, MARY R., and ROBERT W. JACKMAN. *Class Awareness in the United States*. Berkeley, California: University of California Press, 1983. An important study of class identification among Americans based on new comprehensive data sets.

MARX, KARL. *Selected Writings in Sociology and Social Philosophy*. Edited by T. Biltmore and M. Rubel. Baltimore, Maryland: Penguin Books. An introduction to Marx's work on social stratification.

ROSE, STEPHEN J. *Social Stratification in the United States*. New York: Pantheon, 1986. The most recent empirical information regarding the nature and the distribution of inequality in the United States.

SENNETT, RICHARD, and JONATHAN COBB. *The Hidden Injuries of Class*. New York: Random House (Vantage Books), 1973. A sensitive discussion of the subjective experience of social class.

TUMIN, MELVIN M. *Social Stratification: The Forms and Functions of Social Inequality*, 2nd ed. Englewood Cliffs, New Jersey: Prentice-Hall, 1985. An overview of the historical, comparative, and theoretical issues of social stratification.

8

Gender Stratification

THE Matching Exercise (Loewen and Sampson 1986) on the next page has been used to help instructors identify high- and low-scoring students, with the high scorers given the privilege of sitting in front of the class and lowest scorers being assigned seats in the back of the room. If your class took this test, how would the seating arrangement work out?

This exercise obviously rewards students for possessing a kind of knowledge associated with "femininity" and penalizes those who are experts in a "masculine" area. Because it is a reversal of the accustomed way of evaluating skills, it may appear very unfair. But would you be able to argue that a sophisticated and subtle sense of color is of lesser value to human groups than an understanding of the rules of football?

Yet it is a near-universal of culture that whatever men know and do in society is considered superior to that which women do and know. This is the basis of *gender stratification*—a differential evaluation of individuals on the basis of biological sex that leads to unequal claims on the valued resources of the group. Thus we find that most societies throughout history have been stratified by sex, with males enjoying the greater share of power, prestige, and control over property.

Gender stratification is the result of the differential evaluation of social worth on the basis of biological sex.

Matching Exercise*

You have seven minutes to match each color (items 1–8) and each football term (items 9–16) with the description that best fits. Answer every question; feel free to guess. No description is used more than once.

COLORS

____ 1. puce		a.	brilliant yellow
____ 2. taupe		b.	pale light blue
____ 3. teal		c.	pale bluish purple
____ 4. mauve		d.	dark mustard yellow
____ 5. magenta		e.	brownish gray
____ 6. chartreuse		f.	greenish blue
____ 7. ochre		g.	orangish yellow
____ 8. sienna		h.	brilliant yellow green
		i.	deep purplish red
		j.	brownish purple

FOOTBALL TERMS

____ 9. safety

____ 10. screen

____ 11. curl

____ 12. trap

____ 13. touchback

____ 14. lateral

____ 15. touchdown

____ 16. clip

a. to block by throwing one's body across a player's legs from behind

b. a pass thrown parallel to or away from the opponent's goal line

c. to block out a defensive player from the side after he has crossed the line of scrimmage

d. to block an offensive pass-defender so that another defender can blitz the passer

e. downing or holding the ball behind the defender's goal by an eligible member of the offensive team

f. an offensive player is tackled in or loses the ball out of bounds from his own end zone

g. a pass caught behind the line of scrimmage by an eligible receiver who has two or more blockers in front of him

h. the ball is downed by a defensive player behind his own goal after an intercepted forward pass or a kick

i. an eligible receiver runs downfield and then circles into an open area against a zone defense

j. a tackle in which the defensive player's outstretched arm catches the ball carrier by the head and neck unawares

SCORING

A. Number of color terms correct: ____   C. A minus B (enter at right): ____

B. Number of football terms correct: ____   D. Add 8 to C (enter at right): ____

* Answers: 1j, 2e, 3f, 4c, 5i, 6h, 7g, 8d, 9f, 10g, 11i, 12c, 13h, 14b, 15e, 16a

How inevitable is this pattern? What are its possible causes? Can we explain, sociologically, variations in the degree of gender stratification? And what are the realistic probabilities of change in modern societies? In this chapter, we will examine several scenarios of the origins and historical forms of male dominance; describe the current systems of gender stratification; and discuss the possibilities of further structural change, as well as continuing shifts in the attitudes and behavior of both men and women. However, our emphasis will be on the statuses of women: first, because there would be little analysis of gender stratification systems if some women, today and in the past, had not perceived them as unfair; and, second, because the world as seen from a male perspective is well known—it is what, until recently, has been accepted as reality.

But first we must define the concepts of sex and gender.

Sex and Gender

Male and female define biological sex. **Feminine and masculine** are social constructs.

The terms *male* and *female* describe a person's biological sex. *Feminine* and *masculine* are socially constructed genders. Once this distinction between biological and social—between sex and gender—is clear, we can refer to maleness and femaleness as *ascribed* traits, and to femininity and masculinity as *achieved* characteristics that are highly variable from one culture to another and in any society over time.

But gender is more than a set of behavioral norms. People do not have "gender roles" any more than they have "race roles" (Lopata and Thorne 1978). We behave and think and have certain life chances because our language and social structures divide us, on the basis of sex, into distinct categories whose members are assumed to share particular abilities and personality traits. In other words, gender is a structural feature of society, in the same way as is social class.

As with other power relationships, gender is continually redefined and negotiated; men and women can and do rebel and resist (Gerson and Peiss 1985). Precisely because gender is socially constructed, it can never be taken for granted, which is the reason why gender socialization is so intense and why gender deviance is so harshly sanctioned. (Think of what it meant to be called "sissy" or "fag" as a boy, or "dog" or "dyke" as a girl.) We become gendered persons living in a gendered world, thinking gendered thoughts. Depending on the culture, these gendered roles can overlap or be so different that women and men have difficulty understanding one another's experiences.

If gender inequality is not the natural outcome of significant and innate sex differences, it becomes necessary for those who benefit from the system to discover or invent "natural" reasons for its persistence. Thus, the many theories of natural superiority and inferiority that we will deal with in the next section must be seen as rationalizations (justifications) rather than explanations for gender stratification systems (Deaux and Kite 1987, Sayers 1987).

Just how do gender-stratification systems arise and how are they maintained?

A MODEL OF GENDER STRATIFICATION

In all societies, the gender-stratification system tends to favor males, although this is a matter of degree. At one extreme are societies in which women's power is minimal and confined to the household, as in many Moslem countries today. At the other end of the continuum are relatively *egalitarian* social systems in which power differences are narrowed and women have important roles in nonfamily institutional spheres, as in many modern industrial societies. But there is no strong evidence of any society in which women as a category have had greater social power than men (though see Barstow 1978, on Stone Age Turkey).

A second cultural universal is that females are entrusted with child care and other tasks centered on the household. In

We are born with physiological differences, but without socialization, our gender might only be as evident as it is for the infants in this photo. (© Michel Tcherevkoff/The Image Bank)

The traditional female role model centered on child care. It emphasized women's productive functions and highly nurturing behavior. (© William U. Harris)

mal (Hope and Stover 1987). Historically and cross-culturally, this is the case for gathering bands and most foraging groups (Chapter 3). In these societies, both men and women gather food and trap small animals, and both are involved in child care. Resources are shared among all members of the group, and decisions are made by the adults together. And this is probably how human groups existed for many thousands of years before their economic base expanded to include hunting large animals.

Once large-scale hunting developed, the division of labor by sex deepened and sharpened. Men became the hunters because women could not leave their infants for long periods or carry their young for long distances. With the hunt came differences in skills and knowledge, as well as special tools and weapons as the first form of private property. When these differences are based on sex, gender stratification systems develop. Male dominance tends to increase with the amount of private property held by the family—whether it be cattle, land, or children. Where such resources are passed from father to son, *patriarchy* (the rule of men) reaches its high point, most notably in herding and farming societies.

Patriarchy refers to male dominance.

The link between patriarchy and the group's economic organization is illustrated in Figure 8-1 (adapted from Chafetz 1984, Huber 1986).

contrast, males are assigned roles that require moving away from the base camp and that often involve risk. The logic behind this division of labor is related to a mother's need to remain near nursing infants and to the limitations that small children place on physical mobility. Giving men the dangerous tasks is also logical, as fewer men than women are needed to reproduce the next generation. Thus, as long as high birth rates are required for group survival, it is important for males to be socialized to risk taking, and females to nurturing. And for most of human history, infant death rates have been very high and the life expectancy of women very low, so that adult women would spend the greater part of their lives either pregnant or breast-feeding infants (Lerner 1986).

This original division of labor based on the only crucial biological distinction between women and men—the fact that only women bear children—may be a *necessary* cause of gender stratification, but it is not in itself *sufficient* to lead to inequality in power, prestige, and property.

If the group is small and has few resources, any type of stratification is mini-

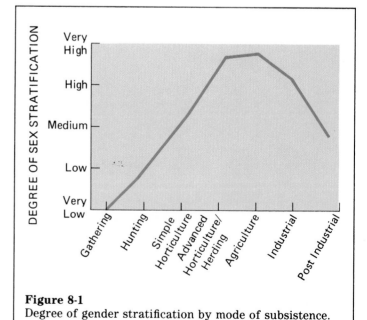

Figure 8-1
Degree of gender stratification by mode of subsistence.

The stereotypes of women as physically weaker is contradicted by a number of activities pursued by women, including service in the Armed Forces. In Israel, for example, all able men are required to serve 3 years; women are required to serve for 2 years. (© Richard Nowitz/Black Star)

Although the general pattern in modern societies is toward egalitarianism, the trend is uneven. It is important to distinguish between formal (declared, official) equality and the actual distribution of prestige, power, and property. In communist countries, for example, official ideology supports gender equality, but women are still assigned primary responsibility for home and children, while taking on poorly paid full-time jobs. Further, occupations with a high percentage of women, even when involving technical skills (such as medicine), are considered of low prestige. Thus, legal equality, although an important first step, does not necessarily eliminate the gender-stratification system (Wolf 1985).

Similar findings are reported for many Western democracies where governments make a conscious attempt to enforce equality, but not everyone changes their accustomed ways. In Norway, for example, despite strong laws against gender discrimination, women still do not receive equal benefits from work, and the Norwegian family remains rooted in traditional, patriarchal norms (Holter 1984).

Before describing gender stratification in our society, let us examine competing theories of sex differences that have been used to justify inequality.

The Nature of Sex Differences

BIOLOGICAL PERSPECTIVES

Most of the biological arguments that were once put forward to explain gender stratification have not stood the test of careful scientific examination. The past few years have seen the publication of extensive critiques of the scientific literature on sex differences (Fee 1983, Bleier 1984, Keller 1985, Sapiro 1985, Fausto-Sterling 1986). This critical literature makes four important points:

(1) Biological theories and research on sex differences have been profoundly biased by patriarchal assumptions. As soon as one claim is disproven, another theory emerges to demonstrate the natural superiority of maleness, from Aristotle's belief that men's brains were simply larger than those of women and Darwin's contention that women were lower on the evolutionary ladder than were men, to the current idea that male dominance is related to some aspects of right/left brain differences (Reinharz 1986, Comini 1987). From this perspective, it would not really matter whether men depended more than women on the right half of the brain or the left; theorists would conclude that whatever capacities that half of the brain had were of higher quality.

(2) The data on sex differences are not very convincing or consistent. Take, for example, the claim that greater body strength and aggressiveness due to male hormones accounts for male superiority. This reasoning cannot account for variations over time and cross-culturally. Gender stratification is not greater in societies with larger average size differences between men or women, or lesser in societies with minimal sex differences in height and weight.

(3) Similarities are far more important and common than differences, although rarely reported. While much has been written about sex differences in the organization of the brain, the similarities in

195

cognitive abilities are massive compared to the slight differences (Kimura 1985). The human brain is a very flexible piece of equipment, and the variation from one person to another, even in the same society, is so great that knowing a person's sex is little help in predicting mental capacity.

(4) It is impossible to isolate the effects of genes and hormones because they involve only tendencies that work themselves out within social environments. In fact, the direction of influence may be the opposite of that commonly assumed. That is, hormone levels often *reflect* rather than cause location in a stratification system. In laboratory studies, the rats that win the struggle for status show a rise in male hormones, while the defeated animals produce lower levels than before the contest. Nor does there appear to be a solid research basis for the idea that female hormone changes have a direct effect on behavior (Greene 1984, Fausto-Sterling 1986).

As for the evolutionary argument that humans carry forward the behavior patterns of their primate cousins, detailed studies of chimpanzees, the apes closest to humans, indicate that aggression in males and submissiveness in females are *less* common than among other primates. Chimpanzees do not live in male-dominated bands; they are relatively noncompetitive; and males and females are roughly similar in size. We have already (Chapter 3) dealt with the myth of man-the-hunter as the original model for gender hierarchies. Rather, it appears that egalitarian gathering represents the earliest human adaptation to the environment.

A NEW VIEW OF SEX DIFFERENCES

The critique of standard science as being based on a male model of behavior implies that there is another way to perceive and behave. This other view sees sex differences as rooted in the social experiences of females and males, not as being fixed in our genes or hormones or evolutionary history. Because it is women who nurture infants and raise children, it is women who develop a sense of connectedness to other people, who are sensitive to emotions, and who rely on experience in contrast to abstract reasoning (Chodorow 1978, Gilligan 1982; but see Rossi 1985,

When you're not locked into the idea that biology determines behavior there are many more options available to you. (© Jon Reis Photography/The Stock Market)

who emphasizes the evolutionary need to reproduce the human species). In contrast, males, because they must separate themselves from their mother in order to become masculine (defined as nonfemale), come to see themselves as isolated individuals, to think in terms of hierarchy and direct cause-and-effect relations, and to equate objectivity with truth (Keller 1985).

Although there is some controversy over the extent to which these differences are rooted in nature (biology) or nurture (society), most scholars agree that the two aspects are intertwined, and that each is influenced by the other. Furthermore, there is increasing agreement that individual and societal well-being depend on being able to continue the virtues of both sets of traits: individuality *and* connectedness, rationality *and* emotion, abstract reasoning *and* personal experience (Diamond and Ackelsberg 1987).

THE DISTRIBUTION OF SEX DIFFERENCES

Even where sex-linked traits are found, it must be kept in mind that the data reported are for *group differences*. That is, when groups of males and females are tested, their measurements will vary *on the average* for those groups. For example, if a researcher is studying acts of nurturance among boys and girls, it is very likely that the total score for girls will be higher than for boys. Let us say that 100 girls produced 600 acts of nurturance in the period under study, whereas 100 boys produced 400. This result does not mean that each girl produced two more nurturant acts than each boy. Rather, when each child's score is arranged along a continuum, the pattern illustrated in Figure 8-2 emerges.

Note that some boys outscored the average girl, and that some girls scored below the average boy. Most of both sexes have scores clustering around 5. Moreover, the difference between the highest- and lowest-scoring girls or boys (0–10) is greater than the difference between the group averages (2). Thus, there is more variation *within* each gender group than between the two sexes. If an observer were to guess which children were more nurturant than others on the basis of sex only, he or she would be correct in six out of ten guesses. By chance alone, an observer would be correct five out of ten times. The added advantage of the sex-linked guess is often only slightly greater than the accuracy to be obtained by picking names from a hat.

A similar diagram would describe almost every other male–female difference that has been systematically studied. In other words, group differences that are often assumed to be absolute are really matters of degree. The effects of sex (or race—and even age, in many cases) on behavior and attitudes are rarely direct; they are largely due to how these ascribed characteristics are viewed by others and how they are used to control access to opportunities and the distribution of scarce societal rewards.

Functional Perspectives on Gender Stratification

Any system of inequality may be justified if it can be shown that those at the top of the hierarchy possess talents and skills that make their success not only possible but necessary to group survival. Those at the lower ranks of the hierarchy are presumed to be without the traits required for leadership. In this perspective, gender inequality is functional for the group because it rewards men for toughness and individualism, which, in the worlds of government and business, are considered superior to caring and connectedness. Conversely, women gain approval for motherhood, homemaking, and caring for husbands.

Because this clear division of labor is thought to reflect innate sex differences, both men and women can achieve personal satisfaction when they follow nature's ground plan. In addition, when they must support a dependent wife and children, men are motivated to remain employed and to work hard (Parsons 1951, Gilder 1973). According to this view, if women were to compete with men in the world outside the home, it might undermine his identity and commitment to work. When each sex has a separate sphere, jealousy is eliminated.

Functionalists are impressed with how female and male traits complement one another: independence/dependence, instrumental orientation/expressiveness, thrusting outward/focused inward. Because these characteristics are thought to follow from differences in reproductive biology and/or the organization of the brain, many functionalists fail to see how these traits are socially constructed and differentially evaluated. But even if it were not in the nature of men and women to have opposite needs and capacities, there are powerful social reasons why such differences would be produced. In many societies, group survival depends on women's single-minded devotion to bearing and raising children. And in most societies—simple or complex—responsibility

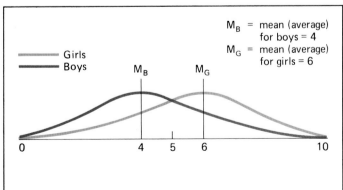

Figure 8-2
Comparison of girls' and boys' scores on acts of nurturance.

for wives and children does strengthen men's commitment to work roles.

Conflict Perspectives on Gender Inequality

From the conflict perspective, sexual stratification has the same basis as any other form of inequality: differential access to the means of production (tools, land, knowledge) and to its products (goods and services).

In general, women's social and personal freedom is related to (1) their *economic* contribution to the well-being of the group and (2) their ability to inherit property. That is why, as seen in Figure 8-1, male dominance is lowest in societies where women provide the major share of food, and highest where land and its products are firmly in the control of men (Blumberg 1978).

In addition to economic power, *beliefs* about what is feminine and masculine influence division of labor and relationships between the sexes. For example, gathering bands with a plentiful food supply tend to have creation myths that emphasize harmony with nature and one another, thus reducing the ideological basis for power differences. In contrast, where the food supply is uncertain and where there is a threat of outside competition, myths emphasize the struggle against nature and one another, in which case control over women is a symbolic means of controlling nature (Sanday 1981).

In all societies, as we have noted several times, beliefs are social products, typically designed to support the existing distribution of power. These beliefs are embedded in *symbols,* in the language and in our cognitive structures, so that we come to perceive male and female as very different categories. If you think of how, in our language, maleness is associated with strength and femaleness with weakness, you can begin to appreciate the power of symbolic controls (Thorne et al. 1983).

Furthermore, when femaleness is defined as deviance from a male standard of desirability, women become a stigmatized category (Schur 1984). As discussed in Chapter 6, the label of deviant serves as a form of *social control,* thereby limiting options. The social control of women can

also be accomplished through laws that treat men and women differently (Rosen 1987) and through the use or threat of the use of force (Sheffield 1987). Thus, from the conflict perspective, whatever the original basis of inequality, once the hierarchy is established, powerful mechanisms of social control—psychological and physical—reinforce it over time.

Most recently, the conflict viewpoint has located gender inequality in women's responsibility for the *social reproduction of labor power* (Vogel 1983, Hartsock 1983). What this means is that, as the functionalists also claim, women are needed primarily to bear and rear the next generation of workers and to keep the current labor force well fed and motivated. So long as women are solely responsible for these tasks, the argument goes, they cannot participate fully in other institutional spheres, nor will they be encouraged to do so (Huber and Spitze 1983, Berk 1985, Hess and Sussman 1984).

This is the reason why one, if not *the,* central goal of the New Feminist Movement is freedom for women to choose their own reproductive strategies (Petchesky 1984), and also why this issue has generated such fierce opposition. If gender stratification is ultimately based on who has control over women's bodies, giving women the right to decide how often and when they will bear children is a profound blow to patriarchal power.

Unlike the functionalists, conflict theorists are less concerned with the origins of stratification systems than with the ways in which structures of inequality are maintained over time. To understand gender stratification, therefore, we must also examine how gender identities are established and reinforced.

> **Social reproduction of labor power** refers to women's role in bearing and raising the next generation of workers.

Socialization to Gendered Identities

Learning about the gendered self and the gendered world is like any other socialization experience, and through the same agents: parents, peers, teachers, and the mass media. No society leaves this process to chance or to some natural unfolding of inborn tendencies. Rather, constant pressures are placed on the growing child, more severe in some societies than others, depending on how much the sexes are thought to differ.

In fact, gender stereotyping begins with expectations for an infant *before* its actual birth. These expectations become social reality when parents respond to the baby's appearance and gestures, as seen in the box at the right. From birth on, children receive very clear gender-typed messages about what "little" or "big" boys and girls are supposed to want and do. Agents of socialization reward conformity and punish deviance. The end product is typically a child and then an adult who fits the cultural definition of feminine or masculine. There is also evidence that, at a very early age, the child becomes an active agent in its own socialization, developing the motivation as well as specific skills for sex-appropriate behavior.

Cognitive structures shape how the mind processes information.

Another way in which socialization pressures work is through *cognitive structures,* that is, in shaping how the mind processes information. According to Rose Laub Coser (1986), the often-observed difference between boys and girls in mathematics skills can be accounted for by differential socialization to anticipated family roles. Girls are encouraged to remain close to home, to limit their explora-

The eye of the beholder sees through social lenses. Is this a little boy or a little girl? (© Pellegrini/International Stock Photo)

The Eye of the Beholder

A research team led by Jeffrey Rubin interviewed the parents of firstborn sons and daughters—fifteen of each sex—as soon as possible following birth. The fathers had been able to view the infant through the windows in the hospital nursery; the mothers had held and fed the child. The parents were asked to "describe your baby as you would to a close friend or relative" and also to fill out a short questionnaire containing descriptive terms for rating their infant: firm—soft, fussy—easy-going, hardy—delicate, cuddly—not cuddly, and the like.

The parents of sons were more likely than the parents of daughters to rate the infant as firm, large-featured, well coordinated, alert, strong, and hardy. The parents of female infants tended to describe their daughters as small, cute, delicate, and cuddly. In most sets of parents, the father gave more extreme ratings to the child than did the mother.

These findings are especially significant in view of the fact that the infants themselves *did not differ significantly* by sex on measures of weight, length, skin color, muscle tone, reflexes, heartbeat, or respiratory rate. In other words, the parents saw in their newborns the characteristics associated with adults of the same sex as the baby. Knowing whether or not the infant was male or female allowed the parents to organize a host of perceptions around that piece of information, regardless of the objective data.

Jeffrey Rubin, Frank Provenzano, and Zella Luria, "The Eye of the Beholder." In *Psychology of Women,* edited by Juanita Williams (New York: Norton, 1979), pp. 134–41.

tion of physical space, and to have few but intense friendships. As a consequence, they do not have the same experiences of expanding control over physical space, of dealing with abstract ideas rather than practical details, and of weaving complex social networks. The result is that boys develop the cognitive abilities associated with mastery in mathematics and science, while girls become rooted in everyday concerns and simple role systems. Coser notes that recent changes in the socialization of girls have resulted in improved performance on tests of math skills, suggesting that sex differences in this cognitive area may disappear over time (see also Eccles and Jacobs 1986, and Baker and Entwhisle 1987).

But differential socialization will be extremely hard to dislodge entirely, so deeply ingrained is it in the structures of everyday life. One recent participant-observation study of elementary schools (Thorne and Luria 1986) found extensive gender segregation among the children and very different kinds of social relations within the groups of boys and girls. The boys come together in group attempts to break the rules; the girls form intimate attachments to one or two close friends. These relations become the basis for adolescent understandings of sexuality and gender identity.

As you remember from Chapter 5, socialization embraces not only internalization of the norms but also formation of a self-image. In general, the accomplishments of men are rated higher than those of women, even when the actual work is comparable. For example, when a scholarly article carried the name of a male rather than a female author, even women students thought it was better written and more informative than the identical article with only the author's name switched (Goldberg 1968, Paludi and Strayer 1985).

One of the most consistent findings in the social-psychological literature is the lower self-esteem and greater self-hatred of female respondents compared to males (Hoelter 1983). Women describe themselves and other women in more negative terms than do men, which is not surprising

as they enact social roles of little power or worth. Even motherhood, although widely praised, offers few societal rewards, while also making women more dependent on the support and protection of men. Although the household is thought to be "women's sphere," where she can reign supreme, the family is not an egalitarian institution, and even there, men have greater power due to their greater earning capacity outside the household (Curtis 1986).

Whatever power and prestige are to be gained from the role of wife and mother must come through one's children, a situation that often leads to overmothering, especially of sons. But in many traditional societies, once a woman has completed her major tasks of bearing and rearing children, her status in the society improves. Middle age often brings personal freedoms and enhanced social power (Brown and Kerns 1985). When her children are grown, a woman has fewer restrictions on her physical movements; she can exert influence on her children's marriage choices and give orders to her daughters-in-law; and even be eligible for roles in the larger community. Whether this improvement in status is due to hormone changes and is therefore built into a universal human pattern of psychosocial development (Guttmann 1985), or simply reflects a lessened need for control over women's sexuality remains a point of de-

It takes a great deal of learning to become the men and women society requires. These young women are making that "extra effort" at a New Mexico beauty school. (© D. Fineman/SYGMA)

bate. But either way, early socialization is always subject to modification through social experiences (see Gerson 1986, for a similar point about contemporary American women).

In the next section we will explore the outcomes of sex-typed socialization and social structures on gender stratification in our society.

Systems of Gender Inequality

The umbrella term "status of women" hides as much as it reveals. In most societies there is no simple status of women, but variations depending on the dimension of stratification—power, prestige, control over property—and the institutional sphere—family, politics, religion, economic system. As we have also seen, women's power within a society can change as she ages. Furthermore, there are great differences *within* the population of women, on the basis of social class, race, and ethnic background. Even though all women may be subordinate to men in the society, women of the higher classes enjoy advantages denied to other women, and in racially stratified societies such as the United States and the Union of South Africa, white women of any social rank share reflected power over women of color. A more accurate term to describe differences between the sexes in the distribution of societal resources, therefore, is *gender inequality* (Mason 1986).

THE POWER DIMENSION

Most positions of power in America—in politics, business, the military, religious and educational institutions—are occupied by white males. This situation is justified (rationalized) by the belief that women do not project images of leadership; that they are not socialized to be comfortable with power; and that, in any event, they do not have the same driving ambition as men do to reach the top. These beliefs take male achievement as the norm, against which women are seen to fall short because of their own failures or basic nature.

In contrast to these views, most recent research on power inequality in politics

Gender inequality refers to the differences between men and women in the distribution of societal resources of power, prestige, and property.

The majority of corporate executives are male. Here, purchasing and supply executives meet to discuss business. (© Junebug Clark/Photo Researchers, Inc.)

and business has examined social structural variables such as informal networks, the sex ratio of the workplace, information channels, support from senior officials, availability of child care, flexible schedules, and so forth (Kantor 1977, Epstein 1983, Sapiro 1983, Carroll 1984, Haas and Perucci 1984, Baron and Bielby 1986). From this perspective, the barriers are in the situations rather than in the individuals. Most obviously, as long as women must assume major responsibility for raising children, they cannot compete on equal grounds with men for positions that are thought to require extraordinary investments of time and energy.

Despite structural obstacles, however, there has been a dramatic rise in the past decade in the numbers of women seeking high positions in politics and business. An equally strong shift has also taken place in public attitudes toward women in these fields.

In Politics. As late as 1985, there were very few women holding national office: two senators, two governors, roughly 5 percent of members of Congress, one or two cabinet-rank officers. But it takes a while for any potential candidate, male or female, to work his or her way up the local and state political party structure, to make the needed contacts, exchange favors, and demonstrate the ability to raise funds. By the mid-term elections of 1986, an unusually large number of women had done just that, winning nomination for Congress **201**

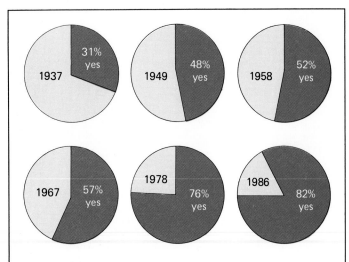

Figure 8-3
Changing attitudes toward women in public life: Percentage of the American population who say they would vote for a woman for president.

Throughout the industrial world, women have increased their political representation. Even in Japan, the most patriarchal of modern societies, a woman was chosen to lead a major political party (*New York Times* 1986). But the last modern state to grant legal equality to women was Switzerland, where women won the right to vote in federal elections only in 1971, and gained equal rights in marriage in 1985. In general, however, women's political presence throughout the world remains quite low and is usually concentrated at the local level and in areas thought to be of special concern to women: education, health, and social welfare. These are also fields for which women are assumed to be uniquely qualified by virtue of their higher capacity for nurturance, in contrast to the more masculine attributes of mastery associated with higher office and areas such as foreign affairs, defense, commerce, and the like (Mueller 1986).

In Business. A similar pattern is found in the world of business, where women now fill one-third of all management posts (compared to 19 percent in 1972), but very few reach the top—only 2 percent of the highest ranking corporate officers are women (*Wall Street Journal* 1986). Nonetheless, women are flocking to graduate schools of business administration, where they now compose 40 percent of the student body, compared to 15 percent in 1976. The number of women with MBAs increased four-fold in the decade 1976–1986, from 5,000 to 21,000. During the same period the entry wage gap between men and women graduates narrowed from four to one thousand dollars.

Because the world of business is not

and governorships. The female candidate is no longer an oddity, and as Figure 8-3 indicates, the proportions of Americans who say that they would vote for a woman for president (or who may simply be unwilling to tell an interviewer that they would not) has risen steadily since the 1930s, and most rapidly in the past two decades.

In the past, the few women in Congress gained their seats by completing the term of a husband who died in office. Today, women are elected in their own right, and they begin their political careers at the local level, on school boards or town councils. It is at these lower levels—state, county, and town government—that the proportion of women in elective office has increased most dramatically, providing the bumper crop of credible candidates in 1986. For example, by 1986, women accounted for 15 percent of mayors and council members in towns of over 10,000 population, compared to only 5 percent in 1976 (National League of Cities 1986).

Yet at the state level, while women comprise over 15 percent of all legislators, they hold only 3 percent of leadership positions (see Table 8-1). A minority within a minority, black women, who represent 6 percent of the total population, held only three-tenths of one percent of elective offices in 1986. Only one black woman now sits in Congress compared to almost two dozen black men.

TABLE 8-1 Percentages of women in selected appointed and elective offices: U.S.

U.S. Senate	2.0%	1987
U.S. House	4.5%	1987
State Legislature	15.5%	1987
Statewide Elective Office	14.6%	1987
State Cabinet Appointees	17.9%	1986
County Governing Boards	8.0%	1984
Mayors & Municipal Council	14.3%	1985

SOURCE: The National Information Bank on Women in Public Office (NIB), a service of the Center for the American Woman and Politics, Eagleton Institute of Politics, Rutgers University.

In 1986, for the first time in Japanese history, a woman, Takako Doi was elected to head a major political party, the Japan Socialist Party even though women hold little over 1% of all the seats in the powerful lower house of Parliament and about 4% of all Parliament seats. (© Kaku Kurita/Gamma-Liaison)

only stratified by gender but by race as well, the proportion of nonwhite women in business schools and executive positions is exceedingly small. Indeed, a recent survey of the nation's 1000 largest companies found only four black senior executives, all men (*New York Times,* May 22, 1987 p. D4). Against such odds, few black or Hispanic women are willing to invest their time and money in executive training. In addition, the limits placed on the careers of white women that we detail in the following paragraphs are doubly constraining for women of color. As a consequence, successful black and Hispanic businesswomen are typically found in self-owned companies and in the fields of cosmetics and fashion.

Although women are rapidly moving into fields once considered exclusive male specialties, the careers of men and women executives still follow different paths. Women executives are typically found in such "feminine" fields as cosmetics, fashion, retailing, public relations, and personnel. The road to corporate power, however, lies elsewhere: in manufacturing, oil and chemicals, financial services, holding companies, and transportation, and, within firms, in production and sales divisions. In terms of directorships on corporate boards, women now occupy close to 4 percent of director chairs in the Fortune

1000 leading companies, and there is typically only one per board (a form of *tokenism*).

According to reporters for the *Wall Street Journal* (Mar. 24, 1986:1), women reach a "glass ceiling" on their way to top management, stopping just short of the inner circle. In part, this is due to the fact that women executives have not yet built up seniority in their firms. But there are a number of other obstacles, including: (1) corporate tradition and prejudice; (2) lack of a sponsor/mentor to guide their career; (3) the belief that women lack ambition and put the welfare of their family above that of the corporation; or, conversely, that men fulfill their family obligations by devoting themselves to work; (4) the fact that "men at the top feel uncomfortable with women beside them" in a business context.

The female executive is in a no-win situation: if she is tough, she is not perceived as womanly, but if she is not tough, she is not worth promoting. Women in management find that they must perform better than men in order to be taken seriously as equals (Pugh and Wahrman 1983, Sutton and Moore 1985). Even so, 61 percent of women executives surveyed by the *Wall Street Journal* report being mistaken for a secretary while attending a business meeting (Rogan 1984). As a consequence,

Tokenism involves the appointment or promotion of one or a few women to positions of power and responsibility in organizations.

An important business meeting about the development of a new office complex. Who are the architects and engineers and who's the secretary? (© LDG PRODUCTIONS/The Image Bank)

many women leave the large companies for smaller firms or start their own businesses. Indeed, since 1975 women have been going into business for themselves at a rate four times that of men. Today, over 25 percent of all small businesses are owned by women. Most, however, are small firms with relatively low profits (Bureau of Labor Statistics 1986). Nevertheless, as owners or executives in small businesses, women have greater control over their working conditions and can mesh their work obligations with family responsibilities. Larger companies have not yet made the changes that would be necessary to retain women managers, such as corporate day care centers, maternity leaves without loss of seniority, or flexible work schedules (Hardesty and Jacobs 1986). If frequent transfers are necessary, married women will find it more difficult to relocate than will married men because a man is more likely to ask his wife to move and change jobs than a woman will ask her husband to look for a new job (Markham et al. 1983). These conditions force many women to choose between career and marriage or between career and parenthood, choices that rarely confront male executives.

Success in the corporate world also depends on informal contacts. Information is exchanged and business conducted on golf courses and in private clubs as well as in offices. To the degree that women are excluded from these settings, they are at a disadvantage in the race to succeed. It is still the case that a majority of private

eating and athletic clubs do not open membership to women (or to black and Jewish men, in many cases). In one case, a woman member of the Texas legislature was shoved out the door of an exclusive club on the grounds that "business was conducted at the noon hour and that women were a distraction (because they) would make the place sound like a gaggle of magpies" (Nazario 1986, p. 21D). To many men, these clubs are the last place they can call all theirs, so that resistance to admitting women members remains very strong. But a number of court cases are challenging this practice on the grounds that so long as business is transacted in these settings, both sexes should be admitted. And, if they are not, then membership dues ought not to be a tax-deductible business expense. Many clubs will then be forced either to admit women or lose members who can no longer afford to join as private persons.

The same wish to exclude women also characterizes men in stereotypically masculine occupations who have recently been forced to adapt to female coworkers. Although women have been effectively integrated into police departments for a number of years, it has been much more difficult for them to be accepted as fire fighters, in part because of the need to share sleeping quarters. In New York City, for example, women fire fighters still report that the men in their company refuse to speak to them, hide or damage their equipment, and subject them to physical harassment (Daley 1986).

PRESTIGE

If prestige is measured by occupational status, we have already noted the growing but still small numbers of women who hold high positions in politics and business. Much the same may be said of medicine, law, college teaching, and science and engineering. Although some institutions may have actively discriminated against female applicants, at least one study indicates that the real cause of the small number of women in professional schools before the 1970s was largely due to socialization-based occupational choice (Cole 1986).

The change since 1970 has been dramatic. For example, women today compose about 30 percent of medical school graduates compared to under 6 percent in 1960; and in law schools, close to 40 percent of recent graduates are women in contrast to 2.5 percent in 1960 (*Statistical Abstract of the United States,* 1987: 148).

But at this point in our discussion, you will not be surprised to learn that women lawyers and physicians tend to be concentrated in the lower-prestige sectors of their professions: family law, for example, rather than corporate mergers, and pediatrics rather than heart surgery. Women are also more likely than men to work in the public sector—as district attorneys or public defenders in the field of law, and as public health or clinic workers in the field of medicine (Epstein 1983, Zimmerman 1987). Changes are occurring, however, as increasing numbers of women law and medical students elect to be trained in the high-prestige specialties.

A similar pattern may be found in the graduate training of Ph.D.s. In 1970, for example, women earned 13 percent of all doctorates; the figure today is over one-third. Despite the increase in numbers, however, women academics are still concentrated in the lower ranks of the faculty and in nontenured positions (American Association of University Professors 1986). Although it will be at least another decade before women are routinely found in senior positions, many have already become department chairs, deans, and presidents of professional societies. Within sociology, however, women are most likely to be found in the less prestigious sub-specialties—e.g., family studies as compared to complex organizations.

Similarly, in science and engineering the numbers of women in technical fields is slowly but steadily increasing, though not to the dramatic extent as in medicine and law. In 1984, women accounted for 25 percent of scientists and only 3 percent of engineers. While the major barriers to graduate training have been largely overcome, equal treatment in the labor market remains a distant goal. Once having earned a degree, women scientists and engineers are more likely than their male colleagues to be unemployed, to work outside their field of expertise, to be denied promotion, and to receive lower salaries (Haas and Percucci 1984, National Science Foundation 1986). In addition, the representation of women in science and engineering is likely to remain low because females are not encouraged to develop the required skills and interests in high school and college (Office of Technology Assessment 1985).

In general, the higher the prestige ranking of an occupation, the fewer the women in it (Bose and Rossi 1983) and the lower the percentage of those women who are nonwhite. Conversely, when an occupation is dominated by women, it is considered low prestige (even if the occupation is medicine, as in the Soviet Union). As women move in large numbers into previously male-dominated fields, not only do the men leave, but the social definition of that occupation changes (Cohn 1985). For example, before 1945, being a bank teller was the path to a management job for young men. After the war, when other types of employment appeared more attractive to men so that banks were forced to hire women, being a bank teller became another dead-end job. In contrast, when babies were delivered by midwives, the task was not considered very prestigious, but once childbirth was taken over by the male medical establishment, obstetrics became a valued profession (Rothman 1982). And where men are "tokens" in a female-dominated field, they are often seen as more competent and worthy of rapid promotion compared to women, as in one study of male nurses (J. Gans 1983). Yet there is some evidence of changing attitudes, at least among college students, whose evaluations of occupational prestige did not depend on the ratio of male to female workers in several professional fields (Johnson 1986).

But most employed women do not have "careers"; they have "jobs," just as most men in the labor force have jobs that are fairly routine and closely supervised, with minimal opportunities for advancement. Indeed, much of the debate over whether or not women are displacing men in the labor force shifts attention away from the fact that the majority of workers today, male and female, are losing ground in terms of wages, job security, and upward mobility (see Chap. 12). However, lower-income white males come to believe that their lack of mobility is due to blacks and women being given preferential treatment, then they will not question the larger stratification system into which they are locked.

PROPERTY

In 1860, New York became the first state to allow a married woman to own property in her own right, to make contracts (but only with her husband's consent), and to become a joint legal guardian of her children. But it took another 110 years for a married woman to be able to establish a credit rating in her own name. Until quite recently, the basic assumption was that because a married woman would be financially supported by her husband, she need not and/or could not own or control resources as an independent person.

LABOR FORCE PARTICIPATION

But it is often forgotten that most women and especially black women in our society have always worked for a living—if not in the paid labor force, then producing goods and services within the home, taking in boarders, tending small shops, and the like. Because these women thought of themselves primarily as housewives, that was how they were listed by the Census Bureau, giving us a highly inaccurate picture of the proportions of working women in the past (Bose 1987).

Full time motherhood has always been a luxury reserved for wives of the well-to-do, and even they often hire others to look after their children. It was only after World War II, when many families moved from cities to the new suburbs of one-family homes, that women were cut off from the stream of adult interactions of small towns and city neighborhoods.

Homemaking and child-care activities expanded to fill the time available to the suburban wife and mother. Birth rates soared from the late 1940s to the mid-1960s, and the economy flourished on the manufacture of appliances for the home: washers, dryers, toasters, television sets, baby furniture, a second car, and so on. In contrast to the economically *productive* households of the past, the modern household is a *consuming* unit only, in which women are charged with maintaining the home, its occupants, and its gadgets.

The kind of productive jobs once available to women at home—serving boarders, taking in wash, dressmaking—have been replaced by factory and office work. Women, like men, have to leave the home to join the productive labor force. And they have, in ever increasing proportions. In 1940, over 27 percent of American women worked outside the home; at the height of the war effort, this figure rose to 35 percent. Not all left the labor force at war's end. In 1955, at the peak of the baby boom, one-third of American women were employed, not much lower than during the war. That percentage has risen each year since. Today, close to six in ten

As the labor force participation of women with young children increases, more women will need child care facilities. What options are available for today's working mothers? (© Steven McCurry/Magnum)

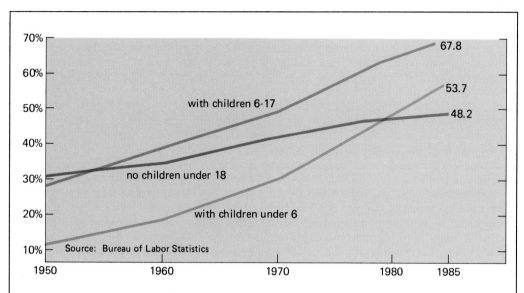

Figure 8-4   Women in the labor force (women's labor force participation, 1950–85). More married women, husband present, with children have been joining the labor force in recent years, and a higher share of women with children than those without children are working or looking for work. Women without children under eighteen at home are older, on average, and less likely to be attached to the work force. (From Daphne Spain and Suzanne M. Bianchi, "How Women Have Changed," *American Demographics*, May 1983, p. 23; *Statistical Abstract of the United States, 1987*, p. 383.)

American women are in the paid labor force: two-thirds of all single women; 55 percent of married women; and 43 percent of the widowed or divorced. The great majority hold full-time jobs. Women workers compose over 44 percent—almost half—of the entire civilian labor force.

In addition to these rising numbers, there has been a major change in the *composition* of the female labor force, from one composed largely of single women up to 1940 to one increasingly dominated by married women. In addition, the labor-force participation of women with small children has risen dramatically since 1970, as seen in Figure 8-4.

In 1986, half of all married women with children under one-year-old were employed, as were 38 percent of single mothers with infants (Hayge 1986). Among single mothers with children under three, 79 percent were in the full-time labor force, as were 84 percent with children ages six to seventeen.

Clearly, most American women are out to work, and while some may withdraw from the labor force for a few years in order to care for small children, the trend

is toward continued employment. Women enter the work force and stay there for several reasons. Those without husbands must earn their own living. Those who are married can enjoy the benefits of a two-paycheck income—one-third higher than the median for families in which the husband is the only wage earner. But money isn't everything. The challenge of the job and social contacts with other workers are very important aspects of women's attachment to paid work (Fox and Hesse-Biber 1985).

Interestingly, during the same period that women's labor force-participation rates have risen so dramatically, those for men have slowly but steadily *declined,* due largely to older men choosing early retirement. Indeed, it appears that the strength of the work ethic has diminished greatly. Most older workers elect to leave the labor force as soon as they are assured an adequate retirement income. (There is sex differentiation here. Recent research suggests that men retire earlier than women, in part because women's life pattern is more varied and in part because their retirement benefits are not as great as they are for men. *New York Times,* Apr. 3, 1986, p. C12.) If these trends continue, the proportions of men and women in the labor force will be roughly equal at ages sixteen to twenty-four, vary most at ages twenty-five to forty-four, and narrow again at ages forty-five to sixty-four. In other words, most American couples in the years ahead will share the world of work, if not the world of home, although some men are increasingly involved in child care (Stein 1984).

Most women who are not in the labor force are also working, though not for pay. They provide a range of needed services for other household members—shopping, food preparation, laundrying, transportation—that does not then have to be purchased from outsiders. In most other modern industrial societies, the importance of this range of service work is recognized by providing tax benefits, pension credits for homemakers, or government payments based on the size of the family. Americans have resisted adopting such programs, perhaps out of the belief that work in the household should be done "for love alone."

THE WAGE GAP

For every woman who enters the labor force in a nontraditional or high-paying position, several others enter at the lower levels (Moore 1986). Furthermore, most employed women in the future will continue to work in low-pay dead-end "pink collar" jobs (Reskin and Hartmann 1986). The overall effect has been to maintain a *gender gap* in earnings that has changed very little since the 1950s. On average, among full-time workers, women earn between sixty to sixty-four cents for every dollar earned by men. The gap is narrowest among new workers, especially college-educated women, and could close even further if they remain in the labor force and work full-time throughout adulthood (Smith and Ward 1985).

An emphasis on the qualities brought to the labor market by individuals, however, cannot account for continued sex differentials in pay for people with similar qualifications in the same occupation. Nor can personal characteristics explain the continued existence of occupations dominated by one sex when there is nothing in the work itself that logically favors one over the other. That is, only about one-third of the gender gap in wages can be explained by *human capital* variables—education, job experience, skill training, work continuity, and the like, or by such psychological components as motivation and commitment (Corcoran and Duncan 1985).

The key factor appears to be *sex segregation* in the workplace, both by occupations and by jobs within a given occupation, as well as within specific work organizations (Harkess 1985, Baron and Bielby 1985, Bielby and Baron 1986, Reskin and Hartmann 1986, Wharton 1986, Tienda et al. 1987). This pattern is also found in other modern industrial societies (see O'Donnell 1985, for Australia; Schmid and Weitzel 1984, for West Germany; and Ruggie 1984, for Sweden and Great Britain). Although the degree of sex segregation in jobs and the workplace has declined slightly in the past fifteen years, most workers are in occupations dominated by members of their own sex. Because occupations are sex segregated, different pay scales can be justified by employers. For example, in 1984 at Yale University, administrative assistants with graduate degrees and reading knowledge of foreign languages, all of whom were women, received annual salaries of $13,000 to $13,600 compared to $18,000 per year for the university's truck drivers, all of whom were male.

Human capital variables are personal characteristics such as education, job experience, skill training, and work continuity.

Sex segregation occurs when women or men are concentrated in a given occupation or in particular jobs within an occupation or work organizations.

The **gender gap** in wages refers to the discrepancy between average earnings of women and men.

SOCIOLOGY & YOU
Sexual Scripts and Gender Roles

Is it really necessary for men and women to participate in the same sexual script in order to get along together?

Sean sauntered up to a group of his friends. "Guess what?" he grinned.

"You just won the World Cup!" countered Jack.

The group laughed.

"So what's up?" asked Jack. "Or is this a quiz show?"

"It's Lynne."

"Yeah?"

"She just asked me out."

"Whoa!" yelled Jack as Bill whistled. Larry said, "Great! Did you accept?"

"Yeah. We're going to her friend's birthday party Saturday night."

Comparable worth or pay equity means similar wages for jobs requiring the same level of skill, training, and responsibility.

In order to lessen such gender gaps in wages, women's rights groups have proposed the principle of *pay equity* or *comparable worth* (Feldberg 1984, Reskin 1984, Steinberg and Haigner 1984, Ladd-Taylor 1985). What this means is that people who occupy jobs that require similar levels of skill, effort, and responsibility, and that are carried out under similar conditions of safety and comfort, should receive similar wages. This position has been vigorously opposed by government officials and business leaders. Nonetheless, several recent court decisions and contracts between state governments and public-employee unions have made pay equity a reality, and it has become "the issue of the 1980s" for many feminists.

At this writing, over half of our state governments are in the process of implementing or studying pay-equity schedules, and in 1986, San Francisco became the first city to vote approval for the idea of equal pay for jobs of comparable worth among its municipal employees.

In the Yale case, a ten-week strike that almost closed down the school ultimately produced a more equitable pay scale, but not without a great deal of resistance from the university administration (claiming that a college is a special place with a special mission that places it above ordinary union negotiations).

Winds of Change

As a result of increased labor-force participation, expanded educational opportunities, and lower fertility rates (with the exception of the period 1947–1965), many American women have gained a sense of independence. And their continued experience with the gender-stratification system has led some to organize for change. The goal of the New Feminist Movement which emerged in the mid-1960s is precisely to challenge gender inequality, in the family and society (Ferree and Hess 1984). Not surprisingly, the far-ranging goals of contemporary feminism have unleashed a powerful backlash. See Chapter 21 for an analysis of the backlash movement. Opposition comes from individual women and men with deep investments in existing gender relations, from employers who would have to change their ways of doing business, and from other groups who benefit from many forms of inequality or have firm ideas about the essential differences between men and women. These people perceive many losses and few gains from any change in the gender-stratification system.

At this writing, it is popularly assumed that the New Feminist Movement has run its course and that the great majority of

---

"You lucked out, guy. Lynne is something. I guess she must really be into you. You'll score big."

"Do you think so?" Sean asked. "I kind of felt she asked me because she needed a date and well, we get along real well—in a sort of non-sexual way."

"Get out!" Bill was vehement. "Any woman who's got what it takes to ask a guy out really wants to make it with him."

Larry looked amused. "That's just wish fulfillment. I'm not saying she doesn't like Sean, but she's not necessarily after his body. I mean, look at it, after all?"

The guys laughed. Sean looked embarrassed.

"Besides," Larry continued, "maybe she just didn't want to show up alone. Women are like that."

"Maybe I shouldn't go." Sean didn't look too happy about this situation.

"Cold feet?"

"No, well, I don't know. If that's what she's after . . . well, I like to make those kind of moves first."

Larry slapped him on the shoulder: "Welcome to the 80s, Sean. Sweet land of confusion."

This textbook has spent considerable time examining the way in which gender roles are learned and how the expectations of behavior of men and women are culturally shaped. It also identifies areas of change and persistence in gender roles. Can you relate what you have learned to the preceding conversation? Which statements seem to be a part of the traditional sexual script? Which statements seem indicative of change? Could you write the female version of this scenario? What do you think Lynne's friends would be saying to her about the fact that she asked Sean out? Would the situation be different if Lynne and Sean were in their thirties rather than their early twenties? What if one of the parties to this encounter were married? Would that change your interpretation of what's going on? How clear are contemporary gender roles to you?

SOURCE: Based on an idea suggested by Beth Jaffe.

The Sociology of Masculinity

Michael S. Kimmel

Michael S. Kimmel is assistant professor of sociology at The State University of New York at Stony Brook. He is the editor of Changing Men: New Directions in the Study of Men and Masculinity *(Sage Publications, 1987),* Men Confronting Pornography *(forthcoming), and* Researching Men's Roles *(a special issue of* American Behavioral Scientist, *May, 1986). He is coauthor of* Against the Tide: Profeminist Men in American History, *a documentary history (Beacon Press, 1988), and his articles on gender, sexuality, and masculinity have appeared in several journals and magazines, including* Gender & Society, Society, Psychology Today, Changing Men, *and in several anthologies.*

When I first mentioned that I was preparing to teach a course on "the sociology of the male experience" my friends and colleagues were intrigued. "Why do you need a separate course on men?" many asked. "Aren't all courses that don't have the word 'woman' in the title implicitly 'about men'?" some wondered. "Isn't this just a way for men to jump on the sex-role bandwagon and, in effect, steal the area away from women?" remarked others.

Each of these statements is partially true. That's the reason why I decided to develop this new course and to educate myself about the sociology of the male experience. It's true that courses not specifically about women are about men, but they are about men only by default. We study men as historical actors—statesmen, soldiers, presidents—or as writers, as psychological "personalities," as members of revolutionary mobs, as classes or status groups, as economic producers or consumers, or filling occupational roles. Rarely, if ever, are men discussed *as men;* rarely is the experience of being a man seen as analytically interesting.

But the core insight of women's studies, it seemed to me, was that gender, like race or class, was a "master status," one of the central organizing principles of social life. Inspired by this, I decided to look at men's lives as gendered lives, as lives in which masculinity was no longer taken for granted, but became the prism through which the life was viewed.

It was like putting on a new pair of glasses. I was seeing the world—a world I thought I knew—in a completely different way. (This is what I understand to be the essential experience of the sociological imagination.) I remembered how architect Louis Sullivan described his ambition as creating "masculine" forms: strong, solid, commanding respect, and how composer Charles Ives criticized a contemporary rival as scoring weak-willed, even "feminine," symphonies that lacked vigor and power. I recalled how President Theodore Roosevelt was praised for his "hard-muscled frame" and his "crackling voice," as a "masculine sort of person with extremely masculine virtues and palpably masculine faults." Or how Ernest Thompson Seton, an organizer of the Boy Scouts of America, described its founding in 1910 as the antidote to a culture that had "turned robust, manly, self-reliant boyhood into a lot of flat chested cigarette smokers with shaky nerves and doubtful vitality." And I also remembered how President Lyndon Johnson, when informed that a liberal senator was going to oppose his policies made a remark suggesting that the senator's anatomy was decidedly not male! I realized that the idea of masculinity had formed a core around which men's experience had revolved; it had become the metaphor by which they understood their experiences. Perhaps its centrality, and the fact that it has been, for so long, the normative gender, has made masculinity so invisible.

With this realization, themes of masculinity were suddenly everywhere I looked, especially in the late 1980s, when men appear so confused about what it means to be a "real" man that scores of books and articles advise us on the subject. My male students were echoing this theme, confessing that they didn't know whether they were expected to be Rambo or Tootsie, Phil Donahue or Clint Eastwood, Ashley Wilkes or Rhett Butler, Alan Alda or Sylvester Stallone.

As a historical sociologist, my impulse is to understand a contemporary phenomenon by examining its historical antecedents. And I soon discovered that the 1980s is not the first historical era in which such confusion about the meaning of masculinity was evident. The issue surfaced in the pivotal decades of the late nineteenth century, when changes in the organization of work following the late-century rapid industrialization, the closing of the frontier, and the perceived "feminization" of American culture (as socialization—home, school, and Sunday School—became increasingly the domain of women) dislodged the definition of masculinity from its traditional moorings. Between 1880 and 1920, advice manuals mushroomed, and the Boy Scouts and Young Men's Christian Association (YMCA) were founded as deliberate attempts to reverse the ennervating trends in American society.

To discover another era of "crisis" of masculinity was intellectually puzzling, but the parallels between then and today are instructive. Today, the rise of multinational corporations and the shift to a service economy (see Chapter 12), themselves phenomena of the globalization of production and the "deindustrialization" of advanced countries, have reshaped both the American economy and the ways in which individuals relate to their work. We also experience the closing of a frontier, as movements of national liberation and decolonization in the Third World seek independence from American influence. And there is renewed concern about the "feminization" of America, a nation grown slothful and indolent, gone "soft" on communism, in which the gains of the women's movement (and not coincidentally the rise of a visible gay culture) are seen as sapping the masculine strength of the nation.

Not all men are reacting against the new definitions of femininity being developed by women in the workplace and the home. And my continuing research project has been to chronicle the history of "pro-feminist" men in American history, those men who actively supported women's claims for equal opportunity, equal education, political participation (suffrage, ERA), sexual autonomy (birth control, abortion), family reforms (divorce, child custody), and against male violence. Here my own experiences came into play, informing my research and my teaching, helping to frame my questions.

My interest in men who supported feminism has its origins in my college years, when I was one of the first male students at Vassar College in 1968–71. I stumbled upon, or more accurately was pushed against the wall by feminist women, whose analysis seemed accurate, even if it did make me uncomfortable. I heard about earlier "Men of Vassar," men like Matthew Vassar himself, who was dedicated to providing an education for women that would be every bit as good as the one men received at Yale or Harvard. And, there was the turn-of-the-century president of the college who organized campus suffrage demonstrations.

I also became involved in the National Organization for Changing Men, a group which supports feminist women and gays and lesbians, and applauds "the insights and positive social changes that feminism has stimulated for both women and men." The organization serves as a national network of men who are active in areas such as counseling men who batter women, enlarging men's options as friends, lovers, husbands, and fathers, and fighting discrimination against gay men and lesbians. I serve as the organization's national spokesperson.

These experiences have also been decisive in my preparation for my course, Sociology of the Male Experience. The class explores what it means to be a man in contemporary American society, what we mean by masculinity—not as a fixed and static role, but as a socially constructed and historically variable set of attitudes and behaviors. I wanted to look at how the meaning of masculinity changes across cultures, in any one culture over time, and over the course of an individual man's life. Like a photograph album, we pause at various pivotal moments—childhood socialization, education, peer relations, sports, the military, sexuality, relationships with women and men, marriage, fatherhood, and aging—to observe how social scientists, historians, and writers and poets had understood those issues. The variations in men's experience—by race, age, class, and sexual orientation—has become one of the course's most significant subtexts.

Mine is only one of a growing number of courses in "Men's Studies," which tap an interest in gender issues generally, and in men's experiences in particular. Perhaps courses like this will become part of the regular curriculum in many colleges and universities, courses in which masculinity is "deconstructed," examined sociologically, and perhaps "reconstructed" within a vision of sexual equality and gender justice.

Americans have rejected radical change and may even be moving back to more traditional patterns of gender relations. Newsmakers refer to a "postfeminist" generation, and a few authors have written books blaming the women's movement for continued inequality (Hewlitt 1986). From a sociological viewpoint, however, vast and probably irreversible changes have taken place and are likely to continue. In this section we examine three of these: changes in men's lives, changes in public attitudes on a range of issues, and the development of feminist scholarship.

CHANGES IN MEN'S LIVES

A commonplace of popular social science is the *idea* of "masculinity in crisis." This is the belief that the traditional "macho" style is too confining for men who seek intimacy rather than dominance in their relationships (Kimmel 1986). While this may be true it is also the case that a series of popular movies and novels with super-tough heroes—characters portrayed by Sylvester Stallone, Chuck Norris, Clint Eastwood, and Charles Bronson—can be seen as an antifeminist statement.

As Kimmel (1986) notes, there have been other historical periods in which traditional definitions of masculinity have been threatened (by economic changes as much as by women's rights activism), with the same predictable reactions: an antifeminist backlash, a reassertion of masculine dominance, and the emergence of a small but important group of men who grasp the possibility of far-reaching change in gender relations.

And, indeed, there is today a small but academically influential "men's movement" that seeks to reduce gender inequality (Doyle 1983, Kimmel 1987). Obviously, it will not be easy to convince men that they have more to gain than lose from changing a system that works to their advantage. The "new man" is one who rises above traditional role expectations and power plays, who is capable of sensitivity, intimacy, and commitment, and who is very supportive of the "new woman." Although the sample studied to date is small, it is evidence that there are men who are more sympathetic than not to the goal of gender equality—often in response to the experiences of their wives and daughters (Astrachan 1986).

The area in which current changes in men's roles is expected to have greatest impact is that of child care. The contributors to a recent collection of scholarly essays on "Men in Families," for example, are in general agreement on the need for men to become more involved in family life—for their own sakes as well as those of their wives and children (Lewis and Salt 1986). The authors cite a variety of data to indicate that men consider their family life as important as their work life, that they expect to spend more time with their children than did their own fathers, and that they support egalitarian marriage relationships.

There is some debate, however, over just how much more involved in child care and homemaking responsibilities even the "new man" can be without support from employers. Actual shifts appear far smaller than commonly thought (Hess and Sussman 1984, Pleck 1987). Nor is there strong data to support the blanket assumption that fathers' involvement in child rearing must have positive effects. The crucial variable is *choice:* what is the preferred arrangement of the parents. As Lamb et al. (1986) state: "Children tend to do best when their parents are able to organize their lives and responsibilities in accordance with their own values and preferences, rather than in accord with a rigid, socially determined pattern" (p. 142).

In actuality, we really do not know much about the potential effects of fathers' involvement in child care because the necessary studies have yet to be undertaken, and because so much of the literature is biased by value judgments and unsupported beliefs about the power of "role models." More important, however, is the fact that men today and in the near future will undoubtedly spend a *smaller* percentage of their lifetime in families with children than did men in previous generations (Eggebeen and Uhlenberg 1985). Age at first marriage is later, as is age at birth of first child; the possibility of divorce is higher (leading to several years in adulthood outside of marriage); and one can expect to live a decade or more after one's children have grown. All of which has decreased the amount of time that men today spend in environments with young children, whatever the potential benefits of such interaction.

Other critics suggest that the "new man" may be a media myth, and that while upper-status men may be more sensitive than their predecessors, they are not more inclined to establish long-term commitments to marriage or parenthood (Ehrenreich 1984). Nonetheless, men's roles in the family are clearly changing:

> I believe that men perceive their roles as being under threat in a world that is different from any in the past. No society has yet come even close to equality between the sexes, but the modern social forces described here did not exist before either. At the most cautious, we must concede that the conditions favoring a trend toward more equality are more favorable than at any prior time in history. If we have little reason to conclude that equality is at hand, let us at least rejoice that we are marching in the right direction. (Goode 1982: 147)

CHANGING ATTITUDES

The impact of the New Feminist Movement can also be seen in changing attitudes toward work, marriage, parenthood, and improving the status of women in general. Typical of most national public opinion polls, data gathered by the Roper Organization in 1970, 1974, 1980, and 1985 show growing levels of support for "efforts to strengthen and change women's status in society today," from 40 percent of women and 44 percent of men in 1970 to 73 percent of women and 69 percent of men in 1985, the first year that women's support exceeds that of men. Support for strengthening women's status is strongest among younger women and those with a college education. Furthermore, 75 percent of all respondents feel that women's roles will continue to change, and 60 per-

What does the body language of each couple tell you about men's and women's role expectations? Given the different historic periods in which they lived, what topics are each couple likely to talk about and what topics are probably taboo? (© Culver Pictures; © Erika Stone/ Photo Researchers, Inc.)

cent feel that women today are looked upon with more respect than was the case only a decade ago.

On the subject of marriage, the percentage of women who feel that "having a loving husband who is able to take care of me is much more important to me than making it on my own" has *declined* from 64 percent in 1974 to 48 percent today. Over the same period, the percentage expressing a preference for combining marriage, career, and children has risen from 52 percent to 63 percent (a figure that rises to 70 percent for women age eighteen to twenty-nine). Although 90 percent of both men and women think that marriage is the best way to live, their idea of an ideal marriage has changed greatly. In 1974, half the sample preferred a traditional ar-

rangement in which the wife was exclusively devoted to homemaking; in 1985, only 37 percent of women and 43 percent of men still preferred that type of marriage. Half of the men and 57 percent of women in 1985 chose a marriage in which husband and wife shared child care, housework, and paid employment.

As for choosing between work inside and outside the home, Tables 8-2 and 8-3 indicate a profound change, especially strong at the younger ages.

In general, it is safe to say that young women today have a very different set of priorities than did young women of the past, and that they are largely supported by their male age peers (Thornton et al. 1983, Mason 1986).

Although combining work and family

TABLE 8-2 Working or staying home

"If you were free to do either, would you prefer to have a job outside the home, or would you prefer to stay home and take care of a house and family?"

	1974	1980	1985
Prefer to Stay Home	60	51	45
Prefer to Have Job	35	46	51
Don't Know	5	3	3

TABLE 8-3 Percentage preferring a job, by age

Age	%
18–29	58
30–39	51
40–49	55
50 +	45

SOURCE: *The 1985 Virginia Slims American Woman's Opinion Poll*, Storrs, CT: Roper Center, 1985: 66–7.

Gender Stratification in Cross-Cultural Perspective

If the United States is far from achieving gender equality, most of the rest of the world has even further to go. While girls and women make up over half of the world's population and account for two-thirds of all labor time, they own less than 1 percent of all property and earn 10 percent of all income (Sarri 1985, Sivard 1985, Tiano 1987).

The situation of women in the Third World (the less economically developed countries of Asia and Africa, and parts of Central and South America) is particularly disadvantaged. Contrary to popular assumptions, the position of women does *not* improve as their societies move into the world economic system. In fact, the few areas of control and autonomy enjoyed by women in traditional societies are eliminated by the introduction of Western capitalist institutions. Most of the new technologies introduced into these societies increase the economic power of men relative to that of women. For example, the emphasis on cash crops for export means that women no longer tend their own garden plots but work as field hands. Agricultural machinery and training are typically provided only to men, and the once-independent women traders of Central Africa have been displaced by more "modern" institutions of exchange (Bossen 1984, Robertson 1984, Blumberg 1986). When women do find paid employment it is as domestic servants or as extremely low-paid workers in global "sweat shops"—clothing and electronics factories in Asia and South America (Nash and Fernandez-Kelly 1983).

Furthermore, many elements of traditional gender inequality survive attempts at modernization. In India, for example, where women are valued as brides according to how much wealth (dowry) they bring to the marriage, bride-burning appears to be increasing at an alarming rate, as men seek to free themselves for additional marriages and additional dowries (Kronholz 1986). And in the People's Republic of China, despite ideological support for gender equality, little has changed in the patriarchal family system of the countryside (Johnson 1983).

Gender equality requires not only ideological commitment but social structural supports—especially for child care and food preparation—and a high evaluation of "reproductive" as well as "productive" labor. The division of labor along gender lines, and the differential social worth of these tasks has reinforced gender inequality on the collective settlements (*kibbutz*) of Israel despite the intention of the founders to ensure equality for all members (Palgi et al. 1983).

Yet there are also ways in which industrial development could improve the chances for gender equality. Most importantly, the spread of education to females and a lowering of fertility rates are essential preconditions for the rise of a feminist movement. Today, organized efforts to improve the status of women are found in all developed nations and increasingly in the Third World (Chafetz and Dworkin 1986).

SOURCES: Kay Ann Johnson, *Women, the Family, and Peasant Revolution in China*, Chicago: University of Chicago Press, 1983; Michal Palgi, Joseph Rafael Blasi, Menachem Rosner, and Marilyn Safir (Eds.), *Sexual Equality: The Israeli Kibbutz Tests the Theories*, Norwood, PA: Norwood Editions, 1983; Laurel H. Bossen, *The Redivision of Labor: Women and Economic Choice in Four Guatemalan Communities*, Albany, NY: State University of New York Press, 1984; June Nash and Maria Patricia Fernandez-Kelly, *Women, Men, and the International Division of Labor*, Albany, NY: State University of New York Press, 1984; Claire C. Robertson, *Sharing the Same Bowl: A Socioeconomic History of Women and Class in Accra, Ghana*, Bloomington, IN: Indiana University Press, 1984; Rosemary Sarri, *World Feminization of Poverty*, 1985; Ruth L. Sivard, *Women . . . A World Survey*, Washington, DC: World Priorities, 1985; Rae Lesser Blumberg, "Gender Stratification and Economic Development: Paradigm and Praxis at the Intersection of Social Structure, Human Lives, and the African Food Crisis," paper presented at the 81st Annual Meeting of the American Sociological Association, New York, August 1986; June Kronholz, "Amid Social Progress, Bride-Burning Appears on the Rise in India," *Wall Street Journal*, Aug. 21, 1986, p. 1 ff.; Janet S. Chafetz and Anthony G. Dworkin, *Female Revolt: The Rise of Women's Movements in World and Historical Perspectives*, Totowa, NJ: Rowman & Littlefield, 1986; Susan Tiano, "Gender, Work, and World Capitalism: Third World Women's Role in Development," in Beth B. Hess and Myra Marx Ferree, *Analyzing Gender: A Handbook of Social Science Perspectives*, Newbury Park, CA: Sage, 1987.

obligations does lead to "role overload," there are compensations: a widening set of role choices is thought to account for the great improvement in the mental health of married women over the past decade or so (Kessler and McRae 1982). Multiple role identities enhance a sense of self-worth in both men and women and reduce symptoms of anxiety and distress, even among women trying to "have it all" (Thoits 1986). Self-reliance and self-esteem are also related to successful strategies for coping with stress (Patterson and McCubbin 1984).

THE IMPACT OF FEMINIST SCHOLARSHIP

Not only are men and women today revising gender beliefs and behaviors, but there has also been a quiet revolution in the world of scholarship. Women and men who entered graduate school at the beginning of the new wave of feminism are now established academics engaged in research of interest to them. In large part, that research has looked at previously neglected aspects of their fields of study, particularly the hidden world of women. In one field after another this new view has led to important changes in theory and practice—in both biological and social sciences.

For example, looking at history from "the bottom up," that is, from an emphasis on the activities of ordinary people, provides a very different picture from focussing on generals and diplomats. Historical periods long considered great steps forward in human liberation were so only for men; no one bothered to ask what was happening to women during the golden age of Greece or the Italian Renaissance (Kelly 1984).

There is still a long way to go before a more accurate model of self and society can be developed, but the rethinking of accepted wisdom is well advanced (Stacey and Thorne 1985). This reshaping of knowledge will work its way into textbooks, become the new "truth," and enter into people's consciousness. Far from being played out, the spirit of the new feminism has produced a vision of a society in which gender inequality, along with that based on race and class, is no longer tolerable.

Summary

In this chapter we explore the causes and consequences of gender stratification. Real and perceived sex differences are the basis for inequality in all but the most simple gathering bands, despite the fact that the similarities between the sexes far outweigh the differences. From a functional perspective, gender differences promote personal well-being, provide for a natural division of labor, and serve the needs of the society as a whole. In contrast, a conflict analysis of gender stratification centers on power inequalities, male dominance, and female subordination.

Socialization to gendered identities begins early and continues across the life course. The resulting social structures tend to disadvantage women in terms of power, prestige, and property. Even though women's labor-force participation rates have risen dramatically over the past two decades, most women workers remain clustered in low-pay, dead-end jobs. Although attempts to lessen the wage gap have met with limited success, the concept of pay equity has gained increasing support.

With the emergence of the Women's Movement in the United States and elsewhere, systems of gender inequality are under attack throughout the world. Thus far, the changes in women's lives have been greater than those for men, who have more to lose under conditions of gender equality. Recent attitude surveys indicate major shifts in expectations of work and marriage among both young women and men. Profound changes have also occurred in the field of knowledge, as feminist scholarship has revised and broadened the content of one academic discipline after another. Gender equality remains a distant goal, but one that is closer today than it was a decade ago.

Suggested Readings

ANDERSON, MARGARET. *Thinking About Women: Sociological Perspective on Sex and Gender,* second edition. New York: Macmillan, 1988. This book gives significant attention to major feminist and sociological theories on sex and gender as well as integrating issues of race and class throughout the text.

BERNARD, JESSIE. *The Female World.* New York: Free Press, 1981. An ambitious examination of the language, culture, arts, and ethos of the female world. Bernard describes the male impact on the female world; the consequences and pervasiveness of the male ethos; and women's options within this framework.

DOYLE, JAMES A. *The Male Experience*. Dubuque, IA: William C. Brown, 1983. An historical and cross-cultural examination of masculinity in society.

EHRENREICH, BARBARA. *The Hearts of Men: American Dreams and the Flight from Commitment*. Garden City, NY: Anchor/Doubleday, 1983. In a controversial examination of the American middle-class male since 1950, Ehrenreich analyzes the impact and extent of the changes men make in their lives on the emerging women's movement.

HESS, BETH B., and MYRA MARX FERREE, eds. *Analyzing Gender: A Handbook of Social Science Perspectives*. Newbury Park, CA: Sage, 1987. State-of-the-art essays on various dimensions of gender stratification by leading social scientists.

HOCHSCHILD, ARLIE. *Second Shift*. New York: Random House, 1987. A fascinating study of the division of labor between wives and husbands inside and outside the home.

KIMMEL, MICHAEL S., ed. *Changing Men: New Directions in Research on Men and Masculinity*. Newbury Park, CA: Sage, 1987. A stimulating collection of essays on various aspects of men's social roles.

LEWIS, ROBERT A., and ROBERT E. SALT, eds. *Men in Families*. Newbury Park, CA: Sage, 1986. Original essays dealing with men's family and work roles; and men as husbands, fathers, and friends.

LIPMAN-BLUMEN, JEAN. *Gender Roles and Power*. Englewood Cliffs, NJ: Prentice-Hall, 1984. An overview of the relationship of gender to the social institutions of society.

MILKMAN, RUTH, ed. *Women, Work and Protest: A Century of U.S. Women's Labor History*. Boston: Rutledge & Kegan Paul, 1985. An interesting survey of women's labor activism in the United States from the late nineteenth century to the present.

RHIM, SOON MAN. *Women of Asia: Yesterday and Today: India, China, Korea, Japan*. New York: Friendship Press, 1983. A sensitive account of the status of women in traditional Asian societies, changes in their status, and modern political developments.

RUSSELL, DIANA H. *Sexual Development: Rape, Child Sexual Abuse, and Workplace Harassment*. Newbury Park, CA: Sage, 1984. A powerful exploration of major forms of sexual violence based on the most recent social-science research.

TAVRIS, CAROL, and CAROLE WADE. *The Longest War: Sex Differences in Perspective*, 2nd ed. New York: Harcourt Brace Jovanovich, 1984. An overview of the differences between women and men and their implications for society.

9

Age Stratification

H AVE you ever been told to "act your age" or "You can do that when you are older"? Have you observed your parents or grandparents and thought: "They shouldn't do that at their age!"? Statements and thoughts such as these are examples of the importance of age as a dimension of social structure (Riley 1987). In all societies, age is a standard used for entering or leaving social positions.

Because age groups form social strata with particular obligations and re-

sources, we can speak of an *age stratification* system as a component of social structure. This chapter explores the relationship between chronological age and the distribution of power and wealth, as well as changes in social status throughout the life course. Then we focus on the elderly in modern societies, particularly the United States. The chapter continues with a discussion of current problems affecting the elderly, such as income, social security and, especially, health care.

Age stratification refers to the differential distribution of societal resources on the basis of chronological age.

The Importance of Age Stratification

Age is an **ascribed characteristic;** we are a particular age at any one time.

As a status, age is important in three ways. First, like gender, age is an *ascribed characteristic.* At any particular moment, we are a specific age (though we may try to look younger or older) so that age provides a very clear basis for the division of labor. That is, twelve-year-olds are not expected to do some of the things that thirty-year-olds do. Nor are older persons expected to behave as much younger people do. Age becomes a criterion for occupying certain statuses throughout our lives. Age may be formalized as a basis for occupying statuses: for example, in the United States and other industrialized nations, laws control ages for school attendance, employment, serving in the military, voting, election to public office, and marriage. Even such apparently individual behaviors as driving a car, buying liquor or cigarettes, and responsibility for criminal behavior are governed by our age status. Persons are assumed to be incapable of making moral choices until they reach a certain age and, therefore, cannot be held responsible for conduct that would be either tolerated or considered criminal if committed by someone above that age. In contrast, certain behaviors that are illegal for young people are not for those older: e.g., running away from home, refusing to obey parents, or obtaining contraceptive devices without parental approval.

Age is a **transitional status** in that we are constantly moving from one age to another.

Second, unlike gender, age is always a *transitional status.* We are constantly moving from one age to another. Age provides a kind of cultural roadmap of our lives: a notion of where we should be going and what we should be doing at a particular point in our life. Every culture contains norms about what is appropriate behavior at various periods in the life course and defines the usual set of passages or transitions from one age to another (Eisenstadt 1956, Neugarten, Moore, and Lowe 1965, Hogan 1980). Moving from one age status to another is accomplished by socialization to age-appropriate behavior. The expression "act your age" means precisely that: conform to age-based expectations. Role partners reward conformity and disapprove of violation of age-based norms for social behavior. For example, nine-year-old children who cling to their mothers or seventy-five-year-olds who wear skimpy swimwear are violating generally accepted American age norms and both are likely to be negatively sanctioned.

Third, although in every society some age groups are more powerful, more wealthy, and have more prestige than others, the unique aspect of age as a status is that during our lives each of us can expect to occupy positions of varying dominance based on age. All of us were once powerless children, for example, and, for most of us, our power, wealth, and prestige are likely to change as we move from one age status to another. Thus young people who treat the elderly as a minority perpetuate inequalities that will eventually affect their own statuses in later life. As Comfort (1976, p. 4) ironically noted:

> One wonders what Archie Bunker would feel about immigrants if he knew that on his sixty-fifth birthday he would turn into a Puerto Rican. White racists don't turn black, black racists don't become white, male chauvinists don't become women, anti-Semites don't wake up and find themselves Jewish—but we have a lifetime of indoctrination with the idea of the difference and inferiority of the old.

AGE AND SOCIAL STRUCTURE

The **age structure** of the population refers to the number of people of various ages within a society.

The **role structure** of the population refers to the number of roles available to be filled.

Every society contains some elements of age stratification that affect opportunities, experiences, and relationships. Age stratification results from two factors: the *age structure* of the population, or number of people of various ages within the society, and the *role structure,* or number of roles available to be filled. The age structure and the role structure of any society always have the potential to be in or out of balance with one another, depending on the number of people available to fill needed roles (Riley 1976). In some societies, most roles required for economic survival need little training, so that children and old people perform many productive tasks. Moreover, because of relatively high death rates, the labor of all potential producers is valued. Industrialized societies, however, have less need for unskilled labor. The relative scarcity of jobs creates pressures to exclude the elderly and children in favor of young and middle-aged adults. The balance between age and role structures determines the age stratification pattern of any society. Generally, if there are more people, such as the elderly or children, than there are socially productive roles for them to occupy, there will be greater age inequality within a society.

The Social Construction of Age. How do we decide who is old? To an American seven-year-old, a sixteen-year-old sibling is old; to a fourteen-year-old, parents may seem not only old but possible contemporaries of Benjamin Franklin. Age is a relative concept, constructed both personally and socially. Each of us has an idea, based upon our own ages and where we stand in the life course, about what ages are "young" or "old" at any point in time. For example, the late statesman and financier Bernard Baruch, when asked in his eighties to define old, replied that it described anyone fifteen years older than he!

CULTURAL FACTORS. More importantly, age is not only a number but a social construct, defined by norms specific to a given society at a particular time in history. For example, the Nandi of Kenya recognize twenty-eight age-status groups while the Nupe of Nigeria have only three (Eisenstadt 1956). In some societies, a girl or boy is considered an adult at puberty. In other societies, a particular age is chosen regardless of physical maturity; twelve or thirteen is a very common age for crossing the line from childhood to adult status. In the United States today, usually six age groups are recognized: infancy, childhood, adolescence, young adulthood, middle age, and old age.

HISTORICAL CHANGES. The recognition of these age groups is, however, relatively new. Childhood as we now define it emerged only within the last 150 years or so (Aries 1962). Prior to that time, age groups were much broader: infancy-toddler, young adult, and older adult. Those we now consider "children" assumed adult social roles, whether that of king or serf. As a source of cheap labor, children were considered adult workers by the time they entered their teens (Aries 1962). In societies where life expectancy (the average number of years a person can expect to live) is short and physical conditions are demanding, a person may be defined an "elder" by age forty or forty-five.

Demarcations: The Rite of Passage. In many societies, the line between childhood and adulthood is marked by a public celebration—a *rite of passage*. This is a ritual or ceremony that symbolizes the movement from one age status to another; it defines the meaning of this movement or transition and establishes cultural markers both for the society and the individuals involved. For example, when children become legal adults, they are eligible for positions of power and prestige. At some later age, people must give up important statuses. In many societies, where elders control valued resources (such as property, jobs, and their children) until their death, they may never have to give up power. Even today, in some parts of modern societies (rural Ireland, for example), a son must wait for his father's death before inheriting the land that will permit him to support a wife and children, a circumstance that accounts for the very late age at first marriage among Irish men.

Rites of passage, to mark both entry into adulthood and removal of elders from ruling positions, are common in simple societies. In modern societies, there are relatively few formal rites of passage, although such events as school graduations,

A **rite of passage** is a public celebration marking the movement from one age status to another.

Much of everyday life in Modern Society is age segregated: schools, work, social activities, etc. Groups which include several generations, such as the family or this group of friends, are rare. When was the last time you socialized with people who were older or younger than yourself? (© Barbara Kirk/The Stock Market)

A wedding is a rite of passage acknowledging the transition from the single to the married state. It symbolizes the union of 2 families, new loyalties, and new responsibilities. (© Bob Nicklesberg/ Woodfin Camp and Associates)

marriage, and retirement are associated with change of status. But the ages at which people become eligible to marry or to receive retirement benefits are quite variable.

The main point is that every society regulates the flow of people into and out of valued statuses on the basis of age. Definitions of appropriate ages for certain roles are socially constructed and not biologically given. The processes whereby people of different ages are channeled into particular roles produce an age-related hierarchy of power and prestige. This hierarchy, which affects us all, is an *age-stratification system* (Riley et al. 1972).

The Importance of Age Structure

Every society is composed of an *age structure* of persons and an age structure of roles (Riley et al. 1972). The age structure of persons (or age strata) is the number of people in each age category: for example, age fifteen to age twenty, twenty-five to thirty-five, thirty-five to forty-five, and so forth. The age structure of a society may be illustrated as a population pyramid which summarizes the distribution of the population by age and sex. Less modern-

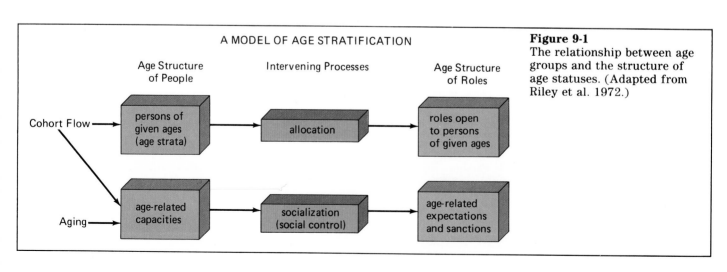

A MODEL OF AGE STRATIFICATION

Figure 9-1
The relationship between age groups and the structure of age statuses. (Adapted from Riley et al. 1972.)

Age Structure of People — Intervening Processes — Age Structure of Roles

Cohort Flow → persons of given ages (age strata) → allocation → roles open to persons of given ages

Aging → age-related capacities → socialization (social control) → age-related expectations and sanctions

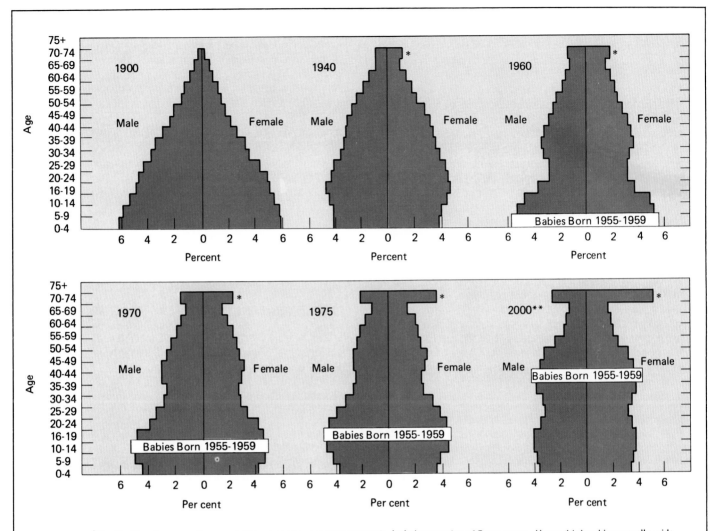

*The final band, representing people 75 years and over on the pyramids, includes a number of 5-age groups. Hence this band is unusually wide

Figure 9-2 Age structure of the U.S. population in 1900 to 2000.

ized societies have differently shaped age structures, with many more children and few elderly (see Chapter 18 for further discussion of population pyramids). Differences between the age structure of the United States in 1900 and in 2000 may be seen in Figure 9-2. These pyramids show the number of males and females of different ages in various decades. By 2030, however, due to the aging of persons born during the "baby-boom" years of 1945–1964, 21 percent or about one in five Americans will be sixty-five or over. This proportion is expected to remain fairly stable (barring unexpected increases in birth rates) until the middle of the twenty-first century because of the low birth rates in the United States that began in 1965 and continue to the present.

BIRTH COHORTS

Each age group is called a *cohort*. A *birth cohort* consists of a group of people born during specific time periods, such as 1950–1955, 1960–1965, and so forth. In Figure 9-2, you can see the aging of the "baby-boom" cohort over time. Birth-cohort members age together through a similar slice of history. Thus, each cohort is different from every other. In any high school class, for example, students are likely to belong

A **birth cohort** consists of a group of people born during a specific time period.

Cohort Effects of the Depression

The concept of cohort increases our understanding of the meaning history may have had for a group of people born within the same time period. Elder and Liker (1982) found that, among women born at the turn of the twentieth century, health in old age reflected the impact of personal and financial losses during the Great Depression. Of course, economic hardship left its mark on everyone, but it interacted with social class to affect health in particular ways. Thus middle-class women, who were most deprived during the depression, ranked well above those of their class who were not deprived in physical health, psychological well-being, and life satisfaction in old age. For the first group, coping with economic stress apparently prepared them to deal more effectively with problems in later life. Lower-class women, however, were less fortunate, for hard times almost universally left a negative imprint upon their lives and health in later life. Economic stress for them meant there was no margin of comfort left. The hardships of the depression took what little reserve they had in the effort to survive.

SOURCE: Glen H. Elder, Jr., and Jeffrey K. Liker, "Hard Times in Women's Lives: Historical Influences Across Forty Years," *American Journal of Sociology* 88 (1982): 241–269.

eth century experienced relatively early school completion, late marriage, and a long period between beginning full-time work and marriage. In contrast, cohorts born during periods of relative economic prosperity, high expenditures for welfare, and low birth rates tended to prolong schooling, to delay entry into the job market, and to be married earlier (Hogan 1981). The effects of the birth cohort interact with social class, ethnicity, and sex to influence the life course itself.

Shifts in the Age Structure of the United States

LIFE EXPECTANCY

Since 1900, the trend in industrialized nations, such as the United States, has been toward increasingly older populations. Although, as discussed more fully in Chapter 18, the proportion of people in each cohort reflects birth rates during specific time periods, the growth in absolute

to the same birth cohort and share common knowledge of music, political events, trends in dress, and so forth. Their parents, however, will be far more diverse in age and experience. In one recent class of students whose average age was eighteen, their parents ranged in age from thirty-seven to sixty-two, representing members of birth cohorts who had been born during the Great Depression of the 1920s and 1930s, cohorts born during World War II, and cohorts born during the post-war "baby-boom" years. The parents will, therefore, have had very different socialization experiences and life chances. They experienced childhood, adolescence, young adulthood, and middle age at different times in history and thus in different social circumstances. Living through different historical conditions speeds or slows down patterns of marriage, schooling, and work, which in turn affect access to wealth, power, and prestige. For example, birth cohorts from the early part of the twenti-

Your birth cohort will have a strong influence on your life. These babies, born in Beijing, China, will all, for example, bear the effects of their government's push to decrease population. (© Alon Reininger/Woodfin Camp and Associates)

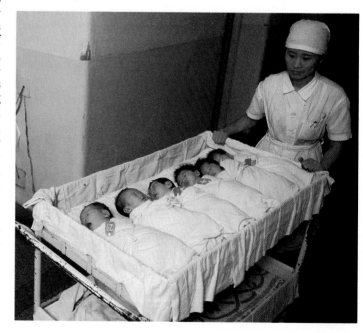

Life expectancy refers to the average number of years one can expect to live as a member of a particular cohort.

numbers of old people reflects changes in *life expectancy* or average years members of a particular birth cohort can expect to live. Each cohort encounters historically grounded opportunities and barriers that affect life expectancy. Thus the life expectancy of young men is affected by war; the life expectancy of infants by contagious disease, and that of women by the number of pregnancies experienced.

Life expectancy is patterned by race and sex as well as by birth cohort. For example, white males born in 1900 had an average life expectancy at birth of forty-seven years while white females averaged forty-nine years. Nonwhites had a lower life expectancy—thirty-three years for men and thirty-four for women. Today, dramatic changes for both blacks and whites and women and men are evident. Life expectancy at birth is now about seventy-two years for white males and close to eighty years for white females. For Afro-Americans, average life expectancy has increased to 65.5 years for men and almost seventy-four years for women.

LIFE SPAN

Life span refers to the biological limits to which our species is able to survive.

Contrary to popular belief, the *life span* or the biological limits to which our species is able to survive, has not increased or decreased since ancient times. What has changed is life expectancy. When Julius Caesar was born some 2,000 years ago, average life expectancy was only twenty-two years. Nor was it much longer by the time George Washington was president when people on the average could expect to live to age thirty-five. Although Washington himself lived to old age, infant and childhood disease, childbirth, and epidemics took their toll among his playmates. Only the hardiest and richest were likely to grow old. Even as late as 1930, only half of all newborns in the United States could expect to live to age sixty-five; today, over three-quarters can. Thus, although the maximum years of life that humans are biologically able to live has not changed, the proportion who live to reach age sixty-five, eighty-five, or even 100 or more has increased dramatically. Although the 1980 Census listed one out of every 7000 Americans as age 100 or over, these data depend on self-reports of age. Thus, according to the Social Security Administration, which

requires proof of age not demanded by the Census, the proportion of people 100 years or older is actually much lower—one in every 14,000 Americans. White females are most likely to reach 100 or more, followed by black females, black males, and lastly, white males.

At the same time that the proportion of older people in the American population is growing, the percentage in the fourteen to twenty-four year age group is shrinking and expected to continue to decline. In 1975, 21 percent of the total U.S. population was between the ages of fourteen and twenty-four. By 1985, that figure had dropped to 18 percent (*Statistical Abstract of the United States,* 1987, p. 14). Based on current birth rates, it will decline to 16 percent by 1995, shrinking by one-quarter the size of the available number of young people to take entry-level jobs (Education Commission of the States 1985). Clearly, the United States, along with other industrialized nations, is undergoing dramatic changes in the age structure of its population. These in turn are likely to change the social fabric of political and social life.

The Age Structure of Roles

The age structure of roles in a society is made up of the statuses and opportunities that are open to people of a given age. For example, as the number of jobs available either expands during economic growth or contracts during a recession, one way to control the flow of workers is to change the age requirements for entering the labor force (by lengthening the period of schooling), or for leaving it (by raising or lowering the age when one receives Social Security).

Family roles are also subject to changing definitions of age-appropriateness. Countries that are trying to control the growth of their population can reduce the birth rate by raising the age of legal marriage, as in the People's Republic of China today. Conversely, where high birth rates are encouraged, as in Eastern Europe, the legal age for marriage will be lowered.

And so it is in other institutions. The age of voting eligibility can be lowered to give growing numbers of jobless young adults a feeling of attachment to the society. In other words, the supply of people and of roles must be kept in balance (Waring 1975). Social institutions must adapt to population shifts, and these institutional changes, in turn, affect the population structure (by encouraging or discouraging births, or by reducing age-related death rates, primarily through health-care policies).

AGE-RELATED CAPACITIES

In many cases, biological factors limit a person's abilities to perform certain roles. Few females under the age of twelve or over the age of fifty can become mothers. The very young and the very old will find it difficult to dig ditches. Professional athletes over the age of forty are rare. But most age limits are culturally and socially defined. Miss America is young because we equate beauty with youth. When airlines first hired stewardesses, there was an upper age limit, which has now been extended, but the minimum age for female flight attendants remains around twenty, and none are in their sixties. The reason is not that the job requires talents that are age-associated, but that attendants are expected to be decorative. Another example of socially defined age limits is the age of consent for marriage, which varies from one place to another, has changed over time, and may be different for females and males. Clearly, societal beliefs about the appropriateness of sexual activity, and not biology, account for these differences.

THE APPEARANCES OF AGE

Of all the physical changes associated with growing old, young people are probably most aware of the changes in appearance. Hair thins and turns gray while wrinkles become pronounced. In American society, changes such as these are greeted with anxiety for, although almost all of us want to live as long as possible, few want to "look old" and will go to extraordinary lengths to appear youthful. Because of the double standard of aging, the cosmetic changes associated with aging have greater impact on women's roles than on men's. For example, age tends to reduce the sexual value of women while enhancing that of men (see Chapter 11 for a discussion of the marriage market). Masculinity has tra-

ditionally been associated with assertiveness, competency, self-control, independence, and power: all qualities enhanced with maturity, if not old age. Femininity, in contrast, has been associated with helplessness, passivity, compliance, noncompetitiveness, and warmth: all qualities often attributed to "good" children. Moreover, feminine "sexiness" has been associated with youthfulness, an indication that women are valued more for their ability to bear children than for the wisdom they might bring to various roles.

Signs of aging often trigger concerns about self-worth among women, concerns that accurately reflect the marriage and work options open to women in midlife. Despite the growing population of "older" women such as Joan Collins and Linda Evans, the dynamic duo of the nighttime soap "Dynasty," their ability to maintain TV stardom has been based precisely on the fact that they "do not look their age." In contrast, John Forsyth, also a "Dynasty" star, looks like an "older man," and indeed is over a decade older than Evans or Collins.

While the media reflect and reinforce this negative image of female aging, increasing numbers of middle-age and older women themselves are defying the stereotype. Midlife women are entering the labor force, returning to college, and experiencing the "empty nest" as a liberation rather than a loss (Giele 1982, Porcino 1983, Baruch and Brooks-Gunn 1984). Divorce and widowhood have increased the ranks of older women living alone, but the vast majority appear to be coping very well and even enjoying their independence (Markson 1983). It is expected that future cohorts of older women, with more years of education and work experience, will be even better prepared for meeting the challenges of aging than are today's elderly.

Nonetheless, many middle-aged women—and a growing number of middle-aged men—perceive that their claims to positions of power, prestige, and property are jeopardized by outward signs of aging. The market for products that disguise or delay the onset of cosmetic change has grown rapidly over the past decade, from face creams that promise to rejuvenate (make young again) the skin while you sleep to highly unusual medical experiments. The search for the fountain of youth, it appears, is never-ending. For example, some decades ago Dr. Paul Niehans

Changes in appearances are probably the most dramatic evidence of aging and both men and women spend a great deal of money to keep their youthful looks. Due to the double standard, however, the cosmetic changes associated with aging have a greater impact on women than on men. (© Adriano Heitmann/ Archive)

in Switzerland developed a cell therapy using lamb embryo cells. Despite the lack of proven values of this treatment, it attracted as customers such public figures as Winston Churchill, the Duke of Windsor, and Chancellor Conrad Adenauer of Germany. Another briefly popular therapy for men consisted of grafts of monkey testicles; an American version of this treatment involved transplanting goat testicles into aging men. There is no scientific evidence that either "therapy" benefited the recipients; however, the practitioners did, indeed, benefit—financially.

More recently, Gerovital H2, developed by Dr. Ana Aslan of Rumania, has become popular. A procaine and vitamin therapy claiming to reverse the aging process, it has been received by thousands of people, many of whom have traveled to the Geriatric Institute in Bucharest to seek rejuvenation. Controlled studies in the United States and Great Britain have failed to demonstrate Gerovital's antiaging properties although it does have a mild antidepressant and antiarthritis effect.

Ginseng, a plant in the same family as English ivy, is also increasingly popular as a youth-restorer. Used for centuries in China and Korea, Ginseng supposedly lowers blood pressure and improves mental activity and organ function (Tok 1978): claims which have not been validated in other studies.

Current searches for prolonging life include use of magnetic fields, lowered body temperatures, drugs such as L-DOPA, vitamin E, vitamin B-12, and so forth. Seeking for eternal vigor continues now as in ancient times: from Ginseng to Gerovital. And this search has become big business.

Structure of Roles, Role Strain, and Role Slack Throughout the Life Course

As we have noted, in any society, the proportion of people available to play socially defined roles is constantly changing, requiring shifts in the age structure of roles in order to maintain a rough balance between people and role. Perhaps this is why the idea of "childhood" as we now know it is relatively new. Until recently, death was very much a part of everyday life. Indeed, popular art of medieval times often included "steps of the ages," or rows of figures illustrating the various ages from birth to death standing on a double staircase. Steps went up one side and down the other, but in the center, ready to meet members of any age group, stood the skeleton of the grim reaper, death (Aries 1962). When life expectancy was so short and death likely to occur at any age, people were drafted into roles such as worker or parent when they were far younger than today. Their contribution was needed to ensure the social and economic functioning of the society. In modern societies, this is no longer the case, and young people are carefully excluded from socially valued roles.

ADOLESCENCE AND YOUNG ADULTHOOD

When people are denied entry into statuses for which they believe themselves eligible, deviance may result. In our soci-

225

Many young people test out their capacities in part-time or summer jobs. Participation in the working world and a self-generated income often increase feelings of self-worth and autonomy. (© Carrie Boretz/Archive)

Role slack occurs when capacities are underdemanded, as in adolescence.

ety, adolescence is a period of *role slack,* that is, a period during which teenagers' capabilities are underdemanded (Education Commission of the States, 1985). For example, at present, people under the age of twenty-one account for more than half of all arrests for property crimes; unwed teens give birth to about 650,000 babies; and a teenager commits suicide every ninety minutes in the United States. In 1982, 26 percent of eighteen-year-olds did not graduate from high school—a 4 percent increase over 1972 figures. At the same time, the unemployment rate for all teenagers is three times higher than for adults, with black youth more than twice as likely to be unemployed as their white age peers, illustrating the effect of both age and race stratification on life opportunities.

Much juvenile delinquency—e.g., driving, drinking, sexual experimentation—can be interpreted as premature attempts to play adult roles. Failure to graduate from high school may result from similar perceptions: the status of student may be perceived as "childish," uninteresting and unlikely to lead to success. School provides no useful roles. Similarly, unemployment rates reflect not only various kinds of discrimination but also the changing demands of the economy for unskilled workers—a major factor in role slack.

Role strain, the overburdened demands of work, marriage, parenthood, and civic responsibility, most often occurs in early adulthood.

In contrast, early adulthood is a time of *role strain,* when the demands of work, marriage, parenthood, and civic responsibility can overburden many people (Goode 1960, Wilensky 1962). It is also a time of high rates of violent crime, and when suicides peak among black men and women. The difficulties of establishing a stable family life and occupational future

are revived at mid-life when many people feel overwhelmed by demands at home and work.

MIDDLE AGE

More recent than the discovery of childhood or adolescence is the recognition of middle age as a distinct period in the life course. In societies with fairly limited life expectancies, little or no attention was paid to midlife. Long life has altered our sense of time, making us simultaneously more aware that it is limited and more interested in measuring it (Stub 1982). Only in the 1970s did the Social Science Research Council call attention to midlife so that it became "in" as a research subject (much to the relief of countless laboratory animals who had hitherto been subjected to experiments to induce premature aging! Greenberg in Davis 1981, p. 113).

Midlife Crisis. One result of the interest in midlife has been the concept of a "midlife crisis," which may sell lots of popular psychology books, but which is not supported by systematic research (Pearlin and Radebaugh 1985). Midlife does bring its strains and problems, but typically not extreme mental disorder. In many other cultures, including modern industrial societies, midlife is not viewed as a period of special crisis (Gaullier 1986). Indeed, there is no equivalent term in French to "midlife" itself.

In America, however, with its great emphasis on competitive achievement in love and work, the particular problems that face middle-aged women and men has led to the social construction of a special life-course phase. For women, the problems are typically framed in terms of various "losses"—of sexual attractiveness, children in the home, and possibly one's husband (through divorce or death). But these assumptions reflect a male-defined view of women. As we have already noted, the great majority of middle-aged women find midlife a highly satisfying period in their lives. There will, of course, be a few women whose world has been so centered on home, children, and husband, that they have no other sources of self-worth; for them, middle age can bring on a crisis of identity that leads to illness and even suicide (for white women).

For men, middle age is likely to bring the realization of "limits"—to strength, to occupational achievement, and to earnings. Most men will adjust their expectations to the new reality, but a few will use the concept of "midlife crisis" to justify major changes in their life-style and marriages—take flying lessons, buy a sports car, divorce and remarry, have an affair. Note, however, that this definition of mid-

Tina Turner and Mick Jagger are both in their forties. Do you think they're having a mid-life crisis? (© Philadelphia Inquirer/Archive)

life crisis is based on the experience of white middle-class men. In the working class, one's occupational ceiling is usually reached before age forty, and the sports car is out of reach.

In actuality, middle age is most often a period of maximum social power. People aged forty-five to sixty-four enjoy the highest levels of income and occupational prestige. Marriage partners who have lasted three decades or more consider themselves as happy as when they were newlyweds. The difficulties of child rearing are in the past; the joys of grandparenting are eagerly anticipated. Yet this is also a period of preparation for the status changes that are an inevitable part of aging in modern societies.

OLD AGE

It is at the oldest age levels that age-related capacities become both a major social and personal issue. What are appropriate norms for behavior in old age? There are almost no role proscriptions except to avoid being "odd" and relatively few prescriptions for preferred role behavior.

Deviance.   Almost all forms of deviant behavior decline with age, from late adolescence and young adulthood on. Although there is evidence of a recent increase in crime by the elderly greater than their increase in the population (Newman et al. 1984), crime rates for other age groups increased as well. Persons aged sixty and over have the lowest arrest and conviction rates for serious crimes. In general, available research indicates that the elderly drink less than the young and are also more likely not to drink at all. Alcoholism, when it occurs in later life, is very often a continuation of a pattern begun in midlife (Whittington 1985). Use of street drugs is also relatively infrequent, although there is some evidence that older people may simply be more adept at concealing their addiction (Whittington 1985). However, it seems likely that the majority of studies on alcoholism and drug use in old age may tell us more about age cohort patterns rather than about old age itself. The now-old were socialized in an era when sterner views about recreational alcohol and drug use prevailed. Patterns of behavior with respect to drug and alcohol use may look different when the birth cohort that grew up in the sixties becomes elderly.

Why is deviance relatively uncommon among the elderly and sometimes ignored when it does occur? Gove (1985) has suggested that certain kinds of deviance that involve risk or physically demanding behavior decreases with age due to both biological and social role changes; as strength declines and hormonal levels fall due to aging, people are less prone to engage in risk-taking behavior. Suicide, nonetheless, is one form of deviant behavior that does increase in old age but only for white males. As shown in Figure 1-1 on p. 000, white male suicide rates rise steadily with age, while those for black men drop after age twenty-five. Note that, contrary to popular belief about the negative impact of retirement, the suicide rate does not increase abruptly at age sixty-five. It is not loss of a job but of a wife that is most clearly associated with high suicide rates among older men. As future cohorts age, it will be interesting to see the degree to which the frequency of what we now define as deviance in old age changes and the extent to which new definitions of deviance emerge.

Incapacity. When is a person "too old" for certain roles? In the past this may have not been difficult to answer for few people lived to be "too old" to lose their value to the group. Old women could still gather food and watch children, and old men could recall needed information. In very simple gathering-and-hunting societies, depending on the availability of food, the few frail elderly are either cared for or abandoned. This does not mean that young adults in such a society are cruel but only that they are conforming to norms designed to increase the chance of group survival (Foner 1984).

As noted in Chapter 8, in agricultural societies the male head of the extended family controls the flow of property throughout the kinship group. Moreover, his political power tends to increase with age through control over both inheritance of property and family members as well as over ceremonial or religious rites. And in many societies, the social power of older women is also enhanced when child rearing is completed.

But regardless of the society and its means of subsistence, the relative power and prestige of both male and female elders has been based almost entirely on their ability to control things of value to their children or to the society as a whole: information, economic assets, and family loyalty (Amoss and Harrell 1981, Gutmann 1980, Keith 1979). It is precisely these sources of control that are lost by the elderly in the course of industrialization. The lowered status of the elderly in mod-

What are appropriate activities and practices in old age? Should the elderly be passive and sedentary or active, involved and in good physical shape as is the case with these two citizens who exercise regularly? Helen Zechmeister, 81 years old, holds 8 national power lifting records; John Turner, age 67, a psychiatrist, lifts weights, jogs and takes long walks just for the health of it! (Photo by © Etta Clark, from the book *Growing Old is Not For Sissies*)

ern societies is thus closely linked to socio-structural changes limiting their ability to command important resources in either the family or the larger society. As a result of their loss of control over resources, elders in industrialized societies are relatively disadvantaged in three dimensions: power, prestige, and property.

Diminishing Power. There has never been a "golden age" in which elders were automatically respected or loved (Nydegger 1985). Rather, respect for the elderly reflected their power over resources and other family members. Nor is there any reason to believe that younger family members enjoyed being powerless any more than they would in the United States today. Although there is a common belief that somewhere, in some far-distant land—China and Japan are frequently mentioned—there were societies dominated by respect for elders, what is ignored is that such honor was often bought at great cost to younger people. Le Vine (1965), for example, has noted the frequency of suicide in traditional China among young married women desperate to escape their tyrannical mothers-in-law in whose households they lived as near-slaves. Moreover, reports on the People's Republic of China today indicate that once elders cease to control property, norms of respect are often ignored. Yet the status of the elderly did not decline sharply under Communist rule and may have even improved as elders provided a source of stability and order during a period of rapid social change (Davis-Friedman 1984). In contrast, the status of poor elderly in capitalist Hong Kong, where there are few governmental programs to support the elderly, where their labor is unneeded, and where they may no longer control resources, is low (Ikels 1984).

Historical Perspectives. Recent work by historians has suggested various trends during the nineteenth century that affected the status of the aged. Some have argued that status losses were due primarily to attitudinal shifts in the regard with which they were held (Fischer 1978, Achenbaum 1978). More recent research links the status of the elderly to widespread social and economic changes which reduced the capacity of older workers to control resources (Gratton 1986). For example, the development of large-scale in-dustry rendered obsolete many of the skill-based occupations at which older workers excelled, while also lowering the demand for family-owned and -run farms (Gratton 1986). By about 1850, cities organized around craft manufacturing and commerce began to be replaced by industrial cities, where younger workers competed for the new jobs. Between 1890 and 1930, during the period of rapid industrialization in the United States, older men (forty-five to sixty-four) in mining and farming maintained their representation in the labor force, but these occupations declined in importance as the proportion of workers in manufacturing and service occupations increased dramatically. At the same time, the ratio of older men in manufacturing and service occupations gradually declined due to the influx of young immigrants willing to work for lower wages and easier to control than older workers.

In other words, older men had a hold in declining industry, but lost footing in those occupations on the upswing. With the introduction of "efficiency experts," older workers were frequently penalized for their relative slowness in assembly-line production compared to younger workers (Gratton 1986). By 1910, more and more elderly relied on public charity as a source of care and older people predominated in homes for the poor.

Along with these economic and social changes came the medical discovery of old age, in which the aging process was defined as an illness without a cure (Haber 1983). A new concept of the life course began to emerge. The growth of industrialization, changes in the organization and control of labor, an abundance of young immigrant workers, and equation of old age with illness combined to set the stage for the definition of old age as a social problem.

This combination of factors—accompanied by increased emphasis on personal freedom and individuality—has tended to diminish the relative esteem in which the elderly are held. Elders' managerial talents, work skills, and ability to act as religious mediators lose meaning in industrialized, activist, youth-oriented societies where change is valued. Most importantly, the increasingly large numbers of old people in the population are not viewed as potential leaders on the basis of their particular technical skills or wisdom. Instead, the elderly are likely to be viewed as symbols of inactivity, poor health, and impending death.

The Elderly in Modern Societies

THEORETICAL PERSPECTIVES

As a result of their loss of control over scarce resources, people aged sixty-five and over in modern societies are relatively disadvantaged in terms of the three dimensions of stratification: power, prestige, and property. From a *functional* perspective, the contributions that older people can make to the society are limited. Most are not in the labor force—a source of income and prestige. Their knowledge and skills may also have become obsolete in an era of rapid technological change.

In *exchange* terms, this loss of status means that the elderly have few "bargaining chips" to use in claiming social resources. Their bargaining power is based chiefly on the care that they once gave their own children and the productive roles that they played earlier in their lives. In exchange, then, adult offspring have an obligation to care for their own parents—an obligation that most do fulfill, voluntarily, with little assistance, and at great financial and emotional cost.

The exchange model also suggests a societal obligation to provide adequate income and health services to the elderly. The United States, alone among modern industrial societies, has not fully met this obligation. Rather, retirement incomes are based on previous work experience and ability to save; medical expenses are only partially covered. Housing programs are minimal and designed to assist private builders, and transportation and social service needs are generally unmet.

From the *conflict* viewpoint, therefore, many of our elderly have to endure the same struggle for resources that they waged when they were younger. The same subgroups are less well off when they are elderly as when they were younger: women, the nonmarried, blacks, and people whose earning levels were relatively low. Particularly disadvantaged are very old women (aged eighty and over), most of whom have outlived their husbands (and even their children), whose only income is

about $400 a month in Social Security payments, and who are very likely to have one or more long-term illnesses.

INCOME AND LABOR FORCE PARTICIPATION

Since the passage of the Social Security Act in 1935, the proportion of retired male workers has increased dramatically. Only about one in five elderly men are employed today as compared to one in two in 1950, and the proportion of a man's life spent in retirement has increased from 3 percent in 1900 to 20 percent in 1980. The decrease in labor-force participation has extended to men in their fifties and early sixties as well: in 1950, over 88 percent of men aged fifty-five to fifty-nine and about 77 percent of those aged sixty to sixty-four were in the labor force as compared to 80 percent and 55 percent, respectively, in 1985. Labor force participation by women aged sixty-five and over has, however, varied little. In 1950 about 10 percent of women sixty-five and over were in the labor force as compared to slightly less than that (6 percent) in 1985. But increasing proportions of women between the ages of fifty-five and sixty-four have entered the labor force: 27 percent in 1950 as compared to 43 percent in 1985.

A major factor contributing to the greater proportion of life spent by men today in retirement is availability of Social Security or other pension income. Despite

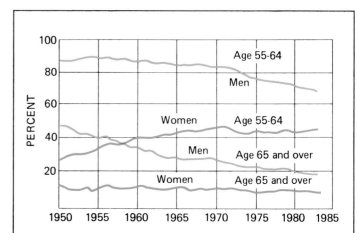

Figure 9-3
Labor Force Participation of Older People, 1950–1984, by Sex. (SOURCE: U.S. Bureau of the Census and Bureau of Labor Statistics.)

Hunger has no age limits. (© George Cohen)

Poverty and the Aged.   Contrary to popular belief, however, poverty rates for the elderly have decreased within the past two decades. As may be seen in Figure 9-4, the poverty rate of those 65 and over has declined from about 29 percent in 1966 to about 15 percent today. And the gap between the old and other groups living in poverty has narrowed significantly.

In addition to the proportion of older people living in poverty, slightly over 8 percent are officially classified as "near poverty," bringing the total of poor elders to somewhat more than one in every five. Being poor in old age is not a result of the aging process but rather a continuation of a life-long pattern in which disadvantaged groups remain poor while the economically advantaged remain relatively well-off. Income is a continuum, with wealthy old people at one end, and poor old people at the other. Most importantly this inequity reflects the low earnings among the now-old and their few or inadequate opportunities to amass savings able to withstand the effect of inflation. Wealth is rarely accumulated in old age.

In the long term, Social Security and other social programs such as Medicare

recent changes in the laws on mandatory (forced) retirement, the general trend has been for men to leave the labor force at increasingly earlier ages. Many workers leave as soon as they are assured of adequate retirement income, or when health factors make retirement necessary. Contrary to common belief, most old people do not want to work till they drop, and retired men do not suddenly fall into a deep depression. Retired workers are typically very pleased to be out of the work force. Nor is their labor needed, for jobs for older workers typically are in declining portions of the economy. Moreover, the unemployment rate for workers aged fifty-five or over in the United States is currently the highest since 1945. Compared to younger workers, older workers once they lose their jobs are also likely to stay unemployed longer, receive less pay on the new job when rehired, and to give up searching for a new job (U.S. Senate 1984). As in the 1900s, expanding industries today tend to be in fields that employ younger rather than older workers (Kaufman and Spilerman 1982).

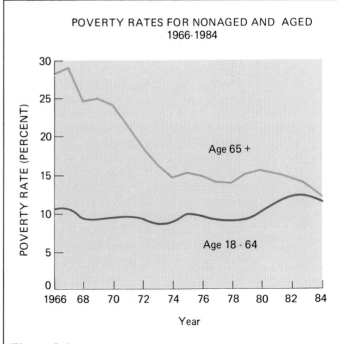

Figure 9-4
SOURCE: U.S. Bureau of the Census. Current Population Surveys, 1967–85.

have had a positive effect on the quality of life of most elders, allowing them to remain independent and to maintain their own homes. Not only are adult children today less dependent upon their parents for resources than in the past, but elders, in turn, no longer have to depend as much as they once did on their children. But Social Security alone usually cannot maintain a retired person's standard of living. Benefits average only 40 percent of preretirement income, and 27 percent or less for people whose incomes were at the ceiling level for Social Security taxes. The average new beneficiary today is paid $467 a month, or $5,604 a year. The highest payment for new beneficiaries is $792 a month or $9,504 per year. The gap between preretirement and postretirement income is closed for some by savings and additional pensions: an estimated 37 percent of retirees with families receive pensions which, when added to Social Security, nearly double the average income of retirees.

Although income in retirement is lower than when one was at work, many expenses are no longer necessary. In general, retired couples between ages sixty-five and seventy-four can manage quite well on a combination of Social Security and other pensions. But once the husband dies—and most men die before their wives—private pensions usually end, and Social Security benefits are lowered. A husband's death becomes a penalty. Thus, whereas only 7 percent of older married men have incomes below the poverty level, the figures for women are two to three times higher because they are more likely to be both widowed and very old.

Although both household and individual incomes are highest during midlife in the United States, households whose head is aged sixty-five to seventy-five have more income per person than those whose head is under age forty-five (see Table 9-1). Husband and wife families over age sixty-five in 1980 actually had a higher level of real income than they had in 1950 at age thirty-five to forty-five (Conference Board 1985). But individual income declines in old age: with people 75+ below any other age group except the youngest. How the elderly use income is the issue.

Old People as Consumers. Recently, numerous businesses have discovered the "graying of America" and have become

TABLE 9-1 The dimensions of income by age of household head*

Age	Average Household Income	Average Individual Income
Total U.S.	$25,211	$ 9,338
Under 35	22,180	8,120
35–50	31,756	9,162
50–55	34,093	11,365
55–60	30,050	11,557
60–65	25,011	11,369
65–70	19,918	9,960
70–75	16,250	9,028
75 & over	13,547	8,467

* Household figures are for 1984, income figures are for the preceding year

SOURCE: Conference Board, 1985.

increasingly aware of the economic potential of older people as consumers. Measures of income commonly used by experts in marketing include *discretionary* household and per capita income. *Discretionary income* is the amount of money, on the average, left over after all necessary expenses, such as food, housing, clothing, and so on, have been paid. Figure 9-5 summarizes the distribution of discretionary income among American families by age of household head.

That older people have been recognized as a distinct market could be a mixed blessing, as there is an emerging tendency to overestimate their wealth. Neither individual nor household income is a perfect measure. Both are averages that obscure the richest and the poorest in each age group. There are many elders with substantial economic resources; there are also many older people, especially very old widowed women and members of minority groups, living in difficult financial situations.

In other words, old age poverty is largely a problem for women, widows, and blacks. When income data on all America's elderly are combined, it appears that poverty is not a major issue. But this claim overlooks the fact that the oldest, and the fastest growing, segment of our population is the very old (those eighty-five years old and over), almost all of whom will be widows living in poverty, or near enough, and whose medical needs are increasingly costly (Hess 1983b).

Discretionary income refers to the amount of money left over after necessary expenses such as food, housing, and shelter have been paid.

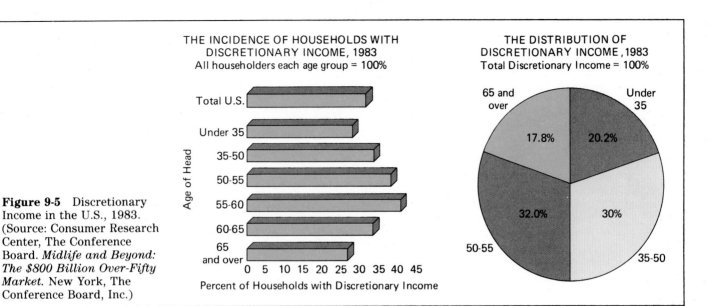

THE INCIDENCE OF HOUSEHOLDS WITH
DISCRETIONARY INCOME, 1983
All householders each age group = 100%

THE DISTRIBUTION OF
DISCRETIONARY INCOME, 1983
Total Discretionary Income = 100%

Figure 9-5 Discretionary Income in the U.S., 1983. (Source: Consumer Research Center, The Conference Board. *Midlife and Beyond: The $800 Billion Over-Fifty Market.* New York, The Conference Board, Inc.)

POLITICAL POWER

A major, still unrealized source of bargaining power, derived from their proportional increase in the population, is the voting strength of the elderly, which could be used to exert political power. Are the elderly forming a potent political force? Consider the 1984 presidential election when Ronald Reagan was reelected by the largest plurality in American history. At age seventy-three, Reagan was the oldest man ever to be elected to the American presidency. As one newspaper noted: "When he was born, the flag that flew over his hometown had 46 stars. William Howard Taft was president. Windshield wipers were just becoming standard equipment on cars." (*Wall Street Journal,* Oct. 9, 1984, p. 1). That an old man would be the leader of a nation is not a new event; for example, Ayatollah Khomeini of Iran was eighty-four and China's Deng Xiaoping, age eighty at the time of Reagan's reelection. What was new was an elderly American president. The evidence suggests that Reagan was reelected despite, not because of, either his age or his political position on social policies affecting the elderly, even though his age was viewed by many voters as a political liability rather than an asset. That chronological age became an issue in the election is an illustration of *ageism,* that is, the acceptance of negative stereotypes of old age as inevitably associated with failing physical health and declining mental capacity. Yet Reagan's reelection

Ageism is the acceptance of negative stereotypes about old age.

victory suggests that personal popularity and ability to inspire confidence can neutralize concerns regarding the assumed disabilities of old age.

Older voters themselves split almost evenly between Reagan and his opponent Walter Mondale, despite the fact that Mondale's record was one of almost total support for programs for the elderly compared to Reagan's relative neglect of such issues. The fact that older people did not vote overwhelmingly for Mondale suggests the weakness of "gray power" as a unified political force. This is all the more remarkable given the attack on programs for the elderly that marked Reagan's first term (1980–1984).

Among the many explanations offered for the growing national debt during the early 1980s was the idea that benefits targeted to older Americans were responsible for busting the budget. In fact, public money for elderly programs accounts for a small fraction of the budget, while the largest program, Social Security, is primarily self-funded through withholding taxes. But this reality was obscured in the great debate over the Social Security system of the early 1980s, an issue that highlights a larger set of struggles over social policy and government spending deeply rooted in American ideology (Estes 1983). It is an issue still to be resolved.

Voting Patterns of the Elderly. Study after study has indicated that voting rates tend to increase with age. In the November 1984

The diversity of the elderly makes it rather difficult to organize around their political interests. Social Security benefits, however, are a common rallying point as we see here at a demonstration aimed at preventing cuts to these benefits. (© George Cohen)

elections, one-third of those who voted were fifty-five years of age or older. Of all age groups, voters fifty-five to sixty-four had the highest participation rate (70 percent) and sixty-five to seventy-four-year-olds the second highest (68 percent voted). Voting participation declines among those seventy-five and over; only 58 percent voted. Among the elderly, white men are the most likely to vote, followed by white women, then black men and black women. Among those elders registered to vote but did not, the two major reasons cited are lack of interest and poor health. Voting rates for people sixty-five and over are second only to those of people aged forty-five to sixty-four, and much higher than for young adults, as seen in Table 9-2.

In any given election, people sixty-five and over account for between 15 to 20 percent of the voters. This proportion may be much higher in districts with many elders (Florida, Arizona, rural areas, and central cities).

But, as the 1984 presidential election illustrates, it would be a mistake to think of older people as a single-interest voting group (Smith and Martinson 1984). Nor do people necessarily become more politically conservative as they age. Birth cohorts will vary in their initial political

While many people think of the elderly in terms of the past, they themselves often have a deep sense of commitment to the present and future. (© Dennis Brack/Black Star)

TABLE 9-2 Percent of age-strata voting in presidential elections 1964–1984

Year	Age Group (Percent Voting)			
	18–24	25–44	45–64	65 and over
1964	50.9	69.0	75.9	66.3
1968	50.4	66.6	74.9	65.8
1972	49.6	62.7	70.8	63.5
1976	42.2	58.7	68.7	62.2
1980	39.9	58.7	69.3	65.1
1984	40.8	58.4	69.8	67.7

SOURCE: Bureau of the Census, *Current Population Reports*, Series P–20, No. 405, Table A. U.S. Government Printing Office, Washington, D.C., 1986.

How Secure is Social Security?

The Social Security system was established in 1935 to encourage older workers to retire and make room for younger workers during the Great Depression. The system provided a monthly check to retired or disabled workers and to the surviving spouse and minor children of dead workers. Social Security is financed by a tax on a part of earned income—half paid by the worker and half by the employer. Although only a small proportion of the labor force was originally covered by the system, it has gradually expanded in coverage and the size of benefits so that Social Security today is the single most important source of income for the great majority of older Americans.

By the 1970s, however, certain problems appeared: due to continued inflation, periods of high unemployment, and a rapid increase in the number of people receiving benefits, the system's surplus was being reduced at a faster rate than predicted. Congress took care of the immediate problem by raising both the Social Security tax rate and the amount of income on which the tax was applied. But the high unemployment of the 1981–1982 recession severely reduced payments into the system, while the number of early retirees continued to rise. The Reagan administration's answer was a Social Security reform package that would have reduced individual benefits, delayed cost-of-living adjustments, and tightened eligibility for disability payments—all of which brought a storm of protest from organizations representing older people.

Eventually, Congress enacted a set of compromise amendments in 1983 that could keep the system in reasonable financial shape through the first half of the next decade. The Social Security tax and the base on which it is paid will both rise slowly; some benefits were reduced and others delayed, but no basic change was made in the system. Yet for the first time since 1935, a basic challenge was

made to the entire concept of a government's responsibility to its nonworking citizens.

The debate over Social Security was in actuality an ideological struggle over the limits of public welfare programs in the United States. On the one hand were the defenders of the Social Security system who pressed their claims that governments, representing the society as a whole, have an obligation to provide for the health and welfare of people who are not wage earners; on the other hand are those believers in private enterprise who have always opposed public programs that transfer money from earners to nonearners, and who would prefer to see Social Security replaced by private pension plans. It is no accident that the strongest attacks on the financial stability of the Social Security system came from publications such as the *Wall Street Journal, Fortune, Business Week,* and *Forbes.*

The fact that the system remained essentially intact, however, did not altogether please some critics from the other end of the political spectrum. Many social scientists would prefer to see the United States adopt a system similar to that of all other modern industrial societies in which old-age benefits are funded from general revenues and offered as an entitlement of citizenship rather than being linked to employment history. In this sense, the American Social Security system is a perfect reflection of the work ethic, described in Chapter 3, as the source of our particular value system.

SOURCES: John Myles, "The Trillion Dollar Misunderstanding," *Working Papers,* July–August 1981, 23–31; S. M. Rosen, "The Social Security Crisis: Poor Economics, Dangerous Politics," *Social Policy,* Summer 1983, 39–40; Beth B. Hess, "Manufacturing Crises in Social Policy: The Withering Away of the Welfare State," Paper presented at the 37th Annual Meeting of the Gerontological Society of America, San Antonio, Tex., November 1984.

attitudes, which are shaped by the historical events of their youth, and modified by further experiences in the society. Crucial issues at a particular life stage can bring dramatic shifts (Campbell and Stratz 1981).

In addition, the elderly, as much if not more than other age strata, have crosscutting identities such as social class, ethnicity, religion, region of the country, and so forth. Sheer numbers of people do not automatically translate into political

power, especially when there are deep social class divisions (Williamson et al. 1982). Again, as the Reagan–Mondale election results indicate, it is not easy to organize older people around political issues. Their diversity is simply too great. Moreover, when efforts are made to influence legislation affecting elders, others in "the aging establishment" often speak for the aged: the thousands of social and health-care workers involved in programs for the elderly, professors and researchers in the

Research on Aging: A Calculated Decision

CHARLOTTE IKELS

Charlotte Ikels is currently assistant professor at Case Western Reserve University and a research associate at Harvard University's Fairbanks Center for East Asian Research. She is the author of Aging and Adaptation: Chinese in Hong Kong and the United States, *1983, and a number of articles. She has also edited a special issue of the* Journal of Cross-Cultural Gerontology *on "Migration and the Elderly."*

My intellectual engagement with aging began while a graduate student at the University of Hawaii when I had to make a very practical choice, that of a dissertation topic. I felt that I had to select a topic that would simultaneously satisfy four different requirements. First was my own interest in illuminating some aspect of Chinese culture. Second, given the nature of our political relationship with the People's Republic of China (the United States had not yet established formal diplomatic relations, but was expecting to in the near future), I had to select an issue that would not be perceived as threatening by the Chinese government. Since the Chinese have long had a reputation of "respecting the elderly," I thought the study of aging would be both "safe" and exciting as my intended informants had lived through a tumultuous historical era and doubtless had seen many changes and faced many challenges. Thirdly, my graduate work as well as that of several others in the Department of Anthropology was being supported by a National Institute of Mental Health Research Traineeship. Ostensibly we were being trained to consider the role of coping skills in facilitating the adaptation of populations to new circumstances or new environments. Doctoral committees interpreted this mandate broadly,

and aging, at least in revolutionary China, fell within the acceptable category. Finally, I had an eye on the future. Specifically, I wanted to work on a topic that would enhance my marketability as a new Ph.D. No matter how intrinsically interesting other topics might have been, I did not feel at that time that I could indulge myself in the luxury of pursuing any of them if there was a strong chance I would wind up unemployed as a result.

Following my first year of course work, I was fortunate enough to do three months of exploratory research in Hong Kong (the resumption of diplomatic ties with the PRC was destined to proceed too slowly for me to conduct my dissertation research in China proper). Enter good luck in the form of the Hong Kong government and the Hong Kong Council of Social Service, an organization of private agencies. By a most fortunate coincidence these two bodies had just begun a joint investigation into the circumstances of the elderly in Hong Kong. I had unparalleled access to specially compiled data from the recent census, to homes for the aged, and to officials variously involved with services for the elderly. It was a very stimulating time; I knew aging was the topic and Hong Kong was the place!

During the nearly two years I spent gathering data, I came to know many Chinese elderly. A few had been born in Hong Kong, but the vast majority had emigrated from adjacent Guangdong Province in China. Having in most cases endured extreme hardships over the years, these older people were, first and foremost, survivors. They had a clear grasp of the realities of life in urban Hong Kong. They did not expect their families to function in accordance with traditional values, and

they generally avoided antagonizing their adult children on whom they realized they would eventually be financially and socially dependent. What they dreaded was the possibility of being separated from their children, a fear that was justified by the migration patterns of the younger generation. Just as the older generation had left China, so the next generation was leaving Hong Kong for destinations in Europe, North America, and Australia. Many elderly faced the dilemma of remaining in a familiar environment without their children or relocating to a totally different cultural setting in order to be with their children.

As I examined issues of aging and adaptation, I began to feel the need for contact with others who had conducted research on aging outside of the United States. Even as a graduate student I had joined the Gerontological Society of America, but its membership seemed primarily interested in problem-oriented research in the United States. Eventually I made contact with a new interest group within the American Anthropological Association known as the Association for Anthropology and Gerontology (AAGE). Through this organization I met numerous people who had done research among non-Western populations and who were concerned about the narrow base on which many theories in American and European gerontology had been constructed. We felt that what were often taken as universals of human behavior were actually responses to the particular circumstances found in Western industrialized societies. We then began developing research designs to explore this issue systematically. Over the years the field that I entered originally as the result of a calculated decision has enriched my life. I also found employment!

field of aging, and adult children of aged parents. In short, the elderly have generally remained more spoken for than speaking for themselves. Few attempts have been made to change the image of elderly from "pushover pussycats to feisty prowling panthers" (Jacobs 1980). The group called the Gray Panthers is a major exception, but its membership remains very low despite its high ideals.

IS THERE A SUBCULTURE OF AGING?

Subcultures are distinctive ways of adapting to our social environment. As you will recall, a subculture is formed when a category of people is treated differently in terms of access to valued statuses and when members of that category perceive their common interests so that they interact with each other far more often than they do with people in other groups. Although some sociologists, such as Rose (1965), have proposed that the aged comprise a subculture in American society, more recent research suggests that age may be relatively less important in determining the ways in which people group themselves than such characteristics as religion, ethnicity, social class, or health. Perhaps the most important question is whether or not our society is becoming increasingly age graded? If so, will chronological age or economic need be the basis for eligibility for public benefits?

Health Care
and the Elderly:
A Contemporary Issue

It is by now a truism to say that health-care costs increase with age. The elderly accounted for over one-third of all health-care expenditures in 1984, and most of this involved terminal illnesses. Old people enter hospitals twice as often and stay almost twice as long as adults under age sixty-five. Those sixty-five and over are also the only age group in the United States to whom national health insurance (Medicare) is provided (see Chapter 17).

The need for and access to the health care system is influenced not only by actual illness but by socioeconomic characteristics, sex, individual preferences, and broader social-structural factors, including the organization of the health-care system itself.

OUTPATIENT CARE

Despite the stated belief that health care should be available to all the elderly, barriers still exist. Although Medicare has resulted in a major increase in the use of hospital services by the elderly, the average number of physician visits has remained unchanged: 6.7 visits in 1964 and 6.6 in 1980 (Davis 1984). National survey data indicate that it is precisely the most ill—very poor elderly—who make fewest physician visits, and that black elderly make significantly fewer visits than whites (Kleinman, Gold, and MacKue 1981). Moreover, blacks of all ages are less likely to have a particular private physician or dentist, reflecting their lower average income (NCHS, Vital and Health Statistics, Series 11, No. 218, 1981).

Medicare pays for approximately 44 percent of all personal health care expenditures for those over sixty-five. Other public programs, including Medicaid, account for 19 percent. The remaining 37 percent is paid by the elderly themselves or by private health insurance (Davis 1984). Not only are the poorest old least likely to have private insurance to supplement Medicare, but those who lack supplemental coverage are less likely to make outpatient physician visits (Link, Long, and Settle 1980, Snider 1980). Use of community-based health-care services is often limited by an older person's inability to deal with agency personnel. Many do not know that they are entitled to services; and most do not have a regular health-care provider. Transportation is another major problem for low-income elderly (Vigel and Palmer 1982, Wolinsky et al. 1983).

Access barriers such as those just described have added to the "axiom of inequality" of health care (Wildavsky 1977) where the rich receive more services than the poor although the latter are more likely to be disabled. Despite the fact that low-income elderly use fewer services, they pay more of their income for what they do get. In 1980, average, out-of-pocket charges for medical care amounted to 15 percent of the 1980 income of elderly persons *below* the poverty level, but only 2 percent of the total for high-income old people (National Medical Care Utilization and Expenditure Survey, Data Report, No. 4, 1984).

INSTITUTIONAL CARE

In Hospitals. Over the past two decades, the number of hospital admissions has increased by over one-third, primarily due to elderly patients. As a consequence, hospital utilization rates are extremely sensitive to the age structure of the society: in this case, to the rapid increase of population age seventy-five and over. For example, patients age eighty and over, regardless of income or health insurance, stay in the hospital an average of twelve days compared to slightly over eight days for patients aged forty to sixty-four (National Center on Health Statistics, 1985).

Because Medicare and Medicaid were designed to cover hospital care rather than medical services in the community, it is less expensive for the patient to be hospitalized than to remain at home. These patients are also the most costly for hospitals, requiring more tests because of their multiple medical problems. Terminal illnesses account for the bulk of medical care costs in most hospitals today. But because Medicare and Medicaid reimbursements are relatively low, many hospitals are caught in a bind: to discharge a patient at the earliest possible moment in order not to lose money, or to retain the patient and be forced to raise bills for younger patients.

In Nursing Homes. Medicare and Medicaid have also affected the use of nursing homes. Although the percent of older people in long-term care has not changed since 1964—approximately five percent of all elderly—the percent in nursing homes as opposed to mental hospitals has shifted dramatically. That is, the increase in nursing home patients since 1964 is not due to the rise in the overall population of old people, but to a shift from public mental hospitals to private profit-making nursing homes.

Medicare does *not* pay for the great majority of nursing-home services, but it does subsidize people who build and sell nursing homes. The patients or their families pay out-of-pocket between $50 and $100 a day. Quality nursing-home care is thus restricted to the wealthy. For the elderly who cannot afford to pay their own way, and who use up all their savings, Medicaid will pay a fixed fee to the nursing home operator. But this amount is so small that most nursing homes either refuse to take Medicaid patients or reserve only a few beds for that purpose.

Who enters a nursing home? Most are women, aged eighty or over, and all but a few are white. Many have never married, and the remainder are widowed, having

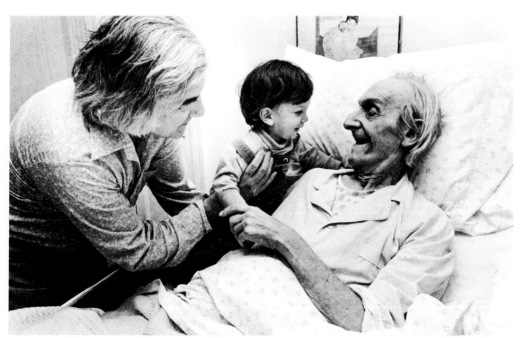

The family group is an important support system at all life stages. It can be particularly essential during periods of hospitalization. (© Abigal Heyman/Archive)

nursed a spouse through a terminal illness. The great majority suffer from several disabling mental or physical conditions (Munley et al. 1980). Very few of those with living offspring are "dumped" into long-term care; the typical pattern is that adult children have tried every alternative before some setback in their lives or severe medical problem for the elderly relative make it impossible to provide care at home. Yet a disproportionately high percentage of nursing home residents have no living children able to delay their entry into the home or to visit them after institutionalization.

The risk of spending one's final days in a long-term care facility rises with age—reaching about one in four at age eighty-five and over. Because this stratum is the fastest growing elderly age group, we can expect both nursing home admissions and overall health care expenditures in the society to continue to rise through the remainder of this century.

FAMILY SUPPORT SYSTEMS

As health-care costs escalate, informal support systems have received more and more attention. Roughly three million older people have chronic physical or mental limitations that require some help at home, and many others have episodes of acute illness, making them temporarily dependent on others. Contrary to popular belief, most of this care is already provided by family members, most often the spouse or children (see Chapter 11). It is more likely that an older disabled man will be cared for by his wife than that she will receive care from her husband. Women, on the average, live eight years longer than men, and men generally marry women younger than themselves. In any case, the primary caregiver is likely to be a woman, whether wife, daughter, or daughter-in-law, many of whom may be approaching old age themselves or are already old.

Regardless of affectional ties, such caregiving is not without stress both for the giver and the recipient. This is true not only in the United States but in other nations, even ones in which the elderly have been traditionally venerated, such as Japan (see Box).

Like the Japanese family, American family caregivers experience role strain as they attempt to keep resources in balance

Caring for the Elderly in Contemporary Japan

A recent best-selling Japanese novel, *The Twilight Years* by Sawako Ariyoshi, focuses on the problems of caring for an impaired elderly relative in Japan today. In this book, the burden of care for Mr. Tachibana's aged father falls chiefly upon his daughter-in-law, Akiko, an employed middle-aged woman, who feels increasingly trapped by the dual responsibility of job and constant care for her father-in-law. When she seeks help from the Department of Social Welfare for the Elderly, the social worker comments: "He's very old isn't he? . . . he's doing fine for a man his age. He lives in such a pleasant environment . . . he has his son, daughter-in-law and grandson living with him. . . ."

"You may be right, of course, but, as I've already mentioned, I work full-time. I've been suffering terribly from lack of sleep since he gets up in the middle of the night. He's so senile I can't leave him at home on his own. . . . (pp. 157–158). I'm sure I'll find some peace of mind if he's admitted to an institution. . . . "

"But don't you think he'd be happier living at home? . . . I appreciate that you work full-time but someone has to make sacrifices" (p. 159).

The social worker comments further that there is no ready solution to problems of caring for an impaired elderly relative; although caregiving tears many families apart, the wife or daughter, or daughter-in-law must cope courageously. Eventually, Akiko's father-in-law dies at home from pneumonia. It never occurred to anyone that the men of the family should assist in direct care.

This controversial novel highlights the point that Japan, like the United States, has found no ideal solution to provide home care to an impaired elderly relative. Cost, eligibility for service to a middle-class family, lack of home health supports from formal agencies, and stress on family members remain unsolved problems in many industrialized nations undergoing rapid demographic change.

SOURCE: Sawako Ariyoshi, *The Twilight Years*. Tr. Mildred Takahara, Kodansha, 1984.

while caring for an older relative: the demands of one's job and other family members, on the one hand, and economic and personal resources to meet these demands on the other. How can families reduce these competing role demands? Several studies have suggested that formal ser-

Even in societies where the elderly have traditionally received more deference than in the U.S. caring for the elderly is problematic. Many people are, for example, surprised to realize that there are homes for the aged, such as the one depicted here, in Japan. (© Fred Ward/Black Star)

vices, providing relief from the daily responsibilities of caretaking, would help (Sussman 1977, 1979, Horowitz and Shindelman 1980). Overwhelmingly, caregivers preferred to have services, such as a homemaker and home-health aide, rather than economic incentives such as cash grants, tax incentives, or food stamps. In a climate of economic restraint when formal services are being reduced, it is important to keep in mind that the informal care system, although valuable, should not be viewed as *the* alternative to formal support services. Only when formal *and* informal services are in place will the elderly be assured the kinds of care they need and want when disabled.

Summary

Age, as an ascribed characteristic, is used as the requirement for entering into or exiting from valued statuses. Social definitions of appropriate ages for role performances lead to age-related hierarchies of power and prestige.

The population of every society has a specific age structure. The resulting population pyramids represent the supply of males and females of different ages available to fill various social roles. Although biological factors set some limits on behavior, age limits are for the most part culturally and socially determined. When persons are excluded from roles that they believe they can fulfill, strain and deviance may result.

Over the life course, there are periods of relative role strain and role slack. Young adulthood and middle age are characterized by many competing role demands, whereas adolescents and the old may be presented with too few challenges.

The social position of the elderly stems from their ability to control things of value to their children and to society: economic assets, family loyalty, and valued information. The elderly are a relatively powerless group in modern societies, though their numbers are increasing and some do occupy powerful and prestigious offices in political and religious organizations.

The great diversity of political views and beliefs among the elderly make political unity based on age status difficult. Legislation providing the basis for survival to most old people has been enacted, but further provisions seem unlikely to be made soon.

Probably the most important contemporary issue for the elderly is health care. Increasing physical disability and decreasing social networks can necessitate substantial caregiving provisions which can be especially problematic for those elderly persons with limited wealth or savings. In many circumstances, the options available—outpatient care, hospital care, nursing-home care, and family support systems—do not provide an adequate solution to the problem.

240

Suggested Readings

CHERLIN, ANDREW J., and FRANK F. FURSTENBERG, JR. *The New American Grandparent: A Place in the Family, A Life Apart.* New York: Basic Books, 1986. The first nationwide study of American grandparents—a portrait of their own lives and links to their families.

CLAUSEN, JOHN. *The Life Course: A Sociological Perspective.* Englewood Cliffs, NJ: Prentice-Hall, 1986. A clearly written and interesting overview of the life course utilizing sociological, psychological, and historical research.

ELDER, GLEN H., JR. *Children of the Great Depression.* Chicago: University of Chicago Press, 1974. A classic study of the Depression Years cohorts and the impact of social-historical events on their lives.

HESS, BETH B., and ELIZABETH MARKSON, eds. *Growing Old in America.* 3rd ed. New Brunswick, NJ: Transaction, 1985. A comprehensive collection of thirty-six articles covering the social aspects of aging: cultural values that relate to the aged, the interplay of individual and societal factors, the changing social status of the elderly, the instability of the adult years, and the politics of aging, particularly the abuses of medicine, mental hospitals, and nursing homes.

MARSHALL, VICTOR W., ed. *Later Life: The Social Psychology of Aging.* Beverly Hills, CA: Sage, 1986. A collection of original essays from a symbolic-interaction approach, emphasizing the ways in which older people are active agents in constructing their social worlds.

MYLES, JOHN. *Old Age in the Welfare State: The Political Economy of Public Pensions.* Highly readable introduction to the "political economy of aging" approach to understanding the status of elderly in modern societies.

VAN TASSEL, DAVID, and PETER N. STEARNS, eds. *Old Age in a Bureaucratic Society.* Westport, CT: Greenwood Press, 1986. An excellent set of essays in the social history of aging, an exciting new field of gerontological study.

10

Racial, Ethnic, and Religious Minorities

Bigotry refers to racial, religious and ethnic intolerance.

THE symbol of the Statue of Liberty welcoming the poor and the huddled masses has often masked difficulties experienced by nonWASP immigrants. These are only a few examples in a long history of racial, religious, and ethnic intolerance (*bigotry*) in the United States:

• During World War II, most of the Japanese-American population of the

United States was interned in detention camps.

• When John F. Kennedy ran for president of the United States in 1960, his first campaign activity was to assure the public that, as a Roman Catholic, he would not be influenced by the pope in matters of U.S. policy.

• In 1976, a Chinese-American teenager was stabbed by another youth in

Brooklyn who said "We don't want Chinks in our neighborhood."

- In 1987, a group of civil rights marchers in a rural county in Georgia were stopped by an angry white crowd. Leading the crowd was a white man who had once been convicted for bombing a black church. Speaking to a cheering crowd, he indicated that he didn't want "niggers bringing AIDS" to the county.

Race, religion, and ethnicity are social categories that influence social placement in any society, but societies vary greatly in the degree to which their population is composed of different racial, religious, or ethnic groups. Some societies, such as those of Denmark, Sweden, and Norway, are *culturally homogeneous;* that is, the members of the society are similar in racial stock, religious observance, and country of origin. Such societies do not experience the difficulties of absorbing many people whose norms and customs differ from those of the majority. Recently, however, even Sweden has been shaken by attacks on "guest workers" from southern Europe and North Africa, imported as unskilled or semiskilled labor.

Other societies are *culturally heterogeneous;* that is, their citizens differ greatly in color and appearance, in beliefs and values, and in language and culture. The Soviet Union has over two hundred such nationality groups within its borders. So, to a lesser extent, do Yugoslavia, Australia, New Zealand, South Africa, Israel, Canada, and the United States. In such societies, social order depends on (1) how the various groups are brought into contact with one another (intergroup relations) and (2) how scarce rewards are allocated. The basic theme of this chapter is the extent to which the ascribed statuses of race, religion, and ethnicity influence placement in the major stratification hierarchies and the experiences of minority groups in the United States.

Minority groups are defined in contrast to the **dominant group** of the population. The dominant group is not necessarily numerically larger. Dominance refers to *control* over central sectors of social life, including the power to define standards of beauty and worth. Thus, although WASPs are a minority of the American population, their influence on our culture, our language, our ideology, and our law has shaped the nation more than the influence of any other group. They are the Americans against whom other groups are measured and evaluated. In contrast to the WASP ideal, those who are not white, northern European, or Protestant have characteristics that not only set them apart but become cues for different, typically unequal treatment.

Cultural homogeneity results from similarity in race, religion, and nationality.

Cultural heterogeneity occurs when a society contains a variety of minority groups.

Dominant groups exercise control over societal resources.

Where diverse ethnic and racial groups attempt to live side by side, a great deal of effort has to go into producing a harmonious cultural mosaic. (© Momatiuk Eastcott/Woodfin Camp and Associates)

Minority-group status involves visible traits, differential treatment, self-image, and shared identity.

There are four elements necessary to defining *minority-group status:*

1. *Visible ascribed traits,* by which most minority group members can be recognized.
2. *Differential treatment* on the basis of possessing these traits.
3. The *organization of self-image* around this identiy.
4. An *awareness of shared identity* with others in the same group.

Members of such groups can be thought of as belonging to *subsocieties.* Participation in a subsociety fills three functions for its members: (1) it provides the in-group identity needed for self-definition; (2) it maintains patterns of primary-group relations (*Gemeinschaft*); and (3) it interprets the broader national society through the particular filter of minority-group traditions (Gordon 1978). Thus, minority-group members can construct a subculture that protects and nurtures those who remain within its network of primary and secondary ties. Belonging to a minority group, however, often makes it difficult to enter the maintstream society.

Ethnicity, Race, and Religion

Ethnicity refers to national background.

The United States contains many ethnic, religious, and racial minorities. *Ethnicity* refers to national background or cultural differences. People and groups vary in how much they retain the customs, language, and surnames of their country of origin.

Religion is a set of beliefs and rituals associated with the sacred.
Race is based on the distribution of biological traits.

Religion is a set of beliefs and rituals associated with the sacred. People of the same religion recognize each other through shared worship (see Chapter 15).

Race is much more difficult to define. Although most of us speak of race as if we were sure of its meaning, it is almost impossible to define the term scientifically. There are two ways to classify racial groups from a biological perspective. The first is based on physical appearance (phenotype), such as skin color, eye shape or hair texture. Your own experience should prove how inaccurate such classifications can be. Negroid and Caucasian types are not pure. Both categories contain people who are light- and dark-skinned, tall and short, long-headed and round-headed, straight-haired and curly-haired. The variation within phenotypes is too large to permit easy classification.

A second method of telling races apart is based on genetic makeup (genotype). This definition is also inexact. Human blood groups are fixed by genotypes, but millions of combinations of blood patterns exist. From a scientific viewpoint, therefore, it is difficult to say that distinct races exist in a biological sense.

Social class, unlike race or ethnicity, is considered an *achieved* status in modern industrial societies. However, by definition, access to positions of power, prestige, and property is controlled by the rules and actions of the dominant group within a society. Members of racial, religious, or ethnic minorities find higher or lower barriers to achievement depending on several factors, including (1) how closely they resemble the dominant culture in appearance and customs, (2) the skills and talents (including education) they bring to the society and (3) the state of the economy. This means that the historical experience of different minority groups in America has varied greatly, so that generalizations are somewhat difficult. For example, despite similarities in their treatment within our dominant institutions, the outcome for Jews and blacks in the United States has been very different. Blacks, because of their greater visibility in white society, are much more likely than Jews to experience barriers to social mobility.

In the United States, ascribed statuses often serve as *caste* boundaries, limiting entry into mainstream positions of prestige and power. Whereas race is a most difficult social boundary to surmount, over time both religion and ethnicity have become less powerful barriers to achievement. A Catholic (Al Smith) could not be elected President in 1928, but John Kennedy was elected in 1960. A recent U.S. secretary of state was Henry A. Kissinger, born in Germany, and a recent head of The National Security Council, Zbigniew Brzezinski, was born in Poland. Jews and Italian-Americans now manage major corporations. New York has had an Italian-American governor and Massachusetts voters twice elected a Greek-American governor. In terms of the ability to achieve high positions in a society, however, some subgroups are more privileged than others as we shall see throughout this chapter.

Models for the Integration of Minority Groups

How can a varied population be welded into a unified whole? To maintain social stability, a common set of values and norms has to be forged, so that the members of different ethnic, racial, and religious groups can interact in an orderly fashion. Several explanations for the integration of minority groups have been proposed, among which are the *melting pot* and *cultural pluralism models*.

THE MELTING POT

The model of the *melting pot* (a concept referring to the melting down of differences) is based on the belief that immigrants could and should, through exposure to the mass media and a common educational system, gradually lose their differences and come to share a common language and culture, enjoying equal opportunities for success in the New World. A popular view in colonial America was that all people were descended from Adam and Eve, the differences among them being the result of specific environments. In time, it was thought, all newcomers would conform to American norms and beliefs, producing a distinct American population.

Despite a strong national belief in the melting pot, and despite the success of the public-school system in teaching a common language and culture to millions of immigrants, ethnic minorities have in many ways remained "unmeltable." Not only was the melting-pot ideology founded on an overly simple theory of human nature, but its supporters overlooked the crucial importance of race, religion, and ethnicity as sources of identity, self-respect, and community. They also assumed that WASP norms, values, and life-styles were the ideals that others must follow.

At the very least, it was hoped that the children of minority-group members would come to share similar norms and values through an education consisting of civics, English, and the memorization of patriotic literature and songs. As one observer commented tongue-in-cheek, "One part ability to read, write, and speak English; one part the Declaration of Independence; one part the Constitution; one part love for apple pie, one part desire and willingness to wear American shoes, and another part pride in American plumbing will make an American of anyone" (Smith 1939, p. 115). In this sense, second- and third-generation immigrants have become strongly attached to American institutions and goals and are often among our most vocal patriots.

To ease their way on the path to upward mobility early in this century, many changed their names to disguise their religious and ethnic background. Elite universities were known to have quotas for "Jews and those whose names ended in vowels." Few minority-group members thought it possible to run for political office, and even fewer were accepted into the management of banks, corporations, or stock exchange firms. Americanization could go only so far in integrating minorities into the larger structures of society.

But, by 1950, recent immigrants and their children comprised a relatively small percentage of the United States population and many differences that had once marked ethnic communities were disappearing. In addition, the foreign-born and their children moved to other parts of the city or to the suburbs. It seemed as if the melting pot had indeed melted down many of the distinctive aspects of ethnicity. But other divisions related to immigration were still evident. Religious affiliation rather than ethnicity began to emerge as the crucial trait by which white Americans identified themselves (Archdeacon 1983). For example, by 1950, British, German, and Scandinavian Protestants frequently intermarried, as did Irish, Italian, and Polish Catholics. Yet while people crossed ethnic lines to choose mates, relatively few crossed religious lines. It seemed that ethnic differences were being melted down in America, but into three pots rather than one (Archdeacon 1983).

This *triple melting-pot* model of intergroup relationships was, however, relatively short-lived. The persistence of ethnicity, race, and religion both as important aspects of personal identity and as barriers to acceptance and achievement led to a reexamination of the ways in

---

The **melting-pot model** of integration assumes that immigrants will lose their cultural uniqueness and become part of the dominant American culture.

The **triple melting pot** suggested that ethnic differences were melting but religious differences, between Catholics, Protestants, and Jews, were not.

Ethnic Identity and the 1980 Presidential Election

What impact does ethnicity have on political actions and attitudes? Using data from the 1980 election, Archdeacon (1983) examined ethnic identity as related to two aspects of political orientation: the proportion of various ethnic and racial groups decribing themselves as "conservative" and the proportion voting for Ronald Reagan. The results of his study appear in the following table.

Proportion Describing Themselves as "Conservative" and Proportion Voting for Reagan in 1980 for Selected Racial and Ethnic Groups

Group	Conservative	Voted for Reagan
German Protestant	42%	72%
British Isles*	41	53
American Indian	36	60
Irish Catholic	35	48
Irish Protestant	33	59
Italian	30	56
Black	26	7
German Catholic	25	36
Hispanic	16	25

* Includes English, Scots, and Welsh

As you look at the table, you will notice that some ethnic groups, such as German Protestants and those from the British Isles, were considerably more conservative than Hispanics. But political conservatism alone did not determine which groups were most likely to vote for Reagan. Nor was ethnicity alone a good predictor of voting behavior, for religion crosscut with ethnicity. Thus German Protestants were both more conservative and were more likely to vote for Reagan than were German Catholics; Irish Catholics, who were slightly more liberal than Irish Protestants, were considerably less likely to vote for Reagan.

Studies such as this suggest that ethnic background and identity interact with other factors, such as religion, age, education, and income—as well as the personal popularity of the political candidate. Poor Italian-Americans and rich ones do not necessarily think alike; Irish Protestants have a history that is different from Irish Catholics, and Native Americans living on a reservation may have a different world view from those who live in cities. In other words, the effect of a particular ethnic heritage on behavior is neither universal nor unchanging.

SOURCE: Thomas J. Archdeacon, *Becoming American: An Ethnic History*. New York: Free Press, 1983.

Cultural pluralism emphasized the special contributions of various immigrant cultures to the diversity of American society.

which groups were absorbed in the social structure of the United States. *Cultural pluralism* became the new ideal.

CULTURAL PLURALISM

Unlike the melting-pot model, in which all differences among groups would be melted down and cease to exist, the cultural-pluralism model emphasized the special contributions of various immigrant cultures to the diversity and vitality of American cultural life—as in a salad bowl in which every ingredient remains distinct yet contributes to the salad. Cultural pluralism implies an acceptance of differences in relatively personal matters such as food, family, religious rituals, and community associations. Members of different ethnicities, racial groups, and religions thus live the most intimate parts of their lives within their own traditions. It does not mean a number of multiple cultures, however, in the proper sense of the world "culture." The United States could not survive in its present form if there were compartmentalized, parallel power systems and a loss of concern with the common good of the nation as a whole.

It was once thought that as a result of urban industrial life and the realization of equal opportunity, later-generation minority-group members would gradually become *less* identified with their ethnic, racial, or religious backgrounds, so that only surface differences would remain. In the 1960s, this belief was challenged, as blacks, Hispanics, and Native Americans protested against continued inequality of opportunity. A new ethnic consciousness was sparked. The discovery and celebration of one's past roots served to mobilize these minority groups for political action. For example, the slogan "Black is beautiful" strengthened the identity of blacks with each other. Formation of such action

We don't know whether these doctors socialize after work, but they do share a set of professional offices and this culturally pluralistic sign. Which ethnic groups do you think live in this neighborhood? (© Eugene Gordon)

groups as the Mexican-American La Raza (literally, "the race"), the American Indian Movement (AIM), and the Congress of Racial Equality (CORE) created bonds of mutual support among people who otherwise felt isolated. Such groups also provided an avenue through which political pressure could be brought to bear on the power structure of American society.

Not only has there been an increased pride in their heritage and uniqueness among blacks, Hispanics, and other disadvantaged groups, but there has also been an increase in ethnic consciousness among other, more advantaged immigrant groups. This has included an appreciation of roots and a protest against lingering inequalities. Slogans such as "I'm proud to be Polish" and "Kiss me; I'm Irish" emphasize the continuing role of ethnic identity in American life. Despite currently high rates of intermarriage among white ethnic groups, a growing number of people identify with only one ethnic group, a trend most pronounced among young adults (Alba and Chamlin 1983). Ethnic identity seems here to stay.

Processes in the Integration of Minority Groups

Minority groups are linked to the larger society in several ways, which form a *continuum* from near isolation (segregation) to a blending into the dominant culture (amalgamation). This continuum is depicted in Figure 10-1.

SEGREGATION

Segregation describes efforts to isolate minorities and may be of two types: *de facto* and *de jure*. *De jure* means "supported by law." *De facto* means "in fact," but not necessarily supported by law. An example of *de jure* segregation is the *apartheid* ("apartness") policy of the Republic of South Africa, where a small minority of whites dominates the country, and the majority—blacks, persons of mixed race, and Asians—have limited freedom of movement, living and working on rural reservations or in selected urban areas. Separate school systems, transportation, and public facilities are established by law for the different races. The quality of nonwhite education, jobs, and housing is distinctly inferior. Such an arrangement is similar to the legally sanctioned separate facilities provided for blacks in the South up to the mid-1960s. Following a series of U.S. Supreme Court decisions, *de jure* segregation in the United States is now prohibited. *De facto* segregation, however, remains not very different from that described by Gunnar Myrdal, a Swedish sociologist who studied racial segregation in the 1940s (Myrdal 1945).

The term **segregation** refers to attempts to isolate minority groups.

De jure segregation is supported by law. **De facto** segregation is the result of custom and personal choices.

EXTENT OF MINORITY CONTACT
WITH MAJORITY CULTURE

Segregation   Accommodation   Acculturation   Assimilation   Amalgamation

LOW   HIGH

A continuum of processes of absorption into the majority culture

Figure 10-1

People in the Republic of South Africa are segregated by race for most of their interactions. Over 300 racial laws force members of each racial group to live in their own areas, use separate hospitals, buses, beaches and educational facilities. (© Alon Reininger/Woodfin Camp and Associates)

ACCOMMODATION

Accommodation occurs when the members of a minority group are aware of dominant norms and values without having internalized them.

Accommodation is the phase in which the members of a minority become aware of the norms and values of the dominant culture but do not necessarily change their own norms and values. They adapt to the dominant culture without fully participating in it. For example, established Cuban residents of Miami have developed businesses and industries within the Cuban community that allow them to remain culturally and linguistically distinct from the English-speaking community. Yet, they have learned to deal effectively with the mainstream social institutions, such as the schools and the political economy. Aware of and able to negotiate the dominant Anglo culture, Miami's Cubans nonetheless remain separate, interdependent, a community-within-a-community (Wilson and Martin 1982, Rumbaut 1986).

ACCULTURATION

Acculturation takes place when minority-group members adopt the dominant values and norms but are not admitted to intimate groupings.

Acculturation, sometimes called *cultural assimilation,* occurs when the people in a minority group adopt as their own the norms, values, and behavior patterns of the dominant society but are still not admitted to more intimate social groups. For example, even Jews who are directors of corporations are rarely invited to become members of elite clubs to which the

WASP business leaders belong (Zweigenhaft 1982).

ASSIMILATION

Assimilation is sometimes called *structural assimilation* to distinguish it from acculturation or cultural assimilation. *Assimilation* describes the entry into the dominant society through friendship and other close associations (see Chapter 4). The rate of assimilation of different minority groups varies both by the degree of their physical differences, such as skin color, and by the degree to which their cultural traits depart from the dominant ideal. It has been easier for light-skinned, English-speaking people to become assimilated in the United States than for darker people or those who do not speak English. The former are more likely to be "melted down" into the dominant culture, though they may still retain a strong ethnic identity, as do many Irish-Americans.

Assimilation occurs when people from minority groups are accepted in major social institutions and more personal groupings.

AMALGAMATION

The final process is *amalgamation,* a process most closely associated with the melting pot. Amalgamation occurs when cultures or races mix to form new cultural and racial types. The prime means of amalgamation is through intermarriage.

Amalgamation is the mixing of minority and dominant groups through intermarriage.

Although the rates of ethnic and religious intermarriage have increased dramatically within the last few decades, *interracial* marriages remain rare, accounting for less than 3 percent of all marriages today.

These five processes highlight the complicated ways in which minority groups become a part of the majority society. Segregation that is maintained by custom still controls large-scale entry into many institutional spheres, as well as into such primary groups as the family. For example, nonwhites are still noticeably underrepresented in major corporations and law firms. In the following section, we examine some of the barriers that prevent minority groups from entering the mainstream of American society.

Barriers to Integration

The three major barriers to the integration of minority groups are *prejudice, discrimination,* and *institutional racism.* Prejudice and discrimination involve individual responses; institutional racism is a widespread structural arrangement.

PREJUDICE

Prejudice involves prejudging members of ethnic, religious, and racial groups.

Stereotypical thinking occurs when a set of characteristics is attributed to all members of a social group.

Prejudice literally means "prejudging" without knowledge. Thus, ethnic, racial, religious, or other social categories are *stereotyped.* A *stereotype* is an image in which a single set of characteristics, favorable or unfavorable, is attributed to an entire group. Stereotypes are overgeneralized; that is, behavior that may be true of some members is taken as typical of the whole group. A stereotype also singles out surface aspects of group behavior without relating them to their underlying causes. Students today will probably recognize some of the stereotypes found in college students of more than fifty years ago:

Jews: shrewd, money-grabbing

Blacks: lazy, happy-go-lucky

Italians: impulsive, passionate

Irish: quick-tempered, witty, stupid (Katz and Braly 1933)

Why do such stereotypes persist? Because there are many intelligent but "ignorant" people; that is, they are flexible and knowledgeable in many ways but close-minded and unbending in others. Knowing why prejudices exist is one way in which stereotypical thinking may be reduced. Holding stereotypes feeds prejudices and prevents us from viewing other people as individuals.

Scapegoating. Prejudice is also reinforced by *scapegoating* or finding someone else to blame for one's misfortune. The term *scapegoating* refers to the biblical practice of sacrificing a goat to appease God for human sins. Scapegoating consists of blaming a particular group for social ills. In Nazi Germany, for example, Jews were blamed for the massive economic problems of the nation. In the United States, at approximately the same time, people who were dissatisfied with economic and political conditions were also likely to express anti-semitic attitudes (Campbell 1947). Scapegoats are not confined to one group. Thus whites who are unhappy with local government frequently blame blacks for their troubles (Campbell 1971). The poor are thought to be responsible for poverty; rape victims are seen as "asking for it"; and jobs are scarce because women are entering the labor force. None of these assumptions is true; each is an example of scapegoating.

Scapegoating refers to finding someone else to blame for one's misfortune.

Jewish concentration camp prisoners at Buchenwald peer out at Allied liberators at the end of World War II. In Nazi Germany scapegoating and genocide went hand in hand. (© UPI/Bettmann Newsphotos)

Roots of Prejudice. How does prejudice arise? Its roots are complex, but like other attitudes and behaviors, prejudice is learned. The author Lillian Smith described how she learned racial prejudice as a child:

> By the time we were five years old, we had learned, without hearing the words, . . . that . . . segregation is right and must not be broken, for we believed God, whom we feared and tried desperately to love, had made the rules concerning not only Him and our parents but . . . negroes. Therefore when we as small children crept over the color line and ate and played with negroes or broke other segregation customs known to us, we felt the same dread of consequences, the same overwhelming guilt we felt when we . . . thought thoughts about God or our parents that we knew we must not think. . . . These were our first lessons. (Smith 1949, pp. 83–84)

Smith's experience as a small child illustrates not only that prejudice is learned most often within a primary group, but that prejudices tend to conform to the norms of the community. Prejudice is thus generally an *institutionalized pattern* rather than a personal quirk.

Function of Prejudice. One major function of prejudice is to improve one's own group position in the stratification system at the expense of another group. Competition for jobs, property, and wealth tends to raise the level of prejudice whenever a minority challenges the dominant group.

DISCRIMINATION

Discrimination is the practice of unequal treatment.

Whereas prejudice is a set of attitudes, *discrimination* is the *practice* of treating people unequally. The two are closely related. That is, prejudice often leads to discrimination. Discrimination, in turn, reinforces prejudice, in a vicious circle that limits opportunity and produces a self-fulfilling prophecy. This vicious circle is shown graphically in Figure 10-2. Note that a visible difference in race, sex, ethnicity, or religion can start off the cycle and lead to either discrimination or prejudice, or both. In any case, opportunity is blocked and a self-fulfilling prophecy is set in motion. Many years ago, for example, when Irish-Americans were poorly educated, they were denied opportunities for training in skills. Therefore, when a job

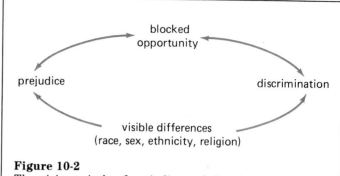

Figure 10-2
The vicious circle of prejudice and discrimination.

opening presented itself they did not have the requisite qualifications. In turn, the belief that the "Irish are stupid" was confirmed.

Yet, prejudice and discrimination are two *separate* dimensions. A person can be prejudiced without acting in a discriminatory way. The person who fears Jews may, for example, vote to admit them to his fraternity if other members are strongly in favor. Conversely, people without prejudice against minority-group members may deny them equal treatment. For instance, real-estate agents with no personal hostility toward blacks may nonetheless steer black buyers away from houses located in white neighborhoods because of a belief that the norms of the community require such discrimination. In short, people's behavior is usually designed to try to ensure approval and validation from others in the groups to which they belong. As Table 10-1 indicates, people can act differently from their attitudes, depending on how the situation is defined. Thus, discrimination can be reduced *without* attitude change by encouraging group norms that define such behavior as unacceptable.

Because it is easier to change behavior than to change attitudes, policies that affect discrimination are more successful in ending segregation than are attempts to reduce prejudice. Individual and institutional discrimination often go hand in hand, especially when norms permit or encourage open displays of hatred.

IMPACT OF DISCRIMINATION

Prejudice and discrimination can destroy life, health, and property. They also affect the self. The victims of prejudice and dis-

Segregated facilities still existed in the U.S. as recently as 1956. There were even segregated units in the military at the time of the Korean War. (© UPI/Bettmann Newsphotos)

maintain its dominant position. This process also makes those who discriminate or hold prejudices less adaptable or open to change. Finally, dominance easily shades into abuses of power.

Fear of Displacement. Prejudice and discrimination are most likely to be displayed by those who are the most threatened by the success of minority-group members. They fear that they may lose status when others gain it. For example, the hostility toward immigrants in the nineteenth and twentieth centuries was most marked among members of the working class, who felt that the entry of new groups into the labor market would reduce their ability to improve their own working conditions. Today, white workers who are in direct competition with blacks in low-paying, low-skilled jobs are more prejudiced against blacks than are white workers in higher-paying jobs (Cummings 1980). Although whites with more education are less likely to hold prejudiced attitudes toward blacks, wealthy whites, especially business owners, benefit the most from prejudice and discrimination because such attitudes and behaviors reduce the ability of black and white workers to organize together in their common interests. As a result, the wages for both whites *and* blacks are depressed because they have not been able to bargain as one group (Bowser and Hunt 1981).

crimination often internalize negative self-images, which lead to low self-esteem. Not only is a toll paid by members of the minority group experiencing prejudice, discrimination, and racism, but there are costs to the majority. In *de jure* segregation, duplicate or parallel facilities, such as separate school systems and restrooms, must be provided. Furthermore, the majority group wastes resources in trying to

INSTITUTIONALIZED RACISM

In many areas of social life, discrimination is built into the entire structure of norms and behavior and reinforced by both formal and informal agents of social control;

TABLE 10-1 An illustration of the relationship between attitudes and behavior

		Attitude	
		Prejudiced	Accepting
Behavior	*Discriminatory*	not only hates having strangers next door but actively attempts to prevent having them (e.g., by crossburning and retaining exclusionary zoning laws).	does not care who lives where but will not fight institutional racism/inequality.
	Nondiscriminatory	does not want strangers next door but will not do anything to prevent their moving in or their continued residence.	does not object to and may even welcome strangers' moving into neighborhood.

Canarsie Against Liberalism

From 1975 to 1977, Jonathan Rieder, then a sociology graduate student, lived in Canarsie, a white, working- and lower-middle-class, predominantly Italian and Jewish, section of Brooklyn, N.Y. A neighborhood of about 70,000 people, Canarsie was torn by racial strife at the time Rieder did his participant-observation study of the fragile community. Although their different cultural backgrounds and strengths had been a source of previous intergroup tensions, Canarsie's Italians and Jews united to defend their way of life.

"Canarsie," Jonathan Rieder noted, "owes its name to the Algonquian word for fort, fenced land, or palisade" (1985, p. 13). And the white ethnics who live in this section of Brooklyn felt they were defending their hard-won gains against two forces: liberal politicians and blacks. Although Canarsians would not describe themselves as racist and, until at least the mid-1960s, were ready to help blacks gain equal opportunity, they viewed the relative gains made by blacks during the 1970s as limiting their own chances for continued social mobility. Rising taxes, the Vietnam War, and inflation during the 1970s led the community to seek scapegoats to explain their economic plight. "Limousine liberal" politicians and the blacks in surrounding neighborhoods became the targets of Canarsie anger. Not only was support withdrawn from politicians viewed as at fault, but violent vigilante action was taken against blacks who tried to move into the neighborhood. Interracial crime fed feelings of bitterness, giving rise to statements such as "You have to protect your body and your children." Small business owners, trade unionists, and other whites drew sharp distinctions between the welfare checks that enabled their own immigrant parents to survive and current recipients of welfare benefits nearly as large as Canarsians' take-home pay. First-time homeowners panicked as blacks began to buy houses in Canarsie. But perhaps most threatening was the integration of neighborhood schools.

Rieder's study of Canarsie paints a vivid picture of both scapegoating and of the fear of displacement. It also brings home the important point that social changes, such as busing, may not always be efficient means to achieve real social integration. This is particularly true when the change is imposed by outside elites who do nothing to provide greater opportunities for the advancement of the relatively disadvantaged of either race. Structural unemployment and limited opportunities continue to promote fear of displacement.

SOURCE: Jonathan Rieder, *Canarsie: The Jews and Italians of Brooklyn Against Liberalism.* Cambridge, MA: Harvard University Press, 1985.

Institutionalized racism occurs when discrimination is built into normative structures and reinforced by formal and informal agents of social control.

Redlining is the practice by banks and other lending institutions of refusing to make mortgage money available for housing in certain neighborhoods.

this is called *institutional racism.* For example, segregated housing patterns are often maintained by the practice of *redlining,* through which banks and other lending institutions refuse to make mortgage money available for housing in racially mixed neighborhoods (see Chapter 19). Few areas of social life are free of institutionalized patterns of discrimination as the routine way in which business is conducted.

Who benefits from institutionalized racism? The answer is complex. In organizational settings it generally produces contradictory, inefficient, and costly behavior. For example, racism harms both white as well as black welfare recipients, but other whites benefit from inequality in employment (Bowser and Hunt 1981). In sum, regardless of individual attitudes and legal norms, there are many *group* pressures that maintain segregation (Pinkney 1987).

Genocide. The most extreme result of prejudice and discrimination is *genocide;* that is, the deliberate attempt to murder an entire category of people. The most well-known example of genocide was the Nazi holocaust during World War II. Today, genocidal attacks are common in parts of Asia, Africa, and the Middle East, committed by friends as well as by enemies of our government.

THE PERSISTENCE OF PREJUDICE AND DISCRIMINATION

Why do prejudice and discrimination continue to exist? From a conflict perspective, both are most likely to occur when there is competition over scarce resources. In Britain, for example, there was little prejudice or discrimination against Blacks, Indians, or Pakistanis until large numbers arrived and began to compete with British workers for jobs at a time of rising unemploy-

Genocide is the deliberate attempt to murder an entire category of people.

ment. For a conflict theorist, prejudice and discrimination benefit the capitalist class by creating divisions within the working class. Inequality is perpetuated as workers of different races or ethnicities fight one another rather than join together to demand higher wages.

From a functionalist perspective, prejudice and discrimination have both positive and negative consequences for a society. Despite their negative impact on minority individuals, prejudice and discrimination help build social solidarity and reaffirm the values of the dominant group. Moreover, prejudice and discrimination may actually aid the economy. The pre-mechanized agricultural South, for example, depended on cheap black labor, while the industrializing northeast exploited the labor power of new immigrants. Discrimination in general ensures a pool of low-skill, low-wage employees for the "dirty work" of society. Few people would choose a career as a street cleaner, ditch digger, or migrant farm worker if other options were readily available. But prejudice and discrimination are also highly dysfunctional in that millions of people are denied the opportunity to contribute fully to society.

Can prejudice and discrimination be eliminated? Racial, ethnic, and religious prejudice and discrimination are deeply embedded in our society. But so, also, are the values of fairness and achievement. These two conflicting themes in American culture create a strain that, as Myrdal (1945) suggested over forty years ago, make social change inevitable. Indeed, the civil rights movement of the 1960s forced many Americans to confront the basic conflict between discrimination and equality—a tension that has echoed through our history, as successive waves of immigrants added to the heterogeneity of our population.

Immigration to the United States

The 100th birthday of the Statue of Liberty reminded us that we are all immigrants. The estimated 2.5 million Native Americans displaced by white settlers in the seventeenth century were themselves descended from immigrants who probably came across a land bridge between Siberia and Alaska (Bouvier and Gardner 1986).

Today, both legal and illegal immigration continue to account for population growth in our society.

By the time of the Revolutionary War, America's population was already racially, religiously, and ethnically diverse. Until the mid-nineteenth century most immigrants were from Northern Europe. By the 1880s, however, the major streams of immigration came from Southern and Eastern Europe. Between 1875 and 1926, about 9 million Italians immigrated to the United States, along with hundreds of thousands of Poles, Hungarians, Slovaks, Czechs, Roumanians, and Jews. Over 3.3 million Russians came to the United States between 1820 and 1950. These Southern and Eastern Europeans, with their different languages, religions, norms, and values, were greeted with fear and scorn. Protestants were hostile to both Jews and Roman Catholics (whom they called "papists"). The newcomers were not only resented for their differences but also because they were willing to work for lower wages than were native-born workers. Laws passed in the 1920s established a quota system limiting immigration from Southeastern Europe and Asia. By this time, also, the demand for workers had declined as the nation headed into the Great Depression (Parrillo 1980).

By 1965, however, the quota system established forty years before was viewed as outmoded, and a new set of immigration laws were enacted. In recent years, as shown in Figure 10-3, immigration is higher than it has been since the 1920s. In fact, immigration has replaced births as the major factor in population growth. There has also been a dramatic shift in the origin of America's immigrants within the last twenty years. Somewhat over 80 percent of legal immigrants admitted to the United States during 1980–1985 were from Latin America and Asia: a marked change from 1921–1960, when people from these regions accounted for only 21 percent of those admitted legally to the United States. As was true 100 years ago, the United States is on the verge of being transformed ethnically and racially. At their current rate of growth, persons of Hispanic origin will increase from 7 percent of the population today to close to 20 percent by 2080, but it is far more likely that over several generations, Hispanic Americans will adopt the same low fertility patterns of other immigrant groups

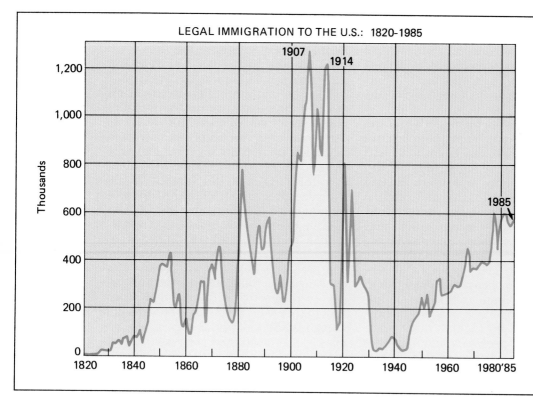

LEGAL IMMIGRATION TO THE U.S.: 1820–1985

Figure 10-3
Legal Immigration to the U.S.: 1820–1985. (Source: Leon F. Bouvier and Robert W. Gardner, *Immigration to the U.S.: The Unfinished Story.* Population Bulletin, 41, 1, November 1986, p. 10.)

(Bean and Swicegood 1985). Over the same period, Asian-Americans are expected to increase their representation in the population from 2 percent to 12 percent (Davis 1982).

How will these post-1980 immigrants be received? In the past, serious disturbances, such as rioting, and extreme discrimination in hiring increased whenever there were major changes in the numbers or countries of origin of immigrants. The widespread dislike for the Irish is an example. It was not uncommon during the nineteenth century for businesses to post signs saying "No Irish Need Apply," or for anti-Irish riots to occur in cities with large numbers of these new immigrants.

There are indications that many of today's new immigrants experience similar rejection. Public opinion surveys find an increasing number of Americans strongly in favor of limiting immigration—49 percent in 1986 as compared to 33 percent in 1965 (Bouvier and Gardner 1986). And, as in the past, native-born Americans are asking such questions as: "Are jobs being taken from American citizens?" "Is Spanish taking over as the nation's second language?" or, perhaps most important, "How will these new immigrants adapt to the cultural mainstream of American soci-

ety?" Yet there are also indications that native-born Americans, many of whose parents or grandparents were immigrants, are far more tolerant of cultural diversity today than were native-born Americans 100 years ago.

Racial Minorities

NATIVE AMERICANS

As the preceding discussion shows, the United States has been heavily populated only in the past two hundred years. And it was not long after the arrival of European settlers that Native American tribes were reduced to a racial and ethnic group "inferior" to the "more civilized" white newcomers. They were all categorized as "Indians," and their widely varying cultures were destroyed. Because white settlers thought of their culture as superior to that of other people, the physical characteristics of all other racial groups were taken as evidence of biological inferiority. Thus, the white colonists rationalized their seizure of land and resources and the destruction of the Native American cultures.

Treaties with Native Americans could be ignored on the grounds that they were not entitled to equal status with white Americans. Whole tribes were, therefore, forceably removed from lands wanted by white settlers. By 1983 about 53 million acres, or 2.4 percent of United States land, was managed in trust by the Bureau of Indian Affairs. These reservations became notorious for their lack of economic opportunities.

In 1983, criticizing the reservations for fostering dependency, the Reagan administration stressed the need for economic self-sufficiency through developing mineral resources and energy reserves. Yet, only thirty-seven of the 283 tribes recognized by the federal government have energy or minerals on their lands, and only twenty-four of these have large amounts (Winslow 1983). Moreover, most tribes own only a small part of their reservations. Nor can self-determination and economic self-sufficiency be achieved easily when the most basic needs, such as adequate education, housing, and health care, have not yet been met.

Native Americans remain the poorest and the most disadvantaged of all racial or ethnic groups in the United States, as shown by death rates from a wide range of diseases far greater than those of the population as a whole. Mortality from alcohol-related causes among Native Americans remains about twenty-two times higher than the national average, and the suicide rate is twice the national average. Unem-

ployment remains high; housing is substandard; and nearly half the hospitals built by the Indian Health Service were built before 1940 and are both understaffed and in need of repairs.

According to the 1980 U.S. Census, there are about 1.4 million Native Americans. The states with the largest Indian population are California, Oklahoma, Arizona, New Mexico, and North Carolina. Contrary to popular belief, only slightly more than half of all Native Americans live on reservations. Many live in metropolitan areas such as Los Angeles, Chicago, Seattle, and Minneapolis–St. Paul. Others are farmers and migrant laborers in the southwest and the north-central regions, and many live in New York State and in New England.

Far from being on the verge of extinction, the Native American population has grown faster than the U.S. population as a whole. New births, however, can account for only a small percentage of the 72 percent increase in Native Americans between the 1970 Census and the 1980 Census. It seems likely that many people who had identified themselves as belonging to some other race or ethnicity in the 1970 Census decided to identify themselves as Native Americans in 1980.

Among Native Americans, a new militancy is evident. There has been a rising tide of political activity, illustrated by the American Indian Movement (AIM). Dem-

A Native American family living on a reservation experiences many barriers to integration within mainstream society. (© William U. Harris)

Combating Radiation Effects: A Navaho Example

Probably few of us realize that the Navahos, who are stereotypically associated with the making of silver jewelry and rugs, have operated uranium mines since the 1950s. In fact, by 1960, small, owner-operated Navaho mines on tribal lands had produced about 6 million tons of uranium. Unfortunately, no safeguards against radioactive contamination were prescribed until fifteen years later when the Environmental Protection Agency was established. (See photo p. 257.)

Over the years, medical personnel had noted the high frequency of birth defects, miscarriages, and stillbirths among Navahos in the mining area. And local residents had observed similar symptoms among the livestock upon which much of the Navaho economy is dependent. When examination of conditions on tribal lands indicated that there were many exposed and radioactive uranium mines and rock dumps, scientists hypothesized a relationship between the radioactivity and these health problems. During the 1980s, researchers began to study the medical records of over 13,000 Navaho infants born between 1964 and 1981. They discovered that birth defects during the 1960s and 1970s were two to eight times higher among Navaho babies than the national or other Native American tribe averages. Clearly, radiation had played a major role.

To learn more about the effects of past industrial development upon their society, Native American students at the Navaho Community College in Shiprock, N.M., are working along with scientists and medical researchers to investigate the role of radiation in birth defects. For example, through an examination of teeth, students have been able to determine the level of radiation to which people in the area have been exposed. Students have also been involved in research on radioactivity among sheep. In addition, special efforts are being made to assist the more than 5,000 Navaho children handicapped as a result of radiation.

The radiation hazard experienced by the Navahos is not unique. Many Americans in different parts of the United States have unknowingly been exposed to industrial hazards. For the Navahos, however, the exposure has been particularly problematic. Many people, uninformed about the danger, used radioactive rocks to build their homes. Unfortunately, efforts to relocate these families were interrupted in the late 1970s when expected federal support did not materialize. The challenge faced by the Navahos is twofold: they must identify and cope with past industrial hazards and develop productive, safe industry in the future.

SOURCE: Based on research, funded by the NIH Minority Biomedical Research Program and the March of Dimes Birth Defects Foundation, conducted by Lora Magnum Shields, Visiting Professor, Shiprock Community College and Alan Goddman, Arizona Department of Health.

onstrations and lawsuits have called attention to the treaties broken by the U.S. government and the unmet needs of the American Indian. Several of the lawsuits have resulted in a return of native lands and/or million-dollar reparation payments. But it has been difficult for Native Americans to create a unified political front because of the great variety among tribes. There is no typical Native American, no one Indian culture, language, religion, or physical type.

BLACKS IN AMERICA

Blacks and Stratification Hierarchies. In 1985, 29 million blacks accounted for 12 percent of the total population of the United States. To what extent have American blacks moved into and up the stratification system?

Power. Although all legal barriers to black voting have been removed, blacks are less likely to vote than whites, partly because of difficulties encountered in registering and voting in the South, but primarily due to lower income and education, which, in turn, are associated with lower voter turnout in general. Also, feelings of powerlessness and alienation reduce the motivation to vote ("What good would it do?").

The number of black elected officials rose dramatically from about one thousand five hundred in 1970 to more than six thousand in 1985. Over half are city or county officials, including the mayors of major cities such as Atlanta, Philadelphia, Los Angeles, and Chicago. An urban black political elite is beginning to emerge. But the current rate of increase is only about one-third of what it was from 1970 to 1976.

Native American students at the Navaho Community College at Shiprock, New Mexico, are working with medical researchers to investigate the effects of radiation on birth defects. Here they're preparing teeth to be analyzed for lead content. (© Lora Magnum Shields)

Although blacks constitute about 11 percent of the country's voting-age population, they still held less than 1.5 percent of the nation's elected offices as of 1985 (*New York Times,* Aug. 6, 1985, p. A16). For their representation to increase, political subdivisions must contain not only many blacks but also a secure and expanding black middle class with funds to contribute to political campaigns (Karnig and Welch 1981). Moreover, black candidates must be able to attract campaign funds and votes from nonblacks. Very few hold high positions in federal or state government, although the proportions have increased slowly, as have the number of judges, mid-level civil servants, and law-enforcement officers. At the moment, these officeholders represent considerably fewer than the 12 percent that would reflect the percentage of blacks in the population. Much of the mobility among blacks has been due to entrance into middle-management jobs in the government sector during the 1960s and 1970s (Oliver and Glick 1982), precisely the jobs currently being cut back at the federal and state levels.

Property. In terms of employment, occupation, income, and wealth, blacks remain disadvantaged compared to whites. Blacks are also likely to have less valuable homes and less housing equity (Parcel 1982), and to pay higher lending rates for home mortgages (Pol, et al. 1982). As the last hired,

blacks are also typically among the first fired when the economy turns downward. Thus, in 1986 annual unemployment rates were twice as high for blacks as for whites.

The incomes of black workers lag behind those of whites. Among families with a full-time worker, the median income for blacks is roughly three-quarters of that for whites. Overall, black incomes are about 56 percent of that for white families. In part, these figures reflect the high propor-

A black political elite is beginning to emerge, although slowly. Here John Lewis, Democratic candidate for Congress, campaigned in Atlanta, Georgia. (© SYGMA)

tion of black families headed by females, many of whom are not in the labor force (see Chapter 8). In 1985, 35 percent of black families fell below the poverty level—nearly three times the rate for white families. And the proportion of black children living in such households has risen dramatically, increasing the racial difference in socioeconomic status.

High unemployment and economic tension have taken their toll among blacks. The suicide rate among young blacks has risen, with those lacking strong family and community ties at highest risk (Davis 1979). Divorce rates have also increased dramatically, often because of discrimination in the work force, racism, unemployment, and the stress associated with trying to survive on very low incomes (Rule 1982). Because the last hired are also younger than those already established in jobs, most black unemployment occurs among young men who are in precisely the age group requiring the economic security to marry, raise families, and become attached to the labor force. In 1986, the proportion of unemployed black teenagers was twice that of white teens. The long-term results of their unemployment cannot be calculated but will probably include social unrest in the years ahead. Yet, whites in general believe that blacks are benefiting from reverse discrimination in employment; they see blacks' opportunity as having greatly improved in recent years, and they tend to deny the structural limits on blacks' opportunities (Kluegel and Smith 1982).

Much has been written about the increasing numbers of black families that have moved into the middle class (Wilson 1980, 1981), but blacks still work harder for fewer rewards. At the same level of education and occupation, black wages are lower than those of whites. In fact, a typical white male high school graduate earns only slightly less than a college-educated black male, largely because of discrimination and the differing employment opportunities for the two races. And black women, as white women, consistently earn less than men of either race (see Table 10-2). Although 40 percent of black workers were in white-collar jobs in 1980, compared to 54 percent of white workers, blacks were still underrepresented in the best-paying jobs. For example, black men and women make up between 3 and 7 percent of engineers, physicians, and lawyers. Blacks have made occupational gains since 1960 but they have not been as significant as those of whites, particularly white males. In science, for example, black scientists are excluded from significant communication channels in their disciplines (Pearson 1985). Blacks remain heavily represented in lower-paying jobs such as postal clerks, health aides, and domestics. And while blacks have made minor gains in business ownership and in home ownership, racial polarization has increased, with an increasing number of whites in the suburbs. For example, the proportion of non-Hispanic whites in cities as diverse as Detroit, New York, Denver, and San Antonio declined by 20 percent or more during the 1960–1980 period (Winsberg 1986). And only 6 percent of all American suburbanites are black.

Prestige. Given the political, income, and occupational data just presented, it is evi-

TABLE 10-2 The impact of higher education on income differences between black and white year-round, full-time workers age 25 and over: 1984, in dollars.

	Median Income			
	Males		Females	
Level of Education	White	Black	White	Black
High school graduate	24,000	16,724	14,733	13,619
1–3 years of college	26,302	21,105	17,114	15,795
4 years of college	32,002	25,110	20,291	20,626
1 or more years of graduate school	37,052	34,133	25,184	23,142

SOURCE: Bureau of the Census, "Money Income of Households, Families, and Persons in the United States: 1984," Series P-60, No. 151, April 1986, Table 33.

dent that sources of personal and social prestige are systematically denied to blacks (Hout 1986). In one area of most rapid gains, education, advancement may be more apparent than real. Between 1965 and 1981, college enrollment of blacks aged eighteen to twenty-four had nearly doubled from 10 percent to 19 percent. However, it took a downswing in the 1980s and leveled off at approximately 10 percent. (See Chapter 14 for further discussion on this point.) Moreover, compared with white high school graduates, a larger proportion of blacks are at two-year colleges and trade schools. Only 8 percent of black adults, compared to 18 percent of whites, have a college degree—the admission ticket to advancement (Reid 1982). And, both black men and women have higher earnings in metropolitan areas with greater government employment, where barriers against discrimination are less (Maume 1985).

How have black executives fared? For them, corporate America has not been the vehicle for satisfaction or mobility. They are underrepresented, unwanted, and made to feel uncomfortable. Despite their MBAs and initial attractiveness to corporate recruiters, many say they are blocked in their climb up the corporate ladder. Even blacks in positions that pay well and sound prestigious have complained that they have been placed in high-visibility, dead-end jobs (Jones 1986). Moreover, many companies have downgraded affirmative action programs in response to conservative governmental policies during the Reagan administration. And black executives may perceive the corporate world as far bleaker than they had hoped, as Figure 10-4 indicates.

Caste or Class? The evidence supports the caste model of black/white stratification in the United States today, although debates over the relative importance of class and race continue. Some analysts (Wilson 1978, 1986) claim that race itself is less important than the overwhelming effects of poverty. Others cite continuing racism as a major factor in perpetuating the cycle of poverty. That blacks have fared poorly in our economic system seems evident. Although blacks have achieved higher levels of education and have greater opportunities for political activity, they remain outside the mainstream stratification system. And their disadvantages have been built into the social structure. For generations, despite their familiarity with American customs and language, blacks were systematically denied the right to vote, to be on juries, and even to be promoted in the military long after newer immigrant groups had achieved these goals (Lieberson 1981). Moreover, as the number of blacks increased, and as more southern blacks migrated to northern cities, their living conditions in the North worsened. Blacks have become more, not less, residentially segregated from the white community. Such increased segrega-

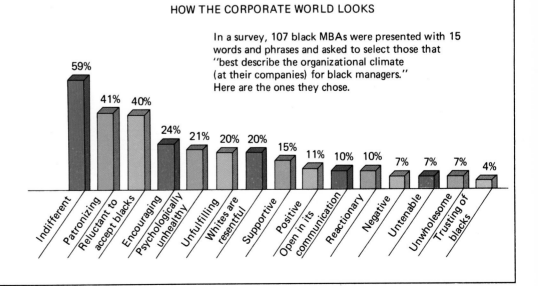

Figure 10-4
Source: Edward W. Jones, Jr., Harvard Business Review, "Black Managers: The Dream Deferred," 1986.

HOW THE CORPORATE WORLD LOOKS

In a survey, 107 black MBAs were presented with 15 words and phrases and asked to select those that "best describe the organizational climate (at their companies) for black managers." Here are the ones they chose.

The effects of poverty and discrimination can continue to produce powerfully debilitating socializing experiences. (© Robert A. Sengstacke/Tri-State Defender Publishing Company, Inc.)

tion has, as the example of Canarsie illustrates, often reflected a desperate attempt by whites to maintain their tenuous economic advantage (Rieder 1985).

The trend in the 1970s toward increased political and economic gains for blacks has been halted and even reversed. The costs of recession, inflation, and cuts in governmental spending for social and educational programs in the United States have been disproportionately borne by the poor in general and blacks in particular. Although affirmative action programs have helped trained and educated blacks, the economic prospects for poor black men or women have not improved (Wilson 1981, 1986). Indeed, although a survey of trends in American attitudes toward racial issues between the 1940s and 1980s shows that, while white Americans increasingly support principles of equality, they are far less enthusiastic about implementing them (Schuman, Steeh, and Bobo 1985). Support for federal job intervention and open housing laws has been consistently low in both North and South. And support for federal intervention to insure school desegregation actually has declined, apparently because of opposition to busing.

Power and control are central issues, for as soon as it appears that blacks may constitute a significant population mass, white resistance becomes more pronounced. Today, as in 1947, "the pervasive gap between our aims and what we actually do is a kind of moral dry rot which

eats away at the emotional and rational bases of democratic behavior" (Presidential Commission on Civil Rights 1947).

ASIANS IN THE UNITED STATES

Like European-Americans, Asian-Americans come from different cultures and religious backgrounds and speak different languages. Yet, a tendency to classify all Asians together has dominated both immigration policy and popular attitudes. In this section, we describe some of the different Asian groups that have immigrated to the United States and the similar and dissimilar problems that they have experienced as a result of both race and ethnicity.

The Asian-American population increased by 142 percent between 1970 and 1980. Despite the growing importance of Asians, the decennial census is the only source of detailed information currently available. Unlike Hispanics, on whom data are collected by the federal government each year, Asians are still too small a category to be captured in sample surveys. The only other source of national data on Asians comes from the Immigration and Naturalization Service, which collects annual information on immigrants. Population projections, however, indicate that during the 1980s, the Asian-American population will grow by 58 percent—from 3.9 million to 5.9 million, and by another 38

TABLE 10-3   Asian-American ethnic groups, 1980

Chinese	894,000
Filipinos	795,000
Japanese	791,000
Koreans	377,000
Indians	312,000
Vietnamese	215,000
Hawaiians	202,000

SOURCE: Statistical Abstract of the United States, 1986, p. 34.

percent during the 1990s to 8.1 million (Bouvier and Agresta 1985). Those people described by the Census Bureau as Asian and Pacific Islanders are diverse, representing different languages, religions, and cultural traditions (see Table 10-3).

Chinese.   In the mid-nineteenth century young Chinese males were imported to work on the transcontinental railroad. Unable to bring wives with them or to send for brides, those who remained in the United States formed an almost exclusively male community. Chinese men were victims of extreme prejudice, discrimination, and open violence until the outbreak of World War II in 1941, when suddenly they became the "good Asians,"

compared to the "evil" Japanese. Restrictive immigration laws were ended, and the Chinese-American population grew rapidly.

According to 1980 U.S. Census data, the number of people of Chinese ethnicity totaled almost 900,000 and surpassed the Japanese as the leading population of Asians. But the Chinese will not retain their top numerical position for long. By 1990, Filipinos are expected to outnumber Chinese. The majority of Chinese live in seven states with California having the highest concentration (40 percent of all Chinese ethnics), followed by New York, Hawaii, Illinois, Texas, Massachusetts, and New Jersey (Hacker 1983). Once the barriers of discrimination were lifted, Chinese-Americans entered colleges and universities in growing numbers. Today, over one-third are college graduates compared to only 17 percent of other Americans.

As may be seen in Figure 10-5, a high proportion of both American- and foreign-born Chinese in the labor force held jobs as managers, professionals, or executives in 1980, and this proportion is growing. The most recently arrived Chinese who came in the five years before the 1980 Census were somewhat less likely than other Chinese to hold high-level positions, probably reflecting language problems, differing

The decade following the end of the Vietnam War brought some 840,000 immigrants from Indochina, mostly refugees. Many came from rural backgrounds with little education and no knowledge of English, factors which have made adaption difficult. On the other hand, they usually came with a network of kin that sometimes provided a necessary support system. (© David Burnett/Woodfin Camp and Associates)

professional standards, and job discrimination. Although residential discrimination still exists in some areas, it has been less difficult for Chinese than for blacks to assimilate culturally or to amalgamate, as the relatively high rates of Chinese-white marriages indicate.

Japanese.   According to one social scientist (Kitano 1976), Japanese immigrants "came to the wrong country and the wrong state (California) at the wrong time (immediately after the Chinese) with the wrong race and skin color, with the wrong religion, and from the wrong country" (p. 31).

The first generation of Japanese-born immigrants who arrived in the early twentieth century were called *Issei* and were not easily assimilated. Yet, their children, born in the United States and known as *Nisei,* were taught the value both of education and of conformity to the norms and expectations of the majority culture. After the outbreak of World War II, the Japanese in North America were forcibly moved from their homes and "relocated." Inasmuch as hostility toward Japan was high in the United States during World War II, Japanese-Americans provided visible targets for its expression. Their appearance, language, and culture were interpreted

The first generation of **Japanese-Americans,** the *Issei,* were not highly assimilated, whereas their children, the *Nisei,* are.

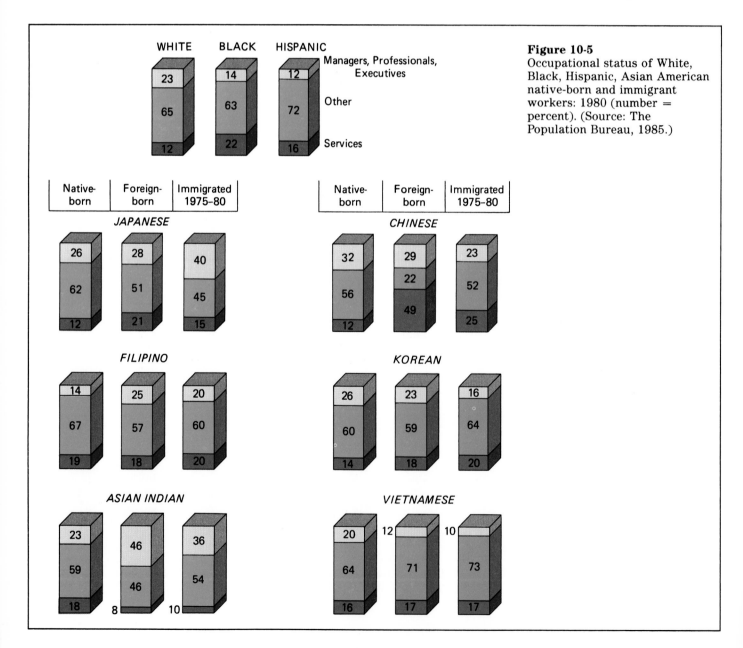

Figure 10-5
Occupational status of White, Black, Hispanic, Asian American native-born and immigrant workers: 1980 (number = percent). (Source: The Population Bureau, 1985.)

The Burakumin: Caste in Japan

SOON MAN RHIM

Soon Man Rhim is professor of sociology and anthropology at William Paterson College. He received his Bachelor of Theology degree at Yonsei University in Korea, an M.A. from Columbia University, and a Ph.D. in sociology at Drew University. He is the author of Women of Asia Yesterday and Today: India, China, Japan, and Korea *(1983) and numerous articles on the sociology of religion and outcasts and religion. He is currently pursuing research on the Burakumin, including a recent field trip.*

In Japan, industrialization has enriched the lives of some but has not changed the conditions of others. Among the 118 million Japanese live a group of 2 to 3 million men, women, and children who are its society's outcasts and constitute Japan's largest minority group. The untouchables are referred to as *Burakumin,* or "hamlet people." The term *Buraku* is currently used euphemistically to refer to a segregated community made up largely of the descendants of Tokugawa Era (1600–1868) outcasts.

The Burakumin of Japan are known to few Americans. Even the Japanese do not like to acknowledge their outcasts. Japan's Burakumin were formerly referred to as *Eta* (literally meaning "full of filth") or as *Hinin* ("non-people") and even as *yotsu* ("four-footed ones"). Today such terms are not used, but the social existence of the untouchables continues unchanged.

The social and economic experiences of the Buraku are quite revealing. Compared to the national averages, the Burakumin have slightly larger family size; less education; a greater proportion of households living below the minimum housing standard; and much greater dissatisfaction with housing conditions. Perhaps most dramatically the average household income for a Burakumin family is 40 percent less than the average annual income for Japanese families. Their health is generally poorer; the disease rate, a complex figure reflecting several illnesses, is three-and-one-half times the national rate. The Burakumin have a higher unemployment rate, and a greater percentage are employed in less "stable" jobs which are more subject to unemployment and layoffs and smaller incomes. In terms of education, their high-school drop-out rate is four times the national average; their attendance is one-half the national average; and two out of five Burakumin have difficulty reading and writing.

The history of the untouchables is traced back to ancient and medieval Japan where various forms of slavery and untouchability existed. Although several competing explanations regarding the racial origins of the Burakumin exist, the consensus among researchers appears to revolve around the occupational origins of these people. The Burakumin are made up of two subdivisions/groups: Eta and Hinin.

The Eta were those engaged in the making and sale of leather goods and other simple handicrafts. They were also animal slaughterers, disposers of the dead (both animal and human), and engaged in other menial labor.

The Hinin occupations included some of the following: beggars, puppet-show men, monkey-masters, shooting-gallery keepers, peep-show men, diviners, dog trainers, snake charmers, story tellers, jugglers, acrobats, executioners, and others.

Those undesirable occupations were often related to the concepts of uncleanness existing in folk belief and intertwined with the native Shinto religion. Shintoism has a pure/impure dichotomy, and practices various types of ritual purification related to blood, death, and dirt. Those people who worked at disposing dead people and animals were regarded as doing unclean work.

The diffusion of Buddhism in Japan, a belief system introduced in the early sixteenth century, reinforced the prejudice against those who dealt with dead animals; Buddhism proscribes and condemns the killing of animals and the eating of meat. Thus, Buddhism is believed to have contributed to segregating and holding in contempt those occupations that involved any such handling of animals—butchering, skinning, bone and leather processing, burying.

Contrary to the original teachings of Gautama Buddha, emphasizing the equality of all humans, Japanese Buddhism has discriminated against the Burakumin. During the feudal Tokugawa period (1600–1868) when Buddhism was the predominant state religion, all persons were required by law to register as parishoners at some Buddhist temple; the outcasts could register only at the True Pure Land Sect. Yet the temples which accepted the outcasts were called polluted temples or temples of the leather workers. And their priests were called polluted priests.

The Burakumin are not physically or culturally different from the other Japanese. Yet, they have remained poverty-ridden, powerless outcasts in their own home society. Most Japanese families are loath to have contact with Burakumin and are careful to check family records to insure that intermarriage with them is avoided. The disclosure of Burakumin ancestry would probably put an end to the marriage plans of a young couple.

as indications of disloyalty to the United States. Over 100,000 West Coast Japanese-Americans were placed in detention camps with guard towers and barbed-wire fences. Their property was confiscated, sold, or stolen. Among the long-term effects of relocation were a reduction in the relative power of men over women in the family, a weakening of control over offspring, and reinforcement of a sense of ethnic identity.

According to the 1980 census, almost 800,000 Japanese-Americans lived in the United States. Most live in five states: the largest percentage in California, then in Hawaii, Washington, New York, and Illinois. Third-generation Japanese-Americans rank highest among all nonwhite groups in educational attainment and income. Their occupational distribution is more varied than that of Chinese ethnics.

Has the pattern of Japanese-American assimilation been similar to that of other minority racial groups, or are they still excluded from the majority society? Although they have experienced rapid social mobility, a racial disadvantage remains. The Japanese value system has promoted economic success, which has led to high rates of upward mobility. Greater mobility, in turn, has been associated with a shift from jobs in the ethnic community to employment in the corporate economy, and to greater assimilation (Bonacich and Modell 1980). For example, third-generation Japanese-Americans have a higher percentage of non-Japanese friends than do first- or second-generation Japanese-Americans. They are also more likely to have non-Japanese spouses, to live in a non-Japanese neighborhood, and to profess non-Japanese religious beliefs (Montero 1981). Moreover, the Japanese are the only Asian-American group to have a higher proportion of childless couples than do whites (Robey 1985). In short, as occupational and financial mobility has occurred, greater cultural, structural, and marital assimilation has taken place.

Can the Japanese-American community remain intact or will it be amalgamated into the majority society? The answer will depend on whether Japanese-Americans develop a broader identity as Asian-Americans. But the most highly educated and most successful Japanese-Americans have become the most cut off from their ethnic background; for example, 40 percent have non-Japanese spouses (Montero

1980, 1981). The irony of this trend toward amalgamation is that the Japanese may lose their roots in the tradition that gave rise to their upward mobility.

The Indochinese. Indochina is a region in southeast Asia that includes Vietnam, Kampuchea (formerly called Cambodia), Thailand, and Laos. In 1960, a total of only fifty-nine immigrants were admitted to the United States from Vietnam, Laos, and Cambodia combined; all but three of these came from Vietnam. However, in the decade following the end of the Vietnam War about 842,000 Indochinese immigrants, primarily refugees, arrived in the United States. About 40,000 more have been admitted each year since 1980, and tens of thousands remain in refugee camps awaiting entry to the United States (Rumbaut 1986, Gardner, et al. 1985). Indochinese now represent more than one Asian-American in five.

Within the Indochinese population, there are marked cultural and linguistic variations. Only about one-sixth came as part of the largely elite first wave of South Vietnamese who brought with them money and skills. In contrast, recent arrivals have been both more numerous and more diverse: Vietnamese "boat people"; lowland Laotians; almost all of the Hmong or Laotian hill tribes; and Kampucheans. Many of these people came from rural backgrounds, had little education or transferable occupational skills, no knowledge

These people have just been sworn in as citizens, an important rite of passage for new Americans. (© Mike Maple/Woodfin Camp and Associates)

The Asian Success Story

For the last few years, the top ten winners in the Westinghouse Science Talent Search have been disproportionately Asian-American high school students. Although Asian-Americans make up less than 2 percent of the American population, in 1985 they comprised 8 percent of undergraduates at Harvard, 19 percent at MIT, and 25 percent at the University of California, Berkeley, and their representation in the most prestigious colleges and universities is growing. Asian-Americans typically score around 520 on the math section of the college admissions Scholastic Aptitude Test, about thirty points higher than whites. Regardless of their parents' level of education or socioeconomic status—two common predictors of academic achievement—Asian-Americans consistently get better grades than other students. Paradoxically, the more English that was spoken in the students' homes, the less well Asian-Americans did in school! Do results such as these indicate that Asian-American students are getting brighter than non-Asian-American students? Do Asians have a genetic advantage, or does their apparent lead in scientific and mathematical skills come from a specific cultural tradition?

The answer would seem to lie in part in the fact that Asian-Americans work harder. For example, in 1982 a careful survey published by the U.S. Department of Education showed the following results on how much time, on the average, students of different ethnic or racial backgrounds spent on homework.

It is, some sociologists have suggested, the Confucian ethic that is a dynamic factor in Asian achievement. Confucius was a Chinese philosopher who lived in the fifth century B.C.; his ideas spread not only through China but also Korea, Japan, and Vietnam. According to the Confucian ethic, people can always improve themselves by proper effort

High school sophomores spending 5 hours or more a week on homework, by racial/ethnic group

Racial/Ethnic Group	%
Asian-Pacific	46
White	29
Black	25
American Indian	22
Hispanic	16

SOURCE: "School Experiences and Performances of Asian-Pacific American High School Students," U.S. Department of Education 1986.

and instruction. People are encouraged to work for the honor of the family, not only for one's self. Asian-American children are expected to study hard, and often are discouraged from dating and other distractions.

The academic and professional success of Asian Americans is similar to that of Eastern European Jews several decades ago. One of the unanswered questions is whether Asian-Americans will continue their high levels of achievement after they are assimilated. Will they be gradually replaced at the head of the class by another ethnic group as were the Eastern European Jews? And what of the growing number of Asian-American children, in particular Koreans, who are being adopted by non-Asians? Will their rates of achievement parallel that of children with Asian parents, or resemble that of the families into which they are adopted?

SOURCES: Fox Butterfield, "Why Asians Are Going to the Head of the Class," *New York Times,* Aug. 3, 1986, section 12, pp. 18–23; Malcolm W. Browne, "A Look at Success of Young Asians," *New York Times,* Mar. 25, 1986; Nancy O'Keefe Bolick, "The New Faces of Adoption," *Boston Magazine,* October 1986, pp. 152–157, 197–198.

of English, and had spent long periods in refugee camps overseas prior to coming to the United States. Moreover, their arrival coincided with inflation, recession, and growing fears of displacement among the native-born population (Rumbaut 1986). Despite government policies that attempted to settle these new refugees throughout the United States, about 40 percent of Indochinese immigrants live in California, and 8 percent in Texas. Vietnamese also cluster in Washington, Penn-

sylvania, New York, Louisiana, and the District of Columbia. Laotians can be found in places as diverse as Minnesota, Rhode Island, and Oregon, with a large concentration of Hmong in agricultural central California.

How have these new immigrants, with their different languages and skills, fared? According to one large survey of refugee families who arrived from 1978 to 1981, two-thirds of the households were receiving some welfare payments and among

Asian students in the U.S. are doing exceptionally well academically, a factor attributed, for the most part, to hard work. (© Wesley Bocxe/Photo Researchers, Inc.)

those who had been in the United States for forty months or more, about half received some welfare payments (Caplan, et al. 1985). Unemployment was 86 percent among adults in these households soon after arrival, but had dropped to 30 percent four years later. Key factors in becoming economically self-sufficient included pre-migration level of English literacy and occupational prestige; being a high school graduate; and having more than one family member employed (Caplan et al. 1985, Rumbaut 1986). However, as Indochinese women tend to have relatively large families (Hmong women have ten times more children under the age of five than do white women, and Vietnamese women two and one-half times more) their labor-force participation is severely limited. Life for many Indochinese is difficult. As one middle-aged Hmong farmer indicated:

> In our old country whatever we had was made or brought in by our own hand; we never had any doubts that we would not have enough for our mouth. But from now on to the future, that time is over. . . . I myself am too dumb/ignorant; any jobs they have require a literate person. . . . We have

the arms and legs, but we can't see what they see, because everything is connected to letters and numbers. . . . I've been trying very hard to learn English and at the same time looking for a job. No matter what kind of job, even the job to clean people's toilets: but still people don't even trust you. . . . I'm looking at me that I'm not even worth as much as a dog's stool. . . . My life is only to live day by day until the last day I live, and maybe that is the time when my problems will be solved. (Rumbaut 1986).

Other Asians.   In 1980, there were about 1.7 million people of other Asian ethnicities in the United States. Filipinos accounted for 45 percent, followed by Asian Indians and Koreans. Koreans showed the most remarkable growth, increasing from 69,999 in 1970 to 377,000 in 1980, a growth rate of 415 percent. The welcome given to the arrival of Asian-Americans, like that of most new immigrants who are not of northern European origin, has been mixed. However, Asians, whether from Korea, India or elsewhere, may be the achievers of the future. An incredible 52 percent of adult Asian Indians and more than one-third of Filipinos are college graduates. (It is important to note that most Asian Indians admitted to this country already had a good educational background upon arrival.)

Ethnic Minorities

The great variety of nationalities is a defining characteristic of American society. To illustrate general themes in the immigrant experiences as well as to introduce you to the fastest-growing ethnic minorities in the United States, our discussion will focus on two recent entrants: Hispanic Americans and Middle-Easterners.

HISPANIC AMERICANS

Hispanic American is a category made up of many separate cultural and racial subgroups bound together by a common language, Spanish (although even language patterns vary by country of origin). In 1986, about 18 million Spanish-speaking people were officially recorded as residing in the United States; and several million others are believed to have entered without official documents. Because of their generally younger ages and high birth rates, it is likely that Spanish-speaking Americans will soon outnumber blacks as the single largest minority group in the United States.

In 1986, the three major ethnic subdivisions within the Spanish-speaking population were Mexican-Americans (Chicanos), roughly 60 percent; Puerto Ricans, 14 percent; and Cubans, approximately 6 percent. The remaining 20 percent were from other Central and South American countries, particularly the Dominican Republic, Colombia, and El Salvador. As Table 10-4 indicates, differences within the Spanish-speaking minority are striking, especially in terms of education and income. Each ethnic group has its own immigration history, cultural patterns, and its own internal diversity. There is a stratification system within the Hispanic population, based not only on indicators of socioeconomic status but also on skin color. Thus, race and ethnicity combine to determine the relative status of Spanish-speaking Americans, both within the stratification system of the wider society and within the hierarchy of the Hispanic subculture. These divisions reduce the likelihood of the development of shared interests necessary to build a unified Hispanic power base.

Mexican-Americans. When the United States acquired its territories in the Southwest, these areas had already been settled by Mexicans. A gradual pattern of economic and social subordination of the Mexicans, as well as Native Americans, developed as white Americans ("Anglos") migrated west (Moore and Parker 1985; Ford Foundation Working Report 1984).

Like many other ethnic groups who have not been accepted by the majority group, Mexican-Americans tend not only to live in particular geographic areas, such as Southern California, South Texas, and New Mexico, but to live in distinctly Mexican neighborhoods, or *barrios*. However, depending on the community in which they live, residential conditions range from highly segregated to almost completely nonsegregated living patterns.

Although the stereotype of the Mexican farm laborer persists, relatively few Mexican-Americans today work on farms, in contrast to the employment pattern of their parents. This change, however, reflects the increasing industrialization of agriculture rather than gains in job status or income. The occupational mobility of Mexican-Americans has been horizontal rather than vertical. That is, the present generation has moved from farm labor into other unskilled jobs, such as work in canning factories. Relatively few have moved into semiskilled or higher-status occupations. Many undocumented workers from Mexico have been employed in low-wage service and manufacturing jobs to keep labor costs low and to prevent unionization (Wilson 1981).

On various measures of social mobility, Mexican-Americans rank below the average for the population as a whole. In gen-

TABLE 10-4 Selected characteristics of persons of Mexican, Puerto Rican, and other Spanish origin, 1985

Characteristic	Mexican	Puerto Rican	Other Spanish*
Age			
under 18	39%	37%	28%
18–64	57%	60%	65%
65 and over	4%	2%	7%
Percent unemployed	12%	14%	9%
Median income	$19,184	$12,371	$21,664
Years of school completed by those age 25 or over			
0–8 years	43%	34%	30%
1–3 years high school	15%	20%	11%
4 years high school	26%	28%	34%
1 or more years college	16%	18%	24%

* Includes Cubans, Central and South Americans.

SOURCE: *Statistical Abstract of the United States*, 1986, table 38, p. 33.

These Mexican-American migrant workers in Salinas, CA are still employed as farm laborers. The majority of Mexican-Americans, however, have moved on to the industrial sector. (© Craig Aurness)

eral they have less education than do non-Hispanics or blacks. The differences in school achievement are primarily due to a conflict of cultures (and language) between home and school. Over time, many drop out of a punishing situation. Although most adults have very high goals for their children's education, their own lack of training locks them into low-paying, dead-end jobs.

The traditional Mexican family is an extended one, with the kinship group being both the main focus of obligation and the source of emotional and social support. Birth rates are relatively high: 20.3 per 1,000 population for Mexican-Americans as compared to 14.2 per 1,000 for non-Hispanic whites. Within the family, gender roles are well defined. Both mothers and daughters are expected to be protected and submissive, and to dedicate themselves to caring for the males of the family. For the Mexican male, *machismo,* or the demonstration of physical and sexual powers, is basic to self-respect.

These traditional patterns protect Mexican-Americans against the effects of prejudice and discrimination, but they also reinforce isolation from the majority culture. An upwardly mobile Mexican-American must often choose between remaining locked into a semi-isolated ethnic world or becoming alienated from family, friends, and ethnic roots (Arce 1981). (See the Vignette on Mexican-American families in Chapter 11.)

Puerto Ricans. Citizens of the United States since 1898, Puerto Ricans began to arrive on the mainland in large numbers in the 1950s because of the collapse of the sugar industry on their island. One-third of the world's Puerto Ricans now reside in the mainland United States. Of the two million mainland Puerto Ricans, 80 percent live in six states: New York, New Jersey, Connecticut, Illinois, Pennsylvania, and Massachusetts. Although about two-fifths of the Puerto Ricans in the continental United States have incomes below the poverty level, their expectations of success are higher than the expectations of those who have remained in Puerto Rico, where the cost of living is about eight times that of Washington, D.C., and the income per person is only three-fifths of that in Mississippi, our poorest state.

Although Puerto Ricans are often grouped with Mexican-Americans, the two populations are very different in history, culture, and racial composition. Puerto Rico's culture is a blend of black and Spanish influences, with a heavy dose of American patterns. This pattern is different in Mexico, where both Spanish and Native American elements combine.

The Puerto Rican experience on the mainland has included a continuing struggle for stability and achievement in education, politics, the arts, and community control. Puerto Ricans have been elected to the U.S. Congress, to state legislatures, and to city councils. In 1983, a Puerto Rican was appointed chancellor of the New York City schools. Growing numbers of Puerto Ricans have moved from the inner city to middle-income, homeowner suburbs, and young Puerto Ricans are entering the fields of law, business, medicine, and teaching (Rogler and Cooney 1986). Yet, others continue to have difficulty on standardized English and math tests, to drop out of school, and to face unemployment. About 44 percent of Puerto Rican families are likely to be headed by a woman with no husband present. Less than four in ten mainland Puerto Ricans of voting age are registered to vote, a circumstance that has limited their political influence. The island of Puerto Rico has been hit especially hard by the economic recession, and within the past few years, the arrival of people from Puerto Rico has increased rapidly, including middle-class, professional, and skilled workers. Many are settling *not* in the New York area, but in the Sunbelt and in Connecticut and Massachusetts. At least 20 percent of the physicians who graduate from Puerto Rico's four medical schools leave to practice on the mainland. Recruitment of bilingual teachers, social workers, and health professionals by mainland employers may be creating a "brain drain" from the island.

Cubans. Cuban immigration to the United States began in large numbers when Fidel Castro came to power in the mid-1950s. Between 1954 and 1978, over 325,000 Cubans were admitted as permanent residents in the United States, especially in the Miami, Florida, area. In early 1980, an additional 115,000 Cuban refugees entered the country in a sudden, somewhat chaotic exodus. Although it is too early to determine how these new Cuban immigrants will fare in the United States, many earlier immigrants have achieved success operating businesses within Cuban communities (Rumbaut 1986).

Of all Spanish-speaking subgroups, the Cubans are older and better educated; are more likely to live in metropolitan areas, though not the central city; and have the highest median income. Much of their success, however, can be attributed to the educational and occupational characteristics with which they entered America; theirs was an upper- and middle-class emigration in contrast to that of the Cuban newcomers of 1980, who were, on the average, younger, less educated, and less skilled. Recent Cuban immigrants have also been received with greater hostility and fear, and they are experiencing barriers to mobility within the established Cuban communities as well as outside.

MIDDLE EASTERNERS

In recent years, a new group of immigrants from the Middle East has begun to emerge as a visible urban minority. The number of immigrants from Middle Eastern countries has averaged more than fifteen thousand annually since 1976. Yet, little is known about them. Parrillo (1983), in a study of the "Arab community" in New Jersey, found substantial diversity among the

The bulk of Cuban refugees came to the U.S. after the Cuban Revolution. They were mostly middle class and became successful in the professions and in business. Most settled in Miami, transforming a declining resort town into a busy commercial center known as "Little Havana." (© Randy Taylor/SYGMA)

new immigrants. They have come from a number of different countries such as Egypt, Syria, Lebanon, Iran, and Jordan and they speak a number of languages. Their religious affiliations include Muslim, Coptic Christian, and Melkite Catholic, and they bring with them diverse cultural norms. Many would not describe themselves as "Arabs." They do not speak Arabic nor identify with Arabic history and culture. The one common denominator of these different ethnic groups is their Middle Eastern origin. The socioeconomic position of the various ethnic groups also varies: the Lebanese, the Syrians, and the Iranians are primarily middle class, other groups mostly working class.

Moreover, some observers claim that the most recent wave of arrivals from the Middle East has not assimilated as readily as earlier immigrants, perhaps because many came as refugees who hope to return to their native countries when political conditions become calmer. In the Detroit area, which now has the largest concentration of Arabic-speaking people outside the Middle East—over 200,000 Lebanese, Palestinians, Yemenis, and Iraqi-Chaldeans— there has been conflict between Middle Easterners and other ethnic groups. In 1985, the mayor of Dearborn, a suburb of Detroit, was elected on a platform promising to deal with "the Arab Problem"; and in Detroit the year before, a near-riot ensued after the shooting death of a black youth suspected of robbing a shop owned by a Chaldean (*New York Times*, June 30, 1986, p. B5). From the limited information available (Parrillo 1985), however, there seems to be little racial tension, juvenile delinquency, or crime within Near Eastern immigrant communities. Tensions are caused by drinking, dating, and language, as younger people become acculturated to the norms of the dominant society and reject traditional values and behavior. As with most other immigrant groups, length of residence in the United States is an important factor both in acculturation and in socioeconomic status.

Religious Minorities

We have dealt at some length with racial and ethnic minorities, and with the ways in which ethnicity and race limit a per-son's opportunities to achieve power, property, and prestige. Religion, too, has affected self-identification as well as access to the good life in America.

PROTESTANTS

The United States is predominantly a Protestant nation numerically and ideologically. Although the framers of the U.S. Constitution refused to establish a state religion, being Protestant was an accepted requirement for economic and political leadership until very recently.

Because Protestantism includes Episcopalian Wall Street brokers as well as African Methodist black sharecroppers, it is difficult to make general statements about social class among Protestants. The various denominations can be roughly ranked in terms of the wealth of their members, their levels of education, and their occupational attainment. In this hierarchy, white Episcopalians are usually at the top. Presbyterians are next, followed by Methodists, Lutherans, and Baptists. A rule of thumb is that the hierarchy of prestige within American Protestantism is from the most formal to the least formal, from the whitest to the darkest members, and from the high socioeconomic status to the low. Data on religion such as that found in Table 10-5 is not routinely collected by the Census and is thus drawn from sample

TABLE 10-5 Percentage of whites with four or more years of college education and with incomes of $25,000 or more; 1977–80 dollars, by religion.

Religion	4+ Years of College	Income $25,000 or more
Protestant, all	14	6
Episcopalian	46	12
Presbyterian	22	11
Methodist	18	8
Lutheran	11	6
Other Protestant	15	10
Baptist	8	6
Catholic, all	13	8
Irish	23	11
Polish	16	7
Italian	12	7
Mexican	5	0
Jews	42	26

SOURCE: Thomas J. Archdeacon, *Becoming American: An Ethnic History* (New York: Free Press, 1983), Tables VIII-1, VIII-2.

surveys which summarizes differences in family income and education for socio-religious groups.

There are also regional variations: In the Philadelphia area, many of the most prestigious and wealthy families are Quaker; in Boston, many are Congregationalists or Unitarians. In Virginia, most are Episcopalian; in Texas, they are likely to be Methodist or Baptist. Historical factors, such as time of migration and the reasons for coming to this country, determine the elite denomination in each region.

Although intermarriage among various Protestant subgroups is high, marriage with Catholics or Jews remains low. According to sample surveys, 83 percent of those who come from Protestant backgrounds have married other Protestants (Archdeacon 1983).

CATHOLICS

Although individual Catholics in U.S. history, such as John Carroll, who signed the Declaration of Independence, have enjoyed high prestige, as a group Catholics were long regarded with suspicion by the Protestant majority. Like the Protestant denominations, Catholicism includes the rich and the poor, from the Kennedys to the most recently arrived Puerto Rican family. There is a stratification hierarchy within American Catholicism that reflects time of immigration and racial and ethnic factors. The internal status system is headed by the Irish and other northern Europeans, followed by southern and Eastern Europeans, with Hispanic groups at the bottom. The proportion of Catholics in the United States has risen dramatically over this century, from about 10 percent of the total population in 1900 to about 25 percent today, due to both immigration and relatively high birth rates.

At one time, because of the different social-class positions of the ethnic groups, it was a source of great agony to both families if an Irish Catholic sought to marry an Italian Catholic. As anti-Catholic sentiment has waned in the society as a whole, so also have many internal divisions within Catholicism, as well as many differences between non-Hispanic Catholics and Protestants in family size, education, occupation, and income (Archdeacon 1983).

To what extent does Catholicism remain a factor in social-class placement? Prob-

The majority of the recent Hispanic immigration practices Catholicism, thereby increasing the ranks of a denomination whose membership was on a slight decline. (© Stephanie Maze/Woodfin Camp and Associates)

ably very little. Discrimination today is more related to race and ethnicity than to religious preference. It had once been thought that the emphasis on community fostered by the parish church would reduce the motivation for individual achievement among Catholics. And for some decades, the closeness of the religious and ethnic group, along with discrimination against Catholics, limited their upward mobility. These barriers now appear to have been overcome, and Catholics are well represented today in politics, business, and higher education.

At the same time, the Catholic Church provides a basis for identity and for the development of primary-group relationships. Despite considerable intermarriage, most Catholics still marry within their faith, and many continue to send their children to parochial schools.

JEWS

Among Jews, as with so many other minority groups, an internal statification system exists, based on time of immigration, **271**

The religious diversity in the U.S. spans a very wide range of beliefs even within any one denomination. Here Orthodox Hassidic Jews, a very traditional branch of Judaism, celebrate a marriage. (© Ted Spiegel/Black Star)

ethnic origin, and social-class background. In general, Jews have enjoyed great success in the educational and economic spheres in the United States. They are over-represented among college graduates and high-income earners.

Jews are, however, less likely to climb up the corporate ladder, the most common route to business success for gentiles. Although part of the corporate elite today, Jews typically enter through investment banking or law, or by starting their own corporations (Domhoff and Zweigenhaft 1983). They are also unlikely to belong to elite corporate social clubs.

Those Jews who overcome the discrimination that still exists in the corporate world become less visibly Jewish. In contrast to other successful Jews, those who sit on corporate boards and belong to non-Jewish social clubs are less likely also to list their membership in Jewish clubs or organizations.

Intermarriage, too, has eroded the Jewish community. Each successive generation of Jews has intermarried to a greater extent than the previous one. Present intermarriage rates are estimated to be around 30 percent (Massank 1978, Cohen 1984) and the Jewish birth rate is the lowest of any ethnic or religious group in the United States. As with the Japanese, the very cultural roots that promoted success are on the verge of being abandoned.

Emerging Themes in Group Relations

In this brief overview of racial, ethnic, and religious minority groups in the United States, several themes are clear. Minorities meet resistance to achieving high status in the stratification system. They are subject to various degrees of prejudice and discrimination. There is a tendency to create status hierarchies even within the minority community, although there are varying degrees of success in transferring these rankings to the stratification system of the society as a whole. Members often rely on the support of the minority community. Their ethnic roots are important in giving identity to minority people in our modern industrial society. Between the first and third generations of immigrants, great changes have occurred in all minority groups in the direction of approximating the patterns of dominant group norms and behavior. Slowly, the effects of religious and ethnic distinctions have been lessened, but these are more surface differences than are those of race or sex.

WHEN MINORITY GROUPS CLASH

If minority groups have similar experiences of discrimination and low status in the United States, why do the most disadvantaged not unite to challenge the control of the dominant groups? One of the rallying cries of the 1960s was the need for a "coalition of the oppressed"; women, blacks, Hispanics, homosexuals, and idealistic young whites. By the 1970s, these elements of a coalition had failed to stick together. In the 1980s, not only has each group tended to go its own way, but it has often found itself in conflict with one or more of the other groups; although at least one 1984 presidential candidate, Jesse Jackson, tried to reconstruct a "rainbow coalition."

A short account is adequate: The women's movement has had some difficulty enlisting minority women in its cause, and gay women claim that their needs are being downplayed. American Jews, once the major source of financial and organizational assistance to the black civil-rights movement, have been deeply offended by black support for the Palestinians. Blacks, on the other hand, have found that Jewish goodwill often stopped short of pushing for their entry into graduate schools of law and medicine, where Jewish young people might have to give up places to aspiring blacks. Competing claims for the control of poverty programs have kept poor blacks and Hispanics from pooling their limited resources. Members of both groups must compete with each other for fewer unskilled jobs in the inner cities. In 1983, riots in Miami, Florida, were fueled by increasing resentment among blacks over the relative economic success of Cubans. Conflicts between various minorities are also fueled by some politicians for their own gain.

When the economy is not growing, support for antipoverty programs evaporates. Status fears are increased, especially among those whose jobs are most threatened. It seems safe today to predict many more instances of clashes, verbal and physical, among minority groups. In a *zero-sum* situation, where one group's gain must be at the expense of another, each will be concerned only with its own goals (Thurow 1980). However, no group alone can muster enough strength to influence the dominant elites; thus, the final result of a splintering of minority groups is a reduction in the possibility of major change in the structure of the American stratification system.

Summary

This chapter has focused on the experiences of racial, ethnic, and religious minority groups in the United States. Although societies vary with respect to their cultural homogeneity or heterogeneity, race, religion, and ethnicity are ascribed characteristics that influence the placement of groups and individuals in the stratification system for every society.

The experiences of minority groups are controlled by the dominant groups of the population. Minority-group status is defined in terms of four major elements: (1) distinctive traits identifying the minority-group members; (2) differential treatment, stemming from that identity; (3) the organization of self-image based on this identity; and (4) an awareness of shared identity with similar others.

How can different groups be welded together to form a nation? The melting-pot model developed from the belief that immigrants could and should, through the influence of a common education and the mass media, lose their differentness and come to share a common language and culture. They would thereby benefit equally from opportunities for success. A second model—that of cultural pluralism—developed from the view that the United States was a nation of nations in which the unique contributions of various immigrant groups to the diversity and vitality of North American culture would be recognized. In actuality, minority groups are linked to the larger society along a continuum ranging from near isolation to a near-total blending into the dominant culture. Segregation, accommodation, acculturation, assimilation, and amalgamation are the major processes of minority-dominant adaptation.

Barriers to integration reflect both individual attitudes (prejudice) and behaviors (discrimination) and institutional patterns of discrimination built into the structure of norms and behavior. Prejudice and discrimination have a strongly negative effect not only on people's lives, health, employment opportunities, housing, and income, but also on their self-images.

The roots of racism in the United States date back to the treatment of Native Americans. Because the white settlers saw their culture as superior to those of other races, the land and the resources of Native Americans were seized, and their many tribal cultures were destroyed.

American blacks have made significant historical gains in political power, economic status, and prestige, especially since 1965, but there are still dramatic differences between the conditions of blacks and whites. These suggest a caste model of racial inequality in the United States. Today, in fact, trends toward increased political and economic roles for blacks have stalled and even reversed as the nation's economic growth has slowed.

The Chinese, who came to work on the transcontinental railroads, and who were once victims of prejudice and discrimination, have begun to assimilate. Many young Chinese have graduated from college or professional schools and have gone into high-prestige occupations.

The Japanese faced similar restrictive policies. During World War II, over 100,000 were sent to detention camps. Japanese-Americans today rank high in terms of educational achievement and income. The most successful Japanese-Americans have become assimilated, abandoning the cultural roots that promoted their success.

Currently, the fastest-growing ethnic minority in the United States are the Hispanic Americans, who represent several distinct cultural and ethnic groups sharing a common language, Spanish. Mexican-Americans, Puerto Ricans, and Cubans make up the three major ethnic subdivisions.

A new, urban group of immigrants from the Middle East is also becoming visible. Although they are often described as *Arabs,* they are linguistically, culturally, and religiously different depending on their country of origin.

Religion is another social category affecting self-image and access to power, prestige, and property. Although the United States is a predominantly Protestant nation, numerically and ideologically, the differences in wealth, education, occupation, and prestige within Protestantism are dramatic. Similar variation exists among Catholics and Jews, reflecting time of immigration, ethnic origin, and social-class background.

Though religious and ethnic distinctions have become less important over time, institutional patterns of racism, as well as personal prejudice and discrimination, continue to reinforce the racial distinctions that perpetuate some of the forms of social inequality in America.

Suggested Readings

ALBA, RICHARD D. *Italian-Americans: Into the Twilight of Ethnicity.* Englewood Cliffs, NJ: Prentice Hall, 1986. An historical and sociological analysis of Italian-Americans.

BALTZELL, E. DIGBY. *The Protestant Establishment: Aristocracy and Caste in America.* New York: Vintage, 1964. This work examines the role of WASPs in American history and their reaction to increasing social diversity.

DAVIS, CARY, CARL HAUB, and JOANNE WILLETTE. *U.S. Hispanics: Changing the Face of America.* Washington, DC: Population References Bureau, 1983. A review of the different Hispanic minorities of the United States.

DELORIA, VINE, JR., ed. *American Indian Policy in the 20th Century.* Norman, OK: University of Oklahoma Press, 1985. A valuable collection of articles which documents the progress of the Native Americans primarily due to the increased input of Indians into the formulation of policy.

GARDNER, ROBERT W., BRYAN ROBEY, and PETER C. SMITH. *Asian Americans: Growth, Change and Diversity.* Washington, DC: Population Reference Bureau, 1985. An overview of the growing Asian population in the United States.

HELMREICH, WILLIAM B. *The World of Yeshiva: An Intimate Portrait of Orthodox Jewry.* New Haven, CT: Yale University Press, 1986. A valuable, insightful look at the daily life, participants, curriculum, and cultural and ethical goals of this social system.

LE MAY, MICHAEL C. *The Struggle for Influence: The Impact of Minority Groups on Poli-*

tics and Public Policy. New York: University Press of America, 1985. This text analyzes a large and diverse number of minority groups in the United States and their similar and different power struggles with the white majority.

LUKAS, J. ANTHONY. *Common Ground: A Turbulent Decade in the Lives of American Families.* New York: Knopf, 1985. This Pulitzer Prize-winning book examines the experience of three different families in Boston in the aftermath of the 1974 order to desegregate the schools.

MOORE, JOAN, and HARRY PARKER. *Hispanics in the U.S.* Englewood Cliffs, NJ: Prentice Hall, 1985. An analysis of the social problems faced by recent Hispanic American immigrants.

PARRILLO, VINCENT. *Strangers to These Shores: Race and Ethnic Relations in the United States,* 2nd ed. New York: Macmillan, 1985. An excellent account of the experiences of the major racial and ethnic groups in the United States, including the older and newer European groups, Native Americans, Asian immigrants, blacks, Hispanics, and other groups comprising the American mosaic.

PENA, MANUEL. *The Texas-Mexican Conjunto: History of a Working Class Music.* Austin, TX: University of Texas Press, 1985. This book examines the roots of a popular form of music among Texas-Mexicans during the 1930s and 1940s which sought to preserve traditional culture and resist assimilation into American society.

PINKNEY, ALPHONSE. *Black Americans,* 3rd ed. Englewood Cliffs, NJ: Prentice Hall, 1987. This book explores the historical, social, and economic conditions facing Afro-Americans in the United States.

SIMON, RITA J. *Public Opinion and the Immigrants: Print Media Coverage 1880–1980.* Lexington, MA: Lexington Books, 1985. A thorough historical documentation of the print media's view of immigration and the policies of restriction they approved.

SIMPSON, G. E., and YINGER, J. M. *Racial and Cultural Minorities: An Analysis of Prejudice and Discrimination,* 5th ed. New York: Plenum, 1985. An important source of data on discrimination which focuses on both theory and research.

WILLIAMS, JAMES D. *The State of Black America in 1986.* New York: National Urban League, 1986. This report examines the social and economic status of Afro-Americans in the United States.

Part IV
Institutional Spheres

The next six chapters examine the major areas of patterned social activities necessary for the survival of people and groups. These are the *institutional spheres* centered on family life, economic activity, political structures, educational institutions, belief systems, and the criminal-justice system. Over the course of human history, as culture and social organization grow increasingly complex, these spheres become separated from their traditional embeddedness in kinship relations. In modern societies, economic, political, educational, religious, and judicial activities take place outside the family system, where people have statuses independent of kinship ties.

This process of institutional specialization is called *structural differentiation,* as each sphere becomes an increasingly complex part of the larger society. Members of modern societies parcel out their days and hours among these differentiated spheres of activity. The chapters in Part IV trace the historical development and current structure of each of these areas: family, work, politics, school, place of worship, and criminal-justice organizations.

11

Courtship, Marriage, and the Family

THINK of the full range of possibilities
and imagine a society in which

• Young people select their own marriage
partners
• All but a few people will marry at least
once

• Couples can choose the number and
spacing of children
• Levels of satisfaction in marriage are
extremely high
• Children and grandparents have more
time together than ever before in
history

- The frail elderly are typically cared for by other family members

Is this some golden age in the past? Or some future Utopia? Actually, these statements describe the contemporary American family system. Despite all that you may have heard about its "breakdown" or even its "death," studies show that family life is alive and well, and in many ways more satisfying than ever before.

But there are several trends that arouse worry among Americans: high divorce rates; increases in unwed teenage pregnancy and in single-parent households; and violence among family members. Critics of the modern family also point with alarm to the growing tendency to delay marriage and childbearing, to lowered fertility rates, and to the rising proportion of young couples who live together without being married. From another viewpoint, however, most of these trends can be interpreted positively as signs of greater personal freedom in intimate relationships. As we shall see, many of the "problems" associated with divorce, single-parent families, and teenage pregnancy are the result of poverty and blocked opportunities, both of which can be offset by public-policy initiatives. And to many social scientists, divorce is as much a solution as a cause of family difficulties.

Because the family was our earliest setting and remains our refuge from the outside world, our primary source of identity and meaning, it is not easy to be objective about it. Nonetheless, from a sociological perspective, the family system of any society must be analyzed in the same way as any other institutional sphere: as a set of socially constructed norms and behaviors centered on some activity crucial for survival of the group. In this case, the essential survival task is the orderly reproduction of new members. The rules that govern courtship, marriage, and family relationships are designed to control sexuality, to pair off potential parents, to maintain order within the household, and to meet human needs for intimacy and care. These rules and roles differ from one society to another and undergo change over time. Family life is neither instinctual nor divinely ordained; the human family is a social system based on arbitrary norms learned in the process of socialization.

In this chapter we first discuss the origins of the human family, describe the many forms it takes throughout the world, and follow the major changes that accompany modernization. The second part of the chapter examines in detail the contemporary American scene and its variety of family structures and range of interpersonal relationships.

Origins of the Family

Humans share biological and behavioral characteristics with other primates—monkeys, chimpanzees, orangutans, and the great apes—that make families possible and even necessary: (1) birth of infants, typically one at a time, at a much earlier stage of development than other animal young, so that they require constant care for many years; (2) gender-based division of labor in which females engage in child care and the males in protection; (3) year-round sexuality leading to continual social interaction between males and females; and (4) preference by females for the more cooperative males (Zihlman 1978, Tanner 1981).

Yet without other traits *not* found in primates, humans could not develop family patterns much different from the loose ties that link chimpanzees. Gough (1971) lists such qualities as language, foresight, self-control, and the ability to plan collectively and to learn new behaviors as the essential bases for close and lasting human relationships. It is incorrect to speak of primate "families" when what is actually being observed is a unit composed of a mother and her children, with a constantly changing set of males on the fringes of the group. Families based on relatively permanent relationships between adult females and males are possible only when more than sexual intercourse is involved. It is crucial, in fact, that sexuality and fertility be brought under control of the group (McLaren 1984). Social life is impossible unless and until sexual drives are governed by cultural and social norms. It seems likely, therefore, that the first and perhaps most powerful set of norms created by human beings were those that limited and channeled sexuality.

FUNCTIONAL EXPLANATIONS

The Incest Taboo. Because they have a reflective mind, human beings can control impulses, including sexual desires and jealousies. Such controls are internalized through a set of rules formed by agreement among members of the group. These rules are called *incest taboos.* Found in every human society, they specify precisely who can mate with whom. Typically, sexual relations between parents and their children and between brothers and sisters are forbidden. Just who else is included varies widely. Although evidence of similar restraints is found in primate bands, incest taboos in human societies are often elaborate and arbitrary, varying from one group to another, and enforced by the weight of public opinion and internalized guilt. Such norms reduce jealousy within both a given family and the group as a whole.

Many scientists also consider incest rules to be the foundation of group survival. By forbidding sexual relations within a given unit, the taboos force sons and daughters to marry *outside* their immediate family. Thus, alliances are made between one family and another. Ties of kinship and obligation bring potential enemies together; the number of cooperative families in a society increases; and the group as a whole is strengthened. Marrying outside the family also reduces the likelihood of mental and physical birth defects by bringing a new gene pool into the breeding group (although this benefit was unknown until the last century).

Exchange Factors. Levi-Strauss (1969) and others have also suggested that the exchange of brides and grooms is the original *social* relationship, serving as an example of all exchanges that bind individuals and families together in enduring social systems. If the leading males in various families agree to give up sexual rights over their sisters and daughters, all other types of exchange follow. Underlying all social relations is the concept of *reciprocity*: A gift obligates the receiver to return something of equivalent value later.

The Principle of Legitimacy. A third basis for marriage and family is described by Malinowski (1929/1962) as the "principle of legitimacy," by which he meant that the function of marriage is to identify one man as being responsible for the protection of a woman and her children, and for their placement in the social system. That is, because simple societies are organized according to kinship, the status of the father typically determines the social position of children (this system of assigning status is known as *ascription*). Note that the "father" does not have to be the biological parent. What is important is a *social father* who assumes responsibility through marriage.

CONFLICT EXPLANATIONS

A functionalist sees important benefits for groups and for individuals in the discovery of the incest taboo, the exchange of brides and grooms, and the concept of social fatherhood. Groups are strengthened, and individual needs are met. However, when a conflict theorist asks who benefits from these arrangements, the answer is clearly that the kinship groups, the heads of families, and men in general rather than women benefit most (Smart 1987).

Incest taboos and the rules regulating mate selection (who can marry whom) are often used to keep property within a given kinship line. For example, brother–sister marriages, as in the ruling families of ancient Egypt, prevented the dividing up of the family's estates. Even today, in many societies, the most desirable marriage choices are among cousins, and for the same reason. In other words, heads of families control group resources by controlling mate selection. Household heads also control the behavior of other family members through force. Thus, although it is condemned as immoral and forbidden by law, incest as a form of sexual abuse, committed primarily by older men on female children, is not as rare as commonly thought, even in our society (Gordon 1986). Historical records and contemporary survey data indicate that incestuous episodes characterize anywhere from 1 to 10 percent of American families (Finkelhor 1979, Herman 1981, Gordon and O'Keefe 1984). Further, contemporary studies indicate that sexual abuse appears to be the major cause of girls' running away from home (Burgess et al. 1986).

The *exchange of marriage partners* among kinship groups is part of a society's

The **incest taboo** forbids sexual relations between certain group members and specifies who can mate with whom.

Reciprocity obligates the receiver of a gift to return something of equivalent value later.

The concept of legitimacy or **social fatherhood** identifies one man as responsible for the protection of a woman and her children and for the children's placement in the social system.

power system. Family rank is advanced or maintained through marriages and the power of males—as fathers or brothers—is shown in their "giving away" the women of their family. The almost universal pattern whereby men, but not women, have certain rights over their kin, has been described by Rubin (1975) as the "traffic in women" that underlies male dominance. For the conflict theorist, the exchange relations that functionalists consider the basis of all social life actually reflect differences in economic and political power rather than the norm of reciprocity.

Similarly, the concept of *social fatherhood* reinforces the superior position of men in most societies. Legitimacy is not very important—that is, high rates of illegitimacy are tolerated—precisely in those societies or social classes where fathers cannot transmit resources or place their offspring in the ongoing social system. These conditions are common in cultures that have been destroyed by outside forces and among the poor in modern societies. Social fatherhood is a form of power.

Kinship in Cross-Cultural Perspective

Throughout this volume, we have stressed the importance of family-based (kinship) relationships in the social structure of simple societies. Yet, kinship systems vary both from one society to another and over time. In general, five characteristics describe kinship systems: how many marriage partners (spouses) are permitted at one time; who can marry whom; how descent and transmission of property are determined; where a couple lives; and what the power relations are within the family. The many differences between traditional and modern patterns are shown in Table 11-1.

CULTURAL UNIVERSALS AND VARIATIONS

These five characteristics determine the family system of a society. Elaborated over time, along with other rules governing

TABLE 11-1   Kinship in cross-cultural perspective

	Traditional Societies	Modern Societies
Number of spouses at one time	One (**monogamy**) or Plural (**polygamy**) **Polygyny**—two or more wives **Polyandry**—two or more husbands	One (**monogamy**)
Choice of spouse	Choices made by parents to enhance family power	Relatively free choice
Line of descent	From males (**patrilineal**) From females (**matrilineal**)	Both equally (**bilateral kinship**)
Couple's home	With groom's family (**patrilocal**) With bride's family (**matrilocal**)	Place of one's own (**neolocal**)
Power relationships	Various degrees of male dominance (**patriarchy**)	Greater equality (**egalitarian**)
Functions of family	All-embracing, to protect the kinship group as a whole	Specialized, to provide a stable environment for child rearing and emotional support
Structure	Extended	Nuclear
Focus of obligation	Blood relationships	Marriage tie and children

courtship, child rearing, divorce, and widowhood, these family systems present a fascinating picture of human variability and adaptability. Indeed, so varied are the courtship and marriage practices of different societies that it is impossible to provide any single explanation for the differences: neither climate, land use, political system, nor population size can systematically account for these variations. The only factor that seems to characterize patterns of mate selection and marriage in preindustrial societies is the protection of the interests of descent groups.

The use of marriage rituals is also universal because the society as a whole has a stake in orderly reproduction. The rituals of the marriage ceremony symbolize the union of separate kinship groups through the exchange of gifts, and the public nature of the marriage signifies the couple's responsibilities to their society. For most people throughout human history, marriage has been less a personal than a familial and societal affair. Many of you have grandparents whose marriages were arranged by family elders, so common has this custom been even in the twentieth century, and it is still preferred in many societies.

Although each society has developed and elaborated its own solutions to the problem of orderly reproduction, there have also been major patterns of change in family systems across time.

The Family in Historical Context

EXTENDED-FAMILY SYSTEMS

Throughout human history and in most of the world today, the needs and interests of family groups outweigh the needs or interests of individuals. The kinship or descent group is often referred to as an *extended family,* that is, a relatively large unit composed of several related households, either a father and his sons and their families, or a mother, her brother, her daughters and their families. Another type of extended family is composed of a man or woman with plural marriage partners in societies that practice *polygamy.*

Extended families have many advantages: shared wealth and power, protection, and a supply of potential grooms and brides for alliances with other families. Horticulture and agriculture, you will remember, are based on human labor and the ownership of land, so that over the thousands of years that farming was the major mode of adaptation to the environment, the extended family was central to survival. Before the rise of the modern nation-state, with public provision for the care of the young and the old, for protection of property rights, and for education of the young, these tasks fell to the kinship group. Without centralized governments

The **extended family** is a relatively large unit composed of several related households.

Polygamy is an extended family composed of a man or a woman with more than one marriage partner.

Polygamy was declared illegal by the Supreme Court in the early 1900s. Despite the law, however, families consisting of one husband, several wives (in this case, four) and their children, still exist in the U.S. today. (© Stephen Wicks/ Black Star)

The nuclear family has both advantages and disadvantages when compared with the extended family. If you could choose either one, which do you feel would be most beneficial to you? (© William U. Harris)

to keep public order, each extended family guarded its own land and protected its members.

NUCLEAR FAMILIES

Each nuclear family is a unit composed of a married pair and their dependent children, living together. In any society, this *nuclear family* is more-or-less closely linked to other nuclear families in the kinship group. In other words, the major distinction is not nuclear *versus* extended, but the degree to which nuclear units in the same kinship line share residence, resources, work, and responsibilities for blood relatives.

In general, extended-family systems are typical of nonindustrial societies and the rural sectors of modern societies. In this sense, extended-family systems are *traditional*, whereas the nuclear family as a relatively independent unit is *modern*. But, nuclear units are also characteristic of many simple societies and were probably quite common in preindustrial Europe (see review by Nydeggar 1985).

In other words, the common belief that the transition to industrialism was marked by an abrupt shift from extended- to nuclear-family systems oversimplifies the historical evidence. Nuclear families actually predate the Industrial Revolution in many parts of Europe and extended kinship groups proved functional in easing the adaptation of family members to the

The **nuclear family** is a unit composed of a married couple and their dependent children.

demands of industrial work schedules (Hareven 1983).

THE FAMILY IN AMERICAN HISTORY

However, as helpful as the extended-kinship group may have been in the early decades of industrialism, it has never been the dominant family form in our society. There was no golden age in American history where people spent most of their lives in households composed of three or more generations. The historical evidence shows quite clearly that the typical household consisted of a husband and wife and their young children, perhaps joined for a few years by a widowed grandparent, but rarely containing other adult relatives (Demos 1970).

Nor is there any strong evidence that past generations of parents and adult children wished to live together any more than they do today. For two centuries and more, young people went "west," leaving their kin behind. Most immigrants from Europe were young, single persons who established families only after arriving in America. Many of these families eventually became extended, as adult children remained with the parental couple, more because they could not yet afford their own home than because of cultural traditions brought from the "old country." In other words, most extended-family households in America have been temporary adjustments. This is still true today, parti-

283

Even in the early history of the U.S. the extended family was more a myth than a reality. Typical households consisted of nuclear families and, possibly, a widowed grandparent. (© Culver Pictures)

cularly among the poor (Angel and Tienda 1982, Scheirer 1983).

FROM TRADITIONAL TO MODERN

Eventually, however, people who live in industrial societies come to share certain "modern" attitudes about individual rights and family obligations, and the balance between the two. The crucial distinction between modern and traditional concerns the primary focus of obligation; is it to the bloodline of extended kin, or to one's marriage partner? What makes a family modern is not its structural isolation but its shift of sentiment inward, to the nuclear unit. For example, if you were to receive two messages simultaneously, one reporting the serious illness of a parent and the other an accident to your spouse, to whose bedside would you go? In most traditional societies, one's duty to a parent, especially to the father, would come before all others.

This shift in attitudes and beliefs tends to appear in most societies as they become industrialized, along with increased support for gender equality. One recent study of factory workers in six countries at different stages of modernization found that men's attitudes toward women's rights and extended family obligations were related to various aspects of industrialism, especially education and higher living standards (Miller 1984). That is, across cultures the impact of increased education and personal well-being is to reinforce support for individual rights against the power of the larger collectivity.

The Modern Family

The difference between traditional and modern family forms has often been described in terms of losses of function for the extended kin group. The nuclear family in a modern society is much less powerful and versatile than was the traditional extended family. Tasks once assumed by extended kin are now performed by outside agencies. In the *economic* sphere, for example, the family is, as a rule, no longer self-sufficient; it is dependent on wages earned outside the home. The Industrial Revolution dramatically changed the relationship between home and workplace (the two became physically and emotionally separate) and, consequently, the relationships among family members. Women and children lost their economic value and became dependent upon the earnings of the husband. As we noted in Chapter 8, the modern family is now primarily a *consuming* unit, highly dependent on the economic system beyond the home, over which the family members have little control.

In the *political* sphere, the rise of the modern centralized state has reduced the need for protection once provided by extended kin. Armies, police forces, and courts replace armed relatives. The public-school system has been created to *educate* people for work in an industrial economy. *Religious* needs are also increasingly met by specialists outside the family setting and family functions become narrower.

As the extended family becomes less and less important as a source of goods and services, the young are freed from control of their elders. At the same time, the challenges of modern life create a need for affection and emotional support that cannot easily be met by family members with whom one has relationships of unequal power or rivalry. Increasingly, then, people look to their marriage partners for such personal rewards. The modern family is specialized for emotional support and for the early socialization of children, that is, to gratify expressive needs rather than performing the instrumental functions of extended families.

Expressive needs are best met by emotional intimacy with a few people. Hence the importance of mate selection, not for the kinship-based needs of the past, but for emotional compatibility. The *romantic love syndrome* (Goode 1959) has emerged as the new basis for choosing a husband or a wife. Although love has always been possible in traditional marriages, it has rarely been the sole reason for choosing a marriage partner. In the modern marriage, by contrast, love is the primary—indeed, the only socially approved—basis for mate selection.

The **romantic love syndrome** involves the selection of a mate on the basis of love rather than kinship-based needs.

MATE SELECTION IN MODERN SOCIETIES

If romantic love is the only legitimate reason for choosing a marriage partner, then people must be free to make their own choices. Parents can no longer arrange marriages for their children, although they can influence such choices directly (by signs of approval or disapproval) and indirectly (by moving to a certain part of town or joining a particular church). But in a modern society, the burden of choice rests with the young people themselves, and each generation of youth has elaborated a set of norms and behaviors—dating rituals—to help them select a mate (Adams 1979).

Although dating rituals change over time in response to other changes in the society, the general pattern begins with a form of group dating among twelve- and thirteen-year-olds, where sets of boys and girls engage in a joint activity such as skating, going to movies, or just hanging out. Gradually, the numbers involved become smaller: perhaps three or four couples together, for comfort and protection; then, by late high school, double or single dating. As in simple societies, gifts are exchanged: bracelets, pins, rings. The difference is that the gifts are exchanged by the dating couple and not by their families. Indeed, the families may be intentionally excluded from these rituals.

Then follows a period of semiengagement prior to the formal wedding announcement. Up to this time, either young person can be released from the relationship, not without pain, but with relative ease. Once the public announcement is made, families and friends and the world at large are witnesses to the intention to marry; larger and more expensive gifts are exchanged. These customs reinforce the process—followed in most societies—of progressively bringing the weight of the community to bear on mate selection. Marriage is still too important to families and societies to be left entirely to the engaged persons.

In contrast to marriage arranged by kinfolk, this pattern of mate selection can be described as relatively "free," but there are many ways in which such choices are channeled by parents and peers. Thus, although theoretically you could choose any one of hundreds of millions of persons of the opposite sex, you are confined to a rather limited subset: the people you actually meet, and those whom you can confidently bring home to dinner. These factors alone automatically exclude all but a small "pool of eligibles"—persons likely to be very similar to you in terms of social background characteristics.

The tendency to select a mate of the same race, religion, social class, ethnic group, educational level, and age as yourself is called *homogamy* (*homo* = "like"; *gamy* = "marriage"). People who are like oneself are easy to be with for a number of reasons. First of all, there is a foundation of shared values and attitudes as a result of similar socialization, which reduces the likelihood of disagreement and misinterpretation. Second, people who agree with us are very rewarding to be with because they reinforce our own sense of rightness. Third, we avoid negative reactions from family and friends.

Homogamy is the tendency to select a mate with similar social background characteristics.

But modern societies provide widened opportunities for meeting people from different geographic areas and social backgrounds—at college, in the armed forces, at the workplace, singles bars, and even through personal advertisements or video dating services. Women, in particular, have greater freedom than in the past to meet and date a variety of men. Thus, increasing numbers of American marriages

Most people marry homogenously; that is, they marry someone who is similar to themselves on dimensions of race, class, and ethnicity. (© Thomas Hopker/Woodfin Camp and Associates)

Heterogamy is the tendency to select a mate with different social background characteristics.

are *heterogamous* (*hetero* = "different") in terms of race, religion, and ethnicity (McCrae 1983, N. Glenn 1984). Heterogamy has its benefits in exposing marriage partners to other ways of thinking and doing, adding an element of variety and challenge to the relationship.

It has been generally assumed that homogamous marriages are somewhat more stable than heterogamous unions, and that cross-racial marriages are especially vulnerable, as are those that encompass wide differences in age, education, and social class. The data, however, are not altogether clear. Regarding age heterogamy, for example, some researchers found that age differences of five years or more are associated with a higher probability of divorce than among couples whose ages are roughly similar (Albrecht and Heaton 1985), while other researchers claim that there are no significant differences in marriage quality directly due to age dissimilarity between spouses (Vera et al. 1985). Because wide age differences are most characteristic of lower social strata, it is economic stress rather than age heterogamy that accounts for differences in marital quality.

In general, as barriers to heterogamy fall, couples are able to adjust and adapt more easily than when such unions were rare and enacted in defiance of strong parental and cultural pressures.

The Marriage Market. When marriages are not arranged by elders, people must make the best bargains they can. The

286

choice of the word *bargain* is intentional because the mate-selection process in contemporary America has many features of a marketplace, in which each potential partner must advertise her or his virtues, just as all merchants promote their goods in order to attract buyers. The goal is to secure the most pleasing partner, as defined by personal taste, cultural ideals, and the expectations of one's parents and peers.

Each person's value in this market is determined by the possession of qualities desired by others. A female's beauty and youth are the traits most often valued by men. In contrast, women most often seek occupational potential in males. This means that over time, a female's value on the marriage market tends to decline, whereas a male's is likely to increase.

Social class is also important. Although most people marry within the same stratum, men can "marry down" because it is their accomplishments that usually determine the couple's place in the status system. A female is urged to marry at the same level as her father's, or at a higher one. This pattern may change as women achieve occupational status in their own right, and as a family's socioeconomic status (SES) is determined by both parents' achievements.

From a functional perspective, the marriage market has traditionally represented a mutually beneficial exchange: Women receive protection, economic support, and social rank; in return, they provide emotional and sexual services, maintain the home, and produce offspring. When one partner feels that the exchange is no longer fair, she or he may try to strike a better bargain with another partner.

But as long as men and women have different levels of social power and resources, the exchanges cannot be entirely fair. From the conflict perspective, then, mate selection takes place under conditions that generally favor men: They have a wider range of choice, do not lose their market value with age, and retain their independence in the world outside the home. These conditions rarely exist for women.

Nonetheless, the relative power of women in the mate-selection process has increased in recent years largely because of their ability to remain economically independent. As a result, the median age at first marriage has risen dramatically: for women, from 20.8 years in 1970 to over 23 years today, and for men, from 23.2 to 25.7 between 1970 and 1986. Looked at another way, in 1970, almost two-thirds of American women were married by age twenty-four; today, only 42 percent are (U.S. Bureau of the Census 1986d). This delay reflects a desire to complete a college education (see Chapter 14) and to establish oneself in an occupation before marriage and parenthood, a stunning reversal of the pattern for women before 1970 as shown in Figure 11-1.

EGALITARIANISM

In general, the modern family is characterized by reduced power differentials between husbands and wives and between parents and children. That is, in the society at large, the power differences between father, mother, and children are not as great as they used to be. This trend, called *egalitarianism,* has its ideological roots in the modern Western emphasis on individual rights. But despite a commitment to equality in the abstract, most Western nations have successfully avoided extending the principle to women as a category, much less to wives and dependent offspring. Egalitarianism is possible when the less powerful gain access to resources of their own, or when the more powerful can no longer determine the life chances of other family members. If the nuclear family is the source of affection and emotional support for its members, these are more likely to flow from mutual respect among equals than from fear or duty between superiors and inferiors.

Marital Power. Egalitarianism between wife and husband is not a necessarily modern phenomenon. In gathering and hunting bands where there is little private property or other bases of stratification, marital power differences are minimal. Inequality appears greatest in agricultural societies where ownership of land is lodged exclusively in the kinship line of males, and in which women and children are bargaining chips in the family's power games. Women's power in marriage, while never greater than that of men, is higher in societies with nuclear- rather than extended-family systems, and in societies where property passes through the female line (Warner et al. 1986).

In contemporary America, as we have seen, education and paid employment enhance women's bargaining power before and during marriage, and there is much evidence to suggest that shared marital power is associated with emotional well-being for both spouses (Mirowsky 1985). Nonetheless, the common pattern in our society remains one of male dominance within the family as well as the broader society (Hiller and Philliber 1986).

Parents and Children. Egalitarianism between parents and children has both mate-

> **Egalitarianism** refers to the reduction of power differences between husbands and wives and between parents and children.

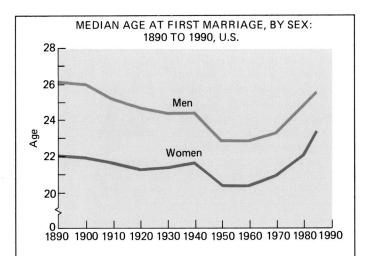

Figure 11-1
Source: U.S. Bureau of the Census. *Current Population Reports,* Series P-20, No. 402, "Households, Families, Marital Status, and Living Arrangements": March 1985 (Advance Report). Washington, D.C.: U.S. Government Printing Office, October 1985, p. 2.

rial and ideological roots. The material conditions include the dramatic drop in infant death rates in modernizing societies (see Chapter 18), in addition to the marked decline in fertility in industrialized societies where children under age fourteen are forbidden to enter the paid labor force. These trends mean that each family will have fewer children than in the past, but the great majority of offspring will survive to adulthood. Thus, parents can now invest more time and emotional energy in each child. The child becomes important in its own right rather than as an economic asset or potential marriage pawn.

Tracing this changing definition of the child in our society, Zelizer (1985) sees the period between 1870 and 1930 as one in which the economically valuable child of preindustrial society is gradually replaced by the "economically worthless but emotionally priceless child." For example, in the nineteenth century, foster parents preferred older boys for their labor value; in the twentieth century, the pattern shifts toward legal adoption, with infants, particularly baby girls, preferred for their sentimental value.

Industrial societies are also characterized by a weakening of ascriptive bases of stratification, so that young people are less dependent on parents for occupational and marital placement. According to modern psychological theories of personal development, maturity involves breaking free from physical and emotional dependency on parents and making one's own way through the occupational system and marriage market. The power of parents to command respect or obedience is limited. Intergenerational affection can no longer be demanded; it must be earned, and this requires a more egalitarian relationship than was possible or necessary in the past.

THE FAMILY CYCLE

Modernization has also brought changes in the timing of family events across the life course. Comparing the typical pattern of American families formed in 1900 with that of a couple marrying today, we can see how extensive these changes are. The 1900 marriage would have followed a rather long courtship period while the husband-to-be established himself economically; and despite the long wait, both would enter marriage with limited sexual experience. The couple would probably have four children, the last being born when the mother was in her mid-thirties. By the time the youngest child was ready to leave home, it was likely that one parent had died. The widowed spouse would survive for a half-decade or more, often living with an unmarried child.

In contrast, couples today enter marriage after a short courtship and relatively long history of sexual experience. The childbearing phase of the family cycle will consist of two offspring, closely spaced, and be completed by the time the mother is age thirty. When the children are in school full-time, if not before, the mother will reenter the labor force. The children will be out of the house—in college or living on their own—when the parents are in their early fifties. Given the great increase in life expectancy during this century, the parents will now enjoy at least *two decades* of being alone together again. This is a dramatic change, a phase of the life cycle—the *empty nest* stage—that did not exist for most couples in the past.

The **empty nest stage** of the family cycle occurs when all the children are out of the house and the parents are alone together again.

SOCIOLOGY & YOU
Picking the One and Only

When asked why they paired off with a particular person, most Americans give the only socially approved answer in a modern society, "because we were in love." Love is our all-consuming obsession, the object of our songs, our writings, our dreams, and our searching. Curiously, however, Cupid rarely strikes at random. Love choices, like other social phenomena, are patterned in fairly predictable ways.

As we note in the text, you will choose from a pool of eligibles who have already been screened on a variety of ascribed and achieved characteristics: race, religion, ethnicity, age, education, and social class. And the chances are higher than not that you will ultimately select someone similar to yourself on most if not all of these traits. Why should these people seem so much more attractive than persons who differ from you in social background?

Among the many factors at work in encouraging homogamy (the tendency to choose a partner similar to oneself) are the following:

Propinquity (geographical closeness). The most obvious limitation on selection of a sexual partner is the

Widowhood Phase. Because life-expectancy gains for women have been greater than those for men, the majority of American wives today will spend a decade or more as widows. In 1985, at ages sixty-five to seventy-four, only 9 percent of men were widowed compared to 39 percent of women, and at ages seventy-five and over, the figures are 23 percent for men and 68 percent for women (U.S. Bureau of the Census 1986c). As described in Chapter 9, these widows are likely to have low incomes and increasingly severe health care needs. Nonetheless, the great majority prefer to live independently of their children. Since the mid-1960s, this independence has been made possible because of liberalization of Social Security benefits and the introduction of Medicare. To the extent that both programs continue to be cut back, many older women will be forced to join the household of an adult child. In contrast, older widowers have been able to maintain independent residences with less difficulty, thanks to their greater economic security, the ability to purchase home health care, and their high probability of remarriage.

The combined effects of later marriage, increased divorce rates, and older women living alone can be seen in Table 11-2. The proportion of households occupied by a married couple has declined, while the proportions of single-person and single-parent households has risen.

MODERN MARRIAGE: DOING IT LESS AND ENJOYING IT MORE?

There are many strains unique to contemporary marriages. If one chooses one's own mate, marries for love and love alone, and is expected to provide emotional support in a relationship that could last for over five decades in the privacy of a nuclear household, can there be any wonder that many couples find the challenge more than they can handle? The currently high divorce rates may simply reflect the very high marriage rates in our society since

likelihood of meeting. Because we typically live in neighborhoods with other people of the same social class, we are introduced to status equals. The same process is at work in our leisure associations, religious affiliations, and possibly our choice of college. The more we interact, the more we find to agree about, and the more we agree, the more we like one another.

Social Pressures. The selection of socially homogeneous partners is also encouraged by significant others. The risk of losing the affection and approval of parents and peers creates a powerful pressure toward conformity with their expectations. An inappropriate love object will suddenly seem less attractive in the face of disapproval from others, although many young people can and have taken such risks. Usually, however, just knowing in advance what kind of person will be seen as an appropriate choice is sufficient to influence your perceptions of who's lovable or not.

Feeling at Home. Not only are people who have been brought up to hold the same values and tastes in a position to reward one another with agreement, but a common socialization simply makes conversation easier. We "feel at home" with people who share our language, we can talk on the same wave length. So often, when speaking with someone of a very different background, we talk past one another—a frustrating experience at best.

Making a Fair Exchange. In the marriage market, like any other arena of free enterprise, potential partners bargain for the best deal. As coldhearted as this may sound, a moment's reflection should suggest that "love" breaks out under some very calculated conditions: we rarely fall in love with people who can give little in return for our affection and time. Somehow, more or less consciously, we have an idea of our own worth and are unwilling to accept an "unfair" exchange.

For some couples, exchanging good looks for money or social status will be seen as a fair deal, as when a young movie starlet marries an older wealthy man. The advantage of a homogamous choice, however, is precisely that one need *not* weigh all the terms of the exchange—the very similarity between the partners tends to minimize such trade-offs.

Nonetheless, as Americans enjoy increased geographic mobility and greater freedom from control of parents, and as we are all influenced by mass media socialization, these pressures toward homogamy will decline. Indeed, ethnicity and religion have already lost much of their force in channeling mate selection, although age and education are more important than in the past. But your choice will rarely be determined by some mysterious overwhelming irresistible force. While the heart may have reasons which reason knows not, it is never totally blind. Good luck!

TABLE 11-2 Household composition, United States, 1970 and 1986 (in percents)

	1970	1986
Family Households	81.2	71.9
Married couple	70.5	57.6
Male headed household	1.9	2.7
Female headed household	8.7	11.5
Nonfamily Households	18.8	28.1
Male only	6.4	12.0
Female only	12.4	16.1

SOURCE: U.S. Bureau of the Census, Current Population Reports, Series P-20, No. 412, "Households, Families, Marital Status, and Living Arrangements: March 1986" (Advance Report). Washington, DC: U.S. Government Printing Office, November, 1986d, p. 3.

World War II—when almost everyone gets married, it is unlikely that they all choose wisely.

Yet social surveys consistently record very high levels of satisfaction in marriage, largely because the people who are not happy have ended the relationship through divorce, desertion, or separation. And perhaps many people find any marriage preferable to not being married.

Marriage in Middletown.   One of the most optimistic reports of contemporary American family life comes from a fifty-year follow-up study of Middletown, a typical midwestern city originally surveyed by

Helen and Robert Lynd in 1924 and 1935 (Caplow et al. 1982). The current researchers found that even in comparison to the 1920s and 1930s, family was the center of people's lives and that generational links were perceived as very strong. These findings are not unique to Middletown; similar results emerge from almost every other recent study of attitudes toward family (Cherlin 1983).

The Middletown research also provides support for several other broad conclusions about the contemporary American family: that married couples increasingly rely upon one another for emotional security; that sexual mores have become less rigid; and that even when women work outside the home, they are still almost exclusively responsible for child-care and homemaking tasks. It appears that as the world around them becomes more stressful and unmanageable, Americans in Middletown and elsewhere turn inward to their home and kin.

Although an introductory chapter cannot cover all aspects of modern marriage and family life, several features require further comment: the benefits of marriage, domestic violence, divorce and remarriage, men in the family, and variations on the "ideal."

The Benefits of Marriage.   The functional perspective and the exchange model suggest that both partners benefit from the

Despite the many problems facing American families today, marriage and family life is alive and well. In fact, most Americans will marry during their lifetime. (© William U. Harris)

division of labor and the emphasis on affection in modern marriages. In return for her devotion to homemaking, a wife receives social status, economic security, and the opportunity to bear legitimate offspring. In return for being cared for and having children to carry on the family line, husbands are motivated to earn adequate incomes. This system also serves societal goals by producing willing workers and stable socialization environments for the young.

From the conflict perspective, however, such a basic harmony of interests cannot be assumed. Not only do family members have individual interests to protect, often at cross-purposes, but the family unit itself is not necessarily well-suited to the modern industrial system. Increasingly, American husbands and wives are sharing economic responsibilities outside the home without any major change in the division of labor within the household, and without the range of public programs available in other industrial societies (e.g., parental leave, day care, home health services, housing subsidies). Within the family, conflicts must be handled without the help of other kin or the community at large. In many respects, therefore, the nuclear household is an emotional hothouse, with all emotions focused on its very few members. (See "Sociology & You" in Chapter 4 on the dual-career family.)

Under these circumstances, family roles are subject to *negotiation,* never fixed and continually redefined. An idealized emphasis on romantic love has diverted attention from the very real contests for control and self-definition that take place in the household. But marriage partners bring very different resources into their struggle to define the relationship. In general, because of their higher incomes and alternative sources of esteem, men are thought to be *less* dependent than women on marriage for their well-being. According to this line of thinking, because women have more at stake in remaining married, they therefore have less power in the relationship.

Indeed, it is commonly assumed that men could do quite well without marriage but that a woman's life would be empty and meaningless without a husband and children. In reality, the data clearly show that marriage is beneficial for both men and women. In contrast to the nonmarried, married people tend to live longer,

report higher levels of personal happiness, and to be in better physical and mental health (Kessler and Essex 1982). There is some controversy among sociologists regarding the relative benefits of marriage for men and for women. Some research shows that marriage is more important to the physical and mental well-being of men (reviewed in Bernard 1982), while other data indicate an advantage for women, at least in terms of mental distress (Thoits 1986). In other words, compared to their nonmarried counterparts, married women are somewhat better off than married men. But when married women are compared to married men, the women's rates of mental distress are higher. For many of these women, employment offers an alternative source of esteem, and their mental and physical health is superior to women who are exclusively homemakers (Verbrugge and Madans 1985). But for others, the combination of homemaking, employment, and child care is a source of role conflict and overload, with negative effects on emotional well-being (Thoits 1986).

Other evidence that conflict is as much a feature of family life as are harmony and cooperation comes from data on domestic (within-the-family) violence and on divorce and separation.

VIOLENCE IN THE FAMILY

The emotional closeness of modern family life has its darker side; people who are intensely dependent upon one another are also very vulnerable. Estimates of the extent of family violence vary widely. The best guess is that between 10 and 20 percent of American households are arenas of interpersonal violence. According to a 1985 national survey, about 16 percent of American couples report at least one violent episode during the year, the same percentage as in 1975. However, there was a decline in incidents of severe abuse over the decade (Straus and Gelles 1986). Similarly, with respect to violence against children, the overall incidence remains high; almost two-thirds of households reported some acts of physical punishment (mostly slapping and spanking); but the percentage reporting severe violence (beating, kicking, threatening with gun or knife) declined from 14 percent in 1975 to about 11 percent in 1985 (Straus and Gelles 1986).

Although some domestic violence is directed against husbands and parents, the

Women are often the targets of physical abuse in a family with violent behavior patterns. (© George Cohen)

most common victims are wives and children (Pagelow 1984). The physical punishment of children has had widespread support historically in America. The early settlers believed that children needed to have evil impulses beaten out of them—"spare the rod and spoil the child"—and even today many parents are willing to allow school authorities to use physical restraints on students. Throughout our history, there has also been considerable sentiment in favor of putting disobedient wives "in their place"; few figures have been more ridiculed than the "hen-pecked" husband. The basic issue in domestic violence, therefore, is the pattern and structure of family authority and not, as commonly assumed, a personal problem of either abuser or victim (Hornung et al. 1981). Research that emphasizes psychological variables—a form of blaming the victim—serves to obscure what most Americans would prefer not to believe—that the family itself can be a cradle of violence as well as a source of comfort and security (Foss 1983).

Roots of Family Violence. A review of the growing body of research on family violence suggests that it is a complex re-sponse to several conditions, both within the household and the general society: poverty and powerlessness, media portrayals of violence against women, ideological supports for male aggression, struggles for self-expression within the family, and the meanings that people give to their actions (Breines and Gordon 1983, Finkelhor and Yllo 1985).

There are also a number of immediate factors that place stress on family members. Both child and wife abuse, for example, are related to low education and occupational prestige, early marriage, and unplanned pregnancy (Gelles and Cornell 1985, Fergusson et al. 1986). In the case of infants, the problem is more often neglect than outright abuse, particularly for teenage unwed mothers who simply do not know what to do or where to turn for support. When their mothering skills are judged by middle-class social workers, the parent is at risk of having the child removed (Pagelow 1984).

There is some research and much speculation on the intergenerational transmission of violence. Does the experience of witnessing family violence or being its victim increase the likelihood of being in an abusive relationship oneself? There does appear to be a link between observing fighting between one's parents and subsequent violence in one's own marriage, either as victim or abuser (Kalmus 1984). The higher rate of spousal violence in remarriages can also be explained as the effect of prior experience rather than a response to the complexities of the reconstituted family (Kalmus and Seltzer 1986). In addition, one large-scale study of teenagers' violence toward parents indicates that this behavior is learned in families where parents used severe physical punishments against their children (Peek et al. 1985). But there is little evidence to support the belief that victimization in childhood leads women in particular to seek out abusive partners (Pagelow 1984).

Dealing with Abuse. Ferraro and Johnson (1983) conducted in-depth interviews with battered women to learn how they actually experienced their victimization. They discovered the rationalizations that permit women to remain in abusive relationships, as well as the ways in which they come to redefine their situation as intolerable. Battering takes place in an emotional and social field that rarely permits any simple solution; one has to admit having made crucial mistakes, and then decide to change the entire course of one's life. It is often easier to find excuses, blame oneself, and look at only the better moments. Often, too, the victim fails to perceive any alternatives. Nonetheless, as Schwartz (1986) points out, the majority of women are not helpless victims; they can and do take charge of their lives.

DIVORCE AND REMARRIAGE

The proportion of marriages that end in divorce has risen steadily over the past two decades but appears now to have reached a plateau. An unknown number of marriages are also dissolved through desertion and separation. Current estimates are that fewer than half of all marriages contracted today will remain intact for thirty years or more (Glick and Lin 1986), and one Census Bureau projection suggests that 60 percent of women now age thirty to thirty-nine will experience at least one divorce (Norton and Moorman 1986). But we must also remember that a large percentage of marriages in the past were ended by the early death of one spouse, so that a child's risk of family disruption has remained relatively stable (Sweetser 1985). The effects of divorce on children's emotional well-being, however, appear to be stronger than those of parental death (Glenn and Kramer 1985).

Why Are Divorce Rates So High?   Divorce is the other side of the coin of romantic love. If one chooses one's own mate on the basis of sexual attraction, marries for emotional support, and expects personal fulfillment, what reason is there to continue in a relationship that provides none of the above and may even be damaging to mind and body? Any marriage system based on expressive needs rather than instrumental goals must provide a way out of unsatisfying unions. Thus, in all but a few modern industrial societies, divorce laws have been liberalized. But there are also some modern nations—the Soviet Union and most of Eastern Europe, for example—in which the divorce rate rose so rapidly that new restrictions were imposed because the birthrate was also plunging (Moskoff 1983). Laws on marriage, divorce, and birth control have always been used to

promote societal goals; the family is too important a social institution to be left to lovers.

Among the many changes in modern societies that increase the likelihood of divorce are the value attached to self-fulfillment, geographic and social mobility, and alternative sources of financial and emotional well-being for women. Furthermore, as divorce becomes more common, it also becomes more acceptable (Thornton 1985). From a symbolic interactionist perspective, Henslin (1985) also notes the dysfunctions of traditional gender typing and separateness of sex worlds (see also Vaughan 1986). For many Americans today, then, divorce is seen as a legitimate *solution* to deeper problems within the marriage.

Risk Factors.   There is a large research literature on the correlates of marital breakdown (for recent analyses, see Fergusson et al. 1984, Glenn and Supancic 1984, Morgan and Rindfuss 1985, Glenn and Shelton 1985, Schaninger and Buss 1986, South and Spitze 1986). In general, the younger the age at first marriage, the higher the risk of divorce, desertion, or separation. Unplanned and premarital pregnancies are also associated with marital breakdown, as are limited educational attainment, low income, husband's unemployment, and geographical mobility. Controlling for other variables, employed women are more likely than their nonemployed counterparts to leave a marriage. Conversely, factors that tend to preserve the relationship are participation at religious services, shared decision making, planned pregnancies, adequate income, and emotional maturity. The rate of marital disruption is higher for blacks than whites, but this difference has narrowed over time, so that most of the recent increase is due to divorce among white couples (National Center for Health Statistics 1985).

Once a couple is married, the most powerful predictor of continued stability is, quite simply, the length of the marriage itself: The longer it lasts, the lower the likelihood of divorce. The bulk of divorces occur in the first five years of marriage, and, contrary to popular belief, there is *no* "second peak" once a couple reaches mid-life and their children have left home. Rather, with each added year, a marriage

The Revolution That Failed

In the 1970s, divorce laws throughout the United States were revised to reflect the idea that the negative effects of divorce would be minimized if conflict and hostility were removed from the divorce process. The concept of "no fault" divorce allowed the courts to dissolve a marriage without having to attach blame to one partner or the other. Judges were also directed to divide marital property between the ex-spouses.

But a ten-year follow-up of the "divorce revolution" of the 1970s found that the new law worked against the interests of women, especially those who had been exclusive homemakers during their marriage (Weitzman 1985). When the marital assets were split, ex-wives were often forced to sell the family home and take half the profits. Judges failed to take into account any special advantages the husband had gained in business training and experience during the marriage. Women who had remained out of the labor force for a decade or more in order to help their husband's careers were given enough money for job training and then expected to fend for themselves. As a consequence, the ex-husband's standard of living rose by 42 percent after divorce, while the ex-wife's dropped a full 73 percent. This income effect persists for many years following divorce (Weiss 1984). In addition, divorced wives are often barred from claims on their ex-husband's pension rights, and they typically lose medical-insurance coverage.

Contrary to popular belief, the vast majority of divorced women do not receive *alimony* (personal support payments) from their ex-spouse. In 1983, alimony was awarded in less than 14 percent of all divorces, and only 77 percent of those awards were even partially honored. The average alimony payment was about $4000 per year, well below the poverty level for one person.

Child-support payments were awarded to fewer than half the divorced women with children under age twenty-one in 1983. Of these, only half received the full amount, and 24 percent received exactly nothing. But as the average yearly payment was about $2300, the nonpayment rate was not a major factor in protecting divorced mothers from poverty (U.S. Bureau of the Census 1985).

The bottom line is that divorce is an economic disaster for millions of women. Solutions to this personal problem and public issue include making divorce more difficult, beefing up enforcement of child-support decrees by attaching the ex-spouse's wages, and encouraging judges to include "career assets"—the advantages built up in business training and experience during the marriage—as part of the family property. In the decade or more of marriage, the wife has usually done her share in building the family assets, providing child-care services, managing and running the home, caring for adults, and acting as a general support system, all without pay. It would seem equitable, then, that she should share in the family assets when the unit is dissolved.

SOURCES: U.S. Bureau of the Census, Current Population Reports, Series P-23, No. 141, "Child Support and Alimony: 1983." Washington, DC: U.S. Government Printing Office, July 1985; Lenore J. Weitzman. *The Divorce Revolution: The Unexpected Social and Economic Consequences for Women and Children in America.* New York: Free Press, 1985; Robert S. Weiss, "The Impact of Marital Dissolution on Income and Consumption in Single-parent Households," *Journal of Marriage and the Family,* 46 (1984): 115–127.

gains in strength as the couple jointly confront and cope with the stresses of modern marriage.

Consequences of Marital Disruption. Although it may be a solution to some problems, the end of a marriage has a number of negative consequences, particularly for children and the women who become single parents (Peterson and Zill 1986, Kobrin and Waite 1984). Although it is possible that half of all American children will spend some years in a single-parent household, the number of children per divorce has actually declined since the mid-1960s, largely because of (1) falling birthrates, (2) the fact that most divorces occur early in a marriage, and (3) the tendency for troubled partners to have fewer children than their more successful counterparts. As a result, there is, on average today, only one child per divorced family.

Remarriage. The great majority of divorced persons remarry, although this rate has declined since 1970. Those who divorce at younger ages tend to remarry in higher proportions and sooner than do older divorced persons. Remarriage rates among women were highest for young mothers and for women who had not graduated high school. In contrast, women without children and those with a college education were less likely to remarry (Glick and Lin 1986). Men's remarriage rates are higher than those for women at all ages. Not only do men have a larger pool of eligibles from which to select, but marriage offers them greater protection against early death. The probability of divorce in remarriage is somewhat higher than that for a first marriage, but appears largely confined to families with stepchildren in the household (White and Booth 1985). Considering the difficulties built into remarriages, especially when children are involved, we should really be amazed that so many do succeed.

TABLE 11-3   Types of households, United States, 1985, in percents (N=86,789,000)

Married couple, children under 18, husband-only wage earner	10
Married couple, children under 18, dual wage earners	17
Married couple, no children, one wage earner/retired	18
Married couple, no children, dual wage earners	13
Single parent household	14
One-person household	24
Other nonfamily households (e.g. nonmarried couples)	4

SOURCE: Computed from Table 17, P. 87, U.S. Bureau of the Census, Current Population Reports, Series P-20, No. 411, "Household and Family Characteristics, March 1985." Washington, DC: U.S. Government Printing Office, September, 1986b.

Varieties of American Families

When Americans think about "the family" they have an image based on ideals of the dominant culture: a nuclear unit composed of a married couple and their minor children, with the husband/father employed outside the home and the wife/mother devoted to child care and homemaking. This is the image of the modern American family enshrined in sociologist Talcott Parsons' functional analysis (noted in Chapter 1).

In actuality, today there is no "American family," but rather a range of household structures that meet people's needs at various points in their lives or that are forced on them by circumstances (see Table 11-3).

In this section we will explore the causes and consequences of these variations.

MINORITY FAMILIES

In contrast to the ideal pattern, ethnic and racial minorities are often characterized by extended households. Although frequently interpreted as a reflection of cultural differences, such households are primarily a response to economic conditions. Poor families of all ethnic and racial groups depend on kinship ties and shared resources for their survival. In most cases of immigrant families, however, the nuclear type is dominant by the third genera-

tion, as acculturation and assimilation take their course.

Hispanic Families in the United States.   Due largely to racial and ethnic prejudice and discrimination, Hispanic families have not been fully integrated into mainstream institutions. As a consequence of their relative isolation, some traditional patterns have been retained. For example, fertility rates for Hispanic women are higher than for American women in general. Within the family, the authority structure remains more male-dominated than is the norm in our society, and Hispanic women are discouraged from assuming roles outside the household. This type of closeness, with its traditionalism and patriarchal control over women, is called *familism.*

In previous studies of the Hispanic family, such familism, patriarchy, and a sense of fatalism (not being in charge of one's fate) were thought to be deeply rooted and "dysfunctional" cultural characteristics that served as barriers to social and economic mobility (e.g. Staples and Mirande 1980). It was also assumed that with further acculturation, this "cultural baggage" would be replaced by more "modern" family structures and relationships.

More recent analyses, however, indicate that these earlier assumptions failed to appreciate the full effects of continued economic segregation (Bridenthal 1981/87). Rather than being a static institution, the Hispanic family, as any other, is deeply influenced by the economic system. And as long as Hispanic and black workers are

Familism refers to family closeness, traditionalism, and patriarchy.

channeled into low-paying employment, often in the nonindustrialized sector (agriculture, food service, janitorial), upward mobility would be highly unlikely regardless of family structure. Thus, it is more fruitful to look at Hispanic family patterns as a means of coping with a harsh and oppressive environment (Baca Zinn and Eitzen 1987).

From this perspective, family structures and relationships are adaptive, and must be examined in the context of the larger society. Referring to the familism and male dominance of Mexican-American families, for example, such "clannishness" can be seen as a defense against the insults of interaction with mainstream institutions (Moore and Parker 1985). Networks of support are crucial among all groups that have been subjected to systematic discrimination and degradation, and familism has proven to be an effective adaptation to exclusion from mainstream institutions and avenues of mobility.

A major reason for egalitarian relationships among black middle-class couples is the greater likelihood of the partners having equivalent education and occupations. (© Black Star)

Black Families. The effects of exclusion from mainstream institutions are most clearly seen in data on black families. Compared to all other Americans, blacks are more likely to postpone marriage or to never marry; to experience divorce, desertion, and separation, and to forego remarriage (Glick 1985, McAdoo 1985). As a result, only 51 percent of black households consist of a married-couple family, compared to 84 percent for white households, while 44 percent are headed by a woman with no husband present, in contrast to 13 percent of white households (U.S. Bureau of the Census 1986b).

The very low marriage rates for black men and women are due in part to difficulties faced by many black men in their role as family provider, and in part to the fact that there are many more black females than black males. The family ideology of black Americans is no different from that of whites; the goals are the same, and expectations of success run high. But social structural conditions make realizing these goals impossible for large numbers of poorly educated, low-skilled black males (Staples 1985, French 1987).

THE STABLE, MIDDLE-CLASS BLACK FAMILY. Two-thirds of high-income black men are in strong and stable marriages. And an increasing proportion of black families do have incomes over the national median—up from 10 percent in 1950 to over 30 percent today.

These middle-class black families differ somewhat from their white counterparts (Peters and McAdoo 1983). Most are composed of *two* adult wage-earners, often both professionals, whose joint income still falls short of that earned by one white professional. Only among black couples under age thirty-five do two wage earners reach an income comparable to that of a white couple. Where only the male is employed, black family income is roughly two-thirds that of white single-earner families. Not only is the typical black middle-class family composed of two full-time workers, but the relationships between husband and wife are typically more egalitarian than in either dual-earner white families or single-earner black families (Ericksen and Yancey 1979). One reason is that the black husband and wife, unlike their white counterparts, are likely to have equivalent education and jobs (Willie 1981).

Yet most attention has focused on the growing number of black families at the lower end of the income spectrum, and especially the inner city female-based household.

THE INNER-CITY BLACK FAMILY: MATRIARCHAL OR MATRIFOCAL? Many scholars object to the word *matriarchy* ("female-

Matrifocal refers to families centered on the woman.

dominated") to describe the black family among the poor. A more accurate term is *matrifocal,* meaning "centered on the woman." The fact that black males are more likely to be unemployed or underemployed makes it difficult for them to enact the traditional role of breadwinner. Moreover, the federal welfare system is arranged so that women with dependent children receive benefits only if there is no adult male in the household. Thus, the family fares better if the husband and father leaves. Many men leave to seek employment elsewhere but cannot afford to move their wives and children to the new location.

As a result, over 40 percent of black families are headed by women. This matrifocal system is held together by the extended line of female kin: mother, daughters, and their children sharing a household and pooling resources. If the women have power within this family group, it is by default, and whenever men join the household, they are typically accorded the status given other males in our society.

Research on the matrifocal family system has taken two directions. One points to the strengths of the matrifocal pattern in maintaining generational continuity, providing services to kin in general, and resisting the negative impact of pressures outside the family. The second details these outside pressures: unemployment, low pay, assignment to demeaning tasks, residential segregation, and other institutionalized patterns of discrimination. In both views, the matrifocal family is a *response* to the conditions of poverty rather than the cause; that is, "an adaptation necessary for survival and advancement in a hostile environment" (Hill 1972). In other words, the causes of family breakdown and reconstruction into female-headed households are largely economic and not a product of some peculiar racial incapacity, as many political leaders would have us believe.

Alternative Life-styles

Other variations on the ideal American family reflect the increasing array of options that have become legitimated over the past several decades: living alone, liv-

ing as a nonmarried couple, voluntary childlessness, single parenting, dual-earner couples, and homosexual households (Macklin and Rubin 1983).

LIVING ALONE

As shown in Table 11-3 the most common (or modal) household type is one person living alone—almost one in every four households! This is a significant increase from 13 percent in 1960. Live-alones are not necessarily more socially isolated than their married age peers, nor do there appear to be negative psychological consequences, provided that this is their chosen life-style (Alwin 1984). The live-alone population consists of three distinct subgroups that differ in age, marriage expectations, and financial resources.

The Never Married. Over the past two decades, there has been a dramatic increase in the number of young people who have been postponing marriage, as can be seen in Table 11-4.

These data are best understood as reflecting changing values and behavior on the part of young people. Today, there are many options as attractive, if not more so, than marriage upon graduation from high school, especially for young women: completing a college education, establishing oneself in the work force, living independently, and taking one's time in selecting a mate (Goldscheider and Waite 1986). In addition, the widespread availability of effective contraception permits an active sex life without marriage. There have also been supportive changes in public attitudes toward singlehood and sex relations

TABLE 11-4 Percentage of men and women remaining single in United States, 1960–1985

	1960	1970	1980	1985
Women				
20–24	28.4	35.8	50.2	58.5
25–29	10.5	10.5	20.8	26.4
Men				
20–24	53.1	54.7	68.6	75.6
25–29	20.8	19.1	32.4	38.7

SOURCE: U.S. Bureau of the Census, Current Population Reports, Series P-20, No. 410, "Marital Status and Living Arrangements: Mar. 1985." Washington, DC: U.S. Government Printing Office, November 1986, Table 1, pp. 16–18.

Demythologizing Families

MAXINE BACA ZINN

Maxine Baca Zinn is professor of sociology at the University of Michigan–Flint's Department of Sociology/Anthropology/Social Work. She is the co-author of Diversity in American Families *(1987) with D. Stanley Eitzen, and has written a number of articles, including "Employment and Education of Mexican-American Women" in the* Harvard Educational Review *(1980) and "Sex Roles and Sexism" in* Social Problems *(1983). She is on the executive board of the ASA Section on Sex and Gender and was visiting scholar at the Center for Research on Women at Memphis State University.*

How is family diversity structured by American society? This has been an ongoing question within my work. My concern with variations in family life stemmed from a disjuncture between my own experience and traditional sociological ideas about racial-ethnic people in general and their families in particular.

As a Hispanic of Mexican descent growing up in the Southwest, I lived among different racial-ethnic groups and observed differences in the ways of life of various peoples. But as an undergraduate sociology student, I was taught that ethnic and cultural differences were deficiencies for minority groups, and that ethnic families and cultures were, therefore, the *cause* of inequality and poverty. This reasoning led to the standard assumption that racial-ethnic families would change and adopt more modern patterns only as they gave up their distinctive cultural characteristics. Widely accepted abstract principles such as this blamed the victims for their place in society.

My graduate training in sociology at the University of Oregon was completed during a period of critical challenge. Along with others in the social sciences, I was acutely aware of the limitations of traditional sociological explanations. Women, minorities, and others were engaged in the critical analysis of the social institutions that foster social inequality and of the social science explanations legitimating that inequality. Coming to maturity during the social upheavals of the late sixties and early seventies, I sought alternative approaches that would combat the myths and stereotypes about racial-ethnic people. Like other minority scholars conducting research on "their" people, I had a special mission.

My first research on family life investigated Hispanic families to show how private lives of families are shaped by the larger society. This structural approach was a needed corrective for traditional approaches that have interpreted the experiences of racial-ethnic people largely in terms of culture. The most prevalent assumption about the Hispanic family has been that it is a cultural holdover from the Mexican past, operating as an authoritarian structure dominated by an autocratic male. I sought to show how structural factors provide compelling insights into the lives of families. I built my case using marital roles and marital power as an illustration. The research examined how power in families was influenced by external forces, most notably women's employment. Focused interviews and participant observation over a year-long period revealed that changes in the family lives of married Hispanic women are closely linked to their involvement in social networks outside family settings. I found power to reside not in Mexican cultural ideals about women's and men's rights, but in economic and other resources that were external to families. Wives' employment gave them power by providing them with extra-domestic resources.

The old model depicted racial-ethnic families as gradually giving way to an acculturated and modern family type. My findings refuted this assumption. Despite ongoing changes in the balance of power between husbands and wives, families did not change in a uniform manner. Instead, they experienced various adjustments and adaptations in response to social networks, labor markets, and other societal conditions. Even as couples adopted modern roles and their marriages became more egalitarian, they held on to Mexican ethnic customs and practices in other areas of family life. They identified themselves as ethnics, valuing ethnic customs in rituals, kinship gatherings, and daily family activities. They were modern and ethnic at the same time.

The emphasis on how social and economic conditions affect racial-ethnic families does not deny the importance of culture in family life. While culture is a vital part of the family, it is neither the determinant of family structure nor does it produce the inequality and subordination of America's minority groups. The focus must be on structural variables.

My research on Hispanic families is part of a growing body of new scholarship about the family lives of racial ethnics, including Blacks, Hispanics, and Asian-Americans. Such work has been important in changing typical conceptions of minorities and their families. However, it does much more than demythologize racial-ethnic families. It addresses the problem of false universalization of the family, or the incorrect generalization that families' experiences change in uniform ways. Insights gleaned from the new scholarship on minority families can be abstracted to family studies in general to provide a more comprehensive and accurate understanding of the forces in society that impinge on families, the behaviors of family members, and the forms taken by family units throughout society.

Rather than a unified whole, "the family" is experienced differently by people in different social classes, different racial and ethnic groups, and by women and men. Understanding families and their diversity compels us to examine how they are related to the larger social world. My co-authored book, *Diversity in American Families,* shows how public issues shape the private lives of a population varied by race, class, and gender. These structured inequalities are key determinants of the diversity of family forms and the differential experiences within families. This book and all of my work in sociology retains the critical stance that I developed entering the academic world as a minority scholar. This means studying families not only from middle-class, white, male viewpoints, which have dominated the study of the family, but from other viewpoints as well.

---

before marriage (Thornton and Freedman 1983, Virginia Slims 1986), even among American Catholics (Smith 1985). However, the glamorous singles scene portrayed in the media is far from the norm for most nonmarried persons, who lead lives little different from their married friends (Stein 1981).

Most of the never married will eventually marry, although it is estimated that as many as 15 percent may remain single, a significant increase from the 7 to 10 percent who never married in earlier cohorts. To some extent, the experience of living alone itself erodes traditional family expectations, at least among young women (Waite et al. 1986). Women who have tasted independence are more likely than other young women to plan to remain in the labor force, to have nontraditional attitudes toward gender roles, and to lower expectations of family size.

While the overall trend is toward leaving the parental home earlier than in the past, a small but growing number of live-alones are returning to the parental nest, due largely to temporary unemployment, divorce, unwed motherhood, or extended graduate study (Glick and Lin 1986). And some will continue to remain in the parental home until they are married (Goldscheider and Goldscheider 1987).

Divorced. Divorced persons account for one-fifth of the live-alone population, and tend to be somewhat older than the never marrieds. As already discussed, remarriage rates differ by age and sex, with more women than men remaining unmarried and establishing single-person households.

Widowed. The third category of live-alones, and the fastest growing subgroup, are elderly widows and widowers. As noted earlier, older people prefer independent residence as long as health and income permit. A major problem for very old women, however, is that their health-care needs increase as their resources decline. There is also today a shortage of suitable and affordable housing as federal programs have been eliminated and as single-room occupancy hotels and boarding houses are being converted to condominiums that most widows cannot afford.

COHABITATION

Not all single persons live alone. In 1985, about 4 percent of American households were composed of a nonmarried couple. This pattern is called *cohabitation* (living together) and is technically defined by the Bureau of the Census as "persons of the opposite sex sharing living quarters" or POSSLQs. The Census does not ask details of the relationship, so that it is possible that some fraction of America's two million cohabiting couples are not also sexual partners. Most cohabitors today are between ages twenty-five to forty-four, in contrast to the years before 1970 when the majority of cohabitors were age forty-five and over (U.S. Bureau of the Census, 1986c, pp. 14–15). Although representing only a small fraction of all households at any given time, cohabitation before marriage has become widespread. One study of all marriage applications in one Oregon county between 1970 and 1980 found that the proportion of applicants who listed identical home addresses had increased from 13 to 53 percent, leading the researcher to speak of "the institutionalization of premarital cohabitation" (Gwartney-Gibbs 1986).

From the studies reviewed by Macklin (1983), cohabitors do not differ greatly

> **Cohabitation** occurs when persons of the opposite sex share living quarters.

from noncohabitors with the important exception of having a lower religious commitment, nor were there any major differences in subsequent marital stability. But because most research on cohabitation uses small or localized samples, the findings are often contradictory. One recent study, for example, found that cohabitation with one's future spouse was associated with *lessened* satisfaction in marriage for both partners (DeMaris and Leslie 1986). Some researchers have found that cohabitation delays entry into marriage (Gwartney-Gibbs 1986), while others find no effect on the timing of marriage (Yamaguchi and Kandel 1985).

The safest conclusion is that cohabitation today appears to be a comfortable option for people seeking to meet needs for intimacy without closing off other possibilities and for divorced women and men who want to live with a new potential partner before they try marriage again (Spanier and Glick 1986).

CHILDLESSNESS

Involuntary Childlessness. Although there have always been married couples without children (10 to 15 percent in modern societies), this has usually been the result of inability to conceive—*involuntary childlessness.* Inadequate diet, health problems, and lack of medical care account for the relatively high rates of childlessness, especially among the poor. Despite the long-term decline in birthrates, bearing children remains a normative expectation of married couples in our society. Therefore, not to bear children is a form of deviance, and childless couples feel stigmatized (Miall 1986). Some will choose to experiment with the many new reproductive technologies such as *in vitro* (in the laboratory) fertilization, artificial insemination, or the use of a surrogate mother. Others will adopt. And still others, a majority, gradually adapt to remaining childless.

How do members of this last group manage their stigmatized identities? According to a study by Miall (1986), a number of protective strategies are used: selective disclosure of medical problems, willingness to admit deviance, and various means of hiding or manipulating information. These techniques are used most actively by women married to infertile men, in an effort to shield their husbands.

Involuntary childlessness refers to the inability to conceive.

In vitro fertilization occurs in the laboratory.

Voluntarily Child-Free Couples. While new reproductive technologies, improved diet, and other medical advances may have reduced the proportion of couples who are involuntarily childless, other trends have increased the proportion who choose to be child free. Women planning on professional careers may postpone both marriage and childbearing until the odds of a safe pregnancy turn against them; some will find that other spheres of activity provide greater rewards than those perceived to come from child rearing. Upwardly mobile couples could feel that parenthood would be inappropriate to their life-style; others will be inhibited by the emotional and financial costs of raising and educating offspring (Houseknecht 1986).

Estimates of the proportion of women who will remain child free in the future range as high as 29 percent, but this includes never-married women (Thornton and Freedman 1983). For married women, the figure could, however, be considerably higher than in the past—perhaps one in five (U.S. Bureau of the Census 1986a). The disruptions of divorce and remarriage also contribute to increased childlessness. While some remarried women may simply delay childbearing, others will continue the child-free life-style experienced before remarriage (Griffith et al. 1984).

SINGLE-PARENT HOUSEHOLDS

The proportion of American families headed by a single parent has doubled since 1970 to over 26 percent in 1985 (U.S. Bureau of the Census 1986d). Slightly over 20 percent of white families with children live in single-parent households compared to 70 percent of their black counterparts. Nine out of ten such families are headed by a woman, 37 percent of whom were divorced, 24.5 percent never married, and 18.5 currently separated. In numbers, this represents 8.5 million families, containing 23 percent of all American children under age eighteen. For the future, it is estimated that 42 percent of all white children and 86 percent of all black children will spend some time in a single-parent household (Bumpass 1985). Roughly one-third of these children never see the absent parent, another 25 percent have contact less than once a month, while only 10 to 12 percent see the other parent several times a week or more frequently (Bianchi and Seltzer 1986).

Voluntary childlessness refers to the decision by a couple not to have children.

The Adoption Triangle

As the overall birthrate in our society falls, so too does the supply of adoptable children, despite the rise in pregnancy among unwed teenagers. In 1982, for example, although an estimated two million couples expressed a desire to adopt, only 141,862 children were actually officially adopted. Sixty-four percent of these children were adopted by a relative, typically a stepparent, leaving only 50,700 children for nonrelative adoption (National Committee for Adoption, 1986).

Analysis of data from a large national survey of women age fifteen to forty-four in 1982 provides a detailed picture of the characteristics of the three major parties involved: the children, the birth mothers, and the adoptive mothers (Bachrach 1986). The shortage of native-born children has led to an increase in foreign-born adopted children, over 60 percent of whom were Korean, and most of the remainder from South and Central America. The great majority of these were girls (boys apparently being more valuable to the birth mothers) and under the age of one year. Increasingly, also, as the supply of healthy infants diminishes, "children with special needs" (older children and those who are handicapped) are being adopted. In spite of the publicity given to groups that aid adopted children in finding birth parents, only about 2 percent of these children make the effort, and all but a few are women.

Adoptive mothers tend to be older, better educated, and of a higher socioeconomic stratum than birth mothers. As a consequence, adoptees are economically better off than children who remain with the biological parent (Bianchi and Seltzer 1986), (which may explain their reluctance to search for the birth mother). The great majority of women who place their children for adoption are white; only 1 percent of premarital births occurring to black women resulted in adoption compared to 12 percent for white mothers. Some of this difference is due to the fact that the white mothers were more likely to have received prenatal counseling; some is due to the higher demand for white infants; and some is due to the availability of family supports for black unwed mothers. In comparison to nonmarried women who choose to keep their infants, the birth mothers who place their children for adoption have an easier time in later life; they are more likely to complete high school, eventually to marry, and to remain above the poverty level.

SOURCES: *Adoption Factbook*, National Committee for Adoption, Washington, DC, 1986; *Working Paper /2*, National Center for Health Statistics, Hyattsville, MD, 1985; Christine A. Bachrach, "Adoption Plans, Adopted Children, and Adoptive Mothers," *Journal of Marriage and the Family*, 48 (1986): 243–253; Suzanne M. Bianchi and Judith A. Seltzer, "Life Without Father," *American Demographics*, 8 (1986): 43–47.

Although the increase in single-parent families appears to have leveled off in the 1980s, there is no question that these statistics indicate a major and probably irreversible change in the distribution of American households. This change is an excellent example of the process described by C. Wright Mills (see Chapter 1) as the translation of personal problems into public issues.

When compared with two-parent families, those headed by one person experience a number of problems, the most severe being low income (Norton and Glick 1986). The single parent is also under stress in having to handle the role obligations of mother and father. Because single parents tend to have lower educational, occupational, and health statuses than do parents in intact families, even employment does not fully solve financial problems. And being employed adds to difficulties in allocating time for necessary activities (Sanick and Mauldin 1986).

The children in single-parent families also experience special difficulties. They must adjust to changed household structure as well as to reduced economic circumstances. And although most will eventually find their way to success in marriage and work, the path is rockier than for other children, and the failure rate somewhat higher. In cases where family income is comfortable and assured, where the custodial parent has satisfying employment, and where social supports—friends, relatives, day-care facilities—are adequate, children from single-parent families do quite well. But these are not the typical conditions.

The limited data on single-parent fathers indicates that they feel comfortable and perform competently in the role (Risman 1986). Compared to single-parent

Many single parents are remarrying to form the "His, Hers, and Ours" version of family life, consisting of the children from both spouses' previous marriages as well as offspring of the current union. What unique advantages and disadvantages does this kind of family have? (© Horii/International Stock Photo)

mothers, however, fathers do enjoy higher incomes and occupational prestige; they can more easily hire household help; and they will remarry sooner. But they also develop warm and intimate relationships with their child, particularly if they fought to have custody. As Risman (1986: 101) concludes:

> . . . childhood experiences and sex role socialization do not create inflexible gender typed behavior patterns. Instead, as structural theory suggests, the situational demands of role requirements influence adult behavior and lead men to mother when they have no wives to depend upon.

But the sheer volume of single-parent households that are characterized by poverty and its negative consequences has raised this phenomenon to a public issue. Scholars in the field of family studies are unanimous in asking for increased societal investment in income supports, job training, child-care assistance, and counseling for single-parent families in need (see special issue of *Family Relations,* January 1986). And in 1987, an overhaul of the welfare system, especially the AFDC program (see Chapter 7) has become a major priority of Congress and the administration (Dowd 1987).

Teenage Parenthood. Many single parents are not legal adults; they are teenagers and even children. Teenage birthrates in the United States have actually *declined*

steadily since 1956, along with birth rates in general, but as a proportion of all births they have increased greatly. What is different today is that more pregnant teenagers who carry their children to term are choosing not to marry and not to place the infant for adoption, electing rather to raise their children as single parents. Almost all the increase in unwed pregnancies since 1980 has been among women age twenty and over. Some of it, however, is attributable to a slight increase in the birthrate for women fourteen and under (The Alan Guttmacher Institute 1986). And while the rate of nonmarital childbearing is considerably higher for blacks than for whites, the difference has been declining over the past decade, as the black rate fell while that for white girls and women rose (National Center for Health Statistics 1986).

The great majority of sexually active teenagers do not use contraception, either because of ignorance or lack of foresight. However, research indicates that talking with parents about birth control increases the likelihood of effective contraceptive behavior (Louis Harris & Associates 1986b) as well as decreasing the likelihood of sexual intercourse (Furstenberg 1986). Effective contraception is also associated with educational level (although many college women remain relatively uninformed) (Gallup 1985) and with egalitarian gender-role attitudes (MacCorquodale 1984).

Thus it should not be surprising that highest rates of teenage pregnancy occur among young people from low SES backgrounds who are having difficulties with school (Robbins et al. 1985, Hogan and Kitagawa 1985). Other high-risk factors include family stress/breakup, large number of siblings, and lack of parental supervision, all of which are associated with poverty. Interestingly, one large longitudinal study (Robbins et al. 1985) fails to support the popular psychological view that poor teenagers use parenthood to bolster their self-esteem or to reduce feelings of powerlessness. Rather, it was found that highly popular students were most likely to be sexually active and therefore at risk of pregnancy.

Increasingly, the general public, the scientific community, and Congress are calling for expanded sex-education programs, and even birth-control centers in the schools (Louis Harris & Associates 1986a,

The Children's Defense Fund is among the organizations trying to educate teens about the consequences of pregnancy. Do you think poster campaigns such as this one are reaching the targeted audience? (© Children's Defense Fund)

It's like being grounded for eighteen years.

Having a baby when you're a teenager can do more than just take away your freedom, it can take away your dreams.

The Children's Defense Fund.

Teen Pregnancy: A Comparative View

Compared with five other modern Western nations—Canada, England, France, Sweden, and the Netherlands—the rate of both teenage births *and* abortions in the United States is twice as high, and increasing yearly. What could account for this? The difference cannot be due to an earlier onset of sexual activity since the age of first intercourse is roughly the same in all modern societies. Nor is it a matter of having children in order to receive welfare income; family-assistance benefits in all other modern societies are more favorable than ours. Moreover, these high rates are not primarily a minority-group phenomenon; the teenage pregnancy and abortion rates of American whites alone are far greater than those of the other countries studied.

One difference we find is that all the comparison countries offer *more* sex education and access to birth control than does the United States. As a consequence, American teenagers have the lowest level of contraceptive information and use. The researchers suggest that a more open and accepting attitude toward teenage sexuality in our society would lead to family planning programs that could reduce the rates of pregnancy and abortion.

SOURCE: The Alan Guttmacher Institute: New York, 1986.

U.S. House of Representatives 1986, National Research Council 1986). One experimental program with a school-based clinic has reported dramatic success in delaying sexual activity among boys as well as girls, and in reducing pregnancy. Not only did the clinic provide information and contraceptive devices, but the program gave the girls, especially, a sense of being in control of their lives (Fine 1986).

The outlook for teenage parents is bleak. Most do not marry and will experience the difficulties of single parenthood already discussed. For the 10 percent who do marry in their teens, the prospect is not much brighter: divorce rates for parents under age eighteen are three times higher than for parents who have a first child after age twenty. Because so few have had prenatal care or counseling, teenagers have limited parenting information and skills, leading to unrealistic expectations that frequently result in neglect or mistreatment of the child (*Psychology Today* 1986).

Inadequate prenatal care, poor diet, and the normal effects of a first birth are associated with low birth weight and other health complications among offspring of teenage mothers. That is, not age *per se* but the socioeconomic circumstances of teenage parents appears to account for the negative health effects for both mother and child (Mackinson 1985).

Teenage motherhood also limits educational plans (Marini 1984, Haggstrom et al. 1986). However, many girls who become pregnant in high school were already low on academic ability and achievement, so that they might not have gone on to college under any circumstances (Haggstrom et al. 1986). Some school districts have introduced special classes for adolescent mothers, but because large numbers will have dropped out before, during, or after pregnancy, more intensive outreach efforts are needed (Roosa 1986).

DUAL-EARNER FAMILIES

Dual-earner families or couples consist of two wage earners.

Dual-earner families have become the new norm. As noted in Chapter 8, a majority of married women are now in the labor force, including over 60 percent of those with school-age children, and one in four of those with preschoolers. Families with two earners have significantly higher median incomes than do those with one earner. Employed wives tend to be in better emotional and physical health than nonemployed wives (although some of this difference may be due to the fact that healthier women will enter the labor force). At the same time, there are conflicting data on the effects of wives' employment on their husband's sense of well-being—some men will feel relief at sharing financial responsibility and enjoying a higher standard of living; others will find it difficult to give up traditional role expectations (Kessler and McRae 1981). Overall, there appear to be few, if any, direct effects of wives' employment on husbands' well-being, and whatever distress may be felt by some husbands is mediated by family income and his proportional contribution (Fendrich 1984).

As for the effects of a wife's employment on the marriage relationship, dual-earner marriages do tend to be less stable than those with one earner (Booth et al. 1984). But these data are difficult to interpret. Wives in less satisfying marriages may be most likely to seek employment; or, being employed and having financial security makes it possible for a woman to leave an unhappy marriage. That is, marriages that are already fragile are most likely to be negatively affected by the wife's employment. But a wife's labor-force participation does require adjustment; the power balance shifts; and there are problems of meshing work and leisure schedules with the demands of homemaking. One problem is finding time to spend together; the more time spent in joint activity, the more satisfying is the marital relationship of dual-earner couples (Kingston and Nock 1987). Yet one recent reanalysis of twenty-seven studies concluded that there were *no* statistically significant differences in marital adjustment between employed and nonemployed wives, or between husbands of employed and nonemployed spouses (Smith 1985).

The wife's gains in mental health and sense of control are partially offset by *role overload* as most employed women also take full responsibility for household and child care tasks (see articles in Hess and Sussman 1984). The typical employed wife spends between seventy and eighty-three hours a week on work inside and outside the home. In this situation, a great deal of role negotiation must take place, as family members come to accept her employment and eventually to take it seriously (Hood 1983). Couples that cannot negotiate a satisfactory adaptation will be under stress. If the wife leaves the labor force, she may become resentful; if she stays, other family members will feel neglected.

This is not a uniquely American situation. In Sweden, where there are strong ideological and legal supports for shared work and domestic roles, men's involvement in child care and homemaking, while greater than that of Americans, remains minimal (Hass 1980). And in the Soviet Union, the domestic pressures on working women are so great that many prefer divorce to spending the extra hours on household tasks expected by their husbands (Blekher 1979). While women in the Soviet Union and the socialist countries of Europe have more outside supports than their American counterparts—day care, health service, strong colleague ties—they also feel overburdened by their home and work responsibilities and complain about not receiving much help from their husbands (Rueschemeyer 1981). In a Canadian sample, husbands of nonemployed women contributed an average of forty-five minutes a day to child care and household tasks, while men married to employed women added an additional five to fourteen minutes (Michelson 1985). More recent evidence suggests that ". . . the smaller the gap between the husband's earnings and his wife's, the greater his relative contribution" to household tasks (Ross 1987).

There are signs of change. Traditional sex role attitudes are related to age and birth cohort, with new cohorts of young adults increasingly approving of shared roles (Thornton, Alwin, and Camburn 1983), especially those in dual-earner families (Stephan and Corder 1985, Harris 1987). As a consequence many young couples will begin marriage with flexible role expectations. But attitudes also change in response to actual situations, so that couples who start out in traditional roles find themselves adopting different behaviors and beliefs during their marriage, depending on their work experience, while others who had expected greater sharing find themselves drifting into traditional patterns.

Although the change in women's roles has been gradual but constant over the past two decades, there is also evidence of important changes taking place, particularly among younger men (reviewed in Stein 1984). For example, one study showed that, compared to their fathers, young men held a more "nurturing" view of fatherhood, with less emphasis on the "provider" role (Pruett 1987). And data from a national survey indicate that husbands of employed women are slowly but surely increasing their involvement in child care and household work (Pleck 1983).

In addition, contrary to the fears of many, their mother's employment has no strong or consistent negative effects on children (see reviews of this literature by Moore et. al. [1984], and Pietrkowski and Repetti [1984]). If the mother is working because she wishes to, if there is support from her husband and others, and if there are adequate child-care arrangements, the children's social and intellectual development is no different from that of children raised by full-time homemakers (Kamerman and Hayes 1982). Indeed, there may even be gains in independence for both boys and girls, and in achievement goals for daughters and for working-class children in general. Some social scientists believe that increased interaction with a nurturing father improves the psychological development of both sons and daughters (Biller 1981, Lamb 1981).

A variation on the dual-earner family is the *dual-career family* (Hertz 1986, Scarf 1987). Hertz interviewed affluent families with median incomes of $90,000 annually. Their joint incomes allowed them to buy the various support services that enabled both husband and wife to advance their careers and to have a comfortable lifestyle. Some stress still existed because ca-

Dual-career families or couples are ones in which both husband and wife have a career.

reers were demanding and couples had to work out a new set of expectations with regard to career and family obligations. And feminists find themselves in a dilemma because this new class of highly paid businesswomen depends on maintaining a large pool of lower-income women who work as domestics and child-care givers.

Given the probably irreversible trend toward wives' employment, and the attitude shifts among their children, it is safe to predict increasingly egalitarian marriages, with a more flexible division of labor both within and outside the home than in our recent past. Among the new family life-styles that could become more common in the future are (1) the family organized around the wife's career—the WASP or "Wife as Senior Partner" pattern (Atkinson and Boles 1984)—in which a husband's job permits greater flexibility, the wife has a high status position, and there are no young children in the household; and (2) the *"commuter marriage"* in which both partners are equally committed to their careers as well as to their marriage, but work in different cities (Gerstel and Gross 1984). The commuter marriage usually involves two separate households with the partners alternating weekend visits. Both these variations on the dual-earner model are extreme departures from normative expectations of the wife's role, and have a number of built-in stresses. However, researchers have found that they also have compensations, including great flexibility in negotiating marital roles.

Commuter marriages are ones in which husband and wife work in different cities and usually have separate households.

HOMOSEXUAL RELATIONSHIPS

Another alternative to the normative ideal is the homosexual life-style. An unknown, and probably unknowable, number of American men and women prefer sexual partners of their own sex. Many do not announce their sexual orientation for fear of stigma or outright legal prosecution. There are also problems of definition. Is homosexuality to be defined strictly in terms of behavior, or is self-definition the key? Many people who are attracted to persons of their own sex do not act on these feelings. Conversely, many people who have had homosexual relations continue to define themselves as basically heterosexual. Furthermore, because sexual identities are socially constructed, our

Homosexuality refers to a sexual preference for a person of one's own sex.

Heterosexuality refers to a sexual preference for a person of the opposite sex.

Gay parents are just as concerned as heterosexual parents about their children's education, health, welfare and development. Sexual preference is merely one aspect of any person, one aspect of any parent. (© Ira Berger/Woodfin Camp and Associates)

conceptions of gay or lesbian are quite modern and related to the social control of deviance in a society in which traditional authorities have been weakened (D'Emilio 1983). In an earlier era, for example, close ties among nonmarried women were seldom interpreted in a sexual framework, nor did the participants think of themselves as "sick" or "evil."

That homosexuality need not be limited to a small proportion of the population is shown by historical and cross-cultural data on societies in which such relationships are fairly common and even obligatory (Herdt 1984). In fact, in a number of these societies, heterosexual relationships, required in order to reproduce the group, often assume secondary importance—the very opposite pattern from what we consider to be "normal." Given the great range of sexual behaviors and the strong impact of culture and socialization, many sociologists today prefer to think in terms of "sexual scripts" (Gagnon and Simon 1973, 1986) that is, culturally approved ways of organizing sexual experiences. (See our discussion of sexual scripts in Chapter 8.) In our society, the dominant script is based on the male heterosexual model, leaving other experiences to be defined as deviant (Schneider and Gould 1987).

Roots of Homosexuality. As we have noted in Chapter 6, Americans tend to look for direct, single-cause answers to questions about nonnormative behavior: genes, hormones, universal psychological processes, and domineering mothers are the most common. But none of these alone is sufficient to explain sexual orientation.

No researcher has as yet shown a direct link between a particular gene or hormone level and homosexual behavior in either men or women. There is some evidence that gender nonconformity in childhood may predict a homosexual outcome for men, but little agreement on the causes of the original nonconformity (Green 1987). Yet even if there is an inborn tendency toward rejecting "normal" sex-typed attitudes and activities, this alone cannot account for the large proportion of adult homosexuals whose childhood behavior was more conforming than not.

Mental health experts have long pointed to a particular family type to explain male homosexuality: a dominant mother and a weak father. This finding, however, reflects biases in psychological theory rather than the family background of homosexuals. The same households produce both heterosexual and homosexual offspring, and it seems equally likely that a brutal father would be as negative a role model as a weak father for many boys. Several researchers have asked psychologists to analyze sets of personality test data in order to distinguish homosexual from heterosexual respondents. In almost every instance, the mental health experts' decisions were no more accurate than if the data sets had been sorted by a nonprofessional (Jay and Young 1979). Nor can most observers identify homosexuals accurately on the basis of speech, dress, or mannerisms. Most homosexuals are totally indistinguishable from the population in general. In 1973, the American Psychiatric Association removed homosexuality from its list of mental disorders (Bayer 1981), although there are periodic attempts to reinstate it.

If homosexuality is not produced by biology or wicked mothers, what processes are involved? A more sociological view is to see homosexuality as learned in the same way as heterosexuality: through experiences, labeling, and the internalization of self-definitions, which, in turn,

make one type of sexual expression more comfortable than the other. Each experience reinforces an identity and reduces the attractiveness of alternative behaviors (Gagnon 1977). For example, a boy who is late in reaching puberty—whose voice remains high-pitched and who has no beard to shave—may be teased by others and filled with self-doubt. These feelings will make it difficult to act out heterosexual roles in the dating situation, where fear of failure could become a self-fulfilling prophecy. Such failures reinforce the doubts. If, by chance, homosexual encounters also prove less anxiety producing, the youngster may well come to prefer these experiences. In other words, a long chain of events, making heterosexuality uncertain and making homosexual activity attractive, must occur, despite overwhelming pressures to conform to the heterosexual ideal. These cultural and social forces are such powerful agents of social control, that the great majority of boys and girls emerge from adolescence as heterosexually oriented adults.

Before actually engaging in homosexual activities the gay or lesbian must pass through a period of narrowing options (Person 1980). The crucial process centers on the acceptance or rejection of a gay or lesbian identity (Weinberg 1983, Kennard 1984). Taking a symbolic interactionist approach, Weinberg (1983) finds, for example, three phases in the construction of a homosexual identity among gay men: suspecting that one might be gay, engaging in homosexual behavior, and ultimately labeling oneself as gay. A similar process appears to underlie the social construction of a lesbian identity, as seen in the growing body of first-person accounts (reviewed in Zimmerman 1984).

Although both lesbians and gay men are subject to stigma and discrimination (Levine 1981, Levine and Leonard 1984), the greater public concern seems to be directed at male homosexuals. *Homophobia*—the exaggerated fear of male homosexuality—is common in societies where women are the exclusive raisers of the young and where males develop deep insecurities over their sexual identity.

Nonetheless, American attitudes toward homosexuality have become more tolerant over the past decade as have attitudes on all things sexual. In one recent survey of college students, for example, a majority disagreed with the statement that "homo-

Homophobia refers to an exaggerated fear of male homosexuality.

sexuality is immoral" (47 percent of male and 60 percent of female students), 81 percent agreed that "sexual preference is someone's own business," and 76 percent agreed that "homosexuals are entitled to the same protection against discrimination as any other minority group" (*USA Today,* May 15, 1986).

Pair Relationships within the Homosexual Subculture.

Contrary to common perception, gay men and lesbians do not typically recreate the gender-role differences found in the broader society of dominant males and passive females. To the contrary, relationships between homosexual partners are most likely to be egalitarian (Peplau 1982, Harry 1984).

Although there is some evidence that gay men engage in a greater variety of sexual experiences, and with more partners, than do lesbians (McWhirter and Mattison 1983), this difference has been greatly exaggerated (Schneider and Gould 1987). The great majority of homosexuals seek intimacy in a stable relationship, but given the narrow pool of eligibles, success is more problematic than for heterosexuals. Despite the heavily publicized behaviors of a minority of gay men and lesbians, the homosexual scene is probably no more violent or sexually exploitive than the heterosexual world. Indeed, many of the extreme aspects of the homosexual subculture have been muted as a result of the AIDS epidemic and a renewed emphasis on "safe sex."

Is Homosexuality a Threat to the Family?

Despite the new gay activism, greater public tolerance, and attempts to ensure basic civil liberties, it is unlikely that the homosexual life-style will attract more than the estimated 4 percent of exclusive homosexuals, with another group drifting in and out of the subculture. (This figure is based on the Kinsey report of the 1950s. There has been no significant survey data of U.S. sexual behavior since then, although a government sponsored Task Force on Homosexuality in the early 1970s concluded that the Kinsey figures still hold [Gebhard 1972].) Opponents of homosexuality seem to imply that the gay life-style is so attractive that other people must fear exposure to it—an attitude that suggests doubts about the strength of their heterosexual identity. A more likely stimulus for increasing the ranks of homosexuals is that

heterosexuality based on gender inequality may become a progressively *less* attractive option, particularly for women.

The debate on gay and lesbian life-styles has been dominated by the assumption that homosexuality is such an overriding identity that it affects every other aspect of a person. This is not necessarily the case. Just as heterosexuality does not obsess most men and women, coloring their every thought and act, the homosexual's choice of sex partner is only one part of a complex social person. The problems of daily life—work, leisure, comfort and safety, companionship, death, and taxes—beset the gay as well as the straight, and in many ways, they are harder for the homosexual to resolve because of discrimination and stigmatization, even within academic sociology departments (Huber et al. 1982).

Additional difficulties have been raised by public fears over AIDS (see Chapter 17) and the personal anguish of having friends and lovers become ill and die.

MEN IN FAMILIES

Traditionally, even in the sociology of the family, mention of husbands and fathers is usually confined to their role as major breadwinner and the contributions of other family members to men's work-related activities. Only recently has a research literature on other aspects of men's family roles emerged (Beer 1983, Pleck 1985, Lamb 1986, Lewis and Salt 1986, Chafetz 1987). Most of this research has focused on the causes, correlates, and consequences of increased participation in parenting and homemaking.

The great majority of men will get married at least once, most will also become fathers, and a higher proportion of men than women, at all ages, will be married and living with a spouse. Clearly, family life continues to provide many comforts and benefits to men, and may bring even more satisfaction to the men who participate most fully (Lewis 1986). There is also a Durkheimian point to be made: family life provides the boundaries and stable environment that protect against anomie. While a single life may be tempting, people can suffer from a lack of social restraints.

The New Father?

As part of the "natural childbirth" movement, increasing numbers of young husbands have joined their wives in birthing courses and taken part in the actual delivery. However, it is doubtful whether this experience creates a father-child bond of special strength, although there may be many other benefits from the feeling of being included in the birth experience (Palkovitz 1986).

A small proportion of new fathers will also assume a major role in caring for the infant (Risman 1987). These men tend to be highly educated, with flexible time schedules, an ideological commitment to gender equality, and married to women in high-status jobs (Russell 1983). Limited data on father-infant interaction indicates that fathers act very much like mothers, but also engage in more vigorous play with both sons and daughters (Ricks 1985). As much as many men might wish to take a more active role in child care, they are inhibited by the demands of outside employment. Employers could, if they valued the loyalty of employees (both men and women), lessen the conflict between work and family responsibilities by providing

The "new father" assumes a major role in caring for his children not only because he wants to but because he can. Reversing traditional role relationships is difficult without being able to change the structure of the situation the partners are in.
(© M. Murdock)

flexible work schedules, parental leave without loss of benefits, and educational programs at the workplace (Pleck 1986, Thorne 1987).

The New Husband.   As few employers offer such supports, and as time spent on family tasks brings lower rewards to men than to women, there has *not* been a major shift in the division of household labor over the past two decades (Coverman and Sheley 1986, Hess and Sussman 1985). Where men have become most active is in the "fun" parts of child care. Pleck (1985) suggests several additional reasons for this minimal increase on the part of men and the continued role overload for employed wives: some women will actively discourage their husbands in order to retain control over this sphere; the men resist because housework is boring and unappreciated; or men could be displaying a "learned helplessness" that relieves them of responsibility.

The day of the "househusband" remains very distant. But if there are few men who are full-time child-care givers or homemakers, there is no question that the division of household labor is becoming increasingly varied. The process of role negotiation can lead to many different outcomes, which can be seen as a strength rather than a weakness of our family system. The strength comes from the possibility that both partners can find a satisfying balance instead of feeling forced to conform to an ideal stereotype.

In all its variety, the American family system has adapted to the conditions of postindustrial society. According to recent survey data, family life continues to be the leading source of satisfaction for most Americans; intimacy and sharing are the goals of relationships; and the vast majority of young people expect to marry and raise children. But the content of these relationships is undergoing vast change: flexible roles, joint involvement in work and homemaking, and shared child care are the preferred patterns, especially among younger respondents (Ethan Allen 1987, Harris 1987). And despite relatively high levels of divorce, delayed marriage, nonmarriage and nonparenthood, current cohorts of Americans will actually spend *more* years than ever before as part of a family—as child, spouse, and parent—thanks to increased life expectancy in all three generations (Watkins et al. 1987).

Summary

Like other institutions, the family system is a set of norms and behaviors. In the family system, these are clustered around the essential activities of reproduction, socialization, protection, intimacy, and care. Family-based relationships are essential features of the social structure of all human societies. Though these kinship systems vary from one society to another over time, they can all be described in terms of five basic characteristics: (1) how many spouses are permitted at one time; (2) who can marry whom; (3) how lines of descent and the flow of resources are determined; (4) where the couple lives; and (5) what the power relations are within marriage and the family.

The major historical change has been from relatively large extended-family systems composed of a number of related households, to the nuclear family system of a married pair and their children. The nuclear family is a less versatile unit than the extended family, as an increasing number of tasks once assumed by the kinship group are now performed outside the home. Yet the stresses and demands of modern life create needs for affection and emotional support which people seek from their marriage partners and their children.

The modern family is also characterized by reduced power differences between husbands and wives and between parents and children. These shifts toward egalitarianism have been influenced by broader liberal trends, legal changes, the influence of psychological theories of child development, and a decline in parents' ability to control the social mobility of their children.

Marriage and parenthood continue to be almost universal among Americans and to be associated with positive feelings. Nonetheless, there is widespread fear for the future of the American family because of the increasing frequency of divorce, a growing awareness of family violence, and the perception of a general decline in adherence to sexual moral codes.

When marriages no longer provide emotional support and personal security, the partners separate and divorce. This is the other side of the coin of relatively free mate selection. An increasing number of contemporary marriages end in divorce, although 80 percent of these men and women remarry. There is evidence that the divorce rate is leveling off, as more young people delay entering a first marriage.

The emotional intensity of modern family life and the cultural glorification of aggressive masculinity both contribute to outbursts of violence within the family, most often directed at women and children. People who have grown up in violent households tend to repeat the pattern in their own families.

The ideal of a one-earner nuclear family is actually represented by a small minority of American households. There has been a dramatic increase in persons living alone, both before marrying and after being widowed. In the years to come, some young singles will never marry, and some married couples will choose not to have children. A growing number of unmarried men and women, of all ages, will live together before or after a marriage. Divorced women—and an increasing number of divorced men—will maintain a single-parent household for several years. And openly expressed homosexuality will continue to represent an alternative life-style for a small fraction of American men and women.

Variety will also result from role negotiations between wives and husbands who have both individual and shared investments in work and family. The result is a diversity of family forms that can be viewed as a positive adaptation to the conditions of modern life.

Suggested Readings

ALLAN, GRAHAM. *Family Life: Domestic Roles and Social Organization*. New York: Basil Blackwell, 1985. A superb analysis of the interplay between economic structures and domestic relations in the modern family.

BERNARD, JESSIE. *The Future of Marriage*. New Haven, CT: Yale University Press, 1982. An informative and lively summary of sociological research on marriage and the family by a noted and eminent expert in the field.

BLUMSTEIN, PHILIP, and PEPPER SCHWARTZ. *American Couples.* New York: William Morrow, 1983. An interesting compilation of data, this book is based on questionnaires and interviews with six thousand American couples.

CHERLIN, ANDREW J. *Marriage, Divorce, Remarriage.* Cambridge: Harvard University Press, 1981. An informal, yet scholarly, analysis of the causes and consequences of recent marriage and divorce trends and differences between white and black family patterns.

FREEMAN, MICHAEL D., ed. *State Law and the Family—Critical Perspectives.* London: Tavistock, 1984. A collection of articles on the attempts to regulate family life and the legal protection of family members in matters such as domestic violence, children's rights, and custody and financial support of children.

LEWIS, ROBERT A., and ROBERT E. SALT, eds. *Men in Families.* Beverly Hills, CA: Sage, 1986. A collection of readings focusing on three major themes: Men as fathers, as husbands, and in family, kin, and friendship networks.

MAYER, EGON. *Love and Tradition: Marriage Between Jews and Christians.* New York: Plenum Press, 1985. A readable book on the impact of intermarriage on the parents, children and the couple, and the decisions and problems that arise in these marriages.

PLECK, JOSEPH H. *Working Wives/Working Husbands.* Beverly Hills, CA: Sage, 1985. An exploration of the division of labor within the household between husbands and wives.

STEIN, PETER J. *Single Life: Unmarried Adults in Social Context.* New York: St. Martin's Press, 1981. Essays and research studies illuminating the many facets of single life, including the never marrieds, the separated, the divorced, and the widowed.

WEITZMAN, LENORE J. *The Divorce Revolution: The Unexpected Social and Economic Consequences for Women and Children in America.* New York: Free Press, 1985. This book documents the beneficial effects of current divorce laws for men and its strangely negative effects for women and for children.

VAUGHAN, DIANE. *Uncoupling: Turning Points For Intimate Relationships.* New York: Oxford University Press, 1986. A carefully crafted examination of dissolving relationships.

12

Economic Systems and the Organization of Work

D UE to World War I hostilities, the anthropologist Bronislaw Malinowski was forced to remain on the Trobriand Islands in the Western Pacific. This gave him the opportunity to study the culture by observing daily life over an extended period. One of the more fascinating activities noted by Malinowski was the periodic arrival of canoes from neighboring islands. The canoes were greeted with elaborate rituals involving the exchange of armbands or necklaces made of shells, which had little intrinsic value but great ceremonial importance. These activities were part of the *kula ring* tra-

dition whereby the shell necklaces were transported from one island group to another in a clockwise direction, while the armbands traveled counter-clockwise. The few men on each island who received these gifts kept them for a short period before fitting out their own canoes and taking the kula items to another island in the prescribed direction, often fifty miles away on the open sea.

Malinowski wondered why the pieces of shell jewelry were considered so very valuable, kept only temporarily, and never exchanged for anything except other necklaces or armbands, at great cost and risk. After many observations, however, Malinowski (1922) realized that the kula objects were a symbolic cover for a high volume of practical trade from one island to another. That is, while the chief kula partners were handing over the armbands and necklaces, other members of the trading party were exchanging yams, coconuts, sago, baskets, mats, vines, and shells that could be used as knives. The kula ring was a vast trading network that distributed goods among the various islands by *barter* (straight exchange).

Barter involves the direct exchange of goods.

The kula ring also served as the mainspring of social stratification. Being one of the few who can participate in kula trade was a sign of high prestige, while their special relationship with kula partners on other islands added to the wealth and power of these "big men."

In this one elaborate custom of the Trobrianders, we can see quite clearly that economic systems do not operate in a cultural or social-structural vacuum. Economic behavior in all societies has a symbolic dimension and is linked to the other institutional spheres of the society—its political structure, patterns of marriage and family, socialization practices, and belief system. This is as true of modern-day Americans as it was of Malinowski's Trobriand Islanders.

Origins and History of Economic Systems

Economic systems originate in the trial-and-error attempts of human groups to survive in specific locations. The groups that failed to find sufficient resources or to motivate members to contribute to the well-being of all will have quickly disappeared.

The term *mode of subsistence* refers to the group's means of adapting to its environment. We assume that for most of human history, small bands subsisted on what could be gathered immediately. Later in human history, other economic systems evolved, each progressively more complex in knowledge and technology: hunting, fishing, herding, horticulture, agriculture, and industrialism. (See Chapter 3, Fig. 3-3.) Over time, many societies undergo change in their mode of subsistence; others remain much as they were centuries ago. Today, across the world, each of these adaptations is still practiced. On our continent, for example, the homeless survive as gatherers, Canadian Eskimos fish and hunt, ranchers of the midwest herd, Mexican villagers practice horticulture, wheat growers are agriculturalists, and many of our cities are highly industrialized. The long-term historical trend, however, has been toward increased division of labor, specialization of tasks, more efficient use of energy, and linkage to the economic systems of other societies.

Once a mode of subsistence is established, the original patterns (folkways) are invested with a sense of sacredness (mores) and ultimately supported by a set of impersonal rules and sanctions (laws). This is the process of *institutionalization* whereby a given adaptation becomes a way of life and affects all other areas of activity.

Institutionalization is the process whereby a given adaptation becomes an established pattern.

Components of Economic Systems

The economic system of any society consists of the norms and patterned activities regulating the production, the distribution, and the consumption of goods (material objects) and services (assistance and knowledge).

An **economic system** consists of the norms and activities regulating the production, distribution, and consumption of goods and services.

PRODUCTION

Primary, Secondary, and Service. Primary production consists of gathering, growing, or mining; that is, taking directly from the earth for immediate use. *Secondary production* involves transforming these raw materials into other objects, i.e. manufacturing everything from bows and arrows and baskets to baby bottles and bombs. Modern societies, however, are characterized by a third level of production: the provision of services. *Service work* includes everyone involved in sales, government, education, homemaking, child care, beauty care, business management, insurance, banking, information processing, transportation, communication, entertainment, sports, and health care.

Primary production includes gathering, growing, or mining. **Secondary production** involves transforming raw materials through manufacturing into other consumable objects. **Service work** refers to providing assistance and/or information.

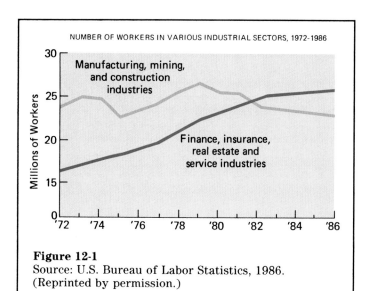

NUMBER OF WORKERS IN VARIOUS INDUSTRIAL SECTORS, 1972-1986

Manufacturing, mining, and construction industries

Finance, insurance, real estate and service industries

Figure 12-1
Source: U.S. Bureau of Labor Statistics, 1986.
(Reprinted by permission.)

As seen in Figure 12-1, the United States is rapidly becoming a "service society" as the proportion of jobs in manufacturing declines relative to those in the service sector. All the growth in the labor force in this decade has been in services and trade (Bluestone and Harrison 1987). In addition, the percentage of the labor force engaged in farming has declined from about 30 percent in 1920 to under 3 percent in the 1980s. Most farming today is performed by machines on large tracts owned by corporations rather than by "family farmers" (Vogeler 1981). (See Chapter 19.)

Not only is the service sector expanding rapidly, but most of these jobs are at the lowest-paying end of the scale, and many are part-time or temporary (Serrin 1986). The most dramatic employment declines have been in the high-pay unionized industrial sector—automobile and steel plants, for example—where production has moved overseas. Thus, while the recovery from the recession of 1982–1983 has been vigorous, with millions of new jobs created, unemployment, underemployment, poverty, and near-poverty are also higher than they were in the late 1970s.

And even some of the newly created jobs, those in clerical work, are in danger of being phased out as computers do more of this type of work (U.S. Office of Technology Assessment 1985; U.S. Bureau of Labor Statistics 1986). At the same time, there has been an increase in employment situations often thought to be exploitative: sharecropping in agriculture, home-based factory work, and temporary workers throughout the service sector (Simpson and Simpson 1983, Wells 1984, Noble 1986, Serrin 1986). These workers are rarely eligible for health insurance, paid vacations, sick leave, or other benefits, and in some cases do not receive Social Security coverage. Overall, for every "high tech" new service job in computing and electronics, many more will be created in the "low tech" fields (fast-food handling, health aide, data processing). (See Table 12-1.)

DISTRIBUTION

Once the goods and services have been produced, each society must develop rules for the distribution of its resources. Whenever a group's resources cannot be allocated equally, the distribution rules become the basis of social stratification.

Primary production in our society is rarely small-scale. Dairy farming, for example, is a major agribusiness. Grazing cows in clovered pastures have been replaced by rows of well-tethered animals. (© John Blaustein/Woodfin Camp and Associates)

TABLE 12-1   Projected job opportunities: 1984–1995 (numbers in thousands)

	Employment		Change 1984–1995	
	1984	1995	Number	Percent
THE OCCUPATIONS WITH THE LARGEST JOB GROWTH				
1 Cashiers	1,902	2,469	566	29.8%
2 Registered nurses	1,377	1,829	452	32.8
3 Janitors and cleaners, including maids	2,940	3,383	443	15.1
4 Truck drivers	2,484	2,911	428	17.2
5 Waiters and waitresses	1,625	2,049	424	26.1
6 Wholesale trade salesworkers	1,248	1,617	369	29.6
7 Nursing aides, orderlies, and attendants	1,204	1,552	348	28.9
8 Salespersons, retail	2,732	3,075	343	12.6
9 Accountants and auditors	882	1,189	307	34.8
10 Teachers, kindergarten and elementary	1,381	1,662	281	20.3
11 Secretaries	2,797	3,064	268	9.6
12 Computer programmers	341	586	245	71.8
13 General office clerks	2,398	2,629	231	9.6
14 Food preparation workers, excluding fast food	987	1,205	219	22.1
15 Food preparation and service workers, fast food	1,201	1,417	215	17.9
16 Computer systems analysts, electronic data processing	308	520	212	68.7
17 Electrical and electronic engineers	390	597	207	52.8
18 Electrical and electronic technicians and technologists	404	607	202	50.0
19 Guards	733	921	188	25.6
20 Automotive and motorcycle mechanics	922	1,107	185	20.1
THE FASTEST GROWING OCCUPATIONS				
1 Paralegal personnel	53	104	51	97.5
2 Computer programmers	341	586	245	71.8
3 Computer systems analysts, electronic data processing	308	520	212	68.7
4 Medical assistants	128	207	79	62.0
5 Data processing equipment repairers	50	78	28	56.2
6 Electrical and electronic engineers	390	597	206	52.8
7 Electrical and electronics technicians and technologists	404	607	202	50.7
8 Computer operators, except peripheral equipment	241	353	111	46.1
9 Peripheral EDP equipment operators	70	102	32	45.0
10 Travel agents	72	103	32	43.9
11 Physical therapists	58	83	25	42.2
12 Physician assistants	25	35	10	40.3
13 Securities and financial services salesworkers	81	113	32	39.1
14 Mechanical engineering technicians and technologists	55	75	20	36.6
15 Lawyers	490	665	174	35.5
16 Correction officers and jailers	130	175	45	34.9
17 Accountants and auditors	882	1,189	307	34.8
18 Mechanical engineers	237	317	81	34.0
19 Registered nurses	1,377	1,829	452	32.8
20 Employment interviewers, private and public agencies	72	95	23	31.7

SOURCE: U.S. Bureau of Labor Statistics, 1985; *Data Users News,* March 1987.

Barter, Reciprocity, Redistribution and Market. Gatherers typically share the day's yield of food among all members of the band. In more complex economic systems, there will be surplus goods or services to exchange within the group or between societies. The simplest means of distributing surplus is by direct exchange or *barter* of goods and services judged to be of equivalent value by the traders, as in the kula ring. The kula also illustrates another common distributive principle: the *rule of reciprocity,* which involves the giving of gifts that obligate the receiver to return something of similar value at some later date.

The **rule of reciprocity** holds that giving gifts obligates the recipient to return something of similar value.

Once a society has reached the degree of complexity that requires a centralized government, the rulers can collect taxes and gifts from other members of the society, as well as tribute from foreigners. The rulers then decide how to *redistribute* this wealth in order to maintain their own power and keep most citizens content. Redistribution takes place in modern societies through social-welfare programs such as Medicare, subsidies to farmers, tax incentives to corporations, and Aid to Families with Dependent Children.

But the major method of distribution in complex societies is the *market system,* in which some general standard (a currency) is used to measure the value of goods and services. The worth of any item then depends on how much currency others are willing to give up for it, which, in turn, depends on how many other buyers and sellers there are in the marketplace.

Theorists of the market system claim that in the long run demand and supply will tend toward balance, leading to the most efficient use of raw material and labor power. In the short run, however, recessions and inflation can upset the play of market forces. And people are not always the rational decision makers of economic theory; their choices may be based on noneconomic factors such as emotions or status needs.

In a **market system** a currency, which is a general standard, is used to measure the value of goods and services.

CONSUMPTION

Literally, to "consume" means "to eat up." How members of a society use and consume goods and services is an important aspect of culture. In most societies throughout human history, the household has been both a unit of production and consumption. The unique feature of industrialism, however, is the separation of

The Kula Ring, studied by Bronislaw Malinowski, was a vast trading network that distributed goods among the various Western Pacific islands by barter. Barter is still an acceptable form of trade in many societies, including our own. (© David Austen/Stock Boston)

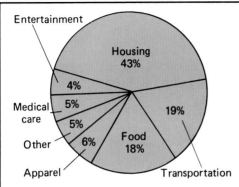

Figure 12-2
How Americans Spend Their Income: Consumption Patterns of American Households, 1982–1984. (Source: Department of Labor, U.S. Bureau of Labor Statistics, *The New York Times*, February, 1987.)

workplace and household. Production takes place outside the household—in factories and offices—and is performed by one or more adult members of the family. The household then becomes primarily a consuming unit, and its nonemployed members become economically dependent on the wage workers. Figure 12-2 illustrates the typical consumption patterns of American households in the 1980s.

Consumption patterns in most societies reflect and create social hierarchies. The classic example of this process is the *potlatch* ceremony of the Kwakiutl Indians of Southwest Canada. At a feast to celebrate an important family event, the host and guests will try to outdo one another in boasting and gift giving, often destroying property in the process. The ultimate test of prestige is the amount of property—blankets, canoes, food, money—a person can give away or throw into the sea or onto a bonfire. The guests, as spectators or receivers of gifts, are under an obligation to recognize their host's high status until they themselves can hold a potlatch of equivalent or greater waste (Benedict 1934, Rohner and Rohner 1970). The New York real estate millionaire, described in Chapter 3, who rented the ocean liner for his child's coming-of-age party can be considered a latter-day Kwakiutl.

The potlatch and similar acts of conspicuous consumption (Veblen 1899, see

The **potlatch** ceremony of the Kwakiutl Indians is an act of conspicuous consumption in which material goods are given or thrown away.

Chapter 1) create webs of obligation as they establish status hierarchies. Only the highest ranked or most wealthy can shower gifts on other people who then owe something in return (loyalty, support in battle, acts of respect). That is the reason why we often feel ambivalent about receiving an unexpected gift.

Although we have shown several parallels between economic behavior in preliterate and modern societies, industrialism brings major changes in patterns of production, distribution, and consumption.

Contemporary Economic Systems

Modern economic systems can be arranged along a continuum representing the degree to which economic activity is regulated by public agencies or left entirely to the marketplace and those who own the means of production. This continuum is represented in Figure 12-3. At one extreme is *free-enterprise capitalism* with minimal political interference. At the other extreme, marked by central planning of production and distribution, is a fully *socialist economic system*. These terms refer to economic systems and are not necessarily linked to a particular political system (see Chapter 13): Capitalist economies can flourish in democratic states (the United States), dictatorships (Chile), and caste societies (South Africa). Conversely, socialist economies are found in both dictatorships (Soviet Union) and democracies (Sweden).

Free-enterprise capitalism is an economic system with minimal political interference.

A **socialist economic system** is marked by central planning of production and distribution.

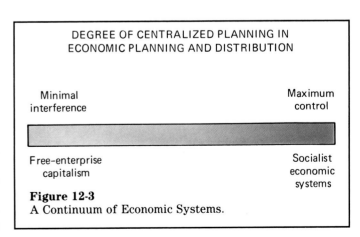

Figure 12-3
A Continuum of Economic Systems.

CAPITALISM

In a capitalist economy, the means of production (land, factories, knowledge, corporations) are privately owned and operated for the profit of the owners. In theory, the free play of supply and demand and competition among producers will drive out the less efficient firms, lead to lower prices, and enhance the well-being of the society and its members. Both owners and workers are motivated by the promise of keeping the fruits of their labors.

In practice, capitalist economies lead to relatively high levels of inequality in power and wealth in the business sector as well as among members of the society. A number of contemporary social scientists have asked why such inequality is tolerated in societies in which all adults have the right to vote; why, in other words, don't the majority of people support greater public control over private wealth (Schott 1984; Przeworski 1985)? Some of the answers were given in Chapter 7; others have to do with the real gains of the working class in advanced capitalist systems. In fact, capitalist societies with democratic political systems have moved progressively away from pure free enterprise: e.g., anti-trust laws, social security, welfare legislation, health insurance for the poor and elderly, education assistance, farm subsidies, and similar programs. At the same time, justifications for capitalism have changed as the economy itself undergoes transformations (Weber 1981).

An emphasis on private profit and short-term gains also encourages speculation. One result of uncontrolled economic activity was the near collapse of the entire market system during the stock market crash and the Great Depression of the 1920s and 1930s. These events led to political intervention in order to reform banking procedures, limit the power of speculators, and control the supply of money. Thus, the economic systems of the United States and other Western nations are best described as *state capitalism* or *welfare capitalism,* essentially free markets within limits designed to ensure social stability.

Some critics claim that these public interventions have actually benefited the business community by protecting owners from their own worst impulses. Public subsidies (direct payments) to farmers, shipping companies, and highway-construction firms, all raise prices to consumers while benefiting owners. This pattern has been labeled "welfare for the rich and capitalism for the poor" (Marshall 1977), as twice as much public money is spent on programs that benefit major corporations as is spent on programs for the poor (Harvie 1983).

Trends Toward Concentration of Power. At the level of the economic system itself, the ideals of free enterprise have been compromised by trends that lessen competition and lead to greater concentration of decision-making power. First is the tendency of larger companies to swallow up competitors in the same line of business (*monopoly*).

Market forces are also limited by the growth of *conglomerates,* where one "holding company" buys controlling interest in companies in a variety of commercial sectors. This central firm does not itself manufacture anything, but its Board of Directors makes decisions that affect several areas of the economy, as shown in the case of RJR Nabisco, Inc. in Figure 12-4.

Along the same lines, *interlocking corporate directorships,* whereby the same individuals sit on the boards of directors of a number of different companies, lead to increasing concentration of power in the hands of a small group of executives (Burt 1983). The interlocks also serve in the long run to decrease competition and increase profits. With the contemporary trend toward mergers, buyouts, and takeovers—largely as a means of enhancing short-term profits for stockholders and speculators—fewer and fewer companies and corporate officers dominate the private sector. When a small group of New York banks, brokerage houses, and insurance companies control the flow of money throughout the economic system, conflict and competition are reduced (Mintz and Schwartz 1981, Useem 1983). At the same time, this concentration of economic power makes the entire economic system more vulnerable to the ups and downs of the business cycle, requiring more intervention by government to stave off crises (Himmelstrand et al. 1981).

The accountability of major American business firms is further eroded by their increasing involvement in multinational economic enterprises (Moran 1985, Newfarmer 1985). Many American firms have

State capitalism or **welfare capitalism** refers to free markets existing within limits designed to ensure social stability.

Monopoly is the tendency of larger companies to acquire competitors in the same line of business. **Conglomerates** exist when one company owns controlling shares in other companies in a variety of business sectors.

Interlocking corporate directorships involve members of one board of directors sitting on the boards of other companies.

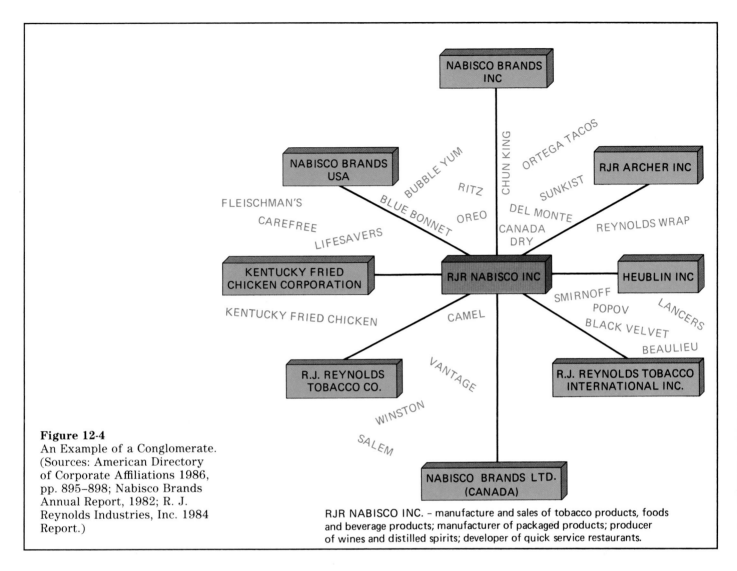

Figure 12-4
An Example of a Conglomerate.
(Sources: American Directory of Corporate Affiliations 1986, pp. 895–898; Nabisco Brands Annual Report, 1982; R. J. Reynolds Industries, Inc. 1984 Report.)

RJR NABISCO INC. – manufacture and sales of tobacco products, foods and beverage products; manufacturer of packaged products; producer of wines and distilled spirits; developer of quick service restaurants.

Multinational corporations are firms with branches and factories in many countries, and whose ownership is not linked to one nation.

branches or manufacturing plants in other countries, just as foreign firms and individuals have increasingly bought into American enterprises. The resulting growth of *multinational corporations* presents problems in loyalty and control. Many multinationals do not fall under the supervision of any one government. Decisions are based solely on corporate goals rather than on the well-being of any one nation. While some economists hail the potential for economic growth in the developing nations that Western business can provide, others fear that an economic imperialism will replace the political imperialism of the past.

In these many ways, the nature of advanced capitalism differs greatly from the original ideal of competing small firms in a perfect market in which only economic criteria influenced decision making. How-

ever, the ultimate collapse of the system, as prophesied by Karl Marx and his followers, has not occurred, either.

SOCIALISM

Socialism is based on the belief that economic activity should be guided by public needs rather than by private profit making. Socialist goals include the reduction of inequality based on inherited wealth or status, and the widest possible distribution of such basic resources as education, health care, and housing. But just as the promise of general prosperity under capitalism remains unfulfilled, so also do the egalitarian ideals of socialism. The real world is considerably more complicated than any of its theoretical representations. And, as Marx and Weber were well aware,

Socialism is based on the belief that economic activity should be guided by public needs rather than private profit making.

economic systems cannot be understood in isolation from other institutional spheres.

Contemporary socialist theory owes much to Karl Marx's critique of capitalism, including his prediction of its long-term flaws and the ultimate transition to socialism. Much of Marx's analysis has not stood the test of time, often because of changes in capitalist economies made precisely to avoid the prophesied outcome. But there is great vitality in the Marxist tradition, especially among contemporary Western sociologists (Stephens 1980, Burawoy and Skocpol 1982, Gouverneur 1983, Levine 1984, Petras 1984). At the same time, there has been a resurgence in pro-capitalist theories by American economists and philosophers (Friedman and Friedman 1980, Gilder 1981, Nozick 1985).

From the Marxist perspective, "forces of production"—modes of subsistence and their relevant skills and knowledge—are best realized under certain political arrangements, belief systems, and family structures. For example, because industrialism needs a disciplined labor force, a religion based on work as a calling and households dependent on a male wage earner are both highly functional. And allowing workers to vote helps to siphon off discontent, provided that the party of the working class remains less than a majority (Przeworski 1985).

When forces of production change—from hunting to agriculture or from farming to factories, for example—the other institutions must also undergo change. The ultimate step in the replacement of capitalism by socialism comes when the workers themselves own or at least control the means of production. At this point, there is no longer a distinction between owners and workers, which was the major division within all historical societies and the source of social conflict. Although the socialist transformation has not yet occurred in most advanced industrial nations, Marxist theories contend that the built-in contradictions of advanced capitalism will eventually lead the working class to organize politically to bring about radical economic changes (Stephens 1980, Levine, 1984).

Contemporary Socialism. Socialism has taken many forms today. At one extreme, in the Soviet Union and Eastern Europe, repressive political systems dominate all aspects of the society. Critics of socialism note that the economies of these societies are very inefficient in their use of material and people, with resulting low rates of productivity and worker morale. However, one detailed study of comparable firms in Hungary and the United States found that it is not necessarily true that socialist workplaces are less efficient than those in an advanced capitalist economy (Burawoy and Lukacs 1985). In addition, many socialist societies have been opening up areas of limited managerial autonomy and even some private enterprise (So 1986).

A less extreme form of economic planning is found in almost all Western countries, and especially Sweden and Denmark, where production remains largely in private hands but the distribution of goods and services is socialized. This sys-

Pictured here is the interior of a Soviet truck factory. To a certain extent, similar production techniques, even within different economic and political systems, will produce a similar work environment. (© SYGMA)

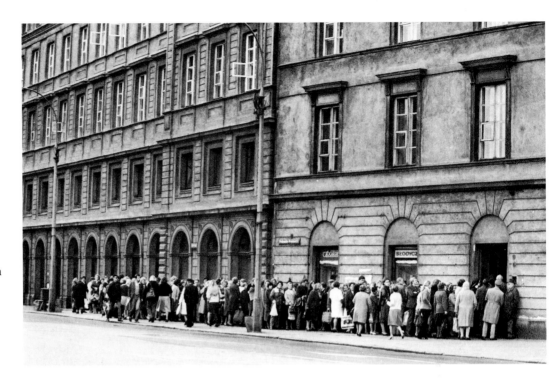

Consumer goods of all kinds are difficult to obtain in many Eastern European countries. Here people line up in front of a bakery in Warsaw. What is the last item you lined up for? (© Jean Pierre Laffont/ SYGMA)

In a **welfare state** production is privately owned but the distribution of goods and services is socialized.

tem is often called the *welfare state* (Flora and Heidenheimer 1981). Higher education, health care, housing for workers and the elderly, and social services are provided in a way that minimizes class and status differences. Paying for the welfare state involves relatively high rates of taxation (half of the national product in Sweden compared to less than one-third in the United States). Yet if we add up what we pay for defense from our tax dollars plus what American families pay out-of-pocket for medical expenses, college costs, and the care of disabled relatives, the total financial burden is at least as high as that paid in taxes by Swedes.

In general, socialist economies are associated with redistributive policies designed to reduce educational and income inequality, at least in those societies with democratic political systems. In the Soviet Union and Eastern European nations, however, inequality remains quite high: not only in the political sector, but in access to housing, higher education, and a wide range of consumer goods. Rural-urban differences are marked, as are gender differentials in occupations and income. As Szelenyi (1983) notes in his study of inequality in housing in Eastern Europe, whereas Americans count on state intervention to modify the unfairness of the market system, citizens in a redistribu-

tive economy may have to depend on greater leeway for free-market forces. Each system has its own brand of inequality.

A final criticism of socialism points out the deadening effects of large and deeply entrenched bureaucracies (see Chapter 4). The expanding number of jobs in government is functional in providing employment for college graduates and the upwardly mobile, but can be dysfunctional when speedy and risky decisions are required. The process of goal displacement often leads to a greater emphasis on protecting one's job than on enhancing efficiency and productivity (Hodges 1981, Shlapentokh 1987).

Work Organization and Commitment

DIVISION OF LABOR

Industrial economies whether capitalist or socialist are characterized by an extreme division of labor and task specialization. In the United States, for example, the Department of Labor publishes a *Dictionary of Occupational Titles* with over 12,000 entries! Such extreme specialization has led social theorists, from Durkheim, Weber, and Marx to Talcott Parsons and Kai

Erikson to see the organization of work in modern societies as potentially threatening to social unity. When each worker does only one small task and participates in the culture in a limited way, it is difficult to generate a sense of shared values and common fate among all citizens.

Durkheim worried about the lack of intermediate groups between the individual worker and the impersonal forces of government and business. Weber spoke of "disenchantment" and "demystification" as modern life becomes increasingly subject to technological controls. And Marx saw it all leading to *alienation,* a feeling of being cut off from the product of one's labor, from other people, and ultimately from oneself. The theme of work and alienation continues to attract sociological attention, as seen in Kai Erikson's 1985 Presidential Address to the American Sociological Association, in which many of Marx's insights were applied to the automated workplaces of today. Erikson (1986) concluded his remarks by suggesting that alienating work affects the human spirit, making us ever more brutal to people who are different from us, and increasingly indifferent even to one another.

The central institution of industrialism is the factory. Factories bring workers out of their homes to one central location where machines and labor power can be used most efficiently and where management can exercise direct control over the work force. The perfect embodiment of the rationalization of work is the assembly line, with each step in the production process separated from other steps and given to one worker. The relationship of the assembly-line worker to the finished product is rendered all but invisible. Contrast, for example, the worker in a shoe factory with a shoemaker. The shoemaker makes an entire shoe, works with the leather, fits it to the buyer, draws on a set of skills, and enjoys a feeling of creative accomplishment in the result. The worker in a shoe factory, however, may only attach a heel to each shoe as it passes down the line, with little sense of personal creativity.

This process has been described as "deskilling" (Braverman 1974) in contrast to the accumulation of artistic skills required of craftspersons in the past. Deskilling is not confined to the factory floor; much white-collar work has been similarly routinized (Wright and Singlemann 1982, Feldberg and Glenn 1983). This is espe-

cially the case where machines increasingly deskill the work and even take over tasks previously performed by human workers (Thompson 1984).

AUTOMATION

The ultimate in impersonal production is *automation,* replacing workers with machines. Although initial costs may be high, in the long run machines are cheaper than people—and easier for management to supervise. Machines do not complain or take coffee breaks; they do not join unions or go on strike; and they do not expect a pension at the end of their worklife. But for many tasks they are not any more efficient than human workers (Howard 1985). In addition, the highly experienced blue-collar workers who actually operate the machines keep their special knowledge of quirks and shortcuts to themselves in order to maintain control of the work process as well as to expand their own free time on the job (Halle 1984).

But management also has ways to protect its interests. Workers who continue to insist on wage increases and improved benefits can be threatened with loss of

Alienation is the feeling of being cut off from the product of one's labor, from other people, and from oneself.

Automation is the replacing of workers with machines.

"Modern Times" with Charlie Chaplin is a classic American film that satirized the human effects of automation and assembly line production. (© The Bettmann Archive, Inc.)

Automation replaces workers with machines, as you can see in this photo of one of the most automated factories in Japan. Their virtue? Neither American, Japanese nor Soviet machines complain, take coffee breaks, join unions, gossip, punch in late, or have interpersonal problems. (© Ethan Hoffman/Archive Pictures)

their jobs by the introduction of computers and robots. In addition, automation can improve management's ability to control and supervise employees (Erickson 1986, G. Marx 1986). Video-camera surveillance, drug testing, wiretaps, computer monitoring, and beepers are all commonly used today to keep track of employees and their activities. And workers appear willing to relinquish their right to privacy rather than lose their jobs in a period of relatively high unemployment.

The fully automated service economy is not very far off; we will explore its consequences in Chapter 22.

WORKER SATISFACTION

Despite the objectively degrading characteristics of most employment, the great majority of American workers claim to be satisfied with their jobs, even among today's better educated labor force (Glenn and Weaver 1982, V. Burris 1983, but see B. Burris 1983, on low-level clerical workers). A number of factors may be at work here: (1) the tendency to lower expectations to fit reality; (2) a wish to avoid the sense of utter failure attached to so crucial a role; (3) alternative sources of satisfaction—in workplace friendships, in trying to outwit management, in the nonwork activities that can be enjoyed with one's wages. In other words, there may be a shift in modern societies from *intrinsic* (built-in) to *extrinsic* (external) satisfactions from the job. Halaby (1986) also suggests that workers accept their subordination when they believe that their employer is acting legitimately.

This trend extends also to white-collar employees. One analysis of "how-to-succeed" manuals over the three decades between 1950 and 1980 found a distinct change in emphasis as middle-class work opportunities narrowed in the 1970s. The 1980 books emphasize finding fulfillment outside the workplace, in leisure activities and personal relationships, which, of course, presents no great threat to employers (Biggart 1983).

Worker satisfaction is highest in jobs where an employee has some control over the work process and is not closely supervised. Such *job autonomy* involves making decisions about the timing and sequence of tasks, exercising one's own judgment, and having a distinct impact on the outcome—all of which contribute to a sense of self-esteem, intellectual flexibility, and low levels of job stress (Kohn et al. 1983, Lorence and Mortimer 1985, Mortimer and Finch 1986). Indeed, the effect of autonomy on worker satisfaction is greater than that of income, although it is usually the case that high-autonomy jobs are in the better-paying occupations. Conversely, dissatisfaction is highest where employees are kept to a tight schedule, closely monitored, where the tasks are repetitive and routinized yet require complex skills, and where the worker feels under pressure. These are the conditions under which employees display the classic symptoms of alienation—feelings of powerlessness, meaninglessness, and isolation (Blauner 1964, Seeman 1972). And at least one large-scale study found such adverse conditions to be more characteristic of large national corporations than of

Job autonomy involves making decisions about the timing and sequence of tasks, exercising judgment, and having an impact on the outcome.

323

smaller and more local firms (Hodson and Sullivan 1985).

THE NEW INDUSTRIAL CONTRACT

Because satisfied workers are also more productive, many employers are experimenting with techniques for enhancing employee morale and increasing their participation in decision making (Simmons and Mares 1983).

At the simplest level, such innovations as *flextime* and *job sharing* give workers more options in meshing their work and family responsibilities. Flextime refers to flexibility in scheduling worktime in contrast to the standard 9 AM–5 PM, five days a week. This is especially helpful for dual-earner parents who need to arrange work hours so that child care is shared and assured. In the case of job sharing, two part-time workers take the place of one full-time employee, also sharing fringe benefits. In general, although there is great variation from one situation to another, these programs have had a modest positive effect on productivity and morale but not enough to persuade most employers to make the necessary changes (see e.g. Ralston et al. 1985).

Quality Circle. A more elaborate method of raising morale and increasing productivity involves a technique imported from Japan: the *quality circle* (QC) or teams of employees and managers who typically meet for an hour a week to discuss how to improve their work performance. Employees feel more positive about their jobs when they see that their suggestions are taken seriously, and management often realizes great savings. QCs have caught on among American companies, and can be found in some form in about half of all companies with more than 500 employees (*Psychology Today* 1986). But even though ordinary workers get to call the bosses by their first names in the QC, all the other hours of the work week are characterized by the basic relationship of industrial production: extreme inequality between employers and employees (Hill 1981).

Workplace Democracy. Indeed, some critics see QCs as "cooling out" devices, a minimal gesture of participation designed to reduce worker discontent, especially in the current era of declining real wages. These social scientists support a much more radical solution: *workplace democracy*, whereby workers become the owners (Bradley and Gelb 1983, Dahl 1985, Russell 1985). Worker-owned firms are still rare in the United States, though more common in Europe and Israel. In many cases, the workers have bought out owners looking for short-term profits or who were ready to abandon the plant in favor of moving their operations abroad or to a part of the United States with cheaper labor (Collins 1983, Rothschild and Whitt 1987, Sirianni 1987).

ESOPs. Workplace democracy is perceived as no less efficient than the system of private ownership and management. In addition, it might encourage social relationships based on cooperation and sharing, while reducing power inequality in the workplace. Short of full workplace democracy some companies have limited

Flextime refers to variations in scheduling worktime.

Job sharing involves one full-time job being performed by two part-time workers.

Quality circle are teams of employees and managers who meet to discuss how to improve their work performance.

Workplace democracy occurs when the workers become the owners.

Although current U.S. quality circles (shown here) are an adaptation of the Japanese model, the U.S. and England had introduced forms of employee participation during WW I and WW II. In the U.S. they were called "workers' councils." The Japanese adapted and perfected the concept, incorporating it into their emerging system of management after WW II. (© Stacy Pick/Stock Boston)

In **employee stock ownership plans** owners contribute company shares as part of workers' benefit packages.

employee stock ownership plans (ESOPs). Under these plans, the owners contribute shares in the company as part of the workers' benefit package; receipt of the stock is usually deferred until one leaves or retires. In the meantime, management has use of the money, plus the tax advantages of their contribution. The workers' investment in the company increases with each year of employment, but only about one-third of ESOPs allow the workers actually to vote their stock (Rosen et al. 1986).

Thus far, ESOPs have proven very successful in terms of both company performance and worker morale. Research by Rosen et al. (1986), however, found that workers did not necessarily work harder because they now owned a share in the profits; rather, the ESOP was seen as a financial benefit much like any other. And in most cases, workers did not participate in management decisions on any level. This should not, however, be taken as evidence of lack of support among workers for participatory democracy in the workplace. Sentiment in favor of worker involvement appears to be highest among employees dissatisfied with both intrinsic and extrinsic rewards from their job, and among union members, suggesting a rather broad base of support (Fenwick and Olson 1986, see also Haas 1986).

In both the United States and other countries, satisfaction with self-management programs is highest for older and better educated workers, those in nonmanual supervisory positions, and members of the dominant ethnic/race group (Taylor et al. 1987).

The most ambitious attempt to institutionalize workplace democracy is taking place today in Sweden, where the Federation of Trade Unions and the government support a Codetermination Law whereby companies place a certain proportion of their stock each year into a "wage-earners fund" controlled by the unions. In another decade or two, the most profitable businesses will be worker-owned and -managed, and by the middle of the next century, the Swedish economy will be fully socialized, in production as well as distribution, and by a gradual and peaceful process (Himmelstrand et al. 1981).

In Sweden and most of Europe, the economic interests of the working class have been represented by a "labor" or

Do They Really Do It Better in Japan?

In April 1986, NBC Television presented a *White Paper* titled "The Japan They Don't Talk About." That's the Japan that is not full of happy workers dressed in company uniforms or doing gymnastics before starting the workday. In actuality, workers with lifetime jobs, extended benefits, and company housing are but a small fraction of the Japanese labor force; they are primarily men employed by the government or a large corporation (Plath 1983). Inequality and gender discrimination characterize the Japanese economy just as they do our own. Hierarchy and bureaucratization are common. Cost of living is high; wages are relatively low. Households are extremely crowded. And the elderly are not necessarily guaranteed a comfortable old age. In short, few American workers would want to change places with their Japanese counterparts.

Nonetheless, there are some similarities. As with American workers, job autonomy has positive psychological outcomes (Naoi and Schooler 1985), and employee morale is highest when workers participate in decision making (Lincoln and Kalleberg 1985). But Japanese workers have even less power relative to management than do American workers. The emphasis on cooperation, group goals, and dependency on employer services ("paternalism") have served to coopt the workers and blunt the effort to unionize. Thus far, government and business forces have effectively limited the powers of workers' organizations.

SOURCES: James R. Lincoln and Arne L. Kalleberg, "Work Organization and Workforce Commitment: A Study of Plants and Employees in the U.S. and Japan," *American Sociological Review,* 50 (1985): 738–760; Atsushi Naoi and Carmi Schooler, "Occupational Conditions and Psychological Functioning in Japan," *American Journal of Sociology,* 90 (1985): 729–752; National Broadcasting Company, *NBC White Paper: The Japan They Don't Talk About,* Apr. 22, 1986; David W. Plath, Ed., *Work and Lifecourse in Japan.* Albany, NY: State University of New York Press, 1983.

"social democratic" political party in a system of class-based parties. In the United States, although there is tendency for capitalists to vote Republican and for manual workers to vote Democratic, the two parties embrace voters and issues across class and status lines. The interests of American workers have been largely represented by self-governing unions.

The American Labor Movement

Among industrial democracies, Japan and the United States are unique in the tameness of their labor organizations, which have been largely coopted by management. From the very beginning, the American labor movement was fiercely resisted by employers and all levels of government, to the point of extreme violence. In 1886, for example, Chicago police opened fire on a rally of workers supporting the radical idea of an eight-hour workday. Several workers were killed and dozens injured. When the police returned the next night to break up a protest demonstration in Haymarket Square, a bomb killed seven officers. Authorities arrested several union organizers for murder even though none had thrown the bomb: four were hanged; one committed suicide; and three were imprisoned. Official violence bred a similar reaction among the workers in many other parts of the country.

In general, however, the resistance of capitalists in business and government was successful in delaying the growth of a broad-based union movement, and then ensuring that the unions, when finally granted the right to organize in 1935, were cleansed of all radical elements (Aronowitz 1983, Griffen et al. 1986, Davis 1986). The result was a labor movement more opposed to "foreigners," women workers, and nonwhites than to the class-based interests of the owners. And within the movement, there was a constant tension between trade unions of skilled craft workers (American Federation of Labor) and the broad-based industrial unions (Congress of Industrial Organizations). Only in 1955 did the two groups join ranks to form the AFL-CIO. But by then, the union movement had already crested.

From a high point of 35 percent in 1945, the proportion of unionized workers in the labor force had fallen to 17.5 percent by 1985. This decline in membership can be traced to a number of broader economic trends: (1) the loss of jobs in "smoke stack" industries such as automobile manufacture and steel milling where unionization had been most successful (Kochan 1985); (2) lack of interest, until recently, in organizing service industries with large numbers of women and black employees (Davis 1986); (3) the success of employer-sponsored welfare plans in blunting unionization (Cornfield 1986); and (4) the actuality and threat of relocating to states and countries without strong labor organizations (Jaffee 1986).

The example of southern textile work-

Early resistance of capitalists and the government to a broad-based union movement in the U.S. was harsh and often violent, as you can see in this wood engraving of the Haymarket Riot in Chicago. Is the relationship between business, government, and labor different today? (© The Bettmann Archive. Drawing by T. de Thulstrup after H. Jeanneret)

ers illustrates many of these factors. Over the past fifteen years, textile mills have been moved from the highly unionized northeastern states to the southern states where unions are weak. Employers are very paternalistic, providing a range of services and appealing to the local patriotism of employees. As a result, workers perceive their self-interest to be the same as management's; and, indeed, their continued employment depends on the health of the company. The most loyal (anti-union) are the better-paid employees with strong local roots. Support for unionizing, in contrast, is strongest among blacks and less-skilled workers who can be easily replaced. Thus, it does not appear that unions will have an easy time organizing the southern textile mills (McDonald and Clelland 1984, Leiter 1986).

Always under attack from management and conservative politicians, the union movement has also been severely criticized from the left for its failure to become a class-based political force in opposition to capitalist control of the society. In this view, not only have union leaders "sold out" to the establishment in order to achieve personal respectability and power (as advisors to presidents, for example) but those who have profited most from unionization—high-skill blue-collar white males—have turned their backs on other workers and on the original goals of the union movement: to improve the status of all workers, reduce inequality throughout the society, and bring democracy to the workplace.

The strength of a labor movement also depends on the willingness of unions to support one another—to engage in sympathy strikes or to refuse to cross a picket line. But American labor today has failed to raise the principle of "worker solidarity" above that of "every union for itself," as seen in the example of the Professional Air Traffic Controllers Association (PATCO) strike of 1981 and its consequences described by Arthur Shostak.

A final criticism of the union movement involves the concept of "goal displacement" (see Chapter 4). Union organizations have themselves become entrenched bureaucracies in which the goal of maintaining the organization has displaced that of serving members. Unlike the past, when union leaders came up from the ranks and had little formal education, today's leadership is as likely as not to come from a comfortable middle-class background, to be college educated, and to earn an income comparable to management personnel. Periodically, rank-and-file members attempt to reform the leadership and direction of their unions. Although such efforts rarely succeed against the joint power of entrenched union officials and their allies among the employers, they do contain the seeds of a more democratic and responsive unionism that could revitalize the entire movement (Nyden 1984).

Yet for all their faults, the unions have had a powerful positive effect on the status of all American workers (Freeman and Medoff 1984). Among the achievements for which organized labor can take credit are the eight-hour day and five-day workweek; health and pension benefits; sick leave and unemployment insurance; the minimum wage; and safer and more sanitary workplaces—none of which were obtained without an extended struggle with capitalists who claimed that the free market in labor would be compromised. And for all their failures, the unions were—and perhaps still are—the only organized force for economic democracy in our society. In philosophy, if not always in action, the unions represent the interests of the great mass of wage earners against the far more powerful forces of industrial capitalism.

But with today's decline in union power, workers are losing ground in wage settlements and fringe benefits; in many cases they are actually agreeing to "givebacks" of previously gained advantages. Even so, union members fare much better than nonunion workers in similar industries. In 1985, for example, the average weekly wages of unionized workers was $444 in contrast to $325 for nonunion workers.

THE FUTURE OF AMERICAN UNIONS

If the union movement is to hold its own and possibly expand, its leaders must find a way to reach previously nonunionized populations: both high- and low-skill service workers, managers, professionals, part-timers, and pink-collar employees. It must also adapt to a labor force that is younger, more educated, less likely to be married, and far more likely to be female than in the past. Forty percent are dual-earner couples and only 10 percent are married men with non-working wives.

Lending Labor a Hand

Arthur B. Shostak

A professor of sociology at Drexel University, Art Shostak enjoys serving as a consultant to the major unions, a program evaluator, a labor educator, a futurist, and a public speaker (he gave 44 commissioned speeches in 1986). His 13 books include The Air Controllers' Controversy, Blue-Collar Stress, Sociology and Student Life, Our Sociological Eye, *and* Modern Social Reforms.

Going back to 1954 when I began my pursuit of a B.S. degree in industrial and labor relations, and continuing on through my '58-'61 Ph.D. graduate program in industrial sociology, I have always sought effective ways of helping organized labor. This is a cause my father briefly served during the Depression when he was an organizer of fellow bread truck drivers. His brother also contributed as a lifelong activist in the New York City teachers union. And even now one of my brothers is an activist in the AAUP/AFT local of college professors at the University of Pittsburgh.

Since becoming an applied sociologist in 1961, I have found five ways of lending a (sociological) hand: (1) As a *teacher* I enjoy trading insights into possible reforms of work with unionists who take my courses at the AFL-CIO's George Meany Center for Labor Studies (Silver Spring, Md.); (2) as a *public speaker* I enjoy popularizing insights from sociology for union-sponsored conferences, workshops, and the like; (3) as a *researcher* I do my best to provide unions with clear and timely answers to pressing sociological questions about childcare centers, drug rehab designs, and so on; (4) as a *writer* I try to find a reading audience among rank-and-filers, union leaders, and staffers, for reform-advocating monographs like *Robust

Unionism, Blue-Collar Stress,* and *Blue-Collar Life,* along with volumes I co-author with unionists, such as *The Air Controllers' Controversy,* and my current writing project, *The Air Controllers' Comeback.*

In my fifth role, that of *survey researcher,* I generally combine the other four, and thereby enjoy myself all the more. For example, in 1980 when PATCO, the union of air traffic controllers, asked me to help clarify what underlay the unprecedented discontent of their 14,000 members, I devised five surveys for use at three month intervals. After collecting the data I explained my computer-based findings to key PATCO activists. When it came time for the union to capitulate or strike, I reported my findings indicating that 78 percent of the respondents had said they would "hit the bricks," (that is, strike) a survey response off by only three percent from the actual turnout. (During the ill-fated strike I reviewed my survey findings as a speaker at various PATCO rallies, and began the scores of interviews that resulted three years later in my co-authored book on this subject.)

Now, when I am frequently asked by students like yourselves why I think this particular social movement is worth all the help sociologists can give it, I dwell on two sets of personal convictions, the first focused on the workplace; the second, outside of it.

Where the workplace is concerned, I believe we will probably always have unions, as we will always have employers distracted from sensitive personnel relations by greed, competition, or callousness. I also believe shop stewards and the grievance process are indispensable buffers between a lone worker and an impersonal managerial powerhouse. And I believe locals are obliged to adequately service members by the threat of a costly decertification

challenge or a raid from a rival labor organization.

Outside of the workplace, I believe labor makes a critical contribution by "bird dogging" every relevant governmental agency (e.g., OSHA–Occupational Safety and Health Administration, the Department of Labor, etc.). I also believe labor helps with its efforts to raise workplace standards in developing nations. And I believe labor's sustained political effort on behalf of the have-nots and the lower middle class (today's "working class") helps provide an indispensable element—an elevating conscience and vision—in our social and economic order.

None of which is to deny the great distance labor still has to go to set its own house in order. Like many of you my heart aches when I read or watch media coverage of labor's various shortcomings. Far too few women and minorities hold powerful office and far too many discouraged bureaucrats keep unions from trying innovations that might revive both sagging morale and membership. Organized crime has too much influence (as it does in the business world), and decades of antagonistic relations undermine efforts at forging new labor-management cooperation on behalf of urgently needed productivity gains. Working as I do, however, on the inside, and working as I have, over a 25-year period, I am more encouraged than ever by the commitment to reform by shop-floor activists and labor leaders alike.

When PATCO, for example, was destroyed in 1981 by the firing of 70 percent of the air controller workforce, many commentators thought this sounded the death knell of the modern labor movement. You and I were told that PATCO replacements would never unionize, as they were the "new" breed of worker—anti-union, self-centered, career-protecting "yuppies." We were told that management would never make the same mistakes twice; that is, it would never repeat the poor personnel practices that had given PATCO such a loyal following prior to the '81 strike. Above all, labor organizers could not mount a classy, modern, and appealing enough organizing campaign to ever win a

majority vote of the post-'81 controllers.

Given the first law of sociology, "things are seldom what they seem to be," the outcome in June of 1987 should have come as little surprise: With an extraordinarily high turnout of 84 percent, the new union of air traffic controllers—one I now hope to serve, as in the past, as a survey

researcher—received a greater than two-to-one margin of victory (70 to 30 percent). What antagonists had heralded as a death knell in '81 appears, just a few years later, to be a symbol of recovery and renewal, a symbol of labor's new possibilities in a post-industrial America . . . and another exciting invitation to sociologists to lend a hand.

Traditional goals and slogans will have to be revised. Wages and job security may be less important than working conditions and benefit packages. New strategies for organizing must also be devised in order to attract white-collar workers who may not think themselves similar to people who carry lunch boxes rather than briefcases to work. Technology can be used to labor's advantage, as can the movement toward power sharing (Early and Wilson 1986, Kuttner 1986). And there *are* signs of revival. Teachers' unions have grown into a major component of the labor movement. Other white-collar workers, not quite ready to consider themselves unionized, are forming "professional associations" to protect their interests. The decrease in union membership appears to have leveled off, but the fate of the American labor movement today may rest in the hands of working women.

Organizing Women Workers. Historically, organized labor in America has been a stronghold of white male fellowship, even though large numbers of working-class girls and women were essential to its growth and ultimate success (Schofield 1983, Strom 1983, Milkman 1985). As early as 1824, female factory employees in Pawtucket, R.I., staged an organized protest against management attempts to lengthen the workday to over twelve hours. Dozens of similar strikes occurred throughout the industrializing northeast in the following decades. Women workers in textile mills and garment sweatshops were among the most militant union supporters in the early years of this century. Women's auxiliaries and groups of workers' wives pro-

vided essential support during many of the landmark strikes of American labor history. Remarkable individual women overcame the barriers of class and gender to become leaders in the cause of labor: Lavinia Wright, Sarah Bagley, "Mother" Jones, Lucy Parker, Elizabeth Gurley Flynn, Mary McLeod Bethune, and Fannie

Mary Harris (1830–1930), otherwise known as "Mother Jones," was an orator, union organizer, and basic "hellraiser" who focused on overall union issues, not just those related to women. Her motto: "Sit down and read. Educate yourself for the coming conflict." (© UPI/Bettmann News Photos)

Sellins among others; several were killed and others jailed for their union activities (O'Sullivan and Gallick 1975).

There were also organizations of reform-minded middle-class women who supported working women's call for higher wages, lower hours, safety and sanitation features, and the right to unionize. Beginning in the 1850s, the settlement house movement, led by Jane Addams and Lillian Wald, provided social services and education to working people and their families.

By the 1950s, however, the American labor movement had become increasingly conservative, and despite the large numbers of women and blacks employed in wartime defense industries, the union leadership remained exclusively white and male, and dominated by representatives of skilled trades: highly patriotic, anti-communist, and traditional on social issues such as women's rights. But it is now precisely those fields in which women predominate that offer the best chance for reversing the decline in union strength. Although it had been commonly assumed that women workers did not want to be unionized, recent research by women scholars suggests that female workers are not passive pawns of employers. They are aware of gender and class exploitation, and they resist victimization as best they can, in offices and on shop floors (Goldberg 1983, Glenn and Feldberg 1984, Lamphere 1985, Ferree 1987).

Indeed, the number of union women is currently increasing at a faster rate than for men. Both here and abroad, unions are beginning to recognize the special concerns of women workers (Cook et al. 1984). Admitting women to leadership positions, however, lags far behind their representation in the unionized labor force. Only in 1987 was a third woman added to the thirty-five-member executive council of the AFL-CIO.

As with men, unionized women enjoy higher wages and greater job security than their nonunion counterparts. In fact, the difference in wages between unionized and nonunionized women workers—34 percent—is greater than between unionized and nonunionized men—21 percent (Sacks 1985). Nonetheless, as long as employed women continue to have primary responsibility for homemaking and child care, often as sole parent, their interests will diverge from those of male workers.

Labor Segmentation

While organized labor has been successful in raising the status of some workers, it has generally failed to reduce inequality within the working class. A major source of *intra*class inequality is the stratification of the economy itself; there are broad differences between "core" and "peripheral" industries. The *core sector* consists of major industries (e.g. heavy manufacturing, chemicals) characterized by large investments in plants and equipment, unionized labor force, monopolies, and high profits. The *periphery,* in contrast, is composed of smaller, relatively competitive low-profit firms (e.g. fast-food shops, clothing manufacture), with a heavy investment in low-pay manual workers (typically nonunion). In general, owners and workers in the core sector enjoy greater political power than those at the periphery (Apostle et al. 1986).

This *dual economy* is complemented by a *split* or *segmented labor market,* differentiated by race and gender. Core workers are disproportionately drawn from a labor pool of white males, while peripheral employers draw heavily on women and low-status minority populations. People with similar years of education and training will receive very different wage returns depending on where they are employed (Tolbert et al. 1980, Kaufman 1986). Thus, the gender and race wage gaps noted in Chapter 7 are a product of labor-force location over and above any individual work-related traits.

The dual economy/segmented labor-market model has been subject to a great deal of modification by more recent analyses of inequality within the working class. The idea of two sectors may be very helpful in isolating firms at the two extremes, but is far less useful for explaining wage and promotion differences among workers in the great majority of firms that have mixed characteristics (Hodson 1983). Within the core and periphery, businesses can vary in terms of organizational complexity (how large, how many layers of management, the technological base) and by their degree of control over the market of their type of goods or service (Baron and Bielby 1984). These differences will affect the chances of an employee's shifting jobs or moving upward in a particular type of firm (Carroll and Mayer 1986).

The **core sector** consists of major industries, large investments in plants and equipment, unionized labor, monopolies, and high profits.

The **periphery** consists of smaller, competitive, low-profit firms employing low-pay, nonunion manual workers.

Dual economy refers to the existence of two separate types of employing firms: core and peripheral.

The **split** or **segmented labor market** is differentiated by race and gender, core workers being primarily white males and peripheral workers being primarily women and minorities.

Another important variable is the diversity of firms within any sector: the greater the diversity, the greater the chances for people with very different skills to find a place and to prosper. Low diversity rewards a limited set of skills so that only some workers succeed, while others fail (Hannon 1986). Using this theory to explain why income inequality within the black population is more extreme than for other minority populations, Hannon (1986) notes the very low range of diversity of businesses in black communities.

One area in which segmentation theory can be expanded, however, relates to the international economy, namely the exchanges between industrialized nations and developing countries in Asia, Africa, and South and Central America—the *Third World*. The industrialized nations are the core and the Third World the periphery in terms of the flow of investment and manufacturing jobs (Dixon and Jonas 1982). In this case, though, some workers in the core will lose their jobs and wage advantages, as seen in the decline of American steel and automobile manufac-

turing in the 1980s. The trend toward "offshore" production, in this view, will lead to lower standards of living for workers in industrialized economies while improving only slightly the income of Third World workers.

Employment and Unemployment

Employment and unemployment rates also reflect the dual economy as well as such other structural factors as the person's occupational status and the state of the overall economy (Schervish 1983). In the event of business-cycle recessions and unemployment, the people most vulnerable to losing jobs and remaining unemployed are those in low-skill positions in highly competitive industries—namely women and blacks (Cummings 1987). These workers compose a "reserve army" of employees who can be shuttled in and out of the labor force as required by employers seeking to minimize their fixed labor costs (Bose, Feldberg and Sokoloff 1987).

This is nothing new; unemployment has been a fixture of working people's lives since the beginning of industrialism in America (Keyssar 1986). Only since the 1930s have there been even minimal forms of assistance to the involuntarily unemployed. With the exception of a few very short periods of recession, unemployment rates between 1945 and 1975 have been under 6 percent. In the recession of 1975 the rate climbed to over 9 percent, dropped to under 6 percent in 1979, and then, shot up to a high of 9.5 percent in 1982–1983. It has remained between 6 and 7 percent even during the recovery period. See Figure 12-5.

JOBLESSNESS

The official unemployment rate, however, seriously underestimates *joblessness.* It does not take into account (1) the people who have become so discouraged with the job search that they have stopped trying, or (2) those who have had to settle for part-time employment. When these workers are added to the officially unemployed (those seeking work) the rate is roughly doubled, or between 14 and 15 percent of the civilian labor force (Morehouse and Dembo 1986).

Increasingly, American multinational companies have established manufacturing plants in Third World countries with substantial supplies of workers whose wages are a fraction of U.S. wages. This results in increased domestic unemployment, the closing of American plants and offices, and increased profits for multinational companies. Here, Malaysian women fabricate computer chips for a multinational corporation. (© Chuck O'Rear/Woodfin Camp and Associates)

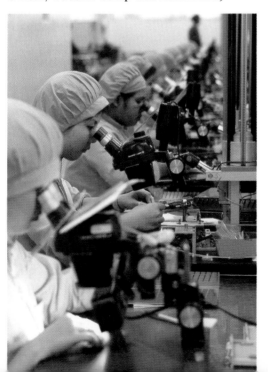

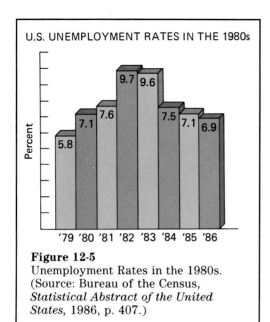

Figure 12-5
Unemployment Rates in the 1980s.
(Source: Bureau of the Census,
*Statistical Abstract of the United
States*, 1986, p. 407.)

who wish to be employed has become an accepted fact-of-life in our society, as there has been little public outrage or political fall-out as a result (Hershey 1986). The unemployment rate has remained high because the number of new jobs has been lower than the number of people entering the labor force (the last of the baby boomers). In addition, the shift to a service economy limits job growth, especially full-time positions. Future trends in employment and unemployment will reflect the growth and decline of the various economic sectors. Table 12-1 details projected job opportunities. See page 315.

PREMATURE RETIREMENT

Another factor in swelling the unemployment rate is the difficulty faced by older blue-collar workers, age fifty-five to sixty-four, in securing new employment once their plants have closed and their jobs moved offshore (Greenhouse 1986). For example, of the eleven million American workers who lost jobs because of plant relocation or shutdown between 1979 and 1980, only 60 percent found new jobs by 1985, mostly in the service sector, and the great majority of these workers were earning less than 80 percent of their previous wages (Noble 1986).

The premature retirement of many older male workers has greatly changed the age structure of the labor force over the past two decades, as seen in Table 12-2.

As labor-force participation rates of men age twenty-five and over have declined,

The official unemployment rate is calculated from a sample of 59,000 households contacted each month by the Bureau of Labor Statistics, but the Bureau also conducts a monthly survey of 250,000 business firms which typically reports a smaller number of employed persons because it does not count people on strike. Neither survey reaches the mass of inner-city or rural unemployed or underemployed. In addition, the official rate excludes anyone who worked for more than one hour for wages in a given month.

Regardless of how or what is calculated, the current historically high post-recession proportion of people without jobs

TABLE 12-2   Labor force participation rates by age and sex, 1965 and 1986*

	Men			Women		
Age Group	1965	Sept. 1986	Percent Change	1965	Sept. 1986	Percent Change
16–19	53.8%	57.6%	+7.1%	38.0%	52.1%	+37.1%
20–24	85.8	86.2	+0.5	49.9	72.7	+45.7
25–34	97.2	94.4	−2.9	38.5	71.7	+86.2
35–44	97.3	94.8	−2.6	46.1	73.8	+60.1
45–54	95.6	91.0	−4.8	50.9	66.3	+30.3
55–64	84.6	67.2	−20.6	41.1	42.3	+2.9
65 and older	27.9	15.1	−45.9	10.0	7.7	−23.0

SOURCE: *New York Times*, 1986.

*The rate for each group is the number of people in the labor force in that group—that is, those employed and unemployed who have looked for work in the past four weeks—as a percent of the civilian noninstitutionalized population in that group.

those for women in all but the oldest age groups have risen dramatically, leading to increasing convergence in the work experience of men and women.

PLANT CLOSINGS

Despite the obvious hardships that plant closings cause for workers and their families, there has been little organized resistance and even less social-science attention, suggesting the power of business interests to define the situation in strictly economic terms (McDonald 1985). Research money is available for studies of how social supports can help relieve the emotional damage of unemployment (Caplan et al. 1986), but apparently not for research on organizing local communities to resist the corporations. So long as most Americans are led to believe that workers are being displaced by the irresistible forces of new technology, they will fail to recognize the true causes: the 1982–1983 recession, the flight of capital to overseas production, poor management, and the drive for short-term profits (Salzman 1985).

YOUTH UNEMPLOYMENT

As difficult as it is for established workers to lose their jobs and have to settle for lower-status employment, the situation of young job seekers is even more bleak. For youth who do not attend college, employment is crucial to maturation, to becoming

PERCENT UNEMPLOYMENT, MALES AGE 18-24, BY RACE: 1972-1985

BLACKS

WHITES

40
30
20
10

'72 '74 '76 '78 '80 '82 '84 '85

Figure 12-6
Source: *The New York Times*, July 20, 1986, Sect. 3, p. 2.

self-supporting and to enjoying a stable family life. Unfortunately, teenage unemployment rates are roughly three times as high as those for adults, and the difference is greatest for black youth. In 1985, while the economy was thought to be fully recovered from the 1982–1983 recession, fewer than four in ten black men age eighteen to nineteen, and only six in ten age twenty to twenty-four were employed. See Figure 12-6.

From their broad-based and in-depth study of inner-city black males in Boston, Chicago, and Philadelphia, Freeman and Holzer (1986) found that there is no single cause or answer to this problem. The young men were as serious about seeking jobs as their white counterparts, but they

Studies of black inner-city youth indicate that the young men are as serious about getting jobs as their white counterparts, but fewer jobs exist and those that do, pay lower wages. Here representatives of Philadelphia's "Crisis Intervention Network" sign up teens for jobs. (© Frances M. Cox/ Stock Boston)

also wanted the same level of pay as white youth and the same opportunity for upward mobility. The real problem was that such jobs were very few and far between in the local area, and many of the young men did not have the means to travel great distances to look for or maintain a job. In comparison to a limited job market, the rewards of street crime are higher and immediate.

Nonetheless, many of these young men continued to fight the odds and to find work that promised some advancement. These youngsters were more likely than the unemployed to come from families in which parents were employed, who did not live in public-housing projects, and who also attended church once a week or more (see also Williams and Kornblum 1985). The researchers note that the solution to black teenage unemployment will involve more than simply offering low-level jobs at below-minimum wages as has been proposed by conservative economists. Much else is needed: stable families, decent housing, adequate schooling, strong community organizations, control of street crime, and containment of the drug culture.

The population of hardcore unemployed also includes many white ethnic and Hispanic youths, female as well as male. But longitudinal data on a representative sample of 12,000 young people who were fourteen to twenty-two in 1979 shows that the problems of black males are far more grave and extensive than for the others (Borus 1984). Racial differences in school leaving and college attendance, the researchers note, are due largely to the greater likelihood of growing up in poverty and in a single-parent household, of receiving little encouragement to remain in school, and of being a teenage parent. These are the conditions that produce "disconnected youth" who may never be able to hold jobs or provide for families (Education Commission of the States 1985). Their problems will ultimately add to the societal burden of crime control, health care, deteriorating urban environments, and generalized fear and racial conflict.

Unemployment not only reduces the national product and adds to the costs of social-welfare programs but takes its toll on the unemployed and their families. According to Brenner (1982), each 1 percent increase in unemployment increases our suicide rate by 4 to 5 percent, the homicide rate by 5 to 6 percent, admissions to mental hospitals by 3 to 4 percent, and infant deaths by 5 to 6 percent. Moreover, because unemployed workers also lose their medical-insurance coverage and cannot afford to continue their policies as individuals, many health needs go unmet.

Other researchers (House 1981, Liem and Rayman 1982) have reported a range of physical and emotional problems among the unemployed, including anxiety, insomnia, depression, ulcers, alcoholism, high blood pressure, and family violence. These problems have been clearly identified as being the consequences and not the causes of unemployment.

Corporate Life

CORPORATE POWER

The sociology of economic systems also embraces the study of corporations as social structures, as well as the life-styles of business elites (see also Chapter 7). The organizational characteristics that affect mobility opportunities for white-collar employees have already been noted: size, complexity, and share of market power. We have also discussed (Chapters 8 and 10) the barriers to reaching the highest levels of corporate power experienced by women, blacks, and Hispanics. And we have mentioned the successes of the American business community in blocking the growth of an oppositional union movement. Corporate elites have also been able to blunt the full effect of laws designed to curb their freedom, as in the case of anti-trust legislation and the petroleum industry (Coleman 1985).

While the American public may always have been somewhat mistrustful of big business, at no time has corporate power been seriously challenged, even during the reform period of the 1930s following the collapse of the stock market and banking system. Today, if anything, corporate power is as dominant as ever, although public confidence in business honesty is quite low. In a 1986 poll, before the "insider trading" scandals, only 24 percent of respondents thought that moral and ethical standards were higher in big corporations than in the federal government (Clymer 1986). In the same poll, most people felt that corporations had failed to help

Ownership in American corporations is spread among 43 million people. Most shares, however, are held by other corporations, banks, and conglomerates. Annual meetings, such as the one shown here, where management reports to shareholders and voting occurs, do not usually provide a true picture of the nature of corporate power. (© William Strode/Woodfin Camp and Associates)

local communities, protect the environment, or see to it that their executives behave legally. Nevertheless, a majority (higher among men and whites) also thought that it was still possible for anyone to work hard in business and become rich, and that personal ability was the key to success. Apparently, faith in the work ethic overrides negative feelings toward big business.

Corporations have shown a remarkable ability to adapt to broad changes in the economic system. While specific firms have risen or fallen as the economy moved through the phases of early, mature, and advanced capitalism, the strength of the business sector as a whole has not diminished. Business elites have been able to find new opportunities for profit, using the money and power already accumulated. Indeed, what at first might appear to have been a major threat to company executives, a "hostile takeover" by outside investors, has typically been turned into an opportunity to make an enormous personal profit—the "golden parachute" that cushions their fall (Hirsch 1986).

CORPORATIONS AND THE COMMUNITY

With the growth of conglomerates and multinationals, and the emphasis today on short-term profits through mergers and takeovers, the links between a large national corporation and the local communities in which its plants and offices are located have become very thin. The owners do not live in the community and may never even have seen it; the plant or office building is simply a piece of property on the company's books to be kept or sold in order to enhance the value of the corporation's stock. As noted earlier in this chapter, the threat of closing or relocating can be used to get workers to agree to give back previously won raises and benefits.

CORPORATE STRUCTURE

The American labor force is spread over close to fifteen million business firms. More than ten million of these firms have only one owner and typically employ fewer than twenty people. Over 1.6 million are owned by two or more partners. But it is the three million *corporations* that compose the bulk of the labor force and the business assets of the society. The 100 largest manufacturing corporations in the United States today account for half of all manufacturing assets in our economy, and the 200 largest account for over 61 percent (*Statistical Abstract, 1986:* 524).

A corporation is a formal organization (see Chapter 4) that is, a legal entity, or actor, in its own right (Coleman 1986). Corporations can enter into contracts, accumulate assets, get into debt, and go bankrupt without its members (owners, managers, or employees) being held personally responsible. Ownership in corporations is widely held: 43 million people own shares in one or more American corporations. Although these data suggest that income from corporate profit is spread across the stratification system, the great majority of stockholders are in the upper portion of the SES hierarchy. Two-thirds of shareowners are people with some col-

Corporations are formal organizations that are legal actors in their own right.

335

lege education, and 60 percent are in the higher-income brackets (*Statistical Abstract, 1986:* 509). Most shares, however, are held by other corporations, including banks and conglomerates.

Corporate power, as noted earlier in this chapter, is also concentrated through the device of *interlocking directorates.* The interlocks not only enhance the power of individuals, but also give manufacturing corporations control over the other resources necessary for its product (Burt 1983, Mintz and Schwartz 1985). These interlocks add to the solidarity of both organizational giants and the class interests of those who own and manage the corporations (Palmer et al. 1986). Although a crucial characteristic of the large corporation in a capitalist economy is the separation between ownership (stockholders) and management (the executives who run the corporation), the difference does not have much effect on the distribution of wealth and power in our economic system.

Corporations often seek to soften their public image by making charitable contributions and supporting local causes, but these gifts amount, on average, to less than 1 percent of income before taxes (*Statistical Abstract, 1986:* 539). One fascinating exception to this average is the relatively high level of charitable giving by companies with headquarters in St. Paul/Minneapolis—over 5 percent of pretax income. This unusual level of charitable giving prompted an in-depth study of the corporate culture of the twin cities by Joseph Galaskiewicz (1985), who found that the basic motivation was *not* to buy the goodwill of local residents or of the consumers of the companies' products, but, rather, to maintain a pecking-order of prestige within the local business community—a form of "corporate potlatch" (Padgett 1986). In other words, companies competed to do good deeds in order to establish or preserve their reputations in the eyes of other corporate managers.

Corporate Cultures. There is a growing body of theory and research on the internal workings of corporations, showing how the particular structure of the firm has a clear and direct effect on the actions of its employees. For example, Rosabeth Moss Kanter (1977) showed how the nature of the job accounted for most of the

differences in motivation and behavior between women and men workers. Any person whose job is closely supervised, with no mobility ladder, will spend a lot of time around the water cooler and leave on the stroke of five o'clock. It just happens that women are more likely than men to have these kinds of jobs. When men have jobs with the same characteristics, they behave in much the same fashion as women in similar occupations.

Another line of research in the sociology of complex organizations looks to characteristics of the firms and their place in the entire market structure to explain different rates of advancement for employees (See Chapter 7). Other sociologists have examined broader historical trends in the relationship between organizations and their economic and societal environments. In one recent study, Fligstein (1987) shows how the top leadership in the largest American corporations has undergone important change in this century. Up to World War II, corporation presidents were most likely to be the individuals who founded the company or who came from the manufacturing division. In the middle decades of the century, the top slots were occupied by people from the sales and marketing departments, and most recently, it is the financial experts who have risen to the highest positions. These shifts reflect major changes in the goals of firms, away from an emphasis on products and the marketplace to the current trend toward increasing profits through acquisitions, mergers, buyouts, takeovers, and other financial schemes.

Corporations are also studied by anthropologists in the same way as any simple society. Concepts such as culture, norms, socialization, rituals, and adaptation to the environment can be applied to what goes on within the bounded world of the business firm. For example, Reynolds (1987) has written a case study of a firm that failed even though it was in the forefront of electronic engineering; the cause, he discovered, was in the lack of fit between the company's declared purpose and procedures ("ideal culture") and the actual way in which everyday business was conducted ("real culture"). Top managers came to believe their own myths about the corporate culture of openness and customer orientation while ignoring the reality that their own rules were made in

Interlocking directorates occur when the same individuals serve on the board of directors of several giant corporations.

private and designed to make a profit at any cost. Eventually, employees withdrew their loyalty and the entire enterprise went bankrupt.

In this brief overview, we have suggested how the basic sociological perspective—a focus on social structure and on context—can illuminate the behavior of corporations as well as that of the role incumbents within them.

Summary

In this chapter, we examine the origins and historical development of economic systems—the group's adaptations to their environment. Economic activities embrace the production, distribution, and consumption of goods and services. Modern industrial societies are increasingly characterized by the growth of the service sector relative to primary production and to manufacturing.

Contemporary economic systems can be arrayed along a continuum representing the degree to which market forces are under public control. At one extreme, free-enterprise capitalism assumes maximum freedom for privately owned enterprises operated for profit. At the other extreme, socialist economies involve public ownership of the means of production and distribution on the basis of citizenship. Most modern economies fall somewhere between the polar types, attempting to blend the efficiency of capitalism with the socially stabilizing effects of equitable distribution.

Modern economies are also characterized by a complex division of labor and "deskilling" of work that some critics believe leads to widespread feelings of alienation, especially among today's better-educated pool of workers. Nonetheless, worker satisfaction remains high as many people shift from expecting intrinsic rewards from their labor to seeing the job as a means of earning income that can then be spent on things that bring pleasure. A number of firms are experimenting with techniques for enhancing worker morale and productivity, from flexible work schedules to employee-ownership plans. The long-range effects of such programs are still unknown.

The American labor movement, unlike its European counterparts, has not established itself as an oppositional force to capitalism. This is due in part to the unique history of American labor and the enormous power of the business establishment. The unions today represent less than one-fifth of the work force, as non-unionized service jobs replace the high-pay unionized sectors of the economy. The future of the unions depends on attracting white- and blue-collar service workers, who have traditionally been difficult to organize. Women workers are probably the most promising resource for a revitalized unionism.

Differentials in pay and career ladders among workers are related to their location in the dual economy and segmented labor market, and most particularly to the type of firm in which they are employed. In general, inequality, especially on the basis of race and gender, is reinforced by the structural characteristics of industries and firms.

The very likelihood of being employed or unemployed is related to these structural factors. The profit-making sector relies on a "reserve army" of low-wage employees who can be hired when times are good and readily dropped in periods of recession. In our society today, the unemployment rate has remained relatively high even after most sectors recovered from the 1982–1983 recession. In addition, another 7 to 10 percent of the work force are without jobs because they have stopped looking, accepted early retirement, or have found part-time employment. Unemployment is especially high among youths age sixteen to twenty-four, reaching to over half of black teenagers. The eventual costs to the society in unstable families, health problems, and crime will be very high.

The chapter closes with a look at the other end of the economic spectrum—the corporate world of power and privilege. Decisions made on the basis of short-term profit to stockholders and corporate executives have direct impact on the viability of local communities and on the life chances of ordinary workers. We review recent research on the corporation as a social actor. Ownership and management remain closely linked to the SES hierarchy, while corporate power becomes increasingly concentrated. Corporations also have a structure and culture that affect employees' behaviors and feelings, as well as their chances for upward mobility.

Suggested Readings

ARONOWITZ, STANLEY. *Working Class Hero: A New Strategy for Labor.* New York: Pilgrim Press, 1983. Far-reaching analysis of the problems of declining membership and power on the part of American unions, their reaction to past industrialism, and a call for a new political alliance between labor and other forces of progressivism and egalitarianism.

BLUESTONE, BARRY, and BENNETT HARRISON. *The Deindustrialization of America.* New York: Basic Books, 1982. A detailed examination of shifts in the American economy as traditional industries decline in importance.

BURT, RONALD S. *Corporate Profits and Cooptation: Networks of Market Constraints and Directorate Ties in the American Economy.* New York: Academic Press, 1987. A structural analysis of economic transaction among monopoly industrial sectors and its influences upon the behavior of corporate leaders.

DEAL, TERRENCE E., and ALLAN S. KENNEDY. *Corporate Cultures: The Rites and Rituals of Corporate Life.* Reading, MA: Addison-Wesley Publishing Co., 1982. An examination of the values, rites, and rituals of corporate life.

KILMON, RALPH, MARY J. SAXTON and RAY SERPA, eds. *Gaining Control of the Corporate Culture.* San Francisco: Jossey-Bass, 1985. This book examines the need for change within corporations and identifies the cultural behavior and influences that contribute to organizational change.

PIORE, MICHAEL J., and CHARLES F. SABEL. *The Second Industrial Divide: Possibilities for Prosperity.* New York: Basic Books, 1984. An important contribution to the industrial policy debate, focusing on a move away from mass-production industries toward more flexible manufacturing methods.

RITZER, GEORGE, and DAVID WALCZAK. *Working: Conflicts and Change.* 3d. ed. Englewood Cliffs, NJ: Prentice-Hall, 1986. An examination of the patterns of conflict within the workplace.

SANTOS, RICHARD. *Hispanic Youth: Emerging Workers.* New York: Praeger, 1985. A timely examination of the problems and prospects for the employment of Hispanic youth. Suggestions for policy implementation are included.

SHERMAN, BARRIE. *The New Revolution: The Impact of Computers on Society.* New York: John Wiley & Sons, 1985. An interesting examination of the role of computers in society and its potential for control.

STANDOHAR, PAUL D. *The Sports Industry and Collective Bargaining.* Ithaca, NY: ILR Press, 1986. An interesting examination of sports as a business. It provides information on contract bargaining, salary negotiation, and free agency.

STINCHCOMBE, ARTHUR L. *Economic Sociology.* New York: Academic Press, 1983. A comparative analysis of ecology, organization, technology, population, and class using herding, agrarian, and industrial economies.

13

The Political System: Power, Politics, and Militarism

P OWER, as defined by Max Weber, is the probability of realizing one's own goals even against the opposition of others. At the societal level, from a functional perspective, power is the ability to govern and maintain order within the group. From the conflict perspective, power is typically analyzed in terms of the "capacity of a social class to realize its objectives" (Poulantzas 1973). Power is a crucial aspect of relationships between people and among groups. Political sociologists study the dynamics of power: Who rules, how is that rule justified, and what are its consequences?

Power

AUTHORITY: TRADITIONAL, CHARISMATIC, AND LEGAL-RATIONAL

By definition, power is a resource that is unevenly distributed among members of a group or among competing groups within any given society. Sociologists are most interested in power that is *legitimated,* that is, exercised with the consent of the governed or in accordance with the norms.

Legitimated power is exercised with the consent of the governed or in accordance with norms.

Authority is legitimated power.

Traditional authority is based on habit and acceptance of the group's customs.

Charismatic authority is based on some extraordinary quality of the leader or the leader's ideas.

Legal-rational authority is based on laws that limit the power of office holders.

Legitimated power is called *authority,* and Max Weber (1922/1958) distinguished three bases of authority: traditional, charismatic, and legal-rational.

Traditional authority is based on force of habit and absolute acceptance of the customs of the group. Weber singled out patriarchy—the rule of men as fathers, husbands, lords, monarchs, and religious leaders—as the ideal form of traditional authority. As there are few restraints on traditional leaders, Weber regarded this type of power as basically irrational because it was not grounded in any special talent for the task or in the reasoned agreement of the powerless.

Charismatic authority is based on some extraordinary quality of the leader or the leader's ideas (*charisma* means "gift"). An emotional bond is forged between the charismatic figure and the followers who believe in the leader's superhuman characteristics and who are willing to follow commands without question (Willner 1984). Among the historical figures with charismatic qualities are such founders of world religions as Moses, Jesus, Muhammad, and Lord Krishna. In this century, most charismatic leaders have also been political leaders—Vladimir Lenin, Franklin Roosevelt, Adolph Hitler, Winston Churchill, George Wallace, Fidel Castro, Charles de Gaulle, and John Kennedy—along with two dominating religious figures: Mahatma Gandhi and Martin Luther King, Jr. (Schweitzer 1984). With a few exceptions—the faith healer Aimee Semple McPherson and Argentina's Evita Peron, for example—women are rarely accepted as leaders to follow without question.

Yet because charismatic authority is based on a unique gift, and because followers act out of blind faith, it too is irrational by Weber's definiton. Often, followers attempt to create a formal organization that embodies the faith and that can carry on the cause after the leader's death (and charismatic leaders, because of the intense emotions they generate, tend to have short lives or to come to a violent end). Weber speaks of this process as "the routinization of charisma" whereby the divine gift is translated into everyday structures of power: the church, the political party, the social movement.

Legal-rational authority, according to Weber, is the least irrational form of power because it is based on an impersonal bond

Both Elizabeth, Queen of England (top) and Margaret Thatcher (bottom) prime minister, have legitimate political authority. The Queen's authority is traditional and rests on custom and heredity; the prime minister's authority as well as that of Mikhail Gorbachev, general secretary of the Soviet Communist Party (pictured to the right of Margaret Thatcher) is legal-rational and derives from the position itself. (© Associated Press/Wide World Photos, Inc.; © Peter Turnley/Black Star)

between ruler and the ruled. Power is limited by laws that apply to all office holders, regardless of personal quality or social status. This form of authority, claims Weber, offers the greatest protection against arbitrary force. Hence, the label "legal-rational."

ORIGINS OF POLITICAL SYSTEMS

As with the other primary institutions of any society, political systems arise out of some basic survival need, in this case the need for internal order and defense against external enemies. To ensure these goals, some members of the group are granted power to define and enforce the norms. In the most simple of gathering bands, all adults could join in this task, mutually approving the rules and sanctioning one another's role behavior. But the more complex the society, the harder it is to have decisions made by the group as a whole. Different degrees of power become linked to some statuses and not to others (Glassman 1986). At the very least, in all but the most simple bands, age and sex become minimal bases for power differences: elders can give orders to juniors, and men to women.

The more complex the society, the greater the need to coordinate the activities of many specialists and to settle disputes between kinship groups or other social units. At some point, loyalty to the society as a whole must supersede family and local allegiances. A governing group becomes the focus of such loyalty, with the power to make rules and enforce them. Such groups range from the tribal councils of preliterate societies to the Congress of the United States. Leaders can be witch doctors, queens or emperors, military dictators, presidents, or general secretaries of the ruling party. As we move along the continuum of cultural complexity, the political system itself becomes elaborated, ultimately involving a web of local and national lawmaking bodies, of courts to settle disputes, officials to enforce the laws, and a military establishment to defend the group.

POLITICAL INSTITUTIONS IN COMPLEX SOCIETIES

The **state** is the political organization of a society.

The political organization of a society is called the *state*. States are organized sets of institutions that govern and defend a given territory. As simple as this definition may seem, there is much debate today on the nature of the state as a sociological entity (Bright and Harding 1984, Carnoy 1984, Alford and Friedland 1985, Evans et al. 1985, Skocpol and Amenta 1986, Block 1987). Up until the 1970s, discussions of political sociology were dominated by one of two oversimplified visions: (1) the functionalist view that industrialization eventually leads to certain social policies in all modern societies, producing a similar form of "welfare state" regardless of other dif-

ferences; and (2) the Marxist view that the state is the political arm of capitalism, engaged in policies that reproduce the stratification system. Today, however, the historical evidence suggests a more complicated picture in which the state operates as a relatively autonomous (self-directing) institutional sphere, with its own history and logic, while also linked to the other institutions.

The new rallying cry is to "bring the state back in" as an independent force in sociological analysis (Evans et al. 1985, Skocpol 1985). Some sociologists would claim that the state has always been an important variable (Coser 1986) and that, in fact, the emergence of a centralized state was a precondition for the development of modern economic systems (Giddens 1985). Similarly, Wuthnow (1985) argues that the success of Protestantism in England, in contrast to France, had less to do with the psychological appeal of the ideas of the Reformation than with the fact that the state bureaucracy in England in the sixteenth century enjoyed relative autonomy from the landed nobility, so that new ideas had an independent resource base. Thus, while few social scientists would claim that the political system is completely independent of the influence of economic elites, the new "state-centered" research focuses on how social policies are often initiated and maintained independently of the class structure.

Politics and Economics. The new state-centered perspective in political sociology was developed in reaction to inadequacies in the traditional Marxist view, which maintained that the state was a captive of the ruling class. However, if governments can function autonomously, then it should be possible for members of the nonruling classes to influence social policy in directions that may not please the economically powerful.

Indeed, many scholars in the Marxist tradition now argue that a socialist transformation of the economy can be best accomplished through democratic political structures (e.g. Carnoy 1984). Conversely, others claim that it is socialism rather than capitalism that is most compatible with democracy. Capitalism, these critics suggest, leads to such inequality that democratic values cannot be realized—in the home, the workplace, or the community (Green 1985). A genuinely egalitarian society would support democratic decision making in all settings, public and private (Bowles and Gintis 1986). Nonetheless, most Americans appear committed to both democracy (in general) and to capitalism, even though the tension between the two is vaguely recognized (McClosky and Zaller 1986).

The empirical evidence on the link between democracy and income equality or inequality is not at all clear, given the wide differences in research designs (Bollen and Jackman 1985). In other words, extending the right to vote does not inevitably lead to a narrowing of income differences in the society, nor does a high level of inequality necessarily undermine democratic political systems (see Chapter 7). Nonetheless, over the course of this century, all capitalist democracies have developed extensive programs for reducing the impact of inequality, if not reducing inequality itself. These policies constitute the "welfare state."

THE WELFARE STATE. The term "welfare" is usually applied to policies designed to help the needy, but the major programs associated with the expansion of the welfare state have little to do with poverty. In the United States, for example, the two largest welfare programs, Social Security and Medicare, provide income support and health insurance for *all* retired workers. In addition, public (government) policy on taxation and expenditures has worked primarily to the benefit of business interests and the upper-income strata (Devine 1985, Gilbert 1986). For example, a tax law that

allows all homeowners to deduct the interest on their mortgage payments in an obvious gift to the top half of the income hierarchy.

Welfare policies in most of Western Europe appear to have had a greater effect on reducing income differences than in the United States, but these countries have also provided all their citizens with a wider array of social benefits, including educational and housing subsidies, than is directly available to Americans. Over time, these programs have become perceived as rights of citizenship.

Although conservative critics complain that such policies are "handouts" that reduce people's willingness to work hard, welfare expenditures have succeeded in maintaining economic and social order in the advanced capitalist democracies—up until the international economic downturn that began in the early 1970s (Heckscher 1984, Offe 1984). Today, most modern societies find it increasingly difficult to maintain their welfare programs, not because welfare destroys the moral fabric of the society but because their economies are no longer expanding sufficiently to handle all the demands placed on the modern state.

As a consequence of these changes in national and international economic systems, sociologists are examining the various alternatives for modern societies. Political conservatives claim that the welfare state must be dismantled as the first step in a return to a market-based economy, where supply and demand will determine

This old-age community, sponsored by the Swedish government, is integrated into the larger society rather than being separated from it. Why is it harder to achieve this kind of integration in most American communities? (© Joseph Rodriguez/Black Star)

the production and distribution of goods and services. Supporters of the democratic transition to socialism look to an even more integrated welfare state in which both the social and economic aspects of policies are considered together, and where cooperation can occur across class lines (Mishra 1984). This might be possible in a country such as Sweden, with a small, basically homogeneous population and a long history of social cohesion and concern. The outlook for the United States, with its weak unions, powerful business sector, racial divisions, and emphasis on individual rather than collective solutions is not at all clear. A return to a market-based economy is highly unlikely, but so is a move toward extending the welfare state.

Totalitarian and Democratic States.

The capacity of governments to act against the interests of economic elites depends on the degree to which non-elites can participate in the process of choosing their rulers. In the last chapter we saw how economic systems can be arranged along a continuum from free enterprise to socialist, according to the degree of central planning. In this chapter we will distinguish political systems on the basis of the extent to which citizens have the right to dissent (to disagree openly with government policies). At one extreme are *totalitarian* states, where the right to dissent is denied. At the other extreme are *democratic* societies where political opposition is guaranteed.

TOTALITARIANISM. As the name implies, totalitarian governments attempt to exercise total control over the society and its members—over behavior and thoughts, over public and private life. Leaders of totalitarian states are called dictators, and they can be civilians (as in the Soviet Union), military figures (as in many parts of South America and Africa), or religious authorities (as in Iran). What they have in common is absolute power that can be maintained only by repressing legitimate opposition. Structurally it does not matter whether the dictatorships are of the "right"—fascist regimes—or of the "left"— communist states. While fascist dictators often rule in the name of a racial or religious elite, communist dictators do so in the name of the masses. In either case, a single political party has exclusive control over the political process. And in both types of state, sociology departments are

among the first academic units to be dismantled.

Totalitarianism is most common in societies without the essential preconditions of democracy: widespread literacy, economic stability, and an egalitarian ideology. But even industrialized democratic states are vulnerable to the appeal of dictators when economic problems become overwhelming, as when a Hitler or Mussolini comes to power. In other cases, fear of communism leads people to accept equally totalitarian leaders, such as ex-President Marcos of the Philippines, or any of a half-dozen other dictators in Asia, Africa, and South America who have seized power with the active assistance of the United States government.

An important aspect of totalitarianism is control over cultural products. The media, schools, and theaters are all carefully supervised; only certain kinds of art and music are considered appropriate. Public meetings are closely watched for any hint of opposition. Books are burned and the people who wrote them are sent to prison. This is as true today in South Africa and Chile as in Poland or the People's Republic of China.

DEMOCRATIC STATES. What distinguishes a *democratic society,* then, is not how many people vote—dictatorships tend to have very high voting turnouts—but whether or not there is a legitimate opposition. In some democracies, however, not all citizens have the right to vote—blacks in South Africa, for example.

In the United States, where women did not receive the vote until 1920 and where the legal rights of black voters were systematically denied well into the 1960s, the basic guarantee of democracy is the First Amendment to the Constitution:

> Congress shall make no law respecting an establishment of religion, or prohibiting the free exercise thereof; or abridging the freedom of speech, or of the press; or the right of the people peaceably to assemble, and to petition the Government for a redress of grievances.

These rights—to speak, to publish, and to assemble peaceably—that we have as citizens, and that cannot be taken away by the government, are called *civil liberties.* Most Americans do not realize that the Bill of Rights—the first ten amendments to the Constitution—is designed to protect citizens against abuse of power by the government.

Under **totalitarianism** governments attempt to exercise total control over society and its members.

Democratic societies protect the right to dissent.

Civil liberties refer to the rights to speak, publish, and assemble.

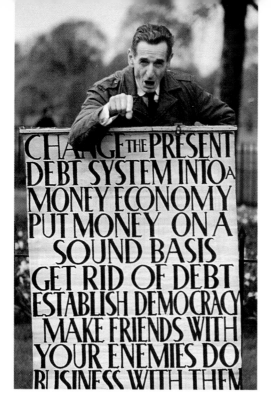

A hallmark of democracy is the guaranteeing of political opposition and the right of dissent. Great Britain is one of the oldest parliamentary democracies and British citizens pride themselves on a political system that forces the debate of issues. The famous "speakers' corner" in London's Hyde Park has been the scene of many such debates. (© Malcom J. Gilson)

National surveys between 1980 and 1986 indicate that the vast majority of Americans do not know what is in the First Amendment, and that only a minority would support the full range of civil liberties (McClosky and Brill 1983, Hearst Corporation 1987). For example, only 18 percent in one sample would allow a group that supports atheism to meet in a civic auditorium, and, in another survey, two-thirds of American adults were certain that the Constitution established English as the official language of our society.

MANIPULATING PUBLIC OPINION

Both totalitarian and democratic governments depend on manipulating public opinion in order to reinforce their claim to legitimacy. Attempts to influence public attitudes can be very subtle, as when the leader's speeches are preceded by the national anthem and accompanied by a display of flags and uniforms.

The flow of information from leaders to citizens is also subject to manipulation through propaganda and censorship.

Propaganda. *Propaganda* refers to the selective release of information thought to be favorable to those in power. In wartime, especially, civilian populations are continually being told how well their side is doing. These messages are important in maintaining high morale, but they also serve to stifle dissent. In peacetime, also, governments are very quick to release reports that put a positive light on the regime's accomplishments. Sometimes propaganda is designed to frighten citizens into supporting government goals, as when misleading reports of Soviet military strength are used to gain public approval for increased defense budgets (Center for Defense Information, 1987).

Censorship. In contrast, *censorship* involves the selective witholding of information. In totalitarian societies, newspapers often appear with blank columns where the government censors have forbidden publication. In democracies, it is far more difficult to censor news, but governments often try to do so by claiming "national security" interests. In the United States, in recent years, the government has stopped publication of books by former members of the Central Intelligence Agency (CIA) about events that took place decades earlier. In 1979, for a brief period, the government was able to stop publication of the *Progressive,* a small-circulation left-wing periodical that carried an article on how to build a nuclear weapon, based solely on material that the reporter was able to find in a public library. As the same information would be available to any foreign agent with a library card, this was hardly a case of national security being compromised. Yet, for a few months, the magazine was stopped from publishing, the first and so far the only instance of "prior restraint" in our history. The First Amendment protects speech until *after* it can be shown to have an unlawful outcome, not before.

Chilling Dissent. More obvious techniques for reducing political opposition include police surveillance, wiretapping, opening mail, and other ways to make people think twice about what they say and with whom they associate. These "chilling" tactics are part of everyday life in totalitarian states,

Propaganda refers to the selective release of information favorable to those in power.

Censorship involves the selective witholding of information.

344

Big Brother Never Sleeps

In 1948, the British author George Orwell wrote a novel called *1984,* which depicted England (called "Oceania" in the book) under totalitarian rule. People were watched by electronic surveillance, and their ideas were subject to "thought control." The term "Big Brother" has come to refer to all the ways in which democratic as well as totalitarian governments, under the pretense of protecting and helping, can exercise complete control over the population.

In 1984, sociologist Gary Marx compared the contemporary American scene with Orwell's vision. He noted that we are quite free of the physical coercion and suppression that characterizes most totalitarian states. But he also suggested that in the past several decades such violent forms of social control have been replaced by more subtle and nonviolent threats to privacy and civil liberties, even in democratic states. "The velvet glove is replacing, or covering, the iron fist" (G. Marx 1986: 137).

Because the state cannot watch everyone all the time, it is far more efficient to influence people through something that they watch or read all the time: the mass media. As we detail in Chapter 20, whoever owns and manages the mass media also controls the production of culture, the source of our beliefs and norms of behavior. In totalitarian societies, the media are state owned and operated; in democracies, a combination of government and private business have similar powers.

But it is the new, state-of-the-art techniques of surveillance that Gary Marx finds most potentially dangerous. This list includes: video cameras in public places and at work; lie detectors; arbitrary drug testing; data banks that contain information on one's health, income, credit-card use, and all other types of personal information; wiretapping, remote-control video and audio taping devices; satellite "eyes in the sky"; electronic "leashes" (ankle loops that emit radio signals) to keep track of persons on parole and probation; magnetic-tape ID cards for employees that monitor movement within the workplace; hot lines for anonymous tips; and even neighborhood watch groups to report suspicious behavior.

This new surveillance, according to Marx, differs from traditional forms of social control in several respects: (1) it can overcome the limits of distance, darkness, or physical barriers; (2) records can be easily stored and combined; (3) equipment replaces people as both information gatherers and agents of control; (4) it allows targeting of entire groups rather than specific individuals; (5) it is aimed at preventing violations through self-policing; (6) the new techniques have low visibility; (7) and they can probe below the surface into areas of life previously not open to observation.

Gary Marx concludes that if totalitarianism ever comes to the United States it will do so by the slow acceptance of the new surveillance and its inevitable outcome in chilling dissent and discouraging nonconformity. No invasion, no revolution, no violent overthrow is necessary. We will become willing participants of our own loss of liberty in our eagerness to catch a thief, find a junkie, plug an information leak, increase productivity, or uncover a traitor.

SOURCE: Gary T. Marx, "The Iron Fist and the Velvet Glove: Totalitarian Potentials within Democratic Structures," pp. 135–162 in James F. Short, Jr. (Ed.) *The Social Fabric: Dimensions and Issues.* Newbury Park, CA.: Sage, 1986.

---

but they have also been used to great effect in our society: against socialists in the 1930s, anyone who got in the way of Sen. Joseph McCarthy in the 1950s, antiwar activists in the 1960s, and religious groups helping refugees from South American dictatorships in the 1980s.

Coercion, Repression, and Genocide. The ultimate in social control is the use of force (*coercion*) to ensure obedience. The threat of force is also highly effective, so that a few well-publicized cases—as in treason trials—will keep most people very quiet. *Repression* involves imprisonment, house arrest, and public execution of "troublemakers," a familiar tactic in all totalitarian states. The final step in ensuring compliance is to do away with opposing groups altogether. *Genocide* refers to killing an entire population, and there are many examples from our century, but none more devastating than the slaughter of six million European Jews by the German government before and during World War II.

Coercion is the use of threat of force to ensure obedience.

Repression involves imprisonment, house arrests, and public executions.

Genocide occurs when entire populations are intentionally destroyed.

We associate coercion, repression, and the imprisonment and execution of troublemakers with totalitarian governments. These practices, however, are not unknown in the U.S. In the '70s, for example, members of the Black Panther party were harassed in a variety of ways. Here a group of party members are shown being stripsearched after a raid on Black Panther headquarters, August 31, 1970 in Philadelphia, PA. (© UPI/Bettmann Newsphotos)

Societal Consequences of Inequality

Societies marked by extreme differences in economic and social power between the few who rule and the many who are controlled by surveillance and coercion are seldom as stable as they appear to be from the outside. Social order is maintained by increasingly repressive measures, which create further hostility among citizens that, in turn, leads to political violence (Muller 1985). In most cases, opposition movements will be physically crushed, but every now and then, the mass of the population will successfully defy totalitarian leaders and overturn the government, much to the surprise of outsiders. In the past decade, popular revolutions in Iran and the Philippines have toppled absolute rulers who had been strongly supported by the United States.

The Shah of Iran and President Marcos of the Philippines are examples of the British historian Lord Acton's famous maxim: "Power tends to corrupt; absolute power corrupts absolutely." No matter how "good" the original intentions of power holders, they soon find that exercising authority becomes an end in itself; they develop an exaggerated sense of their own virtue and of others' inferiority; and, all too often, cannot resist using their power

for personal gain (Kipnis 1976). The greater one's power, the easier it is to become corrupted by its use. The sociological point here is that individual qualities and personality variables are secondary to the influence of being in a position of power. Anyone of us could become corrupt.

"THE IRON LAW OF OLIGARCHY"

Even in organizations that represent "the masses," the leaders, including those who are democratically elected, tend to become cut off from their followers. *Oligarchy* means "rule by a few," and the "iron law" proposed by Robert Michels (1911/1962) states that because decision makers have a crucial interest in being proved correct, they tend to manipulate information in order to gain support. The few who lead have a full-time commitment to their rule; the masses are only periodically concerned. A gap is opened between the rulers and the ruled, and the corrupting influences of power appear. Censorship and propaganda characterize official statements, while the leaders are shielded from bad news by the people who surround them. If the followers are able to create a revolution and overturn their rulers, they will eventually find the process repeated as the new leaders follow the paths of the old because of the same imperatives of power.

Oligarchy is the rule of the few.

Examples of the iron law at work can be seen in the recent history of the United States. Three Presidents, blinded by their landslide election victories, began to see themselves as above the law, could not admit making poor decisions, sought to manipulate public perception, and eventually got caught in the tangled web of deception. Lyndon Johnson pursued an increasingly unpopular war, fed false information to the press and people, was shielded from bad news by his subordinates, and, until the last moment, had no idea of the reality of his situation. Richard Nixon was engaged in an active cover-up of a crime, told lies, and resigned the Presidency only as he was about to be impeached. And Ronald Reagan thought that he could conduct a secret foreign policy in direct contradiction to the will of Congress.

The beauty of democracy is that every two, four, or six years, our rulers must appear before us and justify their actions, in competition with other candidates. Citizens in a democracy can periodically replace one set of leaders with another, so that even if the iron law cannot be repealed, no one can stay in office long enough to become fully corrupted by power. Government may remain in the hands of an elite, but their power is limited by democratic politics (Etzioni-Halevy 1983).

If the modern state is indeed a semi-autonomous institution capable of representing the interests of "the people" against those of the economic elite, and if the best guarantee of protection against corrupt rulers is open elections, then democracy does matter. But democratic institutions are of limited effect unless most members of the society actively participate in the political process.

Political Participation

Political participation in the United States takes place on several levels: running for office, contributing money to candidates, working on campaigns, voting, or doing none of the above.

OFFICE HOLDING

As we saw in Chapters 8 and 10, despite recent gains, few women, blacks, and Hispanics hold public office, elected or appointed. The higher the office, the less likely to find people occupying it who are not white males. In part, this finding is due to the fact that people without economic and interpersonal power are not perceived as strong candidates, and without legitimated authority they remain powerless, as a self-fulfilling prophecy. But there are also structural explanations. One path to becoming a candidate is to have worked your way up the political party organization, working for others and doing favors until you have earned a chance to run for office yourself. At this time, very few blacks and Hispanics have this background experience, and women are only now emerging from the political pipeline—which is how most women candidates in 1986 won their party's nomina-

Annette Strauss, Mayor of Dallas (top), and Henry Cisneros (bottom), Mayor of San Antonio, are two exceptions among office holders. Several other cities have minority mayors. Does yours? (© Phil Huber/Black Star; © Kokojan/Black Star)

tion. The other route to candidacy involves having enough money to mount an effective campaign, a criterion that immediately screens out most women, blacks, and Hispanics.

CAMPAIGN ACTIVITY

Only a small proportion of citizens take an active role in political campaigns as contributors or volunteer workers. Although there are now limits on the amount of individual contributions to a particular candidate or organization, there is no limit on the number of organizations to which one can contribute. This fact has led to the creation of large numbers of *"political action committees"* (PACs) that can use their funds to support causes and candidates, especially the members of Congress who sit on committees that oversee particular areas of activity.

Volunteer workers, however, do not have to be wealthy or even motivated by personal or ideological considerations. Most campaign workers become active when drawn in by friends (Zipp and Smith 1982). The low political involvement of working-class and poor people may reflect not only powerlessness and lack of education but relative isolation from social networks (Zipp et al. 1982). Recruitment is selective, and participation socially structured.

VOTING

The minimal act of political involvement is voting. As can be seen in Table 13-1 and Table 13-2, not all eligible Americans are registered to vote, and not all who are registered exercise the right to vote. Indeed, the trend over the past two decades in registration and voting has been downward. Although the decline appeared to be halted in the presidential election year of 1984, the turnout for congressional elections in 1986 was the third lowest in American history, at slightly over 37 percent (Gailey 1986). This means that fewer than four in ten citizens actually chose the persons who represent their districts and states in the U.S. Congress.

WHO VOTES?

Registration and voting varies by gender, race, Spanish origin, and age. In addition, as seen in Table 13-2, the probability of

Political Action Committees (PACS) are special interest organizations that use funds to support causes and candidates.

TABLE 13-1 Voting-age population in the United States: Percentage of those eligible registered and voting in the 1968 and 1984 presidential elections

	Percentage Registered		Percentage Voting	
	1968	1984	1968	1984
Totals	74.3	68.3	67.8	59.9
White	75.4	69.6	69.1	61.4
Black	66.2	66.3	57.6	55.8
Spanish origin	—	40.1	—	32.6
Male	76.0	67.3	69.8	59.0
Female	72.8	69.3	66.0	60.8
18–20 yr. old	44.2	} 51.3	33.3	} 40.8
21–24	56.4		51.1	
25–44	72.4	66.6	66.6	58.4
45–64	81.1	76.6	74.9	69.8
65+	75.6	76.9	65.8	67.7

SOURCES: Statistical Abstract, 1979, p. 514, adapted from Tables 836 and 837. Current Population Reports, Voting and Registration in the Election at November 1980, Series P. 20, No. 359, Washington, D.C., 1981. Series P. 20, No. 405, Voting and Registration in the Election of November 1984, Washington, D.C., 1986.

being registered and voting is associated with such indicators of social class as education, occupation, and income. As these data are no secret, politicians are well aware that a smaller proportion of blacks and relatively few Hispanics bother to vote. Nor do people eighteen to twenty-four exercise this right with frequency. Itshould be no surprise, then, to discover that party platforms are not constructed around their interests. If policy changes are to come, it will be *after* underrepresented groups show up in the voting booth.

In fact, the black-white voting differential, which was still over 10 percentage points in 1980 was cut in half, to under 5 percent, in 1984, due in large part to the presence of Jesse Jackson on the ballot. These differences in voting rates also reflect the educational, occupational, and income distributions of the two races. If social class is controlled, some black subgroups actually have higher voting rates than comparable whites, especially those who have a high sense of personal control over their lives (Guterbock and London 1983).

WHO DOESN'T VOTE

People who might have the most to gain from government intervention are actually the least likely to vote: victims of

TABLE 13-2 Percentage of voting-age population having registered or voted in the election of 1984 by education, employment, and income

	Registered	Voted
Years of School Completed:		
Elementary	53.4	42.9
High School: 1–3 years	54.9	44.4
High School: 4 years	67.3	58.7
College: 1–3 years	75.7	67.5
College: 4 years or more	83.8	79.1
Labor Force Status:		
Unemployed	54.3	44.0
Agriculture	64.3	55.9
Private wage and salary	66.7	58.6
Self employed	72.4	65.2
Government worker	82.0	75.9
Not in Labor Force	68.1	58.9
Family Income:		
Under $5,000	49.8	37.5
5000–9999	56.8	46.2
10000–14999	62.9	53.5
15000–19999	65.5	57.1
20000–24999	68.7	61.1
25000–34999	74.2	67.0
35000 and over	80.7	74.2

SOURCE: U.S. Bureau of the Census, *Current Population Report,* Series P-20, No. 405, p. 7. U.S. Government Printing Office 1986.

discrimination, the young, the poor, the less educated. The subgroup with the lowest voting rates is people eighteen to twenty-four, many of whom may not have lived in one community long enough to qualify. Young adults are also likely to be in the midst of many status changes—from student to worker, from single to married, from nonparent to parent—so that politics might be a low priority at this time of their lives.

But, as Emile Durkheim would predict, as these young adults settle down to family, work, and community roles, they will become integrated into the ongoing fabric of society, with a stake in social order. The greater the investment in ongoing social systems, the more likely one is to vote, and to enjoy the benefits of public policies. Because so many Americans do *not* vote, the few who do can exert influence far beyond their numbers.

As Figure 13-1 shows, most of our Presidents since 1920 have been elected by fewer than one-third of the voting age population, and before 1920, because women could not vote, a man could become President with the support of little

more than 15 percent of white adults. Note that the Reagan "landslide" of 1984 actually involved fewer than three in ten voters.

Nonvoting may also be seen as another symptom of the withdrawal of the powerless from a system that does not recognize their needs. This effect is strongest among

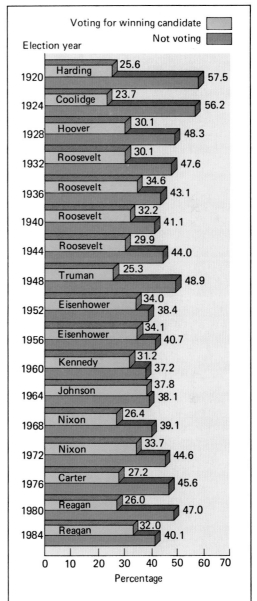

Figure 13-1
Nonvoting Americans. Percentage voting for the winning candidate and percentage not voting, 1920–84 (after universal suffrage). (Source: U.S. Bureau of the Census, series P-23, No. 102, April 1980; series P-20, No. 405, March, 1986.)

both inner-city blacks and white rural poor (Gaventa 1980). Despite much talk about the need to register all possible voters, neither major political party appears interested in empowering the most deprived among us. If politicians were to respond to the needs of the very poor, they would have to support programs that would alienate the majority of nonpoor, which is no way to win elections. Some activists believe that if the poor could be registered as they wait on line in welfare offices or on unemployment lines, they might emerge as a major force in local politics (Piven and Cloward 1983).

The most dramatic change, however, has been in the voting behavior of women. In 1980, for the first time since they gained the right to vote in 1920, women's voting rate exceeded that of men, a trend that continued through the presidential vote in 1984 and the congressional elections of 1986. This fact is doubly important to politicians because adult women also outnumber their male age peers, especially at older ages. Given the overall aging of our population, this means that it will be very difficult in the future for a candidate to win election without paying attention to what have become defined as "women's issues," such as child welfare, workplace equality, health care for the elderly, and world peace.

THE GENDER GAP

Concern with these issues has led to a divergence in the voting choices of men and women, with women showing a higher preference than men for candidates of the Democratic party (Mueller 1987). This "gender gap" of between 6 and 8 percentage points in recent elections is also without precedent. Until 1978, there had been little difference in the choices of women and men voters, although Democrats have traditionally been associated with social-welfare programs and Republicans with concerns such as patriotism, individualism, and protecting private property.

Although the Reagan candidacy in 1984 did attract a majority of women voters, their support was still less strong than that of men. By 1986, however, the gap had widened, with women's votes being credited with the election of pro-feminist candidates across the nation, as well as with the defeat of all four antiabortion state

referenda. According to Brackman and Erie (1986), the gap will persist because of basic structural changes in our society: women's labor-force participation rates, the feminization of poverty, and the group consciousness produced by the women's movement. In addition, Mueller (1987) notes that the concept of the "gender gap" itself has served to focus attention on women's political power. Indeed, she suggests that public-opinion polling has replaced earlier attention-getting tactics such as mass protests and demonstrations.

Political Socialization

The term *political socialization* refers to the influences and experiences that lead people to define their political orientation as either conservative or liberal. Because eighteen-year-olds do not confront the political system as blank slates, the basic question is one of the relative impact of early learning in the home and community compared to adult experiences that lead to a reexamination of attitudes formed in adolescence.

As Figure 13-2 illustrates, the process of political socialization combines elements of both early and later influences. There is a direct link between political attitudes formed by the time one enters college and those held in later adulthood, but intervening experiences also have an effect. In many cases, occupational roles will reinforce earlier attitudes because conservative students tend to choose careers in business and the military, while liberal students turn to human services or academics.

Although it is often assumed that social class should have a profound effect on political orientations, empirical findings

Political socialization includes the influences and experiences that determine one's political orientation.

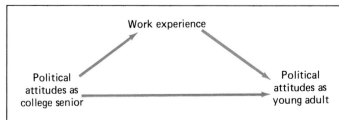

Figure 13-2
A model of political socialization. (Adapted from Lorence and Mortimer, 1979.)

are not that clear-cut. It is important to distinguish (1) attitudes toward "economic" issues such as private ownership, taxation, and budget priorities, from (2) attitudes on "social" issues such as women's rights, school prayer, and racial integration. In general, the upper middle class is most liberal on social issues and the working class the least. On economic matters, the class positions are reversed, with the working class most liberal. These differences, however, appear to be more related to *educational level* than to income or occupation (Zipp 1986). Salaried professionals such as academics and other "knowledge workers," tend to be the most liberal of all occupation/education groups in terms of support for personal freedoms, gender equality, homosexual rights, and racial tolerance (Brint 1984).

The difference between social and economic attitudes is especially visible in data on young upwardly mobile professionals—*yuppies*. Although a minority within their baby-boom birth cohorts, yuppies have captured the attention of the media. One longitudinal study of 1965 high-school graduates found that by age forty, 15 percent met the yuppie criteria: a four-year college education, professional or managerial employment, and relatively high household income (Jennings and Markus 1986). Compared to their non-yuppie age peers, this cohort of yuppies, whose attitudes were deeply influenced by the antiwar and other social movements of the 1960s, remained very liberal on social issues, but turned extremely conservative on economic matters. Because yuppies have very high rates of political participation, they will have an effect on social policy far greater than their numbers.

The data on yuppies illustrate how political attitudes are shaped by historical experiences at certain points in the life course; being a college student in the late 1960s had a strong impact, even on college graduates who would not be classified as young upwardly mobile professionals. As discussed in Chapter 9, members of particular birth cohorts share both life-course experiences and generational concerns that affect political orientations and voting behavior (Braungart and Braungart 1986). People who were adults during the Great Depression share a set of attitudes that they carry into old age, and that are very different from the attitudes of people who were young adults in the 1950s.

Yuppie stands for young upwardly mobile professional.

The Structure of Power in America

A recurring theme in political sociology is the debate over "Who Rules America?" How is power distributed in a *mass society* where traditional authority has been replaced by distant and formal bureaucracies, and where buffer groups such as the extended family, neighborhood, and occupational association no longer stand between individuals and their faceless rulers? The issue is whether there are many different and competing bases of power (the *pluralist model*) or whether decision making is concentrated in the hands of a small group (the *power elite model*).

THE POWER-ELITE MODEL

In 1956, sociologist C. Wright Mills published a book entitled *The Power Elite* in which he traced the social-class backgrounds of leaders in business, government, and other major spheres of influence and authority. It is not necessary to prove a conspiracy among these people or even to show that they are in contact with one another, in order to suggest that the decisions made in one power sector reinforce those made in others. As products of similar class locations and socialization experiences, these leaders will think alike, share a vision of what is fair and good, and act in ways that maintain the existing stratification system. These relationships are shown in Figure 13-3 on p. 352.

The empirical work based on Mills' thesis has centered on identifying a "national upper class" whose (white male) members own most of the nation's wealth, manage its business sector, run its universities and foundations, control the mass media, and staff the higher levels of government, the courts, and political parties (Dye 1983, Domhoff 1983, Useem 1984). The emphasis in recent power-elite research is less on the content of socialization than on the structural links among its members: from schools and clubs to marriages and interlocking directorships.

The ties between the corporate elite described in Chapter 12 and a political "ruling class" have also been researched. This is most obvious in the actual exchange of personnel, as when business leaders become cabinet officers, or as heads of regulatory agencies leave government for jobs

The **power-elite model** assumes that decision making is concentrated in the hands of a small group.

The **power elite** refers to similarity of world views and actions among leaders of business, government, military, and other major spheres of influence and authority.

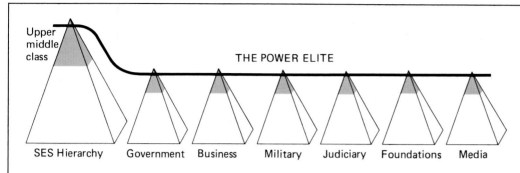

Figure 13-3
The power elite is composed of members of the upper and the upper-middle classes who have achieved the highest possible positions in each of these centers of power.

in the industries they had previously regulated (Domhoff 1983). This traffic in personnel has become so heavy and open to charges of conflict of interest that Congress had to pass a law setting time limits and restricting permissible contact between ex-officials and their successors. Recent studies have examined the flow of campaign contributions, finding that major business contributors have been highly supportive of the conservative economic agenda and its candidates. One study of corporate political contributions between 1974 and 1980 found that 83 percent of the total money went to Republican candidates (Kouzi and Ratcliffe 1983). Similarly, Clawson et al. (1986) found a high degree of unity among corporate contributors in the 1980 congressional elections.

Since the 1980 elections, business interests have been crucial to the rise of the "New Right," a coalition of interest groups with extremely conservative agendas: the anti-gun-control lobby; anti-abortion groups; free-market economists; anti-communists; supporters of school prayer; proponents of military strength; and fundamentalist Protestants (see Chapter 15 on the New Religious Right). The common wisdom among political sociologists had been that the radical right attracted a new class of wealthy businessmen—"Cowboy Capitalists" from the South and West—in contrast to the "old Yankee" capitalists of the North and East associated with more moderate elements within the Republican party. But a recent analysis of contributions to New Right policy organizations such as the Heritage Foundation, the Hoover Institution, and the American Enterprise Institute found that support came from the entire spectrum of the corporate elite (Jenkins and Shumate 1985). The researchers suggest that a continuing squeeze on profits and the decline of anti-

establishment social movements has created a climate in which the entire corporate elite has turned sharply rightward.

Another source of support for the power-elite vision of the world lies in the vast resources of the major American foundations. Foundations are tax-exempt organizations built on endowments from very wealthy families. Funds from the interest on the endowments are used to finance various educational and charitable causes chosen by the trustees and managers of the foundations. As members of the elite strata, shaped by similar schooling and social networks, foundation heads (white males all, until very recently) are not likely to lend their support to persons or organizations whose goal is to overthrow the existing system or to challenge American interests abroad. One intensive study of the overseas programs of the Carnegie, Ford, and Rockefeller foundations, for example, concludes that they have generally reinforced a foreign policy based on the interests of American corporate capital (Berman 1983).

Indeed, assuming that American foreign policy has been dominated by the goals of corporate capitalism, some social scientists have identified an "Atlantic ruling class" composed of economic and political elites in Western Europe and the United States (van der Pijl 1984).

THE PLURALIST MODEL

Critics of the power-elite model suggest that it oversimplifies reality, assumes a greater uniformity among leaders than actually exists (not everyone can graduate from Harvard, Yale, and Princeton—and even their graduates do not always agree on values), and underestimates the sources of conflict within the "ruling class."

Pluralists contend that business inter-

The **pluralist model** assumes that there are many different and competing bases of power.

ests are very diverse; policies that benefit core industries may be disastrous for peripheral firms. Furthermore, the various power sectors are usually in competition for scarce resources, as when the military competes with consumer industries for electronics experts, or when the government competes with private enterprise in providing health care. In the political sphere itself, pluralists point out that power is widely diffused across the three layers of government: local, state, and federal. And within each level, there is a separation of powers among the courts, the legislature, and the executive branch.

The basic assumption of pluralism is that the diversity of interests in mass society ensures that no one group can control decision making throughout the system (Riesman 1950). As shown in Figure 13-4, each power sector serves as a potential buffer against uncontrolled expansion.

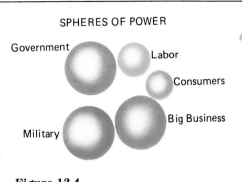

SPHERES OF POWER

Figure 13-4
Model of Countervailing Forces—
Competing power sectors may form coalitions to prevent the uncontrolled expansion of another sector.

Some of the important differences between the elite and pluralist perspectives on power are summarized in Table 13-3.

TABLE 13-3   Two portraits of the American power structure

Power Structure	Power Elite (Mills)	Pluralist (Riesman)
Levels	a) unified power elite b) diversified and balanced plurality of interest groups c) mass of unorganized people who have no power over elite	a) no dominant power elite b) diversified and balanced plurality of interest groups c) mass of unorganized people who have some power over interest groups
Changes	a) increasing concentration of power	a) increasing dispersion of power
Operation	a) one group determines all major policies b) manipulation of people at the bottom by group at the top	a) who determines policy shifts with the issue b) monopolistic competition among organized groups
Bases	a) coincidence of interests among major institutions (economic, military, governmental) b) social similarities and psychological affinities among those who direct major institutions	a) diversity of interests among major organized groups b) sense of weakness and dependence among those in higher as well as lower status
Consequences	a) enhancement of interests of corporations, armed forces, and executive branch of government b) decline of politics as public debate c) decline of responsible and accountable power—loss of democracy	a) no one group or class is favored significantly over others b) decline of politics as duty and self-interest c) decline of effective leadership

SOURCE: Adapted from William Kornhauser, "Power Elite or Veto Groups?" in S. M. Lipset and L. Lowenthal (eds.), *Culture and Social Character* (N.Y.: Free Press, 1961).

The major point of agreement among all analysts of power in mass society is that the great majority of citizens are politically inactive, especially the poor. As noted in Chapter 12, not only the poor but the urban working class are particularly powerless against the economic elites who shut down plants or move their operations to the suburbs or overseas with little warning.

Although the two models are often presented as mutually exclusive, they are best seen as alternative explanations depending on the system under analysis. The power structure of a small town would probably resemble the elite model, with local leaders in frequent contact and making decisions that are mutually beneficial. The power structure of a college or university, however, comes closest to the pluralist ideal, with administration, faculty, staff, and students competing for scarce resources and serving to limit the concentration of power in any one group. For example, when student power has appeared to threaten administrative control, administrators have called on outside reinforcements; faculties are continually testing their power against those of administrations; staff members go out on strike, and faculty members and students may refuse to cross picket lines in defiance of the administration.

But because in most political systems the great mass of people remain uninvolved, elites and other power holders are rarely challenged. In recent decades, there have been new efforts to organize "ordinary" citizens into effective power blocs capable of pursuing local interests and/or fighting against decisions made by politicians or corporations that would negatively affect their communities.

Community Action

In the 1960s, the best-known efforts to organize the powerless were directed by Saul Alinsky in Chicago, Rochester, and other urban areas. Alinsky and his assistants taught inner-city residents how to organize, demonstrate, put economic pressure on local merchants, and to run their own organizations. These activities give people a sense of being in control of their own destinies, a feeling of empowerment.

Saul Alinsky was a driving force in community organization in the '60s. His techniques for eliciting solutions to problems of the powerless and impoverished included startling tactics such as sending dead rats from tenants' apartments to errant landlords. (© Werner Wolff/Black Star)

Although Alinsky's work was soon overshadowed by the urban upheavals of the late 1960s, and the present period of urban neglect (see Chapter 19), he left an important legacy: a body of ideas and techniques for empowering people at the grass roots (or, in this case, asphalt). In the late 1970s, many activists from the antiwar and civil-rights movements turned their attention from trying to influence policy at the highest levels to making a difference at the lowest level, the backyard (Boyte 1980).

As is true of *self-help* groups in general, neighborhood organizations are a means of bridging the enormous gap between isolated individuals or families and the impersonal bureaucratic structures "out there" that govern our lives. This search for community is an enduring theme in sociology, and one that is especially significant in mass society. Organizations that bridge this gap are, in the words of Evans and Boyte (1986), "free spaces" in which people develop a sense of strength and collective identity, learn cooperation, and generate change from the bottom up.

Self-help groups allow people to derive strength from one another in face-to-face interaction.

NEIGHBORHOOD ORGANIZING

Local organizations today tend to be issue-centered: health care, housing, utility rates, trash sites, highway routes, and safety in the streets are frequent focuses for action. Although most of the activists involved in grass-roots organizing are concerned with relatively powerless populations, middle-class neighborhoods also organize, often to resist changes that might be beneficial to the less powerful. Such middle-class organizations have the advantages of sophisticated volunteers and professional help (Fisher 1984). Organizers for the poor often cannot make up in zeal for these differences in resources and political savvy (Henig 1982, Krauss 1987).

Despite intense interest in neighborhood mobilization on the part of social scientists, organizing a community remains an extremely difficult task. And because each local organization has a very narrow immediate agenda, it has been even more difficult to build coalitions across community groups or among geographically separated organizations. One of the leaders in establishing a national network of grass-roots groups has been ACORN—the Association of Community Organizations for Reform Now (Delgado 1986a). Although many local groups have developed the structures and skills required for successful challenges to politics-as-usual, national organizing remains problematic. As analyzed by Delgado (1986b), the future vitality of community organizations (COs) depends on reaching out not only to other COs but to other social movements for democratic change (namely the civil-rights, feminist, and peace movements). In Delgado's words, "The *real* question is not whether [COs] will survive, but whether they will develop the internal structures and external strategies necessary to grow beyond a group of organizations waiting for a movement into a progressive movement for social change" (1986:47).

The Military

A primary characteristic of the state is its monopoly over the use of legitimate force. Governments—whether tribal councils, absolute monarchies, or parliamentary democracies—are expected to settle disputes within the group and thus avoid blood feuds and other socially disruptive behaviors. Governments are also charged with defending the group from outside enemies. To serve these functions as social systems become more complex, two types of specialists emerge: a *police force* for internal order; and a *military* for external defense (Giddens 1985).

The role of police is discussed in Chapter 16. In this section we will examine the military component of our society, the increasing militarization of our culture, and the consequences for world peace and human survival.

THE AMERICAN MILITARY

Until recently, the United States was unique among modern societies in not having a large professional military. Rather, the ideal was the "citizen-soldier," a civilian who could be called on to join a local military unit only when the need arose (Moskos 1986). Examples include the militias of the Revolutionary War and the state National Guard units of this century. But when volunteers were lacking, citizens could be forced—conscripted—into the military, as was the case during the Civil War, both World Wars, and, most recently, the Vietnam War. From 1945 to 1973, conscription (the draft) continued through periods of peace as well as war.

The All-Volunteer Force. With the end of the draft in 1973, a new concept replaced the citizen-soldier ideal: the "economic man" model of military service (Moskos 1986). Military service would no longer be seen as an obligation of citizenship, but as a job, like any other, to which recruits could be attracted by high pay, the chance to travel, educational opportunities, and other special benefits. It was thought that an *all-volunteer force* (AVF) would be smaller and more professional than the citizen army, and that because recruits would make a career of military service, the higher pay scales would be offset by lower turnover rates. The AVF marks a major organizational as well as philosophical change in the American military (Segal and Segal 1983). Although the military remains a *ranked* society, the essence of hierarchy, in which each rank has clear rights over lower statuses and clear obligations toward occupants of higher statuses, the contemporary AVF is a very different

The **all-volunteer force** is composed of people who enter the military as a full-time career.

military establishment from its predecessors in our history.

The expected reduction in active-duty armed forces has taken place—from an average of fifteen per 1,000 population in the 1960s to about nine per 1,000 today (*Statistical Abstract, 1986:* 340). The AVF has also had dramatic effects on the composition of the armed forces. The armed forces today contain increasing proportions of both blacks and women. In addition, a majority of active-duty personnel today are married, many with their spouse and children living on base. Each of these changes is the consequence of societal trends, with clear consequences for both the military and the society as a whole.

Racial Factors. The AVF has a higher proportion of minority personnel—black and Hispanic, particularly—than did the conscripted armed forces. Blacks compose 20 percent of the enlisted (nonofficer) personnel, or almost double their representation in the total population. In fact, the U.S. Army is the most integrated institution in our society—at the lower ranks. Among officers, only 5 percent are black. While some black leaders hail the AVF as an important employment/education opportunity for inner-city youth, others wonder why a disproportionate number of blacks should be expected to die in defense of the society (Halloran 1986). The figures for persons of Spanish origin are considerably smaller, though growing.

The armed forces do provide relatively well-paying and respectable employment for young men and women whose job prospects were already limited by economic and residential trends. While military service removes many black males from the marriage pool in their home communities, it allows many others to afford marriage.

Interracial relations reflect those of the wider society. When blacks and whites are on duty together, segregation is minimal and relationships relatively smooth. Once off duty, or off the post, however, the members of different racial groups tend to go their own ways (Moskos, quoted in Halloran 1986).

Women in the Military. Although there have been women in the American military since the early 1940s, the AVF, under considerable outside pressure, has actively recruited women to its ranks. In general, the educational standards for women enlistees is higher than those for their male counterparts. Today, one in ten members of the armed forces is a woman—12 percent of the Air Force, 10 percent of the Army, 9 percent of the Navy, and 5 percent of the Marine Corps. Gradually, some of these women have worked their way into the officer corps where they command men as well as women. And very gradually they have come to be accepted as colleagues.

Originally, the job categories open to women recruits were limited to the clerical and medical areas. It was thought that women were neither physically nor emotionally suited to most forms of military service, and especially not for combat duty. The military is a particularly male world that rewards strength and bravery and all the qualities that Americans believe distinguish men from women at the most basic level (Rustad 1982, Enloe 1987). If women could perform as well as men, and perhaps even be in a position to give orders, enlisted men (and officers) would lose that competitive edge in proving their manliness. The easiest solution to this problem is simply to close off certain jobs. But even here, the line has become blurred over time. In 1986, the Air Force approved all-women crews for the Minuteman 2 nuclear missile, and the Navy now permits women aboard support ships that could be called into combat. In the absence of combat, restrictions on the work they can do keep women from the highest-paying military jobs, and from the kinds of training that would lead to improved civilian job prospects. Despite some remaining limitations, however, the American AVF has been less openly sexist than other modern military establishments, including the Israeli army (Yuval-Davis 1985).

But the military remains an essentially male world. According to Cynthia Enloe (1983), women's roles have been and always will be outside the central core of the military mystique: the experience of combat. Women can be camp followers (prostitutes), wives of military men, nurses, soldiers with limited duties, or defense-industry workers—all supporting roles that touch on but do not penetrate the world of male bonding that is the essence of militarism.

Looking at the difference among seven cohorts of women who entered the armed services at roughly the same age between 1952 and 1976, Stiehm (1985) found enor-

Women entering the military today, though a small minority, are likely to have experiences and opportunities that are very similar to those of male recruits. Do you think they experience different pressures nevertheless? (© Bettye Lane/Photo Researchers, Inc.)

mous differences in their careers and attitudes as military policy changed dramatically from one cohort to another. The few remaining women of the oldest cohorts had accepted their limited roles, remained childless, and worked their way up to non-commissioned-officer status. The women who entered in the late 1960s were in good position to move into leadership roles with the introduction of AVF. The most recent cohorts have had an experience comparable to that of their male counterparts, similar training, and most of the same job opportunities. They are also likely to be married (usually to military men) and many are also mothers.

Military Families. Few commanders of military bases in the past have had to deal with a community of family men and women. Officers and their wives have typically lived on base, in a world in which the husband's military rank determined the interactions of their spouses (the wives of lieutenants show deference to the wives of captains who defer to the wives of colonels, and so on up the chain of command).

What is new today is the large proportion of *enlisted* personnel who are married and live on base. And in many cases, both partners are in the military. In order to keep people from leaving the military, which increases the costs of maintaining the armed forces, the various services must deal with military families. This means arranging assignments that keep

husbands and wives together, and paying attention to the social-welfare needs of families and children. As a result, each of the services has established family-service centers, and the Army is experimenting with the British system whereby an entire regiment, soldiers and their families, stays together in the same unit at the same place (*Psychology Today* 1986). In addition, the military must develop supportive services for single-parent families and for those in which the mother is on active duty. Yet, as Segal (1986) points out, both the military and the family are "greedy institutions" (Coser and Coser 1972) that demand total commitment. There is, therefore, a potential for conflict between the demands of military service and of family obligation.

MILITARISM AND MILITARIZATION

Militarism refers to a societal emphasis on military ideals and virtues and a glorification of war and warriors. Militarism is associated with heavy expenditures on weapons and training, as well as an aggressive foreign policy. *Militarization* refers to the mobilization of entire societies around militaristic goals. As noted in the previous section, up until the past three decades, the American tradition had been relatively nonmilitaristic. Our military has been under civilian control and our peacetime armed forces quite small. Every so often, the government and media could rouse the population to a fever pitch of

Militarism refers to a societal emphasis on military ideals and a glorification of war.

Militarization occurs when an entire society is mobilized around militaristic goals.

Contemporary American society is characterized by *militarism,* the societal emphasis on military ideals and virtues, the glorification of war, and large expenditures on weapons. In fact, about 30% of our national budget is earmarked for military expenses. (© George Hall/Woodfin Camp and Associates)

military fervor, but conscription has not been very popular despite support for particular wars.

Until recently, the United States was able to avoid the militarism of other modern nation-states by her physical and ideological isolation from the rest of the world. We conducted limited wars against Native Americans, the British, and the Spanish for territory on this continent. And we did not hesitate to invade or create revolutions in those South and Central American countries where U.S. corporations have extensive business interests. But involvement in the European World Wars of this century came reluctantly. Today, however, the United States ranks among the most thoroughly militarized of modern societies.

In part, militarism is an inevitable correlate of the centralized state and the international system of trade, where wars are fought for economic as well as political goals (Galtung 1985). In part, the rise of militarism in America is related to our assuming, at the end of World War II, the role of "leader of the free world." The 1950s saw the beginning of a "cold war" between the United States and the Soviet Union, each fearful of the other's power,

and each convincing its population that the other represented all the forces of darkness ("capitalist dogs" and "communist atheists").

Unable to stop the spiral of fear, each superpower and a host of lesser powers have become dominated by military goals, military values, and military expenditures. Military concerns now outweigh other influences on foreign policy, trade, and aid—all have become weapons in a war between good and evil. This presents a special problem to democratic societies because the military is by nature a totalitarian institution. It becomes increasingly difficult for civilian authorities to control or even question military leaders who operate behind a veil of secrecy labeled "national security." Secrecy, propaganda, and censorship all erode democratic institutions.

Militarism invades the culture: movies, television, and children's cartoon programs all glorify combat as a solution to political and social problems. Indeed, one culture hero of the 1980s, Rambo, defies even the U.S. military because he feels it has been *too soft* on the red menace. Of course, when one's enemies take the law into their hands, they are called "terrorists."

War and military experiences remain basically a male experience. Most boys are exposed to war toys and learn to play with them. This is part of the socialization process that prepares boys to become "real" men. (© Judy S. Gelles/Stock Boston)

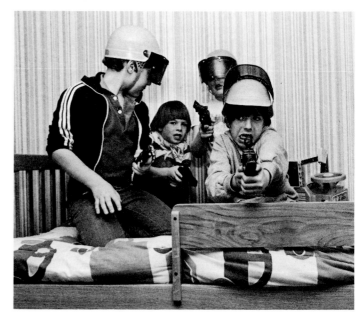

All males who play with war toys are not boys. (© Nancy Moran/SYGMA)

Children's toys and games reflect this new emphasis. In the United States, sales of war toys increased 600 percent between 1982 and 1986. More than 218 million war toys and accessories were sold in 1985—about five for every child in the nation (*Defense Monitor* 1986). Cartoon series featuring robots and action figures with names such as "Ripsaw" and "Twinblade" fill the time slots for children's entertainment. As part of the Reagan administration's goal of deregulating businesses, all guidelines for children's programming were lifted in 1983.

Older children and adults are not immune from the excitement of military things: camouflage suits, shooting galleries, video games, soft air guns, training camps for would-be mercenaries, and magazines such as *Soldier of Fortune* have all enjoyed great popularity in the mid-1980s. From a feminist perspective, militarism and masculinity are intertwined; both are grounded in a glorification of male power and can be seen as logical extensions of the relationships of patriarchy (Enloe 1987).

The greatest impact of militarism, however, will be felt in the area of domestic policy and priorities for federal spending.

The Military-Industrial State.   In his Farewell Address to the Nation in January 1961, President Dwight D. Eisenhower, a military leader of World War II, warned the country about a new threat to democratic government and the pursuit of world peace: the combination of a large permanent military establishment and an immense arms industry (1961/1985). This *military-industrial complex* could, he saw, become an independent power in setting priorities in both our domestic and foreign relations. Supporting such a vast apparatus would take funds from civilian projects, and once in place, the complex would have a vested interest in world conflict rather than peace. In the words of C. Wright Mills (1976) our society would be characterized by a "permanent war economy."

Twenty-six years later, out of a total proposed U.S. budget of one *trillion* dollars, 29 percent (or $293,000,000,000) is earmarked for military expenses. In comparison, roughly one-tenth of the 1987 total is budgeted for education, employment, and social services—an amount that represents a reduction from 1986 spending levels (Office of Management and Budget 1987). Most of the current and future American military budget is devoted to complex weapons systems such as the MX missile ($25 billion), Trident submarines ($67 billion), B1B bombers ($28 billion), and the Strategic Defense Initiative ("Star Wars") at a minimum of $70 billion for research and development. Spending increases have been much more limited for more conventional weapons, and for training and maintaining a peacetime military.

Throughout the world, military spending has escalated since the 1960s until, today, the international trade in armaments is greater than that in food (Worldwatch 1986). The grand total spent on arms worldwide in 1985—$980 billion—is more than the combined income of the poorest half of all nations. In Third World countries, military expenses absorb the money needed to improve agriculture or build industries. In Ethiopia, for example, where famine is widespread, 42 percent of the government budget went to the military (Worldwatch 1986). The chief beneficiaries of this spending are the arms industries of the United States and the Soviet Union (Kurtz 1987).

The cost of weapons also strains the economies of developed nations. Although

The **military-industrial complex** consists of a large permanent military establishment combined with an immense armament industry.

On May 28, 1987, Matthias Rust, a 19-year-old German pilot, flew a single-engine Cessna 172 from Helsinki, Finland into Red Square in Moscow, the capital of the Soviet Union. The intrusion occurred despite the fact that the U.S.S.R. has an Air Defense command of 550,000 personnel in service and over 2,500 interceptor aircraft. Two days later the Defense Minister and the Commander of the Soviet Air Defenses were dismissed from their commands because they "had shown intolerable unconcern and indecision about cutting short the flight of the violator plane without resorting to combat means." Even extreme military surveillance may not achieve its goals. (© SYGMA)

supporters of defense spending claim that this stimulates the whole economy, several recent studies suggest the opposite effect. The countries with the *lowest* percentage of national income devoted to the military have the *most* competitive economies (Kaldor et al. 1986). This is because more money is available for the kind of research and development that increase the productivity of consumer industries. In societies with high military budgets, defense industries can hire scientists away from civilian employment; the systems they produce for the military do not always have affordable consumer uses, so that domestic industries lose their competitive edge. In addition, the money in the pockets of defense workers can create de-

mands that the civilian sector cannot fill, thus fueling inflation. And finally, compared to education, health care, and community services, dollars spent on the military create the fewest new jobs while providing high incomes to a few workers at public expense (Adams 1982, Feagin 1986).

Warfare Welfare. But the military-industrial complex, as Eisenhower foresaw, has great power to persuade Congress and the public that our military needs are paramount. In part, their success depends on continued fear of the power of the Soviet Union and the belief that the Soviets are arming themselves at a faster pace than the United States. In March 1987, for example, the Defense Department issued its sixth annual report on Soviet military power, which found once again that the Soviets have been gaining in almost every military category in preparation for a major conflict with the United States. These reports have been very effective in convincing the Congress and American people to increase the American military budget. The reelection of Ronald Reagan in 1984 was strong evidence of continued public preference for military over domestic spending.

In part, also, the success of the military-industrial complex is a product of the vast amounts of money at stake. Members of Congress compete to win defense contracts for their districts; defense contractors spend a great deal of money on political candidates; retired Pentagon officers take jobs in defense industries. A vast system of "weapons welfarism" has emerged, with little supervision by civilian authorities (Feagin 1986, Melman 1986). As a consequence, vast cost overruns are the norm. Thousand-dollar oil plugs and hundred-dollar resistors add up to hundreds of millions of dollars of taxpayer money transferred to defense contractors. Although forty-five of the top 100 defense companies were under criminal investigation for fraud in 1984, little has been done to change the ways in which defense contracts are awarded.

There are other types of cost attached to this level of military spending. On the one hand, critics of military spending note that as increased numbers of people depend on the military budget for their livelihood, the more difficult it becomes to change priorities. And once the complex weapons systems are in place, the temptation to use them grows, while the sheer number and variety of offensive weapons in every part of the world today raises the possibility of accidental war. On the other hand, supporters of the military buildup claim that the surest guarantee of peace is the ability to punish attackers, so that military strength is a *deterrent* to our enemies. These positions have become the center of a major debate on the causes, the risks, and the consequences of nuclear war (Evans and Hilgartner 1987).

Nuclear War. The arms race that has overtaken so many industrial and developing nations has also spread to the atmosphere. Today's nuclear weapons are faster, more accurate, and far more powerful than imagined only a decade ago. Although only six nations acknowledge having nuclear weapons, another two dozen could be well on their way. Nuclear power reactors and research facilities are a global phenomenon. Compared to the total power of munitions used in World War II, the combined power of the world's *known* stockpile of nuclear weapons is 5000 times greater, as seen in Figure 13-5. Each of the five thousand squares in Figure 13-5 represents all the firepower used over the four years of World War II.

Thus, the sheer volume of potential destructiveness directs attention to the new nuclear arms race. The two leading players, the United States and the Soviet Union, appear to be matching one another in developing weapons and counterweapons, despite the fact that each could now wipe out most of humanity several times over, and all in the space of a few minutes. The rationale is that so long as neither superpower feels that the other has distinct advantage in being able to strike first without suffering equivalent damage, a state of "mutually assured destruction" (MAD) will maintain world peace.

Despite periodic posturing and threats, both superpowers have thus far basically honored a set of treaties that limit testing and deployment The uncertainties of super-power relations, however, have generated peace movements in Western Europe and the United States. Millions of citizens have demonstrated in favor of a *nuclear freeze*—an immediate and mutual stop to all testing and deployment. The counterargument is that since mutuality is highly unlikely, the advocates of a

Nuclear freeze refers to an immediate and mutual halt to all testing and deployment.

Figure 13-5
A single square above represents the TNT equivalent of the munitions used in World War II. An estimated 3 million tons were used in that war. The block of squares represents the TNT equivalent of today's world stockpile of nuclear weapons. Estimated at 16,000 million tons of TNT, these weapons alone have over 5,000 times the destructive power of World War II. (Source: Sivard, 1985: 16.)

Criminology, Justice, and Peace

RICHARD QUINNEY

Richard Quinney, professor of sociology at Northern Illinois University, is certainly the most distinguished criminologist of his generation. He has written extensively, producing fifteen books and fifty articles in the field of criminology. In 1984 he was awarded the Edwin Sutherland Award for his contributions to criminological theory by the American Society of Criminology. In this vignette he speaks of his commitment to social justice and of his eventual transition to Buddhism.

Perhaps this thought about crime and justice began in a landscape of woods and fields, under a sky filled with white clouds, along a ridge that stretched into the far horizon, somewhere in Wisconsin. In long summer evenings in the early 1940s, after the cows had been milked, we would jump on our bicycles and play out the adventures of the Lone Ranger and Tonto, American radio heroes of the day. The narrator's words rang in my ears: *"(The early settlers) have given you a land where there is true freedom, true equality of opportunity. A nation that is governed by the people. By laws that are best for the greatest number. Your duty is to preserve that heritage and strengthen it. That is the duty and heritage of every American."*

And he went on about the man whose adventures we followed: *"This is the legend of a man who buried his identity to dedicate his life to the service of humanity and country. It is the story of the origin of the Lone Ranger."*

With imaginary silver bullets blazing into the sky, I knew that the world stretched far beyond my family's Wisconsin dairy farm. I was truly inspired by what might be done in this life and I truly believed in the "forces of good and evil" as they had been defined for me.

But the ideals I learned in childhood—on the radio, in the one-room schoolhouse, in the Methodist Church, and from my parents—were soon to be tested. I noticed that farm families seemed to lack the opportunities of families in town. I felt discriminated against in high school. I came up against those small town sophisticated kids who made me feel like I was from the backwoods—"farmer" they called me. Law, when it could be observed, did not always appear to be just. One evening in town as I sat beside the hotel, I was initiated into the cruel workings of legal "justice." Bold headlines in the evening newspaper announced the execution of Julius and Ethel Rosenberg. Still proclaiming their innocence after the final refusal of the judge to consider their appeal, they were killed in the electric chair. Earlier that year, Senator Joseph McCarthy, who tried to find the communists in our nation, sent a picture postcard of himself to the farm asking for our vote. The era of the political witch-hunt followed. I was becoming politically aware.

In college and in graduate school—at a time in the 1950s before students were exposed to critical and Marxist ideas—I began to realize that this country was dominated by those with money and power. The laws did not always seem to be for the greatest number, nor for the protection of all. The social activism of the '60s created an awareness that came to be central to the understanding of law, crime, and justice in the United States.

A new criminology developed, shaped by a succession of events: the attempted invasion of Cuba in 1961; the assassination of President John F. Kennedy; the civil rights movement; the emergence of a counterculture; opposition to the Vietnam War and to the Cambodian invasion; a questioning of the foundations of higher education; urban riots against unemployment, poor housing, and social conditions of blacks; and the assassination of Martin Luther King, Jr.

Living through these events I knew that my work in sociology and criminology must reflect what is happening in the real world. I felt that a relevant criminology could be created only when personal ideals provided a vision for an understanding of crime. I attempted to develop a theoretical perspective that would critically examine the established order. Marxist criminology provided an analysis that was, I felt, essential to the understanding of reality in American society, for we had been taught to identify good and evil in ways that legitimized the interests of the ruling class.

My own efforts, however, gradually moved to an analysis based on a spiritual, as well as a materialist, understanding of human existence. Materialism alone has not provided adequate solutions. The official policies and programs of recent years—promoted in the name of criminal justice—have, in fact, removed us even further from reducing the crime problems. The law has been reformulated, offenders have been punished, and knowledge has been quantified.

Yet the United States remains a crime-ridden nation. In spite of all the wealth, economic development, and scientific advances, this country has one of the worst crime records in the world. Something in our analysis has been missing. A criminology must be recreated to be relevant to the present era, and to the one that is emerging. I would like to briefly indicate what the premises of that new criminology might be like based on my journey toward Buddhism, a framework within which I believe we can find the foundations of peacemaking.

Thought, in the Western rational mode, is conditional; it limits knowledge to what is already known.

Yet, in Buddhist thought, each life is a separate spiritual journey into the unknown and the unknowable, beyond the ego-centered self. It is necessary, therefore, to go beyond Western thought. We must see that human existence is characterized by suffering; crime is suffering, and the sources of suffering are within each of us. Only by going beyond the ego-centered self, can we end suffering and live in peace, personally and collectively. Love and compassion and the end of suffering and crime will be attained through quieting of the mind and an opening of the heart, through being aware.

Understanding, service, justice—all these—flow naturally from love and compassion, from mindful attention to the reality of all that is, here and now.

In this way a criminology of *peacemaking,* a nonviolent criminology of compassion and service, will create a just society for the living of peaceful lives.

---

freeze are really asking the United States to make a one-sided (unilateral) bargain. The logic of a freeze—that members of both societies would benefit from reduced military expenditures and a lessening of the risk of death—becomes distorted by the realities of international power politics, internal power struggles within each society, and the particular fears of individual leaders.

The triumph of militarism occurs when political leaders choose military solutions to complex social and economic problems in the world, and thereby escalate the arms race (Kaku and Axelrod 1987). But it is important to realize that the seeds of today's nuclear-war threat were planted at the very beginning of the atomic age when the fear of communism led our political and military leaders to insist on absolute superiority in the development and production of nuclear weapons (Boyer 1985). Government and military leaders also succeeded in convincing the media to play down "hysteria" over the dangers of radioactivity while emphasizing the positive aspects of the nuclear age. As a result, nuclear policy was not fully debated in its formative stages, but left in the hands of "experts" with their own agendas.

Social scientists, along with the great mass of Americans, were slow to recognize all the implications of the atomic nuclear age. But the threat of nuclear extinction has served to focus attention on these issues. As a result, the Sociology of Peace and War is now a recognized specialty within the American Sociological Association. Research topics include the power of the military-industrial complex, the manipulation of public opinion, military personnel as social actors, masculinity and militarism, the dynamics of international cooperation and competition, and the consequences of the arms race. Nuclear war, it appears, is too important to be left to generals and physicists.

Summary

The study of political systems begins with an analysis of power and the legitimate bases of authority in tradition, charisma, or law. As social systems become more complex, governing institutions called the state emerge. In all societies, the political system is linked to other institutional spheres, particularly the economy. A combination of political and economic forces has led to the establishment of the welfare state in most modern societies.

Political systems can be ranged along a continuum from totalitarianism to democracy, depending on the degree to which citizens have rights against the state and can freely engage in dissent from and opposition to their rulers. All governments attempt to manipulate public opinion through the selective control over information—propaganda and censorship—and to chill dissent by surveillance. Although these techniques are dominant in totalitarian systems, the "iron law of oligarchy" suggests that all power holders are tempted to manipulative actions.

In a democracy, citizens participate in

the political process through running for office, working on campaigns, and voting—or not voting. These forms of participation are socially structured, with certain subgroups historically overrepresented as candidates and voters.

Sociologists have developed two models for analyzing the structure of power in our society: the power-elite model and the pluralist model. Each is valuable in explaining some types of power systems. Both point up the fact that the majority of citizens are politically inactive, a situation that may be changing through the spread of community-action groups.

A defining characteristic of the state is its monopoly over the use of legitimate force: the police for internal order; the military for external defense. The American military has historically been based on the ideal of the civilian-solider, but beginning in 1973 the armed forces have been composed of volunteers and an enlarged

professional officer corps. The contemporary American military differs from that of the past in the proportion of blacks, Hispanics, and women in both the enlisted and officer ranks, and in the presence on base of families of enlisted personnel.

Many sociologists have noted a recent trend toward the *militarization* of American society, in which military goals determine foreign policy and domestic budget priorities. The spread of militaristic values in the culture may be seen in children's toys and adult's leisure activities. The military-industrial complex is a dominant feature of our economy and our foreign trade. Around the world, military spending has increased dramatically in the past few decades. As the arms race escalates, especially between the Soviet Union and the United States, so does the possibility of an intentional or accidental outbreak of nuclear war.

Suggested Readings

BERMAN, EDWARD H. *The Influence of the Carnegie, Ford, and Rockefeller Foundations in American Foreign Policy: The Ideology of Philanthropy.* Albany: State University of New York Press, 1983. Shows how large foundations serve as part of a complex network of people and institutions that shape American foreign policy.

DYE, THOMAS R. *Who's Running America?* 3rd ed. Englewood Cliffs, NJ: Prentice-Hall, 1983. An overview of the networks among America's elite through which power and influence are exercised.

FIESE, HANS-PETER, ed. *Since the Prague Spring.* New York: Random House, 1979. Documents and letters that keep alive the long-term struggle for human rights in Eastern Europe. An example of a secular social movement's endurance despite official repression.

MARABLE, MANNING. *Black American Politics: From the Washington Marches to Jesse Jackson.* London: Verso, 1985. An examination of the role of the social-protest movement in electoral politics.

MOORE, BARRINGTON. *Social Origins of Dictatorship and Democracy.* Boston: Beacon Press, 1966. A classic work that analyzes the movements of societies toward either democratic or dictatorial governments.

O'CONNER, JAMES. *Accumulation Crisis.* New York: Basil Blackwell, 1984. A careful analysis of contemporary capitalist society that links political-economic and cultural theory in the explanation of the relationship between the ideology of individualism and current economic crises.

PRZEWORSKI, ADAM. *Capitalism and Social Democracy.* Cambridge: Cambridge University Press, 1985. A stimulating analysis of the persistence of capitalism in spite of the growth of political democracy.

SCHUCK, PETER, and ROGERS M. SMITH. *Citizenship Without Consent: Illegal Aliens in the American Policy.* New Haven: Yale University Press, 1985. An interesting discussion of historical and contemporary issues concerning the rights of citizenship in the United States.

14

Education

I N 1925, a public-school teacher in Dayton, Tenn., named John Scopes, was arrested for teaching Darwin's theory of evolution in violation of state law. After a famous trial, Scopes was found guilty and fined $100. The Tennessee Supreme Court later overturned the conviction on the grounds that the fine was too high, but left the law standing. Sixty-one years later, in 1987,

the Supreme Court of the United States ruled that states could not be required to teach the biblical story of creation along with material on evolution.

• By 1982, over half of all U.S. schools reported receiving objections from community groups regarding materials in the libraries, including some dictionaries (for overly explicit definitions of sexual terms), the story of Robin Hood ("a dangerous advocate of income redistribution"), and the film *Romeo and Juliet* ("encourages drug use"). A major target is teaching materials that deny that there are absolute standards of goodness and truth (Pincus 1984, Hechinger 1986).

- In March 1986, the school board of Winchester, N.H., voted not to renew the contract of a high-school principal who had won national praise for raising the proportion of students going on to college from 10 percent to about half in just five years. The principal was criticized for having a beard, wearing casual clothes, introducing sex-education classes, talking about drug addiction, and trying to use district funds for special-education students. According to his leading critic, "he looks and acts like a tramp" and "the kids . . . he says are emotionally unstable, all they need is a good kick in the butt" (*New York Times,* Apr. 27, 1986, p. 46).

- In June 1986, the U.S. Secretary of Education traveled to Paterson, N.J., to lavish praise on a school principal noted for walking around with a bullhorn and shouting at both students and parents. The principal described parents as welfare cheats and Libyan agents, even suggesting that one woman might be hiding a bomb in her turban (*New York Times,* June 8, 1986, p. E22).

These news items portray a very different educational system from the idealized picture of schools as incubators of intellectual freedom and curiosity. In actuality, the American school system has never really been as sheltered from outside pressures as we would like to believe. As a major institutional sphere of any society, education is linked to other institutional structures: the family, the economy, the polity, and the belief system. Thus, it is not surprising that the past eight years have seen a number of attempts to shape the system to serve the ideological goals of religious and political conservatives. As a consequence, there has been renewed emphasis on content supporting the existing stratification system, and on traditional teach-

The lawyer Clarence Darrow is pictured here to the right of John Scopes (center) after the so-called "monkey trial" of 1925. Scopes was tried for teaching Darwin's theory of Evolution in the public schools. (© UPI/ Bettmann Newsphotos)

ing methods and discipline, including physical punishments. (The United States is one of only five modern societies that still permits students to be hit by school authorities.)

Clearly, parents and outside-interest groups representing a variety of viewpoints perceive the educational system as a major battleground for the hearts and minds of the next generation of adult citizens. Just as blacks and feminists in the 1960s and 1970s criticized the structures and content of education for racist and sexist biases, so, today, powerful backlash forces are pressing for changes that reflect their vision of what is good for children and the society.

Indeed, it is not too strong to speak of the educational system today as "under siege" (Aronowitz and Giroux 1985), attacked from the left, right, and center of the political spectrum. Critics of the left view the schools as agents of socialization to inequality. Critics from the right, as seen in the news items, fear that young people are being given too much freedom of thought and action. And from the center come reports from foundations and national commissions warning of a "tide of mediocrity" about to sweep America out of world leadership (National Commission on Excellence in Education 1983, Carnegie Foundation 1983).

In this chapter we examine the historical role of the American educational system, its functions and dysfunctions, and links with other institutional spheres. We will also explore the social system of the classroom, the structure of higher education (colleges and universities), and current controversies over quality and equality in America's schools.

Many of the functions of education are *manifest,* that is, stated and intended goals such as transmitting the culture to newcomers (whether children or immigrants), training people for adult roles, developing skills, and creating new knowledge.

Schools also serve *latent* functions; that is, there are consequences of the educational process which are not part of its stated or intended goals. The term *hidden curriculum* refers to the other material learned in educational settings, such as ethnocentrism and respect for authority. In contemporary America, for example, one might also learn lessons in sexism, racism, anticommunism, homophobia, competition, and the superiority of non-manual over manual labor.

In addition, school systems in industrial societies are important channels of social placement, serving as gatekeepers to occupations, and sorting students into "winners" and "losers."

Manifest functions of education are its stated and intended goals such as transmitting the culture to newcomers.

Latent functions are the consequences of the educational process which are not part of its stated and intended goals.

The **hidden curriculum** refers to material learned, such as ethnocentrism and respect for authority, which are not part of the official curriculum.

Functions of Education

A major **function of education** is to extend the socialization process begun in the family.

Education extends the socialization process that starts in the family. Because family members often cannot teach all that a child needs to know, other agents of the society take over the task of presenting specialized knowledge. The more complex the society, the less family-bound and more lengthy the educational process.

In simple gathering societies, both boys and girls learn very similar skills by watching and imitating older children or adults. In societies with many specialized occupations, family members may be able to retain control over certain skills, as in apprenticeship programs, but many other occupations are not so easily handed down from parent to child. Still others require long periods of special training. The earliest schools were developed for such jobs: for scribes in Egypt and China, philosophers in Greece, and priests in Judea.

Educational systems in complex societies are also charged with the societal goal of promoting unity within the group. The assumption is that if all children learn the same basics—language, values, beliefs about what is good and right—there will be fundamental agreement on group goals ("value consensus").

TRANSMITTING THE CULTURE

Because our society is so diverse, it is difficult to define "an" American culture, although there are certain broad beliefs and conceptions of the good that are generally shared (see Chapter 3). Achieving such consensus is all the more difficult as the American educational system is based on local control by elected school boards in over 16,000 separate districts representing extremely diverse populations. Thus, the task of presenting a common culture today has primarily fallen on the writers and publishers of textbooks. What is learned by American schoolchildren has been filtered through many layers of potential bias as a result of decisions by textbook writers, by the publishers in the interest of profit making, and by the local school boards that select the books.

As a result, textbooks have become a political battleground, not only through attempts at censorship, but through the threat of loss of income for publishers. Because elementary and high-school books are often adopted statewide, publishing companies are under pressure to produce books that offend the fewest people and that can sell in all parts of the country. One solution is to simply leave out such

In 1986, in what has been called the "Scopes Trial II," in Greenville, Tennessee, a fundamentalist Christian parents group, led by Vicki Frost, shown here, brought suit against the school board for providing students with textbooks that offended their religious beliefs. Among the books parents found objectionable were *The Wizard of Oz,* because it portrayed courage, intelligence, and compassion as personally developed rather than God-given; *Cinderella,* because it mentioned magic; and *The Diary of Anne Frank,* because it suggested that all religions are equal. The lower court ruled in their favor. In August 1987, however, a federal court overturned this decision. (© Rob Nelson/Picture Group)

controversial topics as the women's movement, poverty and hunger, and, of course, evolution (Heard 1982, People For the American Way 1986). Further, what is left in is often presented as colorlessly as possible in the hopes that community groups will not notice (which means that students might not, either).

History textbooks are particularly important because they shape the student's view of this country and its role in the world. Recent surveys of school textbooks, however, indicate that students learn little about the rest of the world and even that little is often oversimplified and/or distorted (Anyon 1979, Brown 1981, Beck and Anderson 1983).

Thus, the culture that is transmitted is a social product, its content shaped by conflict among interest groups, the norms of the local communities, and publishers' need to make a profit. It is also a culture that is heavily biased toward the *status quo* (things as they are), that downplays

368

conflict and dissent, that defines inequality as a personal problem, and that reflects a white middle-class, male-dominated world from which many students are excluded and made to feel inferior (Bourdieu and Passeron 1977, Apple 1982, Freire 1985).

ACCULTURATION OF IMMIGRANTS

As described in Chapter 10, city schools in the early part of this century were thought to be the "melting pots" in which diverse ethnic groups would lose their uniqueness while learning English and the basics of modern industrial society. Because the period from 1880 to 1920 was one of enormous economic growth, absorbing millions of skilled and semi-skilled workers, the schools were able to fulfill this function relatively successfully.

The fact that the same school systems today are having less success with black and Hispanic youngsters must also be viewed in historical perspective. The types of students, their teachers, the physical settings, surrounding community, employment opportunities, and attitudes toward educational authorities are all very different today.

TRAINING FOR ADULT STATUSES

A second major function of formal education is to prepare children to accept their eventual roles in community, family, and workplace. From the first day in school to the last, students are taught the virtues of their society, respect for its leaders, good work habits, and the benefits of conformity.

Young people are also presented with direct and indirect training in traditional family roles. Although schoolbooks today have moved away from the idealized images of suburban family life of only a decade ago, there are limits to how realistically they can portray modern realities without evoking a strong reaction from parents who do not want their children to read about divorce and single parenting, much less teenage pregnancy and domestic violence.

Sex education is another area of fierce debate among parents, religious leaders, and school boards. Rather than offend some parents, most school boards find it safest to confine sex education to a short course on reproductive biology rather than to discussions of the responsibilities and risks of sexual activity (Richardson and Cranston 1981). But given the rising rate of unwed teenage pregnancy and increasing alarm over sexually transmitted diseases, a number of states and local districts are mandating earlier and broader education in sexuality. Opponents claim that such material only encourages early experimentation, and that if a values dimension is added, this gives the school an authority that properly belongs to the family. Despite such opposition, public support for sex education in the schools remains very high and the trend is toward integrating this material into the general curriculum at ever earlier grades.

Socialization to *work roles* is both general (obedience, promptness, discipline) and particular. Typically, *vocational education* is targeted to children of the working class—shop and auto mechanics for the boys, typing and hairdressing for the girls. By convincing students that this is all to which they can aspire, school authorities "cool out" potential competitors for higher-status jobs.

Many critics charge that these latent functions are actually the heart of schooling. Learning to know one's place, to obey superiors, to believe that the system is fair, are lessons that last a lifetime, long after one has forgotten the dates of the Civil War (Best 1983). In this perspective, kindergarten has been described as "boot camp" (Gracey 1977), and high school compared to prison (Haney and Zimbardo 1975).

DEVELOPING TALENT

The manifest function of the American school system is to identify and nurture talent by offering a "free" (publicly financed) education to each child. In modern societies, where achievement is thought to replace ascription as the basis of occupational status, the schools become the crucial link between ability and mobility.

From the functional view, then, schools encourage competition in order to separate the best students from the less able, thus creating a hierarchy of intelligence, or a *meritocracy,* based solely on an individual's innate talent. The underlying assumptions are (1) that school personnel can accurately identify bright and dull students, (2) that standardized tests are an objective means for achieving this goal, and (3) that differences in test scores

Meritocracy is a hierarchy of talent.

As computer literacy becomes increasingly important for adult work roles, more schools and colleges are offering computer training for their students. This training will differ in content and complexity depending on the occupational goals expected of the particular student population. (© Brownie Harris/The Stock Market)

reflect innate differences in intellectual functioning. In other words, the basic premise is that given an equal opportunity to learn, unequal outcomes are due to personal qualities (e.g. Ravitch 1983). In this way, functionalists claim that society as a whole benefits from the skills of its brightest members, while all individuals are helped to find their "natural" level.

CREATING NEW KNOWLEDGE

Modern industrial societies depend on continued production of scientific and technological information. Because knowledge is a form of power, it has always been the monopoly of a few: witch doctors, storytellers, scribes, monks, and in modern societies, academics. In medieval Europe, religious institutions were the centers of knowledge, but with the surge of interest in science during the Renaissance, Reformation, and Age of Enlightenment, nonreligious ("secular") universities gradually became the primary sources of new knowledge.

But the domination of universities is challenged today by private foundations and corporate research and development divisions, which can offer higher pay and better working conditions to professionals. Research is also carried out directly by various departments of government at all levels. As a result, universities have lost some of their power in relation to other societal institutions.

Nonetheless, the research function remains central to the university's mission, and has expanded along with the size of its graduate schools. Graduate students must perform original research to earn their masters and doctorates. Professors must publish a number of research-based books and papers in order to be promoted or receive tenure. Further, the financial lifeblood of many graduate departments today is a share of the research grant money that professors are able to win from government, business, or foundations.

The Conflict Perspective

Each of the major functional assumptions has been challenged from the conflict perspective which focuses on the hidden curriculum rather than the stated claims of educators. From this point of view (superbly analyzed in Giroux 1983) it is argued that:

- schools sort students into winners and losers on the basis of *nonacademic* variables such as race, gender, and social class.
- the educational system is designed to reproduce inequality, in support of an economic system that requires a large and obedient labor force led by a small elite of owners and managers (see also Freire 1986).
- a belief in meritocratic selection leads people who do not succeed to blame themselves for their failure.
- the approved "culture" as reflected in curriculum and textbooks works to *delegitimize* other ways of perceiving.
- middle-class parents are able to secure privileges for their children in contrast to the relative powerlessness of lower-strata parents with children in the same schools (Sieber 1981).

At the microlevel, interaction between students and their teachers and administrators, as well as the very structure of the classroom, reinforce all these tendencies toward rationalizing and maintaining inequality (see the selections in Appel and Weiss 1984).

Critics also charge that standardized tests do not measure an innate intelligence so much as the ability to do well on the tests—which is no small talent since the tests are fairly accurate predictors of school performance. Young people who are well socialized to the dominant culture will therefore have a great advantage.

Both functional and conflict theorists see the educational system as a "filtering process" that channels students into particular programs and academic careers. Where the perspectives differ is: (1) in their explanation of the basis on which educational decisions are made: talent or social background; and (2) for what goals: developing talent or maintaining the social class system.

THE EVIDENCE

In general, children from the middle and upper social strata score higher on standardized tests and are likely to remain in school longer regardless of their test scores, than do other children. Most evidence on the link between individual intellectual skills and social rewards suggests that the United States has a long way to go before the claim of a meritocracy can be supported (Livingstone 1983, Krauze and Slomcyznski 1985).

Tracking.   As compared with only fifteen years ago, students are now assigned to *"tracks"* or programs of varying content and pacing at increasingly earlier ages. A single school class will therefore be divided into several levels that often coincide with social-class background. This track placement, in turn, affects the quality and length of education received by the student (Oakes 1985). These outcomes are not unique to the United States, but are found in other modern industrial societies such as Israel (Shavit 1984) and Scotland (Willms 1986).

Cultural Capital.   The effects of parents' social status on their offsprings' educational attainment (highest grade completed) have been clear and consistent throughout this century (Mare 1981), even though a higher proportion of people attend school for more years with each new cohort of students.

Quite apart from their financial resources, which can be used to purchase tutoring or private schooling, wealthier parents also transmit *cultural capital* (Bourdieu 1984, Dimaggio 1982). Cultural capital refers to a style of talking and thinking, as well as an interest in music, art, and literature that allows a person to move freely among creators of the dominant culture.

Achievement Expectations.   As we noted in Chapter 5, the use of "psychological" rather than physical disciplining techniques by middle-class parents leads to internalized guilt and high-achievement motivation in their children. Further, these parents stress the development of cognitive abilities, high expectations, and a sense of competence (Davis and Kandel 1981, Mercy and Steelman 1982, Looker and Pineo 1983).

Because middle-class parents have more control over their environment, they can make "deferred gratification" pay off, and their offspring know this, in contrast to children from low-income families who

accurately perceive their parents' lack of social power.

Family Size.   Middle-class students also benefit from having fewer siblings than is typical for working-class families. If children develop verbal and cognitive skills through interaction with parents, those from small families will spend more time with parents than with peers and siblings, in comparison to children from large families (Zajonc 1986, but see Ernst and Angst 1983).

Family size often outweighs the effect of social class, as seen in the achievement of working-class youth from small families (Alwin and Thornton 1984, Blake 1985). If this is so, then the general societal trend toward small families should weaken the advantages currently enjoyed by middle-class students.

For all these reasons, then, regardless of ability, youth from the higher social strata compared to other students, do better in school, stay there longer, and are ultimately prepared to move into higher-status occupations. Although family SES appears to have a stronger direct effect on school performance in early childhood than in late adolescence, the advantages tend to be cumulative (Alwin and Thornton 1984).

The Structure of the American Educational System

In all modern industrial societies, education has become increasingly *differentiated* and *specialized*. Where, for example, there was once a one-room schoolhouse, there are now age-graded classes divided among elementary, intermediate, junior high, and high schools.

Knowledge is similarly separated into categories, to be taught by specialists. Eventually, students are expected to choose one distinct package of information (their "major") that will prepare them for the world of work.

Career specialization is most marked at the *post-secondary* (after high school) level. Students who do not go directly to college can select from a number of alternatives: apprenticeship programs, voca-

---

Tracks are programs of varying content and pacing, to which students are assigned.

Cultural capital refers to a style of talking and thinking as well as an interest in music, art, and literature which prepares individuals for membership in the dominant culture.

Post-secondary education takes place after high school.

tional schools, certificate studies, or on-the-job training.

INCLUSIVENESS

The American education system is also *inclusive,* that is, open as opposed to closed or exclusive. Over time, the ages at which children must enter or leave school have been extended, so that almost all children age five to sixteen are currently enrolled.

Unlike many European school systems, the American high school provides a general ("comprehensive") education, although within the schools, students are channeled into college-preparatory and vocational tracks.

In addition, *pre*kindergarten schooling is on the increase, for children of both the poor and the wealthy (Fiske 1986). For disadvantaged children, Head Start and similar programs are designed to remedy the lack of cultural capital in their homes and neighborhoods. For offspring of the well-to-do, early childhood education is seen as a means of encouraging cognitive development. Many schools now run half- and even full-day programs for three- and four-year-olds, which is a great help to both dual-earner parents and single parents. Although it is still too early to assess the long-term effects of such programs, the evidence thus far suggests no harmful consequences (Scarr 1985, Hechinger 1987).

Nor does education stop at high-school or college graduation. Millions of Americans are enrolled in adult education classes, both academic and vocational, and thousands more are part-time college students.

In all, about 60 million Americans age three and over are enrolled in school, including 2.5 million nursery schoolers and 12.5 million college students (Bureau of the Census, No. 409, 1986, p. 20). The numbers in elementary and high schools have dropped sharply as a consequence of the declining fertility rate, while the numbers attending college and preschool have risen modestly.

Educational Attainment. As a result of the trend toward inclusiveness, the percent of young adults (age twenty-five to twenty-nine) who completed high school has risen dramatically since 1940: from 11.5 percent to over 85 percent in 1983. In the same period, the proportion completing four or more years of college rose from 10.2 percent to 22 percent (U.S. Bureau of the Census, 1985b, p. 3).

Indeed, the proportion of Americans age twenty-five and over who have had any college education—about one-third—is the highest in the world. In general, differences in educational attainment *within* our population have declined over the past forty years; that is, the spread has narrowed, with more people clustered around the median (12.6 years).

The American education system is **inclusive,** or open, to almost all children of given ages.

How do you think the typical school day in this small 1912 public school compared to a typical school day in the suburban school pictured on page 377 of this chapter? How does the structure of the school day mirror the structure of the society in which it occurs? (© M. E. Warren Collection/Photo Researchers, Inc.)

IQ, Test Scores, and Race

Some social scientists (for example, Jensen 1981) believe that the abilities measured by standardized tests of intelligence are largely inherited. Therefore, they claim, consistent differences in test scores between white and black children can be used as evidence of a basic inherited difference in intellectual capacity. Most scientists, however, argue that there are few, if any, inborn biologically based differences by race (or religion or ethnic background), even though each person is different from any other. Biological tendencies, remember, are expressed within a cultural and social context, so that measured intelligence is the outcome of the interplay between inherited abilities and learning in particular environments.

Intelligence is not a single trait but a bundle of capacities that people have in different combinations and strengths at various ages. Moreover, reported IQ differences refer to *group* averages and not universal individual differences. There is evidence in some American tests that the items reflect a middle-class, white experience of the world (Taylor 1980).

For all these reasons, conclusions about the intellectual abilities of any racial or ethnic group are probably more *political* than scientific. The IQ controversy has been used to justify different educational treatment of blacks and Hispanics. For example, researchers in California were struck by the many Mexican-American and black children referred to classes for the mentally impaired. Although the youngsters had IQ measurements well below average, they were actually neither feebleminded nor retarded. They could not understand the tests. Most could easily care for themselves, maintain social relationships, and deal with the world outside of school (Mercer 1973). On the basis of interview data, observations, and medical examinations, most of the students were reassigned to regular classes. Nonetheless, IQ tests are still being used to identify and separate the "retarded" in many school districts (Berk et al. 1981).

After a careful review of existing theories and data, Scarr (1981) concluded that inherited differences may account for some variation among American whites in average or better-than-average homes, but the cognitive differences between white and black children are largely due to cultural and lifestyle factors (see also Blau 1981). Recent data from the College Entrance Examination Board (Biemiller 1982) show that the average differences in black and white Scholastic Aptitude Test (SAT) scores become smaller as family income level rises. For both groups, the scores are higher for children from high-income and high-education families, but the black students' scores rise faster than those for whites (Burton and Jones 1982). In addition, contrary to the testmakers' claims, students can improve their SAT scores by taking cram courses.

Other research has shown that early intervention can dramatically affect the subsequent development of intellectual skills, as seen in the longterm gains registered by Head Start children in the United States (Hechinger 1987).

Reviewing national education tests between 1969 and 1980, Jones (1982) found strong gains in the performance of black students, which he attributed to a belief that schooling would lead to career options that simply were not available before, however hard working or bright the student. Other educators agree that federal and state assistance (including hot meals) to low-income school districts and needy children have had a measurable positive effect on school grades and test scores.

Finally, there are differences in "educational technology" and the time spent on instruction and on coverage of challenging material in schools attended primarily by blacks and those attended by nonblacks (Dreeben and Gamoran 1986).

So, also, have differences by race, sex, and age decreased. At the same time, income differences among people with different levels of education have *not* declined. To the contrary, while high-school graduates today earn proportionately more compared to nongraduates than in the past, the differential for college graduates has also risen (U.S. Bureau of the Census, 1985b, p. 11).

For each year in the system, a certain number of pupils drop out for one reason or another. Consider, for example, the career of pupils entering kindergarten in 1969. For every 100 who entered fifth grade in 1974, almost all were still in school for ninth grade, and 89 made it through the 11th grade. During high school, some students dropped out, through academic failure, opportunities for employment, or marriage, but almost three-quarters graduated high school. Almost half of the original 100 entered college, but only half of those completed their studies in four years. Over the following years, half of the dropouts will return, however, and earn the college degree.

These figures are an impressive improvement from fifty years ago when only one-third of the class would graduate high school, or from the 1950s when just half of all high school students earned diplomas. For most of our history, the majority of children received less than eight years of formal schooling. Many immigrant youngsters never attended school, going to work as soon as they were able; and in the American South, no schools at all were provided to black children.

BUREAUCRACY AND EDUCATIONAL INSTITUTIONS

So complex and inclusive has the educational system become that many school districts are organized along the lines of any other large-scale business with multi-million dollar budgets, hundreds of employees, and thousands of clients. The organizational chart of most colleges could as easily be a diagram of Chrysler Motors or the National Broadcasting Corporation. The trustees operate as a board of directors; the president is chief executive officer; the deans are division managers; and department chairs are middle-management supervisors with control over small units of production. Some critics of the American educational system argue that the similarities between running a school and running a business is another way in which the schools reproduce the norms, behaviors, and even the structures of modern capitalism (Bowles and Gintis 1977).

There is, however, a crucial distinction between educational institutions and Chrysler or NBC. Students are not really products, although their achievements (as products of the system) are constantly measured and graded. There is an ongoing tension between students, who wish to be treated as individuals, and the needs of the institution to process large numbers of clients in an orderly way within a specific time period (Appel 1982, Giroux 1983). As schools are bureaucratized, students become numbers on a computer tape. Rules and procedures for grading, promoting,

and graduating become fixed. Administrators and many teachers devote their efforts to keeping the system going and preserving their jobs. The result is another example of *goal displacement,* the tendency for the goals of organizational survival to replace or displace the original goals of education.

PUBLIC AND PRIVATE SYSTEMS

Another structural feature of American education is the existence of two separate school systems: one supported by public taxes and open to all; the other paid for by private fees and selective in admissions.

Approximately 15 percent of American elementary and secondary students are enrolled in private schools.

Parochial Schools. By far the largest number of private schools and students are church-related or *parochial* (the word means "limited," "narrow," or confined to the parish, but has come to refer to religious schools).

And by far the most extensive parochial system in the United States is operated by the Roman Catholic Church: over 9300 elementary and high schools enrolling slightly under three million students. Since 1970, however, the Catholic school system has shrunk by one-third, due in part to the movement of Catholics out of the cities where the schools were located, and their dispersion to the suburbs where there may not be enough families to support a parochial school. In addition, the cost of running these schools has risen dramatically with the hiring of lay teachers, who require competitive salaries, to fill in for the sharp decline in the numbers of nuns and brothers in teaching orders, who received only minimal income. In 1960, three-quarters of the teachers in Catholic schools were members of religious orders; by 1985, fewer than 20 percent were nuns or brothers (*Statistical Abstract,* 1987, p. 132).

In contrast to the Catholic schools, the fastest-growing sector in parochial education today is the American Christian school system operated by conservative Protestant churches, where enrollment doubled between 1970 and 1980 and is still increasing (National Center for Educational Statistics 1983).

Parents send their children to parochial

Goal displacement occurs when organizational survival displaces the original goals of an institution.

Parochial schools refers to private schools operated by religious groups.

As the number of religious who teach declines, students are increasingly likely to have lay teachers even within the parochial setting. Do you think that affects the character of the socialization experience within the school? (© Mark Mittelman/ Taurus Photos)

schools when they feel that the public-school system does not reflect their values. The Catholic school system expanded most rapidly during the period of heaviest Catholic immigration, when parents were dissatisfied with the basically "modern" and Protestant orientation of the public schools (Ralph and Rubinson 1980). American Christian schools today mirror the revival of fundamentalist, traditional beliefs among many Protestants (see Chapter 15). The emphasis is on discipline and unquestioned belief in the absolute truth of the Bible (Peshkin 1986).

But the functions of parochial schools go beyond control of educational content and the insulation of children from competing values and mores; they also channel friendships and ultimately influence mate selection.

Preparatory Schools. These latent functions of private education are especially important in the 20 percent of nonpublic schools that are not church-related or designed for children with special and emotional learning problems. Such schools are places where the sons and daughters of the wealthy receive expensive and academically rigorous educations, in preparation for entry into elite colleges and occupations (hence the term *preparatory*).

Preparatory schools are private schools developed to prepare children of well-off parents for entry into elite colleges.

In a recent study of elite boarding schools (where students live on campus, away from their families), Cookson and Persell (1985) describe the many ways in which this socialization experience prepares students for assuming positions of power in the society—through the curriculum, which builds on and extends the cultural capital of upper-status individuals; the sports programs, which emphasize both competitiveness and teamwork; the role models provided by the teachers, themselves often well-educated members of the upper-middle strata; and, above all, formal and informal rituals that reinforce a sense of superiority and service as members of a privileged class. These elements compose what Cookson and Persell refer to as a "moral education" through which students develop high levels of self-esteem and confidence, and learn to justify their positions of power.

Although there is some evidence that private schools are less exclusive than in the past, close to 30 percent of children from high-income families are enrolled in private schools, compared to one in ten from low-income families, most of whom were enrolled in parochial schools.

Public Schools. The other 85 percent of American schoolchildren attend one of 86,000 elementary and secondary schools financed out of local taxes. The history of public education in America illustrates the interplay of values, economic interests, and educational opportunity. The schools have been transformed by egalitarian social trends in the larger society, and, at other times, influenced by narrower economic or political interests (Carnoy and Levin 1985; Katznelson and Weir 1985).

In the nineteenth century, many public schools were selective in their admissions (Labarree 1984); at the same time large numbers of young people simply failed to attend. Between 1870 and 1940, however, a major effort was made to "professionalize" the public schools—to upgrade the qualifications of teachers, to remove administrative jobs from political influence, and to expand enrollments. The reformers were largely successful in the major cities, with the help of organized labor and in opposition to local business and political leadership (Peterson 1985). The reform movement was less successful in small towns, where public-school authorities were able

375

to resist pressures for change for another decade or so, and to continue to provide unequal services on the basis of a student's race, gender, or social class (Tyack et al. 1984).

Eventually, however, reformists' goals were met, and the public-school system today is characterized by compulsory attendance, acceptance of all but a few severely handicapped children, professionalized (and unionized) teaching staff, and democratically elected school boards.

Educational Quality. Are there major differences in the quality of education offered by public and private schools? One influential study (Coleman et al. 1982) has reported higher achievement-test scores for private-school students compared with those in the public system, but these findings have been criticized by other sociologists (Heyns 1981, Alexander and Cook 1982, Crain and Howley 1982).

Most important is the fact that private schools can select their students, whereas public schools cannot. Furthermore, most private schools place all their students on the academic track, which leads to higher test scores. Because the student bodies are so very different, any comparisons between private and public school test scores is highly questionable. Thus, we do not yet know if the test-score differences reflect the process of selection into the schools or are the product of what is taught and how. As we shall see in a later section, many public schools, even those in low-income areas, can operate as effectively as private schools.

In the Classroom

The functions and structure of schools are macrolevel topics. But schooling actually takes place at the microlevel—in face-to-face interaction among students and teachers in specific classrooms and institutions. These interactions compose the social system of the classroom. Yet this system cannot be understood without reference to the enduring values of our culture: success, achievement, competition, individualism. The goal is to offer "basic training" for adulthood, whether in wealthy suburbs or decaying cities.

SUBURBAN SCHOOLS

The school system of the United States is designed to reward high achievers. From the beginning, children learn that their own success depends on the failure of others. Because there can be few best pupils, students compete with one another; thus the recognition of hierarchy and stratification is built into the school experience.

These lessons are part of the hidden curriculum of the schools throughout the country, particularly in small towns and in the suburbs that grew so rapidly after 1950. Jules Henry (1963) and his students observed suburban classrooms for six years in the late 1950s, noting both the manifest and the latent functions of bits of daily behavior. For example, one boy was having difficulty solving a math problem at the blackboard. He stood in front of the class, paralyzed with anxiety and unable to respond to the teacher's clues as the rest of the children waved their arms for the chance to correct him. Finally, the teacher called on another student, who solved the problem with a great show of triumph—a victory gained at the expense of another pupil's public humiliation.

One recent observational study of over one thousand elementary and secondary classrooms (Goodlad 1983) showed that teaching methods had changed little from those in style decades ago: Teachers talk at pupils; students work on written assignments or answer specific, narrow questions; there is little feedback or guidance from the teacher; and all this is done in an emotionless environment. Such a teaching style reinforces dependence on authority, straight-line thinking, hands-off learning, and passivity (Sirotnik 1983, Bossert 1979). There is little reason to believe that elementary- and high-school classes have changed greatly since this study.

If success depends on self-discipline, conformity to expectations, achievement orientation, and a taste for competition, the suburban schools have been reasonably successful. The suburban high school has, for example, been described as a place where boredom rules and where the student body is fragmented into subcultures of jock, grinds, freaks, greasers, bobos, rah-rahs, hard guys, nerds, and others too bored even to form a subculture (Larkin 1979). This fragmentation of the students works to the advantage of administrators

Both the internal and external space of schools can reflect educational philosophies and approaches to learning. Take a look at this suburban high school building. Some critics have compared high schools to prisons—what do you think? (© Susan McCartney/Photo Researchers, Inc.)

in maintaining order. The inability of students to break out of their peer group and mount an effective challenge to school authorities prepares them for a lifetime of political apathy and obedience, concentrating their energies on personal relationships, in preparation for an equally boring adulthood. One reason why the American high school may appear so characterless is that it operates on much the same principles as the shopping malls that are the students' new recreation centers, with something for everyone, trying to please all tastes (Powell et al. 1985).

RURAL SCHOOLS

Day-to-day activities in a rural Midwest elementary school were studied intensively by anthropologist Norris Brock (1985), who found that the staff ruled almost exclusively by punishment—most often directed at slow learners, especially if they were also poor and black. Brock relates incident after incident in which teachers and their aides ignore or ridicule the work of students they feel ought not to be too bright (see also McCarthy and Hoge 1987 for similar findings in nonrural schools).

In Chapter 5, we noted that punishment is a relatively ineffective technique for

changing behavior, especially if it is not accompanied by rewards for alternative ways of acting. When teachers ignore acceptable behavior and react only to inappropriate acts, students readily learn that doing nothing or even dropping out of school altogether is less painful than staying. The unrewarded children of the poor—whether in rural or urban schools—soon become "turned off" from learning altogether; the costs outweigh the perceived benefits.

URBAN SCHOOLS

Only three decades ago, the school systems of many major cities achieved great success in acculturating immigrants and serving as channels of upward mobility. Due to various population trends to be discussed in Chapter 19, the large cities gradually lost their middle-class residential base, along with employment opportunities and taxable properties. Today, the inner-city school population is largely composed of low-income ethnic and racial minorities.

Unlike in the past, urban schools today must absorb more children of the poor, keep them in school longer, and send them into declining labor markets. The buildings have continued to deteriorate, expe-

College Dreams

In 1981, the principal of a public school in one of the poorest sections of New York City asked an old graduate to give the commencement address to the school's sixty-two sixth graders, about to enter junior high. The speaker, Eugene Lang, a millionaire businessman, had attended the school fifty years earlier, when the neighborhood was composed primarily of white ethnic immigrant families. When Lang rose to address the Class of 1981, he saw mostly the faces of black and Hispanic children, survivors of extreme poverty and family breakup. Realizing the inappropriateness of his prepared remarks about hard work and success— the standard Protestant Work Ethic presentation—Lang threw away his notes, spoke from his heart, and made a promise: he would personally finance the college education of any student who stayed in the system and graduated high school. He also arranged for a guidance counselor to follow the class, and invited the children to come to his office and talk over their plans with him.

Six years later, in a school that had had a dropout rate of close to 75 percent, all but a few of Lang's audience had graduated high school and about half have entered college.

The publicity that followed Lang's offer caught the attention of other wealthy benefactors. In 1986, for example, nine more business people agreed each to adopt an entire class of sixth graders from the most impoverished districts in New York City, offering remedial services, personal guidance, and scholarship aid. In Dallas, Texas, and twenty other major American cities, similar programs have been initiated, bringing help and hope to thousands of students. And in Boston, a group of business organizations has established a fund to provide financial aid to any graduate of the city's public schools who is accepted at college and whose family cannot afford tuition. The corporations also promised to provide a job upon college graduation (Butterfield 1986).

In honor of the Rev. Martin Luther King, Jr., Lang has named his program "I Have A Dream."

The sociological point, of course, is that dropping out and poor academic performance have less to do with innate ability than with the young person's perception that staying in school and doing well will have a positive outcome. Once assured that there was a payoff, something that nonpoor children take for granted, the students in PS 121 improved their academic performance, stayed in school, and passed their college entrance exams. Always, we must look at the structure of opportunity in order to understand individual behavior.

SOURCES: Kathy Hacker, "Deep Pockets Push a Dream Toward Reality," *Chicago Tribune*, Feb. 23, 1986, Sect. 2, p. 1ff; Larry Rohter, "From 6 New Benefactors, 425 College Dreams," *New York Times*, June 21, 1986, Section B, p. 1ff; Fox Butterfield, "Funds and Jobs Pledged to Boston Students," *New York Times*, Sept. 10, 1986, p. 1.

---

rienced teachers have chosen to work in other districts, the neighborhoods are made hazardous by gangs of unemployed youth, and powerless parents have difficultly in imparting a sense of high expectations to their children. Family structure—i.e. two-parent or single-parent—appears to have less effect on a minority child's school success than does the ability of a parent to spend time with the student, to help with homework, and to establish achievement-centered rules in the earliest grades (R. Clark 1983).

But much depends on the atmosphere of the school and the commitment of its staff. The learning problems of most inner-city poor children are not due to lack of ability or to personal flaws, or even to their relatively deprived cultural context. As Edmonds (1979) notes, we already know how to succeed in teaching all the children whose schooling is of importance to us; that this has not been done says more about the public's commitment to educating the poor than about the children themselves.

A number of reports (Rich 1983, Fine 1985, Carnegie Corporation 1986, Clendinen 1986) suggest that the key factors in making urban education work are: (1) strong administrative leadership; (2) a climate of expectation in which no child would be allowed to fall behind; and (3) an orderly but not oppressive atmosphere— precisely the characteristics that give a scholastic advantage to students from private schools (Coleman 1982).

Renewing the school means re-awakening hope that something good will come of the education, that the effort of learning will have a payoff in the form of a decent job at wages above the poverty line.

Until such jobs are available, many youngsters will take the easier route to survival: drop out and live off the streets.

Dropping Out. An observational study by Michelle Fine (1985) of dropouts from a New York City high school points to many factors: unemployment, widespread poverty, urban decay, demoralized teachers, overcrowded schools, lack of minority faculty, the need to work in order to help out the family, impersonal teaching, and being actively or passively encouraged by the authorities to leave. The high volume of dropouts (one-third to one-half of all high-school students in most inner city systems) does clear the schools of "difficult students" but also leaves those youngsters most in need of remedial academic services with no help at all. Only a few of these high-risk students may eventually find an alternative school that provides the intensive support they require (Carnegie Foundation 1983).

While it is fashionable today to call for more "self-help" from members of minority communities, most of the success stories in urban education have relied on continued state and federal funding for school meals, educational equipment, and faculty development. A more recent source of support is the business community, often filling in for the drastically reduced federal commitment since 1980. A potential problem, however, is that school officials may lose control over the content of educational material, which could become slanted toward the special interests of the business group. For example, instructional packets from utility companies extoll the virtues of nuclear power without mentioning possible hazards, and a U.S. Chamber of Commerce publication never refers to monopolies or other distortions of the "free market" (Harty 1981).

TEACHERS' EXPECTATIONS

It has long been assumed that the way in which teachers react to students may influence the pupils' scholastic achievement. In this view, when teachers expect high performance from a child, they tend to interpret whatever the child says in a positive light, which then spurs the pupil to ever higher accomplishments. Conversely, a student from whom little is expected will be discouraged from excelling and will eventually perform at a minimal level. This is an example of the "self-fulfilling prophecy" whereby people (e.g. teachers) behave in a way that ultimately makes their predictions (e.g. a child's academic achievement) likely to come true. The research evidence, however, is not altogether consistent on the strength of this effect or how it is achieved, and the original study (Rosenthal and Jacobson 1968) has not been successfully replicated.

There is, however, ample evidence that teachers often react to a student on the basis of such ascribed characteristics as race, religion, ethnicity, social class, or gender (Wilkinson and Marrett 1985). For example, the research literature on gender stereotyping (Marland 1984) documents the ways in which teachers treat boys and girls differently—to the detriment of both. In the early grades, school personnel tend to favor girls for their ability to sit quietly and for their verbal skills, thus making life very uncomfortable for boys. At higher grades, however, the schools tend to favor boys in terms of career interests and encouragement to explore their environment, which leaves the girls ignored and powerless—at least in working- and lower-middle-class districts.

Higher Education

FUNCTIONS AND STRUCTURE

The primary manifest functions of higher education are: (1) transmission of existing knowledge; (2) production of new information; and (3) preparation of the next generation of scholars. As a consequence of the increasing *specialization of knowledge,* universities are organized into relatively discrete units—departments, programs, schools, divisions—on the basis of particular "bundles" of knowledge (B. Clark 1983). These units enjoy a wide degree of autonomy (self-direction), as only peers can judge another's work. Yet the entire institution must be able to operate as a unified whole, which is the job of the administration. This dilemma leads to some tension between the faculty's need for academic freedom and the administration's concern with institutional survival.

But the administration does not operate in a vacuum. Although private colleges and universities are relatively independent—financed primarily by student fees, alumni gifts, and an accumulated endow-

The increasing **specialization of knowledge** in universities and colleges leads to relatively discrete units of organization.

The Socialization of a Teacher

Margaret L. Andersen

Margaret L. Andersen is Associate Professor of Sociology at the University of Delaware and the author of Thinking About Women: Sociological Perspectives on Sex and Gender *, 2nd ed. (New York: Macmillan, 1988). She teaches courses on the sociology of sex and gender, race and ethnic relations, and women's studies and has received the University of Delaware's Excellence-in-Teaching Award. She serves on the Executive Committee of the Eastern Sociological Society and on several committees of the American Sociological Association.*

My interests as a teacher are focused primarily in the areas of race relations and the sociology of sex and gender. I want students to understand how race, gender, and class shape all of our experiences, not just the experiences of those who are the victims of inequality. I try to help students understand the differences in group experience that inequality creates, at the same time that I emphasize our human commonalities. My classes are centered on the idea that inclusive thinking (the inclusion of race, class, and gender in all of what we think and teach) transforms knowledge, since women and the world's minorities have previously been excluded from much of the content of our teachings. I encourage students to examine their own experiences as a way of seeing how gender, race, and class have shaped their lives. My own experiences illustrate this point.

In 1958, my family moved from the urban neighborhood in Oakland, California, where I had been born, to the small town of Rome in northwest Georgia. Like many young, upwardly-mobile white American men, my father had been promoted in his company; the move was seen as a necessary step on the corporate ladder. I was ten at the time and saw in this move neither the sociological nor historical significance that I would later come to understand. For me, a young girl, the move across country was high adventure, although I wondered what it would be like to live so far from my grandparents and my girlfriend—all of whom lived within the few blocks in Oakland that constituted my childhood universe. For several years following, my parents would pack the car every other summer and we would drive back to California for a visit. In preparation for these trips, my younger sister and I would fill the backseat with dolls, games, and a good supply of license plate bingo cards to pass the long hours of cross-country driving. Excited by the prospect of visiting our grandparents and anticipating the sights we would see along the way, my sister and I saw no pitfalls to the trip except perhaps boredom and periodic sibling squabbles. Mostly, we were eager to be on the road, wondering in what roadside restaurants we would eat, whether we would stay in a motel with a swimming pool, and how many souvenirs our allowances would buy. We checked our progress in the long hours of driving by following the maps—the beginning, for me, of a long-standing love for reading maps. As the trip wore on, we were often cranky, but on the first day of the trip, through rural Alabama, Mississippi and Tennessee, we had no complaints. Two young white girls, happy to play with their Barbies, were off to see Grandma and enjoy whatever adventures came our way.

In what must have been the same period of time, another young girl also made regular summer treks to her grandmother's house. Traveling into, not out of, the South she went with her family and sister from Washington, D.C., to Charleston, South Carolina, where her grandparents lived. She describes these trips:

"The drive to South Carolina allowed us a transition from our country to that one. My father always saw to it that we carried huge provisions—fried chicken, potato salad, toast, ham, buttered bread, unbuttered bread, big Thermos jugs filled with lemonade, and anything else we could possibly want to eat or drink. We even carried bottles filled with plain water and a special container just for ice. As far as possible, the family car was to be self-sufficient. With all those provisions, our summer transition to the South began as a moving feast. We regaled ourselves all along the way, while playing games with license plates, singing songs, and reading the maps. I imagine that the vehicle of our transition had more discipline, as well as more to eat and drink, than most American cars in July. For no matter how many children went with us, disorder in the backseat was out of the question. We made our voyage with the cramped adventure of astronauts. Our parents made our capsule self-sufficient because we would make no pause for refreshment, not from the time we passed the whites-only Marriott Hotel, just across the Potomac, to the time we last turned off U.S. 1 toward Charleston. We even had sufficient water with us to refresh the car's radiator in an emergency; and my father planned ahead of time where to stop for gas. On those trips south we children could not explore gas-station restrooms, as we did on the Pennsylvania Turnpike. We could not break the 550-mile trip in some scenic place to sleep in a roadside motel. We avoided secondary roads; and, if we made a wrong turn through some little town, we consulted our maps for the same reason that we carried so much food and drink: a determination to avoid insult, or worse. I remember the anxiety of my parents when we had to stop once in the middle of a Southern nowhere to change a flat tire."

When I first read Fields' account, I was stunned by what it reveals, not just about Fields' experience, but also about my own. Two young girls recall the excitement of summer visits to their grandparents, but I never imagined that I could not stop at a roadside snack bar, could not swim in a motel pool, or assume that the world was on my side. My white skin protected me from fears of potential violence and harassment; her black skin did not.

Comparing my experience to Fields' reveals the potential for life histories to illuminate social and historical structures that condition our experiences. Students might think about answering the question, "If someone were to write your life history, what would we learn about race, class, and gender relations in this country?" Responses to this question reveal that the social structures of race, gender, and class inequality affect all people, not just those who are victims. Writing such life histories can also engage students in empathetic dialogues about these conflict-ridden and emotional topics. In addition, such an assignment gives voice to the experiences of women and minority students—voices that are typically denied by the rest of the curriculum.

I have found that my training as a sociologist prepares me for the work I do in the classroom because it has made me think about the ways that the experiences of all of us are connected to social institutions. The sociological perspective has also heightened my sensitivity to the world around me. Despite some of the problems in the sociological discipline, namely that it has in the past been constructed through the experience of a few, I have found that an inclusive sociological perspective provides the frameworks for interpreting both individual and collective experiences.

SOURCES: Parts of this essay are excerpted from Margaret L. Andersen, "Race and the Social Science Curriculum: A Teaching and Learning Discussion," *Radical Teacher,* November, 1984: 17–20. Mamie Garvin Fields with Karen Fields, *Lemon Swamp and Other Places: A Carolina Memoir.* New York: Free Press, 1983, pp. xii–xiv.

---

ment fund—they are under nominal control of a board of trustees and are bound by some government guidelines if they receive any federal aid. And even private schools must adapt to the community in which they are located.

Public institutions—state colleges and universities, and the community colleges—in contrast, are funded by tax dollars allocated by state legislatures, and are, therefore, more vulnerable to political pressures than are the private schools. When the survival of the institution depends on the goodwill of the tax-paying public and their elected representatives, the school becomes very sensitive to its outside environment. Thus, many public colleges and universities have invested heavily in programs of special concern to state and local industries. It also helps to have nationally ranked athletic teams (see Chapter 20).

Stratification Within Higher Education. Institutions of higher education in the United States form a ranked hierarchy. At the top are a handful of private universities (e.g. Harvard, Princeton, Yale), followed by elite private colleges (e.g. Amherst, Vassar, Dartmouth), state universities, state colleges, and, at the base, the community colleges. The more highly ranked the institution, the higher are both its fees and standards of admission.

As might be expected, the proportion of students or faculty who are female, minority, or of working-class origins is *inversely* related to institutional prestige; that is, the lower the rank, the more diversified the student body and the faculty.

THE FACULTY

The faculty is also stratified on the basis of *rank:* full professor, associate professor, assistant professor, instructor. Promotions and tenure (job security) depend on years of service and quantity and quality of publications. Teaching skills are rarely a factor except in the community colleges; the higher the academic rank, the *fewer* hours spent in classroom teaching.

Faculties also reflect the *race* and *gender* stratification systems of the larger society. There are very few blacks—perhaps one percent—of the faculty in predominantly white institutions, and only a handful are at the highest ranks. These figures are actually *down* from a peak in the late 1970s, and will not rise soon because the number of blacks in graduate schools has also declined (Staples 1986). Talented men and women of color today can enter a variety of better-paying occupations that do not require a graduate degree.

The question of why there are so few faculty women has been hotly debated. On one hand are those who contend that because the academic status system is based purely on merit, the absence of women in high ranks reflects their lower level of productivity, probably due to competition from their family obligations (e.g. Glazer 1976, Cole 1979). On the other hand, a growing body of research finds little difference in either the quantity or quality of women's and men's productivity, once you take into account the fact that male professors are more likely to have been at their jobs for a longer period of time, and to be at institutions that demand and support scholarly research.

But even if all else were equal, the "merit" system does not operate impartially (Persell 1983, 1984, Theodore 1986). It is easier for male graduate students to find a mentor and to be recommended for posts at high-ranked institutions. Furthermore, papers and publications thought to be authored by a man are judged of higher quality than those of women faculty— even when it's the same paper with just the name of the author changed (*see* Chapter 8).

Despite dramatic gains over the past twenty years in the numbers of women faculty and in their proportion at the higher ranks, women graduate students continue to have difficulty finding senior sponsors (Solomon 1986) or doing so without being subjected to sexual harassment (Glaser and Thorpe 1986).

The New Academic Gypsies. One way to lower the cost of running a college is to use part-time and temporary "adjuncts" in place of full-time faculty (Abel 1984). Adjuncts are hired by the semester, paid by the course, and do not receive fringe benefits such as medical insurance or pension coverage. To make an adequate living, an adjunct would have to teach at four or five different institutions, and spend a great deal of time in travel—hence the label "academic gypsies"—and all for a total income less than half that of a full-time faculty member.

The proportion of faculty who are part-time has doubled in the past two decades—from 20 to 40 percent of the total. As adjuncts tend to be recent PhDs and since women are now graduating in large numbers, a great number of these adjuncts will be women.

The Graying of the Faculty. Because relatively few full-time faculty have been hired over the past decade, the average age of the teaching staff has been rising. In order to open up more opportunities for junior faculty and to cut salary costs, a number of schools are offering inducements for senior faculty to take early retirement (Boase 1986).

Even so, most faculties are top-heavy with older tenured teachers, leading to a possible *shortage* of highly qualified full-time faculty in the next decade (Fiske 1986b). Thus, it is possible that college teaching will once more become an attractive option for young intellectuals. By the time you finish graduate school, there may be many colleges competing to hire you!

There has a been a dramatic decline in the number of new full-time professors; the ranks of the tenured are getting older. Does this have any impact for students? (© Bruno J. Zehnder/Peter Arnold, Inc.)

College Choices

Remember how you sweated out the Scholastic Aptitude Tests (SATs)? Spent long hours looking over catalogues, talking with friends, assessing family finances, and trying to decide what you wanted to do with the rest of your life? And then waited nervously for word from the colleges you selected—hoping for a fat rather than a thin envelope?

These agonies have become a yearly *rite of passage* for over half of America's high-school graduates. Yet the process whereby colleges and students are matched is not at all well understood. It appears that almost everyone who wants to attend college could find a place, including most of those who did not apply, but that the young people who select themselves out of postsecondary education have made a realistic appraisal of their chances of graduating whatever the basis for this assessment may be (Manski and Wise 1983).

With the exception of a few hundred elite institutions, most American universities and colleges are not highly selective in their admissions policies, which means that the SATs really do not make that much difference. According to some critics, because the tests have about the same validity as your high-school record in predicting college performance, they are a waste of time, money, and emotional energy (Owen 1985, Hechinger 1986). Your high school record would do as well.

Just what the tests actually measure is also a matter of debate. It cannot be innate intelligence if cram courses can produce dramatic changes in test scores (see Owen 1985 for a review of this research). Conversely, if the tests only measure the ability to take the test, and that is precisely the same ability needed to pass college courses, then test scores are important data for college admissions offices.

But scholastic ability as measured by SAT scores and high-school grades is only one standard for acceptance. Admissions officers also take into account an applicant's participation in extracurricular activity, special talents (in athletics or music, for example), race and ethnicity, the impression made during an interview, letters of recommendation, and financial need. There are actually many factors involved in acceptance.

At the most selective institutions, it helps to have parents or siblings who are alumni, and a preparatory-school background (Persell and Cookson 1985). "Cultural capital," as measured by the parents' occupational environment, is also associ-

ated with admission to high-ranked schools (Karen 1986). Nonetheless, most elite institutions today do strive for diversity within their student body: by race, region of the country, social class, and field of interest. Admission to Harvard and similar schools, therefore, does not depend solely on academic ability, but involves weighing a number of factors, only some of which favor offspring of the elite. There is some access for the non-elite.

But the assumption that college admissions is a simple function of the applicant's personal characteristics overlooks the *structural* factors that may determine who goes where. A structural analysis, such as that provided by Karen (1986) in his study of admissions to Harvard University, focuses on the interaction among members of the admissions office. It is they who judge the relative importance of an applicant's qualifications, and who make the final decisions to accept or reject on the basis of their perceptions of the long-term interest of the university that employs them and to whom they owe primary loyalty.

It is always hoped that the chosen applicants will do well in college and in their subsequent careers, thus justifying the admission decision and adding to the school's prestige. But there is little clear-cut evidence linking academic performance with later life success. Much depends on how "success" or "excellence" are defined. Both Klitgaard (1985) and Astin (1985) suggest a "value-added" approach to evaluations of higher education. That is, students should be admitted on the basis of their potential contribution to the society as a whole, and schools should be judged on how well they have been able to develop the talents of a range of students, rather than in counting how many graduates earn high incomes or have high status occupations. How would you wish to be judged?

Sources: Alexander A. Astin, *Achieving Educational Excellence: A Critical Assessment of Properties and Practices in Higher Education,* San Francisco: Jossey-Bass, 1985; David Karen, "The Politics of Admission to Elite Colleges: The Case of Harvard," Paper presented at the 56th Annual Meeting of the Eastern Sociological Society, New York City, April 1986; Fred M. Hechinger, "How Should Colleges Pick Students?," *New York Times,* June 24, 1986; Robert Klitgaard, *Choosing Elites: Selecting the Top Universities and Elsewhere.* New York: Basic Books, 1985; Charles F. Manski and David A. Wise, *College Choice in America,* Cambridge, MA: Harvard University Press, 1983; David Owen, *None of the Above: Behind the Myth of Scholastic Aptitude,* Boston: Houghton Mifflin, 1985.

THE STUDENT BODY

In 1987, approximately 12.4 million men and women were enrolled in one of over 3000 degree-granting institutions of higher education in the United States. While this represents an increase of almost 40 percent since 1970, the number of college students may decline slightly in the next five years, as a reflection of lowered fertility since the late 1960s. But since college enrollments have not shown the same steep drop as those for elementary and high school, from where have the new collegians come? Some are high-school graduates who would not have been able to afford higher education before the opening of community colleges; others are having difficulty in finding jobs with adequate pay and mobility prospects without a college degree; and a large number are "nontraditional" students in terms of their age.

Increased Diversity. All these trends lead to more diversity within the student body than in the past. Over half of today's high-school students are going directly to college, compared to only 24 percent in 1960, and within a few years of high-school graduation, another 10 percent will enter college (Riche 1986). But the most dramatic recent increases in enrollments have come from the entry of older (twenty-five and over) part-time students, most of whom are women. Between 1972 and 1985, enrollments rose 53 percent for students age twenty-five to twenty-nine; 122 percent for those age thirty to thirty-four; and 112 percent for people age thirty-five and over (National Center for Educational Statistics 1986).

As a result, more than one-third of all college students today are age twenty-five and older, raising the median age of college students to over twenty-one, the age at which most students in the past had already graduated! Today, also, almost four in ten college students are part-time, primarily in community colleges and urban campuses.

Another major shift in the composition of the student body since 1965 is the increased presence of nonwhites, from under 10 percent of the total to about 15 percent today. But while Asian enrollments continue to rise, those for blacks and Hispanics have declined. The proportion of blacks on campus leveled off in the 1980s at between 9 to 10 percent (lower than their representation in the total college-age population), due largely to federal reductions in financial aid coupled with rising tuitions that price out a majority of black and Hispanic youth from four-year residential colleges (Adolphus 1984, *New York Times,* Dec. 4, 1986).

Although black enrollments have doubled since 1980, many of these students are in two-year rather than four-year colleges, and close to one-third attend predominantly black schools (Staples 1986). Being enrolled in a largely black college is not necessarily disadvantageous for black men, who tend to have higher "intellectual-performance" scores than their female classmates in these schools or than black men at predominantly white institutions. In contrast, black women do best in white coeducational schools. According to Fleming (1984), in a male-dominated and racist society, black men will feel most in charge on black coeducational campuses, while women of color feel less powerless on white coeducational campuses.

In contrast to the overall decline in black and Hispanic enrollments, *highly qualified* minority students are heavily recruited by elite institutions that want to diversify their student body. In these cases, some minority students are accepted by many selective schools and will make their choice based on their impression of the college's commitment to minority students (Wald 1986). Thus, schools with a history of racism will continue to attract few minority students.

It also appears that black enrollments in graduate schools of law and medicine have declined since 1980, again largely due to cutbacks in federal assistance (Shea and Fullilove 1985). The absence of minority students will be most strongly felt by white institutions, as the majority of black medical students and faculty remain concentrated in a few primarily black medical schools in the South.

The enrollment gains of women and blacks since 1965 can be traced to pressures on the schools from civil-rights organizations. Thus far, no similar groups have pushed for increased admission of working-class youth in general (Karen and McClelland 1983). Indeed, the trend since the early 1980s has been in the opposite direction, as federal financial aid to low- and moderate-income students has been drastically reduced while the cost of a

TABLE 14-1 Fees for tuition, room, and board: 1988 selected private colleges and universities

Bennington	$17,999
Harvard/Radcliffe	17,100
Dartmouth	17,091
Yale	17,020
MIT	16,970
Columbia	16,630

SOURCE: *New York Times*, May 12, 1987, p. B7.

college education has risen steadily. As seen in Table 14-1, fees at some elite institutions in 1988 were equal to *half* of the median income of all American households. Although the cost of attending a state university is roughly half that of private schools, families with more than one child to educate can be severely pressed for funds (see Michalak 1986, on future costs).

Does It Pay To Go To College? Given these very high fees for private colleges—far higher than in any other modern industrial society, where higher education is largely subsidized by government—does it pay to go to college? Is the investment in education worthwhile? You bet. At the very least, employers take your diploma as a sign of ambition and self-discipline. And the degree from a private institution carries that much more clout, saying something about family background and personal achievement.

In general, college education is a key variable in determining social status, especially life-style. And it even pays off immediately in dollars. In 1986, the average starting salary for college graduates at 230 major companies was $21,060, ranging from over $27,000 for engineers to slightly under $20,000 for majors in sales/marketing.

There are, however, marked differences by race and sex in the money return for a college degree. Women graduates who are employed full-time earn roughly two-thirds the income of men graduates, although this difference has narrowed to 75 percent in the most recent cohort of graduates. Black male college graduates will earn about 80 percent as much as their white peers. The income difference between black and white women, however, is only 5 percent.

The longer you stay in school, the higher will be your eventual income return. In general, median household income is directly related to length of schooling, as shown in Table 14-2.

HIGHER EDUCATION AND SOCIAL STRATIFICATION

Higher education is a primary factor in the maintenance of the social-stratification system of any modern society (Foster 1983, Useem and Karabal 1986). Although it must be noted that at the elementary and secondary level the American system is *less* stratified than in most European countries (Rubinson 1986), the post-secondary system, while extensive, is highly stratified.

In both the United States and England, graduates of preparatory schools and selective private colleges and universities are disproportionately represented among the religious, economic, political, and social elites. In other European countries, a few public universities with very rigorous admission standards serve the same function. In France, however, reproduction of advantage is primarily direct, through the actual handing on of business ownership, rather than through the educational system (Robinson and Garnier 1985). Even in Sweden, social-class background interacts with educational attainment to produce income differences (Winn 1984).

The process of educational stratification is similar in communist countries as well. Contrary to the ideals of equal opportunity and selection by merit, entry into the leading institutions of higher education is tilted toward the offspring of highly placed officials and Communist Party

TABLE 14-2 Median income for year-round full-time workers, age 25 and older, by education: 1985

Years of School Completed	Median Income
Elementary School	$18,645
Four Years of High School	23,863
1–3 Years of College	26,960
Four Years of College	32,822
More Than Four Years of College	39,335

SOURCE: U.S. Bureau of the Census, Current Population Reports, Series P-60, No. 154, "Money Income and Poverty Status of Families and Persons in the United States, 1985 (Advance Data)," Washington, DC: U.S. Government Printing Office, August 1986, p. 13.

members: "The higher the level of study, the greater is the difference among social groups" (Zaslavskaya, quoted in Taubman 1986).

Attending *any* college is more strongly associated with family income than with high-school grades (*Chronicle of Higher Education,* 1983, 1986, Lerner 1986). As Table 14-2 indicates, attendance at an elite institution is beyond the means of the vast majority of American households, without some scholarship assistance.

The financial crunch is even affecting institutions traditionally commited to "open admissions" and minimal tuition charges, such as The City University of New York (CUNY) and the community colleges. Fees are rising and admissions becoming somewhat more selective. The CUNY experiment in open admissions—accepting all applicants—has proven costly in terms of resources devoted to remedial programs (i.e. remedying the failures of the high schools and bringing students up to college level) but surprisingly successful educationally. By 1984, half the entrants had graduated college, although most took longer than four years to do so because they had to work to support themselves (Lavin, Alba, and Silberstein 1981).

The overall trend today, however, is away from equal educational opportunity and toward strengthening the link between family income and length of schooling, in effect reproducing the stratification hierarchy from one generation to another.

COMMUNITY COLLEGES

Two-year public colleges were originally designed in the 1960s to fill two very different goals; they were expected to relieve some of the pressures of the expected baby-boom enrollments on the state university system, and to provide local industries with a reliable source of trained workers. Responding to both needs, community colleges became the academic growth industry of the 1970s. Today, there are almost one thousand two-year public colleges, enrolling about four million students.

Community colleges are of many types. Some, in cities and industrial areas, are primarily institutions of "higher voc ed" (Pincus 1980), in which low-income students are prepared, at taxpayers' expense, for entry-level jobs in local industry.

Other community colleges, in suburbs and wealthier areas, have maintained their college-transfer programs, but primarily for their white, middle-class students. Even there, most students today are enrolled in the "career" courses: secretarial, computer science, business and accounting, mechanical technology, nursing, and the like. These areas receive most of the colleges' budget and generate high levels of community support, especially from local employers. Thus, claim critics of the community college system, the schools actually *limit,* rather than expand, students' opportunities, "cooling out" the losers by giving the impression that they have had a chance to better themselves (Pincus 1983).

The tension between the promise of upward mobility provided by the community college and the limits set on such mobility are illustrated in Weiss' (1985) study of the school culture constructed by black students at an urban community college. The students are caught in the bind of wishing to escape ghetto poverty, an individualistic goal, and the pull of their group ties to one another. Many subcultural attitudes and values tend to undermine academic success, about which most were skeptical to begin with. The few who can break their ties to the community will be the ones to succeed academically—but at great personal cost.

Nonetheless, community colleges have many advantages—low tuition, convenient locations, part-time programs, evening and weekend courses—that can make two years of college a reality for many people who otherwise would not have perceived themselves as college students. Thus, the student body is far more varied in terms of race, ethnicity, and social class than the typical four-year college. It also contains a large number of people who need remedial help in order to handle college-level material. This means that much of the school's resources must be devoted to "catch-up" work rather than to expanding academic programs. As a consequence, transfer rates to four-year colleges have been lower than originally expected. The gap between the two- and four-year schools is especially large for minority students who compose 25 percent of the students at the community college but less than 10 percent at four-year institutions.

Several programs designed to improve the transfer rate have been studied by the

For millions of Americans, education continues throughout adulthood through evening and weekend college classes as well as non-degree adult education classes. In fact, the fastest growing segment of the educational marketplace is the adult student. (© Blair Seitz/ Photo Researchers, Inc.)

Ford Foundation (1987), including closer cooperation with local high schools to prepare students before entry, more rigorous course offerings at the community colleges, scholarships for honors students, and stronger coordination with neighboring four-year colleges. There is no doubt that if the trustees and administrators of community colleges make transfer rates a standard of their own success, thousands more will be able to achieve a full college education. The small classes and close links with professors (rather than with graduate teaching assistants as in most four-year schools) actually offers the community college student a rare opportunity for intellectual stimulation.

Although often cited as a problem, the great diversity of students and faculty at the community college level can be considered a major virtue. The community college is certainly more reflective of the heterogeneity and democratic ideals of our society than are most other colleges and universities. Supporters of the system feel strongly that something of value will be lost if the community colleges evolve into either the higher vocational education or post-secondary remedial schools. Achieving high academic goals while retaining an open door admissions policy is a formidable task, and many community colleges have succeeded, with honors.

Current Controversies

COMPETING PHILOSOPHIES

Throughout the twentieth century, there has been tension between two competing philosophies of education. Should the goal of schooling be to liberate a young person's creative capacities or to instill the values and skills demanded by the marketplace?

Open Classrooms.   The former position is illustrated by the *open classroom* movement of the 1960s, based on the belief that once the physical structure of the classroom was opened up, children's minds would follow. Freed of the constraints of sitting in rows on little chairs facing a distant teacher's desk, many children blossomed intellectually and socially. Other children, however, could not handle the lack of structure, and many teachers were unprepared for the difficulties presented by such an individualized learning atmosphere. Above all, parents were upset by the seeming disorganization of the open classroom, and by the idea that children should be "happy" in a setting that ought to be defined as "work."

Although the reformers (Herndon 1965, Kozol 1967, Silberman 1970) were espe-

The **open classroom** is based on the belief that, freed of structural restraints in the classroom, children will develop intellectually and socially.

cially interested in developing the talents of poor children, the open classroom was primarily successful in middle-class suburban districts where parents supported the goal of creativity.

Back-to-Basics. But by the early 1970s, countertrends were already under way. As standardized test scores continued to fall, and as concerns over poor children faded, public opinion shifted toward the traditional view of schools as training grounds for obedience and marketable skills.

Rejecting the belief that closed environments produced closed minds, support for a *back-to-basics* approach came from many sources. Parents of impoverished students wanted their children prepared for mainstream jobs. Working-class parents wanted more discipline in the classroom. And political and religious conservatives took the opportunity to attack teachers' unions and what they considered to be the evil effects of "secular humanism"—the belief that human reason and goodwill could solve personal and social problems without divine intervention. Conservatives were particularly upset over the introduction of sex education in the public schools at the same time that organized prayer was held unconstitutional.

The back-to-basics philosophy is strongly reflected in the positions taken by the Reagan administration's Department of Education: emphasizing the need for discipline (including physical punishments by school authorities), calling for a return of school prayer, and supporting efforts to weaken the power of the teachers' unions.

The **back-to-basics** trend emphasizes discipline, respect for authority, and traditional subject matters.

QUALITY AND INEQUALITY

Another major controversy in contemporary education centers on the perceived conflict between educational *quality,* or what some people call the "pursuit of excellence" in individuals, and *equality,* using the schools to promote social justice. These two goals need not be mutually exclusive, but have come into conflict because of the limited resources available to the schools, and because many Americans seem to believe that individual talents are not evenly distributed across racial and ethnic groups (see Kingston 1986).

Schooling and Racial Equality. The issue of racial equality illustrates the enduring tension between different aspects of the American value system: recognition of individual merit on the one hand, and social justice on the other. Should the goal be equality of opportunity or can we aim for a rough equality of outcomes? Can there ever be equal opportunity in education without major changes in neighborhood and family structures? In addition, controversy over racial integration of the schools has revived political conflict between broad national goals and the tradition of local control of schools (J. L. Hochschild 1984).

School Desegregation and Integration. The value struggle between the goals of social justice and individual freedom has centered on the schools as both creators of inequality and as potential channels of equal opportunity. Before 1954, school systems in the American South systematically denied educational opportunity to black students and teachers by drawing district lines that kept the races apart and then investing three to four times more money on white schools (Ravich 1983). In response to a legal challenge, the Supreme Court in 1954 declared that a racially seg-

In the struggle between segregation and integration, the competing goals of individual freedom and social justice have been played out in American schools. (© Alex Webb/Magnum)

regated school system created by local authorities was, in and of itself, a violation of the constitutional guarantee of equal treatment under the law and that such systems must be dismantled "with all deliberate speed."

Almost thirty-five years later, after much deliberation and very little speed, the record on desegregation is mixed. Southern school districts have gradually changed. But thousands of white children were taken out of the public-school system and placed in private schools. However, it is not clear whether this "white flight" was an immediate response to fears of school desegregation or simply part of the steady migration to the suburbs that had been going on since the end of World War II (see Chapter 19). The falling proportion of white students in public schools is also due in part to declining fertility among whites in general after 1965.

In the North, where separation had not been legally imposed, the schools were also becoming racially segregated as white families moved from city to suburb. Thus, by 1980, schools in most large Northern cities were predominantly nonwhite, in contrast to the almost totally white schools in the surrounding communities. In other words, racial segregation of the schools has *increased* in many areas since 1970 (Orfield 1983), even while public-opinion surveys indicate increased support of the goal of desegregation (Smith 1981). In other districts, however, racial balance has clearly improved (U.S. Commission on Civil Rights 1987).

Local opposition to school desegregation, especially when accompanied by busing, remains very strong, as has been the case in Boston for over a decade (Buell and Brisbin 1982). Such resistance is most intense in "defended neighborhoods," defined by Buell (1982) as areas within the city where community tradition and ethnic *gemeinschaft* are still quite powerful. Most often members of the working class, these whites feel that their way of life has been threatened by politicians who live safely away from the turmoil. It is typically poor working-class areas that are targeted for integration.

Yet, there are a number of cities in which school districts have been successfully integrated, thanks to cooperation of many community groups, local political leaders, and the business community

(Willie and Greenblatt 1981). Further, desegregated schools can benefit both black and white students (Daniels 1983, Center for Social Organization of the Schools 1985, Winerup 1985). Indeed, early conflict over desegregation can ultimately *lower* racial tension by uniting the black community behind their youth, in support of peaceful change (Crain and Mahard 1982). There is also evidence, however, that local conflict over school integration actually reinforces the *status quo* by siphoning off working-class white frustration while leaving the real power structure intact (Monti 1985).

But even in integrated school districts, black students can be rendered invisible through tracking and other ways of dividing the student body (Rist 1981, Oakes 1985). Some critics of the schools see standardized tests as a means of "objectively" resegregating classrooms within the school, for both students and teachers (Pressman and Gartner 1986).

Solutions. Under threat of court order, school systems have undertaken various approaches to reducing segregation and to stemming white flight.

MAGNET SCHOOLS. One way to keep white youngsters in inner-city schools is to offer an unusual educational experience. Magnet schools, as the term implies, attempt to attract students with special interests to a particular program offered only in that school, such as music and art, science, athletics, or specific teaching techniques that many parents will consider worth the bus trip.

GRADE DIFFERENTIATION. Another way to divide children into desegregated units is to have specific schools for different grades. That is, School X is for all kindergarteners through second-graders in the district; School Y is for the third through the sixth grades; and School Z is the intermediate school. Thus, all children will have some years in their neighborhood school and other years away, so that the burden of busing is more equally distributed.

MERGING SCHOOL DISTRICTS. If whites are in the suburbs and nonwhites are in the cities, one integration method involves the merging of school districts, so that both sets of children are in the same district, with busing to create racial balance among all the schools in the new district.

Magnet schools are designed to attract students by offering specialized educational programs.

Grade differentiation divides a district's students into separate schools for given grade levels.

ENRICHMENT OF NONWHITE SCHOOLS. If integration cannot be achieved, then an enrichment of the inner-city schools can at least provide equal, if separate, education. This course of action requires the willingness of all citizens to support extra taxes for the benefit of nonwhite children.

Programs for the Handicapped. How fair is an educational system that teaches only those who can come to school and meet the expectations of classroom teachers? If the constitutions of most state governments guarantee a free public education for all, what are school districts to do about their physically and mentally handicapped youngsters? For many years, the physically handicapped have been coached at home for a few hours a week. Emotionally disturbed youngsters have either been labeled uneducable or sent to special classes, and the mentally retarded have rarely received all the educational services that they need. Only recently have the parents of handicapped children organized to exchange information, to file lawsuits, and to protest to school boards. This pressure has resulted in legislation ordering an appropriate education for the more than eight million handicapped young people in the United States, of whom fewer than half are actually receiving such services. Of those in "special education" programs, only one in five is a fulltime student, with the majority receiving less than 10 hours of instruction per week. Forty-two percent are classified as "learning disabled," which can cover a wide range of specific diagnoses. Another 26 percent are "speech impaired," 17 percent have been labeled mentally retarded, and 8.4 percent as "emotionally disturbed" (*Statistical Abstract,* 1987, p. 129).

The major problem, of course, is that special education is relatively expensive. The classes must be small and the teachers carefully trained; equipment must be purchased; and regular evaluations must be provided. When communities feel burdened by taxes, the local school budget is often the first to be cut, and as most parents do not have handicapped youngsters, special education is apt to be defined as a "frill." If state law protects the special programs, cuts must be made elsewhere; the result may be conflict between the parents of handicapped children and other taxpayers (Anderson 1982).

Mainstreaming makes the school experience different for both the handicapped and the non-handicapped by breaking the pattern of isolation that often exists between these groups. Mainstreaming is particularly helpful in providing less restrictive educational experiences for those who are handicapped. (© Richard Hutchings/Photo Researchers, Inc.)

MAINSTREAMING. Another technique involves integrating handicapped children into the regular school program. Not only does this method normalize the experience of the handicapped, but it also lets other students interact with those who differ from them. But mainstreaming is hard to implement. Without more help—both for training and for classroom aides—many teachers cannot cope, and the nonhandicapped and their parents feel cheated. In some cases, mainstreaming has increased negative attitudes and has added to the strain on the handicapped; in other instances, the actual and potential benefits have outweighed these drawbacks.

Mainstreaming involves integrating handicapped students into the regular school program.

A Report Card for the Educational System

As might be expected of so varied an institution with so many personal and societal functions, the American educational system has received both high marks and failing grades:

Successes

- The establishment of a universal and comprehensive school system in a nation of students from many backgrounds and needs.
- Basic assimilation tasks performed by the elementary schools in the first half of the twentieth century.
- A post-secondary educational system with a wide range of options, potentially available to most high-school graduates.

Failures

- Inequality is still built into the dual and parallel school systems. The social class structure is reproduced by the length and the type of schooling that the student's family can afford. Even as the educational level of all groups has risen, the relative position of racial and ethnic subgroups has remained unchanged.
- In the United States since the mid-1960s, there has been a *general* decline in the scores of high-school students on standardized achievement tests, although the downward trend appears to have leveled off.
- Millions of Americans cannot write or read well enough to address a letter correctly or to understand a bus schedule.

Prospects for the Future

Can the American educational system build on its successes and overcome its failures? Much depends on what are defined as successes and failures. What some would consider its greatest failure—inequality of educational opportunity—others see as its great glory: recognition of individual merit. And while some people call for a return to a "common core" of Western knowledge, others claim that this is the same elitist view of the world that underpins all forms of inequality.

In the process of idealizing the past, we forget that there never was a golden age when schools performed their functions without conflict. To the contrary, until recently, many children were never enrolled, others received minimal training, and the schools have always been a battleground for opposing political and economic interests.

Today's criticism from all directions, however, does suggest a higher level of discontent than in the past. If so, the trend for the remainder of this century is likely to be toward *pluralism*—greater diversity among schools. Some schools will feature open classrooms, others a more traditional structure. Some will appeal to artistic students, others to budding scientists, and so forth. The major question is whether these will be public schools or operated as private, profit-making businesses with the assistance of taxpayer money in the form of tax deductions, shared busing, textbook loans, or outright tuition credits.

THE VOUCHER SYSTEM

One sign of the trend toward pluralism and private ownership is the revival of the *voucher* concept. Originally the brainchild of liberals concerned with empowering parents of poor inner-city youth, voucher plans are now supported by conservative religious groups and economic elites seeking an alternative to the public-school system.

In a voucher plan, school-tax monies in a given district are redistributed to families as certificates ("vouchers") worth a particular sum of money that can be used for tuition in a school of the parents' choice. This approach encourages the establishment of a variety of educational facilities, so that, theoretically, each child can be placed appropriately. In effect, public tax dollars could and would be used to finance religious and preparatory schools—a distinct advantage for the parents who already send their children to private schools. The gains for low-income families are less obvious.

The 1985 version of this plan supported by the Reagan administration, for example, would replace all federally funded educational assistance to low-income students with a voucher worth roughly $600, which the parents can then apply to any type of school (Flanders and Meier 1986). Unfortunately for lower-income parents, $600 will not go very far, especially without easy transportation.

The **voucher system** would allow families to spend a given sum of tax money for any type of schooling available.

Illiteracy

Despite our nation's enviable record in educating a higher proportion of its population for more years than any other nation, a large number of Americans remain unable to read or write adequately enough to function in a modern industrial society.

Just how many people are *illiterate* is a matter of some debate. The most recent Bureau of the Census report (1986) places the illiteracy rate at 13 percent of American adults, or roughly 26 million persons age fourteen and over. This is in sharp contrast to a 1979 estimate of one-half of 1 percent, which was based on whether or not a person had completed fifth grade. The census data are based on actual literacy tests taken by a random sample of 3400 in 1982.

Other researchers put the figure even higher. Kozol (1986), a critic of the American educational system, uses the figure of 60 million, or one-third of all adults, as being incapable of handling such important tasks as reading the labels on aspirin bottles or the want ads in newspapers or even instructions for public transportation. Not only do these people lead marginal lives, unable to take part in mainstream activities, but they cannot help their children to develop cognitive abilities. As a consequence, the children enter the school system without the minimal skills needed to learn to read or write—so they, too, become non-readers, perhaps not totally illiterate, but certainly not able to function fully in an information society.

According to a recent report from the Department of Education, most Americans age twenty-one to twenty-five are able to read as well as the average fourth grader, which is the technical measure of literacy. Beyond that, however, there is widespread "functional illiteracy," with four-fifths of the sample unable to handle a bus schedule, and nine-tenths incapable of correctly filling out a mail-order form—and these are our most recently educated adults (Kirsch and Jungeblut 1986)!

Native-born whites compose the largest group of functional illiterates, but their illiteracy rate is only 16 percent, compared to 44 percent for black adults, and 56 percent for Hispanic adults tested in English (Rohter 1986). Obviously, many non-English speakers are fully fluent in their native language, and large numbers of blacks are able to communicate effectively in "Black English."

Regardless of which numbers turn out to be accurate, the level of illiteracy in our society is shockingly high. The costs—in illness, crime, unemployment, poor workmanship, wasted talent—is not easy to calculate, although Kozol claims it runs $20 billion per year. The societal response has been almost nonexistent: $100 million in the federal government budget, or about $2 for each person who could use remedial help.

SOURCES: Jonathan Kozol, *Illiterate America,* New York: Anchor Press, 1986; Larry Rohter, "The Scourge of Adult Illiteracy," *New York Times,* Apr. 13, 1986, p. 33–36, Special Supplement on Education; U.S. Bureau of the Census, "Illiteracy: 1982," Washington, DC: U.S. Government Printing Office, 1986; Irwin Kirsch and Ann Jungeblut, "Literacy: Profiles of America's Young Adults," Washington, DC: National Assessment of Educational Progress, September, 1986.

Another possibility is that public-school districts will respond to this threat by themselves diversifying. That is, various schools will specialize in certain programs and teaching techniques, just as the private or alternative schools do now. But it is just as likely that the public schools, particularly in the inner cities, will have to educate only the most difficult students, with ever-declining resources, while the private and parochial schools continue to screen out the hard-to-teach.

TEACHING AS A PROFESSION

Much of the current debate about the quality of American education has focused on the teachers. On the one hand, they—and their unions—are blamed for the fact that test scores appear to have declined at the same time that teachers' pay has increased and their teaching load decreased. On the other hand, teacher salaries are actually below those that similarly trained persons could earn in almost any other field. In 1986, even letter carriers had higher weekly median earnings (Bureau of Labor Statistics 1986).

One blueprint for the future (Carnegie Corporation 1986) proposes "transforming teaching from an occupation into a profession" by upgrading educational qualifications, instituting a system of national certification, increasing salaries, and providing more autonomy in the classroom. The goal is to improve student performance and rescue the public-education system from its critics on both left and right.

HIGHER EDUCATION

The trend toward specialization and training in specific skills in U.S. education is also seen at the college level, where the proportion of students enrolled in the humanities and the social sciences has declined. The most popular fields of study today are linked to specific occupations: business, prelaw, and computer programming. Student activism on behalf of social causes such as civil rights and international peace has also declined in favor of vocational goals and self-interest. A rare exception was the few, far-between, and short-lived protests against university investments in South Africa in 1986.

Both the student body and the faculty are becoming specialists in ever narrower bodies of knowledge, following the general pattern of specialization and upgrading of skills in the society as a whole. Yet, there is an element of "deskilling" involved in such limited concentration in one academic area, just as there is in the workplace (see Chapter 12). A return to the broader goal of a general education in all aspects of the culture seems unlikely in a society entering the postindustrial age. But there are signs of change; some colleges are reemphasizing general education requirements in addition to specialized knowledge. Combining these goals is a major challenge to higher-education leaders today.

Summary

Educational institutions are formal extensions of socialization, designed to transmit the culture, train people for adult statuses, develop talent, and generate new knowledge. In modern industrial society, educational systems are complex and extensive, covering the years from nursery school to graduate school. Functionalists claim that the educational system is a meritocracy where objective standards are applied and individuals can rise on the basis of their innate talent. Conflict theorists see the schools as a mechanism for reproducing the ruling elites.

The American educational system includes both a public and private sector. Most private schools are parochial, i.e. under religious control; others are exclusively preparatory institutions for the children of the upper strata.

In the classroom, children are systematically prepared for their adult roles. Although suburban, rural, and urban schools serve very different student bodies, some features are common. The urban schools, however, present special problems because students do not see any benefits to remaining in school.

Higher education is a stratified system of colleges and universities. Within schools, faculties are also stratified by academic rank. Over the past twenty years, both faculty and student body have become increasingly diverse in terms of race, ethnicity, social class, and gender, but higher education still serves to reinforce the existing divisions of wealth and power.

Current controversies focus on liberal versus conservative views of the functions of education and the perceived conflict between quality and equality, as most vividly illustrated in the struggle over racial integration of the schools.

Although the American educational system has many achievements to its credit—ours is the most educated population in the world—problems remain. Prospects for the future include increased pluralism among schools, continued diversity among students of higher education, and enhanced professionalism among elementary and secondary teachers.

Suggested Readings

ARONOWITZ, STANLEY, and HENRY A. GIROUX. *Education Under Seige: The Conservative, Liberal and Radical Debate over Schooling.* South Hadley, MA: Bergin & Garvey, 1985. An examination of the contemporary problems facing the school systems and the factors that shape them.

CARNOY, MARTIN, and HENRY M. LEVIN. *Schooling and Work in the Democratic State.* Stanford, CA: Stanford University Press, 1985. This book analyzes the democratic process operating within the school system and shows how this process can serve to undercut the repressive nature of the workplace.

COHEN, ARTHUR, and FLORENCE BREWER. *The American Community College*. San Francisco: Jossey-Bass, 1982. A comprehensive portrait of the structure and the processes of community colleges which discusses the three essential elements: students, faculty, and administration.

COOKSON, PETER W., JR., and CAROLINE HODGES PERSELL. *Preparing for Power: America's Elite Boarding Schools*. New York: Basic Books, 1985. An in-depth study of elite preparatory schools that examines the relationship between education and social class.

FLEMING, JACQUELINE. *Blacks in College: A Comparative Study of Students' Success in Black and in White Institutions*. San Francisco: Jossey-Bass, 1984. A descriptive account of factors that contribute to the success of black students focusing on psychosocial adaptation and intellectual performance as conditions for future success.

KOZOL, JONATHAN. *Illiterate America*. Garden City, NY: Anchor Press, Doubleday, 1985. This book presents the plight of illiterate Americans and calls for a national plan of action to solve the problem.

PESHKIN, ALAN. *God's Choice: The Total World of a Fundamentalist Christian School*. Chicago: University of Chicago Press, 1986. An ethnography that explores the beliefs and behaviors of students who attend Christian schools.

SOLOMON, BARBARA MILLER. *In the Company of Educated Women: A History of Women and Higher Education in America*. New Haven, CT: Yale University Press, 1985. An historical analysis of women's access to and experiences in higher education from colonial times to the present.

THOMAS, GAIL E., ed. *Black Students in Higher Education: Conditions and Experiences in the 1970's*. Westport, CT: Greenwood, 1981. A comprehensive collection of papers on the status of black students in higher education. The essays highlight academic experiences and progress and distribution in undergraduate, graduate, and professional schools.

15

Belief Systems: Religions and Ideologies

MEMBERS of the Hagan tribe of Papua New Guinea divide the world into two realms: the wild and the tamed. They believe that a girl child's upper teeth develop first because they grow downward, pointing to the earth to which Hagan women become rooted. Boys tend to cut their lower teeth first, symbolizing eventual growth upward toward the sky and manliness (Strathern 1980, p. 206).

• The Tewa Indians of New Mexico believe that they originated in the waters of a Northern lake, and once on land, divided into two groups that traveled along parallel paths to the Southwest. The idea of duality—of everything having both a human and a supernatural aspect—is central to their way of thinking and to their social organization. The concept affects their very behavior (Ortiz 1969).

- Many societies recognize people, called *shamans,* who have special talents for dealing with the supernatural. Among the Tapirape of Brazil, shamans are believed to derive their power from dreams, to go into trances from which they can cure the ill, and to be able to turn themselves into birds and travel across both time and space. Shamans are a source of guidance (Wagley 1977).

- The Aztecs of Mexico had a very complex set of beliefs and rituals, with 5000 priests in their capital city whose goal was to delay the end of the world. In order to please the gods, the priests had to offer up a beating heart every day of the year, and several on special days according to a very intricate calendar. It is estimated that 15,000 persons a year were ritually sacrificed, their hearts removed, and the remainder of their bodies eaten by members of the society; possibly this compensated for the loss of other animal protein due to rapid population growth (Harner 1977, Harris 1985).

- In 1986, in the United States, hundreds of followers have left their homes and families in order to live near a forty-year-old woman psychic (a person in touch with other worlds) named J. Z. Knight, and thousands of others pay $400 a session to hear her transform herself into a 35,000-year-old wise man named Ramtha. Ramtha becomes a link with the past. Knight is only one of several dozen entrepreneurs of a new type of spiritualism in this country that offers believers the hope of success in this world (Lindsey 1986).

These are only five examples of the many thousands of different sets of beliefs and rituals devised by members of human groups to regulate and give meaning to their lives. While other people's beliefs may seem quite strange to us, what would an Aztec think about the story of Adam and Eve?

In this chapter we define and examine the essential characteristics of such systems of ideas and ceremonies, with special emphasis on recent trends in the United States.

The Sociological Study of Belief Systems

At the beginning of Chapter 3, you were asked to create culture and social structure on a deserted island to which your sociology class had been miraculously transported during a nuclear attack. At some point, members of the group would begin to retell the story of their amazing good fortune, find explanations for their having been chosen to survive, praise themselves for the rules they have created, and decide that they have a great mission to perform. In essence, you would produce a *belief system*—ideas about the meaning of life that are shared among a group of believers.

If the group had also agreed that some divine force was guiding their destiny, we would call this particular kind of belief system a *religion.* Because not all belief systems are based on faith in a supernatural power, we have used the broader term for the title of this chapter, although most of the material does concern religions.

Because belief systems involve faith and emotion, they may seem unsuitable for critical analysis. But sociologists do study belief systems and have been interested in them from the very beginning. August Comte and Emile Durkheim, as well as Karl Marx and Max Weber all had a great deal to say about religion, though what each had to say was quite different. Comte was a man of the Enlightenment who wanted to substitute the scientific study of society, a *secular ideology,* for what he saw as the superstition and irrational faith of the past. Weber and Marx were fascinated by the interplay among religious beliefs, the behaviors encouraged by such beliefs, and the economic system of the particular society. And Durkheim saw belief systems as a celebration of society itself.

DURKHEIM

According to Durkheim, ideas about the ultimate meaning of life and the ceremonies that express these beliefs arise out of the collective experience of the group. If all social institutions are a product of a group's trial-and-error attempts to survive, then belief systems, too, must originate in society itself. What other frame

A belief system is a set of shared ideas about the meaning of life.

Religion is a belief system based on the concept of a divine force guiding destiny.

Secular ideologies are belief systems based on worldly rather than divine forces.

This group of Afghanistani "freedom fighters" (rebels) prays as they prepare for another attack against Soviet soldiers occupying their homeland. God has been on many sides. (© P. Issot-Sergent/ Gamma-Liasion)

of reference was available to the earliest humans?

First, beliefs, like language or any other symbol system, depend upon *agreement among minds* for their meaning. Second, the content of belief systems—the ideas expressed, objects worshipped, ceremonies enacted, and values held sacred—all express the *shared fate* of believers. It is through their belief systems, said Durkheim, that people experience the abstraction *society* and reinforce their commitment to one another.

For Durkheim (1912/1961), *all* systems of belief, regardless of specific form or content

"... have the same objective significance and fulfill the same function everywhere. ... There are no religions that are false. All are true in their own fashion; all answer, though in different ways, to the given conditions of human existence." (pp. 15, 17)

WEBER

In *The Protestant Ethic and the Spirit of Capitalism* Weber related the rise of capitalism in the nineteenth century to the

development of Calvinism. He demonstrated how the demanding values of this religion and the underlying anxieties it generated about salvation proved very compatible with the demands of capitalist investment. (The main ideas of this work have been discussed in Chapter 3 with respect to the American value system.) Weber also studied Buddhism, Hinduism, Christianity and Judaism. In every instance his concern was the interrelationship of religious beliefs and the history and structure of the society in which they developed.

Thus, sociologists do not question the truth of any belief system—all are true to those who believe. Rather, we ask "What happens because people believe it?" This is an empirical question; it can be answered by systematic observation. Even though belief systems deal with ultimate issues that are not subject to empirical verification, we can objectively examine the *origins* and *consequences* of belief. The sociology of religion begins with the assumption that beliefs are social products, an essential part of culture, the content of which varies from one time and place to another. That is, like all knowledge, beliefs about the ultimate nature of reality de-

Death raises questions and anxieties for which even relatively secular societies must provide explanation and ritual. How do our modern funerals compare with this simple burial in Guatemala? (© Antoinette Jongen/Black Star)

velop within specific social contexts, reflect certain power relationships, depend on the faith of believers, and cannot be falsified (Hargrove 1984). But we can ask why people believe what they do, and what happens because of it.

DEFINING BELIEF SYSTEMS

Are there universal aspects of all belief systems, whether religious or secular? What, for example, would be the common elements of cannibalism, Calvinism, Confucianism, and communism? And how are individual needs meshed with social necessity?

According to one well-known sociological formula (Yinger 1969), religion is found where (1) people are aware of the continuing problems of daily life; (2) where people have constructed explanations and rituals around this awareness; and (3) where specific role incumbents are assigned the task of maintaining the awareness and the ritual. This formulation links all three levels of sociological analysis: individual awareness/need; shared ceremonies and beliefs at the cultural level; and group interaction at the level of social structure.

A belief system exists, therefore, wherever the human need for meaning leads to the construction of beliefs and rituals that characterize a community of believers. The precise content is irrelevant so long as the beliefs reduce individual anxiety and produce social cohesion.

Functions of Belief Systems

Systems of belief and ritual thus fill both individual and group needs. They are systematic attempts to interpret a broad range of earthly (and otherworldly) phenomena. As you yourself may have noticed, people turn to worship at times of great personal misery or happiness. These are often also points at which the unity of groups are placed under strain.

Many religions also serve a "cooling-out" function by softening anger at injustice. The poor, especially, need to feel that something better awaits them if not in this world, at least in the next one. And it clearly serves the interest of the nonpoor to have the less fortunate members of their society direct their sense of injustice elsewhere. If oppressed people can be convinced that it is the will of God, or Allah, or some other divine power that they should bear their fate quietly in return for rewards after death (when "the last shall be first"), social order is not threatened. This is the context of Karl Marx's statement that religion serves as the "opiate" (pain killer) of the masses, lulling them into believing that their condition is divinely ordained and cannot be changed by organized effort. Using this perspective, many contemporary conflict theorists see religion as a powerful support for the privileged classes.

MANIFEST AND LATENT FUNCTIONS

Rituals such as Communion, Bar/Bat Mitzvot, rain dances, even human sacrifice and witch hunts, have both manifest and latent functions. The open and declared purposes are typically the need to activate ceremonies that are thought to influence uncontrollable aspects of life—the future of the young person, natural disasters, evil in the world, outside enemies. The latent function of rituals is to reinforce tradition and give people an immediate experience of group unity. Thus, while a rain dance may not bring rain, it does, for a moment at least, relieve personal and social stresses produced by extended periods of drought. Similarly, the search for "enemies of the people" during political witch hunts such as that conducted by Senator Joseph McCarthy in the 1950s periodically reassures Americans that they are safe from the "red menace" of Communism. (See section on civil religion, p. 409.)

DYSFUNCTIONS OF BELIEF SYSTEMS

Most belief systems assume that one and only one creed reflects the truth. In other words if each belief system is *the* Word, then others must be false. Moreover, those who possess the one and only truth often feel obligated to spread it.

Thus, there is always potential conflict among those who hold different beliefs. Because there is little room for compromise, religious wars have often been among the most bloody and long-lasting. Western history is filled with religious persecution, forced conversion, and wholesale slaughter, even though most faiths proclaim mercy and brotherhood, at least among believers. Belief systems tend to unify the faithful but to divide them from all nonbelievers, who, by definition, are unfaithful and therefore not to be tolerated.

Within a given society, the presence of two religions is often associated with conflict, as, for example, in Northern Ireland today. The United States has avoided major *sectarian conflict* (interreligious strife) by making tolerance of religious differences a legal and moral principle. Article VI of the Constitution of the United States says that "no religious test shall ever be required as a qualification to an office or public trust...." The First Amendment states, "Congress shall make no law respecting an establishment of religion, or prohibiting the free exercise thereof." But the First Amendment has not always checked anti-Catholic and anti-Jewish passions; U.S. history has had many episodes of religious persecution and discrimination. The Ku Klux Klan, for example, was organized to save the nation

Sectarian conflict refers to interreligious strife.

This boy's bar mitzvah, celebrated at the Wailing Wall in Jerusalem, Israel, helps bridge a life transition to adulthood. It also reinforces Judaic religion and tradition for his kin and community. (© Yoran Lehmann/Peter Arnold, Inc.)

from the "foreign" influence of Catholics and Jews as well as blacks (Parrillo 1985).

These examples illustrate a major sociological principle: The same social pattern can be both adaptive (functional) and maladaptive (dysfunctional), depending on the context and the specific group involved. What is functional for a subgroup may not be so for the larger society. Thus, a belief system can increase solidarity within one group, but it can also lead to conflict in a society with different sets of beliefs and believers. Nor do religions always relieve personal anxiety; but if people were less afraid of violating taboos or of losing their faith, they might be less anxiety-ridden and less in need of religious comfort in the first place (Radcliffe-Brown 1964).

Nonetheless, in all human societies, a minimal set of beliefs exist (1) to provide a meaning for life; (2) to explain the unknown; (3) to reduce the tensions of important transitions in the life course; and (4) to generate a sense of solidarity among the believers.

Structure of Belief Systems

Every religion or ideology has three essential components based on these personal and societal needs:

An **origin myth** is the story of how the group began.

1. An *origin myth* (the word *myth* indicates not falsity but the fact that the events being described happened much earlier and cannot be verified) is a tale of how the group began, such as the biblical story of the Creation. An origin myth creates a history that makes sense of the present.
2. In the present, there are *rules of conduct* to be followed: proscriptions (prohibitions) and prescriptions (recipes for the good life) to guide the individual. These codes of conduct reinforce social order, as, for example, the Ten Commandments or most of the Koran, the holy book of Islam.
3. The third element of belief systems is a vision of the future: a mission such as spreading the good word, waiting for the second coming, or leading the revolution. The sense of destiny unifies all

true believers and gives meaning to both individual existence and human history.

The same three elements are found everywhere: in the religions of simple as well as complex societies, among believers in scientific explanation as well as followers of mysticism, among astronomers as well as astrologists. And among militant anti-religionists.

MARXISM AS A SECULAR IDEOLOGY

The writings of Karl Marx, along with those of the Soviet leader Lenin (1870–1924), form the basis of a secular ideology called *Marxism,* which gives its believers the same certainty that Christianity or Judaism brings to others. As the official ideology of the Soviet Union, the People's Republic of China, Cuba, and many countries in Eastern Europe, Marxism contains all the elements of any belief system: an explanation of history, a guide for behavior in the present, and a vision of the ultimate triumph of justice. The strength of these beliefs among followers in many nations has led one critic to speak of "Marxism as a World Religion" (Boli 1981).

In the Soviet Union, as in any other society, beliefs are designed to support the existing order, to reinforce the authority of the leaders, and to motivate the citizens to sacrifice for the good of the group. The Soviet leaders have sought to replace traditional religious ceremonies with new secular ones, especially at important moments in the life course: birth, marriage, and death. Special rituals also mark the entry into and the exit from youth groups, school, the military, and the workplace (Lane 1981). Important events in Marxist-Leninist history are celebrated as holidays in which the society as a whole is honored. The goal of all these rituals in the Soviet Union, as in other societies, is to legitimize the political system. The difference is that Marxism is a purely secular belief system, whereas most others are based on a faith in divine forces. Thus, a belief system that began as a revolutionary call to end the oppression of traditional religions has itself become the official ideology of a totalitarian state. A Marxist funeral in Moscow is only the most recent form of a ritual developed by members of the earliest human populations. At least 100,000 years

Marxism, like many political ideologies, celebrates its heroes and past achievements, reinforces the authority of current leaders, and motivates citizens to sacrifice for the nation and the group. Here placards of Karl Marx and Ho Chi Minh are raised at a parade commemorating the anniversary of the fall of Saigon, Vietnam. (© Matsumoto/SYGMA)

before *Homo sapiens,* our Neanderthal cousins placed their dead in proper graves, positioned the body, and left offerings of seeds and flowers. These burial sites are evidence of the very early emergence of belief systems.

Origins and Cross-Cultural Perspectives

The explanation of religion as a phenomenon rooted in social structure and the material world, does not always satisfy those who seek a more spiritual and individual (rather than social) basis for religion. Through the years, philosophers and social scientists have suggested a number of other factors such as: awe over the power of nature, fear of death, the need to interpret dreams, guilt over the wish to kill one's parents, and original sin. Some

sociologists speak of a human need for *transcendence,* to escape the limits of one's own senses and to feel that one's life has significance beyond daily experience (Berger 1965).

These possible sources, however, cannot explain the endless variety of belief systems or how they change over time. For this type of analysis we must follow Durkheim and Weber and pay attention to the group's particular culture and social structure. Do gathering bands, for example, tend to develop belief systems different from those of agricultural tribes? If the origins of belief lie in the uncertainties of human existence, then we would expect differences simply on the basis of varying modes of subsistence. In line with that thinking, anthropologist Marvin Harris (1985) suggests that the kinds of gods people worship reflect the nature of social relationships within the society. In simple gathering or hunting bands, the gods, like the people they guide, are basically an egalitarian bunch, with little distinction between male and female. These gods were important in creating the group but they leave daily life largely to the skills of the native population and to lesser divinities. In contrast, in agricultural societies, especially those with centralized states and well-defined social classes, the gods themselves are highly stratified and insist on strict obedience to standards of conduct and morality.

It is also probable that divine beings were once thought of in feminine terms. The link between the fertility of nature and that of humans should lead to the worship of female forces, and, indeed, among the earliest objects of a clearly religious nature there are tiny statues of females in an advanced state of pregnancy.

There is also evidence that important ritual functions were performed by women, such as the vestal virgins in ancient Europe, druid priestesses in Britain, and members of women's cults in early Roman history (Pace 1985). Statues of a mother goddess from ancient Crete and wall paintings from Stone Age Turkey (Barstow 1978) suggest an even more central role for women, not only in religious ritual but in the society as a whole. Indeed, there is evidence of widespread mother worship throughout the world, from prehistoric to contemporary societies (Preston 1983).

Yet the major world religions today are

Transcendence refers to the need to go beyond the limits of one's own senses and feel that life has meaning beyond one's daily experiences.

This statue, thought to have originated 40,000 years ago in the Upper Paleolithic Era, was found in a cave in Austria. Called the "Venus of Willendorf," it is one of the earliest religious objects linking the fertility of nature and humans. (© Art Resource Center)

strikingly dominated by male imagery: the Father reigns supreme, through chosen Sons. The leaders of biblical Hebrews were called *patriarchs.* Today, in some branches of Judaism, patriarchy is still a dominant feature. (See section on "Women in the Pulpit" later in this chapter.) Christianity is also extremely masculine in its doctrine, symbols, and power structure. Islam is almost exclusively male-oriented, forbidding women to enter the main body of the mosque. Although the major Eastern religions—Buddhism, Hinduism, and Shintoism—are less openly masculine, women's role in ritual is very limited. These regularities in belief and practice, originating in *agricultural* societies of the Near and Far East still reflect the male-dominated social systems of the time and place of their emergence.

Yet, despite such similarities, it is the diversity and richness of beliefs and rituals that fascinate the social scientist. Because of the wide range of events that are not always under human control in pre-industrial societies, ritual life is more elaborate and complex than in modern societies (which are, in this respect, more simple than many other cultures).

SACRED AND PROFANE

In all societies, there are two very different sets of behaviors and objects. One set is considered *sacred,* and is invested with holy, divine, mystical, or supernatural force. The other realm is the *profane,* which is earthly and understandable in its own terms. Just which behaviors and objects go into which category is a matter of wide variation among all the world's religions and ideologies. Sacredness is not built into any object; it is a characteristic imposed by the group. Thus, what would to one group simply be two pieces of wood joined together becomes "the cross" with all its mystical significance to another. And sacred burial places of the Plains Indians are just so much good pasture land for Midwest farmers.

Sacred behaviors and objects are invested with holy, divine, mystical, or supernatural force.

Profane behaviors and objects are not holy, but earthly and understandable on their own.

RELIGIOUS ROLES

In all societies, certain people are placed in charge of the sacred items and ceremonies. Indeed, religious roles are among the very first to emerge in human history ("the second oldest profession"). Shamans, witch doctors, priests and priestesses, ministers, rabbis, and Islamic mullahs are all religious specialists whose duties include protection of sacred things and places.

MAGIC

People throughout the world also attempt to control the supernatural. *Magic* refers to behaviors designed to manipulate unseen forces, whereas religion involves coming to terms with a superior power.

Magical formulas, words, and gestures are used to reduce uncertainty. Among the Trobriand Islanders of the South Pacific, for example, fishing in the calm waters of a lagoon requires little in the way of ceremony, as success depends only on skill; but when the same men and boats venture into the ocean beyond the lagoon, where high winds can make fishing hazardous,

Magic refers to behavior designed to manipulate unseen forces.

Many religions have sought to keep women away from holy places in an attempt to maintain purity. This sign appears at the entrance of a Hindu Temple in Bali. Since most of the members of this community would have been socialized to the norm, for whom do you think the sign was written? (© Eugene Gordon)

the departure of the vessels is marked by solemn rituals (Malinowski 1925/1955).

Magic is used whenever an outcome cannot be predicted by rational, "scientific" knowledge. The fact that magic is more common in preliterate than in modern societies can be explained by differences in the supply of scientific explanations, not in the mental capacities of preliterate or modern people. Besides, even we "moderns," when faced with the unpredictable, cross our hearts, stroke a rabbit's foot, light candles, or pray. Any of you who has watched a professional baseball game can recognize such magic-based behaviors as rubbing charms, crossing oneself, tapping the bat three times, or any of the repeated series of tics and twitches displayed by pitchers and batters.

Belief Systems and Social Change

Because belief systems deal with the eternal (either truth is everlasting or it is not truth), most religions are by nature con-

servative, supportive of the *status quo* if not openly reinforcing existing political and economic inequality. Yet religions and secular ideologies can also be agents of social change (Ackerman 1985). New movements are continually being formed within established belief systems, even in simple societies. Typically, a charismatic leader introduces changes in the traditional practices which, over time, become the basis for a new religion. Both Jesus and Muhammad were such leaders.

Max Weber was especially concerned with the independent effect of ideas on social relationships. In his comparative studies of religion and society, Weber showed how certain beliefs create a mindset that can have specific economic and political consequences (Weber 1922-3/1957). We have already discussed (Chapter 3) Weber's analysis of how the central themes of early Protestantism reinforced the motives and behaviors essential to the rise of capitalism (see Woodrum 1985 for a similar insight into Japanese Americans).

Religious traditions have sometimes been used to justify resistance to authority, as in contemporary Poland where the Catholic Church, with the support of the Pope, has become a symbol of challenge to the Communist regime. When, however, after many decades of papal support for military and civilian dictatorships in Central and South America, a new breed of Catholic clergy has developed a "liberation theology" on behalf of oppressed peasants, traditional church leaders have denounced them for being too secular.

PRIESTS AND PROPHETS

The dual nature of belief systems—as support for the *status quo* or as an agent of change—is captured in Max Weber's distinction between the *priestly* and the *prophetic.*

In general, priestly functions involve dealing with the specific tradition of the faith in which the priest is a trained and ordained leader. In religious terms, the priest is a conservator (saver) and, in political terms, often supports the existing structure of power. The *prophet,* on the other hand, is a charismatic figure, usually risen from the ranks of untrained laypersons, and is a witness to a revelation calling for a new order. As the bringer of this new order, the prophet is by definition at

Priestly functions deal with specific traditions of the faith.

The **prophet** is a charismatic figure, witnessing a revelation calling for a new order.

odds with established authorities. The prophet can be a simple teacher of the new law, as was Jesus, or could seize political power, as did Muhammad. In other words, priests represent traditional values and may actually be the heirs of a prophetic movement. Prophets disrupt the social order and, as disturbers of the peace, leave themselves vulnerable to passions both for and against their prophecy.

Whereas Karl Marx emphasized the priestly, conservatizing functions of religion, Max Weber studied the dynamic aspects of belief systems and the relationship between a religion and other institutional spheres. Weber spoke of the *routinization of charisma,* whereby the prophet's work is transformed into a worldly organization. The resulting bureaucracy often becomes the deadening structure described by Marx. Thus, many religions begin as forces of social and political change but, if successful, eventually become the new establishment.

There is a basic tension between religion and its emphasis on the holy, on the one hand, and the world as it is, full of imperfection and temptations, on the other. Jealousy, hate, lust, greed, and other assorted human passions always threaten to turn people away from thinking about the perfect good. Religious leaders must continually warn and threaten the less faith-ful. Some religions, claimed Weber, survive by maintaining an otherworldly stance; that is, the members group themselves in religious communities separate from the rest of society (as, for example, the Hutterites and the Amish of modern America). Or as Confucians and Orthodox Jews do, believers create two spheres of activity with different rules for each. Orthodox Jews, for example, can hold a job and be devoted to secular business concerns for part of the day but, in the rest of their activities, follow a purely religious way of life.

NATIVISTIC REVIVALS

In times of deep or rapid social and political change, the power of established authorities is weakened. These are the historical moments when charismatic figures are likely to emerge and find a mass following. This was the case for the Old Testament prophets, the Ayatollah Khomeini in Iran, and Wovoka of the Plains Indians a century ago.

The Ghost Dance Religion. By the late 1880s, the buffalo had disappeared from the Great Plains. Native American tribes were forced onto reservations as white settlers took their land and destroyed the Indians' culture base. For a short period in

The **routinization of charisma** occurs when the prophet's work is transformed into a worldly organization.

Participating in the Ghost Dance was to have provided protection against the encroaching white settlers. This movement ended, however, at the Battle of Wounded Knee where U.S. troops decimated Chief Sitting Bull's forces. (© J.O. Milmoe)

1870, a version of the very sacred Ghost Dance swept through the tribes. In 1889, when disorganization and anger were widespread among the Plains Indians, the Ghost Dance religion was revived under the influence of Wovoka, a prophet who claimed that the dance would bring back dead ancestors and fill the land with animals for hunting.

The dance spread rapidly, along with hatred for whites and a renewed pride in Indian ways. A particularly enraged group of Dakotas under Chief Sitting Bull fought against the U.S. Army and was thoroughly routed in a battle at Wounded Knee. Although the Ghost Dance religion persisted for a few more years, Native American cultures and societies were effectively destroyed.

Nativistic revival movements arise when a culture is disintegrating under the impact of profound change.

The Ghost Dance is an example of the *nativistic revival movements* that arise when a culture is disintegrating under the impact of profound change. In the Pacific Islands, disrupted by colonialism and World War II, islanders have built airstrips for the arrival of planes (remembered from the war) full of material goods that will restore traditional power. These *cargo cults* express a yearning for the wholeness of the past, and magical reliance, quite literally, on the "God in the Machine" (Worsley 1968).

Modernization

Modernization refers to the spread of industrialization and urbanization and the growth of the world economy.

Today, however, the most powerful source of social change is *modernization*: the spread of industrialization and urbanization, and the growth of a world economy. Kin-based production is replaced by cash-crop agriculture or the assembly line; traditional authority is challenged at all levels; family members migrate to where they can find jobs; and tribes and clans are expected to be loyal to an arbitrarily imposed nation-state. Few societies can absorb all these changes without a great deal of personal stress and social strain. People feel that they have lost control over their lives. The "old ways" of doing things no longer work, but the "new ways" are unclear, and this is as true of some regions of the United States as of the developing nations (Marty 1987).

The destabilizing effects of such rapid and thorough-going change have led to several modern nativistic revivals, most notably the rise of "Islamic fundamentalism" in Iran, under the Ayatollah Khomeini. In reaction to the *anomie* produced by the Shah of Iran's attempt to turn his country into a modern state in the space of a few decades (a process that took hundreds of years in the West), the people rebelled under the leadership of religious authorities who called for a rejection of all western influences and a return to the strict faith of the past. Women were told to give up modern clothing and wear the traditional black shawls and veils; boys and girls were once more forbidden to attend school together; and the authority of fathers and mothers was restored.

It is possible that the recent surge of Christian revivalism in the United States also reflects widespread feelings of powerlessness in the face of profound economic and social changes that have transformed small-town life and threatened the taken-for-granted structures of control in the family and community (see p. 416).

SECULARIZATION

The transition from traditional to modern societies in the West also involved the triumph of reason, science, and technology—a reliance on the powers of individuals to solve human problems. These traits are components of *secularization,* with its focus on this world, in contrast to faith in sacred powers.

Secularization involves the triumph of science, technology, and rationality over the forces of faith and reliance on divine powers.

Science, of course, need not be viewed as being in opposition to faith; no matter how much we know scientifically, there are always questions that science cannot answer. Although many scientists claim that the universe was created 15 billion years ago with a "big bang," they still cannot tell us about the moment *before* that great explosion. Or the moment before that. At some point, we are faced with possibilities that cannot be scientifically proven or disproven (Hammond 1985).

Nonetheless, the areas of life in which technical mastery has replaced faith and magical practices are ever-widening. The integrative functions of religion have been taken over by political structures and economic organizations, so that families and stable local communities centered on places of worship are no longer the dominant sources of social control (Wilson 1982, Turner 1983). And while faith and ritual may be important for individuals in time of personal stress, most members of modern societies base their decisions on a rational calculus of means and ends, costs and benefits, rather than relying on the commands of religious authorities.

It is this modern way of thinking (the *secular mind*) that most conflicts with religion. The belief that human beings themselves can change the conditions of their lives, without reliance on divine interaction, is the greatest challenge to traditional faith. If a machine breaks down it does little good to pray for it to resume operating, but there is much to be gained from reading the technical manual and making the correct adjustments.

The secular spirit, moreover, is marked by an emphasis on *consumption*, on enjoyment of the here and now, and on a vision of the good life on earth rather than in the hereafter. Central, also, to the secular orientation is a focus on the *individual*. Note that these characteristics reflect the thrust of the Protestant work ethic so crucial in the development of modern capitalism. Yet, as we will see later in this chapter, it is precisely these traits that most disturb the new prophets of Protestant revivalism, who have defined "secular humanism" as the great enemy because it denies the power of God and divine providence in this world.

The concept of secularization has also come under serious criticism from contemporary scholars, who note that the idea itself reflects the positivist bias of modern social science (Hadden 1987). In addition, cross-cultural studies suggest that generational and cultural factors affect religious commitment differently even in industrialized societies (Sasaki and Suzuki 1987). For example, the secularization process has been fully realized in the Netherlands,

partially in the United States, and only minimally in Japan.

The modern era is also characterized by *world religions,* representing the triumph of a few major faiths in spreading across the world, absorbing other religions, and converting millions (see Table 15-1).

Organized Religion and Religious Behavior in America

RELIGIOUS AFFILIATION

About six in ten Americans are formally linked to (affiliated with) a religious congregation. These figures are somewhat misleading, however, since some churches count children and others count only adults. Roman Catholics comprise the single largest body of believers, with close to 53 million members. All Protestant denominations combined, however, account for about 80 million individuals, well over half of all church members in America. In 1986, there were an estimated 5.9 million members of Jewish congregations, 4 million members of the Eastern Church, 1 million other types of Catholic, and 200,000 Unitarians and non-Christian believers, excluding Muslims and Hindus, and about 100,000 Buddhists (Goldman 1985, Jacquet 1987).

These figures represent a slight rise from the previous year and continue a trend of very slow growth in church membership in the 1980s, at the same rate as the population as a whole (Roozen 1986, Jacquet 1987). This increase is not across the boards, however; the Roman Catholic Church and the major established Protestant denominations have experienced slow declines, while new smaller sects have gained.

The Roman Catholic population in the United States will continue to grow at a faster rate than that of Protestants or Jews, largely because of immigration of young adult Hispanics, with their relatively high birth rates. As these new migrants become acculturated, however, they will tend to follow the pattern of previous Catholic ethnic groups whose fertility rates have declined to the same level as the Protestant majority. In the process, many Catholic couples practice birth con-

---

TABLE 15-1 Members of world religions as a percentage of the world's population: estimates for the year 2000

Religion	Number	Percent of Total
Muslim (Islam)	1,201,000,000	19.2
Roman Catholic	1,169,000,000	18.7
Protestant	400,000,000	7.0
Buddhist	359,000,000	5.7
Eastern Orthodox	153,000,000	2.4
Jewish	20,000,000	.3
All others	2,918,000,000	46.6

SOURCE: Jacquet, 1985.

Religions of the East

In contrast to religions originating in the Near East—Judaism, Christianity, and Islam—the major belief systems of Southeast Asia and the Far East are more concerned with thought than with action, are oriented to nature, and are polytheistic (accepting many gods). The questions posed by such religions as Buddhism, Hinduism, Shintoism, and Confucianism are these: "What is my place in the universe?" "Which path shall I take to happiness?" "What is the way of harmony?" "What is life?" The element of searching and seeking in these questions is very different from the insistence on received doctrine of Islam, Judaism, or Christianity: "*This* is the way!"

Three elements of Eastern religion that appeal to young people in the United States today are (1) the emphasis on self-discipline (not unlike early Calvinism); (2) a belief in the unity of all life, that is, humans with nature, past with present, and one person with another, all linked together in one chain of life; and (3) the higher value placed on experience than on intellect, whereby knowledge comes from an opening of the mind to feeling and intuitive understanding.

Hinduism, Buddhism, Confucianism, and Shintoism, however, have very different histories and doctrines.

The great theme of *Hinduism* is that of an everlasting cycle of life in which all things are reincarnated (born over and over again), and the grand goal of human existence is to transcend this endless cycle through meditation, which brings perfect peace from earthly desires.

Buddhism is based on a knowledge of correct conduct through suffering and contemplation, with the goal of *nirvana*, a complete emptying of the self so that Buddha's insights can enter and free the person from the cycle of reincarnation.

In contrast, *Confucianism* is founded on a reverence for the past and is full of rules of behavior, much as are Western religions. The key concept is *piety* (respect and righteousness), first expressed in the family as the worship of one's ancestors and obedience to one's parents, and then extended to the state. Subjects shall respect their kings, children their parents, wives their husbands, and younger children their elders. Friend to friend is the only egalitarian relationship in the Confucian system.

Shintoism, the native religion of Japan, is based on the belief that divine forces of nature *(kami)* exist in the sun and the moon, rivers, trees, and animals. Shinto has been greatly influenced by Buddhism and Confucianism and has proved to be open to a variety of elements (including faith healing).

---

trol in ways still forbidden by the Church. In 1985, for example, 83 percent of Catholics between ages eighteen to thirty-nine favored use of artificial birth control (*New York Times,* Nov. 25, 1985). The normative conflict between Church teaching and personal conduct has caused large numbers of young couples to stop attending mass, although most remain "communal Catholics," deeply aware of their religious identity and fully expecting to rejoin the Church at a later date (Hout and Greeley 1987).

Although a majority of Catholics also disagree with official doctrine on women as priests, allowing priests to marry, permitting divorce and remarriage, and favoring legal abortion, eight in ten feel that one can disagree with the Pope and remain a good Catholic (*New York Times,* Nov. 25, 1985, Smith 1984). A far more serious problem for the Roman Catholic Church is the steep decline in persons entering holy orders and the consequent graying of the clergy. Between 1966 and 1986, for example, the number of Catholic nuns dropped from 181,421 to 113,658, with very few new recruits. Half of American nuns today are over age sixty-two. And although the number of priests increased by 9,000 during the same period, this is far below the number needed to serve a growing Catholic population (*Official Catholic Directory,* 1986). Worldwide, since 1969, 100,000 Catholic priests have left holy orders, leaving only 400,000 active male clergy (*New York Times,* Oct. 10, 1986).

IMPORTANCE OF RELIGION

National survey data continue to show that about 56 percent of Americans say that religion is "very important" in their lives. This is up slightly from 52 percent in 1978, but significantly lower than the high

Types of Religious Organizations

Before we discuss contemporary religious groups and secular ideologies, a short vocabulary lesson is necessary. Social scientists distinguish among churches, ecclesia, denominations, sects, and cults.

CHURCH
• an association of believers with a clear structure of offices and places of worship, that is, with a high degree of institutionalization.

Churches are recognized parts of the social system. Thus, we can speak abstractly of the Catholic Church or the Protestant Church in America. This usage is more general than reference to a specific church, such as the First Baptist Church of Boston. Although Jews worship in temples and Muslims in mosques, we can also speak of the Jewish or Muslim church as a religious body.

ECCLESIA
• a state or established church wherein most members of the society are members of the one church, and the church hierarchy and political leadership are mutually protective of each other's interests.

For example, the Anglican church is the established church of England; Judaism is the state religion of Israel; Catholicism of Italy; and Islam of Egypt. Typically, political authorities are more powerful than religious leaders in modern societies; but there are a few instances of *theocracy*, in which religious leaders also control the political apparatus, such as Iran under the ayatollahs after the fall of the shah in 1979.

DENOMINATION
• an organized religious group *within* a church, as for example, the Methodist and Baptist branches of Protestantism, or the reform movement in Judaism.

Denominations have their own hierarchy, ritual style, and version of the truth. Often, denominations have developed through *schism* (division) within an established church, out of which a new religious group is formed that varies somewhat, but not entirely, from the mother church.

SECT
• a group that separates from a denomination, usually over a matter of religious interpretation and practice.

Evangelicals within Protestant denominations often build their own places of worship while remaining a part of the larger religious body. Over time, a sect may attract enough members and find sufficient differences with the established hierarchy to become a full-fledged denomination. Among Muslims, for example, local conditions have produced many different versions of Islam. This has caused much conflict in the Muslim world since each claims to hold the truest version.

CULT
• religious groups even smaller in number and less organized than sects. Cults are often based on immediate emotional experience rather than on the thought-out ideology of most world religions. Ecstatic (emotional, revelation-oriented) practices such as snake handling, talking in tongues (glossolalia), and uncontrollable body movements are frequent features of cult behavior. There are also secular (nonreligious) cults, such as those centered on self-improvement (e.g., Scientology).

---

of 75 percent in 1952. Protestants were more likely (61 percent) than Catholics (56 percent) or Jews (25 percent) to say religion is "very important." Women, nonwhites, older people, those from small towns, and in the lower educational and income strata are most likely to endorse the importance of religion in their lives (Gallup Poll 1984). Over 90 percent of all Americans say that they believe in God, 85 percent claim personally to embrace the Ten Commandments (which suggests some cognitive dissonance given other data on adultery and untruthfulness), and 75 percent say that they pray every day (Briggs 1984).

ATTENDANCE

Despite such strong expressions of faith, however, actual attendance at religious services has declined by 20 percent since 1955, and remained at a plateau of about 40 percent in the 1980s (Jacquet 1987). Many who do not attend services will, however, listen to religious programming on radio or television.

As participation in organized prayer is highest among women and the elderly, the decline in attendance at services could reflect cohort differences, with today's younger people remaining less involved throughout their lives. Alternatively, age and gender differences in religious behavior could also indicate that the life events that turn people toward the church—marriage and parenthood, a death in the family, divorce, and occupational problems—have not yet been fully experienced by young adults. Possibly, both trends are at work. In other words, aging remains associated with increasing rates of religious observance but each incoming cohort does so at a lower level than the one before.

Declining attendance and church membership is also related to the steady increase in religious *intermarriage* in our society. Potential conflict between spouses of different religious backgrounds can be minimized by reducing the importance of religion in their lives (Glenn 1982). Intermarriage appears to be a special problem for the already small Jewish population, with estimates ranging as high as one-third over the past two decades. More accurate recent demographic studies, however, put the figure at under 30 percent, and note that many non-Jewish spouses convert to Judaism, so that the net loss of members is minimized (Massarik 1978, Cohen 1984). In addition, the leavers tend to have been only marginally identified with Judaism, while the converts are generally more religious than the average Jew by birth (Cohen 1984, Silberman 1985).

Religious commitment takes place in a social network in which personal relationships are more important than ideology or specific doctrines (Stark and Bainbridge 1980). Because young people today are more likely than those of the past to attend college, to travel, and to meet people from different backgrounds, it should not be surprising that ties to traditional faith are weakened. Young adults, especially those with liberal political attitudes, account for almost all of the increase in those checking "none of the above" when asked about religious affiliation (Hadaway 1980).

Religious behavior in America, then, has been greatly affected by all the secularizing currents of modern life. At the same time, paradoxically, there has been a trend toward making public life sacred.

CIVIL RELIGION

Our society is almost unique in the variety of religions it embraces. It *is* unique in the range of religious expression protected by custom and law. As befits a nation founded by survivors of sectarian persecution, our Constitution guarantees religious tolerance, erecting a wall between Church and State.

But how, under conditions of religious pluralism, can the need for establishing a unifying system of beliefs at the societal level be met? Sociologist Robert Bellah (1970, 1975) found the functional equivalent of a common faith in the *American civil religion,* in which our nation and its institutions are seen as divinely blessed, with a moral mission in the world, and guided by ethical standards derived from the Puritan emphasis on good citizenship. In other words, civil religion is a secularized Protestant morality, best exemplified in the sense of civic responsibility found among small-town business leaders (Hughey 1983) and WASP elites in the Northeast (Baltzell 1979). But with the decline of both types of elites in the mid-twentieth century, much of this moral force has been lost, and the line between ethical and nonethical behavior—in business and government, as well as personal life—has been blurred.

Nonetheless, this "universal religion of the nation" has served the essential functions of any belief system: to legitimize and sanctify (make sacred) the social order and to integrate its members, despite differences of faith (Gehrig 1981). The intermix of nationalism and religion is visible both when we make secular holidays sacred, as on the Fourth of July, and when we transform sacred holy days into commercial orgies, as at Christmas. No politician running for office will fail to call upon "God's will or wisdom"; our currency is stamped "In God We Trust"; and we pledge allegiance to "one nation under God." The civil religion even has its own integrating rituals that reaffirm collective values, e.g. periodic political witch-hunts against sinners such as communists or atheists or anyone who can be defined as "un-American" (Bergesen 1984). In sum, the civil religion becomes an ideological umbrella under which diverse religious communities can huddle.

Other analysts are less optimistic. Several decades ago, Will Herberg (1960) foresaw a loss of authentic spiritual commitment in a vague sea of secular piety, where simply having a religious affiliation was more important than fully living one particular set of beliefs. This outcome can be

American civil religion is a set of unifying beliefs that sees America as divinely blessed, with a moral mission and guided by ethical standards.

seen in the wide differences between the proportion of Americans who say they believe in God and the percentage who actually attend religious services.

Another criticism of the "civil religion" comes from those who fear that religious symbolism has been coopted by political and economic leaders in order to justify controversial policies. The civil religion may be in place, but the social unity beneath it has already crumbled (Demerath and Williams 1985). Indeed, even Bellah himself (1975), observing the use of religious appeals to support the Vietnam War, remarked that "the American civil religion is an empty and hollow shell" (p. 142). Sometimes, too, the distinction between sacred and secular in national politics is blurred as when President Reagan claimed that the United States must be prepared to fight the Soviet Union because "there is sin and evil in the world and we are enjoined by Scripture and the Lord Jesus Christ to oppose it with all our might" (*New York Times*, Mar. 9, 1983, p. A18).

Politics is not the only sphere in which the line between Church and State has been obscured. Business leaders today often conduct "prayer breakfasts" before

A "prayer breakfast" may lead off a business meeting. What functions does such a ritual perform for the participants? (© Paul Fusco/Magnum Photos, Inc.)

going to work and making decisions based on their firm's need to show a short-term profit. And in professional athletics, members of the Sports World Ministry conduct locker room services to ask God's support for their efforts.

SECULARIZATION AND MAINSTREAM RELIGION

The great paradox of contemporary American religion is this: amid widespread religiosity, in which the nation itself is rendered sacred, the *mainstream churches* have experienced declines in membership and influence. (The term "mainstream" refers to such regularly established religious bodies as the Roman and Eastern Catholic churches, the major Protestant denominations, and the three recognized branches of Judaism.) According to sociologist Robert Wuthnow (1985), religious divisions in our society today are not between churches or among denominations, as in the past, but between religious liberals and conservatives *within* each church (see also Hertel and Hughes 1987). These opposing camps, furthermore, are linked to clear-cut differences in social background and, therefore, to different locations in the social structure as well as different reactions to the broad currents of political and economic change. In general, compared to religious liberals, the conservatives are older, from small towns in the Midwest or South, upper-working or lower-middle class, and likely to have been dislocated by shifts in the economy.

In order to attract or maintain the commitment of their liberal members, mainstream churches have tried to become "more relevant," particularly to the interests of younger congregants. But such changes as the use of English in place of Latin or Hebrew, replacing hymns with folksongs, and calling the pastor by his or her first name have done little to attract younger people and much to alienate older worshippers who derive comfort from traditional usage.

These observations lend weight to Peter Berger's (1969) claim that people seek a profoundly moving experience from their religious devotions; they wish to rise above the humdrum of daily life. In fact, the more routinized one's everyday experience, the greater the need for transcendence through faith. Berger suggests that secularized services cannot meet this need

Mainstream churches are the established religious bodies of the major denominations.

because the very nature of secularism is earthbound. People want to understand the everlasting, not the here and now. They do not want to be presented with moral dilemmas, but to be insulated from them. For precisely these reasons, as we will see in a later section, the fastest-growing religious sectors lie outside the mainstream churches.

Another explanation of the enduring importance and persistence of religious beliefs and behaviors in a secular age is provided by the researchers who revisited the city of "Middletown" fifty years after it was first studied by Robert and Helen Lynd in 1924. Caplow and his colleagues (1983) found that the residents of this typical middle-American city were actually more involved in religious life than was the case five decades earlier. At the same time, they were more caught up in the pleasures of modern life, more educated, wealthier, and more tolerant of others—all traits that should have reduced religious involvement.

The researchers turned to the insights of the French traveler Alexis de Tocqueville (1830), to make sense of these contradictory findings. 150 years ago De Tocqueville was struck by the high levels of religious interest present in such a materialistic society. He appreciated the importance of religious pluralism and the separation of Church and State, but he also noted that people need some type of moral restraint on selfishness. Since government lacks this type of authority in a democratic society, citizens cling to religion to set limits on their behavior.

BLACK CHURCHES IN AMERICA

Religion has always been a major resource for the oppressed, but the black churches in America are of special importance as the only institution over which blacks themselves have had full control. Most American blacks are Protestant, members of diverse Baptist sects or "African" variants of other mainstream denominations; a small percentage are Roman Catholic; and a growing number are affiliated with Black Muslim congregations. There is also a popular Black Spiritual movement that won converts among the newly arrived Southern migrants to Northern industrial centers in the early part of this century (Baer 1984).

The particular structure and forms of

The black church is a significant source of social and emotional support for the black community as well as a source of social change for the society as a whole. (© Eve Arnold/Magnum Photos, Inc.)

black religious life in America, even today, can be understood only within the context of the pervasive racism of the larger society. The black churches do more than offer hope to the deprived; they are places where a sense of pride is nurtured, and where people can organize for social change and provide help to one another (Smith 1982, Mukenge 1983, Baer 1984, Gilkes 1985). The black churches are especially important as agents of integration—not into the broader society, but *within* the black community. It should be no surprise, then, to find that all but a few of the leaders of the Civil Rights Movement in the 1960s came from the ranks of clergy.

The leadership role of black churches was made possible, first, by their almost total segregation from outside control and, second, by the fact that the church was the only avenue of upward mobility for those talented and ambitious young people who were systematically excluded from high-prestige occupations in the larger society. (However, now that gifted men and women of color can have careers in law, medicine, business, and academics, proportionately fewer enter religious studies.)

Black churches have also been characterized by a relative openness of leadership roles to women (Gilkes 1985, Briggs 1987). To the extent that the church has been the historical center of black communities, the bearer of a distinct tradition, **411**

Discovering What "Everybody Knows"

CHERYL TOWNSEND GILKES

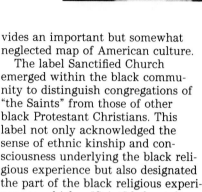

Cheryl Townsend Gilkes is the John D. and Catherine T. MacArthur Assistant Professor of Sociology and Black Studies at Colby College. An ordained Baptist minister, she is also the assistant dean of the Congress of Christian Education for the United Baptist Convention of Massachusetts, Rhode Island, and New Hampshire. She gratefully acknowledges the support of the Center for Research on Women at Memphis State University in the writing and manuscript preparation of this essay.

If you grew up in a black community, "everybody knows" about the Sanctified Church. However, given the social barriers of institutional racism, what "everybody knows" in the black community is not often shared in the larger society. Thus aspects of life that are distinctive and especially interesting are not explored as additional dimensions of human experience within a particular group but are treated instead as deviant and negatively problematic with respect to the larger group. Rather than modifying existing theories and concepts to include the experiences of black people, social scientists have tried to fit the black experience into already existing categories that connote a deviant approach to social life rather than try to understand such patterns in their own right.

Nowhere in the literature on black churches did the term Sanctified Church exist as an organizational fact. The terms for these churches were labeled "sects" and "cults"— terms that separated these churches from their very real connections to the larger black Protestant tradition. This led to their exclusion from much of the community and religious research. The churches were so stigmatized by their "sect" and "cult" status that the role of the largest of these denominations, the Church of

God in Christ, was totally ignored in accounts of the Memphis garbage workers strike in 1968. The fact that Mason Temple, the denomination's headquarters church at that time, was the site of Martin Luther King Jr.'s last sermon had been overlooked and discounted. Among the limited writing about the Sanctified Church was an essay by Zora Neale Hurston, written around 1928 and not published until 1982, and several accounts of the origins of gospel music in the black community. Previous sociological literature focused entirely on these churches as deviant and as isolated congregations, even when observation contradicted these descriptions.

Although the intellectual origins of my research go much deeper into several ideological and theoretical debates, the very real origins of this project rest with my father, who agreed with W. E. B. Du Bois that sociological research was especially useful for an understanding of the black experience. To distinguish myself from previous work, however, I began my research from the perspective of what "everybody knows." Thus my approach emphasizes the continuities among these independent denominations and (1) congregations formed by black people in the post-Reconstruction South, (2) their direct organizational descendants formed in the urban South and later the urban North, and (3) the independent black Methodist and Baptist denominations and congregations formed prior to and immediately after the Civil War by slaves and free black people. My interest in the Sanctified Church also reflected the close intellectual kinship between qualitative sociology and anthropology. Religion is, after all, an important dimension of culture. It organizes the social responses to the spiritual and uncontrollable. In a pluralistic society, religion provides identity and solidarity for moral constituencies. Organized religion pro-

vides an important but somewhat neglected map of American culture.

The label Sanctified Church emerged within the black community to distinguish congregations of "the Saints" from those of other black Protestant Christians. This label not only acknowledged the sense of ethnic kinship and consciousness underlying the black religious experience but also designated the part of the black religious experience to which a "Saint" belonged.

Perhaps the most important finding in this research, which is still in progress, has been the discovery of the importance of the Sanctified Church to women. These churches not only depended upon women for their organizational, economic, intellectual, and spiritual strengths, but they were sometimes founded in direct response to the needs and problems of women. The roles of women were of such magnitude that they often erased the stereotypical images of these churches as congregations of the uneducated and of the backward rural peasants. Furthermore, when larger and more mainstream denominations adopted more masculinist approaches to women's roles, the Sanctified Church provided opportunities for a wide variety of women who sought to exercise their "gifts." Although the majority of the denominations of the Sanctified Church affirm the centrality of male authority, women head some of these denominations and a number of their congregations.

I followed the lead from what "everybody knows"; but did not stop there. I developed questions and hypotheses from my readings of church programs and organizational histories and from my observations at conventions and church meetings. The prominent visibility of women in these histories led me to ask the questions that opened up the oral and written records of these churches and connected these materials to the social forces surrounding the black experience. Perhaps the most important sociological discovery for me, however, the one that exemplified the importance of a sociological perspective that grows out of or emerges from the situation itself, rather than from others' definitions of it, was the one that came when my father read my article "'Together and in Harness': Women's

Traditions in the Sanctified Church." He sat down at the dining room table, turned to my article, which was heavily underlined and annotated with marginal notes, and described his amazement at the approach I had taken. He noted that much of what I had said about women in the article had been in front of his eyes growing up—even

within his own family—but that he had never really noticed or attached importance to it. "These women were really important," he said. I smiled when I realized that I had "discovered" that what "everybody knows" is our most critical context of sociological discovery and reconstruction.

and catalyst of collective action, women have been important figures, even though men retained nominal (in name) authority. The social/cultural functions of the church have allowed women to carve out an area of autonomy in face of both racism and sexism (in the black as well as white society).

As long as most blacks continue to experience barriers to achievement in mainstream institutions, the church has a vital mission, and there seems to be little lessening of its central role in the black community. Indeed, as outside sources of support continue to be reduced, the church may once again have to function as an all-purpose social welfare agency.

Contemporary Trends

FOUR DECADES OF CHANGE

The 1950s and the "Death of God." The period of social stability, cultural blandness, and personal prosperity in America from 1945 to the early 1960s produced many false assumptions: that economic growth would be endless, that democracy would sweep the world, and that the American Dream was available to all willing to work for it. As Max Weber predicted, the world was demystified and rationally mastered, and all problems seemed capable of technological solution.

Out of these perceptions came the thesis that "God is dead," and that nonrational religious experiences—revelations, possession by the Devil, speaking in tongues, and the like—were holdovers from a superstitious past that would soon disappear altogether as mainstream churches be-

came more humanistic (concerned with personal dignity) and oriented toward this world and its problems. Religious holy days had become commercial holidays, and the civil religion appeared to be triumphant.

The 1960s and Social Activism. By the early 1960s, the churches seemed to lack a mission: no heathens to conquer, not many souls to save, few Princes of Darkness to battle. Then came the challenge of the civil rights movement in the United States. Black leaders sought and found allies among those who had long preached brotherhood and justice—members of the religious establishment. That the civil rights movement was spearheaded by black clergy added special impact to their plea for religious support, and the mainstream churches responded positively. No civil rights demonstration in the 1960s was without it ranks of nuns, rabbis, priests, and ministers. The National Council of Churches budgeted several million dollars for its Commission on Race and Religion (CORR), which organized the mammoth march on Washington in August 1963, lobbied for civil rights legislation, and conducted summer programs in Mississippi in 1964 ("the ministry of reconciliation"). The passage of the Civil Rights Act of 1964 owes much to the pressures exerted by the mainstream churches.

No sooner had the churches responded to the demands for equality and justice for blacks than the moral dilemmas of the Vietnam War became apparent. Again, many clergy—though fewer than for the civil rights movement—joined antiwar demonstrations. Altogether, the 1960s were a decade of social activism unparalleled in modern church history. Younger clergy, especially, were exhilarated by their role in the fight against racism and what they saw as an unjust war.

Their parishioners were less thrilled. While church leaders were engaged in protest, rank-and-file church members grew upset about decisions being taken without their consent. Many disapproved of the causes to which their clergy were drawn, resenting the time, money, and effort diverted from local needs.

The 1970s and Back to the Pulpit.

By the end of the 1960s, membership in the National Council of Churches had declined, contributions had decreased dramatically, lawsuits were threatened questioning the council's tax-exempt status, and several public opinion surveys showed that most citizens felt that the clergy should not engage in direct attempts to change society (Hadden 1969).

Off the streets and back to the pulpit, many ministers, priests, and rabbis redefined their mission as service to their particular congregation or parish rather than to abstract concepts or to groups outside their immediate responsibility. The dilemma of choosing between serving one's flock, the primary responsibility of a minister, and serving the broader goals of peace and justice was resolved in favor of saving souls. The prophetic functions that had inspired the clergy in the 1960s gave way to an emphasis on priestly duties and to a return to a more local orientation.

Into the 1980s and New Awakenings.

For those clergy still dedicated to social activism, there were several new causes. The National Council of Churches' Interfaith Center on Corporate Responsibility has been in the forefront of campaigns to make American corporations aware of the ethics of their investments and business practices abroad, especially in the case of South Africa (Ermann and Clements 1984). "Liberal" Protestant denominations such as the Episcopal and Methodist have also expressed concern over the environment, in contrast to "conservative" Protestant sects and the Baptist and Mormon churches that continue to emphasize a biblical belief in "mastery over nature" (Hand and Van Liere 1984). As environmental and antinuclear issues are less divisive than antiwar and civil rights activism, they offer the clergy an opportunity to be socially conscious without upsetting their congregants.

Catholic priests have become active in efforts to defeat the Equal Rights Amendment and to overturn the Supreme Court decision that legalized abortion. In addition, recent statements by the American Catholic Bishops Conference have strongly condemned economic inequality and the development of nuclear weapons. Unfortunately for the bishops, most legislators who are against abortion and women's rights issues also favor a nuclear buildup and less government assistance to the poor.

The church basement is usually the site of the shelter or soup kitchen for the homeless. American clergy have also provided refuge for illegal political escapees from Central America. Social issues are once again becoming the center of religious concern and debate. (© George Cohen)

WOMEN IN THE PULPIT

Another new direction that has brought some turmoil into church affairs is the increasing insistence of women on full participation in all aspects of religious life, including admission to the clergy (Lehman 1985, Briggs 1987). Despite long and strong resistance, the ruling bodies of mainstream churches have eventually decided to ordain women. Over half of all Protestant denominations now have women in the ministry, as do the Reform and Conservative branches of Judaism.

Greatest resistance has come from the Orthodox branch of Judaism and the Catholic Church. In Orthodox Jewish synagogues, women must remain in a special section, screened off from the main sanctuary, lest they distract the men from their sacred tasks. Some changes, however, have occurred in Roman Catholic practices, in part to compensate for the shortage of ordained priests and in part to accommodate the demands of women for a more active role in the ritual. Today, for example, in many parishes, women (nuns and laypersons) have taken part in all priestly functions except hearing confessions and consecrating the communion bread and wine.

Nonetheless, among the older and more conservative Catholic clergy, the idea of women's participation in central rituals remains unacceptable. In 1986, for example, the bishop of Pittsburgh ordered that women be excluded from the Holy Thursday ceremony commemorating Jesus washing the feet of the Apostles at the Last Supper, on the grounds that since the original participants were all men, so also should be those present at the reenactment (*New York Times,* Mar. 16, 1986). But whereas such a decree might have been accepted without a fuss in the past, Catholic women, including many nuns, actively protested.

Today, women account for a least one-fourth of all students at theological seminaries, where they tend to be academically superior to the male students, owing largely to greater motivation and fewer competing avenues for achievement (Austin 1983). When women were first ordained, they had difficulty finding pulpits of their own; most took jobs on college campuses or in the administrative offices of their denomination, or as assistant clergy. Now that worshipers have had a

Despite a lengthy resistance, the mainstream Protestant churches, as well as Reform and Conservative branches of Judaism, have decided to ordain women. What do you think are the sources of the resistance to women clergy? (© David Alpern)

decade or more of getting used to seeing women in the pulpit, a majority of newly ordained women have been accepted as leaders of their own congregations (Carroll et al. 1983).

In a related development, women who have received theological training are rethinking their religious traditions, reinterpreting sacred documents to include women's experience, and reconstructing rituals (Daly 1984, Ruether 1983, 1985, Fiorenza 1985). Although this effort has stirred controversy, particularly among those who believe in the literal wording of scripture, it has also spurred a reexamination of texts and practices by mainstream scholars, both male and female.

Other feminists, giving up on the possibility of changing the established religions, have rediscovered pre-patriarchal beliefs and rituals and woven them into a "women's spirituality movement" (Walker 1985). Female-centered and female-controlled, the women's spirituality movement incorporates a variety of images of female power as givers and protectors of life, from the early fertility goddesses to the beneficial witches whose knowledge of herbs and healing comprised medical information for most of human history.

Even with the return to a priestly emphasis in the 1970s and 1980s and selective involvement in social issues, the mainstream Protestant churches did not regain their previous strength in terms of membership, contributions, and leadership of the religious establishment in America. Rather, spiritual enthusiasm and belief-system creativity have taken place outside the mainstream: (1) in the rise of fundamentalist Protestant sects from the mid-1970s on; (2) in the emergence of a wide variety of cults (Robbins and Anthony 1982); and (3) in the spread of radical liberation theology in the Third World (Cox 1985).

FUNDAMENTALIST PROTESTANTISM

The most fascinating development on the current American religious scene is the revival of Protestant fundamentalism. This is a "back-to-basics" approach to religion. *Fundamentalists* believe that every word of the Bible must be taken literally; that a true believer must spread the good word and live a clean life; that Satan is alive in the world; that a fearful destruction will precede the return of the Messiah; and that there is a clear structure of authority from God to His chosen ministers and then to the husband as head of the family (Barnhart 1987).

Because these traditional beliefs no longer fit the image of "modern" mainstream Protestantism, fundamentalists were gradually pushed to the fringe of the Protestant establishment, where they organized independently of the major denominations. As a result, most fundamentalist congregations today are technically *sects,* unaffiliated with any nationally organized church. But over the past two decades, as participation in mainstream denominations declined, membership in independent fundamentalist sects has risen sharply.

One explanation for the revival of fundamentalism emphasizes its functions for people who believe that they are losing control over their way of life (Page and Clelland 1978). Such *status anxiety* is easily transformed into the type of moral

outrage that is at the heart of fundamentalist doctrine (Lipset and Raab 1981). This interpretation is supported by data on the sociodemographic characteristics of people attracted to fundamentalism— Southerners and Midwesterners who grew up in small towns, women, the elderly, and persons with relatively low educational and occupational statuses (Hunter 1983, Cardwell 1984). These are subgroups whose sense of mastery has been eroded by secularization and by the shift from local to national economic and political decision making.

But explaining social movements in terms of individual feelings of alienation or loss of certainty is not completely satisfying to sociologists. Social facts, remember, must be analyzed at the level of social structure. In the case of fundamentalist sects, their power to define American morality had been lost many decades earlier, with the repeal of Prohibition and their rejection by the new Protestant establishment (Simpson 1983). Nor had there really been much change in the kind of life-style fears that have dominated fundamentalist thinking since the 1950s (Miller nd.). What, then, accounts for the reawakening of fundamentalism in the 1980s? The most obvious answer is that fundamentalist leaders took advantage of public distress over the manifest failures of modernism.

The 1960s and 1970s offered one example after another of the breakdown of social order—student protest, antiwar demonstrations, riots, assassinations, civil rights activism, the women's movement, homosexual marches, the ambiguous ending to the Vietnam War, and the Watergate scandal. These events could be traced to a single cause: the spread of "secular humanism," that spirit of the modern age that places human beings rather than God at the center of life. The only aspect of life not out of control was faith in the old-time religion. But the "new" old-time religion differs from the traditional version in two important structural features: its intense involvement in electoral politics, and the emergence of "prime-time preachers."

The New Christian Right. Because of their vulnerable position as unaffiliated sects, fundamentalist churches had historically been strong supporters of the separation of church and state. It was a major shift, therefore, when, only a decade ago, funda-

Fundamentalists represent a back-to-basics approach to religion, namely that every word of the Bible is God's word.

Sects are congregations not affiliated with any nationally organized church.

mentalist leaders joined forces with extremely conservative political action groups to form the "New Christian Right" (NCR) (Liebman and Wuthnow 1983). By combining their mailing lists, media know-how, and funding sources, two groups that had previously been considered "too extremist" to have much effect on public policy, suddenly became a powerful force in electoral politics (Miller 1986). The name of one of the early umbrella organizations, Moral Majority, has even become a household word, as well as a target of negative feelings, leading to a name change in 1986: Liberty Federation.

Thus, the rise of the New Christian Right can be best explained in terms of "resource mobilization"—the ability to raise money, to activate existing networks of churchgoers and local activists, and to forge alliances with a large number of single-interest groups (see Chapter 21 for a more detailed discussion of resource mobilization theory)—rather than in terms of any great change in people's religious and political ideologies. Support for the fundamentalist moral/political agenda is not confined to people with status fears. Large contributions have come from such wealthy families and corporations as the DuPonts, the Hunt brothers of Texas, Pepsico, Mobil Oil, and the founders of the Coors beer company (Koenig and Boyce 1985, Magrass 1986).

The New Christian Right gained legitimacy in the 1980 election, when the candidates it supported won the White House and a dozen seats in the U.S. Senate. Once the line between church and state had been blurred, NCR leaders were quick to define the "Christian" position on a range of issues, not all of which appear directly religious, including women's and gay rights (against), nuclear power (for), sex education (against), defense spending (for), antipoverty programs (against), aid to the Nicaragua rebels (for), and gun control (against).

But there are also signs that the NCR is not as powerful or monolithic as the media and movement leaders suggest (Guth 1983, Shupe and Stacy 1983). With so many special interests at stake—both political and religious—some conflict is inevitable, and rivalry among leaders can be expected. Nor are followers all of one mind or always totally obedient. It is not accurate to lump all religious conservatives together without regard to different contexts, or to assume that they uncritically accept the entire list of "Christian positions" (Flowers 1984; Hall 1985, Messner et al. 1985, Rose 1985).

Prime-Time Preachers. Although technology has brought us "the electronic ministry" there is no technical reason why the religious airwaves should today be dominated by fundamentalist ministers. Again, resource factors are important: the ability to raise money, to purchase television time or to construct an independent media network. Important, too, is the failure of mainstream denominations to take advantage of the new medium. Television is not friendly to intellectual discussions of moral ambiguities by graduates of establishment theological seminaries. The fundamentalist preachers understand the value of showmanship and of a single clear message in language that most viewers can immediately grasp, and in the earthy accents of the South and Midwest rather than the upper-class diction of Eastern establishment private schools.

The causes of the trends that distress so many viewers are distant and complex—changing labor markets, the shift to a service economy, the decline of American influence abroad, falling birth rates, and the rise of modern feminism. It is comforting to believe that one's personal problems can be solved by a return to faith and to traditional gender roles. It is even more comforting to believe that what ails society can also be cured by religious prescriptions. Thus, what began as an effort to save souls has become a crusade to purify the nation, a crusade whose success depends, paradoxically, on that triumph of modern technology—the electronic media.

EVANGELICALISM

Although the term *evangelical* is often used interchangeably with "fundamentalist," it is useful to distinguish the two forms of Protestantism. While all fundamentalists are evangelicals, not all evangelicals share the fundamentalists' extremely conservative positions on political and social issues (Hunter 1987).

Evangelicals stress the personal witnessing of God's presence coupled with an obligation to spread "the word." The con-

Evangelical refers to an emphasis on the personal witnessing of God's presence.

Pray TV

The numbers are mind-boggling. Perhaps as much as $2 billion worth of airtime, more billions in contributions from viewers, an audience of 61 million for at least some time each month, a nationwide network of radio and television stations, hundreds of thousands of letters every day, millions of WATS line calls each week. There can be no doubt that the electronic ministry is big business, and growing each year.

Pray TV's media "stars" are gifted users of the medium, with colorful personalities, backed by scenery and music that accentuate their message. The pioneers of the field were Billy Graham and Oral Roberts, both relatively moderate compared to today's leading televangelists: "Pat" Robertson, Jimmy Swaggart, Jim Bakker, and Jerry Falwell. Throughout the telecasts, viewers are given 800 numbers for phoning in pledges, questions, and comments. The phone calls not only generate money but also names to be added to the mailing lists that are the major resource of the New Christian Right.

The most popular and powerful of the younger generation of prime-time preachers is Robertson, who now operates the twenty-four-hour cable TV Christian Broadcasting Network (CBN), with 30 million subscribers. Although from an elite background, Robertson went through a period of poverty before finding his calling as a religious broadcaster and founder of the 700 Club. Today, CBN, with 4000 employees, also operates a university and law school. And Robertson has offered himself as a candidate for President of the United States, claiming that secularists have ". . . taken the Holy Bible from our young and replaced it with the thoughts of Charles Darwin, Karl Marx, (and) Sigmund Freud" (*Star Ledger*, Sept. 18, 1986).

Jimmy Swaggart is closer to the stereotype of a revivalist Protestant preacher, with dramatic attacks against Catholicism as well as communism. In addition to his weekly TV program, Swaggart holds services at his Family Worship Center in Louisiana, runs a Bible College, and cuts records as a gospel singer.

Before his involvement in a sex scandal, Jim Bakker and his wife appeared daily on his twenty-four-hour cable Praise the Lord (PTL) Network, which reaches 13 million households. Bakker's major project is a religious theme park and family resort, Heritage USA, on 2500 acres in South Carolina. The project cost $150 million to build, and $30 million to operate each year. In 1985, Heritage USA hosted 5 million visitors. During the summer the park features a passion play with a cast of 100 and three camels.

Jerry Falwell has the highest name recognition among prime-time preachers. His congregation in Virginia claims 21,000 members, and his Liberty University enrolls 7000 students. Falwell appears weekly on both cable and commercial television. His political influence is such that Vice President Bush was a featured speaker at the founding of Liberty Federation.

Sources: Jerry D. Cardwell, *Mass Media Christianity*, Lanham, MD, University Press of America, 1984; William E. Schmidt, "TV Minister Calls His Resort 'Bait' for Christianity," *The New York Times*, Dec. 24, 1985, p. A–8; "Power, Glory, and Politics: Right Wing Preachers Dominate the Dial," *Time* Magazine, Feb. 17, 1986, pp. 62–69.

Born again means having an experience that changes one's life through the acceptance of the Lord.

cept of being *born again* is central to the Protestant evangelical doctrine; it means having an experience that changes one's life through acceptance of the Lord. A public announcement of this rebirth brings the weight of the community of believers to bear on future conduct, as when members of the congregation stand up and announce their renewed commitment.

The enthusiasm of their witnessing and the relatively lower social status of members have historically set American evangelical churches apart from the more liberal mainstream Protestant denominations, but not quite so distant as the fundamentalist sects. There are many evangelicals, such as Jimmy Carter, former President of the United States, who do not insist upon a literal interpretation of the Bible, who oppose the arms race, support women's rights, and are involved in social activism on behalf of the poor.

As with the fundamentalist sects, evangelical congregations have enjoyed a recent surge in membership. Further, evangelical tendencies have also been noted in Roman Catholicism, with the emergence of a "Charismatic" movement (Paloma 1982, Bord and Faulkner 1983), and in Orthodox Judaism, with renewed interest in expressive Hasidism.

Yet there is some question about evangelism's staying power. Some critics suggest that too many compromises with modernism have eroded its claim to represent unchanging truth (Hunter 1983) while others believe that moderate evangelism provides an attractive alternative to the anti-intellectualism of fundamentalism, on the one hand, and the failure of liberal Protestantism to meet the need for transcendence, on the other (Briggs 1982).

THE NEW CULTS

Another source of competition with mainstream religion is the variety of cults attracting both young and older adults. Although numerically and politically less important than the fundamentalist movement, the cults have attracted a great deal of attention because of the sometimes unusual behavior of believers and because of the fear generated among parents of young converts. Some of the modern cults are offshoots of fundamentalism; others derive from Eastern religions; still others center on the supernatural or, at the opposite extreme, one's own self. In addition, several expressly political cults have emerged among relatively powerless minorities.

The Bhagwan's followers, dressed in red and orange, had a fervent belief in his ability to show the correct path. However, not long after this photo was taken, the commune of Rajneeshpuram in eastern Oregon collapsed because of lawsuits stemming from fraud and theft of the group's resources and internal politics. The Bhagwan was deported. (© James Mason/ Black Star)

The cults that have received most media attention are those based on non-Western belief systems: Transcendental Meditation, Zen Buddhism, Yoga, Hare Krishna, and dozens of smaller groups centered on total obedience to a *guru* or "wise one." One of the more unusual of the latter cults was the group attracted to the guru Bhagwan Shree Rajneesh that sought to build an entire community in the hills of eastern Oregon in the early 1980s. Hundreds of followers, dressed in orange and red, would line the streets of the new town and bow as Bhagwan drove by each day in one of his ninety-seven Rolls Royces. Bhagwan's brand of Eastern mysticism appealed to well-educated middle-class men and women in their thirties willing to sacrifice material success in order to build the holy city of Rajneeshpuram. The enterprise collapsed in 1986 when several Rajneesh leaders were accused of fraud and theft of the group's resources and the Bhagwan himself was declared an illegal alien (Fitzgerald 1986).

But the cult that appears to have stirred the sharpest reaction from the general public is the Unification Church of the Rev. Sun Myung Moon, whose followers are known as Moonies.

The Great Moonie Debate. The Unification Church claims a membership of 45,000 primarily young adults, one-third of whom are engaged in full-time work for the church (Goldman 1985). The church's doctrines combine elements of Christianity with strong support for capitalism and the American military; its practices emphasize hard work, self-discipline, and communal living. Where Unification theology departs from standard Christianity is in the belief that because Jesus failed to bring the millenium, a second Messiah, born in Korea—the birthplace of Reverend Moon—is about to fulfill the Biblical prophecy.

Parents of recruits have difficulty understanding how their children can willingly cut themselves off from previous ties in order to live in group dormitories and devote all their energies to making money for a Korean who says that he has spoken with Jesus, Moses, and Buddha. Because this behavior seems irrational, the only explanation that parents (or the mass media or mainstream religious leaders) can accept is that innocent youngsters have been brainwashed, weakened by poor

Marriages within the Unification Church are sometimes carried out on a massive group level. In fact, in 1982, 5000 members of the church were married by the Rev. Moon in New York's Madison Square Garden. The Church continues to thrive and has a dedicated following of members who tithe regularly to support it. (© Bettina Cirone/Photo Researchers, Inc.)

diets, and held against their will. Therefore, some parents feel that it is perfectly legitimate to try to kidnap the children and "deprogram" them (Robbins and Anthony 1982). Further, if it can be shown that recruits were not freely exercising their First Amendment rights of religious choice, the Unification Church and similar cults need not be recognized as legal religious bodies, with all the immunities and tax exemptions that follow (Robbins 1983).

But there is *not one* systematic study of the Unification Church, or of most other cults to which young people are attracted, that supports these charges (Melton and Moore 1982, Robbins 1983, Selengut 1983, Barker 1984, Flowers 1984, Streiker 1984, Stark and Bainbridge 1985). To the contrary, the research indicates that people are introduced to cults through their interpersonal networks, that they are not physically coerced into joining, and that the vast majority of recruits eventually leave of their own free will (Streiker 1984, Beckford 1985).

The Cult Experience. What, then, does explain the attraction of cults for young Americans? Unlike members of funda-

mentalist sects, recruits are not drawn from small-town middle-America, or from powerless or relatively deprived subgroups, but tend to be well-educated children from higher-than-average-status homes. Jewish young people from upwardly mobile and highly acculturated families are greatly overrepresented among cult members.

Rather than perceiving cults as some exotic and unnatural phenomenon, most researchers place them well within the American historical tradition of religious pluralism (Melton and Moore 1982, Flowers 1984). And rather than viewing joiners as helpless victims, social scientists ask such questions as: why did cults flourish in the late 1970s and early 1980s; what functions are filled by membership; what does the experience mean to the believer; and who benefits?

The answers that most observers agree upon are that cults:

- emerge in reaction to extreme *secularization* in the wider society (Stark and Bainbridge 1985);
- attract young people who are not yet embedded in family and work roles by offering *acceptance* and *belonging* (Streiker 1984);
- replace parental authority with the *authority* of the charismatic leader;
- provide an "alternative reality" through which personal experience can be understood and shared (Selengut 1983);
- emphasize *immediate experience* that has not been filtered through the intellect or the views of parents (Cox 1977).

Nor is it only among the joiners that we should seek explanations. As Stark and Bainbridge (1985) note, our children are not deceived or stolen by cults; they join new religions because parents and secular institutions (and mainstream churches) have not filled the need for transcendence. New religions draw from those who are structurally available for recruitment, namely people not already firm in their faith. Or, in the case of Moonies in England (Barker 1984), recruits may have actually come from very religious households. They failed, however, to find any subsequent supports for their faith in the largely secularized mainstream churches. Here are young people who want desperately to believe, and who, therefore, are

One of the most visible of the newer religions is the Hare Krishna movement which came into popularity in the 60s and still exists today. Most recruits are white, middle class Americans, many of whom are college dropouts. In exchange for their dedication they receive a complete personal transformation, including new clothes, hairstyles, and, of course, a new belief system. (© Baldev/ SYGMA)

predisposed to accept the certainty and authority of the Unification Church.

It is not only the young who thirst for simple and clear answers to the problems of daily life in a rapidly changing society. There are cults for older people, too.

Out-of-This-World Cultism. From the beginning of recorded history to the present, there have been periodic predictions of the end of the world. The most recent versions involve invasions from outer space by creatures in unidentified flying objects (UFOs). Many Americans, of all ages, also believe in astrology, possession by the Devil, haunted houses, and other out-of-this-world phenomena, though few actually join cults centered on such beliefs.

When Prophecy Fails. Cult leaders who have predicted the end of the world on a specific date have thus far been wrong (though they may yet be correct). What happens to a group when prophecy fails? In a classic study of a doomsday cult, researchers found that group members were faced with *cognitive dissonance*— the mental discomfort of holding mutually exclusive perceptions: "The world will end" and "It didn't" (Festinger et al. 1966). To relieve the dissonance, we must modify one perception or the other.

In the case of a failed prophecy, you could give up the belief altogether, but this involves rejecting an important part of your life. Or, you could try to convince yourself that the world had indeed ended but that this was taking a different form

Cognitive dissonance occurs when a person must deal with mutually exclusive ideas and perceptions.

than expected. The third and most common way of reconciling conflicting perceptions is to rework the connection between them. True believers can attribute the failure to human error, a miscalculation of the date, or a lack of faith strong enough to convince higher powers to proceed with the plan. Thus, cargo cultists, ghost dancers, and members of prophetic sects can continue to believe even though empirical evidence contradicts their expectations.

The problem of cognitive dissonance arose in 1987 when one of the most popular TV evangelists, Jim Bakker, resigned his PTL ministry after a local newspaper reported that he had paid blackmail to hush up a one-night sexual affair. It was also announced that Bakker's wife, gospel singer Tammy Faye, had been treated for drug addiction. The millions of people who sent money to PTL each month were faced with the task of reconciling their faith in the Bakkers with the undeniable facts of infidelity, drug abuse, and the possibility that their contributions were used as hush money. One resolution to this dilemma, in keeping with the gospel preached by the Bakkers, was to assign blame to the Devil. PTL followers believe that the spirit of Satan is at work in the world and will be until the Second Coming. Therefore, it is not too difficult for them to attribute Tammy Faye's drug problem and Jim Bakker's sexual episode to "dark forces" and "sinister designs" beyond the control of mortals.

Indeed, a survey of regular viewers of TV evangelists, in the week after Bakker's

421

Jim Bakker and Tammy Fay Bakker, once powerful leaders in the PTL, are now struggling to regain as much credibility as possible in the light of their "fall from grace." Do you think Eden is retrievable? (© Nancy J. Pierce/Black Star)

resignation, found that 43 percent felt that the Devil was responsible (Hevesi 1987). A similar proportion said that Bakker must take responsibility for not resisting the temptations of Satan. Many in this second group solved their dissonance problem by suggesting that there was a divine plan that would make everything all right in the end. Others felt that this was really a test of their faith; the more difficult it was to forgive, the greater the necessity for keeping the faith. Few believers have been able to relinquish fully a set of beliefs and behaviors so central to their lives.

Self-Awareness Cults. The fastest-growing type of cult in our society today is devoted to the cultivation of the self, to developing one's capacities for making money and being successful in work and love. This collection of groups has recently been called the "New Age Movement" (Lindsey 1986) and embraces believers in many kinds of occult (supernatural) forces, such as psychic healing, reincarnation (rebirth in another body), and talking to the dead through mediums.

Another branch of the self-awareness or New Age Movement has its origins in the human-potential movement and the work of psychologists Carl Rogers and Abraham Maslow in the 1950s. The combination of mysticism and self-improvement in organizations such as Scientology, National Training Institutes, Silva Mind Control, and Lifespring, have attracted a largely middle-class and increasingly middle-aged following. Indeed, many large corporations now pay for their managers to take seminars on expanding consciousness, altered states of mind, meditation, hypnosis, even fire walking, in the hopes that the executives will become more productive.

Political Cults. Public fear and fascination are periodically aroused by the headline-producing actions of the members of political cults: The Black Panthers, the Symbionese Liberation Army (SLA), and the People's Temple are perhaps the three most striking recent examples. All three were rooted in the civil rights agitation of the 1960s, becoming increasingly militant as the pace of improvement in the conditions of poor blacks became increasingly slow. Shoot-outs, imprisonment, and internal quarrels eventually reduced the strength of the Panthers and the SLA.

The People's Temple, however, grew in numbers, wealth, and commitment throughout the 1970s. A biracial group of believers in the charismatic Rev. Jim Jones, many of the members of the People's Temple followed their leader to Guyana in South America, where they established the community of Jonestown, based on a mixture of Christianity and Marxism.

In November 1978, the world was shocked to learn of the mass suicide in Guyana of 911 adults and children, members of the People's Temple. In an effort to explain such an unbelievable event, most analysts examined the personality of Jim Jones or the characteristics of his followers—both of which were unusual. But however interesting these details might be, they can explain only why some people chose to join the People's Temple; nothing in these personal data can account for mass suicides of almost one thousand people.

Sociologists Rose Laub Coser and Lewis Coser (1979) chose to focus on the *structural* elements of the People's Temple and the settlement of Jonestown, which they defined as a utopian commune, one of many such attempts to create an ideal community amid a social order perceived as corrupt or immoral. Moreover, communes (like some families) tend to become *greedy institutions,* absorbing all the energy, passion, and loyalty of their members, leaving them completely at the mercy of their leaders.

In contrast, social historian Gillian Lindt (1984) objects to the use of the term "cult" for the People's Temple whose roots were in the social gospel of liberal Protestantism and the expressive rituals of the black spiritualist movement. By emphasizing its "cult" characteristics, the media managed to give an added dimension of menace not only to the Jonestown story but to all religious minorities that disturb the mainstream majority. Lindt traces the development of the People's Temple from a well-intentioned multiracial community

Greedy institutions absorb all the energy and loyalty of their members and leave them at the mercy of their leaders.

Walking on Fire

The hottest seminars of 1986 taught people—for $125 a throw—to walk on coals. Seminar leaders claimed that the power of positive thinking would protect against pain and burning. In reality, as experiments by McCarthy and Leikind (1986) demonstrate, anyone can walk on coals without training and without harm, provided one steps quickly. Embers are poor conductors of heat even though the coals themselves are very hot. The seminars are designed to make people feel better about themselves (which may not be worth the risk to slow walkers). The researchers suggest that the greater danger is that seminar participants may be convinced by their success as fire walkers to spend even more money on other seminars, including one on "neurolinguistic programming," which claims to cure you of drug addiction or painful illness within minutes.

Source: William J. McCarthy and Bernard J. Leikind, "Walking on Fire: Feat of Mind?" *Psychology Today,* February 1986, p. 10–12.

in the 1960s to an isolated outpost under an authoritarian charismatic leader. So powerful was Jones' vision and so ready to believe were his followers, that their mutual self-destruction was only the other side of the coin of faith.

The 1978 mass suicide of almost 1000 members of the People's Temple in Jonestown, Guyana was a dramatic example of the almost hypnotic power of a "greedy institution." (© P. Ledru/SYGMA)

Summary

All belief systems have certain elements in common: ideas about the meaning of life, rituals, and a community of believers. The beliefs relieve personal anxiety and bring members of the group together.

Every belief system has three essential elements: an origin myth, rules of conduct, and a vision of the future. This is true both of religions based on faith in supernatural powers and of secular ideologies based on human efforts in this world. According to sociologists, the particular beliefs of any group emerge from its ongoing life and reflect the social order itself.

Every society distinguishes the sacred from the profane and constructs rituals that help people over major transitions and times of danger. The major dysfunctions of belief systems are the potentials for sectarian conflict within the society and for misunderstanding other societies.

Modernization and secularization have had profound effects on contemporary religious practices and organizations. The secular way of thinking emphasizes scientific explanations and rationality, thus challenging beliefs in divine forces and values based on faith. Nonetheless, religious beliefs remain important to the overwhelming majority of Americans. Our tradition of religious tolerance has led to the institutionalization of a "civil religion" in which patriotism and faith are blended.

Over the past four decades, involvement in secular affairs by church leaders has undergone several major changes. The stability of the 1950s was followed by the call to social activism of the 1960s. Then came a decade of emphasis on the priestly duties of tending one's own flock and, today, the challenges to mainstream churches presented by the growth of fundamentalist sects and the new cults.

The fundamentalist Protestant challenge comes from members of the social strata most threatened by the many changes taking place in our society, and it has become a powerful force in conservative politics. The cults attract a younger, more highly educated group of believers, who are attracted by the companionship and acceptance of other young people, by the certainty of the beliefs, and by the authority of the leader. For all believers, a supportive group context is crucial for maintaining motivation and commitment to the cause.

Suggested Readings

BARKER, EILEEN. *The Making of a Moonie*. London: Basil Blackwell, 1984. An assessment of the various reasons why people join the Unification Church and a critique of the tactics associated with the Moonies.

BALTZELL, E. DIGBY. *Puritan Boston and Quaker Philadelphia*. New York: Free Press, 1979. An ASA award-winning book, this is an outstanding and insightful comparative study of the role of elites in Boston and Philadelphia with rich historical data.

BERGER, PETER L. *The Sacred Canopy: Elements of a Sociological Theory of Religion*. New York: Doubleday, Anchor, 1969. An elegantly written examination by one of the leading figures in the field of the complex relations between religion and society and of the increasingly private nature of belief and faith.

COX, HARVEY. *Religion in the Secular City*. New York: Simon and Schuster, 1984. An examination of religion in the 1980s with an emphasis on resurgent fundamentalism and television evangelism.

DURKHEIM, EMILE. *The Elementary Forms of Religious Life*. New York: Free Press, 1912/ 1965. The classic analysis of the functions of religious beliefs and religious rituals, what they represent, and how they contribute to the integration of the social order.

FOSTER, LAWRENCE. *Religion and Sexuality: The Shakers, Mormons, and the Oneida Community*. Urbana and Chicago: University of Illinois Press, 1984. A detailed study of the religious beliefs and sexual practices of these sects and the expansions of women's participation in public life.

16

Law, Crime, and the Criminal Justice System

I N 1987, sixteen executives of major Wall Street firms were arrested by federal agents and charged with selling cocaine and trading the drug for stocks, information, and lists of preferred customers.

• According to the U.S. Consumer Products Safety Commission, in 1987, 200 people a year die from injuries related to malfunctioning cigarette lighters.

• In 1987, while walking down a well-lit street in Cambridge, Mass., a thirty-four-year-old man, recently released from prison for robbery, was shot and killed by former friends whom he had implicated in the crime.

• In 1987, details about the undercover sale of arms to Iran and diversion of profits to Nicaraguan rebels were made public. A congressional committee investigated possible illegal actions by government officials, including the President himself.

• In 1987, a retired social worker, age eighty-one, revealed her role as an undercover agent for the New York special prosecutor for nursing homes. Posing as "a little old lady about to be placed in a nursing home by her son," she visited four nursing homes, two of which were subsequently indicted for soliciting bribes totalling $55,000 to secure her admission to their facilities.

What do these different news items—involving drugs, violence and revenge, greed, and politics—have in common? Their one common denominator is that they describe illegal or criminal acts. These examples illustrate the variety of crimes and criminals, as well as some of the reasons why a particular case comes to public attention.

As the diverse nature of these acts indicates, there is no one cause of crime or criminality: a point of particular interest to sociologists. As discussed in Chapter 6 (Conformity and Deviance), every society has its rules. It also has its deviants and agents of social control. The amount of crime in any society depends on two factors: first, the range of conduct controlled by law; and second, the effectiveness of agents of social control.

How does crime differ from other types of deviance? As you will remember from Chapter 6, the range of behaviors likely to be defined as deviant varies from time to time and place to place. But only a few acts arouse such strong feelings that they are forbidden by law. People who commit illegal acts are targets of formal and official sanctions, including arrest, prosecution, and punishment. This chapter focuses on different types of crime in the United States, and the ways in which crime and criminals are controlled through police, courts, jails, and prisons.

The Role of Law

In modern societies, the *law* of the state or province is the formal code of rules enforcing conformity. In simple societies, these are matters of custom and informal sanctions. Social norms become laws when their violation is controlled by action exercised in a socially approved, predictable way by an authorized third party. That is, norms are enforced by impersonal agents of the people as a whole who are empowered to act as accuser and judge.

A difference is usually made between *criminal* and *civil law*. Conduct believed to be against the interests of the society or the state is sanctioned under *criminal law*. Conduct against the interests of pri-

> **Criminal law** provides sanctions against conduct believed to be against the interests of the society or state.

vate persons is punishable under *civil law*. This distinction is not as neat as it sounds. For example, consider the act of assault, which is directed against a specific person but which is also a threat to the public interest, as people want to feel safe from attack. Assault, therefore, involves both a criminal and a civil violation of law (Quinney and Wildeman 1977).

The criminal law is one set of rules and regulations in society. It overlaps norms of the family, the church, and other institutional spheres. Many criminal behaviors were so defined before the days of Moses in the Bible. Others like dope pushing, airline hijacking, and income tax evasion are relatively new additions. What is a crime in one time and place is not necessarily a crime in another. For example, before the American Civil War, slavery was legal in many states. Today, not only is slavery against the law, but anyone treating another person as a slave is likely to go to prison.

There has probably never been a society without crime. Emile Durkheim pointed out that crime is necessary to all societies for its *latent functions* in producing social cohesion and setting the boundaries of acceptable behavior. What varies is the definition of crime, which is largely a result of which groups have sufficient power to enact their norms into law.

The concept of crime as a wrong against society is very old, although punishment was often left to the injured person or her or his family rather than to agents of the state. Retaliation, or "an eye for an eye," was an early and exact form of social control. This rule, although bloody, ensured that the punishment would be no greater than the harm done and was actually a first step in creating the balance scales of justice. With the rise of nation-states, the right to punish wrongdoers was taken away from the individuals and their families and became a state monopoly. When sanctions are applied universally to all who commit a given act, we can speak of the *rule of law*.

HOW NORMS BECOME LAWS

At least three ideas have been proposed to explain how norms become laws: (1) *social injury*; (2) *consensus*; (3) *conflict*. The **social injury model** is based on the commonsense idea that all laws are passed

> **Civil law** provides sanctions against violations of the interests of private persons.

> The **social injury model** sees laws as a means of protecting members of the society.

to protect people in a particular society. Laws are intentional attempts to reduce behavior that is harmful to the public welfare or morals or to the interests of the government or national security. But this approach fails to answer two questions. First, what is harmful behavior? Second, who decides what is harmful?

The *consensus model* is based on the belief that norms become laws because they reflect a general agreement about appropriate behavior. Laws thus become a barometer of social values within a society. Conflicts typically revolve around relatively unimportant issues. The consensus model is a *functionalist* explanation, based on the work of Emile Durkheim. As you will recall, the functionalist perspective emphasizes social cohesion. Although conflict and competition may occur among groups, such contests eventually result in the strengthening of the social norms that are contained in laws.

In contrast to the functional model, *conflict* theorists propose two major approaches to explain the establishment of laws. The first is the *economic view,* stemming from the work of Karl Marx. According to Marx, conflict is necessary in societies as they are currently organized economically and can only be overcome after massive social changes. The conflict that Marx considered important was that between social classes—those who controlled the means of production and those who did not. Basic to Marx's view of crime is that those who own the means of production, for example, capitalists in the United States, also control the political process. They use this power to enact and enforce laws supporting their own economic interests and to check the interests of the lower classes. Laws also benefit the upper strata in the labor market, as when certain lower-class behaviors are designated as illegal and unwanted surplus workers are removed from the labor force and sent to jail. Crime itself implies a power relationship: to commit a crime is often to impose power upon others, whereas to be punished for a crime is to be subject to the power of others (Hagan and Palloni 1986). At the same time, crime creates jobs for other members of the community: judges, lawyers, legal scholars, crime-detection experts, and some psychologists, psychiatrists, and sociologists.

Quinney (1977) and other contemporary conflict theorists have argued that the government uses its power to control lower-class people's opposition to their enforced poverty. That is, that the legal system serves the interests of the ruling class instead of the interests of all people. Quinney summarized the conflict perspective on how laws are created as follows. First, because societies contain different economic interests and because views of right and wrong vary immensely, both individuals and groups want to maximize their own self-interests by passing laws. Second, groups and individuals differ in their access to power within a society. Third, many activities that are dangerous to the public are rarely labeled as criminal (for example, unsafe bridge design, wars, and radioactive waste disposal); most laws are enforced because they reflect the political, economic, and ideological interests of specific power groups (for example, laws against loitering or defacing property). In short, *economic power* determines what becomes law.

From this viewpoint, control of crime

At one time dumping garbage was hardly a problem, let alone a serious crime. Garbage and sanitation are now the focus of considerable legislation. Dumping must be legal; it must be done at certain places in specified ways. How does this balance individual interests with the interests of the group as a whole? (© John Maher/Stock Boston)

Margin notes:

The **consensus model** is based on the idea that norms become laws because they reflect customs and general agreement about appropriate behavior.

Conflict models assume that laws serve the interests of the dominant class.

may also be a profitable financial investment. As Quinney and Wildeman (1977) suggested, "A major part of the law and growing social-industrial complex is what we can call the 'criminal justice-industrial complex.' Criminal justice, in all its aspects, is becoming one of the last remaining capital-investment industries. That industry finds it profitable to invest in crime is one of the final contradictions of the capitalist system" (pp. 117–18). This industry includes prisons, guards, police staffs, lawyers, judges, social workers, and others. The criminal justice system may serve corporate interests better than it serves individual interests (Hagan 1982).

For example, owner and managers can use organizational resources to commit crimes involving more money and victims than can people in statuses without such authority (Hagan and Palloni 1986). Thus, corporations and their executives use deceptive advertising or informal price-fixing to obtain money from customers (victims), much as the lower stratum criminal may use a gun, knife, or fists.

A variation on this theme is proposed by the *culture conflict* school. Rather than emphasizing the economic differences among groups, culture conflict theorists stress differences in *values*. From this viewpoint, economic class interest is only one division within a society. When the community has competing factions and custom can no longer maintain conformity, law is imposed by the most powerful interest group (not necessarily the majority). Table 16-1 summarizes the types of criminal behavior explained by each of these three theoretical views.

Each perspective emphasizes a different aspect of the legal system. Yet, any given system is the outcome of the interplay of consensus, conflict, and the need for order.

The **culture conflict model** stresses value differences and a belief that the laws reflect the values of the most powerful groups.

Crime in the United States

CRIME IN THE STREETS

Fear of crime is common in American society, especially in urban areas. By 1983, 45 percent of Americans reported they were afraid to go out alone at night within a mile of their homes, and 13 percent were afraid to go out during the day (*New York Times,* Feb. 23, 1983). Most feared are *street crimes,* that is, acts that directly threaten one's person or property. It is often said that fear of crime is largely a fear of strangers. Yet, while almost half of all violent crimes are committed by total strangers, a similar proportion involves friends, acquaintances, or relatives, including spouses and ex-spouses (U.S. Department of Justice, 1987).

Fear of crime is influenced by such factors as the public's perception of the volume of crimes committed in their area, by the proportion of minority-group members living in the city (Liska et al. 1982), and by a person's sex and age. Paradoxically, although women and the elderly are most fearful of street crime, 70 percent of victims of violent crimes by strangers are men. Violent crime is also predominantly targeted against younger persons; the average age of victims during 1982–1984 was twenty-seven. More than three-fourths of victims of violence by strangers were under age thirty-five; only 3 percent were age sixty-five or over (U.S. Department of Justice, 1987).

In contrast to popular opinion, most violent crimes committed in the United States involve victims and offenders of the same race (U.S. Department of Justice, 1987). Nor are most violent crimes committed at

Street crimes are actions that directly threaten persons or property.

TABLE 16-1 A model of theoretical perspectives as they relate to types of criminal behavior

Behavior	Explained by Theoretical Perspective		
	Social Injury	Consensus (Functionalist)	Conflict
Dreaded by most (for example, murder)	Yes	Yes	Yes
Threat to many vested-interest groups (for example, power-elite groups)	No	Yes	Yes
Threatening special-interest groups (for example, nuclear plant sit-in)	No	No	Yes

The police have the right to use coercive force, including firearms, to control behavior. As with all rights, however, there are limits as to how they can be exercised. (© Eugene Gordon)

night; about half occur between 6 A.M. and 6 P.M.—a proportion, incidentally, which does not vary by whether or not the offender is known to the victim (U.S. Department of Justice, 1987). In this section, we shall examine some of the most common types of crime in the streets and in the home.

Measuring Crime. In the United States, two major data sources are used to determine the extent of crime. The first is the *Uniform Crime Reports,* compiled by the Federal Bureau of Investigation from monthly and yearly information submitted by city, state, and county police units. Eight categories, selected because they are regarded as among the most serious law violations, form the basis of the FBI Crime Index: (1) murder and nonnegligent manslaughter; (2) forcible rape; (3) robbery; (4) aggravated assault; (5) burglary; (6) larceny; (7) motor vehicle theft; and (8) arson. Not included in the index are confidence games, embezzlement, forgery, and other nonviolent crimes. As you can see in Table 16-2, which summarizes rates per 100,000 population for 1985, among these *index crimes,* those involving property—particularly larceny/theft and burglary—are most commonly reported.

Note that the index crimes are those

Uniform Crime Reports are compiled by the FBI from city, state, and county police information.

Index crimes include murder, forcible rape, robbery, and aggravated assault.

most often committed by the poor and powerless. Crimes typically associated with the more affluent, discussed later in this chapter, are not included in this list.

How useful are these statistics in assessing the extent and increase or decrease in crime? Although the *Uniform Crime Reports* are widely used by the police and the

TABLE 16-2 Rates of selected crime index offenses per 100,000 population in the United States, 1985

Crime	Rate per 100,000
Larceny/theft	2,901
Burglary	1,297
Motor vehicle theft	462
Aggravated assault	303
Robbery	209
Forcible rape	37
Murder/manslaughter	8

(*Note:* arson, the eighth index crime, is not included in the table inasmuch as rates per 100,000 were not calculated. During 1985, 86,455 cases of arson were committed according to FBI reports: 56 percent of which involved the malicious fire-setting of a building; 26 percent the burning of a motor or other vehicle; and the remaining 18 percent "other.")
SOURCE: *Statistical Abstract of the United States, 1987,* Table 261, p. 155, and Table 280, p. 163.

mass media, they have two major short-comings: (1) Not all crimes are reported to the police, for many victims do not want to take the time and effort to lodge a complaint. Some may fear revenge while others do not feel that reporting the crime will do any good. Thus, official statistics greatly underestimate the number of crimes. (2) The data reported by various local units are not always comparable. States and municipalities differ in crime definitions, in reporting techniques, in their willingness to do the paperwork, and in deliberate falsification to increase or maintain budget appropriations for the reporting unit.

Nonetheless, the data do roughly indicate the number of crimes considered most serious by officials and the types of activities in which law-enforcement agencies are engaged. Because of their unreliability, however, they are *not* very useful in the assessment of changes in the volume of crime. Official crime rates do describe the amount of criminal activity that comes to the attention of the police and how it is labeled.

To add to the information provided in the *Uniform Crime Reports,* the Department of Justice conducts a *National Crime Survey* of close to 50,000 randomly selected households. Twice a year, the adults in these households are interviewed about any incidents in which they have been the victims of crime, whether reported or not. These data on victimization give a more accurate picture of the amount of crime than do the official reports, but there is no way to tell the extent to which respondents conceal, exaggerate, or minimize their experiences.

Typical data from the victim survey are shown in Table 16-3. As you can see, blacks are more likely than whites to experience serious violent crime, burglary, and motor vehicle theft. People in cities, where the majority of blacks live, run higher risks of victimization than people who live in suburbs or rural areas. This is why, at each income level, black households are more likely to be burglarized than are white households.

Although we cannot know how much crime goes unreported or how much re-

The **National Crime Survey** is based on samples of U.S. households and businesses.

TABLE 16-3 Percent of households touched by crime by selected characteristics, 1985

Percent of Households Touched by:	Race of Household Head			Annual Family Income				Place of Residence		
				Low	Medium		High			
	White	Black	Other	Under $7,500	$7,500–$14,999	$15,000–$24,999	$25,000 or more	Urban	Suburban	Rural
Any NCS crime	24.8%	26.5%	24.7%	22.9%	24.2%	24.6%	29.1%	29.6%	25.8%	19.5%
Violent crime	4.6	5.8	4.2	5.9	4.7	4.5	4.8	6.0	4.8	3.6
Rape	.1	.2	.2	.3	.1	.1	.1	.2	.1	.1
Robbery	.8	2.0	1.2	1.2	1.0	.8	.9	1.7	.9	.3
Assault	3.9	4.0	3.0	4.9	3.7	3.8	4.1	4.5	4.0	3.3
Aggravated	1.4	1.8	1.1	2.1	1.2	1.3	1.4	1.6	1.5	1.2
Simple	2.8	2.5	2.1	3.4	2.7	2.6	2.9	3.2	2.8	2.3
Total theft	17.7	17.2	17.8	14.0	16.9	17.8	21.8	20.2	18.9	13.6
Personal theft	11.7	10.0	13.0	8.1	10.3	11.3	15.5	12.9	12.7	8.6
Household theft	8.0	9.4	6.6	8.1	8.5	8.4	8.6	10.1	8.2	6.3
Burglary	5.1	6.9	4.7	7.0	5.5	4.8	5.1	6.8	4.9	4.4
Motor vehicle theft	1.3	1.9	1.3	1.0	1.1	1.4	1.7	1.9	1.4	.7
Serious violent crime[a]	2.2	3.8	2.4	3.3	2.3	2.1	2.3	3.3	2.4	1.5
Crimes of high concern[b]	7.5	9.8	7.5	9.4	7.7	7.3	7.9	10.1	7.5	5.9

Note: Detail does not add to total because of overlap in households touched by various crimes.
[a] Rape, robbery, aggravated assault.
[b] A rape, robbery, or assault by a stranger or a burglary.
SOURCE: U.S. Department of Justice, *Bureau of Justice Statistics,* "Households Touched by Crime, 1985," June 1986, p. 3.

ported criminal activity remains unrecorded, data from the *National Crime Survey* suggest that most crimes are not reported. Of the more than 37 million crimes that took place in 1983, for example, only 35 percent were reported to police. The crimes most likely to be reported were motor vehicle theft (69 percent) and aggravated assault (58 percent); the least likely was household larceny/theft (25 percent) (U.S. Department of Justice, December 1985). Reporting was most common for crimes where: (1) the victim has been seriously physically injured; (2) the value of property theft is $250 or more; (3) the victim is twenty years of age or older; and (4) the victim has at least some high school education (U.S. Department of Justice, 1985).

Interestingly, in 1986, the *Uniform Crime Reports* indicated a slight rise in crimes, while the *National Crime Survey* showed a continued decline. The difference is probably due to the fact that fewer households are being victimized, but the victims are more willing than in the past to report the crimes. In addition, because most crime is committed by young men, crime rates ought to vary with the proportion of males age fifteen to twenty-four in the general population. Thus, the rise in crime rates of the 1960s and 1970s is a direct outcome of the influx of Baby Boomers into the at-risk age groups. Conversely, the recent declines in victimization rates can be accounted for, in large part, by the aging-out of the Baby Boom cohorts (Cohen and Land 1987).

Homicide.   One of the most violent crimes is homicide. The typical homicide victim in the United States is a black male. In 1983, the homicide rate per 100,000 people was 51.4 among black males and 11.3 among black females as compared to 8.6 among white males and 2.8 among white females. Typically, too, victims are young; homicide ranks as the second leading cause of death in the eighteen- to twenty-four-year age group in the United States. Homicide victims and their killers are most likely to come from the same racial or ethnic background. The victim and killer are likely to know each other as well: in 1984, only 18 percent of the homicides reported to the police in the United States were known to be committed by a stranger (Bureau of Justice Statistics, 1987b).

Despite high rates of homicide, handguns are readily accessible in most large American cities. In fact, Bernhard Goetz (pictured here), nicknamed the "subway vigilante," became a folk hero to some people, by brandishing his illegal revolver and shooting four black teenagers on a New York subway. Is anticipated self-defense a good reason for carrying an illegal weapon? (© Tony Mangia/SYGMA)

American males are particularly at risk of homicide when compared to men in other nations. In per person terms, about ten American men die by violence for every Japanese, Austrian, West German, or Swedish man; fifteen American men are killed for every Swiss or Englishman; and somewhat over twenty for every Danish male (Currie 1982). Why? Is it, as President Reagan proposed in 1981, that some men are prone to evil? If so, why should "the nature of man" (or woman) vary by national boundaries so that Americans are particularly prone to violence?

Many answers have been proposed for the high rate of homicide in the United States, including the strong tradition of violence surrounding racial conflict, the labor movement, and the settlement of the west. Yet other nations with similar histories—Australia, Canada, and New Zealand are three examples—have far lower homicide rates. Some criminologists claim that the homicide rate could be decreased by restrictions on the sales of handguns. Fifty-nine percent of the murders in the United States in 1985, for example, involved the use of a gun, most often a handgun. Firearms were also used in 21 percent of the aggravated assaults and 35 percent of the robberies reported to the FBI in 1984 (*Statistical Abstract of the United States, 1987,* p. 158–161).

Yet the evidence that gun ownership is a cause of criminal violence remains controversial. According to a 1982 national survey, the typical handgun owner is male, white, Protestant, middle-class, and southern (*Society,* 1982). These people are neither the typical homicide victims nor offenders, although use of firearms in murder, aggravated assault, and robbery is higher in the South than in other regions of the nation (*Statistical Abstract of the United States, 1987,* p. 161).

Other sociologists refer to a *subculture of violence* in the United States in which physical aggression is the norm (Wolfgang and Ferracuti 1967). Poor young males, especially in ethnic groups stressing masculine honor, are more likely to learn to solve arguments through violence than are young people from middle-class homes. Indeed, according to FBI data, the single most common factor in murders in 1985 was an argument. Yet there is an element of blaming the victim in the theory of subcultural violence. The high rates of homicide among young black males, and, to a lesser extent, young black females, indicates unbearable levels of frustration, poverty, and blocked opportunity. To term this a subculture of violence may be descriptive but it is not explanatory. Economic inequality and discrimination appear more important than poverty itself, or the percentage of blacks in the population of an area or region of the country: "If there is a culture of violence its roots are pronounced economic inequalities, especially if associated with ascribed position" such as that of race (Blau and Blau 1982, p. 114).

Property Crimes. The number of crimes against persons is relatively small compared to the number of property crimes. In 1985, over 3 million burglaries, almost 7 million larceny/thefts, and about 1 million motor vehicle thefts were reported to the police, and, as you will recall from earlier in this chapter, these figures underestimate the actual event of property crime. To prevent such victimization, about one-third of American homes and two-thirds of our workplaces have some type of crime prevention device. Crime has, in fact, turned many homes into fortresses.

Property crimes are most likely to be reported to police when they take place in large cities and least likely to be reported when they occur in rural areas. The relationship between population size and the probability of victimization is in part due to the anonymity that the city provides (see Chapter 19). But the impersonality of urban life cannot explain variations in property crime from one city to another. Why, for example, are report rates in Phoenix, Ariz., higher than in New York City? Undoubtedly, differences in the reporting procedures of local departments is a factor.

Sociologists are also examining the possibility that variations in the probability of victimization by age group, marital status, social class, and place of residence can be partly explained by patterns of *normal* activity. That is, as more people spend more time outside the home—at work or at leisure—they will be at risk of becoming victims, especially if these "routine activities" take place where there are motivated offenders relatively unsupervised by

Property crimes, such as burglaries, larceny, and theft, are much more prevalent than crimes against persons.

Growing up in poor urban neighborhoods does not mean you'll take up a life of crime. These young men are members of the Guardian Angels, a volunteer organization, which has received national acclaim for its work patrolling the streets and subways of New York. (© Eve Arnold/Magnum)

When securing property, someone is locked out. It has also been suggested that someone is locked in. (© Bill Gallery/Stock Boston)

agents of social control (Cohen and Felson 1979, Miethe et al. 1987, Messner and Blau 1987). Recent evidence confirms these relationships, at least for property crimes.

There is also evidence that crimes such as grand larceny and burglary are most frequent in communities where there are marked differences in levels of economic power and in income (Jacobs 1981). Who commits these crimes? Those who are confronted with wealth that they themselves cannot achieve by legitimate means are apparently the most likely offenders; they are not, however, always the poorest of the poor (Jacobs 1981). In general, with the exception of burglary (a more specialized and "professional" crime), property crimes are committed by young men with limited education who are disproportionately drawn from minority groups. At least, these are the people who are arrested and taken to court. Relatively few middle-class thieves are processed through the courts. When detected, middle-class offenders are more likely to be labeled as mentally disturbed and sent into psychiatric treatment, or, if juveniles, sent to special schools.

At every age, males are more likely to be arrested and charged with a crime than are females, although female arrests for petty crimes have increased over the last fifty years or so (Steffensmeier and Cobb 1981).

FEMALE CRIMINALS

Until recently, very little had been written about the female offender. Many *fewer women* than men have been arrested and imprisoned. In 1985, women accounted for only about 17 percent of those arrested in the United States. The proportion of prisoners who are women is about 5 percent, a fact contributing to the very high cost of their incarceration.

Several theories have sought to explain the relative lack of female criminals. These include such contradictory ideas as that the female offender is a biological or psychological oddity, rebelling against the natural passivity of her sex; that she is basically more vicious and cunning and thus less likely to be detected; that she is more conforming, more moral, more religious, and thus not easily tempted; and that she has little social support from peers for criminal activity as well as limited opportunity.

It has also been proposed that differences in the types and patterns of crimes by women result from gender socialization. Adler (1979) commented that we all go crazy or criminal along the well-worn, gender-linked paths; we cannot understand the female (or for that matter, male) offender except in the context of his or her social role. It is difficult to commit a major crime, such as burglary or armed robbery,

Many **fewer women** than men are arrested and imprisoned.

if one has not been trained to move with stealth or to handle a gun. The types of crimes in which women have been involved include prostitution, larceny (primarily shoplifting), vagrancy, and domestic violence—all linked to gender role (Figueira-McDonough et al. 1981).

Has the women's movement changed the nature of female criminality? U.S. data show a gradual increase in the proportion of women arrested within the last decade. The increase, however, has been almost entirely accounted for by greater female participation in such minor property crimes as larceny, fraud, and forgery. Relatively few women are arrested now or have been arrested in the past for violent offenses such as assault or homicide.

Exaggerated protection of women (chivalry) has become unimportant in crime reporting. Moreover, police are *more* likely to arrest females than males suspected of property crimes (Visher 1983). Younger, black, or hostile women are also at greater risk of arrest than are those who are white or older, or who fit traditional gender-role stereotypes (Visher 1983).

As women are probably no more or less moral than men, the rise in female rates of larceny, forgery, and other property crimes appears to reflect increased opportunities to commit such acts rather than any basic personality changes. In addition, women who are arrested for criminal activity rarely express feminist sentiments. On the contrary, the few crimes of violence committed by women are closely tied to their roles as mothers, wives, and lovers. Traditional gender roles still dominate the lives of both female and male offenders.

For example, one of the few studies of women who have been convicted of embezzlement and fraud found that most were motivated by the need to support their families (Zeitz 1981). In contrast, men convicted of embezzlement or fraud tended to be motivated by desires for prestige or to cover mistakes.

ORGANIZED CRIME

The *Godfather* movies sum up what many Americans know about organized crime: It is Sicilian-led, run by close-knit families, and ruled by a patriarch who exerts almost complete control over his family and who demands secrecy while loyal lieutenants kill troublesome enemies in restaurants,

warehouses, and barbershops. The words *Mafia* and *Cosa Nostra* have become synonymous with the concept of organized crime in America.

It is both difficult to define criminal syndicates or organizations and to separate fact from fiction. The major sources of information are congressional hearings, court testimony, data from informants, and journalistic accounts. The simplest definition of *organized* or *syndicated crime* is continued organized endeavors to accumulate wealth in defiance of the law.

Organized crime has three major characteristics: (1) its members supply goods and services not otherwise available, such as loans, gambling, and narcotics; (2) in order to carry out illegal activities without interference, they bribe and otherwise corrupt public officials and others in positions of power; and (3) violence is used to enforce agreements.

Organized crime is neither a new nor a solely Sicilian phenomenon in the United States. It is not an alien conspiracy, but as much a part of the American scene as apple pie (Block and Chambliss 1981). When immigrants found that the streets of urban America were not paved with gold, and when discrimination and prejudice reduced their access to legitimate economic opportunities, illegal activity provided a ready, if crooked, ladder of social mobility. Later immigrant groups found that crime often brought success. In the United States during the late nineteenth century, organized crime was dominated by Irish and Germans. By the turn of the century, Eastern European Jews had emerged as gang leaders, and by the late 1920s, Italians had begun to displace the others in syndicated crime. Because they were among the last large wave of European immigrants, Italians found it particularly difficult to break out of the slums. Crime has always been an attractive alternative to poverty in the urban ghettos of America.

If the syndicates are ladders of social mobility, then blacks and Hispanics, as the minorities most likely today to be excluded from legitimate opportunity structures, should have become increasingly involved in organized crime. Limited evidence suggests that this is true, although the black and Hispanic operations remain primarily in narcotics, gambling, protection, and extortion. As white ethnic criminals move into legitimate businesses, their

Organized or **syndicated crime** is committed by members of formally structured groups operating outside the law.

low-prestige illegal activities are handed over to the newest immigrants.

Although we tend to think of organized crime as most common in large cities in the northern states, the Sunbelt has begun to rival the North in the level and sophistication of such activity. The Dixie version of organized crime is a loose confederation of burglars, operators of credit-card and real-estate frauds, drug smugglers and distributors, contract killers, operators of prostitution and pornography rings, and car thieves (King 1982). Unlike the organized crime in much of the Northeast, organized criminal activity in the Sunbelt is not dominated by any particular ethnic group. Southern rural residents and urban dwellers, as well as people from other states, make up this new criminal class (King 1982). As in the past and in other parts of the United States, organized crime is a route to social mobility in the South.

For obvious reasons, the amount of money amassed and invested by organized crime is unknown. With their wealth, crime syndicates can manipulate the value of shares on the stock market, control prices of retail goods, evade regulation of the quality of goods produced, avoid paying income taxes, secure government contracts without competitive bidding, and influence trade unions. The combination of investment in legitimate businesses and the corruption of officials is possible only because of vast amounts of working capital.

CRIME IN THE SUITES: WHITE COLLAR AND ORGANIZATIONAL CRIME

White-collar crimes are illegal activities committed by persons of high status, usually by nonviolent means, for their own benefit.

White-collar crime is a term coined by Edwin Sutherland (1949) to describe those crimes committed by respectable, high-status persons in the course of their employment. Although we have subtitled this section "White-collar and Organizational Crime," we want to stress that although the two are often confused with each other, they are separate. *White-collar crime* consists of illegal acts, without the use of violence, either to obtain or to avoid the loss of money or property or to secure a professional or business advantage. *Organizational crime* refers to illegal actions undertaken by legitimate corporations and their officials—bribery, price fixing, and tax evasion—for corporate rather than personal advantage.

Organizational crimes are carried out in one's role as employee to achieve corporate goals.

For example, if you have ever made a copy of a videotape, record, music cassette, or computer program without authorization from the holder of the copyright, you have committed a white-collar crime. If, in the course of normal business activity you approve the production of an automobile with a known defect, you have committed an organizational crime. To class both types of criminal activity as "white collar" simply describes the middle-class nature of the crimes (for gain, no violence) and the criminals (white collar, business suit).

White-Collar Crime. White-collar crime, like any other crime, is caused by the coincidence of three necessary conditions: motivation, neutralization of social controls, and opportunity (Coleman 1985). Motivated by a desire for individual profit, white-collar criminals typically are people with access to the resources needed to commit their crimes (opportunity) and in situations where the probability of being caught is relatively small (neutralization of social controls). The bank executive who embezzles funds, the physician who performs unnecessary surgery, the businessperson who pads expenses, the teacher who conceals a second source of income from the Internal Revenue Service, and the promoter of fraudulent land schemes are all white-collar criminals.

The extent of white-collar crime in the United States is unknown because the crimes are extremely difficult to detect, often have no identifiable victims, and involve fairly complex financial dealings. Although white-collar crime does not arouse the degree of fear created by crime in the streets, it has a powerful impact. Hundreds of thousands of citizens are affected, and mistrust of business and public officials is generated as the costs of multimillion dollar frauds are passed on to the public. Billing on government contracts for services that were not performed, cutting back on construction materials to increase profits, doubling the bill to insurance companies, and filing false income-tax returns ultimately raise prices and lower the standard of living of all citizens (Geis 1982).

White-collar crime, like any other kind of crime, is defined differently from time to time. As a recent historical example, until 1967 the physician in the United States who performed an abortion—except when the mother's life was in dan-

White-Collar Crime: Ponzi's Pyramids

Each era has produced its own master swindlers whose illegal activities have netted them millions of dollars. One of the oldest swindles involves paying high cash returns to early investors in a get-rich scheme, before leaving the scene with the rest of the money. A master of this method in the 1920s was an American financier names Charles Ponzi, who took in over $15 million on the slogan "50% return in 45 days, double your money in 90." Small investors flocked to make their killing. Ponzi's investments included a brokerage firm, a mansion, a limousine, and an excellent wine cellar. Exposed by an article in the *Boston Post*, Mr. Ponzi was indicted on eighty-six counts of larceny and mail fraud, for which he served a ten-year sentence (Slocum 1962). Similar schemes emerge every year, including the version for 1987.

One recent variation on a Ponzi scheme is a game called "airplane." For an initial investment of $1500 to $2500, a player becomes one of eight passengers on the imaginary airplane, along with four flight attendants, two copilots, and a pilot who pockets the passengers' money and leaves the ship. Each of the two copilots then becomes a pilot, taking half the attendants and passengers from the original plane to form a new aircraft. Each passenger must now find another person to invest in the scheme. Once this is done, the pilots take their money and leave, the flight attendants move up to copilot and the copilots become commanders of two different planes. Depending on how many people join the pyramid, the earliest sets of passengers stand a good chance of becoming pilots and realizing a big profit. Late joiners, however, are likely to lose their investment, especially if the authorities have discovered the scheme by this time and arrested the pilots (Neuffer 1987).

risk of detection. To the average victim of white-collar crime, the means of redress are so technical, lengthy, and expensive that most find it easier to ignore the crime than to fight. After all, no one got mugged (Johnson and Douglas 1978).

Organizational Crime. As we have noted, organizational crimes differ from white-collar crimes in two important ways. First, they are not committed for personal gain but in one's role as an employee or a corporate decision maker. For example, the executives of Lockheed, Exxon, and some two hundred other American firms who regularly bribed agents of foreign governments in defiance of U.S. law were corporate criminals, acting to fulfill organizational rather than purely personal goals.

Second, organizational crimes may be punished under civil, criminal, or administrative law. Organizational crimes thus broaden the definition beyond criminal law, which is the only legal sanction against ordinary criminals (Schwartz and Ellison 1982). The major penalty of trial, probation, and imprisonment used to control white-collar and street criminals cannot be used against corporations or

The highly successful and well-respected financier, Ivan Boesky, was found guilty of insider trading and stock manipulation. This white-collar crime was only one in a large number of its kind discovered in the boardrooms of Wall Street in '86 and '87. (© David Burnett/Press Images)

ger—could be prosecuted. Today, that doctor is engaged in the legitimate practice of medicine. Changes in social norms have redefined many other professional behaviors. On the other hand, technology, the mass media, and economic prosperity have created the possibility of new forms of white-collar crime: consumer fraud while catering to status needs or appealing to greed, or using a computer to gain access to other people's data or to falsify bank accounts. The increasing complexity of modern society both widens the white-collar criminal's options and narrows the

Business Scams

Dishonest schemes in the corporate world take many forms, most of which are difficult to detect or to prove. These range from petty frauds to stock swindles. Some common scams include the following.

BID RIGGING
Bid rigging occurs when potential competitors act together to prepare and submit bids for contracts. The alleged competitors decide which company will put in the low bid and subsequently pay off the companies who supposedly lost out.

INSIDER TRADING
Insider trading is carried out by senior executives and corporate officers of publically traded companies who use information not generally available to the public to buy and sell company shares thereby profiting without the usual competition.

STOCK MANIPULATION
Stock manipulation describes the buying and selling of shares to create a false appearance of active trading to push prices higher. The stock manipulators then sell their own shares for large profits. It also describes giving out false information to inflate or deflate stock prices.

CORPORATE TAX FRAUD
Almost everyone recognizes the notion of income-tax fraud. Relatively few of us are aware that corporations often cheat on their taxes by claiming exemptions and mislabeling expenses.

FRANCHISING FRAUDS
Franchising frauds occur when the owner of the name of the business fails to deliver promised goods or services to the buyer(s) of a franchise. Instead, substandard equipment is installed, or shoddy goods supplied. In its simplest form, the franchiser simply steals the money.

BANKRUPTCY FRAUD
Bankruptcy fraud describes the stealing or hiding of the assets of a business before declaring bankruptcy. Another form of bankruptcy fraud is the purchase of an economically healthy business which is declared bankrupt after its owners have sold goods obtained on credit, thus avoiding payments to creditors.

---

businesses. Although its officers and employees may be jailed, a corporation cannot be put behind bars (Clinard and Yeager 1980). In general, businesses and corporations that break the law are handled by government regulatory agencies, such as the Environmental Protection Agency, the Food and Drug Administration, and the Federal Trade Commission. The complex legal procedures surrounding the control of organizational crime, plus the attention given to street crime in the media, have perpetuated the image of "real crime" as being homicide, burglary, larceny, or other individual acts against people or their property.

Is organizational crime really crime as we generally define it? Some people have argued that it is only natural for businesses or agencies to attempt to get an advantage or to protect their own interests. Pollution, bribery, price fixing, corporate frauds, and tax violations are widespread and may not violate traditional community norms. Yet, these acts unnecessarily threaten the health, the economic well-being, and the lives of far more people than do murder, robbery, or rape. Giant corporations have so much wealth and political power that their operations affect the lives of almost all of us, from birth to death. They can manipulate public opinion through the media. Their behavior influences and shapes our foreign relations and can disrupt the political process through illegal campaign contributions and outright bribery.

How widespread is organizational deviance? Nobody really knows, for its very nature encourages concealment. Moreover, greater resources are spent detecting and prosecuting crime in the streets than crime in the suites. The form and content of the legal system in the United States tends to protect organizations and their property against the acts of individual people rather than protecting people from organizations (Hagan 1982). Only rarely is an organization prosecuted under criminal law.

In a study of 582 corporations, Clinard and Yeager (1980) found six main types of illegal corporate behavior. These included: (1) administrative violations, such as failure to recall a defective product; (2) environmental violations, such as major oil and chemical spills and air and water pollution; (3) financial violations, like illegal political contributions, bribery, overcharging customers, and tax violations; (4) labor violations, including discrimination in employment, unfair labor practices, occupational safety and health hazards, and wage and hour offenses; (5) manufacturing violations, such as production of defective or dangerous products; and (6) unfair trade practices, including price-fixing, fee-fixing, and other practices designed to eliminate competition or to mislead the public. This long list of types of violations has an even longer list of government agencies that are responsible for sanctioning such behavior.

Despite the relatively recent attention to corporate crime, it is neither new nor isolated. Of the corporations studied by Clinard and Yeager (1980), about 42 percent had multiple cases charged against them in a one-year period, and 13 percent accounted for over half the violations. Illegal acts were most likely to be committed by large corporations, with oil, motor vehicle, and drug companies particularly frequent offenders. A study by Etzioni (1985), focusing on *Fortune* magazine's 1984 list of America's 500 largest industrial corporations over the 1974–1984 period indicated that 62 percent of the corporations were involved in one or more illegal incidents, and the top 100 corporations in the United States accounted for more incidents than all the others combined.

Since corporations cannot go to jail, the stiffest penalty, other than jailing its officials, are fines. The effects of fines in most cases are small, as most corporations gain more than they lose financially from the offense. A $25,000 fine for a corporation whose annual revenue is several billion is hardly a stiff penalty. Furthermore, a stiff fine may be reduced if a donation that is tax deductible is made to worthwhile causes. For example, although Allied Chemical was fined $13.2 million for polluting the James River with Kepone, its fine was reduced to $5 million when the firm donated $8 million for research and programs on the effects of the chemical.

Since the early 1980s, the federal government has intensified its attack on organizational crime. The body of laws addressing organizational crime has also expanded. Thus, the Racketeer Influenced

and Corrupt Organizations Act (RICO), which was passed in 1970 to control organized crime, has now been extended to include other businesses. The Bank Security Act of 1970 requires banks and brokers to report most cash and foreign currency transactions of $10,000 or more, and the Comprehensive Crime Control Act, passed in 1984, gave authorities new weapons to prevent fraud against banks.

Crimes related to environmental or safety regulations, however, have not been a significant target. Rather, the attack has focused on defense procurement, money laundering, and bank and securities fraud. The list of corporate crimes that have come to light is extensive. Because of the large stakes involved in the stock market, the Federal Securities and Exchange Commission has focused on criminal use of insider information—privileged data used by executives to trade stocks for their own as well as corporate benefit.

The billions of dollars spent by the Department of Defense on weapons since 1980 have been accompanied by such practices as cost overruns, rigged bids, kickbacks, duplicate billing, falsified documents, security breaches, and outright bribery. In 1985, forty-five of the nation's top 100 defense contractors were under active criminal investigation; others have settled their cases; and for still others, the evidence has been too difficult to pursue. The very complexity of the government agencies charged with overseeing the vast military program almost invites abuse. Other contributing factors include the relatively low salaries of the government workers compared to their counterparts in defense industries, and the lack of time or skill to do a competent job of supervision.

The sociological point here is that corruption and corporate crime in the defense industry has more to do with the structure of the situation than with the personalities of the individuals involved.

The Profit Motive. Two incidents that shocked many Americans in the 1980s were the tragic 1986 accident to the space shuttle *Challenger* and the numerous suits against A. H. Robins Pharmaceutical Company brought by users of an intrauterine contraceptive device (IUD), the Dalkon Shield. What do these very different events have in common? They both reveal deliberate suppression of information and the loss of life for corporate gain.

When the *Challenger* began its fatal seventy-three-second flight, engineers from Morton Thiokol Incorporated, the subcontractor for the solid-fuel booster rockets, were aware that the synthetic rubber seals between the rocket's joints could fail in cold weather. The evening before the launch, Thiokol's vice president for engineering recommended against the flight. But thirty minutes later, after being asked to "put on my management hat" by the corporation's senior vice president, he reversed his decision. In the trade-off between profits over safety, pressure from corporate users and from NASA, in favor of launching, won out, and warnings by the engineers were ignored.

A. H. Robins executives also ignored information. After purchasing the rights to market the Dalkon Shield in 1971, the company learned that the shield was both ineffective and dangerous. Yet the product continued to be advertised and marketed, and the physician who developed it continued to receive royalties. By 1974, Robins was forced by the government to withdraw it from the market; nevertheless the company continued to sell the device abroad. Only in 1984 did Robins recall all shields still in use. Meanwhile, numerous users had experienced unwanted pregnancies, miscarriages, and chronic inflammation of the pelvis; at least thirty-three women had died. Many women sued the company that failed to inform them or their physicians of the hazards. In an attempt to avoid payment of these and anticipated future claims, Robins filed for bankruptcy.

Both the Thiokol and the Robins cases illustrate a lack of corporate accountability. The corporate structure itself is oriented toward profit and away from liability and thus it is almost a standing invitation to irresponsible conduct (Mintz 1985). Moreover, within the corporate structure, the usual constraints on behavior such as religion, conscience, and criminal codes are relaxed. The protection offered by the relative anonymity of corporate structure permits executives to avoid confronting any contradiction between what is good business and what is accepted personal morality. But is the person who assaults people from an office chair any less a criminal than the one who accosts them in an alley (Mintz 1985)?

Neither Thiokol, NASA, nor Robins is alone in lacking corporate accountability. By the early 1930s, for example, there was reliable evidence that workers in the asbestos industry were developing incurable lung disease; by the 1960s, studies showed that asbestos was a danger to anyone who came in contact with it. Yet the industry's largest company, Manville Corporation, had systematically concealed these findings. When, ultimately, juries began to award compensation for injury and damage, Manville Corporation filed for bankruptcy. The list could go on.

Government experts estimated that violations of various tax, fraud, bribery, pollution, and other federal laws by the nation's thousand largest corporations cost the economy billions of dollars (Clinard and Yeager 1980). If corporate America pays only a very small share of the costs

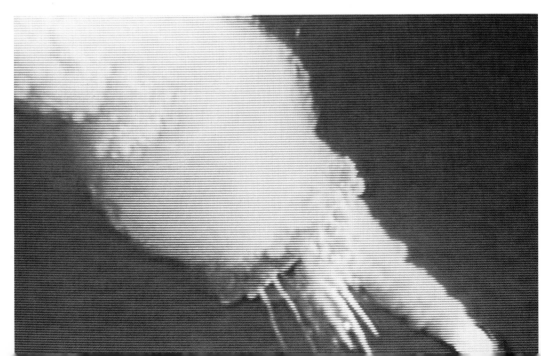

The tragic death of six U.S. astronauts and a civilian teacher in the 1986 Challenger explosion revealed the power of the profit motive and political pressure over the value of human life. Which model of society is most helpful in understanding the supremacy of profit? (© Owen/Black Star)

of running the United States, individual citizens must replace every revenue dollar lost.

Bribery, too, is widespread both in government and in corporations. The line between legal and illegal bribery is often thin—so thin that the late Senator Paul Douglas refused to accept any gift or payment worth more than five dollars. Bribery, like love, is easy to recognize but difficult to define; few societies have eliminated all gifts to those in power (Noonan 1985).

The complexities of corruption in government and the private sector were highlighted in the 1987 congressional investigation of arms sales to Iran, a violation of our government's own policy, and the subsequent diversion of some of the profits to rebels seeking the overthrow of the government of Nicaragua, which violated a congressional ban on such aid. Because both policies were of questionable legality if carried out by officials of our government, the White House staff used private-sector fund raisers and arms dealers. The legal details will take years to unravel, but the primary defense of those involved has been the claim that they were carrying out the President's policy even if not precisely ordered to use illegitimate means. This reasoning is basically the same as that of executives who commit violations of the law in pursuit of the broader objectives of their organization.

Because organizational deviance has not been much reduced by laws or regulation from outside, or by policing from within, we must conclude that the benefits outweigh the costs of such activity. Organizational crime, like any other, provides goods and services at a profit to the organization. Unless the demand for such benefits declines or alternative sources are found, such activities will continue.

CRIMES WITHOUT VICTIMS

Crimes without victims are sometimes known as *vice,* or *crimes against morality.* That is, they are not directed against a person or against property but are believed to endanger the moral fiber of society. Yet, moral standards in complex societies are mixed and constantly changing. What offends one group's morality may be acceptable to another group. Because those involved in such offenses as pornography, prostitution, gambling, drug use,

Crimes without victims violate moral standards, but those involved are willing participants.

and sex acts between consenting adults have themselves chosen to be participants, many people have argued that these acts should be decriminalized. From this perspective, the prosecution of such behavior wastes the time and the resources of police and court personnel, and it serves only to stigmatize the few who are arrested.

Victimless crimes are also likely to lead to the corruption of law-enforcement personnel. Vice squads are the most vulnerable unit in any police department. The range of discretionary power here is often so great that the officer can be bribed to arrest X and not Y, or to raid one home and not another. There is also the possibility that the officer's subjective evaluation of different kinds of people will dictate who is picked up on vice charges. For example, if a police officer is told to get rid of the prostitutes on Forty-second Street in New York City, where there are more prostitutes than the officer can arrest at one time, what criteria will he or she use: appearance, skin color, personal feelings? If someone pays the officer to leave some "girls" alone, and enough can still be arrested to please the superior officers, is any harm done? In all these ways, the ideal of equal treatment under the law is systematically and regularly violated by the very agents of the law. That victimless crimes remain on the statute books reflects a complex set of economic, political, and moral issues.

Prostitution. As described in Chapter 6, prostitution is a "safety valve" deviance, condemned but tolerated in a wide variety of societies throughout the world. Although there are some male prostitutes, whose clients are primarily homosexual, the occupation is predominantly female. With the exception of a few legalized brothels in the state of Nevada, prostitution is illegal in the United States. It is impossible to know how many men and women are in the business of selling sex; they range from people who walk the streets, to students and homemakers working on a part-time basis, to expensive dates arranged by an escort service. But it is likely that the great bulk of prostitution in the United States is controlled by organized crime.

Despite the enormous volume of illegal sexual activity, only about 100,000 arrests for commercialized sex were made in 1985, almost all of them involving young women, many being arrested several times during the year. It is rare that a prostitute's customer is also arrested. Clearly, prostitution is a profitable business with a low probability of arrest—for the buyer, the seller, and the people who "protect" the prostitute for a share of her income.

Because prostitution flourishes despite its illegality many legal scholars claim that this and other victimless crimes actually reduce respect for the law in general. In fact, in 1985, a study commission of the Canadian government recommended that most forms of prostitution be removed from the criminal code, and that local authorities be given the power to license and regulate brothels. The commission also concluded that current laws, similar to those in the United States, victimized and dehumanized women, failed to protect them from abuse by their customers or protectors ("pimps"), and generally supported the sexist notion that men's sexual needs had to be met (*McLeans* 1985).

On the other hand, there are many groups that benefit from periodic attempts to enforce the laws: politicians and other moral entrepreneurs (see Chapter 6); police vice units that are paid to arrest prostitutes; officers who take bribes; and the judicial system that collects the fines. But in all the condemning, with the exception of the Canadian report (which was not all that well received) little systematic attention has been paid to the roles of men in perpetuating the sexual degradation of women, many of whom turn to prostitution when more legitimate means of earning a living are unavailable. In fact, there is an increasing tendency, even among some feminists, to tolerate prostitution so long as it is freely chosen and the women are not exploited by clients, pimps, or law enforcement officials. An organization called COYOTE (an acronym for Call Off Your Old Tired Ethics) is attempting to change the laws to protect the rights of prostitutes, to provide health care, and generally to improve working conditions, just like any other trade union.

Pornography. As you browse through magazine racks, books, or video tapes—or even turn on the television set—you will undoubtedly see sexually detailed materials that would not have been openly displayed in the United States only two decades ago. The production, sale, and possession of such products was against the law. These rules were relaxed in the 1970s, following the report of a presidential commission that found little evidence linking pornography to antisocial behavior.

In 1986, however, President Reagan established a new commission on pornography specifically charged with finding ways to contain the spread of pornography. In sharp contrast to the 1970 report, the new commission issued findings of a clear link between exposure to "sexually explicit" material and the level of sexual violence in the society. The commission then recommended raising the criminal penalties on the production and distribution of obscene materials. What accounts for such a dramatic reversal in a mere sixteen years?

In part, the difference in findings reflects the composition of the two panels, with the 1986 commissioners specifically selected for their known opposition to pornography. In addition, the choice of witnesses was similarly skewed, with 77 percent in favor of increased censorship (Lynn 1986, Mosher 1986).

To what extent are the newer findings valid? Is there a proven causal link between exposure to pornography and subsequent sexual violence? The evidence is

The regulation of pornography is difficult, in part, because the definition of what constitutes pornography varies and, in part, because it is a $7 billion industry with strong interests in maintaining itself. (© P. Chauvel/SYGMA)

actually very tentative, and, if there is any relationship, it is due to the violence in the pornographic material rather than to its sexual content (Donnerstein 1986). Most Americans, however, in 1970 and today, believe that the link exists—but for other people, if not themselves. As far as data on rape, the *National Crime Survey* found no increase in the period between 1973 and 1984 (*Statistical Abstract* 1987, p. 159), even though the volume of readily available sexually explicit material increased greatly over the decade. Adult bookstores can be found in most communities; X-rated videos are sold in conventional shops; and cable television has a "blue" channel in many areas of the country.

If proving a link between pornography and antisocial behavior of any kind has been problematic, it has been even more difficult to establish a workable definition of "obscenity." American courts have used a number of standards over the past 125 years, beginning with a set of concepts borrowed from British law that asked whether the material *tended* to corrupt people *whose minds were open* to such immoral influences and who were *likely to see* the material. Note the problems (1) in finding evidence that the intent of the producers was to corrupt, (2) in showing the degree to which a person's mind is open to such influence, and (3) in proving that the material was likely to fall into that person's hands.

Similar definitional traps characterize later attempts to distinguish what is obscene from what some people might label art. Included here are such concepts as whether or not the work appeals to "prurient interests" (lustful thoughts); whether or not it has "redeeming social value" (can be considered a work of art by a legitimate creative talent); whether it would be considered obscene by the yardstick of "prevailing community standards"; and, most recently, replacing the prevailing community standard by what the "reasonable man (sic)" might think.

The basic argument against censorship of pornography rests on the freedom of press guarantee of the First Amendment. If no direct harm can be proved, the material should fall under protected speech. If young children are abused by the producers of pornography there are other statutes under which people can be prosecuted.

Many feminists, who tend to be strong believers in civil liberties, however, find themselves caught in a bind on the pornography issue because so much of the material is degrading and exploitive of women. Paradoxically, it is the expressions of sexuality—which many women are now claiming for themselves in contrast to a male-defined reality—that are likely to be suppressed rather than the images of extreme violence.

But so long as a market exists that cannot be supplied legitimately, pornography—however defined—will be produced and distributed by people willing and able to defy the law.

Gambling. As with prostitution and pornography, many Americans feel that gambling corrupts public morals. Arguments against gambling include its links to organized crime, the bribery of government officials, and the destruction of family life. Although it is impossible to know how many people engage in illegal gambling, the desire to try to get something for almost nothing is widespread. Many others enjoy the thrill of risk taking when high stakes are involved. Of the millions who could have been caught, there were only 28,000 gambling arrests in 1985.

Despite the fact that gambling is considered sinful by many, churches have for many years conducted Bingo games to raise needed funds. State governments, too, have found it easier to run off-track betting parlors or establish lotteries than to raise taxes. It appears that asking people for money in a straightforward manner is more dangerous to politicians than enticing them into partial sin. From a sociological perspective, state lotteries are dysfunctional in a number of ways: bettors are victimized by exceedingly poor odds of winning, social values are eroded, and the economic benefits to local governments are questionable. What is really happening, according to some critics (Abt 1985), is that money is being taken from the poor, who are the major buyers of lottery tickets, to pay for programs that ought to be funded by general taxation. The lottery does not raise new revenue but replaces other, more equitable, sources of funding.

In addition, because of the very low chance of winning and the relatively low payoff for most games, legal gambling has

What is the difference between legalized and illegal gambling? Whose interests does each serve? Who are the winners? Who are the losers? (© Leif Skoogfors/Woodfin Camp and Associates)

not crowded out such illegal operations as the "numbers game," which operates on the same principle but with a better payoff and tax-free winnings. It appears that the latent consequence of legalized gambling has only broadened the market for the illegal variety.

Drug Use. Another controversial victimless crime is the use of illegally purchased drugs, although the supporters of tougher laws argue that the users are victimized by their very dependence on drugs. The link between drug use and street crimes has also been cited as a reason for maintaining strict drug laws. Much of this relationship disappears, however, when the social status of the user is taken into account. In other words, whereas many poor criminals are drug users, many middle-class users do not commit crimes. Although the number of people addicted to narcotic drugs is unknown, several studies indicate that the rates of addiction are higher among physicians and nurses than among the poor. The poor addict is, however, more visible.

Because there is so much popular mythology about drug use, it is difficult to give a short review of what is actually known. To begin with, most research evaluating the impact of drug use has been poorly designed, and data on the effect of marijuana, heroin, cocaine, and other substances have been politicized both by those who support a tighter control of drugs and by those who support decriminalization or legalization. What *is* clear is that the illegal drug market is a primary source of income for organized crime.

The rapid rise in the use of cocaine and related drugs has increased demand for treatment of addicts as well as punishment of dealers. Publicly funded drug-treatment services have been swamped: many have long waiting lists. Relatively little scientific information has been gathered about addiction to crack, and physicians are divided about the most effective way to break the pattern of its use. Drug rehabilitation has become big business as numerous corporations, such as Avon Products (best known for cosmetics), have established profit-making chains of rehabilitation centers. Costs of treatment in these facilities is high; in 1986, for example, charges ran as high as $21,000 for a six-week treatment period (*Newsweek,* June 30, 1986, p. 53). High costs have not been confined to private residential treatment programs; because of "irregularities" in salary and travel expenses, the government had to suspend a million-dollar grant to the National Partnership to Prevent Drug and Alcohol Abuse, an organization once chaired by Nancy Reagan. Clearly, drug use is a multi-million dollar business, hurting some and benefitting others, and attracting a variety of both public and private entrepreneurs.

Juvenile Delinquency

Juveniles may come to the attention of the law enforcement system for three reasons: (1) they have committed a crime; (2) they are neglected or abused; or (3) they

Juveniles come to the attention of law officials because they have committed a crime or status offense, or been neglected or abused.

This young male "runaway" can be prosecuted for a status offense, an act which would not be a violation if committed by an adult. Is there a purpose to this dual system of classification? If so, whose interest does it serve? (© Stephen Shames/Visions)

A **status offense** is an act that would not be considered a violation if committed by an adult.

have committed a *status offense.* A status offense is an act that would not be considered a violation of the law if committed by an adult. Being a truant from school, violating curfew laws (being out late at night), using alcohol or tobacco, running away from home, being a potential runaway, and being ungovernable (incorrigible) are all status offenses.

According to FBI data for 1985, children under the age of fifteen accounted for 28 percent of the arrests for curfew violations, 43 percent of the arrests of runaways, 23 percent of the vandalism arrests, and 26 percent of the arrests for arson. The remainder were persons age fifteen and over. Since there is some disagreement on the age at which one ceases to be a juvenile, the upper limits to this category fluctuate. In forty of the fifty states, those below the age of eighteen at the time they committed the offense are under the jurisdiction of the juvenile court system. In six states, an individual ceases to be a juvenile at age seventeen; and in two states at age sixteen. In still another state, the age is twenty-one if the offender is attending high school or vocational school, and eighteen if not attending school. Still another state sets age nineteen as the end of the period in which a person is regarded as a juvenile before the law. In certain instances, however, those legally

defined as juveniles may be tried as adults if the offense is serious enough. In other instances, trials can be held and courts continue to supervise a juvenile beyond the specified age. To make matters even more complex, a different age could apply in cases involving adoption or failure to support a child, or for "persons in need of supervision" (PINS). Even the minimum age at which the death penalty may be imposed shows considerable variation among states, from a low of ten years to a high of eighteen years of age.

Many of the differences in the age at which one is considered adult reflect long-established norms as well as the efforts of various interest groups. For example, "age of reason," a term used by lawyers to describe the age at which a child is capable of acting responsibly, has commonly been defined as seven years; below that age, a child is conclusively presumed to be incapable of committing a crime. In general, according to legal tradition, a child between ages seven and fourteen is assumed to be incapable of committing a crime although evidence to the contrary can be offered. Variations in law regulating age at marriage reflect beliefs about sexuality, family formation, and ability to support and care for children as well as regional and subcultural differences. Older students in some states may recall when people could purchase liquor at age eighteen but could not vote until age twenty-one; their parents or grandparents may remember when drivers' licenses had no fixed age limit.

Who is arrested as a juvenile delinquent? Data consistently indicate that American males are three times more likely than females to be arrested. Although more white than nonwhite young people are arrested, blacks and Hispanics are disproportionately represented among the arrested. That children from low-income and working-class homes have higher rates of arrest than those from higher-income homes could reflect either a real difference in delinquent activity, fewer financial or family resources, or the tendency for police and other authorities to label poor youth as lawbreakers. Indeed, when self-reports of delinquent behavior are compared with official records, the data indicate that much self-reported delinquency by higher-strata white juveniles is never included in police reports (Thornberry and Farnsworth 1982). If re-

444

ported, offenses by those with more resources are typically dealt with informally before any charge or arrest is brought.

Table 16-4, compiled from FBI data, shows the percentages of juveniles and adults arrested in 1985 by age and offense. Reading across the table, you can see that 1 percent of arrests for murder and nonnegligent manslaughter were of people under age fifteen: 8.3 percent were under age 18, which means that 7.3 percent were between the ages of fifteen and seventeen. In comparison, 32.9 percent of the arrests for murder and nonnegligent manslaughter were of young adults aged eighteen to twenty-four and 48.3 of arrests for this crime were aged twenty-five to forty-four. (As you read across the table, you will note that crime is primarily an activity of younger adults.)

THE JUVENILE COURT SYSTEM

The **juvenile court system** is separate from the adult system and was designed to protect children and adolescents from the stresses of labeling and severe punishment.

There are two separate court systems in the United States: one for juveniles and one for adults. The adult system will be described more fully later in the chapter. The *juvenile court system* was specifically designed to keep children and adolescents from undergoing the stress of adult courtroom procedures and the effects of labeling. The emphasis is on treatment rather than punishment. Because the juvenile court judge was supposed to represent the interests of the child, legal safe-

guards such as those mandated for adults were not considered necessary. Over the past twenty years, however, the U.S. Supreme Court has reduced the informality of the juvenile-justice system. Precisely because the juvenile court was informal, there was little uniformity in decisions reached by judges. Moreover, previous decisions affect later ones, even when offense and extra-legal factors are controlled (Thornberry and Christenson 1984, Henretta et al. 1986). In addition, the penalty for each successive offense tends to escalate for repeat offenders whether or not this is in their best interests (Henretta et al. 1986).

Today, although each state has its own pattern of juvenile justice, every defendant has the following legal rights: (1) to know the nature of the charges; (2) to have legal counsel; (3) to question witnesses; and (4) to avoid self-incrimination. In every state, appeal procedures have also been established. These rights, however, do not extend to status offenses such as truancy, running away, or unmanageability.

During 1983, about 1.2 million delinquency cases were disposed of by juvenile courts, or about forty-four cases per 1,000 population age ten to seventeen in the United States. Over three-quarters of these cases involved males. An additional 196,000 cases concerned dependent and neglected children. (*Statistical Abstract*

TABLE 16-4 Persons arrested, by charge, sex, and age: 1985 [Represents arrests (not charges) reported by 11,249 agencies (reporting 12 months) with a total 1985 population of 203 million as estimated by FBI]

Charge	Total (1,000)	Percent Distribution							
		Male	Under 15 yr.	Under 18 yr.	18–24 yr.	25–44 yr.	45–54 yr.	55–64 yr.	65 yr. and over
Total arrests	10,290	82.6	5.7	17.1	32.4	41.9	5.2	2.5	.9
Serious crimes	2,125	78.6	12.2	30.8	30.9	32.3	3.3	1.8	.9
Murder and nonnegligent manslaughter	16	87.6	1.0	8.3	32.9	48.3	5.9	3.2	1.4
Forcible rape	32	98.9	5.2	15.1	30.4	47.3	4.7	1.8	.7
Robbery	121	92.4	6.5	25.0	40.3	32.7	1.3	.4	.2
Aggravated assault	263	86.5	4.3	13.8	30.3	47.2	5.5	2.4	.9
Burglary	382	92.6	14.2	38.0	35.4	24.7	1.3	.4	.1
Larceny—theft	1,179	69.0	14.2	32.8	28.3	31.5	3.8	2.3	1.3
Motor vehicle theft	116	90.7	9.5	38.0	35.2	24.5	1.5	.5	.2
Arson	17	86.9	26.3	41.2	21.9	30.0	4.5	1.9	.5
All other nonserious crimes	8,165	83.6	4.0	13.6	32.8	44.4	5.6	2.7	.9

SOURCE: *Statistical Abstract of the United States 1987,* Table 279, p. 163.

1987, p. 171). How many juveniles are being held in custody? Custodial facilities for juvenile offenders are of many different types and include detention centers, shelters, reception and diagnostic centers, training schools, halfway houses, and work camps. In 1985, about 80,000 juveniles were in public or private residential facilities at an average per capita cost of $25,200 in public custody and $23,800 in private custody (*Statistical Abstract* 1987, p. 171).

The Police and Law Enforcement

Police in every society are people who have been given the general right to use coercive force to control behavior (Klockars 1985, Bagley 1985). They have this right because citizens or vested interest groups call upon law-enforcement personnel to deal with situations in which "something ought not to be happening about which something needs to be done NOW!" (Klockars 1985). As formal agents of social control, police are empowered by the state to detect and limit criminal behavior. As informal agents, they make on-the-spot decisions about which offenses and offenders will receive attention and how they will be processed and with what offense they will be charged. From the perspective of conflict theorists, the police in any society are hired by the rich and powerful to keep disruptive people and ideas under control. From a functionalist view, the government represents the people; thus, police use force only on imperfectly socialized people who threaten social order.

The police and other government law-enforcement agents, such as the FBI, are relative newcomers to the American scene. In the seventeenth and eighteenth centuries, crime detection and control were relatively simple processes. Law and order were maintained by constables, sheriffs, justices of the peace, private citizens, and privately employed guards. As the size and diversity of the population increased, city police forces were established to promote public order among immigrant workers. Within the past fifty years or so, American per capita police expenditures adjusted for inflation nearly quadrupled, peaking in 1978 (Bureau of Justice Statistics 1986). Those cities with the highest crime rates spend more per capita for police protection than cities with lower crime rates.

The *police are enforcers* of rules rather than definers or moral entrepreneurs. As you will recall from Chapter 6, enforcers do not necessarily have any personal stake in the law to be upheld. In contrast, moral entrepreneurs are crusaders with a heavy investment in the social control of behavior that they consider morally offensive (Becker 1973). As enforcers, police are bureaucrats whose duties are defined by their position within a complex organization. Whether the police officer views an act as moral or immoral, dangerous or harmless, should not matter; they are neither legislators or reformers. Their job is to uphold the law.

Actual police work, however, is extremely complex. Police bureaucracies are unique in many respects. The status of police officer requires not only conformity to organizational rules but also initiative and risk taking on the job. Far more than any other public employees, police are under constant pressure from several sources. Police on the street must be ready to use coercive force in unexpected situations; detectives solve crimes only if citizens provide them with enough clues; and the basic bureaucratic police structure is deeply divided between workers and bosses who have different interests and beliefs (Reiner 1985). Street police, for example, believe that police in management positions have little, if any, understanding of what work on the beat is like (Reuss-Ianni 1983).

The individual officer's status is thus unclear. Partly connected to civilian life as a private citizen, partly connected to a bureaucratic organization where many rules are difficult to enforce, and partly connected to the criminal world, the police often find that they are not well liked in the community. Their spouses and children often find themselves cut off from most of the officer's life—a situation made worse by irregular hours and shifts. Perhaps it is not surprising that family violence and marital problems are high among police families (Alex 1976).

POLICE CORRUPTION

Corruption refers to acts that violate public trust and involve deliberate support of

---

*The **police** in every society have the right to use coercive force to control behavior.*

*The **police are enforcers** rather than definers of rules.*

illegal activity. Tendencies toward corruption are built into the law-enforcement system, as we noted in discussing victimless crime. Police work often requires reliance on informants, entrapment (luring someone into committing an offense), and other forms of trickery. Such tricks may range from the radar trap and unmarked car of the highway patrol to the undercover work of an agent infiltrating the Ku Klux Klan. Then too, the tension between administrators and front-line personnel within law-enforcement bureaucracies encourages patrol officers and detectives to pursue their own personal versions of police work so that they become moral entrepreneurs rather than enforcers (Punch 1985). Since the police have the power to arrest offenders, lawbreakers often offer bribes. In police slang, those who accept small bribes or engage in minor forms of misconduct are "grass eaters"; those who receive large payments or gains from organized crime are "meat eaters." The opportunities for corruption exist; it only remains for someone to take them.

When, if ever, do morally good ends justify either corruption or unethical or illegal means of reaching these ends? This is a very old question, rooted both in philosophy and the values of each society.

Adult Court Systems

The judicial process has three principal participants: the *prosecutor* (district attorney); the *defense attorney;* and the *judge.* Many others, including the defendant, appear in supporting roles. The prosecutor represents the interests of society and any injured parties. The defense attorney represents the accused; and the judge personifies the law and impartial justice. The statue of Justice, found in many courthouses, is blindfolded—she does not see differences of color or gender or class—with a sword in one hand that stands for swift justice, and a scales in the other hand, referring to the rights of the accused against the overwhelming power of the state.

Although one cornerstone of the American legal system is the right to a jury of one's peers, most cases are settled by guilty pleas or by the release of the suspect due to a lack of solid evidence. Of the few cases that go to trial, the majority of accused people choose to appear before a judge without a jury.

The judicial process in the United States is complicated by several parallel court

The three major parties in the criminal justice system are the **prosecutor,** the **defense attorney,** and the **judge,** each representing different interests.

The criminal justice system involves the prosecutor, the defense attorney, and the judge. Although television shows focus on the deliberation and reactions of jurors, only a small proportion of all cases involves a trial with a jury. (© Charles Steiner/SYGMA)

An Ex-Convict's View of Plea Bargaining

James Sykes (not his real name) was released in 1985 from a state penitentiary where he had served sixteen years of a life sentence for the murder of a six-year-old child. He is now forty years old and is employed in an unskilled job. He has consistently denied that he committed the crime. Discussing his conviction he said:

"I didn't even know the kid. See, what happened was that I used to go to this bar and get drunk. There were these two brothers, and we would all get drunk and fight. I was wild and they was wild. We'd threaten each other and fight, but we'd only fight til we fell down. Then we'd threaten to get each other, . . . you know, to kill each other. But then this kid in his family got killed and they arrested me. . . . I didn't even know the kid and I'm no kid killer. It wasn't his kid. . . . I was out on the street and the cops picked me up. They didn't search me. They picked up two teen age kids, boys, that night too. These two kids, they said they had seen me near where the murder took place that night. Then the next day the cops said they found a knife in the cruiser that they'd brought me in with. The judge said, "Didn't you search him before you put him in the cruiser?" The cops said no, which was true, they hadn't. And the judge said, "Was the cruiser locked?" They said no, and he said, "Well, anybody could have put it there, overnight, couldn't they? Why didn't you search him when you should of?" And they didn't have no good answer.

". . . The judge was fair; he asked those two boys who said they seen me if they could identify me and they said, yes, down to the shoes I was wearing. So the judge had them try to identify my shoes, and they couldn't. They finally told the judge that the cops had told them to identify me. . . . And then the D.A. brought in Johnny Walter, who owned the store where I was supposed to have bought the knife. He said I had bought it there. The judge asked him, "How can you tell?" Johnny, who was always a crook, said, "I remember." And the judge said, "How can you tell—you sell hunting knives. This looks like it came from Woolworth's." And he dismissed Johnny as a witness, saying, "I don't want to see you in this court testifying never again." Johnny was lucky he got off; he used to sell even machetes and switchblades against the law. But, he must have been about eighty years old even then.

". . . No, I didn't have no real lawyer, not my lawyer anyway. He was court-appointed, and he was bucking for power. Everybody he defended got convicted. Now he is the district attorney. They didn't have nothing on me that would stick, but the lawyer put in a plea bargain for second degree. So I done sixteen years time and am on parole for the rest of my life."

How much of Mr. Sykes's story is correct is unknown. His account, however, illustrates a frequent objection to plea bargaining—that it can be used to convict a suspect when the evidence appears to be insufficient to secure a conviction.

Excerpted from an interview with a paroled offender by one of the authors (Markson 1987). All names and specific identifying information have been changed.

---

systems. Not only is there a separate system for adults and one for juveniles, but thre is also one set of courts for federal offenses and another one for violations of state laws. And, as noted earlier, there are civil as well as criminal wrongs. In addition, each system has lower and higher courts, with the latter hearing appeals from the former, and above all the layers and separate systems, sits the Supreme Court that can hear appeals from all the lower benches if a constitutional issue or federal/state conflict is involved. The very complexity of the system, while often a source of frustration and annoyance, is designed to ensure that the scales of justice are not overbalanced by the state.

PROCESSING THE CRIMINAL

Just as the judicial system is complex, so is processing the person accused of a crime. At every step in the process, decisions are made that influence the fate of the suspect. For example, blacks arrested for homicide are more likely to be charged with first-degree murder when the victim was white than are either blacks or whites arrested for the murder of someone of the same race (Radelet 1981). After being arrested and charged with a crime, the suspect who cannot afford bail money goes to jail to await trial. During this time, the accused might be advised to plea-bargain ("cop a plea"), that is, plead guilty to a

Plea bargaining is an agreement between the prosecution and the accused to reduce the charges if the defendant pleads guilty.

lesser charge. *Plea bargaining,* an agreement between the prosecution and the accused to reduce the charges if the defendant pleads guilty, is very controversial. Its critics claim that it is used to the disadvantage of the poor and the uneducated. Its supporters claim that it is better than having to release a suspect when the evidence is not strong enough for conviction on the more serious charge. By pleading to a lesser charge, the accused is promised a lighter sentence; the prosecutors can clear cases and secure convictions, which indicate success in controlling crime; and the public is spared the costs of a trial.

What determines the type of sentence given to an offender? Although the range of penalties for each crime is set by law, judges have some flexibility. Public demands for fixed and firm penalties are often opposed by criminologists who feel that they will lead to greater inequalities in the system. It has also been noted that judges with few choices in sentencing are likely to send people to prison rather than to use probation, parole, or order victim restitution (Nagel 1980).

Traditionally, judges have been given considerable leeway in sentencing, including open-ended or indeterminate sentences (three to six years, for example) with parole boards responsible for deciding an offender's actual release date. Within recent years, however, this system has been attacked as inconsistent and unfair. Critics claim that both social class and race, for example, affected sentencing so that poor people and blacks are more likely than others to receive stiffer sentences for similar crimes (Kleck 1981, Unnever 1981). And, among both males and females, blacks are more likely than whites to be in prison on any given day as well as ever to serve a prison sentence in their lifetime (Bureau of Justice 1985). It is also worth keeping in mind the differential application of penalties according to other status characteristics of the offender. For example, although 1,027 corporate executives were tried during 1955–1975, only 5 percent received a prison sentence (Clinard and Yeager 1980). And even when such offenders serve time, they are likely to be sent to the so-called country-club prisons, designed for low-risk inmates. Justice may be blind, but she has an excellent sense for wealth, power, and prestige differences.

In contrast, more conservative critics argue that sentences are too short and that parole boards released prisoners too early. As a result, some states now have set determinate or fixed sentences for certain types of crimes. Proponents of determinate sentencing believe that fixed penalties will reduce racial, social-class, and geographic disparities and may also make penalties stiffer. Critics of determinate sentencing have charged that both judges and attorneys will avoid harsher sentences by turning to plea bargaining, thus letting the offender off with a lesser charge.

PUNISHMENTS AND CRIME

Will harsher penalties reduce the volume of criminal activity in the United States? In 1985, the *National Crime Survey* estimated that 22 million American households had experienced rape, robbery, assault, burglary, or theft. Add another million or more white-collar crimes and an uncountable number of crimes without victims, and you can see that we could be talking about over 30 million or one-third of American households. Yet, in the same year about 245,000 new inmates entered our prison system.

Clearly, if only 1 percent of criminal acts lead to imprisonment, the chances of avoiding arrest and conviction are very high. Even if each prisoner received an

What do you think is going through the minds of these inmates? (© Jean Gaumy/Magnum)

extra-heavy sentence, crime would still pay because the risks of *any* punishment are so slim. As we have seen, the vast majority of crimes go unreported; of reported crimes, perhaps 85 percent are unsolved. Of the 15 percent of "alleged perpetrators" arrested, most have their charges dismissed or reduced through plea bargaining, and others are released under probation (Anderson 1985). For every 100 arrests, an average of four cases go to trial, and about 30 percent of these result in an acquittal (*Justice Facts, 1985,* p. 15). And for every 100 persons sentenced, only seventy-one spend any time in jail or prison. The twenty-six persons in jails serve an average sentence of nine months; and the forty-five sent to prison serve an average sentence of under seven years (*Ibid,* p. 23).

Yet, when it comes to allocating money for the criminal justice system, most of the public and their legislators favor harsher sentences and building more jail cells. Even if the amount spent on prisons were to double, however, this would represent, at best, locking up another 1 or 2 percent of all possible criminals. The most logical conclusion is that crime would not be significantly reduced by building more prisons or passing laws that increase criminal penalties. According to the director of the Bureau of Justice Statistics, ". . . even with the recent increases in prison populations, the probability of a criminal being sent to prison may not have been as high in 1985 as it was in 1960" (*New York Times,* May 11, 1987, p. A13). Investing money in police departments, the courts, the district attorney's office, and probation officers would probably bring a far greater reduction in the volume of crime.

In the past, the single most important factor in determining the size of a prison population has been the number of cells available: the more cells available, the more people sentenced to prison (Nagel 1980). Since 1979, with the opening of 138 new state prisons and renovation and expansion of numerous others, nearly 5.4 million square feet of state prison space have been added. Not surprisingly, given both an increase in determinate sentencing, in prison space, and in public pressure for longer prison terms, the inmate population has grown. By 1984, the total increase in prison space (29 percent) had been exceeded by a 45 percent growth in

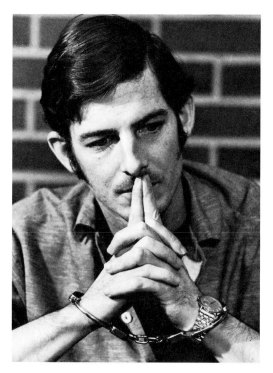

This man, John Spenkelink, was executed on death row in Florida. As more inmates await this fate, the controversy over the death penalty continues. Is it "an eye for an eye" or is it deterrence? (© Ken Hawkins/SYGMA)

the number of prisoners (Bureau of Justice Statistics 1986). Overcrowding was greatest in prisons in Southern and Western states—areas where tax dollars for construction of new penal facilities is least likely to be supported by taxpayers.

THE DEBATE OVER THE DEATH PENALTY

Throughout human history, some deviance has been considered so disruptive of social order that the offenders have been banished or executed. *Capital punishment* is another term for the death penalty (from the Latin *capo,* head). Until 1967, in the United States, capital punishment, by firing squad, hanging, or the electric chair, was an accepted part of our criminal justice system. In 1967, the Supreme Court heard a challenge to the death penalty on the grounds that it was (1) "cruel and unusual punishment" and therefore forbidden by the Eighth Amendment to the Constitution, and also (2) that because the execution rate for black offenders was

Capital punishment is another term for the death penalty.

ten times higher than that for whites, the "equal protection" clause of the Eighteenth Amendment was violated. The Court did not rule on the cruel and unusual punishment issue, but did ban capital punishment in existing cases because it was being applied in an arbitrary manner. The Court thus left open the possibility of reinstating the death penalty if the states could set uniform standards and safeguards against unfairness.

In the following years, one state after another enacted death-penalty legislation designed to meet the Court's test of fairness. But no executions took place until after 1976, when the Court upheld the revised legislation in three separate cases, and capital punishment was once more the law of the land. As you can see in Figure 16-1, the number of death-row inmates began a steep rise, and although the first execution did not take place until 1983, after lengthy appeals, eighteen people

were put to death in 1985, a figure that has also risen sharply each year since. Close to forty states now have capital punishment statutes and over 1600 persons, almost all men and all convicted of murder, are under sentence of death. The states with the greatest number of inmates on death row are Florida (259), Texas (242), California (195), Georgia (109), and Illinois (103) (*New York Times,* April 23, 1987, B12).

The last major challenge to the death penalty was turned back by the Supreme Court, on a five-to-four vote, in early 1987. In this case, the challengers once more presented social science data demonstrating that the death penalty was still being applied differently according to the race of the murdered person. After controlling for all other variables, the researchers found that a defendant who killed a white was 4.3 times more likely to be sentenced to death than was a person who killed a black, and the odds for execution rose

Figure 16-1
Source: Bureau of Justice Statistics, "Capital Punishment, 1985," October 1986, p. 2; NAACP, Legal Defense Fund, July 9, 1987.

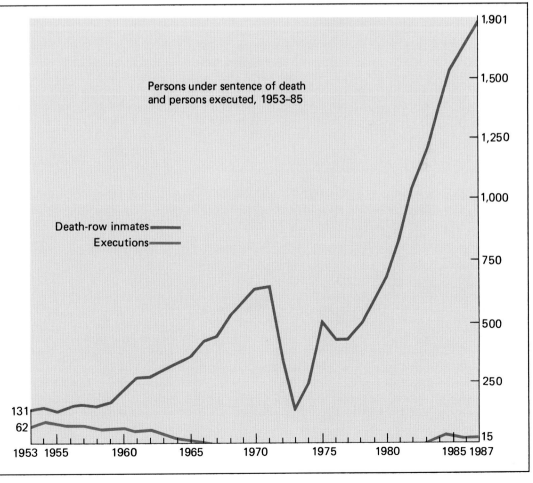

Persons under sentence of death and persons executed, 1953–85

Death-row inmates
Executions

only slightly higher if it was a black who murdered the white (Baldus et al. 1987). Clearly, white lives are more valued than black ones. Although the Court acknowledged the validity of the statistics, five justices held that the data did not prove an intent to discriminate.

It appears, then, that the death penalty is here to stay for the near future. Only the Union of South Africa, among all modern industrial nations, has joined us in approving capital punishment. And the American public does approve by an overwhelming margin—over 80 percent in recent polls. Popular support for the death penalty is based on two beliefs: (1) that it deters crime; and (2) that the state is justified in seeking retribution for a serious crime.

DETERRENCE. Reported increases in crime rates and widespread public fear have revived the belief that the harshness of a penalty will deter potential criminals or will ensure that one person, at least, will never commit another crime.

Opponents of the death penalty are quick to note that evidence to support the deterrence thesis is less than convincing. Indeed, most studies show no statistically significant murder-rate reduction due to use of capital punishment (Bailey 1980, Bowers et al. 1984). Moreover, because most murders are crimes of passion committed against members of one's own family or friends, it is difficult to estimate how many would have been avoided through rational calculation about the punishment. According to one survey, popular support for capital punishment is based more on general political and social attitudes and beliefs than on responses to crime-related concerns or experiences (Tyler and Weber 1982).

RETRIBUTION. People who support retribution view executions as a visible means of redressing (balancing out) a social wrong. Somehow, the members of a society feel avenged when they can see that a crime has not gone unpunished, regardless of whether the punishment has a deterrent effect on other would-be criminals. In other words, imprisonment or the death penalty is not used to control the wrongdoer as much as to satisfy the general public's desire for retribution. This view enlarges on Durkheim's point that punishment reaffirms the moral norms of the community. It solidifies the group against the threat of evil, and it reaffirms

the essential virtue of those who do not need to use violence to secure success.

Nonetheless, there are some people, such as sociologist Michael Radelet, who continue to argue that executions in the United States are cruel and unusual punishment, no more effective than imprisonment, and applied arbitrarily.

PRISONS AND JAILS

Close to 1.5 percent of the adult population of the United States is under some form of supervision by the criminal justice system. The great majority—two-thirds—are in the community under probation. Close to 550,000 are in state or federal prisons; another 120,000 are serving their short-term sentences in local jails; and 260,000 are out of prison on parole (Bureau of Justice Statistics, 1986, 1987). These numbers are all-time highs and represent a political response to the public perception that crime is out of control. As we have seen, however, crime rates were already on a downward path due to the aging of Baby Boom cohorts. Nonetheless, America's jails and prisons are now overflowing with inmates.

The history of prisons or incarceration (from the Latin "to place behind walls") in America has been influenced by two opposing philosophies, both of which can be derived from our Protestant value system: *rehabilitation* and *punishment*. To rehabilitate means to return to a previous state, and is based on a belief in the power of repentance and salvation. Punishment rests on the dual assumptions that evil must be painfully removed from the sinner and that victims must be avenged. As it is almost impossible to punish and rehabilitate at the same time, the meaning of incarceration in our society has fluctuated between these two principles. At this moment, the public appears to believe that rehabilitation is a form of "coddling," and that the solution to crime is to put people in prison and "throw away the key." Hence, a prison population that is growing at a faster rate than the population as a whole, and also at a faster rate than the public is willing to spend tax monies to house and supervise.

These trends have added the problems of overcrowding and underfunding to the tensions that are an inevitable part of any *total institution*.

Rehabilitation means restoration to a former state of health.

Studying the Death Penalty

Michael L. Radelet

Michael L. Radelet is currently an associate professor of sociology at the University of Florida. He is the author of a dozen major studies on the death penalty, including one which documents over 300 cases in which people convicted of homicide were later found to be innocent (Stanford Law Review, 1987).

In 1979, when I arrived in Florida after seven years of studying medical sociology, I had no interest in or knowledge of the death penalty. Nor did I have any strong opinions about it. Like other college students, I had some general plans for the future, but futures seem to be constructed by compromises between our plans and the opportunities that present themselves. When I learned that a Jacksonville legal secretary needed a sociologist to analyze data she had collected and to ascertain if the death penalty was being applied with a racial bias, I decided to do it simply because it sounded quick and easy—exactly what new professors need if they hope to earn tenure. In those days, I was naive; I thought the results might show no racial disparities, and made sure that everyone knew that I would publish my findings no matter what they were.

One of the strongest attractions of sociology is that through it one gets to learn about some very interesting groups. People on death row are frequently nasty and dangerous, but they all share one positive trait: they are fascinating. As I read more about capital punishment, and being sensitive to being called an ivory-tower intellectual, I began to write to one of the men on death row. Later I visited him, and did so twenty more times before he killed himself a year later. For the next four years, I paid monthly visits to another condemned inmate; he was executed in

1985. Through these visits I got to know dozens of condemned men and their families. In many respects, my visits to the prison taught me more than my visits to the library.

More than anything else, it was these families that made me take a stand opposing the death penalty (Radelet et al. 1983). Their agony, coupled with the data emerging from my research that showed racial bias in the administration of the death penalty (Radelet 1981), far outweighed in my mind any justifications for the penalty voiced by its supporters. Prisoners suffer, and given that in most states the alternative to the death penalty is life imprisonment without parole, eliminating the death penalty will not mean that its potential victims will not suffer. As I see it, the death penalty usually injures the prisoner's family more than the prisoner himself. I cannot believe that the only thing we as a society can do for the families of homicide victims is to double the number of innocent families who mourn the loss of a loved one.

Given this perspective, my involvement in capital punishment quickly grew beyond the purely academic. In the last few years I have had to sprinkle the ashes of one dead inmate in Africa, deliver the worldly goods of another to his family in Canada, store the inherited possessions of a couple more in my closets, and sit with a few families while their loved one was meeting his maker. Holding the hands of mothers as their sons are being executed and being the recipient of bulk discounts at local funeral homes has strengthened my resolve to learn more and to teach others about this issue. Often it is depressing work, but I am convinced that it would be far more difficult to sit and watch in passive silence.

Does publicly standing opposed to

the death penalty violate ethical principles about "objectivity"? As I see it, objectivity is not the same as neutrality, and *not* to shout out at what one sees as a moral outrage is in itself a moral outrage. After all, when I lecture about racism in my sociology courses, I do not feel obliged to offer equal time to the Ku Klux Klan. Sociologists need to have informed perspectives, but these perspectives need not be neutral.

Others, of course, will see things differently. That, too, is part of the excitement that sociology has to offer. It seems to me that on an issue like capital punishment, one's position, pro or con, is less important than simply taking a stand, learning how to defend it, and respecting the opinions of those who differ. What turns me off are those who are apathetic or who take a position without bothering to learn much about it.

Sociology is a discipline that teaches, among other things, compassion for the powerless. There are an endless number of issues these days in which compassionate people can become involved: women's rights, institutional racism, abortion, child abuse, drug abuse, crime and prisons, unwanted pregnancies, nuclear war and energy, and even the death penalty, to name a few. Sociology can teach compassion for those less fortunate, the value of making a commitment to act to change things, and the competence to make one's voice heard—no matter what stand on what issue one chooses to take.

SOURCES: Radelet, Michael L. "Racial Characteristics and the Imposition of the Death Penalty," *American Sociological Review* 46(1981): 918–927; Radelet, Michael L., Margaret Vandiver, and Felix M. Berardo, "Families, Prisons, and Men with Death Sentences: The Human Impact of Structured Uncertainty," *Journal of Family Issues,* 4(1983): 593–612.

Total institutions, such as prisons and jails, control and monitor all aspects of inmates' lives.

Prisons as Total Institutions.

Prisons and jails are *total institutions* (Goffman 1961) in which diverse human needs are handled by a bureaucratic organization that promotes group living. Prisons and jails have certain features in common with military bases, monasteries, mental hospitals, and nursing homes, which are also total institutions. As Goffman defined it, a total institution is a place where there is a breakdown of the barriers that usually separate sleep, work, and play. Ordinarily, these activities are carried out in different places, with different role partners, and under different authorities. In the total institution, all aspects of life are conducted under the same authority and in the same physical location. Moreover, the total institution encourages batch living, where each person must carry out his or her activities in the presence of others, where everyone is required to do the same thing, and where all activities are closely scheduled and predictable, based on the needs of the institution and its staff. Inmates are stripped of their preprison identities: They are put in uniforms, shaved (if they are males), given a number, and subjected to other ceremonies of degradation and depersonalization.

Although total institutions may be classified according to their purpose—the protection of the inept, the isolation of dangerous persons, the rehabilitation of the ill, and so forth—they are all designed to resocialize and change people and their sense of themselves (Goffman 1961). Every total institution is a *minisociety* for its residents, and prisons are no exception. Although there is immense variety among prisons, ranging from the maximum-security walled prison of Sing Sing to the minimum-security prison farm of Chino, Calif., all share certain characteristics: (1) restriction of personal freedom; (2) limited choice of work; (3) impersonality; (4) social distance between prisoners and prison officers and guards; and (5) organization as primarily a single-sex setting.

These structural aspects of the prison give rise to a subculture among inmates that is very different from that of the prison personnel. The subculture of prisoners includes such rules for behavior as playing it cool, doing one's own time, not getting involved, being tough, never informing on fellow inmates, and not sympathizing with officials or accepting their word. Inmates construct a definition of the situation that rationalizes their conduct and reinforces the values of their subculture.

Both staff and inmates must adjust to the requirements of institutional order. Prison norms are, however, inconsistent with rehabilitation, for the discomforts and irritations of the present occupy the almost exclusive attention of everyone (Conrad 1973). Very few can be resocialized to the norms of straight society because exposure to prison norms limits both the opportunity to learn skills for legitimate success in the outside world and contact with their families.

Prison Conditions Today.

With the current overcrowding of U.S. prisons, few funds can be devoted to educational and job-training programs, even if rehabilitation was a popular concept. What the inmates do learn are definitions of the situation that are not favorable to success in the community, to which all but a few return, and usually within two years. Without skills to help them become stable citizens, half will be back in prison at some time in their lives. The term used to describe repeat offenders is *recidivist,* literally, "one who has fallen again"—a concept that perfectly evokes our Puritan past.

Lack of privacy, the brutality of guards and other inmates, loss of contact with families, boredom, poor food and medi-

About 530,000 Americans are in state and federal prisons today. Can you picture yourself in an 8 ft. × 8 ft. space for most of the day, month after month, year after year? (© R. Benyas/Black Star)

cal care, and persistent daily discomforts have turned many American prisons into "jungles."

What makes conditions in prison so difficult? Are prison officials brutal by nature? Or is it the prisoners themselves who, by their past histories, have shown that they need to be restrained with harsh measures? Both of these questions are based on the belief that there is a tendency, or *predisposition,* among certain persons to act in certain ways. An alternative approach is the *situational view;* it is the social situation and the particular statuses and roles assigned to persons that produce certain kinds of behavior. In Chapter 4, we described the experiment in which young, mentally healthy male volunteers, all similar in personality traits and attitudes, were randomly assigned the role of prisoner or guard. The experiment had to be halted within a week because of emotional breakdowns among the "prisoners" and cruel behavior among the "guards." The mock prison experiment provides insight into the real world of the prison. One's status in the social structure of the prison—prisoner or guard—influences one's behavior and one's beliefs about oneself and others.

Against the background of the mock prison experiment, such events as prison riots become more understandable. One of the most savage prison riots in U.S. history occurred in the New Mexico State Penitentiary in 1980, leaving thirty-three inmates dead and eighty injured, as well as $82 million worth of damage to the prison. As analyzed by Useem (1985) the New Mexico riot illustrates how structural characteristics affect inmate and guard behavior. Between 1970 and 1975, the prison had a rehabilitation strategy based on job training and employment placement. In 1975, funds for these activities were cut back in favor of increasing the inmate population. Inmate violence increased as the men felt cheated by the authorities. With over 1100 men in space designed for 850, tempers flared, and the prisoners split into warring subgroups. The custodial staff could not maintain control. Unable to vent their rage outward, the inmates turned on one another.

Prison violence will undoubtedly increase as overcrowding continues. According to the Bureau of Justice (1986), by 1984 the average amount of living space per inmate in state prisons was under sixty square feet—to which the prisoner was confined for an average of eleven hours per day. To get a feel for this type of confinement, walk off a square with eight feet on either side, put chalk marks on the floor and stay within those lines for one entire day. Perhaps more difficult would be to live in a space three times larger, but with two other people there every moment.

There are a number of solutions to overcrowding. Some, such as additional smaller and more secure prisons, are enormously expensive to build and staff, and probably not very cost effective in reducing recidivism. Other alternatives are much less expensive but unlikely to meet public demand for harsh punishment. Some of these, used successfully in Europe, include (1) community-based programs for nondangerous offenders; (2) small correctional facilities where inmates can gain work experience and income from which taxes can be deducted to pay the cost of incarceration; (3) homelike surroundings that the inmates can decorate as they choose, and where they can wear civilian clothing and engage in activities that reinforce a noncriminal identity; (4) short-term visits home or extended visiting from relatives, particularly wives and children.

At the moment, the major solution to overcrowding has been the courts, where in one state after another judges have decided that current conditions represent unsafe as well as cruel and unusual punishment. Under court orders to reduce the prison population immediately, state authorities have freed inmates close to their release date and placed the less dangerous on parole. Although the same results could have been accomplished by lighter sentences at the beginning, it would be politically impossible at this time.

Jails. Local jails house three different populations. Some are people being held between arrest and arraignment (having a judge decide whether or not the accused should be held for trial); others are awaiting trial (usually only people unable to raise bail money), or on trial; and the remainder are convicted persons serving terms of under one year or waiting to be transferred to a prison.

From a sociological point of view, the jail, even more than the prison, demon-

> The **predispositional view** assumes that there is a tendency among certain persons to act in certain ways.
>
> The **situational view** assumes that the social situation and statuses and roles assigned to persons produce certain kinds of behavior.

strates the subtle uses of the criminal justice system as an agency of social control, because most of its inmates have not yet been convicted of any crime. Rather, many are there because they offend the public's sense of appropriate behavior (Irwin 1985). They have drunk too much, been rowdy in public, talked back to a police officer, or were suspected of doing drugs or selling sex. In addition, the question of who remains in jail and who is sent home with a promise to appear in court is usually answered on the basis of social status and resources.

Summary

Every society has rules that are considered so important to social order that their violation is severely sanctioned. These laws may reflect the consensus of the group or the interests of the powerful. In the United States, most attention has been paid to street crime because it is associated with violence and the possibility of physical harm. We discuss how such crimes are measured and the risks of being victimized. In addition, recent changes in patterns of female crime and organized crime are explored.

Not all violations of the criminal law take place on the streets. In terms of the money involved and the lives touched, crime in the suites—white-collar and organizational crime—is far more widespread in America than is street crime. Business scams, corporate greed, and government/industry corruption are increasingly publicized although criminal penalties remain lighter for white-collar than for street criminals. In addition, crimes without victims provide opportunities for corruption of people in all social statuses.

The chapter deals with problems of police work and law enforcement, including the judicial system and its complexity. Questions of punishment and crime arise in the context of criminal sentencing in general and the death penalty in particular. Harsher sentences appear to have less effect on the crime rate than does the probability of being caught. In the course of the judicial process, most offenders avoid being brought to trial, and very few are ultimately sentenced to prison. Prison life is extremely dehumanizing and most ex-convicts eventually return to a life of crime. Overcrowding and prison violence will continue as long as we insist on "locking 'em up" without providing a range of educational and resocializing experiences that will ease the transition to living in the community.

Suggested Readings

ARCHER, DANE, and ROSEMARY GARTNER. *Violence and Crime in Cross-National Perspective*. New Haven: Yale University Press, 1984. A detailed analysis of crime and violence in 110 countries. This cross-cultural data base compares different categories of crime, e. g. homicide, assault, robbery, theft, and rape.

GEIS, GILBERT. *On White-Collar Crime*. Lexington, Mass: Lexington Books, 1982. These twelve papers discuss and analyze the various aspects of white-collar crime, as well as corporate power, and the abuse of power.

HANSON, BILL, et al., eds. *Life with Heroin: Voices from the Inner City*. Lexington, Mass.: Lexington Books, 1985. An interesting study of heroin addicts whose lives and patterns of drug use do not fit the stereotypes generally presented in the media.

HEIDONSOHN, FRANCES. *Women and Crime: The Life of the Female Offender*. New York: New York University Press, 1985. An important contribution to the understanding of female offenders. This book discusses the self-images of these women, their treatment within the legal system, and the explanations offered to explain their behavior.

JACKSON, GEORGE. *Soledad Brother: The Prison Letters of George Jackson*. New York: Coward-McCann, 1970. This dramatic firsthand account illuminates the experiences of those who defy the agents of law enforcement.

MAEDER, THOMAS. *Crime and Madness: the Origins and Evolution of the Insanity Defense*. New York: Harper & Row, 1985. An historical study of the insanity defense and its importance to criminal law.

MANN, KENNETH. *Defending White Collar Crime: A Portrait of Attorneys at Work.* New Haven: Yale University Press, 1985. A detailed account of American white-collar criminal attorneys and the critical importance of information control in defense of their clients.

QUINNEY, RICHARD. *Class, State and Crime: On the Theory and Practice of Criminal Justice,* 2nd ed. New York: Longman, 1980. A conflict-perspective approach to the study of crime by a leading sociologist.

REIMAN, JEFFREY H. *The Rich Get Richer and the Poor Get Prison,* 2nd ed. New York: John Wiley & Sons, 1984. Using a conflict perspective, this book analyzes the differences in the treatment of defendants from different classes.

Part V
Contemporary Issues

Part V covers a range of issues that vitally affect the quality of life in our society and the entire world. In Chapter 17 we examine the topics of *health* and *health care*. The social aspects of health and health care compose a relatively new and extremely active field of sociological study. Illness and wellness are socially structured, as is the organization and distribution of health-care facilities.

The dynamics of *population* growth and distribution are explored in Chapter 18. The sheer number of people in any society, as well as their distribution by gender and age, have implications for individual lives and for the stability of the society as a whole.

The development of cities, the residential dispersion of our population, and the particular conditions of *urban, suburban,* and *rural life* in America today are the subject matter of Chapter 19. Much has been written recently about the "crisis of the cities" and the negative features of urbanization, but cities remain vital centers of modern societies. The future of the American city is important to all of us—whether we live in cities, suburbs, or rural areas.

The last chapter in this section considers the new scholarship on *popular culture.* We pay special attention to the role of the mass media in creating reality and setting the agenda of social issues; to popular music as a manifestation of important social trends; and to the place of sports in American culture.

17

Health, Illness, and the Health-Care System

WHAT does sociology have to do with questions of health and medical treatment? Aren't people healthy or ill depending on biological factors, and isn't the practice of medicine based on hard scientific evidence? Quite the opposite. As you will see, definitions of health and illness, the distribution of diseases, questions of treatment and access to health care, and the boundaries of health professions—all are strongly influenced by culture and social structure. Indeed, so deeply are health issues affected by the variables used in sociological analysis that medical sociology is today the largest subfield in American sociology.

Take, for example, some of the leading news stories of recent years: AIDS, surrogate motherhood, genetic experimentation, organ transplants, chemical warfare, the cost of health care, reproductive rights, teen suicide, and definitions of death. Each of these stories is as much a sociological as a medical phenomenon. And each also raises moral or ethical concerns that cannot be settled by an appeal to "impartial" science.

Patterns of health and disease vary from one society to another, from one historical era to another, and by the level of economic and technological development. Modern industrialism, like any other major change in the mode of subsistence, introduced both new and unforeseen medical problems as well as the means of treating various disorders.

For example, the rapid urbanization of nineteenth century London led to inadequate sanitation and polluted water supplies causing a major cholera epidemic that killed large numbers of city dwellers. Today, the threats are less immediately obvious. Soldiers involved in atomic bomb tests during World War II are believed to be at higher than average risk of developing cancer many decades later, as are Vietnam veterans who were exposed to Agent Orange. The widespread use of chemicals such as dioxin in pesticides and herbicides has been linked to cancer, miscarriages, and birth defects in civilian populations.

Thus, although both health and illness are simple words, they have different meanings for different people in different time periods and societies. Both health and illness are culturally and socially defined. That is, what may be considered normal or healthy by one society may be viewed as abnormal by another. This is not to say that disease is not real or that particular causes of illness cannot be identified. Rather, members of a society tend to develop norms about whether a specific condition is to be treated as an illness or as a normal part of life. In some societies, for example, people with epilepsy have been regarded as possessed with magical powers; in others, as cursed by God; and in today's society, as suffering from a treatable medical disorder. Moreover, depending on the society, healers can be priests of the gods, lawmakers, magicians, pharmacists, barbers, or scientifically trained physicians.

Yet all diseases share certain undesirable results inasmuch as they may be personally painful, interfere with usual role performance, or both. In every known society, the definition of health problems and responses to them have been organized, although in various ways. More-

over, some diseases are culturally defined as respectable, e.g., heart disease, or as disreputable, e.g., herpes. This chapter will focus on the definitions and distribution of health and illness and upon the organized social responses to control disease that have developed in American society.

Patterns of Health and Illness

Although many indicators of the quality of life among people in preindustrial, industrial, and postindustrial societies have been developed, one of the most important is the health status of the population. Health is closely linked not only to the level of industrial development of a country but also to the age and sex composition of its people and to the distribution of wealth, power, and prestige. Diseases and illness, including mental illness, are not distributed in the population at random. Rather, they are unevenly distributed by age, sex, social class, place of residence, race, ethnicity, occupation, and habits such as smoking and drinking.

SOCIAL EPIDEMIOLOGY

The study of the patterns of the occurrence of specific diseases, disabilities, and defects within a population is known as *epidemiology.* Social epidemiologists are particularly concerned with the distribution of illness in a social context, that is, how life-styles relate to the occurrence of diseases. Social epidemiologists analyze the relationships among a specific disease agent (such as bacteria or viruses), the individual, and the social and physical environment. For example, why is black-lung disease most prevalent among miners, cancer among asbestos workers, and drug addiction among doctors and nurses?

Epidemiological studies have increased our knowledge of the patterns of both illness and health and have explained the differing rates of illness within a population. For example, in 1854, a London physician, John Snow, observed that there were sharp differences in the numbers of people who contracted cholera in the different districts of the city. Although the

Epidemiology is the study of the patterns of occurrence of illness in a population.

cause of the disease was unknown, he was able to trace the epidemic to the sources from which those people with the highest incidence of plague got their water. When these water sources were closed down, the plague was halted.

More complex epidemiological studies have illuminated the factors influencing contagion and disease resistance. Tuberculosis, for example, is due to a particular bacterium, but its contagiousness has been found to depend not only on exposure to the germ but on general social conditions and the state of health of the person who has been exposed. The rise of the Industrial Revolution and increased migration from rural to urban locales produced dramatic changes in life-styles such as overcrowding, close physical contact among many people, poor hygiene, malnutrition, and bad sanitation. Vast increases in the numbers of people contracting and dying of tuberculosis soon followed. The identification of the social factors associated with tuberculosis led to their correction, and the disease began to disappear as a major killer. Changes in life-style were thus directly involved in both the rise and the decline of this disease.

Incidence and Prevalence of Diseases.

When John Snow charted the number of new cases of cholera in London, he used one of the major tools of epidemiology: *incidence rates.* An incidence rate describes the number of *new* cases of a disease that occur within a specific population during a stated time period. Incidence measures give us a picture of how new cases are distributed in the population, and they provide a basis for studying the origins of a disease. By knowing how a disease first occurs among a particular group of people and who contracts the illness, we can find clues about its occurrence.

The second major tool used by epidemiologists in studying disease is *prevalence rate.* The prevalence rate describes *all* known cases of a disease, regardless of when they began, in a particular population within a specified time. Prevalence rates reflect the total amount of disease present in a particular population at a particular time, whereas incidence rates refer only to the new cases observed in a specific time period. Measures of prevalence are most useful in revealing the extent of various health problems so that provision of health care can be planned.

The **incidence rate** is the number of new cases of a disease within a population during a stated time period.

The **prevalence rate** is the number of all the known cases of a disease in a population, regardless of when they began.

They are not very useful in the study of the causes of disease.

An example may clarify the distinction between incidence and prevalence rates. Let us assume that we are interested in the frequency of cancer resulting from job-related exposure to radiation. If we looked at the incidence rates, our figure would probably be rather low because of increased safeguards in the industries that use radioactive materials. Prevalence rates would yield a higher figure because many people were exposed in the past to levels of radiation that were far greater than those considered permissible today. Knowledge of the prevalence rate would give us an idea of the magnitude of the problem and would help us to plan cancer-treatment facilities. Knowledge of the incidence rate for various years would enable us to assess whether present industrial safeguards have successfully reduced or eliminated radiation-related cancers. It would also improve projections for the future.

THE SOCIAL DISTRIBUTION OF ILLNESS

The four basic factors in social epidemiological research are age, sex, race and ethnicity, and social-class membership. Each of these is related to differences among people in their health, illness, and death rates among subgroups.

Age. The most striking fact about age in the United States and other industrialized nations is the great increase in life expectancy at birth that has occurred during this century. *Life expectancy* at birth is the average number of years that a person can expect to live (see also Chapters 9 and 16). In 1900, the average number of years that an American could expect to live was forty-seven; by 1986, this number had risen to seventy-five. This increase has been influenced by significant improvements in living and work conditions, as well as in diet and sanitation. Improved medical technology, such as antibiotics and new surgical techniques, have also been important, although to a lesser extent than major advances in public health.

The net result of increased life expectancy is that most people in industrialized nations today die not from infectious diseases such as tuberculosis, the number two killer in 1900, but from chronic (long-term, irreversible) diseases, most of which

Life expectancy is the average number of years a person can expect to live.

The life expectancy of this little girl is much greater than that of her grandmother. What social factors are likely to affect her life expectancy? (© William U. Harris)

are neither infectious nor contagious. Children under the age of six are most likely to die of acute infectious diseases, adolescents and young adults as a result of accidents, homicide, and suicide, and older people of chronic illnesses. Table 17-1 summarizes the major causes of death in the United States in 1900 and in 1986. As you can see from the table, chronic diseases have almost replaced infections as leading causes of death.

TABLE 17-1   The five major causes of death in the United States, 1900 and 1986, ranked from highest to lowest

1900	1986
1. Pneumonia and influenza	1. Heart diseases
2. Tuberculosis	2. Cancer
3. Gastroenteritis	3. Stroke and related disorders
4. Heart diseases	4. Accidents
5. Stroke and related disorders	5. Pneumonia and influenza

SOURCE: National Center for Health Statistics, *Monthly Vital Statistics Report,* Vol. 36, No. 1, April 29, 1987, p. 8–9

It is estimated that half of the American population today suffers from some form of chronic illness, 11 percent of whom are limited in some major activity (Institute of Medicine/National Research Council, 1985). Although respiratory problems and headaches are the most common acute complaints of both younger and older adults, we tend to develop chronic diseases as we age (Verbrugge 1986). It is thus not surprising that older people are more likely than the young to develop heart diseases, arthritis, declines in vision and hearing, and to be more disabled by such difficulties. Almost four in ten people sixty-five and over experience some limitation in ability to work, keep house, or engage in other major activities, as compared to slightly more than two in ten people aged forty-five to sixty-four, and less than one in ten of those under age forty-four (Institute of Medicine/National Research Council, 1985). When elders are ill, they are likely to require more medical care, and when hospitalized, to stay there longer than do younger patients (Verbrugge 1986).

Yet old age, as you will recall from Chapter 9, is not inevitably linked with poor health. Nor is age itself an indicator of poor health. The frequency with which people report daily health problems does not increase dramatically with age. According to national health surveys, 69 percent of elderly American men and 70 percent of elderly American women report good to excellent health compared to 79 percent of middle-aged men and 78 percent of middle-aged women (Verbrugge 1986). In a study conducted by one of the authors, some very old inner-city, low-income elderly were apparently in better health than people fifteen years their junior. Rather than age, the number of medications received (a rough indicator of severity of illness) and living in public housing (an indicator of low income) were associated with frequent illness requiring medical attention (Markson et al. 1984). Some very old people—including several over 100 years old—survived precisely because of their basic good health.

Surprisingly, although the United States currently spends more of its domestic gross national product (GNP) on health than any other industrialized nation, Americans do not have as long an average life expectancy at birth as do people in other industrialized nations. Although

Age alone is no reason to expect illness. An active life-style and positive attitude help maintain health. But how may life-style and attitude be affected by cultural definitions of aging in our society? (© Rae Russell)

there is some relationship between the number of people per physician and life expectancy, this ratio alone does not explain the differences. The Dutch, the Swedes, and the Australians have a longer life expectancy at birth than do Americans, although the number of people per physician is about the same in all four nations. And the Japanese, who have about 200 people more per physician than Americans, can expect to live on the average two years longer. How can these differences be explained? The answer lies with the organization, access, and cost of health care, which are discussed later in this chapter.

Sex. The life expectancy of females in industrialized societies is much higher than that of males—about eight years in the United States today. The percentage of males dying at any age is greater than the percentage of females, for all causes except diabetes. Moreover, the gap between male and female life expectancy is widening, suggesting that women have greater biological resistance to infectious and chronic diseases (Hazzard 1983). It is *not* true that men die because they work harder than women and are therefore under greater stress. Rather, males have higher death rates from conception on, and are more likely than females to develop "killer" diseases in adulthood.

Yet, a consistent finding in social epidemiology is that women have both a higher incidence and a higher prevalence of physical and mental illness than men. They are also more likely to use the services of physicians and of hospitals. Why, if women are ill more often, do they live longer?

Several explanations, linking gender roles to illness behavior, have been proposed, including the views (1) that women are more likely than men to stop work because of poor health; (2) that the traditional feminine role may have certain built-in strains that make women ill; or (3) that women have more interest in and knowledge of health and thus notice changes in the state of their bodies more quickly than men. In short, women are more likely than men to engage in illness behavior, including reporting symptoms, using health-care services, and experiencing disability or discomfort (Verbrugge 1986).

Yet there is also evidence that gender-role differences in some illness behavior are relatively unimportant (Davis 1981, Marshall et al. 1982). Rather, when the particular disease is held constant, sex plays a minor role in illness behavior. For example, among people seeking treatment for cancer, there are no sex differences regarding the stage at which women and men first report for treatment (Marshall, Gregorios, and Walsh 1982). Moreover, much of the recent research on illness has shown a direct link between women's employment status and their health. Several studies have indicated that there are higher rates of reported illness among homemakers than among women working outside the home (Nathanson 1980, Verbrugge 1981). Employed women are also less likely than homemakers to take time away from their regular activities if they do become ill and are more likely to return to normal activities sooner. Clearly, gender role and severity of illness interact to produce patterns of illness.

Race and Ethnicity. One reflection of social inequality in the United States is the difference in health among various racial and ethnic groups. Blacks, Mexican-Americans, Puerto Ricans, and Native Americans continue to have lower life expectancies than other Americans. Their poorer health is a result of a complex set of factors, including generally lower income,

464

overcrowded housing, fewer sanitary facilities, limited access to health facilities, as well as prejudice and discrimination.

Not only is their life expectancy lower, but some diseases have a higher incidence and prevalence among minority groups. For example, Native Americans, especially those living on reservations, still suffer frequently from typhoid fever, diphtheria, and other illnesses now uncommon among the general population. Indeed, Native Americans may be in the poorest health of all Americans, having not only higher rates of infections, but also more illness due to alcoholism, malnutrition, and untreated ear infections, all of which are associated with their poverty.

Mexican-Americans have a high incidence of flu, pneumonia, and tuberculosis, and blacks are more likely than whites to have pneumonia or flu. The illness experience of these minorities illustrates the complex relationships between health and life-style. Although there are a few types of illness to which certain racial or ethnic groups are connected biologically, such as Jews to Tay–Sachs disease or blacks to sickle-cell anemia, most of the illnesses found among minorities are a result of their disadvantaged economic status in the United States.

Consider the incidence of high blood pressure (hypertension), associated with stroke and heart disease. Although all its causes are not yet fully understood, high blood pressure is heightened by diets high in food fats, and by stress and anxiety. Blacks of both sexes and all ages have higher blood pressure readings and are more likely to develop heart diseases than are whites. Furthermore, low-income blacks have higher hypertension rates than do their high-income counterparts (Livingston 1985). It seems likely that poverty and poor diet, blocked social mobility, and anger and frustration play a major role in the incidence of hypertension. Coping resources may be fewer: "Lower class blacks are more likely than are middle and upper class blacks to perceive their life experiences as exceeding the resources at their disposal" (Livingston 1985, p. 173). There is, however, a small but significant percentage of hypertension among blacks not explained by their living situation, suggesting that racism itself has not only social and psychological but also physical consequences (Schnall and Kern 1986).

What of other ethnic groups in the United States? The information, although scant, suggests distinct differences in illness patterns associated with ethnicity. For example, alcoholism is low among Jews and Italian-Americans but high among Irish-Americans. Chinese- and Japanese-Americans rarely develop heart dis-

Race is a factor in high blood pressure. What aspects of the living situation of blacks contributes to hypertension? (© William U. Harris)

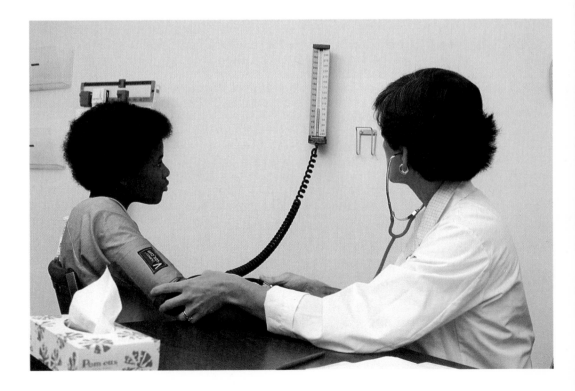

ease. Yet, Japanese-Americans die much more often from heart disease than do Japanese living in Japan. This difference is narrowing, however, as diet in Japan includes more meat and animal fats, a circumstance indicating that cultural rather than biological factors are involved.

Social Class. Social-class differences in life expectancy and illness have been observed for centuries, and a vast body of evidence indicates that those in the lower strata die younger and have more illness than those in the higher strata. For example, among every age group, a greater proportion of those below the poverty level have at least one chronic illness (Andersen 1983). Poverty, overcrowding, exposure to toxic substances, and limited access to medical care all play a part in the greater illness, greater disability, and premature death of persons in the lower socioeconomic classes (Ross and Duff 1982).

> **Lower socioeconomic status** is generally associated with poor health and shortened life expectancy.

Yet, other factors may also be important. For example, the occurrence of such stressful events as unemployment, the death of one's spouse, and divorce have been found to be associated with the onset of illness or disease. This relationship is not as simple as it first appears, however, as social supports often cushion the impact of stressful life events. Among men with high blood pressure, for example, those with a larger family support network were able to maintain a risk-reduction life-style after diagnosis and to lower their blood pressure in comparison to men without support networks, even when other factors were controlled (O'Reilly 1986). Moreover, family, friendship, and marital support networks can alter the impact of stressful life events. For example, unemployed men without strong support networks were more likely to have symptoms of physical illness, to be depressed, and to have higher levels of cholesterol (a chemical in the body associated with heart disease) than were unemployed men with close ties to family and friends (Gore 1978). Findings such as these emphasize the importance of the macro and micro effects of social-class membership on health and well-being.

But perhaps the most fascinating example of the interplay between social and medical variables is that of AIDS (Acquired Immune Deficiency Syndrome), often considered the modern equivalent of the great plagues of the past (Feldman and Johnson 1986).

SOCIAL CHARACTERISTICS OF AN EPIDEMIC: THE CASE OF AIDS

In the five years since 1979, when it was first recognized as a disease, the incidence of acquired immune deficiency syndrome (AIDS) roughly doubled every six months. By the end of 1985, it was estimated that 1 million Americans were already infected with the AIDS virus, a number that could double or triple by the end of the century. About 40 percent of these will eventually develop AIDS and die as a consequence of the failure of the immune system to resist other infections (Boffey 1986). Other estimates indicate that these projections may be low due to underreporting and failure to take into account ARC, or AIDS-related complex, a disease that is sometimes fatal itself and almost always a precursor of AIDS (*Newsweek,* Nov. 24, 1986, p. 31). Even if these other infections were treated successfully, the resistance of AIDS victims is so poor that another illness usually follows until one occurs that cannot be treated, and death results.

In the few years since AIDS has been recognized, researchers have discovered the virus that causes it, developed a test for identifying antibodies, and found a drug that seems to control some symptoms. But finding a *cure* may be more difficult, for the AIDS virus targets the entire immune system, thus making it basically unlike other conditions. Any cure must not only destroy viruses but also increase immunity.

Who is most likely to develop AIDS? Current estimates suggest that more than 90 percent of the victims will be members of the two main risk groups: homosexuals and intravenous drug users. AIDS, which is transmitted by an exchange of body fluids, can also be transmitted through conventional heterosexual sex. It *cannot* be acquired from touching a person with AIDS or from a bus or toilet seat or from food served in a restaurant. Nonetheless, AIDS victims have lost their jobs (although a 1987 Supreme Court decision ruled that workers could not be fired on the basis of infectious disease). A 1986 Gallup poll indicated that the percentage of people who would avoid known or suspected homosexuals had increased, and

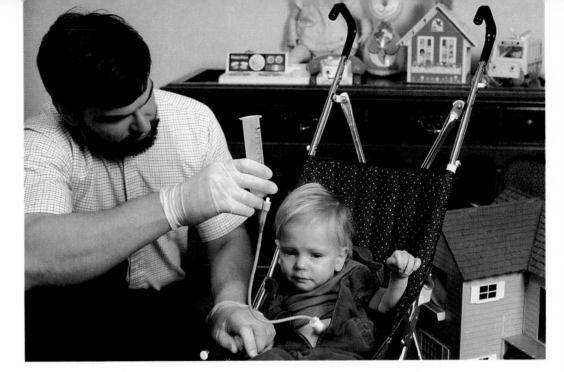

Children may contract AIDS at birth or through blood transfusions. (Blood screening for AIDS did not begin until 1985.) Many communities have tried to ostracize these children by boycotting school classes and even resorting to violence. Are persons with AIDS becoming the new lepers? (© Alon Reininger/Woodfin Camp and Associates)

that the proportion who would avoid places where homosexuals may be present has also risen. In addition, some health-care personnel, including physicians, nurses, nurses' aides, and dentists, have refused to provide even basic care to AIDS victims (Lieberson 1983, Wertz et al. 1986). Because AIDS is transmitted through blood, some Americans fear that they may be endangered by giving blood, even though disposable needles make the risk of any infection almost impossible.

Despite the widespread public concern about AIDS, its victims do not receive widespread sympathy. As of 1987, 43 percent of the public felt that children with AIDS should not be allowed to stay in school (*New York Times,* May 22, 1987, p. 84). In another survey, 54 percent felt that people with active cases of AIDS should be required to enter quarantine at a public health facility (*Newsweek,* Nov. 24, 1986). Why are AIDS victims dreaded, despite evidence that the disease cannot be spread by casual social contact?

The answer lies in the social characteristics of the majority of known victims of the illness (Altman 1986). The disease was first diagnosed in a socially devalued group—homosexual men with previous histories of multiple partners and sexually transmitted diseases. Its incidence among homosexual men led it to be initially called GRID (Gay Related Immunodeficiency Disease). This also provoked conservative religious critics of homosexual life-styles to view it as just retribution for deviance—"God's way of spanking." Some

homosexuals in turn regarded the AIDS controversy as a deliberate attack upon the emergent gay liberation movement (Lieberson 1983). Many victims of AIDS have been understandably hesitant to indicate they had the disease. It was not, for example, until after the death of film star Rock Hudson that it was known that he had AIDS or that he was homosexual. Similarly, the cause of death for the pianist/entertainer, Liberace, was not reported as AIDS until after a compulsory autopsy. Such is the power of social stigma.

As long as AIDS was considered the "gay plague," requests for research funds were generally ignored. It is by now clear that AIDS is not exclusively a disease of homosexual men. Indeed, shortly after the discovery of numerous cases of AIDS among homosexual men, two other socially devalued groups were observed to have the disease: drug users and Haitians. Drug users, primarily heroin addicts, contract the disease through contaminated needles, and Haitians, the majority of whom were neither homosexual nor drug users, through blood rites associated with voodoo. Because of the low social value accorded these AIDS victims, funds for their disability benefits or medical care were not initially available, despite the fact that the average patient is unable to work and faces huge expenses.

Given the enormous cost of treating AIDS patients, it is likely that the disease will cause an explosive increase in health-care costs. It was not until 1983—four **467**

"Safe Sex" on Campus

How can the incidence of AIDS be reduced? Some nations, such as France and Britain, have begun massive media campaigns advising the use of condoms to ensure "safe sex." In the United States, the Surgeon General has been outspoken in supporting such an educational campaign, although numerous political and religious groups have opposed supporting any solution other than complete abstinence. By 1987, colleges and universities had begun to distribute "safer sex kits." Dartmouth College, for example, distributed a kit containing pamphlets on safe sex and AIDS, and various barriers to the exchange of body fluids. At other schools, safe sex kits have been more controversial. Boston University's dean of students, for example, criticized a plan to distribute condoms to students, on the grounds that the university's responsibility is to educate rather than endorse sexual activities. "If a student is responsible enough to make decisions about whether he or she should engage in sex, I would like to think that student is responsible enough to buy the necessary protection available. . . . My bottom line response to anyone who is that immature to say, 'I'm embarrassed to go into a drugstore and buy a condom' I say, 'Keep your damn pants on'" (*The Daily Free Press,* Mar. 26, 1987, p. 1, p. 5).

For many students and young and middle-aged adults, AIDS may change the rules of the dating game. The available evidence on AIDS indicates strongly that those who have long-term relationships with faithful partners are at little risk of the disease—as long as they do not receive a transfusion of contaminated blood or use intravenous drugs.

Fear of AIDS has altered sexual behavior among unmarried heterosexuals and within the homosexual community (Fox 1987). In addition total sales of condoms doubled in dollar sales between 1980 and 1986, and special brands have been designed to appeal to female consumers. The effect of AIDS on dating behavior is thus an ongoing illustration of the impact that a disease may have, not only on health but on other aspects of life as well.

epidemic has also raised questions about discrimination in health care. Insurance claims filed by AIDS patients at one hospital are often rejected as "preexisting disorders" (although similar claims by cancer patients are not), and gay rights advocates suggest that insurers "bank on the fact that the life span of your typical lawsuit is longer than the life span of the typical person with AIDS" (*Newsweek,* Nov. 24, 1986).

A recent increase in research funds and benefits reflects in part the discovery that AIDS has been found in people with hemophilia, an inherited blood disease requiring frequent transfusions, and among newborn infants, children, and married heterosexual couples.

AIDS is also an international problem. In Central Africa, for example, according to World Health Organization estimates, at least 50,000 people have died from the disease since its appearance in the late 1970s. Known in some African nations as "the slim disease" because of the weight loss associated with AIDS, it is possible that several million people carry the virus, which has been spread there primarily through heterosexual rather than homosexual contact. The discovery that AIDS may be neither associated with homosexuality, multiple sex partners, drug use, or deviant religious beliefs has begun to alter both attitudes and funding for research.

Yet a number of questions remain unanswered. Is there a cure for AIDS within the foreseeable future? How will the costs of care for AIDS victims be met and by whom? How successful will public education campaigns for "safe sex" be in reducing its incidence? For these questions to be answered, careful scientific research and social planning rather than an attitude of blaming AIDS victims for their condition are needed.

years after the AIDS epidemic began— that its victims were granted almost automatic disability benefits under federal programs; prior to that time, many waited up to two years to become eligible, by which time most of them had died. The AIDS

Health and Illness as Social Identities

In American society, health is highly valued and is essential to a wide variety of social roles characteristic of industrialized societies. As Kalish (1976) pointed out, if there can be said to be a common religion in the United States, it is health, and its

Health and **illness** are **concepts** that describe adaptations to everyday life and the meanings that we give to living.

high priests are physicians. Yet, as noted at the beginning of this chapter, *health* and *illness* are not entities in themselves. Rather, they are *concepts* used to describe a process of adaptation to the changing demands of everyday life and the meanings we give to living (Mechanic 1978). Although we generally have no problem in identifying serious or incapacitating illness, basic to any definition are beliefs about what states of physical or mental well-being are or are not desirable. For example, in some societies, fat people are envied as attractive; in others, they are regarded as suffering from mental and physical disease. Nor are definitions of health and illness fixed. Both are constantly being redefined as new knowledge and technology are introduced, as the relative power of social institutions fluctuates, and as mechanisms of social control change.

These changes in the definition of illness shape and are shaped not only by the values of a society but by its social institutions because people occupying roles in various institutional spheres have vested interests in the changes. For example, in the United States today, slimness is highly valued and is associated with youth and

physical attractiveness. Moreover, physicians, psychologists, drug manufacturers, and owners of exercise clubs profit from the definition of obesity (being overweight) as a disease to be treated. Although there are no universally agreed-upon causes or results of being fat, it is considered both a medically and a socially undesirable condition requiring intervention. Competition among various vested-interest groups about the best ways to control this disorder still continues.

Not all diseases are points of controversy. There is little argument about whether tuberculosis, smallpox, malaria, and measles are illnesses, or about the most appropriate methods of treating them. The underlying causes of these diseases are relatively easy to identify in terms of current knowledge, and the institution of medicine is generally granted exclusive treatment rights. But conditions such as alcoholism, drug abuse, depression, and bed-wetting are much less agreed-upon; they are physical or behavioral deviations from the norm that pose personal or social problems for the individual and/or for the community. Moreover, there are situations in which behaviors thought to threaten the norms are defined

Wellness has become an important concept and physical fitness is an essential part of it. However, some people think that in modern urban America fitness and weight loss have been elevated to a fetish. What do you think? (© T. Zimberoff/ SYGMA)

Sociologist as Partisan:
Doing Movement Research

MARTIN P. LEVINE

Now an associate professor of sociology at Bloomfield (N.J.) College, Martin P. Levine was active in the gay liberation movement. He remained active after becoming a sociologist, helping to organize and lead both the Sociologists Gay Caucus and AIDS Network. He has also published extensively on the victimization of lesbians and gay men, and is the editor of Gay Men: The Sociology of Male Homosexuality.

Political commitments often shape sociological practice; in other words ideological concerns and beliefs frequently influence a sociologist's choice of research topics. This is certainly true for me. I have been active in various movements for sexual and gender liberation for most of my life. These affiliations, in turn, shape the work I do as a sociologist.

To a great extent, activism led me to become a sociologist. As an undergraduate, I participated in both the women's and gay liberation movements. From these experiences I learned to question prevailing assumptions about femaleness and homosexuality. At that time, people believed that femininity was a manifestation of women's nature and homosexuality was a mental illness. The movements disputed these claims, arguing that they were sexist and homophobic. To feminists, the role of women was socially constructed. To gay activists, homosexuality was a healthy variant of sexual expression.

The courses I took in sociology corroborated these beliefs. Sociologists taught me that gender roles and psychopathology are cultural constructions, signifying that societies define for themselves the behavioral expectations associated with being female or being psychologically disturbed. They base this assertion on the enormous variation in definitions of femininity and mental illness among cultures. To sociologists, then, nature plays an insignificant role in organizing women's status, and there is nothing inherently pathological about homosexuality.

Sociologists also validated other movement tenets. Activists claimed that sexism and homophobia significantly reduce the life chances of women, lesbians, and gay men. Sociologists substantiated this position in their research, documenting how these forces led to pervasive social, economic, and political discrimination against women and homosexuals. I was hooked, and decided to apply to graduate school for a doctorate in sociology. This training, I believed, would facilitate my work as an activist.

Subsequent experiences proved me right. Over the course of my career as a sociologist, I repeatedly used the training for movement purposes. My work on employment discrimination and antigay and lesbian violence illustrates this point. Lesbian and gay activists have long maintained that there is widespread violence and job discrimination against homosexuals. The lack of systematic evidence on the extent of these problems, how-

ever, stymied their efforts to redress the issues through legal remedies. Opponents typically argued that the lack of such evidence proved that the problem was insignificant. There is thus no need for special protections.

Movement activists approached me with the problem, asking that I collect and assemble what was known about the issue. After examining the sociological literature on homosexuality, I discovered some evidence of employment discrimination and violence against lesbians and gay men. These findings became the basis for the reports and journal articles that were widely circulated within the movement.

This research played a role in the struggle to obtain lesbian and gay civil rights bills. At legislative hearings across the nation, activists cited my findings concerning the extent of discrimination and violence. On a number of occasions, I was invited to testify as an expert witness, presenting my research in front of the New York City Council and the United States House of Representatives.

In the last few years, my work has taken on a new meaning. Though it still reflects activist commitments, it now also commemorates the dead. AIDS has decimated my friendship circle, killing many acquaintances. I have promised that I will honor their lives, using my skills as a sociologist to educate about lesbianism and male homosexuality. What I teach and what I research thus honors their memories.

as diseases, as in the cases of homosexuality in the United States until recently or of political disagreement with the government in the Soviet Union.

Clinical Models of Illness and Disease

It seems clear that the terms *illness, health,* and *disease* are used in many different ways. Although most sociologists define health or illness from a nonclinical, social-system viewpoint, other scientists use clinical models. Two clinical models, the *pathological* and the *statistical,* are most commonly used in definitions of physical and mental illness today. Both of these are designed to identify abnormalities in a way that will direct diagnosis and treatment (Mercer 1972).

The *pathological model* describes diseases by the biological symptoms that accompany them and focuses on defining the nature of "abnormal" functioning within an organism. This is the most commonly used model in medicine today. Specifically, the pathological model (1) seeks biological explanations within the individual; (2) often assumes that each illness has one specific cause rather than multiple causes (for example, that a particular germ causes tuberculosis); and (3) emphasizes what is wrong with a person rather than what is right.

The pathological model has been particularly useful in the study of acute physical illness, but it has limitations in the study of more complex disorders. Many long-term or chronic illnesses have multiple causes: biological, social, and environ-

mental. Moreover, explanations of disease often require an understanding of the society and the social structure in which people live. For example, researchers have observed that fat adults often were fat children. This finding has led to biological explanations, such as a search for excess fat cells that develop in early childhood and affect weight in adulthood. Yet, equally valid questions, such as "Why do we value chubby babies but not chubby adults in our society?" and "What social factors encourage thinness or fatness in adulthood?" tend to be overlooked in the pathological model.

By contrast, the *statistical model* defines health or illness in terms of the average of a population. Imagine a bell-shaped curve—the so-called normal distribution in statistics (also used by professors who are "grading on a curve"). "Normal" or "average" is just that, the arithmetical average of the population being studied. In a particular group or population, the eyesight that the majority have or their scores on an intelligence test are thus defined as "normal." People with unusually high or low scores are abnormal; that is, they deviate from the majority. Unlike the pathological model, the statistical model does not necessarily imply "healthy" or "good," although it may become value-laden (as in the case of intelligence). Some of the differences between the two models are presented in Table 17-2.

Believing that disease, or illness, fits the statistical model has several results. First, it emphasizes the largest groups in a population and defines them as normal, and it underemphasizes smaller groups and defines the members as ill. For example, Mercer (1973) found that Mexican-American children were much more likely to be

The **pathological model** focuses on biological symptoms and abnormal functioning in an organism.

The **statistical model** defines health or illness in terms of the average of a population.

TABLE 17-2 The pathological and the statistical models of disease

Pathological Focus	Statistical Focus
Abnormality is the focus.	The average of a group is defined as normality.
The individual is the focus.	The group is the focus.
Culture and group are not considered: explanation is biological.	Findings do not go beyond the group and are based on a specific group or population.
Cause–effect model.	Cause not included in model.

SOURCE: Adapted from Jane Mercer, *Labeling the Mentally Retarded,* Berkeley, Calif.: University of California Press, 1973.

defined as mentally retarded by social institutions dominated by Anglos than were either black or white non-Hispanic children. Their behavior and school performance differed from those of the majority. Yet, within their own community, these children were considered normal, and as adults they showed no signs of retardation. The Mexican-American children had norms for child development that were not held by the majority. This example also shows that a definition of illness may be valid only for the group of people from which it was developed. The majority of a population defines what is normal, but what the majority are like may differ from group to group. Thus, when a study moves from one culture or population to another, the majority must be reexamined and illness must be redefined.

The statistical model is less limited than the pathological model. In the pathological model, some physical malfunction or abnormality must be shown if an illness is to be diagnosed. In the statistical model, however, this is not the case, for one can alter the percentage of the population to be described as ill by either redefining as "normal" behaviors or characteristics once considered sickness (for example, homosexuality or the smoking of marijuana by college students), or by defining as medical problems behaviors previously considered unproblematic (for example, overactivity in children).

The statistical and pathological models of illness are important because each of them affects the society in which it prevails. A society in which certain behaviors, such as drug use, mental illness, or alcoholism, are seen as illnesses is clearly different from one in which they are viewed as sins or crimes. Generally, the broader the definition of illness and the more conditions or acts there are that are viewed as symptoms of disease, the more powerful are health institutions. Physicians and other health personnel assume roles as agents of social control that were once occupied by priests, parents, or law-enforcement personnel. Forms of behavior, activities, or symptoms once considered deviant become *medicalized;* that is, they are treated as medical problems. Accordingly, occupations and institutionalized patterns rise and fall and resources shift as beliefs about the nature of health and illness change. Moreover, whether behavior is viewed as illness requiring treatment or as deviance alters what roles we play, how others act toward us, and how we act and feel about ourselves.

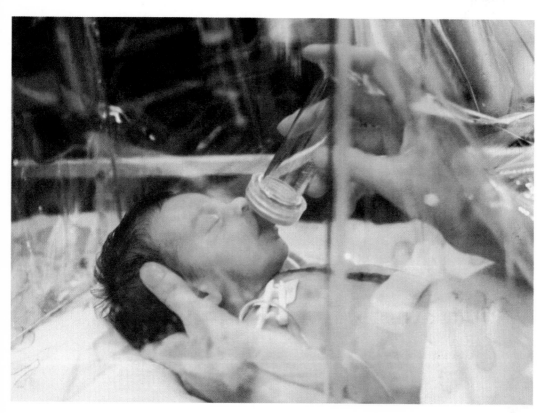

New technology makes it possible to keep alive higher and higher risk babies, a factor in the growing field of neonatology. Some critics feel this has medicalized the life process itself. (© SYGMA)

The box on the next two pages describes how the birth process has become medicalized and how the health establishment can become an instrument of social control.

THE SICK ROLE

Is there a particular role assigned to the sick? A functionalist would probably answer yes. Parsons (1951), for example, suggested that good health among most members of a society much of the time is necessary if people are to play their usual social roles. Illness, to the extent that it reduces one's ability to play these roles, also reduces the functioning of the group. Instead of contributing to the well-being of the group, the sick drain away resources from it by requiring help from others. Sickness thus must be socially controlled, according to Parsons: otherwise, social stability would be threatened. Over three decades ago, Parsons and Fox (1952) proposed that illness was particularly disruptive in the nuclear American family of the 1940s and 1950s, which they saw as having two main functions: the socialization of children and the emotional support of adults. Because the family functioned primarily as an emotional rather than as a productive unit, its members were likely to feel many role strains that made illness an attractive state into which to withdraw. Thus, the father who was expected to be the primary earner might seek a rest from the rigors associated with his job through sickness; the child, a return to dependency and to being the center of attention; and the mother, relief from having to manage human relationships or a way of reacting to being excluded from the life open to men. If any member of the family becomes ill, role relationships are changed. A sick father draws attention away from the children, a sick child draws attention away from the father, and a sick mother results in loss of support for both father and children. Given these negative effects of illness on social functioning, formal social-control mechanisms develop to reduce the impact of illness and to discourage staying sick. Although this theory was developed to describe the typical middle-class nuclear family of the 1940s and 1950s, it remains relevant when we consider the impact of illness on the family as a social system and the way in which the illness is managed.

Regardless of the pattern of division of

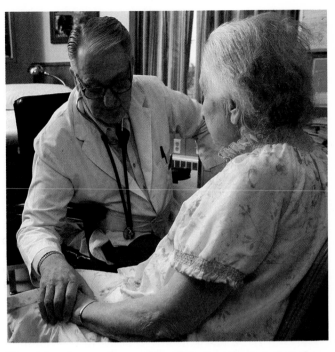

The sick role usually requires giving up control over the treatment of the illness to socially sanctioned experts. In the case of the elderly this may increase their feelings of dependency. (© Charles Harbutt/Archive)

labor within any given family, the sudden illness of one member presents a crisis—the upset in the usual balance of roles—among both well and sick members. Like sudden death, illness within the family may be a script with which we are familiar but few of us know the lines. These are learned through experience, and the precise script will vary according to the roles of each family member and resources available to them.

One way to control the negative effects of illness, Parsons (1951) proposed, is through the *sick role*. The sick role has the following characteristics: (1) through no personal fault, the sick person cannot function in her or his usual capacity; (2) accordingly, she or he is exempted from normal responsibilities; (3) in return, because illness is an undesirable state, the patient is obliged to seek competent help from disease specialists; and (4) to follow the instructions of physicians or other therapists in order to get well as soon as possible. Unlike most other roles, the sick role is a semideviant one. That is, the sick person is excused from normal role behaviors *only* as long as he or she works at getting well. Obeying medical instructions and treatment replaces normal activ-

The expectation of a person in the **sick role** is that he or she cannot function as usual, is exempt from normal responsibilities, is expected to get medical help, follow a physician's instructions and get well as soon as possible.

The Medicalization of Childbirth

In 1900, the majority of children in the United States were born at home. Since 1966, the proportion of all births occurring in hospitals has been 98 percent or higher, and over 95 percent have been attended by physicians. Moreover, an increasing proportion of births occur through medical intervention—labor induced through drugs, Cesarean section, and other procedures introduced by the physician. The use of fetal monitors, enabling health personnel to chart the heart beat of the unborn child prior to delivery, are routine in even uncomplicated deliveries in many hospitals. How did childbirth increasingly become a medical procedure?

The answer lies in part in the political struggle of the medical profession for dominance over health issues. Birth in colonial America followed the British tradition of women relatives and friends gathering with a midwife in the home to provide help and emotional support. Childbirth was not usually a "medical" problem; indeed, many physicians believed that caring for pregnant women was beneath their dignity. During the nineteenth century, however, belief in the value of science and technology paved the way for physicians to extend their authority; they opposed the use of midwives in childbirth, describing them as "old, gin-fingering and guzzling," "filthy and ignorant," "un-American," "pestiferous," and "vicious." Increasingly, a medical vocabulary was used to define childbirth.

Not only was a vigorous medical campaign mounted to discredit midwives but also a strong effort was made to relocate birthing from the home to a hospital setting. Hospital-based births were financially profitable to hospitals and more conve-

nient for physicians. Births also redefined the image of the hospital—from a place where the poor and dying were treated to a place of hope. Furthermore, shifting birth to a hospital enabled teaching hospitals to train medical students, interns, and residents in obstetrical procedures. By 1935, the percentage of births in hospitals had increased to about one-third. Increasingly, birth became defined as basically dangerous, requiring medical management. Techniques designed for abnormal births became routine, and as additional technologies and drugs became available for use in childbirth, physicians adopted them.

Although feminists and childbirth reformers have protested the medicalization of childbirth, their impact has been deflected by physicians and hospitals. Birthing rooms and childbirth classes have been instituted in hospitals, but without reversing the trend toward medicalization. For example, during the 1965–1983 period when birthing rooms and childbirth classes became standard at many hospitals, Cesarean sections increased from 4 percent to 20 percent of all births. The tendency for women to delay the start of their families until they were in their thirties, has also enhanced the use of medical technology in birth, as these "old mothers" are viewed as relatively high risk. Despite documentation of the risks associated with medical intervention in routine childbirth, techniques designed for the abnormal birth situation are now extended to cover most other births.

Indeed, the physician who does *not* intervene in the course of an apparently normal birth may run the risk of censure by colleagues or the threat of a malpractice suit. In 1985, a British physician,

ity, but the sick role is not expected to be a long-term role.

The Growth of American Medicine

The American health-care system as we know it evolved primarily within the past 100 years in response to changes in technology, pressures of competing interest groups, and felt social needs. Although hospitals can be traced back to ancient Greece, it was not until late in the nineteenth century that they provided care to

large numbers of people. Nor were hospitals healthy places in which to receive care; antiseptic procedures were almost unheard of, and physicians often came directly into wards and operating rooms from the morgue without washing. Relatively few medical practitioners had formal instruction in the basic sciences; many lacked any medical training. Technology was limited and treatments such as bloodletting often did patients more harm than good.

As odd as it may seem to us today, physicians in the nineteenth century were "a weak traditional profession of minor economic significance," bitterly divided, torn by internal quarrels about the nature

Wendy Savage, was suspended from her medical practice on the grounds of alleged incompetence. She held the unpopular view that each woman should be allowed a normal delivery unless there was a strong personal preference by the mother to the contrary. Accused by her colleagues of malpractice, it was only after both a lengthy public campaign and legal action that she was permitted to resume her position. Her "crime" was apparently not that a stillbirth occurred but rather that she did not practice "defensive medicine." As Savage summed up the issues of her suspension, they included five points:

• Birth and power—who controls childbirth?
• What kind of services do women want—and who is going to decide on the kind of care that is offered to them?
• Accountability—of hospitals, public authorities, and of doctors.
• Incompetence—how is it defined? Who measures it?
• Disciplinary procedures for doctors—can they be improved? (Savage, 1986, pp. 174–175).

Savage commented: "Within the last forty years we have seen in this country a complete take-over of the whole process of birth by obstetricians.... Only 2 percent of women still have their babies at home.... This major change in childbirth patterns in society has been followed by increased medicalisation of birth and rising rates of intervention, without good scientific evidence that these high rates are necessary (p. 175).... Accepting that the woman should have control over her own fertility by means of access to contraception and abortion on her terms, not those of the medical profession, and understanding that the woman should have choice about the way her pregnancy and labour is conducted, seems to be deeply threatening to some obstetricians—of both sexes" (p. 176).

As the "Savage Enquiry" indicates, even health professionals who challenge the medicalization of a natural condition may face serious consequences, for such opposition raises questions about the way in which medicine is organized, the training of doctors, and the power of physicians.

The example of childbirth illustrates a key aspect of medicalization. Sociologist Irving Zola (1986) noted that medicine is "the new repository of truth, the place where absolute and often final judgments are made by supposedly morally neutral and objective experts . . . accomplished by medicalizing much of daily living (p. 379). . . . It is the battleground, not because there are visible threats and oppressors, but because they are almost invisible: not because the perspective, tools and practitioners of medicine and the other helping professions are evil, but because they are not . . . the danger is greater, for not only is the process masked as a technical scientific, objective one, but one done for our own good" (p. 388). Or, briefly put, how much should social control be medicalized?

SOURCES: Rose Weitz and Deborah A. Sullivan, "The Politics of Childbirth: The Re-emergence of Midwifery in Arizona," *Social Problems*, 33, 3, 1986, 163–175; Wendy Savage, *A Savage Enquiry*, London: Virago Press, 1986; Irving Zola, "Medicine as an Institution of Social Control," in Peter Conrad and Rochelle Kern, *The Sociology of Health and Illness*, 2nd edition, New York: St. Martin's Press, 1983, pp. 379–389.

of illness and its treatment, and financially insecure (Starr 1983). By the middle of the twentieth century, physicians were prosperous, unified professionals, in control of the market for health care. Indeed, since 1950, physicians' fees have increased 75 percent faster per year than prices for other goods and services. Between 1985 and 1986, physicians' fees increased over 7 percent as compared to a 1.7 percent overall increase in U.S. prices (*New York Times,* July 16, 1986).

Not only did the power and wealth of physicians increase steadily within the last few decades but the frequency and types of services provided by physicians expanded dramatically. At the same time hospitals became the central institution in the delivery of health services. As a result, expenditures for health care have also risen. In 1985, for example, Americans spent $425 billion—10.7 percent of our gross national product or $1,721 per person—on health care (Friedland 1987). How did these changes come about?

THE RISE OF MEDICAL DOMINANCE

The development of modern health care as an industry was initially stimulated by work in social epidemiology and the rise of the public-health movement in the nineteenth century as well as by scientific discoveries such as the germ theory of disease, anesthetics, and immunizations. By 1910, with the publication of a landmark study, *The Flexner Report,* the reorganization of medical training and the professional independence and dominance over health of physicians was set in motion. Significant recommendations of the Flexner report that were to transform American medicine included: (1) basic training of physicians must include two years of biological and physical sciences plus two years of closely supervised hospital experience; (2) medical schools should be affiliated with universities to have access to their science faculties and laboratory facilities; and (3) medical school graduates must pass a rigorous licensing exam before being able to practice. As medical diploma mills were driven out of business by the new medical universities, the general quality of American medicine improved; quarrels within medicine decreased; and admission requirements to the recently reformed medical schools were set. The Flexner report was influential in establishing the scientific basis of medicine, increasing both the authority of the physician and the demand for medical care in a society where science is highly valued (Starr 1983).

Not only was the stage set for an increased demand for health care, but supply was governed as well. Entry into the practice of medicine was restricted by both training and licensing requirements established by professional organizations such as the American Medical Association. Self-regulation is a primary characteristic of American medicine, at least as old as the Flexner report, which viewed the new, "scientific" medicine as a kind of gentlemen's club, from which women, blacks, Jews, and other ethnic minorities were to be systematically excluded (Ehrenreich and English 1980). Following the expansion of medical schools at universities, the smaller institutions that had trained blacks and women were forced to close. Admission to the accredited medical colleges was almost exclusively restricted to white males—a pattern that continued until the 1970s (Ehrenreich and English 1980). Whereas, in some American cities in 1900, women accounted for almost 20 percent of all physicians (Walsh 1977)—that percentage dropped dramatically within the next few decades as women were

channeled into nursing, social work, teaching, and public-health work (Morantz-Sanchez 1985). It was not until the 1970s, when antidiscrimination legislation was enforced, that admission policies were revised. Yet less than one in five practicing physicians in the United States today is female or nonwhite.

The New Medical Industrial Complex.

As all-powerful and autonomous as American physicians have been throughout most of this century, there are signs today of a major power shift in the delivery of health care. The solo practitioner or small group practice is gradually being replaced by profit-making companies that own chains of hospitals, nursing homes, medical office centers, and walk-in clinics. In these facilities, the physician ceases to be self-employed and becomes a salaried employee of the corporate owners.

Today, one-third of all hospitals in the United States are now part of multi-unit chains, a kind of medical Woolworth's, in which nonmedical administrative decisions are made at the regional or national level rather than locally. In some cases, physicians have responded by forming their own companies and contracting their

Scientific and technological advances have changed the profession of medicine. Open heart surgery, for example, requires a team of skilled personnel as well as millions of dollars worth of medical equipment. Such services can only be provided by a large medical complex. (© Bill Strode/SYGMA)

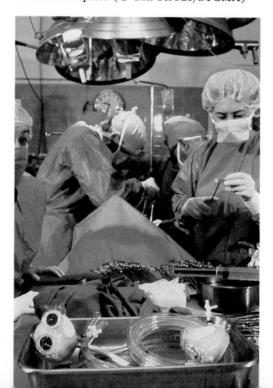

Women Physicians: Still Second-Class Citizens

How have the careers of women physicians differed from those of men? From 1910 to the 1960s, women experienced widespread discrimination in medical school admissions, internships, and residencies. Women physicians were held in low esteem by both male and female patients. But by 1979, one-fourth of American medical school students were female: affirmative action had opened more professional opportunities to women, and the feminist movement had encouraged many women to seek physicians of the same gender.

Yet women physicians still do not reap the same rewards that men do from equal levels of both motivation and professional accomplishments. Marriage, for example, is a positive factor for the careers of male physicians but is often a drawback for women in medicine. This is especially true for women with children, who are often forced to limit the professional socializing so important to success in either private practice or academic medicine. They have the responsibilities of wife and mother as well as their careers and little time for the informal social contacts that make one a member of the "old boys" network. Ironically, their lesser participation in informal social activities is frequently viewed as a lack of commitment to their professional careers.

Sociologist Judith Lorber (1984) notes that the paradoxical problem faced by women in medicine is similar to the one faced by women in other male-dominated occupations, that is, the necessity to organize as a group to challenge their treatment as an undifferentiated group. For Lorber "the ultimate goal is not for women to join men in inner circles imbued with the male perspective . . . but for the establishment of new values which reflect the needs and priorities of all members of society— female and male, old and young, rich and poor" (p. 115). As the proportion of women in medicine increases and the very nature of medical practice changes, it will be interesting to see the extent to which this goal will be realized.

SOURCE: Judith Lorber, *Women Physicians: Careers, Status, and Power*, New York: Tavistock, 1984.

---

services out to local hospitals, or by establishing their own health-care clinics. All these trends suggest considerable conflict within the medical establishment over control of the delivery of health care, involving salaried v. autonomous physicians, doctors v. hospitals, nonprofit v. for-profit medical centers, health-care providers v. insurance companies, and, increasingly, various levels of government regulators (Starr 1983). The result will undoubtedly be a more varied system than in the recent past, offering greater choice to the consumer. A potential problem is the reinforcement of the tendency toward one health-care system—private and profit-making—for the affluent and another— public and underfunded—for the poor.

Adding to the changes taking place in American medicine is the rising number of physicians. In 1950 there were only 145 medical doctors for every 100,000 Americans; by 1983, there were 228 per 100,000; and by 1990, there could be as many as 250, or an "excess supply" of thirty to seventy thousand physicians (McArdle 1987). Some observers also predict that there will be a shortage of physicians in some specialties, such as family practice

and general psychiatry, and an oversupply in more highly paid fields such as obstetrics/gynecology and surgery (McArdle 1987). The oversupply of physicians in some specialty areas could reduce professional unity and increase conflict as doctors compete with one another for a dwindling supply of patients. Other analysts predict a "counter-revolution in which medical staffs reassert their positions both in supervising patient care and in sharing in net income" (Pauly 1987, p. 59).

NURSING: A PROFESSION IN FLUX

Although we tend to think of physicians as the major providers of health care, *nurses* comprise the largest group of health workers in the United States today. The roots of nursing as a profession are several. Nursing has been linked to the development of Christianity, in which caring for the sick was considered a religious act. During the Middle Ages, for example, nunneries often provided the equivalent of hospital care for the poor. Some nursing care was also provided by members of the nobility who felt an obligation to care for the less privileged. During wartime, in the past, often

Nurses comprise the largest group of health workers in the United States.

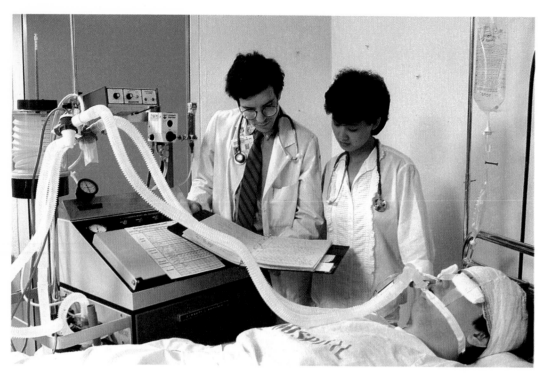

Traditionally doctors have been men and nurses have been women. While this is changing, it is still the primary pattern. How is this related to the underevaluation of the nursing profession? (© Barbara Kirk/The Stock Market)

the only care available for those wounded in battle was given by women camp followers. The history of modern nursing dates from 1854, when an Englishwoman, Florence Nightingale, organized a group of women from affluent families to care for the wounded and sick soldiers of the Crimean War.

The history of nursing is closely linked to the history of the feminine role. Indeed, the very term "nurse" implies the traditional definition of a mother's relationship with her offspring: nurturance. Until relatively recently, the majority of health care in Western societies was provided by women who were the midwives and healers for most of the population. They were not, however, permitted to undertake formal study and their ability to treat the sick was often viewed as the result of witchcraft. As early as the thirteenth century women were prohibited from studying medicine, and any woman who had medical knowledge and had not studied medicine was regarded as a witch—the perfect catch-22 (Ehrenreich and English 1980).

With the rise of medicine as a male-dominated profession, the role of the nurse was defined as that of helper to the physician. The profession of nursing became an almost exclusively female occupation, in which obedience to authority was stressed. Nurses were also often regarded

as sexual objects; despite the rigid rules of personal conduct enforced by most schools of nursing in the late nineteenth and first half of this century, the myth that nurses were sexually available because of their close contact with the human body persists even today. Some analysts, like Mauksch (1972), have suggested that physicians view nurses much as whites once viewed blacks: that the nurse is happiest working for him, that the doctor loves and understands her needs best, and knows what is best for her.

Today, many doctors and most nurses would challenge this view, so that nursing is a profession in flux. Two-thirds of American nurses work in hospital settings and are part of its bureaucratic structure, where they also receive and implement the orders of physicians. Traditionally, nursing roles have consisted of both socioemotional and technical tasks, involving complex technical procedures as well as attention to the patient's physical and psychological discomfort and needs. The nurse in a hospital setting must negotiate among these various, sometimes competing, role expectations. As hospitals have become the focal point for delivery of a wide variety of health-care services, however, many of the traditional bedside tasks of nurses have been delegated to less-trained personnel. As new procedures and equipment are introduced nursing has become more technologically oriented. It is increasingly common for the nurse to lead a team of nonprofessionals who provide the direct care.

As part of the push toward professionalization, nursing organizations have sought to raise the prestige accorded to its members. Training has been upgraded, with greater emphasis placed on a four-year college or university bachelor-degree program rather than a two- or three-year hospital-based school of nursing. As the qualifications for nursing degrees have risen, nurses are less willing to perform many unskilled or semi-skilled tasks. The women's movement, too, has encouraged nurses to challenge many of the traditional assumptions about their handmaiden-to-the-physician role, and to press for higher pay and more recognition.

The rise in costs of health care plus the increasing specialization within the medical profession has also encouraged the development of new types of expertise among nurses. The *nurse administrator* and the *nurse practitioner* are two new career directions for nurses that require training beyond the bachelor's level. A nurse practitioner is a registered nurse who has received advanced training in a medical specialty. There are obstetrical nurse practitioners, pediatric nurse practitioners, geriatric nurse practitioners, and family nurse practitioners, among others.

Some nurse practitioners have gone into independent private practice, where they take patient medical histories, give physical examinations, do x-rays and lab work, institute preventive measures, provide emotional support, and treat illnesses. The nurse practitioner is an illustration of the movement toward greater autonomy and greater responsibility, authority, and expertise within the field of nursing. Although the future directions of nursing are not yet clear, it is obviously a changing profession, seeking new areas in which nurses may exercise their skills and enjoy more autonomous work roles, although not without opposition from physician organizations.

Such opposition, coupled with relatively low pay, heavy work loads, high responsibility but little autonomy, have gradually reduced the appeal of nursing as an occupation. So many other avenues of accomplishment are open for women today that enrollments in nursing programs have dropped off dramatically, as shown in Figure 17-1. Increasing numbers of young men, however, are entering nursing, though this is hardly enough to offset the overall decline in enrollment. As a result, the current shortage of registered nurses for hospital staffing throughout the country and in all medical specialties will become even more severe in the years ahead. Short-term solutions include allowing less-trained personnel to assume some nursing

The **nurse administrator** and the **nurse practitioner,** new careers paths, require training beyond the bachelor's level.

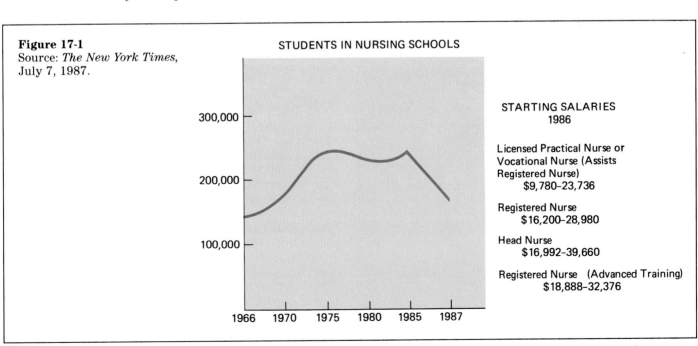

Figure 17-1
Source: *The New York Times,* July 7, 1987.

STUDENTS IN NURSING SCHOOLS

300,000

200,000

100,000

1966   1970   1975   1980   1985   1987

STARTING SALARIES
1986

Licensed Practical Nurse or
Vocational Nurse (Assists
Registered Nurse)
$9,780–23,736

Registered Nurse
$16,200–28,980

Head Nurse
$16,992–39,660

Registered Nurse   (Advanced Training)
$18,888–32,376

tasks, recruiting graduates of foreign nursing schools, hiring part-time and temporary workers, closing hospital wings, and asking current staff to work overtime (Lewin 1987). The long-range solution, which few medical leaders are yet willing to embrace, would be to raise entry pay, improve promotion opportunities, permit more autonomy in patient care, and remove traces of traditional patriarchal attitudes: in other words, to get serious about professionalizing nursing. In the meantime, nurses are joining other non-physician health workers in organizing and unionizing in order to improve their pay and working conditions.

PHYSICIAN ASSISTANTS

Physician assistants are personnel who perform a wide range of duties usually performed by physicians.

The term *physician assistant* (PA) covers health workers who perform a wide range of duties, including taking patient case histories, performing physical examinations, drawing blood, caring for wounds, and other tasks usually performed by physicians. Programs to train PAs are relatively new and began during the Vietnam War when thousands of military medical corps personnel were trained to care for the sick and wounded. The concept of the physician assistant was viewed by orga-

Physician's assistants and nurse practitioners sometimes establish independent practices which provide basic medical care to their patients. Since many routine and preventive measures can be taken care of in this way, why would these practices be opposed by physicians? (© Michal Heron/Woodfin Camp and Associates)

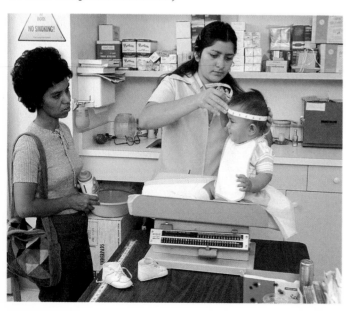

nized medicine as both a way to use this special training and to provide needed medical staffing. The first program to train civilian physician assistants was established at Duke University in 1965 and, unlike nursing, was comprised primarily of males. There are now over sixty PA programs accredited by the American Medical Association and enrollment remains predominantly male.

Many physician assistants are absorbed into private medical practices by physicians who add PAs to their staff as "physician extenders," often charging their regular fees for visits conducted by a PA and pocketing the difference between the PA's salary and the fee charged (Sidel and Sidel 1986). Today, however, physician assistants have become less necessary as "extenders" as the supply of physicians has grown. Large numbers of physician assistants, like nurse practitioners, have established their own independent practices—often to open opposition from local medical groups. At best, neither the PA nor the nurse practitioner will ever achieve the power, prestige, or wealth of a physician.

Not unexpectedly, there are conflicts between the physician-assistant and the nurse-practitioner programs involving relative status, hierarchy, and funding, as the primarily female field of nursing and the newer, predominantly male PAs compete for position. Both nurse practitioners and physician assistants possess similar skills. The extent to which their training and ability to administer and deliver health care will overlap the territory traditionally controlled by the medical profession remains to be seen.

MARGINAL HEALTH PRACTITIONERS

There are also a variety of marginal health professions, that is, not in the mainstream of the American health-care system. These include chiropractors; osteopaths; Christian Science practitioners; and midwives. Traditionally all these professions shared a distaste for the medical doctor's use of drugs, although their approaches to the treatment of illness are quite varied.

For example, *chiropractic,* or the treatment of disease through manipulation of the body—particularly the spine—was founded in 1895 as a drugless and nonsurgical alternative to medicine. Since the foundation of the first chiropractic college in the United States, chiropractors have

Chiropractic is the treatment of disease through manipulation of the body, especially the spine.

been greeted with hostility and ridicule by other medical professionals. Yet chiropractors must pass rigorous licensing procedures, often the same basic science exams as MDs. The chiropractor, however, is seen as a "quack," and evidence of success in curing low back pain and muscular disorders without drugs has generally been discounted by the medical establishment. Chiropractors are typically denied the right to treat patients in medically dominated hospitals. Not surprisingly, the status of the chiropractor is lower than that of the MD, although chiropractic has become increasingly popular among people who are interested in holistic health and other alternatives to conventional medical practitioners.

Osteopaths
receive training in mainstream medicine as well as body manipulation techniques.

Like chiropractic, *osteopathy* began as an alternative to nineteenth-century medicine, with its sometimes fatal drugs and surgery. Originally emphasizing the relationship of muscles and bones to all other systems of the body, osteopaths today receive training in mainstream medicine as well as in body-manipulation techniques. Unlike the chiropractor, osteopaths' practice is not limited by law, and they function as conventional physicians. In some states, doctors of osteopathy and doctors of medicine practice on the same hospital staff and refer patients within each others' professional networks. In other states, the status of the osteopath in comparison to the doctor of medicine remains relatively low. Although also opposed by the American Medical Association for many years as "quacks," osteopaths have gradually been absorbed into conventional medicine. Yet many osteopaths are opposed to the loss of their identity as a distinct profession. Whether osteopathy will cease to exist separate from medicine within the next few decades is uncertain.

An entirely different kind of health-care provider is exemplified by the Christian Science practitioner. Christian Science in general denies the existence of sickness and emphasizes the importance of mind and spirit. Christian Science practitioners are concerned with healing a wide range of conditions through prayer—not only poor health, but family and business problems, social injustices, intellectual limitations, psychological tensions, and moral confusion. Trained by a Christian Science teacher, practitioners have the right to practice in the majority of the United States. Like many other healers from a variety of backgrounds, Christian Science practitioners emphasize health rather than illness, and people's potential to control their bodies.

The Growth of Hospitals

Paralleling the physician's dominance of medical practice has been the growth of hospitals as major health-care centers. In 1873 there were only about 100 general hospitals in the United States, many of which were owned by state or local governments or by religious organizations. Today, *hospital ownership* falls into three broad categories: (1) for-profit or (proprietary) private; (2) nonprofit private; and (3) public.

As noted previously, the growth of hospitals in the early part of this century had been greatly encouraged by physicians who wanted them as teaching and research sites. Moreover, as medicine became increasingly recognized as a healing art, more people who could afford it sought medical care. To meet the growing need, nonprofit community hospitals, providing acute and surgical care and supported by patients' payments, were founded. As a result, physicians gained critical power, for only they could order the admissions that filled the beds. Concerned that their incomes might be threatened, physicians used organizations such as the American Medical Association to limit the number of free clinics and to prevent public health officials from offering direct medical care (Starr 1982).

Hospital ownership is either public, nonprofit private, or for-profit (proprietary) private.

PROPRIETARY CHAINS

Today, however, the rapid growth of the for-profit (proprietary) hospital networks has posed a profound challenge to the survival of traditional community-based nonprofit medical facilities. In 1986, a few dozen corporations accounted for 13 to 14 percent of the nation's hospital beds, and in some states—Florida, Texas, and Virginia, for example—proprietary chains own between 30 and 40 percent of all hospitals (Mullner et al. 1986, National Academy of Science 1986). In addition to purchasing and constructing facilities, proprietary corporations also hold contracts to manage an increasing number of nonprofit hospitals. Proprietary chains received their early momentum from the purchase of smaller community hospitals that were having financial problems due to the rising cost of care coupled with limited ability to raise revenues from the public and patients. By centralizing their purchasing and other administrative tasks, the chains claimed to be able to lower overhead costs while bringing businesslike efficiency to the task of providing health care. The major argument against the proprietary chains is that the quality of care is likely to be sacrificed to the goal of turning a profit for shareholders.

The evidence at the moment suggests little difference in quality of care between profit-making and nonprofit facilities. The proprietaries have not performed noticeably better either medically or administratively, nor have costs been lowered by virtue of competition (Ermann and Gabel 1985, National Academy of Science 1986). In fact, the for-profit rates are about one-fourth higher than those charged by nonprofits. This is so for at least three reasons: (1) high markups for services, above the actual cost increases; (2) more expensive laboratory and pharmacy costs; and (3) the need to pay off construction costs over a short period of time, especially in cases of overbuilding.

But the major source of profit for the proprietaries has been their ability to refuse care to people who cannot pay. The for-profits do not provide the same level of charity care as the community-based nonprofits, and since over 35 million Americans have no health insurance, many people are locked out of the for-profit system. While the proprietaries have not promoted competition in price, they have stimulated a market for recruiting doctors to their staffs. The typical for-profit can offer a steady, and high, salary, rent-free offices, paid nurses and secretarial assistance, centralized billing, and even country-club membership (Dallek 1986). Few nonprofits can compete in this league. Money is not the only inducement. Among physicians recruited to for-profit hospitals was a well known surgeon who was attracted to Humana Heart Institute in Louisville, Ky., by the guarantee of 100 heart transplants without all the regulations required in other hospitals (Dallek 1986).

Critics of the for-profits suggest that our health system is increasingly dominated by the Yuppie ethic, which may be phrased simply as "who says you can't have it all?" Accordingly, an "all-frills Yuppie Health Care Boutique System" designed for paying patients has emerged (Friedman 1986). Hospitals, physicians, and other providers offer a range of services: wellness and health-education programs, same-day surgery, home health care, private rooms, and even gourmet meals. Those who use such alternative services tend to be highly educated, white-collar professionals, aged twenty-five to forty-five, and often dual-career couples. Wellness programs, for example, are most popular among people with graduate education: same-day surgery is most preferred by college graduates and those with advanced degrees; extended-hour services are most often used by professionals who are college graduates, and so forth (Jensen 1986). The poor, however, remain unserved or rejected by this "designer-jean" health-care market.

THE PUBLIC HOSPITAL

To what extent are uninsured or poor patients dumped into public hospitals by private for-profit and nonprofit hospitals? If health care is a commodity to be sold at a profit then it must follow the laws of the marketplace. As one Humana Health Care senior vice president put it: "Health care is a necessity, but so is food. Do you know of any neighborhood grocery store where you can walk out with $3,000 worth of food that you haven't paid for?" (Dallek 1986, p. 56)

Dumping of patients on public hospitals by private for-profit and nonprofit hospitals has indeed been documented in several states. Leaders of the profit sector say that while they will provide acute-care services, uninsured patients are encouraged to transfer to public hospitals once their conditions are stabilized. But public hospital officials claim that they receive uninsured or poor patients in very critical conditions (Reinhold 1986). For example, three profit-making hospitals in Texas recently refused to treat an uninsured laborer who needed emergency care for very severe burns received while he was working; he simply did not have the deposit they required, which ranged from $500 at one hospital to $1,500 at another. He was finally treated at a public hospital seventy miles away where he required nineteen days of acute care and major skin graft surgery because of the delay (Dallek 1986).

The public hospitals, while providing much needed services to the poor and indigent, bears the cost of these services. Two categories of health care are evolving: one for Americans with insurance and money, and one for the uninsured and poor. (© Eugene Gordon)

In Illinois, according to a 1986 report, 89 percent of the patients transferred from the emergency rooms of other Chicago hospitals to Cook County Hospital were black or Hispanic, 81 percent were unemployed, and 25 percent were in an unstable medical condition (Reinhold 1986).

It seems clear that two categories of medical care are evolving: one for those with insurance and money, and one for the uninsured. Medicaid, the main source of medical care for the poor, covered less than 40 percent of the poor in 1984 as compared to 70 percent when the program developed in the 1960s. And public hospitals admit a disproportionately large number of the poor and the uninsured at the same time that they face reductions in federal programs, limited local revenues, and increased demands for services as more people are turned away from the proprietaries (Hughes and Lee 1986).

Three Models of Health-Care Delivery

The challenge to any nation's health-care system is meeting the health needs of its population most effectively and effi-ciently. Many systems do not provide optimum care for various reasons, usually related to social and political values. As noted earlier in this chapter, the norms and values of each society determine the level of funding, the institutions developed to deliver service, and the ways in which scarce resources will be allocated. Such seemingly neutral acts as performing an organ transplant, eliminating environmental pollution, or advising people to reduce salt intake in their diets all reflect basic values and and beliefs about health care, its organization, and financing.

Although most of us take the American health-care system for granted, its organization is unique among industrialized nations. The United States remains the only industrialized nation except South Africa without a national health insurance program. After the passage of Medicaid (designed to cover health care for the poor) and Medicare (for the elderly) in 1965, dozens of different proposals for universal national health insurance were introduced into Congress and defeated. During the Reagan administration with its general orientation toward reduction of governmental spending on social programs, increased "privatization" and cooperation between the public and private sectors was heavily emphasized (Roper 1987). In addition, the prestige and income of physicians in the United States is almost unparalleled in any other industrialized nation.

Although many models for the organization of health care have been proposed, three are particularly relevant to American patterns of present and future health service: (1) the professional model; (2) the national health service or central-planning model; and (3) the national health insurance model.

THE PROFESSIONAL MODEL

Most common today in the United States, the *professional model* is based on the power and influence that physicians exercise over the practice of medicine. Most physicians today still operate essentially as entrepreneurs: that is, as members of solo or partnership practices loosely tied to other physicians or to large employers through referrals, social networks, hospital affiliations, and medical society membership.

Payment for health care in the professional model is *fee-for-service,* where fees

The **professional model** is based on physicians' control of health care.

are set by members of the profession on the basis of the customary charges within a given area and medical specialty. Regulatory boards are dominated by physicians and are focused on the activities of individual doctors rather than on the profile of medicine as a whole. Emphasis on monitoring the quality of care traditionally has been on controlling inputs into the system through medical training and licensure. The licensing of physicians and hospitals is controlled by the profession itself. The geographic distribution of physicians has been determined by training and practice opportunities and individual perferences rather than by any consideration of the health needs of Americans on a national basis.

A recent variation on the professional model is the *Health Maintenance Organization* (HMO), an almost uniquely American pattern of health-care delivery in its combination of private enterprise and group insurance features. The HMO is an organization that provides a full range of medical care to people who pay a fixed yearly sum in advance. In turn, subscribers agree to use the physicians and hospitals that are members of that HMO. Unlike the fee-for-service system, HMOs make money when people do *not* use its services. The emphasis is on preventive medicine—teaching people to take better care of themselves and to avoid illness. Furthermore, when medical costs are prepaid, people are more likely to see a physician at an early stage of an illness, reducing the eventual cost of treatment. If the HMO can sign up large numbers of subscribers, the law of averages should work in its favor, as very few people under the age of sixty-five are likely to be gravely ill.

HMOs thus tend to reduce medical costs in general, provide a wide range of services at minimal expense to subscribers, and in some cases, permit member physicians to conduct a full private practice. Both the number of HMOs and the number of subscribers have grown rapidly since 1980, as shown in Figure 17-2. In 1985 alone, HMOs grew by 42 percent and membership by 26 percent (Rankin 1986). Most dramatic has been the increase in HMOs owned by nationwide for-profit corporations. As with proprietary hospitals, it was assumed that competition among HMOs could produce high-quality and cost-effective health care. Premiums for HMO membership are in the same range or lower

> The **health maintenance organization** (HMO) is based on prepayment for health care by patients who agree to use member physicians and hospitals.

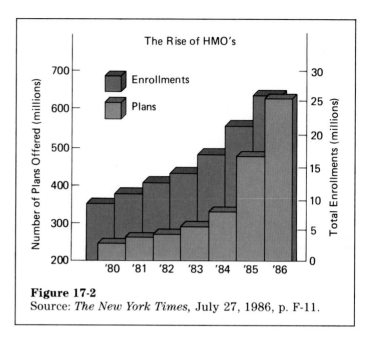

Figure 17-2
Source: *The New York Times*, July 27, 1986, p. F-11.

than for most traditional health insurance plans, and subscribers are saved deductibles, copayments, and filling out insurance forms.

Individual practice associations (IPAs) have grown faster than other types of HMOs. In an IPA, physicians accept patients under a prepayment arrangement but are also free to accept fee-for-service reimbursement. Patients visit participating physicians in their own offices rather than going to the clinic-like centralized facility of some HMOs. By June 1985, there were an estimated 181 IPAs with an enrollment of nearly 4.7 million (Friedland 1987). A third variant of the HMO model is the *preferred provider organization* (PPO), an agreement between health-care providers and third-party payers to provide fee-for-service health care at a discount. The PPO describes a broad set of arrangements between providers, third-party payers, and employers, but in most cases, people subscribing to a PPO may choose any physician or hospital but are given financial incentives to choose among "preferred providers." These providers gain an increased pool of patients and often process insurance claims faster. PPOs have also grown dramatically since the early 1980s; in 1982, only thirty-three were in operation but by 1985, there were 195, and an increasing number of employers are forming PPOs (Friedland 1987). Unlike the traditional HMO, PPOs do not make prepayment arrangements with

> In **individual practice associations** (IPAs) physicians accept patients under a prepayment arrangement but can also accept fee-for-service reimbursement.

> The **preferred provider organization** (PPO) is based on agreement between health-care-providers and third-party payers to provide health care at discount.

members, and thus, providers assume little monetary risk.

How effective is the HMO? A 1984 study indicated that hospital use among HMO members was 40 percent lower than among people with conventional fee-for-service physicians, and 20 percent lower than among people with a 5 percent co-payment (Friedland 1987). Although some researchers maintain that HMOs provide at least as good care as fee-for-service medicine, others argue that HMOs avoid using specialists or expensive lab tests and may not only ration care but also require lengthy waits for elective surgery (Rankin 1986). Some HMOs have collapsed from financial mismanagement, and others have been criticized for setting up restrictive membership, so that poor health risks are screened out. The result is that those people most in need of health services are not eligible for service. For example, relatively few HMOs serve primarily poor minority groups or the elderly, even though the costs of providing care to these groups and their patterns of use are not very different from those of the more economically advantaged (Steel, Markson, et al. 1982, Markson, Crescenzi, and Steel, in press).

THE CENTRAL-PLANNING MODEL

The **central-planning model** is based on public control over health care.

In contrast to the professional model is the *national health service* or *central-planning model,* based on the notion of public control over the planning and allocation of health staffing and resources. Within the central-planning model, all medical care is provided through noncompetitive, geographically organized health systems. A central-planning agency or health authority is responsible for the coordination of health resources, including the practitioners and the facilities within a defined region. Although the pattern of such health systems varies from country to country, many resemble the "planetary" form of organization developed in Sweden, where there is one health center per 15,000 people that revolves around a district hospital (1 per 60,000–90,000 population), in turn revolving around a central hospital. The central hospital answers to the regional medical center (1 per 1,000,000 population), which is responsible to a government agency or agencies.

In sum, services in the central-planning model are organized on the basis of population and governmental estimates of service needs. Physicians are incorporated into the system either on a salary or by formal contract. The geographic distribution of physicians is controlled through regulation, assessed needs, and vacant positions. Although fee-for-service is not discouraged and physicians may see private patients, this practice is the exception. Payment for health care may be from a variety of sources, including government insurance and appropriations, private health insurance, and consumer out-of-pocket expenditures. In Sweden, for example, national, county, and municipal funds; compulsory national health insurance; and direct payments by patients—all finance health care, whereas in England, health care is almost entirely financed on the national level through general tax revenues.

One major criticism of the central-planning or "socialized medicine" model is that it encourages people to "overuse" the service, leading to long delays for elective surgery. Another criticism is that physicians are overworked and underpaid, which lowers morale and reduces the motivation to study medicine. However valid these points may be, in none of the European nations with centrally planned health services have voters chosen to change the system.

THE NATIONAL HEALTH INSURANCE MODEL

National health insurance places the financing of health care under government control.

A third model is the *national health insurance model.* National health insurance essentially places only the financing of health care under governmental control, most often through universal health insurance in which premiums are paid by income taxes, or through other revenues. Based on the premise that health care should be equally accessible to all, national health insurance covers most medical expenses for all citizens of the nation. Canada and West Germany are two countries with such policies. In many national health insurance systems, a *corporatist model* has developed to counterbalance the priorities of consumers and providers. In the corporatist model, the role of government is threefold: to set rules for health-care practice; to establish and administer health-insurance policies; and to arbitrate disputes. A major difference between the national health service or central-planning model and the corporatist

In the **corporatist model** of national health insurance the government balances the interests of the medical profession with those of consumers and removes the profit motive.

model is that in the corporatist model, the government does not run the health-care system. Rather, the role of the state is to balance interests of the medical profession with those of consumers and to remove the profit motive from health insurance in an effort to contain costs.

The form of national health insurance adopted by Canada, for example, is financed from income taxes and has resulted both in increased access to care and to health-care cost containment. Lower administrative costs, elimination of private profit in health insurance, and a national policy of cost control have made Canadian health-care costs, on the average, $100 per person per year cheaper than in the United States (Lee 1982, Marmor 1982). At the same time Canada also has a fee-for-service private-enterprise system for those who wish to pay for it.

Financing and Organizing Health Care

The controversy surrounding the organizing and financing of health care in the United States is considerable. Supporters of greater government intervention in the health-care area have argued that planning at the national level is necessary because individual providers have vested interests that may not coincide with the needs of the general population. Consumers are neither well informed nor foresighted enough to plan and save for their health needs. Moreover, without national health insurance and governmental regulation, the regional and class differences in health services that now exist in the United States cannot be overcome. For example, Mississippi has fewer than half the physicians and dentists per 100,000 population than does Massachusetts.

Those who oppose further government intervention argue that it would lower the quality of care and limit professional autonomy. They argue that physicians, because of their technical expertise, are in the best position to assess the need for health services, and the laws of the marketplace will discourage exploitation by the greedy. The consumer, not an agency or a regulatory board, is in the best position to plan for financing his or her own health care.

A major issue closely related to how health care should be organized is its financing. Health-care expenditures have increased over 800 percent since 1960, while the consumer price index increased 110.6 percent during the same period (Friedland 1987). By 1986, health-care expenditures were over $425 billion—almost 11 percent of the gross national product, as may be seen in Figure 17-3 which shows national health expenditures as a percentage of gross national product for selected years.

Why have health-care costs increased so rapidly? A variety of reasons have been put forward, including technological advances ranging from sophisticated diagnostic testing devices to heart bypass surgery and organ transplants. Some of these procedures require substantial outlays of money; yet other changes, such as computerization of laboratory testing and new antibiotics, reduce both the demand for labor-intensive medical care and the need for hospitalization. The growth and aging of the population, too, have contributed to the rise in health-care expenditures inasmuch as the incidence of illness and death is greatest among the elderly. Those sixty-five and over tend to spend about three-and-one-half times as much per person on medical care as do younger population groups (Davis 1985). Only 9 percent of the elderly account for 70 percent of Medicare expenditures (U.S. General Accounting Office, 1984).

But technology and an older population are only partial explanations. A comparison of health-care expenditures in the United States and in England in the last

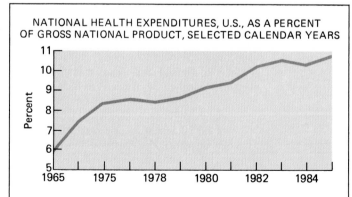

Figure 17-3
Source: U.S. Department of Health and Human Services, Health Care Financing Administration.

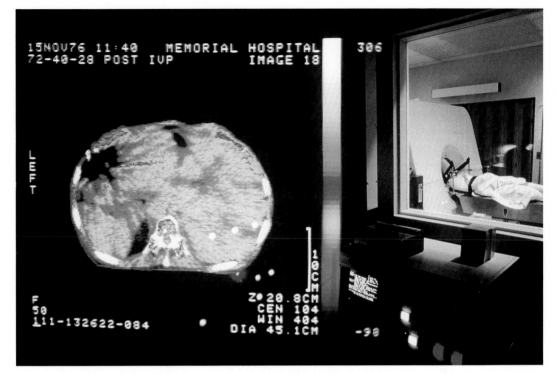

One of the major reasons for increasing health care costs is the high cost of sophisticated medical technology such as this CAT scan device. Some people feel such diagnostic services should not be available to those who cannot pay for them. What do you think? (© Dan Moody/Black Star)

few years indicates that England spent almost 5 percent less of its gross national product on health care than did the United States; that its per-person spending for health care was much lower; that its infant mortality rate was lower; and that the number of hospital admissions was lower. Several factors account for the relatively unremarkable health-care record of the United States. These include the high administrative costs of U.S. insurance plans, alleged medical waste and mismanagement, including unnecessary medical procedures, and fraud. Marketing inefficiencies also result in increased costs. For example, most health care in the United States is financed after the event by third-party insurers, based on provider charges, a procedure which may not encourage cost-effective practices, as patients and physicians are insulated from the effects of their choices (Friedland 1987). An additional estimated $78 billion in waste is generated annually by administrative overheads, half of which could be saved if the United States adopted methods of managing finances that have been used by other nations for decades (Sager 1986). Contrary to common beliefs about national health services, such as in Britain, costs are relatively low, and the health of subscribers greatly improved. In fact, by most measures, the health status of British and Americans are about equal, with a slight advantage for the British (Sager 1986). Furthermore, research demonstrates that the British National Health System delivers care more equitably (Stevens 1983).

American physicians' fear of malpractice suits leads to defensive medicine, which also increases costs. According to a study by the American Medical Association, 40 percent of physicians participating in a survey in the early 1980s indicated that they prescribed additional diagnostic tests to avoid possible malpractice suits. These increased tests may contribute $15.1 billion annually to the costs of health care (American Medical Association 1984). And finally, medicine is not an exact science. Norms for medical practice are set by practitioners in a geographical area rather than by consensus on best practice. Thus residents of Boston, Mass., are only half as likely to have their tonsils removed as people in Springfield, Mass.—only ninety-five miles away (Wennberg and Gittelson 1982). And in one part of Maine, 20 percent of women over age seventy-four have had a hysterectomy as compared to 70 percent in another part of the state. In another area the rate of surgery for hemorrhoid operations was about 3 times the state aver-

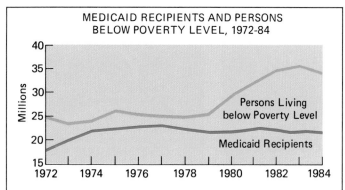

MEDICAID RECIPIENTS AND PERSONS BELOW POVERTY LEVEL, 1972-84

Persons Living below Poverty Level

Medicaid Recipients

Figure 17-4
Source: Marian Gornick; Jay N. Greenberg, Ph.D.; Paul W. Eggers, Ph.D.; and Allen Dobson, Ph.D., "Twenty Years of Medicare and Medicaid: Covered Populations, Use of Benefits, and Program Expenditures," *Health Care Financing Review,* 1985 Annual Supplement: 13–59.

Because hospital charges and utilization rates have increased dramatically since the introduction of Medicare, various plans to "cap" (set a ceiling on) hospital costs and to control use have been suggested, all of which share two common factors: (1) establishment of *prospective* reimbursement rates for specific services, that is, rate setting *prior* to their actual delivery; and (2) placement of hospitals at possible financial risk if they do not cap costs (Stern and Epstein 1985).

Under the original Medicare regulations, hospitals were reimbursed according to "reasonable cost" based on the actual cost figures provided by the hospital for care of particular patients. In contrast, a *prospective payment system* for Medicare patients based on diagnosis-related groups (DRGs) rather than "reasonable costs" was phased in nationwide by the end of 1985. Under this new system, hospitals will be paid by Medicare on a per-case basis with different fixed payments for each of 467 different DRGs. As you will recall, both treatment received and length of stay for patients with the same condition and degree of severity have varied widely among hospitals as when elderly patients with the same illness who are treated in urban hospitals stay longer per admission than those treated in rural hospitals. With the introduction of DRGs, payment rates are simplified: that is, hospitals are reimbursed in advance on the basis of diagnosis and anticipated hospital stay. The hospitals with costs *below* the DRG rate can keep the difference as profit. Hospitals spending

The **prospective payment system** is based on fixed payment diagnosis-related groups (DRGs) rather than "reasonable costs."

age! (Wennberg et al. 1984) A similar pattern has been noted throughout the United States. Apparently what determines the difference in rates is, at least in part, a function of the number of hospital beds and surgeons in a given area—more beds lead to more medical admissions and more surgeons lead to more operations.

The rapidly rising cost of health care in the United States today is a critical policy issue. As presently financed, Medicare for the elderly is expected to run out of funds within the next decade. And, as may be seen in Figure 17-4, the gap between those living below the poverty level and Medicaid recipients is widening rather than dwindling.

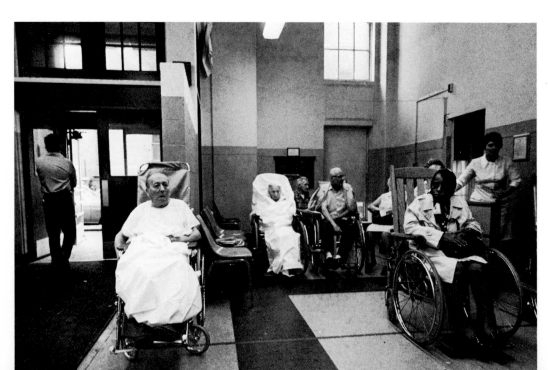

While treatment financed by Medicare may be problematic, it does, nevertheless, ensure medical care. If funds do run out, as expected, what will be the consequences for patients such as these? (© Norman Hurst/Stock Boston)

above the rate will lose the excess expenditure. Thus, if the DRG rate for a patient with diabetes is set at $200 per day for ten days, facilities in which diabetic patients are discharged earlier will profit, while facilities with patients who stay longer will lose revenue.

The introduction of DRGs has been controversial. Opponents of DRGs argued that this policy will encourage early discharge of patients and restrict admission of very poor or very ill patients (Stern and Epstein 1985). Those favoring DRGs claim that efficiency will be improved and unnecessary services will be eliminated without compromise of quality (Schweiker 1982). The actual long- and short-range effects of DRGs remain to be seen. It seems likely, however, that such a major change in one part of the hospital system—reimbursement—will have an impact on the system as a whole and perhaps affect all aspects of the organization and health care.

Several more sweeping solutions to runaway health-care costs proposed by the House of Representative Select Committee on Aging, include: (1) employment of more nurse practitioners and physician assistants to perform the routine procedures; (2) medical treatment in smaller, local facilities rather than in large, expensive medical centers; (3) encouraging physicians to enter family practice rather than specialties; and (4) developing care outside of hospitals (*New York Times,* May 6, 1984, p. 35). These or similar proposals, shifting the locus of care to nonphysicians and to the community, would change both the current structure and costs of medical care and make health-delivery systems more similar to those of nations such as Canada and Sweden.

Summary

Each stage of economic development and technology has its own pattern of health and illness and its own ways of treating them. Health and illness are socially and culturally defined, and what may be considered normal or healthy in one society may be viewed as abnormal in another. Health and illness are linked to the level of industrial development of a country, to its norms and values, and to its population's characteristics.

Epidemiology is the study of the patterns of occurrence of illness in a particular population. Measures of incidence and prevalence are used by epidemiologists to give an idea of the magnitude, the increase, or the decrease of specific diseases within a stated period of time. Age, sex, race and ethnicity, and social class are important factors in epidemiological studies. All of these have been found to interact with each other as well as with the severity of a disease to produce particular patterns of health or illness.

The relative social regard given to people who have certain kinds of diseases affects not only the treatment they receive but the amount of time and money spent in attempting to find causes and cures for their ailments. Health and illness are constantly being redefined as a result of changing norms, shifts in the mechanisms of social control, and changes in the relative power of social institutions.

Two different models, with potentially different outcomes for the management of disease, are commonly used in medicine today: the pathological and the statistical models. Generally, the broader the definitions of illness and the more conditions viewed as symptoms of disease, the more powerful are health-care institutions. Certain types of behavior once regarded as deviant then become medicalized, and physicians assume roles as social-control agents that may previously have been occupied by priests, law-enforcement officers, and others. In turn, sick people may be assigned a new role—the sick role—so that their behavior can be controlled.

The American health-care system as we know it, however, is relatively new. The dominance of the physician has occurred within this century, during which control over teaching standards and over entry into the profession of medicine has been introduced. The profession of medicine has developed a strong self-regulatory system, not only exercising control over its own practitioners but influencing the way in which other health professions operate. Hospitals as major care-giving facilities are relatively new as well; their development parallels that of medicine.

Various models of health care have been proposed. Most common in the United States is the professional model, based on physicians' control of health care. In contrast, the central-planning model is based on public control over health care. The third model, the national insurance, places the financing of health care under government control, sets rules and policies, and arbitrates disputes.

Controversy about the organizing and financing of health care in the United States continues as health-care costs rise. Yet, power over the vast industry that is the health-care system may be shifting. Medical-industrial complexes of profit-making corporations have entered the health arena. Whether physicians will control or be controlled by such corporations—and by the government—will be determined in the years to come.

Suggested Readings

BECKER, HOWARD S., BLANCHE GEER, EVERETT HUGHES, and ANSELM STRAUSS. *Boys in White: Student Culture in Medical School.* Chicago: University of Chicago Press, 1961. A classic study of the socialization of students into the medical profession.

CHIVIAN, ERIC, SUZANNA CHIVIAN, ROBERT JAY LIFTON, and JOHN MACK, eds. *Last Aid: The Medical Dimensions of Nuclear War.* San Francisco: Freeman, 1982. A detailed description of the horrifying medical, physical, environmental, and psychological consequences of a nuclear war by experts in the field.

COLOMBOTOS, JOHN, and CORINNE KIRCHNER. *Physicians and Social Change.* New York: Oxford University Press, 1987. An important contribution to our understanding of physicians and the socialization process by which they acquired their values and attitudes.

CONRAD, PETER, and ROCHELLE KERN, eds. *The Sociology of Health and Illness,* 2nd edition. New York: St. Martin's, 1983. Individual articles in this collection will acquaint students with basic issues in health-care policy and with the specific relationships between social structure and organization and the health of populations.

ROTHMAN, BARBARA KATZ. *The Tentative Pregnancy: Prenatal Diagnosis and the Future of Motherhood.* New York: Viking, 1986. This book explores the impact of reproductive technology on women's decisions to abort and the subsequent experience of the "tentative pregnancy."

FISHER, LAWRENCE E. *Colonial Madness: Mental Health in the Barbadian Social Order.* New Brunswick, NJ: Rutgers University Press, 1985. A fascinating ethnography of how colonial dominance and exploitation have created a context within which those who engage in individual patterns of resistance are viewed as "mad."

LEWIN, ELLEN, and VIRGINIA OLESEN, eds. *Women, Health and Healing: Toward a New Perspective.* New York: Tavistock, 1985. An informative collection of articles which illustrate how medical ideas influence social policies and women's health. The articles discuss reproduction, occupational health, and women as domestic providers of health care.

STARR, PAUL. *The Transformation of American Medicine.* New York: Basic Books, 1983. A penetrating analysis of the origins, history, and future of American medicine from the perspective of politics, the economy, and the social structure of American society. Winner of the Society for the Study of Social Problems, C. Wright Mills Award.

WAITZKIN, HOWARD. *The Second Sickness: Contradictions of Capitalist Health Care.* Chicago: University of Chicago Press, 1986. An important critique of the American health care system.

18

Population: People and Their Environment

WHAT effect will being born after 1965 rather than five years earlier have on the rest of your life? A great deal. The period 1945 to 1964 is known as the Baby Boom years. People born before or after these dates are likely to face a very different set of problems and possibilities from those encountered by people born during those two decades. One of the most important factors shaping the course of your life is, very simply, the number of other people who were born at the same time that you were. The size of your *birth group* (cohort) affects such outcomes as education, if and when you marry, the number of children you have, lifetime income, and occupational mobility.

Baby boomers, for example, have suffered from two problems. The first drawback was the sheer number of age peers. For example, members of the Baby Boom had to cope with overcrowded classrooms and teacher shortages. In the labor market, many found

The **birth group** or **cohort** refers to the number of other people who were born at the same time that you were.

that jobs and promotions were not easy to get. The huge number of new workers, all competing for work meant that baby boomers would have fewer choices.

A second difficulty is that Baby Boomers had the bad luck to begin their careers just as the American economy entered a period of economic stagnation. From 1945 until 1973, the American economy was expanding steadily, and wages grew an average of almost 3 percent each year. In the mid-1970s wage growth ended, with the result that a man aged twenty-five in 1973 is lucky to have the same earning power today as he did then (Levy and Michel 1985). Two oil price shocks leading to higher energy prices, slowdowns in productivity, and changes in the distribution of occupations (See Chapter 12) have compounded the financial problems of Baby Boomers. The proportion of young families with incomes of $35,000 or more is no higher today than it was in 1973 (adjusted for inflation). Moreover, in 1973, a larger proportion of young families had reached this income on one salary (Levy and Michel 1985). People born during the Baby Boom can expect to earn less over their lifetimes than is the case for earlier or later smaller cohorts of workers. As a large cohort caught between two smaller ones, Baby Boomers will find their lives affected even in old age. They will make heavy demands on the social security and health-care system at a time when the still-employed labor force is expected to be much smaller than it is today.

Are members of the Baby Boom generation embattled workers or glamorous yuppies as they are so often portrayed? Widely viewed in the media as the generation that can have it all, they have maintained high levels of consumption through such adaptations as postponement of marriage, dependence on two earners, and reluctance to have children. Even the relative political conservatism of this birth group is thought to reflect their fear of shrinking opportunities for economic security (Levy and Michel 1985). In these many ways, our destinies are shaped by the number of births and the distribution of age groups in the society.

In this chapter, we shall examine some of the changes in population that affect not only our own lives but the structure of societies. To most Americans, population problems are associated with other, less modern nations. For example, one thinks of overpopulation in developing Third World countries, famine in Africa, and the large number of infant deaths in Asia. But the life chances of people and the social structure of the United States are just as linked to the growth, composition, and distribution of the population as is true of more crowded and less economically developed societies. All are affected by population changes, which, in turn, influence economic, political, family, religious, and educational systems.

As noted in Chapter 12, based on the nature of its economic system, a society can be described as *preindustrial, industrial,* or *postindustrial.* In the *preindustrial* society, fishing, agriculture, and mining are the dominant modes of subsistence. In an *industrial* society, machine technology for the manufacture of goods is dominant. The *postindustrial* society is characterized by increased growth in the service sector, including finance, trade, transport, recreation, health, education, and government. If labor and capital are the chief features of industrial economies, the production of information and knowledge is the hallmark of postindustrial economies. As you will see in this chapter, changes in the size, the composition, and the distribution of populations are closely linked to industrial development. *Demography* (from the Greek *demos,* "people") is the study of the characteristics and the patterns of change of human populations. Before examining these shifts, let us define some of the basic terms and sources of data used by demographers.

Demography is the study of the characteristics and the patterns of human populations.

Basic Demographic Concepts

Demographers commonly use two types of numbers to describe populations: *absolute numbers* and *relative numbers. Absolute numbers* are the actual count of people, of births, deaths, marriages, and so forth. For example, the statement that 16.5 million Canadians live in urban areas gives a characteristic of the population in absolute numbers. Although useful, absolute num-

Absolute numbers are actual counts of people, births, marriages, deaths, and so forth.

bers have their limitations. The United States, for example, has a population about ten times larger than that of Canada, so that a comparison of the absolute number of urban residents in Canada with the absolute number in the United States would tell us little about similarities or differences between the two nations. Demographers therefore often use *relative numbers,* such as percentages, rates, and ratios, that summarize statistical information and control for differing population size. Relative numbers are especially useful when we compare the behavior of a given population at two or more points in time, or when we contrast two or more

Relative numbers such as percentages and rates allow comparisons of different size populations.

societies at the same time. Some of the more common demographic terms are defined in Table 18-1.

Sources of Data Used by Demographers

CENSUS DATA

The desire to count the number of people who were born, who died, or who resided within a geographic area is very old. Although we do not know when the first population statistics were collected, an-

TABLE 18-1 Commonly used demographic terms

CRUDE BIRTH RATE: the number of births within a specified time period divided by the total population within that time period, multiplied by 1,000. This may be visualized as:

$$\frac{\text{total number of births, U.S., 1988}}{\text{total U.S. population, 1988}} \times 1,000 = \text{birth rate, 1988}$$

CRUDE DEATH RATE *(mortality rate):* The number of deaths within a specified time period divided by the total population within that time period, multiplied by 1,000. Thus:

$$\frac{\text{total number of deaths, U.S., 1988}}{\text{total U.S. population, 1988}} \times 1,000 = \text{U.S. death rate, 1988}$$

LIFE EXPECTANCY: the average length of life remaining to a person at a given age, typically at birth.

NATURAL INCREASE: the birth rate minus the death rate.

FERTILITY RATE: the number of live births within a specified time period divided by the population of women between the ages of fifteen and forty-nine (the years most likely to be childbearing), multiplied by 1,000. Thus,

$$\frac{\text{number of live births, U.S., 1988}}{\text{number of U.S. women aged 15 to 49, 1988}} \times 1,000 = \text{U.S. fertility rate, 1988}$$

(The fertility rate is a more refined measure of births than the birth rate, which is based on the total population of all ages and both sexes, rather than only on women likely to give birth.)

INFANT MORTALITY RATE: the ratio of deaths to live births of children below one year of age in the population, that is,

$$\frac{\text{no. of deaths below age 1 in 1988 in the U.S.}}{\text{no. of live births in 1988 in the U.S.}} \times 1,000 = \text{U.S. infant mortality rate, 1988}$$

(The infant mortality rate is regarded as a sensitive indicator of health and economic development. It is also important in determining life expectancy.)

MIGRATION: the movement of people into (immigration) or out of (emigration) a given geographic area. (Migration is an important variable in the growth or the decline of regional or national populations.)

NET MIGRATION: the difference between the in-migration (immigration) and the out-migration (emigration) for a geographic area within a specified time period.

POPULATION GROWTH: the sum of natural increase (birth minus deaths) and net migration.

DEMOGRAPHIC TRANSITION: the change from populations characterized by high birth and high death rates; to high birth and low death rates; to low birth and low death rates and population stability (zero population growth). (This transition typically accompanies industrialization.)

A **census** is an inventory of the entire population at a given time in a specific area.

A census is taken **every ten years** in the United States.

cient Greece, Rome, and Egypt all gathered information about their populations, often for taxation or military purposes. A *census* is an inventory of the entire population at a given time; it provides valuable information about each person in a specified geographic area.

Today, in the United States, a census is required by law *every ten years.* The first census in the United States was taken in 1790, the most recent in 1980. Although everyone is required by law to answer census questions, the information is, not surprisingly, subject to error. Some people find its questions too difficult to answer; others, despite guarantees of confidentiality, are concerned about privacy; and some (especially the very poor) are difficult to locate and thus are never counted. A typical national census in the United States has been estimated as having about a 3 percent error; in other words, its information is about 97 percent accurate. Censuses taken in developing nations, where the population may be more difficult to locate and where illiteracy is greater, are much less accurate.

The information collected in a census reflects the complexity of the society and its values. What is asked also reflects the uses to which the information will be put. For example, in the first U.S. Census in 1790, the questions were few and the publication of the results was immediate. Census takers nailed the information they had collected to store walls, so that each citizen could be sure the information was accurate. Only five questions were asked of each household: number of free white males sixteen years of age or older, number of free white females, number of free white males under sixteen, number of other free (nonwhite) persons, and number of slaves. This simple information showed the number and the location of potential voters and nonvoters by race, sex, and age.

By 1890, not only had the complexity of the questions increased, but they mirrored national concerns of that era about the mortality, the physical characteristics, and the health of the population, including such questions as "Are you a tramp, syphilitic, or habitual drunk?" and requesting the head size (large, average, or small) of any mentally retarded persons in the household. The 1980 U.S. Census focused on information of practical use to the government and of endless fascination

to social scientists, such as housing, income, family size, and other components of quality of life.

SAMPLE SURVEYS

Sample surveys, or minicensuses, based on a small but representative sample of the population, provide updated information that supplements the census. Such surveys provide relevant information at a relatively low cost and within a short time. In the United States, for example, data on unemployment are gathered monthly from a panel of approximately sixty thousand households. Information on household composition and living arrangements is updated yearly from the same survey.

Sample surveys are based on a small but representative part of a population.

VITAL STATISTICS

Vital statistics are records of births, deaths, divorces, marriages, and other significant events that are recorded as they occur. Such records were traditionally collected by parish churches and, in some parts of Europe, date back to the eleventh century. It was not until the late nineteenth century, however, that most western European countries began systematic civil (governmental) registration of these events. In the United States, vital statistics are collected at the local and state levels and are summarized by the federal government. Unfortunately, not all areas are equally thorough or accurate in their record keeping, so that U.S. data on marriages and divorces, for example, are actually estimates.

Vital statistics are records of important events such as births, marriages, and deaths.

MIGRATION STATISTICS

Another source of information used by demographers is *migration statistics.* Some nations keep very close counts of both internal and international migration. The United States collects information primarily on immigration into this country. These data are useful in measuring the changing characteristics of the population as well as gains or losses of population through international migration.

Migration statistics measure the population flow within a society as well as the movement in or out of it.

POPULATION PROJECTIONS

What do the following statements have in common? "According to Census estimates . . . ," "When world population reaches 6 billion . . . ," "The proportion of

Population projections are estimates of future growth of a nation, state, or other geographic area.

Hispanics and Asians in the population by 2020 will be . . ." They are all *population projections,* that is, estimates of future growth of a nation, state, or other geographic area. Projections are an important demographic tool, but no population projection is perfect, for none of us can see the future or accurately predict the behavior of millions of people. As Haub has commented, "The Weather Bureau makes forecasts, not the Census Bureau. With considerable confidence, weather people can say that, in the past, when the meteorological situation was thus-and-so . . . the weather behaved in a certain manner. . . . They do have a detailed model to go on that basically stays the same" (Haub 1986, p. 8). Demographers do not, unfortunately, have as predictable information with which to work. They can only make reasonable guesses about future population patterns, based on estimates of death rates, birth rates, and net migration. Events, such as wars, disease, famine, changes in the economy, and shifts in the availability of birth control, coupled with poor or missing data, can make even the most careful projection fall short of the mark. The projection itself is not wrong; what is wrong are the assumptions behind it. Perhaps the most famous example of erroneous assumptions in modern history was the projection of the length of time the Baby Boom would continue in the United States. Demographers assumed it

There are many ways to look at this planet. You may see the earth from your own place on it and look outward to what seems like far and distant places and people; or you can see it as an ecosystem containing a multiplicity of interdependent inhabitants of which you are only one. (© Allen Lee Page/The Stock Market)

was a short-lived, post-World War II upswing in the birth rate; instead, it lasted twenty years. The projections were mathematically correct but the assumption behind them was not.

To avoid being locked into a single set of predictions that may prove to be wrong, demographers often make several projections, based on different assumptions. Figure 18-1 shows several projections for American population growth, each of

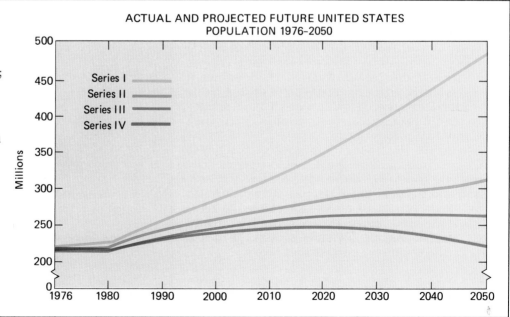

Figure 18-1
United States population—projections to 2050. Series I is the highest birth rate estimate; Series IV, the lowest; Series II and III are intermediate, with III closest to zero population growth and II similar to current birth rates. (From U.S. Bureau of the Census, *Statistical Abstract of the United States, 1980,* Washington, D.C.: U.S. Government Printing Office, 1980.)

ACTUAL AND PROJECTED FUTURE UNITED STATES
POPULATION 1976–2050

Series I
Series II
Series III
Series IV

Predicting Life Expectancy: The Case of Anna and Andy

In 1984, twins—Andy and Anna—were born in the United States. Although they were born only moments apart, at birth Anna had a life expectancy of seventy-eight years and Andy seventy-one. This is because demographic data show that, on the average, females live longer than males in the United States. But are these estimates accurate? Even without knowing anything further about the lifestyles or behavior of Anna and Andy, some demographers would say that both twins can expect to live even longer, depending on the kinds of assumptions that are made about progress against mortality.

For example, if we assume that a lowering of death rates at each age continues at the same pace as in the 1970s, Anna's life expectancy at birth will increase to age ninety, and Andy's to age eighty-one. And, if progress continues at the same rate and both twins have a same sex child at age twenty-five, Anna's daughter can expect to live to age ninety-four, Andy's son to age eighty-five. Their grandchildren may live even longer: if Anna's daughter also has a daughter at age twenty-five, this granddaughter could expect to live to age ninety-seven. Andy's grandson could expect to live to age eighty-nine.

What different assumption could be made that would reverse the male-female difference in life expectancy in the above example? If an acceleration of progress against causes of death is used in projecting their life expectancy, Anna could expect to live to age ninety-three. But Andy's life expectancy would increase to age ninety-seven—four years greater than Anna's. How could this be? The answer is both complex and simple. During the 1970s, male life expectancy increased at a greater rate than it did among women. Thus, although females still lived longer, males made greater gains in chances of survival. Projecting this higher rate into the future results in a longer life expectancy for Andy than for Anna.

The figure 18–2 which appears to the right of this box summarizes the three estimates just described for Anna and Andy. As you can see, assumptions made about factors influencing life expectancy drastically change the results. In actuality, few demographers expect mortality rates to continue their decline. The safer guess is that death rates will remain close to current levels.

(Based on John M. Owen and James W. Vaupel, "Life Expectancy," *American Demographics*, pp. 37–38, November 1985.)

which is based on a different guess about fertility rates and net migration. Within the next thirty years or so, you will have the opportunity to see not only which assumptions were the most accurate but which factors—birth rates, death rates, and net migration—affected patterns of population increase in the United States.

The Growth of Populations

How many people have ever lived on Earth? The best estimate is 50 billion, even though it is difficult to pick a date and say "here's where humanity began" (Westing 1981). For nearly 97 percent of human history, the world population remained under 5 million, kept in check largely by high death rates. Then, from about 1750 on, the world's population began a rapid rise, reaching 1 billion by 1830. In July 1987, the world population passed 5 billion, accounting for one in ten persons who have ever lived! And as you read this, 158 people are being born each minute.

What accounts for such a steep and swift rise? Populations size is closely related to the food supply and level of technology of the group. Although the shift from a gathering/hunting mode of subsistence to horticulture and farming meant a more secure

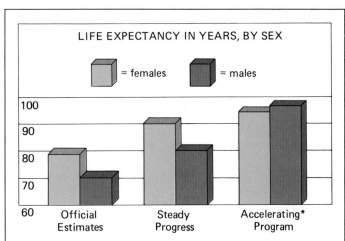

*The accelerating program assumes an extreme drop in male mortality.

Figure 18-2
If mortality rates continue to decline as they did between 1960 and 1980, children born today could expect to live, on average, well into their nineties.
(Source: Owen and Vaupel, p. 38.)

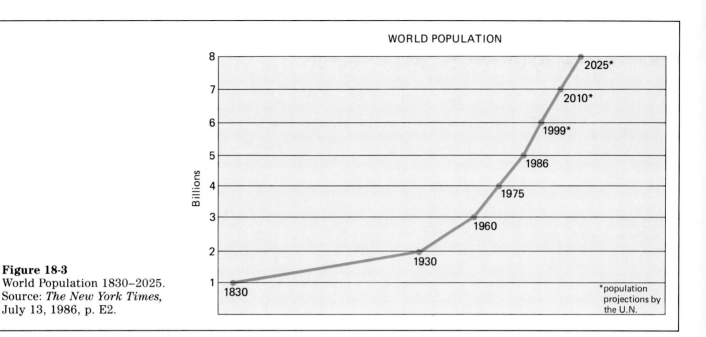

WORLD POPULATION

Figure 18-3
World Population 1830–2025.
Source: *The New York Times*,
July 13, 1986, p. E2.

food supply, capable of supporting larger numbers of people, world population grew only slightly over the tens of thousands of years of basic agriculture. It is with the Industrial Revolution of the past 250 years that such a sustained increase in population has taken place, as you can see graphically in Figure 18-3.

This increase occurred first in the industrializing societies, where public-health advances in sanitation (sewers, indoor toilets, boiling water, sterilizing instruments, and pasteurizing milk) and changes in agricultural technology combined to increase food supply and to lower death rates. Population growth takes place when death rates decline while birth rates remain high. This is what happened in industrializing societies in the eighteenth and nineteenth centuries, triggering a major change in population dynamics.

The Demographic Transition

The **demographic transition** is a result of lower death rates, which led to an increase in the world population.

The term *demographic transition* refers to the historical stage through which industrializing societies passed in which a population kept in balance by high death and high birth rates was temporarily thrown off balance before reaching a new equilibrium with low death and low birth rates.

In the first phase of the transition, lower mortality leads to population growth in two ways. First, people are subtracted from the population at a slower rate. Second, more births occur because of the

Some observers say that the low natural increase in American society has affected the value of children. As there are fewer and fewer children they become more precious. Do you think this is true in every type of society? (© J. Guichard/SYGMA)

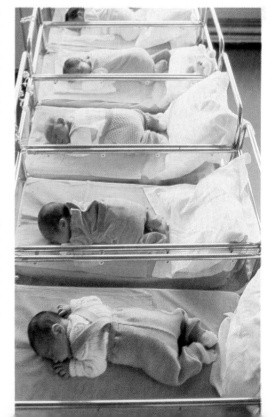

Malthus and Exponential Population Growth

The first stage of population growth, characterized by high birth rates and lower death rates, is sometimes called the *Malthusian period of population growth*, after the British clergyman Thomas Malthus (1766–1834). A demographer, a social reformer, and an opponent of contraception, Malthus suggested that there was a close relationship between the number of people and the amount of food available. Observing the high birth rates in late-eighteenth-century England, Malthus predicted that the number of people would soon overtake the available food supply because population increases in a *geometric progression*, doubling itself every twenty-five years. Agricultural production, however, increases in an *arithmetical progression*, adding a constant quantity to present production every twenty-five years. Thus, Malthus predicted runaway population growth, in which a population of 1 million would increase to 2 million after twenty-five years, 4 million after fifty years, 8 million after seventy-five years, and so on, to about 1,000 billion after five hundred years. Food, however, would merely increase by adding the quantity

current produced every twenty-five years, so that after five hundred years it would be no more than twenty times greater than at the present time. Population would grow a millionfold; food production only twentyfold. Geometric increase of population is called *exponential growth*.

Malthus proposed that positive checks to halt this population disaster must be taken and advocated celibacy and late marriage; otherwise, harsher, natural restraints like war, famine, disease, and malnutrition would limit population growth through death. Although Malthus correctly predicted the rise of population at a swift rate, he did not realize that improved technology would cause agricultural production to increase much more rapidly than he predicted, nor did he realize that couples might voluntarily limit the size of their families through means other than sexual abstinence. However, the concern about rapid population growth and its effect on agriculture, natural resources, and quality of life initially voiced by Malthus remains a major issue today.

greater number of people who survive through their childbearing years. If, at the same time, food production and living standards are improved, dramatic gains in life expectancy occur.

It typically takes several decades before birth rates also begin to fall for reasons that will be detailed later in this chapter. Briefly, however, as parents realize that most of their children will survive to adulthood, they need bear only the desired number. The trend toward lowered fertility is especially strong among urban couples for whom a large family can be a barrier to upward mobility and higher standards of living. Children, who are economic assets in an agricultural society because of their value as labor, are a major expense in an industrial society.

In the third phase of the demographic transition, when birth rates have fallen along with death rates, the population is once more in balance and there is little or no *natural increase*. The United States today, for example, has a very low rate of natural increase—about seven people per 1,000 population in 1987. Fertility has stabilized at 1.8 children per woman, or just

below the *population replacement level* of 2.1 births needed to replace the parents (the extra .1 in 2.1 is a demographer's correction for the fact that some people will die before reaching childbearing age, and others will have no children). The condition of no natural increase is also called *zero population growth* (ZPG).

It is somewhat confusing to realize that ours is a ZPG society at the same time as the Census Bureau announces that the annual *number* of births has risen steadily from 1970 to 1986. This paradox is a result of the fact that the Baby Boomers are now in their childbearing years, adding to the number of births, but the average born to each woman will be slightly under two. In other words, there is no "Baby Boomlet," but only an echo boom from the original large cohorts. When the Baby Boom generation grows out of prime childbearing ages, the rate of natural increase in the United States will probably decline still further—to as low as four persons per 1,000 population in the year 2000. Unless, of course, there should happen to be a new Baby Boom, something very few demographers foresee in the near future.

Natural increase refers to the difference between birth rates and death rates.

The **population replacement level** occurs when the average number of births per woman reaches two.

Zero population growth takes place when each couple produces only two offspring.

Overpopulation

Overpopulation means that there is imbalance between the number of people and the ability of the group to support them.

In the second phase of the demographic transition, when death rates fall without a comparable reduction in births, a population could outstrip its resources. *Overpopulation* refers to an imbalance between the number of people and the ability of the group to support them. Note that the term is relative; a large population is not itself a problem, but becomes one only when there is insufficient food, shelter, or work.

Throughout the Third World, where over 90 percent of the world's population is concentrated, overpopulation is a threat to social stability. In many countries, infant death rates, although high, have been greatly reduced through the introduction of public health programs and medical technology. Yet fertility remains high; with an average of between 6 and 8 children per woman in Moslem countries and most of Africa. About 40 percent of the population in most developing countries is under age fifteen. Put another way, 90 percent of today's population growth takes place in the world's poorest nations, bringing further pressure upon already strained political and economic systems.

Furthermore, at current rates, the population of the developing world is expected to double within the next three decades.

The young are a major segment of the poor in Third World countries. Like these urban dwellers in Mexico City, they face the prospect of lifelong poverty. (© Steve Benbow/ Woodfin Camp and Associates)

Table 18-2 summarizes many of the demographic differences between developed and developing countries.

FACTORS AFFECTING HIGH FERTILITY

However dysfunctional for the group as a whole, high *fertility* is often a rational choice for parents. In societies without public programs for the care of the elderly, one's children are the most reliable form of social security in old age. In most agricultural economies, the children can produce more than they consume, even though some will starve to death when the land is poor (which becomes an argument for having many children).

This is an example of the classic "dilemma of the commons," the commons being the piece of land in English towns that belonged to the village as a whole and on which anyone could graze their cattle. But if each villager tried to maximize individual profit by putting as many cattle as possible on the commons, the animals would soon chew up the edible grass and the commons could no longer support any of them. In other words, if each family looks out for its own security by bearing many children, the group as a whole will eventually run out of resources.

High fertility is also encouraged in societies characterized by patriarchal values, in which a man's prestige depends on the size of his family. In many of the same

---

TABLE 18-2 World population highlights 1987

World Population: 5,026,000,000
World Total Fertility Rate: 3.6 children per woman
    Developed countries: 2.0
    Developing countries: 4.1
Population of People's Republic of China: 21 percent of world total
World Birth Rates: 28 per 100,000 population
    Developed countries: 15
    Developing countries: 32
World Infant Mortality Rate: 81 per 1,000 live births
    Developed countries: 16
    Developing countries: 90 (97 if China excluded)
World Rate of Natural Increase: 1.7 percent per year
    Developed countries: 0.5
    Developing countries: 2.1
Projected world population:
    Year 2000: 6,158,000,000
    Year 2020: 7,992,000,000

SOURCE: *1987 World Population Data Sheet,* Population Reference Bureau, Washington, D.C.

countries, religious beliefs also work to deny women access to family-planning information and services. Despite claims that women achieve fulfillment through childbearing, fertility rates tend to decline whenever women are given a choice. Their range of choice is likely to widen as leaders of developing nations, in a reversal of previous policy positions, appear to be eager to introduce population controls (*New York Times,* May 31, 1987, p.E 30). At the same time, however, the United States has cut funding for overseas as well as domestic family-planning programs on the grounds that they might encourage abortion.

Components of Population Change

The population of any society is determined by three factors: deaths, births, and migration. When births exceed deaths, a population grows. When fertility rates are lower than mortality rates, the population declines. When more people migrate into a society than leave, population grows; when more leave than enter, population declines. In the United States today, for example, while the overall fertility rate is very low, population decline has been delayed by the entry of young adult immigrants from Asia and South and Central America with relatively high traditional birth expectations.

MORTALITY (DEATH) RATES

As we have noted in Chapters 9 and 17, because mortality rates at young ages have been greatly reduced in industrial societies, life expectancy has increased dramatically. For people born before 1750 in Europe, average life expectancy was about thirty years—roughly the same as in ancient Rome, two thousand years earlier! The primary causes of such high mortality were wars, epidemic diseases, and famine. Food shortages were common, lowering resistance to diseases. The Irish potato famine of the 1840s, for example, not only reduced population through illness and death, but also through out-migration as hundreds of thousands of young people left the country for America and England.

Up until recently, death was likely to occur at any age. Today, in modern industrial societies, it is almost exclusively associated with old age. Whereas in 1900 only 42 percent of Americans could expect to live until their sixty-fifth birthday, three-fourths will do so today. But the picture is very different in the less-developed na-

In our society, we tend to expect death to occur only in old age. In previous times, death was seen as a "natural" occurrence at any age. How do you think that has affected our attitudes about living?
(© G. Rancinan/ SYGMA)

TABLE 18-3 Infant mortality, life expectancy, and per capita GNP for selected nations

Country	Infant Mortality Rate Per 1,000 Live Births	Life Expectancy at Birth	Per Capita GNP (U.S. 1985 $)
Industrialized nations			
Japan	5.5	77	11,330
Sweden	6.8	77	11,890
Switzerland	6.9	76	16,380
Canada	7.9	76	13,670
Netherlands	8.0	76	9,180
United Kingdom	9.4	74	8,390
United States	10.5	75	16,400
Developing Nations			
China	61.0	66	310
Saudi Arabia	79.0	72	8,860
India	101.0	55	250
Nigeria	124.0	37	760
Ethiopia	152.0	41	110
Afghanistan	182.0	39	*

* Information not available.

SOURCE: *1987 World Population Data Sheet,* Population Reference Bureau (abridged by authors).

tions, as shown in Table 18-3, which presents average life expectancy, infant mortality rates, and the per capita gross national product (GNP) as a measure of living standards, for selected industrialized and developing societies.

Social Class. A major factor associated with mortality is social class. Life expectancy is influenced by income and education. For example, in the United States, among families with incomes of under $3,000 per year and where the household head has less than eight years of formal education, the infant mortality rate is about 140 percent above the national average. Studies of Native Americans highlight some of the links between socioeconomic status and life expectancy. On the Indian reservations, although the birth rate is twice that of the general population, infant mortality is also much higher, and six times as many children die of tuberculosis.

Inequality in power, wealth, and prestige within a nation results in different distributions of infant mortality and life expectancy. For example, Saudi Arabia has many poor people; it also has a middle class and a few very rich. The rich have a life isolated from the conditions of the very poor. When national averages are taken, as in Table 18-3, the well-off people obscure the plight of the poor. In countries such as Afghanistan or Ethiopia, where the overwhelming majority of the population is very poor and plagued by famine, war, and disease, the results are much plainer. Everyone dies relatively young.

To summarize, although life expectancy has increased in most nations of the world, this increase is most maked in the modern, industrialized societies. Those nations still undergoing the transition from a preindustrial to an industrial mode of subsistence continue to have higher rates of infant mortality and lower life expectancies than modernized countries because of the lower standards of living, poor sanitation, and low incomes. They also suffer from less efficient agricultural production and lack of money to buy food and technology from other countries.

BIRTH AND FERTILITY RATES

The number of children that a woman bears in her lifetime and the timing and spacing of her pregnancies have major effects on her children's chances of survival. Women who start childbearing in their teens or continue past their midthirties are at a relatively higher risk of

Infant Mortality in the United States

Infant mortality rates may be as important as ups and downs in the economy and the GNP (Gross National Product) in charting the well-being of a nation and its people. As you will recall, the infant mortality rate describes the number of babies out of each thousand born alive who die before reaching the age of one. For the world as a whole, roughly one child out of every ten does not live to see its first birthday. There is, however, considerable variation among nations. How does the United States compare with other countries?

According to 1987 data, about 10.5 infants died for each 1,000 live births in the United States. Compared to other industrialized nations, the U.S. rate was relatively high. Canada, for example, had an infant mortality rate of 7.9; Sweden, 6.8; and Iceland, 6.2. Indeed, all of Northern and Western Europe, with the exception of Austria and Belgium had lower infant mortality rates than the United States. Even Japan and Taiwan had lower rates than the U.S.

What explains the relatively high infant mortality in such a rich nation as ours? In the United States as throughout the world, infant deaths are highest in poor areas. Low family income, overcrowding, lack of sanitation, and exposure to poisonous substances make it likely that a child will develop a fatal disease during the first year of life.

In addition, prenatal care reduces infant death. Throughout much of Europe, prenatal care is not only encouraged but subsidized. For example, Swedish women average sixteen visits to the doctor during their pregnancies while American women average less than twelve. Almost one-quarter of American women receive no medical care during the first three months of pregnancy and close to 6 percent receive care only in the last three months or not at all. Low birth weight, too, contributes to infant mortality, and low birth weights are most commonly associated with lower socioeconomic status and lack of prenatal care. Yet it is precisely low-income women with minimal access to health care who are most likely to give birth in the United States today.

What can be done about infant mortality? Nations with the greatest success in reducing the rate of infant deaths have also shown that effective programs are not necessarily expensive. Such remedies as health education, more even distribution of food resources, better sanitation, improving the status of women, and targeting public spending for maternal and child health care can help to reduce infant mortality significantly.

(SOURCES: *Statistical Abstract of the United States*, 1987; *1987 World Population Data Sheet*, Population Reference Bureau Inc., Washington, D.C.)

having their children die in infancy. In addition, short intervals between births are associated with higher-than-normal infant mortality rates because a woman's body needs time to recover from pregnancy and to rebuild nutritional reserves.

Social scientists and demographers have been intrigued by the decline in both births and fertility that has accompanied the transition to industrialization. Recall that *birth rates* are calculated by dividing the total number of births within a given time by the total population, and *fertility rates,* considered a more accurate measure, are calculated by dividing the total number of births by the number of women of childbearing age. Most demographers have concluded that the higher survival rates of children provided a reason for limiting family size. It was no longer necessary to have large families to ensure that one or two children would live to adulthood. Furthermore, as modes of economic

production became more complex, and increasing levels of education were required for social mobility, having many children became a liability. Child-labor laws reduced their ability to contribute to family income, and compulsory education laws required that children be supported until a certain age. Then, too, improved contraceptive techniques became widely available in most industrialized nations as early as the 1880s.

Although we tend to think of contraception as a new invention, attempts to limit family size in one way or another have characterized most societies throughout history. The relatively late age of marriage common in Western Europe until the last century was one such restraint. Other methods included infanticide (the killing of infants), particularly of females; abandonment; and starvation. Eighteenth-century European observers noted that the deaths of children were often welcomed;

parents wished openly and loudly for their children to die or to leave home. Small-pox, a major cause of infant and child-hood mortality, was actually known as the "poor man's friend" (van de Walle and Knodel 1980). Earlier generations of parents were not unfeeling or heartless; it's simply that, contrary to popular belief, children were not always viewed as an asset, either to the nobility, to the farmer with limited wealth, or to the landless industrial worker. Lacking more effective methods of birth control, infanticide by neglect, death through disease and child abuse relieved women from the excessive strain of working all day in industry and agriculture, and at the same time assuming all child-care duties. Infant mortality also relieved men from the support of very large families.

Smaller family size was not necessarily related to industrialization. Although both birth rates and fertility rates declined in England only after considerable urbanization and industrialization had taken place in the late nineteenth century, a similar decrease occurred at about the same time in Hungary, which was less industrialized.

Indeed, the first sign of fertility decline occurred in nonindustrialized France a century earlier, when most of the population was rural, poor, and Catholic. This fact suggests that economic development is a sufficient, though not necessary, cause for fertility to decline. Also important are social values.

In most Western nations, one hundred years ago, women who married in their early twenties and survived their child-bearing years could expect to bear six to eight children, four to six of whom would probably live to marriageable ages themselves. Yet, the birth rates tended to be somewhat lower than we might expect because many women married rather late, and others died or were widowed during their childbearing span. Nor did all women marry. We associate remaining single with being modern, but between 10 and 25 percent of Western European women a century or so ago remained unmarried, as compared to somewhat under 10 percent today. A typical demographic pattern in Western Europe in the mid-nineteenth and the twentieth centuries is illustrated in Figure 18-4.

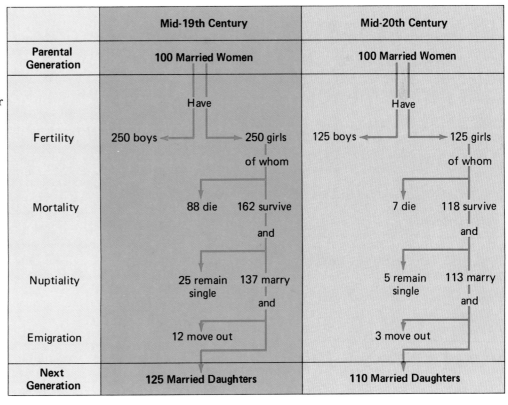

Figure 18-4
Typical demographic patterns in Western Europe, mid-nineteenth and twentieth centuries. (From Etienne van de Walle and John Knodel, "Europe's Fertility Transition: New Evidence and Lessons for Today's Developing World," in *Population Bulletin* 34[6], 1980, Fig. 1, p. 4.)

	Mid-19th Century	Mid-20th Century
Parental Generation	100 Married Women	100 Married Women
Fertility	Have / 250 boys ← → 250 girls / of whom	Have / 125 boys ← → 125 girls / of whom
Mortality	88 die 162 survive / and	7 die 118 survive / and
Nuptiality	25 remain single 137 marry / and	5 remain single 113 marry / and
Emigration	12 move out	3 move out
Next Generation	**125 Married Daughters**	**110 Married Daughters**

Fertility and Adoption: The Effects of Personal Values on Population Trends

WILLIAM FEIGELMAN AND
ARNOLD R. SILVERMAN

William Feigelman (Ph.D., SUNY at Stonybrook) is professor and chairperson of the department of sociology at Nassau Community College (Long Island, New York) and editor of Sociology Full Circle, *4th edition (Holt, Rinehart & Winston, 1985). His current research deals with teenage drug use and the treatment of multi-drug abusers.*

Arnold Silverman (Ph.D., University of Wisconsin) is also a professor of sociology at Nassau Community College. He has written in the area of social problems with a special emphasis on race relations. They have co-authored Chosen Children: New Patterns of Adoptive Relationships *(Praeger 1983).*

It is often said that the selection of social-research issues is sparked by the personal interests of the researchers. William Feigelman and Arnold R. Silverman's work on the social biases linked with adopting stigmatized children is consistent with this assertion.

After much consideration—and with an effort to live consistently with their politically liberal and humanitarian ideals—the Feigelmans decided to add their second (and last) child by adoption instead of by procreation. Knowledgeable about the problems of third-world countries, and especially familiar with Latin American conditions, they decided to adopt a Colombian child.

Once the adoption was completed, the Feigelmans felt the usual boastful pride of parents of an adorable, healthy, infant daughter. At the same time, these feelings were mixed with a sense of uncertainty and vague confusion about their nontypical mode of family formation.

For Arnie and Ruth Silverman, the 1972 defeat of George McGovern's presidential campaign represented a turning point, bringing to an end a period of intense political involvement. Tired of that futile and demanding struggle, they turned their attention to family life and professional careers. The Silvermans started to think about raising a family. Arnie also began to consider issues of family and parenting as a new area for his research. His interest in adoption grew as initial attempts to conceive a child had not been successful.

Normal office conversations between colleagues about family lives soon provoked a more serious discussion of this new and seemingly uncharted area of "intercountry" (foreign) adoptions. Eventually, the two researchers, with grant assistance from the National Institute of Mental Health and Research Foundation of the State University of New York, studied some 700 adoptive families and followed them over a six-year period.

During a formative stage of the research Silverman started attending meetings of a local adoptive parent self-help group. One of the meetings provided an important orientation to the study. A lawyer who addressed the group of adoptive parents on the subject of the adopted child's original birth certificate, offered information about when it is needed and how it could be obtained. In many states a second birth certificate is issued at the time of adoption, naming the adoptive parents as the mother and father. The original birth certificate—listing the child's birth parents—is often unavailable to the adopting parents. When the lawyer's presentation was completed, one parent rose and declared "We were given our child's original birth certificate and I'll tell you what we did with it; we burned it!" This statement was followed by thunderous applause and shouts of approval from most of the audience.

In thinking about this incident, we realized the tremendous importance of stigma in some adoptive relationships. Many adoptive parents feel stigmatized by their own infertility. Although adoption made it possible for them to realize their wish to become parents, it also reminded them of what they considered to be their "failure"—their inability to procreate.

The impact of infertility on parent-child relationships in adoption was a theme that also showed up in the analysis of the survey results. Compared to adoptive parents who are able to have natural offspring, infertile couples wanted to adopt children who resembled those that would have been born to them, especially in terms of race and ethnic background. In addition, infertile parents were more reluctant to celebrate the fact of adoption and, although they rarely concealed the fact, they did not advertise it or see it as positively as did fertile parents. They also felt less enthusiastic about their child's right to search for birth parents. In contrast, fertile adoptive parents were willing to adopt older children or those with visibly different racial backgrounds. They sent out cards to announce their adoption and generally rejoiced in what they understood as an enormously positive experience. These couples were more relaxed about their adopted child's right to search for birth parents.

The research took place when adoption was a lively issue for both families. Without the personal involvement and the contact with adoptive parents and children it is unlikely that the meanings of the data would have come to be understood as deeply as they were.

As you will note in the figure, when women in the nineteenth and twentieth centuries are compared, it is obvious that, despite fairly high levels of mortality, nonmarriage, and international migration, substantial population growth took place. The rate of population growth in Europe and America, however, has been slowly but steadily declining since the mid-eighteenth century. Although women began to limit the number of children they bore, most of their offspring would survive to adulthood.

Fertility declines in industrial nations are not only a response to changing economic realities; they are also a consequence of shifts in social mores and values—from a traditional family-centered orientation to an emphasis on the individual and personal fulfillment. As described in Chapter 11, all these trends have led to (1) a tendency to delay marriage and childbearing, (2) widespread use of contraception (especially sterilization), and (3) an increase in single-parent households, which are likely to have only one child (van de Kaa 1987). In effect, the "birth dearth" of late industrial societies is determined by a variety of forces, and in the absence of any countertrends, most demographers predict continued low fertility rates, at least in societies where women have gained power over their reproductive choices (Westhoff 1986). It is important to remember that it was the Baby Boom that was exceptional and not today's declining birth rates, which is merely an extension of two centuries of fertility decline in the West.

The Second Demographic Transition. So steeply has fertility declined in Europe and North America that some demographers speak of a "second demographic transition" from a low- or no-growth population to one that is actually in decline (van de Kaa 1987). Most European countries are experiencing sustained low fertility—from a low of 1.3 children for West German women to a high of 1.8 for British women. Only Ireland, at 2.5 children per woman, has a fertility rate high enough to replace the parent generation (*1987 World Population Data Sheet*).

Population decline has led to varied political responses, with conservatives alarmed over a loss of national strength, and liberals generally pleased with the degree to which women are able to make their own reproductive choices (Teitlebaum and Winter 1986). In the United States and other modern societies, opposition to women's rights is in part a response to these population fears, as seen most vividly in the case of Romania.

MIGRATION

Migration is the third important component that directly affects the size of a population. Why do people migrate? Peterson (1975) has proposed several broad reasons, including (1) *primitive migration,* which occurs when people cannot cope with natural or climatic forces, such as drought, famine, or lack of water; (2) *impelled* or *forced migration,* typically due to political pressures, such as were experienced by the Jews in Nazi Germany in the 1930s, or Central Americans escaping dictatorships today; (3) *free migration,* in which individual choice plays a role, such as in the movement westward in the United States; and (4) *group migration* or *mass migration,* in which many people, sharing a common characteristic such as ethnicity or religion, relocate. The Irish in the nineteenth century and such religious sects as the Hutterites, the Mennonites, and the Amish are illustrations of entire groups forced to move to improve their living standards or to maintain a particular way of life.

These migration categories often overlap. Most migrants may leave their place of origin for more than one reason. For example, communities of Hutterite migrants from Europe came to North America not only to maintain a way of life (group migration) but also to avoid religious persecution (impelled or forced immigration).

Who migrates? Although much depends on the historical period and the distance traveled, demographers have observed that when the distance is great and when migration has a pioneering quality, the migrants are predominantly young, unmarried males. In general, migrants tend to be young, unattached adults who lower the age structure of the country they enter while raising that of the place they leave. Figure 18-5 illustrates some of the pushes and pulls of migration.

The migration of young Irish men and women during the potato famine of the 1840s, for example, added greatly to the American birth rate over the following

Primitive migration occurs when people cannot cope with natural or climatic forces.

Impelled or **forced migration** is typically due to political pressures.

Free migration is one in which individual choice plays a role.

Group migration or **mass migration** involves the relocation of people who share a common characteristic such as ethnicity or religion.

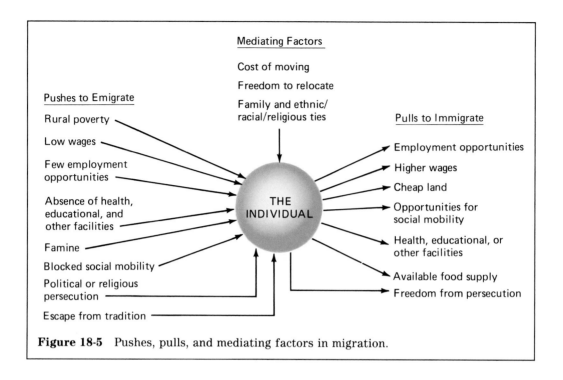

Mediating Factors

Cost of moving

Freedom to relocate

Family and ethnic/racial/religious ties

Pushes to Emigrate

Rural poverty

Low wages

Few employment opportunities

Absence of health, educational, and other facilities

Famine

Blocked social mobility

Political or religious persecution

Escape from tradition

THE INDIVIDUAL

Pulls to Immigrate

Employment opportunities

Higher wages

Cheap land

Opportunities for social mobility

Health, educational, or other facilities

Available food supply

Freedom from persecution

Figure 18-5 Pushes, pulls, and mediating factors in migration.

two decades, masking the beginning of the long-term decline. At the same time, their leaving helped reduce overpopulation in Ireland where other forms of birth control were forbidden by a powerful church. Although it was expected that most would return, the majority did not, and periodic migrations became the primary mechanism for Irish population control.

The many other waves of immigration that shaped our society are analyzed in Chapter 10. The most recent of these—largely Asian and Hispanic—like the European Catholics before them, have partially counterbalanced the overall trend toward lowered fertility rates. But it will not be long before they, too, adopt mainstream patterns—in family size as well as other aspects of the culture.

Composition of the Population

Although fertility, mortality, and migration are all important factors, they are affected by and reflect two basic population characteristics: *age* and *sex*. Both these variable are directly related to fertility, mortality, and migration. Only women of a

certain age can bear children, and older people (or in some nations, infants) are much more likely to die than the members of other age groups, and young adults are most likely to migrate.

POPULATION PYRAMIDS

Demographers often summarize age and sex distributions by *population pyramids.* Differences in the age and sex composition of economically developed countries, such as the United States or Sweden, and less developed nations, such as Mexico or India, may be observed in the population pyramids shown in Figure 18-6. As you look at these population pyramids, notice that a vertical line divides the number of males, shown on the left side of the chart, from the number of females, shown on the right. The figures on the scale at the bottom give the numbers (in millions) of people of each sex. Horizontal bars represent age groups in five-year intervals.

The pyramids in Figure 18-6 illustrate the demographic differences among societies experiencing rapid growth, slow growth, and no growth.

Note that there are more older people and fewer children in the developed than in the developing regions. How does this pattern affect people's lives? The lower

Population pyramids represent summaries of age and sex distributions.

birthrates and the higher life expectancies in all the industrialized nations suggest that greater public attention will have to be given to the needs of the elderly and less to those of the young. Some analysts of the future have suggested that this changing population pyramid means that the children of tomorrow will grow up in a society which is far less child-centered than today's. Parents may be less permissive and less concerned with the needs, wants, and gratification of their children. Childhood could become more structured and demanding and adolescence less prolonged (Toffler 1980).

That changes in the population pyramid affect a society and its socialization practices have been recently noted in China, a nation that has deliberately attempted to restrict couples to one child. Traditional patterns of socialization have changed as families have become smaller, so that children receive more attention and are clev-

erer, more imaginative, and healthier—and more likely to be spoiled brats.

In both the developed and the developing nations, population pyramids are affected by the three basic processes described in the previous section: births, deaths, and migration. Immigration and emigration may produce bulges or dents in the age and sex structure of receiving and sending countries. Special conditions also affect population pyramids; for example, in the USSR, the many deaths that occurred during World War II affected the marriage rate, the birth rate, and the sex composition of the population for several decades.

The population profile for Sun City, Ariz., a retirement community, resembles a cyclone more than a triangle due to the ratio of young to old. An interesting exercise would be to compare the population pyramid for your college with that of the surrounding community.

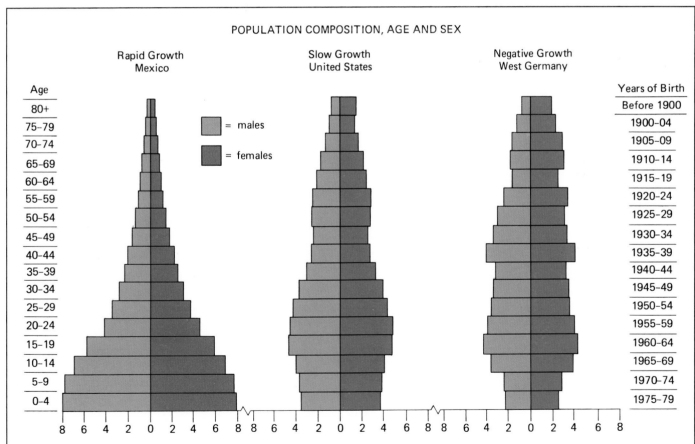

Figure 18-6 Source: *World Population: Fundamentals of Growth*, Population Reference Bureau, Inc., 2213 M Street N.W., Washington, D.C., 1984.

In Search of a Baby Boom: The Fetus as Social Property

In 1966, alarmed by a birth rate of 14 births per 1,000 population, the Romanian government abruptly ended legal abortion and announced a national goal of increasing both the birth rate and its national population by 30 percent in 1990. Today, although the birth rate remains at 14 per 1,000, contraceptives have been banned and can be neither manufactured nor imported. The legal age of marriage was lowered to 15. Employed women up to age forty-five are required to undergo monthly gynecological examinations at work to detect and monitor possible pregnancies. Women must participate in the program in order to receive other medical care. Legal abortion is reserved for medical emergencies. Moreover, unmarried people over the age of twenty-five and married people who are childless without a valid medical reason must pay an additional 30 percent tax on income.

Official policy dictates childbearing as part of good citizenship. As the president of Romania stated in 1986: "The fetus is the socialist property of the whole society. Giving birth is a patriotic duty, determining the fate of our country. Those who refuse to have children are deserters, escaping the laws of national continuity." (Population News, 1987: p. 3). Yet many Romanians apparently avoid this "patriotic duty"; an estimated 40 percent of the women pregnant in 1985 had illegal abortions.

To combat illegal abortions, a special unit has been established within the State Security Police to monitor each pregnant woman every month until childbirth. An equal interest in the fate of the living is not apparent. Ambulance rescue squads responding to an emergency routinely ask the caller for the age of the sick person. If the afflicted person is old, medical assistance arrives late. Clearly, it is more than a concern for human life that is involved in setting Romania's population policy. First, although it is one of the most populous countries in Eastern Europe, Romania has far fewer people than the Soviet Union. At the same time, Romania has attempted to maintain its own foreign policy, separate from other nations in the Soviet bloc. A larger population might, according to some observers, make the Romanian government feel more secure in its ability to withstand pressure from other nations. In addition, a larger labor force may help its lagging economy and provide recruits for its military.

Although much of the world is plagued by the problem of reducing its birth rate, Romania is only one of several nations trying to increase the birth rate. For example, within the fifteen republics in the Soviet Union, birth rates have been either stable or declining in the Eastern industrialized areas, compounding a labor shortage and leaving

WHY AGE AND SEX ARE IMPORTANT

Dependency Ratios. The combination of births, deaths, and net migration at any particular point in time produces a certain number of males and females within each age group. Knowledge of the age and sex structure of a population permits calculation of the *dependency ratio,* that is, the ratio of those under fifteen or over sixty-five years of age to people aged fifteen to sixty-four. The dependency ratio is often used as a measure of the economic well-being of a nation, as it describes the ratio of income earners (or potential earners) to those not producing income. Because only those in the labor force pay taxes and earn income to support children or the elderly, a nation with a very high proportion of old or young must raise productivity in order to support its members.

The **dependency ratio** is the ratio of those earning an income to those not earning an income.

Age, Sex, and Life-styles. Knowing the age and sex composition also allows us to understand various aspects of social, political, and economic life. For example, when the proportion of males in a population is greater than that of females, different life-styles and types of social control emerge. In the frontier West, most of the local population were unmarried males, so that high levels of drinking, fighting, and prostitution were likely to occur, creating problems for law enforcement. In family-oriented cities and suburbs, where the sex ratio is about equal, social and economic behavior is family-oriented. Moreover, the sheer number of partners available to men and women at a given point in time may change sexual norms and behavior, patterns of marriage and family breakup, and the social structure itself. Guttentag and Secord (1983) proposed that when women are scarce, norms develop that stress resource-rich land short of people. Although to give birth to a tenth child makes a Soviet woman a certified Mother Heroine, families in the cities of the Soviet north typically remain limited to one child. At the same time, however, among the Moslem and Asian populations in the central and western parts of the Soviet Union, the birth rate has grown rapidly. In Tadzhikistan, in central Asia, for example, the birth rate is the highest in the Soviet Union—about thirty-nine per 1,000—and there are over 32,000 Mother Heroines. But in Lithuania, in the eastern part of the USSR, the birth rate is only about sixteen per 1,000, with a mere thirteen Mother Heroines.

The Soviet government has offered incentives designed to encourage population growth in its eastern provinces: cash for each baby, extended maternity leaves, free food, and free schools. Rather than employ such economic incentives, Romania has used repressive measures to increase birth rates. How well have these two policies worked? For Romania, not very well: at its present rate of population growth, it will not double in size for another 178 years. And ironically, economic incentives in the USSR have primarily subsidized precisely those portions of the nation where the birth rate has always been high and where as many as half the people are under the age of sixteen.

In contrast, the People's Republic of China, with over one billion citizens, is engaged in a massive campaign to lower fertility by half! Couples are encouraged to have only one child by a mixture of economic incentives and repressive measures. One-child families receive tax benefits and other advantages, the age of legal marriage has been raised to over 21, contraceptives are widely available, and mothers are under pressure to terminate future pregnancies. The policy has been more effective among modern, educated city-dwellers than among the less well-educated peasants and farmers who hold more traditional values and for whom having children remains a social and economic asset.

These extreme cases illustrate one central point: in all societies, including our own, reproduction is never simply a matter of individual choice. Societies attempt to control the size of their population through subtle and not so subtle policies that influence the desire for children, that determine access to health care, and that affect the possibility of in- or out-migration.

SOURCES: "How Romania Governs its Fertility," *Population News*, February 1987, pp. 3–4; Serge Schmemann, "Russia Wants a Baby Boom of its Own," *New York Times*, July 22, 1985; *1986 World Population Data Sheet*, Population Reference Bureau, Inc.; H. Yuan Tien, "China's One-Two Fertility Debate," *Population Today*, April 1986, pp. 6–8.

---

monogamy and the restriction of women to the home. When men are scarce, these norms change, so that men are less likely to want to commit themselves to a lifelong marital relationship. Many women thus remain unmarried so that their labor-force participation is a necessity. Thus do age and sex ratios influence life-styles, attitudes, and sex roles.

Birth Cohort. As you will recall from Chapter 9, another key aspect of the age structure of a society is the *birth cohort*, that is, the people born within a certain time period. Each birth cohort varies in its original composition, and it changes as a result of mortality associated with sex, social class, ethnicity, and race. The Baby Boom example at the beginning of this chapter shows how the members of a particular age cohort share a common history that affects their entire lives. The in-

terplay among birth cohort, opportunity structure, and social change is illustrated by their fate.

GROWTH AND DISTRIBUTION OF THE U.S. POPULATION

In 1610, the population of the United States included a handful of white Europeans and an uncounted number of Native Americans. With 4.5 million people by 1790, the United States had more than doubled its inhabitants by 1820. In 1900, the U.S. population was roughly 76 million. Today, our population stands at about 244 million, more than three times higher than it was at the turn of the century. Two sources of growth were important: (1) *net increase,* or the excess of births over deaths; and (2) *immigration.* Immigration has been a significant factor:

between 1820 and 1985, more than 52.5 million immigrants settled in the United States (*Statistical Abstract of the United States 1987,* Table 7, p. 11).

The history of the united States has also been one of *population redistribution.* Originally, the American population lived primarily in rural areas and farming was the major mode of production. With industrialization, people moved from the countryside to the cities. The percentage of people living in rural areas has sharply declined even within this century, and the proportion of people living in the outlying areas of central cities has increased markedly. This redistribution of population is a result of changes in the modes of production.

> The **population redistribution** occurs as people move from one area to another.

Geographic Mobility.   Geographic mobility or *internal migration* is an important part of demographic change in the United States. It has a major impact on population distribution as people move between cities and suburbs, metropolitan and non-metropolitan areas, states, and regions. Knowing the characteristics of people who move allows us to assess the consequences of migration for both the areas they leave and those to which they move.

> **Internal migration** is a major part of demographic change.

How mobile are Americans? Surprisingly, although we tend to think of ourselves as a nation of frequent movers, the rate of moving has decreased in recent years. About 17 percent of the population moved between 1983 and 1984 compared to 21 percent between 1960 and 1961. The majority of moves are short-distance: about two out of every three people who moved between 1983 and 1984 remained in the same county, and nine out of ten stayed in the same region of the United States. The majority of people who relocated were young: over four in ten were between the ages of twenty and twenty-nine (*Current Population Reports,* series P-20, no. 407, 1986).

Where do people go? People living in the North moved least and were more likely to remain in the same county or same state than were movers in the South or West. Central cities tended to lose population; of those moving from central cities, about three times as many went to the suburbs as to more rural areas. The most dramatic population growth, however, was in the Sunbelt states (see Figure 18-7). During the 1970s and early 1980s, both the Midwest and Northeast—the Snowbelt re-

gions—lost population to the South and the West—primarily to Sunbelt states. But by 1983–1984, the southern region of the United States was the only area experiencing growth through internal migration. Although all regions of the United States gained population through immigration from abroad, the South and West were the most favored destinations.

The Rise of the Sunbelt.   In the 1960s, migration to the Sunbelt states began to account for the most important streams of interstate migrants. Over one third of all Americans now live in the fifteen states that make up the Sunbelt. The number of people in the Sunbelt increased by 22 percent from 1970 to 1980. This is nearly triple the rate of population increase in the rest of the country.

Why the sudden attractiveness of the South and the Southwest, when for most of this century, migrants had streamed out of the South into the industrialized North? By 1950, the Snowbelt states had entered a postindustrial era, and many industries moved to the South, which had lower taxes and a pool of nonunionized workers for labor-intensive, low-wage manufacturing, such as in the textile and clothing industries. Union membership in the Sunbelt is about one half that of the United States as a whole, and most Sunbelt states have "right-to-work" (antiunion) laws. Thus, workers there have been willing to work for lower wages than those in the northern and north-central states. After years of living in a largely economically underdeveloped region, Sunbelt workers were less concerned with high wages than with simply having jobs.

Many Snowbelt residents were attracted to the newly expanding areas of the

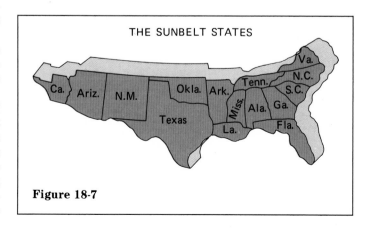

THE SUNBELT STATES

Figure 18-7

Atlanta, Georgia has experienced a great deal of new development in commerce, manufacturing, and real estate. It is one of the thriving cities of the Sunbelt and with one of the busiest airports in the U.S. Atlanta is also the home of major league baseball, football, and basketball teams. (© Mike Yamashita/Woodfin Camp and Associates)

United States despite generally lower wages. Employment opportunities have been greater, the environment has been relatively free of urban blight, and taxes and energy costs have been lower. The Sunbelt has promised a more rural, less congested, cleaner environment in which to live and raise children—precisely the initial attraction of the suburbs when compared to the older, industrial cities. Even large Sunbelt cities have offered a more relaxed way of life. In addition, for many, particularly older people, the warmer climate is a major benefit.

The inmigration of people and the economic prosperity of the Sunbelt initially resulted in a more even distribution of income among the regions of the United States. But as the South and West have increasingly inherited much of the economic and political power of the North and North-Central regions, they have also inherited some of the problems of Snowbelt cities: crime, congestion, and physical decay. For example, most of the Sunbelt has yet to catch up with the nation as a whole in per capita wealth. In only three states, California, Arkansas, and Virginia, was the 1985 median family income higher than the national average. Moreover, throughout the Sunbelt, a higher percentage continues to live in poverty than in the United States as a whole.

There is also a growing gap among the subregions that make up the Sunbelt. The ethnic and racial composition of inmigrants varies from state to state. For example, more than half of all Hispanic Americans lived in Florida, Arizona, Texas, New Mexico, and Southern California in 1980. Asians account for a growing proportion of the population in Texas and California, while Cubans, Latin Americans, Caribbean Islanders, and Haitians are an increasing population in Florida. Income differentials among states are noticeable as well. For example, per capita income in Mississippi in 1986 remained the lowest in the United States. Neighboring Arkansas, in contrast, had the highest per capita income of any of the Sunbelt states. Similarly, the percentage of people living in poverty varied widely among Sunbelt states. Although the South has the largest number of top wealth holders in the United States, and California has the highest number of millionaires, income differences among people within each state are vast: for example, California, Virginia, and Arkansas had a lower percentage of people living below the poverty level than the national average. Moreover, the population of the Sunbelt is growing at different rates. The southeastern states and Southern California may have passed their peak of population growth although for different reasons. The Southeast, with the highest percentage of the labor force engaged in manufacturing, has generally not adapted to the rapid changes of a postindustrial economy, while rising labor costs and housing prices in California have made it less attractive for internal migration.

Rising rates of unemployment in the Sunbelt suggest that the region is no longer recession-proof. Only seven of the fifteen Sunbelt states had unemployment rates lower than the national average in 1985. Yet for the remainder of the 1980s, it seems likely that the lure of the Sunbelt as a whole will continue, and its population **511** will increase as that of the Northeast and Middle West declines.

Population Patterns in Modern and Developing Nations

How can population statistics provide information about the economic organization and the degree of modernization of a particular society? In this context, it is more useful to think in terms of *nations* rather than societies. Nations are distinct political entities on which data are more or less routinely collected, but a society is not necessarily identical with political boundaries. For example, Nigeria contains several societies, each with its own culture, language, and social structure.

MODE OF SUBSISTENCE

The higher the proportion of the labor force engaged in agriculture, the more likely is a society to be preindustrial. There is, however, variation in the mode of subsistence in developing, industrial, and postindustrial countries. If we compare several Latin American countries with the United States we can see a decrease in the proportion of people employed in agriculture over an eleven-year period, indicating movement away from an agricultural economy. Yet, there are marked differences among the countries that give clues about their level of industrialization. The United States, a *postindustrial* nation, has by far the lowest proportion of its labor force in agricultural work, and even this percentage is declining. Argentina and Chile, both of which have industrial economies, rank next. Mexico, Bolivia, and Paraguay have begun to industrialize at a relatively rapid rate; agricultural employment declined by 10 percent or more during 1965–1982. The Dominican Republic, although gradually industrializing, still had over half of its labor force employed in farming, thus much closer to the ideal type of preindustrial society: its primary mode of subsistence is land-based.

The introduction of industry is only one factor in the uprooting of village populations. In their efforts to modernize, developing countries require a supply of unskilled labor for such tasks as road building and other public works. Young men from villages are offered minimal wages and housing in work camps, and once having left home become part of the unskilled labor pool that drifts to large cities, moving from one job to another, with long periods of unemployment in between.

Sitting in traffic seems to be an international experience. How different is this traffic jam in Lagos, Nigeria from the one in your favorite North American town?
(© W. Campbell/SYGMA)

For people who remain in farming, other major changes have taken place over the past three decades. As developing societies become part of an international economic system, local production is replaced by an emphasis on a single "cash crop" that can be used in international exchange to bring dollars to the nation. Villages and families cease to be self-sufficient, no longer tending their traditional variety of foods and animals. Local farmers are now dependent on the world market, where a sudden drop in the price of the primary cash crop—tea, coffee, or sugar, for example—means instant poverty. Even in good times, the revenues from cash crops may not be sufficient to support a large family. This becomes another source of landless peasants who drift toward population centers in search of employment.

The result of all these trends is a gradual depopulation of the countryside and a massive influx of young people into cities.

URBAN–RURAL POPULATION

The proportion of the population that resides in cities (urban) or in the countryside (rural) also tells us about a nation's level of modernization and technology. Less economically developed countries are far more likely to have higher concentrations of people in rural areas and villages precisely because they are less industrialized. *Urbanization* describes the rise in the proportion of the total population concentrated in cities and suburbs (see Chapter 19). Although urban concentration is a rough indicator of industrialization, it does not tell us how city dwellers earn their living. For example, both the United States and Argentina are urbanized, yet the United States is postindustrial, with much of its labor force employed in service occupations rather than manufacturing. Measures of urbanization, therefore, do not allow us to distinguish an industrial from a postindustrial country.

Nonetheless, migration from rural to urban areas gives us an indication of social and political pressures that occur as people stream into the cities. More than 40 percent of world population currently lives in urban areas, and by the early part of the twenty-first century, more than *half* the world's population is expected to live in cities. Most of the world's largest cities are now in developing countries and are grow-

Urbanization describes the rise in the proportion of the total population concentrated in cities and suburbs.

TABLE 18-4 Supercities of the twenty-first century (ranked by largest estimated population)

	Population in 2000	Change from 1980
1. Mexico City, Mexico	31.0 mil.	Up 107%
2. São Paulo, Brazil	25.8 mil.	Up 91%
3. Shanghai, China	23.7 mil.	Up 66%
4. Tokyo–Yokohama, Japan	23.7 mil.	Up 19%
5. New York (N.Y.–N.J.), United States	22.4 mil.	Up 11%
6. Peking, China	20.9 mil.	Up 83%
7. Rio de Janeiro, Argentina	19.0 mil.	Up 78%
8. Bombay, India	16.8 mil.	Up 102%
9. Calcutta, India	16.4 mil.	Up 86%
10. Jakarta, Indonesia	15.7 mil.	Up 115%

SOURCE: Population Reference Bureau, Inc., 1982.

ing to sizes never before known in the history of the world. For example, Mexico City, with over 15 million people, is predicted to have twice as many people by the year 2000. Table 18-4 summarizes the ten world supercities expected to contain a total of 215.4 million people or about 35 percent of the world population in 2000.

As you can see in the table, only one of these supercities is located in the United

Urban growth in developing countries sometimes results in massive overcrowding and an increase in poverty. Modernization increases an already great disparity in incomes. (© Diego Goldberg/SYGMA)

States; 8 of the 10 are in developing nations. Urban problems are taking a new dimension. Within the next fifty years, the mainly rural character of Third World countries will vanish and they will have to plan for cities of immense size. The current rate of urban population growth in Africa is 5 percent, implying a doubling of its urban population every fourteen years. The current figure for East Africa is about 6.5 percent, a doubling time of about ten years. Such extreme rapid urban growth has never been seen before.

Experts differ about whether urban growth is a blessing or a curse. Those who think urban growth is a blessing point out that higher rates of urbanization are associated with economic growth and increased life expectancy. The facts however, obscure important differences among people. Income is distributed unevenly among urban dwellers, and measures of national economic growth often ignore the plight of those who remain outside urban areas. Moreover, the housing shortage in many large cities is already overwhelming; according to World Bank estimates, one fourth of the urban population in most African and Asian cities cannot afford even minimal housing. Card-

board crates, sheets of plastic, tin cans, leaves, bamboo, and earth are the main sources of building materials. Some people simply live on the streets.

As large numbers of people stream into these cities, problems of pollution, unemployment, overcrowding, housing, crime, and urban sprawl are likely to increase. All of these make social order and political stability increasingly problematic. The rural surplus population may become an urban surplus population; that is, an informal work sector of street vendors, sidewalk repair shops, prostitutes, shoe shiners, and other marginal occupations. But urban life is essential to the social nature of the modern world. Emphasis should be on creation of urban environments where people could enjoy an economically and socially enriched life. This is a challenge for which few of these nations have sufficient resources.

Population, Resources, and the Environment

At present, demographers estimate that the world population is expanding at the rate of 153 people a minute, 9,180 an hour, 220,320 a day and 80 million a year. The fastest expansion is occurring in poor, less developed nations—the very places where food, housing, sanitation, and economic opportunity are in shortest supply. As the population of the world expands at a rapid rate, the fear that food supplies and natural resources will be exhausted and that the air and water will be polluted has occupied both scientific ad popular attention. For example, the number of news stories about the environment has risen dramatically since 1970 when they began to replace civil rights as a source of popular concern in our society. The 1986 meltdown at the Chernobyl nuclear power plant in the Soviet Union highlighted the global dimensions of this issue, while adding to the Soviet's problems as one of the most heavily polluted nations in the world. Deforestation, water and air pollution, smog, and acid rain confront leaders in the Soviet Union and the United States alike, as they do people in many other parts of the world.

Yet it is an oversimplification to believe that changes in the environment are new

The city usually generates new and different jobs by virtue of its size and complexity. But who would have imagined that a subway needed a subway pusher such as these in Tokyo? How would you write the job description? (© J. P. Laffont/SYGMA)

Calcutta, India, another super city where growth has been a double-edged sword. (© Jehangir Gazdar/Woodfin Camp and Associates)

events. There has been a long history of human depletion of the natural environment. Beginning with hunting, gathering, and agriculture, natural vegetation was replaced with crops, lands were overgrazed, and forests cut down. As people began to build cities, they changed the environment still further, using up natural resources and spewing waste into the air and water in the drive toward industrialization.

The forces regulating human populations change as people adapt to their environments in different ways. As discussed earlier, the last few centuries have been characterized by improvements in public health and a general rise in the standard of living. New farming and transportation technology expanded the food supply and decreased the danger of famine. These and other changes allowed the population to increase at an unparalleled rate.

But deaths caused by war and natural disasters—drought, earthquakes, and floods—have also proportionately increased. For example, when a cyclone struck the Bay of Bengal in 1985, tidal waves caused the deaths of 5,000 to 10,000 people in Bangladesh. Because Bangladesh is so densely populated, the islands

swept away by the tidal waves were the only place available for many to live. Therefore, even after the cyclone, dangerous areas such as these remain heavily inhabited. There is simply no place else for the poor to go (*Population Education Interchange,* 1986).

The famine in Africa highlights similar problems. The drought which caused the famine that killed so many people would not have been so severe had there not already been a heavy strain on both the land and the people. Poor land use and continued cutting down of trees encouraged extension of the desert into previously workable land. When coupled with rapid population growth in the region, the stage was set for high death tolls. Massive food aid shipments have been required since 1983 to reduce the famine that took the lives of hundreds of thousands of Africans in six nations in the early 1980s. But wars, lack of transportation, and corruption have kept much of the food from reaching the most needy.

Some scientists have argued that people have already far exceeded the earth's car-

According to one view, scenes such as this one of Ethiopia's famine are likely to become all too familiar in the future. Famines are expected to increase in the poorest nations of Africa and Asia while the affluent countries store excess food or dump it to protect price structures. (© David Burnett/Woodfin Camp and Associates)

rying capacity, that is, the maximum population that the earth can support indefinitely. Given this depletion, a "crash," or dramatic reduction in population cannot be avoided and will lead to both revolutionary changes in life-styles and loss of many of the conveniences people in industrial and postindustrial societies take for granted (Catton 1980). According to this and similar arguments, sometimes termed the *"doomsday approach"* by critics, natural resources will drop dramatically during the last decades of the twentieth century, leading to rapid declines in production and in food. Pollution will continue to accompany industrial growth, and overpopulation will continue to cause instability in developing nations, even as millions starve to death.

According to the **doomsday approach** natural resources will drop dramatically during the last decades of the twentieth century, leading to rapid declines in production and in food.

Not all demographers believe that such a crash is inevitable. Some, like Simon (1980), have proposed that much of the information about population growth, natural resources, and the environment is "false bad news." According to this optimistic view, the world supply of land available for agriculture has actually increased, and the scarcity of natural resources, including food and energy, has decreased. The problem is in distributing these increased resources to where they are needed. A growing world population, while initially lowering production, will eventually produce higher per-worker productivity and ultimate raised standards of living. "Bad news," however, is more likely than good news to capture the attention of the media (Simon 1980).

Moreover, politics play a large role. Africa's famine is not due solely to drought and rapid population growth. Political instability and war disrupt farming and increase the number of refugees who are crowded into a relatively small area. Ethiopia's present food crisis was greatly worsened by two decades of civil war. Since independence, over twenty wars have occurred in central Africa, and more than seventy leaders have been assassinated or ousted.

International trade policies also play a role. For example, North America emerged as a major worldwide supplier of grain during the 1970s, but its agricultural exports dropped off sharply during the 1980s. Why? The reasons are complex: a worldwide weak economy, heightened overseas competition, and a strong dollar.

The net result has been a sharp drop in food exports from both the United States and Canada. Yet stockpiles of grain in the United States grew so large that by mid-1986, government estimates indicated that there was enough surplus wheat stored in the United States to make twelve loaves of bread for every person in the world. At the same time people are starving.

What will the future hold? Predicting the effects of a rapidly growing population and its impact on the environment is complicated by the fact that there are so many uncontrollable variables involved. With respect to food supply, soil erosion, dwindling water supplies, and other hazards could threaten the agriculture of not only developing but industrialized nations. Yet new technologies are always possible. The extent to which such technological advances may benefit the global population is an unresolved political question.

SOCIOLOGY & YOU
The Impact of Demography On Your Everyday Life

You have probably realized by now that social forces influence your life in many ways, and that most of your very private concerns are in fact shared by millions of other Americans. Most of us have to ask such questions as "What occupation shall I follow?" and "What is the best way to prepare for it?" "Where will I wind up living?" "Will I rent or own?" "How can I assure myself of a long, healthy life?" "Shall I marry and do I want to have children and if so, when?" Sociologist Robert Kennedy, in a delightful book, *Life Choices: Applying Sociology* (1986) suggests that when millions of Americans face the questions of life, death, occupation, parenthood, and residence, their collective answers add up to national rates of migration, mortality, fertility. These factors, plus the flow of immigration into the United States, determines the total number of people with whom you'll share your future, and with whom you'll compete to attain many of your hopes and goals. You will be cooperating and competing with your birth cohort (agemates) for many things—education, jobs, housing, material and nonmaterial resources, energy, clean air, and water.

In this chapter we present the population pyramid of the United States in 1986 showing the age and sex dis-

As the world population increases, we can anticipate an increased demand for energy. This future demand will have a major impact on the economy and individual life-styles. Attempts at conservation, however, are responsive to changes in the supply of oil. During the shortages of the late 1970s, when gasoline prices rose dramatically, Americans bought smaller, more fuel-efficient cars, supported a fifty-five mile-an-hour speed limit, and took other conservation-minded actions. But when it appeared that there was a glut of oil in the mid-1980s, car manufacturers began to produce larger, less fuel-efficient models, the speed limit was raised, and no one turned off the lights.

But oil is a limited resource; it took millions of years to create oil deposits and once we use them up, alternative sources of energy will have to be found. Coal, however, is also a limited resource, and one whose mining, moving, and burning has serious environmental consequences. *Acid rain* is the name given to the deposits of sulphur and other chemicals emitted from industrial smokestacks. Because such industries are concentrated in the northern part of the United States, much of the rain drifts over the border into Canada, where it has become a major political issue and source of ill will between the two nations.

The other major energy alternative, nuclear power, has its negative features, as the Chernobyl accident vividly illustrated. Clouds of radioactive material floated across vast expanses of Europe, contaminating crops and animal feed, and perhaps seeping into water supplies that will affect people for many decades ahead. The possibility of further accidents, both as a result of faulty technology and human error, has produced a growing movement of anti-

Acid rain refers to the deposits of sulphur and chemicals emitted from industrial coal smokestacks.

tribution of the total population. The number of people born the same year as you were is an example of a social phenomenon that has and will have a great impact on your life, but one over which you have no control. Let's take a quick look at one area in which the size of your age cohort is important: housing opportunities.

Birth cohorts have a close link with housing trends because most people enter the home-buying market in their late twenties. Since 1976 the average age of the first-home buyer has been about twenty-eight (Kennedy 1986: 26). Many people in their early or mid-twenties may want to own their own home eventually but chances are they are renting or still living with their parents. It takes some years to save for initial down payments.

Exactly how does the cohort influence available housing? In the mid-1970s, when the Baby Boomers entered the housing market to buy their first home, their greater numbers (compared to earlier cohorts) suddenly increased the demand for housing. Older housing stock was repaired and kept serviceable; the number of units built before 1940 declined only slightly between 1970 and 1980. Therefore, the housing available to the Baby Boom cohort was a little older than that available to the Depression era babies ten years earlier.

Prices also changed. While the Depression babies found home prices moderate, the Baby Boomers found a situation where rates of inflation increased dramatically by the late 1970s. Between 1975 and 1980 the general consumer price index increased by 53 percent

while the cost of the new privately owned, one-family house increased by 64 percent. Because the Baby Boomers were competing with each other for scarcer housing, they drove up the prices higher than would have been the case had there been fewer of them. As the prices for first homes increased, the proportion of first-home buyers who used savings and investments as the only source of their down payments declined from almost three-fourths to one-half between 1976 and 1980. Many turned to their families for financial assistance; others borrowed heavily. And the less fortunate were priced out of the market altogether, and forced to lower their housing aspirations. Renting became a more affordable way to meet their housing needs. To own one's home, a couple required a higher income than could be earned by a single worker. One solution, then, was to have wives continue to work after marriage, so that while, in 1960, young wives were typically full-time homemakers, by 1980 the majority were in the labor force. Although women remained and advanced in the labor force for a number of reasons, their motivations were, at least in some part, influenced by the desire to improve the family's housing situation with the goal of home ownership, a key element in social status and a sense of economic security in our society.

How many people were born in the same year as you were? In what year will you be (or were you) thirty years old? How do you think the size of your birth cohort is affecting your life choices?

The barge Mobro, loaded with 3,000 tons of garbage, left Long Island City, N.Y. with its cargo on March 22, 1987. Seven states and three foreign countries refused permission to dump the garbage in their landfills. Finally on September 2, 1987, the cargo was incinerated in Brooklyn, a few miles from its origination point. It was then buried. Total cost of this cruise—over $1 million. (© UPI/Bettmann Newsphotos)

nuclear energy activists in Europe and the United States. At the moment, the construction of nuclear energy facilities in our country has been brought to a standstill, less because of opposition from environmentalists than because of the current steady supply of relatively cheap coal and oil.

A final problem area concerns the disposal of waste—not only all the chemical, radioactive, and other poisonous materials generated by industry, but the normal garbage produced by a modern population. Americans were vastly entertained in 1987 by the saga of a barge full of trash from a New York town that traveled up and down the Atlantic Ocean looking for a dumping place. In many cases, disposing of garbage and waste through burying it has resulted in deadly materials ultimately reaching the underground water supply. Burning produces air pollution.

Possibly, some technique for using nonradioactive waste to produce energy will be developed. But in the meantime, the thought of modern societies buried under their own refuse brings into clear focus the basic issue of the fit between populations and their environments. Perhaps no other issue is less glamorous or more important for your generation to solve.

Summary

Demographers study the characteristics and the distribution of populations. Censuses, sample surveys, vital statistics, and migration statistics are the major sources of the data used by demographers. A census is an inventory of the entire population of a country; in the United States, one is conducted every ten years. Vital statistics are records of births, deaths, divorces, marriages, and other important life events. Migration statistics are counts of movements within a society or in and out of a country.

Changes in population size are linked to the availability of food and the level of technology. Population growth increased slowly over the many thousands of years before the Industrial Revolution, which set the stage for a dramatic and sustained rise in the world population. The first stage of the demographic transition is characterized by lowered death rates, accompanied by continuing high birth rates leading to a surge in population growth. Several decades later, as birth rates decline, the pace of natural increase in the population also slows.

Mortality rates, birth and fertility rates, and migration are the major components of population change. Mortality declines at the youngest ages are reflected in large increases in life expectancy (the average number of years one can expect to live) that ultimately lead to reductions in birth rates. Immigration and emigration patterns also affect the age distribution of the population in both the receiving and the sending societies. The age and sex composition of a society are summarized by demographers in population pyramids shaped by the combination of births, deaths, and overall migration at a specific point in time.

There are substantial regional differences in population growth in the United States. The Sunbelt region has attracted migrants from other states, whereas the Snowbelt areas have lost population. A number of economic, social, and personal factors underlie this trend, though the most recent data indicate a slowing down of the Sunbelt's rapid economic growth. In general, also, U.S. cities have been losing population to their suburban fringe areas.

The past two decades have been a period of increasing concern over famine, air and water pollution, and the depletion of natural resources. Many scientists predict social unrest and reduced standards of living, whereas others speak of technological breakthroughs. But there is evidence that worldwide fertility and birth rates have declined and that population control is being accepted in many developing nations. Nonetheless, the world's population continues to increase by several hundred thousand people a day, though at a slower rate than a decade ago, and world hunger may become even more widespread. In developed nations, environmental problems center on energy, pollution, and waste disposal.

Suggested Readings

BOGUE, DONALD I. *The Population of the United States: Historical Trends and Future Projections.* New York: Free Press, 1985. This book provides an overview of our population, its social and economic characteristics as well as the history of racial and ethnic variation.

GUTTENTAG, MARCIA, and PAUL F. SECORD. *Too Many Women? The Sex Ratio Question.* Beverly Hills, CA: Sage 1983. In a very readable book, the authors argue that the number of opposite-sex partners available to men and women at any given historical time will lead to changes in sexual behavior and mores; marriage, family and divorce patterns; and women's consciousness regarding traditional and modern roles.

KENNEDY, ROBERT E. *Life Choices: Applying Sociology.* New York: Holt, Rinehart and Winston, 1986. This book provides a life-course perspective for age-related demographic projection of the Depression, Baby Boom, and Baby Bust cohorts. It discusses educational attainment, occupation, marriage and childbearing, home ownership and retirement prospects.

TEITELBAUM, MICHAEL S., and JAY M. WINTER. *The Fear of Population Decline.* Orlando: Academic Press, 1985. A fascinating historical account of the beliefs of western politicians and leaders concerning the decline of national and racial populations.

WARD, KATHRYN B. *Women in the World Economic System: Its Impact on Status and Fertility.* New York: Praeger 1984. An informative and important study that analyzes the impact of Third World women's labor force participation on fertility rates.

19

Urban, Suburban, and Rural Life

L ONDON, England, is covered with a thick, biting fog that makes breathing both difficult and hazardous to health. A famous statistician, John Graunt, has just published the first convincing statistics on mortality due to air pollution. The time is 1690, and the cause of the air pollution is coal. Coal—the technology greeted as the fuel for the future during the seventeenth century—had deposited a persistent and dangerous cloud over the city.

In the seventeenth century, as today, scholars sought solutions to the unanticipated and disturbing side effects of technology on urban life. For example, someone invented a smokeless stove, claimed to be so constructed that "coal steept in Cats-piss makes not the least ill scent" (Justel, in Brimblecombe 1987). Another proposed solution was that industries should move out of London into what we now call industrial suburbs. Clearly, problems of population density, use of resources, technological change, and their effects on city and country life are not unique to the twentieth century.

Regardless of the century or stage of economic development of a society, urban, suburban, and rural life-styles are socially constructed. As forms of social organization, however, city and country life are relatively recent. Up until ten thousand years ago when agriculture began to replace hunting and food gathering as the primary mode of subsistence, people lived primarily in migratory groups. With the introduction of agriculture, forms of social organization, suited to more stable residential patterns, began to develop, as seen in Figure 19-1. Archaeologists have estimated that cities evolved about six thousand years ago. Although no one yet knows where and when the first city was built, traces of cities, most often located in river valleys and on plateaus, have been found in the Near East, in Asia, and in West Africa. These preindustrial cities were governmental, agricultural, commercial, and religious centers.

What happens to social institutions and social interaction as urban life becomes the major pattern and as rural and village life declines is the subject of this chapter. To understand the impact of the growth of the city on social institutions and value systems, you will also learn about the growth of the city and the suburbs, and about some of the problems associated with urban and suburban life in the United States today.

Urban Versus Rural Life

Differences of opinion about the positive and negative features of urban life are probably as old as the first city. Urban life has been associated with assertiveness, masculinity, intellect, power, and danger; the suburbs and the countryside, with family life, rest, closeness to nature, and safety. Although these life-styles are social inventions, the city has been singled out by critics as the height of artificiality. For example, Thomas Jefferson commented that American cities were "pestilential to the morals, health, and liberties of man" and viewed a then widespread yellow-fever epidemic as a blessing because it would reduce the urban population (Fischer 1976).

Four related themes have dominated debates on the virtues of urban or rural life: (1) the theme of nature versus art, in which the city may be described as either more civilized or more sinful than the countryside; (2) the theme of familiarity versus strangeness, in which the city is associated with the new, the different, and the unexpected, and the rural with familiar things and people; (3) the existence of community, or *Gemeinschaft,* relations in the rural area, as opposed to the impersonal, or *Gesellschaft,* social relations that dominate urban life; and (4) the theme of tradition versus change, in which the countryside is the stronghold of traditional values, and the city is the place where tradition is shattered and new norms developed (Fischer 1976). These four themes illustrate the mixed feelings that people have had toward the city. On the one hand, the city symbolizes freedom, progress, excitement, and change. On the other, it is seen as artificial, lonely, stressful, and ugly. By and large, the evidence suggests that both rural and village life have been romanticized by most Americans who long for the relative simplicity and isolation of the countryside. Yet, most Americans—over three in four—live in what are defined as urban areas.

If city life is so unattractive, how can this pattern be explained? The major reasons for migrating to or remaining in the

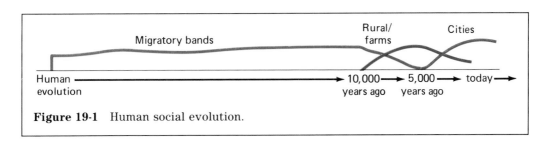

Figure 19-1   Human social evolution.

To some extent our views of both city and country life suffer from exaggeration and myth making. The urban scene is not simply a landscape of empty and anonymous brick and cement, nor was the rural village the quaint, cute and clean scene that has been recreated in this tourist attraction. (© Clif Garboden/Stock Boston; © Aktar Hussein/Woodfin Camp and Associates)

city have been associated with modernization and the division of labor. In industrialized societies, the urban setting has generally provided not only a more complex occupational structure but greater economic opportunity and more and better jobs. Before the Industrial Revolution,

however, our population was widely dispersed in villages and small towns across the continent.

RURAL LIFE

Farm Life. The United States began as an agricultural nation. In 1790, about 93 percent of the American population worked on farms. Even today, when only slightly more than 2 percent of the U.S. population lives on farms, images of the beauty of rural life dominate popular thought. For example, a 1986 *New York Times* poll reported that almost six in ten Americans believe that "farm life is more honest and moral than elsewhere" and over two-thirds think that "farmers have closer ties to their families than elsewhere." Yet relatively few Americans live on farms today, for both the number of farms and the percent of people engaged in farming has declined dramatically within the last sixty years. In 1920, there were about 6.5 million farms in the United States; by 1986, there were only 2.2 million. As you can see in Table 19-1, although the number of farms has declined by about 66 percent, the average number of acres per farm has increased by over 300 percent. As tractors and other power-driven equipment have reduced the number of farmers and farm laborers required for agriculture, larger farms have become common and migration from the farms has increased.

There are, however, considerable differences among farm residents who now account for slightly over 2 percent of the U.S. population. According to Census definitions, not all farm residents are farmers; that is, the term "farm population" describes a broader residential group than people who make their living through agriculture. In 1985, for example, only half of all employed farm residents reported agriculture as their main employment. In fact, about one-third of all farm residents in the labor force were employed in a service industry, with another 20 percent in manufacturing (Bureau of the Census, 1986). Conversely, many farmers do not reside on farms; about 30 percent of farm operators and managers lived off farms in 1985 and were not counted in government statistics as farm residents.

The declining number of people making their living by agriculture is due in part to recent financial stresses. From a purely

TABLE 19-1   The changing farm in the U.S.

	Number of Farms (in millions)	Average Farm (in acres)	Agricultural Acreage (in billions)
1910	6.40	137	0.879
1920	6.52	147	0.959
1930	6.55	151	0.990
1940	6.35	168	1.065
1950	5.65	213	1.202
1960	3.96	297	1.176
1970	2.95	374	1.102
1980	2.43	429	1.042
1986	2.21	455	1.007

SOURCE: *Statistical Abstract of the United States 1987,* p. 621, Table 1097.

economic view, investing in farming is risky. Unlike most other businesses, farming is unique in that both economic factors (food prices, farm subsidies) and natural forces (rainfall, temperature) affect the success or failure of agriculture as a business. In addition, farming is heavily influenced by government regulation and deregulation, irrigation projects, credit policies, and various price-support programs.

Although thousands of farmers have gone bankrupt or have left the land to make a living elsewhere, those with large farms and few debts have done very well. On average, *corporate* farms covered over 2,000 acres and enjoyed annual sales of

$527,000 in 1982. In comparison, the average *family* farm in the United States in 1982 covered 330 acres, with sales of about $40,000 (*Statistical Abstract of the United States, 1987,* p. 623). Increasingly, farming is dominated by **agribusiness,** where a relatively small proportion of farmers, using sophisticated technology, produce a large percentage of the food consumed here and sold abroad. The highly regulated and heavily subsidized nature of American agriculture stands in sharp contradiction to the folk myth of the lone, individualistic farmer (Bennett 1986).

Who comprises America's farm population? In 1985, 97 percent of farm residents were white, slightly under 2 percent were black, and a similar proportion were of Spanish origin (*Current Population Reports,* Series P-27, No. 59, 1986). Almost half live in the Midwest; 32 percent live in the South, 14 percent in the West and the remainder in the Northeast. The black farm population is concentrated almost entirely in the South (98 percent), those of Spanish origin in the West and South (92 percent). Blacks have left the farms at higher rates than whites. In 1920, nearly half of the total black population lived on farms compared to just over one-fourth of all whites. Factors relating to the declining number of blacks in farming include smaller acreage, sales of black-operated farms by white owners, and the higher proportion of black farm residents in poverty—about double that for white farm residents.

Agribusiness is a type of farming where relatively few farmers, using sophisticated technology, produce a large proportion of the food consumed domestically and abroad.

While corporate farms are experiencing substantial profits, small farms are suffering major losses. Foreclosures are common as are auctions of farm equipment, such as this one in Missouri. Farmers are being forced off their land in record numbers. (© J. P. Laffont/SYGMA)

Although traditionally, people living on farms have been young, this pattern has changed dramatically since 1940. As of 1985, the median age of farm residents was 36.5 years, significantly higher than the median of 31.4 for the nonfarm population. Yet farm residents are more likely to be married and living with a spouse than nonfarm residents, and they tend to have more children than urban or suburban dwellers. Changes in the structure of farm families are related to economic and political currents affecting agriculture as a business. The time and effort required for successful farming, and all its uncertainties, make farming a less attractive choice for young people than regular wage work in the industrial or service sectors. And, as we have noted, fewer and fewer family farms are being passed on from parents to children.

Despite the relative persistence of traditional beliefs about male dominance in the rural family, farm women are involved in a wide range of work roles and decisions

The family farm was once a model of "gemeinschaft" relationships. Today only 2% of families live on farms. Agribusiness and technology have made dramatic changes. (© Michal Heron/Woodfin Camp and Associates)

(Rosenfeld 1986). Many family farms are equal partnerships between husband and wife (Bennett 1986); and in one recent study, over half of the farm women interviewed in a national survey indicated they could continue farming if something happened to their husbands (Rosenfeld 1986).

Rural and Village Life. Rural areas encompass more than just the people who live and work on farms. According to the Census definition, anyone who lives in an incorporated area with fewer than 2500 inhabitants is a "rural resident." Up until the 1920s, these villages were centers of economic and social life for the scattered farm population. But between 1920 and 1960, millions of rural people left such communities to move to the growing industrial cities, where jobs were plentiful and where young people could find a life of their own. The depopulation of rural America was reinforced during the period of interstate highway construction, when the smaller communities were completely bypassed and isolated.

Left behind were older people and those still engaged in agriculture. Rural villages typically contained at least a post office, a church, and gas station/general store. Some inhabitants earned a living by repairing farm equipment or selling seed and fertilizers; others were employed in nearby towns or cities. By 1970, however, the stream of people moving to the cities from the countryside had not only slowed but by the end of the decade, a reverse migration was under way—jobs and people were beginning to move out of cities and into the countryside. Although the black rural population increased between 1970 and 1980 for the first time in several decades, the movement out of cities and suburbs (areas adjacent to the city) was primarily a white phenomenon (Lichter et al. 1985). We will discuss the reasons for these migration patterns in a later section of this chapter.

Thus, while rural villages had been losing population or remaining stable during the 1950s and 1960s, two-thirds experienced population increase in the 1970s (Johansen and Fuguitt 1984). Today, over one in four Americans lives in a rural area, especially in the South and Midwest. In other words, we are witnessing a *deconcentration* of our population, as people and businesses enjoy increasing flexibility

The Death and Life of a Small Community

John Stephenson, a sociologist who has studied villages both in Kentucky and in Scotland, suggested that "there is much to be learned about the life and death of small communities through the study of their histories, their rewards of daily life, and what is happening to their populations, whether they are located in the Blue Ridge mountains of the U.S. or the Highlands of Scotland." Is village life dying? To answer this question, Stephenson studied the village of Ford, a small community of 150 people in Scotland. In existence for over 300 years, Ford once had more than 1,000 inhabitants, but over the last 100 years or so, people moved away as the town declined both economically and socially. This extensive outmigration to more urban areas, coupled with closing of the town's school in the early 1970s, drastically reduced the ranks of village natives. Almost no native-born inhabitants remain in the community today.

Yet, in the early 1980s, Ford was in the process of repopulation: "almost everyone who lives here now was born somewhere else" (p. 123). These newcomers have been drawn to Ford for a variety of reasons. Some people have moved to the community because of old family ties to the locale; others are Scots who have been attracted to it as a desirable place to live and work; still others have moved from urbanized central Scotland and England in search of a more peaceful life-style. Although sharp social divisions and rivalries exist among these three groups, social and community life has been revitalized. Shared identity with the village of Ford and the very diversity and competition among different factions of newcomers have transformed the community, creating new social institutions and informal social networks.

Stephenson's study highlights two significant, and often neglected points about rural communities. First, change in the character of a small town does not necessarily worsen the quality of life or the strength of social ties. Second, contrary to romantic belief, rural life is not synonymous with traditional ways of doing things. Rather, large-scale changes within even a very small community may produce new social bonds, enabling an apparently dying community to survive and adapt to a changing society. The greatest threat to the vitality of the town of Ford, according to Stephenson, may be from tourists in search of a "quaint village." To attract tourist dollars, Ford's residents might try to recreate a "traditional village" that no longer exists in fact, thereby weakening their new vitality.

SOURCE: Based on John Stephenson's, *Ford: A Village in the West Highlands of Scotland.* Lexington: University Press of Kentucky, 1984.

in where to locate (Frey 1987). Employers no longer need to be near raw materials, transportation facilities, or pools of low-skill workers. Modern communications can link widely dispersed businesses. And when the jobs move out of urban areas, so do the employees who can afford to relocate. The new rural dwellers, however, are very different from the country folk of the past. Many rural areas now feature small housing developments or mobile-home parks; others contain split-level homes on several acres, whose residents enjoy a life-style very similar to that of the city or suburb they recently left.

Some rural areas, however, remain locked in poverty, and others have become new slums. In general, rural poverty rates have always been higher than for more urbanized areas; in the South, for example, both white and black country dwellers are among the poorest, least educated of Americans, with extremely high infant mortality rates and a very low life expectancy. The new rural slums are most likely to be found in the Southwest, where migrant workers, unemployed Anglos and Mexican-Americans are huddled in small communities, without proper sanitation, clean water, or adequate health care. In one part of the Rio Grande Valley, where 250,000 people live in 400 rural slums, these conditions have led to the spread of infectious diseases usually associated with developing nations (*Newsweek,* June 8, 1987, pp. 27–28).

Although it is generally thought that social networks (that is, supportive friendship and family ties) are stronger among rural residents than city dwellers, this is not always the case today, or possibly in the past as well. Although the majority of

Like urban poverty, rural poverty tends to be hidden. Both poor whites and blacks in the rural south have high infant mortality rates, little education, low life expectancy and impoverished living conditions. To many this seems a major social contradiction in the most affluent country in the world. (© J. P. Laffont/SYGMA)

studies do show that kinship interaction is higher among rural than city families, the relationship may have less to do with rural residence per se than with age, education, occupation, migration history, and race. For example, inner-city black women have more extensive supportive networks than their white counterparts, but among rural people, the pattern is reversed (although black mothers had the closer kin ties even in the countryside, they had very few others upon whom to call for help). For both black and white low-income rural mothers, links to professional support systems were largely nonexistent (Gaudin and Davis 1985).

Growth of the City

URBANIZATION

Urbanization involves the concentration in cities of large numbers of people of differing occupations and backgrounds.

A major step in the process of modernization has been *urbanization,* or the concentration in cities of large numbers of people with different occupations and backgrounds. *Urbanization* has three major characteristics: (1) density of population, and either (2) the size of the population in a geographic area, or (3) varieties of statuses. Generally, the more people with different ascribed and achieved status within a defined geographic space, the more likely we are to describe the area as urban. In the urban setting, visible symbols of power, prestige, and wealth—the size of one's home, the neighborhood in which one lives, the car one drives, and the clothing one wears—are more important in defining a person's status and identity than in more rural localities. In the countryside or the small town, one's family history, economic position, and personal characteristics are well known by others. Visible status symbols have far less meaning.

Urbanization does not hinge on some magic numbers or concentration of people or absolute size. Rather, it is a matter of degree (Wirth 1938, Redfield 1947, Davis 1959). For example, in many agricultural villages in India, the average number of people per room is greater than that found in some of the largest cities. Yet, they are not urbanites. The geographic area in which they live, the size of the village population, and the degree of division of labor are all too small. Some of the differences between rural and highly urbanized

Moscow's skyline reveals prominent symbols of power, prestige, and wealth. The capital of the Soviet Union records the transition of power from the Russian Czars to Soviet Bolsheviks. The Kremlin, seen here, is the seat of Soviet power. (© Pablo Bartholomew/Gamma-Liaison)

TABLE 19-2 Rural and urban life*

Characteristic	Rural ——————————— Urban
Heterogeneity of population	Low ——————————— High
Availability of formal organizations and services	Low ——————————— High
Division of labor	Low ——————————— High
Potential anonymity of individual	Low ——————————— High
Major nature of social relationships	*Gemeinschaft* ——————————— *Gesellschaft*
Major type of social control	Informal ——————————— Formal
Degree of status ranking on the basis of visible symbols	Low ——————————— High

* An *ideal type* of rural society is described under the heading "Rural," and an *ideal type* of urban society is described under the heading "Urban." As ideal types are rarely seen in real life, the lines between "rural" and "urban" indicate that there is a continuum on each of the dimensions listed.
SOURCE: Adapted from Edgar R. Butler, *Urban Sociology: A Systematic Approach* (New York: Harper and Row, 1976), p. 266.

life are shown in Table 19-2. As you can see from the table, rural life is simpler and more informal. The division of labor is limited, and most people are likely to know each other.

Urban growth began to explode during the late 1700s and developed rapidly thereafter. In 1800, the population of London, England, was almost 1 million, Paris was over half a million, and Vienna was about 200,000. By 1900, ten world cities had at least 1 million inhabitants: London, Paris, Vienna, Moscow, St. Petersburg (now renamed Leningrad), Calcutta, Tokyo, New York, Chicago, and Philadelphia. And today the number of people living in cities outnumbers the entire population of the world 150 years ago. Figure 19-2 summarizes patterns of urbanization from 1900 to 2020 throughout the world.

Statistical Definitions of Urbanization. Although sociologists disagree about the definition of the term *urban,* demographers have used *population size* as a yardstick. This approach has several advantages. One is the availability of accurate data on population size in many countries. Moreover, because large communities are more diverse and provide more opportunities for different life-styles, occupations, and living arrangements, population size may affect other aspects of social life.

Knowing the size of the population of a city thus allows us to make some guesses about what life is like there. Keep in mind, however, that what may be a reasonably accurate guess about life-styles and behavior in one part of the country or in one nation might not be accurate about an-

Population size is used as a measure of urbanization by demographers.

other. Social norms and values remain more important factors than the size of the population.

The Bureau of the Census describes as urban any city, town, or village with 2,500 inhabitants or more. The United States has more than seven thousand such localities. Often, metropolitan areas such as San

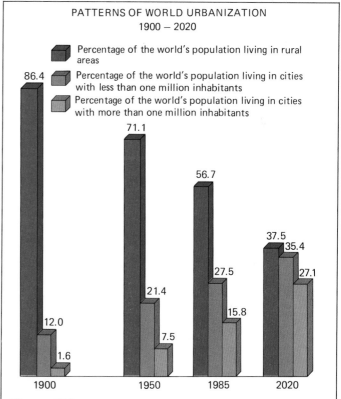

PATTERNS OF WORLD URBANIZATION
1900 – 2020

Percentage of the world's population living in rural areas

Percentage of the world's population living in cities with less than one million inhabitants

Percentage of the world's population living in cities with more than one million inhabitants

86.4

71.1

56.7

37.5   35.4

27.5   27.1

21.4

15.8

12.0

7.5

1.6

1900   1950   1985   2020

Figure 19-2
From data reprinted in J. John Palen, *The Urban World* (3rd edition) New York: McGraw Hill, 1986, p. 5.

Francisco, Boston, New York, and Washington, D.C., spill beyond their municipal divisions and include smaller cities and towns, and even some rural and semirural areas. To describe such units, demographers have introduced the term *metropolitan area.*

Metropolitan Statistical Area (MSA) is the term used by the Bureau of the Census to describe a geographical area with a large population center, together with neighboring communities which have a high degree of economic and social integration with that center. As of 1986, there were 281 metropolitan and standard metropolitan areas, up from 172 in 1950. Metropolitan areas now include places as different as New York City and Laredo, Tex. Each metropolitan statistical area must include at least: (1) one city with 50,000 or more inhabitants; or (2) an urbanized area of at least 50,000 inhabitants *and* a total MSA population of at least 100,000 (75,000 in New England). The Census definition also requires that an MSA include as "central county (ies)" the county in which the central city is located plus adjacent counties with at least 50 percent of their population in the urbanized area. Additional "outlying counties" are included if they meet certain requirements such as ease of commuting to the central city, population,

> A **metropolitan statistical area** is a geographical area with a large population center together with neighboring communities which have a high degree of economic and social integration with that center.

and density. This is a relatively new definition of a metropolitan area and reflects changes in the nature of urban life. In the new metropolitan area, people may be spread out in a way that does not support our beliefs about what usual urban life is like (e.g., overcrowded, busy, crime-ridden). But the life-styles of those residing in metropolitan areas are linked by shared business and industrial patterns.

URBANISM

Urbanization and **urbanism** are related concepts. The term *urbanization* is generally used to describe the size, the density, and the variation of a population within a specific location. *Urbanism* refers to a way of life, in which the traditional life-styles associated with village life are replaced by individualistic norms and styles of behavior (Redfield 1941).

Many sociologists have been disturbed by what they see as the potentially harmful effects of city life. For example, Louis Wirth (1938), in a classic essay on urbanism, proposed that the density and the variety of large cities have negative psychological and social consequences. Urban life exposes people to too much stimulation. As a result of the complexity of city life, primary-group ties are increasingly

> **Urbanism** refers to a way of life in cities which emphasizes individualistic norms and styles of behavior.

The similarities among cities do not usually obliterate the uniqueness of each one. San Francisco, like other metropolitan areas in the U.S., has a thriving central commercial and administrative area. It also has a style all its own, recognizable in these Victorian houses seen against the San Francisco skyline. (© Howard Millard)

Washing Dirty Linen in Public

Do impersonal, special-function settings in the city promote isolation, or do people structure social interaction in these settings to fit their own needs and preferences? To answer these questions, Regina Kenen studied sociability among users of laundromats located in different types of neighborhoods in San Francisco and New Jersey. The laundromats studied were in the areas of the city most likely to show the more alienating qualities of urban life described by such theorists as Milgram and Wirth.

She found that how people behave in laundromats varies according to the social class and the ethnicity of the customers. Among primarily middle-class laundromat users, norms of *polite inattention* govern interaction among strangers. Among those who come alone to wash their clothes, the conversation is limited to such communications as "Excuse me," or "You dropped something." Many customers leave the laundromat after putting their clothes in the washer; others leave the scene mentally, standing next to their machines and staring into space; still others read or knit. All these techniques discourage conversation with strangers. Many customers also create spatial barriers between themselves and other users whenever possible, such as sitting in a chair away from others or piling possessions on a vacant chair next to them.

Customers entering with friends or family put their surroundings into the background and interact with one another but avoid conversation with strangers. In the middle-class laundromat, customers apparently view sociability as difficult. The norms seems to be to play it safe by avoiding all interactions with strangers.

In sharp contrast to the polite inattention of middle-class laundromat customers is the sociability among the users of a laundromat in a Chicano neighborhood. Customers of this laundromat look at each other when they enter, and both men and women spend a lot of time talking to each other. People come in from the street to chat with one another, to use the telephone, or to smoke. Social life is an almost continuous flow between apartments, the street, and the laundromat. Strangers, acquaintances, and friends talk among the soapsuds.

In urban settings, people inhabit spaces in different ways. Behavior in the laundromat appears to be more influenced by the larger sociocultural context than by the laundromat's physical setting. Customers bring their own expectations of intimacy or isolation.

SOURCE: Regina Kenen, "Soapsuds, Space, and Sociability," *Urban Life*, **11**(2), (1982): 163–83.

difficult to maintain. People are engaged in temporary and segmented roles. In turn, both social control mechanisms and informal support networks are loosened. Left to face their difficulties alone, city dwellers are at high risk of suicide, alcoholism, mental illness, and criminality. More recently, this view has been supported by Milgram (1970), who claimed that the urban environment produces a "psychic overload" that is difficult for most people to handle easily.

How true is this picture of urban life? Not very, it seems. Even in the impersonal setting of public places, such as the laundromat, people structure their use of space and social interaction to fit their norms and life-styles (see Box). They also sometimes create new forms of "instant community" for the brief period during which they share similar locations and tasks.

Nor is there evidence that mental illness is more common in the city than elsewhere (Srole 1980) or that deaths from

alcoholism are higher (Gove, Hughes, and Galle 1979). Primary group ties are not weakened. Indeed, there are *no* differences in the amount or quality of social ties among more and less urban residents (Fischer 1982). Nor is urbanism associated with lowered social support; if anything, urban dwellers tend to have extensive and diverse social networks (Fischer 1982). As Dewey (1960) pointed out, over two decades ago, urbanism is *not* a way of life confined to the city. Rather, it is a trait associated with *whole societies* and not simply the degree of urbanization.

An urbanized society is characterized by patterns of behavior, social structure, and ideologies that are worldly, dynamic, civilized, and highly literate (Dewey 1960). Members of ruralized societies, on the other hand (even those living in cities), value ritual, tradition, kinship loyalty, and stability. For example, in Europe before 1700, towns of under 5,000 inhabitants performed basic urban economic functions—marketing, specialized production, services—and in even smaller towns, the seasonal pattern of baptisms was sharply different from that of the surrounding countryside, suggesting that there were marked social differences between the countryside and the city despite small-city size (Dyer 1981). In nonindustrial societies today, as in the preindustrial past, life is largely ruralized: there are few differences in social institutions, quality of life, and intellectual vitality between the city and the country.

In modernized nations, urban-rural differences have once more decreased. Whether you live in New York City, San Francisco, Okracoke, N.C., or Grand Island, Neb., you are living in an urbanized society. Even the loneliest farm is reached by information from big cities via television, films, books, videos, radio, and newspapers. Interaction between city and rural residents has also been promoted by national highway systems. Although the term *urbanism* has generally been used to describe the ways of thinking or acting of city-dwellers, it is more than that. Urbanism means *cosmopolitanism* (from the Greek *kosmos,* or world), where newer ideas, values, and technology flow from metropolitan to rural areas and are spread throughout a society. Similar notions of reality are shared by urban, suburban, and rural residents. Urbanism is thus closely linked with the economic dynamism that

Cosmopolitanism refers to the spread of newer ideas, values, and technology throughout a society.

occurs when cities interact densely with one another which in turn promotes their expanding influence (Jacobs 1984).

The Development of the American City

The growth of the city has been particularly dramatic in the United States. In 1790, there were only 3.9 million people, or an average of 4.5 people per square mile. Values and belief systems were dominated by traditional, rural patterns except in a very few cities. There were *no* cities with a population as large as 50,000, and only 5 percent of the people lived in towns of more than 2,500. By 1870, the United States population was 25 percent urban, and by 1920, 50 percent. In 1987, the total population was approximately 243 million, or about 81 people per square mile, three-fourths of whom live in urban areas as defined by the Census.

The population is not evenly distributed among the different geographic regions of the United States. For example, the island of Manhattan in New York City has an average density of 75,000 people per square mile, and 24 million others live within a ten-mile radius.

Because so many people are concentrated in relatively small geographic areas,

The concentration of many people in relatively adjacent areas has led to the development of supermetropolitan areas linked economically, socially, and by transportation. For example, the San Francisco–Los Angeles shuttle connects two west coast cities in less than one hour. It makes neighbors of people who might never have known each other in another era. (© John Blaustein/ Woodfin Camp and Associates)

TABLE 19-4 Regional migration between 1983 and 1984, in thousands

	People Moving In	People Moving Out	Net Gain or Loss
Northeast	487	578	−91
Midwest	820	1,102	−282
South	1,399	973	+426
West	834	887	−53

SOURCE: "Geographical Mobility: March 1983 to March 1984." U.S. Bureau of the Census, *Current Population Reports,* Series P-20, No. 407.

A **megalopolis** consists of overlapping metropolitan areas with many social, economic, and transportation links.

increased attention has been paid to the supermetropolitan region, characterized by social, economic, and transport links between overlapping metropolitan areas. Often called a *megalopolis* (from the Greek, *mega,* "large," and *polis,* "city"), one such stretch is "Bo-Wash," an almost continuous area of urban and suburban communities extending from north of Boston to just south of Washington, D.C., and from the coast of the Atlantic Ocean to the Appalachian foothills—a large region indeed.

Although predicted by some urban scholars to be the wave of the future, the megalopolis has grown more slowly during the last decade than expected, as the United States population has shifted from the large metropolitan areas of the northeastern and north-central areas to the promises of sun, fun, and expanding industrialization of the Sunbelt states, as may be seen in Table 19-4.

REASONS FOR THE RAPID GROWTH OF CITIES

Sociologists generally agree that several conditions are required for the growth of cities: (1) an agricultural base able to produce food surpluses that can support both the rural and urban population; (2) an efficient transportation system; and (3) the provision of jobs and services in urban areas that will attract people from the countryside. Increases in agricultural productivity allowed urban populations to grow and created additional demands for agricultural products. In turn, new markets were created in rural areas for urban products (Hohenberg and Lees 1985). The result was a take-off in self-sustaining urban growth.

Urbanization is thus closely tied to modernization and industrialization, machine technology, and division of labor. In small-scale, primarily rural societies, there are few specialized land uses in either city or country. When separate areas are set aside for particular uses, these are generally clustered.

In today's metropolitan center, however, specialized land use is the norm, often enforced by zoning regulations that control whether neighborhoods will be designated as industrial, business, multifamily, or single-family areas. As such planned use of land has increased, competition and conflict among various interest groups about the most appropriate ways in which land should be used have also increased.

THE ECOLOGY OF THE URBAN SCENE

As the United States and other industrialized nations have moved from being primarily agricultural to being manufacturing and service societies, the use of land has changed dramatically. The term *human ecology* was coined by Robert Park in 1921 to describe the physical relationship between people and land use (Park and Burgess 1921). Studies since the 1920s show that cities in most Western, industrialized nations have developed according to one of three basic models of urban ecology: (1) the *concentric zone;* (2) the *sector* and; (3) the *multiple nuclei.*

The *concentric-zone model* (Burgess 1925) describes the city as a series of circles built around a central core (Zone 1), which contains the cultural center and the business district. Just beyond the central core lies the zone of transition (Zone 2), encompassing both industrial and business activity and residential slums, rooming houses, cheap hotels, and other run-

Human ecology focuses on the physical relationship between people and land use.

The **concentric-zone model** describes the city as a series of circles built around a central core.

This urban garden was cultivated in an abandoned lot in a zone two area of a major U.S. city. It became a symbol of community, defiance and city pride for those who contributed to it, and a source of pleasure to all except the wrecking crew that destroyed it to make room for a new high rise development. (© Jim Anderson/Woodfin Camp and Associates)

down dwellings. Zone 3 contains housing for blue-collar workers as well as shops designed to meet their needs. Zone 4 is comprised of shopping centers and single-family houses, where white-collar workers reside and shopping centers develop. Zone 5, the commuter's, is bounded by the richer residences of Zone 4, but it also includes suburbs, estates for the wealthy and the near rich, industrial plants, and local workers' housing. Based largely on Chicago and similar, older industrial cities, the concentric-zone model describes the spatial arrangement of many large cities.

Pittsburgh and New Orleans, however, resemble more closely the *sector model* (Hoyt 1939), in which certain physical aspects of the city, such as transportation routes, unusual scenic beauty, or geographic barriers modify the shape and the growth pattern of cities. Cities thus become divided into a number of sectors, radiating from the central business district. Those areas best suited for industry or trade because of their location expand in one sector, residential areas along another route.

The third model of urban ecology is the *multiple-nuclei model* (Harris and Ullman 1945). Unlike the concentric-zone and sector models, the multiple-nuclei approach assumes that the city has not just one but several nuclei or centers, each of which is devoted to a different activity. Similar land uses tend to cluster, and like attracts like. Thus, one nucleus may be devoted entirely to banking activities, another to manufacturing, another to government buildings, and so forth. Specialized facilities within a given area attract

The **sector model** focuses on certain physical aspects that shape the growth pattern of cities.

The **multiple-nuclei model** assumes that the city has several centers each devoted to a different activity.

532

those who need and support it, and the city becomes differentiated.

PROCESSES OF URBANIZATION

Despite such variety in growth patterns, classical social ecologists such as MacKensie (1925) have noted processes common to urbanization in many societies: (1) *concentration;* (2) *segregation;* (3) *invasion;* and (4) *succession.*

Concentration, the first phase of urbanization, occurs when many people settle in a relatively small space. This phase leads to overcrowding, in turn promoting a decentralization of activities, so that people and industries spread from the center of the city to outlying areas.

With the decentralization of activities comes *ecological differentiation,* in which specific activities become geographically identified with particular areas of the city and are physically isolated from others. In this fashion, the city develops a distinct financial district, a retail-trade center, and a residential sector, each separate from the others.

Cities are never static. Any differentiated area is open to *ecological invasion* by new activities or populations. For example, industries may overlap a residential neighborhood, a warehouse district may be converted into luxury condominiums, or a traditionally black neighborhood may be resettled by Puerto Ricans. Once this process of ecological invasion is more or less complete, *succession* has occurred; that is, one activity or group of people has replaced another.

From a conflict perspective, this de-

Urban concentration occurs when many people settle in a relatively small area.

Ecological differentiation involves the distribution of specific activities in separate areas of the city.

Ecological invasion occurs when new populations or activities come into a differentiated urban area.

Succession is the completed cycle of ecological invasion.

scription of urban development has been criticized as deterministic. That is, technology and land uses have been treated as almost inevitable processes in urbanization rather than as being the result of social inequality and conflict (Tabb and Sawers 1978). Conflict theorists have proposed that the present physical forms of the city merely reinforce and reflect economic, ethnic, and racial stratification (Gordon 1978, Castells 1978). In short, rather than being a gradual, social evolutionary process, urbanization is shaped by political and economic forces. In contrast to the functional explanations offered by traditional demographers, a conflict approach highlights changes from the commercial to the corporate city.

FROM COMMERCIAL TO CORPORATE CITY

The commercial city was organized around craft manufacturing, commerce, transportation, or politics.

In the United States before 1850, cities were organized around craft manufacturing, commerce, transportation, or politics. These early urban centers more closely resembled the medieval city than today's metropolis. Dominated by informal street life and a random placement of streets, shops, and housing, unplanned arrangements of buildings and people promoted informality and spontaneity in social relationships. Only as land became more expensive did the urban pattern of rectangular or square city blocks develop and specific land uses become identified.

By 1850, the commercial city began to be replaced by the *industrial city*, dominated by the factory, the railroad, and the slum. The large industrial city is particularly suited to two functions: (1) economy of scale; that is, many workers can be employed within a single factory or a series of factories, and a surplus labor pool can be built up within the city to meet expanding needs; and (2) enforcement of labor discipline. In the large city, the working classes were more isolated from the middle and upper social strata than they were in smaller cities. As economic and residential differences increased and social informality decreased, the industrial city became an ethnically, racially, and economically segregated place to live.

The large industrial city was dominated by factories, railroads, and slums.

The industrial city just described was relatively short-lived. By the twentieth century, industrial plants were being built in vacant areas outside the central city.

Whole *industrial suburban cities,* such as Gary, Ind., which was developed by United States Steel, emerged. The decentralization of industry was aided by the availability of electrical power lines, trucks and highways, and the automation of manufacturing, processes that developed even more rapidly after World War II. The introduction of assembly-line production demanded a different kind of industrial plant. The old three- or four-story factory of the industrial city was replaced by the vast, cost-efficient one- or two-story building, where many employees could work on an assembly line on the same floor. Between 1899 and 1901, industrial employment in twelve of the thirteen largest industrial districts in the United States increased 100 percent faster in new, outlying industrial suburbs than within the city itself (Ashton 1978).

Industrial suburban cities developed in vacant areas outside central cities due to economic, political, and labor-related reasons.

Although technology promoted the development of the city, conflict theorists have been quick to point out that the suburbanization of industry predated many technological innovations. Gordon (1978) has proposed that the suburbanization of industry was designed to reduce or prevent labor–management conflict. As the trade union movement organized in

The inner city is no longer the main source of industrial jobs. Plants, such as this one in North Carolina, have moved to the suburbs for more space and lower costs. How has this served the suburban residential community? (© Chip Henderson Photography by Steve Muir/Woodfin Camp and Associates)

the heart of the industrial city, factory owners found it to their advantage to build isolated mills or plants in new suburbs. This strategy reduced the likelihood of contact between their employees and labor union organizers and workers in other factories. Relocating industries from the central city had other economic advantages for the owners: reduced taxes and shorter commuting time. Flight from the city to reduce municipal tax payments persists today as industries have increasingly moved out of central cities, and out of the Northeast altogether.

Industrial growth outside the central city was also promoted by a shift in the political power base. The old commercial city and the early industrial city had been largely controlled by political leaders closely related to the social and economic elite. As the central cities grew, migrants from rural areas and from abroad streamed into the city. The old economic elite found its power reduced by new political machines, dominated by and seeking votes from these newcomers. The inability to control political machines that depended on urban workers' votes provided other incentives for owners to relocate industry beyond the city limits.

THE GROWTH OF THE CORPORATE CITY

Corporate cities developed when manufacturing was decentralized and economic power was consolidated in smaller towns and cities.

The *corporate city* began to develop as manufacturing was decentralized and control over investment money was concentrated in the hands of a few major banks in the early 1900s. Not until the 1920s, however, was economic power centralized enough for skyscraper business and financial districts to be developed within the central city. Two parallel transformations took place in the urban area. While industry was relocating to the outskirts of the city, the old downtown shopping-district was gradually taken over by office buildings serving as power points for the administration of industry and the development of service industries such as banks and life insurance companies.

The typical corporate cities of the United States, however, are not the old industrial centers, such as New York, Detroit, or Chicago, but the newer cities in the Sunbelt, such as Dallas, Phoenix, Atlanta, and Houston. With few visible factory districts within the city, the working

class scattered, and suburban shopping malls replacing the downtown shopping area, the corporate city most resembles the fragmented metropolis of the multiple-nuclei model.

With a few exceptions, the central city is no longer the source of technological change. Rather, industrial parks in suburbs and strip cities are more likely to produce such change. Silicon Valley, a large area well outside the city limits of San Francisco, and Route 128, beyond the first ring of suburbs of Boston, are two such sites, where mass industry and large labor pools have been replaced by high-level technology firms employing white-collar technicians and managers who live nearby, another dimension of urban depopulation (Peterson 1985).

Some analysts have suggested that given the development of "mobile capital" by multinational corporations, regions and smaller communities have little control over urban development (Sawers and Tabb 1984). Decisions made in closed corporate boardrooms tend to benefit private interest and often result in great social damage to the public. Unemployment, underemployment, widening socioeconomic inequality, regressive taxes, and pollution are common consequences of decisions made for corporate gain at the cost of both employees and community residents (Sawers and Tabb 1984). From a conflict perspective, urban planners have failed to design a human urban city because they are caught up in serving the needs of corporations to maximize profits at the expense of quality of life (Boyer 1983).

In any event, newer urban centers are very different from our highly populated cities, such as Chicago, New York, and other old industrial cities ringed by dependent suburbs. Sprawling, relatively small cities with no clearly defined center—such as Yuba City, Calif.; Benton Harbor, Mich.; or Houma-Thibodaux, La.—are more characteristic of contemporary metropolitan development. Since the 1980 Census, at least thirty-eight new metropolitan areas of the sprawling type, with a total of almost 5 million people, have been designated by the federal government.

Not only are new forms of urban areas emerging, but differences between the residents of the older, central cities and those of the surrounding suburbs have become more pronounced.

The Suburbs

A *suburb* is part of the metropolitan area beyond the political boundaries of the city but closely linked to it economically and socially. The word suburb comes from the Latin, *sub* (under or outside) and *urbs* (city walls). Although suburban growth is a major feature of modern industrial societies, suburbs also existed in ancient and medieval cities, when the very poor were forced to live outside the city gates. Today it is the relatively wealthy who populate the areas beyond the metropolitan centers.

Although a particular suburb or suburban neighborhood might look like a homogeneous expanse of single-family houses, alike as peas in a pod, the entire suburban scene today is characterized by extreme diversity and by a greater degree of residential segregation in terms of social class and race than is found in most cities. Racial segregation is particularly severe. Although large numbers of blacks joined the exodus from the central city in the 1970s, their experience in suburbia has been vastly different from that of white suburbanites. As we noted in Chapter 10, institutionalized racism in the real-estate and mortgage markets establish and ensure residential segregation. As few whites choose to live in integrated suburbs, the value of property held by black homeowners fails to increase as rapidly as that of white homeowners in white neighborhoods (Lake 1981). Thus, although the blacks who move to the suburbs are gener-

To many people, a house in the suburbs represents the same "little piece of land" and autonomy that the pioneers sought in the journey to the frontier. (© Brett Froomer/The Image Bank)

ally better off economically than those who remain in the city, they are "steered" to areas that are less attractive than those available to whites in the same income categories.

Because the outflow of whites has been far greater than that of blacks, and because the more affluent of either race have moved out fastest and farthest, many metropolitan areas have come to resemble a doughnut, in which the hole is the impoverished central city and the doughnut itself the relatively prosperous suburbs (Lichter et al. 1985). Nonetheless, the suburbs display great income differentials, as seen in Table 19-6.

TABLE 19-6 Twenty suburbs: the richest and the poorest per capita income*

Richest	Suburb of	Income	Poorest	Suburb of	Income
Kenilworth, Ill.	(Chicago)	$48,950	Ford Heights, Ill.	(Chicago)	$4,523
Hunter's Creek, Tex.	(Houston)	47,957	Cudahy, Calif.	(Los Angeles)	5,040
Cherry Hills, Colo.	(Denver)	46,105	Bell Gardens, Calif.	(Los Angeles)	5,187
Mission Hills, Kan.	(Kansas City, Mo.)	46,030	Coachella, Calif.	(Los Angeles)	5,225
Piney Point, Tex.	(Houston)	45,940	Kinlock, Mo.	(St. Louis)	5,529
Bloomfield Hills, Mich.	(Detroit)	44,456	Florida City, Fla.	(Miami)	5,628
Sands Point, L.I.	(New York)	43,494	Huntington Park, Calif.	(Los Angeles)	6,067
Rancho Santa Fe, Calif.	(San Diego)	41,756	Opa-Locka, Fla.	(Miami)	6,320
Nichols Hills, Okla.	(Oklahoma City)	40,772	Compton, Calif.	(Los Angeles)	6,403
Ladue, Mo.	(St. Louis)	40,700	Robbins, Ill.	(Chicago)	6,436

* Projected from 1983 Census Bureau Figures.
SOURCE: *New York Times,* Apr. 30, 1987, p. A 18.

GROWTH OF THE SUBURBS

Suburbanization resulted from the expansion of the highway system, the spread of housing developments, and the dispersion of industry.

Suburbanization began to increase in the late nineteenth century as a result of both relocation of industry to the suburbs and technological change (Binford 1985). Before the automobile, the streetcar made limited suburban development possible. Land speculators built streetcar lines from the center of the city to outlying districts, where they had bought land in order to attract people anxious to escape the noise and filth of the city (Ashton 1978). Once the new development had been sold, the land speculators encouraged municipalities or private corporations to buy the streetcar line.

A major factor in the spread of suburbia was the mass production of automobiles that began in the 1920s. In 1900, only 10 percent of the American population lived in suburbs; by 1929, the population of suburbs was growing twice as fast as that of central cities. The construction of new highways with public funds also made suburban life more convenient for commuters.

There is, however, no single explanation for the rapid suburban growth within the last four decades. Rather, it is the outcome of an interactive process in which living conditions, political factors, racial and ethnic tensions, taxation, relocation of industry, and technological change contributed to suburban expansion. This interaction is shown graphically in Figure 19-3.

After World War II, suburbs expanded rapidly as upwardly mobile veterans took advantage of low-cost mortgage programs and publicly financed higher education. Today, more Americans live in suburbs than in central cities or nonmetropolitan areas, and many never leave their suburb except to go to work. Between 1970 and 1980, the population in the central cities declined, and the suburban population increased, outnumbering the urban centers that had spawned them by three to two.

What is the lure of suburban life? One major reason for the growth of suburbs is a shift in money investment patterns so that new industries and retail trade centers have increasingly located outside the central city. By the early 1980s, the amount of office space in suburbia was greater than that in city central business districts, and by 1985, 57 percent of all office space in the United States was in the suburbs (Hughes 1986). Although the suburban office vacancy rates are higher than those in central cities, it is anticipated that businesses will be increasingly attracted to suburban locations. At least three factors have stimulated suburban industrial growth: the growing importance of the service sector in the economy of the United States, federal tax legislation, and the interstate highway system (Hughes 1986). In addition, foreign competition and the energy glut have taken a severe toll on several industries: Energy lost about 98,000 jobs, and high technology has gained a relatively small number. Manufacturing lost over 1 million jobs, while the number of workers in finance, health care, and retail trade, among other services, increased by 2.8 million between 1984 and 1985 alone. The occupations where employment is increasing can be as easily located in the suburbs as in the cities—and at far less cost.

Various changes in federal tax and regulatory policy have redirected money from production facilities into commercial real

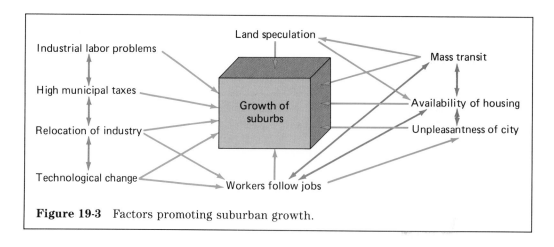

Figure 19-3 Factors promoting suburban growth.

"Main Street U.S.A.," where people meet to exchange greetings, gossip, and shop, has been almost completely replaced by the mall, a sprawling complex of stores and recreational architecture where people meet to exchange greetings, gossip, and shop. How have things changed? (© Billy Barnes/ Click–Chicago)

estate development. Special tax treatment for limited real-estate partnerships, changes in banking laws, such as the removal of ceilings on interest rates, and tax write-off provisions have all stimulated the development of office parks outside central cities. At the same time, federally subsidized interstate highways provided easier access to the new suburban offices where rents may be one-third to one-half less than in the central city. Not only are rents lower, but labor may be cheaper as well. Many suburban companies employ an educated, largely female, labor force willing to accept lower wages. In short, the largest number of jobs are being created in the suburbs where unemployment is the lowest.

ADVANTAGES OF SUBURBAN LIFE

Several generations ago, supporters of suburban life claimed to have the best of both worlds: being close enough to the city to take advantage of cultural and educational activities, yet enjoying the wholesomeness, peace, and calm of rural life (Fischer 1982). American life has separated public and private spheres (Popenoe 1985), family and social pursuits, and male and female activities (Saegert 1980). The suburbs emphasize these differences, as well as providing an opportunity to own a single-family dwelling and to raise a family in an outdoor environment.

Suburban life is dominated by its family orientation (domesticity). In 1980, 34 percent of all married couples with children lived in suburbs as compared to 23 percent who lived in cities. Twice as many single-parent households headed by women were in the city as in the suburbs, and more unrelated persons shared households in the city than in the suburbs.

The advantages, then, of suburban life are several. The suburbs are more removed from the noise and the crowding of the city, yet relatively close to its activities. There is also more room for leisure pursuits, outdoor activities, and raising children. Less anonymous than the city, neighborhoods are more homogeneous as people of like backgrounds and interests choose similar residential areas. Home ownership is usually made possible by the availability of mortgage money for single-family dwellings, a deeply valued goal of many Americans.

During the 1940s through the 1960s, middle-class members of the Baby Boom generation comprised the largest youth population in the history of American suburbs. Yet in young adulthood, many of these suburban-reared Baby Boomers rejected the homogeneity of their environment and sought the excitement of city life. During the 1970s, the "swinging singles and mingles" life-style of youthful Baby Boomers stimulated development of urban condominiums, small luxury apartments, two-bedroom townhouses, and reconverted lofts. Long-forgotten urban neighborhoods were rediscovered and revitalized by Yuppies (young upwardly mobile professionals) who transformed urban areas as diverse as Boston, St. Louis, Hoboken, N.J., and Norfolk, Va.

537

But as members of the Baby Boom generation reached mature adulthood, increasing numbers returned to the suburbs. Between 1980 and 1984, more than 5.8 million people have moved to suburbia. And, according to some projections, married-couple households headed by people aged thirty-five to fifty-four, whose incomes are traditionally highest of all, will account for 8.1 million or 56 percent of the total increase in households by 1995 (Sternlieb and Hughes 1986). Such couples are likely to seek conventional housing in family-oriented, suburban neighborhoods.

After fleeing their parents' suburban life-style, why are members of the Baby Boom seeking to reestablish the very pattern they had rejected? The answer in part lies in the decentralization of office space. Across the nation, as increasing numbers of industries have located in suburban office parks, middle-class professionals have relocated as well. Not only are office rents cheaper, but some firms deliberately locate in areas that require less commuting on the part of their executives. Low-income office employees, then, must do the traveling from their urban homes to work in suburbs in which they cannot afford to live.

A second factor in the move back to suburbia is quality of life. It appears that Baby Boomers are leaving central cities for the same reasons their parents did: larger living quarters, a better life-style for their children, and a sense of community. Many young couples are relieved to escape the "beer cans, broken glass, chicken bones in all the parks," higher crime rates, and pollution that characterize many central cities. And many have found that they prefer to live in a neighborhood where there are other people very much like themselves. Precisely because of the homogeneity of suburban housing developments, it is easier to know the social status of one's neighbors. As one Baby Boomer who moved to suburbia commented, "In the city, you don't know if a guy is making $50,000 or $500,000. Not that it's important. Out here, where you stand is a little more visible. You know the guy is driving a late-model car . . . if they're sending their kids to private schools and you say, 'Yeah, they're doing OK'" (*Newsweek,* July 21, 1986, p. 54).

The return migration of urban professionals has altered the character of many suburbs. The new residents often require two incomes to maintain their life-style, so that residential streets may be relatively quiet, with parents at work and small children in day care. Increasingly, the suburbs offer many of the amenities (pleasures) previously associated only with urban life—orchestras, theaters, good restaurants, elegant shops. The "big world" is now readily accessible through cable television, VCRs, and satellite dishes.

DISADVANTAGES OF SUBURBAN LIFE

Yet for all of its advantages, suburban life also has negative aspects. Public transportation is generally poor, sometimes nonexistent, so that a second, even a third car is required to visit friends, to drive to work, and to pick up children.

Services may also be difficult to reach. Transportation to the central city is often limited, so that cultural and educational opportunities, although relatively near, are often inaccessible. Although hospitals, shopping plazas, office parks, and restaurants are abundant in many suburbs, they, too, are inaccessible by foot. Nor are there many services for different age groups. Much suburban development has been planned for couples with small children, so that playgrounds and barbecue pits abound. Yet, as the suburban population has aged, teenagers, singles, the elderly, and one-parent families are often left out of the planning equation. Ideologically and ecologically, suburbia remains the stronghold for rearing young children in a dual-parent family (Ridgeway and Wilson 1981).

The very sameness of the suburb, initially one of its attractions for many home buyers, has proved to be a disadvantage for some. As more and more suburbs have developed and become established communities, they have also become increasingly stratified according to income, ethnicity, and race. Despite a tendency for suburbs to become employment communities, a status hierarchy of "good" versus "mediocre" versus "poor" suburbs remains.

Because of their internal homogeneity, the suburbs have often been criticized as promoting conformity. Conformity *is* more likely in suburbia, but whether suburbia promotes conformity or conformists select suburbia remains an open question. The sameness of suburban life is reinforced by the lack of opportunity for

Growing Up Black In Suburbia

Although slow racial integration in the suburbs began in the 1970s, minorities still make up a relatively small proportion of suburbanites: about 9 percent of the suburban population in the Northeast and less than 7 percent in the Midwest. What is it like to be a member of a minority group growing up in suburbia? According to one black 1987 high-school graduate, it is difficult because people in the town and school system never saw beyond the color of his skin.

Nigel Jones, a resident of the town of Weston, Mass.—a suburb of Boston with the highest median income in the state and one of the best public-school systems in the nation—was chosen as commencement speaker for his high-school graduating class. One of seventeen black students graduating, he was the only black Weston resident receiving a diploma. The other black students in his class lived in Boston and commuted daily to Weston High as part of a program called METCO, designed to promote greater racial balance between central-city and suburban schools. Focusing on his personal experience of being black in a primarily white community and school system, Jones commented: "I am invisible . . . a statistic . . . a barrier to college admission . . . a symbol of a good black boy. I am anything and everything but a human being, an individual with personal ambitions, emotions, and desires."

Jones used the following illustration to indicate the unconscious racist attitudes held by many town residents: "How do I know I am invisible? When the [town] policeman came to the door, he told my stepmother that he had reports that there had been a black man in a beat-up car sitting in the driveway. . . . I was the black man in the driveway. The driveway is ours." He questioned whether the police would have been called by neighbors had they seen a white teenager sitting in a car in his driveway.

Not surprisingly, Jones' graduation speech was the subject of debate in his home suburb. The chief of police indicated that he had not heard any reports of racist actions by members of the police; the chair of the Board of Selectmen stated that he did not know of any racism in the town. A member of the School Committee, in contrast, indicated that he had no reason to doubt the validity of Jones's comments.

In his graduation address, Jones also noted that black students at his school, in general, are not as academically skilled as white students—". . . not because of any intrinsic deficiency, as some of the faculty of Weston may believe. If you took any fifty kids from South Boston or Dorchester (both low-income inner-city Boston areas with primarily white students) and placed them in the highly academic environment of Weston High, you would get the same results. It's a socioeconomic problem, not a racial one." The high school principal agreed with Jones's analysis of class differences as a factor that separates students in this suburban community.

How racist is Weston and the thousands of suburbs similar to it? Weston, like many other suburbs, prides itself on its liberalism. Yet relatively few members of minority groups live there. Suburbs in the Northeast and Midwest are more likely to be racially segregated than suburbs of the newer urban areas in the Sunbelt. Thus, while overt prejudice is absent, a number of factors—subtle and unconscious—will make growing up in suburbia qualitatively different for blacks, Asians, or Hispanics than for members of the dominant group. That is, because of the emphasis on sameness that has been part of suburban life, minority group members experience a sense of apartness both at school and in the community.

Based in part on Donna Scaglione, "Weston's Invisible Truth," *The Tab*, June 16, 1987, p. 11.

young people to meet people different from themselves. It has been suggested that suburban schools sustain a narrow view of the world that prepares students to live in a conforming, bureaucratic society (see Chapter 13).

The sprawl of suburban development is also creating other problems. Traffic jams now afflict suburban workers as well as commuters. Environmental issues are also of growing concern, inasmuch as many suburban areas have not anticipated the problems of congestion, pollution, and destruction of natural beauty associated with rapid growth. Many new office parks are ugly; others lack on-site shops or services, making life both inconvenient and dull for workers. The price of inadequate planning may be that suburbs lose the charms that initially attracted residents.

In some communities, citizens have organized to limit further growth. For example, over twenty communities around San Francisco have enacted laws to slow the pace of development, and some suburbs have barred construction of new office parks until traffic congestion issues are resolved.

QUALITY OF LIFE

Suburban life is a series of trade-offs in which men and women have qualitatively different experiences. In a study of relatively wealthy urban and suburban couples, Saegert (1980), found that the average urban woman differed from her suburban counterpart in placing a higher value on working outside the home (whether or not she was employed). Suburban dwellers of both sexes were more satisfied with their home as a place to raise children, to do work they enjoyed, and to have fun, and as a space to use freely. City residents of both sexes were more involved in work-related and cultural pursuits. The domestic nature of the suburbs seems evident.

There are other differences in quality of life for men and women in the suburbs. For example, men are generally more likely than women to want to move from the central city; for them, suburban life represents both a status symbol and a retreat. Women are more likely than men to find themselves bored, and to report that their spouses spend less time with them, the children, and other family mem-

bers. These gender-related differences cut across socioeconomic lines, so that both white-collar and blue-collar women have reported that moving from the central city to suburbia has reduced rather than increased the number of close ties with family and friends (Saegert 1980).

Suburban women, like rural women, must rely more often on their own resources and on their immediate families for pleasure and amusement. In this context, it is interesting to note the large increase in the proportion of suburban wives who, sooner or later, seek outside employment. Just as the city has been blamed for producing psychic overload, suburbia has been accused of producing psychic underload (Popenoe 1977). If there is a crack in the picture window, it may have been caused by boredom (Ridgeway and Wilson 1981).

The Urban Crisis: Poor Cities, Rich Suburbs

To understand today's urban "crisis"—the increasing poverty of the cities in contrast to the growing wealth of the suburbs—it is necessary to pull together many of the points already made in this chapter. The story begins with the first wave of movement from the cities to the suburbs, in the late 1940s, which was brought about by two programs subsidized by all taxpayers: (1) low-interest mortgages to veterans of

This section of the South Bronx in New York has come to be a symbol of the legacy of urban decay. Against a backdrop of rubble, renewal, and renovation, politicians often visit to promise improvements. What purpose does this strategy serve? (© Thomas Hopker/ Woodfin Camp and Associates)

World War II, that made suburban home building attractive to developers and affordable to young couples; and (2) a massive federally funded highway construction program that linked the suburbs to the central city where most of the movers were still employed and where they looked for entertainment and shopping.

But it was not long before shopping facilities and other amenities followed the people; huge malls on the suburban fringe replaced central-city department stores. During the 1960s, a second ring of suburbs opened up; families could afford two cars, gasoline was inexpensive; the tax laws encouraged home buying; and more people moved out of the cities than moved in. By the 1970s, not only the people and shops, but also the jobs had relocated outside the city limits, as service employment replaced manufacturing. Unlike manufacturing plants, office buildings do not generate smoke or other pollutants, and they can be located in the suburbs as well as the cities. By 1980, then, there was very little to link the suburbs to the cities.

As a consequence of these trends, each reinforcing the other, the cities gradually lost their higher-income families, taxable businesses and privately owned real estate, and jobs. Factories and stores are abandoned, and absentee landlords allow rental housing to deteriorate. The city government can do little to stem the tide because the tax base has shrunk. Without funds to pay police and teachers, public safety and school quality are reduced. The more dangerous the city becomes, the less attractive to remaining families and businesses. The kind of entry-level manufacturing jobs so abundant for previous generations of urban workers are no longer available, while the city schools have failed to prepare students for higher-skilled, better-paying service employment. In New York City, for example, although there was a small gain in the number of jobs between 1980 and 1986, employment in manufacturing declined by 22 percent while skilled service increased by almost the same proportion (Herbers 1986). The lack of fit between available jobs and the skills of workers leads to high unemployment among minority teenagers and young adults, rising crime rates, family dissolution, abandoned housing (landlords walk away from buildings in which no one can afford to pay rent), and destroyed neighborhoods. Figure 19-4 graphically

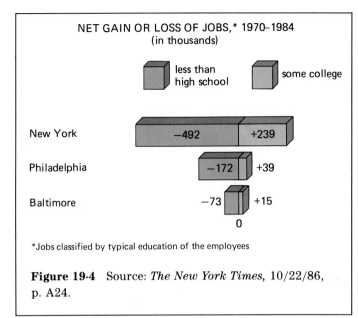

NET GAIN OR LOSS OF JOBS,* 1970–1984
(in thousands)

less than high school   some college

New York   −492   +239
Philadelphia   −172   +39
Baltimore   −73 +15
                    0

*Jobs classified by typical education of the employees

Figure 19-4   Source: *The New York Times*, 10/22/86, p. A24.

summarizes the net loss of jobs for people with limited education in three major American cities between 1970 and 1984.

Thus, the same spiral that leads to the growth and economic health of the suburbs has a downside in the continuing economic and social decline of the cities.

The depopulation of American cities has sharply increased the level of racial inequality in our society, with the inner cities growing blacker and the most distant suburbs whiter (Peterson 1985). At the same time, political power at the state level has shifted from the once densely populated cities to the suburban and rural communities. A majority of state legislators represent relatively well-off districts and will not readily vote to tax their constituents in order to help the urban poor. In contrast to the 1960s, when the economy was expanding, there has been little real economic growth in the 1980s and one major recession. At the same time, Americans elected a federal administration pledged to reduce all forms of assistance to the poor. The urban underclass, therefore, has had to absorb a decline in both economic opportunity and assistance programs.

Most of the processes we have mentioned in accounting for the urban crisis were not the result of any conspiracy or intentional effort to impoverish cities and enrich the suburbs. The actual outcome was a latent consequence of many individual decisions that produced mutually reinforcing trends. Assisting returning veterans in realizing the American dream of owning their own home, for example, was a widely supported policy in the 1940s. Few policy makers considered the long-term implications of the program and the fact that it favored the men who could afford the down payments. Who could blame a merchant for closing down a department store that was losing money because of high rent, heating expenses, loss of customers, and lack of parking space, especially if a smaller shop in a suburban mall would bring higher profits? If high-level executives prefer to work near home, in attractive and safe surroundings, and at lower rents, is it not in the best interest of stockholders that the corporation move to the suburbs? And what state legislator from a suburban district would be reelected on a platform of saving the inner cities?

In other words, people acting out of their own best interests create impersonal trends that have great impact on the social system—on the structure of the job market, for example, or on schools and housing. But there have also been intentional actions that have hastened the downward spiral of the cities, particularly in the area of housing.

URBAN HOUSING

The kind of "institutionalized racism" that we noted in Chapter 10 has done much to reduce the stock of livable housing in the cities. The practice of *redlining* whereby banks refuse mortgage or home-improvement loans in certain areas of the city (those blocks marked in red lines on a city map) guarantee that people cannot upgrade the quality of their housing. As property values in the redlined area decline, some landlords will abandon the dwelling rather than pay taxes, others will hire someone to commit arson in order to collect insurance. Local merchants will leave the neighborhood, along with any other residents who can afford to move. The whole process of neighborhood destruction does not take long, as the blocks likely to be redlined are those already occupied by relatively poor minority families. The mortgage officers can claim that they are protecting their own jobs by acting in the best interests of the bank's shareholders and depositors in not making

risky loans. In other words, the racist outcome is a result of "good business practices." And the self-fulfilling prophecy is realized.

But there are also other business practices, often illegal, that intentionally produce segregated neighborhoods. *Blockbusting* occurs when real estate agents purposely create a sense of panic in stable white neighborhoods, by selling or renting a home to a black family. Once the black family is visible, the agents approach other residents, hint that property values will now decline rapidly, and urge the home owners to sell at once. As one realtor's calling card said, "Don't wait until it's too late!" (Gottlieb 1986). The real-estate agent offers to buy the house on the spot, at well under the market price, and subsequently sells it to an upwardly mobile black family at well over its actual value. In these cases, the neighborhood may not decline physically, but the goal of creating stable integrated neighborhoods will be frustrated.

The low-income city resident, then, must deal with absentee landlords in the case of rental units, or with uncooperative lending institutions in the case of owner-occupied housing. Nor can they look to local, state, or federal agencies for much help. The city government does not have the resources to operate, much less repair, the rental housing they have repossessed for back taxes. State government, as we have already noted, is dominated by suburban interests, and the federal government is itself responsible for the destruction of city neighborhoods in the name of "urban renewal" (which became a code word for "black removal" and the construction of subsidized office buildings rather than low-income housing).

Most recently, over the past decade, the Federal Housing Administration has engaged in a multimillion dollar scheme of fraud and bribery that transformed inner-city neighborhoods into deserted wastelands—and all with taxpayer money! Real-estate operators would bribe FHA officials in order to secure federally insured mortgage loans for clients who stood little chance of meeting payments on their already run-down homes. When the owners had to default and abandon their homes, the properties became targets of arson or squatters (illegal residents). The former residents are made homeless and their houses destroyed, while the real-estate

Community Development Corporations: Their Rise and Decline

During the 1960s, Community Development Corporations (CDCs) were created to give local communities control over their own economic development and to institutionalize the collective power of community members within a competitive capitalist economy. Based on a model developed by the Ford Foundation and funded by federal money, community development corporations were intended to be a "third sector" that could accomplish what the public and private sector had not: revitalization and renewal of deteriorating inner-city areas. Some urban analysts argued that the decline of central cities was due to the uneven flow of income between low income neighborhoods and the rest of the metropolitan area. These urban areas were, in effect, "colonies" that exported cheap labor to other portions of the city and imported goods from the outside. Most low income residents spent more money in stores owned by large chains or absentee owners outside their neighborhoods than they spent in their own area. Public services, which would have lowered the flow of money out of the community, were almost nonexistent, and the more needy the urban neighborhood, the fewer the available services. For example, when the difference between what residents paid in taxes and what they received in services was compared in New York City, there was a gap of about $76 million between taxes paid and services in Bedford-Stuyvesant, a poor black neighborhood, compared to Borough Park, a white, middle-class neighborhood. Clearly, low-income, minority neighborhoods were being shortchanged on public services.

Neighborhood-based, community development corporations offered a variety of services. Some focused on housing and development of small businesses, others on tenant rights, still others on opposition to urban renewal which would disrupt existing neighborhood life. Some CDCs organized human services, legal aid, and even cable television programming for local residents. In 1981, the Reagan administration cut funds for community development corporations. To survive, CDCs have sought other sources of support: foundation grants, operating revenues from their own businesses, small contributions, and "syndicates" or tax shelters for investors in real estate. Recent changes in the federal tax law, however, have made investment in community development projects less attractive than they were in the past. Furthermore, seeking private investment has changed the ways in which many community development projects operate. Community development workers often find themselves acting as landlords who must evict poor tenants in order to meet the expenses of the corporation. Recruitment of staff, especially fund raisers, from outside the neighborhood has also created tension between local residents and professional staff. Increasingly, the organizations have been forced to choose between ideology and economic survival.

Although the community development corporation model can play a useful role in revitalizing an area, popular support that could empower them no longer exists. Today, CDC projects tend to be small-scale operations that are unlikely to succeed without large-scale social change and a redistribution of resources within the broader national economy.

Based on "Evaluating CDC's: Can They End Urban Decay?" *Dollars and Sense*, December 1986, pp. 19–21.

agents pocket the insured payments from the United States government (Gottlieb 1986).

Many people who look at the state of urban housing are quick to blame the residents ("Why can't they keep the place in decent shape?"), but in most cases there is very little that a single person or family can do to improve neighborhood housing, especially when there are a lot of people who make a profit from urban decay.

It seems clear that cities that developed during the industrial phase of a society do not adapt easily to a postindustrial economy. The resources that make a city prosper as a manufacturing center are not as important in a predominantly service economy. Surrounded by richer, primarily white, middle-class suburbs, urban residents in decaying cities are limited in their abilities to expand or to change the nature of the central city. There is neither money nor space to do so. Industry and capital have moved out to more attractive areas, leaving behind urban social problems. Table 19-7 summarizes the changes in ethnic composition of the city, which is still characterized by "white flight." The concentration of the poor, minority groups, the elderly, and female-headed households is a *consequence,* not a cause of the problems of older cities.

TABLE 19-7 Distribution of population, by percents, in central city, metropolitan ring and non-metropolitan areas, White, Black, and Hispanic, 1970–1980

	White		Black		Hispanic	
	1980	1970	1980	1970	1980	1970
Central city	27.0	27.8	59.7	58.2	53.1	50.0
Outside central city	47.5	40.1	22.3	16.1	35.0	32.8
Outside SMSA*	25.5	32.1	18.0	25.7	11.9	17.2

* Standard Metropolitan Statistical Area.
SOURCE: Donald Bogue, *The Population of the United States.* New York: Free Press, 1985, Figure 3–10, p. 136; *Statistical Abstract of the United States,* 1986, p. 19.

Overcrowding (usually defined as more than one person per room in a dwelling unit) is also frequent in low-income, female-headed, or minority inner-city housing, as is the lack of such essentials as a flush toilet, hot water, central heating, a complete kitchen, and easy access to the dwelling unit from outside. Yet, inner-city housing is not cheap by any means, and poor people spend a larger percentage of their income on housing than do the non-poor. In the United States, more than two-thirds of female-headed households and one-third of all minority households spent over 25 percent of their income on rent.

THE OTHER CITY

Although the inner city is disproportionately home to the poor, most major American cities are also characterized by sections of extreme wealth—the "gold coast," "Park Avenue," or whatever the local name for the high-rent district. New York, Chicago, Boston, Philadelphia, Minneapolis, San Francisco, and other "old" cities remain centers of finance, communication, and the arts and there is a certain flair and excitement to city life when you can afford it. The past decade has seen a major increase in the construction or conversion of luxury urban housing, often with tax write-offs for the developers as cities strive to retain some high-income families and facilities.

In many of these cities, there are also abandoned or deteriorating areas that had once been well-to-do neighborhoods, with solidly built housing stock. Some of these buildings can be purchased at very low prices—sometimes only the back taxes owed by the former owner. And because of

their central location, such housing is especially appealing to the Yuppies who still work in the city but who cannot yet afford luxury housing.

Gentrification. The word "gentry" originally referred to land-owning nobility. Today, *gentrification* refers to the process whereby deteriorating property is purchased and renovated by middle- and high-income urban residents. Some gentrifiers are people who have left the suburbs and moved back into the cities; others are professional couples upgrading their housing; still others are highly paid single people who enjoy the vitality of urban life. The old housing is usually stripped to its base and totally renovated and redecorated. When an entire block is gentrified, sidewalks are redone, street lighting improved, and the quality of life substantially improved. However, because no new housing is produced for the previous tenants, the upgrading of one neighborhood is counterbalanced by greater residential crowding in another section.

A classic example of redlining followed by gentrification in Boston's South End has been repeated in countless other urban areas. In the late 1960s and early 1970s, what had been a stable white ethnic neighborhood of well-built brick row houses (two- and three-story houses attached to one another) close to the central business district was gradually abandoned as banks refused to renew mortgages or grant improvement loans. The older residents moved out, and the houses remained vacant until they were purchased by real-estate developers in the 1980s and converted into high-price rentals or condominiums (housing units that are privately

Gentrification refers to the migration of middle- and upper-income people into urban centers and their renovation of existing housing.

Older and newer structures co-exist, epitomizing the economic and political changes impacting the city. (© Gale Zucker/ Stock Boston)

owned but with common facilities and expenses shared by all residents of the same building or group of homes).

The market for gentrified housing has remained strong, leading developers to buy up abandoned housing and harass low- and middle-income tenants into leaving other buildings that can then be converted for high profit. This problem is not unique to large cities; the growing suburban centers are also experiencing a shortage of suitable housing for the high-income executives moving into the area. Here, too, low-income tenants find their rents suddenly doubled and tripled; evictions are common; and when the current residents have left, the buildings are torn down or completely transformed into luxury apartments and townhouses. This renovated housing is well beyond the reach of the vast majority of American families. In Boston's South End, for example, two-bedroom condominiums were selling for $250,000 in 1987, and a single-family renovated brownstone for $425,000.

In the 1970s it was hoped that gentrification would not only bring the affluent middle class back to the cities but also revitalize neighborhoods, bring needed jobs, improve the tax base, and ultimately upgrade housing for the less wealthy. Gentri-

fication, however, has had only limited effects on the well-being of the city as a whole. Existing communities have been broken up, the original residents forced into cheaper, substandard housing, and the fragile shell of economic strength in the gentrified neighborhoods has done little to relieve the core of urban poverty. Thus, at least one unintended consequence of gentrification has been a lowered quality of urban life for all residents.

Homelessness. It is difficult, for obvious reasons, to know how many Americans are homeless at any given time, but there is no question that the population of people who live on the streets has increased dramatically (see Chapter 6). Although the homeless population once consisted largely of "skid row" male alcoholics, today's street people are far more varied, including large numbers of unemployed young people, elderly women, and entire families. They are found not only in the older cities of the North and East, but in the growing Sunbelt cities of the South and West where many workers had migrated in search of employment before the oil boom went bust.

Sociological studies of the homeless have been largely in the demographic tradition: who, where, why? For example, Rossi et al. (1987) studied the homeless of Chicago with a survey of 722 people living in shelters and on the street. Over three-fourths were men, with an average age of forty, and a median income of about $100 per month, mostly from welfare and disability benefits. Only one in five had worked the previous week and the majority had been out of work for three years or more. On average, they had been homeless for close to one year. Although their educational attainment was not notably low—most were high-school graduates—they did differ from the general population in three crucial respects: (1) their extreme poverty; (2) their numerous disabilities, both physical and mental; and (3) their high levels of isolation—more than half had never married and were also alienated from family and friends.

Similar demographics have been reported from five other major metropolitan studies: the homeless are overwhelmingly male, a majority under age forty; largely white, although blacks are overrepresented; and primarily transient (Snow and Anderson 1987, Table 1). There is little evidence to support another common misperception that the homeless prefer life on the streets and find eating at soup kitchens preferable to paying for a meal. To be sure,

many homeless have refused offers to sleep at public shelters; but this is often because the shelters are filthier and more dangerous than the streets. There are some homeless who do wish to be left alone under any circumstances. The great majority, however, appear to be on the streets as a result of factors over which they have little control—job markets, the housing shortage, their own poor health, and widespread public indifference.

From a symbolic interaction perspective, the homeless, as with any population at the bottom of the status system, are faced with the task of constructing an identity as a person of worth in the face of universal stigmatization. To study this topic, Snow and Anderson (1987) conducted a year-long field study of 168 homeless people in Austin, Tex. Among the basic devices used in "identity work" were: (1) "Distancing" talk that disassociated the person from other homeless people, from the demeaning work roles available to them and from the very institutions upon which their survival depends—soup kitchens, shelters, and churches; (2) Selective "embracement" of some role identities, interpersonal relationships, and a religious attachment—e.g., people who called themselves "bums," but also "loyal friend" and claimed closeness to a particular belief

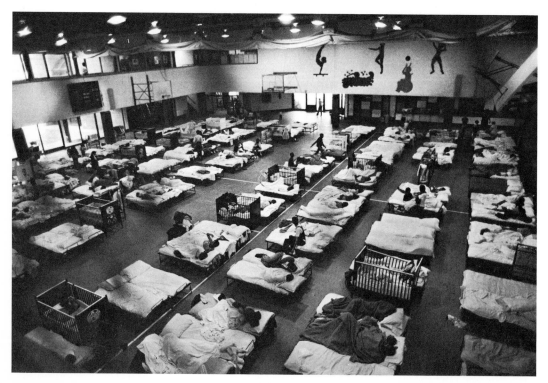

A "home of one's own" becomes a cot for the night for only a few of at least one million urban homeless. Meanwhile shelters have become a controversial issue as communities shout, "Not in this neighborhood!" What would be your solution to the problems of the homeless? (© George Cohen)

Homelessness in America: Identifying the Problems, Seeking the Solutions

RUSSELL K. SCHUTT AND
GERALD R. GARRETT

Russell K. Schutt and Gerald R. Garrett are, respectively, associate professor and professor in the department of sociology at the University of Massachusetts in Boston. They have authored and co-authored a number of articles and reports about the homeless and are currently preparing a full-length text for publication. They have also developed a video tape, Working with the Homeless: A Video-Based Training Experience, *for shelter staff. Schutt has written* Organizations In a Changing Environment *as well as articles on the sociology of law and teaching research methods. Garrett has conducted research on the homeless in New York, Seattle, and other U.S. cities in the 1960s and 1970s and has coauthored (with Howard M. Bahr)* Women Alone.

Over the course of a year, millions experience an episode of homelessness and many more narrowly avoid homelessness by doubling up with family or friends. At any one time in the mid-1980s, at least one-quarter million Americans are homeless. With the wisdom of hindsight, large-scale homelessness in America appears to be a predictable consequence of earlier social policies: gentrification of central cities and rising housing costs; declining welfare benefits and other income supports; deinstitutionalization of mental-health treatment and inadequate implementation of a community-based system of mental-health care. However, when large numbers of homeless persons first became evident in city centers, government agencies and private charities were caught unprepared. Many emergency shelters were established quickly—by 1984, 1800 shelters provided over

90,000 beds—but these shelters were ill-equipped for the case management and health-care services that many of their guests required.

The City of Boston began the Long Island Shelter for the Homeless in 1983. While the primary concern of the shelter was the provision of food and beds, staff soon implemented a system of intake interviewing in order to identify the other needs of their guests. On a brief, open-ended intake form, case managers recorded information about guests' economic resources, social supports, and physical and mental health. By 1985, the influx of forms from the thousands of homeless persons who came to the shelter began to overwhelm the shelter's ability to report on the needs of all its guests. At this point Sister Debbie Chausse, an administrator at the Long Island Shelter and a University of Massachusetts sociology graduate, turned to her alma mater for help in "computerizing the Shelter's intake records."

Since I (Professor Schutt) was scheduled to teach a graduate course in Computer Applications in Social Analysis, I viewed the shelter's request as an opportunity to give my students a worthwhile experience in applied research. I talked with the shelter staff about their experiences with the intake form. Computer Applications students then began to develop a system for coding the forms. We soon discovered that there were many inconsistencies in the interviewing methods used by different shelter case managers. In order to improve case management and recordkeeping, a more structured interview instrument would be required.

The shelter project took on the dimensions of a major research effort. I turned to Professor Garrett, a sociologist who had conducted numerous

studies of the homeless in the 1960s and 1970s, for assistance. Together, we submitted a proposal for funding to our university and received a research grant that allowed us to enlarge the project. More intake forms were coded and entered into a computer data base and an arrangement was made for regular processing of a random sample of intake records. A graduate class in interviewing under Professor Garrett conducted in-depth interviews with shelter users; this in turn stimulated further improvements in the intake interview form. A second grant funded the project for another year; since then, graduate assistants and student interns have "kept the data coming."

The computerized intake information has become a valuable resource for both shelter staff and government policymakers. Shelter nurses and case managers use the intake forms in medical-social review sessions. City and state officials use statistical reports on Long Island's guests to help set policy directions. Articles from our research have contributed to the literature on the problems of the homeless and services for them. In addition, several students in our Graduate Program in Applied Sociology have developed theses in conjunction with their work on the project.

We have also used our research on Boston's homeless as a basis for developing training materials for those who work with this population. We received a grant that supported a national conference entitled "Homelessness: Critical Issues for Policy and Practice."

The discipline of sociology, we believe, provides the integrated approach necessary for understanding this problem and for assisting those who struggle to lessen its traumatic impact.

system and; (3) "Fictive storytelling," not altogether accurate stories about one's past, as well as fantasies about the future.

These three techniques allowed the homeless to weave a sense of self and to negotiate an identity through their conversations with others. Rather than passively accept a stigmatized identity imposed from outside, these men and women attempted to control the social construction of their own reality.

WHAT CITIES DECLINE?

Is the decline of the central city unavoidable? The answer seems to be no. The differences among central cities and suburbs are not as great as the differences between major cities in the Sunbelt and those in the northern industrial belt. Major cities in the South and West seem to be doing considerably better than large cities in the North in a number of categories, including employment, income, and racial patterns. Data from the 1980 Census for the nation's twenty-two largest cities and their suburbs, eleven in the North and eleven in the South and West, show that all but one of the eleven northern cities declined in population between 1970 and 1980 while the suburban population in all but two of these cities increased. In contrast, only two of the Sunbelt central cities (San Francisco and New Orleans) lost population, and all had an increased number of suburban residents.

Before 1978, the competitive edge of urban centers in the Northeast was weakened by a poor business climate and other negative features of large- and medium-sized metropolitan areas. After 1978, the overall economic position of the Northeast improved due to increased defense expenditures in the region, and the decentralization of population and industry into the suburbs. The Midwest, however, has remained disadvantaged economically and jobs have declined. In contrast, the South experienced a large gain in blue-collar jobs as well as in white-collar and service positions. Smaller metropolitan central-city counties grew even during the recession of the early 1980s, as did both the central cities and suburban counties in the South's largest metropolitan areas. Finally, the West has both a favorable industrial mix and other features that have resulted in steady growth of the region

(Kasarda, Irwin, and Hughes 1986). As may be seen in Table 19-8, demographers have predicted that by the year 2030, the South should have almost as many jobs in the finance, insurance, real-estate and services, government, and utilities sectors as the Northeast and Midwest combined. What is the likely effect on migration trends?

A Tale of Two Cities.   New York City and Phoenix, Ariz. provide an interesting tale of two cities. New York has ten times as many people as Phoenix on less land area. From 1970 to 1980, New York lost 10 percent of its population, while Phoenix gained by 33 percent. New York families had an average income in 1980 that was about $3,000 lower than the national average: Phoenix families had an average income almost $1,000 higher than the national average. Only 6 percent of the families in Phoenix were headed by a single mother as compared to a third of those in New York. New York lost 25 percent of its blue-collar jobs between 1970 and 1980 while Phoenix gained by 41 percent. Over 20 percent of the people living in Phoenix had moved there within the last five years, but less than 9 percent of those in New York had come to the city during that time. In New York, the population contains a larger percentage of blacks, Hispanics, and elderly than in Phoenix. Moreover, the suburbs of the two cities are very different. In New York, the suburban family income was almost $10,000 more than among city families. In Phoenix, family income in the suburbs was only about $500 higher than for city families. New York is an example of the "doughnut complex" where the poor central city is the hole, surrounded by rich suburbs.

WHAT CITIES WILL GROW?

According to current trends in urban development, the most dramatic growth is anticipated in the South and West. Among the fifty metropolitan areas that are expected to grow most rapidly between 1985 and 2005, eighteen are in the South, nineteen are in the West, eight are in the Northeast, and five are in the Midwest. The metropolitan area of Washington, D.C., is expected to gain more people than any other metropolitan area, outstripping Houston and Anaheim–Santa Ana. The metropolitan areas expected to grow most

TABLE 19-8 By 2030, the South should have almost as many jobs in the finance, insurance, real estate and services, government, and utilities sectors as the Northeast and Midwest combined

(Employment by industrial sector and region, 1985 and 2030, in thousands)	1985		2030		Percent Change 1985–2030
	Number	Percent Distribution	Number	Percent Distribution	
SOUTH					
Total	37,994	100.0%	56,008	100.0%	47.4%
Primary	1,698	4.5	1,393	2.5	−18.0
Secondary	8,118	21.4	10,259	18.3	26.4
Retail, wholesale	8,315	21.9	13,086	23.4	57.4
Finance, insurance, real estate	1,957	5.2	3,528	6.3	80.3
Services, government, utilities	17,906	47.1	27,742	49.5	54.9
NORTH*					
Total	49,860	100.0%	54,742	100.0%	9.8%
Primary	1,647	3.3	1,462	2.7	−11.2
Secondary	11,621	23.3	10,009	18.3	−13.9
Retail, wholesale	10,757	21.6	11,632	21.2	8.1
Finance, insurance, real estate	3,124	6.3	3,863	7.1	23.7
Services, government, utilities	22,711	45.5	27,776	50.7	22.3
WEST					
Total	21,688	100.0%	31,267	100.0%	44.2%
Primary	1,066	4.9	1,230	3.9	15.4
Secondary	4,097	18.9	5,290	16.9	29.1
Retail, wholesale	4,630	21.3	6,541	20.9	41.3
Finance, insurance, real estate	1,289	5.9	2,452	7.8	90.2
Services, government, utilities	10,606	48.9	15,754	50.4	48.5

* Northeast and Midwest census regions combined.
SOURCE: John D. Kasarda, Michael D. Irwin, Holly L. Hughes, "The South is Still Rising," *American Demographics,* June 1986, Figure 2, p. 35.

rapidly are those that will gain the most jobs in the years ahead.

Although northern central cities contain a high proportion of blacks (ranging from 22 percent in Boston and Columbus, Ohio, to 70 percent in Washington, D.C.) and very small proportions in the suburbs, Sunbelt cities generally had a more equal distribution of these minorities in the city and suburbs. The blacks who are moving South are younger and better educated than blacks who already live there; 61 percent had at least a high-school diploma as compared to only 45 percent of black southern natives. But the economic condition of blacks in the South still lags far behind that of whites despite the boost new, more-educated blacks have begun to bring to the region.

The Future of Cities

Analysts of the problems of the city, such as housing, crime, and unemployment, have proposed a variety of solutions. Con-servative writers, such as Banfield (1974), believe that urban ills stem from too much government intervention in the private market. According to this view, the assumption that all people are created equal has led to programs that merely increase the problems of the city; a policy of *benign neglect* is needed, which will lead to the disappearance of these problems over time.

In sharp contrast to this approach, conflict theorists claim that the very structure of American social and economic institutions makes it impossible to solve these problems. Capitalism is based on scarcity and surplus, and on the idea that to preserve current power relations, it is necessary to maintain an unequal distribution of goods and wealth. Therefore, only radically different approaches to the problems of the city will directly affect the poor, as the programs developed to date are by definition inadequate, a mere drop in the bucket that muddies the basic conflict between rich and poor.

Any large city faces the problem of how to pay for necessary services when jobs and taxable incomes cross the city line into other towns. As more affluent families flee to the suburbs and as industry withdraws from the central city, the tax base of the central city is reduced. The central city can no longer support the services that its residents require, whereas the suburbs can pay for more services than their population needs. To restore the balance between the central city and its suburbs and to reduce competition between nearby locales for industry and tax dollars, *regionalization* has been proposed as a solution that would recognize the interdependence among the units in the total metropolitan community. *Regionalization* is the formation of areawide governing bodies to handle areawide problems such as water supply, sewage, highway construction, parks, property assessment, and transportation. Local municipalities might remain responsible for such services as schools and fire departments.

Although regionalization is not a new concept (Boston attempted to regionalize in 1896), it has not been popular in the United States. Even when the metropolitan area is located within one county, agreements among the various municipal governments are difficult to negotiate and implement.

Existing local governmental structures would also have to be changed. There are ongoing experiments in regionalization in several American cities today, although an awareness of the common fate facing neighboring cities and towns is not widespread among citizens or politicians. And, regional interdependence may be resisted.

For all of their problems, the cities are likely to survive in one form or another. There are goods, services, opportunities for economic and social mobility, and cultural variety that can be found only in the city. These aspects of city life will continue to make them attractive places to live and work.

What will the city of the future be like? Doxiadias (1968) has suggested that by 2150, there will be a *eumenopolis* (from the Greek for "worldwide city"). The *eumenopolis* is essentially a strip-city development, interconnected nationally, continuously, and worldwide. Can you imagine a eumenopolis extending from Toronto through New York City and Washingon, D.C., to Atlanta or Miami?

Several patterns of future city development are shown in Table 19-9. Each type of city highlights an issue, a problem, or an opportunity faced by most major cities today (Shostak 1982). The first type of city, Conflict City, is characteristic of many of the old, industrial cities in the United States today. The second, Wired City, represents the extension of high-tech, whereas Neighborhood City is a vision of thrifty recycling, fresh ideas, and grass-roots ventures. Conservation City is dominated by energy requirements; that is, urban space is used to minimize energy costs and to maximize a pleasant life-style. In International City, ideas, people, and products circulate with freedom. Resi-

Regionalization is the formation of areawide governing bodies to handle common problems such as water supply, sewage, highway construction, parks, and transportation.

The eumenopolis is a continuous series of cities interconnected nationally and worldwide.

Stanley Tigerman, a contemporary architect/planner, is known for designs that offer urban solutions for the future. What kinds of patterns of behavior do you think this cityscape, designed by Tigerman, would generate? (© Stanley Tigerman/Balthazar Korab LTD)

dents here are citizens of the world rather than rooted in local ties. Regional City envisages new forms of government that go beyond municipal boundaries. The last, Leisure City, is associated with shorter work years; dual incomes; smaller, better-off households; and a commitment to recreation in the expanding amount of free time.

Whether the city of the future will take the shape of any of the proposals in Table 19-9 depends on a willingness to plan for residential development. Thus far, the United States has not had a comprehensive urban planning policy. Instead, there has been a set of

uncoordinated, often contradictory, essentially random public policies and programs.... Thus if in the past urbanization has been governed by any conscious public objectives at all, these have been, on the one hand, to encourage growth, apparently for its own sake; and on the other, to provide public works and public welfare programs to support piecemeal, spontaneous development. (Berry 1973, p. 119)

How we construct cities of the future will be closely related not only to the economic situation but, more importantly, to our social structure and value system (Gottdiener 1985, Hayden 1984).

TABLE 19-9 Cities in the twenty-first century: Some possible scenarios

Scenarios	Implementation Factors
I. Conflict City	Achieved by drift, inaction, and response to crisis; opposed by proaction residents, but supported by civic cynicism, lethargy, lack of political vision, and class and race hostility.
II. Wired City	Promoted by commercial pressure on competitive firms and the lure of vast profits in new information services; opposed by technophobes and companies vulnerable to telecommunication breakthroughs.
III. Neighborhood City	Promoted by historical appreciation for small-scale community advantages; opposed by modernists who perceive the city as a single operational entity; opposed also by those who see neighborhoods as narrow bastions of self-defeating ethnic and racial isolation.
IV. Conservation City	Promoted by ecology and environmental conservation pressures and partisans; opposed by cultural hostility to "beehive" living arrangements, and by traditional pride in the right to wide options in land development.
V. International City	Promoted by commercial pressure on competitive firms and the need to secure new jobs for the local labor force; opposed by a provincial culture and a tradition of urban insularity and ethnocentrism.
VI. Regional City	Promoted by recognition of inadequacy of city resources to meet problems with larger scope, and by the need to achieve economies of scale and central political direction; opposed by boosters of traditional political boundaries.
VII. Leisure City	Promoted by a steady contraction in the average work year, and by a steady rise in joblessness and in dual income, smaller, better-off households, and by prorecreation culture; opposed by a Calvinist Work Ethic culture, by those who see leisure undermining the productivity of the local work force, and by those who fear "the devil will make work for idle hands," as in the case of an undereducated permanent caste of unemployables.

SOURCE: Arthur Shostak, "Seven Scenarios of Urban Change," in Gary Gappert and Richard V. Knight, eds., *Cities in the Twenty-first Century, Vol. 23, Urban Affairs Annual Reviews,* (Beverly Hills, Calif.: Sage, 1982, p. 90).

Summary

In this chapter, we have looked at what happens to social institutions and social interaction as urbanization becomes the norm. Although city life has been criticized as strange and different, impersonal, untraditional, and more artificial than that of the countryside or suburbs, the lifestyles associated with all three locales are social constructs. The variety of the city promotes social differentiation, creativity, and change.

Despite the romantic view held by most Americans on the virtues of country life, most people live in urban areas. Since World War II, more and more people have begun to live in suburbs, popular for their relative peace and quiet, their spaciousness, their encouragement of leisure pursuits, and their advantages for raising children. But suburban life also has drawbacks: Transportation is generally poor, services may be difficult to reach or not available at all, and the very sameness that initially attracted people to suburbia may produce conformity and boredom, especially among teenagers, the elderly, and middle-aged women.

The older American cities have been beset by problems in the last few decades, including a shrinking population, smaller tax bases, high rates of unemployment, and the relocation of industry. Many major cities have attempted to counter these difficulties by subsidizing new construction, promoting gentrification, and seeking new sources of capital. It seems unlikely, however, that the old, industrial city will prosper until further social changes are made.

Various ways in which the city of the future might be constructed have been proposed, all of them designed to reduce some of the problems of present-day cities. The future of American cities depends on the decisions made by the voters, the legislators, and the owners of capital. City planning, like all other social planning and deliberate social policy, reflects a series of choices among competing values and interests. Decisions about size, location, type of construction, transportation, parks, schools, and use of space to promote or reduce social interaction will reflect both the power interests and the norms and values of the society in which these decisions occur.

Suggested Readings

BUSS, D. M., and F. S. REDBURN. *Shutdown or Youngstown: Public Policy for Mass Unemployment.* Albany, N.Y.: State University of New York Press, 1983. An examination of the impact of a plant closure in a "one-factory town."

FISCHER, CLAUDE S. *To Dwell Among Friends: Personal Networks in Town and City.* Chicago: University of Chicago Press, 1982. Fischer reexamines the assumptions people have about the negative effects of urbanization on social and moral life. Basing his analysis on the SMSA sample of Oakland and San Francisco, the author finds no differences in the quality of social ties among urbanites as compared to non-urbanities. Yet, he did find stronger friendship ties and networks in the city.

GEIST, WILLIAM. *Toward a Safe and Sane Halloween and Other Tales of Suburbia.* New York: Time Books, 1985. An interesting insight into suburban life in the United States.

HARTMAN, CHESTER. *America's Housing Crisis: What is to be Done?* Boston: Routledge & Kegan Paul. 1983. A collection of essays on the state of the housing crisis in the United States and the need for federal intervention.

JACOBS, JANE. *The Death and Life of Great American Cities.* New York: Random House, 1961. A classic analysis of the problems of urban planning, urban renewal, and life in American cities.

SAWERS, LARRY, and WILLIAM K. TABB, eds. *Sunbelt/Snowbelt: Urban Development and Regional Restructuring.* New York: Oxford University Press, 1984. This book examines the underlying forces which transform the economy and structure of regions and cities.

20

Popular Culture: Mass Media, Popular Music, and Sports

O N the weekend of July 4th, 1986, Americans celebrated the rededication of the Statue of Liberty. With the exception of a few minutes of "newsworthy" material available to all television networks, exclusive rights to broadcast the four-day entertainment extravaganza were sold to the highest broadcasting bidder. The entertainment included a performance by 200 Elvis Presley look-alikes and the release of 5000 homing pigeons billed as doves of peace. At one point the producers seriously considered asking Richard Nixon, the former president of the U.S. who was forced to resign, to be the keynote speaker [President Aquino of the Philippines was too busy running her country, and the Jewish human rights activist Elie Weisel would not perform on the Sabbath (Dowd 1986).]

The organizing committee also sold the rights for an advertiser to become an "official" sponsor of the events. Among the many commercials that linked products with Liberty Weekend was one that featured people whose work or play required them to raise their arms and who were thankful for the protection provided by a particular deodorant; the final shot showed the Statue of Liberty with her arm raised too.

Whatever else Liberty Weekend involved—patriotism, pride, community—it was also a prime example of *popular culture:* a product designed for mass consumption. And since this is America, the product was highly commercialized. Liberty Weekend, like Disneyland or Atlantic City, represents the blending of profit making and entertainment that characterize popular culture in the United States.

Other recent examples of American popular culture include the following:

- Rambose, a nightclub in Houston, Tex., where the staff wear military fatigues and the decor includes sandbags, camouflage netting, and machine gun emplacements. Every night, customers raise their hands in a one-finger gesture to Russia, Nicaragua, Cuba, or Libya.

- Babyland General Hospital, home of the original Cabbage Patch Kids, whose employees, dressed as nurses and physicians, regularly "deliver" dolls wrapped in bunting and displayed at the Delivery Room window.

- The garage sale, organized for "fun and profit" (Herrmann and Soiffer 1984).

- The bidding war by Hollywood movie companies for rights to the hottest true family story of 1986: the one about the thirteen-year-old girl who asked the police to arrest her parents for drug use.

The weekend celebration of the rededication of the Statue of Liberty was a recent example of popular culture which combined profit making and entertainment. Do you think our founding fathers would have attended the festivities? (© Robert McElroy/Woodfin Camp and Associates)

The Study of Popular Culture

Popular culture is both what people do in their leisure time and the products designed for mass consumption.

Although we have defined *popular culture* as products designed for mass consumption, other scholars prefer a broader definition: popular culture is, they say, whatever people do when they are not at work or asleep, that is, in their *leisure* time. Denisoff and Wahrman (1983), for example, use the blanket term *entertainment* to cover the variety of products studied by students of popular culture, everything from comic strips to striptease shows, from baseball cards to Boy George, and the thousands of other items of mass consumption that reflect a society's culture, its values, and patterns of thought.

Popular culture in America is also big business. It provides employment and wealth to those who produce it, the opportunity for self-expression and pleasure to those who consume it, and endless fascination to those who study it. In other words, popular culture has two aspects: (1) the human impulse to play, to be creative, and to let one's imagination roam (Biesty 1986); and (2) the needs of an advanced capitalist economy to generate new markets and to make money at it (Rojek 1985).

In this chapter, we can only skim the surface of this fast-growing field of study (Mukerji and Schudson 1986). We will examine the role of popular culture in mass society, questions of control and social class, and the processes whereby fun and games are institutionalized. We will take an in-depth look at three major subfields: the mass media, popular music, and sports.

Popular Culture in Mass Society

FUNCTIONAL PERSPECTIVES

As a species, humans may have benefited from their impulse to play and to create things of beauty (artistry). Leisure-time activities reduce personal anxiety and relieve tension. For the group as a whole, creating things that give pleasure to others bring members together. Many forms of play and games also represent the solidarity of the tribe or village, and even the nation (as in the modern Olympic Games). In other words, the popular culture supports social order by providing entertainment for individuals and by unifying the group.

These individual and group benefits become very important in modern societies, where leisure time is often defined as the pause that refreshes weary workers. Because play is an end in itself, we say that it is *expressive*. It is done to express or satisfy certain human needs. Work, on the other hand, is a means to another goal. Thus, work is *instrumental*. Popular culture, therefore, is an expressive outlet that balances the demands of instrumental obligations and duties. In this sense, popular culture is especially functional in societies with an intense commitment to instrumental roles: "The harder we work, the harder we play." When many different products are provided for leisure consumption, people who are discontented or overworked can be "cooled out" with fun and games, instead of directing their anger toward employers or other authorities.

Play as Work. There is also another way in which popular culture can be considered supportive of the American value system. The "work ethic" described in Chapter 3 is in part based on the early Puritan distrust of fun and games as sinful. Pure enjoyment still makes some of us feel guilty. But if play is made to seem like work, the discomfort is lessened (Lewis 1982). Play can be transformed into work if winning is the goal, or if play is defined as a money-making activity. "How-to" books that promise to improve your golf game or tennis stroke are written as if they were operating manuals for a machine. Do this and that correctly and you will succeed. This is the same goal-directed way of thinking that characterizes the work ethic: If all the right steps are taken in the precise order, a given goal can be achieved. Jogging to the point of exhaustion is work, not pleasure. Only after single-minded devotion to a hard day's play or work has one truly earned that glass of foaming beer. Thus, even leisure is subject to the same process of "scientific management"

as work in modern society—another example of what Max Weber called the "iron cage" of technology (Andrew 1981).

Mass Culture as a Unifying Element.   Those elements of the popular culture that are produced and distributed through the mass media (radio, television, magazines, and newspapers) make up a *mass culture* that creates common unifying values and attitudes in large, heterogeneous (mixed) societies. Because industrial society is based on specialization and the separation of occupational and status groups, the popular culture may be the only culture shared by most members. Whatever else divides us, the World Series and the Super Bowl bring us together (Goethals 1981).

CONFLICT ANALYSIS

The terms *popular* and *mass culture* suggest something that emerges out of the personal creativity of "the people." Yet, the production of culture, like any other activ-

Mass culture refers to elements of popular culture that are produced and distributed through the mass media.

Our Puritan heritage teaches us that self-discipline, even in eating (or, perhaps, especially in eating) will set us on the right path. Do you think this old advertisement is far from contemporary concerns? (© Culver Pictures)

I Say
Genuine Joy
Genuine Appetite
Genuine Health and therefore
Genuine Complexion

All come from eating the GENUINE
Kellogg's
TOASTED CORN FLAKES
NONE GENUINE WITHOUT THIS SIGNATURE
W. K. Kellogg
THE KIND WITH THE FLAVOR—MADE OF THE BEST WHITE CORN.

Graham Crackers, Grape-Nuts, Corn Flakes, and Original Sin

Among the most interesting aspects of popular culture are the health and fitness fads that periodically sweep the country. Social historian Harvey Green has analyzed these trends and showed how they are shaped by broader currents of change in the society. The history of physical fitness fads is greatly enlivened by the larger-than-life eccentrics who led various health reform movements.

Particularly fascinating are the three men who founded the food empires that still dominate our breakfast tables: Sylvester Graham, C. W. Post, and J. H. Kellogg. Graham's crackers were a "natural" food answer to widespread fears about the negative health effects of city life and factory work for the urban masses. In addition, members of the newly emerging class of white-collar workers, fearful that they might be "feminized" by the shift from manual to nonmanual labor, were reassured that their masculinity could be preserved by eating natural foods.

C. W. Post, too, was keenly aware of the differences between manual and nonmanual workers; his Grape-Nuts were originally marketed as "brain food" for middle-class employees. Post and others were also worried about declining birth rates in the white middle class, in contrast to the high fertility of recent immigrants and American blacks. All types of health foods were being promoted in the early 1900s to restore virility to WASP middle-class males.

But the most unusual character in the history of health foods was J. H. Kellogg, who had a Puritanical obsession with original sin and the evils of unbridled sexuality. His breakfast products—especially Corn Flakes—were good for you because they reduced the sex drive; eat enough of them and you would be freed of sin.

What the three had in common, along with so many other health and fitness leaders throughout our history, was a very American belief in individual responsibility for one's state of physical and moral health. Ill health, therefore, could not be the fault of working conditions or blamed on employers. Such an emphasis on the individual also works against collective efforts to improve the workplace or to narrow life-style differences between middle- and working-class families.

SOURCE: Harvey Green. *Fit for America: Health, Fitness, Sport and American Society.* New York: Pantheon, 1986.

---

ity, is socially structured. Who are the artists and entertainers, the creators of products? Where and how do they work? Who pays them? Who consumes their products? What are the standards of success, and who defines them? Who benefits?

The major issue from the conflict perspective is that of control over the *production of popular culture*—the issue of cultural hegemony that we referred to in Chapters 3 and 7. If the elements of popular culture are not entirely spontaneous creations, then some people and groups must decide what is made and for whom, as well as what vision of the world is portrayed in them. From this perspective, popular culture is manufactured in the same way as any other product: there are industries that turn out movies, television and radio programs, newspapers and magazines, records and rock bands, sports events, books, and even art exhibits.

Conflict theorists are also interested in another form of control: Who defines what is real or good? And when does what is

> Control over the **production of popular culture** is a major concern for sociologists in the conflict tradition.

good become "what we think is good for you"? This is the activity of "gatekeepers" and "tastemakers"—particular people whose social position permits them to open or close the gates to success, and to impose their standards of goodness. Gatekeepers and tastemakers form a cultural elite, and are typically drawn from the ranks of the educated middle class.

A final concern of conflict theorists is the possibility of using popular culture as a means of opposing the established order. An authentic popular culture should emerge from the daily experience of people rather than being imposed on them by others. In this sense, musical styles have been an important channel of protest or comfort for groups outside the mainstream. For example, the sounds and lyrics of soul, country-and-western, reggae, and the blues frequently express the pain of life's losers. The 1960s are remembered today for the music of protest as much as for the street demonstrations that captured the headlines.

Culture and Class.   When we try to examine what people do in their leisure time, the range of possibilities is enormous: Some listen to rock music, others to grand opera; some read *Playgirl* or *Penthouse,* others *Ms* or *GQ;* some play sandlot baseball, others sail yachts. In a society as mixed as ours in terms of race, religion, ethnicity, and social class, there will be great differences in the expression of the popular culture. For example, blacks and whites enjoy different types of popular music; Irish men spend more time in bars than do Jews; white middle-class men are the major market for pornography; and women of all ages and social classes buy paperback romances. There are also regional cultures, particularly between North and South and the East Coast and the West Coast. For example, one study of regional differences in leisure-time activities found a greater emphasis on home-, family-, and church-centered activities among southerners as compared with the rest of the nation (Marsden et al. 1982).

Aspects of popular culture also show great variation by social class. The leisure-time activities of the well-to-do are very different from those of the less affluent. This difference is partly a consequence of having more money to spend, and partly a result of having been socialized to contrasting ideas of fun and play.

Working-class leisure patterns have long been a center of struggle between workers and their employers (Rosenzweig 1983). In the early days of the factory system, leisure and work were combined, as when employees drank and gambled on the job. By the end of the nineteenth century, employers succeeded in tightening discipline, and drinking moved into the saloon, the haven of working-class men. By the 1920s, the saloons gave way to the movie house, another setting controlled by the middle class. Rosenzweig (1983) suggests that the conflict over leisure diverted workers' attention from other economic issues, and accounts for the late development of American unionism, its lack of radicalism, and the failure of workers to form a class-based political party.

In Chapter 7 we saw how the *consumption* of products of popular culture is used to measure social status (Sobol 1982). Analysts of popular culture often make a distinction between the items enjoyed and sponsored by the affluent—*elite culture*—and those enjoyed by the majority—*mass culture.* There is a strong element of snobbery in many descriptions of this difference, with elite culture seen as more

Elite culture consists of items enjoyed and sponsored by the wealthy.

A number of taste cultures exist in the U.S. appealing to different publics. For some, an evening with the American Ballet is wonderful while others prefer the thrill of the circus. Do you think these taste cultures are mutually exclusive? (© Jack Vartoogian; John Marmaras/Woodfin Camp and Associates)

pure and worthy, and mass culture as watered down and vulgarized—the difference, for example, between attending the ballet or a barn dance.

Criticisms of Mass Culture. Mass culture has been attacked on many grounds: (1) that it appeals to the lowest levels of taste; (2) that it generates a false sense of reality and dulls critical thinking; (3) that it corrupts the standards of elite culture by offering instant fame and fortune to crowd pleasers; and (4) that it really is not "art" because it is produced only for profit (Denisoff and Wahrman 1983, J. Blau 1986).

These arguments echo a long-standing fear by American elitists that "too much" democracy undermines standards of excellence, a theme that is still heard in discussions of mass education (e.g., open admissions lowers the value of a college degree). It is not difficult to find easy targets of ridicule: Mother's Day cards as poetry, movie soundtracks as serious music, television game shows as displays of intellectual skill, or professional wrestling as athletics.

But there is also a darker vision: mass audiences as passive receivers of entertainment rather than as active agents of their own fate, thus leaving them vulnerable to the appeals of dictators. The theme of mass culture ("bread and circuses") as a sign of moral and social decay has a long tradition in Western thought (Brantlinger 1983). How often have you heard the argument that pleasing the masses was the cause of the fall of the Roman Empire? Or that barbarians are always at the gates, ready to destroy civilized peoples?

In Defense of Mass Culture. Contemporary students of popular culture tend to view the distinction between elite and mass culture in less sharp and value-laden terms. Throughout most of Western history, both ordinary citizens and the wealthy and powerful enjoyed many of the same pastimes and entertainments. Although De Fleur (1982) distinguishes a spontaneous and anonymous folk art from the conscious creations of talented artists who were employed by royalty or the church, the mass of citizens were able to enjoy sacred music, church art, public architecture, and dramatic performances. In modern society, however, certain pleasures become the exclusive privilege of the

wealthy, who turn them into status symbols.

There has also been a great deal of crossover between elite and folk culture. Styles filter both up and down. For example, elites often set standards of dress and adornment that quickly appear in less expensive copies. Conversely, musical forms with great mass appeal are frequently adapted by classical composers. Nor are the audiences for elite and mass culture so sharply separated; individuals typically have both "high" and "low" tastes.

Recent research (J. Blau 1986) also demonstrates that, contrary to mass society theory, elite cultural forms (e.g., art museums, opera, ballet and theater companies, orchestras) are actually more evenly distributed across the nation than are most forms of popular culture (e.g., craft fairs, movie houses, nightclubs, bands and dance halls). That is, high culture has become somewhat democratized while mass culture remains regionalized. The fear that commercialized popular art forms would replace or debase elite forms has not been realized: both forms flourish in some areas, and neither in other parts of the country.

Some critics of artistic elitism go so far as to suggest that contemporary mass culture displays more diversity and creativity than does high culture. Compare, for example, popular music to contemporary classical compositions, or subway-car "graffiti" to what is being shown as serious modern art.

Taste Cultures. The validity of *all* forms of popular culture has been most forcibly argued by Herbert Gans (1974). Gans uses the term *taste cultures* to suggest the great variety of culture publics, without implying value judgments. If we can subscribe to the principle of cultural relativism when comparing entire societies (see Chapter 2), it is also possible to describe differences among taste cultures without claiming that any is superior to the others. Far from being a passive homogenized mass, consumers of popular culture are an extremely varied population. Contrary to mass society theory, consumers are active participants in interpreting their experience (Gottdiener 1985).

The Production of Culture. In contrast to an earlier emphasis on the individuals who create and consume popular culture,

Taste cultures include a great variety of culture publics, without implying value judgments.

Americans and the Arts

Americans have often been stereotyped as indifferent to "the arts"—live theater, classical music performances, art museums, ballet—preferring soap opera to grand opera. But public opinion data suggests otherwise. According to a 1984 national survey, when going to the movies and attending popular music concerts are also considered, three-fourths of the respondents indicated that the arts gave them "pure pleasure" and over 90 percent felt that the arts were important to the quality of life in their community.

Most people who attend artistic events are consumers of a variety of art forms. As you might expect, people who go to museums, live theater, and classical music concerts come from the higher-income and -education strata, are likely to live in or near large cities, and to be middle-aged (Blau 1986b). Not only do they have the time and money to attend, but they also have developed the "cultural capital" or tastes that attract them to such leisure pursuits.

In contrast, pop music primarily appeals to a younger audience: 82 percent of persons age eighteen to twenty-nine attended at least one popular music concert in 1984, compared to 63 percent of persons age thirty to forty-nine. Movies are also most heavily attended by young adults, with 96 percent of persons eighteen to twenty-nine having made at least one visit to a movie house in 1984.

Attendance at artistic events has risen steadily over the past few decades, even though home entertainment has been made easier with VCRs and cable TV, and despite a drop in the median hours available for leisure pursuits from 26.2 in 1973 to 18.1 in 1984. It appears that more Americans, especially women, are working longer hours than in the past, so that, on an individual basis, consumption of the arts has declined, but since more people than ever before are attending one or more such events, the overall percentage has risen.

As for personal participation in the arts, this, too, has increased. The most common forms of involvement are (1) playing a musical instrument, photography, painting, and creative writing for the young and better educated, and (2) craftwork such as needlepoint, weaving, and pottery making for older, predominantly female residents of small towns.

In sum, the arts are alive and well across America, with the expected social-class differences, but also with a great deal of crossover and overwhelming general support.

SOURCE: *Americans and the Arts*, New York: Louis Harris and Associates for Philip Morris, Inc., 1984; reported by Martha Farnsworth Riche in *American Demographics*, July, 1985, pp. 42–44.

Production of culture refers to the organizational chain that determines the creation, distribution, and consumption of cultural products.

many sociologists today are focusing on structural aspects of the *production of culture:* organizations, markets, industries, distribution chains, and other systems that determine what is finally produced and offered to the public (DiMaggio 1977, Ryan 1985). In this view, popular culture is the outcome of a three-way interaction among: (1) the objects produced; (2) the profit-making producers and distributors of those objects; and (3) the social groups that consume them. Just what is produced, how it is marketed, and who buys it are all related to basic economic variables such as control over markets, dealing with competition, avoiding regulation, and generating consumer demand (Ryan 1985). Yet because sociologists are also interested in the meaning that people attach to the products they desire and purchase, the study of mass culture must have a symbolic interactionist dimension (Gottdiener 1985).

Like any other facet of culture, popular culture is learned and shared. This process takes place within families, peer groups, social classes, and particular subcultures. But by far the most important element in the production and spread of popular culture—the condition that makes mass culture possible—is the existence of mass media in modern societies.

The Mass Media

Media is the plural of *medium,* which means a channel through which something is carried (transmitted). *Mass media* refers to the agents of communication in a mass society: (1) the print media—books, magazines, and newspapers; and (2) the electronic media—television, radio, and recordings. These are our equivalents of

Mass media are channels of communication in a mass society, primarily the print and electronic media.

the storytellers and singers who were the earliest media of information and entertainment. In modern societies, such face-to-face communication is replaced by mass-produced items for use by a wide public. This means that the products must be acceptable to many people, so that the economic requirements of mass production become at least as important as the quality of the product.

This mass-produced cultural product is what critics have condemned as masscult, or as *kitsch,* a word that means common (vulgar) and simple (De Fleur 1982). It is very easy to poke fun at television game shows, cowboy movies, and paperback romances for their vulgarity and lack of sophistication. But sociologists are analysts of culture, not art critics. The topics of interest to us are the manifest and latent functions of the mass media. The manifest functions include selling products and making a profit, as well as providing entertainment and information. The latent functions, because they are often hidden and unintended, are more difficult to analyze. How do mass communications support the status quo? What values and behaviors are encouraged? What status groups are either coopted or cooled out? Is popular culture manufactured by dominant groups in their own interests? How do the conditions under which popular culture is manufactured affect the product? These are the questions we examine in the following sections.

GENERAL CHARACTERISTICS

Importance of Mass Media. First it is necessary to establish the importance of the mass media in the daily lives of most Americans. What do people do in their leisure time? A well-publicized national survey of leisure in America (United Media Enterprises 1982) asked respondents what they do everyday or almost every day. (See Table 20-1.)

Clearly, television, newspapers, radios, and books were the primary means of entertainment and information for an overwhelming majority: 99 percent of American homes have at least one radio (average: five), and 98 percent have a television set (average: two), which is typically turned on for almost seven hours per day. (The big story, of course, was that twice the percentage of Americans worked

in the garden than had sex on a frequent basis.)

The mass media are also important elements of the economic system, employing close to one million workers, and accounting for tens of billions of dollars in payrolls alone. In addition, about $70 billion will be spent this year on advertising in the print and electronic media, particularly on ads for foods, automobiles, beauty aids, and over-the-counter medicines. The American mass media are crucial for raising the level of consumer demand that is the basis of our industrial system. Media images reinforce both the desire for specific goods and the belief that consumption itself is an American virtue (Ewen and Ewen 1982).

Advertising revenues are the only source of income for most radio and television stations, and a major source for newspapers and magazines. In this respect, the American system is almost unique.

Public Versus Private Ownership. Throughout most of the world, television and radio stations are owned and operated by government agencies, and in many nations, so also are newspapers and book-publishing companies. As a result, information and entertainment can be largely controlled by political leaders, either through direct acts of censorship and propaganda, or through more subtle means when the producers of information and entertainment are part of the bureaucratic apparatus itself (Dubin 1986).

TABLE 20-1 How Americans spend their leisure time

Activity	% Doing Daily
Watch television	72
Read a newspaper	70
Listen to music at home	46
Talk on the phone to friends	45
Exercise or jog	35
Spend the evening talking to someone	30
Read a book	24
Pursue a hobby	23
Work in the garden	22
Engage in sexual activities	11

While the radio has been a significant factor in most of our lives, think of how media technology in this area has changed. How has this affected listening patterns and the listener? (© UPI/Bettmann Newsphotos; Mike Maple/ Woodfin Camp and Associates)

In contrast, the mass media in the United States are commercial enterprises, owned and operated by profit-making corporations. The few exceptions are college-run stations, the Public Broadcasting System, and some local nonprofit stations—all with limited audiences and financial dependence on government grants or viewers' subscriptions.

The diversity of American media, and their separation from the state, have long been considered essential to the First Amendment guarantee of free speech in particular and democratic policies in general. The government has had to regulate access to the airwaves only because there is a limited number of broadcast bands, whereas theoretically everyone could own a printing press (de Sola Pool 1983).

But if the American mass media are relatively free of political interference, they nonetheless operate under a number of powerful economic constraints. Because most media are businesses, success depends as much on attracting advertisers as audiences. The risk of losing advertising revenue can influence decisions about what to produce. The trick is to offend the fewest possible advertisers and publics, which accounts for both the sameness and the blandness of media offerings.

At the same time, because of the size and heterogeneity of our population, there is an audience for a variety of specialized media products—magazines for every type of sports interest, for various age groups, for women who work and those who are full-time homemakers, for stock-market analysts and soldiers of fortune; cable television channels for sports fans, music lovers of all types, pornography addicts, news freaks, and religious followers; and a radio program for every taste.

Media Goliaths.   The major trend that has reduced the variety and independence of various mass media is the increasing likelihood of *crossmedia ownership* (Bagdikian 1983). This refers to the fact that the same owner(s) might have controlling interests in radio stations, television outlets, and newspapers. The result is that a few locally powerful people can control the flow of information and entertainment in an entire community.

At the national level, major media giants such as the Columbia Broadcasting System (CBS) or the New York Times Company are also involved in the production of books and records as well as television and radio programs. For example, a company such as Gulf & Western, which only holds stock in other organizations, controls movie-making and distributing companies, the theaters that show the films, and the book publisher with tie-ins to the film. Thus, the same group of executives can make decisions affecting a number of media (Dreier 1982). That "show biz" has become Big Business can also be

Crossmedia ownership occurs when the same owner(s) control interests in several media at the same time.

seen in the mergers *within* as well as between movie studios and television companies, leading to increased concentration of power in the entertainment industry (Cieply and Barnes 1986).

Most recently, the three major national television networks have been sold to corporate owners: NBC to General Electric, ABC to Capital Cities, and CBS to a family whose fortune was made in real estate. It is expected that the primary emphasis of the new owners will be on bottom-line profits, leading to the sacrifice of quality programs and features that do not attract a large audience. The effects of the new ownership can already be seen in a scaling back of the very expensive newsgathering operations required for their evening news programs. In some major cities, these national newscasts are now shown at 6:30 rather than the more popular hour of 7:00 so that local stations can schedule the far more profitable game shows at the later time. In general, as long as they are accountable to nonmedia managers, the major networks will be under pressure to avoid great risks in programming. Nonetheless, efforts to control the growth of media goliaths by invoking federal antitrust regulations has been resisted by the Reagan administration (Jones 1986).

EFFECTS OF THE MASS MEDIA

Most criticism of the mass media is based on the assumption that what people see and read and hear strongly affects their attitudes and behavior. This assumption is shared by critics on both the left and the right of the political spectrum—each fearing what the "other side" might be doing, while trying to have their own views widely broadcast. Whereas some claim that the media reinforces social inequality, others see television as the great equalizer.

Postman (1983), for example, claims that television is dangerous to our political and social health because it focuses on trivialities and dulls our capacity to think critically. Thus, audiences become addicted to a quick entertainment "fix," even while watching the news or presumably "educational" programs. Similarly, from a structural analysis of how prime-time television programs are chosen and produced, Gitlin (1983) concludes that their focus on personal rather than public issues deflects attention from social problems, while lull-

ing viewers into believing that all problems can ultimately be solved.

Although it is difficult to believe that the media do *not* have a direct impact on attitudes and behaviors, the research findings are unclear. Feminists and members of other minority groups have drawn attention to the potentially damaging effects of media portrayals of women, blacks, and the elderly, or, worse, of their absence altogether (Tuchman et al. 1978, Arluke and Levin 1982, Courtney and Whipple 1983, Cantor 1987). Yet there is very little empirical evidence to support the belief that television has a large or enduring effect on behavior (Ball-Rokeach et al. 1984).

Even advertising, an activity whose rationale is its influence on behavior, appears to have little power in producing sales for specific products, although it indirectly reinforces capitalism by encouraging viewers to even higher levels of consumption (Schudson 1984). Ironically, media executives and advertising personnel have a vested interest in proving a link between media exposure and viewer response, but both deny any causal connection when the issue is media violence.

Antisocial Behaviors. Most of the research on media effects has centered on the issue of violence and the possibility that media portrayals contribute to the level of antisocial behaviors in the society. Yet, as Cantor (1982) asks: If there were no portrayals of sex on the media, would it disappear from our behavioral repertoire?

The research evidence here, too, is not at all clear. On the one hand are several government-sponsored reviews of the social-science literature that give qualified support to the idea that televised violence is related to aggressive behavior among some children (Surgeon General 1972, Withey and Abeles 1980, National Institute of Mental Health 1982). But these effects were largely short-term and varied considerably among different types of children.

The government reports paid special attention to the ongoing research of Gerbner et al. (1981), who found that "heavy" consumers of television think that the world is a more dangerous place than do "light" viewers. Heavy viewers are more fearful and mistrustful of others and have an exaggerated view of the real level of crime and violence. Other studies (reviewed in

Comstock 1980) report laboratory experiments in which children's immediate behavior was influenced by their having watched different types of films. But the laboratory is not the real world.

Evidence from the real world and for adults comes from the work of Phillips (1982—1983, Bollen and Phillips 1982) on the effects of mass-media reports of violence on United States homicide and suicide rates. For example, Phillips' research design indicates that homicides tend to rise immediately following well-publicized heavyweight prize fights, and suicides increase in the ten days following the widely reported suicide of some famous person. However, every one of these claims has been modified or refuted by other research. Stack (1984), for example, using other measures of mass-media attention in addition to control variables, found no support for Phillips' theory of imitative suicides. Rather, unemployment rates and season of the year (Spring is apparently a difficult time for unhappy people) explained most of the variation in suicides.

Furthermore, one recent study of the link between exposure to television violence and committing violent acts found that the relationship was in fact *negative*. That is, among population groups with high levels of television viewing, rates of violent crimes are relatively low (Messner 1986). The research suggests that because television viewing is something people do in the privacy of their homes, they are not out on the streets being influenced by peers to engage in criminal behavior. In a study of Swedish adolescents, Roe (1983) found that students who were having trouble at school were not attracted to television but to their peer groups, rejecting the adult world and its artifacts. It was the better students who used television to enhance their knowledge of the adult world and add to their cultural capital.

Two other recent studies also conclude that the evidence linking media violence to antisocial behavior is very weak. Cullingford (1984) argues that children do not really pay much attention to what they watch, and that they are quite capable of separating reality from make-believe. And Gunther (1985) notes that "violence" is too broad a concept to be helpful in research; when behavior is more closely specified, direct cause and effect is almost impossible to prove. Both the viewing and the subsequent behaviors take place in social contexts, with great variation in how people define their situation.

The television networks have also responded with studies and research reviews of their own (Milavsky et al. 1982, American Broadcasting Company 1983). Their major point is that academic researchers have been much more cautious in their conclusions than the government reports suggest. It appears that the viewing, listening, reading public is not as passive as often assumed. Choices are made within very complex fields of influence. Neither children nor adults give television their full attention; in fact, radio and television are frequently used as background "noise" for other activities.

A MODEL OF MASS COMMUNICATION

The simplest model of the variables involved in mass communications is presented in Figure 20-1. Media audiences have a two-way relationship with both their sources of information and society as a whole. People's dependence on the media for information varies with the stability of their society; that is, at times of rapid social change or events beyond their control, people seek out information to clarify their perceptions. And when media reports only increase the confusion (ambiguity or lack of clarity), people become even

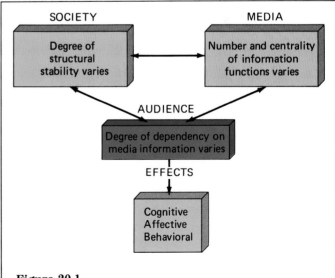

Figure 20-1
Society, media, and audience: Reciprocal relationships. (Adapted from Melvin L. DeFleur and Sandra Ball-Rokeach, *Theories of Mass Communications*, 4th ed., New York: Longman, 1982, p. 243.)

more dependent on the media. The ultimate impact on attitudes (cognitive effects), feelings (the affective dimension), and action (behavior) are the result of this process, which then feeds back into the social system and the media. Most sociologists view communications as a *social* process in which the media and other social forces interact to construct reality (McCormack 1980).

Agenda setting refers to the list of topics that come to the attention of the public.

Agenda Setting. Where the media have their strongest effect then, is *indirectly,* by setting the agenda—the list of topics that come to the attention of the consuming public. By their choice of what to cover and for how long, newspapers, television, and magazines create reality. The women's movement, for example, became a "hot item" in the early 1970s, even though feminist organizations had been at work for years; today, the media speak of a "post-feminist era" when, in actuality, there has been no decline in public support for most goals of the movement.

The agenda-setting approach to mass communications is very popular among social scientists today because it combines an emphasis on media power with an appreciation of the active role of the consumer (Roberts and Bachen 1982). The majority of readers and viewers are not passive sponges, but active selectors of what they see and read. This information is cognitively organized, usually into preexisting slots in our minds. But because the media provide us with material that has already been partly preprocessed by reporters and editors, who determine the relative importance of the stories they choose to cover, its influence is especially strong where people have no other way of knowing what is happening, primarily those with limited social contacts or personal experience (Grabner 1984). We must, therefore, be aware of the contexts in which consumers do their watching, listening, and reading, as well as the context in which media products are created. These considerations are most crucial in analyzing media presentation of the news.

ALL THE NEWS THAT FITS

It is often assumed that newspapers, news magazines, radio newscasts, and the televised nightly news present "*the* news," that is, pure factual information. Most media sociologists would disagree, as indicated in the titles of their work: "Writing News and Telling Stories" (Darnton 1975); *Making News* (Tuchman 1978); *Manufacturing the News* (Fishman 1980); and *Inventing Reality* (Parenti 1985). The basic theme of these studies is that the gathering and presentation of the news is shaped by social contexts, primarily the environments in which reporters work and in which editors make decisions about what stories to cover and broadcast. The crucial questions become: "Where are the cameras and reporters?" "What deadlines must be met?" and "How can the material be made understandable to the public?"

There are also space and time limits set by each medium: twenty-two and one-half

When the cameras set up to shoot, there is always a direction and a framework. The audience does not end up seeing a random selection of images. Have you ever attended an event and later seen it on TV? Did you feel the presentation provided a true reflection? (© George Hall/Woodfin Camp and Associates)

Living With Television

TODD GITLIN

Todd Gitlin, a former journalist, is professor of sociology and director of the Mass Communications Program at the University of California at Berkeley, where he received his Ph.D. in 1977. He teaches courses on the mass media and the sociology of culture and knowledge. He is the author of a number of books and articles dealing with the media, including Inside Prime Time *(New York: Pantheon, 1983),* The Whole World is Watching: Mass Media in the Making and Unmaking of the New Left *(University of California Press, 1980) and most recently,* The Sixties: Years of Hope, Days of Rage *(New York: Bantam, 1987). He also edited* Watching Television *(New York: Pantheon, 1987). The following vignette is based on an interview with Todd Gitlin in the April/May 1987* Media File.

Television is very much part of most children's lives today. Studies by Nielsen indicate that the average household has a TV turned on more than seven hours each day. While children are not necessarily and constantly glued to the tube, much of their experience comes to them through television. This represents a generational change.

I'm a member of the transitional generation; I was already ten by the time we got a television. Before our family had a TV, there was one little friend in the building who had one. We would gather round as if it had some central ceremonial/ritual function, watching "Howdy Doody" and "I Remember Mama," two popular shows of the time. I remember watching the 1950 World Series when I was seven and crowds of people huddled around the new model TVs displayed in the RCA Building in New York City. So I have the ex-perience of pre-television, I have the experience of television as a special thing, a virtual shrine, and I have the experience of being taken over by television, from ages ten to six-teen. I have, therefore, some respect for the power of the contraption. I fought back by writing parodies of "Perry Mason" and "Have Gun, Will Travel," on the principle that writing is a kind of self-defense against the predictable.

When I was in college, television news became problematic to me because I became passionately concerned about politics. I remember the TV depiction of the Birmingham, Ala. civil-rights demonstrations in the spring of 1963. I had already taken sides in my mind, yet my attitudes were solidified by the images of the police unleashing dogs on peaceful demonstrators.

My political activism led me into Students for a Democratic Society (SDS), a national student protest organization. I was national president of SDS in 1963 and 1964. At the time I got involved in SDS it was an organization of a few hundred members nationally. We didn't think much about media. We didn't think much about being publicly known. It was very much an organization put together on a face-to-face basis through intense personal relations, direct appeals and conversions. SDS only came to take media seriously when we set about to organize against the Vietnam War in 1965; that was the watershed. Before the march on Washington and the war in Vietnam, SDS was only one left-wing student organization, among others. After Apr. 17, 1965, we were intimately involved in trying to galvanize a national movement around what was now a national issue.

We had to go, not only into the streets, but into the cameras. We rapidly developed a new self-consciousness about ways you could lose control or risk losing control when you went before the cameras. There was a sense that you could not work on the large political stage unless you engaged the camera. There's no way to extricate yourself from the media spotlight. You don't have a choice about whether the terrain exists. The media is an institution. It exists and is powerful. That doesn't mean you want to play its game by its rules. What you try to do is enter into the thing as much as possible on your terms. Activists have not taken the media seriously enough as an object for public policy. Many complain about the nature of programming on network TV, but there's little systematic discussion of what sort of media would be preferable.

As for news, the media acts plucky and independent, but, by and large, they let the White House set the agenda. The media offer rituals of reassurance rather than conducting a serious democratic debate. We are seeing a new wave of serious study and criticism of TV and popular culture in general, yet I still observe reluctance at many colleges and universities to expand the study of mass communication. Many people in the social sciences and humanities think that the researchers are somehow succumbing to the general rot by studying it. These disciplines feel embattled by popular culture; they feel they should keep the flame burning for true value. That means disdaining television as something beneath attention. That's a big mistake. Television is here to stay; it can't be wished away. How to contend with it is an issue that belongs in the curriculum of colleges and universities.

minutes on the televised evening news; a fixed number of pages, depending upon advertising revenues, for newspapers and magazines; and three to five minutes per hour of radio time. Stories must then be sifted and shaped to meet these constraints.

For example, of the thousands of events that take place throughout the world every minute, only a dozen or so will become that day's "news." Much depends on where the half-dozen major news services have their equipment and reporters. In addition, most national and international news comes to reporters in the form of official handouts from carefully cultivated sources within governments. These are then passed along without critical commentary. When reporters become too critical, their news sources dry up. As a result of this dependence on official sources, the press often fails to uncover major stories, such as the secret sales of weapons to Iran between 1985 and 1987, and the illegal diversion of those profits to rebels in Nicaragua. Hundreds of people, including bellhops in Teheran and plane crews in Central America, knew what was happening long before the American press (Pear 1987). Our reporters depended for information on their contacts in the State Department and the White House, where officials were either ignorant themselves or refused to spill a secret. It was left to an obscure magazine published in Lebanon to inform Americans of what their government was doing, but even then, much of the American press refused to believe the story because it ran counter to what reporters expected of our government. In the case of Democratic presidential candidate Gary Hart, however, one newspaper conducted a "stake-out" in order to gain information on his sex life. After some hesitation, other media picked up the story and the candidate soon dropped out of the race.

Thus, what finally emerges as "the news" is a *negotiated reality:* the end product of decisions made by reporters and their editors concerning what is newsworthy, what people want to hear about, where the news crews are, and what information has been given by sources. In brief, news is what those who control the media decide is news.

Framing. Once a story has been selected it must be made understandable to the public. *Framing* involves placing a story into a preexisting frame of reference (Tuchman 1978) as when the story of the Catholic bishops' opposition to nuclear warfare was reported as if it were a prize fight—Bishops v. Reagan—rather than as part of a crucial debate on the morality of governments (Mankoff 1983). In one detailed study of how the media handled the presidential election campaign of 1980 (Robinson and Sheehan 1983), the researchers found that campaign issues were generally ignored in favor of reporting that treated the event as a horse race. When President Reagan met with Party Chairman Gorbachev, newspaper headlines spoke of "round one" or "one on one" at the summit. And, in 1987, Lt. Col. Oliver North was described by NBC's Tom Brokaw as scoring "a hole in one" in his confrontation with Congress. Clearly, the imagery of sports provides a ready frame of reference for the American public.

Framing is also accomplished through the use of code words such as "underdog," "radical," or "distinguished," which carry a strong evaluative component. Citizens of countries that our government does not like are referred to as "terrorists" when they do the same things as the "freedom fighters" that our government supports.

Formatting. News stories are also *formatted,* that is, constructed with a lead line setting up the issue, details in the middle, and a neat wrap-up at the end. No dangling ends disturb the public; whatever is wrong with the world can be set right, usually on the confident word of a government official. Even on those rare occasions when the media take the lead in creating a crisis of confidence, as during the Watergate affair, the bottom line is reassuring: not that a President had committed illegal acts and was almost impeached, but that "the system worked" (Gitlin 1980, Lang and Lang 1983). So quickly were the negative features of the episode forgotten, that Richard Nixon today is regularly sought out—and well rewarded—by the media for his expert opinion on the state of the world.

MEDIA POLITICS

There is growing debate about whether or not news work is influenced by the social background or political bias of the overwhelmingly white male college-educated

Framing involves the placing of news stories into a preexisting frame of reference to make it understandable to the public.

Formatting of news stories involves the design and construction of their presentation to the public.

elite who own, manage, and staff the mass media. On the one hand, political conservatives claim that network newscasts display a distinct liberal slant. Attacks from the political right include an unsuccessful attempt led by Senator Jesse Helms to buy controlling stock in CBS in 1985, and the constant criticism of all types of programming by an organization called Accuracy in Media.

On the other hand, a number of sociologists suggest that any bias in the media tilts in favor of the existing systems of power and inequality (Gans 1979, Paletz and Entman 1981, Parenti 1985, Qualter 1985). From this perspective, the media play down potentially troublesome issues, are too respectful of powerful elites, create an illusion of public unity, and generally advance the class-based interests of their owners. Such "ideological hegemony" is often very subtle, as when the media combine reports of workers' strikes in Poland with high praise for the Solidarity movement, while portraying striking U.S. postal employees as without legitimate grievances (Rachlin 1986).

Although one systematic study (Robinson et al. 1985) of all policy-related programs on the three major networks in the first three months of 1983 showed little systematic bias in what was reported or how it was presented, the debate continues and may even grow more intense in the years ahead.

Popular Music

In this brief section, we can only indicate the ways in which popular music—perhaps the aspect of popular culture with which you are most familiar—illustrates the sociological concept of the *production of culture*. It is tempting to think of all forms of music and art as spontaneous expressions of one person's particular talents, and to perceive the artist as someone set apart from others. But all culture is created in a social context—in a particular society at a given historical moment, within a circle of friends, audiences, potential purchasers, gatekeepers, and critics. All these factors determine what gets produced, how it is distributed, and how it is evaluated.

Popular music is possibly the art form

The Video Road to Vietnam

Media critic J. Fred MacDonald has recently published a carefully documented study of how, over several decades, American television has openly promoted anti-communism in basically the same way as Soviet media promote anti-Americanism. During the 1950s, when Senator Joseph McCarthy and other right-wing crusaders accused the networks of harboring traitors, the owners of the three major networks immediately fired everyone whose name was even casually mentioned—actors, writers, reporters, staff.

In the 1950s, the networks wholeheartedly supported the Korean War, withholding information at the request of the CIA and the Pentagon, and censoring film clips of the damage inflicted on Korean civilians by American troops. The closest the American public came to the battlefield was the television program, "MASH," where everything became a joke anyway.

Networks are heavily influenced not only by government officials but also by major advertisers who benefit from any material that shows capitalism in a better light than socialism. Anti-communism, therefore, serves the interest of economic as well as political elites.

MacDonald also details how ordinary programming carried out the Cold War themes of hostility toward anything remotely Eastern European. Thus, he claims, the public was well softened up for accepting and supporting the war in Vietnam. Our children are brought up to see only communists as the enemy; our politicians are elected on "get-tough-on-Commies" platforms; the "red menace" fills our TV screens and movie houses—just as much today as in the McCarthy era three decades ago.

SOURCE: J. Fred MacDonald. *Television and the Red Menace: The Video Road to Vietnam.* New York: Praeger, 1985.

that is most influenced by its context. Rhythms and lyrics emerge from the immediate experience of composers and performers, reflecting subcultural differences, speaking to the issues and themes of each historical period. But not every song is recorded, and not every record is played on the air or stocked in music stores. Sociologists are interested in the chain of events that transform one person's inspiration into an object of culture. The famous country-music singer Waylon Jennings, for example, became a particular type of artist, not because of some inner necessity, but because of the peculiar characteristics of studio recording in Nashville and the changing nature of the record market in the late 1970s (Denisoff 1983). Similarly, a study of Hollywood music composers shows how careers are shaped by the way in which films are produced rather than by differences in artistic merit (Faulkner 1983). Each type of music is produced within a peculiar organization of workers and markets, so that it is possible to speak of the "industrialization" of that art form.

The gatekeepers for popular music in America are the disc jockeys who decide what gets played over the air, affecting, in turn, which records become best-sellers and which artists become superstars. DJs respond to a number of influences: their own personal taste; their perception of audience tastes; and their interpersonal contacts with artists, producers, and distributors (Chapple and Garofalo 1978). In addition, musical reputations and incomes in America are also dependent on the actions of the major copyrighting companies (BMI and ASCAP) who control licensing

Howard Stern combines the role of disc jockey and media personality. Unlike many public gatekeepers who try not to offend, he broadcasts with a free-wheeling approach that critics say is offensive and defamatory. But his fans are as loyal as his critics and sponsors continue to support him. (©Ken Regan/Camera 5)

and fee collection (Ryan 1985). These are the individuals and organizations that shape the popular music scene. Presumably, music and artists who do not conform to gatekeeper standards simply never get a hearing.

RACE, ROCK, AND RAP

As might be expected, popular music has not avoided the racism that affects other forms of popular culture and the society as a whole. Despite the fact that most modern rock has its origins in black music, and despite the presence of a few black superstars, the vast majority of people who earn high incomes from popular music—as composers, musicians, arrangers, record-company executives, agents, and concert managers—are white (Pareles 1987b). The popular-music industry operates under the same constraints as any other business. Profits depend on pleasing large numbers of consumers. Concert audiences and record buyers in America are predominately white and tend to be attracted to white artists, regardless of the music itself.

The degree of "institutionalized racism" in popular music today is probably less obvious than in the early days of rock when black music was not accepted by the general public or widely recognized until it was performed by such entertainers as Elvis Presley, Pat Boone, or the Beatles who "covered" black artists such as Fats Domino, Chuck Berry, and The Miracles. Today, there are a number of black performers who can attract a basically white audience, especially those who "look" or "sound" white and who stick to non-political themes.

For a brief period in the 1960s it appeared that the division between white and black popular music was being narrowed as civil-rights activists of both races joined in protest over racial inequality (Garofalo 1987). But some observers suggest that the gap had widened again in the early 1980s due to two developments (Rockwell 1984). The first was the decision by record producers and distributors to target specific audiences. Thus, in place of the old top-40s list there are now specialized sales charts, with black music only one small segment of the market. The second change was the emergence of Music TeleVision (MTV), in which the color of the performer could not be ignored or hidden. These two trends could reduce the

Run-DMC, a popular black rap group, has toured with the Beastie Boys, a white rock group that has adapted the rap format for some of its songs. While this "crossover" extends the exposure of black groups to white audiences, some black artists feel it decreases their appeal to black audiences. (© Neal Preston/Camera 5)

opportunities for black performers to reach a wide audience.

Other trends, conversely, could increase the exposure of black artists. Affirmative action has added to the number of minority personnel in the business end of the industry, while audience "crossover" appears also to have increased. One recent example of crossover is the growing popularity among white adolescents of rap music, an art form that emerged from the world of inner-city black male teenagers (Toop 1984, Pareles 1987a). "Rapping" involves increasingly exaggerated and boastful verbal contests, and the music that accompanies it has a hard-rock sound. The lyrics often reflect the basic sexism of adolescent males in general, and the violence of slum life in particular. But both the rhythm and words appear to have struck a responsive chord across racial lines.

SEXISM AND SADISM

Sex and violence in popular music are not confined to rap music. Certain types of popular music have always been perceived as "masculine," as representing a forcefulness and tempo and drive associated with men. The lyrics of these pieces typically reflect a world in which women are perceived as sex objects, or as dangerous, or somehow standing in a man's way. Album covers featuring bruised and bound women were quite popular in the late 1970s.

While some women artists also play on these themes, suggesting that they love to be brutalized, most have found success in the softer, more romantic forms of blues, ballads, and country music. The success of a handful of female superstars, however, should not be mistaken for feminist progress. Not only does the industry remain dominated by white males, including the performers' agents and managers, but the thrust of the lyrics remains basically unliberated. Story lines typically involve a woman who has been abandoned or mistreated by her lover; nevertheless, she wants him back and is willing to forgive all, because nothing is worse than being alone.

There are trends, however, that suggest an increased feminist influence on popular music. One is the emergence of women's rock groups and soloists with openly liberated agendas in their music and its lyrics. The other trend concerns a change in the messages conveyed in country-music lyrics. A content analysis of songs from 1970 to 1981 finds signs of rebellion (Vander Mey and Bryant 1986). For example, Loretta Lynn now sings about leaving a cheating husband and about wanting no more babies, and some stations refused to play her song "The Pill."

Conversely, a hit song of 1986 has Madonna singing of the joys of teenage pregnancy and begging her father not to preach at her. This record and its MTV version have been widely praised by anti-abortion groups, and no radio or television station has refused to play it.

The general trend in the early 1980s, however, was toward a moderating of the overt and often violent sexism of the 1970s **569**

Controversy surrounds the effect of song lyrics on teenage listeners. Here, Mrs. Gore and Mrs. Baker, members of the PMRC, testify at a Senate Committee hearing on rock and roll music. Do you think record lyrics should be protected by the First Amendment? (© Pamela Price/Picture Group)

(Palmer 1985). Mick Jagger, who boasted that women were "under my thumb" now sings that "she's the boss." The lyrics of male performers today, particularly the younger ones, seem to be less macho and more concerned with their relationships with women, most likely reflecting genuine dilemmas in their own lives. It will be interesting to see if these more gentle voices of the 1980s can continue to be heard above the clanking of hard metal from some of the hottest, most violent, and sexist groups of the late 1980s.

The question, "Does any of this have any effect on listeners or viewers?" however, remains unresolved—and largely unresearched in a systematic way. If violence on television in general does not appear to have any lasting or strong consequences for behavior, there is little to suggest that song lyrics or MTVs have a direct effect. Moreover, recent research indicates that "concept videos" contained 19 percent less violence than prime-time TV programs (Jaeger 1987). Nonetheless, citizen groups have become aroused over the issue. In 1985, several wives of legislators in Washington formed the Parents Music Resource Center (PMRC), and together with the national Parent-Teacher Association (PTA), won an agreement from record companies that the companies would put labels on their records—much like the warning on cigarette cartons—announcing that the lyrics involved sex, violence, or substance abuse. The two groups based their actions on consumers' rights to know the contents of a product, and 70 to 80 percent of the public supported the idea (Harrington 1986). Voluntary compliance however, has been less than wholehearted. Record companies often put the message in very small print—one and one-sixteenth of an inch—or simply note "explicit lyrics" on the covers.

Do listeners pay much attention to lyrics or are they mainly moved by the beat of a song? One recent study found that the listening audience was more attracted to the music than to the lyrics, frequently misunderstanding the text of the songs (Prinsky and Rosenbaum 1987). However, lyrics can probably be ignored to a greater degree than the impact of listening *and* seeing provided by MTV, but thus far the only restraints on MTV are those of the marketplace in general. Here, clearly, is an area ripe for systematic sociological study. At the moment we have only a few beginnings along with the hunches of parents and the unsupported pronouncements of mental health workers.

Sports

Sport is an important leisure activity in all societies—a source of entertainment and an expression of cultural values and themes. Sports differ from play in being organized by sets of rules. In this sense, sports can be distinguished from non-organized athletic activities such as hiking, fishing, and jogging.

We follow Edwards (1974) in defining sports as:

- activities with clear standards of performance;
- involving physical exertion through competition;
- governed by norms defining role relationships;
- typically performed by members of organized groups;
- with the goal of achieving some reward;
- through the defeat of other participants.

By this definition, *sports* are not spontaneous expressions of the human impulse to play, but a form of structured social behavior with values, norms, statuses, and roles. Furthermore, sports are linked to other institutional spheres and to the major stratification hierarchies (Coakley 1986, Gruneau 1983, Boutillier and San Giovanni 1983, Eitzen and Sage 1986).

As with other institutions in modern industrial society, sports are characterized by increasing specialization of roles (e.g., the "designated hitter"), bureaucratic or-

Sports are a form of structured social behavior with values, norms, statuses, and roles.

Who's the Boss?

"The boss" of popular music is a most improbable figure in this age of glitz and hype: a genuine blue-collar hero who prefers privacy to publicity, who wears no jewelry or fancy costumes, and whose themes are the everyday concerns of working-class Americans. Bruce Springsteen sings about jobless veterans, plant closings, the search for self-respect, and other insults of social class—but does so with such upbeat music that the effect is far from depressing.

Yet Springsteen's lyrics also appear to have touched a responsive chord among white teenagers and many of their elders. In this respect, he carries on the tradition of American protest music—from black spirituals and the ballads of the union movement to the powerful songs of the 1960s: "We Shall Overcome" and "Blowin' in the Wind." But Springsteen departs from this tradition in not offering political solutions to the problems he so carefully details. Thus, presidential candidate Ronald Reagan referred glowingly to Springsteen's 1984 album, "Born in the USA," mistaking its title and red, white, and blue album cover for an exercise in Rambo-like patriotism rather than as an ironic twist on the impossibility of achieving the American Dream.

ganization (NCAA, NFL, etc.), quantification ("stats"), secularization, and gradual equality of opportunity (Guttmann 1978). Sports also reflect and reinforce important social and cultural themes, as seen in an-

Football, at both the amateur and professional levels, is a well-organized sport with important social functions for both participants and spectators. Can you imagine our society without organized football or baseball or basketball? How would life be different? (© All Sport Photography, U.S.A., Mike Powell/Woodfin Camp and Associates)

thropologist Clifford Geertz' (1973) in-depth analysis of the Balinese cockfight. The cockfight, an aspect of popular culture, is linked to social stratification, to personality development, and to the value system of the society. In other words one can understand Balinese culture through the symbolism of this particular sport.

For Americans, sport embodies the values of work, competition, manliness, and commercialism. In other countries, the organization of sports reflects different national problems and goals. In developing societies, for example, soccer teams often perform an integrating function that weak national governments cannot (Lever 1983). And in the communist countries of Eastern Europe, the ideals of nonelitism and general participation are expressed in Spartakiads, amateur athletic meets in every town, open to all, with awards for everyone.

AMATEUR SPORTS IN THE UNITED STATES

By definition, amateurs are not paid to perform; playing the game is its own reward. For much of Western history, sports were an aristocratic pastime, as only the

This Spartakiad took place in 1987 in the town of Leipzig (German Democratic Republic); 35,000 gymnasts participated in a 2½ hour sport program. (© Eastfoto)

affluent could afford to play without compensation. Today, amateur athletics in the United States are associated with working-class activities organized at the community level—softball or bowling leagues, for example—or with college and university athletic programs.

College Sports. Up to the 1960s, college athletic programs came close to the elitist ideal of amateurism, in which the sons of the middle and upper classes combined the rigors of physical competition with academic studies on their way to a comfortable adulthood. As the universities grew in size and as a large national audience for sports telecasts was developed, the nature of college athletics underwent a radical change.

Universities today are multi-million dollar enterprises, with buildings and grounds to maintain, faculty and staff to pay, and thousands of students to house and feed. As student fees cover only a small part of these costs, institutions of higher education have been forced to look for other sources of income: allocations from state legislatures, alumni donations, and payments for televising sports events (over $100 million worth in 1986). Teams with winning records can enhance all three sources of income. Their games are more likely to be televised, which also reinforces alumni loyalty and influences state legislators to increase university funding. The state university teams provide a symbolic focus of identity and solidarity among state residents (Deegan and Stein 1978).

As a result, college athletic programs have become big business, not only self-supporting but often a money-maker for the rest of the school (Hart-Nibbrig and Cottingham 1986). In 1986, the 100 universities with top-level football teams raised and spent more than $1 billion for their sports programs (Goodwin 1986). Athletic departments at these universities operate as separate entities, with their own budgets and staff. Head coaches, between their salaries and endorsements and television appearances, can earn two or three times as much as the president of the university or the governor of the state, and are far better known. The pressure to field a winning team becomes intense, taking precedence over other concerns such as the academic rank of the school or the intellectual development of athletes.

Athletic talent is widely recruited, and scholarship assistance is readily available. But many student athletes are ill prepared for college life and are not offered much help in overcoming academic deficiencies, even though their skills are valuable to the school (Purdy et al. 1982). In 1986 and 1987, following several well-publicized cases of unethical and/or illegal conduct in the recruitment and retention of student athletes, the National Collegiate Athletic Association announced stricter academic standards for accepting and retaining athletes. The new standards, however, are still far below those for other students, and practice, travel, and playing time absorb weekdays as well as weekends. For many college athletes, educational goals are secondary to gaining the training necessary for recruitment to professional sports, although, as shown in Table 20-2, the odds of success are extremely low.

Not only will very few college athletes enjoy even a brief career in professional sports, but it is unlikely that their sports training will contribute to future success in any but military occupations (DuBois 1980; Lapchick 1986).

Olympic Games. Amateur status is also required for participation in the Olympic Games, although most nations have found ways to subsidize their athletes. The need to prove the superiority of their political system has led many countries to barely disguised means of supporting Olympians—with state-funded jobs in the Soviet Union and Eastern Europe, and by private contributions and federal support for training facilities in the United States.

In recent years, however, commercial interests have intruded on the games as athletes become walking (or skiing, or running) advertisements for the equipment

In recent years athletes all over the world have become living advertisements for various products. The Spanish bullfighter, Louis Reina, for example, stunned his audience when he appeared in the ring with advertising on his sequined suit. He displayed the letters AKAI, the name of a Japanese electronics firm, on his arms and legs. (© Reuters/ Bettmann Newsphoto)

manufacturers who donate products in return for the possibility of having their sneakers, skis, or headbands appear on television. And although an athlete cannot be directly paid for her or his preparation and participation in the games, an Olympic victory is an immediate stepping-stone to a professional contract. Very few American Olympic skating stars, for example, have not joined professional ice shows following their amateur success.

Amateur athletics are alive and well in the United States today, but the lure of professionalism has been gradually eroding the ideal of sport for the sheer joy of doing well. Not only do professional sports offer fame and fortune, they more fully express the American sports ethic.

TABLE 20-2 Major league career opportunities, 1985

	Baseball	Football	Basketball
High School Players	400,000	600,000	600,000
College Players	25,000	40,000	17,000
Major League Players	600	2,400	300
Rookies per year	100	250	60
Average Length of Career (years)	7.5	4.5	5

SOURCE: Stanley D. Eitzen and George H. Sage, *Sociology of North American Sport,* 3rd ed. Dubuque, Iowa: W. C. Brown, 1986, p. 254.

SPORTS AND AMERICAN VALUES

Sports and the Work Ethic. A number of cultural values are embodied in the way in which sports are organized in America and in how Americans think about athletics. The ideology of sport embraces such virtues as competition, achievement, courage, self-control, discipline, dedication, success, teamwork *and* individual responsibility. Sound familiar? These are all elements of the *work ethic* described in Chapter 3.

Although sport is often defined as the opposite of work, there are many ways in which sports are just like work—both are governed by the need to achieve, involve trained skills and the division of labor, are based on competition, and are even divided into specific segments (innings, quarters, rounds). Socialization to sport is actually socialization to modern industrial society (Rigauer 1981).

Sometimes the need to win becomes an obsession, as in the observation of Coach Vince Lombardi that "winning isn't everything, it's the *only* thing." This is certainly a far cry from the amateur ideal of playing your best regardless of the outcome. To some degree, the idea that losing represents personal failure is bound up with our traditional conceptions of gender roles.

Sports and Manliness. Sports in America are also considered the great test of masculinity. The qualities ascribed to winners (whether female or male) are those associated with manliness in our culture: strength, courage, coolness under pressure, and self-reliance. Team play is socialization to the exclusive world of the locker room. The strength of these feelings can be seen in the violent reactions of some professional ball players when women reporters were first allowed into locker rooms on the same basis as male sportswriters; the athletes intentionally dropped their towels and shouted obscenities. As late as 1986, one ball player sent a package with a dead rat to a woman reporter.

Although being a "jock" is the royal road to high status among adolescent boys, the long-term benefits are less clear. School athletes are under great stress because of the strictness of their training, the pressures to win at any cost, the fear of injury, and the neglect of studies that will be of greater use than athletic skills in the adult labor force (Stein and Hoffman 1981). There are also interpersonal consequences: the need to defeat others can inhibit the capacity to form intimate ties, especially with women, thus reducing the chances of marital success (Sabo and Runfola 1980). In addition, people who perceive the world as full of either winners or losers find it difficult to compromise; if one's own self-esteem depends on always being the winner, the give-and-take of marriage can be very threatening.

Yet manliness through sports remains an important element in the socialization of boys, as indicated in the goals of Little League, Inc.:

> . . . to help and voluntarily assist boys in developing qualities of citizenship, sportsmanship, and manhood. Using the disciplines of the native American game of baseball, to teach spirit and competitive will to win, physical fitness through individual sacrifice, the values of team play and wholesome well-being through healthful and social association with other youngsters under proper leadership.

We should not wonder that many parents objected strongly to court orders to permit girls to join Little League teams. Imagine having your son struck out by a girl pitcher! Presumably, also, there are some parents who shudder at the thought of their daughters becoming socialized to the values that underlie the Little League philosophy.

Sports as Big Business. Another way in which our culture has shaped sports is through "industrialization." Ball players are bought and sold like any other business property, and moved from one city to another in the pursuit of profit. The players have also benefited from "the sports industry," with baseball players, for example, earning an average of $371,000 in 1985 compared to about $29,000 in 1970 (Standohar 1986). Television networks offer hundreds of millions of dollars to sports leagues for broadcast rights but earn the money right back by charging advertisers hundreds of thousands of dollars for one-minute commercials.

The owners make money not only by attracting customers to see their highly paid superstars, and by charging fees for various concessions (parking, food, drink, souvenirs), but through tax write-offs and subsidies. Most baseball owners pay no taxes and have their stadiums rebuilt by city governments too fearful of losing the team to stand up to the owners (Eitzen and Sage 1986). Today's owners tend to be rather different from those of the past, who came from sports backgrounds and were essentially super-fans. The new breed are business people looking more for an investment than a hobby (Standohar 1986).

When sport becomes expensive mass entertainment, it is necessary to win at any cost, to keep fans in their seats and television cameras on the field. Raising the stakes may also raise the level of violence—among the customers as well as the players.

Sports Violence. A number of factors, from the cultural to the physical, have been cited as contributing to the upsurge in sports violence: cultural acceptance of violence as a means of resolving disputes; an exaggerated sense of masculine honor; fear of defeat; media coverage that appears to glorify or legitimize violence; a weakening of the norms of civility among spectators; ready availability of beer; sports betting; and the physical discomforts and ugliness of many arenas and stadiums (Goldstein 1983, Smith 1983, Bredemeier and Shields 1985).

To some extent, both players and spectators set sports apart from other activities, with a morality of its own, where aggressiveness is part of the game and the individual can be completely self-centered, while responsibility for good conduct is placed on referees and umpires (Brede-meier and Shields 1985). For the player, violence is a form of self-protection, provided that no lasting injury is done; there is an understanding among players concerning the limits of "fair" fighting, and it is in the interest of each to remain within the norms.

Nonetheless, injuries have become more frequent and severe in recent years for several reasons: the heightened level of competition and "must win" philosophy; the use of steroids in weight-training programs, producing oversize players; the development of lighter equipment in the interests of speed; and the adoption of artificial playing surfaces that place greater strain on leg muscles and provide less cushion for falls. As a result, the average playing career of a professional football player has declined from 4.6 years in 1983 to 3.6 years in 1986 (*Sports Illustrated,* Nov. 10, 1986).

For the fans, various social-psychological processes may be at work: copycat aggression when the players are seen to get away with it; the opportunity to be anonymously aggressive and act out feelings that would be unacceptable in other contexts; and a need to define one's turf. All of these feelings are intensified by excessive drinking. It would be a mistake, however, to think of fan violence as a particularly modern phenomenon—think of the Romans and their circuses! Indeed, the historical trend has been toward a lessening of uncontrollable spectator mobs, although there may be a reversal of this civility among audiences today (Guttmann 1986).

Forty persons died and about 300 were injured when a group of British soccer fans charged the Italian section in a Brussels, Belgium, stadium before the start of an England-Italy soccer match. Although the media and European governments berated the British hooligans, research by sociologists indicates that there were complex reasons for fans' violence, including low wages and high unemployment in Britain. (See Box p. 576) (© S. Franklin/SYGMA)

Football Hooligans

In 1985, a soccer match between an Italian and an English team ended in a riot in which forty persons died and 100 were injured. Some weeks later, another soccer riot broke out in, of all places, the People's Republic of China. But these were only two examples of a widespread phenomenon: "football hooliganism," fan violence at international matches.

Contrary to the views of government officials and the media that such outbursts are the irrational products of sick minds, the researchers begin with the sociological assumption that such behavior is meaningful and stems from social structural forces. To call the rioters "uncivilized" is simply one more way in which the ruling elites dismiss the real grievances of people whose behavior frightens them.

The English fans who follow their local teams to Europe (at very inexpensive excursion rates) are typically young white working-class males whose normal life-style is one of compulsive masculinity and fighting. The local football (soccer) team becomes a focus of loyalty and nationalistic pride.

Rather than take out their frustrations over low wages and high unemployment rates against their own government, the English fans turned on the "foreigners" in the neighboring stands. Not only does the British government escape the wrath of these young men, but officials can turn around and blame the working-class lads for their own misfortunes.

The structure of soccer stands also contributes to the potential for violence. Fans are herded into sections without seats, pressed together, with only a flimsy partition separating them from the other team's fans. A lot of drinking, many verbal exchanges between people who cannot understand one another's language, the discomfort of being in a foreign country, and the need to prove one's manhood, all feed the likelihood of violence. When the stands collapse or catch fire (probably due to a carelessly thrown cigarette) many lives can be lost.

SOURCE: John Williams, Eric Dunning, and Patrick Murphy, *Hooligans Abroad: The Behavior and Control of English Fans in Continental Europe.* London: Routledge & Kegan Paul, 1984.

Suggested solutions to the problem of fan violence include banning the sale of beer, improving the physical appearance of the stadiums, changing the rules so that scoring occurs more often, raising ticket prices so that lower-income fans are priced out, and reducing violence among the players (Goldstein 1984). But these are all solutions based on a psychological mode of reasoning which locates the problem within or between individuals rather than in the broader social system. For a more sociological viewpoint, recent work by English sociologists on "football hooliganism" is illuminating (see Box).

SPORTS AND STRATIFICATION

Sports are both democratic and highly stratified. There is something for everyone, from sandlot ball to polo. Professional sports are largely populated by working-class youth, and their audiences are primarily drawn from working- and lower-middle-class households. At the same time, control over what is played by whom under which rules remains with the dominant elites, who also reap the financial rewards of commercialized sports (Gruneau 1983).

Some sociologists, such as Eitzen and Sage (1986) claim that sports are oppressive in terms of race, gender, and social class. First, the sense of "good times" and well-being derived from competitive sports are based on defeating others. Second, once people accept the bureaucratic rules of sports, and associate these with good feelings, people will not question bureaucratic controls in other spheres. Even the language of sports has been adapted to the workplace—"game plan," "teamwork," "time out," "huddle," and so forth. Third, it is an illusion to believe that your leisure activities are under your own control. In reality, our tastes and opportunities are shaped by others, just as the flow and timing of televised sports are based on network needs.

Social-Class Considerations. Social-class background determines who participates in various types of sports. Activities that require expensive equipment or facilities, extensive training, and long periods of practice—tennis, golf, sailing, skiing, polo, competitive swimming, and ice skating—are mostly enjoyed by the well-to-do. Low-income and minority athletes are most likely to take up boxing, wrestling, track, basketball, baseball, and other sports that involve minimal outlays for equipment and that can be practiced anywhere.

We can see, therefore, that the relative distribution of athletes by social class and race is not a function of their abilities, but is due to variations in resources and opportunities. It is as rare to have an upper-class white on a professional basketball team (e.g., Bill Bradley) as it is to find a black on the professional golfers' tour (e.g., Calvin Peete).

Racism. The dramatic expansion of professional sports in the past three decades has opened the gates of opportunity for many talented minority athletes. It may be difficult to believe today, but there were no black major-league baseball players until Jackie Robinson joined the Brooklyn Dodgers in 1947, to the open hostility of his teammates and spectators. Because entry into professional basketball and football is typically linked to college training, few minority youth were found in these ranks until the 1960s.

The increasing number of black and Hispanic athletes in college and professional sports has led some observers to conclude that democratization is a necessary outcome of the commercialization of sport because success depends on selecting players by talent rather than on the basis of prejudice or sentiment. Nonetheless, there are still fields in which minority athletes are underrepresented, such as golf, tennis, and swimming—the "country club" sports.

And even within the sports that are today dominated by black and Hispanic players, racism is not altogether absent. The dilemma facing many owners and athletic directors is that to attract customers, the team must win; if minority players are most talented, they should be recruited or hired. At the same time, if fans identify with players of their own race, and the vast majority of paying spectators are white, an all-black team could lose money while winning games, which seems to be happening in basketball (Lapchick 1984).

One common solution to the problem of using minority players without alienat-

How are these children's recreational activities shaped by their social class membership? (© Sepp Seitz/Woodfin Camp and Associates; Jean-Yves Ruszniewski/ Photo Researchers)

ing fans is to practice *stacking* (Edwards 1973). Stacking is based on the importance of different positions on a ball team; some are more central than others, involving greater responsibility and/or control over other players. In football, the central positions are quarterback, kicker, and center; in baseball, pitcher, catcher, second base, and shortstop. As late as 1983, 99 percent of quarterbacks, 98 percent of kickers, 93 percent of pitchers, and 86 percent of catchers were non-Hispanic whites (Eitzen and Sage 1986, p. 273).

The further from the center, the more removed from decision-making roles, the greater the proportion of minority players.

Stacking involves the selective use of white players in central or decision-making positions.

577

Data from the rosters of all twenty-six major-league baseball teams in 1984 further suggests that only the most outstanding black players are selected, while marginal whites are selected over marginal blacks and Hispanics (Phillips 1984, Mendonca 1984).

Another, more subtle form of racism can be found in the commentaries of sports reporters. All too often, the reporters describe a white player as using intelligence and hard work to reach the top, while black athletes are described as having "natural" skills. As the black basketball player, Isiah Thomas, recently remarked about the impression created by these unconscious stereotypes: "When (Larry) Bird makes a great play, it's due to his thinking and his work habits. It's not the case for blacks. All we do is run and jump. We never practice or give a thought to how we play. It's like I came dribbling out of my mother's womb" (Ponder 1987). Despite these lingering reminders of racism within professional sports, however, there can be no doubt that athletics has increasingly served as a channel of upward mobility for a small number of minority youth.

Upward Mobility. Sports and other entertainments have long been successful routes out of poverty for a few unusually talented and lucky individuals. A study of the racial, religious, and ethnic backgrounds of well-known singers, comedians, and sports figures in the United States would find that Irish names predominated in the early part of this century, followed in the decades between 1920 and 1960 by Jews and Italians (many of whom shortened or Americanized their names). By the late 1960s, blacks began to appear in more than token numbers, to be followed, in turn, by Hispanic athletes and entertainers.

The extremely high salaries of today's superstars, however, may give an inaccurate impression that major changes are also occurring in the overall distribution of wealth, power, and prestige in America. This is not so.

Minority-group members can achieve fame and fortune in entertainment precisely because the major stratification hierarchies are *not* disturbed. The major decisions that affect our society are not made in the left field of Yankee Stadium or on a Las Vegas stage, but at the Pentagon, in the U.S. Senate, and on Wall Street,

where one can search in vain for more than a token black or Hispanic. True, a few white males—Ronald Reagan, Bill Bradley, and Jack Kemp, for example—can use their entertainment fame to reach public office, but the influence of most athletes and film stars is limited to endorsements.

In addition, entertainers are, by definition, people who perform for the pleasure of others, and who, therefore, are economically dependent on those willing to pay for their services. There is a sense in which all "social actors" are dependent on their audiences, but in the case of athletes/entertainers, the essential social relationship of master and servant is maintained, even while the financial status of the two may be reversed. Indeed, the limited successes of blacks and Hispanics in sports have not even translated into real power within that sphere. Very few are managers or coaches, and even fewer are front-office personnel, broadcasters, or athletic directors at colleges. For all the changes of the past four decades, control of amateur and professional athletics

Harry Edwards, Professor of Sociology at the University of California–Berkeley, a prominent sport sociologist and long-time activist on behalf of minority athletes, was named special consultant to Baseball Commissioner Peter Ueberroth in the spring of 1987. Edwards' task is to identify managerial and front-office jobs for minority athletes who have retired from active sports. (© AP/Wide World Photos) (See Box p. 579.)

From Olympic Boycott to the Commissioner's Office

The absence of black and Hispanic managers and white collar employees of sports organizations was brought to public attention in early 1987 when one front office employee, in a televised interview, suggested that blacks do not have the "natural equipment" to be managers. In the ensuing uproar, the Commissioner of Baseball announced that he would require each club to file an affirmative action plan within a month. A special consultant was added to the Commissioner's own staff—Prof. Harry Edwards, professor of Sociology at the University of California, Berkeley, a long-time activist on behalf of minority athletes as well as a leading figure in the sociology of sport.

After completing his Ph.D. at Cornell University, where he was a Woodrow Wilson Scholar, Harry Edwards first hit the headlines with a campaign to have black American athletes boycott the 1968 Olympic Games in Mexico City as a protest against racism throughout the world and as a gesture of solidarity with the civil rights movement in the United States. Although the boycott attempt failed, a few athletes did make symbolic statements, most notably two black sprinters who raised closed fists while standing on the winners' stands during the playing of our national anthem. The episode shocked the sports world, and the two athletes' careers were ruined.

Edwards continued his academic career at Berkeley, teaching courses on race relations, family, and the sociology of sport. He has published many papers and edited a number of books on the subject of minority athletes. In addition, he has worked directly with many sports organizations, including the San Francisco 49ers football team and the Golden State Warriors of the National Basketball Association. Edwards attempts to instruct management in the sociological perspective, locating players in a social and cultural context, and stressing the importance of anticipating problems before they arise.

As special consultant to the Commissioner, Prof. Edwards' newest task is to help find front office and managerial jobs for minority athletes who have left active sports. In contrast to retired nonwhite players, white athletes, regardless of their skills as players, have little difficulty moving into nonplaying jobs with the clubs—as scouts, or as coaches and managers of farm teams. As Edwards puts it, he will be looking for "...that bright, committed young player who might not become great enough to be a Reggie Jackson or a Dave Winfield or a Rickey Henderson, but (who) loves the game. How do we keep him around long enough in a viable and developing pool so he can step into a middle-range, middle-paid job to become more knowledgeable about the game and learn... Somebody kept the white players around to learn the dynamics of the game, not only on the field but in the clubhouse and at the country club and conventions"—that is, where the real power is found.

SOURCE: *The New York Times*, June 13, 1987.

remains firmly in the hands of upper-income white males.

WOMEN AND SPORTS

If sports in America represent the ultimate in masculine ideals, it is not surprising that attempts to broaden opportunities for women have been deeply resented and resisted. In 1972, however, the Education Act was amended to include a clause (Title IX) forbidding discrimination on the basis of sex in all schools receiving federal funds. But few schools, even today, have programs for female athletes that come close to those for males in terms of funding, facilities, coaching, or practice time. Colleges and universities claim that anything taken from the men's programs would cost millions in lost television revenues and alumni donations (Boutillier and San Giovanni 1983).

The success of Title IX depends primarily on the federal government's willingness to enforce the law. When the law is enforced, as was the case in the 1970s, opportunities for girls and women improved dramatically. In 1970, only 300,000 high-school girls played on school athletic teams; by 1979, two million girls did so. Before Title IX, there were no colleges that awarded athletic scholarships to women; in 1983, there were over 10,000 women's athletic scholarships. Before Title IX, there were almost no women's national collegiate championships; in 1983, the NCAA sponsored thirty national championships for women (Packwood 1984). In 1984, however, the Reagan administration argued successfully before the Supreme

Court that Title IX referred only to specific programs receiving federal funds. Since athletic programs do not receive such funding, colleges and universities are no longer under an obligation to provide equal opportunity to female athletes.

Absence of Encouragement. Another barrier to girls' and women's participation in organized athletics is the persistence of myths about potentially harmful effects on their reproductive systems (Coakley 1986). Actually, the appropriate research in sports medicine and physiology was conducted only *after* participation rates surged. The facts appear to be that, under supervised training, female athletes, no less than their male counterparts, realize many benefits in physical health and psychological well-being from testing their strength, endurance, and courage. More difficult to deal with, perhaps, is the lingering fear of being considered "unfeminine" or somehow "unnatural." Professional women athletes are continually being forced to deal with rumors and innuendos about their sexual preference. As a result of all these pressures, few young girls receive the encouragement, training, and institutional supports that would prepare them for athletic success. More so than boys and men, girls and women become attached to sports through supportive networks (Coakley 1986). Thus, the absence of encouragement is more detrimental for women than for men. For those who do persevere, however, the rewards are typically less than for boys and men: fewer and smaller trophies for amateurs, less prize money for professionals.

The sports in which school girls have come to excel are track, gymnastics, and basketball—activities that require little equipment or other financial outlay. At the high-school level, practice times for girls' teams are scheduled after those for boys, when the playing fields are in poorer condition. Before Title IX, many school districts would provide uniforms and equipment for boys' teams only.

Methany (1977) argued that female athletes are encouraged to compete in "ladylike" sports, such as those stressing grace and beauty (figure skating, swimming, skiing, and tennis) or that do not involve physical contact (track, softball, and volleyball). Even in these fields, until very recently, there were few role models and even fewer people willing to train and coach girls and women. Parents are also less likely to encourage an athletic daughter than to support a son's sports interests, regardless of skill level. However, because parents and coaches expect girls to have less athletic talent and desire than boys, they are also more permissive of displays of feeling and emotion, which is actually very helpful in learning skills and in relieving the pressures of competition. In comparison to the sports world of boys and men, a lowered emphasis on winning and record breaking makes girls' and women's sports even more open and less elitist (Coakley 1986). A recent study of college athletes and physical-education majors (Theberge 1982) showed that men placed more emphasis on winning and less on the enjoyment of playing than did women.

Sports Equity. Nonetheless, despite the lack of strong federal enforcement, the idea of sport equity has slowly made its way into the public consciousness, and the performance of female athletes have continued to improve dramatically. While they do not swim or run as fast as men, the time gaps are growing smaller and smaller. The fastest women runners and swimmers today would have beaten the male champions of a decade ago (Boutillier and San Giovanni 1983).

The two fields in which women have a long history of professional accomplishment are golf and tennis, and in both of these sports, television coverage and prize money have increased greatly in the past five years. Although women remain far less likely than men to earn millions of dollars in golf and tennis prizes, it is no longer an impossibility.

The Olympic Games movement has also contributed to an awakening awareness of women's athletic accomplishments. Each Olympics has recognized more and more women's events, while the nationalistic fervor that grips viewers spills over to their women's teams. In 1984, in Los Angeles, American women won the first gold medals of the games in an event just opened up to them—road-cycling. Women competed on even terms with men in the equestrian (horse-riding) events, winning two of the three medals awarded. Most dramatic of all was the sight of the first Olympic marathon for women, an event previously closed to them on the assumption that they were too "fragile" for such a test of endurance.

In the 1984 Olympics women participated for the first time in the marathon run, won by Joan Benoit of the U.S. Her winning time was faster than that of Emil Zatopek, the legendary Czech runner, in winning the 1952 Olympics. (© UPI/Bettmann Newsphotos)

Olympic spectators and the television audiences saw women excel in sharp-shooting, field hockey, basketball, and other so-called masculine skills. They saw women who could have been their own wives, daughters, mothers, and sisters engaged in the single-minded pursuit of their personal best, as cool and courageous as any of the male competitors. And they cheered, and cheered, and cheered. It would be very difficult ever again to argue that women athletes do not need or deserve the encouragement, coaching, and facilities available to their male counterparts. As long as Americans value their standing in international athletics, public support for sports equity can only increase. The larger the pool of potential champions, the more likely it is that a winner will emerge—and winning, for many Americans, is everything, even if the champion is not "one of the boys."

But strong prejudices remain. For many men—and women—sport is the last field of achievement that males can consider all their own, embodying all that they value, making them in some way unique.

Despite all these barriers, the number of women participating in intercollegiate athletics grew fivefold between 1971 and 1984. During the same period, however, the proportion of women coaches for these teams declined from 90 percent to 50 percent. The trend has been toward folding women's athletics into the overall athletic program, with all the potential for recruiting violations, illegal substance use, and hidden cash payments that besets the men's programs (Alfano 1985). From the sociological perspective, it will be interesting to see if women's sports remain fundamentally different in goals and style from the male version, or whether the imperatives of funding and winning will shape attitudes and behaviors regardless of gender.

Summary

In this chapter we examine selected aspects of contemporary popular culture. Popular culture in mass society serves many functions for individuals and for the group as a whole. People are informed and entertained, the essential values of society are reinforced, and people are brought together in shared rituals. From the conflict perspective, questions are raised about control over the production of culture and about which values and whose power is maintained.

Mass culture has been criticized for its vulgarity and openness to political manipulation. It has also been defended by supporters of cultural pluralism and praised for the variety of taste cultures that characterize our society.

Popular culture is transmitted through the mass media. Most Americans depend on these media for their entertainment and information. The trend today is toward increasing centralization of ownership.

An ongoing debate continues over the effects of the media on attitudes and behavior, but there is little evidence that these effects are direct. Indirectly, the media are important in setting agendas and bringing selected issues to public attention. Most models of mass communication are based on a complex interplay among the society, its media, their audiences, and the contexts in which people receive its messages.

Media messages, including the news, are negotiated realities, produced under specific constraints, including the need for most mass media to be profit making. Whether consciously or not, the media reflects certain views of the world and are thus politically important.

The area of popular music reflects many of the "social production" variables that affect all popular culture: the time, the place, the economic structures, and the audience in which the art form is created and distributed.

Sports are another important aspect of our popular culture. Both amateur and professional sports express deeply held cultural values about work and manliness, and both are strongly influenced by considerations of the marketplace. The current trend toward commercialization has made sports both more democratic and more closely linked to the major stratification hierarchies of race, social class, and gender.

Suggested Readings

BALL-ROKEACH, SANDRA J., MILTON ROKEACH, and JOEL W. GRUBE. *The Great American Values Test: Behavior Belief Through Television.* New York: Free Press, 1984. An empirical study of the impact of television on egalitarian and pro-environmental values, beliefs, and behavior.

BECKER, HOWARD S. *Art Worlds.* Berkeley: University of California Press, 1982. A highly readable and insightful analysis of the social production of art and the institutional settings in which art is created, evaluated, and distributed.

BOURDIEU, PIERRE. *Distinction: A Social Critique of the Judgment of Taste.* Cambridge: Harvard University Press, 1984. A fascinating ethnography on the class-based nature of our tastes in books, music, sports, food, and clothes.

BOUTILLIER, MARY, and LUCINDA SAN GIOVANNI. *The Sporting Woman.* Champaign, Ill.: Human Kinetics Publishers., 1983. A very interesting and timely analysis of women in sports.

BRANTLINGER, PATRICK. *Bread and Circuses: Theories of Mass Culture as Social Democracy.* Ithaca: Cornell University Press, 1983. An historical examination of the different forms of mass culture and its impact on public participation in cultural life.

COAKLEY, JAY J. *Sport in Society: Issues and Controversies,* 3rd ed. St. Louis, Mo.: C. V. Mosby, 1986. A very fine undergraduate text in the sociology of sports.

EITZEN, D. STANLEY, and GEORGE H. SAGE. *Sociology of North American Sports,* 3d. ed. Dubuque, Iowa: Wm. C. Brown, 1986. An excellent overview of the field including sports and culture, youth, education, religion, mass media, social stratification, racism, and sexism.

EPSY, RICHARD. *The Politics of the Olympic Games: With an Epilogue.* 1976–1980. Berkeley: University of California Press, 1981. A unique treatment of the contemporary Olympic games as a significant international political event. Epsy traces the political aspects of sports and sports organizations since World War II.

GRABER, DORIS A. *Processing the News: How People Tame the Information Tide.* New York: Longman, 1984. An empirical analysis of how people make sense of the media and the ways in which they interpret, accept, and ignore the information presented.

KOPPES, CLAYTON R., and GREGORY D. BLACK. *Hollywood Goes to War: How Politics, Profits and Propaganda Shaped World War II Movies.* New York: Macmillan, The Free Press, 1987. This book explores the film industry's response to America's entry into World War II. It includes a discussion on the role of Office of War Information and government censorship in films made during that period.

KUHN, RAYMOND. *The Politics of Broadcasting.* New York: St. Martin's Press, 1985. A comparative study of the relationship between government and broadcasting media in Western Europe, North America, Japan, and Australia.

LANG, GLADYS ENGEL, and KURT LANG. *The Battle for Public Opinion: The President, the Press and the Polls During Watergate.* New York: Columbia University Press, 1983. An extensive analysis of the ways in which television defines and structures political crises and shapes public opinion.

MARTORELLA, ROSANNE. *The Sociology of the Opera.* Amherst, Mass.: Bergin Press, 1982. A study of performers and performances, including the influence of economics on the selection of repertory.

MEYROWITZ, JOSHUA. *No Sense of Place: The Impact of Electronic Media on Social Behav-* *ior.* New York: Oxford University Press, 1985. A provocative examination of the impact of media on the social construction of relationships in our society.

RYAN, JOHN. *The Production of Culture in the Music Industry: The ASCAP-BMT Contro-* *versy.* Lanham, Md.: University Press of America, 1985. An examination of power and expansion within the music industry, tracing the history and organization of two major music-licensing firms in the United States.

Part VI
Social Change

Although the rate of change will vary greatly between simple and complex societies, no culture or social structure remains forever unchanged. In previous chapters, to probe various aspects of society, we have had to slice into ongoing social systems and present a series of snapshots—moments frozen in time. But each snapshot is just one frame in a constantly changing reel. Cultures and social systems are always in the process of change: What was normative yesterday might be deviant tomorrow, and today's deviance becomes tomorrow's norm.

Some changes come from within a society as a result of seemingly spontaneous creativity, while other changes are consciously pursued by organized groups. Chapter 21 describes these dynamic aspects of social life, with special attention to *social movements* that promote or resist major institutional changes.

The book closes with Chapter 22, a review of the broad currents of cultural and social change across time. The focus is on *modernization* as the master process through which recent history has unfolded. However, at all periods, cultures and social structures have been influenced by contact with other groups, by conquest, or by human curiosity and inventiveness. Because social systems are human creations, and because we are capable of developing new forms of social life, society is an ever-changing collection of values, norms, and relationships.

In showing you how societies are constructed, we have also given you the intellectual tools for reconstituting social systems. It is our hope that your introduction to sociology will encourage you to work toward a society that embodies your highest ideals of justice and fairness.

21

Collective Behavior and Social Movements

D ID you hear about the child who died after biting into a poisoned Halloween apple? The barber who choked to death from a ball of hair scraps? The missing women who were sold to Near Eastern harems? Did a classmate tell you that her sister's boyfriend knows someone who had found a worm in a cola bottle? Or maybe you've been picking out the green M&Ms because they make you feel sexy? These are all examples of "urban legends" (Brunvand 1986), stories that are widely spread—and believed—but that are totally without basis in fact.

If urban legends are untrue, why are people ready to believe them? And why are there so many stories of harm to children, freak accidents, contaminated food, kidnappings, and unusual techniques for enhancing the sex drive? These questions lead us to the sociology of collective behavior, a category of analysis that studies such varied events as crazes and fads, panics and mass hysteria, mobs and crowds of all types, the effects of rumor and public opinion, social movements, and even revolutions. From a sociological viewpoint, these "happenings" are not random or chance events, but reflect ongoing tensions in the social structure, or play on fears generated in the culture. Take the example of the "Halloween sadist," that anonymous giver of treats who supposedly wishes to hurt innocent children. In one careful study of all such incidents reported in leading newspapers from 1958 to 1984, Best (1985) found that *no* deaths or even severe injuries to children could be traced to anonymous givers of Halloween treats. The only recorded deaths involved one child who ate heroin found in a relative's house and another whose father intentionally laced the treat with cyanide. Otherwise, all cases mentioned in the press turned out to be hoaxes, many of them perpetrated by the presumed "victim," who becomes the center of national attention.

Urban legends reflect generalized fears about the danger of modern life.

Best (1985) suggests that *urban legends* reflect generalized fears about the danger of modern life, with the "Halloween sadist" myth being a product of the special tensions of the 1970s. This was a period of growing fear of crime, drugs, and child abuse. The "Halloween sadist" embodied all these evils, and the legend took on a life of its own, featured in the media every October along with warnings to children not to eat anything that is not wrapped or sealed. As noted by Brunvand (1986), who has collected *three* volumes of urban legends, he could run TV announcements during the Super Bowl saying that the stories are hoaxes, and some listeners would still repeat the original legend.

The fears and fantasies that become the makings of urban legends are often exploited in the headlines of the more sensationalist press. (© William U. Harris, created by Robin Roy)

gradually emerge as events unfold and participants give meaning to their behavior. Any temporary gathering of people has the potential for collective response and action (McPhail and Wohlstein 1986).

There is no easy formula for specifying what is or is not collective behavior; it is largely a matter of degree. Spontaneous behavior is seldom as random as it appears, nor are highly structured activities immune from collective protests from within (Lyng and Kurtz 1985). In some instances, what appear to be spontaneous outpourings are carefully manipulated by authorities, as in the case of political rallies in Cuba (Aguirre 1984) or of the Iranian "student" takeover of the American Embassy in Teheran in 1979.

As a minimal definition, *collective behavior* refers to noninstitutionalized activities that are both cause and consequence of flux or change in the established order. In this chapter we will be able to present only a brief overview of the fasci-

Defining Collective Behavior

The activities that fall in the category of "collective behavior"—from urban legends to prison riots—are a bit of a mixed bag. What makes them objects of sociological analysis is that they involve persons responding to the same situation, whether or not in actual contact. Collective behavior is more loosely structured and less purposeful than most other forms of social action, and tends to occur outside normal institutionalized channels. But no situation remains unstructured for long; norms

Collective behavior refers to noninstitutionalized activities that are both cause and consequence of flux or change in the established order.

nating variety of behaviors that fall within this definition.

Types of Collective Behavior

One way to make sense of the diversity of collective behaviors is to arrange types of activity along such dimensions as (1) spontaneous versus structured forms; (2) short-term versus long-term commitments; (3) expressive versus instrumental goals; and (4) unconscious versus conscious motives. For example, a continuum of spontaneity might look like the one in Figure 21-1.

HYSTERIA, PANICS, AND RUMOR

In general, events that are spontaneous are also short-lived, expressive, and lacking in clear-cut goals. Examples of behaviors at this end of the continuum are (1) mass hysteria (uncontrollable outbursts of emotion); (2) panics (actions caused by sudden overwhelming fear); and (3) rumors (the spread of unconfirmed information). These types of collective behavior appear to be so unpredictable that they are often also described as *irrational*. But while difficult to predict, such behaviors are not totally random. There are social and historical causes for much of what seems to be irrational and spur-of-the-moment.

HYSTERIA. Most cases of mass *hysteria,* for example, can be traced to environmental stress. The seventeenth-century New England schoolgirls who claimed to be possessed by witches were no doubt suffering from a combination of boredom and puberty in a sexually repressive society (Boyer and Nussbaum 1974). Nor were their targets randomly selected; accused witches were usually older unmarried women in marginal social statuses who were feared for their nonconformity and whose social networks were not strong.

Today, outbreaks of mass hysteria typically involve schoolchildren and women assembly-line workers—both being relatively powerless groups, engaged in extremely boring work, and who have cultural permission to act "irrationally." The hysterical episode breaks up the dullness of their days, provides relief from pressure, and brings them to the center of attention. Although social isolates are often the first to display symptoms, the hysterical reaction spreads quickly through informal networks (Colligan et al. 1982).

Panics are typically grounded in real fears and anxieties, as illustrated in the famous "Men from Mars" radio broadcast of 1938 (see Box, p. 589). Similar fears surface today in periodic "sightings" of unidentified flying objects (UFOs), none of which has yet been shown to be of extraterrestrial origin. Yet some people believe that an invasion is near, and have spent millions of dollars on "survival camps" (Myers 1983).

Hysteria is an uncontrollable outburst of emotion.

Panics are actions caused by sudden overwhelming fear.

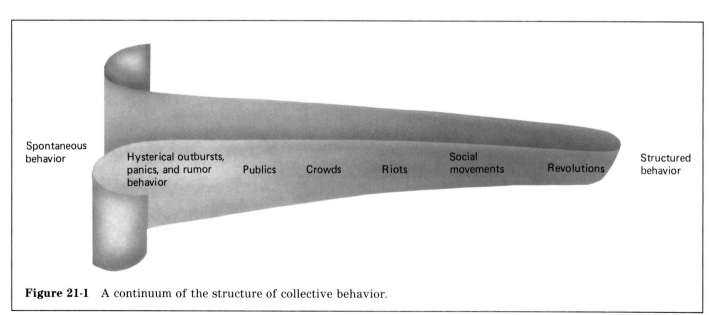

Spontaneous behavior

Hysterical outbursts, panics, and rumor behavior

Publics

Crowds

Riots

Social movements

Revolutions

Structured behavior

Figure 21-1 A continuum of the structure of collective behavior.

The Martians Are Coming

At 8:00 P.M. on Sunday, October 30, 1938—Halloween—actors of the Mercury Theater began their radio presentation of H. G. Wells's novel *The War of the Worlds*. Although some listeners knew they were hearing a radio play that dealt with science fiction, much of the audience had tuned in ten minutes after the program began because a competing radio show was featuring a rather poor singer. What they heard was an actor who sounded exactly like a radio announcer under stress, telling them that an unidentified flying object had landed in Grover's Mill, New Jersey, and that Martians had fought a battle with United States troops in the Watchung Mountains before moving on to New York City, whose population had been quickly overcome by poison gas, and where, by the time of the half-hour station break, only one survivor was left—all in less than thirty minutes!

The second half of the program was never broadcast. Panic had swept the entire country. Millions of people fled their homes to avoid the Martians; bus and train terminals were mobbed; phone lines were swamped; and rumors of casualties circulated widely. Yet, only one person had actually been injured in the panic.

The incident brought instant fame to Orson Welles and his Mercury Theater. It also proved how willing people were to believe the unbelievable, a state of mind that was probably helped by real fears based on the Great Depression at home and the rise of the Nazis in Germany abroad.

SOURCE: Material on the radio broadcast is from John Houseman, "The Men from Mars," *Harper's Magazine*, Vol. 197 (December 1948), pp. 74–82.

Rumors are the spread of unconfirmed information.

RUMOR. As shown in the example of urban legends, unverified information from anonymous sources can pass quickly from one person to another. A rumor is a group product; it exists only at the level of interaction. Although some rumors may be intentionally planted, most are unconscious distortions of normal communication that reinforce existing anxieties and prejudices, as when legends about contaminated hamburgers confirm our worst fears about what goes on in fast-food outlets (Rosnow and Kimmel 1979).

In a social-psychological perspective, the life of a rumor resembles the children's game of "pass it on," where, with each telling, some details are exaggerated and others forgotten, as each person shapes the story to her or his existing attitudes and expectations. In one famous experiment, white students were shown a picture of a white man threatening a black man on a subway train; as one student described the picture to the next, the situation was soon reversed, with the black threatening the white, because this version was more compatible with their preexisting view of the world (Allport and Postman 1947).

From a purely sociological perspective, however, it is important to note that rumors typically originate among persons of low prestige or who are relatively isolated, and then spread through the most convenient networks (Koenig 1985). Rumors are a way of striking back and of becoming noticed. Identifying an "enemy" often enhances the solidarity of the group.

Rumors are especially important in crowd situations where people are milling around with no means of testing the truth of what they are told. Under these circumstances, any reasonable definition of the situation will be accepted. For example, when people waiting to get into a rock concert hear the rumor that there are not enough seats for all ticket holders, they have been known to stampede the gates, trampling and injuring one another. In this case, the rumor makes sense because many people believe that concert promoters will do anything to make a profit.

MINOR FORMS OF COLLECTIVE BEHAVIOR

Some types of collective behavior are important primarily for what they tell us about popular taste at a particular moment. Three of these—crazes, fads, and fashions—can be classified according to how long they last, how widely they spread, and their social significance, if any.

Crazes are periodic outbursts of unexpected and often playful or absurd behavior, such as walking pet rocks, piling into a phone booth, or playing Trivial Pursuit.

Crazes are periodic outbreaks of unexpected and often playful or absurd behavior.

Nudity of one kind or another was symbolic of the rebellious '60s and early '70s; "streaking" was a craze of that era. Alf, a space alien puppet with his own TV sitcom, was a craze of the '87–'88 season. Do you think Alf is indicative of any broader trends in our society? (© Charles Wendt/Boulder Daily Camera; NBC Color Photos)

These activities are usually designed to relieve boredom rather than to make a profound social statement, but social scientists can read something into almost any behavior. For example, in the early 1970s, several incidents of "streaking" (running

naked in public) were interpreted as protests against conventional mores.

Fads last longer than crazes and also appeal to a wider audience. Break dancing, box radios, disco roller skating, earth art, and diamond-shaped signs on the rear windows of automobiles are recent examples of fads.

Fashions are more enduring, widespread, and socially significant than either crazes or fads. Trendsetters define what is "in" and networks of influence carry the message. The direction of influence can be from the top down, as with "designer" clothes being copied in less expensive versions, or from the masses up, as with blue jeans or punk rock.

Dress and body adornment carry important information about a person's social status, in modern as well as preliterate societies (Rubinstein 1985). In a society without an hereditary aristocracy, it may be necessary for the higher strata to be distinguished from the lower in some very visible way. Conversely, it could be argued that mass production in our society permits a democratization of dress that obscures the reality of social-class differences, thus reinforcing the myth of classlessness. In an authentic classless society, fashion could be subversive—thus, in the People's Republic of China until recently, all citizens, male and female, educated or illiterate, were encouraged to wear the same type of simple, functional clothing. In a caste society, however, fashion would be unnecessary, as status distinctions are very clear without different adornment (Blumer 1974).

Fashion may also serve to establish individuality, as when an item of dress or adornment becomes a personal statement, a way of standing out from the crowd. This function is especially significant in a society such as ours where lip service is paid to individualism but people who are too different, i.e., individualistic, are pressured to conform.

PUBLICS

Unlike the other collective behaviors discussed in this chapter, a *public* is composed of people who are not in the same place at the same time, but who react similarly to a common stimulus. For example, Richard Nixon's concept of the *silent majority* referred to an assumed public that strongly supported the Vietnam

Fads last longer than crazes and appeal to more people.

Fashions are more enduring, widespread, and socially important than fads.

A **public** consists of people who are not in the same place at the same time, but who react similarly to a common stimulus.

War but that did not take to the streets to demonstrate its approval of his policies. He felt that he spoke to this public.

All advertising is designed to create a public for a product, whether it is a bar of soap or a politician. Other publics consist of people who have some preexisting common interest—the environment, gun control, abortion, or civil rights, for example—and whose opinions may be formed individually but whose commitment can be activated by events reported in the media.

An unorganized public can become an *interest group* when its members feel strongly enough to move beyond letter writing and to seek out others with similar feelings. This potential for action in publics increases the power of the media. The importance of publics in modern societies cannot be overestimated. Until recently, it was very difficult, if not impossible, to reach all the members of the society simultaneously; today, it can be done in a moment by radio and television. Ultimately, mass society is based on the willingness of publics to support the social order. (How public opinion can be shaped and manipulated was also discussed in Chapter 13.)

> An **interest group** develops when members of a public seek others with similar feelings about an issue.

CROWDS

In contrast to the loosely linked collective behavior involved in hysteria, panics, rumors, and expressions of public opinion, crowds are typically characterized by greater mass, greater consciousness, and *emergent* qualities; that is, crowds can turn into organized groups. Crowds of various types are closer to being authentic social groups than are the collections of individuals who pass along rumors or become hysterical.

A *crowd* is a temporary gathering of people that is brought together by some common concern or activity, and in which there is an awareness of the presence of others. The scope of a crowd is therefore limited to the people in it then and there. Yet, a crowd is not a group in the sense of having structure, such as a division of labor with patterned roles. Rather, members of the crowd cease to be distinct persons when they blend into the mass. Under these circumstances, people can literally as well as figuratively become "lost in the crowd" and therefore be released from the norms that typically regulate behavior.

> A **crowd** is a temporary gathering of people brought together by some common concern or activity.

Types of Crowds. There are many different kinds of temporary collections or *aggregates* of people, from shoppers in a supermarket to a lynch mob. Some encounters are too brief and others too structured to be considered examples of crowd behavior. Both casual and conventional crowds test the limits of our definition.

A *casual crowd* is an accidental gathering of people who are following individual goals in the same place at the same time (e.g., shoppers, travellers, strollers) and who then share a common focus—as witnesses to an accident, for example—that makes them aware of one another. At the

> A **casual crowd** is an accidental gathering of people.

Rock concert audiences often turn into expressive crowds like these heavy metal fans in Russia who have been caught up in the spirit of the music and the moment. (© Ricki Rosen/Picture Group)

A **conventional crowd** is composed of people who are gathered as spectators or audiences at events governed by established norms.

An **expressive crowd** shows strong feelings with outbursts of emotion.

Acting crowds have some goal beyond mere expression of emotion.

Race riots, the most common type of mob action in the United States, were most often directed against a specific group, such as blacks or Chinese.

other extreme, a *conventional crowd* is composed of people who have intentionally gathered together at events governed by established norms, such as religious services, sports events, or theater performances. Here, behavior is highly patterned and, therefore, highly predictable.

But both casual and conventional crowds can be transformed into acting and expressive crowds (Blumer 1951). An *expressive crowd* emerges when participants are gripped by feelings that overwhelm customary normative controls. Spectators at sports events have been known to tear up the turf on a playing field, and people have been trampled at religious rallies. In contrast, the *acting crowd* has a goal beyond the mere expression of emotion. Fueled by the belief that only action outside the norms can accomplish those goals, the acting crowd could easily become a rioting mob.

RIOTS. Far from being rare, riots have occurred with some regularity in American history, from the Boston Tea Party to contemporary riots in prisons. By far the most common type of mob action in the United States has been the *race riot*. Thousands of blacks were lynched in the South before, during, and after the Civil War; hundreds, perhaps thousands, of Chinese "disappeared" in the West. White mobs burned and looted black sections of

several northern cities in the 1860s and the 1940s; and acting crowds of white parents damaged buses and threw objects at black schoolchildren in Boston and elsewhere in the 1970s. The black ghetto riots of the mid-1960s—in Cleveland, Detroit, the Watts section of Los Angeles, and Rochester, New York—were not race riots in the same sense as those just mentioned. Black mobs did not attack white residential areas; they directed their violence at white-owned business within the ghetto and at other symbols of white control of the political and economic life of the inner city. Even as late as 1980, black rioters in Miami remained within their part of the city, although by this time there were few nonblack targets in the area. The Miami riots also involved resentment over favoritism to Hispanics in the operation of public programs (Dunn and Porter 1983).

Not all mob action is negatively evaluated in the United States; much depends on who is involved and who does the judging. Students, blacks, and prisoners are usually defined by the media as rioters. Strikers, desegregation protesters, or National Guard troops that are out of control are rarely described as rioters, although identical behaviors are being observed. Victory parades after successful sports events are allowed to spill over, to disrupt traffic, and to damage property—as exam-

Riots are common throughout the world. While they may be spontaneous expressions of feelings which have no legitimate outlet elsewhere, they may also be incited for political reasons by groups which manipulate others for their ends. (© Gamma Liaison)

ples of "high spirits" and community pride rather than uncontrolled crowd behavior (Snow et al. 1981).

DEMONSTRATIONS

Demonstrations are carefully prepared, require legal permissions, have widespread publicity, and require local organizing and attention to details.

At the most organized, least spontaneous end of the continuum of crowds are *demonstrations.* An effective demonstration requires a great deal of planning: parade permits, publicity, buses, banners, portable toilets, entertainment, and speakers. The purpose of the demonstration is twofold: (1) to show the public and politicians that the particular cause has widespread support, and (2) to bring the "true believers" together and reinforce their commitment. Organizers announce a massive rally at some crucial site such as a nuclear power plant, the state house, or the area near the Capitol in Washington. Having announced the event, organizers must then make sure that tens of thousands of people take part. The size of the crowd becomes a crucial factor: if fewer than expected show up, opponents will say that the cause is dead.

COMMON ELEMENTS OF CROWD BEHAVIOR

Given the many ways in which crowds can vary—in size, duration, cohesion, and goals—are there any common elements? Turner and Killian (1972) list the following characteristics that are found to some degree in all crowds:

• Lack of certainty about what should be done
• A feeling that something should be done
• The spread of this feeling among participants
• Creation of a particular *mood* based on this uncertainty
• Openness to suggestions about what to do
• Relaxation of customary restraints on behavior

Because crowd behavior is relatively unstructured and variable, outcomes are less predictable than for other social interactions. It should not be surprising, therefore, that the models for understanding collective behavior in general and crowds in particular have been varied and somewhat incomplete.

Models of Collective Behavior

What turns an otherwise ordinary collection of people into a group of hysterical twitchers or a destructive mob? Early theories of collective behavior were framed primarily in a social-psychological perspective, with an emphasis on individual motivations and perceptions. One popular theory, proposed by Gustave Le Bon (1896), explains crowd behavior in terms of people losing their identity and sense of personal responsibility, becoming vulnerable to suggestion, and being swept up in a contagious emotion.

A more sophisticated version of Le Bon's *social* contagion thesis is Blumer's (1951) *emotional reaction model.* An initial stage of aimless milling around is followed by a focusing of attention on a single theme or leader. This emerging definition of the situation is reinforced as members of the crowd interact, creating a circular reaction that continually raises the intensity level. Thus, the crowd is primed for action, often sparked by a rumor.

The **emotional reaction model** focuses on how the intensity of crowds develops.

From a more sociological perspective, the crowd is seen as a field for evolving relationships and norms. That is, through their interaction, participants gradually develop a set of meanings—an "emergent construction of reality" (Wright 1978)—that makes sense of their actions.

THE "VALUE ADDED" MODEL

In a more systematic model, proposed by Neil Smelser (1968), each one of six steps leads to the next, thus narrowing the range of alternatives. The six conditions that are necessary *and* sufficient to produce some form of collective behavior are:

The **"value added" model** consists of six conditions which are necessary and sufficient to produce collective behavior.

(1) *Structural conduciveness.* Social institutions are organized to encourage or discourage collective behavior. In the Soviet Union, for example, an antigovernment rally would be highly unlikely.
(2) *Structural strain.* Tension is introduced into the situation because of inequalities that are seen as unfair, as unjust, and as due to social structural conditions. Residents of inner cities and members of minority groups are, for example, structurally situated to

Encounters with Unjust Authority

Social order depends on most people, most of the time, conforming to the norms that govern institutionalized roles. Under what conditions will people come to the decision that they can no longer obey the rules? This is a question that has long intrigued social scientists. Some, such as Tilly (1985), turn to history for examples of ordinary people engaged in collective protest against the established powers, and then reconstruct the precise conditions that led to their rebellion.

Also beginning with historical examples—a sit-down strike, a student protest, and a police/black Muslim encounter—William Gamson and his associates (1982) devised an experiment to examine how basically conforming people come to define authority as "unjust" and refuse, as a group, to follow orders. The researchers found their subjects through a newspaper advertising for assistance in market research for a company called the Manufacturers' Human Relations Consultants (MHRC). Subjects were divided into thirty-three groups of six to ten people, and presented with a "problem" facing one of MHRC's clients—a large oil company that was being sued by an employee who had been fired for living with a woman to whom he was not married. Subjects were asked to help the oil company by making videotaped statements harmful to the employee, and then by signing a document that could be used as evidence in court.

In only half (sixteen) of the cases did everyone in the groups refuse to sign the document, even though all subjects were being asked to do something that was dishonest. In the remainder of the groups, people behaved as they were asked to by the authority figures, even though very little "official" pressure was exerted on them (they were, after all, paid volunteers). The groups that engaged in collective resistance differed from the conforming groups in the following respects:

- They were already mistrustful of large oil companies.
- They contained some members with special abilities in organizing group action.
- They were able to create a sense of group loyalty.
- They found ways to neutralize the tendency to comply.
- They justified their resistance by defining the demands of authority as clearly "unfair."

From this low-key experiment, as well as from the more dramatic study of obedience to authority among individuals reported in Chapter 4, we can appreciate how difficult it is to break the habit of following orders—whether alone or in a group. Furthermore, as history demonstrates time and again, established authorities are not reluctant to use their monopoly of legitimate force to destroy protest movements: soldiers fight peasants, private police break up strikes, the National Guard shoots students, cattle prods are used on blacks, houses are firebombed—all in the name of "law and order."

SOURCE: William A. Gamson, Bruce Fireman, and Steven Rytina, *Encounters with Unjust Authority*, Homewood, IL: Dorsey, 1982.

experience the conditions leading to a sense of injustice.

(3) *Growth and spread of a generalized belief* occurs as people seek explanations for their intolerable situation. The source of strain is identified: "the power elite," "them." Through their shared definitions of the situations, individuals are prepared for joint action.

(4) *Precipitating factors* are dramatic events that support the generalized belief. The events need not have actually occurred; a rumor will spark crowd reaction if the rumored event fits the generalized belief. Most of the urban violence of the 1960s, for example, was fueled by incidents of police brutality that were further fed by rumor.

(5) *Mobilization for action* comes when a leader emerges to give a sense of direction to those crowd participants willing to take part in the proposed activity ("Let's go!" "Get 'em!").

(6) *Social control factors* are the responses of the authorities. Crowds can be encouraged or discouraged from a given course of action by the way in which a situation is handled by politicians, police, the courts, and the media. The use of force can crush or anger a crowd. Authorities can respond by acknowledging the griev-

Strong authoritarian rule coupled with anti-union activity has helped give the South Korean economy a $6.7 billion trade surplus. It has also created an opposition faction from students, workers, and, increasingly, the middle class. Precipitating factors, such as police brutality, provoked this opposition to erupt into riots, like this one in Seoul in May of 1987. (© Anthony Suau/ Black Star)

ances and acting to reduce further strain, or attempts can be made to isolate the protest's leaders. The ultimate fate of the collective action is shaped by the interaction between participants and the agents of social control.

RESOURCE MOBILIZATION

Social-psychological theories attempt to explain why and which individuals engage in noninstitutionalized behaviors. But the questions that sociologists ask are very different: Why does a particular social protest emerge when it does? What accounts for its success and failure? Theories of individual motivation cannot answer these questions.

Over the past decade, a basically sociological approach to collective behavior has emerged: the *resource mobilization model.* In this view, social movements and protest activities are not abnormal events that attract alienated or marginal people but part of the ongoing processes whereby resources are distributed within the society (McCarthy and Zald 1977, Tilly 1978). The focus is on the movement as a whole rather than on individuals. This approach to collective behavior emphasizes (1) the organizational resources available to protesters, and (2) the tactics used by agents of social control (Zald and McCarthy 1978). Neither shared grievances nor generalized beliefs—both social-psychological variables—are sufficient to explain the emergence of protest activity; nor are participants necessarily the most alienated members of the society. To the con-

trary, isolated individuals by definition are located outside the interpersonal networks through which people are recruited to collective action.

Resource mobilization theorists assume that in modern industrial societies there will always be grounds for protest. Issues can emerge from free-floating discontent and anxiety without any preexisting specific grievance or ideology, as when local residents demonstrate against waste-disposal facilities that they fear might contain toxic materials. But the model also views participants as rational decision makers who have weighed the various costs and benefits of taking collective action, and who have decided that the goals of the protest are worth the time and effort required to fight for them.

Just which protests emerge at particular historical moments, and how successful they are, depends less on the virtue of the cause than on the ability of the protesters to mobilize their forces and to overcome the agents of control (Freeman 1983). The enormous variety of protest actions and their varying outcomes are illustrated in Tilly's (1986) massive historical study of social conflict in France between 1598 and 1984. As both Tilly (1986) and Markoff (1985) note, the nature of rural protests in France was greatly influenced by the spread of a centralized state bureaucracy and the economic changes produced by capitalist development. At the local level, however, the important factors were community solidarity, communications networks, and the relative strength of the forces of the government and economic elites.

The **resource mobilization model** stresses the supports available to protesters, as well as the tactics used by social control agents.

595

Although the resource mobilization model has replaced earlier individualistic approaches, a number of scholars are now attempting to flesh it out with field studies of specific protest movements, paying attention to both group-level and social psychological variables. For example, Shlay and Faulkner's (1984) analysis of problems in organizing tenants focuses on the power differential between landlord and renters that is built into the law and accepted by the protesters. Although a tenants' union was eventually created, participants ultimately failed to improve the quality of their housing, although some individuals gained a sense of efficacy in the process.

Both group and personal incentives for joining a protest were examined in a study of labor negotiations in the Netherlands (Klandermans 1984). The researcher found that people's willingness to join in collective action depended on what they thought other people would do and how these others would react to their own decision whether or not to participate. This formulation, however, overlooks the social and organizational contexts in which such choices are made, as well as the cognitive and ideological factors that influence commitment to a cause (O'Brien and Fugita 1984, Ferree and Miller 1985, Schrager 1985).

As Schrager (1985) and Ferree and Miller (1985) point out, people are mobilized to participate in collective action primarily through networks of friends or coworkers: their decisions are not always based on a simple calculation of costs versus benefits. Furthermore, attitudes and behavior interact in very complex ways, so that the definition of the situation (what is a cost or a benefit, and what are the chances of success) will change with the level of participation. And as one study of neighborhood association members indicates, sometimes the most active members will be those who are most *pessimistic* about the commitments of others, and who therefore feel that they had better do it themselves (Oliver 1984).

Thus, an increasingly sophisticated resource mobilization model is gradually emerging. Its central focus remains the ability of groups to activate resources (membership, funding, public support), to maintain participants' commitment over time, and to resist counterattacks by established institutions. At the same time, the theory embraces social-psychological processes that explain individual participation without reducing these to simplistic cost/benefit analyses.

With these theoretical considerations in mind, let us turn to a detailed analysis of the class of events most frequently analyzed by sociologists: the social movement.

Social Movements: Beliefs and Action

Social movements are organized attempts to introduce or to resist social change. McCarthy and Zald (1977) distinguished among social movements, social movement organizations, and social movement industries.

A *social movement* is defined as "a set of opinions and beliefs in a population" expressing a preference for changing either the elements of the social structure or its system for allocating scarce rewards. A social movement may also be organized around a desire to resist such changes. A *countermovement* is a set of opinions and beliefs in a population that is opposed to the goals of a social movement.

Social movement organizations are the formal structures designed to achieve the goals of a movement or a countermovement.

Social movement industries arise when a number of organizations can unite around a single issue.

Contemporary social movements—including those for equality for blacks, women, and homosexuals, and for and against abortion rights, nuclear power, or the legalization of marijuana—involve large numbers of people on each side of the issue, specific formal organizations set up to realize these goals, and coalitions with other organizations, thus creating a movement industry.

Countermovements must be analyzed in relation to the movements against which they emerged, that is, as part of a *dialectic process*. *Dialectic* refers to the conflict of opposites that ultimately leads to a new status quo, which, in turn, brings new challenges, and so on through time. Movement and countermovement are therefore linked in a dynamic relationship that creates a changed environment. Moreover, countermovements share many

Social movements are organized attempts to introduce or resist social change.

Countermovements are opinions and beliefs in a population that oppose the goals of a social movement.

The **dialectic process** refers to the conflict of opposites that leads to a new status quo.

characteristics of social movements in general. Mottl (1978) identified a four-stage life cycle for countermovements very similar to the model of development for social movements presented later in this chapter.

1. Resistance to change.
2. Mobilization of protest.
3. Transformation to militancy.
4. Return to the status quo if successful; continued low-level resistance if not.

CLASSIFYING SOCIAL MOVEMENTS

Social movements can be classified by duration, by goals, and by tactics. In terms of *duration,* Blumer (1974) distinguishes *general* or long-term secular changes from *specific* movements that are limited in time and place. An example of a general movement would be the gradual extension of equal rights to women in modern societies. Specific movements within this broad current include the campaign for the vote in the early decades of this century and the reproductive choice movement of the past twenty years. But specific countermovements have slowed the general trend at various periods, as we shall discuss later in this chapter.

Goals of social movements range from limited change to a complete overthrow of the social structure, and from total resistance to change to dropping out of the system altogether. In general, *tactics* (actions taken to achieve desired results) will be determined by the goals.

* *Reform Movements* call for changes within the existing system. For example, extending the Fourteenth Amendment's guarantee of equal treatment to blacks, homosexuals, and the disabled involves relatively simple legislative or judicial actions. The tactics selected are those most likely to influence politicians, judges, and public opinion in general: demonstrations, law suits, electioneering, use of the media, and endorsements by leading figures in government or popular culture (see Cohn and Gallagher 1984, for an analysis of media effects on public perception of gay-rights activism, and Scotch 1984, for legal strategies on behalf of the civil rights of disabled persons).

* *Revolutionary Movements,* at the opposite end of the spectrum, aim for fundamental changes in values and institutions. Such a radical goal justifies extraordinary tactics, designed to attract public attention and to spread fear and

Goals of social movements range from limited change to a complete overthrow of the social structure.

Reform movements seek fundamental changes in values and institutions.

Revolutionary movements call for radical structural change in the society.

Revolutionary terrorist groups generally lack any resources other than violence or threat of violence to gain their ends. The publicity achieved through their actions brings their cause to the attention of the general public which would otherwise ignore them. The results of bombings such as this one in Paris cannot be ignored. (© Gamma-Liaison)

uncertainty. Although not all revolutionary movements engage in acts of violence, forms of terrorism such as hijacking, kidnapping, and fire bombing are quite common today throughout the world: in the Near East, especially, but also in Ireland, Western Europe, and in the late 1960s, the United States.

Resistance movements are designed to stop change and to restore traditional values and norms.

- *Resistance Movements* are designed to stop change and to restore what are referred to as "traditional" values and norms. Examples include the Ku Klux Klan, which gained many supporters between 1860 and 1920 in response to widespread fears that the white Anglo-Saxon Protestant majority was imperiled by blacks and Catholic and Jewish immigrants. In the 1980s, the rise of the New Christian Right (see Chapter 15) represents a "backlash" movement to the recent gains of the feminist, gay rights, and children's rights movements.

Utopian movements seek an ideal society for true believers.

- *Utopian Movements* seek an ideal society for a select group of true believers with the hope that their example will be a guide to change in the broader social system. Ironically, the word "utopia" means no place, recognition that a perfect society may be impossible, though the concept has captured the imagination of thinkers for centuries (Alexander and Gill 1984). And there have been many attempts to create just such a community, though few have been successful over time.

Utopian idealism in contemporary America is most clearly associated with the social organization of the *commune,* in which members share common living quarters and pool the rewards of economic production. Major problems center on leadership, the control of sexuality, and commitment to the group, which is the reason why religiously oriented communes have the best survival record (Kanter 1972, Zablocki 1980).

PHASES IN THE DEVELOPMENT OF SOCIAL MOVEMENTS

A number of models have described the "natural history" or life course of social movements (Hopper 1950, Zald and Ash 1969, Blumer 1974). Although different terms are used, all these models distinguish four major phases characterized by: (1) personal discontent and vague unrest in the society; (2) a focusing of concern and the emergence of information networks; (3) development of formal organizations; and (4) acceptance of the movement's goals or its gradual decline through membership loss.

Phase One. Widespread unrest is usually linked to some condition in the wider society: economic crises, wars, migration, technological change, and so forth. Some social movements—nativistic revivals, for example (Chapter 15)—emerge when a traditional way of life is threatened. Other movements arise not at the lowest ebb of a group's fortunes, but when conditions actually appear to be improving. The gap between expected benefits and actual gains creates a *revolution of rising expectations* (Davies 1962).

At such times, people's feeling of being deprived may be absolute or relative. *Absolute deprivation* is a lack of basic necessities for survival. This kind of deprivation often leads to such feelings of powerlessness that individuals withdraw even from collective action. *Relative deprivation* occurs when people compare their condition unfavorably to that of others thought to be like oneself. For example, American blacks are not comparing themselves to blacks in Africa but to whites in this society with the same level of education and skills, and their sense of frustration fuels protest.

These feelings, however, remain vague and unfocused in the early stages of a social movement. The initial impulse is to blame failure on fate or personal shortcomings. The type of leader likely to emerge at this period is the *prophet* (to believers) or the *agitator* (to agents of social control).

Phase Two involves the realization that many others share your feelings of anger or injustice. But recognizing that you are not alone does not automatically lead to a social movement. To transform personal problems into public issues requires an *ideology* that explains the structural sources of discontent, provides an alternative view of reality, and offers a plan of action. This is the stage at which information networks are crucial to linking individuals, and where the media has a major role in legitimating the claims of movement leaders. These leaders tend to be charismatic, attracting public attention while giving voice to the yearnings of the discontented.

The **revolution of rising expectations** refers to the gap between expected benefits and actual gains.

Absolute deprivation is a lack of the basic necessities of survival.

Relative deprivation occurs when people feel unfairly treated in comparison to others thought to be their equals.

In *Phase Three* movement participants are able to mobilize the resources required to sustain formal organizations: money, mass membership, and social tolerance (or at least the absence of open repression). The transformation to a social movement organization also involves reinforcing charismatic leadership with managers and administrators. In Max Weber's terms charisma is "routinized" and the movement partially "demystified."

No matter how high the level of discontent or how righteous the cause, a social movement will succeed only to the extent that it can make alliances with other groups, resist cooptation, avoid conflict within its own ranks, and maintain the commitment of members over the long haul. To accomplish these goals, movement organizations tend to become bureaucratized with power centralized in a small group of leaders (Gamson 1975). It also helps if opposition groups are disorganized or vulnerable to accidents, as in the case of nuclear energy plants (Walsh 1986). In other words, the fate of a social movement is determined less by the virtues of its goals than by the ability of its leaders to mobilize resources from within its own ranks and from the larger social system.

The fate of the movement is decided at *Phase Four.* Success takes the form of *institutionalization,* when the movement's beliefs become part of the taken-for-granted world, and its goals are embodied in stable organizations.

Bishop Desmond Tutu, pictured above, the Secretary General of the Council of South African Churches, has led an unrelenting yet pacifist struggle against apartheid in South Africa. Although Tutu was awarded the Nobel Peace Prize for his work, he has been considered an agitator by the South African government. (© William Knosi/Gamma-Liaison)

The four phases are summarized in Table 21-1.

The other possible outcome for a social movement is defeat. Early successes often provoke powerful countermovements. For

TABLE 21-1 Model of social movement development

	1 Preliminary	2 Focusing of Concern (Crystallization)	3 Organization (Mobilization)	4 Institutionalization
Phase				
Characteristics	Widespread but isolated feelings of discontent and deprivation	Recognition that others share feelings	Centralization of power Mass membership	Public recognition and acceptance of ideas
Challenges	Media access Grass-roots organizing	Ideological development Communications network	Organization survival Avoiding internal conflicts Maintaining members' commitment	Organizational legitimation Benefiting members Resisting cooptation
Structure	None	Local units (cells)	National organizations Alliances with other groups	Bureaucracy
Leadership	Prophet or agitator	Charismatic leader	Managers (priests)	Bureaucrats

example, a socialist movement in the United States in the 1930s was effectively crushed by a combination of government repression, public fear, and internal disputes. The Women's Christian Temperance Union (WCTU) enjoyed the victory of the Prohibition Amendment before experiencing total defeat with its repeal—less than fourteen years later (Blocker 1985).

In other cases, only some movement goals are realized. Partial success creates problems in maintaining member commitment. Leaders must continually emphasize the unmet goals while opponents claim nothing more needs to be done. Manipulation of public opinion is a crucial factor at this point. Today, for example, both the civil-rights and the women's movements are fighting the public perception that their major goals have already been accomplished.

Substantive successes are often hazardous to the health of a social movement. The coalition formed to press for women's suffrage in the United States all but disappeared overnight once the Nineteenth Amendment was ratified in 1920. The struggle to gain the vote was the only issue holding the coalition together, and it was not until four decades later that a new feminist movement emerged to tackle the unfinished business of the suffrage movement.

Goal displacement occurs when movement goals are displaced by the goal of maintaining formal structures.

There are other dangers in becoming successfully organized, most notably *goal displacement,* whereby maintaining the formal structure of the new organization replaces the original goals of the social movement. As leadership passes from charismatic leaders (prophets) devoted to the cause to bureaucrats (priests) whose loyalty is to the organization, the threat of a new ruling elite is raised (see Chapter 13 on the "iron law of oligarchy"). In these many ways, then, organizational success and its consequences can corrupt the original goals of the movement.

SOCIETAL REACTIONS TO SOCIAL MOVEMENTS

The success or failure of a social movement also depends on outside variables. Groups in power often support a movement's goals, convinced of the movement's legitimacy or power. Politicians are quick to pick up winds of change, as witnessed in the 1970s by increasing support of the antiwar movement and declining support for civil rights and the Equal Rights Amendment.

In general, agents of social control can use two basic strategies: *repression* and *cooptation.* Jailing, deportation, harassment, and the ultimate use of armed force have all been used to repress movements defined as subversive. These tactics have been very effective in destroying left-wing movements and militant racial organizations (such as the Black Panthers), but they have been only moderately and temporarily effective against right-wing movements, such as the American Nazis or the Klan, reflecting value judgments made by political leaders and law enforcement officials regarding the potential harm of a movement.

Cooptation is the process of bringing opponents of the system into the established leadership structure. A black civil-rights leader who becomes a presidential adviser or a feminist appointed to a judge-

Repression of a social movement includes jailings, deportation, harassment, use of armed forces, and death.

Cooptation is the process of bringing opponents of the system into the established leadership structure.

The Black Panther party was originally organized as a self-defense group to curb police brutality. Due to their insistence on maintaining arms for self-defense, combined with their revolutionary program, members were constant targets of police departments throughout the country. Later evidence showed that police harassment was part of a search and destroy mission under federal direction. (© UPI/ Bettmann Newsphotos)

ship becomes part of the power elite against which she or he had previously fought. A few visible acts of cooptation can give the impression that the movement's goals have been accomplished, thus reducing public support for further gains, and also thinning the ranks of movement leadership.

Contemporary Social Movements

Social movements typically appear in clusters. The underlying conditions that make protest necessary and possible usually fuel more than one social movement. Ideas and strategies flow from one group to another. Often, the same people have multiple interests in change-oriented activism. It should be no surprise, therefore, that at certain historical moments, a variety of social movements will flourish simultaneously.

A DECADE OF PROTEST: 1963–1973

One such period in recent American history was the span from the early 1960s to the early 1970s. The period's undercurrent of activism among college students (a relatively rare phenomenon in American history) began with the Free Speech Movement on the Berkeley campus of the University of California and the rise of the New Left (Breines 1982), and ended less than a decade later with National Guard troops firing at students at Kent State University in Ohio and at Jackson State University in Mississippi.

At the same time, a massive Civil Rights Movement, forged within black communities at the local level, came to national attention (Blumberg 1984, Morris 1984). By the mid-1960s, a New Feminist Movement was also emerging, partly sustained by women who had first been mobilized by the New Left and the Civil Rights Movements (Ferree and Hess 1985, Katzenstein and Mueller 1987). Members of all these movements were soon joined by other students, religious leaders, politicians, and large numbers of previously inactive citizens in protesting the conduct of the war in Vietnam. Also taking root during these years were the Gay Rights Movement (D'Emilio 1983), the Children's Rights

Movement (Thorne 1987), and the movements against both nuclear power and nuclear war (Price 1982).

COUNTERMOVEMENT ACTIVISM

As each of these movements involved profound challenges to established values and authorities, each was also met by organized resistance. Student protest was the easiest to control because of constant turnover in personnel, the fact that students are together only part of the year, their vulnerability to parental pressure, and the willingness of authorities to use force. Countermovement violence was also directed at civil rights demonstrators—in the form of police dogs, cattle prods, hoses, tear-gas cannisters, stays in southern jails, and, ultimately, lynching or assassination.

Gay Rights activists and antiwar demonstrators have been physically attacked by the police and by "hard hats" carrying the American flag. Women's Movement advocates, however, are most frequently ridiculed or trivialized, while antinuclear groups must compete against the political and financial power of major business interests. In general, violence by countermovement or "backlash" activists has been less effective than their manipulation of the law and the media (McAdam 1983, Barkan 1984).

Despite the great strength of countermovement forces, however, the major social movements of the 1960s and early 1970s were able to mobilize sufficient resources to achieve important goals. As noted elsewhere in this book, the structure of *de jure* segregation has been dismantled; public support for homosexual civil rights has not diminished, even in the face of great fear over AIDS; women's rights have been partially secured; and the war in Vietnam was ultimately forced to a close.

Out of the interplay of movement and countermovement come some gains, some failures, and much unfinished business. Each of these movements has its unique history, its special problems and strengths or weaknesses, its triumphs and tragedies. Social movements are hostages to time, and as history is always being rewritten, analyses of social movements undergo revision and reinterpretation. Latent or unforeseen consequences emerge; battles can be won but wars lost; short-term gains will

Demonstrators against apartheid in South Africa experience countermovement violence from the police on a regular basis. (© David Turnley/Black Star)

activate backlash forces, while counter-movement tactics produce changes in movement goals.

To illustrate many of these problems and processes, we examine in some detail two very different contemporary examples of collective activism—the Civil Rights Movement and the antifeminist backlash movement.

THE CIVIL RIGHTS MOVEMENT

Looking back over twenty-five years of organized civil rights activity from a resource mobilization perspective, a number of recent studies have added new depth to what had become an overly simplified view of this crucial social movement (Barkan 1984, Blumberg 1984, Farmer 1984, Killian 1984, Marger 1984, Morris 1984, Exum 1985, Jenkins and Eckert 1986, McAdam 1986).

Emergence and History: 1955–1965. The modern black civil rights movement took form in the early 1950s, when the legal, political, and economic climate for blacks had measurably improved. The black vote was beginning to look attractive to liberal/left candidates. Expanding opportunities led to a *cognitive liberation* in which the idea of collective protest could be seriously considered (McAdam 1982). Local communities now had the resources necessary to support activism: leadership (largely through the church), a small but stable middle class, and networks of students in primarily black colleges (Morris 1984).

Cognitive liberation occurs when the idea of collective protest can be seriously considered.

602

The first protest activities were not, as commonly believed, spontaneous outbreaks of the most deprived, but carefully rehearsed challenges to Southern custom and law. Rosa Parks knew exactly what she was doing when, in 1955, she refused to move to the back of the bus in Montgomery, Ala., and the conductor obliged her by calling in the police. The arrests of Ms. Parks and the black leaders who came to her defense led to a well-organized boycott of Montgomery buses and white-owned businesses that ended only when the courts ruled that segregated buses were unconstitutional.

Similarly, the students who defied the law and sat down at a "white only" lunch counter at a Woolworth's store in Greensboro, N.C., in 1960, were part of a network of student activists, trained by local civil rights units. The spread of localized protest throughout the South in the late 1950s, although largely organized in advance, did have its spontaneous and emergent side, especially when protesters needed to respond quickly to changes in strategy by the white establishment (Barkan 1984, Killian 1984).

Although it seems difficult to believe today, it was only a generation ago that it was illegal in many parts of the country for blacks and whites to use the same schools, restaurants, or other public facilities. Only in 1954 did the Supreme Court strike down the doctrine of "separate but equal." In 1957, President Eisenhower sent troops to Little Rock, Ark., to enforce school desegregation, and Congress passed a largely symbolic Civil Rights Act. The political situation became more favorable with the Kennedy election in 1960, but it was not until Lyndon Johnson committed the full powers of the Presidency that comprehensive civil rights legislation was enacted in the mid-1960s (Blumberg 1984).

By this time, movement leaders had forged a national coalition able to mobilize the mass of black citizens as well as white sympathizers. Funding from mainstream churches and foundations began to flow into "moderate" civil rights organizations. Black and white professionals offered legal and organizational assistance—not without danger, as a number of civil rights activists were murdered during this period, and many others spent time in jail. In general, the people who volunteered for "high-risk" activism were those who had taken part in other civil rights protests, who were members of many organizations, and who had strong network ties with other activists (McAdam 1986). As the demonstrations grew larger and larger, media coverage expanded, and public opinion grew steadily more favorable.

Goals and Tactics. From the very beginning, the goal of the movement was clear and simple, and reformist: to extend the protections of the Constitution to black Americans. Having preempted the moral high ground, movement leaders chose to adopt the strategy of nonviolent "civil disobedience." *Civil disobedience,* as perfected by Mahatma Gandhi in India, involves a peaceful refusal to obey "unjust" laws in the name of a higher morality. When opponents are provoked to violence, the moral virtue of the movement is highlighted in contrast to the brutality of authorities.

For these reasons, the protest demonstration (along with business boycotts) became a favored tactic of civil rights organizers. Large rallies and marches drew reporters and TV cameras, especially if there was also the threat of danger. Mass demonstrations send a message to politicians, strengthen the commitment of participants, and afford some protection against counterdemonstrators. When they also trigger a violent response, federal authorities are forced to intervene in support of the protesters, thus lending legitimacy to movement goals (McAdam 1983).

The most massive—and peaceful—civil rights march took place in Washington in 1963, and is best known today as the occasion for Rev. Martin Luther King Jr.'s "I Have a Dream" speech. It is important to remember, however, that this highpoint of the movement came after one full decade of organizing at the local level, and that

Civil disobedience involves peaceful refusal to obey unjust laws in the name of a higher morality.

In March of 1965 Dr. Martin Luther King (shown in center with his wife Coretta Scott King) led thousands of civil rights demonstrators on a 50-mile march from Selma to Montgomery, Alabama. (© UPI/ Bettmann Newsphotos)

The Movement: Personal Commitments and Accounts

ALDON MORRIS

Aldon Morris is associate professor of sociology at the University of Michigan. His book, The Origins of the Civil Rights Movement, *was co-winner of the 1986 American Sociological Association Award for best book in sociology. Currently, he is conducting research, along with Dr. Shirley Harchett, on the "Black Power" phase of the Civil Rights Movement and on the contemporary black church. He is president of the Association of Black Sociologists.*

Human societies and human interactions have always fascinated me. I seldom take social reality for granted. The fact of cultural variability is nothing less than amazing. The ways in which societies survive, change, engage in conflict, build structures of inequality, generate culture and great human liberation movements are complex and difficult to understand. On the interpersonal level, individuals interact with each other and even their own consciousness. As individuals interact they have social experiences that make them laugh, cry, or be angry, reflective, and even embarrassed.

The wonderful task of the sociologist is to study and generate knowledge concerning the human drama at both the societal and interpersonal levels. Which aspect of the human drama a sociologist studies and writes about is heavily conditioned by that person's own life experiences. It is no accident that I study social movements in general and the United States Civil Rights Movement in particular. My decision to study social movements is directly linked to the fact that I grew up in American society as a member of an oppressed and exploited racial group. As a young black person I quickly came to realize that racial discrimination and inequality were, in fact, real and had devastating consequences for members of the black community. This was a problem that perplexed and worried me for it was difficult to conceive of ways to change this wretched situation.

Then, as if by magic, the Civil Rights Movement exploded upon the American scene. All of a sudden black people, along with some whites, were marching for racial justice by the thousands and being cursed, beaten, and jailed for their dignified protest against racial injustice. Some even gave their lives while many others were prepared to do likewise.

The Civil Rights Movement caught my interest immediately. I saw it as a force capable of transforming race relations in America. Even as the attack dogs were lunging at demonstrators throughout the South during the 1960s, I wondered about the origins, development, and personalities of this ground-breaking movement. While completing my graduate studies in sociology I decided that my first research objective was to produce a major study of the Civil Rights Movement—an examination of how the movement came about and developed over time. I also wanted to know whether the movement achieved its goals of social change and racial equality.

My research provided answers to a number of significant sociological questions. First, I discovered that the Civil Rights Movement did not occur suddenly or spontaneously. To the contrary, I found that there had always been a black movement for change in this country and that these historic protest streams converged in the 1960s, producing a dynamic and more powerful movement for change. Sociologically, then, movements appear to be part of ongoing struggles rather than spontaneous occurrences. Second, I found that ordinary grass-roots people working through mass-based community organizations constituted the real power behind the movement. This finding suggests that during certain historical periods the actions of ordinary people can bring about important societal change. Third, my research demonstrated how social movements actually function as vehicles of social change. Fourth, my research challenged the common view that the white community, especially northern liberals, financed the modern Civil Rights Movement. In response to the question, "From where did the money come?" I found that the overwhelming majority of local struggles that constituted what we call the Civil Rights Movement were actually financed by the black community itself. Local people dug deep into their pockets to finance their own efforts of liberation. It is as if they clearly understood the words of the black abolitionist Frederick Douglass, who declared, "He who would be free must himself strike the first blow." Thus, oppressed people can act to free themselves.

Fifth, my research makes it clear that black women were also crucial to the rise and success of the Civil Rights Movement. They assumed both leadership and behind-the-scene roles. This should not be surprising because black women have always been in the forefront of the black liberation struggle. The nature of the brutal oppression of Afro-Americans has always prevented black women from being exclusively relegated to the domestic sphere. Throughout the history of black people in America, black women have had to assume work roles outside the home and household. And, due to the disenfranchisement of the black male, they have often been the active voice in the church and community. (See "Discovering What 'Everybody Knows'" by Cheryl Townsend Gilkes in Chapter 15.) Building on their rich tradition of activism, black women played those pivotal roles that made the movement strong and focused.

The Civil Rights Movement was

able to overthrow legally enforced racial segregation and it was successful in its quest for voting rights in the South. Moreover, this movement changed American politics forever. It provided a model for all oppressed groups to follow. Thus the modern women's, students', farmworkers' and handicapped movements all drew their inspiration from the Civil Rights Movement using many of its tactics in their respective strategies. Nevertheless, this powerful and important movement was not successful in its goal of eliminating economic inequality between blacks and whites. There is still a great deal of disparity between these two groups on most economic indices. Correcting this imbalance may well be the task of the next great social movement in America.

In the meantime the human drama continues to unfold in all of its magnificence. Sociologists will never find themselves without opportunities to exercise the sociological imagination. The human drama itself and their roles within it provide their laboratory.

---

outside (white) support, while essential, was never sufficient to ensure success (Morris 1984). Indeed, because white support was typically directed to the most moderate civil rights organizations, this form of patronage may have encouraged goal displacement (Jenkins and Eckert 1986).

Organizational Dilemmas. Despite major gains in the late 1960s, three decades of civil rights activism have failed to eliminate discrimination in jobs, housing, and education, nor has the equal protection of the laws become a full reality. Episodes of violence by blacks in the late 1960s provided a rationalization for the withdrawal of ideological and material support from many civil rights organizations, although the most moderate groups remained well funded (Haines 1984, Marger 1984).

The movement was greatly weakened in 1968 by the assassination of Reverend King who had served as a charismatic focus for various groups within the movement as well as for white sympathizers. As Max Weber would have predicted, overreliance on a charismatic leader at the expense of building a strong organization carries a great risk. No figure of comparable stature except, perhaps, the Reverend Jesse Jackson in the 1980s, has been able to unite the various factions within the Civil Rights Movement or appeal so strongly to the conscience of whites.

In addition, once the civil rights laws were passed, the focus shifted to enforcement by the courts and government agencies, both of which are subject to political pressure, which is heavily weighted toward the white majority. As a consequence, legislative gains in the 1970s were relatively minimal, and since the election of Ronald Reagan in 1980, federal enforcement has been in the hands of officials who openly oppose the programs enacted in the 1970s. The burden of protecting black civil rights has fallen on the courts, but almost all new appointments to the federal judiciary since 1980 have been extremely conservative white males known for their lack of sympathy for civil rights initiatives.

In addition, a new generation of Americans has grown up with little knowledge of the world before 1965. Both black and white youth show a general ignorance of recent history, and older people may have become bored with the subject. When the limited gains of the civil rights movement brought blacks into direct competition with whites for jobs and homes, especially in a period of high unemployment, antiblack feeling has resurfaced across the country.

The Future. Without a unified national leadership, lacking the commitment of the federal government, and about to lose support in the federal courts, the Civil Rights Movement today is facing its greatest challenge since the 1930s. In addition, public opinion has also shifted sharply, with most Americans today believing that blacks have only themselves to blame for not taking advantage of the equal opportunity to succeed.

Where do civil rights leaders go from here? One direction—increasingly urged by critics of the current leadership—is to stop relying on outside forces and to attempt to rebuild the community structures that gave birth to the movement in the 1950s, namely the church and neighborhood organizations. (See vignette, Chapter 15.) Another direction is to strengthen and consolidate black political influence—through voter registration drives and running candidates for state and national office.

THE ANTIFEMINIST COUNTERMOVEMENT

The contemporary social movement with the greatest potential for changing every aspect of the social system is the New Feminist Movement (Ferree and Hess 1985, Katzenstein and Mueller 1987). It is not surprising, therefore, that it has also produced a very powerful backlash movement. The resource mobilization perspective warns us, however, that widespread fear of change is not sufficient to create a social movement: such feelings have to be given an ideological framework; funds must be raised; potential participants identified; and an organizational structure established.

These conditions have been brilliantly met by the architects of the antifeminist movement. If we look at the two central crusades of the contemporary Women's Movement—passage of an Equal Rights Amendment (ERA) and securing reproductive choice—opponents of women's rights have roundly defeated the former and are progressively restricting the latter, even though public opinion polls show widespread support for both. The crucial difference is that the minority who oppose the ERA and legalized abortion feel more strongly and are more willing to devote time and energy to their cause than are the majority who favor such rights in the abstract. This is so, in part, because it is easier to convince people that they have something to lose from change than to show how they could gain (Conover and Gray 1983, Mansbridge 1986). The potential gains are imaginary while the perceived losses are real.

Who Joins? Women who oppose feminism, when compared to supporters, are more likely to be married, involved in church activities, not in the labor force, to have large families, to come from rural backgrounds, and not to have completed college (Mueller and Dimieri 1982, Burris 1983, Brown 1984, Luker 1984, Scott 1985).

These are clearly women whose security—economic and emotional—is rooted in traditional roles and who realistically have much to fear from changes that they feel could release their husbands from the obligation to protect and support them (Spitze and Huber 1982).

Contrary to some theoretical expectations, therefore, women who actually join antifeminist groups are not isolated or alienated; to the contrary, as noted above, they are deeply embedded in primary relationships centered on home and church. Many may also be attracted to the countermovement out of "status discontent" or "status anxiety," as they perceive a loss of social class advantages to which they feel entitled. Status and class concerns have fueled today's countermovement activists in much the same way as in the earlier, less successful antisuffrage movement (Marshal 1986). According to Wood and Hughes (1984), the motivation of countermovement participants can be adequately explained by their cultural environment and socialization experiences as indexed by age, sex, place of residence, and religious affiliation.

In addition to differences in social background characteristics, a number of recent studies have explored the worldviews of both supporters and opponents of the ERA and reproductive rights (e.g., Falik 1983, Brown 1984, Luker 1984, Smith and Klugel 1984, Scott 1985). Not surprisingly, antifeminist views are part of a cluster of values and attitudes that emphasize conformity and self-control, obedience to authority, extreme gender differences, strong religious commitment, and intolerance of ambiguity. As the worldview of feminists is diametrically opposed, the two groups have difficulty finding a common language, which makes conversation, much less compromise, virtually impossible (Luker 1984).

Mobilization Dilemmas. How can one organize women to oppose a women's rights movement; or convince homemakers that they should become active in the public sphere, as well as secure sufficient resources to challenge what appeared to be a powerful and broad-based social movement? According to Marshall (1985), these three "mobilization dilemmas" were solved largely through the genius of Phyllis Schlafly, the charismatic leader of STOP-ERA.

In the ERA period, profeminist mobilization, such as this demonstration, was more common. The success of the Antifeminist Movement in blocking ERA has convinced some people that they will lose rather than gain as a result of change. (© Bettye Lane/ Photo Researchers, Inc.)

The first dilemma involves the manipulation of meaning. To avoid being perceived as "anti" women, the countermovement had to define its positions as "pro" something of extreme importance to women; namely, the family. By calling themselves profamily, opponents of ERA immediately imply that feminists are "antifamily" and maybe not really women at all, but nonsexual, antisexual, or possibly, homosexual.

Schlafly also organized a network of local chapters of an organization called the Eagle Forum. Members receive a newsletter and information packets to use in taking stands on a broad range of "moral" issues in their communities. Eagle Forum chapters were a key element in the crushing defeat of several state-level Equal Rights Amendments in the 1970s, including such "liberal" states as New York and New Jersey, where public opinion polls showed overwhelming support for an ERA just weeks before the election. The Eagle Forum was able to mobilize its members and sway voters at the last moment with this information distribution effort.

Schlafly's most important strategic move, however, was to link the Eagle Forum and STOP-ERA to the many other organizations—religious, political, and economic—that became known as the New Christian Right (see Chapter 15). This coalition included conservative orga-

nizations with broad-based agendas as well as a number of special interest groups not specifically concerned with feminist issues—e.g., activists *against* gun control, disarmament, taxes, unions, the welfare system, and "giving away" the Panama Canal, and *for* nuclear power, prayer in the schools, and a strong military. The masterstroke came when the anti-ERA "profamily" coalition joined forces with the antiabortion "prolife" movement, even though many antiabortion activists do not support the rest of the New Right agenda (Petchesky 1981). In a triumph of resource mobilization, STOP-ERA could draw upon a vast array of potential supporters, establish a strong funding base, and achieve legitimacy as part of the political groundswell that brought Ronald Reagan to the White House.

The Future. In general, it is difficult for either a social movement or countermovement to maintain the commitment of activists over long periods of time. New rallying goals must be found, and both feminists and antifeminists have a long shopping list of causes. Long-term trends that favor antifeminists are the aging of our population, the spread of religious fundamentalism, the proportional increase of Catholics in the population, the revival of militaristic nationalism, fears about the effects of declining birth rates, and lessen-

TABLE 21-2 Support for efforts to strengthen women's status: 1970 and 1985, in percents

	1970		1985	
	Favor	Oppose	Favor	Oppose
Total Women	40%	42%	73%	17%
Marital Status				
Single	53	33	84	8
Married	38	45	70	19
Divorced/Separated	61	27	84	11
Widowed	36	41	61	24
Race				
White	37	46	72	18
Black	60	20	78	11
Age				
18–29	46	39	80	12
30–39	40	44	76	16
40–49	39	43	76	16
50 and over	35	45	64	22
Education				
Less than High School	36	38	63	21
High School Graduate	38	45	72	17
College	44	40	79	14

SOURCE: *The 1985 Virginia Slims American Women's Opinion Poll,* Conducted by the Roper Organization, Inc., University of Connecticut, Storrs, CT., 1985, pp. 16–17.

ing of male support for efforts to improve women's status. But there are also secular trends that favor feminism: higher levels of educational attainment for women, continued high rates of labor-force participation, and, despite media claims that the movement is dead, widespread public support for movement goals. A 1986 Gallup Poll, for example, found that 56 percent of female respondents considered themselves to be feminist (59 percent of women who worked outside the home, 48 percent of full-time homemakers, and 64 percent of nonwhite women). A full 71 percent felt that the Women's Movement has done "fairly well" or "very well" in improving their lives (Gallup 1986).

Further, as seen in Table 21-2, the younger the adult age group, the higher the support for efforts to change and strengthen women's status in our society. Perhaps when members of this "silent majority" begin to feel that some of the rights they have taken for granted are being threatened by the countermovement, they, too, will be available for mobilization. However, women who both maintain households and work outside the home do not have much energy or time for social movement participation.

Summary

A range of activities, from crazes and fads to organized efforts at basic change, falls under the label of collective behavior. Such events can be classified in terms of duration, goals, tactics, and structure. Hysteria, panics, and rumors are at the short-lived, more spontaneous end of the continuum, while crowds—temporary gatherings of people engaged in a common activity—are more structured but have emergent qualities and are, therefore, capable of transformation.

Several theoretical perspectives have been used to explain collective behavior. Many of the early models centered on social-psychological processes and individual motivations. Most recently, the resource mobilization perspective has dominated the field, with its emphases on organizational variables and rationality.

Social movements are organized efforts to bring about change, whether simple reform of existing institutions or a revolutionary overhaul of the entire system. Social movements typically develop through four phases: (1) an early period of general unrest and personal discontent; (2) crystallization of concern and building of networks; (3) emergence of organizations to promote change; (4) adoption of move- ment goals in whole or part, or collapse of the movement.

Resistance to change is often channelled into countermovements with similar problems of resource mobilization. The interplay between movement and countermovement creates a dynamic dialectic that can be illustrated in the case of two contemporary examples of collective activism: the Civil Rights Movement and the antifeminist countermovement.

Suggested Readings

APTER, DAVID E., and NAGAYO SAWA. *Against the State: Politics and Social Protest in Japan.* Cambridge, Mass.: Harvard University Press, 1984. A rich and detailed account of the resistance of local farmers and radical students against the building of a new international airport.

BARNES, DONNA K. *Farmers in Rebellion: The Rise and Fall of the Southern Farmers' Alliance and People's Party in Texas.* Austin: University of Texas Press, 1984. An historical account of the organization of poor farmers against the Texas agricultural system in the 1880s.

BLUMBERG, RHODA LOIS. *Civil Rights: The 1960's Freedom Struggle.* Boston: Twayne, 1984. A well-written introduction to the Civil Rights Movement which deals with the sit-ins, freedom rides, and voter registration drives as well as the urban riots and rise of the Black Power Movement.

EXOM, WILLIAM H. *Paradoxes of Protest: Black Student Activism in a White University.* Philadelphia: Temple University Press, 1985. An interesting case study of the Black Student Movement and its efforts to address feelings of isolation and alienation within a white institution.

FERREE, MYRA MARX, and BETH B. HESS. *Controversy and Coalition: The New Feminist Movement.* Boston: Twayne, 1985. A very readable, comprehensive new analysis of the American feminist movement from the 1960s to the present.

FISHER, ROBERT. *Let the People Decide: Neighborhood Organizing in America.* Boston: Twayne, 1984. An historical overview of neigh- borhood organizing in the United States between 1880 and 1980 around three main areas: social work, political activism, and neighborhood maintenance.

FREEMAN, JO, ed. *Social Movements of the 60's and the 70's.* New York: Longman, 1983. A useful collection of articles which examine the rise and decline of some of the social movements of that era.

NYDEN, PHILIP W. *Steelworkers Rank and File: The Political Economy of a Union Reform Movement.* New York: Praeger, 1984. A fascinating study of rank-and-file insurgency since the end of World War II and the ways in which the members rebelled against the union leadership to gain a voice in the union.

PIVEN, FRANCES FOX, and RICHARD A. CLOWARD. *Poor People's Movements: Why They Succeed, How They Fail.* New York: Vintage, 1979. An insightful examination of the successes and failures of four protest movements: those of unemployed workers, industrial workers, and the civil rights and welfare rights movements.

SMELSER, NEIL J. *Theory of Collective Behavior.* New York: Free Press, 1963. This is a sociological classic, presenting a systematic, step-by-step model of collective behavior and social-movement development. This volume is an important starting point for any theory of social protest.

TILLY, CHARLES. *From Mobilization to Revolution.* Reading, Mass.: Addison-Wesley, 1978. A well-written analysis of collective action, social conflict and revolution over the past five centuries.

22

Modernization, Technology, and Social Change

F OR many generations, a hunting-and-gathering tribe called the Teuso lived in the mountains of east-central Africa. Nomadic bands of Teuso tracked big game in a cycle that led them past food-gathering and watering sites and back to their main grounds. The Teuso were careful never to take more from the land than necessary, so that there would be enough animals and plants for the following year. The Teuso were careful to maintain a balance between population and resources and were well adapted to their geographic and physical environment. Moreover, when first visited by anthropologist Colin Turnbull, the Teuso were an open and friendly people. Their society, like most hunting-and-gathering cultures, was characterized by a high

level of cooperation and informal, open social relationships. Few distinctions were made on the basis of wealth, power, or sex. Women made important contributions to economic security and were recognized accordingly.

The peaceful and open society of the Teuso was drastically changed after World War II, when new countries were formed in central Africa. The leaders of these emerging nations sought to unify the vastly different cultural, social, and linguistic tribal societies within their new geographic boundaries. As part of this process, the Teuso, now called the Ik, found that the newly established government had turned their traditional hunting grounds into a national park. Although hunting in these lands had been at the center of their way of life, the Ik were forbidden by law to pursue the game that had once been their source of food. Instead, government officials attempted to change the Ik into farmers who would stay in one place, rather than living as migratory hunters and gatherers. The land allocated for Ik farming was a rocky area with little rainfall. Because the tribe had no tradition or technology suitable for farming, disaster was certain.

Indeed, when Turnbull revisited the tribe in the 1960s, he found that the Ik had become an unfriendly, uncharitable, inhospitable, and generally mean people (Turnbull 1972). All ties of affection and pity had disappeared. Threatened with starvation, each member of the society acted in terms of immediate self-interest, even grabbing bits of food from a child or an ill person.

What had happened? Major changes in the mode of subsistence among the Ik had affected every other aspect of life, *including personality*. The rapid changes forced on the Ik disrupted the culture and the social structure that they had developed to cope with their environment.

Yet, even if all the members of a society were to resist any change from within and insist that everything be done as it always had been done, there would still be forces beyond their control that would produce change. Climate changes can alter the mode of subsistence. Famine and disease reduce the population. Wars and invasions destroy social structures. Contact with other societies introduces new and different cultural traits. No culture, not even that of simple societies, is exactly the same today as it was five hundred or even five years ago. *Social change* is the process through which values, norms, institutions, social relationships, and stratification systems alter over time. This chapter describes the causes and effects of social change at both the macrolevel of culture and social structure and the microlevel of personality. The Ik are only one example of a society and its people undergoing social change.

Social change is the process through which values, norms, institutions, stratification systems, and social relationships alter over time.

Sources of Change

Social change comes about through processes and events that are either internal or external to a society. Some common ways in which such changes occur include (1) environmental events, (2) invasion, (3) cultural contact, (4) innovation, and (5) population shifts.

Environmental changes include both (1) natural events, such as earthquakes, disease, and climate shifts, and (2) situations produced by people, such as pollution, overuse and overkill of natural resources, and wars. Any one of these environmental factors could produce changes in the economic base and social ties of a group. When a flood occurred in Buffalo Creek, as you recall from Chapter 4, not only were homes destroyed but the entire social structure of the community was altered (Erikson 1976).

Invasion of one group's territory by other tribes, colonial powers, or economic interests is another major source of social change, and may require adaptation to new customs and beliefs, or result in geographic relocation of a group, with

Environmental changes include both natural and socially produced events.

Invasion occurs when one group or nation's territory is overrun and controlled by another.

In 1945, after the defeat of the Axis powers, the Japanese began to have extensive contact with American culture through the presence of GIs (seen here looking at the Japanese parliament building in Tokyo). Over 40 years later, it's difficult to say which culture has been affected to a greater extent by this contact. (© Reuters/Bettmann Newsphotos)

Social Change: A Fictional Film Account

A recent film, *The Gods Must be Crazy*, described the social change that can result in a society from the introduction of a single item from the outside world. While flying over a remote portion of the Kalahari desert in South Africa, a pilot in a light plane finished the bottle of soda he was drinking and threw it out the window. It fell to the ground in an area inhabited by !Kung Bushmen, a nomadic group of people with virtually no possessions or sense of private property (see Chapter 3). No one in this small, remote society had seen a soda bottle before and, because it came from the sky, they believed that it must be a unique gift from the gods. When the bottle was first found, it was a novelty, and people of all ages enjoyed admiring it, playing with it, and speculating about its purpose. It was not very long, however, before arguments and conflict arose among group members about who would possess the bottle and for what purpose. The harmony of this hitherto peaceful society was disturbed by the introduction of a new item of technology. As in the case of the Ik, ties of affection were broken, and communal sharing disrupted.

To recapture the social stability that existed prior to the introduction of this new item, one of the !Kung men took the bottle and tried to give it back to the gods from which it was believed to have come. Thus began a long journey, in which this lone individual made contact with other societies, was confused by their norms and values, and enraged by other people's inability to understand why introduction of this item of technology had altered the basic culture and social structure of his tribe.

This film, while a fictional and humorous account of the effects of diffusion, provides a poignant illustration of culture contact and social change.

Culture contact with people from other societies, in which one group learns how the other has coped with the tasks of survival, is a frequent source of change. For example, through everyday activities, one tribe may accidentally meet another, or contact will be deliberately made for the purpose of trade or exchanging marriage partners. Culture contact can also be imposed by explorers or invading armies, a significant factor throughout history.

Innovation—something new—is used to describe both discovery and invention, for the two processes are often interrelated. A discovery involves the awareness of some aspect of nature that already exists but had not been recognized before, such as the laws of relativity, the infection theory of disease, or Jupiter's moons. Inventions involve the combination of existing parts of culture in a new way, such as in the design of a personal computer or the writing of electronic music.

Population shifts, or changes in the size and composition of the population, are another source of change. The size of different age groups and the sex composition of a population produce important social change. For example, in Chapter 18 you read about the effects of the large Baby Boom generation on every institutional sphere across the life course: from crowded classrooms to clogged avenues of upward mobility, and their eventual strain on the pension and social security system in old age.

Perhaps *diffusion* is the most important process of change. Diffusion describes the process by which new ideas, actions, technology, beliefs, and other items of culture spread from person to person, group to group, and society to society. A few vital innovations in culture were probably necessary for survival of the species. Fire, the wheel, animal traps, and ways of keeping track of the seasons, for example, have been discovered in only one or two places and then diffused by culture contact throughout the inhabited world. A common example of diffusion today is that of consumer goods. Coca-Cola, hamburgers—even MacDonald's and Burger King—are often the first cultural items from the United States to which non-Americans are introduced, and their American names entered directly into the language of these nations. Similarly, most Americans have their first contact with Japanese culture when they buy an automobile or a stereo,

Culture contact involves learning from people from other societies.

Innovation refers to both the discovery and invention of something new.

Population shifts are changes in the size and composition of the population.

Diffusion describes the process by which new ideas, actions, technology, and beliefs of a culture spread from one person, group, or society to another.

changes in the mode of subsistence. For example, when European settlers colonized South Africa, they not only displaced the native residents but altered their economies and created a stratification system based on color. Historically and culturally distinct tribes were essentially homogenized by the white colonists as "blacks" serving the economic interests of whites. As a consequence, many native Africans have been ghettoized. Similar experiences have faced native populations in South America and Southeast Asia.

What does the Soviet Union and the United States have in common? Until recently, few would have answered "heavy metal," but this group of Soviet "metallist" in Moscow attest to the diffusion of our popular culture throughout the world. (© Ricki Rosen/ Picture Group)

and their first words in Japanese may be Toyota or Toshiba.

Not all cultural items that are diffused are equally likely to be accepted, however. Technology is generally most easily diffused, for it is relatively simple to determine whether a new technique is more efficient than an old one. For example, it is not too difficult to demonstrate that a gun is more effective than a spear in hunting game. In contrast, nonmaterial items of culture, such as beliefs and values, are much less readily adopted, as the Chinese have recently discovered since their takeover of Tibet. Although monasteries have been closed or neglected, the Tibetans persist in a Buddhist rather than Marxist belief system. After all, who can quickly tell whether one set of beliefs is more effective than another?

But even enhancing a group's standard of living might not be welcome if the new technique is believed to involve radical changes in other aspects of culture. The diffusion of a new item of culture has many results, somewhat like the ripples created by throwing a stone into a pond. A major change in one institutional sphere affects all relationships among people in the group and may be fiercely resisted. People often fear both the immediate and long range impact of social change. During

the early days of the factory system, for example, new equipment was literally sabotaged by workers who threw sabots (the French word for wooden shoes) into the machinery. Although automation and the introduction of new technology in general have, in the long run, created more jobs than they have destroyed, the new jobs have not always been in the same industries. Moreover, new types of employment often fail to emerge until after a period of profound dislocation and transition. Even a relatively simple change in material culture, such as the use of a gun compared to a spear in hunting, requires dramatic changes in all the rituals surrounding the old way of hunting. In addition, shifts in power relations within the group will eventually alter its system of social stratification.

A particularly violent form of diffusion occurs when one group is conquered by a more powerful one, and traditional patterns are destroyed while innovations are forcibly imposed. The *colonization* of Asia, Africa, and South America was often accompanied not only by introduction of new technology but by efforts to convert the natives to Western morals and beliefs. In the United States, white settlers frequently destroyed Native American cultures, in many cases intentionally, as a

Colonization involves the violent conquering of the indigenous group by a more powerful invading group.

Automation Stops at the Office Door in Japan

Although Japan is known throughout the world for its use of robotics and technology, the typical Japanese office is still likely to be a smoke-filled room filled with grey metal desks overflowing with stacks of paper and files. Conspicuously absent are desk computers, cellular telephones, wall-to-wall carpeting, and office machines. For example, in the financial-district office of Hitachi Credit Corporation, one floor above the new Hitachi computer showroom, clerks use abacuses (counting beads) and enter numbers into ledgers by pencil, much as they did in 1945. Although billions have been spent in Japan to modernize factories, research labs, and engineering departments, little effort has been made to introduce technology into offices. In the United States, the ratio of office workers to desk top computers is seven to one; in Japan it is twenty-six to one. While robots build cars in Nissan Motor Company factories, office personnel produce market projections with pencil and paper, often spending weeks of overtime recalculating by hand production costs and changes in currency rates.

Why have the Japanese been hesitant in modernizing their offices when they are among the world leaders in automation? The answer lies in part in the Japanese language. Written Japanese contains thousands of ideograms (that is, symbols representing an idea rather than a word). It was not until 1979 that computers were developed that could handle these symbols. Although Japanese-language printing machines were available before then, only highly trained secretaries were able to operate them.

A second reason for the reluctance of Japanese to automate offices is mistrust. Many office workers are uneasy when confronted with a keyboard—so much so that this reaction has been nicknamed "keyboard allergy." Moreover, many office workers maintain extensive personal files, for they feel uneasy unless they have their own private copy of every document.

Still another factor is the Japanese management system. Unlike most bureaucracies in the United States, Japanese corporations encourage generalists rather than specialists within the organization. Departments make decisions based on informal consensus among members rather than upon open, formal analysis of a problem. Thus, before an idea has reached top management on paper or been stored in a computer, the decision has already been made.

This example illustrates the many ways in which cultural differences affect the diffusion of technology.

(Based on Stephen Kreider Yoder, "No Computers Need Apply," *Wall Street Journal*, June 12, 1987, 29D.)

way of reducing the power of native leaders. Other times this destruction was accidental, the result of ethnocentric beliefs that our ways were vastly superior to those of simpler societies. Nor has violent diffusion been confined to the distant past. When the U.S.S.R. invaded Afghanistan in 1980, already fragile tribal societies were further divided and modes of subsistence altered. Clearly, whether diffusion is imposed through conquest or adapted voluntarily, it is a powerful force for change.

ACCELERATION IN CHANGE

Once innovations are diffused and accepted, a group increases its cultural base; that knowledge, in turn, encourages further discoveries and inventions. The likelihood of innovation is directly related to the size of the culture base. In other words, the more culture items there are to work with, the greater the probability of recombining elements into something else. This is why the *rate of change* is higher in complex than in simple societies. Inventiveness is not related to differences in intelligence among the peoples of the world. Rather, it is associated with the accumulated knowledge of the group. This is the reason that, over the broad course of human history, social change has occurred at an increasingly accelerated pace. There is a Latin saying that "pygmies placed on the shoulders of giants see more than the giants themselves." This saying describes the innovative advantages of those living in modern societies (Merton 1967). Less developed societies sometimes enjoy advantages that allow them to overtake more developed societies at a later date. For

The **rate of change** is directly related to the size of the culture base; the greater the base, the greater the chances of further change.

example, analyses of developing nations of the Third World show dramatic differences in levels of development, income distributions, patterns of trade dependency, and demographic trends that are linked to the length of time since these nations began industrializing. And societies that shifted their mode of subsistence more recently may have higher, rather than lower, GNPs (gross national products) (Nolan and Lenski 1985).

The term *cultural lag* (Ogburn 1922) describes the tendency for parts of culture to change and adapt at different rates after the introduction of a new technology. Take the case of the introduction of the mass-produced automobile in the United States in the 1920s whose effects on other parts of American society are still being felt. The distribution of the population between city and suburb, patterns of work and leisure, and even dating behaviors, have been dramatically changed by the ability of most people to own their own cars. The physical environment has also been altered, as superhighways, drive-in theaters, and shopping malls sprawl across the land. Moreover, the full effects of pollution from fuel emissions may not be felt for many decades. Even relatively minor technological innovations, such as the de-

velopment of the VCR, have had far-reaching effects, changing not only the recreational habits of millions of Americans but creating new industries.

One model, designed to explain the various aspects of cultural lag between the introduction of a new technology and the many other adaptations that follow in every area of social life is the technology diffusion model (Coates 1983), which is shown in Figure 22-1 on page 616. As you can see, the first result of technological change is that of *adoption,* where people substitute the new, more efficient, technology for an old one. The second step is *accommodation,* in which one institutional sphere undergoes internal changes in order to make more efficient use of the new technology. In the third step, other areas of social life develop new functions and internal organizational changes in response to the technology. New institutions could also be created at this time. In stage four, an institution may become obsolete, be replaced, or change radically. Thus, the introduction of a major new element of culture leads to changes in all areas of life. Change reverberates throughout the system.

Using Figure 22-1, can you plot the many institutional transformations that

Computer technology, once used primarily for industrial ventures, is now a part of almost every facet of our lives. Here guitarist-composer Pat Metheny demonstrates the Synclavier II synthesizer. (© Jack Vartoogian)

have followed the introduction of mass-produced automobiles in the United States? Or consider the many consequences of the personal computer (pc) in millions of American households, offices, and schools.

Before the pc, large and expensive computer systems had been gradually taking over data processing functions for government, corporations, research institutions, and libraries. But the pc brought such systems within the reach of individuals, schools, and small businesses. Manual typewriters and paper files were rendered obsolete; many workers had to learn the new technology to keep their jobs, amid widespread fears of "being replaced by a machine." New industries emerged: for creating programs, instructing users, servicing the equipment, and thinking up ever more sophisticated functions for existing computer systems. Electronic mail and bulletin boards bring instantaneous communication, bypassing such traditional gatekeepers as librarians. Anyone who can learn the program and pay for computer time can have immediate access to vast information banks. Your college library is probably wired into these data banks, and many books will already have been replaced by material that is stored and retrieved electronically.

Despite its many advantages in reducing work time and expanding one's range of information, the personal computer has been resisted by many who fear its long-term effects—much like the French saboteurs of the early Industrial Revolution or their English counterparts, followers of Ned Ludd (called Luddites), who destroyed their new machinery in the hopes of saving their jobs. What do you think might be some of the long-range effects of the personal computer—on work habits, the division of labor in the home, educational systems, shopping, entertainment, or any other area of social activity?

Social Change and Modernization

GENERAL AND SPECIFIC CHANGE

The course of social change in any society depends on specific historical events. For example, the rise of the African nation-states transformed the Teuso into the Ik; a

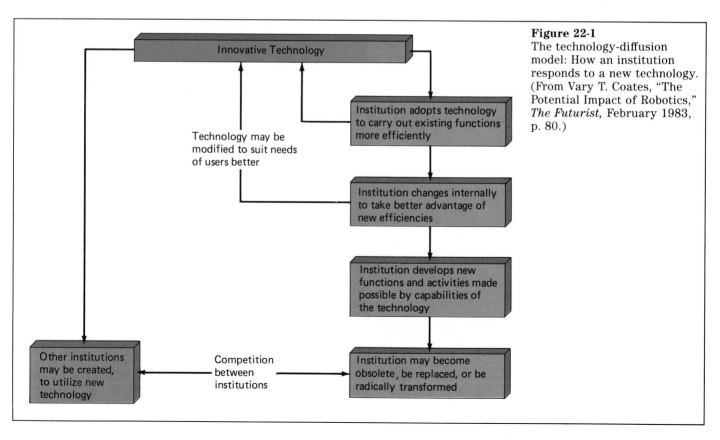

Figure 22-1
The technology-diffusion model: How an institution responds to a new technology. (From Vary T. Coates, "The Potential Impact of Robotics," *The Futurist,* February 1983, p. 80.)

Innovative Technology

Institution adopts technology to carry out existing functions more efficiently

Technology may be modified to suit needs of users better

Institution changes internally to take better advantage of new efficiencies

Institution develops new functions and activities made possible by capabilities of the technology

Other institutions may be created, to utilize new technology

Competition between institutions

Institution may become obsolete, be replaced, or be radically transformed

The traditional and modern exist together even in contemporary society. Libraries now provide information "online" via computer databases and compact disks and in the "stacks" via standard hard copy. Do you think both forms of information will continue to coexist? (© Tom Tracy/Black Star)

Cumulative social change is the gradual development from simple to more complex societies.

chance meeting with a trapper from another society forever altered the way of life for the Tasaday; and three hundred years of immigration, territorial expansion, and industrialization have reshaped the United States.

Sociologists have long sought to discover the overall direction of social change to find some basic principle or law that has operated over the many thousands of years of human history. The basic model we have used in this book assumes that there has been a *cumulative trend,* that is, a general development from simple to more complex societies, from small bands of gatherers, with their limited material culture, to the social and technological complexities of American society today. Many types of societies may exist at the same time, however. For example, China had a highly differentiated social structure when much of Europe was inhabited by small bands of hunters and gatherers. Even in the United States today, there are many different ways of life, ranging from the industrial cities and suburbs of the Northeast to the relatively simple rural farming communities of the Amish. Yet, when the history of all known societies is added together, there is a general cumulative trend. In other words, certain technologies and types of knowledge do not develop without a set of prior conditions. It would be impossible for the automobile as we know it to have been invented without

some notion of a combustion engine, or for open-heart surgery to succeed without a knowledge of sterile procedures.

Not all social institutions become more complex as societies become more intricate, however. For example, family and belief systems are more complex in simple societies than in modern ones, where both institutions have been considerably reduced in scope. When kinship ties and religious authorities no longer control everyday behavior, other social institutions develop or change to handle these tasks. In American society today, the government, the educational institutions, and the nuclear family carry out socialization and social-control tasks that once were managed by kinship networks and religious organizations (see Chapters 11, 13 and 14).

THE RISE OF THE NATION-STATE

The *nation* as a separate unit of social organization is relatively new as the major source of group identity, shared beliefs, values, and loyalty. For most societies throughout human history, nationality meant little. Rather, residential locale, kinship, and ascribed status were the bases for social cohesion. *Nationalism* is a belief shared by many people that they have something in common (such as language, history, or beliefs) powerful enough to make them seek political unity. It has become a tool welding together peoples in one geographic area only within the last four hundred years or so. Nationalism provides a sense of a "we group" with which very different individuals and subgroups may identify. It may also speed processes of economic development and social change.

Although the existence of strong, relatively stable monarchies promoted the rise of nationalism in Europe, at least two other factors favored the concept of the nation-state as a basis for political authority and self-identity: (1) *capitalism* and (2) *colonialism.* Indeed, for many countries, the growth of capitalism coincided with the emergence of nationalism. As capitalistic economies developed, there was a search for wider markets and for raw materials to be exploited, especially by England, France, Germany, the Netherlands, and Spain.

With the discovery of the New World, traders and settlers from Europe entered territories whose peoples had little sense

The **nation** is a distinct unit of social organization providing group identity, communality, and loyalty.

Nationalism is a consciousness of shared identity among the members of a politically distinct territory.

617

of national identity. Many lands, like the United States, had native populations organized into tribal, geographically isolated, and culturally and linguistically different societies. The lack of national identity among the native population of these new lands encouraged greater nationalistic feeling within those European countries that claimed and colonized other continents. More integrated forms of social organization were developed, along with patterns of mutual loyalty and dependency between the colonists and the sending nation. Thus, the stage was set for the development of a nationalism that went beyond allegiance to the local community, region, or clan.

This has not been the pattern among Third World societies, however. By 1950, four nations—the United Kingdom, the United States, Germany, and France—owned about 85 percent of all the capital invested outside of their countries (Chirot 1986). Moreover, about 86 percent of the population in Africa and 42 percent of the population in Asia were under the political rule of colonialists (Chirot 1986). In the early 1950s, however, a new wave of nationalism developed in precisely those countries dominated by European and American economic and political power only a few years before. As a new, native middle class formed in Third World nations, its members learned not only the general rules and uses of colonial nationalism, but the bitter fact that their own career aspirations were limited by it. Not surprisingly, the new nationalism was filled with non-Western content and anticolonial sentiment. For the Third World, nationalism became a liberation movement in which the common element was not language, culture, shared social institutions, or economic expansion, but anticolonialism.

By encouraging the breakup of old stratification and authority patterns, the new nationalism has stimulated diversified, independent economic growth. Yet, because of the internal variation and the old tribal loyalties of many Third World nations, nationalism has different meanings to various social classes and cultural groups within the same country. This difference has created instability in some developing nations. That is, although the established middle classes tend to favor independence without radical change, the old elites often want a return to an ideal-ized past, while intellectuals and workers press for radical social change. All of this has led to the instability of governments in Africa, Asia, and Central and South America today, quite apart from tensions between the superpowers (the U.S.A. and U.S.S.R.).

VARIATIONS IN CHANGE

Although nationalism has been a recent, powerful factor in social and cultural change, it does not determine the history of any particular society. Some societies undergo rapid social change, whereas others remain relatively untouched. Human history is a graveyard of vanishing cultures. The Tasaday may disappear for want of marriage partners; the Ik will disintegrate because of lack of social bonds; and the heirs of the warriors of the Great Plains live in poverty on reservations. Throughout the world, societies that have survived for thousands of years are faced with the prospect of adapting to new circumstances, including nationalism.

In the Near East, previously isolated herding and farming societies are in the process of rapid and sudden growth, modernization, and nationalism. Saudi Arabia

Robots range in type from the almost fantasy-like skeleton pictured here to the more common industrial robots on the assembly line. They are expected to impact on almost every facet of our lives. Have you ordered yours? (© Gregory Heisler/The Image Bank)

Will Robots Change Society?

Most people think of a robot as something from *Star Wars* or *Buck Rogers*—an android that walks, talks, sees, thinks, and looks like C3PO or R2D2. Yet most of the robots developed so far are far less exotic. They are industrial machines that can be programmed to do a number of simple, repetitive tasks usually done by human workers or to assist handicapped people in activities of daily living. Like people, robots can be moved from one job to another and can learn new tasks. Unlike people, they can work two or three shifts a day, six or seven days a week, and do not take coffee breaks, vacations, sick leave, expect to be paid, or argue with management. Nor are they affected by industrial hazards such as radioactivity, toxic wastes, or pollution.

Robots are a relatively recent phenomenon in the United States. While estimates of the number of jobs that can be filled by robots varies, some analysts have suggested that by 2005 robots will occupy somewhat over 3 million of today's industrial jobs (Coates 1983). What impact could this have on the labor force?

In 1985, 5,796 robots were shipped by seventy-two manufacturers in the United States at a total value of over $317 million. Robots are currently classified by their primary industrial function. According to the very wordy Census definition, a robot is "a reprogrammable multi-functional manipulator designed to move materials, parts, tools, or specialized devices through variable programmed motions for the performance of various tasks" (*Statistical Abstract of the United States 1987*, p. 745). Currently, robots are used primarily for welding and assembling parts. At least one company, however, has developed a robotic pet—a battery-operated cat who obeys simple commands—apparently designed for people who want a pet without being concerned about cleaning the litter box.

Because robots thus far have been designed for specialized use and are both costly and complex, some analysts have predicted that the development of robotics will create more jobs than would be lost. According to this view, new job skills and retraining of existing workers will be required as robotics expands. Other views are less optimistic. For example, at present, women and non-whites account for about 4 million semiskilled and unskilled blue-collar workers who are precisely the people most likely to be displaced by wide-spread use of industrial robots. Moreover, since women and nonwhites are less likely than white males to be represented by unions and often have less education, fewer job skills, and are less geographically mobile, they will bear the impact of industrial innovation. In addition, those states with the heaviest concentration of industries that are most likely to use robotics are Snowbelt states with already high rates of poverty and unemployment.

If the technology of the future is not accessible to the average worker, a society could arise that is made up of a busy elite of professionals and a useless majority unable to master the major tools of the society: an elite of "gods" doing the work and a majority of "clods" getting in the way. An extreme example of such a society was described by the novelist Kurt Vonnegut, in *Player Piano* where the gods are PhDs in engineering in control of an almost automated world, the clods are either in the army where they march endlessly or engaged in digging purposeless ditches and filling them once again.

Nobody knows, of course, what the full impact of robots will be, but like any other technical innovation that drastically alters the mode of subsistence, they are likely to produce widespread social change over a long period of time.

Based in part on James C. Albus, "Robots in the Workplace," *The Futurist*, February, 1983, pp. 22–27; Vary T. Coates, "The Potential Impact of Robotics," *The Futurist*, February, 1983, pp. 28–32; *Statistical Abstract of the United States 1987*, Table 1340, p. 745. See also "Factories in Space: The Role of Robots," *The Futurist*, May/June 1987, pp. 23–29, and "The Future of Personal Robots," *The Futurist*, May/June 1986, pp. 22–26.

is one example. The rate of change may be more than the existing culture can support, so that a countermovement (Islamic fundamentalism), seeking a return to traditional ways, has developed, as in Iran in the early 1980s.

Within a given culture, not all change is toward increased complexity. Some cultures emerge from prehistory to become sophisticated nation-states before undergoing a long period of decline and returning to a more simple structure. For example, ancient Egypt had a highly specialized and differentiated social structure; yet, for many centuries thereafter, it existed as an unorganized, basically agricultural territory controlled by a succession of other nations. But, as in the Egyptian case, some of these societies have experienced a rebirth as modernizing nations.

In other words, each society has its unique pattern of development: It has its own history and specific rate of change. No two societies are alike in all respects, and the probabilities of further growth are not predetermined but are subject to historical forces. In addition, technology can produce instant changes in lifestyles.

FROM THE PREINDUSTRIAL TO THE POSTINDUSTRIAL SOCIETY

What do such different countries as the Soviet Union and the United States have in common that can shed light on social change and trends in contemporary societies? Because these two countries have different languages, cultures, forms of economic organization, and political ideologies, the answer would seem to be "Very little." Yet both are examples of the modern society built on the notions of rationality and the bureaucratization of authority. Strange as it may seem, the political ideology of a nation may have little to do with modern social structure. Rather, *modernization* is a social process through which a society becomes more internally differentiated and complex, and in which science and technology guide change. As societies become modernized, they tend to converge; that is to become more alike with respect to social structures, status hierarchies, and power and authority relationships. Nonetheless each society retains its unique historical and cultural features.

Within the past thirty years, many studies have been made of the process of modernization, describing the shift from preindustrial, agricultural modes of subsistence to industrialized ones. The sociocultural change associated with modernization has two important aspects: (1) *mobilization,* in which old patterns of social, economic, and psychological commitments are weakened and people become available for socialization to new patterns; and (2) *social differentiation,* that is, a shift from diffuse to specialized roles (Eisenstadt 1966).

Modernization is linked to three other trends discussed in earlier chapters: urbanization, industrialization, and secularization. Modern societies are composed of large numbers of workers and consumers, engaged in the production and the distribution of specialized goods and services and guided by rational-legal norms. Max Weber used the term *rationality* to refer to a type of social action in which the traditional and emotional bases for behavior are replaced by belief in a logical relationship between means and ends. Typical of industrialized societies, this highly practical view stresses the introduction of predictable and systematic procedures, the backbone of which is a cause-effect model. Rationality has led to new technologies in the economic system, including the replacement of physical labor by machines. Rationality as a basis for political and economic authority, according to Weber, paved the way for the rapid social change that characterizes modern societies.

Yet, legal-rational power is a relatively new idea, whose development parallels the rise of European industrial society and of the nation state. To understand how the sociocultural changes associated with modernization occur, recall some of the contrasts between *preindustrial* and *industrial* societies. Preindustrial societies have economies based on primary production (gathering, hunting, herding, and farming). Industrial societies have an economic and social organization based on machine technology and large-scale systems of production. The development of capitalist economies in the sixteenth century, coupled with technological, cultural, and political systems that encouraged profit, gave some countries great advantages in economic development.

Investment and risk taking spread Western financial power throughout the world. As a result, a few industrialized nations dominate the rest of the world economically and politically. These dominant Western nations are now beginning to enter a new phase of economic development.

POSTINDUSTRIALIZATION

How do postindustrial nations differ from others? Essentially, they are an extension of trends found in industrial nations but with different emphases. In postindustrial societies, science and technology are emphasized more heavily than manufacturing and productive capacity (Bell 1973). Thus, while the index of steel production is a commonly used method to assess the rates of economic growth in an industrial

Modernization is a process through which a society becomes more internally differentiated and complex, and in which science and technology guide change.

Mobilization involves the weakening of previous patterns of social, economic, and psychological commitments making people receptive for socialization to new patterns.

Social differentiation involves a shift from diffuse to specialized roles.

Rationality replaces traditional and emotional bases for behavior with the belief in a logical connection between means and ends.

Alternatives to Bureaucratic Management

How do size, technology, and division of labor affect power over an organization's process and product? How satisfied are workers with bureaucratic life? Can democratic organizational forms survive economically and socially? Numerous organizations throughout the United States and elsewhere have been concerned with these questions. As a response to the growing bureaucratization of work, attempts have been made to develop more participatory work organizations.

For example, thousands of grass-roots worker cooperatives and collectives have been created in the United States in recent years. These grass-roots organizations are radically different from the bureaucratic model described by Weber; that is, they have replaced authority based on status incumbency with consensual, democratic authority that belongs to the workers as a whole. In addition, as described in Chapter 12, two attempts to create more extensive democratic workplaces are: (1) quality-of-work life projects within large corporations, and (2) employee involvement in ownership (ESOPs).

The results of these experiments have been mixed. For example, the majority of studies on alternatives to bureaucracy have indicated that size, technology, and division of labor are important factors. In large organizations where skills and responsibilities cannot easily be shared, the bureaucratic structure described by Weber is likely to persist or be recreated. Development of work teams, committees, and rotation of personnel into and out of various leadership positions can, however, increase broader work participation and feelings of satisfaction among workers. Nor are the effects of worker-owned businesses or worker participation in decision-making on economic or social survival of an enterprise clear. Studies designed either to prove or disprove the merits of the economic performance of alternative organizations have often been poorly designed.

Can alternatives to the bureaucracy succeed? The idea that democracy in the workplace inevitably reverts to "the iron law of oligarchy" (see Chapter 13) is not new. Nevertheless, reversion to oligarchy is not inevitable. Much depends upon the specific organization. New forms of work organization are constantly being developed. The form an alternative organization takes, who benefits, and whether or not it will survive as an economically profitable and socially stable entity depends upon which groups are involved and remain involved in their development over time.

(Based on Joyce Rothschild and Raymond Russell, "Alternatives to Bureaucracy: Democratic Participation in the Economy," *Annual Review of Sociology*, 12, 1986, pp. 307–328.)

---

nation, the percentage of scientific and technical workers in the labor force and the amount of funds spent on research and development are more meaningful descriptions of change to a postindustrial one. If industrial society may be defined by the quantity of goods produced, postindustrial society is defined by its capacity to handle and transmit information.

The changes in every institutional sphere that would result from the movement toward an "information society" could amount to a "quiet revolution," affecting every aspect of our lives. The driving force behind *postindustrial society* is the rapid development of information technology. Accordingly, a premium is placed on knowledge, technical skill, and managerial abilities as bases of power. For example, the acquisition of capital is no longer as important as in industrial society. Nor is ascribed status necessary for access to power or wealth. Instead, education and skill provide ready routes to wealth, power, and prestige (although ascribed status and informal social networks based on stratification remain important factors).

The major problem for postindustrial societies is not economic growth but efficient organization and codification of knowledge. There are many observable results of this concern with knowledge and technical skill. Although there is a new technical elite, this elite is at present largely dependent on industrial and government support and subsidy. This, in turn, has created problems in management: Who owns science and technology and the scientists? While the knowledge of scientists is vital to a rapidly changing postindustrial society, their authority and power remain vaguely defined. Moreover, as Max Weber predicted, large formalized bureaucracies control an increasing share of economic assets and public decisions.

The key element in **postindustrial society** is the rapid development of information technology, placing a premium on knowledge, technical skills, and managerial abilities.

And, although the power and importance of science and technology have risen, so has the power of the bureaucrat. Science and technology are objects of management—not always to the satisfaction of scientists or the general public.

Risks in Postindustrial Technology

As technology increases, so do the risks associated with its use. No matter how hard we try to make technology safe, there will always be accidents. Even the simplest equipment or product can be accidentally misused or have unanticipated consequences. Accidents may be large or

Developments in biotechnology often outpace discussion of their social ramification or possible ethical considerations. Herbicide-resistant plants, such as the tobacco plants here, may be a positive innovation. But could there be drawbacks? (© Fred Ward/Black Star)

small, ranging from cutting one's finger on a kitchen knife to exposure to radiation or side effects from a drug. To what extent are some types of accidents more likely to occur than others? And how could they be prevented?

Perrow (1984, 1986) has argued that most of our current technological systems with catastrophic potential also have a high potential for accidents. Focusing on internal organizational characteristics as well as those of the industrial system itself, Perrow (1986) identified four characteristics of the internal system of an organization affecting safety behavior: (1) its rate of growth (gradual or rapid); (2) length of experience with the technology needed to understand its hazards; (3) centralized or decentralized organizational structure; and (4) ability of the organization to conduct crisis training and drills. Industry characteristics, such as the amount of information in the unit, how it is shared, separation of supervision and sponsorship, and independent inspection also affect safety.

For example, industrial and medical *biotechnology* (e.g., genetic engineering) has several system characteristics that increase the likelihood of accidents. First, biotechnology has increased rapidly with little past experience to draw on. Trials cannot be gradual. In some cases either new forms of life are released or they are not. Competition among laboratories is keen. Regulation or inspection by outside agencies is minimal or nonexistent and, at best, confused. Information flow is often restricted because of the desire to make a profit and to put out a product before the competition. Moreover, there are few strong groups outside the industry advocating safety regulation (Perrow 1986).

Once an accident occurs, how is the catastrophe handled? Very badly, it seems. Accidents that have already occurred in our chemical industry, the space program, and nuclear-power facilities suggest that the built-in risks of technological systems have been underestimated, concealed whenever possible, or initially explained as errors of human operators, rather than as system failures. In addition, several independent investigations have disclosed a pattern of mismanagement associated with risk taking, as well as a history of prior near-catastrophes. When such mistakes are uncovered, formal penalties are usually mild, and any changes that are introduced are relatively minor and do not prevent future occurrences (Perrow 1986). The nuclear accident at Chernobyl in the Soviet Union in 1986 is one example. The threat of nuclear-power disaster is not new. Some years ago, a Nobel Prize-winning physicist, Hans Bethe, stated that a nuclear meltdown was impossible in a plant about to be opened in Detroit. Yet that is exactly what happened, threatening the entire city. And in 1979, although the danger of zirconium-water reactions in nuclear-power plants was discussed, scientists again said there was no danger. This is, however, precisely what caused the nuclear meltdown at Three Mile Island and the explosion at Chernobyl. The point here is that nuclear-power plants, like many other significant new technologies, are indeed "risky business" (Perrow 1986). The full extent of risk may be unknown precisely because the technology is new and investment in its development is substantial.

Risk taking is inherent in the development of new technologies. But many managers may have lost contact with the technologies they are supposed to be managing. For example, compared to the rest of the postindustrial world, American managers are less likely to have a technical background than those in Europe or Japan, while engineers and scientists may believe so strongly in untried technologies that they plunge ahead without assessing the nontechnological consequences (Thurow 1987). Moreover, some technologies turn out to be failures for a variety of reasons. In the recent past, for example, there has been great excitement about solar energy, gasahol, electric cars, picture telephones, and computer shopping for routine household goods. All these technologies promised to alter various aspects of our daily lives. So far none has lived up to its initial promise.

How can the balance between innovative technology and its potential risks be reduced? Anything is liable to failure: designs, products, operators, training, even the environment. Blind faith in technological "fail-safe controls" is a delusion (Hirshhorn 1984). When emergencies occur, as they inevitably will, and automatic controls malfunction as they did at Chernobyl and in the NASA space shuttle *Challenger* accident, human intervention is needed. To avoid the potential for death and destruction, responsible decision mak-

When emergencies occur and "fail-safe systems" malfunction, human intervention is needed. In the case of the Chernobyl nuclear power plant, the chief administrators of the plant were negligent in their responses to the emergency and, as their subsequent trial revealed, were in fact performing unauthorized experiments without adequate safeguards at the plant. More than 100,000 Soviet citizens were dangerously exposed to radiation and a number of the firemen who entered the contaminated plant have already died. (© Robert Gale/SYGMA)

ing in both the public and private sector, and constant vigilance are required. Prompt, correct, and decisive human intervention is needed to prevent catastrophe. Breadth of knowledge, diagnostic ability, team cooperation, and ability to intervene quickly are human traits that cannot yet be equaled by systems controlled primarily by computer programs or "fail-safe" systems (Hirshhorn 1984). Without this human intervention, unanticipated and catastrophic social change will continue to occur as a side-effect of technological innovation.

The Self and Social Change

What happens to the self when social change occurs? Among the Ik described at the beginning of this chapter, changes in the mode of subsistence were also associated with drastic changes in personality and sense of self. From warm, open people, the Teuso turned into the hostile and cruel Ik. They provide a vivid example of the fact that the self is always a product of a particular type of social structure. Change in a society thus not only consists of structural, economic, and cultural shifts but also involves psychological changes. Our very selves and our positions in the social structure are mutually reinforcing. For example, from a conflict perspective, the mode of production shapes the self. The alienation that results from a worker's relationship to the modes of production under industrialism is part of his or her very being, so that people in supervised work have different personality profiles than those in more self-directed jobs.

As described in Chapter 5, much of the self is molded by the actions and the reactions of others toward us. The variety—and sometimes the unpredictability—of others' reactions to us is far greater in modern, urban societies than in the relative stability of isolated simple societies or even in villages or farms within a modern society. Complex societies also provide a greater range of roles than are available in tradition-based or developing nations. This can be a mixed blessing. On the one hand, shifts from traditional primary relationships (*Gemeinschaft*) to relationships based on rational self-interest (*Gesellschaft*) permit us more personal freedom and allow us to live in a variety of social worlds. On the other hand, the range of choices in a complex society requires that each of us must constantly read, process, and select among the cues given us by others to an extent not required in simpler societies.

Modern, urban societies, according to sociologist Georg Simmel (1950), promote a different kind of consciousness, a "blasé attitude" or indifference to many of the people and the events around us. This indifference is a type of survival mechanism, developed to screen out the constant stimulation of other people, sights, smells, noises, and activities that are part of modern life. There are also "side effects" to the rational-legal power that dominates modern, urban society. As Weber noted, rationality involves mathematical measurement of the performances of each worker. In the process of rational calculation, each worker becomes a little cog in a big machine, preoccupied with how to become a bigger, more important cog. What then becomes of the individual?

The effect of social structure on personality has been described in a classic study by David Riesman (1950). Contrasting three different ideal types, each associated with a particular level of industrial development, Riesman identified the *tradition-directed* person, whose behavior is governed by customs; the *inner-directed* person, whose behavior is governed by an internal gyroscope and who is the prototype of the capitalist or the worker in industrial society; and the *other-directed* person, who is equipped with a psychological radar which scans the environment for appropriate messages to guide behavior. The other-directed person, suggested Riesman, is characteristic of postindustrial society. Constantly anticipating new roles and aware of the need to adapt swiftly, the other-directed person differs from the other two types in being less certain of how to behave under all, or even most, circumstances. He or she is constantly reacting and adapting to others.

The reactive-adaptive (other-directed) self is a mixed blessing. The ability to adapt ourselves to a variety of situations allows us to anticipate and prepare for changing roles. Yet, it may also result in anxiety and a crisis of the self. The self is constantly being constructed and reconstructed to fit varying statuses and roles; who and what one is is not readily identifiable. Consumer goods become commodities that establish status, part of what Goffman has called one's "identity kit" or "I am what I wear and use."

In sum, personality is mobilized as a resource in modern society, and the self is rationalized. Success, achievement, conscious control, and self-improvement are primary goals. The self, as the "me" orientation that dominated the United States in the 1970s illustrates, becomes treasured above all else as an object to be used to achieve desired ends.

The **tradition-directed person**'s behavior is governed by custom.

The **inner-directed person**'s behavior is governed by an internal mechanism typical of industrial society.

The **other-directed person,** typical of the postindustrial society, constantly reacts and adapts to the expectations of others.

Accepting Change

As we have noted, not all change is immediately accepted, nor are diffused traits, however superior they may appear to be,

Dress, clothing, and body adornments are used both to convey status and other aspects of identity. If you are what you wear, what are you in this clothing? (© Jim Wilson/Woodfin Camp and Associates)

People with a **vested interest** in the status quo benefit from existing arrangements.

universally welcomed. The new item must be compatible with the existing culture of the receiving society. Innovations must be seen as meeting a need or as conferring a benefit that outweighs the cost of changing behavior. Moreover, in any society, there are people with a *vested interest* in maintaining the status quo, that is, who derive power, prestige, or wealth from the existing arrangements, and who typically are people with great influence in the group. No African witch doctor could have resisted medical missionaries any more thoroughly than members of the American Medical Association fought against Medicare for the elderly between 1945 and 1965. Or one might ask why it took so long for automobiles produced in the United States to be equipped with emission-control devices and why the American automobile industry lagged so far behind other nations in producing compact, more fuel-efficient vehicles. And why does the auto industry continue to resist the use of automatically inflatable air bags that would save thousands of lives each year? In other words, what vested interests are preserved in resisting change?

Change is promoted or resisted by people who occupy statuses in social systems.

Some statuses are more influential than others, so that the people who occupy them are more likely to be *agents of change.* If the tribal chief or shaman (wise person) adopts an innovation, others in the tribe are likely to follow. In any society, there are *trend setters* and *gatekeepers* who can influence the direction of charge.

Although in modern societies the media play a significant part in the introduction of new items, formal and informal interpersonal channels of communication remain as important for Americans as for Australian aborigines. *Social networks* carry the message from one person to another. In an early study of the diffusion of innovation in medicine, Coleman et al. (1957) found that a new drug was more readily adopted by physicians who were more profession-oriented and more integrated into a network of local physicians than by physicians who were relatively isolated from their medical peers and were patient-oriented. Both types of physicians had been exposed to information about the new drug at the same time, but the rate of prescription of the product varied by the doctor's role in her or his social and professional networks. The first to support

Agents of change occupy statuses through which they can influence the direction of change.

the drug, because of their reputations as professional leaders, gave the weight of their prestige to its use. Others followed, with the most isolated physicians being the last to adopt it.

The acceptance of specific social changes thus depends on many factors, including (1) the extent to which the new trait or idea is consistent with what already exists in the culture; (2) the felt costs of adopting the new item or giving up old ways of thinking and behaving; (3) resistance by those with a vested interest in the status quo; (4) a general fear of the long-term effects of change; and (5) the influence of events producing change.

Andy Warhol, now considered an influential artist for his "pop art" productions, was once thought to be the heretic of the art world—scorned and jeered by all but a small following. Now, his works of art, such as this one, are highly esteemed and worth a great deal of money. (© Albright Knox Gallery)

Indeed, not all agents of change are appreciated. Many are labeled as troublemakers or heretics and are subjected to social control and negative sanctions, including ridicule as well as imprisonment, assassination, and execution. When such forces of social control are brought into play, broad currents of change are temporarily slowed. The effectiveness of agents of change depends largely on the context in which they act rather than the importance of their ideas. For example, the idea that the earth was the center of the universe remained official church doctrine throughout the Middle Ages despite evidence from astronomers to the contrary. Those who attempted to shake this belief were dealt with harshly.

As a modern example, the Czechoslovak government, in 1987 placed five organizers of a music group, the Jazz Section, on trial. Their offenses were the introduction of non-socialist modern music, i.e., American jazz, a possible source of corruption of Czech youth, and the publication of uncensored literature, an "illegal economic activity." All five members of the group were convicted of the charges against them, although the sentences were relatively light. Perhaps ironically, Czechoslovakia was the homeland of Franz Kafka, a brilliant novelist of the absurd.

Types of Change

There are also important variations in the *pace* and the *extent* of change required by the introduction of new elements into an ongoing social system.

GRADUAL OR INCREMENTAL CHANGES

Some changes are part of a broad trend whose final impact is unknown. Alterations in social life proceed by small steps, or increments. *Gradual* or *incremental change* may long go unnoticed until a major transformation has occurred. For example, the agricultural revolution of prehistory was not a sudden, dramatic shift in the mode of subsistence but a long, gradual process affecting all institutional spheres. The same can be said of the Indus-

Gradual or **incremental change** is a long process in which one modification is followed by another.

trial Revolution, some elements of which were evolving in Europe long before the introduction of factories. The cumulative outcome, however, is a radical departure from the past. A silent revolution may be occurring today as computers grow in a sophistication and a power that will have widespread effects in the United States and elsewhere.

In general, the trends in modern society have been toward increased political participation, civil liberties and civil rights, sexual privacy, and educational attainment. But these results of incremental change are not as inevitable as was once thought. Modern industrial states can also be marked by political repression and a reduction in personal choice and freedom, as in Eastern Europe and the Soviet Union today. In the United States, long-term changes in the status of women, increased tolerance of religious and other minorities, and more family privacy appear to be firmly established, although subject to temporary setbacks. An examination of public opinion polls from 1970 to 1986 shows that we have witnessed conservative weather in a liberalizing climate. That is, within the long-term trend toward more liberal attitudes, the direction of change is sometimes reversed. Such shifts could also be the beginning of a climate change.

The movement of birth cohorts and their flow through the social system are also important sources of unplanned change, particularly in modern societies, where the social system itself undergoes rapid alterations. Thus, even if cohort characteristics did not change greatly, cohort members would be moving through a different set of structures than did those who preceded them or who will follow. In fact, the causes and the effects of changes are interactive; that is, the cohort modifies the social system and the culture, while also being influenced and shaped by the existing structures.

Another type of gradual unplanned change occurs in belief systems. The members of a society at any one historical moment see the world through the lens of a particular model of reality (Kuhn 1962). This world view organizes reality as, for example, the concept of an unchanging natural universe did in medieval thought: "This is exactly how it was at the moment of Creation," the philosophers thought. Gradually, however, bits and pieces of in-

formation accumulated that did not conform to this model, and a new view of the natural universe emerged, one that introduced the concept of evolution through natural selection. This new interpretation of reality was developed by several different observers at the same time because the evidence was so compelling. Similarly, the theory of relativity marked a major shift in world view. And some would say that still another change will occur as the idea of eternal progress that is so much a part of the Western mind gives way to a conception of the limits of social change.

REVOLUTIONARY CHANGE

Revolutionary change involves a "sudden, basic transformation of a society's political and socioeconomic (including class) structure" (Skocpol 1979, p. 5). But revolutions do not simply happen. They arise from revolutionary situations. Just what situations at which historical moments are ripe for revolution is an old question with no simple answer.

The most influential modern theory of revolution has been that of Karl Marx. As described by Skocpol (1979), Marx's theory has three main elements: First, each revolution is historically grounded in a certain type of society; therefore, there can be no general theory of revolution. Second, organized movements for social change can succeed only where a revolutionary situation exists because of irreconcilable class conflict within the society. Third, because class conflict defines the revolutionary situation, the revolution is completed only when the power of the dominant class(es) is destroyed.

Skocpol (1979) modified Marx's model in light of actual events. Modern revolutions have occurred not, as Marx had predicted, in industrial capitalist countries but in agricultural societies under pressure from outside forces. Moreover, the internal problems that make revolution possible have been political (competing power blocs) rather than economic (defined in Marxist terms as class conflict). And although the revolutionary mass has historically been composed of peasants rather than an urban working class, it has been not the oppressed workers, or even the peasants, but members of the educated elite who have assumed leadership and

Revolutionary change brings basic alterations in the political and socioeconomic structure of a society.

established the new state organizations. Finally, it is not the class system that changes as much as the political structure. These alterations in the distribution and functions of the state organization may, in turn, lead to dramatic changes in the social-class and economic systems.

From her study of the French, Russian, and Chinese revolutions, Skocpol (1979) concluded that the state structure—the political system—should be viewed as more than merely the governing arm of the economic ruling class. Further, if we are to understand modern revolutions, we must take into account the international military rivalry among the industrial states and between the industrialized and the developing nations within a capitalist world economy. That is, the specific society undergoing change is itself embedded in larger systems of interacting states.

Social Changes and World Systems. It is increasingly difficult today—and probably has been since the fifteenth century—to consider changes within any society without referring to broader trends in what Wallerstein (1974) called the "world system." The term *world system* refers to the economic and political relationships among societies, particularly between the industrial states and the less-developed nations. Modern industrial societies can be considered the economic "core" of the world system, and the less-developed nations are the "periphery," providing raw materials for the core countries and then becoming a market for their manufactured goods. This was the logic of colonialism, but in a postcolonial world, raw materials must now be paid for rather than taken, and markets must be won in competition with other exporters.

Third World countries possessing essential raw materials are now in a position of unaccustomed strength in their dealings with industrial societies. The oil-producing nations are a good example. Their monopoly over a scarce resource has permitted them to raise prices on the world market. These raised prices have led to a heavy outflow of money from the core nations, as well as to major changes in lifestyles and industrial growth within both the core and the oil-exporting societies— changes that are politically destabilizing.

But most peripheral societies do not have a needed raw material. Most are extremely poor, overpopulated, and poli-

> The **world system** consists of the economic and political relations among industrial and less-developed nations.

tically unstable. The distribution of the world's wealth has become increasingly imbalanced. The poor nations grow poorer and the wealthy ones wealthier. This process is a major source of political instability in the underdeveloped nations of Asia, Africa, and Central America. As a result, these areas of the globe are potential trouble spots in the rivalry between the United States and the Soviet Union for world influence.

In this new analysis, revolutions need not be deliberately planned; they will eventually arise from strains in the social structure. For example, a totalitarian regime in an agricultural society could be threatened from outside and no longer be able to suppress peasant revolts. But each specific revolt will have its own history within this general pattern. Thus, revolutions in modern industrial societies would probably be very different from those of the past or from those in developing nations. The outcome, however, is likely to be the same everywhere: increased centralization of power and bureaucratization when the new order is stabilized, as well as mobilization of the masses to support the revolution. One authoritarian state is succeeded by another: Only the faces are

---

SOCIOLOGY & YOU
Work in the Year 2000

The text you've been reading identifies a number of social trends and patterns that have and will continue to have influence on many aspects of your life. Sociologists can and do make projections based on the best current data and certain assumptions about future trends. It seems fitting, therefore, that in this last chapter on social change, we look into the near future to see how it might affect your plans. In this limited space we'll focus on the future of the U.S. work force.

The structure of the labor market of any society affects the quality of life of its citizens. Knowledge of labor market trends can be used to increase our competitiveness in the world economy and to deal with long-standing domestic problems or, without appropriate action by the public and private sectors, these trends could have dramatic negative impacts on the economy, our society, and its workers. An identification and analysis of those trends is, therefore, of great personal as well as public importance.

changed. The long-term effects of the recent popular uprisings in the Philippines and South Korea remain to be seen. Will the Philippine government be able to remain democratic or will it eventually give way to dictatorships supported by the military? And will the South Korean government concede to democratic reform or will it maintain its stronghold?

Revolutionary Events, Situations, and Outcomes. Revolutionary situations are different from revolutionary outcomes. According to Tilly (1978, 1986), a *revolutionary outcome* occurs when one set of power holders is displaced by another. A *revolutionary situation* exists when (1) two or more political units claim control over the state; (2) these interests cannot be reconciled; and (3) the opposition party receives support (money, loyalty, and soldiers) from a sizable segment of the population. Such is the case in Northern Ireland today. The revolution ends when only one claimant remains. Tilly identified a range of *revolutionary events,* from a *coup,* in which one segment of the elite displaces another, to a *silent revolution,* in which a revolutionary outcome takes place with

> **A revolutionary situation** occurs when two or more political units claim control over the state, these interests cannot be reconciled, and the opposition party receives support from a sizable segment of the population.

very little overt hostility, to the *great revolution* (for example, the American or French or Russian Revolution).

As for the long-term effects of the revolutionary event, these also vary by time and place. Tilly noted that there are very few examples of moral rebirth as a result of the revolutionary experience; people soon return to their usual round of activities. Such short-term gains may even be erased over the long run (for example, women's rights in the early days of the Russian Revolution), whereas short-term setbacks are ultimately followed by broad-scale transformation (the French Revolution). The general conclusion, then, appears to be that revolutions are much more complex than Marxist theory suggests, that outcomes have positive and negative elements, and that the costs may be very high indeed.

Theories of Change

Does change take place along a single path (*unidirectional*), leading to some predestined goal, the Kingdom of Heaven, for

---

Much of the following discussion is based on W. Johnston's *Work Force 2000 Report,* a cooperative effort between the Department of Labor, Congress, unions, and business organizations. Representatives of these groups sought to identify work trends to the year 2000, in order to assure "decent jobs and a decent society for all Americans." Most of these trends have been fully discussed in preceding chapters of this book. Here are some of the projections:

- Both the population and the workplace will grow very slowly between the present and the year 2000. There could even be a shortage of workers for the first time since World War II.
- There will be both a relative and absolute decline in the number of young workers (ages sixteen to twenty-four) entering the labor market. Businesses, colleges, and the military will compete for eighteen-year-olds.
- However, the population of low-income and minority youth, historically the group with the highest unemployment rate, will increase.
- With the overall decrease of young workers, the average age of the work force will rise dramatically.

- More women will enter the work force so that by the year 2000, over 47 percent of the work force will be women, while 60 percent of working-age women will be at work.
- Immigrants will represent a major source of new citizens and workers.
- Overall, then, most of the growth in the labor force will come from women, minorities, and immigrants, who will continue to hold relatively unrewarding jobs.
- The number of single-parent and two-income families will increase, as will demands for support services such as child care, flex time, choice of benefits, and so forth.
- Greater growth in employment is expected in the South and West, with slower gains in the Midwest.
- The rapid turnover and change of ownership of industries and firms will require workers to adjust more quickly and more often, with some changing jobs five or six times during their work lives.
- Among the fastest growing occupations at the high-skill level are paralegals, computer programmers and analysts, and medical technicians.

Sociology, Social Change, & You

KATHRYN P. GRZELKOWSKI

Kathryn P. Grzelkowski (Ph.D., Indiana University) has returned to academia to teach, to write, and to develop training programs in sociological practice for students who want to work as sociologists in nonacademic settings. She is now an associate professor of sociology at the University of Maine. She continues to maintain her focus in sociological practice with memberships on the ASA Standing Committee on Sociological Practice, the Society for Applied Sociology, and the Association for Humanist Sociology.

Many of you have come to this class in introductory sociology because you had to; it is required for your major. Some of you signed up because you're curious and interested in the field of sociology; and others because it filled a slot in your schedule. You, as a class and as individuals, are therefore very diversified in your interest in, commitment to, and involvement with sociology. Taking the symbolic interactionist approach, we can guess that this course has had different meanings for each of you—that some subjects have been more relevant to you than others; that some ideas suddenly illuminated your personal relationships, or helped you understand why you and others feel dependent and depersonalized in certain environments (e.g., in school, or through discrimination), or gave you a way to interpret and explain some issues that you have found puzzling in the past. Whatever meanings this semester of sociology has carried for you, you are now nearing the end. Do you exhale a sigh of relief, say "Now that's behind me," and forget about this investment in your educational career? Or do you take something of sociology away with you to draw from and apply in the future—something from one of the many topics covered?

Throughout my career as a sociologist, I have worked toward merging sociological knowledge with active efforts for change in everyday life. After a few years of teaching, I moved into the public and private nonprofit sectors where I practiced sociology for ten years, as (1) a director of an agency advocating services for children with special needs, (2) a chief planner in a state department of mental health, mental retardation and corrections, (3) academic director of a private nonprofit, community-oriented, off-campus learning program for college students, and (4) consultant to the Public Defender's Office, Santa Barbara, Calif. During this time I made a conscious choice that I not only wanted to "put sociology to work," but that I wanted to contribute my professional expertise toward building more humanly oriented relationships within the institutions and communities in which people live.

The premise of a humanistic approach is that people can both feel that they have control and exercise that control over their own lives. Therefore, the humanist sociological approach led me to develop specific sociological rationales and action proposals for social change such as: (1) moving mental-health patients from twenty-bed wards in an institution to five-person-group homes in the community (i.e., to normal "family" units that can provide personalized support); (2) using evidence in a murder trial from the defendant's family life and community experiences in challenging the application of the death penalty; (3) working with local grass-roots organizations to consolidate their marketing power against price-setting by local home-heating-oil distributors; (4) developing community self-help organizations to decrease local dependency on large-scale, outside conglomerates for economic well-being; and (5) using a classroom format where stu-

dents take as much control as possible over their own learning, including shared decision making in the requirements for the course and the method(s) of grading.

In all of these fairly diverse areas my sociological knowledge and perspectives have also guided my analysis and insights into the way that people will respond and interact, and therefore, assisted me in implementing these approaches. For example, in the case of the price-setting problem mentioned above, we could anticipate from our studies of power relationships, that the oil distributors would tighten up their efforts to maintain fixed prices at a high-profit level, and that trying to use the courts was simply beyond the financial means of this relatively poor community. But our analysis also told us that the community had two sources of power: (1) the numbers of persons purchasing fuel (but feeling powerless as individuals), and (2) some independent companies within reasonable distance outside the community. Once many persons in the community agreed to work cooperatively and to purchase fuel through a newly established Fuel Buying Collective, it was economically possible for an outlying oil company to bid on the contract at a lower price than the coalition of local distributors. The success of this cooperative action energized the community to search for new ways of empowering its members. The next project for the Fuel Buying Collective was to find alternative heating sources e.g., solar heating, in order to lessen dependency on expensive and ever-depleting oil fuel. So from this initial action, further social change was emerging.

This semester you have read about some ways that we can organize ourselves in a society that strips people of their sense of control, freedom to choose, and even their responsibility. You have also read about social structures—community, schools, work environments, churches, among them—which we perceive as meeting our life-support needs, and yet which perpetuate inequality, conflict, and social injustices. In this chapter you have read about some of the ways that sociologists approach social change.

I, as a person who has combined sociology with many different aspects of work, would challenge you with two questions: "So what?" and

"What now?" Ask yourselves: Can sociology be useful to me in the future? How can I *use* what I have learned throughout this semester in my family, at work, in my community? How can I apply sociological perspectives to better understanding and making informed decisions related to the environment, to government policies both at home and abroad, to the best kinds of living environments and interpersonal relationships for the future?

Just as each of you had different attitudes toward sociology coming into this course, so each of you can realize different applications of sociology to your lives and the world around you. From the examples I have given of some of my applied sociological work, you can see that sociology is not just scientific research, but a living discipline. Put it to work for you in your everyday life, and in those areas where you seek social change.

---

example? Or has the direction been a progressive decline from some Golden Age? Or does change occur in a circular fashion as civilizations rise and fall? You have probably heard popular versions of each of these theories of social change.

Evolutionary Theories of Change. In late-nineteenth-century England, *unidirectional theories* of evolutionary progress were very popular. The path upward ran from savagery, represented by the simple societies discovered by British colonizers, to high civilization, represented, of course, by Victorian England (Spencer 1860/1896). Some Americans might make the same claim for the United States today as a nation chosen by God to lead the free world against its enemies. The belief that one's social system is superior to that of other people provides a basis for the economic exploitation of less-developed societies.

Cyclical Theories of Change. Similarly, the notion that cultures are like organisms, developing from birth to ultimate decline, fit into the intellectual currents of early-twentieth-century Western culture, in which many disciplines emphasized biological functioning, and in which there was a feeling that European civilization was decadent and corrupt. The German philosopher Oswald Spengler summed up this view in *The Decline of the West* (1928). His deep pessimism was justified by the rise of Hitler in Germany and Mussolini in Italy in the 1920s and 1930s, and a

decade of war. But European civilization has proved far sturdier than Spengler's theory predicted. Cultures do flourish and decline over long periods, but there is little evidence that *cyclical theories* of social change have much predictive value.

A more sociological theory of cyclical change was proposed by Sorokin (1941), who suggested that world history has alternated between periods of rationality and order, on the one hand, and letting go, on the other.

Although cyclical views of change have enjoyed a brief vogue, the two theories of social change that stimulate most interest among contemporary social scientists are related to the two macrosocial perspectives of functionalism and conflict. A coming together of these two positions has been a connecting thread throughout this volume, and nowhere is the blending of these two approaches more apparent than in the analysis of change.

Classical Models. Many of sociology's classical theorists have proposed two-part schemes to describe the cumulative direction of social structural change. Durkheim, for example, contrasted *mechanical solidarity* in simple societies, where every member was interchangeable with others, to the *organic solidarity* of modern societies brought on by an increasing division of labor, so that members play complementary roles and are bound together by ties of interdependence.

Tönnies' concepts of *Gemeinschaft* and *Gesellschaft* reflect a similar model of

Unidirectional theories assume that social change occurs in one direction only.

Cyclical theories of change are based on the view that society resembles a living organism, going through phases of growth and decline.

change: a trend from close primary relationships as the basis of social life to the more varied, fragmented, temporary, and role-specific mode of modern life. The same general process was described by the anthropologist Redfield (1941) as a drift from *folk communities* toward *urban society*. In all these schemes, structural complexity is associated with population density and the specialization of tasks.

The *neoevolutionary model* that we have used in this text is a more sophisticated version of these developmental schemes. *Neoevolutionary theory* makes no assumptions about the superiority of one form or another. Nor is the term *progress* used to describe differentiation. It would be very difficult to claim that modern Americans are any more happy, fulfilled, or intelligent than any other people. (Being a Tasaday might not appeal to many of us, but then, few Tasaday might wish to be one of us).

The neoevolutionary model of cumulative change described by Service (1963) and others (see Lenski and Nolan 1983) is based on four simple propositions: (1) the mode of subsistence is basic; (2) changes in technology lead to new adaptations that typically support larger populations; (3) increased density leads to the specialization and coordination of tasks; and (4) the need to create order among different kinds of workers leads to more complex organizations and the emergence of distinct institutional spheres (see Figure 22-2).

Critics of the neoevolutionary model do not object to its assumptions of cumulative change and increasing structural complexity. It is the additional assumption made by functional theorists that institutional arrangements tend toward balance and internal adjustment that is severely questioned. If, as functional theory suggests, social systems change in the direction of increased equilibrium or the smooth working of the system's parts, whatever disturbs a system is considered a dysfunctional intrusion from outside. In other words, functional theory minimizes the possibility that strain may arise from *within* the system, generated precisely from existing institutional arrangements.

The Conflict Model. The *conflict view* focuses on the recurrent and lasting sources of tension and struggle among individuals and groups within any society. The chapters in Part III, "Social Differences and Inequality," detailed the many ways in which power, prestige, and property are unequally distributed in the United States. When inequality is perceived as unfairness, disadvantaged groups may organize to increase their share of scarce resources. Persons and groups that benefit from the status quo will struggle to maintain their power. At any given moment, social systems consist of competing interest groups, so that conflict is built into social organization.

It seems to us that the conflict perspective does not contradict the model of social and cultural change that we have developed from functional and neoevolutionary sources. Rather, conflict theory *completes* the model because it specifies the sources and the processes of change in the social system. Only by looking at the specific circumstances that give rise to discontent and change in any society can we understand why some social systems last and others decay and why some undergo gradual and relatively peaceful change, whereas others experience violent revolution.

For Karl Marx, the competing groups within industrial society were the social classes and their relationship to the means of production, namely, the owners and those who sold their labor. Marx thought that eventually the conditions of modern work would be so alienating that the workers would revolt against the owners of capital. Yet, as we have seen, the working

Neoevolutionary theory traces changes in cultural and societal complexity without making value judgments about the superiority of one society over another.

The **conflict view** of social change stresses the recurrent and enduring sources of strain among the groups within society.

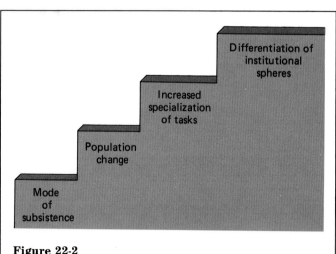

Figure 22-2
Steps in the structural differentiation of society.

Predicting the Future—Not Always Right

Although all of us wonder what the future will hold, it is difficult to predict with accuracy. Some of the erroneous predictions of the future by experts include the following:

On the environment and radioactive waste: "All the waste in a year from a nuclear power plant can be stored under a desk." [Ronald Reagan as quoted in the Burlington (Vt.) *Free Press,* Feb. 15, 1980.] And "A nuclear power plant is infinitely safer than eating, because 300 people choke to death on food every year" (Dixie Lee Ray, governor of Washington and former chair of the Atomic Energy Commission, 1977).

On nuclear war: "Dig a hole, cover it with a couple of doors and then throw three feet of dirt on top. . . . It's the dirt that does it. . . . You know, dirt is just great stuff. . . . If there are enough shovels to go around, everybody is going to make it" (Thomas K. Jones, Deputy Undersecretary of Defense for Research and Engineering, Strategic and Theater Nuclear Forces, explaining to journalist Robert

Sheer how the American people could survive a nuclear war, 1981).

On space travel: "The whole procedure . . . presents difficulties of so fundamental a nature that we are forced to dismiss the notion as essentially impracticable. . . . [Richard van der Reit Wooley, British Astronomer, March 14, 1936; and "Space travel is utter bilge" (ibid, 1956).]

(Note that less than two years after Dr. Wooley's 1956 statement, the Soviets launched the first artificial satellite.)

"Man will never reach the moon regardless of all future scientific advances" (Dr. Lee DeForest—inventor of the audion tube—1957).

On politics: "Because of the greatness of the Shah, Iran is an island of stability in the Middle East" (Jimmy Carter, President of the United States, Dec. 31, 1977).

(For these and other predictions, see Christopher Cerf and Victor Navasky, *The Experts Speak,* New York: Pantheon, 1984.)

---

classes of the world have not become revolutionary; quite the opposite, in fact. Ronald Reagan, a candidate closely linked to capitalist interests, received almost half of all working-class votes in the United States in 1984, an outcome that Marxists would claim to be the result of "false consciousness" among the workers. Ironically, perhaps, the workers of Communist Poland have been more militantly class-conscious in recent years than those in the United States, pressing their interests against the current controller of the means of production, which happens to be the Communist Party.

But Marx's theory of social change does not rely on the necessity of violent revolution. Viewing human history in its totality, Marx saw a *dialectical process of change.* At any given moment, the social system of interconnected parts makes up a status quo, or *thesis,* out of which competing or warring elements emerge to challenge the given order of things. These forces of opposition are called the *antithesis.* Because inequality is a feature of all past and present social systems, antithetical movements are a constant fact of social life. Out of the conflict between thesis and antithesis—the power of vested

interest and the forces of protest—comes a new social order: *synthesis.*

A Unified Model of Change. To synthesize the neoevolutionary and the conflict models, we propose that general change can be best explained in terms of changes in the economic base of society. Groups that do not experience shifts in modes of subsistence are not likely to undergo changes in other institutional spheres—unless, of course, they are invaded. But where subsistence modes do undergo change, other social patterns are ultimately affected. Some changes, as in the case of the Ik, are disastrous. Other societies are more fortunate and adapt to the new conditions at a more complex level of organization. Such has been the pattern of history.

Change *within* a given society, however, can be analyzed in terms of class-based interests. The outcome of any conflict depends on the power of those with vested interests to subvert, coopt, or suppress movements for change. Because ruling elites are typically stronger than protesters, rapid and radical change is generally resisted successfully. However, gradual, almost unnoticed changes within a society may occur, so that over a long

In the **dialectical model, thesis** is represented by the status quo, **antithesis** is the force of opposition. **Synthesis** emerges from the conflict between those two.

period of time, different patterns in the social and cultural fabric of a group become obvious. The gains of the women's movement, for example, although slow and incremental, have ultimately brought major institutional changes to our society.

The Future: What Next?

What can we expect in the future? Both social change and the problems of the future will be, in part, results and reactions to current technology and the institutionalized patterns of social relationships. In the past, the United States and other major industrialized nations have relied on cheap raw materials from preindustrial nations. As a result, industrialized society has developed social and economic institutions based largely on waste and the depletion of the world's resources. Americans in particular are used to the idea of disposables—one car, radio, dress, shoe, cup, or whatever quickly replaced by another newer model. Repairing items is for many people a lost art.

Yet, there is growing evidence that scarcity can be anticipated in a number of areas—scarcity caused by the demands of technology and by the widespread modification of the environment. For example, there are limits to the supply of water and fossil fuels that may have far-reaching implications for almost every economic system. We could delay these potential shortages by reducing our use of water and fossil fuels, by manufacturing longer-lasting goods, and by planned recycling. But this solution, too, has its costs. Longer-lasting goods lead to increased unemployment. After all, fewer workers would be required to turn out fewer but longer-lasting products. Likewise, there is a trade-off between our need for imported sources of energy, such as oil, and balance-of-trade payments. The point here is that many social analysts claim that there is no single, one-time solution to problems that we can expect to face in the foreseeable future.

Nor can the future itself be accurately foreseen. Yet, the restructuring of society is proceeding at this very moment and will change our social relationships and ourselves. Various visions of the future have been proposed, all of which emphasize the importance of technological change. For

Computerized banking has produced vast changes not only in the kinds of financial interactions people have, but in where they have them. Who would have predicted sidewalk banking with a machine that asks questions and thanks you for your responses? (© Eugene Gordon)

example, the rise of computer technology has led some futurists to predict a society in which technology will become too complex for the average person to understand. According to this view, a kind of "gods and clods" division of labor will develop, in which a small group of highly educated engineers and scientists control technology, while the remainder of the population is engaged in meaningless make-work (see box "Will Robots Change Society?"). Others, such as Naisbitt (1982), foresee a multiple-option society, in which the range of personal choices is expanded by "high tech/high touch" developments. That is, technological innovations will be accompanied by compensatory human responses. The United States is moving toward an information society in which short-run interests are giving way to longer time frames, in which self-reliance and the importance of informal social relationships will increase, and dependency on bureaucratic organizations decline.

Attempts to describe the future in detail are almost always wrong. The most accurate way to anticipate the direction of social change is through an understanding of past and current events. Within your lifetime, numerous social changes have occurred. New technologies have developed, and the shift from an industrial to a postindustrial economy has become marked. Numerous revolutions have been fought and are still going on. Shifts in the political climate of the United States have occurred. Social movements have been born, died, or persisted. Fads and fashions in dress, music, and foods come and go rapidly.

What will the future hold? And what will American society—and the rest of the world—be like in fifty years? The answers depend on crucial choices that you will be involved in making during the half-century ahead. A sociological perspective—that is, an awareness of how you are shaped by and shape the world in which you live—is essential to your informed participation in the design of the future. If social systems are human constructions, they can be deconstructed and reconstructed. We have given you the tools for such an analysis; it is a matter of choice whether or not you use this knowledge to work for change and in what directions.

Summary

Social change is a fundamental process which alters values, norms, institutions, stratification systems, and social relationships. There are many sources of change: environmental events, invasion, cultural contact, innovation, and population shifts. Diffusion is, perhaps, the most important process of social change.

Rates of change vary; they may be rapid or slowly incremental. Cultural lag describes the tendency for some parts of society to change at different rates than others.

The process of modernization in Western Europe has been accompanied by the rise of the nation-state, a development favored by the existence of stable monarchies, the growth of capitalism, and increasing colonialism.

Industrial society is characterized by rational-legal authority and bureaucratic organizational society. Postindustrial society extends the trends of its previous stages while emphasizing science and technology. The knowledge industry becomes important. One of the chief concerns of postindustrial society is the monitoring of technologically sophisticated industries that have high potential for accidents.

Change in society also involves psychological changes. Modern societies promote and reward personality characteristics that are different from those rewarded in traditional societies. Not all components of change are welcomed. Change is accepted or resisted depending on people's vested interests in the status quo.

Change may be gradual and incremental, with one modification following another, or revolutionary, bringing fundamental alterations in social structures. Evolional, cyclical, classical, and conflict models seek to explain broad social changes requiring a sociologically informed citizenry.

Suggested Readings

CALDICOTT, HELEN. *Missile Envy: The Arms Race and Nuclear War,* Rev. ed. New York: Bantam, 1986. A penetrating and sobering analysis of the dynamics of the arms race.

CHIROT, DANIEL. *Social Change in the Twentieth Century,* 2d ed. New York: Harcourt Brace Jovanovich, 1986. A world-systems approach to understanding core and periphery relations among nations. Details the decline of American dominance and suggests the future course of economic and political influences.

HAWKES, NIGEL, et al. *Chernobyl: The End of the Nuclear Dream.* New York: Vintage, 1987. A very readable and fascinating account of the events surrounding the Chernobyl disaster and international reactions to the incident.

LAUER, ROBERT H., ed. *Perspectives on Social Change,* 4th ed. Boston: Allyn and Bacon, 1988. A useful overview of theory and research on social and cultural change.

LIPSET, SEYMOUR MARTIN, ed. *The Third Century: America as a Post-Industrial Society.* Chicago: University of Chicago Press, 1979. These sixteen essays, primarily from a functionalist perspective, examine the nature and the implications of postindustrial society.

MOORE, BARRINGTON, Jr. *The Social Origins of Dictatorship and Democracy.* Boston: Beacon, 1966. Classic study of the conflicts and coalitions among various social classes that produced the modern nation-state in its various forms. Marxist and Weberian perspectives powerfully integrated.

MOORE, WILBERT E. *World Modernization: The Limits of Convergence.* New York: Elsevier, 1979. An important book by a leading analyst of social change, examining global development from the perspective of modernization theory.

ROZMAN, GILBERT, ed. *The Modernization of China.* New York: Free Press, 1981. An assessment of the historical and contemporary trends toward modernization from a structural perspective that includes the international context, politics, economic growth, social integration, and knowledge and education.

SKOCPOL, THEDA. *States and Social Revolution.* New York: Cambridge University Press, 1979. An important study of the precondition for revolution from the author's analysis of the French, Russian, and Chinese revolutions.

TILLY, CHARLES. *From Mobilization to Revolution.* Reading, Mass.: Addison Wesley, 1978. The classic analysis of revolution. Tilly pulls together historical analyses to develop a model of revolutionary situations and outcomes.

Glossary

Absolute Deprivation is a lack of the basic necessities of survival.

Absolute Numbers are actual counts of people, births, marriages, deaths, and so forth.

Accommodation occurs when the members of a minority group are aware of dominant norms and values without having internalized them.

Through **Accommodation**, one institutional sphere makes internal changes to better use the new technology.

Acculturation takes place when minority-group members adopt the dominant values and norms but are not admitted to intimate groupings.

Achieved Statuses are positions occupied as a result of choice, merit, or effort.

Acid Rain refers to the deposits of sulphur and chemicals emitted from industrial smoke-stacks.

Acting Crowds have some goal beyond mere expression of emotion.

Through **Adoption** people substitute the new technology for an older one.

Affective personality factors refer to feelings and emotion.

Age Stratification is the process whereby people of different ages are channeled into roles, producing an age-related hierarchy of power, prestige, and property.

The **Age Structure** of the population refers to the number of people of various ages within a society.

Ageism is the acceptance of negative stereotypes about old age.

Agenda Setting by the media refers to the list of topics that come to the attention of the public.

Agents of Change occupy statuses through which they can influence the direction of change.

Agents of Socialization are people and organizations responsible for teaching rules and roles.

Agribusiness is a type of farming, where relatively few farming businesses, using sophisticated technology, produce a large proportion of the food consumed domestically and abroad.

Ahistorical functional analysis fails to explore the historical context and change over time of social patterns.

Alienation is the feeling of being cut off from the product of one's labor, from other people, and from oneself.

The **All-Volunteer Force** is composed of people who enter the military as a full-time career.

Amalgamation is the mixing of minority and dominant groups through intermarriage.

American Civil Religion is a secular faith which sees America as divinely blessed, with a moral mission, and guided by Puritan-derived ethical standards.

The **American Ethos** refers to a set of core values guiding the beliefs and behaviors of Americans.

The **American Health Care System** evolved in response to changes in technology, pressures of competing interest groups, and felt social needs.

Anomie refers to situations in which norms are absent, unclear, or confusing.

Anthropology is the study of nonmodern societies or of subgroups within modern societies.

Anticipatory Socialization involves rehearsing prior to assuming a role.

Antithesis (see **Dialectical Model**).

Apartheid is a system of laws in South Africa which upholds white supremacy and separates the majority of blacks from the minority of whites.

Artifacts or material culture consists of tools and other human-made objects.

Ascribed Characteristics are those over which a person has no control, such as sex, age, race, ethnicity, and religion.

Assimilation occurs when people from minority groups are accepted in major social institutions and more personal groupings.

Authority refers to socially legitimated power.

Automation is the replacing of workers with machines.

The **Back-to-Basics** trend in education emphasizes discipline, respect for authority, and traditional subject matters.

Backstage interaction is free of public performance constraints.

Barter involves the exchange of goods.

Behaviorism concentrates on the study of observable activity as opposed to reported or inferred mental and emotional processes.

A **Belief System** is a set of shared ideas about the meaning of life.

Bigotry refers to racial, religious, and ethnic intolerance.

Biological Determinism is based on the belief that biological factors explain differences in behavior by sex, race, religion, and ethnicity.

A **Birth Cohort** consists of a group of people born during a specific time period.

Blockbusting occurs when real estate agents purposely create a sense of panic in a stable white neighborhood by selling or renting to a black family.

Blocked Opportunity Structures result from the lack of fit between culturally learned aspirations and the limited possibilities of achieving success.

Born Again means having an experience that changes one's life through the acceptance of the Lord.

Boundary Maintenance refers to the ways subcultures/subgroups protect themselves from outsiders.

Boundary Setting occurs when shared norms and values set the limits of acceptable behavior.

Bundles of Knowledge refers to the increasing specialization of knowledge in universities and colleges leading to discrete units of organization.

Bureaucracy is a formal organization designed to accomplish large-scale administrative tasks through systematic coordination of the work of many people.

Capital Punishment refers to the death penalty.

Career Contingencies involves a series of social factors that determine outcomes for people by opening up or closing off certain options.

Case Histories provide in-depth information from a few cases.

Caste Systems are based on ascribed characteristics, with minimal movement across stratum boundaries.

A **Casual Crowd** is an accidental gathering of people.

Censorship involves the selective withholding of information.

A **Census** is an inventory of the entire population at a given time in a specific area. A census is taken every ten years in the United States.

The **Central-Planning Model** is based on public control over health care.

Charismatic Authority is based on some extraordinary quality of the leader or the leader's ideas.

Chiropractic is the treatment of disease through manipulation of the body, especially the spine.

A **Circuit of Agents** includes both informal networks and formal agents.

Civil Disobedience involves peaceful refusal to obey unjust laws in the name of a higher morality.

Civil Law provides sanctions against violations of the interests of private persons.

Civil Liberties refer to the rights to speak, publish, and assemble.

Class Awareness refers to the recognition that differences in income, occupational prestige, and lifestyle are reflections of one's own class position.

Class Consciousness occurs when class awareness becomes the central organizing point of self-definition and political actions.

Class Immobility occurs when social class status is reproduced from one generation to another.

Coercion is the threat of force or use of force to ensure obedience.

Cognitive personality factors refer to how people think and process information.

Cognitive Development refers to changes over time in how we think.

Cognitive Dissonance occurs when a person must deal with mutually exclusive ideas and perceptions.

Cognitive Liberation occurs when the ideas of a social movement can be seriously considered.

Cognitive Structures shape how the mind processes information.

Cohabitation refers to persons of the opposite sex sharing a residence.

Collective Behavior refers to noninstitutionalized activities that are both cause and consequences of flux or change in the established order.

A **Collectivity** is a group of persons acting together.

Colonization involves the violent conquering of the indigenous group by a more powerful invading group.

The **Commercial City** was organized around craft manufacturing, commerce, transportation, or politics.

Commuter Marriages are ones in which husband and wife work in different cities and usually have separate households.

Competition results when situations are defined as ones in which scarce resources will go only to some.

Compromise involves giving up extreme demands to achieve limited goals.

The **Concentric-Zone Model** describes the city as a series of circles built around a central core.

Conflict occurs when parties try to destroy or disable their opponents.

The **Conflict Model** examines disagreement, open hostility, and struggle over power and resources in a society.

The **Conflict View** of social change stresses the recurrent and enduring sources of strain among the groups within society.

Confrontations test the limits of acceptable behavior.

Conglomerates exist when one company controls other companies in a variety of business sectors.

The **Consensus Model** reflects the idea that norms become laws because they reflect customs and general agreement about appropriate behavior.

Conspicuous Consumption is the open display of wastefulness designed to impress others.

Constants are characteristics that do not change from one person to another and do not change over time.

Content Analysis counts the number of references to a given item in a sample of publications.

A **Conventional Crowd** is made of people who are gathered as spectators or audiences at events governed by established norms.

Conversion is an experience that transforms anxiety and confusion into inner calm and certainty.

Cooperation is the sharing of resources in order to achieve a common goal.

Cooptation occurs when members of a dissenting group are absorbed by the dominant group.

The **Core Sector** consists of major industries, with large investments in plants and equipment, unionized labor, monopolies, and high profits.

Corporate Cities developed when manufacturing was decentralized and economic power was consolidated in smaller towns and cities.

In the **Corporatist Model** of national health insurance, the government balances the interests of the medical profession with those of consumers.

Corporations are formal organizations that are legal actors in their own right.

Correlation refers to the effect of one variable on another, how change in one is related to change in another.

Cosmopolitanism refers to the spread of new ideas, values, and technology throughout a society.

Countercultures refer to alternative life-styles for those not conforming to the dominant norms.

Countermovements are opinions and beliefs in a population that oppose the goals of a social movement.

Crazes are periodic outbreaks of unexpected and often ridiculous behavior.

Crimes Without Victims violate moral standards, but those involved are willing to participate.

Criminal Behavior involves actions which break the law.

Criminal Law provides sanctions against the conduct believed to be against the interests of the society or state.

Cross-Cultural Comparisons examine relationships among variables in different societies.

Cross-Media Ownership occurs when the same owner(s) control interests in several media at the same time.

Cross-Sectional Studies take place at one time only.

A **Crowd** is a temporary gathering of people brought together by some common concern or activity.

Cultural Capital refers to a style of talking and thinking and an interest in music, art, and literature which prepares individuals for membership in the dominant culture.

Cultural Hegemony refers to control over the production of values and norms by those in power.

Cultural Heterogeneity refers to a society whose members are very different in race, religion, values, appearance, language, and culture.

Cultural Homogeneity refers to a society whose members are similar in race, religion, values, appearances, language, and culture.

Cultural Lag refers to the tendency for parts of culture to change and adapt at different rates after the introduction of a new technology.

Cultural Pluralism emphasized the special contributions of various immigrant cultures to the diversity of American culture.

Cultural Relativism involves an effort to understand the world as seen by members of other societies.

Cultural Universals are basic elements found in all cultures.

Cultural Variability reflects the variety of customs, beliefs, and artifacts devised by humans to meet universal needs.

Culture is the blueprint for living of a group whose members share a territory and language, feel responsible for each other, and call themselves by the same name.

The **Culture Conflict Model** stresses value differences and assumes that the laws reflect the values of the most powerful groups.

Culture Contact involves learning from people from other societies.

Cumulative Social Change is the gradual development from simple to more complex societies.

Cyclical Theories of change are based on the view that society resembles a living organism, going through phases of growth and decline.

De Facto segregation occurs in fact and is supported by custom rather than law.

Deferred Gratification is the postponing of current pleasure to achieve future goals.

Definition of the Situation is the process by which people define and interpret and evaluate the social context to select appropriate attitudes and behaviors.

Deindividualization is the process of removing a person's civilian identities.

Deinstitutionalization involves the release of people in mental hospitals into the community.

De Jure segregation is supported by law.

Delinquent and Criminal Subcultures originate in the differences between aspirations and blocked opportunity structures.

Demand Mobility refers to societal-level factors affecting mobility rates.

Democratic Societies protect the right to dissent.

The **Demographic Transition** is a result of lower death rates, which led to an increase in the world population.

Demography is the study of the characteristics and the patterns of human populations.

Demonstrations are usually carefully organized and orchestrated protest actions.

The **Dependency Ratio** is the ratio of those earning an income to those not earning an income.

Dependent Variables are influenced by independent variables.

Desocialization is learning to give up a role.

Deviant Subcultures are supportive peer groups and networks for deviants.

Deviants are people who violate norms of expected behavior.

In the **Dialectical Model, Thesis** is represented by the status quo; **Antithesis** is the force of opposition. **Synthesis** emerges from the conflict between those two.

The **Dialectic Process** refers to the conflict of opposites that leads to a new stability.

Differential Association is a theory that states that deviant behavior is learned through primary groups and involves the same learning processes as nondeviant behavior.

Diffusion describes the process by which new ideas, actions, technology, and beliefs of a culture spread from one person, group, and society to another.

Discretionary Income refers to the amount of money left over after necessary expenses such as food, clothing, and shelter have been purchased.

Discrimination is the practice of unequal treatment of people on the basis of their group membership.

The **Disenchantment of the World** occurs as science replaces faith and fantasy.

Dominance refers to control over central factors of social life.

Dominant Groups exercise control over societal resources.

Doomsday Approach maintains that natural resources will drop dramatically during the last decades of the 20th century, leading to rapid declines in production and in food.

A **Double Bind** situation develops when the child receives two contradictory messages.

The **Dramaturgical View** of interaction sees all role partners as actors performing roles in a social setting or stage.

Dual-Earner Families or couples consist of two wage earners.

Dual Economy refers to two separate types of employing firms: core and peripheral.

The **Dyad,** or two-person group, is intimate, has a high exchange of information, and presents great possibilities for total involvement and conflict.

Dysfunctional patterns reduce the capacity of a system to adapt and survive.

Eccentric Behavior is behavior not viewed as disruptive or threatening to the social order.

Ecological Differentiation or urban segregation occurs when specific activities occur in set areas of the city.

Ecological Invasion occurs when new populations or activities come into a differentiated urban area.

An **Economic System** consists of the norms and patterned activities regulating the production, distribution, and consumption of goods and services.

Egalitarianism refers to the trend to eliminate power differences between husbands and wives and between parents and children.

The **Ego** represents the aspects of self linked to the real world.

Elite Culture refers to items enjoyed and sponsored by the affluent.

The **Emotional Reaction Model** focuses on how the intensity of crowds develops.

Empirical Referents are items that can be measured and counted.

Employee Stock Ownership Plans refer to owners contributing company shares as part of workers' benefit packages.

The **Empty Nest Stage** of the family cycle occurs when all the children are out of the house and the parents are alone together again.

Environmental Changes include both natural events and social situations.

Epidemiology is the study of patterns of occurrence of illness in a population.

Ethnicity refers to national background or cultural differences.

Ethnocentrism is the belief that one's own culture is the best and the consequent judging of other cultures by that standard.

Ethnomethodology involves probing beneath the "taken-for-granted" reality.

The **Eumenopolis** is a continuous series of cities interconnected nationally and worldwide.

Evangelical refers to an emphasis on the personal witnessing of God's presence.

Experiments come closest to the scientific ideal of control over variables.

Expressive behavior is valued in its own right.

An **Expressive Crowd** shows strong feelings with outbursts of emotion.

Expressive Roles are oriented toward the expression and release of group tension.

Extended Family is a family unit that consists of two or more nuclear families (married couples with their dependent children) that share economic and social responsibilities.

Extraneous Variables are outside the stated hypothesis.

Fads last longer than crazes and appeal to more people.

False Consciousness of the world develops when people's perception of their social situation does not fit their objective condition.

Familism refers to family closeness, traditionalism, and patriarchy.

Fashions are more enduring, widespread, and socially important than fads.

Fee for Service are fees based on typical charges within an area and medical specialty.

Feeling Rules shape how, when, with whom, and where an emotion is expressed.

Feminine and **Masculine** refer to social constructs; *female* and *male* are biological terms.

The **Feminization of Poverty** refers to the fact that a majority of the adult poor are women.

Fertility refers to the number of children per family.

Field Experiments are designed by social scientists and conducted in the everyday world.

Flextime refers to the sharing of one full-time job by two part-time workers.

Folkways are customs transmitted from one generation to the next.

Foraging is the picking for immediate consumption of readily available foods.

Forced Migration (see **Impelled Migration**).

Formal Agents of Social Control are people in social roles specifically devoted to norm enforcement.

Formal Organizations are social structures characterized by formality, ranked positions, large size, relative complexity, and long duration.

Formalization Stage (see **Mobilization**).

Formatting of news stories involves the construction of their presentation to the public.

Framing involves the placing of news stories into an existing frame of reference to make it understandable to the public.

Free-Enterprise Capitalism is an economic system with minimal political interference.

Free Migration is one in which the individual's choice plays a role.

Frontstage interaction occurs in full view of the public.

A major **Function of Education** is to extend the socialization process begun in the family.

Fundamentalists represent a back-to-basics approach to religion, namely that every word of the Bible is God's word.

Games are organized and more complex forms of role-taking.

Gatekeepers are formal agents who regulate entry into treatment agencies.

Gathering is a more systematic way of finding food, transporting, storing, and preserving it.

Gemeinschaft refers to small, traditional communities, characterized by primary-group relationships and intergenerational stability.

The **Gender Gap** refers to the discrepancy between average earnings of women and men.

Gender Inequality refers to the differences between men and women in the distribution of societal resources of power, prestige, and property.

Gender Stratification is the differential evaluation of social worth on the basis of biological sex.

Generalized Others are widely held expectations of persons in a given status.

Genocide refers to killing an entire population.

Genogram is a diagram that provides a graphic picture of a family system and its relationships.

Gentrification refers to the migration by middle- and upper-income people into urban centers and their renovation of existing housing.

Gesellschaft refers to societies characterized by contractual relationships, where social bonds are voluntary and are based on rational self-interest.

A **Gesture** is a symbol shared by group members.

Goal Displacement occurs when the members of an organization are more interested in perpetuating the organization than in performing the tasks for which it was originally designed.

Goals are objectives of a social movement, ranging from limited change to a complete overthrow of the social structure.

Grade Differentiation divides a district's students into separate schools for given grade levels.

Gradual or **Incremental Change** is a long process in which one modification is followed by another.

Greedy Institutions absorb all the energy and loyalty of their members and leave them at the mercy of their leaders.

A **Group** is any collection of people bound together by a distinctive set of shared social relationships.

Group Differences are usually reported by researchers studying sex-linked traits.

Group Migration and **Mass Migration** are situations in which many people, sharing a common characteristic such as ethnicity or religion, relocate.

The **Health Maintenance Organization** (HMO) is based on prepayment for health care by patients who agree to use member physicians and hospitals.

Heterogamy is the tendency to select a mate different in terms of race, religion, ethnicity, social class, education, and age.

Heterosexuality refers to a preference for a partner of the opposite sex.

Hidden Curriculum refers to material learned, such as ethnocentrism and respect for authority, which is not part of the official curriculum.

Historical Records such as documents, papers, and letters identify relationships among variables over time.

Historical Societies have left written records.

Homicide, or murder, is one of the most violent crimes.

Homogamy is the tendency to select a mate of the same race, religion, social class, ethnic group, educational level, and age.

Homophobia refers to strong fear of male homosexuality.

Homosexuality refers to a preference for a partner of one's own sex.

Hospital Ownership is either public, nonprofit private, or for-profit or proprietary private.

Human Capital variables refer to differences in education, job experience, skill training, and work continuity.

Human Ecology focuses on the physical relationship between people and land use.

Humanist Sociology is based on the belief that sociologists must become actively involved in social change.

Hypotheses are specific statements derived from a theory about relationships among variables.

Hysteria is an uncontrollable outburst of emotion.

The **"I"** is the creative acting part of self, while the **"Me"** consists of the internalized attitudes of others.

The **Id** represents instinctual desires.

The **Ideal** types of Erikson's eight stages are descriptions of the very best or worst outcomes.

Ideal Culture reflects the highest virtues and standards of a society.

Ideological Hegemony refers to control of cultural symbols such as beliefs, values, and ideas by the ruling class.

Immigration refers to the number of people from other countries settling in the host country.

Impelled and **Forced Migration** are typically due to political pressures.

The **Incest Taboo** forbids sexual relations between certain group members and specifies who can mate with whom.

The **Incidence Rate** is the number of new cases of a disease within a population during a stated time period.

The American education system is **Inclusive**, or open, to all children of given ages.

Incremental Change (see Gradual Change).

Independent Variables have the greatest impact, come first in the chain of events, and/or are relatively fixed.

Index Crimes are those most often associated by the public with lower-class criminals.

In Individual Practice Associations (IPAs) physicians accept patients under a prepayment arrangement but can also accept fee-for-service reimbursement.

The Industrial Revolution represents a mode of subsistence based on the factory system of production.

Industrial Suburban Cities developed in vacant areas outside central cities due to economic, political, and labor-related reasons.

Influence is the ability to persuade others to follow one's will.

Informal Primary Groups develop within bureaucracies to meet personal needs.

In-Groups are the primary or secondary groups to which we belong.

In Vitro fertilization occurs in the laboratory.

The Inner-Directed Person's behavior is governed by an internal mechanism typical of industrial society.

Innovation refers to both the discovery and invention of something new.

Instinctual Behavior refers to an unbroken chain of drive arousal leading to tension-relieving action.

Institutional Racism occurs when discrimination is built into normative structures and reinforced by formal and informal agents of social control.

Institutionalization is the process whereby a given adaptation becomes a way of life and affects all other areas of activity.

Institutionalization of a Social Movement occurs when its beliefs are accepted and its goals are embodied in stable organizations.

Institutionalized Evasion of Norms occurs within organizations as a permanent, unofficial part of the system which may be tolerated as part of getting the job done.

Instrumental behavior is a means to some other goal.

Interaction Processes refers to how role partners agree on the goals of their interaction, negotiate behaviors, and distribute resources.

An Interest Group develops when an organized group of people seek others with similar feelings about an issue.

Intergenerational Mobility involves status change between parents and their adult children.

Interlocking Corporate Directorship involves members of one Board of Directors sitting on the boards of other companies.

Culture is Internalized in the mind of the child through parental expectations.

Internal Migration refers to geographical mobility within a nation.

Intragenerational Mobility involves status changes during a person's own adulthood.

Invasion occurs when one group's or nation's territory is overrun and controlled by another.

Involuntary Childlessness refers to the inability to conceive.

The Iron Cage is a new type of "prison" developed by technology and modern organization.

Among Japanese-Americans, the *Issei,* or first generation, were not highly assimilated, whereas their children, the *Nisei,* are.

Jargons are special languages of subgroups/subcultures.

Job Autonomy involves making decisions about the timing and sequence of tasks, exercising judgment, and having an impact on the outcome.

Job Sharing involves one full-time job being performed by two part-time workers.

Joblessness is greater than the official unemployment rate because it adds those who have settled for part-time work and those who have stopped trying to find employment.

The Juvenile Court System is a separate agency from those for adults and was designed to protect children and adolescents from the stresses of adult courtrooms and to emphasize treatment over punishment.

Key Respondents are carefully selected cases providing information on processes not easily visible but having general application.

Kinesics is the study of nonverbal communication.

Labeling Theory emphasizes the process of defining a person's behavior as deviant.

The Large Industrial City was dominated by factories, railroads, and slums.

Latent Functions are unexpected and unintended consequences.

Laws are norms that govern behavior and are considered essential to group survival. They are planned attempts to reduce behavior harmful to the public good or morals or interests of the government.

Legal-Rational Authority is based on laws that apply to officeholders.

Legitimated Power is exercised with the consent of the governed or in accordance with norms.

The **Life Course** refers to the biological and social sequence of birth, childhood, adolescence, adulthood, old age, and death.

The **Life Course** or "natural history" **of a Social Movement** consists of its major phases.

Life Expectancy refers to the average number of years one can expect to live as a member of a particular cohort.

Life Span refers to the biological limits to which our species is able to survive.

Longitudinal Studies follow a group of respondents over time.

The **Looking Glass Self** suggests that we see ourselves reflected back in the reactions of others.

Lower Socioeconomic Status is generally associated with poorer health and shorter life expectancy.

Macrosystem refers to a social system at a higher level of abstraction.

Macrosystem Analysis focuses on society as a whole and is relatively abstract.

Magic refers to behavior designed to manipulate unseen forces.

Magnet Schools attract bright students by offering specialized educational programs.

Mainstream Churches are the established religious bodies of the major denominations.

Mainstreaming involves integrating handicapped students into the regular school program.

Male and **Female** refer to a person's biological sex. *Masculine* and *feminine* refer to social constructs.

Manifest Functions are open, stated, and intended goals.

In a **Market System** a currency, which is a general standard, is used to measure the value of goods and services.

Mass Culture refers to elements of popular culture that are produced and distributed through the mass media.

Mass Migration (see **Group Migration**).

Mass Media refers to the agents of communication in a mass society; primarily the print and electronic media.

Master Status is the most important status occupied and one that affects almost every aspect of a person's life.

Materialism refers to a desire for owning and consuming goods and services.

Matriarchy refers to female-dominated families.

Matrifocal refers to families centered on the woman.

The **Mean** is the average score for a group of subjects.

The **Means of Production** refer to the tools, land, factories, and wealth that form the economic basis of a society.

Measures of Central Tendency are single numbers that summarize an entire set of data.

The **Median** is the mid-point of an entire set of cases.

Mediation refers to the use of a third party to resolve issues.

Medical-Industrial Complex refers to multi-facility chains of profit-making companies owning chains of hospitals, nursing homes, medical office centers, and walk-in clinics.

A **Megalopolis** consists of overlapping metropolitan areas with many social, economic, and transportation links.

The **Melting-Pot Model** of integration assumes that immigrants will lose their cultural uniqueness and become part of the dominant American culture.

Mentors are teachers who act as guides and sponsors.

Meritocracy is a hierarchy of talent.

A **Metropolitan Statistical Area** is a geographical area with a large population center together with neighboring communities that have a high degree of economic and social integration with that center.

Microsystem Analysis focuses on smaller units such as face-to-face interaction.

Migration Statistics measure the population flow within a society as well as the movement in or out of it.

Militarism refers to a societal emphasis on ideals and a glorification of war.

Militarization occurs when an entire society is mobilized around militaristic goals.

The **Military-Industrial Complex** consists of a large permanent military establishment combined with an immense armament industry.

Minority-Group Status involves visible traits, differential treatment, self-image, and shared identity.

Mobilization, an aspect of sociocultural change, involves the weakening of previous patterns of social, economic, and psychological commitments, making people receptive to new patterns of socialization.

The **Mobilization** or **Formalization Stage of a Social Movement** occurs when members gain the resources required to create an organization, active participation, and social tolerance for its existence.

The **Mode** is the single most common category of cases.

Mode of Subsistence refers to the way in which a group adapts to its environment.

Modeling is the copying of characteristics of persons we want to resemble.

Modernization refers to the spread of industrialization and urbanization and the growth of the world economy. It is a process through which a society becomes more internally differentiated and complex, and in which science and technology guide change.

Monopoly is the absence of competitors in the same line of business.

Moral Reasoning or judgment refers to how individuals apply standards of right and wrong.

Mores are folkways that have acquired a sense of necessity.

Multinational Corporations are American firms with branches and factories in other countries or foreign firms with branches and facilities in the United States that make decisions reflecting corporate goals, not the well-being of any one nation.

The **Multiple-Nuclei Model** assumes that the city has several centers, each devoted to a different activity.

The **Nation** is a distinct unit of social organization providing group identity, communality, and loyalty.

The **National Crime Survey** is based on samples of U.S. households and businesses.

National Health Insurance places the financing of health care under government control.

Nationalism is a consciousness of shared identity among the members of a politically distinct territory.

Nativistic Revival Movements arise when a culture is disintegrating under the impact of profound change.

Natural Experiments involve measuring the same population before and after an event that is assumed to change the situation.

No **Natural Increase** occurs in a population when birth rates fall along with death rates.

Negative Sanctions withhold approval or openly criticize.

Neoevolutionary Theory traces changes in cultural and societal complexity without making value judgments about the superiority of one society over another.

Net Increase is the excess of births over deaths in a population.

Norms are rules of behavior that define acceptable conduct.

The **Nuclear Family** is a unit composed of a married couple and their dependent children.

Nuclear Freeze refers to an immediate and mutual stop of all testing and deployment of nuclear weapons.

The **Nurse-Administrator** and the **Nurse-Practitioner**, new nurse careers, require training beyond the bachelor's level.

Official Data are collected by government agencies.

Oligarchy refers to the rule of the few.

The **Open Classroom** is based on the belief that freed of structural restraints in the classroom, children will develop intellectually and socially.

Operationalizing the variables translates the abstract into an observable.

Organizational Crimes are carried out in one's role as employee and are not for personal gain as in white-collar crime.

Organized or **Syndicated Crime** is committed by members of formally structured groups operating outside the law. Organized crime involves the delivery of illegal services to noncriminal customers, the corruption of public officials, and the use of violence.

An **Origin Myth** is the story of how the group began.

Osteopaths receive training in mainstream medicine as well as body-manipulation techniques.

The **Other-Directed Person**, typical of the post-industrial society, constantly reacts and adapts to the expectations of others.

Out-Groups are groups to which we do not belong.

Overcrowding is usually defined as more than one person per room in a dwelling unit.

Panics are actions caused by sudden overwhelming fear.

Parochial Schools are private schools operated by religious groups.

In **Participant Observation** the researcher becomes part of the interaction under study.

The **Particularistic Fallacy** occurs when a correlation at the group level is applied to individuals.

The **Pathological Model** focuses on biological symptoms and abnormal functioning in an organism.

Patriarchy refers to male dominance of power, prestige, and wealth.

Peers are equals and an important source of information and socialization.

A **Percentage** indicates how many of an item there are in every one hundred.

The **Periphery** consists of smaller, competitive, low-profit firms employing low-pay non-union manual workers.

Personal Troubles are private problems experienced directly by individuals.

The **Prospective Payment System** is based on fixed payment diagnosis-related groups (DRGs) rather than "reasonable costs."

Petty Violations of Norms are trivial and minor violations of rules.

Physician Assistants are personnel who perform a wide range of duties usually performed by physicians.

Play serves to expand a child's repertory of roles.

Plea Bargaining is an agreement between the prosecution and the accused to reduce the charges if the defendant pleads guilty.

The **Pluralist Model** assumes that there are many different and competing bases of power.

The **Police** in every society have been given the right to use coercive force to control behavior. The police are enforcers rather than definers of rules.

Political Action Committees (PACs) are special interest organizations that use funds to support causes and candidates.

Political Socialization refers to the influences and experiences that lead people to define their political orientation.

Polls (see **Survey**).

Polygamy is a family system composed of a man or a woman with more than one marriage partner.

Popular Culture is what people do in their leisure time, and leisure time products designed for mass consumption.

Population Projections are estimates of future growth of a nation, state, or other geographic area.

Population Pyramids represent summaries of age and sex distributions.

The **Population Replacement Level** occurs when the average number of births per woman reaches two.

Population Shifts are changes in the size and composition of the population.

Population Size is used as a measure of urbanization by demographers.

Positive Sanctions are reactions showing the role is well played.

Positivism sees science as value-free and totally objective.

In **Postindustrial Society** the key element is the rapid development of information technology placing a premium on knowledge, technical skills, and managerial abilities.

Post-Secondary Education refers to after high school education.

The **Potlatch Ceremony** of the Kwakiutl Indians is an act of conspicuous consumption based on how much property a person can give or throw away.

Power is the ability to impose one's will on others.

The **Power Elite** refers to similarity of world-views and actions among leaders of business, government, the military, and other major spheres of influence and authority, so that decisions made in one power sector reinforce those made in others.

The **Predispositional View** assumes that there is a tendency among certain persons to act in certain ways.

The **Preferred Provider Organization (PPO)** is based on agreement between health care providers and third-party payers to provide health care at discount.

Prejudice involves prejudging members of ethnic, religious, and racial groups.

Preliterate societies do not have a written language.

Preparatory Schools are private schools developed to prepare children of well-off parents for entry into elite colleges.

Prescriptive Norms dictate what is expected.

Prestige is measured by respect from others.

The **Prevalence** rate is the number of all the known cases of a disease in a population, regardless of when they began.

Priestly functions deal with specific traditions of the faith.

Primary Deviance is behavior that violates a norm.

A **Primary Group** is a small group in which members have warm, intimate personal ties with one another.

Primary Production consists of gathering, growing, or mining.

Primitive Migration occurs when people cannot cope with natural or climatic forces.

The **Principle of Legitimacy**, or social fatherhood, identifies one man as responsible for the protection of a woman and her children and for the children's placement in the social system.

Principled Challenges are deliberate attempts to confront the norm-setters.

Principles of Exchange govern relationships among people as they bargain for desired goods and services.

Probability refers to the accuracy of predicting given events, not what any one person will do.

Production of Culture refers to what is produced, how it's marketed, and who buys it.

Profane behaviors and objects are not holy, but earthly and understandable on their own.

The **Professional Model** is based on physicians' control of health care.

Progressivity is the principle of taxing higher incomes at a higher rate.

Propaganda refers to the selective release of information favorable to those in power.

Property refers to a person's total wealth.

Property Crimes, such as burglaries, larceny, theft, are much more prevalent than crimes against persons.

The **Prophet** is a charismatic figure, witnessing a revelation calling for a new order.

Proscriptive Norms cover forbidden conduct.

The development of the **Psyche** is a process consisting of the interplay among id, ego, and superego.

Psychological Development, for Freud, takes place in well-defined phases or stages.

Psychology is the study of individuals' mental and emotional states, needs, motivation, and behavior.

A **Public** consists of people who are not in the same place at the same time, but who react similarly to common stimuli.

Public Issues are factors outside one's personal control caused by crises in the larger system.

Punishment means the infliction of pain or of a penalty.

Qualitative Research relies primarily on verbal descriptions rather than statistics.

Quality Circle refers to a team of employees and managers who meet to discuss how to improve their work performance.

Quantitative Research utilizes scientific objectivity, including complex statistical techniques.

Race is based on the distribution of biological traits, but it cannot be defined scientifically.

Race Riots, the most common type of mob action in the United States, were most often directed against a specific group, such as Blacks or Chinese.

Random Sampling occurs when all possible respondents have an equal chance of being selected.

The **Rate of Change** is directly related to the size of the culture base; the greater the base, the greater the chances of further change.

Rates indicate the number of times a given event occurs in a specified population.

A **Ratio** compares one subpopulation to another.

Rationality replaces traditional and emotional bases for behavior with the belief in a logical connection between means and ends.

Real Culture refers to actual behavior.

A **Recidivist** is a repeat offender.

Through **Reciprocal Socialization** children modify their parents' view of the world.

Reciprocity obligates the receiver of a gift to return something of equivalent value later.

The **Redistribution of Population** occurs as people move from one type of location to another.

Redlining occurs when banks refuse mortgages or loans in certain designated areas of the city preventing residents from upgrading their housing.

Reductionism involves reducing social life to individual behavior or biology.

A **Reference Group** exerts a strong influence on one's identity, norms, and values, whether or not one actually belongs to that group.

Reform Movements seek fundamental changes in values and institutions.

Regionalization is the formation of areawide governing bodies to handle areawide problems such as water supply, sewage, highway construction, parks, and transportation.

Rehabilitation means restoration to a former state of health.

Reification is the logical fallacy of making a concrete object out of an abstract concept.

Relative Deprivation occurs when people feel unfairly treated in comparison to others thought to be their equals.

Relative Numbers refer to the proportions of certain types of people in the total population.

Reliability refers to whether the measuring instrument yields the same results on repeated trials.

Religion is a set of beliefs and rituals associated with the sacred.

Replication involves repeating a specific study often with different types of respondents in various settings and at other times.

Repression, in psychology, involves the placing of unpleasant and unacceptable emotions below the level of consciousness.

Repression of a Social Movement includes jailings, deportation, harassment, use of armed forces, and death.

Repressive Control Systems ensure high levels of conformity.

Residual Deviance can be mental illness that is less easily identified than more obvious norm violations.

Resistance Movements are designed to stop change and to seek traditional values and norms.

Resocialization is learning that involves a strong break with the past and socialization into dramatically different norms and values.

Resource Mobilization Theory stresses the supports available to protestors, as well as the tactics used by social control agents.

Restrained Control Systems involve less intense use of power.

The **Revolution of Rising Expectations** refers to the gap between expected benefits and actual gains.

Revolutionary Change brings basic alterations in the political and socioeconomic structure of a society.

Revolutionary Movements call for radical structural change in the society.

A **Revolutionary Situation** occurs when two or more political units claim control over the state, these interests cannot be reconciled, and the opposition party receives support from a sizable segment of the population.

Riots involve mob action directed against groups or property.

A **Rite of Passage** is a public celebration marking the movement from one age status to another.

Ritualized Release of Hostility occurs when hostility is expressed under controlled situations.

Rituals are culturally patterned ways of dealing with anxiety-producing events.

Role is the expected behavior of those who occupy a given status.

Role Conflict occurs when one role contradicts or competes with another.

Role Distance is the space placed by a person between the self and the self-in-the-role.

Role Prescriptions are norms for permissible and desirable behavior.

Role Slack, when capacities are underdemanded, most often happens during adolescence.

Role Strain occurs when the roles one occupies demand more than one person can adequately fulfill.

The **Role Structure** of the population refers to the number of roles available to be filled.

The **Romantic Love Syndrome** involves the selection of a mate on the basis of love rather than kinship-based needs.

Routinization of Charisma occurs when the prophet's work is transformed into a worldly organization.

The **Rule of Reciprocity** involves the giving of gifts that obligate the receiver to return something of similar value later.

Rumors are the spread of unconfirmed information.

Sacred behaviors and objects are invested with holy, divine, mystical, or supernatural force.

A **Sample** is a selection from the entire population of interest.

Sample Surveys are based on a small but representative part of a population.

Sanctions refer to reactions that convey approval or disapproval of behavior.

The **Sapir-Whorf Hypothesis** indicates that language shapes the form and content of thought.

Scapegoating refers to finding someone else to blame for one's misfortune.

The **Scientific Method** involves objective observations, precise measurement, and disclosure of results.

Secondary Analysis involves the use of data collected by others.

Secondary Deviance results from the social responses people make to primary deviance.

Secondary Groups are characterized by few emotional ties and by limited interaction.

Secondary Production involves transforming raw materials through manufacturing into other consumable objects.

Sectarian Conflict refers to interreligious strife.

The **Sector Model** focuses on certain physical aspects of the city which shape the growth pattern of cities.

Sects are congregations not affiliated with any nationally organized church.

Secular Ideology is a belief system based on the collective experiences and efforts of a group in this world.

Secularization, the transition from traditional to modern societies, also involves the triumph of science, technology, and rationality.

The term **Segregation** refers to attempts to isolate minority groups.

Self is an organization of perceptions about who and what kind of person one is.

Service Work involves the provision of services to various segments of the population.

Sex Segregation refers to the concentration of women or men in a given occupation or jobs within an occupation or within specific work organizations.

Sexual Scripts are ways in which sexual feelings and behavior are culturally organized.

In the **Sick Role** a person cannot function as usual, is exempt from normal responsibilities, is expected to get medical help, follow their instructions, and get well as soon as possible.

Significant Others are persons whose affection and approval are particularly desired.

The **Situational View** assumes that the social situation and statuses and roles assigned to persons produce certain kinds of behavior.

The **Skinner Box** is a completely controlled environment.

Social Change is a process through which values, norms, institutions, stratification systems, and social relationships alter over time.

Social Controls are techniques for enforcing the norms.

Social Differentiation, as an aspect of sociocultural change, involves a shift from diffuse to specialized roles.

Social Disorganization, which was more likely to occur in large urban centers, was once thought to explain mental illness.

Social Facts are characteristics of the group.

Social Fatherhood identifies one man as responsible for the protection of a woman and her children and for the children's placement in the social system.

Social Function refers to the contribution of an element of social structure to the stability of the whole.

A **Social Hierarchy** is a set of ranked statuses.

The **Social Injury Model** sees laws as a means of protecting members of the society.

Social Integration refers to the degree to which a person is a part of a larger group.

Social Mobility is the movement of persons and groups within the stratification system.

Social Movements are organized attempts to introduce or resist social change.

Social Movement Industries arise when a number of organizations unite around a single issue.

Social Norms are rules of behavior.

Social Reproduction of Labor Power indicates that since it is women who are primarily responsible for bearing and raising the next generation of workers, women are prevented from full participation in other social institutions.

Social Statistics refer to official records and systematic observations from which social facts can be deduced.

Social Stratification refers to hierarchies of statuses based on unequal distribution of power, prestige, and property.

Social Structure describes the ways in which values, beliefs, attitudes, and rules for behavior are patterned to produce relatively predictable social relationships.

A **Social System** is a totality composed of interdependent parts.

Socialism is based on the belief that economic activity should be guided by public needs rather than private profit making.

A **Socialist** economic system is marked by central planning of production and distribution.

Socialization is the process whereby one learns how to behave in a given society and develops a sense of self.

Sociobiology is the study of the inheritance of genetically determined behavior.

Socioeconomic Status (SES) is a measure based on a combination of income, occupational prestige, and education.

A **Sociogram** identifies interaction patterns in studying group structure.

The **Sociological Perspective** focuses on the *totality* of social life, the *content* of social interaction, and on the individual as part of a *group*.

Sociology is the study of human behavior, group life, and of societies.

The **Sociology of Emotions** indicates that emotions are socially constructed, exchanged, and maintained.

The **Sociology of Knowledge** is the study of how the production of knowledge is shaped by the social context of thinkers.

Split Labor Market refers to different kinds of workers for different types of industry. It is differentiated by race and gender, with core workers primarily white males and peripheral workers primarily women and minorities.

Sports are a form of structured social behavior with values, norms, statuses, and roles.

The **State** is the political organization of a society.

State Capitalism or **Welfare Capitalism** occurs when the free play of economic forces are constrained by the state to ensure social stability.

The **Statistical Model** defines health or illness in terms of the average of a population.

Statistical Significance is a technical term that indicates how likely a given finding would occur by chance alone.

Statistics are numerical techniques for the classification and analysis of data.

Status is a position in a social system.

Status Attainment research traces the paths by which people reach their ultimate position in the stratification system.

Status Consistency occurs when a person occupies a similar rank across different hierarchies.

Status Cues such as clothing, speech, and hairstyles enable us to locate people in the prestige hierarchy.

Status Inconsistency refers to occupying different ranks in different hierarchies.

Status Incumbents are people who occupy positions in a social system at a given time.

Status Offense is an act that would not be considered a violation if committed by an adult.

Status Set consists of all the statuses occupied by a person.

Status Symbols are outward signs of social rank.

Stereotypical Thinking occurs when a set of characteristics is attributed to all members of a social group.

A **Stigma** is a morally undesirable trait which tends to be generalized, setting the "deviant" apart from people who consider themselves "normal."

Stratification Systems rank some individuals and groups as more deserving than others.

Street Crimes are actions that directly threaten persons or property.

The **Structural-Functional Model** examines the relationship between the parts and the whole of a social system.

Structured Inequality results from the systematic exclusion of specific groups on the basis of ascribed characteristics.

Subcultures refer to differences in values, beliefs, norms, and behavior among societal subgroups.

Subjective Knowledge derives from an individual's own frame of reference.

Subjective Reality refers to the ideas and feelings we have about the world and is developed through social interaction.

Suburbanization resulted from the expansion of the highway system, the spread of housing developments, and the dispersion of industry.

Suburbs are part of the metropolitan area, often linked to the central city's economic and social activities.

Succession is the completed cycle of ecological invasion.

The **Sunbelt** refers to the 15 states located in the South and Southwestern U.S.

The **Superego** represents internalized norms.

Surveys or **Polls** yield information from a large group of respondents.

A **Symbol** is a sound, object, or event which is given meaning by members of a group.

The **Symbolic Interaction Model** examines how people interact with each other, how they interpret such experiences, and how they organize appropriate responses.

Syndicated Crime (see **Organized Crime**).

Synthesis (see **Dialectical Model**).

Tables consist of figures arranged to clarify relationships among variables.

Tactics are actions taken by social movements to achieve desired results.

Task or **Instrumental Roles** are oriented toward accomplishing tasks.

Taste Cultures refers to the great variety of culture tastes without making judgments about their value.

A **Theory** is a set of logically related statements that seek to explain an entire class of events.

Thesis (see **Dialectical Model**).

Tokenism refers to the appointment or promotion of one or a few women or minority-group members to positions of power and responsibility in organizations.

Total Institutions, such as prisons and jails, control and monitor all aspects of inmates' lives.

Under **Totalitarianism** governments attempt to exercise total control over society and its members.

Totalitarian Societies deny the right to dissent.

Tracks in education refer to programs of varying content and pacing to which students are assigned.

The **Tradition-Directed Person's** behavior is governed by custom.

Traditional Authority is based on habit and absolute acceptance of the group's customs.

Transcendence refers to the need to go beyond the limits of one's own senses and feel that life has meaning beyond one's daily experiences.

Age is a **Transitional Status** in that we are constantly moving from one age to another.

The **Triad**, or three-person group, is more stable than the dyad, and there is a greater division of labor.

The **Triple Melting-Pot** suggested that ethnic differences were melting, but religious differences between Catholics, Protestants, and Jews were not.

Two-Career Families or couples are ones in which both husband and wife have a career.

The **Unconscious** is mental and emotional processes we are not consciously aware of.

Unidirectional Theories assume that social change occurs in one direction only.

Uniform Crime Reports are compiled by the FBI from city, state, and county police information.

Urban Concentration occurs when many people settle in a relatively small area.

Urban Legends reflect generalized fears about the danger of modern life.

Urbanism refers to a way of life in cities which emphasizes individualistic norms and styles of behavior.

Urbanization describes the rise in the proportion of the total population concentrated in cities and suburbs.

Utopian Movements seek an ideal society for true believers.

Validation of Self requires assurance that one is who one claims to be.

Validity refers to whether the measuring instrument is really measuring what it was designed to.

The **Value-Added Model** consists of six steps which are necessary and sufficient to produce collective behavior.

Value Consensus refers to an underlying agreement about the goals of a group.

Value Neutrality, the claims that a researcher can be free of personal bias and judgment, is a foundation of the scientific method in the social sciences.

Values are the central beliefs of a culture that provide a standard by which norms are judged.

Variables are characteristics that differ from one person or group to another and change over time.

Verstehen is the ability to see the world as it might be experienced by others.

People with a **Vested Interest** in the status quo benefit from existing arrangements.

Violent Crimes used in the crime index include murder, forcible rape, robbery, and aggravated assault.

A **Virtual Self** is what society expects of a person in a particular role.

Vital Statistics are records of important events such as births, marriages, and deaths.

Voluntary Childlessness refers to the decision by the couple not to have children.

The **Voucher System** allows families to spend a given sum of tax money for any type of schooling available.

Welfare Capitalism (see **State Capitalism**).

In a **Welfare State** production is privately owned but the distribution of goods and services is socialized.

White-Collar Crimes involve complex financial arrangements and are difficult to detect because they do not involve violence or identifiable victims.

Workfare programs are designed to prepare welfare mothers for permanent positions in the labor force.

Workplace Democracy refers to the workers becoming the owners.

The **World System** consists of the economic and political relations among industrial and less-developed nations.

Yuppies are young upwardly mobile professionals.

Zero Population Growth is no natural increase or decrease occurring in the population.

Bibliography

ABBOTT, JACK HENRY. *In the Belly of the Beast: Letters from Prison.* New York: Vintage, 1982.

ABEL, EMILY K. *Terminal Degrees: The Job Crisis in Higher Education.* New York: Praeger, 1984.

ACHENBAUM, ANDREW. *Old Age in the New Land.* Baltimore: Johns Hopkins University Press, 1978.

ACITELLI-DONOGHUE, ANNA. "The Origin and Development of the Japanese Pariah." In John D. Donoghue (ed.), *Pariah Persistence in Changing Japan: A Case Study.* Washington, D.C.: University Press of America, Inc., 1978.

ACKERMANN, ROBERT JOHN. *Religion as Critique.* Amherst, Mass.: University of Massachusetts Press, 1985.

ACOCK, ALAN C., and THEODORE FULLER. "The Attitude-Behavior Relationship and Parental Influence: Circular Mobility in Thailand." *Social Forces* 62(4) (1984): 973–994.

ADAMS, BERT N. "Mate Selection in the United States." In Wesley Burr, Reuben Hill, F. Ivan Nye, and Ira Reiss (eds.), *Contemporary Theories About the Family,* pp. 259–267. New York: Macmillan, 1979.

ADAMS, GORDON. *The Politics of Defense Contracting: The Iron Triangle.* New Brunswick, N.J.: Transaction Press, 1982.

ADLER, FREDA. "Changing Patterns." In Freda Adler and Rita James Simon (eds.), *The Criminology of Deviant Women.* Boston: Houghton Mifflin, 1970.

ADOLPHUS, STEPHEN H., ed. *Equality Postponed: Continuing Barriers to Higher Education in the 1980s.* New York: College Entrance Examination Board, 1984.

AGRESTA, ANTHONY. "The Fastest Growing Minority." *American Demographics* 7 (1985):30–33.

AGUIRRE, B. E. "The Conventionalization of Collective Behavior in Cuba." *American Journal of Sociology* 90(3) (1984):541–565.

AKERS, RONALD. *Deviant Behavior: A Social Learning Approach,* 3rd ed. Belmont, Calif.: Wadsworth, 1985.

ALBA, RICHARD D., and MITCHELL B. CHAMLIN. "A Preliminary Examination of Ethnic Identification Among Whites." *American Sociological Review* 48 (1983): 240–247.

————, and REID GOLDEN. "Patterns of Ethnic Marriage in the United States." *Social Forces* 65 (1986):202–223.

————, DAVID E. LAVIN, and RICHARD A. SILBERSTEIN. *Right Versus Privilege: The Open-Admissions Experiment at the City University of New York.* New York: Free Press, 1981.

ALBUS, JAMES C. "Robots in the Workplace." *The Futurist* (February 1983):22–27.

ALEX, NICHOLAS. *New York Cops Talk Back: A Study of a Beleagured Minority.* New York: John Wiley, 1976.

ALEXANDER, JEFFREY C. *The Modern Reconstruction of Classical Thought: Talcott Parsons.* Berkeley, Calif.: University of California Press, 1984.

ALEXANDER, JEFFREY C., ed. *Neofunctionalism.* Beverly Hills, Calif.: Sage, 1985.

ALEXANDER, KARL, and MARTHA COOK. "Curriculum and Coursework: A Surprise Ending to a Familiar Story." *American Sociological Review* 47 (October 1982): 626–640.

ALEXANDER, PETER, and ROGER GILL, eds. *Utopias.* London: Duckworth, 1984.

ALFANO, PETER. "Women's Sports: Problems Amid the Progress." *The New York Times,* December 15, 1985, p. D1.

ALFORD, ROBERT R., and ROGER FRIEDLAND. *Powers of Theory: Capitalism, the State, and Democracy.* New York: Cambridge University Press, 1985.

ALFRED, RICHARD L. "Community Colleges and Education in the 1980s." *Educational Digest* 50 (March 1985):51–53.

ALTMAN, DENNIS. *AIDS in the Mind of America: The Social, Political, and Psychological Impact of a New Epidemic.* Garden City, N.Y.: Anchor, 1986.

ALWIN, DUANE F. "Trends in Parental Socialization Values: Detroit, 1958–1983." *American Journal of Sociology* 90(2) (1984):359–382.

————. "Living Alone." *ISR Newsletter* (Autumn 1984):3–4. Ann Arbor, Mich.: Institute for Social Research.

————. "Religion and Parental Child-Rearing Orientations: Evidence of a Catholic-Protestant Convergence." *American Journal of Sociology* 92(2) (September 1986): 412–420.

————, and ARLAND THORNTON. "Family Origins and the Schooling Process: Early versus Late Influence of Parental Characteristics." *American Sociological Review* 49(6) (1984):784–802.

AMERICAN DEMOGRAPHICS. "Targeting Metropolitan Growth." (August 1985):50.

AMERICAN MEDICAL ASSOCIATION SPECIAL TASK FORCE ON PROFESSIONAL LIABILITY AND INSURANCE. "Professional Liability in the '80s" (Report I). Chicago: American Medical Association, October 1984.

AMOSS, P. T., and S. HARRELL, eds. *Other Ways of Growing Old.* Stanford, Calif: Stanford University Press, 1981.

ANDERSEN, MARGARET L. *Thinking About Women: Sociological and Feminist Perspectives,* 2nd ed. New York: Macmillan, 1988.

ANDERSON, DAVID C. "Lock 'Em Up! (All 1 Percent)." *The New York Times,* September 23, 1985, p. 18.

ANDERSON, D. S., and A. E. VERVOORN. *Access to Privilege: Patterns of Participation in Post-Secondary Education.* Canberra: Australian National University Press, 1983.

ANDERSON, R., and O. W. ANDERSON. "Trends in the Use of Health Services." In Howard E. Freeman, Sol Levine, and Leo G. Reeder (eds.), *Handbook of Medical Sociology,* pp. 371–391. Englewood Cliffs, N.J.: Prentice-Hall, 1979.

ANDERSON, SUSAN. "Goals on Handicapped Meet Wide Resistance." *The New York Times,* November 14, 1982, p. B12.

ANDREW, ED. *Closing the Iron Cage: The Scientific Management of Worth and Leisure.* Montreal: Black Rose Books, 1981.

ANGEL, RONALD, and MARTA TIENDA. "Determinants of Extended Household Structure: Cultural Patterns or Economic Need?" *American Journal of Sociology* 87(6) (May 1982):1306–1383.

APPEL, MICHAEL. *Education and Power.* London: Routledge & Kegan Paul, 1982.

————, and LOIS WEISS, eds. *Ideology and Practice in Schooling.* Philadelphia: Temple University Press, 1984.

APOSTLE, RICHARD, DON CLAIRMONT, and LARS OSBERG. "Economic Segmentation and Politics." *American Journal of Sociology* 91 (1986):905–931.

ARCE, CARLOS. "A Reconsideration of Chicano Culture and Identity." *Daedalus* 110(2) (Spring 1981):177–191.

ARCHDEACON, THOMAS J. *Becoming American: An Ethnic History.* New York: Free Press, 1983.

ARIES, PHILLIPE. *Centuries of Childhood: A Social History of Family Life.* New York: Knopf, 1962.

ARIYOSHI, SAWAKO. *The Twilight Years,* Mildred Takahara (trans.). Kodansha, 1984.

ARNEY, WILLIAM RAY. "Maternal-Infant Bonding: The Politics of Falling in Love with Your Child." *Feminist Studies* 6(3) (1980):547–570.

ARONOWITZ, STANLEY. *Working Class Hero: A New Strategy for Labor.* New York: Pilgrim Press, 1983.

————, and HENRY A. GIROUX. *Education Under Siege: The Conservative, Liberal, and Radical Debate over Schooling.* South Hadley, Mass.: Bergin & Garvey, 1985.

ASHTON, PATRICK J. "The Political Economy of Suburban Development." In William K. Tabb and Larry Sawers (eds.), *Marxism and the Metropolis: New Perspectives in Urban Political Economy.* New York: Oxford University Press, 1978.

ASTIN, ALEXANDER A. *Achieving Educational Excellence: A Critical Assessment of Programs and Practices in Higher Education.* San Francisco: Jossey-Bass, 1985.

————. *American Freshmen: 20-Year Trends.* Los Angeles: University of California Higher Education Research Institute, 1986.

ASTRACHAN, ANTHONY. *How Men Feel: Their Response to Women's Demands for Equality and Power.* New York: Anchor/Doubleday, 1986.

ATKINSON, MAXINE P., and JACQUELINE BOLES. "WASP (Wives as Senior Partners)." *Journal of Marriage and the Family* 46 (1984):861–870.

————, and BECKY L. GLASS. "Marital Age Heterogamy and Homogamy, 1900 to 1980." *Journal of Marriage and the Family* 47 (1985):685–691.

ATWATER, LYNN. *The Extramarital Connection: Sex, Intimacy, and Identity.* New York: Irvington, 1982.

AXEL, HELEN. *A New Generation of Workers.* New York: The Conference Board, 1985.

BACHMAN, JERALD G., and PATRICK M. O'MALLEY. "Black-White Differences in Self-Esteem: Are They Affected by Response Styles?" *American Journal of Sociology* 90(3) (1984):624–639.

BACHRACH, CHRISTINE A. "Adoption Plans, Adopted Children, and Adoptive Mothers." *Journal of Marriage and the Family* 48 (1986):243–253.

BAER, HANS A. *The Black Spiritual Movement: A Religious Response to Racism.* Knoxville, Tenn.: University of Tennessee Press, 1984.

BAGDIKIAN, BEN H. "Who Pays for the News?" In David Manning White and John Pendleton (eds.), *Popular Culture,* pp. 52–62. Del Mar, Calif.: Publishers, Inc., 1977.

————. *The Media Monopoly.* Boston: Beacon Press, 1983.

BAGLEY, CHRISTOPHER. *Racial and Ethnic Composition.* New York: Bantam, 1985.

BAILEY, WILLIAM C. "Deterrence and the Severity of the Death Penalty: A Neglected Question in Deterrence Research." *Social Forces* 58(4) (June 1980):1308–1332.

BAILLOD, JURG, and ISODOR WALLIMAN. "From Pre-Industrial Office Work to the Age of Micro-Electronics." *Humanity and Society* 9 (November 1985):428–442.

BAKER, DAVID P., and DORIS ENTWISLE. "The Influence of Mothers on the Academic Expectations of Young Children:

A Longitudinal Study of How Gender Differences Arise." *Social Forces* 65(3) (1987):670–694.

BALES, ROBERT F. *Interaction Process Analysis.* Reading, Mass.: Addison-Wesley, 1950.

BALL, RICHARD E., and LYNN ROBBINS. "Marital Status and Life Satisfaction Among Black Americans." *Journal of Marriage and the Family* 48 (1986):389–394.

BALL-ROKEACH, SANDRA J., and MURIEL G. CANTOR. *Media, Audience, and Social Structure.* Beverly Hills, Calif.: Sage, 1986.

————, MILTON ROKEACH, and JOEL W. GRUBE. *The Great American Values Test: Influencing Behavior and Belief through Television.* New York: Free Press, 1984.

BALTZELL, E. DIGBY. *Puritan Boston and Quaker Philadelphia.* New York: Free Press, 1979.

BANFIELD, EDWARD C. *The Unheavenly City Revisited.* Boston: Little, Brown, 1974.

BARKAN, STEVEN E. "Strategic, Tactical and Organizational Dilemmas of the Protest Movement Against Nuclear Power." *Social Problems* 27(1) (October 1979):19–37.

————. "Legal Control of the Southern Civil Rights Movement." *American Sociological Review* 49(4) (1984): 552–565.

BARKER, EILEEN. *The Making of a Moonie.* London: Basil Blackwell, 1984.

BARNHART, JOE EDWARD. *The Southern Baptist Holy War.* Austin, Tex.: Texas Monthly Press, 1987.

BARON, JAMES N., and WILLIAM T. BIELBY. "The Organization of Work in a Segmented Economy." *American Sociological Review* 49 (1984): 454–473.

————, and WILLIAM T. BIELBY. "Organizational Barriers to Gender Equality: Sex Segregation of Jobs and Opportunities." In Alice S. Rossi (ed.), *Gender and the Life Course,* pp. 233–251. Hawthorne, N.Y.: Aldine, 1985.

BARRON, JAMES. "Some Units of Jaycees Rebel Against Admitting Women." *The New York Times,* September 10, 1984, p. 14.

BARSTOW, ANNE. "The Uses of Archeology for Women's History: James Mellaart's Work on the Neolithic Goddess at Catal Hüyük." *Feminist Studies* 4(3) (October 1978): 7–18.

BARUCH, GRACE, and JEANNE BROOKS-GUNN, eds. *Women in Midlife.* New York: Plenum Press, 1984.

BAYER, RONALD. *Homosexuality and American Psychiatry: The Politics of Diagnosis.* New York: Basic Books, 1981.

BAYLEY, DAVID H. *Patterns of Policing: A Comparative International Analysis.* New Brunswick, N.J.: Rutgers University Press, 1985.

BEAN, FRANK D., and GARY SWICEGOOD. *Mexican-American Fertility Patterns.* Austin: University of Texas Press, 1985.

BECK, RACHELLE, and NANCY ANDERSON. *Learning About Central America: What U.S. Children's Books and Texts Teach.* New York: Council on Interracial Books for Children, 1983.

BECKER, HOWARD S. *Outsiders: Studies in the Sociology of Deviance.* New York: Free Press, 1973.

BECKFORD, JAMES A. *Cult Controversies: The Societal Response to the New Religious Movements.* London: Tavistock, 1985.

BEEGHLEY, LEONARD. "Social Structure and the Political Disenfranchisement of the Poor." Paper presented at the 80th annual meeting of the American Sociological Association, Washington, D.C., August 1983.

BEER, WILLIAM R. *Househusbands: Men and Housework in American Families.* New York: Praeger, 1983.

BELL, DANIEL. *The Coming of Post-Industrial Society.* New York: Basic Books, 1973.

BELLAH, ROBERT N. "Civil Religion in America." In Robert N. Bellah, *Beyond Belief: Essays on Religion in a Post-Traditional World.* New York: Harper & Row, 1970.

————. *The Broken Covenant: American Civil Religion in a Time Trial.* New York: Seabury Press, 1975.

BENEDICT, RUTH. *Patterns of Culture.* Boston: Houghton Mifflin, 1934. *"Continuities and Discontinuities in Cultural Conditioning."* *Psychiatry* 1(2) (1938):161–167.

BENNETT, JOHN W. *Of Time and the Enterprise: North American Family Farm Management in a Context of Resource Marginality.* Minneapolis: University of Minnesota Press, 1986.

BENNETT, NEIL G., and DAVID E. BLOOM. "Marriage Patterns in the United States." *NBER Working Paper #1701,* September 1985, pp. 1–31.

BENSMAN, JOSEPH, and ISRAEL GERVER. "Crime and Punishment in the Factory." *American Sociological Review* 28 (1963):588–598.

————, and ROBERT LILIENFELD. *Between Public and Private: Lost Boundaries of the Self.* New York: Macmillan, 1979.

BERGER, JOSEPH. "Religious Surge Found Among 'Baby Boomers.'" *The New York Times,* November 19, 1986, p. 9.

BERGER, PETER L. *The Sacred Canopy.* Garden City, N.Y.: Doubleday, 1969.

————, and THOMAS LUCKMAN. *The Social Construction of Reality.* Garden City, N.Y.: Doubleday, 1966.

BERGESEN, ALBERT. *The Sacred and the Subversive: Political Witch-Hunts as National Rituals.* Storrs, Conn.: Society for the Scientific Study of Religion, 1984.

BERK, SARAH FENSTERMAKER. "Women's Work and the Production of Gender." Paper presented at the 80th annual meeting of the American Sociological Association, Washington, D.C., August 1985.

BERMAN, EDWARD H. *The Influence of the Carnegie, Ford, and Rockefeller Foundations on American Foreign Policy: The Ideology of Philanthropy.* Albany: State University of New York, 1983.

BERNARD, J. L., S. L. BERNARD, and M. L. BERNARD. "Courtship Violence and Sex Typing." *Family Relations* 34 (1985):573–576.

BERNARD, JESSIE. *The Female World.* New York: Free Press, 1981.

————. *The Future of Marriage.* New Haven, Conn.: Yale University Press, 1982.

BERRY, BRIAN J. R. *The Human Consequences of Urbanization: Divergent Paths in the Urban Experience of the*

20th Century. New York: St. Martin's Press, 1973.

BEST, JOEL. "The Myth of the Halloween Sadist." *Psychology Today,* November 1985, pp. 14–15.

BIANCHI, SUZANNE M., and JUDITH A. SELTZER. "Life Without Father." *American Demographics* 8 (1986):43–47.

————, and DAPHNE SPAIN. *American Women in Transition.* New York: Russell Sage Foundation, 1986.

BIELBY, DENISE DEL VENTO, and WILLIAM T. BIELBY. "Work Commitment, Sex-Role Attitudes, and Women's Employment." *American Sociological Review* 49 (1984):234–247.

BIELBY, WILLIAM T., and JAMES N. BARON. "Men and Women at Work: Sex Segregation and Statistical Discrimination." *American Journal of Sociology* 91 (1986):759–799.

BIEMILLER, LAWRENCE. "Board Says Minority-Group Scores Helped Push Up Averages on SAT." *Chronicle of Higher Education* 25(8) (October 20, 1982):1.

BIERSTEDT, ROBERT. *American Sociological Theory: A Critical History.* New York: Academic Press, 1981.

BIESTY, PATRICK. "If It's Fun, Is It Play? A Meadian Analysis." In Bernard Mergen (ed.), *Cultural Dimensions of Play, Games, and Sport,* pp. 61–72. Champaign, Ill.: Human Kinetics, 1986.

BIGGAR, JEANNE C. "The Sunning of America: Migration to the Sunbelt." *Population Bulletin* 34(1) (May 1979):3–42.

BIGGART, NICOLE WOOLSEY. "Rationality, Meaning and Self-Management: Success Manuals, 1950–1980." *Social Problems* 30 (1983):298–311.

BILLER, HENRY. "The Father and Sex Role Development." In Michael E. Lamb (ed.), *The Role of the Father in Child Development* (2nd ed.). New York: John Wiley, 1981.

BINFORD, HENRY. *The First Suburbs: Residential Communities on the Boston Periphery, 1815–1860.* Chicago: University of Chicago Press, 1985.

BIRDWHISTLE, RAY. *Kinesics and Context.* Philadelphia: University of Pennsylvania Press, 1970.

BLACK'S LAW DICTIONARY, 5th ed. St. Paul, Minn.: West Publishing Co., 1979.

BLAKE, JUDITH. "Number of Siblings and Educational Mobility." *American Sociological Review* 50(1) (1985): 84–94.

BLAU, JUDITH R. "The Elité Arts, More or Less de rigueur: A Comparative Analysis of Metropolitan Culture." *Social Forces* 64(4) (1986):875–905.

————. "High Culture as Mass Culture." *Society* (May–June 1986):65–69.

BLAU, JUDITH R., and PETER M. BLAU. "The Cost of Inequality: Metropolitan Structure and Violent Crime." *American Sociological Review* 47 (1982):114–129.

————, and OTIS DUDLEY DUNCAN. *The American Occupational Structure.* New York: John Wiley, 1967.

————, and W. RICHARD SCOTT. *Formal Organizations.* San Francisco: Chandler, 1962.

BLAU, PETER. *Exchange and Power in Social Life.* New Brunswick, N.J.: Transaction Press, 1986.

BLAU, ZENA SMITH. *Black Children/White Children: Competence, Socialization, and Social Structure.* New York: Free Press, 1981.

BLAUNER, ROBERT. *Alienation and Freedom.* Chicago: University of Chicago Press, 1964.

BLEIER, RUTH. *Science and Gender: A Critique of Biology and Its Theories on Women.* New York: Pergamon Press, 1984.

BLEKHER, FEIGA. *The Soviet Woman in the Family and in Society.* New York: Wiley, 1979.

BLOCK, ALAN A., and WILLIAM J. CHAMBLISS. *Organizing Crime.* New York: Elsevier/North Holland, 1981.

BLOCK, FRED. *Rethinking State Theory.* Philadelphia: Temple University Press, 1987.

BLOCKER, JACK S. "Separate Paths: Suffragists and the Women's Temperance Crusade." *Signs* 10(3) (1985): 460–476.

BLUESTONE, BARRY, and BENNETT HARRISON. "The Grim Truth About the Job 'Miracle.'" *The New York Times,* February 1, 1987, p. F3.

BLUMBERG, RAE LESSER. *Stratification: Socioeconomic and Sexual Inequality.* Dubuque, Iowa: Wm. C. Brown, 1978.

————. "Gender Stratification and Economic Development: Paradigm and Praxis in the Intersection of Social Structure, Human Lives, and the African Food Crisis." Paper presented at the 81st annual meeting of the American Sociological Association, New York, August 1986.

BLUMBERG, RHODA LOIS. *Civil Rights: The 1960 Freedom Struggle.* Boston: Twayne, 1984.

————. *Organizations in Contemporary Society.* Englewood Cliffs, N.J.: Prentice Hall, 1987.

BLUMENFELD, HANS. "The Urban Pattern." *The Annals of the American Academy of Political and Social Science* 352 (March 1964):74–83.

BLUMER, HERBERT. "Collective Behavior." In Alfred McLung Lee (ed.), *New Outlines of the Principles of Sociology.* New York: Barnes & Noble, 1951.

————. "Social Movements." In R. Serge Denisoff (ed.), *The Sociology of Dissent,* pp. 74–90. New York: Harcourt Brace Jovanovich, 1974.

BOASE, PAUL H. "Early Retirement and the Graying of the Academy." *Thought and Action* 2(1) (1986):89–100.

BOFFEY, PHILIP M. "AIDS in the Future: Experts Say Deaths Will Climb Sharply." *The New York Times,* January 14, 1986, pp. C1, C9.

————. "Major Study Points to Faulty Research at Two Universities." *The New York Times,* April 22, 1986, p. C1.

BOGUE, DONALD J. *The Population of the United States: Historical Trends and Projections.* New York: Free Press, 1985.

BOLI, JOHN. "Marxism as World Religion." *Social Problems* 28 (1981):510–513.

BOLICK, NANCY O'KEEFE. "The New Faces of Adoption." *Boston Magazine,* October 1986, pp. 152–157, 197–198.

BOLLEN, KENNETH A., and ROBERT W. JACKMAN. "Political Democracy and the Size Distribution of Income." *American Sociological Review* 50 (1985):438–457.

————, and DAVID P. PHILLIPS. "Imitative Suicides: A National Study of the Effects of Television News Stories."

American Sociological Review 47(6) (1982):802–809.

BOLLES, RICHARD. *What Color Is Your Parachute?* Berkeley, Calif.: Ten Speed Press, 1987.

BONACICH, EDNA. "Advanced Capitalism and Black/White Relations in the U.S.: A Split Labor Market Interpretation." *American Sociological Review* 41(1) (1975):34–51.

BOOTH, ALAN, DAVID R. JOHNSON, LYNN WHITE, and JOHN N. EDWARDS. "Women, Outside Employment, and Marital Instability." *American Journal of Sociology* 90 (1984): 567–585.

BORCHERT, WOLFGANG. *The Man Outside.* New York: New Directions, 1971.

BORD, RICHARD J., and JOSEPH E. FAULKNER. *The Catholic Charismatics: The Anatomy of a Modern Religious Movement.* University Park: Pennsylvania State University Press, 1983.

BORUCH, ROBERT F., and JOE S. CECIL. *Solutions to Ethical and Legal Problems in Social Research.* New York: Academic Press, 1983.

BORUS, MICHAEL E., ed. *Youth and the Labor Market: Analyses of the National Longitudinal Study.* Kalamazoo, Mich.: Upjohn Institute for Employment Research, 1984.

BOSE, CHRISTINE E. "Dual Spheres." In Beth B. Hess and Myra Marx Ferree (eds.), *Analyzing Gender: A Handbook of Social Science Research.* Newbury Park, Calif.: Sage, 1987.

————, ROSLYN FELDBERG, and NATALIE SOKOLOFF. *Hidden Aspects of Women's Work.* Westport, Conn.: Greenwood Press, 1987.

————, and PETER H. ROSSI. "Gender and Jobs: Prestige Standings of Occupations as Affected by Gender." *American Sociological Review* 48 (1983):316–330.

BOSSEN, LAUREL H. *The Redivision of Labor: Women and Economic Choice in Four Guatemalan Communities.* Albany: State University of New York Press, 1984.

BOSSERT, STEVEN T. *Tasks and Social Relationships in Classrooms: A Study of Instructional Organization and Its Consequences.* New York: Cambridge University Press, 1979.

BOUDON, RAYMOND. *The Unintended Consequences of Social Action.* New York: St. Martin's Press. 1982.

BOURDIEU, PIERRE. *Distinction: A Social Critique of the Judgement of Taste.* Cambridge, Mass.: Harvard University Press, 1985.

————, and JEAN CLAUDE PASSERON. *Reproduction in Education, Society, and Culture.* Beverly Hills, Calif.: Sage, 1977.

BOUTILIER, MARY A., and LUCINDA SANGIOVANNI. *The Sporting Woman.* Champaign, Ill.: Human Kinetics, 1983.

BOUVIER, LEON F. "America's Baby Boom Generation: The Fateful Bulge." *Population Bulletin* 35(1) (April 1980): 3–35.

————, and ROBERT W. GARDNER. "Immigration to the U.S.: The Unfinished Story." *Population Bulletin* 41(1) (November 1986):10.

BOWERS, WILLIAM J., GLENN L. PIERCE, and JOHN F. MCDEVITT. *Legal Homicide: Death as Punishment in America, 1964–1982.* Boston: Northeastern University Press, 1984.

BOWLES, SAMUEL, and HERBERT GINTIS. *Democracy and Capitalism: Property, Community, and Contradictions of Modern Thought.* New York: Basic Books, 1985.

————. *Schooling in Capitalist America.* New York: Basic Books, 1976.

BOWSER, BENJAMIN P., and RAYMOND G. HUNT. *Impact of Racism on White Americans.* Beverly Hills, Calif.: Sage, 1981.

BOYER, M. CHRISTINE. *Dreaming the Rational City: The Myth of American City Planning.* Cambridge, Mass.: MIT Press, 1983.

BOYER, PAUL. *By the Dawn's Early Light: American Thought and Culture at the Dawn of the Atomic Age.* New York: Pantheon, 1985.

BOYER, PAUL, and STEPHEN NISSENBAUM. *Salem Possessed: The Social Origins of Witchcraft.* Cambridge, Mass.: Harvard University Press.

BRACKMAN, HAROLD, and STEVEN P. ERIE. "The Future of the Gender Gap." *Social Policy* (Winter 1986):5–10.

BRADLEY, KEITH, and ALAN GELB. *Worker + Capitalism = The New Industrial Relations.* Cambridge, Mass.: MIT Press, 1983.

BRAITHWAITE, JOHN. *Inequality, Crime and Public Policy.* Boston: Routledge & Kegan Paul, 1979.

————. "The Myth of Social Class and Criminality Reconsidered." *American Sociological Review* 46(1) (1981): 36–57.

BRANTLINGER, PATRICK. *Bread and Circuses: Theories of Mass Culture and Social Decay.* Ithaca, N.Y.: Cornell University Press, 1983.

BRAUNGART, RICHARD G., and MARGARET M. BRAUNGART. "Life-Course and Generational Politics." *Annual Review of Sociology* 12 (1986):205–231.

BRAVERMAN, HARRY. *Labor and Monopoly Capital.* New York: Monthly Review Press, 1974.

BREAULT, K. D. "Suicide in America: A Test of Durkheim's Theory of Religious and Family Integration, 1933–1980." *American Journal of Sociology* 92 (1986):628–656.

BREDEMEIER, BRENDA JO, and DAVID L. SHIELDS. "Values and Violence in Sports Today: The Moral Reasoning Athletes Use in Their Games and in Their Lives." *Psychology Today,* October 1985, pp. 23–32.

BREINES, WINI. *Community and Organization in the New Left, 1962–1968: The Great Refusal.* South Hadley, Mass.: J. F. Bergin, 1982.

————, and LINDA GORDON. "The New Scholarship on Family Violence." *Signs* 8 (1983):490–531.

BRIGHT, CHARLES, and SUSAN HARDING, eds. *Statemaking and Social Movements: Essays in History and Theory.* Ann Arbor: University of Michigan Press, 1984.

BRIGGS, KENNETH. "Mainstream U.S. Evangelicals Surge in Protestant Influence." *The New York Times,* March 14, 1982, pp. 1, 50.

————. "Religious Feeling Seen Strong In U.S." *The New York Times,* December 9, 1984, p. 30.

BRIGGS, SHEILA. "Gender and Religion." In Beth B. Hess and Myra Marx Ferree (eds.), *Analyzing Gender: A Handbook of Social Research.* Newbury Park, Calif.: Sage, 1987.

BRIM, ORVILLE G., JR. "Male Mid-Life Crisis: A Comparative Analysis." In Beth B. Hess (ed.), *Growing Old in America* (2nd ed.), pp. 147–163. New Brunswick, N.J.: Transaction Books, 1979.

————, and JEROME KAGAN, eds. *Constancy and Change in Human Development.* Cambridge, Mass.: Harvard University Press, 1980.

BRIMBLECOMBE, PETER. *The Big Smoke: A History of Air Pollution in London Since Medieval Times.* London: Methuen, 1987.

BRINT, STEVEN. "'New Class' and Cumulative Trend Explanations of the Liberal Political Attitudes of Professionals." *American Journal of Sociology* 90 (1984):30–71.

BRODEUR, PAUL. *Outrageous Misconduct: The Asbestos Industry on Trial.* New York: Pantheon Books, 1985.

BRODY, JANE E. "Influential Theory on 'Bonding' at Birth Is Now Questioned." *The New York Times,* March 29, 1983, pp. C1, C8.

BROWN, JUDITH K., VIRGINIA KERNS, et al. *In Her Prime: A New View of Middle-Aged Women.* South Hadley, Mass.: Bergin & Garvey, 1985.

BROWN, A. LEE. *Rules and Conflict: An Introduction to Political Life and Its Study.* Englewood Cliffs, N.J.: Prentice-Hall, 1981.

BROWN, RUTH MURRAY. "In Defense of Traditional Values: The Antifeminist Movement." In Beth B. Hess and Marvin B. Sussman (eds.), *Women and the Family: Two Decades of Change,* pp. 19–36. New York: Haworth, 1984.

BROWNE, MALCOLM W. "A Look at Success of Young Asians." *The New York Times,* March 25, 1986.

BRUBAKER, ROGERS. *The Limits of Rationality: An Essay on the Social and Moral Thought of Max Weber.* Dorchester, Mass.: Allen & Unwin, 1983.

BRUNVAND, JAN HAROLD. *The Mexican Pet: More 'New' Urban Legends.* New York: Norton, 1986.

BUELL, EMMETT H., JR., and RICHARD A. BRISBIN, JR. *School Desegregation and Defended Neighborhoods.* Lexington, Mass.: Lexington Books, 1982.

BUMPASS, LARRY. "Some Characteristics of Children's Second Families." *American Journal of Sociology* 90 (1984): 608–622.

BURAWOY, MICHAEL. "The Resurgence of Marxism in American Sociology." *American Journal of Sociology* 88 (Supplement, 1982):S1–S30.

————, and JANOS LUKACS. "Mythologies of Work: A Comparison of Firms in State Socialism and Advanced Capitalism." *American Sociological Review* 50 (1985): 723–737.

BURGESS, ERNEST W. "The Growth of the City." In Robert E. Park, Ernest W. Burgess, and R. D. McKenzie (eds.), *The City.* Chicago: University of Chicago Press, 1925.

————, ed. *Aging in Western Societies.* Chicago: University of Chicago Press, 1960.

BURRIS, VAL. "Who Opposed the ERA? An Analysis of the Social Bases of Antifeminism." *Social Science Quarterly*

65(3) (1983):305–317.

BURRIS, VAL. "The Social and Political Consequences of Overeducation." *American Sociological Review,* 48 (August 1983):454–467.

BURSTEIN, PAUL. *Discrimination, Jobs, and Politics: The Struggle for Equal Employment Opportunity in the United States since the New Deal.* Chicago: University of Chicago Press, 1985.

BURT, RONALD S. *Corporate Profits and Cooptation: Networks of Market Constraints and Directorate Ties in the American Economy.* New York: Academic Press, 1983.

BURTON, N. J., and L. V. JONES. "Recent Trends in Achievement Levels of Black and White Youth." *Educational Researcher* 11(4) (1982):10–14.

BUSCH, LAWRENCE, and WILLIAM B. LACEY. *Science, Agriculture, and the Politics of Research.* Boulder, Colo.: Westview Press, 1983.

BUTLER, EDGAR R. *Urban Sociology: A Systematic Approach.* New York: Harper & Row, 1976.

BUTTERFIELD, FOX. "Why Asians Are Going to the Head of the Class." *The New York Times,* August 3, 1986, Sec. 12, pp. 18–23.

————. "Funds and Jobs Pledged to Boston Students." *The New York Times,* September 10, 1986, pp. 1 ff.

CALVIN, WILLIAM H. *The Throwing Madonna: Essays on the Brain.* New York: McGraw-Hill Book Co., 1985.

CAMERON, KENNETH N. *Marxism: The Science of Society.* South Hadley, Mass.: Bergin & Garvey, 1985.

CAMPBELL, ANGUS. *White Attitudes Toward Black People.* Ann Arbor, Mich.: Institute for Social Research, 1971.

CANNON, LYNN WEBER, and BONNIE THORTON DILL. "Trends in Middle Class Identification Among Black Americans from 1952 to 1978." Paper presented at the annual meeting of the Society for the Study of Social Problems, Toronto, August 1981.

CANTOR, MURIEL. "Popular Culture and the Portrayal of Women: Content and Control." In Beth B. Hess and Myra Marx Ferree (eds.), *Analyzing Gender: A Handbook of Social Research.* Newbury Park, Calif.: Sage, 1987.

CAPLAN, ROBERT D., AMIRAM VINOKUR, and CINDY WILLIAMS. "Coping with Job Loss." *ISR Newsletter* (Autumn 1986). Institute for Social Research, University of Michigan.

CAPLOW, THEODORE, et al. *All Faithful People: Change and Continuity in Middletown's Religion.* Minneapolis: University of Minnesota Press, 1984.

CARDWELL, JERRY D. *Mass Media Christianity: Televangelism and the Great Commission.* Lanham, Md.: University Press of America, 1984.

CARNEGIE CORPORATION OF NEW YORK. "A Nation Prepared: Teachers for the 21st Century." New York: Carnegie Corporation, 1986.

CARNEGIE QUARTERLY. "The Urban School Principal: The Rocky Road to Instructional Leadership" 31(1) (Winter 1986).

CARNOY, MARTIN. *The State and Political Theory.* Princeton, N.J.: Princeton University Press, 1984.

————, and HENRY M. LEVIN. *Schooling and Work in the Democratic State*. Stanford, Calif.: Stanford University Press, 1985.

CARRERA, MICHAEL. *The Facts, the Acts and Your Feelings*. New York: Crown, 1981.

————. "Some Reflections on Adolescent Sexuality." *Siecus Report* 11(4) (March 1983):1–2.

————. "Reconceptualizing Adolescence." *Siecus Report* 12(4) (March 1984):10.

CARROLL, GLENN R., and KARL ULRICH MAYER. "Job-Shift Patterns in the Federal Republic of Germany: The Effects of Social Class, Industrial Sector, and Organizational Size." *American Sociological Review* 51 (1986):323–341.

CARROLL, JACKSON W., BARBARA HARGROVE, and ADAIR T. LUMMIS. *Women of the Cloth: A New Opportunity for the Churches*. New York: Harper & Row, 1983.

CARROLL, SUSAN J. *Women as Candidates in American Politics*. Bloomington, Ind.: Indiana University Press, 1985.

CASE, JOHN, and ROSEMARY C. R. TAYLOR, eds. *Coops, Communes, and Collectives: Experiments in Social Change in the 1960's and 1970's*. New York: Pantheon, 1979.

CASTELLS, MANUEL. "The Wild City." *Kapital State* 4–5 (Summer 1978):2–30.

CASTLEMAN, CRAIG. *Getting Up: Subway Graffiti in New York*. Cambridge, Mass.: MIT Press, 1982.

CATHOLICS FOR A FREE CHOICE. "U.S. Population and Development Policy: A Religious Perspective." Washington, D.C.: CFFC.

CATTON, WILLIAM R. *Overshoot: The Ecological Basis of Revolutionary Change*. Urbana: University of Illinois Press, 1980.

CAVIN, SUSAN. *Lesbian Origins*. San Francisco: Ism Press, Inc., 1985.

CENTERS, RICHARD. *The Psychology of Social Class*. Princeton, N.J.: Princeton University Press, 1949.

CERF, CHRISTOPHER, and VICTOR NAVASKY. *The Experts Speak*. New York: Pantheon, 1984.

CHAFETZ, JANET S. *Sex and Advantage: A Comparative Macro-Structural Theory of Sex Stratification*. Totowa, N.J.: Rowman & Allenheld, 1984.

————, and ANTHONY G. DWORKIN. "In the Face of Threat: Organized AntiFeminism in Comparative Perspective." *Gender and Society* 1(1) (1987):33–60.

————, and ANTHONY G. DWORKIN. *Female Revolt: The Rise of Women's Movements in World and Historical Perspective*. Totowa, N.J.: Rowman & Littlefield, 1986.

CHAPPLE, STEVE, and REEBEE GAROFALO. *Rock 'n' Roll Is Here to Pay: The History and Politics of the Music Industry*. Chicago: Nelson Hall, 1978.

CHERLIN, ANDREW J. "Changing Family and Household: Contemporary Lessons from Historical Research." *Annual Review of Sociology* 9 (1983):51–66.

————. *The New American Grandparent: A Place in the Family, a Life Apart*. New York: Basic Books, 1986.

————, and PAMELA BARNHOUSE WALTERS. "Trends in United States Men's and Women's Sex-Role Attitudes: 1972 to 1978." *American Sociological Review* 46 (1981): 453–460.

CHESNEY-LIND, MEDA. "Women and Crime: The Female Offender." *Signs: Journal of Women in Culture and Society* 12(1) (1986):78–96.

CHODOROW, NANCY. *The Reproduction of Mothering*. Berkeley: University of California Press, 1978.

CHRISTENSON, R. L., and TERENCE T. THORNBERRY. "Unemployment and Criminal Involvement: An Investigation of Reciprocal Causal Structures." *American Sociological Review* 49 (1984):398–415.

CIEPLY, MICHAEL, and PETER W. BARNES. "Movie and TV Mergers Point to Concentration of Power to Entertain." *Wall Street Journal*, August 21, 1986, pp. 1 ff.

CLARK, BURTON R. *The Higher Education System: Academic Organization in Cross-National Perspective*. Berkeley, Calif: University of California Press, 1983.

CLARK, REGINALD M. *Family Life and School Achievement: Why Poor Black Children Succeed or Fail*. Chicago: University of Chicago Press, 1983.

CLAWSON, DAN, ALAN NEUSTADTL, and JAMES BEARDEN. "The Logic of Business Unity: Corporate Contributions to the 1980 Congressional Elections." *American Sociological Review* 51 (1986):797–811.

CLENDINEN, DUDLEY. "Urban Education that Really Works." *The New York Times*, April 13, 1986, Sect. 12, p. 68.

CLEVELAND, CEIL. "Jonestown and the People's Temple Five Years Later: A Social Historian's View." *Columbia Magazine*, April 1984, pp. 11–19.

CLINARD, MARSHALL B., and PETER C. YEAGER. *Corporate Crime*. New York: Free Press, 1980.

CLINARD, MARSHALL, and ROBERT MEIER. *Sociology of Deviant Behavior*. New York: Holt, 1979.

CLYMER, ADAM. "How Americans Rate Big Business." *The New York Times Magazine*, June 8, 1986, p. 69.

COAKLEY, JAY J. *Sport in Society*, 3rd ed. St. Louis: C. V. Mosby, 1986.

COATES, VARY T. "The Potential Impact of Robotics." *The Futurist* (February 1983):28–32.

COCKBURN, ALEXANDER. "Some Radical Notions About Fighting Drugs." *Wall Street Journal*, September 11, 1986, p. 31.

COHEN, ALBERT K. *Delinquent Boys*. New York: Free Press, 1955.

COHEN, LAWRENCE, and MARCUS FELSON. "Social Change and Crime Rate Trends: A Routine Activity Approach." *American Sociological Review* 44(4) (1979):588–608.

COHEN, LAWRENCE E., and KENNETH C. LAND. "Age Structure and Crime: Symmetry versus Asymmetry and the Projection of Crime Rates Through the 1990s." *American Sociological Review* 52 (1987):170–183.

COHEN, STEVEN M. "Jews, More or Less." *Moment*, September 1984.

COHN, SAMUEL. *The Process of Occupational Sex-Typing: The Feminization of Clerical Work in Great Britain*. Philadelphia, Penn.: Temple University Press, 1985.

COHN, STEVEN F., and JAMES E. GALLAGHER. "Gay Movements and Legal Change: Some Aspects of the Dynamics of a Social Problem." *Social Problems* 32(1) (1984):72–86.

COLE, STEPHEN. "Sex Discrimination and Admission to Medical School 1979–1984." *American Journal of Sociology* 91 (1985):549–560.

COLE, STEPHEN, JONATHAN R. COLE, and GARY A. SIMON. "Chance and Consensus in Peer Review." *Science* 214 (4523) (November 20, 1981):881–886.

COLEMAN, JAMES. "Population Stability and Equal Rights." *Society* 14 (May 1977):34–36.

————. "Responsibility in Corporate Action: A Sociologist's View." In Klaus J. Hopt and Gunther Teubner (eds.), *Corporate Governance and Directors' Liabilities,* pp. 69–91. Berlin: de Gruyter, 1985.

————, ELIHU KATZ, and HERBERT MENZEL. "The Diffusion of Innovation Among Physicians." *Sociometry* 20 (1957):253–269.

COLEMAN, JAMES S., THOMAS HOFFER, and SALLY KILGORE. *High School Achievement: Public, Catholic, and Private Schools Compared.* New York: Basic Books, 1982.

COLEMAN, JAMES WILLIAM. "Law and Power: The Sherman Antitrust Act and Its Enforcement in the Petroleum Industry." *Social Problems* 32 (1985):264–274.

————. "Toward an Integrated Theory of White-Collar Crime." *American Journal of Sociology* 2 (1987):406–439.

COLEMAN, LERITA, and TONI ANTONUCCI. "Women's Well-being at Midlife." *Institute for Social Research Newsletter.* Ann Arbor: University of Michigan, Winter 1982.

COLEMAN, RICHARD P., and LEE RAINWATER, with KENT A. MCCLELLAND. *Social Standing in America: New Dimensions of Class.* New York: Basic Books, 1978.

COLLEGE BOARD COST BOOK, 1987. New York: The College Board.

COLLIGAN, MICHAEL J., JAMES W. PENNEBAKER, and LAWRENCE R. MURPHY. *Mass Psychogenic Illness: A Social Psychological Analysis.* Hillsdale, N.J.: Lawrence Erlbaum, 1982.

COLLINS, GLENN. "A Study Assesses Traits of Women Who Kill." *The New York Times,* July 7, 1986, p. C18.

————. "As Nature Grays, a Mighty Advocate Flexes Its Muscles." *The New York Times,* June 15, 1986, p. C1.

COLLINS, RANDALL. *Sociology Since Midcentury: Essays in Theory Cumulation.* New York: Academic Press, 1983.

————. *Three Sociological Traditions.* New York: Oxford University Press, 1985.

————. "The Potential Contribution of Sociology of Emotions to Sociological Theory." *Sociology of Emotions Newsletter* 1(1) (1986):1–2; 1(2) (1986):2.

————. "Is 1980's Sociology in the Doldrums?" *American Journal of Sociology* 91(6) (1986):1336–1355.

COMFORT, ALEXANDER. "Age Prejudice in America." *Social Policy* 7(3) (1976):3–8.

COMINI, ALESSANDRA. "Posters From the War Against Women." *The New York Times Book Review,* February 1, 1987.

CONFERENCE BOARD, CONSUMER RESEARCH CENTER. *Midlife and Beyond: The $800 Billion Over-Fifty Market.* New York: The Conference Board, Inc., 1985.

CONOVER, PAMELA J., and VIRGINIA GRAY. *Feminism and the New Right: Conflict over the American Family.* New York: Praeger, 1983.

CONRAD, JOHN P. "Corrections and Simple Justice." *The Journal of Criminal Law and Criminology* 64(2) (1973): 208–217.

CONRAD, PETER, and ROCHELLE KERN, eds. *The Sociology of Health and Illness,* 2nd ed. New York: St. Martin's, 1986.

COOK, ALICE H., VAL R. LORWIN, and ARLENE KAPLAN DANIELS, eds. *Women and Trade Unions in Eleven Industrialized Countries.* Philadelphia, Penn.: Temple University Press, 1984.

COOKSON, PETER W., JR., and CAROLINE HODGES PERSELL. *Preparing for Power: America's Elite Boarding Schools.* New York: Basic Books, 1985.

COOLEY, CHARLES HORTON. *Human Nature and the Social Order.* New York: Scribners, 1902.

————. *Social Organization: A Study of the Larger Mind.* New York: Scribners, 1909.

CORCORAN, MARY E., and GREG J. DUNCAN. "Why Do Women Earn Less?" Institute for Social Research, University of Michigan, 1985.

CORNFIELD, DANIEL B. "Declining Union Membership in the Post-World War II Era: The United Furniture Workers of America, 1939–1982." *American Journal of Sociology,* 91 (1986):1112–1153.

COSER, LEWIS. *Greedy Institutions.* New York: Free Press, 1972.

COSER, ROSE LAUB. "Cognitive Structure and the Use of Social Space." *Sociological Forum* 1 (1986):1–26.

————, and LEWIS COSER. "Jonestown as a Perverse Utopia." *Dissent* (Spring 1979):158–163.

COURTNEY, ALICE F., and THOMAS WHIPPLE. *Sex Stereotyping in Advertising.* Lexington, Mass.: Lexington Books, 1983.

COVELLO, VINCENT T., ed. *Poverty and Public Policy: An Evaluation of Social Science Research.* Cambridge, Mass.: Schenkman, 1980.

COVERMAN, SHELLEY, and JOSEPH SHELEY. "Change in Men's Housework and Child-Care Time, 1965–1975." *Journal of Marriage and the Family* 48 (1986):413–422.

COX, HARVEY. *Religion in the Secular City: Toward a Postmodern Theology.* New York: Simon & Schuster, 1985.

————. *Turning East.* New York: Simon & Schuster, 1977.

CRAIN, ROBERT L., and WILLIS D. HAWLEY. "Standards of Research." *Society* (January–February 1982):14–21.

————, and RITA E. MAHARD. "The Consequences of Controversy Accompanying Institutional Change: The Case of School Desegregation." *American Sociological Review,* 47 (December 1982):697–708.

CULLINGFORD, CEDRIC. *Children and Television.* New York: St. Martin's, 1984.

CUMMINGS, SCOTT. "White Ethnics, Racial Prejudice and Labor Market Segmentation." *American Journal of Sociology* 85(4) (January 1980):938–950.

————. "Vulnerability to the Effects of Recession: Minority and Female Workers." *Social Forces* 65 (1987): 834–857.

————, and DEL TAEBEL. "The Economic Socialization of Children: a Neo Marxist Analysis." *Social Problems* 26(2) (December 1978):198–210.

CURRIE, ELLIOTT P. "Crimes Without Criminals: Witchcraft and Its Control in Renaissance Europe." *Law and Society Review* 3(1) (August 1968):7–32.

—————. "Crime and Ideology," Part 1. *Working Papers* (May–June 1982):26–35. Part 2 (July–August 1982): 17–25.

CURTIS, RICHARD F. "Household and Family in Theory on Inequality." *American Sociological Review* 51 (1986): 168–183.

CURTISS, S. *Genie: A Psycholinguistic Study of a Modern World "Wild Child."* New York: Academic Press, 1977.

DAHL, ROBERT A. *A Preface to Economic Democracy.* Berkeley: University of California Press, 1985.

DAILY FREE PRESS (Boston University). "AIDS." March 26, 1987, pp. 1, 5 ff.

DAILY RECORD. "New York Report: Sociologist Slams Lotteries." November 23, 1985, p. 20.

DALEY, SUZANNE. "Sex Bias Lingers in Firehouses of New York." *The New York Times,* December 8, 1986, pp. 1 ff.

DALLEK, GERALDINE. "Hospital Care for Profit." *Society* 23(5) (1986):54–59.

DALY, MARY. *Pure Lust: Elemental Feminist Philosophy.* Boston: Beacon Press, 1984.

DANIELS, LEE A. "In Defense of Busing." *The New York Times Magazine,* April 17, 1983, p. 8.

DANNEFER, DALE. "Adult Development and Social Theory: A Paradigmatic Reappraisal." *American Sociological Review* 49(1) (February 1984):100–116.

DARRITY, WILLIAM A., JR., and SAMUEL L. MYERS, JR. "Does Welfare Dependency Cause Female Headship? The Case of the Black Family." *Journal of Marriage and the Family* 46 (1984):765–780.

DAVIES, JAMES C. "Towards a Theory of Revolution." *American Sociological Review* 27(1) (February 1962): 5–19.

DAVIES, MARK, and DENISE B. KANDEL. "Parental and Peer Influences on Adolescents' Educational Plans: Some Further Evidence." *American Journal of Sociology* 87 (1981): 363–387.

DAVIS, CARY. "The Future Racial Composition of the United States." *Intercom* (September–October 1982):8–10.

DAVIS, JAMES A., and TOM SMITH. *General Social Survey Cumulative File, 1972–1982.* Ann Arbor, Mich.: Inter-University Consortium for Political and Social Research, 1984.

DAVIS, KAREN. "Equal Treatment and Unequal Benefits: The Medicare Program." *Milbank Memorial Quarterly (Health & Society)* 53(4) (1975):449–488.

—————. "Medicare Reconsidered." In D. Yaggy (ed.), *Health Care for the Poor and Elderly.* Durham, N.C.: Duke University Press, 1984.

DAVIS, KINGSLEY. "Final Note on a Case of Extreme Isolation." *American Journal of Sociology* 456 (January 1940): 554–565.

—————. *Human Society.* New York: Macmillan, 1949.

—————. "The Origin and Growth of Urbanization in the World." *American Journal of Sociology* 60 (1955): 429–437.

—————, and WILBERT E. MOORE. "Some Principles of Stratification." *American Sociological Review* 10 (April 1945):242–247.

DAVIS, MIKE. *Prisoners of the American Dream: Politics and Economy in the History of the U.S. Working Class.* New York: Schocken, 1986.

DAVIS, R. "Black Suicide in the Seventies: Current Trends." Paper presented at the annual meeting of the American Sociological Association, Boston, August 1979.

DAVIS, RICHARD H. *Aging: Prospects and Issues.* Los Angeles: UCLA Press, 1981.

DAVIS, WADE. "Hallucinogenic Plants and Their Use in Traditional Societies." *Cultural Survival Quarterly* 9(4) (1985):2–5.

DEACON, DESLEY. "Political Arithmetic: The Nineteenth-Century Australian Census and the Construction of the Dependent Woman." *Signs* 11(1) (1985):27.

DEAUX, KAY, and MARY E. KITE. "Thinking About Gender." In Beth B. Hess and Myra Marx Ferree (eds.), *Analyzing Gender: A Handbook of Social Science Research.* Newbury Park, Calif.: Sage, 1987.

DEEGAN, MARY JO. "Early Women Sociologists and the American Sociological Society: Patterns of Exclusion and Participation," *The American Sociologist* 16 (1981):14–24.

—————. "The Golden Era of Women Sociologists." Paper presented at the annual meeting of the Association for Humanist Sociology, Philadelphia, November 1986.

—————, and NANCY BROOKS, eds. *Women and Disability: The Double Handicap.* New Brunswick, N.J.: Transaction Press, 1987.

DEEGAN, MARY JO, and MICHAEL HILL, eds. *Women and Symbolic Interaction.* Boston: Allen and Unwin, 1987.

—————, and MICHAEL STEIN. "American Drama and Ritual: Nebraska Football." *International Review of Sport Sociology* 3 (1978):31–44.

DEFENSE INTELLIGENCE AGENCY. *Soviet Military Power.* Washington, D.C.: Department of Defense, March 1987.

DELAMATER, JOHN. "The Social Control of Sexuality." *Annual Review of Sociology* 7 (1981):263–290.

DELGADO, GARY. "Community Organizing." *Social Policy* (Spring 1986):40–47.

—————. *Organizing the Movement: The Roots and Growth of ACORN.* Philadelphia: Temple University Press, 1986.

DELLA FAVE, L. RICHARD. "The Meek Shall Not Inherit the Earth: Self-Evaluation and the Legitimacy of Stratification." *American Sociological Review* 45 (1980):955–971.

DEMARIS, ALFRED, and GERALD R. LESLIE. "Cohabitation with the Future Spouse: Its Influence upon Marital Satisfaction and Communication." *Journal of Marriage and the Family* 46 (1984):77–84.

DEMERATH, J. N., III, and RHYS H. WILLIAMS. "Civil Religion in an Uncivil Society." *Annals of the American Academy of Political and Social Science* 480 (1985):154–166.

D'EMILIO, JOHN. *Sexual Politics, Sexual Communities: The Making of a Homosexual Minority in the United States.* Chicago: University of Chicago Press, 1983.

DEMOS, JOHN. "Old Age in Early New England." In John Demos and Spence Boocock (eds.), *Turning Points: Historical and Sociological Essays on the Family,* Vol. 84, pp. 284–287. Chicago: University of Chicago Press.

—————. *Entertaining Satan: Witchcraft and the Culture of Early New England.* New York: Oxford, 1982.

—————. *A Little Commonwealth: Family Life in Plymouth Colony.* New York: Oxford University Press, 1983.

DENISOFF, R. SERGE. *Waylon: A Biography.* Knoxville, Tenn.: University of Tennessee Press, 1983.

DENISOFF, R. SERGE, and RALPH WAHRMAN. *An Introduction to Sociology,* 3rd ed. New York: Macmillan, 1983.

DENZIN, NORMAN K. "Toward a Phenomenology of Domestic, Family Violence." *American Journal of Sociology* 90 (1984):483–513.

—————. "Behaviorism and Beyond." *Contemporary Sociology* 15(4) (1986):553–556.

DERSHOWITZ, ALAN M. "Increasing Community Control over Corporate Crime: A Problem in the Law of Sanctions." *Yale Law Journal* 71 (1961):238–306.

DE SOLA POOL, ITHIEL. *Technologies of Freedom: On Free Speech in an Electronic Age.* Cambridge, Mass.: Harvard University Press, 1983.

DEVINE, JOEL A. "State and State Expenditure: Determinants of Social Investment and Social Consumption Spending in the Postwar United States." *American Sociological Review* 50 (1985):150–165.

DEWEY, RICHARD. "The Rural-Urban Continuum: Real but Relatively Unimportant." *American Journal of Sociology* 66 (1960):60–66.

DIAMOND, IRENE, and MARTHA ACKELSBERG. "Gender and Political Life: New Directions in Political Science." In Beth B. Hess and Myra Marx Ferree (eds.), *Analyzing Gender: A Handbook of Social Science Research.* Newbury Park, Calif.: Sage, 1987.

DIMAGGIO, PAUL, and JOHN MOHR. "Cultural Capital, Educational Attainment and Marital Selection." *American Journal of Sociology* 90(6) (1985):1231–1257.

DIXON, MARLENE, and SUSANNE JONAS, eds. *The New Nomads: From Immigrant Labor to Transnational Working Class.* San Francisco: Synthesis Publications, 1982.

DOLLARS and SENSE. "Evaluating CDC's: Can They End Urban Decay?" December 1986, pp. 19–21.

DOMHOFF, WILLIAM G. *Who Rules America Now?: A View for the '80s.* Englewood Cliffs, N.J.: Prentice-Hall, 1983.

—————, and RICHARD L. ZWEIGENHAFT. "Jews in the Corporate Establishment." *The New York Times,* April 24, 1983, Sec. 3, pp. 2 ff.

DONNERSTEIN, EDWARD I., and DANIEL G. LINZ. "The Question of Pornography." *Psychology Today,* December 1986, pp. 56–59.

DOOB, ANTHONY N. "Deviance: Society's Side Show." *Psychology Today* 5 (October 1971):47–51, 113.

DOOLIN, JOSEPH. An untitled study of homelsss men in Boston (unpublished dissertation data). Boston University, Department of Sociology, 1987.

DORN, DEAN. "The First Day of Class: Problems and Strategies." *Teaching Sociology* 15(1) (January 1987):61–72.

DOUGLAS, JACK D. *Investigative Field Research.* Beverly Hills, Calif.: Sage, 1976.

—————, and JOHN M. JOHNSON, eds. *Business and Professional Deviance.* Philadelphia, Pa.: Lippincott, 1978.

—————, and FRANCES CHAPUT WAKSLER. *The Sociology of Deviance: An Introduction.* Boston: Little, Brown, 1982.

DOWD, MAUREEN. "Pigeons, Elvises, Immigrants: Staging Patriotism for the 4th." *The New York Times,* June 12, 1986, p. 1.

DOXIADIS, C. A. *Urban Renewal and the Future of the American City.* New York: Oxford University Press, 1968.

DOYLE, JAMES A. *The Male Experience.* Dubuque, Iowa: Wm. C. Brown, 1983.

DREEBEN, ROBERT, and ADAM GAMORAN. "Race, Instruction, and Learning." *American Sociological Review* 51 (1986): 600–669.

DUBIN, STEVEN C. "Artistic Production and Social Control." *Social Forces* 64(3) (1986):667–688.

DUBOIS, PAUL. "The Occupational Attainment of Former College Athletes." *International Review of Sport Sociology* 15(1) (1980):93–107.

DUNCAN, GREG J., with RICHARD D. COE, MARY E. CORCORAN, MARTHA S. HILL, SAUL D. HOFFMAN, and JAMES N. MORGAN. *Years of Poverty, Years of Plenty: The Changing Economic Fortunes of American Workers and Families.* Ann Arbor, Mich: Institute for Social Research, 1984.

DUNN, MARVIN, and BRUCE PORTER. "Miami 1980: A Different Kind of Riot." Report to Ford Foundation, New York, 1983.

DURKHEIM, EMILE. *The Division of Labor in Society* (1893). New York: Free Press, 1984.

—————. *The Elementary Forms of the Religious Life* (1912). New York: Collier Books, 1961.

—————. *Suicide* (1897). New York: Free Press, 1966.

DYE, THOMAS. *Who's Running America? The Conservative Years,* 4th ed. Englewood Cliffs, N.J.: Prentice Hall, 1986.

DYER, C. "Seasonality of Baptisms: An Urban Approach." *Local Population Studies* 27 (1981):26–34.

EARLY, STEVE, and RAND WILSON. "Do Unions Have a Future in High Technology?" *Technology Review* (October 1986): 57–65.

ECCLES, JAQUELYNNE S., and JANIS E. JACOBS. "Social Forces Shape Math Attitudes and Performance." *Signs* 11 (1986): 367–380.

EDMONDS, RONALD R. "Some Schools Work and More Can." *Social Policy* (March–April 1979):28–32.

EDWARDS, HARRY. *Sociology of Sport.* Homewood, Ill.: Dorsey, 1973.

EGGEBEEN, DAVID, and PETER UHLENBERG. "Changes in the Organization of Men's Lives: 1960–1980." *Family Relations* 34 (1985):251–257.

EHRENREICH, BARBARA. *The Hearts of Men.* New York: Anchor/Doubleday, 1983.

—————. "A Feminist's View of the New Man." *The New York Times Magazine,* May 20, 1984, pp. 36 ff.

—————, and DEIRDRE ENGLISH. *For Her Own Good: 150 Years of the Experts' Advice to Women.* Garden City, N.Y.: Anchor/Doubleday, 1980.

EHRMAN, M. DAVID, and WILLIAM H. CLEMENTS II. "The Interfaith Center on Corporate Responsibility and Its Campaign Against Marketing Infant Formula in the Third World." *Social Problems* 32(2) (1984):185–196.

EISENSTADT, S. N. *From Generation to Generation.* Glencoe, Ill.: Free Press, 1956.

—————, ed. *Post Traditional Societies.* New York: W. W. Norton, 1974.

—————. *Tradition, Change and Modernity.* Melbourne, Fla.: Kreiger, 1983.

EITZEN, D. STANLEY, and GEORGE H. SAGE. *Sociology of North American Sport,* 3rd ed. Dubuque, Iowa: W. C. Brown, 1986.

ELDER, GLEN H., JR., and JEFFREY K. LIKER. "Hard Times in Women's Lives: Historical Influences Across Forty Years." *American Journal of Sociology* 88 (1982):241–269.

EMMONS, CHARLES, and STEVE GILCHRIST. "Conventionalized Frenzy: Hardcore Punk Concerts as Collective Behavior." Unpublished paper presented to Eastern Sociological Society, Baltimore, March 1983.

ENDICOTT REPORT, 1986. Evanston, Ill.: Northwestern University, 1986.

ENLOE, CYNTHIA. *Does Khaki Become You? The Militarization of Women's Lives.* Boston: South End Press, 1984.

—————. "Feminist Thinking About War, Militarism, and Peace: Theorizing in Dark Times." In Beth B. Hess and Myra Marx Ferree (eds.), *Analyzing Gender: A Handbook of Social Science Research.* Newbury Park, Calif.: Sage, 1987.

EPSTEIN, CYNTHIA FUCHS. *Women in Law.* New York: Anchor/Doubleday, 1983.

—————. "Symbolic Segregation: Similarities and Differences in the Language and Non-Verbal Communications of Women and Men." *Sociological Forum* 1(1) (1986):27–49.

—————, and ROSE LAUB COSER, eds. *Access to Power: Cross-National Studies of Women and Elites.* George Allen & Unwin, 1981.

ERICKSEN, JULIA, WILLIAM L. YANCEY, and EUGENE P. ERICKSEN. "The Division of Family Roles." *Journal of Marriage and the Family* 41(2) (1979):301–313.

ERIKSON, ERIK H. "Youth, Fidelity and Diversity." In Erik H. Erikson (ed.), *Youth: Change and Challenge.* New York: Basic Books, 1963.

—————. *Childhood and Society,* rev. ed. New York: W. W. Norton, 1964.

ERIKSON, KAI. "On Work and Alienation." *American Sociological Review* 51(1) (1986):1–8.

ERIKSON, KAI. *The Wayward Puritans.* New York: John Wiley, 1963.

—————. *Everything in Its Path: Destruction of Community in the Buffalo Creek Flood.* New York: Simon & Schuster, 1976.

ERMANN, D., and J. GABEL. "Multi-Hospital Systems: Issues and Empirical Findings." *Health Affairs* 3 (1984).

ERNST, CECILE, and JULES ANGST. *Birth Order: Its Influence on Personality.* New York: Springer-Verlag, 1983.

ESKILSON, ARLENE, and MARY GLENN WILEY. "Parents, Peers, Perceived Pressure, and Adolescent Self-Concept: Is a Daughter a Daughter All of Her Life?" Paper presented at the 56th annual meeting of the Eastern Sociological Society, New York City, April 1986.

ESPING-ANDERSON, GOSTA. *Politics Against Markets: The Social Democratic Road to Power.* Princeton, N.J.: Princeton University Press, 1985.

ETHAN ALLEN. *The Ethan Allen Report: The Status and Future of the American Family.* Danbury, Conn.: Ethan Allen, Inc., 1987.

ETZIONI, AMITAI. "Shady Corporate Practices." *The New York Times,* November 15, 1985, p. A35.

ETZIONI-HALEVY, EVA. *Bureaucracy and Democracy: A Political Dilemma.* Boston: Routledge & Kegan Paul, 1983.

EVAN, WILLIAM M., and STEPHEN HILGARTNER, eds. *The Arms Race and Nuclear War.* Englewood Cliffs, N.J.: Prentice-Hall, 1987.

EVANS, PETER B., DIETRICH RUESCHEMEYER, and THEDA SKOCPOL, eds. *Bringing the State Back In.* New York: Cambridge University Press, 1985.

EVANS, SARA M., and HARRY C. BOYTE. *Free Spaces: The Sources of Democratic Change in America.* New York: Harper & Row, 1986.

EVERHART, ROBERT B. *Reading, Writing, and Resistance.* Boston: Routledge & Kegan Paul, 1983.

EVERSOLL, DEANNA. "A Two-Generational View of Fathering." *The Family Coordinator* (October 1979):503–508.

EWEN, STUART, and ELIZABETH EWEN. *Channels of Desire: Mass Images and the Shaping of American Consciousness.* New York: McGraw-Hill, 1982.

EXUM, WILLIAM H. "Climbing the Crystal Stair: Values, Affirmative Action, and Minority Faculty." *Social Problems* 30(4) (April 1983):383–399.

FALIK, MARILYN. *Ideology and Abortion Policy Politics.* New York: Praeger, 1983.

FAMILY RELATIONS. "The Single Parent Family" 35 (1986).

FARMER, JAMES. *Lay Bare the Heart: An Autobiography of the Civil Rights Movement.* New York: Arbor House, 1984.

FAULKNER, ROBERT R. *Music on Demand: Composers and Careers in the Hollywood Film Industry.* New Brunswick, N.J.: Transaction, 1983.

FAUSTO-STERLING, ANNE. *Myths of Gender: Biological Theories about Men and Women.* New York: Basic Books, 1986.

FAVER, CATHERINE A. "Women, Career Orientations, and Employment." *Psychology of Women Quarterly* 8 (1983): 193–197.

FEAGIN, JOE R. *Subordinating the Poor.* Englewood Cliffs, N.J.: Prentice-Hall, 1975.

—————. *Social Problems: A Critical Power-Conflict Perspective,* 2nd ed. Englewood Cliffs, N.J.: Prentice-Hall, 1986.

FEATHERMAN, DAVID L., and ROBERT M. HAUSER. *Opportunity and Change.* New York: Academic Press, 1978.

FEIGELMAN, WILLIAM, ed. *Sociology Full Circle,* 4th ed. New York: Holt, Rinehart, Winston, 1985.

FEIGELMAN, WILLIAM, and ARNOLD R. SILVERMAN. *Chosen Children: New Patterns of Adoptive Relationships.* New York: Praeger, 1983.

FELDBERG, ROSLYN. "Comparable Worth: Toward Theory and Practice in the United States." *Signs* 10(2) (1984): 311–328.

————, and EVELYN NAKANO GLENN. "Technology and Work Degradation: Effects of Office Automation on Women Clerical Workers." In Joan Rothschild (ed.), *Women, Technology and Innovation.* New York: Pergamon, 1982.

FELDMAN, DOUGLAS A., and THOMAS M. JOHNSON, eds. *The Social Dimensions of AIDS: Method and Theory.* New York: Praeger, 1986.

FELDMAN, JACOB J. *The Dissemination of Health Information: A Case Study in Adult Learning.* Chicago: Aldine, 1966.

FELLMAN, SANDI. *The Japanese Tattoo.* New York: Abbeville Press, 1986.

FENDRICH, MICHAEL. "Wives' Employment and Husbands' Distress: A Meta-analysis and a Replication." *Journal of Marriage and the Family* 46 (1984):872–880.

FENWICK, RUDY, and JON OLSON. "Support for Worker Participation: Attitudes Among Union and Non-union Workers." *American Sociological Review* 51 (1986):505–522.

FERGUSSON, DAVID M., L. JOHN HORWOOD, KATHERYN L. KERSHAW, and FREDERICK T. SHANNON. "Factors Associated with Reports of Wife Assault in New Zealand." *Journal of Marriage and the Family* 48 (1986):407–412.

————, L. J. HORWOOD, and F. T. SHANNON. "A Proportional Hazards Model of Family Breakdown." *Journal of Marriage and the Family* 46 (1984):539–545.

FERNANDEZ, ROBERT M., and JANE KULIK. "A Multilevel Model of Life Satisfaction: Effects of Individual Characteristics and Neighborhood Composition." *American Sociological Review* 46 (1981):840–850.

FERRARO, KATHLEEN J., and JOHN M. JOHNSON. "How Women Experience Battering: The Process of Victimization." *Social Problems* 30 (1983):325–339.

FERREE, MYRA MARX. "She Works Hard for a Living: Gender and Class on the Job." In Beth H. Hess and Myra Marx Ferree (eds.), *Analyzing Gender: A Handbook of Social Science Research.* Newbury Park, Calif.: Sage, 1987.

FERREE, MYRA MARX, and BETH B. HESS. *Controversy and Coalition: The New Feminist Movement.* Boston: Twayne, 1985.

————, and FREDERICK D. MILLER. "Mobilization and Meaning: Toward an Integration of Social Psychological and Resource Perspectives on Social Movements." *Sociological Inquiry* 55(1) (1985):38–61.

FESTINGER, LEON, HENRY W. RIECKEN, and STANLEY SCHACTER. *When Prophecy Fails.* New York: Harper & Row, 1966.

FIALKA, JOHN J. "Social Security Trying to Stop Checks to Dead." *The Wall Street Journal,* January 31, 1983, pp. 31, 54.

FIELDS, MAVIE GARVIN with KAREN FIELDS. *Lemon Swamp and Other Places: A Carolina Memoir.* New York: Free Press, 1983.

FIGUEIRA-MCDONOUGH, JOSEPHINA, ALFREDA INGLEHART, ROSEMARY SARRI, and TERRY WILLIAMS. "Women in Prison, Michigan: 1968–1978." *JSR Newsletter* (Autumn 1981): 4–5.

FINE, GARY ALAN. *Shared Fantasy: Role Playing Games as Social Worlds.* Chicago: University of Chicago Press, 1983.

FINE, MICHELLE. "Dropping Out of High School: An Inside Look." *Social Policy* 16(2) (1985):43–50.

————. "School-based Health Clinics." Paper presented at the annual meeting of the Association for Humanist Sociology, Philadelphia, November 1986.

FINKELHOR, DAVID, and KERSTI YLLO. *License to Rape: Sexual Abuse of Wives.* New York: Holt, Rinehart & Winston, 1985.

FINLAYSON, ANN. "A New Proposal for Prostitution," *Maclean,* May 6, 1985, p. 48.

FINSTON, MARK. "Weekend 'Rambos' Shoot to Thrill." *The Newark Star Ledger* (N.J.), July 22, 1985, p. 19.

FIORENZA, ELISABETH SCHUSSLER. *Bread Not Stone: The Challenge of Feminist Biblical Interpretation.* Boston: Beacon Press, 1985.

FIREY, WALTER, CHARLES J. LOOMIS, and J. ALLAN BEEGLE. "The Fusion of Urban and Rural." In Jean Labutut and Wheaton J. Lane (eds.), *Highways in Our National Life.* Princeton, N.J.: Princeton University Press, 1950.

FISCHER, CLAUDE. *The Urban Experience.* New York: Harcourt Brace Jovanovich, 1976.

————. *To Dwell Among Friends: Personal Networks in Town and City.* Chicago: University of Chicago Press, 1982.

FISCHER, DAVID HACKETT. *Growing Old in America.* New York: Oxford University Press, 1978.

FISH, VIRGINIA KEMP. "Hull House: Pioneer in Urban Research during Its Creative Years." *History of Sociology* 6 (1985):33–54.

————. "The Hull House Circle: Women's Friendships and Achievements." In Janet Sharistanian (ed.), *Gender, Ideology, and Action: Historical Perspectives on Women's Public Lives,* pp. 185–226. Westport, Conn.: Greenwood Press, 1986.

FISHER, ROBERT. *Let the People Decide: Neighborhood Organizing in America.* Boston: Twayne, 1984.

FISHMAN, MARK. *Manufacturing the News.* Austin: University of Texas Press, 1980.

FISHMAN, PAMELA. "Interaction: The Work Women Do." *Social Problems* 25(4) (1978):397–406.

FISHMAN, WALDA, and C. GEORGE BENELLO, eds. *Readings in Humanist Sociology: Social Criticism and Social Change.* New York: General Hall, Inc., 1986.

FISKE, EDWARD B. "Colleges Scrambling to Avert a Possible Faculty Shortage." *The New York Times,* March 16, 1986, p. 1.

————. "Colleges' Tuition Up 7% to 8%; Total Bill

Can Exceed $16,000." *The New York Times,* April 7, 1986, pp. 1 ff.

FITZGERALD, FRANCES. "Rajneeshpuram." *The New Yorker,* September 22 and 29, 1986.

FLANDERS, RICKIE, and DEBORAH MEIER. "TEACH: 'Reaganizing' the American Schools." *Dissent* (Spring 1986): 142–145.

FLEMING, JACQUELINE. *Blacks in College: A Comparative Study of Students' Success in Black and White Institutions.* San Francisco: Jossey-Bass, 1984.

FLIGSTEIN, NEIL. "The Intraorganizational Power Struggle: Rise of Finance Personnel to Top Leadership in Large Corporations, 1919–1979." *American Sociological Review* 52 (1987):44–58.

FLORA, PETER, and ARNOLD J. HEIDENHEIMER, eds. *The Development of Welfare States in Europe and America.* New Brunswick, N.J.: Transaction Books, 1981.

FLOWERS, RONALD B. *Religion in Strange Times: The 1960s and 1970s.* Macon, Ga.: Mercer University Press, 1984.

FONER, ANNE. "The Polity." In Matilda White Riley, Marilyn E. Johnson, and Anne Foner (eds.), *Aging and Society,* Vol. 3, *A Theory of Age Stratification.* New York: Russell Sage Foundation, 1972.

————, and DAVID KERTZER. "Transitions over the Life Course." *American Journal of Sociology* 85(5) (1978): 1081–1104.

————, and KAREN SCHWAB. *Aging and Retirement.* Belmont, Calif.: Wadsworth, 1981.

FONER, NANCY. *Ages in Conflict.* New York: Columbia University Press, 1984.

FORBES. "The Forbes Four-Hundred," October 27, 1986.

FORD FOUNDATION REPORT. *Transfer: Making It Work.* New York: Ford Foundation, 1987.

FOSS, J. E. "The Paradoxical Nature of Family Relationships and Family Conflict." In M. A. Straus and G. T. Hotaling (eds.), *The Social Causes of Husband-Wife Violence.* Minneapolis: University of Minnesota Press, 1983.

FOX, MARY FRANK, and SHARLENE HESSE-BIBER. *American Women at Work.* Palo Alto, Calif.: Mayfield, 1983.

FOX, ROBIN. "Report to International AIDS Conference." Washington, D.C., June 5, 1987.

FRANKLIN, BENJAMIN. *Poor Richard's Almanac* (1784). New York: David McKay, 1970.

FREEMAN, HOWARD E., RUSSELL R. DYNES, PETER H. ROSSI, and WILLIAM FOOTE WHYTE, eds. *Applied Sociology: Roles and Activities of Sociologists in Diverse Settings.* San Francisco: Jossey-Bass, 1983.

FREEMAN, JO, ed. *Social Movements of the Sixties and Seventies.* New York: Longman, 1983.

FREEMAN, RICHARD B., and HARRY J. HOLZER, eds. *The Black Youth Unemployment Crisis.* Chicago: University of Chicago Press, 1986.

————, and JAMES L. MEDOFF. *What Do Unions Do?* New York: Basic Books, 1984.

FREIRE, PAULO. *The Politics of Education: Culture, Power, and Liberation,* Donald Macedo (trans.). South Hadley, Mass.: Bergin & Garvey, 1985.

FRENCH, HOWARD W. "Report Cites Fewer Men in Black Neighborhoods." *The New York Times,* March 7, 1987, p. 31.

FREUD, SIGMUND. *Civilization and Its Discontents* (1930), James Strachey (trans.). New York: W. W. Norton, 1962.

FREY, WILLIAM H. "Migration and Depopulation of the Metropolis: Regional Restructuring or Rural Renaissance?" *American Sociological Review* 52 (1987):240–257.

FRIEDLAND, ROBERT B. "Financing Long-Term Care." In Frank B. McArdle (ed.), *The Changing Health Care Market.* Washington, D.C.: Employee Benefit Research Institute, 1987.

————. "Introduction and Background: Private Initiatives to Contain Health Care Expenditures." In Frank B. McArdle (ed.), *The Changing Health Care Market.* Washington, D.C.: Employee Benefit Research Institute, 1987.

FRIEDMAN, EMILY. "The All-Frills Yuppie Health Care Boutique." *Society* 23(5) (1986):42–47.

FRIEDMAN, MILTON, and ROSE FRIEDMAN. *Free to Choose: A Rational Statement.* New York: Harcourt Brace Jovanovich, 1980.

FURSTENBERG, FRANK F., JR. "Sex Education and Sexual Experience Among Adolescents." *American Journal of Public Health* 75(11) (1986):1331–1332.

————, and GRAHAM B. SPANIER. *Recycling the Family: Remarriage after Divorce.* Beverly Hills, Calif.: Sage, 1984.

FUTURIST. "The Future of Personal Robots," 20(3) (May/June 1986).

————. "Factories in Space: The Role of Robots," 21(3) (May/June 1987):29.

GAGNON, JOHN. *Human Sexualities.* Glenview, Ill.: Scott, Foresman, 1977.

————, and WILLIAM SIMON. *Sexual Conduct: The Social Sources of Human Sexuality.* Chicago: Aldine, 1973.

GAILEY, PHIL. "Voter Turnout is Estimated at 37.3%, Lowest Since 1942." *The New York Times,* November 8, 1986, p. 8.

GALASKIEWICZ, JOSEPH. *Social Organization of an Urban Grants Economy.* New York: Academic Press, 1985.

GALLIE, DUNCAN. *Social Inequality and Class Radicalism in France and Britain.* Cambridge: Cambridge University Press, 1983.

GAMSON, WILLIAM A. *The Strategy of Social Protest.* Homewood, Ill.: Dorsey, 1975.

————, BRUCE FIREMAN, and STEVEN RYTINA. *Encounters with Unjust Authority.* Homewood, Ill.: Dorsey Press, 1982.

GANS, HERBERT J. *The Levittowners.* New York: Vintage, 1967.

————. "The Positive Functions of Poverty." *American Journal of Sociology* 78(2) (September 1972): 275–289.

————. *Popular Culture and High Culture.* New York: Basic Books, 1974.

————. *Deciding What's News.* New York: Pantheon, 1979.

GARDNER, ROBERT W., BRYANT ROBEY, and PETER C. SMITH. "Asian Americans: Growth, Change and Diversity." *Population Bulletin* 49(4) (1985): entire issue.

GARFINKEL, HAROLD. *Studies in Ethnomethodology.* Englewood Cliffs, N.J.: Prentice-Hall, 1967.

GAROFALO, REEBEE. "The Impact of the Civil Rights Movement on Popular Music." Paper presented at the Annual Meeting of the Popular Culture Association, Montreal, Canada, March 1987.

GAUDIN, JAMES M., and KATHERYN B. DAVIS. "Social Networks of Black and White Rural Families: A Research Report." *Journal of Marriage and the Family* (November 1985):1015–1023.

GAVENTA, JOHN. *Power and Powerlessness: Quiescence and Rebellion in an Appalachian Valley.* Urbana: University of Illinois Press, 1980.

GEBHARD, PAUL. "Incidence of Overt Homosexuality in the U.S. and Western Homosexuality." In John M. Livingood (ed.), *Task Force on Homosexuality: Final Report and Background Papers.* National Institute of Mental Health. Washington, D.C.: U.S. Government Printing Office, 1972.

GEERTZ, CLIFFORD. *The Interpretation of Cultures.* New York: Basic Books, 1973.

GEHRIG, GAIL. *American Civil Religion: An Assessment.* Storrs, Conn.: Society for the Scientific Study of Religion, 1981.

GEIS, GILBERT. *On White Collar Crime.* Lexington, Mass.: Lexington Books, 1982.

GELLES, RICHARD J., and CLAIRE PEDRICK CORNELL. *Intimate Violence in Families.* Beverly Hills, Calif.: Sage, 1985.

GENERAL ACCOUNTING OFFICE. *Homelessness: A Complex Problem and the Federal Response.* Washington, D.C.: U.S. General Accounting Office, 1986.

GERBNER, GEORGE, LARRY GROSS, MICHAEL MORGAN, and NANCY SIGNORIELLI. "Violence Profile No. 12." Mimeo, Annenberg School of Communications, University of Pennsylvania, Philadelphia, April 1981.

GERSON, JUDITH M., and KATHY PEISS. "Boundaries, Negotiation, Consciousness: Reconceptualizing Gender Relations." *Social Problems* 32(4) (1985):317–331.

GERSON, KATHLEEN. *Hard Choices: How Women Decide About Work, Career, and Motherhood.* Berkeley, Calif.: University of California Press, 1986.

GERSTEL, NAOMI, and HARRIET GROSS. *Commuter Marriage: A Study of Work and Family.* New York: Guilford Press, 1984.

—————, CATHERINE KOHLER RIESSMAN, and SARAH ROSENFIELD. "Explaining the Symptomatology of Separated and Divorced Women and Men: The Role of Material Conditions and Social Networks." *Social Forces* 64 (1985): 84–101.

GIDDENS, ANTHONY. *The Nation State and Violence,* Vol. 2, *Contemporary Critique of Historical Materialism.* Berkeley, Calif.: University of California Press, 1985.

—————. "The Future of Sociology." Paper presented at the 56th annual meeting of the Eastern Sociological Society, New York City, April 1986.

GIELE, JANET Z., ed. *Women in the Middle Years.* New York: John Wiley, 1982.

GILBERT, NEIL. *Capitalism and the Welfare State: Dilemmas of Social Benevolence.* New Haven, Conn.: Yale University Press, 1986.

GILDER, GEORGE. *Wealth and Poverty.* New York: Basic Books, 1981.

GILKES, CHERYL TOWNSEND. "'Together and in Harness': Women's Traditions in the Sanctified Church." *Signs* 10(4) (1985):678–699.

GILLIGAN, CAROL. *In a Different Voice: Psychological Theory and Women's Development.* Cambridge, Mass.: Harvard University Press, 1982.

GIORDANO, LORRAINE. "Beyond Taylorism: Computerization and QWL Programs in the Production Process." Unpublished ms. New York University, Dept. of Sociology, 1987.

GIROUX, HENRY A. "Theories of Reproduction and Resistance in the New Sociology of Education: A Critical Analysis." *Harvard Educational Review* 53(3) (1985):257–293.

GITLIN, TODD. *Inside Prime Time.* New York: Pantheon, 1983.

—————. *The Whole World is Watching: Mass Media in the Making and Unmaking of the New Left.* Berkeley: University of California Press, 1980.

GLASS, JENNIFER, VERN L. BENGTSON, and CHARLOTTE CHORN DUNHAM. "Attitude Similarity in Three-Generation Families: Socialization, Status Inheritance, or Reciprocal Influence?" *American Sociological Review* 51 (1986):685–698.

GLASSMAN, RONALD. *The Political History of Latin America.* New York: Funk & Wagnalls, 1969.

—————. *Max Weber's Political Sociology.* Westport, Conn.: Greenwood Press, 1984.

—————. *Democracy and Despotism in Primitive Society.* Port Washington, N.Y.: Kennicott Press, 1984.

GLAZER, NONA Y., ed. *Old Families/New Families.* New York: St. Martin's, 1976.

GLENN, EVELYN NAKANO. "Reconstructing the Family." In Beth B. Hess and Myra Marx Ferree (eds.), *Analyzing Gender: A Handbook of Social Science Research.* Newbury Park, Calif.: Sage, 1987.

GLENN, NORVAL D. "A Note on Estimating the Strength of Influences for Religious Endogamy." *Journal of Marriage and the Family* 46 (1984):725–728.

—————, and KATHRYN B. KRAMER. "The Psychological Well-Being of Adult Children of Divorce." *Journal of Marriage and the Family* 47 (1985):905–912.

—————, and BETH ANN SHELTON. "Regional Differences in Divorce in the United States." *Journal of Marriage and the Family* 47 (1985):641–652.

—————, and MICHAEL SUPANIC. "The Social and Demographic Correlates of Divorce and Separation in the United States: An Update and Reconsideration." *Journal of Marriage and the Family* 46 (1984):563–576.

—————, and PATRICIA ANN TAYLOR. "Education and Family Income: A Comparison of White Married Men and Women in the U.S." *Social Forces* 63(1) (1984):169–183.

—————, and CHARLES N. WEAVER. "Further Evidence on Education and Job Satisfaction." *Social Forces* 61 (1982): 46–55.

GLICK, PAUL C. "Black Families." In James M. Henslin (ed.), *Marriage and Family in a Changing Society*, pp. 120–132. New York: Macmillan, 1985.

————, and SUNG-LING LIN. "More Young Adults Are Living with Their Parents: Who Are They?" *Journal of Marriage and the Family* 48 (1986A):107–112.

————, and SUNG-LING LIN. "Recent Changes in Divorce and Remarriage." *Journal of Marriage and the Family* 48 (1986B):737–747.

GOETHALS, GREGOR T. *The TV Ritual: Worship at the Video Altar.* Boston: Beacon Press, 1981.

GOETZ, JUDITH P., and MARGARET D. LE COMPTE. *Ethnography and Qualitative Design in Educational Research.* Orlando, Fla.: Academic Press, 1984.

GOFF, COLIN H., and CHARLES E. REASONS. *Corporate Crime in Canada: A Critical Analysis of Anti-Combines Legislation.* Englewood Cliffs, N.J.: Prentice-Hall, 1978.

GOFFMAN, ERVING. *The Presentation of Self in Everyday Life.* Garden City, N.Y.: Doubleday, 1959.

————. *Asylums,* Garden City, N.Y.: Doubleday, 1961.

————. *Stigma: Notes on the Management of Spoiled Identity.* Englewood Cliffs, N.J.: Prentice-Hall, 1963.

————. *Relations in Public.* New York: Basic Books, 1971.

————. "The Interaction Order." *American Sociological Review* 48 (1983):1–17.

GOLDBERG, PHILIP. "Are Women Prejudiced Against Women?" *Trans-Action Society* 5 (1968):32–38.

GOLDBERG, ROBERTA. *Organizing Women Office Workers: Dissatisfaction, Consciousness, and Action.* New York: Praeger, 1983.

GOLDBERG, STEVEN. "Reaffirming the Obvious." *Society* 23(6) (1986):4–7.

GOLDMAN, ARI. "Moon's Jailing May Have Eased Things for His Flock." *The New York Times,* July 28, 1985, p. E7.

GOLDSCHEIDER, CALVIN, and FRANCES K. GOLDSCHEIDER. "Moving Out and Marriage: What Do Young Adults Expect?" *American Sociological Review* 52 (1987):278–285.

GOLDSCHEIDER, FRANCES KOBRIN, and LINDA J. WAITE. "Sex Differences in the Entry into Marriage." *American Journal of Sociology* 92 (1986):91–109.

GOLDSTEIN, JEFFREY H., ed. *Sports Violence.* New York: Springer-Verlag, 1983.

GOLEMAN, DANIEL. "Studies Point to Power of Nonverbal Signals." *The New York Times,* April 8, 1986, pp. C1 ff.

GOODE, WILLIAM J. "The Theoretical Importance of Love." *American Sociological Review* 24(1) (February 1959): 38–47.

————. "A Theory of Role Strain." *American Sociological Review* 25 (1960):483–496.

————. *The Celebration of Heroes: Prestige as a Social System.* Berkeley: University of California Press, 1977.

————. "Why Men Resist." In Barrie Thorne and Marilyn Yalom (eds.), *Rethinking the Family,* pp. 131–150. New York: Longman, 1982.

GOODWIN, MICHAEL. "When the Cash Register is the Scoreboard." *The New York Times,* June 8, 1986, Sec. 5, pp. 1 ff.

GORDON, DAVID M. "Capitalist Development and the History of American Cities." In William K. Tabb and Larry Sawers (eds.), *Marxism and the Metropolis: New Perspectives in Urban Political Economy.* New York: Oxford University Press, 1978.

GORDON, LINDA. "Incest and Resistance: Patterns of Father-Daughter Incest, 1880–1930." *Social Problems* 33 (1986): 253–269.

————, and PAUL O'KEEFE. "Incest as a Form of Family Violence." *Journal of Marriage and the Family* 46 (1984):27–34.

GORDON, MILTON. *Human Nature, Class and Ethnicity.* New York: Oxford University Press, 1978.

GORE, SUSAN. "Social Support and Health Consequences of Unemployment." *Journal of Health and Social Behavior* 19 (1978):157–165.

GORECKI, JAN. *Capital Punishment: Criminal Law and Social Evolution.* New York: Columbia University Press, 1983.

GORNICK, MARIAN, JAY N. GREENBERG, PAUL W. EGGERS, and ALLEN DOBSEN. "Twenty Years of Medicare and Medicaid: Covered Populations, Use of Benefits, and Program Expenditures." *Health Care Financing Review* (1985 Annual Supplement):13–59.

GOTTDIENER, M. "Hegemony and Mass Culture: A Semiotic Approach." *American Journal of Sociology* 90(4) (1985): 979–1001.

————. *The Social Production of Urban Space.* Austin: University of Texas Press, 1985.

GOTTLIEB, MARTIN. "F.H.A. Case Recalls Bushwick in '70s." *The New York Times,* February 2, 1986, p. 35.

GOUGH, KATHLEEN. "The Origin of the Family." *Journal of Marriage and the Family* 33(4) (Nov. 1971):260–270.

GOUVERNEUR, JACQUES. *Contemporary Capitalism and Marxist Economics.* Totowa, N.J.: Barnes and Noble, 1983.

GOVE, WALTER R. "Sex, Marital Status, and Mortality." *American Journal of Sociology* 79 (July 1973):45–67.

————. "Sex Differences in Mental Illness Among Adult Men and Women." *Social Science and Medicine* 12–3B (1978):187–198.

————, MICHAEL HUGHES, and OMER R. GALLE. "Overcrowding in the Home." *American Sociological Review* 44 (February 1979): 59–80.

————, and JEANETTE TUDOR. "Adult Sex Roles and Mental Illness." *American Journal of Sociology* 78(4) (January 1973):812–835.

GRABER, DORIS. *Processing the News: How People Tame the Information Tide.* New York: Longman, 1984.

GRACEY, HARRY L. "Learning the Student Role: Kindergarten as Academic Boot Camp." In Dennis Wrong and Harry Gracey (eds.), *Readings in Introductory Sociology,* pp. 243–253. New York: Macmillan, 1977.

GRAMSCI, ANTONIO. *The Modern Price and Other Writings.* New York: International Publisher, 1959.

GREELEY, ANDREW M. *The American Catholic.* New York: Basic Books, 1977.

GREEN, HARVEY. *Fit for America: Health, Fitness, Sport and American Society.* New York: Pantheon, 1986.

GREEN, PHILIP. *Retrieving Democracy: In Search of Civic Equality.* Totowa, N.J.: Rowan & Allenheld, 1985.

GREEN, RICHARD. *The "Sissy Boy" Syndrome and the Development of Homosexuality.* New Haven, Conn.: Yale University Press, 1987.

GREENE, BOB. "Bar Wars. *Esquire,* November 1986, pp. 61–62.

GREEN, J. G. *The Social and Psychological Origins of the Climacteric Syndrome.* Brookfield, Vt.: Gower Publishing Co., 1984.

GREENHOUSE, STEVEN. "The Average Guy Takes It On the Chin." *The New York Times,* July 13, 1986, Sect. 3, pp. 1 ff.

————. "Surge in Prematurely Jobless." *The New York Times,* October 13, 1986, p. D1.

GREENO, CATHERINE G., and ELEANOR E. MACCOBY. "How Different is 'The Different Voice'?" *Signs* 11(2) (1986): 310–316.

GRIFFIN, LARRY J., MICHAEL E. WALLACE, and BETH A. RUBIN. "Capitalist Resistance to the Organization of Labor Before the New Deal: Why? How? Success?" *American Sociological Review* 51 (1986):147–167.

GRIFFITH, JANET D., HELEN P. KOO, and C. M. SUCHINDRAN. "Childlessness and Marital Stability in Remarriages." *Journal of Marriage and the Family* 46 (1984):577–586.

GRUNEAU, RICHARD S. *Class, Sports, and Social Development.* Amherst: University of Massachusetts Press, 1983.

GRUSON, LINDSEY. "Alternative Schools Revived." *The New York Times,* April 8, 1986, pp. C1 ff.

GRZELKOWSKI, KATHRYN. "A Journey Toward Humanistic Testing." *Teaching Sociology* 15(1) (January 1987):27–32.

GUILLEMIN, JEANNE. "Federal Policies and Indian Politics." *Society* 17(4) (May–June 1980):29–34.

GUNTHER, BARRIE. *Dimensions of Television Violence.* New York: St. Martin's, 1985.

GUPTA, MAHESH. "A Basis for Friendly Dyadic Interpersonal Relationships." *Small Group Behavior* 14(1) (February 1983):15–33.

GUTERBOCK, THOMAS M., and BRUCE LONDON. "Race, Political Orientation, and Participation: An Empirical Test of Four Competing Theories." *American Sociological Review* 48 (1983):439–453.

GUTH, JAMES L. "The New Christian Right." In Robert C. Liebman and Robert Wuthnow (eds.), *The New Christian Right,* pp. 31–45. New York: Aldine, 1983.

GUTMANN, DAVID L. "Parenthood: Key to the Comparative Psychology of the Life Cycle." In Nancy Davan and L. Ginsberg (eds.), *Developmental Psychology: Normative Life Crises.* New York: Academic Press, 1975, pp. 167–184.

GUTTENTAG, MARCIA, and PAUL F. SECORD. *Too Many Women: The Sex Ratio Question.* Beverly Hills, Calif.: Sage, 1983.

GUTTMANN, ALLEN. *From Ritual to Record: The Return of Modern Sports.* New York: Columbia University Press, 1978.

————. *Sports Spectators.* New York: Columbia University Press, 1986.

GWARTNEY-GIBBS, PATRICIA A. "The Institutionalization of Premarital Cohabitation: Estimates from Marriage License Applications, 1970 and 1980." *Journal of Marriage and the Family* 48 (1986):423–434.

HAAS, AIN. "Social Bases of Support for Workplace Democracy." *Work and Occupations* 13 (1986):241–263.

HAAS, LINDA. "Domestic Role Sharing in Sweden." Paper presented at American Sociological Association annual meetings, N.Y.C., August 1980.

————. "Role Sharing Couples: A Study of Equalitarian Marriages." *Family Relations* 20:289–96.

HAAS, VIOLET B., and CAROLYN C. PERRUCCI, eds. *Women in Scientific and Engineering Professions.* Ann Arbor: University of Michigan Press, 1984.

HABER, CAROL. *Beyond Sixty-Five: The Dilemma of Old Age in America's Past.* Cambridge: Cambridge University Press, 1983.

HACKER, ANDREW. *U/S: A Statistical Portrait of the American People.* New York: Viking, 1983.

HACKER, KATHY. "Deep Pockets Push a Dream Toward Reality." *Chicago Tribune,* February 23, 1986, Sec. 2, pp. 1 ff.

HADAWAY, C. KIRK. "Changing Brands: Denominational Switching and Membership Change." In Constant H. Jacquet, Jr. (ed.), *Yearbook of American and Canadian Churches,* 1980. Nashville, Tenn.: Abingdon, 1980.

HADDEN, JEFFREY K. "Toward Desacralizing Secularization Theory." *Social Forces* 65 (1987):587–611.

HAGAN, JOHN. "The Corporate Advantage: A Study of the Involvement of Corporate and Individual Victims in a Criminal Justice System." *Social Forces* 60(4) (June 1982):993–1017.

————, and CELESTE ALBONETTI. "Race, Class, and the Perception of Criminal Justice in America." *American Journal of Sociology* 88(2) (1982):329–355.

HAGGSTROM, GUS W., DAVID E. KANOUSE, and PETER A. MORRISON. "Accounting for the Educational Shortfalls of Mothers." *Journal of Marriage and the Family* 48 (1986): 175–186.

HAINES, HERBERT H. "Black Radicalization and the Funding of Civil Rights." *Social Problems* 32(1) (1984):31–43.

HALABY, CHARLES N. "Worker Attachment and Workplace Authority." *American Sociological Review* 51 (1986): 634–649.

HALL, ELAINE J. "Religious Conservatism and Abortion Attitudes: Some Unexpected Findings." Paper presented at the 56th annual meeting of the Eastern Sociological Society, New York City, April 1986.

HALL, ROBERT L., MARK RODEGHIER, and BERT USEEM. "Effects of Education on Attitude to Protest." *American Sociological Review* 51 (1986):564–573.

HALLE, DAVID. *America's Working Man: Work, Home, and Politics among Blue-Collar Property Owners.* Chicago: University of Chicago Press, 1984.

HALLORAN, RICHARD. "Women, Blacks, Spouses Transforming the Military." *The New York Times,* August 25, 1986, pp. 1 ff.

HAMMERSLEY, MARTYN, and PAUL ATKINSON. *Ethnography: Principles in Practice.* London: Tavistock Publications, 1983.

HAMMOND, PHILIP E., ed. *The Sacred in a Secular Age.* Berkeley: University of California Press, 1985.

HAND, CARL M., and KENT D. VAN LIERE. "Religion, Mastery-Over-Nature, and Environmental Concern." *Social Forces* 63(2) (1984):555–570.

HANE, MIKISO. *Peasants, Rebels and Outcasts: The Underside of Modern Japan.* New York: Pantheon Books, 1982.

HANEY, CRAIG, and PHILIP G. ZIMBARDO. "It's Tough to Tell a High School from a Prison." *Psychology Today* (June 1975):26 ff.

HANNON, MICHAEL. "Organizational Diversity and Social Inequality." Paper presented at the 81st annual meeting of the American Sociological Association, New York City, August 1986.

HAREVEN, TAMARA K. *Family Time and Industrial Time.* New York: Cambridge University Press, 1983.

HARGROVE, BARBARA, ed. *Religion and the Sociology of Knowledge: Modernization and Pluralism in Christian Thought and Structure.* New York: Edwin Mellen, 1984.

HARKESS, SHIRLEY. "Women's Occupational Experiences in the 1970s: Sociology and Economics." *Signs* 10 (1985): 495–520.

HARLOW, HARRY F., and MARGARET K. HARLOW. "Effects of Various Mother-Infant Relationships on Rhesus Monkey Behaviors." In B. M. Foss (ed.), *Determinants of Infant Behavior,* Vol. 4, pp. 15–36. London: Methuen, 1977.

HARNER, MICHAEL J. "The Ecological Basis for Aztec Sacrifice." *American Ethologist* 4(2) (1986):117–135.

HARRIS, CHAUNCY, and EDWARD ULLMAN. "The Nature of Cities." *Annals of the American Academy of Political and Social Science* 242(3) (1945):7–17.

HARRIS, LOUIS, AND ASSOCIATES. *Americans and the Arts.* Reported by Martha Farnsworth Riche. *American Demographics* (July 1985):42–44.

————. *Inside America.* New York: Vintage, 1987.

HARRIS, MARVIN. *Culture, People, Nature: An Introduction to General Anthropology,* 4th ed. New York: Harper & Row, 1985.

HARRISON, BENNET, CHRIS TILLY, and BARRY BLUESTONE. *Smaller Slices of the Pie.* Washington, D.C.: Center on Budget and Policy Priorities, 1986.

HARRY, JOSEPH. *Gay Couples.* New York: Praeger, 1984.

HARTMANN, HEIDI I., ed. *Comparable Worth: New Directions for Research.* Washington, D.C.: National Academy Press, 1985.

HART-NIBBRIG, NAND, and CLEMENT COTTINGHAM. *The Political Economy of College Sports.* Lexington, Mass.: D. C. Heath, 1986.

HARTSOCK, NANCY C. M. *Money, Sex, and Power: Toward a Feminist Historical Materialism.* New York: Longman, 1983.

HARTY, SHEILA. "Hucksters in the Classroom." *Social Policy* 12(2) (September–October 1981):38–42.

HASTINGS, PHILIP K., and DEAN R. HOGE. "Religious and Moral Attitude Trends Among College Students." *Social Forces* 65 (1986):370–377.

HAUSER, ROBERT M., PETER J. DICKINSON, HARRY P. TRAVIS, and JOHN KOFFEL. "Structural Changes in Occupational Mobility Among Men in the United States." *American Sociological Review* 40 (1975):585–598.

————, and DAVID L. FEATHERMAN. *The Process of Stratification: Trends and Analysis.* New York: Academic Press, 1977.

HAYDEN, DELORES. *Redesigning the American Dream: The Future of Housing, Work and Family Life.* New York: W. W. Norton and Co., 1984.

HAYGE, HOWARD. "Working Women with Children." *Monthly Labor Review,* February 1986.

HAZZARD, WILLIAM. "Mechanisms of Sex Differential in Longevity." Paper given at Combined Medical Grand Rounds, Boston University School of Medicine and University Hospital, Boston, October 18, 1983.

HEALY, KEVIN. "The Cocaine Industry in Bolivia—Its Impact on the Peasantry." *Cultural Survival Quarterly* 9(4):24–26.

HEATON, TIM B., STAN L. ALBRECHT, and THOMAS K. MARTIN. "The Timing of Divorce." *Journal of Marriage and the Family* 47(3) (1985):631–639.

HECHINGER, FRED M. "Censorship Rises in Nation's Public Schools." *The New York Times,* January 3, 1984, p. C7.

————. "How Should Colleges Pick Students?" *The New York Times,* June 24, 1986, p. C5.

————, ed. *A Better Start: New Choice for Early Learning.* New York: Walker & Company, 1987.

HECKSCHER, GUNNAR. *The Welfare State and Beyond: Success and Problems in Scandinavia.* Minneapolis: University of Minnesota Press, 1984.

HENIG, JEFFREY R. *Neighborhood Mobilization: Redevelopment and Response.* New Brunswick, N.J.: Rutgers University Press, 1982.

HENRETTA, JOHN C., CHARLES E. FRAZIER, and DONNA E. BISHOP. "The Effect of Prior Case Outcomes on Juvenile Justice Decision Making." *Social Forces* 65(2) (1986): 554–562.

HENRY, JULES. *Culture Against Man.* New York: Random House, 1963.

HENSLIN, JAMES M. "Why So Much Divorce?" In James M. Henslin (ed.), *Marriage and Family in a Changing Society,* pp. 424–439. New York: Macmillan, 1985.

HERBERG, WILL. *Protestant, Catholic, Jew.* Garden City, N.Y.: Doubleday, 1960.

HERBERS, JOHN. "Urban-Rural Data: Confusing Census." *The New York Times,* December 9, 1982.

————. "Conflict Is Found in Views on Needy." *The New York Times,* February 14, 1983.

————. "Census Data Reveal 70's Legacy: Poorer Cities and Richer Suburbs." *The New York Times,* February 27, 1983, pp. 1, 28.

————. "Sun Belt Cities Prosper as Those in North Decline." *The New York Times,* February 28, 1983, p. B8.

————. "Big City Ringed by Suburbs Giving Way to Sprawl of Small Metropolitan Areas." *The New York Times,* July 8, 1983, p. B4.

————. "Grass Roots Groups Go National." *The New York Times Magazine,* September 4, 1983, pp. 22 ff.

————. "Mismatch in Jobs and Skills is Found in Survey of Cities." *The New York Times,* October 22, 1986, p. A24.

HERDT, GILBERT H., ed. *Ritualized Homosexuality in Melanesia.* Berkeley: University of California Press, 1984.

HERITAGE, JOHN. *Garfinkel and Ethnomethodology.* Cambridge, Mass.: Polity, 1984.

HERMAN, EDWARD S. *Corporate Control, Corporate Power.* New York: Cambridge University Press, 1981.

HERNDON, JAMES. *The Way It Spozed to Be.* New York: Simon & Schuster, 1965.

HERRMANN, GRETCHEN M., and STEPHEN M. SOIFFER. "For Fun and Profit: An Analysis of the American Garage Sale." *Urban Life* 12(4) (1984):397–421.

HERSHEY, ROBERT D., JR. "High But Stable, U.S. Unemployment Is Gaining Acceptance." *The New York Times,* October 14, 1986, p. A28.

HERTEL, BRADLEY R., and MICHAEL HUGHES. "Religious Affiliation, Attendance, and Support for 'Pro-Family' Issues in the United States." *Social Forces* 65 (1987):858–876.

HERTZ, ROSANNA. *More Equal Than Others: Women and Men in Dual-Career Marriages.* Berkeley: University of California Press, 1986.

HESS, BETH B. "New Faces of Poverty." *American Demographics* 5 (May 1983A):26–31.

————. "Aging Policies and Old Women: The Hidden Agenda." pp. 319–332 in Alice S. Rossi (ed.), *Gender and the Life Course.* New York: Aldine, 1985.

————. "Manufacturing Crises in Social Policy: The Withering Away of the Welfare State." Paper presented at the 37th annual meeting of the Gerontological Society of America, San Antonio, Texas, November 1984.

————, and ELIZABETH W. MARKSON. *Aging and Old Age.* New York: Macmillan, 1980.

————, and MARVIN SUSSMAN, eds. *Women and the Family: Two Decades of Change.* New York: Haworth, 1984.

————, and JOAN WARING. "Changing Patterns of Aging and Family in Later Life." *The Family Coordinator* 27(4) (October 1978):303–314.

————, and JOAN WARING. "Family Relationships of Older Women: A Woman's Issue." In Elizabeth W. Markson (ed.), *Older Women: Issues and Prospects,* pp. 227–252. Lexington, Mass.: Lexington Books, 1983.

HEVESI, DENNIS. "TV Followers See Devil's Hand in Bakker's Fall." *The New York Times,* April 13, 1987, p. B9.

HEWITT, JOHN. *Self and Society: A Symbolic Interactionist Social Psychology,* 3rd ed. Boston: Allyn & Bacon, 1984.

HEWLETT, SYLVIA ANN. *A Lesser Life: The Myth of Women's Liberation in America.* New York: William Morrow, 1986.

HEYNS, BARBARA. "Policy Implications of the Public and Private School Debates." *Harvard Educational Review* 51(4) (November 1981):519–525.

HIGGINBOTHAM, ELIZABETH, and LYNN WEBER CANNON. "Woman and Mobility: Integrating Race and Gender into an Analysis of Upward Mobility in America." Paper presented at the 81st annual meeting of the American Socio-logical Association, August, 1986, New York, NY.

HIGHTOWER, JIM. "Hard Tomatoes, Hard Times: Failure of the Land Grant College Complex." *Transaction* 10(1) (Nov.–Dec. 1972):10–22.

HILL, MARTHA S., SUE AUGUSTYNIAK, GREG J. DUNCAN, GERALD GURIN, PATRICIA GURIN, JEFFRY K. LIKER, JAMES N. MORGAN, and MICHAEL PONZA. *Motivation and Economic Mobility.* Ann Arbor, Mich.: Institute for Social Research, 1985.

HILL, ROBERT. *The Strength of Black Families.* New York: Emerson Hall, 1972.

HILL, STEPHEN. *Competition and Control at Work: The New Industrial Sociology.* Cambridge, Mass.: M.I.T. Press, 1981.

HILLER, DANA V., and WILLIAM W. PHILLIBER. "The Division of Labor in Contemporary Marriage: Expectations, Perceptions and Performances." *Social Problems* 33 (1986): 191–201.

HIMMELSTRAND, ULF, GORAN AKRNE, LIEF LUNDBERG, and LAR LUNDBERG. *Beyond Welfare Capitalism: Issues, Actors, and Forces in Societal Change.* London: Wm. Heinemann, 1981.

HINDELANG, MICHAEL J. "Sex Differences in Criminal Activity." *Social Problems* 27(2) (1979):143–156.

————, TRAVIS HIRSCHI, and JOSEPH G. WEIS. "Correlates of Delinquency: The Illusion of Discrepancy Between Self-report and Official Measures." *American Sociological Review* 44(6) (1979):995–1014.

HIRSCH, PAUL M. "From Ambushes to Golden Parachutes: Corporate Takeovers as an Instance of Cultural Framing and Institutional Integration." *American Journal of Sociology* 91 (1986):800–837.

HOCHSCHILD, ARLIE RUSSELL. *The Managed Heart: Commercialization of Human Feelings.* Berkeley: University of California Press, 1983.

————. "Emotion Work, Feeling Rules and Social Structure." *American Journal of Sociology* 85:551–575.

HOCHSCHILD, JENNIFER L. *The New American Dilemma: Liberal Democracy and School Desegregation.* New Haven, Conn.: Yale University Press, 1984.

HODSON, RANDY. *Workers' Earnings and Corporate Economic Structure.* New York: Academic Press, 1983.

————, and TERESA A. SULLIVAN. "Totem or Tyrant? Monopoly, Regional, and Local Sector Effects on Worker Commitment." *Social Forces* 63 (1985):716–731.

HOELTER, JON W. "Factorial Invariance and Self-esteem: Reassessing Race and Sex Differences." *Social Forces* 61 (1983):834–846.

HODGES, DONALD C. *The Bureaucratization of Socialism.* Amherst: University of Massachusetts Press, 1981.

HOGAN, DENNIS P. "The Transition to Adulthood as a Career Contingency." *American Sociological Review* 45(2) (April 1980):261–276.

————. *Transitions and Social Change: The Early Lives of American Men.* New York: Academic Press, 1981.

————, and EVELYN M. KITAGAWA. "The Impact of Social Status, Family Structure, and Neighborhood on the Fertility of Black Adolescents." *American Journal of Sociology* 90 (1985):825–854.

————, and MICHELE PAZUL. "The Career Strategies of Black Men." *Social Forces* 59 (1981):1217–1228.

HOHENBERG, PAUL M., and LYNN HOLLEN LEES. *The Making of Urban Europe 1000–1950.* Cambridge, Mass.: Harvard University Press, 1985.

HOLMES, T. H., and MINORU MASUDA. "Life Change and Illness Susceptibility." In David R. Heise (ed.), *Personality and Socialization,* pp. 434–449. Chicago: Rand McNally, 1972.

————, and R. H. RAKE. "The Social Readjustment Rating Scale." *Journal of Psychosomatic Research* (1967).

HOLTER, HARRIET. *Patriarchy in a Welfare Society.* Oslo: Universitetsforlaget, 1984.

HOMANS, GEORGE C. *The Human Group.* New York: Harcourt Brace Jovanovich, 1950.

————. *Social Behavior: Its Elementary Forms.* New York: Harcourt Brace Jovanovich, 1961.

HOMBS, MARY E., and MITCHELL SNYDER. *Homeless in America.* Washington, D.C.: Community for Creative Non-Violence, 1982.

HOOD, JANE C. *Becoming a Two-Job Family.* New York: Praeger, 1983.

HOOTON, ERNEST ALBERT. *Crime and the Man.* Cambridge, Mass.: Harvard University Press, 1939.

HOPE, KEITH. "Vertical and Nonvertical Class Mobility in Three Countries." *American Sociological Review* 47 (1982):99–113.

HOPE, MARJORIE, and JAMES YOUNG. *The Faces of Homelessness.* Lexington, Mass.: Heath, 1987.

HOPPER, REX D. "The Revolutionary Process." *Social Forces* 28 (March 1950):207–279.

HORNUNG, CARLTON A., and CLAIRE McCULLOUGH. "Status Relationships in Dual-Employment Marriages: Consequences for Psychological Well-being." *Journal of Marriage and the Family* 43(1) (1981):125–141.

HOROWITZ, IRVING LOUIS. "The Life and Death of Project Camelot." *Transaction* 3(1) (Nov.–Dec. 1965):3 ff.

HOUSE, JAMES S. "Social Structure and Personality in Social Psychology." In Morris Rosenberg and Ralph Turner (eds.), *Sociological Perspectives.* New York: Basic Books, 1981.

HOUT, MICHAEL. "Opportunity and the Minority Middle Class: A Comparison of Blacks in the United States and Catholics in Northern Ireland." *American Sociological Review* 51 (April 1986):214–223.

————, and ANDREW M. GREELEY. "The Center Doesn't Hold: Church Attendance in the United States, 1940–1984." *American Sociological Review* 52 (1987):325–345.

HOWARD, ROBERT. *Brave New Workplace.* New York: Viking, 1985.

HOWERY, CARLA B., ed. *Teaching Applied Sociology: A Resource Book.* Washington, D.C.: American Sociological Association, Teaching Resources Center, 1983.

HOYT, HOMER. *The Structure and Growth of Residential Neighborhoods in American Cities.* Washington, D.C.: U.S. Government Printing Office, 1939.

HUBER, BETTINA. *Embarking on a Career with an Under-graduate Sociology Major.* Washington, D.C.: American Sociological Association, 1982.

HUBER, JOAN. "Trends in Gender Stratification, 1970–1985." *Sociological Forum* 1 (1986):476–495.

————, JOHN GAGNON, SUZANNE KELLER, RONALD LAWSON, PATRICIA MILLER, and WILLIAM SIMON. "The Task Group on Homosexuality Report." *The American Sociologist* (August 1982).

————, and GLENNA SPITZE. *Sex Stratification: Children, Housework, and Jobs.* New York: Academic Press, 1983.

HUGHES, JAMES W., and GEORGE STERNLIEB. "The Suburban Growth Corridor." *American Demographics* (April 1986): 34–37.

HUGHES, ROBERT G., and PHILIP R. LEE. "Public Prospects." *Society* 23(5) (1986):60–65.

HUGHEY, MICHAEL. *Civil Religion and Moral Order: Theoretical and Historical Dimensions.* Westport, Conn.: Greenwood Press, 1983.

HUNTER, JAMES DAVISON. *American Evangelicism: Conservative Religion and the Quandry of Modernity.* New Brunswick, N.J.: Rutgers University Press, 1983.

HYMAN, HERBERT H. "The Psychology of Status." *Archives of Psychology* 37 (1942):15.

INCIARDI, JAMES. "The War On Drugs: Heroin, Cocaine, Crime and Public Policy." *The New York Times,* March 15, 1987, pp. 1 ff.

IKELS, CHARLOTTE. *Aging and Adaptation: Chinese in Hong Kong and the United States.* Cambridge, Mass.: Harvard University Press, 1983.

INSTITUTE OF MEDICINE, NATIONAL RESEARCH COUNCIL. *America's Aging: Health in an Older Society.* Washington, D.C.: National Academy Press, 1985.

IRWIN, JOHN. *The Jail: Managing the Underclass in American Society.* Berkeley: University of California Press, 1985.

JACKMAN, MARY R., and ROBERT W. JACKMAN. *Class Awareness in the United States.* Berkeley, Calif.: University of California Press, 1983.

————, and MICHAEL J. MUHA. "Education and Intergroup Attitudes: Moral Enlightenment, Superficial Democratic Commitment, or Ideological Refinement." *American Sociological Review* 46(6) (1984):751–769.

JACOBS, DAVID. "Inequality and Economic Crime." *Sociology and Social Research* 66 (1981):12–28.

————. "Competition, Scale and Political Explanation for Inequality: An Integrated Study of Sectoral Explanations at the Aggregate Level." *American Sociological Review* 47 (October 1982):600–614.

————, and DAVID BRITT. "Inequality and Police Use of Deadly Force: An Empirical Assessment of a Conflict Hypothesis." *Social Problems* 26(4) (April 1979):403–412.

JACOBS, JANE. *Cities and the Wealth of Nations.* New York: Random House, 1984.

————. *Death and Life of Great American Cities.* New York: Random House, 1961.

JACOBS, RUTH H. "Portrait of a Phenomenon—The Gray

Panthers: Do They Have a Long-Run Future?" In Elizabeth W. Markson and Gretchen R. Batra (eds.), *Public Policies for an Aging Population,* pp. 93–103. Lexington, Mass.: Lexington Books, 1980.

JACQUET, CONSTANT H., JR. *Yearbook of American and Canadian Churches, 1985.* Nashville, Tenn.: Abingdon Press, 1985.

——————. *Yearbook of Canadian and American Churches, 1987.* Nashville, Tenn.: Abingdon Press, 1987.

JAFFE, DAVID. "The Political Economy of Job Loss in the United States, 1970–1980." *Social Problems* 33 (1986): 297–315.

JAFFEE, JEROME. "Jaffee Defends Disorder Label for Habitual Smokers." *Psychiatric News* (October 6, 1975):35, 39.

JANOWITZ, MORRIS. *Professional Soldier: A Social and Political Portrait.* New York: Free Press, 1960.

JAY, KARLA, and ALLAN YOUNG. *The Gay Report.* New York: Summit Books, 1979.

JENCKS, CHRISTOPHER, et al. *Who Gets Ahead? The Determinants of Economic Success in America.* New York: Basic Books, 1979.

JENKINS, J. CRAIG, and CRAIG M. ECKERT. "Channeling Black Insurgency: Elite Patronage and Professional Social Movement Organizations in the Development of the Black Movement." *American Sociological Review* (1986):812–829.

——————, and TERI SHUMATE. "Cowboy Capitalists and the Rise of the 'New Right': An Analysis of Contributors to Conservative Policy Formation Organizations." *Social Problems* 33 (1985):130–145.

JENNINGS, M. KENT, and GREGORY B. MARKUS. "Yuppie Politics." *ISR Newsletter* (Spring/Summer 1986):5–7.

JENSEN, JOYCE. "Health Care Alternatives." *American Demographics* (March 1986):36–38.

JOHANSEN, HARLEY E., and GLENN V. FUGUITT. *The Changing Rural Village in America.* Cambridge, Mass.: Ballinger Press, 1984.

JOHNSON, KAY ANN. *Women, the Family, and Peasant Revolution in China.* Chicago: University of Chicago Press, 1983.

JOHNSON, NORRIS BROCK. *West Haven: Classroom Culture and Society in a Rural Elementary School.* Chapel Hill: University of North Carolina Press, 1985.

JOINT ECONOMIC COMMITTEE, U.S. CONGRESS. *The Conception of Wealth in the United States,* July 1986.

JONES, ALEX S. "Antitrust Action Urged for Press." *The New York Times,* April 12, 1986, p. 7.

JONES, EDWARD W., JR. "Black Managers: The Dream Deferred." *Harvard Business Review* 64(3) (1986):84–93.

JONES, ELISE F., et al. "Teen-Age Pregnancy in Developed Countries: Determinants and Policy Implications." *Family Planning Perspectives* 17(2) (March/April 1985):53–63.

JONES, GARETH STEDMAN. *Languages of Class: Studies in English Working Class History 1832–1982.* New York: Cambridge University Press, 1983.

KADUSHIN, CHARLES. "Mental Health and the Interpersonal Environment: A Reexamination of Some Effects of Social Structure on Mental Health." *American Sociological Review* 48 (1983):188–198.

KAGAN, JEROME. *The Nature of the Child.* New York: Basic Books, 1984.

KAKU, MICHIO, and DANIEL AXELROD. *To Win a Nuclear War.* Boston: South End Press, 1987.

KALDOR, MARY, MARGARET SHARP, and WILLIAM WALKER. "The Effects of Military Spending." *Lloyd's Bank Review,* November 1986.

KALISH, RICHARD. "The Effects of Death Upon the Family." In Leonard Pearson (ed.), *Death and Dying.* Cleveland: Case Western Reserve University Press, 1969.

——————, and D. K. REYNOLDS. *Death and Ethnicity.* Los Angeles: University of Southern California Press, 1976.

——————. *Death, Grief, and Caring Relationships.* Monterey, Calif.: Brooks/Cole, 1981.

KALMUSS, DEBRA. "The Intergenerational Transmission of Marital Aggression." *Journal of Marriage and the Family* 46 (1984):11–19.

——————, and JUDITH A. SELTZER. "Continuity of Marital Behavior in Remarriage: The Case of Spouse Abuse." *Journal of Marriage and the Family* 48 (1986):113–120.

KAMERMAN, SHEILA B., and C. D. HAYES, eds. *Families That Work: Children in a Changing World.* Washington, D.C.: National Academy Press, 1982.

KANDEL, DENISE B. "Drug and Drinking Behavior Among Youth." *Annual Review of Sociology* 6 (1980):235–285.

KANTER, ROSABETH MOSS. "Why Bosses Turn Bitchy." *Psychology Today* 9(1) (1976):56–59.

——————. *Men and Women of the Corporation.* New York: Basic Books, 1977.

——————. *Work and Family in the United States: A Critical Review and Agenda for Research and Policy.* New York: Russell Sage, 1977.

KAREN, DAVID. "The Politics of Admission to Elite Colleges: The Case of Harvard." Paper presented at the 56th annual meeting of the Eastern Sociological Society, New York City, April 1986.

——————, and KATHERINE E. MCCLELLAND. "Trends in Access to Higher Education: Class, Race, and Sex." Paper presented at the annual meeting of the American Sociological Association, Detroit, August 1983.

KARNIG, ALBERT K., and SUSAN WELCH. *Black Representation and Urban Policy.* Chicago: University of Chicago Press, 1981.

KARP, DAVID A., and WILLIAM C. YOELS. *Experiencing the Life Cycle: A Social Psychology of Aging.* Springfield, Ill.: Charles C. Thomas, 1982.

KASARDA, JOHN D., MICHAEL D. IRWIN, and HOLLY L. HUGHES. "The South is Still Rising." *American Demographics* (June 1986):33–35, 38–70.

KASL, S. V. "Work and Mental Health." In J. O'Toole (ed.), *Work and the Quality of Life,* pp. 171–196. Cambridge, Mass.: MIT Press, 1974.

KASPAR, ANNE S. "Consciousness Re-evaluated: Interpretive Theory and Feminist Scholarship." *Sociological Inquiry* 56(1) (1986):30–49.

KATZ, DANIEL, and K. W. BRALEY. "Racial Stereotypes of 100 College Students." *Journal of Abnormal and Social Psychology* 28 (1933):280–290.

KATZNELSON, IRA, and MARGARET WEIR. *Schooling for All: Class, Race, and the Decline of the Democratic Ideal.* New York: Basic Books, 1985.

KAUFMAN, DEBRA R., and BARBARA L. RICHARDSON. *Achievement and Women: Challenging the Assumptions.* New York: Free Press, 1982.

KAUFMAN, ROBERT L. "The Impact of Industrial and Occupational Structure on Black-White Employment Allocation." *American Sociological Review* 51 (1986):310–323.

—————, and SEYMOUR SPILERMAN. "The Age Structures of Occupations and Jobs." *American Journal of Sociology* 87 (1982):827–851.

KEITH, JENNIE. "The Ethnography of Old Age: Introduction." *Anthropological Quarterly* 52 (1979):1–6.

KELLER, EVELYN FOX. *Reflections on Gender and Science.* New Haven, Conn.: Yale University Press, 1985.

KELLY, JOAN. *Women, History, and Theory: The Essays of Joan Kelly.* Chicago: University of Chicago Press, 1984.

KENEN, REGINA. "Soapsuds, Space and Sociability." *Urban Life* 11(2) (1982):163–183.

KENNARD, JEAN E. "Ourself Behind Ourself: A Theory for Lesbian Readers." *Signs* 9 (1984):647–662.

KENNEDY, ROBERT E. *Life Choices: Applying Sociology.* New York: Holt, Rinehart & Winston, 1986.

KERBO, H. R. "Characteristics of the Poor: A Continuing Focus in Social Research." *SSR* 65 (1981):323–331.

KERCHKHOFF, ALAN C., RICHARD T. CAMPBELL, and IDEE WINFIELD-LAIRD. "Social Mobility in Great Britain and the United States," *American Journal of Sociology* 91 (1985): 281–309.

KESSLER, RONALD C., and MARILYN ESSEX. "Marital Status and Depression: The Importance of Coping Resources." *Social Forces* 61 (1982):484–500.

—————, and JAMES A. MCRAE, JR. "Trends in the Relationship Between Sex and Psychological Distress: 1957–1976." *American Sociological Review* 46 (1981):443–452.

—————, and JAMES A. MCRAE, JR. "The Effects of Wives' Employment on the Mental Health of Married Men and Women." *American Sociological Review* 47 (1982): 216–227.

—————, and HORST STIPP. "The Impact of Fictional Television Suicide Stories on U.S. Fatalities: A Replication." *American Journal of Sociology* 90(1) (1984): 151–167.

KEYSSAR, ALEXANDER. *Out of Work: The First Century of Unemployment in Massachusetts.* New York: Cambridge University Press, 1986.

KILLIAN, LEWIS M. "Organization, Rationality and Spontaneity in the Civil Rights Movement." *American Sociological Review* 49(6) (1984):770–783.

KIMMEL, MICHAEL S. "The 'Crisis' of Masculinity in Historical Perspective." Paper presented at the 81st annual meeting of the American Sociological Association, New York, August 1986.

—————, ed. *Changing Men: New Directions in Research on Men and Masculinity.* Newbury Park, Calif.: Sage, 1987.

KIMURA, DOREEN. "Male Brain, Female Brain: The Hidden Difference." *Psychology Today,* November 1985, pp. 50–58.

KING, WAYNE. "New Criminal Class is Flourishing in Sunbelt." *The New York Times,* December 12, 1983, pp. 1, 15.

KINGSTON, PAUL WILLIAM. "Theory at Risk: Accounting for the Excellence Movement." *Sociological Forum* 1 (1986): 632–656.

—————, and STEVEN L. NOCK. "Time Together among Dual-Earner Couples." *American Sociological Review* 52 (1987):391–400.

KIPNIS, DAVID. *The Powerholders.* Chicago: University of Chicago Press, 1976.

KIRSCH, IRWIN S., and ANN JUNGEBLUT. *Literacy: Profiles of America's Young Adults.* Washington, D.C.: National Assessment of Educational Progress, 1986.

KITANO, HARRY. *Japanese Americans.* Englewood Cliffs, N.J.: Prentice-Hall, 1976.

KITCHER, PHILIP. *Vaulting Ambition: Sociobiology and the Quest for Human Nature.* Cambridge, Mass.: MIT Press, 1985.

KLANDERMANS, BERT. "Mobilization and Participation: Social-Psychological Expansions of Resource Mobilization Theory." *American Sociological Review* 49(5) (1984): 583–600.

KLAUS, MARSHALL H., and JOHN H. KENNELL. *Parent-Infant Bonding,* 2nd ed. St. Louis: C. V. Mosby, 1982.

KLECK, GARY. "Racial Discrimination in Criminal Sentencing: A Critical Evaluation of the Evidence with Additional Evidence on the Death Penalty." *American Sociological Review* 46 (1981):783–805.

KLEINFIELD, N. R. "The Art of Selling to the Very Rich." *New York Times,* June 15, 1986, Section 3, p. 1 ff.

KLITGAARD, ROBERT. *Choosing Elites: Selecting the Top Universities and Elsewhere.* New York: Basic Books, 1985.

KLOCKARS, CARL B. "The Dirty Harry Problem." *The Annals of the American Academy of Political and Social Science* 252 (1980):33–43.

—————. *The Idea of Police.* Beverly Hills, Calif.: Sage, 1985.

KLUEGEL, JAMES R., and ELIOT R. SMITH. "Whites' Beliefs About Blacks' Opportunities." *American Sociological Review* 47 (1982):518–532.

—————, and ELIOT R. SMITH. "Affirmative Action Attitudes: Effects of Self-interest, Racial Affect, and Stratification Beliefs on Whites' Views." *Social Forces* 61 (1983): 797–824.

KOBRIN, FRANCES E., and LINDA J. WAITE. "Effects of Childhood Family Structure on the Transition to Marriage." *Journal of Marriage and the Family* 46 (1984):807–816.

KOCHAN, THOMAS A., ed. *Challenges and Choices Facing American Labor.* Cambridge, Mass.: MIT Press, 1985.

KOCHEN, MANFRED, and KARL W. DEUTSCH. *Decentralization: Sketches Toward a Rational Theory.* Cambridge, Mass.: Oelgeschlager, Gunn and Hain, 1980.

Koenig, Thomas, and Tracey Boyce. "Corporate Financing of the Christian Right." *Humanity and Society* 9(1) (1985):13–28.

Kohlberg, Lawrence. *The Philosophy of Moral Development.* Vol. 1: *Essays on Moral Development.* New York: Harper & Row, 1981.

Kohn, Alfie. "How to Succeed Without Even Vying." *Psychology Today,* September 1986, pp. 22–28.

Kohn, Melvin L. "Bureaucratic Men: A Portrait and an Interpretation." *American Sociological Review* 36 (June 1971):461–474.

————, and Carmi Schooler. *Work and Personality: An Inquiry into the Impact of Social Stratification.* New York: Ablex Press, 1983.

Komarovsky, Mirra. *Dilemmas of Masculinity.* New York: W. W. Norton, 1976.

Korpi, Walter. *The Democratic Class Struggle.* Boston: Routledge & Kegan Paul, 1983.

Kouzi, Anthony, and Richard E. Ratcliff. "Politics and the Corporate Wallet: Political Contributions by Corporate Officers." Paper presented at the annual meeting of the Society for the Study of Social Problems, Detroit, Mich., August 1984.

Kozol, Jonathan. *Illiterate America.* New York: Anchor/Doubleday, 1986.

Krauss, Celene. "From the Grass Roots: A Practical Critique of Politics." Paper presented at the annual American Sociological Association Meeting, Chicago, August, 1987.

Krauze, Tadeusz. "How Far to Meritocracy? Empirical Tests of a Controversial Thesis." *Social Forces* 63(3) (1985):623–642.

Kronholz, June. "Saga of 'Lost' Tribe in Philippines Shows Marcos Era's Dark Side." *Wall Street Journal,* September 15, 1985, pp. 1 ff.

————. "Amid Social Progress, Bride-Burning Seems on the Rise in India." *Wall Street Journal,* August 21, 1986, pp. 1 ff.

Kuhn, Thomas S. *The Structure of Scientific Revolutions.* Chicago: University of Chicago Press, 1962.

Kurtz, Lester. *The Nuclear Cage; A Sociology of the Arms Race.* Englewood Cliffs, N.J.: Prentice-Hall, 1987.

Kushner, Howard I. "Women and Suicide in Historical Perspective." *Signs* 10(3) (1985):537–553.

Kuttner, Robert. "Unions, Economic Power & the State." *Dissent* (Winter 1986):33–44.

Labaree, David F. "Academic Excellence in an Early U.S. High School." *Social Problems* 31(5) (1984):558–567.

Ladd-Taylor, Molly. "Women Workers and the Yale Strike." *Feminist Studies* 11(3) (1985):464–484.

Laing, Ronald D. "Mystification, Confusion, and Conflict." In Peter J. Stein, Judith Richman, and Natalie Hannon (eds.), *The Family: Functions, Conflicts and Symbols,* pp. 240–252. Reading, Mass.: Addison Wesley, 1977.

Lake, Robert W. *The New Suburbanites: Race and Housing in the Suburbs.* New Brunswick, N.J.: Center for Urban Policy Research, Rutgers University, 1981.

Lamb, Michael. "Second Thoughts on First Touch." *Psychology Today* (April 1982):9–11.

————, ed. *The Father's Role: Applied Perspectives.* New York: Wiley, 1986.

————, Joseph H. Pleck, and James A. Levine. "Effects of Increased Paternal Involvement on Children in Two-Parent Families." In Robert A. Lewis and Robert E. Salt (eds.), *Men in Families,* pp. 141–155. Beverly Hills, Calif.: Sage, 1986.

Lamphere, Louise. "Bringing the Family to Work: Women's Culture on the Shop Floor." *Feminist Studies* 11 (1985): 519–540.

Lane, Christel. *The Rites of Rulers: Ritual in Industrial Society—The Soviet Case.* New York: Cambridge University Press, 1981.

Laner, Mary R. "Prostitution as an Illegal Vocation: A Sociological Overview." In Clifford D. Bryan (ed.), *Deviant Behavior: Occupational and Organizational Bases.* Chicago: Rand McNally, 1974.

Lang, Gladys Engel, and Kurt Lang. *The Battle for Public Opinion: The President, the Press, and the Polls During Watergate.* New York: New York University Press, 1983.

Larkin, Ralph W. *Suburban Youth in Cultural Crisis.* New York: Oxford University Press, 1979.

LaRossa, Ralph, and Jane H. Wolf. "On Qualitative Family Research." *Journal of Marriage and the Family* 47(3) (1985):531–541.

Larson, Oscar R., Gilbert W. Gillespie, Jr., and Frederick H. Buttel. "Sources of Social Class Identification Among Farmers." *Rural Sociology* 48(1) (1983):82–103.

Lawrence, Robert Z. "The Middle Class is Alive and Well." *The New York Times,* June 23, 1985, p. F3.

LeBon, Gustave. *The Crowd.* New York: Larlin, 1969/1895.

Lee, Richard B. *The !Kung San: Men, Women, and Work in a Foraging Society.* Cambridge: Cambridge University Press, 1979.

————. *The Dobe !Kung.* New York: Holt, Rinehart & Winston, 1984.

Lee, Sidney S. "Health Policy, A Social Contract: A Comparison of the United States and Canada." *Journal of Public Health and Policy* (1982):293–301.

Lehman, Edward C. *Women Clergy: Breaking Through the Gender Barriers.* News Brunswick, N.J.: Transaction Press, 1985.

Leiter, Jeffrey. "Reactions to Subordination: Attitudes of Southern Textile Workers." *Social Forces* 64 (1986): 948–974.

Le Masters, E. E. *Blue-Collar Aristocrats: Life Styles at a Working Class Tavern.* Madison: University of Wisconsin Press, 1975.

Lemert, Edwin M. *Human Deviance, Social Problems, and Social Control.* Englewood Cliffs, N.J.: Prentice-Hall, 1967.

Lenski, Gerhard. *Power and Privilege: A Theory of Social Stratification.* New York: McGraw-Hill, 1966.

————. "Marxist Experiments in Destratification: An Appraisal." *Social Forces* 57(2) (December 1978):364–383.

————, and PATRICK D. NOLAN. "Trajectories of Development: A Test of Ecological-Evolutionary Theory." Paper presented at the American Sociological Association annual meeting, Detroit, August 1983.

LERMAN, HANNAH. *A Mote in Freud's Eye: From Psychoanalysis to the Psychology of Women.* New York: Springer Publishing Co., 1986.

LERNER, GERDA. *The Creation of Patriarchy.* New York: Oxford University Press, 1986.

LERNER, RICHARD M. *On the Nature of Human Plasticity.* New York: Cambridge University Press, 1984.

LERNER, STEVE. "Rich Kids." *Common Cause Magazine,* March/April 1986, pp. 15–19.

LEVER, JANET. *Soccer Madness.* Chicago: University of Chicago Press, 1983.

LEVI-STRAUSS, CLAUDE. *Elementary Structures of Kinship.* Boston: Beacon Press, 1969.

LEVINE, ANDREW. *Arguing for Socialism.* London: Routledge & Kegan Paul, 1984.

LEVINE, MARTIN P., ed. *Gay Men: The Sociology of Male Homosexuality.* New York: Harper & Row, 1979.

————. "Employment Discrimination Against Gay Men." In Peter J. Stein (ed.), *Single Life: Unmarried Adults in Social Context,* pp. 268–273. New York: St. Martin's Press, 1981.

————, and ROBIN LEONARD. "Discrimination Against Lesbians in the Work Force." *Signs* 9 (1984):700–710.

LEVINSON, DANIEL. *Seasons of a Man's Life.* New York: Alfred A. Knopf, 1978.

LEVY, CHARLES J. "ARVN as Faggots: Inverted Warfare in Vietnam." *Society* 8 (1971):18–27.

LEVY, FRANK, and RICHARD C. MICHEL. "Are Baby Boomers Selfish?" *American Demographics* (April 1985):38–41.

LEWIN, TAMAR. "Sudden Nurse Shortage Threatens Hospital Care." *The New York Times,* July 7, 1987, pp. 1 ff.

LEWIS, LIONEL S. "Working at Leisure." *Society* 19 (July–Aug. 1982):27–32.

LEWIS, OSCAR. *Four Families: Mexican Case Studies in the Culture of Poverty.* New York: Basic Books, 1959.

LEWIS, ROBERT A., ed. *Men in Difficult Times: Masculinity Today and Tomorrow.* Englewood Cliffs, N.J.: Prentice-Hall, 1981.

————, and ROBERT E. SALT, eds. *Men in Families.* Beverly Hills, Calif.: Sage, 1986.

LEWONTIN, RICHARD C., STEVEN ROSE, and LEON KAMIN. *Not in Our Genes: Biology, Ideology, and Human Nature.* New York: Pantheon, 1984.

LICHTER, DANIEL T., GLENN V. FUGUITT, and TIM B. HEATON. "Racial Differences in Nonmetropolitan Population Deconcentration." *Social Forces* 64(2) (December 1985):487–498.

LIEBERSON, JONATHAN. "Anatomy of an Epidemic." *New York Review of Books,* August 18, 1983, pp. 17–22.

LIEBERSON, STANLEY. *A Piece of the Pie: Blacks and White Immigrants Since 1880.* Berkeley and Los Angeles: University of California Press, 1981.

LIEBMAN, ROBERT C., and ROBERT WUTHNOW, eds. *The New Christian Right: Mobilization and Legitimation.* New York: Aldine, 1983.

LIEM, RAMSEY, and PAULA RAYMAN. "Health and Social Costs of Unemployment: Research and Policy Consideration." *American Psychologist* 37(10) (1982):1116–1123.

LIGHT, DONALD. *Becoming Psychiatrists: The Professional Transformation of Self.* New York: W. W. Norton, 1980.

LIN, NAN, JOHN C. VAUGH, and WALTER M. ENSEL. "Social Resources and Occupational Status Attainment." *Social Forces* 59(4) (1981):1163–1181.

LINCOLN, JAMES R., and ARNE L. KALLEBERG. "Work Organization and Workforce Commitment: A Study of Plants and Employees in the U.S. and Japan." *American Sociological Review* 50 (1985):738–760.

LINDORFF, DAVID. "Exposing Corporate Negligence," *Maclean,* June 30, 1986, p. 29.

LINDSEY, ROBERT. "Isolated, Strongly Led Sects Growing in U.S." *The New York Times,* June 22, 1986, pp. 1 ff.

————. "Spiritual Concepts Drawing a Different Breed of Adherent." *The New York Times,* September 29, 1986, pp. 1 ff.

LIPSET, SEYMOUR MARTIN, ed. *Harriet Martineau: Society in America.* New York: Doubleday, 1962.

————, and EARL RAAB. "The Election and the Evangelicals." *Commentary* 71 (March 1981):26–32.

LISKA, ALLEN E., JOSEPH J. LAWRENCE, and ANDREW SANCHIRICO. "Fear of Crime as a Social Fact." *Social Forces* (1982):760–770.

LIVINGSTON, IVOR L. "The Importance of Socio-Psychological Stress in the Interpretation of the Race-Hypertension Association." *Humanity and Society* 9 (May 1985):168–175.

LIVINGSTONE, DAVID W. *Class Ideologies and Educational Futures.* Barcombe, England: Falmer Press, 1983.

LOEWEN, JAMES W., and SAMUEL F. SAMPSON. "Getting Gender on Their Minds: A Classroom Exercise on Sex Roles." *Teaching Sociology* 14 (1986):185–187.

LOGUE, JOHN. "Will Success Spoil the Welfare State?" *Dissent* 32 (1986):96–104.

LONGINO, CHARLES F. *The Oldest Americans.* Washington, D.C.: Andrus Foundation/AARP, 1986.

LOOKER, E. DIANNE, and PETER C. PINEO. "Some Social Psychological Variables and Their Relevance to the Status Attainment of Teenagers." *American Journal of Sociology* 88 (1983):1195–1219.

LOOMIS, CAROL J. "The Limited War on White Collar Crime." *Fortune,* July 22, 1985, p. 96.

LOPATA, HELENA Z., and BARRIE THORNE. "On the Term Sex Roles." *Signs* 3 (1978):718–721.

LORBER, JUDITH. *Women Physicians: Careers, Status, and Power.* New York: Tavistock, 1984.

LORENCE, JON, and JEYLAN T. MORTIMER. "Job Involvement Through the Life Course: A Panel Study of Three Age Groups." *American Sociological Review* 50 (1985):618–638.

LUKER, KRISTIN. *Abortion and the Politics of Motherhood.* Los Angeles: University of California Press, 1984.

LUMSDEN, CHARLES J., and EDWARD O. WILSON. *Genes, Mind, Culture: The Coevolutionary Process.* Cambridge, Mass.: Harvard University Press, 1981.

LYND, ROBERT S., and HELEN MERRELL LYND. *Middletown: A Study in American Culture.* New York: Harcourt, 1929.

LYNG, STEPHEN G., and LESTER R. KURTZ. "Bureaucratic Insurgency: The Vatican and the Crisis of Modernism." *Social Forces* 63(4) (1985):901–922.

LYNN, BARRY W. "The New Pornography Commission: Slouching Toward Censorship." *SIECUS Report* 14(5) (1986):1–6.

MACCORQUODALE, PATRICIA L. "Gender Roles and Premarital Contraception." *Journal of Marriage and the Family* 46 (1984):57–63.

MACDONALD, J. FRED. *Television and the Red Menace: The Video Road to Vietnam.* New York: Praeger, 1985.

MACKENSIE, R. D. "The Scope of Human Ecology." *Publications of the American Sociological Society* 20 (1925).

MACKLIN, ELEANOR. "Nonmarital Heterosexual Cohabitation: An Overview." In E. Macklin and R. Rubin (eds.), *Contemporary Families and Alternative Lifestyles,* pp. 49–74. Beverly Hills, Calif.: Sage, 1983.

————, and ROGER RUBIN, eds. *Contemporary Families and Alternative Lifestyles.* Newbury Park, Calif.: Sage, 1983.

MACLEOD, DAVID I. *Building Character in the American Boy: The Boy Scouts, YMCA, and Their Forerunners, 1870–1920.* Madison: University of Wisconsin Press, 1983.

MAGRASS, YALE R. "The Boy Scouts, the Outdoors, and Empire." *Humanity and Society* 10 (February 1986): 37–57.

————. "Money Changers in the Temple." *Humanity and Society* 10 (May 1986):197–203.

MAKINSON, CAROLYN. "Health Consequences of Teenage Fertility." *Family Planning Perspectives* 17 (1985): 132–134.

MALINOWSKI, BRONISLAW. *Argonauts of the Western Pacific.* New York: Dutton, 1922.

————. "The Principle of Legitimacy: Parenthood, The Basis of Social Structure." In Rose Laub Coser (ed.), *The Family: Its Structure and Functions.* New York: St. Martin's, 1964.

MALONE, KAREN. *HMOs as an Alternate Mode of Care for the Elderly.* Washington, D.C.: Urban Institute, 1979.

MALONEL, PATRICK. "British Medicine/American Medicine: Leaning Closer but Still an Ocean Apart." *New Physician* 28 (December 1979):20–24.

MANNING, PETER, LAWRENCE LIN, and PAUL ROCK REDLINGER, eds. *Politics and Drugs: The Invitational Edges of Corruption.* New York: E. P. Dutton, 1976.

MANSKI, CHARLES F., and DAVID A. WISE. *College Choice in America.* Cambridge, Mass.: Harvard University Press, 1983.

MARCUSE, PETER. "Why Are They Homeless?" *The Nation,* April 4, 1987, pp. 426–428.

MARE, ROBERT D. "Change and Stability in Educational Stratification." *American Sociological Review* 46 (1981): 72–87.

MARGER, MARTIN N. "Social Movement Organizations and Response to Environmental Change: The NAACP, 1960–1973." *Social Problems* 32(1) (1984):16–30.

MARINI, MARGARET MOONEY. "Women's Educational Attainment and the Timing of Entry into Parenthood." *American Sociological Review* 49 (1984):491–511.

MARKHAM, WILLIAM T., PATRICK O. MACKEN, CHARLES M. BONJEAN, and JUDY CORDER. "A Note on Sex, Geographic Mobility, and Career Advancement." *Social Forces* 61 (1983):1138–1146.

MARKOFF, JOHN. "The Social Geography of Rural Revolt at the Beginning of the French Revolution." *American Sociological Review* 50(6) (1986):761–781.

MARKS, MITCHELL LEE. "The Question of Quality Circles." *Psychology Today,* March 1986, pp. 36 ff.

MARKS, STEPHEN. "Multiple Roles and Role Strain: Some Notes on Human Energy, Time, and Commitment." *American Sociological Review* 42 (December 1977):921–936.

MARKSON, ELIZABETH W. "Family Roles and the Impact of Feminism on Women's Mental Health Across the Life Course." *Marriage and Family Review* 7(3/4) (Fall/Winter, 1984):215–232.

————. Interviews conducted by author, 1987.

————, (ed.). *Older Women: Issues and Prospects.* Lexington, Mass.: Lexington Books, 1983.

————, CAROLINE C. CRESCENZI, and KNIGHT STEEL. "Utilization of Health Services by Low Income Inner City Elderly." Paper given at North Eastern Gerontological Society meeting, Newport, R.I., May 6, 1983.

————, CAROLINE CRESCENZI, and KNIGHT STEEL. "Impact of Prospective Reimbursement on Health Care by the Inner City Old." Final Report to the Medical Foundation, Boston, Mass., 1987.

MARKUSEN, ANN R. "City Spatial Structure, Women's Household Work, and National Urban Policy." In Catherine Stimpson et al. (eds.), *Women in the American City,* pp. 20–41. Chicago: University of Chicago Press, 1980.

MARLAND, MICHAEL, ed. *Sex Differentiation and Schooling.* London: Heinemann Educational Books, 1984.

MARMOR, THEODORE R. "Canada's Path, America's Choices: Lessons from the Canadian Experience with National Health Insurance." In Peter Conrad and Rochelle Kern (eds.), *The Sociology of Health and Illness* (2nd ed.). New York: St. Martin's, 1986.

MARSDEN, PETER R., JOHN SHELTON REED, MICHAEL D. KENNEDY, and KARDI M. STINSON. "American Regional Cultures and Differences in Leisure Time Activities." *Social Forces* 60 (1982):1023–1049.

MARSHALL, ELIOT. "Unemployment Comp Is Middle-Class Welfare. *The New Republic* (February 19, 1977):16.

MARSHALL, JAMES R., DAVID I. GREGORIO, and DEBRA WALSH. "Sex Differences in Illness Behavior: Care Seeking Among Cancer Patients." *Journal of Health and Social Behavior* 29 (1982):197–204.

MARSHALL, LORNA. *The !Kung of the Nyae Nyae.* Cambridge, Mass.: Harvard University Press, 1976.

MARSHALL, SUSAN E. "Ladies Against Women: Mobilization Dilemmas of Antifeminist Movements." *Social Problems* 32(4) (1985): 348–362.

MARSHALL, VICTOR W. *Later Life: The Social Psychology of Aging.* Beverly Hills, Calif.: Sage, 1986.

MARTORELLA, ROSANNE. *The Sociology of Opera.* South Hadley, Mass.: J. F. Bergin, 1982.

MARTY, MARTIN E. *Modern American Religion,* Vol. 1. Chicago: University of Chicago Press, 1987.

MARX, KARL. *The German Ideology* (1846). New York: International Publishers, 1939.

MARX, GARY T. "The Iron Fist and the Velvet Glove: Totalitarian Potentials Within Democratic Structures." In James F. Short, Jr. (ed.), *The Social Fabric: Dimensions and Issues,* pp. 135–162. Newbury Park, Calif.: Sage, 1986.

————. "The Decline of Privacy and Autonomy in the Coming Maximum Security Society." Paper presented at 36th annual meeting of the Society for the Study of Social Problems, New York City, August 1986.

MASON, KAREN OPPENHEIM. "The Status of Women: Conceptual and Methodological Issues in Demographic Studies." *Sociological Forum* 1 (1986):284–300.

MASSARIK, FRED. "Rethinking the Intermarriage Crisis." *Moment,* June 1978.

MASSEY, DOUGLAS S. "Understanding Mexican Migration to the United States." *American Journal of Sociology* 92 (1987):1372–1403.

MAUKSCH, HANS O. "Nursing: Churning for Change?" In Howard E. Freeman, Sol Levine, and Leo G. Reeder (eds.), *Handbook of Medical Sociology,* pp. 206–230. Englewood Cliffs, N.J.: Prentice-Hall, 1972.

MAUME, DAVID J., JR. "Government Participation in the Local Economy and Race- and Sex-Based Earnings Inequality." *Social Problems* 32(3) (1985), 285–299.

McADAM, DOUG. *Political Process and the Development of Black Insurgency, 1930–1970.* Chicago: University of Chicago Press, 1982.

————. "Tactical Innovation and the Pace of Insurgency." *American Sociological Review* 48(5) (1983): 735–754.

McADOO, HARRIET PIPES, ed. *Black Families.* Beverly Hills, Calif.: Sage, 1981.

————. Marie Ferguson Peters Lecture, presented at School of Family Studies, University of Connecticut, May 3, 1985.

McARDLE, FRANK A., ed. *The Changing Health Care Market.* Washington, D.C.: Employee Benefit Research Institute, 1987.

McCARTHY, FRED J. *Television and the Red Menace: The Video Road to Vietnam.* New York: Praeger, 1985.

McCARTHY, JOHN D., and DEAN R. HOGE. "The Social Construction of School Punishment: Racial Disadvantage Out of Universalistic Process." *Social Forces* 65 (1987): 1101–1119.

McCARTHY, JOHN D., and MAYER N. ZALD. "Resource Mobilization and Social Movements: A Partial Theory." *American Journal of Sociology* 82(6) (May 1977):1212–1241.

McCARTHY, WILLIAM J., and BERNARD J. LEIKIND. "Walking on Fire: Feat of Mind?" *Psychology Today,* February 1986, pp. 10–12.

McCLOSKY, HERBERT, and ALIDA BRILL. *Dimensions of Tolerance: What Americans Believe About Civil Liberties.* New York: Russell Sage, 1983.

————, and JOHN ZALLER. *The American Ethos: Public Attitudes toward Capitalism and Democracy.* Cambridge, Mass.: Harvard University Press, 1986.

McDONALD, JOSEPH A. "Plant Closing Research: What's Going on Here?" *Humanity and Society* 9 (1985):108–122.

————, and DONALD A. CLELLAND. "Textile Workers and Union Sentiment." *Social Forces* 63 (1984):502–521.

McCRAE, JAMES A., JR. "Changes in Religious Communalism Desired by Protestants and Catholics." *Social Forces* 61(3) (March 1983):709–730.

McKINLEY, JOHN B., and SONYA M. McKINLEY. "The Questionable Contribution of Medical Measures to the Decline of Mortality in the United States in the 20th Century." *Millbank Memorial Quarterly* (Health & Society Issue) 55(3) (1977):405–428.

McLANAHAN, SARA. "Family Structure and the Reproduction of Poverty." *American Journal of Sociology* 90 (1985):873–884.

McLAREN, ANGUS. *Reproductive Rituals.* New York: Methuen, 1984.

McPHAIL, CLARK, and RONAL T. WOHLSTEIN. "Collective Locomotion as Collective Behavior." *American Sociological Review* 51(4) (August 1986):447–463.

McWHIRTER, DAVID P., and ANDREW A. MATTISON. *The Male Couple: How Relationships Develop.* Englewood Cliffs, N.J.: Prentice-Hall, 1984.

MEAD, G. H. *Mind, Self, and Society.* Chicago: University of Chicago Press, 1946.

MECHANIC, DAVID. *Medical Sociology.* New York: Free Press, 1978.

MELMAN, SEYMOUR. *Profits Without Production.* New York: Knopf, 1983.

MELTON, GORDON, and ROBERT L. MOORE. *The Cult Experience: Responding to the New Religious Pluralism.* New York: Pilgrim Press, 1982.

MELVILLE, MARGARITA B., ed. *Twice a Minority: Mexican American Women.* St. Louis, Mo.: C. V. Moseby, 1980.

MENAGHAN, ELIZABETH G., and MORTON A. LIEBERMAN. "Changes in Depression Following Divorce: A Panel Study." *Journal of Marriage and the Family* 48 (1986): 319–328.

MENDONCA, LENNY. "A Research Project on Sport and Racism." *Journal of Sport and Social Issues* 7(2) (1983):

MERCER, JANE. *Labeling the Mentally Retarded.* Berkeley: University of California Press, 1973.

————. "Who Is Normal? Two Perspectives on Mild Mental Retardation." In E. Gartly Jaco (ed.), *Patients, Physicians, and Illness,* pp. 56–75. New York: Free Press, 1972.

————, ed. *The Other Half: Women in Australian Society.* Ringwood, Australia: Penguin, 1977.

MERCY, JAMES A., and LALA CARR STEELMAN. "Familial Influence on the Intellectual Attainment of Children." *American Sociological Review* 47 (August 1982): 532–542.

MERTON, ROBERT K. "Patterns of Influence: A Study of Interpersonal Influence and of Communications Behavior in a Local Community." In Paul F. Lazarsfeld and Frank N. Stanton (eds.), *Communications Research, 1948–1949*. New York: Harper & Row, 1949.

—————. *Social Theory and Social Structure*. New York: Free Press, 1957.

—————. *On the Shoulders of Giants: A Shandean Postscript*. New York: Harcourt Brace Jovanovich, 1967.

—————. "Manifest and Latent Functions." In *Social Theory and Social Structure* (rev. ed.). New York: Free Press, 1968.

—————. "The Matthew Effect in Science." In Norman W. Storer (ed.), *The Sociology of Science: Theoretical and Empirical Investigations*. Chicago: University of Chicago Press, 1973.

MESSNER, STEVEN F. "Television Violence and Violent Crime: An Aggregate Analysis." *Social Problems* 33(3) (1986):218–235.

—————, and JUDITH R. BLAU. "Routine Leisure Activities and Rates of Crime: A Macro-Level Analysis." *Social Forces* 65 (1987):1035–1052.

—————, CHERYL NIECZKOSKI, and PAMELA FARRELL. "Disapproval of Non-Traditional Life Styles, Religiosity, and Support for Prayer in the Public Schools." Paper presented at the 56th annual meeting of the Eastern Sociological Society, New York City, April 1986.

METHANY, ELEANOR. "Symbolic Forms of Movement: The Feminine Image in Sports." In George Sage (ed.), *Sport and American Society*, pp. 289–301. Reading, Mass.: Addison-Wesley, 1977.

MIALL, CHARLENE E. "The Stigma of Involuntary Childlessness." *Social Problems* 33 (1986):268–282.

MICHALAK, JOSEPH. "Eluding the Tuition Blues." *The New York Times Education Supplement*, April 13, 1986, pp. 19–21.

MICHELS, ROBERT. *Political Parties* (1911) (trans. Edan and Cedar Paul). New York: Collier, 1962.

MICHELSON, WILLIAM. *Environmental Choice, Human Behavior, and Residential Satisfaction*. New York: Oxford University Press, 1977.

MIETHE, TERANCE D., MARK C. STAFFORD, and J. SCOTT LONG. "Social Differentiation in Criminal Victimization: A Test of Routine Activities/Lifestyle Theories." *American Sociological Review* 52 (1987):184–194.

MILGRAM, STANLEY. "Some Conditions of Obedience and Disobedience to Authority." *Human Relations* 18 (1965): 57–75.

—————. "The Experience of Living in Cities." *Science* 167 (March 1970):1461–1468.

—————. *Obedience to Authority*. New York: Harper & Row, 1973.

MILKMAN, RUTH, ed. *Women, Work, and Protest: A Century of U.S. Women's Labor History*. Boston, Mass.: Routledge & Kegan Paul, 1985.

MILLER, ELEANOR M. *Street Woman*. Philadelphia: Temple University Press, 1986.

MILLER, KAREN A. "The Effects of Industrialization on Men's Attitudes Toward the Extended Family and Women's Rights: A Cross-National Study." *Journal of Marriage and the Family* 46 (1984):153–160.

—————, MELVIN L. KOHN, and CARMI SCHOOLER. "Educational Self-Direction and Personality." *American Sociological Review* 51 (1986):372–390.

MILLER, WESLEY E., JR. "The New Christian Right and Its Preexistent Network: A Resource Mobilization Explanation." *Humanity and Society* 10 (May 1986):179–195.

MILLMAN, MARCIA. *Such a Pretty Face*. New York: W. W. Norton, 1980.

MILLS, C. WRIGHT. *The Power Elite*. New York: Oxford University Press, 1956.

—————. *The Sociological Imagination*. New York: Oxford University Press, 1959.

—————. *The Causes of World War Three*. Greenwich, Conn.: Greenwood Press, 1976.

MINER, HORACE. "Body Ritual Among the Nacirema." *American Anthropologist* 58 (June 1956):503–507.

MINTZ, BETH, and MICHAEL SCHWARTZ. "The Structure of Intercorporate Unity in American Business." *Social Problems* 29 (1981A):87–103.

—————, and MICHAEL SCHWARTZ. "Interlocking Directorates and Interest Group Formation." *American Sociological Review* 46 (1981B):851–869.

MINTZ, MORTON. *At Any Cost: Corporate Greed, Women, and the Dalkon Shield*. New York: Pantheon Books, 1985.

MIRANDE, ALFREDO. "Chicano Families." In James M. Henslin (ed.), *Marriage and Family in a Changing Society*, pp. 133–138. New York: Macmillan, 1985.

MIROWSKY, JOHN. "Depression and Marital Power: An Equity Model." *American Journal of Sociology* 91 (1985): 557–592.

MISHRA, RAMESH. *The Welfare State in Crisis: Social Thought and Social Change*. New York: St. Martin's, 1984.

MOLLENKOPF, JOHN H. "The Postwar Politics of Urban Development." In William K. Tabb and Larry Sawers (eds.), *Marxism and the Metropolis: New Perspectives in Urban Political Economy*. New York: Oxford University Press, 1978.

MONTERO, DARREL. *Japanese Americans: Changing Patterns of Ethnic Affiliation over Three Generations*. Boulder, Colo.: Westview Press, 1980.

—————. "The Japanese Americans: Changing Patterns of Assimilation over Three Generations." *American Sociological Review* 46 (1981):829–839.

MONTI, DANIEL J. *A Semblance of Justice: St. Louis Desegregation and Order in Urban America*. Columbia: University of Missouri Press, 1985.

MOORE, JEAN W. "Isolation and Stigmatization in the Development of an Underclass: The Case of the Chicano Gangs in East Los Angeles." *Social Problems* 33(1) (October 1985):1–12.

MOORE, JOAN. *Mexican Americans*. Englewood Cliffs, N.J.: Prentice-Hall, 1976.

MOORE, KRISTIN A., JAMES L. PETERSON, and FRANK F. FURSTENBERG. "Parental Attitudes and the Occurrence of

Early Sexual Activity." *Journal of Marriage and the Family* 48 (1986):777–782.

————, DAPHNE SPAIN, and SUZANNE BLIANCHI. "Working Wives and Mothers." In Beth Hess and Marvin Sussman (eds.), *Women and the Family: Two Decades of Change.* New York: Haworth, 1984, pp. 77–98.

————, and MARTHA R. BURT. *Private Crisis, Public Cost: Policy Perspectives on Teenage Childbearing.* Washington, D.C.: The Urban Institute Press, 1982.

————, and LINDA J. WAITE. "Marital Dissolution, Early Motherhood, Early Marriage." *Social Forces* 60 (1981): 20–40.

MOORE, LYNDA L. *Not as Far as You Think: The Realities of Working Women.* Lexington, Mass.: D. C. Heath, 1986.

MORAN, THEODORE H., ed. *Multinational Corporations: The Political Economy of Foreign Direct Investment.* Lexington, Mass.: Lexington Books, 1985.

MORANTZ-SANCHEZ, REGINA MARKELL. *Women Physicians in American Medicine.* New York: Oxford University Press, 1985.

MORE, DAN T. "Will Robots Save Democracy?" *The Futurist* (August 1981):14–19.

MOREHOUSE, WARD, and DAVID DEMBO. *The Underbelly of the U.S. Economy: Joblessness and the Pauperization of Work in America.* New York: Council on International and Public Affairs, 1986.

MORENO, J. L. *Who Shall Survive?* Boston: Beacon Press, 1934/1953.

MORF, MARTIN. "Eight Scenarios for Work in the Future." *The Futurist* (June 1983):24–29.

MORGAN, S. PHILIP, and RONALD R. RINDFUSS. "Marital Disruption: Structural and Temporal Dimensions." *American Journal of Sociology* 90 (1985):1055–1079.

MORRIS, ALDON. *The Origins of the Civil Rights Movement: Black Communities Organizing for Change.* New York: Free Press, 1984.

MORTIMER, JEYLAN T., and MICHAEL FINCH. "The Development of Self-Esteem in the Early Work Career." *Work and Occupations* 13 (1986):217–223.

MOSHER, DONALD L. "Misinformation on Pornography: A Lobby Disguised as an Educational Organization." *SIECUS Report* 14(5) (1986):7–10.

MOSKOFF, WILLIAM. "Divorce in the USSR." *Journal of Marriage and the Family* 45(2) (May 1983):419–425.

MOSKOS, CHARLES C. "Citizen Soldier Versus Economic Man." in James F. Short, Jr. (ed.), *The Social Fabric,* pp. 243–254. Beverly Hills, Calif.: Sage, 1986.

MOSS, NANCY, and STEPHEN ABRAMOWITZ. "Beyond Deficit Filling and Developmental Stakes: Cross-disciplinary Perspectives on Parental Heritage." *Journal of Marriage and the Family* 44(2) (May 1982):357–366.

MOTTL, TAHI L. "The Analysis of Countermovements." *Social Problems* 27(5) (June 1978):620–635.

MOYNIHAN, DANIEL PATRICK. *The Negro Family: The Case for National Action.* U.S. Dept. of Labor, Washington, D.C., 1965.

Ms. "Hot Commodities," June 1985, p. 20.

MUELLER, CAROL MCCLURG. *The Politics of the Gender Gap: The Social Construction of Political Influence.* Newbury Park, Calif.: Sage, 1987.

————, and THOMAS DIMIERI. "The Structure of Belief Systems among Contending ERA Activists." *Social Forces* 60(3) (1982):657–675.

MUKENGE, IDA ROUSSEAU. *The Black Church in Urban America: A Case Study in Political Economy.* New York: University Press of America, 1983.

MUKERJI, CHANDRA. *From Graven Images: Patterns of Modern Materialism.* New York: Columbia University Press, 1983.

————, and MICHAEL SCHUDSON. "Popular Culture." *Annual Review of Sociology* 12 (1986):47–66.

MULLER, EDWARD N. "Income Inequality, Regime Repressiveness, and Political Violence." *American Sociological Review* 50 (1985):47–61.

MULLNER, ROSS M., ODIN W. ANDERSON, and RONALD M. ANDERSEN. "Upheaval and Adaptation." *Society* 23(5) (1986): 37–42.

MURAKOSHI, SUEO, and YOSHIO MIWA. *Discrimination Against Buraku, Today.* Osaka, Japan: Buraku Kaiho Kenkyusho, 1986.

MURDOCK, GEORGE. "The Common Denominators of Cultures." In Ralph Linton (ed.), *The Science of Man and the World Crisis.* New York: Columbia University Press, 1945.

MYLES, JOHN. "The Trillion Dollar Misunderstanding." *Working Papers* (July/August 1981):23–31.

MYRDAL, GUNNAR. *An American Dilemma.* New York: Harper & Row, 1945.

NAGEL, WILLIAM. "Stream of Consciousness: A View of Prisonia." *Psychology Today* 14(3) (1980):78.

NAISBITT, JOHN. *Megatrends: Ten New Directions Transforming Our Lives.* New York: Warner Books, 1982.

NANCE, JOHN. *The Gentle Tasaday.* New York: Harcourt Brace Jovanovich, 1975.

————. *Lobo of the Tasaday: A Stone Age Boy Meets the Modern World.* New York: Pantheon, 1982.

NAOI, ATSUSHI, and CARMI SCHOOLER. "Occupational Conditions and Psychological Functioning in Japan." *American Journal of Sociology* 90 (1985):729.

NASH, JUNE, and MARIA PATRICIA FERNANDEZ-KELLY. *Women, Men, and the International Division of Labor.* Albany, N.Y.: State University of New York Press, 1984.

NATANSON, MAURICE. *The Journeying Self.* Reading, Mass.: Addison-Wesley, 1970.

NATHANSON, CONSTANCE. "Illness and the Feminine Role: A Theoretical Review." *Social Science and Medicine* 9 (1975):57–62.

————. "Social Roles and Health Status Among Women: The Significance of Employment." *Social Science and Medicine* 14A (1980):463–471.

NATIONAL ACADEMY OF SCIENCE. *For-Profit Enterprise in Health Care.* Washington, D.C.: National Academy of Science, 1986.

NATIONAL BROADCASTING COMPANY. *NBC White Papers: The Japan They Don't Talk About.* April 22, 1986.

NATIONAL CENTER ON HEALTH SERVICES RESEARCH (NCHSR/ HCTA). "Hospital Studies Program, Hospital Cost and

Utilization Project." Research Note #6. Washington, D.C.: NCHSR, 1985.

NATIONAL CENTER FOR HEALTH STATISTICS. *Working Paper 2.* Hyattsville, Md.: National Center for Health Statistics, 1985.

——————. *Monthly Vital Statistics Report,* 36(1) (April 29, 1987).

NATIONAL COMMITTEE FOR ADOPTION. *Adoption Factbook.* Washington, D.C.: National Committee for Adoption, 1986.

NATIONAL LEAGUE OF CITIES. "Report on Women Office Holders." Reported in *Star Ledger* (N.J.), September 30, 1986, p. 10.

NATIONAL RESEARCH COUNCIL. *Risking the Future: Adolescent Sexuality, Pregnancy, and Childbearing.* Washington, D.C.: National Academy Press, 1986.

NATIONAL SCIENCE FOUNDATION. *Women and Minorities in Science and Engineering.* Washington, D.C: NSF, 1986.

NAZARIO, SONIA L. "Gentlemen of the Club." *Wall Street Journal,* March 24, 1986, p. 21D.

NEUFFER, ELIZABETH. "'Airplane': High Stakes Chain Letter." *The New York Times,* April 7, 1987, p. B7.

NEUGARTEN, BERNICE L., and GUNHILD HAGESTAD. "Age and the Life Course." In Robert H. Binstock and Ethel Shanas (eds.), *Handbook of Aging and the Social Sciences* (2nd ed.). New York: Van Nostrand, 1983.

——————, JOAN W. MOORE, and JOHN C. LOWE. "Age Norms, Age Constraints, Adult Socialization." In B. Newgarten (ed.), *Middle Age and Aging,* pp. 22–28. Chicago: University of Chicago Press, 1968.

NEWCOMB, THEODORE. *Personality and Social Change: Attitude Formation in a Student Community.* New York: Dryden, 1943.

NEWFARMER, RICHARD. *Profits, Progress, and Poverty: Case Studies of International Industries in Latin America.* South Bend, Ind.: University of Notre Dame Press, 1985.

NEWSWEEK. "Back to the Suburbs." April 21, 1986, pp. 60–62.

——————. "Crack: The Road Back." June 30, 1986, pp. 52–53.

——————. "Return to the Suburbs." July 21, 1986, pp. 52–54.

——————. "Future Shock: The AIDS Epidemic." November 24, 1986, pp. 30–39.

——————. "In Texas, a Grim New Appalachia." June 8, 1987, pp. 27–28.

THE NEW YORK TIMES. "The Long Road to Success at City University." April 8, 1984, p. E6.

——————. "The Influence of Religion." September 9, 1984, Sec. 4, p. 1.

——————. "Poll Finds Churchgoing Holds Steady in 1984." December 20, 1984, p. 20.

——————. "Church Members Up Less Than 1%." June 19, 1985, p. A20.

——————. "Halt of Income Study Opposed." July 9, 1985, p. A16.

——————. "Study Finds Desegregation is an Effective Social Tool." September 17, 1985, p. C1.

——————. "Swiss Grant Women Equal Marriage Rights." September 23, 1985, p. A6.

——————. "Ban on Women at a Church Ceremony is Protested." March 16, 1986, p. 29.

——————. "The Loaded Question." April 3, 1986, p. A24.

——————. Educational Supplement. April 13, 1986, pp. 68–70.

——————. "Principal's Methods Divide New Hampshire Town." April 27, 1986, p. B1.

——————. "Catholics Find Funds for Aging Nuns and Priests Insufficient." May 30, 1986, pp. 1 ff.

——————. "Bullhorn Behavior." June 8, 1986, p. E22.

——————. "William S. Woodside on the Corporate Roles." July 13, 1986, p. E8.

——————. "Woman Chosen to Head Japan Socialist Party." September 7, 1986, p. A6.

——————. "Coming of Age on the Ocean." September 16, 1986, p. B1.

——————. "Race and Region: A Death Row Census." April 23, 1987, p. B12.

——————. "Tuitions at New Peak, Heating Cost Debate." May 12, 1987, pp. 1 ff.

——————. "Survey Finds Support for AIDS Patients." May 22, 1987, p. B4.

——————. "Third World Nations Finally Embracing Population Control." May 31, 1987, p. E30.

NOBLE, KENNETH B. "Impact of Youth Job Projects is Declared Limited by Panel." *The New York Times,* November 13, 1985, p. A20.

——————. "Study Finds 60% of 11 Million Who Lost Jobs Got New Ones." *The New York Times,* February 7, 1986, pp. 1 ff.

——————. "Factory Homeworkers Fear Change in Job Law." *The New York Times,* August 20, 1986, p. A8.

——————. "High Court to Decide Whether Death Penalty Discriminates Against Blacks." *The New York Times,* 1987, p. A12.

NOCK, STEVEN, and PETER H. ROSSI. "Household Types and Social Standing." *Social Forces* 57(4) (June 1979): 1325–1345.

NOLAN, PATRICK D., and GERHARD LENSKI. "Technoeconomic Heritage, Patterns of Development, and the Advantage of Backwardness." *Social Forces* 64 (1985):341–358.

NORTON, ARTHUR J., and PAUL C. GLICK. "One-Parent Families: A Social and Economic Profile." *Family Relations* 35 (1986):9–17.

——————, and JEANNE MOORMAN. "The Divorced Generation." Report of paper presented at the annual meeting of the Population Association of America. *American Demographics* (July 1986):11.

NOZICK, ROBERT. *Philosophical Explanations.* Cambridge, Mass.: Harvard University Press, 1985.

NYDEGGER, CORINNE N. "Family Ties of the Aged in Cross-Cultural Perspective." In Beth B. Hess and Elizabeth W. Markson (eds.), *Growing Old in America.* New Brunswick, N.J.: Transaction Press, 1985.

NYDEN, PHILIP W. *Steelworkers Rank-and-File: The Politi-*

cal Economy of a Union Reform Movement. New York: Praeger, 1984.

OAKES, JENNIE. *Keeping Track: How Schools Structure Inequality.* New Haven, Conn.: Yale University Press, 1985.

O'BRIEN, DAVID J., and STEPHEN S. FUGITA. "Mobilization of a Traditionally Petit Bourgeois Ethnic Group." *Social Forces* 63(2) (1984):522–537.

O'DONNELL, CAROL. *The Basis of the Bargain: Gender, Schooling, and Jobs.* Winchester, Mass.: Allen & Unwin, 1985.

OFFE, CLAUS. *Contradictions of the Welfare State.* Cambridge, Mass.: MIT Press, 1984.

OFFICE OF MANAGEMENT AND THE BUDGET. *Budgets for 1986–1992.* Washington, D.C.: OMB.

OFFICE OF TECHNOLOGY ASSESSMENT. "Survey of College Freshmen 1984." Washington, D.C. Reported in *The New York Times,* December 26, 1985, p. A15.

OFFICIAL CATHOLIC DIRECTORY, 1984. New York: P. J. Kenedy & Sons, 1985.

OGBURN, WILLIAM T. *Social Change: With Respect to Culture and Original Nature.* New York: B. W. Huebsch, 1922.

OLIVER, MELVIN L., and MARK A. GLICK. "An Analysis of the New Orthodoxy on Black Mobility." *Social Problems* 29 (1982):511–523.

OLIVER, PAMELA. "'If You Don't Do It, Nobody Else Will': Active and Token Contributors to Local Collective Action." *American Sociological Review* 49(5):601–610.

ORFIELD, GARY. *Public School Desegregation in the United States, 1968–1980.* Washington, D.C.: Joint Center for Political Studies, 1983.

ORTIZ, ALFONSO. *The Tewa World.* Chicago: University of Chicago Press, 1969.

ORWELL, GEORGE. *Animal Farm.* New York: Harcourt, 1954.

————. *1984.* New York: New American Library, 1949.

OSTLING, RICHARD N. "Power, Glory—and Politics." *Time,* February 17, 1986, pp. 62–69.

OSTRANDER, SUSAN. *Women of the Upper Class.* Philadelphia: Temple University Press, 1984.

O'SULLIVAN, JUDITH, and ROSEMARY GALLICK. *Workers and Allies: Female Participation in the American Trade Unions.* Washington, D.C.: Smithsonian Institution Press, 1975.

OVERBECK, JOHANNES. *Population and Canadian Society.* Toronto: Butterworth, 1980.

OWEN, DAVID. *None of the Above: Behind the Myth of Scholastic Aptitude.* Boston: Houghton Mifflin, 1985.

OWEN, JOHN M., and JAMES W. VAUPEL. "Life Expectancy." *American Demographics* (November 1985):37–38.

PACE, ERIC. "Women's Cults of Antiquity: The Veil Rises." *The New York Times,* April 30, 1985, pp. C1 ff.

PACKWOOD, BOB. "Discrimination Aided." *The New York Times,* April 20, 1984, p. A27.

PADGETT, JOHN F. Review of Galaskiewicz. *Contemporary Sociology* 15 (1986):818–821.

PAGE, CHARLES H. "Young Turks in Sociology: Yesterday and Today." *Sociological Forum* 1(1) (1986):166–168.

PAGE, ANN L., and DONALD CLELLAND. "The Kanawha County Textbook Controversy: A Study of Politics of Lifestyle Concerns." *Social Forces* 57(1) (1978).

PAGELOW, MILDRED DALEY. *Family Violence.* New York: Praeger, 1984.

PALEN, J. JOHN. *The Urban World,* 3rd ed. New York: McGraw-Hill, 1986.

PALETZ, DAVID L., and ROBERT M. ENTMAN. *Media Power Politics.* New York: Free Press, 1981.

PALGI, MICHEL, JOSEPH RAFAEL BLASI, MENACHEM ROSNER, and MARILYN SAFIR, eds. *Sexual Equality: The Israeli Kibbutz Tests the Theories.* Norwood, Pa.: Norwood Editions, 1983.

PALKOVITZ, ROB. "Fathers' Birth Attendance, Early Contact and Extended Contact with Their Newborns: Critical Review." *Child Development* 56, No. 2 (1985):392–406.

PALMER, DONALD, ROGER FRIEDLAND, and JITENDRA V. SINGH. "The Ties That Bind: Organizational and Class Bases of Stability in a Corporate Interlock Network." *American Sociological Review* 51 (1986):781–796.

PALMER, ROBERT. "What Pop Lyrics Say to Us Today." *The New York Times,* February 14, 1985, Sec. 2, p. 1.

PALOMA, MARGARET. *The Charismatic Movement: Is There a New Pentecost?* Boston: Twayne, 1987.

PALUDI, MICHELE A., and LISA A. STRAYER. "What's in an Author's Name? Differential Evaluations of Performance as a Function of Author's Name." *Sex Roles* 12 (1985): 353–361.

PARCEL, TOBY L. "Wealth Accumulation of Black and White Men: The Case of Housing Equity." *Social Problems* 30(2) (December 1982):199–211.

PARELES, JON. "Defiance and Rage Hone a Debut Rap Album." *The New York Times,* May 10, 1987a, Sec. 2, p. 20.

————. "Who Decides the Color of Music?" *The New York Times,* May 17, 1987b, Sect. H, p. 32.

PARENTI, MICHAEL. *Inventing Reality: The Politics of the Mass Media.* New York: St. Martin's, 1985.

PARK, ROBERT E., ERNEST W. BURGESS, and RODERICK D. McKENZIE, eds. *The City.* Chicago: University of Chicago Press, 1925.

PARKINSON, C. NORTHCOTE. *Parkinson's Law.* Boston: Houghton Mifflin, 1957/1980.

PARRILLO, VINCENT N. "Arab American Immigrant Communities: Diversity and Parallel." Paper presented at the Eastern Sociological Society meeting, Baltimore, March 1983.

————. *Strangers to These Shores: Race and Ethnic Relations in the United States,* 2nd ed. New York: Wiley, 1985.

————, JOHN STIMSON, and ARDYTH STIMSON. *Social Problems.* New York: John Wiley, 1985.

PARSONS, TALCOTT. *The Social System.* New York: Free Press, 1951.

————. "The American Family: Its Relations to Personality and the Social Structure." In Talbott Parsons and Robert F. Bales (eds.), *Family Socialization and Interaction Process,* pp. 3–21. Glencoe, Ill.: Free Press, 1955.

WORLD ALMANAC BOOK OF FACTS, New York: Scripps Howard, 1986.

WORLDWATCH INSTITUTE. *State of the World, 1985*. Washington, D.C.: Worldwatch Institute, 1986.

WORSLEY, PETER. *The Trumpet Shall Sound,* 2nd ed. New York: Schocken Books, 1986.

WRIGHT, ERIK OLIN, et al. "The American Class Structure. *American Sociological Review* 47(6) (1982):709–726.

————, and JOACHIM SINGLEMANN. "Proletarianization in the Changing American Class Structure." *American Journal of Sociology* 88 (1982):S176–209.

WRIGHT, SAM. *Crowds and Riots: A Study in Social Organization*. Beverly Hills, Calif.: Sage Publications, 1978.

WRONG, DENNIS. "The Oversocialized Conception of Man in Modern Sociology." *American Sociological Review* 26 (1961):183–193.

WUTHNOW, ROBERT. "State Structures and Ideological Outcomes." *American Sociological Review* 50 (1985): 799–821.

————. "American Democracy and the Democratization of American Religion." Paper presented at the 80th annual meeting of the American Sociological Association, Washington, D.C., August 1985.

YAMAGUCHI, KAZUO, and DENISE B. KANDEL. "Dynamic Relationships Between Premarital Cohabitation and Illicit Drug Use: An Event-History Analysis of Role Selection and Role Socialization." *American Sociological Review* 50 (1985):530–546.

YANKELOVICH, DANIEL. *New Rules: Searching for Self-fulfillment in a World Turned Upside Down*. New York: Random House, 1981.

YEATES, MAURICE, and BARRY GARNER. *The North American City*. New York: Harper & Row, 1976.

YINGER, J. MILTON. *Countercultures*. New York: Free Press, 1982.

YODER, STEPHEN KREIDER. "No Computers Need Apply." *Wall Street Journal,* June 12, 1987, p. 29D.

YOSHINO, I. ROGER, and SUEO MURAKOSHI. *The Invisible Visible Minority: Japan's Burakumin*. Osaka, Japan: Buraku Kaiho Kenkyusho, 1977.

YUVAL-DAVIS, NIRA. "Front and Rear: The Sexual Division of Labor in the Israeli Army." *Feminist Studies* 11 (1985): 649–676.

ZABLOCKI, BENJAMIN. *Alienation and Charisma: A Study of Contemporary American Communes*. New York: Free Press, 1980.

ZAJONC, ROBERT B. "Mining New Gold from Old Research." *Psychology Today,* February 1986, pp. 47–50.

ZALD, MAYER N., and ROBERTA ASH. "Social Movement Organizations." In Barry McLaughlin (ed.), *Studies in Social Movements,* pp. 461–485. New York: Free Press, 1969.

————, and JOHN D. MCCARTHY, eds. *The Dynamics of Social Movements: Resource Mobilization, Social Control, and Tactics*. Cambridge, Mass.: Winthrop, 1979.

ZAKARIYA, SALLY BANKS. "Another Look at the Children of Divorce: Summary Report of the Study of School Needs of One-Parent Children." *Principal* (Sept. 1982):34–38.

ZBOROWSKI, MARK. "Cultural Components in Response to Pain." *Journal of Social Issues* 8 (1952):16–30.

ZEITZ, DOROTHY. *Women Who Embezzle or Defraud: A Study of Convicted Felons*. New York: Praeger Publishers, 1981.

ZELIZER, VIVIANA. *Pricing the Priceless Child: The Changing Social Value of Children*. New York: Basic Books, 1985.

ZELNICK, N., J. KANTER, and K. FORD. *Sex and Pregnancy in Adolescence*. Beverly Hills, Calif.: Sage Publications, 1981.

ZERUBAVEL, EVIATAR. *Hidden Rhythms: Schedules and Calendars in Social Life*. Chicago: University of Chicago Press, 1981.

————. "Easter and Passover: On Calendars and Group Identity." *American Sociological Review* 47 (April 1982):284–289.

ZIHLMAN, ADRIENNE L. "Women in Evolution." Part II: "Subsistence and Social Organization Among Early Hominids." *Signs* 4(1) (1978):4–20.

ZIMBARDO, PHILIP, CURTIS W. BANKS, CRAIG HANEY, and DAVID JAFFE. "The Mind Is a Formidable Jailer." *The New York Times,* April 8, 1973.

————, EBBE B. EBBESEN, and CHRISTINE MASLACH. *Influencing Attitudes and Changing Behavior*. Reading, Mass.: Addison-Wesley, 1977.

ZIMMERMAN, BONNIE. "The Politics of Transliteration: Lesbian Personal Narratives." *Signs* 9 (1984):663–682.

ZIMMERMAN, MARY K. "The Women's Health Movement: A Critique of Medical Enterprise and the Position of Women." In Beth B. Hess and Myra Marx Ferree (eds.), *Analyzing Gender: A Handbook of Social Science Research*. Newbury Park, Calif.: Sage, 1987.

ZINN, MAXINE BACA, and D. STANLEY EITZEN. *Diversity in American Families*. New York: Harper and Row, 1987.

ZIPP, JOHN F. "Social Class and Social Liberalism." *Sociological Forum* 1 (1986):301–329.

————, and JOEL SMITH. "A Structural Analysis of Class Voting." *Social Forces* 60 (1982):738–759.

ZOLA, IRVING. "Culture and Symptoms: An Analysis of Patients' Presenting Complaints." *American Sociological Review* 31 (1966):615–630.

————. "Medicine as an Institution of Social Control." In Peter Conrad and Rochelle Kern (eds.), *The Sociology of Health and Illness* (2nd ed.). New York: St. Martin's, 1986.

ZWEIGENHAFT, RICHARD L. "Recent Patterns of Jewish Representation in the Corporate and Social Elite." *Contemporary Jewry* 6 (1982):36–46.

Name Index

Subject Index